MASTERPLOTS

Combined Edition

FIFTEEN HUNDRED AND TEN

Plot-Stories and Essay-Reviews

from the

WORLD'S FINE LITERATURE

Edited by

FRANK N. MAGILL

Story Editor

DAYTON KOHLER

VOLUME THREE — GUA-MAG

SALEM PRESS

INCORPORATED

NEW YORK

GUARD OF HONOR

Type of work: Novel
Author: James Gould Cozzens (1903-   )
Type of plot: Psychological realism
Time of plot: Three days during World War II
Locale: An Air Force base in Florida
First published: 1948

Principal characters:

> MAJOR GENERAL IRA N. "BUS" BEAL, Commanding General of the Ocanara Base
> SAL BEAL, his wife
> COLONEL NORMAN ROSS, Air Inspector on General Beal's staff
> CORA ROSS, his wife
> CAPTAIN NATHANIEL HICKS, an officer in Special Projects and an editor in civilian life
> SECOND LIEUTENANT AMANDA TURCK, a WAC
> LIEUTENANT COLONEL BENNY CARRICKER, General Beal's co-pilot
> BRIGADIER GENERAL NICHOLS, assistant to the Commanding General of the Air Force
> LIEUTENANT EDSELL, a writer, assigned to Special Projects
> LIEUTENANT LIPPA, a WAC, in love with Lieut. Edsell
> LIEUTENANT WILLIS, a Negro pilot
> MR. WILLIS, his father

Critique:

Within the complex structure of a large Air Force base in wartime, James Gould Cozzens has evoked a world in miniature in which many of the major conflicts of life are discussed. In a flat but cogent style the author delineates the problems that attach to power relationships, to authority and suppression. Indirectly the book is a profound indictment of the self-willed agitator and nonconformist; directly, it is a striking revelation of the way various types rise to and deal with the crises of life.

The Story:

The huge and sprawling Air Force base at Ocanara, Florida, was almost a world in itself. At its head was Major General "Bus" Beal, a hero in the Pacific theater in the early days of the war and still, at forty-one, an energetic and skillful flyer. To keep the operation of the base running smoothly, the general relied heavily on his Air Inspector, Colonel Norman Ross, who brought to his military duties the same resourcefulness that had characterized his career as a judge in peacetime. And Judge Ross needed all

GUARD OF HONOR by James Gould Cozzens. By permission of the publishers, Harcourt, Brace & Co., Inc. Copyright, 1948, by James Gould Cozzens.

his acumen to do the job.

Landing his AT-7 one night at the Ocanara Airstrip, the general came close to colliding with a B-17. The B-17, piloted by Lieutenant Willis, one of the Negro fliers recently assigned to Ocanara, had violated the right of way. Lieutenant Colonel Benny Carricker, General Beal's co-pilot, struck and hospitalized Lieutenant Willis and in return was confined to quarters by General Beal. The incident, while small, triggered a complex of problems that, in the next two days, threatened to destroy the normal operations of the base. On the following day several of the Negro fliers, incensed by Lieutenant Willis' accident and further outraged at the fact that a separate service club had been set up for them, attempted to enter the white officers' recreation building. This action came close to starting a riot.

To complicate Colonel Ross's difficulties further, tension had developed between the Air Force base and some leading citizens of the town. Alone of General Beal's staff, Colonel Ross felt the hazards of the situation. For the others— in particular for Colonel Mowbray and his assistant, Chief Warrant Officer Botwinick—the difficulties seemed ephemeral and routine. Even General Beal was of little aid to Colonel Ross, for he was brooding unhappily over the arrest of Colonel Carricker, and was further troubled by the recent suicide of an old friend.

Among the members of the Air Force base itself other forces were working to enlarge and compound the difficulties. For Lieutenant Edsell, the hospitalization of the Negro pilot was the springboard for agitation, and he helped arrange for a visit of Lieutenant Willis' father to the base hospital. Only a few of the base personnel understood the difficulties Colonel Ross faced and the skill with which he operated. Those who did, like Captain Nathaniel Hicks, were too concerned with their own problems to be of much assistance.

On the day Mr. Willis was to visit his son, the Ocanara Base was host to another unexpected visitor, Brigadier General Nichols, the personal representative of the Commanding General of the Air Force. To the embarrassment of all concerned, General Nichols' purpose in coming to Ocanara was to award Lieutenant Willis a medal for bravery.

Whatever Colonel Ross may have dreaded from the visit, he was relieved to find General Nichols a not unsympathetic man, for the general had trained himself into a stoical and tolerant frame of mind. He understood the situation at a glance, and at the awarding of the medal at the hospital he conducted himself so well that Mr. Willis himself was charmed.

On the following day the base prepared for a birthday celebration. In honor of General Beal's forty-first year, Colonel Mowbray had organized a military parade which was to include not only marching men and WACS, but planes flying in formation and parachute drops. General Nichols shared the reviewing stand with General Beal and his staff. In the nearby field, near a lake, Captain Hicks and his friend from the WAC detachment, Lieutenant Turck, were posted as observers.

Soon the parade began, and from their observation post Captain Hicks and Lieutenant Turck saw hundreds of parachutists begin the slow descent into a simulated conflict. Then tragedy struck. A group of parachutists, having ill-timed their leap, dropped into the lake instead of hitting the field. In horror, Captain Hicks saw them struggle briefly in the water and then sink.

When knowledge of the disaster reached General Beal's office there was a moment of furious commotion. Charges and countercharges were flung about with abandon. To Colonel Ross it seemed that fate had ordained nothing but problems for him and for Ocanara. But it was now that General Beal shook himself out of his gloom and took command, directing rescue operations with precision and

1184

skill and revealing at the same time that throughout the hectic few days that had passed he had not been unaware of the conflicts going on.

That night Colonel Ross accompanied General Nichols to the plane that was to return him to Washington. Reviewing the difficulties of the past three days, the colonel saw that General Nichols was right: one could only do one's best and, for the rest, trust the situation to right itself.

GUEST THE ONE-EYED

Type of work: Novel
Author: Gunnar Gunnarsson (1889-)
Time: c. 1900
Locale: Iceland
First published: Af Borgslaegtens Historie, 1912-1914; abridged in translation as *Guest the One-Eyed,* 1920

Principal characters:
ØRLYGUR À BORG, a well-to-do landowner
ORMARR ØRLYGSSON, his son
KETILL ØRLYGSSON, Ormarr's brother
GUDRUN (RUNA), Pall à Seyru's daughter
ALMA, the daughter of Vivild, a Danish banker
ØRLYGUR THE YOUNGER, son of Ketill and Runa
SNEBIORG (BAGGA), an illegitimate girl

In his fiction Gunnar Gunnarsson provides novels of traditional form and nobility, made particularly fascinating by their Icelandic setting. The atmosphere of the ancient sagas pervades his books, putting his characters into association with the past while making the present none the less convincing. The drama of the novels is essentially moral, and the ethical dilemmas into which the characters fall are neither gross nor abnormal. Gunnarsson is adept at re-creating the Icelandic character and the Icelandic atmosphere; the human beings about whom he writes move with dignity and passion across barren, stony, but none the less attractive northern plains. One is reminded of Thomas Hardy's dark novels in which the brooding moors take on the pessimism and the courage of people challenged by fate.

Although Gunnarsson retains a tragic view of life, regarding human beings as helpless before forces more powerful than themselves, he never loses sight of the alleviating influences of love, humor, and tradition. Generation succeeds generation in his novels, and although individuals fall, families persevere, so that Icelandic traditions are strengthened and, in turn, strengthen those who share them. *The History of the Family at Borg*—in the original *Af Borgslaegtens Historie*—is a four-part novel of this enduring type.

Guest the One-Eyed, abridged in English translation, is the story of the family at Borg, of a father and his two sons, and of the illegitimate child of one of his sons. The Borg farm, portrayed as a refuge for anyone who needed help, is the home of Ørlygur the Rich, an energetic and compassionate Icelandic farmer sometimes spoken of as "the King" because of the vast number of servants he retains and the hundreds of cattle and horses and sheep he owns. Ørlygur hopes that one of his sons, either Ormarr or Ketill, will become the master of Borg, but Ormarr is interested in playing the violin and Ketill decides to become a priest. The issue is resolved when Ormarr, after throwing away an opportunity to become a world-famous concert violinist and after achieving a remarkable financial success as a shipping magnate, returns to Borg in search of a new challenge.

Gunnarsson quickly creates extremes of character in Ormarr and Ketill. Ormarr is sensitive, intelligent, perceptive, creative, and honest, while Ketill is devious, jealous, destructive, blasphemous, and dishonest. As the parish priest, secretly eager to seize control of the property at Borg, Ketill preaches a series of sermons which slowly encourage the peasants to believe that a great sin has been committed by one of the community leaders. Finally Ketill charges his own father with being the father of a child born to Runa, the daughter of a poor farmer, Pall à Seyru. The charge is coupled with the suggestion that Ørlygur also persuaded Ormarr to marry Runa in order to hide his crime of passionate lust. The depth of Ketill's depravity finally becomes evident to the citizens of the community when Ørlygur, with convincing simplicity and wrath, reveals that the priest who would condemn his own father is himself the father of Runa's child.

The elements of melodrama are here, but the effect is that of tragedy. To have been able to portray such extremes of character—for Ormarr sacrifices his own concerns to marry Runa, while Ketill sacrifices his own family to win power and wealth—without making the characters mere devices for the development of plot is evidence of Gunnarsson's skill as a novelist.

The author's audacity, so successful as to become a sign of his eminence as a writer, leads him to create a complete reversal in the character of Ketill. Ketill, the cold, scheming Icelandic Judas, becomes someone very much like Christ. Repenting his sins, Ketill leaves Borg and, having rejected the idea of suicide, becomes a wanderer, dependent for his board and lodging on the Icelandic farmers to whom he brings simple, soul-restoring messages of love and compassion. He regards himself as a guest on earth, and "Guest" becomes his name. He has lost his eye in saving a child from a burning farm; hence, he is "Guest the one-eyed."

There is no more difficult task in literature than the portrayal of a saintlike character. Readers are ready to accept the fact of evil, and there is no act so base that one cannot readily believe man capable of it. But extreme selflessness, Christlike love, is an ideal, hinted at in the scriptures, and hardly to be found in the community of men. The novelist presuming to create a character who, having been in the depths of sin, becomes a lovable, living incarnation of virtue, is a writer confronting himself with the final challenge of his craft. Gunnarsson took up that challenge; *Guest the One-Eyed* is his victorious response.

The novel has at once the character of a myth and the character of a modern saga. When Ketill finally returns to Borg, known only as Guest the one-eyed, he carries with him the memory of the curses that everyone has put on Ketill, whom all believe dead. His reconciliation with his family—something almost beyond hope, even for a saint, since Ketill's lying charge from the pulpit had both killed his father and driven Ketill's wife mad—is partly the result of his having destroyed the old Ketill by his life as a wanderer, but it is also a result of the readiness of the Icelanders to forgive for the sake of the family, that union of strength which makes life in Iceland possible.

Guest the One-Eyed ends affirmatively with the prospective marriage of Ørlygur the younger, Ketill's son, and Bagga, the beautiful illegitimate daughter of the woman of Bolli who, like Ketill, had known the fire and ice of passion and repentance. Gunnarsson's pessimism is concerned with man's lot on earth, with his struggle and his ultimate death; but it is not a discouraging pessimism that extends to the spirit of man. Iceland may be stony, misty, barren and demanding, but it is also a land of sunshine and changing moods, like the characters about whom Gunnarsson writes.

GULLIVER'S TRAVELS

Type of work: Simulated record of travel
Author: Jonathan Swift (1667-1745)
Type of plot: Social satire
Time of plot: 1699-1713
Locale: England and various fictional lands
First published: 1726-1727

Principal character:
LEMUEL GULLIVER, surgeon, sea captain, and traveler

Critique:

It has been said that Dean Swift hated Man, but loved individual men. His hatred is brought out in this caustic political and social satire aimed at the English people, representing mankind in general, and at the Whigs in particular. By means of a disarming simplicity of style and of careful attention to detail in order to heighten the effect of the narrative, Swift produced one of the outstanding pieces of satire in world literature. Swift himself attempted to conceal his authorship of the book under its original title—*Travels into Several Remote Nations of the World, by Lemuel Gulliver.*

The Story:

Lemuel Gulliver, a physician, took the post of ship's doctor on the *Antelope,* which set sail from Bristol for the South Seas in May, 1699. When the ship was wrecked in a storm somewhere near Tasmania, Gulliver had to swim for his life. Wind and tide helped to carry him close to a low-lying shore where he fell, exhausted, into a deep sleep. Upon awaking, he found himself held to the ground by hundreds of small ropes. He soon discovered that he was the prisoner of humans six inches tall. Still tied, Gulliver was fed by his captors; then he was placed on a special wagon built for the purpose and drawn by fifteen hundred small horses. Carried in this manner to the capital city of the small humans, he

was exhibited as a great curiosity to the people of Lilliput, as the land of the diminutive people was called. He was kept chained to a huge Lilliputian building into which he crawled at night to sleep.

Gulliver soon learned the Lilliputian language, and through his personal charm and natural curiosity he came into good graces at the royal court. At length he was given his freedom, contingent upon his obeying many rules devised by the emperor prescribing his deportment in Lilliput. Now free, Gulliver toured Mildendo, the capital city, and found it to be similar to European cities of the time.

Learning that Lilliput was in danger of an invasion by the forces of the neighboring empire, Blefuscu, he offered his services to the emperor of Lilliput. While the enemy fleet awaited favorable winds to carry their ships the eight hundred yards between Blefuscu and Lilliput, Gulliver took some Lilliputian cable, waded to Blefuscu, and brought back the entire fleet by means of hooks attached to the cables. He was greeted with great acclaim and the emperor made him a nobleman. Soon, however, the emperor and Gulliver fell out over differences concerning the fate of the now helpless Blefuscu. The emperor wanted to reduce the enemy to the status of slaves; Gulliver championed their liberty. The pro-Gulliver forces prevailed in the Lilliputian parliament; the peace settlement was favorable to Blefuscu. But Gulliver was now in disfavor at court.

He visited Blefuscu, where he was received graciously by the emperor and the people. One day, while exploring the empire, he found a ship's boat washed ashore from some wreck. With the help of thousands of Blefuscu artisans, he repaired the boat for his projected voyage back to his own civilization. Taking some little cattle and sheep with him, he sailed away and was eventually picked up by an English vessel.

Back in England, Gulliver spent a short time with his family before he shipped aboard the *Adventure,* bound for India. The ship was blown off course by fierce winds. Somewhere on the coast of Great Tartary a landing party went ashore to forage for supplies. Gulliver, who had wandered away from the party, was left behind when a gigantic human figure pursued the sailors back to the ship. Gulliver was caught in a field by giants threshing grain that grew forty feet high. Becoming the pet of a farmer and his family, he amused them with his human-like behavior. The farmer's nine-year-old daughter, who was not yet over forty feet high, took special charge of Gulliver.

The farmer displayed Gulliver first at a local market town. Then he took his little pet to the metropolis, where Gulliver was put on show to the great detriment of his health. The farmer, seeing that Gulliver was near death, sold him to the queen, who took a great fancy to the little curiosity. The court doctors and philosophers studied Gulliver as a quaint trick of nature. He subsequently had adventures with giant rats the size of lions, with a dwarf thirty feet high, with wasps as large as partridges, with apples the size of Bristol barrels, and with hailstones the size of tennis balls.

He and the king discussed the institutions of their respective countries, the king asking Gulliver many questions about Great Britain that Gulliver found impossible to answer truthfully without embarrassment.

After two years in Brobdingnag, the land of the giants, Gulliver escaped miraculously when a large bird carried his portable quarters out over the sea. The bird dropped the box containing Gulliver and he was rescued by a ship which was on its way to England. Back home, it took Gulliver some time to accustom himself once more to a world of normal size.

Soon afterward Gulliver went to sea again. Pirates from a Chinese port attacked the ship. Set adrift in a small sailboat, Gulliver was cast away upon a rocky island. One day he saw a large floating mass descending from the sky. Taken aboard the flying island of Laputa, he soon found it to be inhabited by intellectuals who thought only in the realm of the abstract and the exceedingly impractical. The people of the island, including the king, were so absent-minded they had to have servants following them to remind them even of their trends of conversation. When the floating island arrived above the continent of Balnibari, Gulliver received permission to visit that realm. There he inspected the Grand Academy, where hundreds of highly impractical projects for the improvement of agriculture and building were under way.

Next Gulliver journeyed by boat to Glubbdubdrib, the island of sorcerers. By means of magic, the governor of the island showed Gulliver such great historical figures as Alexander, Hannibal, Caesar, Pompey, and Sir Thomas More. Gulliver talked to the apparitions and learned from them that history books were inaccurate.

From Glubbdubdrib, Gulliver went to Luggnagg. There he was welcomed by the king, who showed him the Luggnaggian immortals, or stuldbruggs—beings who would never die.

Gulliver traveled on to Japan, where he took a ship back to England. He had been away for more than three years.

Gulliver became restless after a brief stay at his home, and he signed as captain of a ship which sailed from Portsmouth in August, 1710, destined for the South Seas. The crew mutinied, keeping Captain Gulliver prisoner in his cabin for months. At length, he was cast adrift in a long boat off a strange coast. Ashore, he came upon and was nearly overwhelmed by disgusting half-human, half-ape creatures who fled in terror at the approach of a horse. Gulliver soon discovered, to his amazement, that he was in a land where rational horses, the Houyhnhnms, were masters of irrational human creatures, the Yahoos. He stayed in the stable-house of a Houyhnhnm family and learned to subsist on oaten cake and milk. The Houyhnhnms were horrified to learn from Gulliver that horses in England were used by Yahoo-like creatures as beasts of burden. Gulliver described England to his host, much to the candid and straightforward Houyhnhnm's mystification. Such things as wars and courts of law were unknown to this race of intelligent horses. As he did in the other lands he visited, Gulliver attempted to explain the institutions of his native land, but the friendly and benevolent Houyhnhnms were appalled by many of the things Gulliver told them.

Gulliver lived in almost perfect contentment among the horses, until one day his host told him that the Houyhnhnm Grand Assembly had decreed Gulliver either be treated as an ordinary Yahoo or be released to swim back to the land from which he had come. Gulliver built a canoe and sailed away. At length he was picked up by a Portuguese vessel. Remembering the Yahoos, he became a recluse on the ship and began to hate all mankind. Landing at Lisbon, he sailed from there to England. But on his arrival the sight of his own family repulsed him; he fainted when his wife kissed him. His horses became his only friends on earth.

GUY MANNERING

Type of work: Novel
Author: Sir Walter Scott (1771-1832)
Type of plot: Historical romance
Time of plot: Eighteenth century
Locale: Scotland
First published: 1815

Principal characters:
COLONEL GUY MANNERING, a retired army officer
JULIA MANNERING, his daughter
CAPTAIN BROWN, a soldier
LUCY BERTRAM, an orphan girl
CHARLES HAZLEWOOD, Lucy's suitor
SIR ROBERT HAZLEWOOD, his father
GILBERT GLOSSIN, holder of the Bertram property
DIRK HATTERAICK, a smuggler
MEG MERRILIES, a gipsy
DOMINIE SAMPSON, tutor to the Bertram children

Critique:

Certainly one of the greatest abilities of Sir Walter Scott was his flair for making people seem real, especially those drawn from the lower social ranks. No doubt his human touch was based on his own genuine love for people of all walks of life. In *Guy Mannering*, this familiarity with the ways and foibles of human nature is evident throughout. His peasants, tradesmen, and outcasts are not too ignorant or coarse to have fine sensibilities. Indeed, it was the loyalty of the old gipsy, Meg

Merrilies, which was primarily responsible for the happy outcome of this novel. Through these people Scott gave his readers an appreciation of the real values of life.

The Story:

Guy Mannering, a young English gentleman traveling in Scotland, stopped at the home of Godfrey Bertram, Laird of Ellangowan, on the night the first Bertram child, a boy, was born. Mannering, a student of astrology, cast the horoscope of the newborn babe and was distressed to find that the child's fifth, tenth, and twenty-first years would be hazardous. The young Englishman puzzled over the fact that the boy's twenty-first year would correspond with the thirty-ninth year of the girl Mannering loved, which was the year the stars said would bring her death or imprisonment. An old gipsy, Meg Merrilies, also predicted danger for the new baby. Mannering, not wishing to worry the parents, wrote down his findings and presented them to Mr. Bertram, first cautioning him not to open the packet until the child had passed by one day his fifth birthday. Then he departed.

Young Harry Bertram grew steadily and well. He was tutored and supervised by Dominie Sampson, a teacher and preacher retained by his father; and at times the child was also watched over by the gipsy Meg, who had great love for the boy. The child was four years old when the laird became a justice of the peace and promised to rid the countryside of gipsies and poachers. After he had ordered all gipsies to leave the district, old Meg put a curse on him saying that his own house was in danger of being as empty as were now the homes of the gipsies. On Harry's fifth birthday the prediction came true, for the boy disappeared while on a ride with a revenue officer hunting smugglers. The man was killed and his body found, but there was no trace of the child. All search proving futile, he was at last given up for dead. In her grief, his mother, prematurely delivered of a daughter, died soon afterward.

Seventeen years passed. Old Mr. Bertram, cheated by his lawyer, Gilbert Glossin, was to have his estate sold to pay his debts. Glossin planned to buy the property without much outlay of money, for the law said that when an heir was missing a purchaser need not put up the full price, in case the heir should return and claim his inheritance. Before the sale Guy Mannering returned and tried to buy the property, to save it for the Bertram family, but a delay in the mails prevented his effort and Glossin got possession of the estate. Old Mr. Bertram died before the transaction was completed, leaving his daughter Lucy homeless and penniless.

During these transactions Mannering's past history came to light. Years before he had gone as a soldier to India and there married. Through a misunderstanding he had accused his wife of faithlessness with one Captain Brown, who was in reality in love with Mannering's daughter, Julia. The two men fought a duel and Brown was wounded. Later he was captured by bandits, and Mannering assumed that he was dead. When Mannering's wife died eight months later, the unhappy man, having learned she had not been unfaithful, resigned his commission and returned with his daughter to England.

On learning that he could not buy the Bertram estate and allow Lucy to remain there with the faithful Dominie Sampson, Mannering leased a nearby house for them. He also brought to the house his daughter Julia, after he learned from friends with whom she was staying that she had been secretly meeting an unknown young man. What Mannering did not know was that the man was Captain Brown, who had escaped from his bandit captors and followed Julia to England and later to Scotland. Both Julia and Lucy were unhappy in their love affairs. Lucy loved Charles Hazlewood, but since Lucy had no money Charles' father would not permit their marriage.

Captain Brown, loitering near the house, met old Meg Merrilies, who took a great interest in him. Once she saved his life, and for his thanks made him promise to come to her whenever she sent for him. A short time later Brown encountered Julia, Lucy, and Charles Hazlewood. Charles, thinking Brown a bandit, pulled a firearm from his clothing. In his attempt to disarm Charles, Brown accidentally discharged the weapon and wounded Charles. Brown fled.

Charles would have made little of the incident, but Glossin, desiring to gain favor with the gentry by whom he had been snubbed since he had bought the Bertram property, went to Sir Robert Hazlewood and offered to apprehend the man who had shot his son. Glossin, finding some papers marked with the name of Brown, used them in his search. He was momentarily deterred, however, when he was called to interview a prisoner named Dirk Hatteraick. Dirk, a Dutch smuggler, was the killer of the revenue officer found dead when the Bertram heir disappeared. Dirk told Glossin that the boy was alive and in Scotland. Because Glossin had planned that kidnaping, many years before, it was to his advantage to have the young man disappear again. He was even more anxious to get rid of the Bertram heir forever when he learned from Dirk that the man was Captain Brown. Brown —or Harry Bertram— would claim his estate, and Glossin would lose the rich property he had acquired for almost nothing. Glossin finally captured Brown and had him imprisoned, after arranging with Dirk to storm the prison and carry Brown off to sea, to be killed or lost.

Old Meg, learning of the plot in some mysterious way, foiled it when she had Harry Bertram rescued. She also secured Mannering's aid in behalf of the young man, whom she had loved from the day of his birth. Bertram was taken by his rescuers to Mannering's home. There his story was pieced together from what he remembered and from the memory of old Dominie Sampson. Bertram could hardly believe that he was the heir to Ellangowan and Lucy's brother. His sister was overjoyed at the reunion. But it would take more than the proof of circumstances to win back his inheritance from Glossin. Mannering, Sampson, and Sir Robert Hazlewood, who heard the story, tried to trace old papers to secure the needed proof.

In the meantime old Meg sent Bertram a message reminding him of Brown's promise to come should she need him. She led him into a cave where Dirk was hiding out and there told him her story. She had kidnaped him for Dirk on the day the revenue officer was murdered. She had promised Dirk and Glossin, also one of the gang, not to reveal her secret until the boy was twenty-one years old. Now she felt released from her promise, as that period had passed. She told Bertram to capture Dirk for the hangman, but before the smuggler could be taken he shot the old gipsy in the heart.

Dirk, taken to prison, would not verify the gipsy's story, and his sullenness was taken as proof of Bertram's right to his inheritance. Glossin's part in the plot was also revealed, and he too was put into prison to await trial. When the two plotters fought in the cell, Dirk killed Glossin. Then Dirk wrote a full confession and cheated the hangman by killing himself. His confession, added to other evidence, proved Bertram's claim, and he was restored to his rightful position. Successful at last in his suit for Julia Mannering, he settled part of his estate on his sister Lucy and so paved the way for her marriage with Charles Hazlewood. The predictions had come true; Mannering's work was done.

GUY OF WARWICK

Type of work: Poem
Author: Unknown

Type of plot: Chivalric romance
Time of plot: Tenth century
Locale: England, Europe, the Middle East
First transcribed: Thirteenth century

Principal characters:

GUY, a knight of Warwick
FELICE LA BELLE, Guy's mistress
HERHAUD OF ARDERN, Guy's mentor and friend
ROHAUD, Earl of Warwick
OTOUS, Duke of Pavia
MORGADOUR, a German knight
REIGNIER, Emperor of Germany
SEGYN, Duke of Louvain
ERNIS, Emperor of Greece
LORET, Ernis' daughter
THE SOUDAN OF THE SARACENS
TIRRI, a knight of Gurmoise
ATHELSTAN, King of England
COLBRAND, a Danish giant

Critique:

Guy of Warwick was penned by more of an anthologist than a poet. Undoubtedly French in origin, this metrical romance is made up of episodes from earlier romances, epics, and sagas. The story was frequently rewritten throughout the Middle Ages, later reprinted in many languages, immortalized in a play in 1620, and even adapted into a popular children's adventure story in the nineteenth century. In order to learn of all of Guy of Warwick's adventures, the reader would need to consult the earlier French poems, the English epics, the Irish translations, innumerable exempla, and patches of many other heroic poems and related legends. The best edition of the work is by the late scholar Julius Zupitza (1844-1895), who collated the very early Auchinleck manuscript (believed to have been written 1330-1340) with the most complete manuscript, now preserved in Caius College, Cambridge (c. 1400).

The Story:

It was love for a woman that prompted Guy to inaugurate his long series of remarkable exploits. Guy, son of the steward to Rohaud, Earl of Warwick, was a very popular and handsome young squire. As the earl's principal cupbearer, he was instructed, on one fateful occasion, to superintend the service of the ladies during dinner. Gazing on Felice la Belle, Rohaud's beautiful and talented daughter, he fell desperately in love with the fair maiden. When he first declared himself to her, he was rejected because of his lowly birth and lack of attainments. Later, however, when from lovesickness he was close to death, Felice, following the advice of an angel, offered him some encouragement. If he became a knight and proved his valor, she would reward him with her hand in marriage.

After receiving knighthood, Sir Guy set out to prove his valor. Accompanied by his mentor, Herhaud of Ardern, he spent an entire year attending tournaments throughout Europe. Pitted against some of the most renowned knights of Christendom, Guy was indomitable; in every encounter he took the prize. His reputation now established, he returned to Warwick to claim his reward from Felice. This fair lady, however, had decided to raise her standards. After acknowledging his accomplishments, she notified him that he must become the foremost knight in the world before she would marry him.

True to the laws of chivalric love, Guy returned to Europe to satisfy the fancy of his mistress. Again visiting the tournaments, again he was, without exception, victorious. But misfortune awaited him in Italy. His high merit having excited their envy, seventeen knights, led by Otous, Duke of Pavia, laid an ambush for the English champion. Before Guy won the skirmish, two of his closest companions were dead, and his best friend, Herhaud, appeared to be slain. As Guy, himself grievously wounded, began his return journey to England, he was filled with remorse for having allowed the wishes of a haughty lady to lead him to this sad result; but in Burgundy, where he was performing his customary deeds of valor, his spirits were considerably improved by his discovery of Herhaud, alive and disguised as a palmer.

As the two friends continued their journey homeward, they learned that Segyn, Duke of Louvain, was being attacked by Reignier, the Emperor of Germany, who wrongfully claimed the duke's lands. Assembling a small army, Guy defeated two armies that were sent against Segyn. With a larger force, the emperor then encircled the city in which Guy, Segyn, and their followers were quartered. During this blockade Reignier, on a hunting trip, was surprised by Guy, who led the unarmed emperor into the city. There, in the true spirit of chivalry, a rapprochement was brought about between the ruler, Reignier, and his vassal, Segyn.

Soon after rendering these good services to Segyn, Guy found another occasion for the exercise of his talents. Learning that Ernis, Emperor of Greece, was besieged by the mighty forces of the Saracen Soudan, Guy levied an army of a thousand German knights and marched to Constantinople. Received with joy, he was promised for his efforts the hand of Princess Loret, the emperor's daughter. After repelling one Saracen attack, Guy

took the offensive and left on the field fifteen acres covered with the corpses of his enemies. But his greatest threat came from one of his own knights, Morgadour, who had become enamored of Loret. Knowing that the Soudan had sworn to kill every Christian who should fall within his power, Morgadour duped Guy into entering the enemy camp and challenging the Saracen monarch to single combat. Ordered to be executed, the resourceful Guy cut off the Soudan's head, repelled his attackers, and made his escape.

The emperor, because of his great admiration for the English knight, hastened arrangements for the wedding of Guy and Loret. Guy, somehow having forgotten Felice, was agreeable to the plan, until, seeing the wedding ring, he was suddenly reminded of his first love. A true knight, he resolved to be faithful to Felice and to find some excuse for breaking his engagement to Loret. Another altercation with Morgadour ended with Guy's slaying of the treacherous German. Using the pretext that his continued presence in the court might lead to trouble between the Greeks and Germans, Guy took his leave.

Guy planned an immediate return to England, but he was destined to perform further deeds of knight errantry before being reunited with his beloved Felice. While traveling through Lorraine, he met an old friend, Sir Tirri, who was being persecuted by their mutual enemy, Duke Otous. The duke had abducted Tirri's fiancée. Guy wasted no time in rescuing the girl, but Otous did not give up easily. After attempting and failing to defeat Guy on the battlefield, he resorted to foul means and succeeded in capturing both Tirri and his fiancée. Guy, combining trickery with valor, killed the felon duke and freed the lovers.

Just one more incident delayed Guy's return to England. Unintentionally entering the game preserve of the King of Flanders, he was confronted by the king's son and found himself compelled to kill the dissentious prince. In an ensuing encounter with the wrathful father, Guy was forced to slaughter fourteen knights before he could make his escape. Arriving in his native country, Guy, in accordance with chivalric practice, repaired to the court of King Athelstan. He was honorably received, and almost immediately the king enlisted his services to kill a troublesome dragon. After a long and fierce battle, Guy in triumph carried the monster's head to the king.

Guy's homecoming was the less joyous upon his learning of the death of his parents, but this sorrow was compensated for by his immediate marriage to Felice. They were married only forty days, barely time to conceive a son, when Guy's conscience, troubled over the mischief he had done for the love of a lady, forced him on a penitential pilgrimage. His bereaved wife placed on his finger a gold remembrance ring and sorrowfully watched him depart for the Holy Land.

So great a warrior, however, could not escape his reputation or his duty. He interrupted his devotions to kill an Ethiopian giant and to assist Tirri again, this time by slaying a false accuser.

When the pious warrior returned to England he found King Athelstan besieged by King Anlaf of Denmark. It had been agreed that the outcome of the war should be determined by single combat between Colbrand, a Danish giant, and an English champion. In a dream King Athelstan was advised to ask the help of the first pilgrim he met at the entrance of the palace, and the aging Guy of Warwick was that pilgrim. In this last and most famous of his fights Guy, shorn of his weapons, appeared certain of defeat. In his extremity he snatched up a convenient ax, fiercely assailed the giant, cut him to pieces, and thereby saved the English kingdom.

Guy paid one last visit to his own castle, where he discovered Felice engaged in acts of devotion and charity. Without having revealed his identity to her, he went off to the forests of Ardennes. When death was near, he dispatched the gold remembrance to his wife and begged her to supervise his burial. Arriving in time to receive his last breath, the faithful Felice survived him by only fifteen days. She was buried in the same grave as her warrior husband.

GUZMAN DE ALFARACHE

Type of work: Novel
Author: Mateo Alemán (1547-1613?)
Type of plot: Picaresque romance
Time of plot: Sixteenth century
Locale: Spain and Italy
First published: 1599, 1604

Principal characters:
    GUZMÁN DE ALFARACHE, a rogue
    A MULETEER
    A COOK
    A CAPTAIN OF SOLDIERS
    DON BELTRAN, Guzmán's uncle
    A CARDINAL
    A FRENCH AMBASSADOR
    SAYAVEDRA, another rogue and Guzmán's friend
    GUZMÁN'S FIRST WIFE
    GUZMÁN'S SECOND WIFE
    SOTO, a galley prisoner

To readers of Alemán's own day *The Life and Adventures of Guzmán de Alfarache* was a book much more popular than Cervantes' *Don Quixote*, its contemporary. Thirty editions of the novel appeared within six years of its publication and its vogue quickly spread to France and England, where in 1622 James Mabbe translated it into English under the appropriate title of *The Rogue*. Alemán's novel, published in two parts in 1599 and 1604, is typically Spanish: realistic, comic, often coarse. As in other picaresque narratives, Guzmán de Alfarache travels extensively and moves from the highest ranks of society to the lowest, all the while living by his wits and commenting freely on the follies and vices of mankind. Yet Guzmán is not wholly bad; his career is forced upon him by the realization that in his own world he must either trick or be tricked. Being young and high-spirited, he chooses the first course. What sets *Guzmán de Alfarache* apart from other examples of the picaresque novel, however, is the writer's use of philosophical and moralizing digression. Alemán loses no opportunity to comment on human character or behavior, and in his discursive passages he reveals his own outstanding qualities: frankness, pessimism, broad humor, wit, humility of faith, and practical common sense. It is unfortunate that many modern readers have found his discourses dull or distracting. Viewed as their author intended them, they provide a reading of life itself, an obbligato accompaniment to a story which is, in narrative outline and in character drawing, one of the best and most diverting of the picaresque romances.

The Story:

The ancestors of Guzmán de Alfarache lived in Genoa, upstart noblemen who had grown rich in trade. Like others of his family, Guzmán's father was a dealer on the exchange, resorting even to usury in order to add to his wealth, although he piously heard mass every morning and owned a rosary with beads as large as hazelnuts. His love of money led him into his greatest adventure, for when a partner in Seville became bankrupt and carried away some of the money belonging to Guzmán's father, the Genoese took ship for Spain in an attempt to recover some of his lost property. On the way the ship he sailed in was captured by Moorish pirates and the merchant was sold into slavery in Algiers. Seeing no other way out of his difficulty, he embraced the faith of Allah and so was able to marry a rich Moorish widow. Secretly, he took possession of her money and jewels and fled with them to Seville. There, after some time, he found his former partner, recovered most of his debt, made his peace with the Church, and settled down to live the life of a gentleman, trading in money for his profit and gambling for his pleasure.

Being prosperous at the time, he bought two estates, one in town, the other at San Juan de Alfarache. One day he saw the mistress of an old knight and fell in love with her. The lady was not unwilling to share her favors between her two lovers, so that Guzmán could say in later life that at the time of his birth he had possessed two fathers. When the old knight died, the woman carried away all his property and a short time later married Guzmán's true father. The merchant did not long survive, but died a bankrupt, impoverished by his gambling and love of rich living. Left penniless, Guzmán decided to seek his fortune elsewhere. Calling himself Guzmán de Alfarache, after his father's country estate, he started out at fourteen to see the world.

Unused to walking, he soon tired and slept supperless that night on the steps of a church not far from Seville. The next morning his way led him to a wretched inn, where the hostess cooked him a breakfast omelet of eggs filled with half-hatched chicks. He ate the mess ravenously, but before he had traveled a league from the inn he became violently ill. A passing muleteer laughed heartily when Guzmán told his story and in his glee he invited the boy to ride with him. As they rode along the muleteer told how the hostess of the inn had tried the same trick on two lively young fellows who had rubbed her face in the omelet and daubed her with soot.

Meanwhile Guzmán and the muleteer had found two friars by the roadside. Since they were on their way to Caçalla, they were willing to hire two of the carrier's mules. That night the travelers stopped at a village inn where the landlord fed them a freshly-killed young mule instead of veal. The next morning, after discovering the deception, Guzmán and the muleteer threw the whole inn into an uproar. During the confusion two alcaldes appeared and took the rascally landlord into custody. Guzmán and the muleteer left the town in great haste.

Some distance beyond the village they were overtaken by several constables looking for a page who had stolen from his master. Mistaking Guzmán for the page, they seized him, and when the muleteer tried to interfere they bound him as well. After the prisoners had been severely beaten, the constables, convinced of Guzmán's innocence, allowed the travelers to continue on their way. To help Guzmán and the carrier to forget their aching bones, one of the priests told the romantic story of Ozmin and Daraxa, a tale of the Moorish wars.

By the time the story ended they were in sight of Caçalla, where they parted company. For Guzmán's transportation and lodging the muleteer demanded more than the boy could pay. The two friars decided at last upon a fair price, but the reckoning left Guzmán without enough money to buy his dinner that day.

Hungry but ashamed to beg, Guzmán took the road to Madrid. For a time he followed two travelers in the hope that they would offer him some of their dinner when they stopped to eat, but they ignored him. A poor Franciscan friar came by, nowever, and shared with the boy his loaf of bread and piece of bacon. That night an innkeeper gave Guzmán a bed in a stable and the next morning hired him to feed the horses of the guests. Guzmán soon learned to cheat in measuring oats and straw. Deciding at last that the life was too lazy for him, he left the inn and started once more for Madrid.

His coppers soon spent, he was forced to beg, but with such poor luck that it was necessary for him to sell the clothes off his back in order to live. By the time he reached Madrid he looked like a scarecrow. Unable to find work because of his poor appearance, he fell in with some beggars who taught him knavery of all kinds.

For a time he became a porter, hiring himself to carry provisions which purchasers had bought at market. In this way he met a cook who persuaded him to turn scullion. Like the other servants, Guzmán learned to steal from his master. One day he took a silver goblet. His mistress, discovering the loss, gave him money to buy another like it. Guzmán returned the goblet and kept the money, which he soon lost at cards. He continued his petty thefts until his master caught him selling provisions and cuffed him out of the house. Then he went back to carrying baskets in the market. Among his customers was a trusting grocer who one day put into his basket more than twenty-five hundred gold reals. Escaping through side streets, Guzmán fled into the country, where he lay hidden until the hue and cry had died down. With his riches he planned to visit his father's kinsmen in Genoa.

When he thought the coast clear, Guzmán headed for Toledo. On the way he fell in with a young man from whom he bought an outfit of clothing. Freshly attired, he lived like a young gentleman of fortune. He had little luck in his gallantries, however, and his love intrigues always ended with his being fleeced or made ridiculous by ladies he courted. He left Toledo with few regrets when he heard that a constable was looking for a young man recently arrived from Madrid.

At Almagro, Guzmán found a company of soldiers on their way to Italy. Hoping to leave his past troubles behind him, he enlisted. Before long he became the captain's crony, and the two spent their nights in gaming and wenching. Finding himself without funds, Guzmán resorted to his old habits of roguery; at the same time he was reduced to serving the captain who had formerly treated him as an equal. The captain was perfectly willing to profit by Guzmán's wits. In Barcelona they gulled a miserly old jeweler. Guzmán took to him a gold reliquary of the captain's and offered it for sale. After much haggling they agreed upon a price of one hundred and twenty crowns and the jeweler promised to bring the money to the dock. When Guzmán had the coins in his hand, he cut the strings which held the reliquary around his neck and handed the jewel to the old man. Then, after passing the money to a confederate, he shouted that the jeweler was a thief. Because the strings of the reliquary had been cut, and no money was found on Guzmán's person, his story was believed. Guzmán and the captain kept both the money and the jewel.

Having no further use for Guzmán's services, the captain decided to abandon the rogue after the soldiers arrived in Genoa. Turned loose with a single coin, Guzmán applied to his rich relatives for aid. But they refused to receive him and gave him only curses and blows. Don Beltran, his uncle, did take the boy into his house, but only for the purpose of setting the servants on him and having them toss him in a blanket until he was shaken and bruised. The next morning, swearing revenge on his deceitful relative, Guzmán started for Rome.

There he turned professional beggar and lived by his wits, having learned how to make bones appear disjointed and to raise false sores that resembled leprosy or ulcers. Only once was he beaten for his mendacity. One day a kind-hearted cardinal noticed an evil-looking ulcer on Guzmán's leg. Out of pity he had the beggar taken to his own house and given medical attention. The doctor summoned to attend him soon discovered Guzmán's trick, but he kept silent in order to mulct some of the prelate's gold. The sore cured, Guzmán became a page in the cardinal's household. There he lived daintily enough, but he was unable to refrain from stealing conserves and sweetmeats kept in a chest in the cardinal's chamber. Caught when the lid of the chest fell on his arm, trapping him, he received a beating. Even then the cardinal did not discharge him, but at last the churchman could stand his thieving and gambling no longer and Guzmán was dismissed.

His next employment was in the household of the French ambassador, to whom he was page, jester, and pimp, a rascal whose boisterous pranks helped to clear the ambassador's table of parasites who abused the Frenchman's hospitality. The ambassador, planning an intrigue with the wife of a Roman gentleman, made Guzmán his go-between. Learning that the page had seduced her maid, the matron determined to teach him and his master a lesson. One night, while he waited for her answer to the ambassador, she allowed Guzmán to stand for hours in a drenching rain. Blundering about in the darkness of a backyard, he fell into a pigsty. The next day, dressed in his best, he went to complain to his sweetheart about his treatment. While he was strutting before her, a boar escaped from its pen, ran between his legs, and carried him through the muddy streets of Rome.

Guzmán became the laughingstock of the town. One day, as some urchins were taunting him, another young man came to his assistance. He and his rescuer, a waggish young Spaniard named Sayavedra, became close friends. Anxious to escape ridicule, Guzmán decided to go to

Siena to visit a friend named Pompevo. While he tarried in Rome to make his farewells, he sent his trunks on ahead. Great was his dismay when he arrived in Siena and learned that his trunks, filled with clothing, money, and jewels, had been stolen. Sayavedra had preceded him to Siena, passed himself off as Signor Guzmán, and with his confederates made off with the real Guzmán's valuables. After a search Sayavedra was arrested, but the stolen property could not be recovered; it had passed into the hands of a rich thief-master named Alexandro Bentivoglio. Making the best of a bad situation, Guzmán refused to bring charges against the wretched Sayavedra.

Since his guest was low in funds, Pompeyo proved only an indifferent host, and at last Guzmán decided to go to Florence. Not far from Siena he overtook Sayavedra again. When the thief begged for pardon, Guzmán was filled with pity for the rascal and readily forgave him. Together they planned to have Guzmán pass as the nephew of the Spanish ambassador, Sayavedra as his page. Being without shame, they played on the credulity of all whom they met in Florence. Guzmán was about to marry a rich young widow when a beggar whom he had formerly known revealed the impostor's true identity, and he and his page were forced to flee the city.

They went next to Bologna, where Guzmán began a suit to recover his property from Bentivoglio. For his pains he was thrown into jail, from which he was released, penniless again, only after he had withdrawn his charges. Aided by Sayavedra, Guzmán cheated two men at cards, and with the money he won they traveled to Milan. In that city they entered into a conspiracy to defraud a wealthy merchant. Although he himself was arrested as a swindler, Guzmán convinced the city officials of the merchant's dishonesty, and a large sum of money gained by their scheme lined the rogues' pockets once more.

About that time Guzmán devised a plan to revenge himself on his Genoese relatives. Arriving in that city, he let it be known that he was Don Juan de Guzmán, a gentleman of Seville, recently come from Rome. Not recognizing the young beggar whom they had cuffed and insulted several years before, his relatives outdid themselves to honor their wealthy kinsman. On the pretext that a Castilian gentlewoman of his acquaintance was to be married, he borrowed jewels from Don Beltran to dress the bride, giving in security two trunks which the old man believed filled with silver plate. Pretending to be temporarily out of funds, he also secured a large loan from a cousin in return for a spurious gold chain. Then, having taken passage with a trusted sea captain, he and Sayavedra sailed for Spain. During the voyage Guzmán was greatly grieved when his friend became delirious with fever and jumped overboard.

Not wishing to tarry in Barcelona, Guzmán went to Saragossa. There he courted an heiress until the jealousy of her other admirers and his unwise dalliance with her kitchenmaid caused him to leave that city and go to Madrid. Eventually he married, only to learn too late that his wife's father was without a fortune. Before long Guzmán himself was declared a bankrupt and imprisoned. His wife died of shame. Disgusted with the world, he decided to study for the Church.

Shortly before he was to take orders he met a handsome woman who became his second wife. They returned to Madrid, where the wife attracted the attentions of so many wealthy men that for a time their affairs prospered, but in the end they were publicly disgraced and banished. From Madrid they went to Seville. Guzmán's mother they found still alive but stricken in years. There he lived by his wits in a household of quarrelsome women until his wife did him a great favor and ran away with an Italian sea captain. A short time later he and his mother parted in friendly fashion. Later, with the help of a gullible friar, Guzmán became steward to a gentlewoman whose husband was in the Indies. Old habits were too strong for him, and he began to rob his mistress. His thefts being discovered, he was sentenced to the galleys for life.

Because of his smooth tongue and pleasant ways, he was able to make himself a favorite with the officers, thereby arousing the jealousy and hate of his fellow prisoners. When several of them robbed him, the theft was discovered and the culprits were flogged. A short time later the captain's kinsman was robbed, and Guzmán, accused by another prisoner named Soto, was beaten until he was almost dead. Guzmán was soon to have his revenge. Discovering Soto's plot to seize the ship and escape to the African coast, he revealed the plan to the captain. Soto and the chief conspirators were executed. The grateful captain struck off Guzmán's chains and gave him full liberty aboard the galley while awaiting the pardon which had been petitioned of the king. Guzmán, repenting the rogue's life he had led, resolved to mend his ways in the future.

HAJJI BABA OF ISPAHAN

Type of work: Novel
Author: James Morier (1780-1849)
Type of plot: Picaresque romance
Time of plot: Early nineteenth century
Locale: Persia
First published: 1824

> *Principal characters:*
> HAJJI BABA, a rogue
> OSMAN AGHA, a Turkish merchant
> ZEENAB, a slave girl

Critique:

The Adventures of Hajji Baba of Ispahan is a combination of travel book and rogue story, and it does for Persia very much what Le Sage's *Gil Blas* did for Spain. Persia, even in this day of broad travel, has never been widely viewed by Americans. Moreover, the Persia of the time of Napoleon Bonaparte was a Persia that has now disappeared. Customs and manners are as much a part of Morier's entertaining narrative as the picaresque humor of Hajji Baba's adventures and the satire of the rogue's shrewd comments on human nature.

The Story:

Hajji Baba was the son of a successful barber of Ispahan. By the time he was sixteen he had learned the barber's trade, as well as a store of bazaar tales and quotations from the Persian poets. With these he entertained the customers who came to his father's shop, among them a wealthy Turkish merchant named Osman Agha, who was on his way to Meshed to buy goatskins of Bokhara. So taken was this merchant with Hajji Baba that he begged the young man to accompany him on the journey. With his father's blessing and a case of razors, Hajji Baba set out with his new patron.

Before the caravan had been many days on its way it was attacked by a band of Turcoman robbers. Osman Agha had prudently sewed fifty gold ducats in the skullcap under his turban, but when the caravan was captured he was stripped of his finery and the skullcap was tossed in a corner of the robber chief's tent. The robbers spared Hajji Baba's life when they learned he was a skilled barber, and he became a favorite of the

1199

wife of the chief. One day he persuaded the foolish woman to let him borrow Osman Agha's cap. He ripped the gold pieces from the lining and hid them, against the time when he might escape from his captors. Osman Agha had been sold to some camel herders.

Hajji Baba traveled with the robbers on their raids throughout the region. One of these raids was on Ispahan itself, from which the robbers carried away a rich booty. But at the division of the spoils, Hajji Baba got only promises and praise.

One day the robbers encountered the armed escort of a Persian prince. When the others fled, Hajji Baba gladly allowed himself to be taken prisoner by the prince's men. They mistook him for a Turcoman, however, and cruelly mistreated him, stripping him of his clothes and his hidden gold. When he complained to the prince, the nobleman sent for the guilty ones, took the money from them, and then kept the gold himself.

Hajji Baba went with the prince and his train to Meshed, where he became a water vendor, carrying a leather bag filled with dirty water which he sold to pilgrims with assurances that it was holy water blessed by the prophet. With money so earned, he bought some tobacco which he blended with dung and then peddled through the streets of the holy city. His best customer, Dervish Sefer, introduced him to other dervishes. They applauded Hajji Baba's shrewdness and enterprise and invited him to become one of their number. But one day a complaint was lodged against him on account of the bad tobacco he sold, and the authorities beat his bare feet until he lost consciousness. Having in the meantime saved a small amount of money, he decided to leave Meshed, which seemed to him an ill-omened city.

He set out on his way to Teheran. On the road a courier overtook him and asked him to read some letters the messenger was carrying. One was a letter from a famous court poet, commending the bearer to officials high at court. Hajji Baba waited until the courier was fast asleep, took the messenger's horse, and rode away to deliver the courier's letters. Through these stolen credentials he was able to obtain a position of confidence with the court physician.

Hajji Baba remained with the physician, even though his post brought him no pay. He soon found favor with Zeenab, the physician's slave, and sought her company whenever he could do so without danger of being caught. Then the shah himself visited the physician's establishment and received Zeenab as a gift. Hajji Baba was disconsolate, but he was soon made happy by a new appointment, this time to the post of sub-lieutenant to the chief executioner of the shah. Again he received no pay, for he was supposed to get his money as other members of the shah's entourage did, by extortion. It was soon discovered that Zeenab was in a condition which could only be regarded as an insult to the shah's personal honor, and Hajji Baba was summoned to execute the girl. Soon afterward suspicion fell on him for his own part in the affair, and he fled to the holy city of Koom.

In Koom he pretended to be a priest. The shah made a pilgrimage to the city, and during his visit the chief priest presented Hajji Baba's petition to the ruler. Hajji Baba explained that he had acted in all innocence because he had no idea of the high honor to be conferred upon Zeenab. The shah reluctantly pardoned Hajji Baba and allowed him to return to Ispahan.

He arrived to discover that his father had died and that his fortune had disappeared. Hajji Baba sold his father's shop and used the money to set himself up as a learned scribe. Before long he found service with Mollah Nadan, a celebrated priest, who planned to organize an illegal but profitable marriage market. Hajji Baba was supposed to find husbands for women the mollah would provide. When Hajji Baba visited the three women for whom he was supposed to find husbands, he discovered them all to be ugly old hags, one the wife of his former master, the physician, who had recently died. Later, Hajji Baba discovered his first master, Osman Agha, who had finally escaped from the Turcomans and regained some of his fortune. Hajji Baba tricked Agha into marrying one of the three women.

Mollah Nadan undertook to gain favor by punishing some Armenians during a drought, but he incurred the shah's wrath and he and Hajji Baba were driven from the city. Mollah Nadan's property was confiscated. Hajji Baba stole back into the city to see if any of the mollah's property could be saved, but the house had been stripped. He went to visit the baths, and there he discovered Mollah Bashi, who had been taken with a cramp and had drowned. Hajji Baba was afraid that he would be accused of murder, as Mollah Bashi had helped to bring about Mollah Nadan's ruin. But the slave attendant failed to recognize Hajji Baba in the darkness and Hajji Baba escaped, dressed in the mollah's robes. On the horse of the chief executioner he set out to collect money owed to Mollah Bashi. In the clothes of the mollah and riding a fine horse, he cut a dashing figure until he met Mollah Nadan and was persuaded to change robes with him. Mollah Nadan was arrested and charged with the death of Mollah Bashi. Hajji Baba, who had kept the money he had collected, decided to become a merchant.

He encountered the caravan of the widow of Mollah Bashi. She was taking her husband's body to Kerbelai for holy burial. When the leader of the caravan revealed that Hajji Baba was suspected of the murder, he began to fear for his life. But about that time a band of marauders attacked the caravan, and in the confusion Hajji Baba escaped. In Bagdad he reëncountered his old master, Osman Agha, and with him proceeded to invest the money he had available. He bought pipe sticks and planned to sell them at a profit in Constantinople.

There a wealthy widow sought him out and he decided to marry her, first, however, intimating that he was as wealthy as she. He married her and began to live on her income. But his old bazaar friends, jealous of his good luck, betrayed him to his wife's relatives. Thrown out as an imposter, he was obliged to seek the help of the Persian ambassador. The ambassador advised him not to seek revenge upon his former wife's relatives, as they would surely murder him in his bed. Instead, he found use for Hajji Baba in an intrigue developing among representatives of England and France. Hajji Baba was employed as a spy to find out what the foreign emissaries sought in the shah's court.

Here at last Hajji Baba found favor. He discovered that his life among cutthroats and rogues had admirably fitted him for dealing diplomatically with the representatives of foreign countries, and he was finally made the shah's representative in his own city of Ispahan. He returned there with considerable wealth and vast dignity, to lord it over those who had once thought his station in life far below their own.

HAKLUYT'S VOYAGES

Type of work: Travel narratives
Author: Richard Hakluyt (c. 1553-1616)
Type of plot: Adventure and exploration
Time of plot: c. 517 to 1600
Locale: The known world
First published: 1589

Critique:

This work is an anthology of the explorations and travels of British adventurers down to the author's own time. The accounts are bold and vigorous, usually giving only the main events of the journeys, many of them written by the men who made the voyages. Published by Hakluyt in refutation of a French accusation that the English were insular and spiritless, the book is of value in several lights. It gives faithful accounts of many sixteenth-century exploratory journeys; it is an index to the temper of Elizabethan England; and it reflects the enthusiasm for travel literature which was so prevalent at the time of the original publication.

The Stories:

The first group of voyages give thirty-eight accounts of travel and exploration made by Britons up to the end of the sixteenth century. The first stories go back to the medieval ages, for the narrative which begins the work is that of a probably mythical voyage by King Arthur of Britain to Iceland and the most northern parts of Europe in 517.

The first ten narratives deal with voyages made before 1066, the year of the Norman Conquest. They include such journeys as the conquest of the isles of Man and Anglesey by Edwin, King of Northumberland, in 624, the trips of Octher into Norway and Denmark in 890 and 891, the voyage of Wolstan into Danish waters in the tenth century, the voyage of King Edgar, with four thousand ships, about the island of Britain, and the journey of Edmund Ironside from England to Hungary in 1017.

The other voyages described are those taken after the Norman Conquest. The first of these is an account of a marvelous journey made by a company of English noblemen to escort the daughter of King Harold to Russia, to marry the Duke of Russia in 1067. The next account is of the surprising journey of an unknown Englishman who traveled as far into Asia as Tartaria in the first half of the thirteenth century.

One notable voyage describes the adventures of Nicolaus de Linna, a Franciscan friar, to the northern parts of Scandinavia. The twenty-second voyage was that of Anthony Jenkinson who traveled to Russia from England in order to return Osep Napea, the first ambassador from Muscovia to Queen Mary of England, to his own country in 1557.

Surprisingly, almost half of the journeys described in this first collection are those made to Russia by way of the Arctic Ocean, around northern Scandinavia. It is not ordinarily realized that there was any traffic at all between England and Russia at that time, because of the difficulty of both water and land transportation between the two countries.

The final narrative of the first group tells of the greatest event of Elizabethan England, the meeting of the British fleet with the great Armada which Philip II of Spain had sent to subdue England and win for Spain the supremacy of the seas.

The second group of voyages describe trips taken to the region of the Straits of Gibraltar and the countries surrounding the Mediterranean Sea. Eleven of these accounts describe trips made before the Norman Conquest in 1066 and fifty-two describe trips made after that date. The earliest story is that of Helena, the wife of a Roman emperor and a daughter of Coelus, one of the early kings of Britain. Helena, famous as the mother of Constantine the Great, who made Christianity the official religion of Rome, traveled to Jerusalem in 337 because of her interest in the early Christian church. She built several churches there and brought back to Europe a collection of holy relics. One of the relics was a nail reputed to be from the True Cross. It was incorporated some time later into the so-called Iron Crown of Lombardy.

Another voyage which took place before the Norman Conquest was that of a man named Erigena, who was sent by Alfred, King of the West Saxons, to Greece. Alfred was one of the most cultured of British kings in pre-medieval times and very much interested in the classic civilizations. His emissary, Erigena, went as far as Athens in 885, a long voyage for those ancient times.

Several of the post-Conquest voyages were trips made by Englishmen to help in the recovery of Jerusalem from the Saracens during the Crusades. Among the best known are those of Richard the First, often called the Lion-Hearted, and of Prince Edward, son of Henry III, who went to Syria in the last half of the thirteenth century.

Another story is a narrative of the voyage of the English ship, *Susan,* which took William Hareborne to Turkey in 1582. Hareborne was the first ambassador sent by a British monarch to the ruler of Turkey, who was at that time Murad Khan.

Another interesting voyage was that of Ralph Fitch, a London merchant. Between the years 1583 and 1591 he traveled to Syria, to Ormuz, to Goa in the East Indies, to Cambia, to the River Ganges, to Bengala, to Chonderi, to Siam, and thence back to his homeland. It was rare for people to travel, even in the spice trade, as far as did merchant Fitch during the sixteenth century.

A third group of voyages are accounts connected with the exploration and discovery of America. The first account is of a voyage supposedly made to the West Indies in 1170 by Madoc, the son of Owen Guined, a prince of North Wales. It is also recorded that in February of 1488 Columbus offered his services to Henry VII of England and petitioned that monarch to sponsor a voyage to the westward seas for the purpose of discovering a new route to the East Indies.

Bartholomew, brother of Columbus, repeated the request a year later, but was refused a second time by the English king.

Several voyages described are those made to America for the purpose of discovering a Northwest Passage to the Orient. The early voyage of Cabot is among them, as well as the voyages of Martin Frobisher and John Davis. Frobisher made three voyages in search of the Northwest Passage, in the three successive years between 1576 and 1578. John Davis also made three fruitless efforts to find the passage in the years from 1585 to 1587. All of these were an important part of the colonial effort in Hakluyt's own time.

Several exploratory trips to Newfoundland and the Gulf of the St. Lawrence River are also related, the earliest the voyage of Sir Humfrey Gilbert to Newfoundland. The ship *Grace* of Bristol, England, also made a trip up the Gulf of St. Lawrence, as far as Assumption Island. There are also accounts of trips made by explorers of other European nations in the New World, such as the journeys made in Canada as far as Hudson's Bay by Jacques Cartier in 1534 and 1535.

There are full accounts of all the voyages made to Virginia in the sixteenth century and the two unsuccessful attempts by Sir Walter Raleigh to found a colony there in 1585 and in 1587.

Another group of stories tell of both English and Spanish explorations of the Gulf of California. The voyage of Francis Drake is given, particularly that part of his around-the-world trip during which he sailed up the western coast of America to a point forty-three degrees north of the equator and landed to take possession of what he called Nova Albion, in the name of his monarch, Queen Elizabeth, thus giving the British a claim to that part of the New World.

Also described is a voyage taken under orders of the viceroy of New Spain by Francis Gualle. Gualle crossed the Pacific Ocean to the Philippine Islands, where he visited Manila. From there he went to Macao in the East Indies and to Japan, and returned from the Orient to Acapulco, Mexico, in the 1580's.

Another group of stories contain short accounts of trips by Englishmen to various parts of Spanish America. Among these were trips to Mexico City as early as 1555, barely a quarter of a century after it had been conquered by Cortez, as well as to the Antilles Islands in the West Indies, to Guiana, to the coast of Portuguese Brazil, to the delta of the Rio Plata, and to the Straits of Magellan.

Every schoolboy knows the stories of the first two voyages made to the Straits of Magellan and thence around the world, first by Magellan himself and then by Sir Francis Drake. The third man to sail through the Straits and then to proceed around the world is one of the forgotten men of history. Hakluyt gave the credit for this trip to Thomas Cavendish, an Englishman who circled the globe in the years 1586 to 1588.

THE HAMLET

Type of work: Novel
Author: William Faulkner (1897-   )
Type of plot: Psychological realism
Time of plot: Late nineteenth century
Locale: Mississippi
First published: 1940

Principal characters:
   WILL VARNER, chief property owner in Frenchman's Bend
   JODY, his son
   EULA, his daughter
   V. K. RATLIFF, a sewing machine salesman
   AB SNOPES, a newcomer to Frenchman's Bend
   FLEM SNOPES, his son
   ISAAC SNOPES, an idiot relative
   MINK SNOPES, another relative
   LABOVE, schoolteacher at Frenchman's Bend
   HENRY ARMSTID, a farmer

Critique:

Although more like a collection of long short stories than an integrated novel, this book displays Faulkner's genius in presenting the ironic humor in the folk legends of Mississippi. Yet Faulkner makes these tall tales, in spite of their definite locale, seem characteristic of almost any section of rural America. Some of the incidents are strung out over too many pages, but the author's skillful style carries them along successfully. He withholds the climax, the final irony of each episode, until the tale is fully exploited. In Flem Snopes, Faulkner has created one of his major characters—a man who is stubborn, arrogant, and ruthless in his drive for property and power.

The Story:

In his later years Will Varner, owner of the Old Frenchman place and almost everything else in Frenchman's Bend, began to turn many of his affairs over to his thirty-year-old son Jody. One day, while Jody sat in the Varner store, he met Ab Snopes, a newcomer to town, and Ab arranged to rent one of the farms owned by the Varners. Jody then found out from Ratliff, a salesman, that Ab had been suspected of burning barns on other farms where he had been a tenant. Jody and his father concluded that Ab's unsavory reputation would do them no harm. Jody became afraid, however, that Ab might burn some of the Varner property; as a sort of bribe, he hired Ab's son, Flem, to clerk in the store.

From Ratliff came the explanation of why Ab was soured on the world. Ab's principal grievance grew out of a horse-trading deal he once made with Pat Stamper, an almost legendary trader. Ab drove a mule and an old horse to Jefferson and, before showing them to Stamper, he skillfully doctored up the old nag. Stamper swapped Ab a team of mules that looked fine, but when Ab tried to drive them out of Jefferson the mules collapsed. To get back his own mule Ab spent the money his wife had given him to buy a milk separator. Stamper also forced him to purchase a dark, fat horse that looked healthy but rather peculiar. On the way home Ab ran into a thunderstorm and the horse changed from dark to light and from fat to lean. It was Ab's old horse, which Stamper had painted and then fattened up with a bicycle pump.

Will Varner's daughter, Eula, was a plump, sensuous girl who matured early. The new schoolteacher, Labove, fell in love with her the first day she came to the schoolhouse. An ambitious young man, Labove rode back and forth between Frenchman's Bend and the University, where he studied law and played on the football team. One day he attempted to seduce Eula after school had been dismissed; he failed and later was horrified to discover that Eula did not even mention the attempt to Jody. Labove left Frenchman's Bend forever.

As she grew older Eula had many suitors, the principal one being Hoacke McCarron, who literally fought off the competition. When the Varners found out that Eula was pregnant, McCarron and two other suitors left for Texas. Flem Snopes then stepped in, married Eula, and went off on a long honeymoon.

The Snopes clan which had gathered in the wake of Ab and Flem began to have troubles within the family. The idiot boy, Isaac, was neglected and mistreated; when he fell in love with a cow, his behavior became a town scandal. Mink Snopes, another relative, was charged with murdering Jack Houston, who had impounded Mink's wandering cattle. Flem stayed away from town throughout this trouble. When Mink was brought to trial, Flem, who might have helped him, ignored the whole case. Mink was sent to jail for life.

Flem came back from his honeymoon accompanied by Buck Hipps, a Texan, and a string of wild, spotted horses. The Texan arranged to auction off these horses to farmers who had gathered from miles around. To start things off, the Texan gave one horse to Eck Snopes, provided that Eck would make the first bid on the next one. At this point Henry Armstid and his wife drove up. Henry, in spite of his wife's protests, bought a horse for five dollars. By dark all but three of the horses had been sold, and Henry was anxious to claim his purchase. He and his wife were almost killed in trying to rope their pony. Hipps wanted to return the Armstids' money. He gave the five dollars to Henry's wife, but Henry took the bill from her and gave it to Flem Snopes. Hipps told Mrs. Armstid that Flem would return it to her the next day.

When the other purchasers tried to rope their horses, the spotted devils ran through an open gate and escaped into the countryside. Henry Armstid broke his leg and almost died. Eck Snopes chased the horse that had been given him and ran it into a boarding-house. The horse escaped from the house and ran down the road. At a bridge it piled into a wagon driven by Vernon Tull and occupied by Tull's wife and family. The mules pulling the wagon became excited and Tull was jerked out of the wagon onto his face.

The Tulls sued Eck Snopes for the damages done to Vernon and to their wagon; the Armstids sued Flem for damages to Henry and for the recovery of their five dollars. The justice of the peace was forced to rule in favor of the defendants. Flem could not be established as the owner of the horses, and Eck was not the legal owner of a horse that had been given to him.

One day Henry Armstid told Ratliff that Flem was digging every night in the garden of the Old Frenchman place, which Flem had acquired from Will Varner. Ever since the Civil War there had been rumors that the builder of the house had buried money and jewels in the garden. Henry and Ratliff took a man named Bookwright into their confidence and, with the aid of another man who could use a divining rod, they slipped into the garden after Flem had quit digging. After locating the position of buried metal, they began digging, and each unearthed a

bag of silver coins. They decided to pool their resources and buy the land in a hurry. Ratliff agreed to pay Flem an exorbitant price. At night they kept on shoveling, but they unearthed no more treasure. Ratliff finally realized that no bag could remain intact in the ground for thirty years. When he and Bookwright examined the silver coins, they found the money had been minted after the Civil War.

But Armstid, now totally out of his mind, refused to believe there was no treasure. He kept on digging, day and night. People from all over the county came to watch his frantic shoveling. Passing by on his way to Jefferson, Flem Snopes paused only a moment to watch Henry; then with a flip of the reins he drove his horses on.

HAMLET, PRINCE OF DENMARK

Type of work: Drama
Author: William Shakespeare (1564-1616)
Type of plot: Romantic tragedy
Time of plot: c. 1200
Locale: Elsinore, Denmark
First presented: 1602

Principal characters:
HAMLET, Prince of Denmark
THE GHOST, Hamlet's father, former King of Denmark
CLAUDIUS, the present king
GERTRUDE, Hamlet's mother
POLONIUS, a courtier
OPHELIA, his daughter
LAERTES, his son

Critique:

Whether *Hamlet* is considered as literature, as philosophy, or simply as a play, its great merit is generally admitted; but to explain in a few words the reasons for its excellence would be an impossible task. The poetry of the play is superb; its philosophy, although not altogether original with Shakespeare, is expressed with matchless artistry. The universality of its appeal rests in large measure on the character of Hamlet himself. Called upon to avenge his father's murder, he was compelled to face problems

of duty, morality, and ethics, which have been the concern of men throughout the ages. In Hamlet himself are mirrored the hopes and fears, the feelings of frustration and despair, of all mankind.

The Story:

Three times the ghost of Denmark's dead king had stalked the battlements of Elsinore Castle. On the fourth night Horatio, Hamlet's friend, brought the young prince to see the specter of his father, two months dead. Since his father's untimely death, Hamlet had been grief-stricken and in an exceedingly melancholy frame of mind. The mysterious circumstances surrounding the death of his father had perplexed him; then too, his mother had married Claudius, the dead king's brother, much too hurriedly to suit Hamlet's sense of decency.

That night Hamlet saw his father's ghost and listened in horror to what it had to say. He learned that his father had not died from the sting of a serpent, as had been supposed, but that he had been murdered by his own brother, Claudius, the present king. The ghost added that Claudius was guilty not only of murder but also of incest and adultery. But the spirit cautioned Hamlet to spare Queen Gertrude, his mother, so that heaven could punish her.

The ghost's disclosures should have left no doubt in Hamlet's mind that Claudius must be killed. But the introspective prince was not quite sure that the ghost was his father's spirit, for he feared it might have been a devil sent to torment him. Debating with himself the problem of whether or not to carry out the spirit's commands, Hamlet swore his friends, including Horatio, to secrecy concerning the appearance of the ghost, and in addition told them not to consider him mad if from then on he were to act queerly.

Meanwhile Claudius was facing not only the possibility of war with Norway, but also, and much worse, his own conscience, which had been much troubled since his hasty marriage to Gertrude. In addition, he did not like the melancholia of the prince, who, he knew, resented the king's hasty marriage. Claudius feared that Hamlet would take his throne away from him. The prince's strange behavior and wild talk made the king think that perhaps Hamlet was mad, but he was not sure. To learn the cause of Hamlet's actions—madness or ambition—Claudius commissioned two of Hamlet's friends, Rosencrantz and Guildenstern, to spy on the prince. But Ham-

let saw through their clumsy efforts and confused them with his answers to their questions.

Polonius, the garrulous old chamberlain, believed that Hamlet's behavior resulted from lovesickness for his daughter, Ophelia. Hamlet, meanwhile, had become increasingly melancholy. Rosencrantz and Guildenstern, as well as Polonius, were constantly spying on him. Even Ophelia, he thought, had turned against him. The thought of deliberate murder was revolting to him, and he was constantly plagued by uncertainty as to whether the ghost were good or bad. When a troupe of actors visited Elsinore, Hamlet saw in them a chance to discover whether Claudius were guilty. He planned to have the players enact before the king and the court a scene like that which, according to the ghost, took place the day the old king died. By watching Claudius during the performance, Hamlet hoped to discover for himself signs of Claudius' guilt.

His plan worked. Claudius became so unnerved during the performance that he walked out before the end of the scene. Convinced by the king's actions that the ghost was right, Hamlet had no reason to delay in carrying out the wishes of his dead father. Even so, Hamlet failed to take advantage of his first real chance after the play to kill Claudius. He came upon the king in an attitude of prayer, and could have stabbed him in the back. Hamlet did not strike because he believed that the king would die in grace at his devotions.

The queen summoned Hamlet to her chamber to reprimand him for his insolence to Claudius. Hamlet, remembering what the ghost had told him, spoke to her so violently that she screamed for help. A noise behind a curtain followed her cries, and Hamlet, suspecting that Claudius was eavesdropping, plunged his sword through the curtain, killing old Polonius. Fearing an attack on his own life, the king hastily ordered Hamlet to England in company with Rosencrantz and Guildenstern, who carried a warrant for Hamlet's death. But the prince discovered the orders and altered them so that the bearers should be killed on their arrival in England. Hamlet then returned to Denmark.

Much had happened in that unhappy land during Hamlet's absence. Because Ophelia had been rejected by her former lover, she went mad and later drowned. Laertes, Polonius' hot-tempered son, returned from France and collected a band of malcontents to avenge the death of his father. He thought that Claudius had killed Polonius, but the king told him that Hamlet was the murderer and even persuaded Laertes to take part in a plot to murder the prince.

Claudius arranged for a duel between Hamlet and Laertes. To allay suspicion of foul play, the king placed bets on Hamlet, who was an expert swordsman. At the same time, he had poison placed on the tip of Laertes' weapon and put a cup of poison within Hamlet's reach in the event that the prince became thirsty during the duel. Unfortunately, Gertrude, who knew nothing of the king's treachery, drank from the poisoned cup and died. During the contest, Hamlet was mortally wounded with the poisoned rapier, but the two contestants exchanged foils in a scuffle, and Laertes himself received a fatal wound. Before he died, Laertes was filled with remorse and told Hamlet that Claudius was responsible for the poisoned sword. Hesitating no longer, Hamlet seized his opportunity to act, and fatally stabbed the king. Then the prince himself died. But the ghost was avenged.

A HANDFUL OF DUST

Type of work: Novel
Author: Evelyn Waugh (1903-   )
Type of plot: Social satire
Time of plot: Twentieth century
Locale: England
First published: 1934

Principal characters:
    TONY LAST, owner of Hetton Abbey
    BRENDA LAST, his wife
    JOHN, their son
    MRS. BEAVER, an interior decorator
    JOHN BEAVER, her son
    JOCK GRANT-MENZIES, Tony's friend
    DR. MESSINGER, an explorer
    TODD, a half-caste trader who loved Dickens

Critique.

This novel, which portrays the decline of the English landed aristocracy, is full of foolish people who find their lives to be no more than "a handful of dust." The contrasts between the Gothic magnificence of Hetton Abbey, the lives of Brenda and Tony, and the aspirations of the successors to Tony's property, are effective instruments for bringing out the meaning of the story. The author writes finished dialogue; the narrative moves smoothly from beginning to end.

The Story:

John Beaver lived in London with his mother, an interior decorator. Beaver was a worthless young man of twenty-five who moved in the social circles of his mother's wealthy customers. He was not well liked, but he was often invited to parties and weekends to fill a space made vacant at the last moment.

One weekend Beaver was invited to Hetton Abbey by its young owner, Tony Last. Tony lived in the old Gothic abbey with his wife, Brenda, and his young son, John. It was Tony's dream that some day he would restore his mansion to its former feudal glory. Brenda was bored with her husband's attachment to the past, however; she found relief in her weekly trips to London.

Beaver's stay at Hetton Abbey was rather dull, but Brenda liked him and did her best to entertain him. On her next trip to London she saw him again and asked him to take her to a party. At first Beaver seemed reluctant; then he agreed to escort her.

Beaver and Brenda left the party early, creating some idle gossip. In a way, the gossipers were correct, for Brenda had definitely decided to have an affair with Beaver. She returned home to the unsuspecting Tony and told him that she was bored with life in the country. She said that she wanted to take some courses in economics at the university in London. Tony, feeling sorry for her, allowed her to rent a one-room flat in a building owned by Mrs. Beaver. Brenda moved to London and returned to Hetton Abbey only on weekends.

One day, when Tony went to London on impulse, he found that his wife already had engagements. He was forced to spend the evening getting drunk with his bachelor friend, Jock Grant-Menzies.

Tony's escapade bothered his conscience so much that when Brenda returned for the weekend she was able to persuade him to let Mrs. Beaver redecorate in modern style one of the rooms of the old house.

Brenda's conscience bothered her also. She tried to interest Tony in a girl she brought down for a weekend, but it was no use. He only wanted to have his wife back home. However, he still trusted her and suspected nothing of her intrigue in London.

Things might have gone on that way indefinitely if young John Last had not been killed by a horse while he was fox hunting. Tony sent Jock up to London to break the news to Brenda. At first Brenda thought that Jock was speaking of John Beaver's death, for he was out of town. When she learned the truth, she was relieved, realizing for the first time how much she cared for Beaver.

With young John dead, she felt that nothing held her to Tony any longer. She wrote, telling him everything, and asked for a divorce. Stunned, Tony could not believe that Brenda had been false to him. At last he consented to spend a weekend at Brighton with another woman to give her grounds for divorce.

Brenda's family was against the divorce and attempted to prevent it. Then, when they saw that the divorce would go through, they tried to force Tony to give Brenda more alimony than he had planned. He refused, for he could raise more money only by selling Hetton Abbey. The proposal angered him so much that he changed his mind about the divorce. He would not set Brenda free.

Tony, wishing to get away from familiar faces, accompanied an explorer, Dr. Messinger, on an expedition to find a lost city in the South American jungles. During the voyage across the Atlantic Tony had a short affair with a young French girl from Trinidad. But when she learned that he was married she would have nothing more to do with him.

Once the explorers had left civilization behind them, Tony found himself thinking of what was going on in London. He did not enjoy jungle life at all; insect bites, vermin, and vampire bats made sleep almost impossible.

When Negro boatmen had taken Tony and Dr. Messinger far up the Demarara River, they left the explorers in the hands of Indian guides. Then the expedition struck out into unmapped territory.

Meanwhile, back in London, Brenda no longer found Beaver an ardent lover. He had counted strongly on getting a considerable amount of money when he married Brenda; now Brenda could get neither the money nor a divorce.

Brenda began to grow desperate for money. She asked Mrs. Beaver for a job, but Mrs. Beaver thought that it would not look well for her to employ Brenda. A short time later Beaver decided to accompany his mother on a trip to California.

At last Tony and Dr. Messinger came to a river they believed must flow into the Amazon, and they ordered the Indians to build canoes. The Indians obeyed, but they refused to venture down the river. There was nothing for the white men to do but to continue the journey without guides. Soon after they set out Tony came down with fever. Dr. Messinger left him on shore and went on alone to find help, but the explorer drowned when his boat capsized. Tony in his delirium struggled through the jungle and came by chance to the hut of a trader named Todd, who nursed him back to health but kept him a prisoner. Tony was forced to read the novels of Dickens aloud to his captor. When some Englishmen came in search of Tony, the trader made them believe his captive had died of fever. Tony faced lifelong captivity to be spent reading over and over Dickens' novels to the illiterate half-caste, for no white man could travel in the jungle without native help.

Beaver left for California. Brenda knew that their affair was over. No news came from Tony in South America. Without his permission, Brenda could not draw upon the family funds.

Then Tony was officially declared dead, and Hetton Abbey became the property of another branch of the Last family. The new owner of Hetton Abbey bred silver fox. Although he had even fewer servants than his predecessor and had shut off most of the house, he still dreamed that some day Hetton Abbey would again be as glorious as it was in the days of Cousin Tony.

He erected a memorial to Tony at Hetton Abbey, but Brenda was unable to attend its dedication. She was engaged elsewhere with her new husband, Jock Grant-Menzies.

HANDLEY CROSS

Type of work: Novel
Author: Robert Smith Surtees (1803-1864)
Type of plot: Humorous satire
Time of plot: Nineteenth century
Locale: England
First published: 1843; enlarged 1854

Principal characters:
JOHN JORROCKS, a wealthy grocer
MRS. JORROCKS, his wife
BELINDA, his niece
PIGG, his huntsman
CAPTAIN DOLEFUL, a master of ceremonies

Critique:

Handley Cross is a fairly typical example of nineteenth-century English sporting tales. The novel contains little plot and little attempt at dramatic motivation, but to an enthusiastic fox hunter Handley Cross is fascinating because of its gusty hunting tales and the single-minded devotion of its characters to the sport. Jorrocks, appearing in a number of Surtees' works, is dear to devotees of the hard-riding, hard-drinking sporting set.

The Story:

For years Michael Hardy had been the leader of the hunt in Sheepwash

Vale. While he did not pay quite all the expenses of the sport, his personality and vigor kept fox hunting popular in the district. Michael was one of the old school; his hounds were unkenneled and boarded here and there, and the horses were mostly pickups. At his death it seemed that fox hunting could no longer be accounted an attraction in the county.

There were some other difficulties. The village of Handley Cross was rapidly growing. Having discovered by chance the curative values of the local spring, a reprobate physician named Swizzle had set up as a spa doctor, and in a few years Handley Cross became a fashionable watering place. Swizzle was a perfect doctor for many people. He invariably prescribed game pie and rare beef for his patients, and advised two quarts of port wine at dinner. He became a familiar sight in the village, as he buttonholed his patients on the street and inspected their coated tongues and gouty joints. With this new fame as a health resort hotels and souvenir stands sprang up to bring life to the sleepy village.

But there is no good proposition without competition. Another shady practitioner, a sanctimonious doctor named Mello, moved in. He bought land with a small spring on it, poured epsom salts in the water every night, and set up a rival establishment. In no time the town was divided into Melloites and Swizzleites. The important change, however, was in the social life of Handley Cross.

Captain Doleful, a lean, hypocritical half-pay captain, appointed himself master of ceremonies for the town. With the help of august Mrs. Barnington, the social arbiter of the fashionable set, balls and teas soon became popular and social eminence became the goal of the visiting gentry.

In a resort so fashionable it was unthinkable not to have a hunt club. Captain Doleful and some other worthies attempted to carry on after Michael

Hardy died, but their efforts were unsuccessful. For one thing, the leaders of the hunt rode in gigs, conveyances unthinkable in Hardy's day. In addition, the townspeople were too poor or too parsimonious to hire a whipper-in and a huntsman. Worst of all, subscribers to the hunt were often slow in paying; soon there were not enough funds to pay for damage done to crops and fences.

The fashionables decided that the only solution was a real master of the hunt, one not too elegant for a small spa but rich enough to pay the difference between subscriptions and expenses. A committee headed by Captain Doleful and the secretary Fleeceall decided to invite John Jorrocks, whose fame had spread far, to become master of the hunt. Accordingly a letter was sent, and the negotiations were soon brought to a conclusion, for Jorrocks was an easy victim.

After a life devoted to selling tea and other groceries, Jorrocks was a wealthy man. He had turned to hunting as a hobby, and in spite of his Cockney accent and ample girth, he was soon accepted in the field. Although he had the bad habit of selling cases of groceries to his fellow huntsmen, in Surrey Jorrocks soon became a fixture among the sporting set. Now, he was to be master in his own right. Captain Doleful secured a lodge for him, and the date was set for his arrival in Handley Cross.

On the appointed day, the four-piece band turned out and the whole town assembled at the station. Several of the villagers carried banners bearing the legend "Jorrocks Forever." When the train pulled in, Captain Doleful looked through the first-class section but found no Jorrocks. The second-class carriages produced no Jorrocks. Finally, on a flat car at the end of the train, he found Jorrocks and his family snugly sitting in their own coach with the horses already hitched. Loud were the cheers as the new hunt master drove through the streets of Handley Cross.

1211

Jorrocks was soon installed in his new lodging with Mrs. Jorrocks and Belinda, his pretty niece. Belinda added greatly to Jorrock's popularity.

The new hunt master looked over his kennels and the few broken-down hacks in the stable. Besides building up both the pack and the stud, he had to have a real huntsman. He finally hired Pigg, chiefly because his skinny shanks and avowed delicate appetite outweighed his speech of such broad Scots that few could understand what he said. Jorrocks was quickly disillusioned about his new huntsman. When Pigg ate his first meal in the kitchen, there was a great uproar. Hurrying in, Jorrocks found Pigg greedily eating the whole supper joint and holding the other servants at bay. And Pigg could drink more ale and brandy than Jorrocks himself.

Many were the fine hunts that winter. Because Pigg was skillful and Jorrocks persistent, the collection of brushes grew fast. One night Jorrocks was far from home, separated from his trusty Pigg and the pack, and caught in a downpour of rain. He turned into the first gate he saw and knocked. An efficient groom took his horse and two flunkies politely conducted the dripping Jorrocks to his room. On the bed were dry clothes, in the small tub was hot water, and on the table was a bottle of brandy. Jorrocks peeled off his clothes and settled into the tub. He had just started on his third glass of brandy when some one knocked. Jorrocks ignored the noise for a while but the knocker was insistent.

At last a determined voice from the hall demanded his clothes. Jorrocks quickly got out of the tub, put on the clothes which did not fit, and took a firm, possessive grip on the brandy bottle. Then he shouted forcefully that he would keep the clothes.

When Jorrocks came down to dinner, he was surprised to be told that he was in Ongar Castle. His unwilling host was the Earl of Bramber, whose servants had mistaken Jorrocks for an invited guest and by mistake had put him in the room of a captain. Jorrocks looked at the angry captain, who was wearing an outfit of his host. Only Jorrocks' Cockney impudence could have brazened out such a situation.

At last the company sat down to dinner. As usual, Jorrocks drank too much, and while giving a rousing toast to fox hunting he fell fast asleep on the floor He awoke immersed in water. Calling lustily for help, he struck out for the shore. When a flunky brought a candle, he saw that he had been put to bed in the bathhouse and that while walking in his sleep he had fallen into the small pool. But Jorrocks was irrepressible; in the morning he parted from the earl on good terms.

After a hard-riding winter, spring finally spoiled the hunting and the Jorrocks family left for London. Pigg stayed in Handley Cross to dispose of the dogs and horses. Captain Doleful bought Jorrocks' own mount for twenty-five pounds. When the horse became sick and died soon afterward, parsimonious Doleful sued Jorrocks for the purchase price. The court decided in favor of Jorrocks, holding that no one can warrant a horse to stay sound in wind and limb.

Jorrocks' business associates looked on his hunting capers as a tinge of madness. That fall Jorrocks was heard to exclaim in delight at the sight of a frostbitten dahlia; it would soon be fox hunting time. But at last Jorrocks was committed by a lunacy commission for falling victim to the fox hunting madness. In vain Jorrocks sputtered and protested; his vehemence only added to the charge against him. Poor, fat Jorrocks spent some time in an asylum before an understanding chancellor freed him. Luckily he regained his freedom before the hunting season was too far gone.

HANDY ANDY

Type of work: Novel
Author: Samuel Lover (1797-1868)
Type of plot: Comic romance
Time of plot: Nineteenth century
Locale: Ireland
First published: 1842

Principal characters:
ANDY ROONEY, a young Irish boy
SQUIRE EDWARD EGAN, his employer
MURTOUGH MURPHY, an attorney
SQUIRE GUSTAVUS O'GRADY, a rival landlord
EDWARD O'CONNOR, a gentleman and poet

Critique:

Written as a series of anecdotes published in twelve monthly installments, *Handy Andy* is not a cohesive novel insofar as plot is concerned. It is, on the other hand, excellent in character portrayal and atmosphere. The quality likely to hold the modern reader is its droll wit. Rich in Irish folkways, peppered with clever Irish tales, enhanced by Irish songs, *Handy Andy* is more than a series of tales revolving around a political issue, a stupid lout of a boy, and a lovable hero. Accused of flattering his countrymen, Lover replied that as an Irishman he was compelled to present his land as he saw it.

The Story:

Andy Rooney was, from the day he was born, a mischievous troublemaker. When he was old enough to work, his mother took him to Squire Egan of Merryvale Hall, who hired him as a stableboy. His literal mind and naïve ways frequently caused his superiors much agitation.

One day Squire Egan sent Andy to the post-office to get a letter. Thinking the postage unduly high, Andy stole two other letters in order to get his money's worth. The squire's letter was from Murtough Murphy, an attorney, and it concerned a forthcoming election for a county seat held by Sir Timothy Trimmer, who was expected to die before long. Murphy warned Egan that although he could be certain of most of the votes in the election, Squire O'Grady of Neck-or-Nothing Hall

was likely to support the Hon. Sackville Scatterbrain, another candidate. It happened that one of the purloined letters was addressed to Gustavus O'Grady. Peering through the envelope, Egan made out some unflattering words about himself. In anger he threw the letter into the fire. To cover up his error he burned the other letter also and then told Andy that he destroyed them to protect such a foolish gossoon from detection.

Andy could never get anything straight. When Squire Egan sent him on an errand to get a document from Murtough Murphy and Mrs. Egan sent him to the apothecary shop, Andy left Murphy's paper on the counter of the store and took up, instead, O'Grady's packet of medicine. The apothecary then unknowingly gave O'Grady the document from Murphy. On receiving O'Grady's medicine, Squire Egan was insulted and challenged Murphy to a duel. O'Grady, insulted at the contents of Murphy's legal document, challenged M'Garry, the apothecary. The matter was soon straightened out; Handy Andy fared the worst.

Edward O'Connor was a gallant cavalier. Well-educated and gifted as a poet, he was a favorite among the men of the community. He was in love with Fanny Dawson but had not declared himself as yet. A misunderstanding between Fanny's father and Edward had resulted in the young man's banishment from the Dawson house. After the quarrel Major Dawson maintained an intense dislike for the poet. Although she brooded over the absence of her lover, Fanny was forced to obey her father's wishes.

While walking one night, Andy, after stumbling over a man stretched out in the middle of the road, hailed a passing jaunting car. The driver, learning that the drunken man was his brother, stayed behind to care for him and asked Andy to drive his carriage. The passenger, Mr. Furlong, said he was on his way to visit the squire. Assuming that he meant Squire Egan, Andy took Furlong to Merryvale Hall. But Furlong had wanted to see O'Grady on election business. Egan, continuing to deceive the visitor, sent for Murphy, and the two men contrived to pump as much information from Furlong as they could.

When the truth was revealed, Furlong set out for Neck-or-Nothing Hall. There he met with more mischief. O'Grady was in a terrible mood, for he had discovered that the letter announcing Furlong's arrival had gone astray. The climax came when O'Grady's daughter Augusta happened into Furlong's room while he was dressing. A moment later O'Grady's knock at the door sent her hiding under the bed to avoid discovery. O'Grady caught her, however, and insisted that Furlong marry her.

The Hon. Sackville Scatterbrain arrived in time for the nomination speeches, a lively affair with a great deal of shouting and much merriment. On election day Egan supporters succeeded in irritating O'Grady, who had no sense of humor and plenty of temper. Thinking the crowd too boisterous, O'Grady aroused the people by sending for the militia. When he ordered the militia to fire into the angry mob, Edward O'Connor rode into the crowd to disperse it and prevent the militia from firing. Impressed by his bravery, the militia captain refused to fire. O'Grady then challenged O'Connor to a duel. O'Connor wounded O'Grady. When the Hon. Sackville Scatterbrain won the election, Squire Egan began a suit to dispute its result.

Larry Hogan, one of O'Grady's employees, had learned about the purloining of O'Grady's letter, which Squire Egan had burned, and he hoped to put his knowledge to use by intimidating the squire. One night Andy happened to overhear Larry, who was very drunk, talking about his scheme. Confused, Andy went to Father Phil, his confessor, for advice. It so happened that the priest was attending to the nuptials of Matty Dwyer and James Casey. At the wedding feast Casey failed to appear. Fearing that his daughter would be disgraced, Jack Dwyer asked if any of the guests present would marry Matty. Andy boldly offered himself and the marriage was performed. After the couple had been left alone in their new cottage James Casey arrived, accompanied by a hedge-priest who performed a second ceremony. Andy, protesting, was dragged outside and tied to a tree.

O'Grady died from the ill effects of the wound O'Connor had given him. Because the dead man had been deep in debt and unpopular in the community, his body was in danger of being confiscated. To prevent such an action, the family made two coffins; one, the true coffin, was to be buried secretly at night. O'Connor, stumbling upon the scene of the clandestine burial, was struck with remorse at his own deed, but young Gustavus O'Grady forgave his father's slayer, who in return pledged himself to lifelong friendship with Gustavus.

When a beggar warned Mrs. Rooney that someone was plotting to carry off her niece Oonah, Andy disguised himself as the young girl. Kidnaped, he was taken to Shan More's cave, where Andy's wild entreaties so aroused the pity of Shan More's sister Bridget that she took the distressed captive to bed with her. Discovering her error in the morning, Bridget lamented her lost honor, which Andy righted by marrying her. Too late Andy discovered that he really loved Oonah and that he had married a woman of bad reputation.

It was learned that Lord Scatterbrain, disguised as a servant named Rooney, had married Andy's mother, only to desert her before Andy's birth. After the death of the old nobleman—the Hon. Sackville Scatterbrain, his nephew, did not dispute the succession—Andy became his heir, with a seat in the House of Lords. Off to London he went to learn fine manners and to enjoy his new estate. Shan More and Bridget followed to demand a settlement for the deserted wife. To escape the vulgar and persistent pair, Andy gladly gave Bridget some money.

Major Dawson met with an accident which resulted in his death. With the major gone, all obstacles between Fanny Dawson and Edward O'Connor were removed, and O'Connor was finally able to enter the Dawson house and to marry his Fanny.

Shan More made an attempt upon Andy's life. When the attempt failed Andy went to Shan's den, where he found a wounded man, an escaped convict, who proved to be Bridget's true husband. Rid of his wife, Andy was free to marry Oonah.

HANGMAN'S HOUSE

Type of work: Novel
Author: Donn Byrne (Brian Oswald Donn-Byrne, 1889-1928)
Type of plot: Regional romance
Time of plot: Early twentieth century
Locale: Ireland
First published: 1925

Principal characters:
JAMES O'BRIEN, Lord Glenmalure, Jimmy the Hangman
CONNAUGHT, his daughter
DERMOT McDERMOT, a neighbor
THE CITIZEN, Dinny Hogan the Irreconcilable's son
JOHN D'ARCY, Dermot's cousin, Connaught's husband

Critique:

In *Hangman's House,* Donn Byrne intended to write an Irish novel for Irishmen, people for whom their own country was a passion. An intense love for Irish landscape, horse-racing, coursing, Gaelic balladry, hunting, and the writer's freedom-loving countrymen is evident throughout the book. When the novel appeared, critics may have preferred his *Messer Marco Polo* or *The Wind Bloweth,* but revised judgment is likely to put *Hangman's House* above the latter. The book was written in Dublin in 1922 and 1923, while the country was still being harried by the armed resistance of Republican irreconcilables. The state of Ireland at that time is presented in Byrne's

characterization of the Citizen, a splendid man who had direct control over those who wanted to fight for freedom. The novel has been dramatized for the stage and for motion pictures.

The Story:

Dermot McDermot lived in the most pleasant homestead in the County of Dublin. He was a serious, slight man of twenty-five, taking after his Quaker mother more than his Irish soldier father except in his intense love of Ireland and everything Irish.

Dermot's nearest neighbors were James O'Brien, Lord Glenmalure, and his daughter Connaught. They lived in a rather forbidding-looking house that the country people insisted on calling Jimmy the Hangman's House. James O'Brien had been a violent rebel in his youth, but he had found it to his advantage to make his peace with the English. Becoming Lord Chief Justice of Ireland, he was responsible for the hanging of many Fenians.

When Glenmalure was stricken on the bench, he was forced to retire. His condition becoming worse, he called in doctors from Dublin and then England. One told him that he would live a month, certainly no more than five weeks. Then he secretly sent off a letter to John D'Arcy, Dermot's cousin, son of an old friend called Tricky Mick. Dermot thought D'Arcy a twister; Connaught's father said he had merely made a youngster's mistake. Glenmalure knew John D'Arcy was devious but ambitious, and that he might make his way in politics with Connaught's money and Hangman Jimmy's backing. In the weeks remaining to him, Glenmalure made contacts for D'Arcy and then married him to Connaught. Glenmalure knew Dermot wanted to marry Connaught but would not leave his homestead; he thought Connaught, strong-willed as she was, could guide D'Arcy to a place in the world where she might even get a title.

Glenmalure had been a rebel of the old days, but there were still plenty of young men ready for a war for freedom if the word were given. Those who directed the movement decided there must be no war. They sent back to Ireland the Citizen, a commander of cavalry in the French army, but also the son of old Dinny Hogan the Irreconcilable, who had fled from Ireland and gone to live in France after the last uprising. The Citizen was to spend a year in Ireland, to make sure the young men would keep in line.

He had another reason for going to Ireland. John D'Arcy had married and then deserted his sister Maeve. Her shame caused her death and her son's, and their deaths brought on Dinny Hogan's. Dinny's son was out for revenge.

Glenmalure died the night of Connaught's wedding. She and D'Arcy returned from their honeymoon immediately.

Dermot saw them at the Tara Hunt, one of the best in the country. The Citizen also turned up at the hunt and approached D'Arcy to ask if he had been in Paris in '95. D'Arcy, after swearing that he had never been in Paris, went to the police to expose the Citizen. Connaught could not understand why D'Arcy had lied about being in Paris; she was furious when she heard that he had informed on a hunted man.

Dermot knew D'Arcy feared the Citizen but could not understand why. He also heard that things were not going well at Glenmalure, that Connaught kept a woman relative with her constantly, while D'Arcy spent his time gambling with people who would never have dared enter the house during Glenmalure's lifetime. D'Arcy's backers in politics had reneged after Glenmalure died, and D'Arcy was at loose ends.

On St. Stephen's Day the first steeplechase of the year was held at the Hannastown races. Connaught's Bard of Armagh was entered. Dermot heard that long odds were being placed on him, though the horse should have been considered the best in the field. One of the bookmakers told him that D'Arcy had placed a large bet against the Bard, but that there were many small bets on him that would spell disaster to the poor people if the Bard did not run. On the day of the race Connaught's jockey did not show up. Dermot rode the Bard and won. He and Connaught found D'Arcy sobbing afterward because he had lost heavily. Then Dermot knew his cousin was a weakling. That night D'Arcy killed the Bard.

Connaught left home and even the gamblers refused to play with a man who had killed a horse. Connaught, meanwhile, was miserable in England. Dermot looked for D'Arcy to straighten him out, to offer him money to go away if that seemed best. D'Arcy told him that he had married Maeve. Thinking D'Arcy had been married to Maeve when he married Connaught, Dermot thrashed him and would probably have killed him if an innkeeper had not interfered. Dermot gave D'Arcy money and told him to leave the country.

Connaught came home a short time later to a house of bitterness and gloom. After she and Dermot finally admitted they loved each other, Dermot sought out the Citizen to see if they might not work out some way to keep the shame of D'Arcy's conduct from staining Connaught and yet dissolve that marriage so that he and Connaught could be married. The Citizen told Dermot that Maeve had actually died before D'Arcy married Connaught, though D'Arcy could not have known it at that time. Dermot's hands were tied.

D'Arcy, hearing that Maeve was dead, came back to Glenmalure, and Connaught sought refuge with Dermot and his mother. D'Arcy, finding her there, accused Connaught and Dermot of being lovers. When they admitted their feelings, he threatened to hale them into court, but Dermot's mother prevented him. Connaught went again to England. Knowing that Connaught would do nothing to him, D'Arcy began to sell off all the possessions in the house. Dermot made arrangements in Dublin to be informed whenever those things came on the market and he bought up all of them. One night Dermot decided to pick some of Connaught's own roses and send them to her. As he went toward the house Glenmalure looked empty and forbidding. At the gate he met the Citizen, bent on killing D'Arcy. Dermot, not wishing the Citizen to be soiled with the murder of a twister like D'Arcy, tried to persuade him to go away. But the Citizen was determined. Dermot was afraid to let him go in alone.

Inside they found D'Arcy dressed for travel. The house had been stripped and there was a smell of oil in it. Instead of killing D'Arcy outright, the Citizen allowed himself to be persuaded to a duel with pistols. D'Arcy shot before the signal had been given and wounded the Citizen. Then he smashed a lamp on the floor and dashed upstairs. The lamp started a sheet of fire that swept through the house as Dermot and the Citizen fought their way outside. D'Arcy caught his foot while jumping from a window and was dead when he hit the ground.

Dermot's mother went to Connaught for a while. Dermot had the walls of Glenmalure torn down and a neat cottage built in its place. The Citizen, recovered from his wound, went back to his regiment. Then Connaught came home.

HARD TIMES

Type of work: Novel
Author: Charles Dickens (1812-1870)
Type of plot: Social criticism
Time of plot: Mid-nineteenth century
Locale: England
First published: 1854

Principal characters:
THOMAS GRADGRIND, a schoolmaster and a believer in "facts"
LOUISA GRADGRIND, his oldest daughter
TOM GRADGRIND, Louisa's brother
MR. BOUNDERBY, Louisa's husband, a manufacturer and banker

SISSY JUPE, a waif befriended by the Gradgrinds
MRS. SPARSIT, Bounderby's housekeeper
STEPHEN BLACKPOOL, Bounderby's employee
JAMES HARTHOUSE, a political aspirant

Critique:

This novel was Dickens' first story of outright social protest. Earlier works had contained sections of social criticism, but this was the first motivated entirely by the writer's feelings about contemporary British culture. The novel, appropriately dedicated to Thomas Carlyle, another critic of nineteenth-century British society, was based upon personal observations of life in Manchester, one of England's great manufacturing towns and the original for Dickens' Coketown. The story is loaded with the bitter sincerity of Dickens' dislike for the industrial conditions he found in his homeland. Unfortunately for the value of the novel as a social document, Dickens overdrew his portraits of the industrialists responsible for conditions he abhorred; his industrialists became sheer grotesques and monsters.

The Story:

Thomas Gradgrind, proprietor of an experimental private school in Coketown, insisted that the children under him learn facts and only facts. He felt that the world had no place for fancy or imagination. His own five children were models of a factual education. Never having been permitted to learn anything of the humanities, they were ignorant of literature and any conception of human beings as individuals. Even fairy tales and nursery rhymes had been excluded from their education.

One day, as he walked from the school to his home, Gradgrind was immensely displeased and hurt to find his two oldest children, Louisa and Tom, trying to peek through the canvas walls of a circus tent. Nor did it ease his mind to discover that the two youngsters were not at all sorry for acting against the principles under which they had been reared and educated. Later Gradgrind and his industrialist friend, Mr. Josiah Bounderby, discussed

possible means by which the children might have been misled from the study of facts. They concluded that another pupil, Sissy Jupe, whose father was a clown in the circus, had influenced the young Gradgrinds.

Having decided to remove Sissy Jupe from the school, they set out immediately to tell the girl's father. When they arrived at the inn where the Jupes were staying, they found that the clown-father had deserted his daughter. Gradgrind, moved by sentiment, decided to keep the girl in his home and let her be educated at his school, all against the advice of Bounderby, who thought Sissy Jupe would be only a bad influence on the Gradgrind children.

Years passed, and Louisa and young Tom grew up. Gradgrind knew that Bounderby had long wished to marry Louisa. She, educated away from sentiment, agreed to marry Bounderby, who was thirty years her elder. Tom, an employee in Bounderby's bank, was very glad to have his sister marry Bounderby; he wanted a friend to help him if he got into trouble there. In fact, he advised his sister to marry Bounderby for that reason, and she, loving her brother, agreed to help him by marrying the wealthy banker.

Bounderby himself was very happy to have Louisa as his wife. After his marriage he placed his elderly housekeeper in rooms at the bank. Mrs. Sparsit, disliking Louisa, was determined to keep an eye on her for her employer's sake. After the marriage all seemed peaceful at the bank, at the Gradgrind home, and at the Bounderby residence.

In the meantime Gradgrind had been elected to Parliament from his district. He sent out from London an aspiring young politician, James Harthouse, who was to gather facts about the industrial city of Coketown, facts which were to be used in a survey of economic and social life in Britain. In order to facilitate the young man's labors, Gradgrind had given him a letter of introduction to Bounderby, who immediately told Harthouse the story of his career from street ragamuffin to industrialist and banker. Harthouse thought Bounderby a fool, but he was greatly interested in pretty Louisa.

Through his friendship with Bounderby, Harthouse met Tom Gradgrind, who lived with the Bounderbys. Harthouse took advantage of Tom's love for drink to learn more about Louisa. Hearing that she had been subjected to a dehumanizing education, and feeling that she would be easy prey for seduction because of her loveless marriage to the pompous Bounderby, Harthouse decided to test Louisa's virtue.

Before long Harthouse gained favor in her eyes. Neither realized, however, that Mrs. Sparsit, jealous and resenting her removal from the comfortable Bounderby house, spied on them constantly.

Everyone was amazed to learn one day that the Bounderby bank had been robbed. Chief suspect was Stephen Blackpool, an employee whom Bounderby had mistreated. Blackpool, who had been seen loitering in front of the bank, had disappeared on the night of the robbery. Suspicion also fell on a Mrs. Pegler, an old woman known to have been in Blackpool's company.

A search for Blackpool and Mrs. Pegler proved fruitless. Bounderby seemed content to wait; he said that the culprits would turn up sooner or later.

The affair between Louisa and Harthouse reached a climax when Louisa agreed to elope with the young man. Her better judgment, however, caused her to return to her father instead of running away with her lover. Gradgrind, horrified to see what his education had done to

Louisa's character, tried to make amends for her. The situation was complicated by Mrs. Sparsit. She had learned of the proposed elopement and had told Bounderby. He angrily insisted that Louisa return to his home. Gradgrind, realizing that his daughter had never loved Bounderby, insisted that she be allowed to make her own choice. Harthouse, giving up all hope of winning Louisa, disappeared.

Mrs. Sparsit returned to act as Bounderby's housekeeper during Louisa's absence and tried to reinstate herself in Bounderby's confidence by tracing down Mrs. Pegler. To her chagrin, Mrs. Pegler turned out to be Bounderby's mother. Bounderby was furious, for his mother disproved his boasts about being a self-made man. Meanwhile Louisa and Sissy Jupe accidentally found Blackpool, who had fallen into a mine shaft while returning to Coketown to prove his innocence of the robbery. After his rescue he told that Tom Gradgrind was the real culprit. When the young man disappeared, his sister and father, with the help of Sissy Jupe, found him and placed him, disguised, in a circus until arrangements could be made for spiriting him out of the country.

Before he could escape, however, Bounderby's agents found Tom and arrested him. With the aid of the circus roustabouts he was rescued and put on a steamer which carried him away from the police and Bounderby's vengeance.

Mrs. Sparsit, who had caused Bounderby all kinds of embarrassment by producing Mrs. Pegler, was discharged from his patronage, much to her chagrin. Bounderby himself died unhappily in a fit a few years later. The Gradgrinds, all of them victims of an education of facts, continued to live unhappily, unable to see the human side of life.

HARMONIUM

Type of work: Poetry
Author: Wallace Stevens (1879-1955)
First published: 1923

In the case of Wallace Stevens the proper understanding of his early poems as a new dimension of poetic reality was for the most part an exercise in hindsight. This is not the same thing as saying that at any time in his career he lacked the attention of serious criticism or a body of appreciative, well-wishing readers, only that he was sometimes admired for the wrong reasons.

Harmonium was published in 1923, at a time when the French Symbolists—Baudelaire, Mallarmé, Verlaine, Rimbaud, Laforgue—were being assimilated as influences and models, and the Imagist movement had not yet run its course. Because Stevens exhibited the tangential imagery, elisions, and regard for symbolic order of the first group and the concentrated exactness of the second, most readers found little in his poetry to link it with the native tradition. Instead, they seized upon the exotic and ornate qualities of his verse as if these were its final effect rather than a means to an end. Stevens appeared to be, at first reading, a poet whose purity of vision and absolute integrity insulated him from the material concerns of his society. Eliot in England and Joyce in Paris occupied just such positions of isolation and authority. Closer home, the author of "Le Monocle de Mon Oncle," "The Comedian as the Letter C," and "Peter Quince at the Clavier" seemed to provide a similar image of the dedicated artist.

But Stevens, as it later developed, was neither a master of décor for decoration's sake—the literary dandy and Whistler in words, as some called him—nor the alienated poet such as the period demanded. An aesthetic-moral writer of the highest order, he had already in *Harmonium* charted those areas of experience and precept which were to comprise the whole body of his work: the re-creation of the physical world in bold and brilliant imagery, the relation of imagination to reality, the nature and function of art, the poet's place in modern society, problems of structure and style. Stevens was not a poet of growth but of clarification, and his later books merely ordered and refined his vision and techniques. Unlike most poets, who achieve only a temporary balance between temperament and environment, he created a total world for his imagination and his belief in the nourishing power of art. Perhaps the greatest service he provided was to show by example the possible in poetry if man is to find a source of imaginative faith in an age of disbelief or to establish once more a sustaining relationship with the world about him. *Harmonium* "makes a constant sacrament of praise" to poetry—the imaginative ordering of experience—as the supreme fiction.

The unmistakable signature of these poems is the richness of their diction, the use of words not common to English poetry, at least in these plain-speaking times, a parade of brightly colored images and startling turns of phrase. Such words as fubbed, coquelicot, barque, phosphor, gobbet, fiscs, clavier, pannicles, girandoles, rapey, carked, diaphanes, unburgherly, minuscule, ructive, shebang, cantilene, pipping, curlicues, and funest reveal the poet's delight in the unusual and the rare. But as R. P. Blackmur pointed out long ago, Stevens' poetic vocabulary was not chosen for affected elegance, coyness, or calculated obscurity. These words give an air of rightness and inevitability within the contexts that frame them; it is not the word itself but its relationship to other words in the poem that gives to Stevens' poetry its striking qualities of style. It is the same with his images, the strategic effectiveness of "barbaric glass," "poems of plums," "venereal soil," "golden quirks and Paphian caricatures," "rosy chocolate and gilt umbrellas," "oozing cantankerous gum," "women of primrose and purl," "the emperor of ice cream," in conveying a luxuriance of sense impressions. This diction of odd angles of vision and strange surfaces gives the impression of language revitalized as if it were the invention of the poet himself. It becomes a part of what Stevens once called "the essential gaudiness of poetry," and it is capable of a variety of effects, as the following examples show.

The mules that angels ride come slowly
    down
The blazing passes from beyond the
    sun.
            ("Le Monocle de Mon Oncle")

or:

Chieftain Iffucan of Azcan in caftan
Of tan with henna hackles, halt!
            ("Bantams in Pine-Woods")

or:

            . . . and not to think
Of any misery in the sound of the wind,
In the sound of the leaves,

Which is the sound of the land
Full of the same wind
That is blowing in the same bare place

For the listener, who listens in the
    snow,
And, nothing himself, beholds
Nothing that is not there and the noth-
    ing that is.
            ("The Snow Man")

Stevens' diction and imagery are not so much the verbalization of a mode of thought but in themselves a way of thinking. His poetry belongs to the order of solipsism, that philosophical theory which holds that the self is the only object of verifiable knowledge and that all things

are re-created in the image of man in the act of perceiving the world. In his best poems this is the effect toward which Stevens' floating images tend, so that from the world of his verse one emerges with altered perspective. There is in it a different way of seeing, a rearrangement of the familiar pattern of experience by which poetry is no longer a way of looking at life but a form of life. Thus his images point to a passionate drive toward material comfort and rich living, as opposed to spiritual sterility in a world of waste and excess. In *Harmonium* the poles of his world become "our bawdiness unpurged by epitaph" and "the strict austerity of one vast, subjugating, final tone." He is aware of tradition corrupted and a world fallen into disorder, a realization of man dispossessed of unity between himself and his universe, of nature violated, of old faiths gone. Out of his knowledge he writes these lines on a Prufrock theme:

In the high west there burns a furious
    star.
It is for fiery boys that star was set
And for sweet-smelling virgins close to
    them.
The measure of the intensity of love
Is measure, also, of the verve of earth.
For me, the firefly's quick, electric
    stroke
Ticks tediously the time of one more
    year.
And you? Remember how the crickets
    came
Out of their mother grass, like little
    kin,
In the pale nights, when your first
    imagery
Found inklings of your bond to all that
    dust.

For a secular poet like Stevens, poetry was to become the "supreme fiction" and the imagination "the one reality in this imagined world," a way of imposing order on the chaos of experience. This is the theme of "Anecdote of the Jar," one of the simplest but most meaningful of the poems in *Harmonium*:

> I placed a jar in Tennessee,
> And round it was, upon a hill.
> It made the slovenly wilderness
> Surround that hill.

Here is the desire to impose order on the wildness of nature and, indirectly, of the world. It is not the image of the jar that is of first importance in the poem, but the act of placing the jar on such an eminence that it commands the landscape, so that

> It took dominion everywhere.
> The jar was gray and bare.
> It did not give of bird or bush,
> Like nothing else in Tennessee.

Stevens puts Keats' Grecian urn to other uses than those of contemplation or revelation.

This "rage for order" is worked out in more elaborate detail in "The Comedian as the Letter C." A fable in six parts, the poem is Stevens' most ambitious work before "Notes Toward a Supreme Fiction" on the relation of imagination to reality and the poet's place and function in society. It is characteristic of his self-satire that he should picture the poet as a picaresque mountebank trying to reconcile imagination to actuality. In Part I, "The World without Imagination," Crispin the subjectivist sets sail upon the sea of life, to discover that the romantic imagination which has given him eminence within his own limited milieu is a world preoccupied with things and therefore lacking in imagination. Romanticism being equated with egotism, Crispin in the second section, "Concerning the Thunderstorms of Yucatan," decides that the only reality lies in the senses. His love for the exotic ends when he is brought to a realization of the overwhelming and destructive powers of nature. The third division, "Approaching Carolina," follows Crispin through a realm of the imagination, symbolized by moonlight that is the antithesis of the sun, which lights up reality. Turning from the moon as a mere reflection of reality, Crispin in Part IV, "The Idea of a Colony," enters a

new phase of art based on the community and regional ties. Disillusioned, he turns in Part V, "A Nice Shady Home," to domesticity, and like Candide he digs in his own garden; he will become a philosopher. Part VI, "A Daughter with Curls," deals with the final wisdom Crispin found in his return to earth:

> Crispin concocted doctrine from the rout.
> The world, a turnip once so readily plucked,
> Sacked up and carried overseas, daubed out
> Of its ancient purple, pruned to the fertile main,
> And sown again by the stiffest realist,
> Came reproduced in purple, family font,
> The same insoluble lump.

Art, Stevens implies, cannot be made this or that, or be pursued like a chimera; it exists, separate and complete, in its own substance and shape.

There are times when Stevens' search for some standard of ultimate reality and the forms that it may take in poetry leads him away from concrete particularities into the realm of abstract speculation. If he appears at times more concerned with meaning than with being, the reader may also recognize in his work the power of a contemplative writer who insists upon the need of discipline in life as in art. As a modern, he sees the gap between the potential and the actual; consequently he must try to uncover causes, to create a way of seeing that his readers may share.

Stevens himself achieves the supreme, fictive mood of contemplation and understanding in "Sunday Morning," his best poem and one of the great poems of the century. Here in the spectacle of a woman eating her late breakfast on a Sunday morning we have a picture of modern boredom and uncertainty. The woman sits in external sunlight but also in the moral darkness of an age that has lost faith in the spiritual nature of man: "Why should she give her bounty to the dead?" The poet's answer is that happiness lies in the perception of nature, which in its recurrent changes and seasons creates an immortality in which man may share.

> We live in an old chaos of the sun,
> Or old dependency of day and night,
> Or island solitude, unsponsored, free,
> Of that wide water, inescapable.
> Deer walk upon our mountains, and
> the quail
> Whistle about us their spontaneous
> cries;

> Sweet berries ripen in the wilderness;
> And, in the isolation of the sky,
> At evening, casual flocks of pigeons
> make
> Ambiguous undulations as they sink,
> Downward to darkness, on extended
> wings.

Harmonium reveals a poet of moral and humane temper. Stevens' poems, disciplined and perfectly articulated, reflect a limited but significant picture of the modern sensibility.

HARP OF A THOUSAND STRINGS

Type of work: Novel
Author: H. L. Davis (1896-   )
Type of plot: Historical-philosophical romance
Time of plot: Late eighteenth and early nineteenth centuries
Locale: The American prairie country, Tripoli, and Paris
First published: 1947

Principal characters:
MELANCTHON CRAWFORD,
COMMODORE ROBINETTE, and
APEYAHOLA, called Indian Jory, founders of a prairie town
JEAN-LAMBERT TALLIEN, a French revolutionist
THÉRÈSE DE FONTENAY, whom he loved
RENÉ DE BERCY, her fiancé
ANNE-JOSEPH THÉROIGNE, in love with de Bercy
MONSIEUR DE CHIMAY, a wealthy aristocrat and merchant

Critique:

Harp of a Thousand Strings is a novel linking the personalities and events of the French Revolution to the development of the American West. Behind this story of the naming of a prairie town lies the author's theory that the incidents of history are never final, that although they may change form or significance they continue to move like a slow groundswell from country to country among people who have been affected by history's erosions and accretions. History itself is the thousand-stringed harp of the title, an instrument capable of endless vibrations and echoes. In order to present his theme of the reverberations of history, the writer made his novel contrapuntal

in design. The American frontier, the Barbary wars, and the French Revolution are introduced briefly for thematic effect, later to be alternated and recombined. The pattern is one of triads. The three settings, America, Tripoli, and France; the three Americans, each corresponding to one of the drives in Tallien's career; the three choices Tallien must make and their consequences—all are essential to the craftsmanship and design of this unusual and rewarding historical novel.

The Story:

Old Melancthon Crawford had been one of the founders of a prairie town in the Osage country. In his last years his eccentricities became so marked that relatives had him sent back to his birthplace, a Pennsylvania village he had always hated, where they could keep an eye on him and the disposal of his property. After his departure on the eastbound stage Commodore Robinette and Apeyahola, a Creek Indian whom the settlers called Jory, climbed to the prairie swell where Crawford's trading post had stood. Talking about the past, they thought back to a decisive night the three had in common, a night when Tripoli was being bombarded by American naval guns during the war with Barbary pirates.

Under cover of the bombardment the three Americans, prisoners escaped from the pasha's dungeons, had taken refuge in a warehouse belonging to Thurlow and Sons, Boston merchants. Young Crawford was all for carrying away some loot he found in a storeroom, but Apeyahola and Robinette, the wounded sailor, were against the idea. During the argument Monsieur Tallien entered the warehouse. One-time Citizen President of the French National Convention, now an obscure consular official under Napoleon, he was there to keep an appointment with a Paris associate of Thurlow and Sons. To pass the time while waiting, he told the tale of his rise and eventual ruin because of his love for the notorious Thérèse de Fontenay. Crawford, Robinette, and the Indian made a strange audience. Tallien told his story, however, because he saw each young American marked by one phase of his own career: vengeance, ambition, love.

Jean-Lambert Tallien, protégé of the old Marquis de Bercy, was intended for a career in law. During a visit to the de Bercy estate he watched Anne-Joseph Théroigne being carried forcibly away because she had attracted the interest of René, the young marquis, soon to marry the lovely Countess Thérèse de Fontenay. While Tallien stood watching the disappearing cart that carried Anne-Joseph, René rode up with the countess

and haughtily ordered the student to open a gate. At Tallien's refusal the young nobleman raised his whip. Tallien struck the marquis' horse. The animal threw his rider and dragged him, unconscious and bleeding, by one stirrup.

Tallien hid in the woods while angry villagers hunted him with guns and pitchforks. Father Jarnatt, the parish priest, saved the fugitive and sent him off to Paris to seek his fortune in journalism. These things happened in the year the Bastille fell.

In Paris, Tallien again met Anne-Joseph Théroigne, by that time a roughtongued, rabble-rousing virago, the friend of Robespierre and members of the Jacobin Club. It was she who helped Tallien to establish L'Ami des Citoyens, the revolutionary newspaper with which he placarded Paris. Because of her he led the assault on the Tuileries during the August riots. Later he became a deputy to the National Convention and a commissioner to the provinces. Anne-Joseph helped his rise in public favor because she expected to find him useful. Still loving René de Bercy, she had secretly aided his escape to England. Through Tallien she hoped eventually to locate Thérèse de Fontenay, whom she hated.

A man and a woman muffled in native costume entered the warehouse. The man was Monsieur de Chimay, who had come ashore from a French ship to arrange some trade business with Tallien. The woman was not introduced. Since they could not leave the warehouse before the bombardment ended, Tallien continued his story.

One day he heard his name called from a cartload of prisoners. In the wagon was Thérèse de Fontenay, whom he had never forgotten. Hoping to protect her from Anne-Joseph's fury, he denounced the virago for her help to de Bercy and thrust her into an angry mob that stripped and beat her. The woman, never recovering from that brutal treatment, lived mad for many years.

1224

Thérèse was imprisoned in the Carmes. Through spies Tallien tried to take measures for her safety. At last, to save her life, he overthrew Robespierre and ended the Reign of Terror. Telling his story, he made it all sound simple; the others had to guess at the bribes, the promised reprisals, all the scheming of those three anxious days while he held prisoners the influential citizens of Paris and executed the *coup d'état* of Thermidor. Although he knew that Thérèse was involved in a plot for an émigré invasion, he married her later that year.

But choices made for her sake led to other choices that he neither expected nor wanted. Jealous of Captain Belleval, an officer attentive to Thérèse while she was in prison, he arranged to have the captain betrayed to the rebels of the Vendée. When the émigrés finally landed at Quiberon, all were captured. At the same time the peasant who had betrayed Belleval was taken prisoner. In his effort to save the peasant's life Tallien quarreled with General Hoche over the disposition of the other prisoners, and in the end he was forced to declare them enemies of the state and order their execution. Among those who perished was René de Bercy, who chose death with honor rather than accept Tallien's offer of escape to England.

When Tallien returned to Paris and told Thérèse, haltingly, what had happened, she said only that she knew at last what a life was worth. Months later Monsieur de Chimay arrived from London with some of de Bercy's keepsakes. De Chimay was in trade, an associate of the powerful Thurlow firm and a friend of Ouvrard, the influential banker who had become Thérèse's lover. Thérèse saw in the two men a power she could use to undermine that of her husband.

The shelling had ended; Tallien became silent. When he and de Chimay withdrew to transact their business, the woman gave the three Americans a case containing two pistols and a knife, each decorated with the crest of a hand holding a flower. For a moment she drew aside her veil and they saw the face of Thérèse de Fontenay. The Americans went out toward the harbor, each marked by a symbol of Tallien's defeat, but carrying with them also a memory of Thérèse's beauty.

Years later Robinette and Apeyahola, ragged and gaunt, were traveling overland from the Mississippi. Wanted by the authorities, the commodore because of an affair of gallantry in Spanish territory and for taking part in the Gutiérrez insurrection, Apeyahola for a murder in Georgia, they found carved on a tree the design of a hand holding a flower. That crest marked their trail to Crawford's trading post in the Indian country. There they stayed, philanderer, murderer, and thief. When the time came for them to name the village growing up around the old trading post, each remembered the woman they had seen briefly by candlelight in a dingy warehouse. So, out of the turmoil and blood of the French Revolution, Thérèse de Fontenay gave her name to a new town on the American prairie.

THE HARP-WEAVER AND OTHER POEMS

Type of work: Poetry
Author: Edna St. Vincent Millay (1892-1950)
First published: 1922

Ten years before she was awarded a Pulitzer prize for *The Harp-Weaver and Other Poems,* Edna St. Vincent Millay's first and best-known poem, "Renascence," appeared in *The Lyric Year,* an anthology of one hundred poems by as many poets. The Vassar undergraduate, Vincent Millay, as her family and friends then called her, scored a signal victory in her contribution to the anthology, the freer form and the liberal spirit of her work standing out against the stilted Victorian verse and sentimentality found in most of the selections.

"All I could see from where I stood," the first line of "Renascence," begins a poem as regular in meter, rhythm, and rhyme as those by her romantic predecessors. But the new hedonism and the sharp, almost brittle metaphors based on both land- and seascapes create a quite different effect. The pain of omniscience, the poet's burden, is the theme. The imagery is dazzling in its exalted movement to a sensuous climax in which life is celebrated through all the senses.

"Renascence" was a promise of things to come, for the personal lyric was Miss Millay's forte. Her sonnets and her ballads, held in such beautiful balance in *The Harp-Weaver,* are always exact in craftsmanship, capturing at times the innocence of childhood and the sadness of lost ecstasy.

The title poem, "The Ballad· of The Harp-Weaver," appearing at the end of the second section, brings into an almost medieval form saddened innocence and lyric tragedy. Written mostly in the traditional four-line ballad stanza with alternating rhymes, the poem varies subtly in meter and end-stopping to include occasional stanzas with a fifth line and shifting rhyme schemes.These last lines create the panic, the pain, and finally the exaltation of deep feeling. The narrative tells in the first person the story of a young boy of the slums living with his widowed mother who can do nothing to make a living and has nothing to sell except "a

harp with a woman's head nobody will buy." In a fifth line, "she begins to cry" for the starving boy. This was in the late fall; by the winter all the furniture had been burned and the boy can do no more than watch his school companions go by, for he has no clothes to wear. He is disturbed by his mother's attempts to comfort him, to dandle him on her knee while "a-rock-rock-rocking," and to sing to him "in such a daft way." The counterpoint of the harp with a woman's head and "a wind with a wolf's head" suggests the lingering pain after the first panic. The final exaltation, however, is remarkable. A mystical event occurs: the mother weaves clothes for the Christ child, just the size of her own boy, and perishes at the harp, "her hands in the harp strings frozen dead." This odd juxtaposition of the Madonna and the Magi themes with the dance of death demonstrates Miss Millay's versatility and expertness with language.

Part V of the volume, "Sonnets from an Ungrafted Tree," creates its effect by quite opposite methods. This sequence concerns a woman who prosaically watches her unloved husband die and then tries to pick up the empty pieces of her own unloving life He had befriended her in school. when she would have accepted anyone, by flashing a mirror in her eyes; after his death she has a flash of awareness that he had loved her deeply, though he was in no way remarkable in living or in loving. Whatever heat was in this strange body which slept and ate beside her is now gone, the whole unclassified. The impact of this fact makes of these 238 lines a taut though expressionistic drama in which the unreality of the death is emotionally heightened by the very real, familiar objects which express the widow's desolation.

These macabre themes do not go unrelieved in Miss Millay's book. The opening lyric is the keynote to the first part, and "My Heart, Being Hungry" connects this volume with the earlier "Renascence." The lean heart feeds on "beauty where beauty never stood," and "sweet where no sweet lies," symbolized by the smell of rain on tansy. She continues the theme of the bitter-sweet, light-dark, the opposites of nature which make of the humblest experience something like pain, a pain of sensitive awareness of the tears of things. Always, however, there is pure aesthetic pleasure gained from deep-felt realizations, of

A rock-maple showing red,
Burrs beneath a tree

even in deepest grief, she says in "The Wood Road." In spite of the world's negations, the positive things endure. "The Goose-Girl" summarizes this belief:

Spring rides no horses down the hill,
But comes on foot, a goose-girl still.
And all the loveliest things there be
Come simply, so, it seems to me.
If ever I said, in grief or pride,
I tired of honest things, I lied;
And should be cursed forevermore
With love in laces, like a whore
And neighbors cold, and friends unsteady,
And Spring on horseback, like a lady!

In the second section Miss Millay divides her poems between the goose-girl and the lady, the first poem, "Departure," reflecting both. The adolescent girl, busy with her sewing, is pensive, even in despair over half-felt longings:

It's little I care what path I take,
And where it leads it's little I care:
But out of this house, lest my heart break,
I must go, and off somewhere.

She indulges in the pleasant emotion of self-pity, of her dead body found in a ditch somewhere, an adolescent drama which is interrupted by her mother's friendly query, "Is something the matter, dear?" An old legend retold in "The Pond" presents a suicide who picked a lily before she drowned, a grasp even in death after the beautiful.

The extremely short third section con-

tains all these motifs and some strange new ones. "Never May the Fruit Be Plucked" extends the imagery of "My Heart, Being Hungry" to suggest that "He that would eat of love must eat it where it hangs," and that nothing tangible can be taken away forever. "The Concert" extends the internal monologue of the sewing girl, this time a new departure from rather than toward life and love. "Hyacinth," however, is something new and wonderfully strange:

I am in love with him to whom a hyacinth is dearer
Then I shall ever be dear.
On nights when the field-mice are abroad he cannot sleep:
He hears their narrow teeth at the bulbs of his hyacinths.
But the gnawing at my heart he does not hear.

This gnawing at the heart is at least a real emotion, while in "Spring Song" a modern nothingness has replaced the reawakening season. The refrains suggest that modern life has driven out spring with its "Come, move on!" and "No parking here!" The poem ends:

Anyhow, it's nothing to me.
I can remember, and so can you.
(Though we'd better watch out for you-know-who,
When we sit around remembering Spring).
We shall hardly notice in a year or two.
You can get accustomed to anything.

Part IV, the most conventional, is made up of twenty-two unrelated sonnets. These are rather academic in theme and tone, containing as they do echoes of Elizabeth Barrett Browning and John Keats. The first and last illustrate this point, though there are many sonnets in between which point to Miss Millay's individuality. In the first she prophetically reveals the sadness of life after the loss of a beloved. In the last she celebrates the glimpse of sheer beauty that was Eu-

clid's in the "blinding hour" when he had
his vision

> Of light anatomized. Euclid alone
> Has looked on beauty bare. Fortunate
> they
> Who, though once only and then but
> far away,
> Have heard her massive sandal set on
> stone.

The Harp-Weaver presents a poet with
vision unclouded by the didacticism which
mars some of her later work, for these
poems vibrate with an inner fervor that
needs no relationship to the political or
social scene.

HAVELOK THE DANE

Type of work: Poem
Author: Unknown
Type of plot: Adventure romance
Time of plot: Tenth century
Locale: England and Denmark
First transcribed: c. 1350

> *Principal characters:*
> HAVELOK, a prince
> GODARD, his guardian
> GOLDEBORU, a princess
> GODRICH, her guardian
> GRIM, a fisherman

Critique:

Medieval romances in general follow a
pattern, and *Havelok* is no exception. The
hero is noble, brave, and pure; the heroine
is noble, beautiful, and pure. There is a
convenient supernatural element which
helps along the plot. Virtue is rewarded
and villainy is punished. *Havelok,* in spite
of its adherence to the formula, is one of
the more interesting of the romances to
read, for it is reasonably concise and
coherent. Its spirit of adventure hardly
ever flags, and the plot is complicated
enough to produce some feeling of suspense.

The Story:

Athelwold was a good king. No one
dared offer him a bribe, and throughout
all England people were at peace. He was
a particular guardian to widows, children,
and innocent maidens. A messenger might
go peacefully from town to town with a
hundred pounds of gold in a sack. Athelwold's only heir was a young daughter,
still a baby.

When Athelwold knew that his death
was upon him, he prayed for guidance and
then summoned his earls and barons to
his side. There was loud lamenting at the
approaching end of their honored king.
But Athelwold's chief concern was for his
daughter's care. It was decided that
Godrich, Earl of Cornwall, would be the
most trustworthy to bring up the princess.
Godrich swore a great oath to safeguard
the infant Goldeboru and to hold her
lands in trust until she could reign.

But Godrich watched the growing girl
with envious eyes. She was fair to look
upon, and Godrich could not bear to think
of the day when she would be his sovereign. Acting then the part of a traitor, he
took her secretly from Winchester to
Dover and placed her in a remote castle.
To guard the entrance he set his most
trusted thanes with orders to let no one in
to see the princess.

In Denmark, King Birkabeyn lay near
death. He had reigned long and wisely,
but he was leaving his son Havelok and

his two little daughters without protection. He thought of his faithful friend, Godard, a rich man who was the most respected noble in the kingdom. Godard swore a great oath to guard the children well and to see that Havelok came into his inheritance when he became a man. After being shriven, Birkabeyn died content.

Godard was also a false-hearted traitor. On the seashore he cruelly slit the throats of the two tiny girls and then seized Havelok. The boy, terrified at what he had been forced to witness, begged for mercy. Instead of killing Havelok straightway, Godard called for Grim, a fisherman, and commanded him to bind the prince and cast him into the sea with an anchor around his neck. Anxious to please his lord, Grim seized the boy and bound him tightly. Then he took him home to wait for night.

As Havelok dozed on the rude bed in the fisherman's hut, a great light shone from his mouth. Grim's wife was frightened and called her husband. Grim, awed, freed Havelok from his bonds. Bundling his wife, his five children, and Havelok aboard his fishing boat, he set sail for England. The group went up the Humber to land in a likely cove. Since then the place has been called Grimsby.

For twelve years Havelok grew rapidly. He was an active boy and a prodigious eater. Luckily, Grim was a good fisherman, and he could trade his catches at the market in Lincoln. Corn and meat could be bought there, and ropes for the nets. Havelok, who helped Grim in all his labors was especially good at peddling fish.

A great famine came upon the north of England. The crops withered and the fish fled English shores. Day after day Grim's family became poorer. Havelok, touched by the suffering of his foster family, resolved to seek his fortune in Lincoln. Although he could ill spare it, Grim cut a cloak from new sailcloth for Havelok and wished him well. The prince set out for town with his new cloak, but he had neither shoes nor hose.

In the town Havelok starved for three days. No one would hire him and he could find no food. At length he heard a cry for porters. Looking quickly around, he saw the earl's cook with a catch of fish to carry. In his eagerness Havelok knocked down eight or nine other porters to get to the cook first. Strong as a bull, the youth carried the fish to the castle. The next day the cook cried again for a porter, and this time Havelok carried a huge load of meat.

In the castleyard the cook greatly admired the strong fellow. He gave Havelok bread and meat, as much as he could hold, and engaged him as a steady helper. Eating regularly and working hard, Havelok became widely known for his strength. On a certain feast day the retainers held a stone-putting contest. A group of men brought in a stone so huge one man could barely lift it. Havelok easily heaved it many yards.

Godrich, hearing of Havelok's fame, decided to use the youth in his scheme to gain control of the kingdom. Thinking him only a churl, Godrich had Goldeboru brought from Dover and ordered Havelok to marry her. Both young people objected, but Godrich had his way.

Havelok took his sorrowing bride back to Grim's cottage. That night the groom slept soundly but the bride stayed wakeful from shame at being mated to a churl. All at once a light issued from Havelok's mouth and a voice told Goldeboru of her husband's birth and destiny. Awaking Havelok, she advised him to go at once to Denmark to claim his throne.

In the morning Havelok persuaded the three Grim brothers to go with him on the trip to Denmark. Arriving in that land, the impoverished group met Ubbe, a noble who bought a ring from Havelok. Ubbe, greatly taken with Havelok and his beautiful bride, offered them a cottage for the night. The couple accepted gratefully, and soon were asleep after their long voyage.

In the night a band of robbers tried to break in after overpowering the guard set by Ubbe. When Havelok awoke, he set about him valiantly. He seized the door bar and slew robbers right and left. This feat won him more admiration. Ubbe assigned the young couple to a rich bower for the rest of the night. When Ubbe stole in for a look at his guests, he was astonished to see a light streaming from Havelok's mouth and a cross marked on his shoulder. By these signs he knew that Havelok was Birkabeyn's son and heir to the Danish throne.

Calling all the barons of Denmark together, Ubbe dubbed Havelok a knight and proclaimed him king. The assembled nobles passed judgment on Godard, the traitor, who was brought before Havelok, flayed, and hanged on a gallows with a great nail through his feet.

Now master of Denmark, Havelok sailed with a strong force to England to seize that kingdom from Godrich. The battle was joined near Lincoln. Although Godrich fought valiantly and wounded Ubbe, he was finally captured by the wrathful Danes. The false Earl of Cornwall, bound hand and foot, was brought before Havelok for judgment. Godrich was put upon an ass and taken into Lincoln, where his crime was proclaimed. Then he was taken to a nearby green and burned to death.

Havelok married one of Grim's daughters to the cook who had befriended him and made the man Earl of Cornwall. Grim's other daughter was married to the Earl of Chester. As for Havelok and Goldeboru, they lived together long and ruled wisely. Their union was blessed with fifteen children.

A HAZARD OF NEW FORTUNES

Type of work: Novel
Author: William Dean Howells (1837-1920)
Type of plot: Novel of manners
Time of plot: The 1880's
Locale: New York City
First published: 1890

Principal characters:
BASIL MARCH, editor of a literary magazine
MR. FULKERSON, sponsor for the magazine
CONRAD DRYFOOS, publisher of the magazine
MR. DRYFOOS, Conrad's father, a newly rich millionaire
HENRY LINDAU, a socialist

Critique:

Although the structure of this novel is unwieldy and complex, many lovers of Howells' fiction consider it their favorite, perhaps because of the author's deft characterization of a number of varied personalities, more than one usually finds in a Howells novel. Howells, like Basil March in the novel, moved to New York City after a residence of many years in New England, and this novel is the result of that move and the new experiences it brought to Howells, both as a person and as a novelist. In *A Hazard of New Fortunes,* perhaps more than anywhere else in Howells' fiction, the author's own dissatisfaction with America and his interest in social improvement are to be found. In the preface to a later edition of the book, Howells expressed the belief that he had written it when he was at the apex of his powers as a novelist.

The Story:

In his youth Basil March had wished for a literary career. Family responsibilities turned him, however, to the insurance business, a field in which he proved to himself and his employers that he was

1230

but mediocre. After eighteen years with his firm, his employers decided to replace him and put him into a somewhat meaningless position. Rather than be so embarrassed, March resigned. Fortunately for him and his family's future, Mr. Fulkerson, a promoter of syndicated newspaper material, who had met the Marches years before, proposed that March take over the editorship of a new literary magazine that he was promoting. March at first demurred at Fulkerson's proposal, but the promoter, certain that March had the necessary taste and tact to be successful, finally persuaded him to take the position.

Mrs. March and their children had always lived in Boston, and so when the prospect of moving to New York City appeared, even though it meant a career for the husband and father, they needed considerable persuasion. At last Mrs. March was convinced that the removal to the larger city was imperative. She and her husband went to New York to find a flat in which they could make themselves comfortable. After many days of searching, Mrs. March returned to Boston, leaving her husband to make a decision about the editorship. He did so a short time later.

March's problems in connection with a staff did not prove as difficult as he had imagined. Fulkerson, the promoter, had engaged an artist, Angus Beaton, to serve as art director, procured a cover sketch for the first issue, and made all the financial arrangements with the magazine's backer, Mr. Dryfoos, who had recently made a fortune for himself through the control of natural gas holdings. Mr. Dryfoos, who was trying to win his son away from a career as a minister, had undertaken to finance the magazine in order to give his son Conrad a chance to enter business as the ostensible publisher of the periodical. Foreign articles and reviews were to be handled by an old German socialist, Henry Lindau, who had been March's tutor and whom the younger man had met accidentally in New York.

Despite March's fear and lack of confidence, the new magazine, *Every Other Week,* was a success from the very first issue; both the illustrations and the material caught the public fancy. On the periphery of the activities concerning the magazine, however, there were many complications. The Dryfoos family, who had been simple farm folk, wanted to be taken into society; at least the two daughters wanted to enter society. In addition, Christine, the older daughter, fell in love with the art editor, who was not in love with her. Fulkerson, the promoter, had also fallen in love. He was busy paying court to a southern girl who boarded at the same house he did, and the girl's father, a Virginia colonel, was after Fulkerson to have the magazine print at least a portion of his great work extolling the merits of slavery.

Because the magazine had been a success, Fulkerson suggested that for publicity purposes they should give a dinner party for members of the staff and the press. Mr. Dryfoos, who was asked to pay the bill for the proposed affair, vetoed the idea, but he agreed to have a small dinner party at his home for several of the men connected with the magazine. Among the guests was Henry Lindau, who had struck the millionaire's fancy because he had lost a hand fighting in the Civil War. Dryfoos did not realize that Mr. Lindau, who was doing the foreign language work for the magazine, was a socialist. At the dinner party the personalities and the principles of the men clashed openly. The next day the millionaire told Basil March bluntly that the old man was to be fired. March wished to stick by the old German socialist, but Mr. Lindau forced the issue by refusing to do any more work for the capitalistic owner of the magazine.

Another crisis occurred a short time later when Mr. Dryfoos and his son, who hated being a businessman rather

1231

than a minister, had an open clash of wills. The situation became so acute that the father, calling one day when his son was alone in the office, struck the young man in the face. Outside the office, the father also had trouble with his daughter, Christine, for he had forbidden his house to the art editor of the magazine, with whom she was in love.

At that time there was a streetcar strike in New York City. Young Conrad Dryfoos was very much in sympathy with the strikers, many of whom he knew as a result of his church work among the poor and sick of the city. At the instigation of a young woman whom he loved, he went out upon the streets to try to bring peace among the rioting strikers and the police. He saw Mr. Lindau, the aged, one-armed socialist, being beaten by a policeman; when he ran to interfere, he was struck by a stray bullet and was killed.

Mr. Dryfoos was heartbroken at the loss of his son, particularly because he felt that he had mistreated the young man. When he learned that his son had died trying to save Mr. Lindau from the policeman's club, he decided to accept the old man as a friend and to take care of him for the rest of his life. The decision came too late, however, for the old man died as a result of the beating he had received. In a last effort to show his change of heart, Mr. Dryfoos had Mr. Lindau's funeral conducted in his own home.

Still wishing to try to make his family happy, Mr. Dryfoos then swallowed his pride and went to see Angus Beaton, the artist. Confessing that he was sorry to have caused the young people unhappiness, he invited Beaton to resume his calls on Christine. The young man eventually pocketed his pride and called, but in spite of her love for him Christine rejected his suit forcibly and scratched his face.

A few days later, Mr. Dryfoos resolved to take his wife and daughters to Europe. Before he left, he went to the offices of the magazine, where everyone had been wondering what the fate of the publication would be and whether Conrad Dryfoos' death had destroyed his father's interest in the periodical. Mr. Dryfoos magnanimously consented to sell the periodical to Fulkerson and March at a low figure and with very low interest on the money they needed in order to purchase it. Both March and Fulkerson were extremely happy about the turn of events. March saw his future secure at last, and he also saw that he would have a free hand in shaping the editorial policy. Fulkerson was happy because he too foresaw a prosperous future. As the result of his expectations, he was able to marry and settle down.

Some months afterward they learned that the Dryfoos family had been taken up promptly by at least a portion of Parisian society. Christine Dryfoos had even become engaged to a penniless but proud French nobleman.

HEADLONG HALL

Type of work: Novel
Author: Thomas Love Peacock (1785-1866)
Type of plot: Comedy of manners
Time of plot: Early nineteenth century
Locale: Wales
First published: 1816

> Principal characters:
> SQUIRE HEADLONG, the host
> MR. FOSTER, the optimist
> MR. ESCOT, the pessimist
> MR. JENKISON, champion of the status quo

Critique:

Headlong Hall is a novel of talk, a satire on the pseudo-philosophers of the nineteenth century. There is virtually no plot and no character development. In fact, the characters seem to be merely abstract personages uttering pat phrases assigned to them by the author. But beneath the surface there is always keen awareness of the ridiculous in human behavior, dramatically presented by a writer who was intellectually wise enough to be tolerant of society's weaknesses.

The Story:

Squire Harry Headlong differed from the usual Welsh squire in that he, by some means or other, had become interested in books, in addition to the common interests of hunting, racing, and drinking. He had journeyed to Oxford and then to London in order to find the philosophers and men of refined tastes introduced to him in the world of literature. Having rounded up a group of intellectuals, he invited them to Headlong Hall for the Christmas holidays.

Three of the men formed the nucleus of his house party. The first was Mr. Foster, an optimist. To him everything was working toward a state of perfection, and each advancement in technology, in government, or in sociology was all for the good. He believed that man would ultimately achieve perfection as a result of his progress. Mr. Escot, on the other hand, saw nothing but deterioration in the world. The advances which Mr. Foster saw as improvement, Escot saw as evidences of corruption and evil which would soon reduce the whole human race to wretchedness and slavery. The third man of the trio was Mr. Jenkison, who took a position exactly in the middle. He believed that the amount of improvement and deterioration balanced each other perfectly and that good and evil would remain forever in status quo.

These philosophers, with a large company of other dilettantes, descended upon Headlong Hall. Among the lesser guests was a landscape gardener who made it his sole duty to persuade the squire to have his estate changed from a wild tangle of trees and shrubs into a shaved and polished bed of green grass. Mr. Foster thought the grounds could be improved; Mr. Escot thought any change would be for the worse, and Mr. Jenkison thought the scenery perfect as it was.

There were ladies present, both young and old, but they did not join in the philosophical discussions. Many of the talks occurred after the ladies had left the dinner table and as the wine was being liberally poured, for Squire Headlong was aware that the mellowness produced by good burgundy was an incentive to conversation. The discussions took various turns, all of them dominated by the diametrically opposed views of Foster and Escot and soothed by the healing words of Jenkison. Escot harped constantly upon the happiness and moral virtue possessed by the savages of the past, virtue which lessened with each encroachment of civilization. As the savage began to build villages and cities and to develop luxuries, he began also to suffer disease, poverty, oppression, and loss of morality. With this thesis Foster could not agree. He pointed to the achievements of civilization in fields other than those of a materialistic nature. Shakespeare and Milton, for example, could not have achieved their genius in the primitive life Escot applauded. Escot, refusing to concede an inch, pointed to Milton's suffering, stating also that even if one man did profit from the so-called advancements, fifty men regressed because of them. Mr. Jenkison agreed that the subject left something to be said on either side.

Between these learned discussions the gentlemen spent their time in attempts to fascinate the ladies. Escot had once been the suitor of one of the guests, but he had offended her father during an intellectual discussion and had fallen out

1233

of favor. He attempted now to regain his former place in her affection by humoring the father. During these periods of respite, the guests also entertained one another with singing and recitations, the selections being those they themselves had composed.

The squire, planning a magnificent ball, invited the whole neighborhood to be his guests. At the ball the wine flowed freely, so that even Foster and Escot forgot some of their differences. Escot, although he disapproved of any but aboriginal dances, danced often with the lady of his choice. Foster, of course, thought the modern dance the utmost in refinement and an expression of the improved morality of man. Jenkison could see points both for and against the custom. During the evening Squire Headlong was reminded by a maiden relative that should he not marry soon there would be no one to carry on the name that had been honored for many centuries. As his name implied, the squire was not one to toy with an idea once it had entered his mind. Fixing on the lady of his choice in a matter of minutes, he proposed and was accepted. Then he arranged three other matches in an equally short time. Foster and Escot were aided in choosing brides and in getting permission from the father of Escot's beloved. Foster's bride, related to the squire, presented no obstacle. Seizing on another man, the squire told him of the plan and promptly chose a bride for that hapless individual.

Within a matter of days the weddings took place. Then the guests dispersed, after promising to gather again in August. Foster and Escot tried to the last to convince each other and the rest that only one philosophy was the true one, but Mr. Jenkison was not to fall into either of their traps. He would join them again in August, still convinced that there was merit in both their arguments. Neither was right or wrong, but each balanced the other, leaving the world in its usual status quo.

THE HEART IS A LONELY HUNTER

Type of work: Novel
Author: Carson McCullers (1917-   )
Type of plot: Psychological realism
Time of plot: The 1930's
Locale: A Georgia mill town
First published: 1940

Principal characters:
MR. SINGER, a mute
MICK KELLY, an adolescent girl
BIFF BRANNON, a café proprietor
JAKE BLOUNT, a frustrated, idealistic workingman
DR. COPELAND, a Negro physician

Critique:

To read *The Heart Is a Lonely Hunter* as a novel of social criticism is to misinterpret the subtle yet precise art of Carson McCullers. Her true theme in this remarkable first novel is that sense of moral isolation, expressed in terms of loneliness and longing, which is both the social evil of the modern world and the inescapable condition of man. Four different but related stories illuminate Mrs. McCullers' theme through the experiences of Mick Kelly, Biff Brannon, Jake Blount, and Dr. Copeland. These people are drawn to Mr. Singer, the mute, because his physical infirmity seems to set him apart in the same way that their own

1234

sense of separation from the social community makes their lives incomplete. Mrs. McCullers is one of the most distinguished among our younger novelists, a writer whose fiction has both substance and significance.

The Story:

In a small town in the South there were two mutes, one a grossly fat Greek, the other a tall, immaculate man named Mr. Singer. They had no friends, and they lived together for ten years. After a lingering sickness the Greek became a changed man. When he began to be obscene in public, the cousin for whom he worked sent him to the state insane asylum. After that Mr. Singer was desolate.

He took all his meals at the New York Café owned by Biff Brannon. Biff was a stolid man with a weakness for cripples and sick people. When Jake Blount, a squat man with long, powerful arms, came to town, he went on a week-long drunk at Biff's expense. Biff had to find out what bothered Jake. Finding Mr. Singer eating at the café, Jake decided that he was the only person who could understand the message he was trying to give. One night Mr. Singer took Jake home with him. It was not until after he had slept that Jake realized Mr. Singer was a mute. He still felt, however, that the mute could understand him.

Mr. Singer had taken a room at the Kellys' boarding-house, where the daughter Mick, just entering her teens, was a gangly girl, always dressed in shorts, a shirt, and tennis shoes. She loved music and would go anywhere to hear it. Some nights she went to a big house in town where she could hear symphonic music through the open windows while she crouched in the shrubbery. At home no one realized what she wanted, until Mr. Singer moved there and let her talk to him when she was lonely.

Mick decided, after entering Vocational School, that she had to have some friends. Planning a dance, she invited only high school students. The house was decorated with tinsel. Mick borrowed an evening dress and high-heeled shoes from one of her sisters.

On the night of the party a throng of children arrived and separated into noisy groups. When Mick handed out the prom cards, the boys went to one side of the room, the girls to the other. Silence descended. No one knew how to start things. A boy finally asked Mick to prom with him. Outside the house all the neighborhood children had gathered. While Mick and Harry walked around the block, the neighborhood children joined the party. By the time Mick got back, the decorations were torn, the refreshments gone, and the invited and the uninvited guests mixed up so badly that the party was bedlam. Everyone congregated on the street to run races and jump ditches, the partygoers forgetful of their nearly-grown-up state. Mick finally called off the party after she had been knocked breathless on a jump she could have made easily in her tennis shoes.

Portia worked for the Kellys. Her father was Dr. Copeland, the only colored doctor in town. He was an idealistic man who had always worked hard to raise the standards of the Negro people. One dark night Mr. Singer had stepped up and helped him light a cigarette in the rain. It was the first time a white man had ever offered him help or smiled at him. When he told Portia about a deaf-mute boy patient of his, she assured him that Mr. Singer would help him.

Jake, who had found a job with a flying-jenny show, tried to rouse the workers. He spent each Sunday with Mr. Singer, explaining that he had first wanted to be an evangelist until he had been made aware of the inequality in the world. He had unintentionally insulted Dr. Copeland twice, but he was one of the first to talk about doing something for Willie, Dr. Copeland's son.

Willie had been sentenced to hard labor for knifing a man. At the prison camp he and two others tried to run away. They were put in a cold shack for three days with their bare feet hoisted up by a looped rope. Willie lost both feet from gangrene. Dr. Copeland, trying to see the judge about the case, was severely beaten up by a white crowd around the court house and put in jail. Mr. Singer and Portia obtained his release on bail, and Jake went with Mr. Singer to Dr. Copeland's house. There he argued the ethics of the case with the doctor all night, Jake too hysterical to be logical, the doctor too sick.

There was a peacefulness in Mr. Singer's face that attracted Mick. She followed him whenever she could. He bought a radio which he kept in his room for her to listen to. Those were hours of deep enjoyment for her. She felt that she had music in her that she would have to learn to write down.

She fascinated Biff. After his wife died, he watched Mick begin to grow up, but he seldom spoke to her. He was equally quiet with Mr. Singer when he visited at the Kelly boarding-house. Mr. Singer considered Mick pitiful, Jake crazy, Dr. Copeland noble, and Biff thoughtful; but they were always welcome to his room.

On his vacation Mr. Singer went to see his Greek friend. He took beautiful presents along with him, but the Greek was petulant over anything but food. Only there did Mr. Singer take his hands out of his pockets; then he wore himself out trying to tell the Greek with his hands everything he had seen and thought since the Greek went away. Although the Greek showed no interest, Mr. Singer tried even harder to entertain him. When he left, the Greek was still impassive.

Mr. Singer's board was the only steady money the Kellys could depend on. When one sister got sick, the loss of her salary threw the whole family in a quandary. Mick heard that a job was opening at the five-and-ten-cent store. The family in conclave decided she was too young to work. The fact that for the first time they were talking about her welfare prompted her to apply for the job. She got it, but each night she was too tired for anything but sleep.

It was again time for Mr. Singer to go to see his Greek friend. Laden down with presents, he made the long trip. When he reached the asylum office, the clerk told him the Greek was dead. Stricken, he found his way back to the town, left his luggage at the station, went to his room, and put a bullet through his chest.

Mr. Singer's death left his four friends confused. Dr. Copeland, still sick, brooded over it.

Jake Blount joined in a free-for-all at the flying-jenny grounds and, after hearing that the police were looking for him, left town.

Mick did not sleep well for weeks after the funeral. All that she had left was Mr. Singer's radio. She felt cheated because there was no time, no money, no feeling anymore for music, but she could never decide who had cheated her.

And Biff, who had watched Mr. Singer with Jake and Mick, was still puzzling over the relationships he had studied. He wondered whether, in the struggle of humanity, love might be the answer.

HEART OF DARKNESS

Type of work: Short story
Author: Joseph Conrad (Teodor Józef Konrad Korzeniowski, 1857-1924)
Type of plot: Symbolic romance
Time of plot: Late nineteenth century
Locale: The Belgian Congo
First published: 1902

Principal characters:
MARLOW, the narrator
MR. KURTZ, manager of the Inner Station, Belgian Congo
THE DISTRICT MANAGER
A RUSSIAN TRAVELER
KURTZ'S FIANCÉE

Critique:

In one sense, *Heart of Darkness* is a compelling adventure tale of a journey into the blackest heart of the Belgian Congo. The story presents attacks by the natives, descriptions of the jungle and the river, and characterizations of white men who, sometimes with ideals and sometimes simply for profit, invade the jungles to bring out ivory. But the journey into the heart of the Congo is also a symbolic journey into the blackness central to the heart and soul of man, a journey deep into primeval passion, superstition, and lust. Those who, like the district manager, undertake this journey simply to rob the natives of ivory, without any awareness of the importance of the central darkness, can survive. Similarly, Marlow, who is only an observer, never centrally involved, can survive to tell the tale. But those who, like Mr. Kurtz, are aware of the darkness, who hope with conscious intelligence and a humane concern for all mankind to bring light into the darkness, are doomed, are themselves swallowed up by the darkness and evil they had hoped to penetrate. Conrad manages to make his point, a realization of the evil at the center of human experience, without ever breaking the closely knit pattern of his narrative or losing the compelling atmospheric and psychological force of the tale. The wealth of natural symbols, the clear development of character, and the sheer fascination of the story make this a short story that has been frequently praised and frequently read ever since its publication in 1902. *Heart of Darkness* is, in both style and insight, a masterful short story.

The Story:

A group of men were sitting on the deck of the cruising yawl, *The Nellie,* anchored one calm evening in the Thames estuary. One of the seamen, Marlow, began reflecting that the Thames area had been, at the time of the invading Romans, one of the dark and barbarous areas of the earth. Dwelling on this theme, he then began to tell a story of the blackest, most barbarous area of the earth that he had experienced.

Through his aunt's connections, Marlow had once secured a billet as commander of a river steamer for one of the trading companies with interests in the Belgian Congo. When he went to Belgium to learn more about the job, he found that few of the officials of the company expected him to return alive. In Brussels he also heard of the distinguished Mr. Kurtz, the powerful and intelligent man who was educating the natives and at the same time sending back record shipments of ivory.

The mysterious figure of Mr. Kurtz fascinated Marlow. In spite of the ominous hints that he gathered from various company officials, he became more and more curious about what awaited him in the Congo. During his journey, as he passed along the African coast, he reflected that the wilderness and the unknown seemed to seep right out to the sea. Many of the trading posts and stations the ship passed were dilapidated and looked barbaric. Finally, Marlow arrived at the seat of the government at the mouth of the river. Again, he heard of the great distinction and power of Mr. Kurtz who had, because of his plans to enlighten the natives and his success in gaining their confidence, an enormous reputation. Marlow also saw natives working in the hot sun until they collapsed and died. Marlow had to wait for ten impatient days at the government site because his work would not begin until he reached the district manager's station, two hundred miles up the river. At last the expedition left for the district station.

Marlow arrived at the district station to find that the river steamer had sunk a few days earlier. He met the district manager, a man whose only ability seemed to be the ability to survive. The district manager, unconcerned with the fate of the natives, was interested only in getting out of the country; he felt that Mr. Kurtz's new methods were ruining the whole district. The district manager reported also that he had not heard from Kurtz for quite some time, but had received disquieting rumors about his being ill.

Although he was handicapped by a lack of rivets, Marlow spent months supervising repairs to the antiquated river steamer. He also overheard a conversation which revealed that the district manager was Kurtz's implacable enemy, who hoped that the climate would do away with his rival.

The steamer was finally ready for use, and Marlow, along with the district manager, sailed to visit Kurtz at the inner station far up the river. The journey was difficult and perilous; the water was shallow; there were frequent fogs. Just as they arrived within a few miles of Kurtz's station, natives attacked the vessel with spears and arrows. Marlow's helmsman, a faithful native, was killed by a long spear when he leaned from his window to fire at the savages. Marlow finally blew the steamboat whistle and the sound frightened the natives away. The district manager was sure that Kurtz had lost control over the blacks. When they docked, they met an enthusiastic Russian traveler who told them that Kurtz was gravely ill.

While the district manager visited Kurtz, the Russian told Marlow that the sick man had become corrupted by the very natives he had hoped to enlighten. He still had power over the natives, but instead of his changing them, they had debased him into an atavistic savage. Kurtz attended native rituals, had killed frequently in order to get ivory, and had hung heads as decorations outside his hut. Later Marlow met Kurtz and found that the man had, indeed, been corrupted by the evil at the center of experience. Marlow learned, from the Russian, that Kurtz had ordered the natives to attack the steamer, thinking that, if they did so, the white men would run away and leave Kurtz to die among his fellow savages in the wilderness. Talking to Marlow, Kurtz showed his awareness of how uncivilized he had become, how his plans to educate the natives had been reversed. He gave Marlow a packet of letters for his fiancée in Belgium and the manuscript of an article, written sometime earlier, in which he urged efforts to educate the natives.

The district manager and Marlow took Kurtz, now on a stretcher, to the river steamer to take him back home. The district manager contended that the area was now ruined for collecting ivory. Kurtz, full of despair and the realization that devouring evil was at the heart of everything, died while the steamer was temporarily stopped for repairs.

Marlow returned to civilization and, about a year later, went to Belgium to see Kurtz's fiancée. She still thought of Kurtz as the splendid and powerful man who had gone to Africa with a mission, and she still believed in his goodness and power. When she asked Marlow what Kurtz's last words had been, Marlow lied and told her that Kurtz had asked for her at the end. In reality, Kurtz, who had seen all experience, had in his final words testified to the horror of it all. This horror was not something, Marlow felt, that civilized ladies could, or should, understand.

THE HEART OF MIDLOTHIAN

Type of work: Novel
Author: Sir Walter Scott (1771-1832)
Type of plot: Historical romance
Time of plot: Early eighteenth century
Locale: Scotland
First published: 1818

Principal characters:
DAVID DEANS, a dairyman
JEANIE DEANS, his daughter
EFFIE DEANS, another daughter
REUBEN BUTLER, Jeanie's betrothed
GEORDIE ROBERTSON, Effie's betrayer, in reality George Staunton
MEG MURDOCKSON, an evil woman
THE DUKE OF ARGYLE, Jeanie's benefactor

Critique:

The story of Jeanie Deans and her great effort to save her sister's life is supposedly based on fact. Fact or fiction, it is an exciting story, told as only Sir Walter Scott could tell it. *The Heart of Midlothian* is filled with suspense, mystery, and romance, and there is a happy ending. Many consider this Scott's greatest novel.

The Story:

The first knowledge Jeanie Deans had that her sister Effie was in trouble came just a few moments before officers of justice arrived at the cottage to arrest Effie for child murder. They told Jeanie and her father, David Deans, that Effie had borne a male child illegitimately and had killed him or caused him to be killed soon after he was born. Effie admitted the birth of the child but refused to name her seducer. She denied that she had killed her baby, saying that she had fallen into a stupor and had recovered to find that the midwife who attended her had disposed of the child in some fashion unknown to Effie. In the face of the evidence, however, she was convicted of child murder and sentenced to be hanged. Jeanie might have saved her sister, for it was the law that if a prospective mother had told anyone of her condition she would not be responsible for her baby's death. But Jeanie would not lie, even to

save her sister's life. Since there was no one to whom Effie had told her terrible secret, there was no defense for her, and she was placed in the Tolbooth prison to await execution.

Another prisoner in the Tolbooth was Captain John Porteous, who was awaiting execution for firing into the crowd attending the hanging of Andrew Wilson, a smuggler. Wilson's accomplice, Geordie Robertson, had escaped, and the officers feared that Robertson might try to rescue Wilson. For that reason, Porteous and a company of soldiers had been sent to the scene of the execution to guard against a possible rescue. Because Porteous had fired into the crowd without provocation, killing several people, he was to be hanged. But when his execution was stayed for a few weeks, a mob headed by Robertson, disguised as a woman, broke into the prison, seized Porteous, and hanged him. For that deed Robertson became a hunted man.

Meanwhile Jeanie Deans, who had refused to lie to save her sister, had not forsaken Effie. When she visited Effie in prison, she learned that Robertson was the father of her child. He had left her in the care of old Meg Murdockson, considered by many to be a witch, and it must have been Meg who had killed or sold the baby. Meg's daughter Madge had long before been seduced by Robertson and had lost her mind for love of him, and Meg had sworn revenge on any other woman Robertson might love. But proving the old woman's guilt or Effie's innocence was not possible, for Robertson had disappeared, and Meg swore that she had seen Effie coming back from the river after drowning the baby.

Jeanie, determined to save her sister, decided to walk to London to seek a pardon from the king and queen. She told her plans to Reuben Butler, a minister to whom she had long been betrothed. Reuben had not been able to marry her, for he had no position other than that of an assistant schoolmaster and his salary was too small to support a wife. Although he objected to Jeanie's plan, he was able to aid her when he saw that she could not be swayed from her purpose. Reuben's grandfather had once aided an ancestor of the present Duke of Argyle, and Reuben gave Jeanie a letter asking the duke's help in presenting Jeanie to the king and queen.

The journey to London was a long and dangerous one. Once Jeanie was captured by Meg Murdockson, who tried to kill her so that she could not save Effie. But Jeanie escaped from the old woman and sought refuge in the home of the Rev. Mr. Staunton. There she met the minister's son, George Staunton, and learned from him that he was Geordie Robertson, the betrayer of her sister. He admitted his responsibility to Effie, telling Jeanie that he had planned and executed the Porteous incident in order to rescue Effie from the prison. But she had refused to leave with him. He had tried many other schemes to save her, including an attempt to force from Meg the confession that she had taken the baby, but everything had failed. He told Jeanie that he had been on his way to give himself up in exchange for Effie's release when he fell from his horse and was injured. He told Jeanie to bargain with the Duke of Argyle, and as a last resort to offer to lead the authorities to Robertson in exchange for Effie's pardon.

George promised not to leave his father's house until Effie was free.

Jeanie at last reached London and presented herself to the Duke of Argyle with Reuben's letter. The duke, impressed with Jeanie's sincerity and simplicity, arranged for an audience with the queen. She too believed Jeanie's story of Effie's misfortune, and through her efforts the king pardoned Effie, with the stipulation that she leave Scotland for fourteen years. Jeanie secured the pardon without revealing George Staunton's secret.

The duke was so impressed with Jeanie's goodness and honesty that he made her father the master of an experimental farm on one of his estates in Scotland, and he made Reuben the minister of the church. Jeanie's heart was overflowing with joy until she learned that Effie had eloped with her lover just three nights after her release from prison. No one knew where they were, as the outlaw's life was in constant danger because of his part in the Porteous hanging.

Reuben and Jeanie were married and were blessed with three fine children. They prospered in their new life, and Jeanie's only sorrow was her sister's marriage to George Staunton. She kept Effie's secret, however, telling no one that George was actually Robertson. After several years, George and Effie returned to London, George having inherited a title from his uncle, and as Sir George and Lady Staunton they were received in court society. Effie wrote secretly to Jeanie and sent her large sums of money which Jeanie put away without telling her husband about them. Even to him she could not reveal Effie's secret.

By chance Jeanie found a paper containing the last confession of Meg Murdockson, who had been hanged as a witch. In it Meg confessed that she had stolen Effie's baby and had given him to an outlaw. Jeanie sent this information to Effie, in London, and before long Effie, as Lady Staunton, paid Jeanie a visit. Effie had used a pretext of ill health to go to Scotland while her husband, acting on the information in Meg's letter, tried to trace the whereabouts of their son. Although it was dangerous for George to be in Scotland, where he might be recognized as Geordie Robertson, he followed every clue given in Meg's confession. In Edinburgh he met Reuben Butler, who was there on business, and secured an invitation to accompany Reuben back to the manse. Reuben, not knowing George's real identity, was happy to receive the Duke of Argyle's friend. Reuben, at that time, did not know that Effie was also a guest in his home.

As Reuben and George walked toward the manse, they passed through a thicket where they were attacked by outlaws. One, a young fellow, ran his sword through George and killed him. It was not until Reuben had heard the whole story of the Stauntons from Jeanie that he searched George's pockets and found there information which proved beyond doubt that the young outlaw who had killed George was his own son, stolen many years before. Because Effie was grief-stricken by George's death, Jeanie and Reuben thought it useless to add to her sorrow by revealing the identity of his assailant. Reuben later traced the boy to America, where the young man continued his life of crime until he was captured and probably killed by Indians.

Effie stayed with Reuben and Jeanie for more than a year. Then she went back to London and the brilliant society she had known there. No one but Jeanie and Reuben ever knew the secret of Effie and George. After ten years, Effie retired to a convent on the continent, where she spent her remaining years grieving for her husband and the son she had never known.

Reuben and Jeanie Butler, who had been so unavoidably involved in sordidness and crime, lived out their lives happily and carried their secret with them to the grave.

THE HEART OF THE MATTER

Type of work: Novel
Author: Graham Greene (1904-   )
Type of plot: Psychological realism
Time of plot: World War II
Locale: British West Africa
First published: 1948

Principal characters:
MAJOR SCOBIE, police chief in one of the colony's districts
MRS. SCOBIE, his wife
MRS. ROLT, shipwreck victim, Scobie's mistress
WILSON, a counter-intelligence agent
YUSEF, a Syrian merchant

Critique:

The fears and hopes, friendships and petty rivalries, loves and hates of Europeans immured in a colony on the African coast afforded Graham Greene, who actually worked in such a place during World War II, the material for this novel. The book continues the study of British people under the influence of our times begun in Greene's earlier work. Major Scobie, like Arthur Rowe in *The Ministry of Fear*, is a relatively friendless man—a type that seems to have fascination for the author. Like Rowe, in the earlier novel, Major Scobie is placed in a position where he can choose between life or death: the high point in both novels is that at which the choice is made. Beyond the immediate story, however, there are larger implications. *The Heart of the Matter,* written by one of the leading Catholic novelists of the day, is actually a religious story, a fable of the conflict between good and evil. It is a drama of the human soul in mid-passage toward Heaven or Hell.

The Story:

For fifteen years Major Scobie, chief of police in a British West African district had built up a reputation for honesty. Then he learned that in spite of his labors he was to be passed over for the district commissionership in favor of a younger man. Those fifteen long years now seemed to him to have been too long and filled with too much work. Worse than his own disappointment was the disappointment of his wife. Mrs. Scobie needed the encouragement that a rise in official position would have given her, to compensate for the loss of her only child some years before and her unpopularity among the official family of the district.

A love for literature, especially poetry, had set Mrs. Scobie apart from the other officials and their wives. Once the difference was discerned, the other Britishers distrusted and disliked her. They even pitied the man whom she had married. Nor were the Scobies much happier than people imagined them to be. Mrs. Scobie hated the life she led, and her husband disliked having to make her face it realistically. Both drank. When she found he was not to be made district commissioner, she insisted that he send her to the Cape Colony for a holiday, even though German submarines were torpedoing many vessels at the time.

Scobie had not the money to pay expenses of the trip. For a previous excursion of hers from the colony he had already given up part of his life insurance. After trying unsuccessfully to borrow the money from the banks, he went to Yusef, a Syrian merchant, who agreed to lend him the money at four percent interest.

Scobie knew that any dealings he had with Yusef would place him under a cloud, for the official British family knew only too well that many of the Syrian's doings were illegal, including the shipment of industrial diamonds to the Nazis. Pressed by his wife's apparent need to escape the boredom of the rainy season in the coast colony, Scobie finally took the chance that he could keep clear of Yusef's entanglements, even though he knew that the Syrian hated him for the reputation of integrity he had built up during the past fifteen years.

To add to Scobie's difficulties, he learned that Wilson, a man supposedly sent out on a clerkship with a trading company, was actually an undercover agent working for the government on the problem of diamond smuggling. First of all, Scobie had no official information about Wilson's true activities; secondly, Wilson had fallen in love with Scobie's wife; and, thirdly, Mrs. Scobie had bloodied Wilson's nose for him and permitted her husband to see her admirer crying. Any one of the counts would have made Scobie uneasy; all three in combination made him painfully aware that Wilson could only hate him, as Wilson actually did.

Shortly after his wife's departure, a series of events began to break down Major Scobie's trust in his own honesty and the reputation he had built up for himself. When a Portuguese liner was searched on its arrival in port, Scobie found a suspicious letter in the captain's cabin. Instead of turning in the letter, he burned it—after the captain had assured him that the letter was only a personal message to his daughter in Germany. A few weeks later Yusef began to be very friendly toward Scobie. Gossip reported that Scobie had met and talked with the Syrian on several occasions, in addition to having borrowed money from the suspected smuggler.

One day word came that the French had rescued the crew and passengers of a torpedoed British vessel. Scobie was with the party who met the rescued people at the border between the French and British colonies. Among the victims was a young bride of only a few months whose husband had been killed in the war. While she recuperated from her exposure in a lifeboat and then waited for a ship to return her to England, she and Scobie fell in love. For a time they were extremely careful of their conduct, until one day Mrs. Rolt, the rescued woman, belittled Scobie because of his caution. Scobie, to prove his daring as well as his love, sent her a letter which was intercepted by Yusef's agents. In payment for return of the letter Scobie was forced to help Yusef smuggle some gems from the colony. Wilson, Scobie's enemy, suspected the smuggling done by Scobie, but he could prove nothing.

Mrs. Rolt pleaded with Scobie to show his love by divorcing his wife and marrying her. Scobie, a Roman Catholic, tried to convince her that his faith and his conscience could not permit his doing so. To complicate matters further, Mrs. Scobie cabled that she was already aboard ship on her way back home from Capetown. Scobie did not know which way to turn. On her return Mrs. Scobie nagged him to take communion with her. Scobie, unable to receive absolution because he refused to promise to give up adultery, took the sacrament of communion anyway, rather than admit to his wife what had happened. He realized that according to his faith he was damning his soul.

The worry over his sins, his uneasiness about his job, the problem of Yusef, a murder that Yusef had had committed for him, and the nagging of both his wife and Mrs. Rolt—all these made Scobie's mind a turmoil. He did not know which way to turn, for the Church, haven for many,

was forbidden to him because of his sins and his temperament.

In searching for a way out of his predicament Scobie remembered what he had been told by a doctor shortly after an official investigation of a suicide. The doctor had told Scobie that the best way to commit suicide was to feign angina and then take an overdose of evipan, a drug prescribed for angina cases. Carefully, Scobie made plans to take his life in that way because he wanted his wife to have his insurance money for her support after she returned to England. After studying the symptoms of angina, Scobie went to a doctor, who diagnosed Scobie's trouble from the symptoms he related. Scobie knew that his pretended heart condition would soon be common knowledge in the colony.

Ironically, Scobie was told that he had been reconsidered for the commissionership of the colony but that he could not be given the post because of his illness. To Scobie, the news made little difference, for he had already made up his mind to commit suicide.

To make his death appear convincing, he filled his diary with entries tracing the progress of his heart condition. One evening he took his overdose of evipan, his only solution to difficulties which had become more than he could bear. He died, and only one or two people even suspected the truth. One of these was Mrs. Scobie, who complained to the priest after he had refused to give Scobie absolution. The priest, knowing of Scobie's virtues as well as his sins, cried out to her that no one could call Scobie wicked or damned, for no one knew God's mercy.

HEARTBREAK HOUSE

Type of work: Drama
Author: Bernard Shaw (1856-1950)
Time: 1913
Locale: Sussex, England
First presented: 1920

Principal characters:

CAPTAIN SHOTOVER, an English eccentric and visionary
LADY ARIADNE UTTERWOOD, and
MRS. HESIONE HUSHABYE, his daughters
HECTOR HUSHABYE, Hesione's husband
ELLIE DUNN, a guest in Captain Shotover's house
MAZZINI DUNN, her father
BOSS MANGAN. an industrialist
RANDALL UTTERWOOD, Lady Ariadne's brother-in-law
NURSE GUINESS, a servant
BILLY DUNN, an ex-pirate and burglar

Heartbreak House has always held an equivocal place in the Shavian canon. Its admirers—and they are many—bracket it with Shaw's best, beside such acknowledged masterpieces as *Man and Superman* and *Saint Joan*. Severer critics see it as an unsuccessful attempt to create a mood of Chekhovian melancholy and fatalism within a framework of political allegory and social satire, a mixture of comedy, tragedy, dialectic, and prophecy that never quite coalesces into unity of theme or structure.

Shaw himself was as much to blame as anyone for some of the misconceptions regarding his play. Always ready, even eager, to instruct his public, in this instance he maintained an attitude of reticence toward his work and appeared hesitant to let it pass out of his hands. Although part of it had been written as early as 1913 and it was in its final form by 1916, the play was not published until 1919. Its first performance was the Theatre Guild production on November 12, 1920. Even then Shaw apparently preferred to let his work speak for itself without mediation on his part, for when asked on one occasion to interpret some of his lines he answered brusquely that he was merely the author and therefore could not be expected to know. Perhaps he was still smarting from the abuse he had received following the publication of his pamphlet, *Commonsense about the War* (1915), read by the jingo-minded wartime public as a piece of pacifist propaganda. Under the circumstances his reluctance to present his most sweeping indictment of a society unable or unwilling to bring its moral judgments and political convictions into balance with its potential of destruction becomes understandable. War, Shaw seems to say, is no longer the trade of the professional soldier or the recreation of the feudal elite; all of mankind is now involved in the common catastrophe and society must perish if it cannot realize its possibilities for good as opposed to its capacities for destruction.

In a way that criticism has not yet fully appraised, *Heartbreak House* presents almost the whole range of Shaw's thought, for few of his plays are more representative or inclusive in the themes and motifs touched upon if not explored: war, love, society, education, religion, politics, and science. The only element lacking is the Shavian principle of the Life Force. As a drama of ideas it looks back to the earlier plays and anticipates *Saint Joan* and *The Apple Cart*. As comment on upper-class life it continues and climaxes the themes Shaw presents in *Getting Married* and *Misalliance*. Shaw himself is present in his various manifestations: the recorder of that verbal interplay which in the Shavian drama often takes the place of conflict, the playwright of ideas, the master of comedy, the maker of epigrams, the teacher, the critic, the philosopher, the parodist, the fabulist, and the poet.

A clue to the meaning of the play is provided in the subtitle: "A Fantasia in the Russian manner on English themes." Following the production of several of Chekhov's plays in London,

Shaw had been studying the work of the Russian dramatist and had seen in at least three, *The Cherry Orchard, The Sea Gull,* and *Uncle Vanya,* exempla of the theme he himself had in mind: the disintegration of a society from within and its final collapse in the face of forces it had previously ignored or denied. Allowances must be made, however, for Shaw's habit of exaggeration where precedents or sources are concerned. Shaw may have begun his play with a similarity of tone in mind—the atmosphere, he said, was the initial impulse—but he ends with effects quite different from those we find in Chekhov. Partly the difference is one of temperament, the great Russian power of enclosing the poetry of all experience in the single instance, partly the fact that the haunted landscapes of Chekhov's world have little in common with those aspects of British middle and upper-class life that Shaw observed so shrewdly. Shaw's people exist only in the light of his ethical and political values; Chekhov's, entirely within the world of their own moral and spiritual blight. The sound of the ax echoing through the twilight at the end of *The Cherry Orchard* is more portentous and meaningful than the bombs which rain fire and death from the sky at the close of *Heartbreak House.*

The essential differences between these two plays are not altogether to Shaw's disadvantage, for *Heartbreak House,* although it lacks the larger expressiveness of Chekhov's theater, exhibits all the intellectual vigor and wild poetry, the clash of ideas and personalities, of disquisitory drama at its best. A thesis play, it is admitted as such in Shaw's preface, where he states that Heartbreak House is more than a title: it is the Europe—or England —of culture and leisure in the period before World War I. As the alternative to Heartbreak House he sees only Horseback Hall, peopled by the gentry who have made sport a cult. In either case, true leadership is lacking in this world of cross-purposes. futile desires, and idle talk. These people have courage of a sort, but they are able to do little more than clench their fists in gestures of defiance as the bombs drop from the sky.

The setting of the play is the Sussex home, built like a ship, of Captain Shotover, an eighty-eight-year-old eccentric and retired sea captain credited by hearsay with selling his soul to the devil in Zanzibar and marriage to a black witch in the West Indies. Cranky, realistic, fantastically wise, he drinks three bottles of rum a day, strives to attain the seventh degree of concentration, and spends his time tinkering with death-dealing inventions. To Ellie Dunn, a young singer arriving as the guest of Mrs. Hesione Hushabye, the captain's daughter, the atmosphere of the house seems as puzzling and unpredictable as its owner. No one bothers to greet visitors; members of the family are treated like strangers; strangers are welcomed like old friends. An elderly servant calls everyone ducky. When Lady Ariadne Utterwood returns for a visit after twenty-three years in the colonies with her husband, Sir Hastings Utterwood, an empire builder, neither her father nor her sister recognizes her. The captain persists in confusing Mazzini Dunn, Ellie's father, with a rascally expirate who had robbed him many years before. Arriving unexpectedly, Boss Mangan, the millionaire industrialist whom Ellie is to marry, is put to work in the captain's garden.

From this opening scene of innocent, seemingly irresponsible comedy the play proceeds to more serious business, and by the end of the first act the characters have assumed their allegorical identities. Lady Ariadne is Empire, the prestige of foreign rule. Hesione Hushabye is Domesticity, the power of woman's love and authority at home. Hector, her husband, is Heroism, a man capable of brave deeds but so tamed by feminine influence that his only escape is through romantic daydreams and Münchausen-like tales of derring-do. Mazzini Dunn is the nineteenth-century Liberal, a believer in progress but too sentimental to be an intellectual force; consequently he has become the tool of Boss Mangan, a figure of capitalistic Exploitation. Randall Utterwood, Lady Ariadne's brother-in-law, is Pride, a Foreign Office official symbolically in love with his sister-in-law and filled with snobbish regard for caste. Looming over these figures is old Captain Shotover, the embodiment of Old England and its genius, no longer the captain of the great Ship of State but the half-cracked, drunken skipper of a house built like a ship, suggesting his own and his country's maritime history. Captain Shotover is the triumph of the play. In spite of his allegorical significance he is always superbly himself, a figure larger than life and yet lifelike, reliving his past and creating his future in terms of his own fantastic logic. These people come together in twos and threes to speak in their own and in their allegorical characters. Childlike resentments, old grievances, brooding frustrations, impossible dreams, and unexpected disillusionments break through their masks in the heavily charged atmosphere that the play generates, but all this sound and fury leads nowhere. *Heartbreak House* is idleness dramatized, impotence of mind and will translated into speech and gesture.

In one sense *Heartbreak House* might be described as the story of Ellie Dunn's education. In the first act, although she is engaged to Boss Mangan, she fancies herself in love with Marcus Darnley, a middle-aged man of romantic background, whom she has been meeting secretly. The discovery that Marcus is Hector Hushabye opens her eyes to reality and deceit. Disillusioned with romantic love, she decides to accept Boss Mangan and his money, only to discover that his millions are nonexistent, that he is simply the capitalist who uses the money other men entrust to him. In the end she decides that she will become the white bride of old Captain Shotover because his seventh degree of concentration holds a promise of peace and happiness beyond desire or despair. This time it is the captain who disillusions her; his seventh degree of concentration is rum. Ellie's education is now complete, and she is free to be as practical or aspiring as she desires.

Suddenly, while these people sit on the terrace and talk out their predicament, planes begin to drone overhead. Boss Mangan and a burglar—who had turned out to be Billy Dunn the ex-pirate now reduced to petty thievery and sniveling confession—take refuge in a gravel pit; a bomb falls and kills them. The others survive. Heartbreak House still stands.

All criticism of *Heartbreak House* reduces itself to a single issue: Can comedy, even brilliantly presented, sustain a theme of tragic significance? Shaw, as he declared, was only the writer. The reader or the playgoer has been left to answer this question for himself.

THE HEAT OF THE DAY

Type of work: Novel
Author: Elizabeth Bowen (1899-   )
Type of plot: Psychological realism
Time of plot: 1942-1944
Locale: London
First published: 1949

Principal characters:
STELLA RODNEY, an attractive widow
RODERICK RODNEY, her son
ROBERT KELWAY, her lover
HARRISON, a British Intelligence agent
LOUIE LEWIS, wife of a British soldier

1246

Critique:

The wartime setting of this book is no more than incidental, for the story treats of contrasting faiths and loyalties which are altogether timeless. Though the general atmosphere is electric with danger, the author muffles the sound of bombs and anti-aircraft guns until they give only a tonal background for the drama of Stella Rodney, Robert Kelway, and the enigmatic Harrison. The problem of Stella Rodney is that of a woman asked to question her own judgment of the man she loves. Miss Bowen is at her best in dealing with complex personal relationships, and here she inspects some barriers to emotional and intellectual harmony that are embodied in a conflict between patriotism and love. Like Henry James, she is interested in the collision of finely-grained personalities; and the very nature of her subject matter demands a style that is sensitive and involved.

The Story:

The first Sunday afternoon of September, 1942, found Harrison sitting at a band concert in Regent Park. But he was not listening to the music. He was, in fact, merely killing time until he could see Stella Rodney at eight o'clock. Thinking of Stella and the awkward subject he must discuss with her, he kept thrusting the fist of his right hand into the palm of his left. This unconscious motion, as well as his obvious indifference to the music, aroused the curiosity of an adjacent listener. This neighbor, Louie Lewis, was a clumsy, cheaply clad young woman with an artless and somewhat bovine expression. Lonely without her soldier husband and entirely a creature of impulse, she offended Harrison by breaking into his reverie with naïve comments which were brusquely rebuffed. Unabashed, she trailed after him when he left the concert, giving up only when he abruptly left her to keep his engagement.

Stella, in her top-floor flat in Weymouth Street, wondered rather idly why Harrison was late. Her attitude of waiting was more defiant than expectant, for she had no love for her visitor. She hardly knew how he had managed to insinuate himself into her life; first, he had turned up unaccountably at the funeral of Cousin Francis Morris, and since then his attentions had shown a steady increase. There had been a subtle shade of menace in his demand that she see him that night, and a curious sense of apprehension had prompted her to consent. As she awaited his knock, her glance flickered impatiently about the charming flat, and she recalled fleetingly the facts that gave shape to her existence: her young son, Roderick, now in the British army; her ex-husband, long divorced and dead; her own war work with Y.X.D.; and her lover, Robert Kelway, also in government service.

When Harrison arrived, he received a cool and perfunctory greeting. His first remarks were hesitant and enigmatic, but he soon launched into words that left Stella wide-eyed with shock and disbelief. Her lover, he told her, was a Nazi agent passing English secrets on to Germany. Harrison himself was connected with British Intelligence and he had been assigned to cover Kelway's movements. There was just one way to save the traitor. Stella must give him up, switch her interest to Harrison. Then Kelway's fate might be averted, or indefinitely postponed.

The blunt proposition unnerved Stella. She refused to believe in Kelway's guilt, for Harrison did not impress her as a man to trust. She played for time, winning

THE HEAT OF THE DAY by Elizabeth Bowen. By permission of the publishers, Alfred A. Knopf, Inc. Copyright, 1948, by Elizabeth Bowen.

a month's delay in which to make up her mind. Harrison sharply advised her not to warn Robert; the slightest change in his pattern of action would result in his immediate arrest. As the interview ended, the telephone rang. At the other end was Roderick, announcing his arrival for leave in London. Upon Harrison's departure, Stella pulled herself together and made quick preparation to receive her son.

Roderick's coming helped a little; temporarily it deprived Stella of the time to worry. Roderick was young and vulnerable, and his father's early abdication had made Stella feel doubly responsible for her son. Roderick wanted to talk about his new interest in life, the run-down estate in Ireland recently bequeathed him by Cousin Francis Morris. The boy was determined to keep his new property, but, until the war was over, the task of looking after it would be largely Stella's responsibility.

Roderick's leave expired. The next night Robert Kelway came to Stella's flat. She gave no hint of her inward agitation, though she casually inquired if he knew Harrison. Gazing at her attractive, considerate lover, Stella silently marveled that he should be a suspect—he, a lamed veteran of Dunkirk! Considering, however, that she knew nothing about his family, she renewed her request that they visit his mother and sister in the country. A subsequent Saturday afternoon at Holme Dene revealed nothing strange about Robert's background. On the night of her return from Robert's home, she found Harrison waiting at her apartment; he confirmed his watchfulness by telling her where she had been, and why.

Roderick's interests intervened by summoning Stella briefly to Ireland. Robert protested at losing her for even a few days and they parted affectionately. In Ireland, Stella's distrust of Harrison received a jolt; he had been truthful, she learned, in telling her that he had been

a friend of Cousin Francis Morris. She resolved that she would acquaint Robert with Harrison's accusation. When she returned to London, Robert met her at the station. Minutes later, in a taxi, she revealed what she had heard; and Robert, deeply hurt, made a complete denial. Later that night he begged her to marry him, but Stella, surprised and disturbed, succeeded in parrying the proposal.

A few nights later Harrison had dinner with Stella in a popular restaurant. She stiffened with apprehension as he told her that she had disobeyed him by putting Robert on his guard. Before Stella could learn what Harrison intended to do, she was interrupted by the untimely intrusion of Louie Lewis, who crudely invited herself to their table after spotting Harrison in the crowd. Nevertheless, Stella managed to intimate that she would meet Harrison's terms if he would save Robert from arrest. Angry at Louie, Harrison made no response; roughly dismissing the two women, he stalked off, leaving them to find their way home through blacked-out London. Louie, fascinated by the superior charm and refinement of Stella, accompanied her to the doorway of her apartment.

Robert was at Holme Dene, so that not until the next night did Stella have a chance to warn him of his danger. In the early morning darkness of Stella's bedroom, they renewed their love and confidence with a sense that it was to be their last meeting. When Robert finally revealed that he was an ardent Nazi, prizing power above freedom, Stella found no way to reconcile their views. Faint footsteps, as of outside watchers, were heard as Robert dressed and prepared to leave. He climbed up the rope ladder to the skylight in the roof, then came back down again to kiss Stella once more. He told her to take care of herself as he hurriedly disappeared through the skylight. The next morning Robert's body was found lying in the street where he had leaped or fallen from the steeply slanting roof.

More than a year passed before Stella saw Harrison. There were Allied landings in Africa; there was the invasion of Italy; there was the ever-growing prospect of a Second Front. Finally Harrison came back. Stella had had questions to ask him, questions about Robert, but now it seemed pointless to ask them. An air of constraint hung over their conversation, a feeling that Robert's death had removed any real link between their lives. Harrison made no romantic overtures; he even seemed faintly relieved when Stella told him that she was soon to be married.

HEAVEN'S MY DESTINATION

Type of work: Novel
Author: Thornton Wilder (1897-   )
Type of plot: Social satire
Time of plot: 1930-1931
Locale: Middle West
First published: 1935

Principal characters:
GEORGE MARVIN BRUSH, a traveling salesman
ROBERTA, a farmer's daughter
GEORGE BURKIN, a peeping Tom
HERB, a newspaper reporter
ELIZABETH, his daughter

Critique:

In George Marvin Brush, Thornton Wilder would seem to have synthesized the American character with its many tragic inconsistencies. One admires George Brush one moment and detests him as a prig the next. The irony and the deceptive simplicity of *Heaven's My Destination* are terrifying. Although George Brush is not the picaresque hero-type, the novel, with its many colorful and unprincipled characters and its episodic form, resembles the picaresque genre.

The Story:

George Marvin Brush, a straight-laced, clean-living non-smoker and non-drinker of twenty-three, was a salesman for the Caulkins Educational Press; his territory was the Middle West. He was the amusement and the despair of all the traveling salesmen in the same territory who knew him. One day Doremus Blodgett, a hosiery salesman, caught George in the act of penning a Bible text on a hotel blotter and invited George up to his room to chaff him. The righteousness of George infuriated Blodgett, but the hosiery man was almost reconciled when George admitted to him that he had once wronged a farmer's daughter.

At another time George withdrew all his savings from the bank. In his attempt to explain to the bank president his plan of voluntary poverty, he insulted that executive by saying that banks owed their existence only to man's fear of insecurity. Being thought mad, George was jailed, but his ingenuousness confounded even his jailers. One of them, after hearing George propound his theories, withdrew his own savings from the bank.

In Oklahoma City George again saw Blodgett and his "cousin," Mrs. Margie McCoy. There he talked of the injustice of his receiving raises in pay, to the utter confusion of Blodgett and Mrs. McCoy. He told them that he had gone through college and had had a religious conversion in order to be of an independent mind. All he wanted, he said, was a perfect girl for his wife, six children, and a real American home. He confessed that he was hindered in his quest for these ideals by his having wronged a Kansas farm girl, one Roberta, whose farm home he had been unable to find since he had left it.

George went from Oklahoma City to the Chautauqua at Camp Morgan, Oklahoma, to see Judge Corey, a state legislator who was interested in textbook contracts. There he was shocked by Jessie, a college girl who believed in evolution; he pestered a distraught businessman who wanted to be left alone; and he turned down Judge Corey's offer of thirty-five thousand dollars and a state job if he would marry the judge's daughter, Mississippi.

From Camp Morgan George went to Kansas City, where he stayed in Queenie's boarding-house with his four wild friends, Herb and Morrie, reporters; Bat, a motion picture mechanic; and Louie, a hospital orderly. Accord lasted between the four and George as long as George did not preach his anti-tobacco and anti-alcohol creeds. They, in turn, restrained their actions and their speech in his presence. Three of them and George, who had a beautiful voice, formed an expert barbershop quartet. In Kansas City George became the victim of an elaborate practical joke arranged by his friends. After they had tricked him into drunkenness, the five went on a rampage. The second step in their plan to lead George to perdition came when Herb tricked George into going to dinner one Sunday at a brothel. Herb represented the house to George as an old mansion, its proprietor, Mrs. Crofut, as a pillar of Kansas City society, and the troop of prostitutes as her daughters. George, completely duped, was impressed by the graciousness of Mrs. Crofut and by the beauty of her daughters. He treated the girls to a neighborhood movie.

Back at Queenie's, George would not believe Herb when his friend told him the truth about Mrs. Crofut's genteel establishment. Irritated by George's priggishness and stupidity, his four friends beat him nearly to death. Later, at the hospital, Louie told George that he ought to live and let live.

Out of the hospital, George continued his book selling. On a train he met an evangelist who said that money did not matter; however, George gave the man money when he learned that the man's family was destitute. In Fort Worth George exasperated a bawdy house proprietor posing as a medium, by telling her that she was a fake.

Having learned that Roberta had taken a job as a waitress in Kansas City, George went there and forced himself upon the girl, who wanted nothing to do with him. He adopted Elizabeth, the daughter of his friend Herb, who died with few illusions about life.

In Ozarkville, Missouri, George angered a father when he talked to the man's young daughter in the street. Then he went to a country store to buy a doll for the girl and became involved in a hold-up. Carrying out one of his strange theories, he assisted the amazed burglar. The storekeeper, Mrs. Efrim, thought that George was out of his mind. Arrested, he was put in jail, where he met George Burkin, a movie director who had been arrested as a peeping Tom. Burkin explained to George that he peeped only to observe unself-conscious human behavior.

George's trial was a sensation in Ozarkville. The little girl and Mrs. Efrim lied in their testimony, and George attempted to explain his theories of life to a confounded court. When he explained what he called ahimsa, or the theory of reacting to every situation in a manner that was the exact opposite from what was expected, the bewildered judge released him, telling him to be cautious, however, because people were afraid of ideas.

After George and Burkin had left Ozarkville in Burkin's car, they picked up a hitchhiker who turned out to be the burglar whom George had tried to help. George attempted to work his radical theory for the treatment of criminals on the burglar, but the man only fled in confused anger. George and Burkin argued about George's theories, Burkin saying that George had never really grown up, and George claiming that Burkin had thought too much and had not lived enough.

Back in Kansas City, George met Roberta and her sister Lottie for the purpose of reaching a decision in his relationship with Roberta. Lottie suggested that the couple marry and get a divorce as soon as possible, so that Roberta could be accepted again by her family. George, however, could not countenance divorce. Being finally persuaded, Roberta married George and the couple moved into a flat over a drug store. But their married life grew more and more trying. George

found himself taking notes for topics that he and Roberta could safely discuss. They competed for Elizabeth's affections. At last Roberta decided to leave George and return to the farm.

George, unhappy, continued to sell books. He lost his faith and began to lead what many people would call a normal life. At length he fell sick and was hospitalized. In the hospital he admitted to a Methodist pastor that he had broken all but two of the ten commandments but that he was glad he had broken them. He shocked the pastor by saying that one cannot get better and better. While in the hospital he received a spoon which had been willed to him by a man whom he had never met but whom he had admired reciprocally through a mutual friend. He recovered, left the hospital, and reverted to his old ways George Brush was incurable.

HEDDA GABLER

Type of work: Drama
Author: Henrik Ibsen (1828-1906)
Type of plot: Social criticism
Time of plot: Late nineteenth century
Locale: Norway
First presented: 1890

Principal characters:
GEORGE TESMAN, a scholar
HEDDA TESMAN, his wife
MISS JULIANA TESMAN, his aunt
MRS. ELVSTED, Hedda's old schoolmate
JUDGE BRACK, a friend of the Tesmans
EILERT LOVBERG, Hedda's former suitor

Critique:

Hedda Gabler has in it most of the elements of good theater which Ibsen painstakingly learned from the popular French playwrights of the last half of the nineteenth century. In Hedda, he created a woman with hardly one redeeming virtue. She is spiritually as empty as she assumes her environment to be. Nearly every great actress of the last half-century

has played Hedda and audiences have always been attracted to her powerful but ruthless personality.

The Story:

When aristocratic Hedda Gabler, daughter of the late General Gabler, consented to marry Doctor George Tesman, everyone in Hedda's set was surprised

HEDDA GABLER by Henrik Ibsen. Published by Charles Scribner's Sons.

and a little shocked. Although George was a rising young scholar soon to be made a professor in the university, he was hardly considered the type of person Hedda would marry. He was dull and prosaic, absorbed almost exclusively in his dusty tomes and manuscripts, while Hedda was the beautiful, spoiled darling of her father and of all the other men who had flocked around her. But Hedda was now twenty-nine, and George was the only one of her admirers who was willing to offer her marriage and a villa which had belonged to the widow of a cabinet minister.

The villa was somewhat beyond George's means, but with the prospect of a professorship and with his Aunt Juliana's help, he managed to secure it because it was what Hedda wanted. He arranged a long wedding tour lasting nearly six months because Hedda wished that also. On their honeymoon George spent most of his time delving into libraries for material on his special field, the history of civilization. Hedda was bored. She returned to the villa hating George. Then it began to look as if George might not get the professorship, in which case Hedda would have to forego her footman and saddlehorse and some of the other luxuries she craved. George's rival for the post was Eilert Lovberg, a brilliant but erratic genius who had written a book, acclaimed a masterpiece, in George's own field. Hedda's boredom and disgust with her situation was complete. She found her only excitement in practicing with the brace of pistols which had belonged to General Gabler, the only legacy her father had left her.

George discovered that Eilert had written another book, more brilliant and important than the last, a book written with the help and inspiration of a Mrs. Elvsted, whose devotion to the erratic genius had reformed him. The manuscript of this book Lovberg brought with him one evening to the Tesman villa. Hedda proceeded to make the most of this situation. In the first place, Thea Elvsted was Hedda's despised schoolmate, and her husband's former sweetheart. The fact that this mouse-like creature had been the inspiration for the success and rehabilitation of Eilert Lovberg was more than Hedda could bear. For Eilert Lovberg had always been in love with Hedda, and she knew it. In the distant past, he had urged her to throw in her lot with him and she had been tempted to do so but had refused because his future had been uncertain. Now Hedda felt a pang of regret mingled with anger that another woman possessed what she had lacked the courage to hold for herself.

Her only impulse was to destroy, and circumstances played into her hands. When Lovberg called at the Tesman villa with his manuscript, George was on the point of leaving with his friend, Judge Brack, for a bachelor party. They invited Lovberg to accompany them, but he refused, preferring to remain at the villa with Mrs. Elvsted and Hedda. But Hedda, determined to destroy the handiwork of her rival, deliberately sent Lovberg off to the party. All night, Hedda and Mrs. Elvsted awaited the revelers' return. George was the first to appear with the story of the happenings of the night before.

The party had ended in an orgy, and on the way home Lovberg had lost his manuscript, which George recovered and brought home. In despair over the supposed loss of his manuscript, Lovberg had spent the remainder of the evening at Mademoiselle Diana's establishment. When he finally made his appearance at the villa, George had gone. Lovberg told Mrs. Elvsted he had destroyed his manuscript, but later he confessed to Hedda that it was lost and that, as a consequence, he intended to take his own life. Without revealing that the manuscript was at that moment in her possession, Hedda urged him to do the deed beautifully, and she pressed into his hand a memento of their relationship, one of General Gabler's pistols—the very one with which she had once threatened Lovberg.

After his departure, Hedda coldly and deliberately thrust the manuscript into the fire. When George returned and heard from Hedda's own lips the fate of Lovberg's manuscript, he was unspeakably shocked; but half believing that she burned it for his sake, he was also flattered. He resolved to keep silent and devote his life to reconstructing the book from the notes kept by Mrs. Elvsted.

Except for two circumstances, Hedda would have been safe. The first was the manner in which Lovberg met his death. Leaving Hedda, he had returned to Mademoiselle Diana's, where instead of dying beautifully, as Hedda had planned, he became embroiled in a brawl in which he was accidentally killed. The second was the character of Judge Brack, a so-phisticated man of the world, as ruthless in his way as Hedda was in hers. He had long admired Hedda's cold, dispassionate beauty, and had wanted to make her his mistress. The peculiar circumstances of Eilert Lovberg's death gave him his opportunity. He had learned that the pistol with which Lovberg met his death was one of a pair belonging to Hedda. If the truth came out, there would be an investigation followed by scandal in which Hedda would be involved. She could not face either a public scandal or the private ignominy of the judge's proposal. So while her husband and Mrs. Elvsted were beginning the long task of reconstructing the dead Lovberg's manuscript, Hedda calmly went to her boudoir and with the remaining pistol she died beautifully—as she had urged Lovberg to do —by putting a bullet through her head.

THE HEIMSKRINGLA

Type of work: Sagas
Author: Snorri Sturluson (1179-1241)
Type of plots: Historical chronicles
Time of plots: Legendary times to twelfth century
Locale: Norway
First transcribed: Thirteenth century

Principal characters:
ODIN, ancestor of the Northmen
ON JORUNDSSON, of Sweden
HALFDAN THE BLACK, of Norway
HARALD THE FAIRHAIRED, his son
AETHELSTAN, of England
HAKON THE GOOD, Harald's son
ERIC BLOOD-AX, Hakon's brother
OLAF TRYGGVESSON, Christianizer of Norway
OLAF THE SAINT
MAGNUS THE GOOD, his stepson
HARALD SIGURDSSON THE STERN, Olaf the Saint's brother
OLAF THE QUIET, Harald's son
MAGNUS BAREFOOT, Olaf's son
EYSTEIN,
SIGURD, and
OLAF, Magnus' sons
MAGNUS SIGURDSSON
HARALD GILLE, Sigurd Magnusson's half brother
INGE,
SIGURD, and
EYSTEIN, Harald's sons

1253

HAKON SIGURDSSON
ERLING SKAKKE, counselor to Inge
MAGNUS, his son

Critique:

The Heimskringla, a collection of traditional sagas of the Norwegian kings, was first transcribed by Snorri Sturluson, an Icelandic bard and chieftain. Interested in the stories handed down by word of mouth in the houses of chieftains in the northern countries, he wrote them down in Old Norse, the language understood by all Scandinavian peoples at that time. Snorri Sturluson began writing in 1220. Beginning with the Yngling Saga, which traces the descent of the Northmen from the legendary god Odin, The Heimskringla contains sixteen other sagas covering the historic period between 839 and 1177. Each saga tells of the life and achievements of one man; in The Heimskringla each man represented is the chief king of Norway at a time when several men usually fought for the title. These are only a few of the hundreds of sagas known to Scandinavian literature. While the time of sagas in general runs from the sixth to the fourteenth centuries, The Heimskringla covers the Viking Age, dating roughly from the eighth century, when Norwegians came into historical significance because of their raiding expeditions, through the years of Norwegian occupation of foreign lands, the Christianizing of their own country, and finally the consolidation of Norway.

The Stories:

In Asaland in Asia near the Black Sea lived Odin, the conqueror of many nations, and a great traveler, whose people believed he would have success in every battle. When a neighboring people beheaded his friend Mime as a spy and sent the head to Odin, he smeared the head with herbs to keep it from rotting and sang incantations over it. Thereafter the head could speak to Odin and discover secrets for him. While the Romans were subduing the world, Odin learned

that he was to rule the northern half. Traveling through Russia and northern Germany, he finally settled in the Scandinavian peninsula. There he appeared handsome to his friends and fiendish to his enemies. He used magic against his foes so that they were helpless in battle against him, for he could change his own shape and wish himself from place to place. He made laws for his people: that the dead should be burned, that blood-sacrifice be made for good harvests, and that taxes be paid yearly. When he was near death, Odin said that he would go to Valhalla and wait there for all good warriors. Then he died quietly in his bed, and afterward the rulers of the northland claimed descent from him.

The sacrifices his people made to Odin were sometimes great. When King On Jorundsson of Sweden was sixty years old, he made an oracular sacrifice of a son to Odin. His answer from Odin was that he would live sixty years longer if he sacrificed a son every ten years. He sacrificed as he was told until he had given up nine out of his ten sons. By that time he was so old and weak that his people refused to let the tenth son be sacrificed, and so On died of extreme old age. After that people dying from weakness of age were said to have On's sickness.

After twenty generations of Yngling rulers in the Scandinavian countries came Halfdan the Black, born about 820, King of Norway. In those days a king was an intermediary between the people and the supreme powers, whose favor he courted by sacrifices. Halfdan was considered a good king because the harvests were plentiful during his lifetime. He died young in a sleighing accident while crossing thin ice. His people begged so hard for his body to insure continued good seasons that finally the body was quartered, and each quarter and the head were sent to separate provinces to spread his good influence.

Harald the Fairhaired was Halfdan's son. He sent some of his henchmen to bring to him a girl to be his concubine, but she refused to bow to a king of any territory so small and sent word that she would consider him when he ruled all of Norway. His attendants thought her attitude warranted punishment; Harald considered it a challenge. Ten years later, after he had conquered all of Norway, he sent for the girl and married her. He had many children by her and other women. When he was fifty years old, he divided his kingdom among his sons and gave them half the revenues.

At that time Aethelstan, King of England, sent Harald a sword. When Harald accepted it, however, Aethelstan's messengers claimed that he was then subject to their king. The following summer Harald sent his nine-year-old son Hakon to Aethelstan to foster, as a foster father was always subject to a real father. Each king tried to outdo the other, but each ruled in his own kingdom until his dying day. When he was seventy-nine years old, Harald died in his bed.

Hakon went from England to Norway when he heard of his father's death. He was then fifteen years old. At the same time the chief Norse king had sailed west to ravage England; he was Hakon's brother, Eric Blood-Ax, so called because he had slain at least four of his brothers. Eric was killed in England and Hakon subdued Norway. Hakon, who had been converted to Christianity while in England, began to practice Christian habits of fasting and prayer in Norway. Although he did not insist on forcing Christianity on his followers, many of them, out of friendship for him, allowed themselves to be baptized. Hakon wanted to forego sacrifices to the gods, but a counselor persuaded him to humor the people who still believed devoutly in blood sacrifice. Known to his country as Hakon the Good, he was killed in battle with

Eric's sons, to whom he left the kingdom.

The years during which Eric's sons ruled Norway were so bad that fish as well as corn were lacking and the people went hungry. Among other petty kings, the sons killed Tryggve Olafsson, whose wife escaped to bring Olaf Tryggvesson to birth.

As a child Olaf Tryggvesson spent six years in slavery before his uncle learned where marauding Vikings had sent him after capturing the boy and his mother as they were on their way to a place of safety in Russia. By the time he was twelve, Olaf himself was a Viking chieftain. After harrying various parts of England he made peace with Aethelred, the English king, and thereafter always kept the peace with England. By that time his aim was to be a crusader, for he had come under the influence of Christianity during his raids on England. Having been converted and baptized by the English priests, he wanted to Christianize his own land as well. He set sail for Norway in 995. Between that date and 1000, when he was decoyed into a one-sided battle with the kings of Denmark and Sweden and lost his life at Svolder, he converted all of Norway as well as many of the outlying islands, either by the force of his own personality, or, when that did not suffice, by force of arms. Norway was a Christian land by the time Olaf died, but there was no Norwegian king strong enough to rule its entirety while the Danes and Swedes laid claim to various parts of the country.

While he was very young, Olaf Haraldsson joined Viking expeditions to England, Jutland, Holland, France, and Spain. In England, where the Norwegians were fighting the Danes who were then in power in England, he was present at the stoning to death of the archbishop who had confirmed Olaf Tryggvesson. It was said that in Spain Olaf Haraldsson dreamed of a fearful man who told him to give up further travel to the Holy Land and to go back to Norway. In 1015 he sailed for Norway to reëstablish Christianity and to regain the throne once held by his ancestor, Harald the Fairhaired. Though he did not have the striking personality of Olaf Tryggvesson, Olaf Haraldsson had persistence enough to spread Christianity by his bands of missionaries, to win control over Norway, and to set up a central government. The latter was his hardest task, as it meant taking away some of the traditional powers of the chieftains. He created a form of justice that worked equally for the chieftains and the common people, and because of their resentment the chieftains rose against him at last. With a superior force they fought him at Stiklestad, in 1030, when he was cut down. His hope for national union and independence seemed doomed until suddenly rumors were spread that miracles had occurred where his body had fallen. People began to give Olaf Haraldsson a new name, Olaf the Saint, and the whole Norwegian people suddenly craved the independence he had fought for.

Olaf the Saint's stepson, Magnus, obtained the title of King of Norway without much trouble. Afterward he made a treaty with King Hardacanute of Denmark to keep the peace as long as they both should live, the one surviving to become the ruler of the other's country. When Hardacanute died, Magnus thereupon became King of Denmark. Since Hardacanute had also become King of England after the death of his father, Magnus laid claim to England when Edward the Good became the English king; but he was prevented from invading England by trouble stirred up in Denmark by a false friend whom he had made earl there. Letters were exchanged between Magnus and Edward over Magnus' claim to England. Edward's reply was so sensible and courageous that Magnus was content to rule in his own land and to let Edward reign in England.

Greater troubles beset Magnus when his uncle, Harald Sigurdsson, returned north after many years in Russia, Constantinople, and the Holy Land. Harald had left Norway after the battle of Stiklestad, when his brother Olaf the Saint was killed. He plundered all through the south lands and at Constantinople joined the royal guard called the Vaeringer. Meanwhile he had collected much booty, which he sent to the Russian king for safekeeping until he should have finished his wanderings. When he tired of life in Constantinople, he traveled north to Russia. There he married Ellisiv, the king's daughter, and then traveled with her and his booty toward Norway. Eventually he made a deal with Magnus. He received half of Norway in return for half his booty. When Magnus, called the Good, died of illness, Harald, in contrast called the Stern, ruled alone. He was a harsh ruler and he met his death in England while trying to unthrone Harald Godwinsson, Edward's successor.

Through these times miracles continued to be credited to Olaf the Saint. Sometimes he appeared to people in dreams, as he did to Magnus the Good just before his death. Sometimes a pilgrimage to his shrine cured people who had been crippled from birth or who had been maimed in fighting. It was even said that Olaf could pull the root of a tongue so that a man whose tongue had been cut out could speak again. His shrine was in Nidaros.

After Harald the Stern, his sons Magnus and Olaf ruled Norway, but Magnus soon died of a sickness. Olaf, called the Quiet, reigned for twenty-six years. There was peace in Norway during that time, and the country gained in riches and cultivation.

Thereafter Olaf's son Magnus and his nephew, Hakon Magnusson, ruled Norway, but Hakon soon died of an illness. Magnus' reign was of ten years' time, most of which he spent in expeditions to reduce the island possessions to full submission to the central government in Norway. Under Magnus, for the first time, the government became a strong power. Because Magnus returned from one of his expeditions to Scotland wearing the Scottish national costume, his people called him Magnus Barefoot. On a foraging expedition, in 1103, Magnus was killed in Ireland before he was thirty years old.

From that time until 1130 peace descended on Norway and the Church increased its powers. In the early days the Norwegian churches had been under the archbishopric of Bremen, but during that time they gained an archbishopric of their own at Lund in Skane. Magnus' sons, Eystein, Sigurd, and Olaf, ruled the country, but Olaf was only a small boy. Those years were also the period of the crusades. Sigurd took men and ships to the Holy Land while Eystein ruled at home. Sigurd was gone three years and gained much glory in England, Spain, Constantinople, and Palestine. He was afterward called the Crusader. When he came back to Norway, he and Eystein were jealous of each other's powers. Olaf died young and Eystein died before Sigurd. Sigurd had strange fancies before he himself died, but he had done much to improve the legal system of the country by increasing the powers of the Things. The congregation of people at the Things became the highest authority in the land, and even the kings argued their cases before those representative bodies.

Neither Olaf nor Eystein had sons. Magnus, Sigurd's son, became king, but his sole rule was threatened by Harald Gille, who came from Ireland and claimed to be Sigurd's half-brother. Harald passed an ordeal by hot iron to prove his paternity. After Sigurd's death Harald was proclaimed king over part of Norway. It was said that Magnus was foolish, but Harald was cruel. A series of civil wars ensued, ending when Harald captured Magnus and had him blinded and otherwise mutilated. Thereafter Magnus was called the Blind. He retired to a monastery. Harald was killed by the order and treachery of Sigurd Slembedegn, a pretender to the throne.

In the days when Harald's sons reigned there were more civil wars. Crippled Inge was the most popular of Harald's three sons. Sigurd and Eystein led separate factions, and so there was always unrest in the country.

In 1152, Cardinal Nicholas came to Norway from Rome to establish an archbishopric at Nidaros, where King Olaf the Saint reposed. Cardinal Nicholas was well loved by the people and improved many of their customs. When the pope died suddenly, Nicholas became Pope Adrian IV. He was always friendly with the Norsemen.

After Sigurd and Eystein had been killed in different battles, Inge ruled alone. He was twenty-six when he was killed in battle with Hakon Sigurdsson, who had claimed Eystein's part of Norway. Hakon was little to be trusted. Erling Skakke, previously a power behind Inge's throne, then took it upon himself to create a strong party which could put upon the throne whomever it chose. None of his party favored Hakon, called the Broad-Shouldered, who was defeated in battle within a year, when he was only fifteen, in 1162.

Erling Skakke's party finally decided to put Erling Skakke's son Magnus on the throne. The child was five years old at the time. He was a legitimate candidate, however, for his mother was a daughter of Sigurd the Crusader. Erling Skakke was jealous of power, yet he gave much of the traditional authority of the throne to the bishops in exchange for their blessing on Magnus as king; and he made an agreement with King Valdemar of Denmark under which he gave Valdemar a part of Norway as a fief under the Danish crown in exchange for peace. It had been a long time since a foreign king had claim to part of Norway. Erling Skakke spent much of his time wiping out the descendants of Harald Gille, and in time he became a tyrant in order to hold the throne safe for his child, Magnus Erlingsson.

HELEN

Type of work: Drama
Author: Euripides (c. 485-c. 406 B.C.)
Type of plot: Romantic adventure
Time of plot: Seven years after the sack of Troy
Locale: Egypt
First presented: 412 B.C.

Principal characters:
HELEN, wife of King Menelaus
MENELAUS, King of Sparta
THEOCLYMENUS, King of Egypt
THEONOE, a prophetess, sister of Theoclymenus

Critique:

There is some disagreement among Greek scholars as to whether *Helen* is a serious play or, because of its anticlimactic happy ending, merely Euripidean self-parody. The line of action seems to build toward tragedy, from which it is averted at the last moment by a *deus ex machina* in the form of the Dioscuri. The story is taken from a tradition established in the sixth century B.C. by the Greek poet Stesichorus, who believed that Paris had carried off to Troy only a phantom Helen fashioned by Hera, while the real Helen was taken to Egypt by Hermes. H. D. F. Kitto praises this play, asserting that it has appropriate rhetoric throughout, consistent characterization, and a faultless plot. Perhaps the only exceptions to its comic tone are the first ode of the chorus and the murder of the fifty Egyptian galley-men.

The Story:

Helen prayed before the tomb of Proteus, late King of Egypt, who had protected her from any dishonor while her husband Menelaus was leading the Greek hosts at the siege of Troy in the mistaken belief that the phantom Helen carried off by Paris, son of the Trojan king, was really his wife. She recalled that when the three goddesses, Hera, Cypris (Aphrodite), and Athena had appeared before Paris and asked him to judge which was the fairest, Cypris had promised him Helen as a prize for choosing her. But Hera, enraged at being rejected, had caused a phantom Helen to be carried off to Troy. In Egypt the real Helen prayed for the safety of her husband and for protection against Theoclymenus, son of Proteus, who was determined to marry her.

She was accosted by Teucer, an exile from Achaea, who brought tidings of the end of the war, the ruin of the Greeks seeking their homelands, the disappearance of Menelaus and Helen, and the suicide of Leda, Helen's mother, who had killed herself because she could not endure her daughter's shame. The anguished Helen then warned Teucer not to seek out the prophetess Theonoe, as he intended, but to flee, for any Greek found in Egypt would be killed. The chorus grieved for Helen, who lamented her miserable fate and threatened suicide. In despair, she took the advice of the chorus and herself sought out Theonoe.

Menelaus, shipwrecked and in rags, appeared before the palace seeking aid, only to be berated and sent off by a portress who warned him that since Theoclymenus had Helen in his possession no Greeks were welcome in Egypt. Menelaus was astounded, for he had just left his Helen secure in a nearby cave. As he stood there in bewilderment, Helen emerged from her conference with Theonoe and confronted amazed Menelaus. Helen could not convince him that she was indeed his wife until a messenger brought word to Menelaus that the Helen he had left at the cave was gone, having

1258

soared away into the air. The long separated lovers then embraced, rejoiced, and told each other of all the adventures that had befallen them. But their immense happiness was darkened by realization of their present plight: Theoclymenus was determined to make Helen his own, and Menelaus was in danger of his life. The two resolved that if they could not concoct some scheme for escape, they would commit suicide rather than be separated again.

Theonoe, aware of the presence of Menelaus, appeared to inform him that, although Hera had relented and was now willing to let him return to Sparta with Helen, Cypris was unwilling to have it revealed that she had bribed Paris to be chosen as the most beautiful of the goddesses. Therefore Theonoe, serving Cypris, felt obliged to expose Menelaus to her brother. Terrified, Helen fell to her knees in tears and supplication, and the enraged Menelaus threatened that they would die rather than submit. Theonoe relented, promised to keep silent, and urged them to devise some way of escape.

After rejecting several of Menelaus' desperate proposals, Helen hit upon a scheme which she put into operation as soon as Theoclymenus returned from a hunting trip. Appearing before him in mourning clothes and addressing him for the first time as her lord, Helen told him in a pitiful voice that a shipwrecked Greek warrior had just brought her word that Menelaus had drowned at sea. She was now ready, she added, to marry Theoclymenus if he would permit proper burial honors, in the Greek fashion, for her husband. Theoclymenus consented and turned to Menelaus, who was posing as the bearer of sad tidings, for instructions concerning Greek burial rites for a king drowned at sea. He was told that there must be a blood-offering, an empty bier decked and carried in procession, bronze arms, a supply of the fruits of the earth, all to be taken out to sea in a large ship from which the widow must commit everything to the waters. The gullible Theoclymenus, anxious to foster piety in the woman who was about to become his wife, agreed to everything, and preparations were made for both a funeral and a royal wedding.

Later, a breathless messenger came running to Theoclymenus with the news that Helen had escaped with Menelaus. He described in detail how the Greek stranger commanding the ship had permitted a large number of shipwrecked sailors to come aboard and how, when the time came to slay the bull, the stranger, instead of uttering a funeral prayer, had called upon Poseidon to allow him and his wife to sail safely to Sparta. The aroused Egyptians sought to turn back the ship, but they were slaughtered by the Greek warriors whom Menelaus had smuggled aboard. Theoclymenus, enraged, realized that pursuit was hopeless but resolved to avenge himself on his treacherous sister, Theonoe. A servant from the palace tried in vain to convince him that he ought to accept what was obviously an honorable treachery. Both the servant and Theonoe were saved from death when the Dioscuri, the twin sons of Zeus, appeared from the sky to restrain his rage and explain to him that Heaven had ordained the return of Helen and Menelaus to their homeland. Theoclymenus was chastened, and the chorus chanted familiar lines about the irony of Fate.

HENRY ESMOND

Type of work: Novel
Author: William Makepeace Thackeray (1811-1863)
Type of plot: Historical romance
Time of plot: Late seventeenth, early eighteenth centuries
Locale: England and the Low Countries
First published: 1852

Principal characters:

HENRY ESMOND, a Castlewood ward
FRANCIS ESMOND, Viscount Castlewood
RACHEL ESMOND, his wife
BEATRIX, their daughter
FRANK, their son
LORD MOHUN, a London rake
FATHER HOLT, a Jacobite spy
JAMES STUART, the exiled pretender

Critique:

Thackeray did not have high regard for the average historian of his day. To present history as he thought it should be presented, he wrote *The History of Henry Esmond,* a novel which contains a blend of fact and fiction. There is fact in the many historical characters of the book. There is fiction in the love story of Colonel Henry Esmond, who was in love with two women. Today's reader is likely to lose patience with Henry Esmond, whose attempts at winning Beatrix are so ineffectual as to be almost ludicrous; but no reader can escape the witchery of Beatrix's charms. In her, Thackeray has created one of the most delightfully puzzling and fascinating coquettes in all English literature.

The Story:

Henry Esmond grew up at Castlewood. He knew there was some mystery about his birth and he dimly remembered that long ago he had lived with weavers who spoke a foreign tongue. Thomas Esmond, Viscount Castlewood, had brought him to England and turned him over to Father Holt, the chaplain, to be educated. That much he learned as he grew older.

All was not peace and quiet at Castlewood in those years, when his lordship and Father Holt were engaged in a plot for the restoration of the exiled Stuart king, James II. When James attempted to recover Ireland for the Stuarts, Thomas Esmond rode off to his death at the battle of the Boyne. His widow fled to her dower house at Chelsea. Father Holt disappeared. Henry, a large-eyed, grave-faced twelve-year-old boy, was left alone with servants in the gloomy old house.

There his new guardians and distant cousins, Francis and Rachel Esmond, found him when they arrived to take possession of Castlewood. The new Viscount Castlewood, a bluff, loud-voiced man, greeted the boy kindly enough. His wife was like a girl herself—she was only eight years older than Henry—and Henry thought her the loveliest lady he had ever seen. With them were a little daughter, Beatrix, and a son, Frank, a baby in arms.

As Henry grew older he became more and more concerned over the rift he saw coming between Rachel Esmond and her husband, both of whom he loved because they had treated him as one of the immediate family in the household at Castlewood. It was plain that the hard-drinking, hard-gambling nobleman was wearying of his quiet country life. After Rachel's face was disfigured by smallpox, her altered beauty caused her husband to neglect her even more. Young Beatrix also felt that relations between her parents were strained.

When Henry was old enough, he went to Cambridge, sent there on money left Rachel by a deceased relative. Later, when he returned to Castlewood on a vacation, he realized for the first time that Beatrix was exceptionally attractive. Apparently he had never really noticed her before. Rachel, for her part, had great regard for her young kinsman. Before his arrival from Cambridge, according to Beatrix, Rachel went to Henry's room ten times to see that it was ready.

Relations between Rachel and the viscount were all but severed when the notorious Lord Mohun visited Castlewood. Rachel knew her husband had been losing heavily to Mohun at cards, but when she spoke to the viscount about the bad company he was keeping, he flew into a rage. He was by no means calmed when Beatrix innocently blurted out to her father, in the company of Mohun, that that gentleman was interested in Rachel. Jealous of another man's attentions to the wife he himself neglected, the viscount determined to seek satisfaction in a duel.

The two men fought in London, where the viscount had gone on the pretext of seeing a doctor. Henry, who suspected the real reason for the trip, went along, for he hoped to engage Mohun in a fight and thus save the life of his beloved guardian. The viscount, however, was in no mood to be cheated out of an excuse to provoke a quarrel. He was heavily in debt to Mohun and thought a fight was the only honorable way out of his difficulties. Moreover, he knew Mohun had written letters to Rachel, although, as the villain explained, she had never answered them. They fought, and Mohun foully and fatally wounded the viscount. On his deathbed the viscount confessed to his young kinsman that Henry was not an illegitimate child, but the son of Thomas, Lord Castlewood, by an early marriage, and the true heir to the Castlewood title. Henry Esmond generously burned the dying man's confession and resolved never to divulge the secret.

For his part in the duel Henry Esmond was sent to prison. When Rachel visited Henry in prison, she was enraged because he had not stopped the duel and because he had allowed Mohun to go unpunished. She rebuked Henry and forbade him to return to Castlewood. When Henry left prison he decided to join the army. For that purpose he visited the old dowager viscountess, his stepmother, who bought him a commission.

Henry's military ventures were highly successful, and won for him his share of wounds and glory. He fought in the cam-

paign of the Duke of Marlborough against Spain and France in 1702 and in the campaign of Blenheim in 1704. Between the two campaigns he returned to Castlewood, where he was reconciled with Rachel. There he saw Frank, now Lord Castlewood, and Beatrix, who was cordial toward him. Rachel herself cautioned Henry that Beatrix was selfish and temperamental and would make no man happy who loved her.

After the campaign of 1704 Henry returned to his cousins, who were living in London. To Henry, Beatrix was more beautiful than ever and even more the coquette. But he found himself unable to make up his mind whether he loved her or Rachel. Later, during the campaign of 1706, he learned from Frank that the ravishing Beatrix was engaged to an earl. The news put Henry in low spirits because he now felt she would never marry a poor captain like himself.

Henry's affairs of the heart were put temporarily into the background when he came upon Father Holt in Brussels. The priest told Henry that while on an expedition in the Low Countries, Thomas Esmond, his father, had seduced the young woman who was Henry's mother. A few weeks before his child was born Thomas Esmond was injured in a duel. Thinking he would die, he married the woman so that her child would be born with an untainted name. But Thomas Esmond did not die, and when he recovered from his wounds he deserted his wife and married a distant kinswoman, the dowager viscountess, Henry's stepmother.

When Henry returned to Castlewood, Rachel informed him she had learned his secret from the old viscountess and consequently knew that he, not Frank, was the true heir. For the second time Henry refused to accept the title belonging to him.

Beatrix's interest in Henry grew after she became engaged to the Duke of Hamilton and learned that Henry was not illegitimate in birth but the bearer of a title her brother was using. Henry wanted to give Beatrix a diamond necklace for a wedding present, but the duke would not permit his fiancée to receive a gift from one of illegitimate birth. Rachel came to the young man's defense and declared before the duke, her daughter, and Henry the secret of his birth and title. Later the duke was killed in a duel with Lord Mohun, who also met his death at the same time. The killing of Rachel's husband was avenged.

The Duke of Hamilton's death gave Henry one more chance to win Beatrix's heart. He threw himself into a plot to put the young Stuart pretender on the throne when old Queen Anne died. To this end he went to France and helped to smuggle into England the young chevalier whom the Jacobites called James III, the king over the water. The two came secretly to the Castlewood home in London, the prince passing as Frank, the young viscount, and there the royal exile saw and fell in love with Beatrix.

Fearing the results of this infatuation, Lady Castlewood and Henry sent Beatrix against her will to Castlewood. When a report that the queen was dying swept through London, the prince was nowhere to be found. Henry and Frank made a night ride to Castlewood. Finding the pretender there, in the room used by Father Holt in the old days, they renounced him and the Jacobite cause. Henry realized his love for Beatrix was dead at last. He felt no regrets for her or for the prince as he rode back to London and heard the heralds proclaiming George I, the new king.

The prince made his way secretly back to France, where Beatrix joined him in his exile. At last Henry felt free to declare himself to Rachel, who had grown very dear to him. Leaving Frank in possession of the title and the Castlewood estates, Henry and his wife went to America. In Virginia he and Rachel built a new Castlewood, reared a family, and found happiness in their old age.

HENRY THE EIGHTH

Type of work: Drama
Author: William Shakespeare (1564-1616)
Type of plot: Historical chronicle
Time of plot: 1520-1533
Locale: England
First presented: c. 1612

Principal characters:

KING HENRY THE EIGHTH
THOMAS WOLSEY, Cardinal of York and Lord Chancellor of England
CARDINAL CAMPEIUS, papal legate
CRANMER, the Archbishop of Canterbury
DUKE OF BUCKINGHAM
DUKE OF SUFFOLK
DUKE OF NORFOLK
GARDINER, the Bishop of Winchester
THOMAS CROMWELL, Wolsey's servant
QUEEN KATHARINE, wife of Henry, later divorced
ANNE BOLEYN, maid of honor to Katharine, later queen

Critique:

In the prologue to *Henry VIII* the audience is advised that this is not a happy play; it should be received in sadness. The description is incomplete and the advice somewhat misleading. True, the play is sad in its reality of ambition, political maneuvering, misunderstanding, and unhappiness, but, as the story progresses, honesty and altruism predominate. And it is difficult to imagine a Shakespearean audience receiving with sadness Cranmer's eloquent prophecy regarding the newborn princess, known to history as Queen Elizabeth. *Henry VIII* vividly pictures British court life in its spectacular pomp and in its behind-the-throne humanity. Many authorities credit John Fletcher with the part-authorship of this play.

The Story:

Cardinal Wolsey, a powerful figure at court during the reigns of Henry VII and Henry VIII, was becoming too aggressive in his self-aggrandizement. Wolsey was of humble stock, which fact accentuated his personal qualities. Since he had lacked the advantages of family and ancestral office, his political prominence was entirely the result of his own wisdom, manner, and persistence. Unscrupulous in seeking his own ends, he had removed any possible obstacle in his climb to power.

One such hindrance to his ambitious designs was the Duke of Buckingham, accused of high treason. When Buckingham was brought before the court for trial, Queen Katharine, speaking in his defense, protested against the cardinal's unjust taxes and informed the king of growing animosity among his people because he retained Wolsey as his adviser. Wolsey produced witnesses, among them Buckingham's discharged surveyor, who testified to Buckingham's disloyalty. The surveyor swore that, at the time of the king's journey to France, the duke had sought priestly confirmation for his belief that he could, by gaining favor with the common people, rise to govern England. In his lengthy and persistent testimony the surveyor played upon earlier minor offenses Buckingham had committed, and he climaxed his accusation with an account of the duke's assertion that he would murder the king in order to gain the throne.

In spite of Katharine's forthright protestations against Wolsey in his presence, and her repeated contention of false testimony against Buckingham, the accused man was found guilty and sentenced to be executed. The duke, forbearing toward his enemies, recalled the experience of his father, Henry of Buckingham, who had been betrayed by a servant. Henry VII had restored the honor of the family by elevating the present duke to favor. One difference prevailed between the two trials, the duke stated; his father had been unjustly dealt with, but he himself had had a noble trial.

Wolsey, fearing reprisal from Buckingham's son, sent him to Ireland as a deputy; then, incensed and uneasy because of Katharine's open accusations, he pricked the king's conscience by questions regarding his marriage to Katharine, who had been the widow of Henry's brother. Wolsey furthered his cause against Katharine by arousing Henry's interest in Anne Boleyn, whom the king met at a gay ball given by the cardinal.

The plan followed by Wolsey in securing a divorce for Henry was not a difficult one. In addition to his evident trust of Wolsey, the king felt keenly the fact that the male children born to him and Katharine in their twenty years of marriage had been stillborn or had died shortly after birth. Consequently, there was no male heir in direct succession.

The cardinal's final step to be rid of his chief adversary at court was to appeal to the pope for a royal divorce. When Cardinal Campeius arrived from Rome as counsel to the king, Katharine appeared in her own defense. But Wolsey had once more resorted to perjured witnesses. Requesting counsel, Katharine was told by Wolsey that the honest and intelligent men gathered at the hearing were of her choosing. Cardinal Campeius supported Wolsey's stand.

In speeches of magnificent dignity and honesty, Katharine denounced the political treachery that had caused her so much

1263

unhappiness. Later, however, Katharine, expelled from the court and sequestered in Kimbolton, was able to feel compassion for Wolsey when informed that he had died in ill-repute; and her undying devotion to Henry was indicated in her death note to him. Altruistic to the last, she made as her final request to the king the maintenance of the domestics who had served her so faithfully. Her strength to tolerate the injustices she had endured lay in her trust in a Power which, she said, could not be corrupted by a king.

But ambition overrode itself in Wolsey's designs for power. His great pride had caused him to accumulate greater wealth than the king's, to use an inscription, *Ego et Rex meus*, which subordinated the king to the cardinal, and to have a British coin stamped with a cardinal's hat. These, among many other offenses, were of little importance compared with Wolsey's double-dealing against the king in the divorce proceedings. Because Wolsey feared that Henry would marry Anne Boleyn instead of seeking a royal alliance in France, Wolsey asked the pope to delay the divorce. When his letter was delivered by mistake to the king, Wolsey, confronted with the result of his own carelessness, showed the true tenacious character of the ambitious climber. Although he realized that his error was his undoing, he attempted to ingratiate himself once more with the king.

He was too late to save himself. He could instigate the unseating and banishment of subordinates and he could maneuver to have the queen sequestered, but Henry wished no meddling with his marital affairs. Repentant that he had not served God with the effort and fervor with which he had served the king, Wolsey left the court, a broken-spirited man. He was later arrested in York, to be returned for arraignment before Henry. He was saved the humiliation of trial, however, for he died on the way to London.

Henry, shortly after the divorce, secretly married Anne Boleyn. After Wolsey's death she was crowned queen with great pomp. Cranmer, the new Archbishop of Canterbury, became Henry's chief adviser.

Jealousy and rivalry did not disappear from the court with the downfall of Wolsey. Charging heresy, Gardiner, Bishop of Winchester, set out to undermine Cranmer's position with the king. Accused as an arch heretic, Cranmer was brought to trial. Henry, trusting his favorite, gave him the royal signet ring which he was to show to the council if his entreaties and reasoning failed with his accusers. Cranmer, overcome by the king's kindness, wept in gratitude.

As he stood behind a curtain near the council room, the king heard Gardiner's charges against Cranmer. When Gardiner ordered Cranmer to the Tower, stating that the council was acting on the pleasure of the king, the accused man produced the ring and insisted upon his right to appeal the case to the king. Realizing that they had been tricked by a ruse which Wolsey had used for many years, the nobles were penitent. Appearing before the council, Henry took his seat at the table to condemn the assemblage for their tactics in dealing with Cranmer. After giving his blessings to those present and imploring them to be motivated in the future by unity and love, he asked Cranmer to be godfather to the daughter recently born to Anne Boleyn.

At the christening Cranmer prophesied that the child, Elizabeth, would be wise and virtuous, that her life would be a pattern to all princes who knew her, and that she would be loved and feared because of her goodness and her strength. He said that she would rule long and every day of her reign would be blessed with good deeds.

HENRY THE FIFTH

Type of work: Drama
Author: William Shakespeare (1564-1616)
Type of plot: Historical romance
Time of plot: Early part of the fifteenth century
Locale: England and France
First presented: 1600

Principal characters:
HENRY THE FIFTH, King of England
CHARLES THE SIXTH, King of France
PRINCESS KATHARINE, his daughter
THE DAUPHIN, his son
MONTJOY, a French herald

Critique:

In *The Life of Henry the Fifth* Shakespeare skillfully combined poetry, pageantry, and history in his effort to glorify England and Englishmen. King Henry himself represents all that is finest in English royalty; and yet when Henry notes on the eve of the battle of Agincourt that he is also a man like other men, Shakespeare shows us an Englishman who possesses that quality of humility which makes great men even greater. Few can see or read the play without sharing, at least for the moment, Shakespeare's pride in England and in things English, and without sensing the vigor and the idealism that are part of the Anglo-Saxon heritage.

The Story:

Once the toss-pot prince of Falstaff's tavern brawls, Henry V was now king at Westminster, a stern but just monarch concerned with his hereditary claim to the crown of France. Before the arrival of the French ambassadors, the young king asked for legal advice from the Archbishop of Canterbury. The king thought that he was the legal heir to the throne of France through Edward III, whose claim to the French throne was, at best, questionable. The Archbishop assured Henry that he had as much right to the French throne as did the French king; consequently, both the Archbishop and the Bishop of Ely urged Henry to press his demands against the French.

When the ambassadors from France arrived, they came, not from Charles, the king, but from his arrogant eldest son, the Dauphin. According to the ambassadors, the Dauphin considered the English monarch the same hot-headed, irresponsible youth he had been before he ascended the throne. To show that he considered Henry an unfit ruler whose demands were ridiculous, the Dauphin presented Henry with some tennis balls. Enraged by the insult, Henry told the French messengers to warn their master that the tennis balls would be turned into gun-stones for use against the French.

The English prepared for war. The Dauphin remained contemptuous of Henry, but others, including the French Constable and the ambassadors who had seen Henry in his wrath, were not so confident. Henry's army landed to lay siege to Harfleur, and the king threatened to destroy the city, together with its inhabitants, unless it surrendered. The French governor had to capitulate because help promised by the Dauphin never arrived. The French, meanwhile, were—with the exception of King Charles—alarmed by the rapid progress of the English through France. That ruler, however, was so sure of victory that he sent his herald, Montjoy, to Henry to demand that the English king pay a ransom to the French, give himself up, and have his soldiers withdraw from

France. Henry was not impressed by this bold gesture, and retorted that if King Charles wanted him, the Frenchman should come to get him.

On the eve of the decisive battle of Agincourt, the English were outnumbered five to one. Henry's troops were on foreign soil and ridden with disease. To encourage them, and also to sound out their morale, the king borrowed a cloak and in this disguise walked out among his troops, from watch to watch and from tent to tent. As he talked with his men, he told them that a king is but a man like other men, and that if he were a king he would not want to be anywhere except where he was, in battle with his soldiers. To himself, Henry mused over the cares and responsibilities of kingship. Again he thought of himself simply as a man who differed from other men only in ceremony, itself an empty thing.

Henry's sober reflections on the eve of a great battle, in which he thought much English blood would be shed, were quite different from those of the French, who were exceedingly confident of their ability to defeat their enemy. Shortly before the conflict began, Montjoy again appeared before Henry to give the English one last chance to surrender. Henry again refused to be intimidated. He was not discouraged by the numerical inferiority of his troops, for, as he reasoned in speaking with one of his officers, the fewer troops the English had, the greater would be the honor to them when they won.

The following day the battle began. Because of Henry's leadership, the English held their own. When French reinforcements arrived at a crucial point in the battle, Henry ordered his men to kill all their prisoners so that the energies of the English might be directed entirely against the enemy in front of them, not behind. Soon the tide turned. A much humbler Montjoy approached Henry to request a truce for burying the French dead. Henry granted the herald's request, and at the same time learned from him that the French had conceded defeat. Ten thousand French had been killed, and only twenty-nine English.

The battle over, nothing remained for Henry to do but to discuss with the French king terms of peace. Katharine, Charles' beautiful daughter, was Henry's chief demand, and while his lieutenants settled the details of surrender with the French, Henry made love to the princess and asked her to marry him. Though Katharine's knowledge of English was slight and Henry's knowledge of French little better, they were both acquainted with the universal language of love. French Katharine consented to become English Kate and Henry's bride.

HENRY THE FOURTH, PART ONE

Type of work: Drama
Author: William Shakespeare (1564-1616)
Type of plot: Historical chronicle
Time of plot: 1400-1405
Locale: England
First presented: 1596

Principal characters:
KING HENRY THE FOURTH
HENRY, Prince of Wales
JOHN OF LANCASTER, another son of the king
EARL OF WESTMORELAND, and
SIR WALTER BLUNT, members of the king's party
HOTSPUR, son of Henry Percy, Earl of Northumberland
THOMAS PERCY, Earl of Worcester, Hotspur's uncle

EDMUND MORTIMER, Earl of March, Hotspur's brother-in-law and
claimant to the throne
SIR JOHN FALSTAFF, a bibulous knight
MISTRESS QUICKLY, hostess of the Boar's Head Tavern in Eastcheap

Critique:

In Part I of *The History of King Henry IV* historical details and dramatic sequences involving affairs of state are secondary to the comic aspects of the plot. Falstaff, Shakespeare's best humorous character, is the figure whose entrances have been anticipated by audiences of every period. Here, within a historical framework, humor exists for its own sake, and in no sense are the humorous details a subplot to the activities of the Crown. Woven into and between the scenes of court and military affairs, the antics of Falstaff and his mates created a suitable atmosphere for showing Prince Henry's character. He entered into their tricks and zaniness with an abandon equal to the irresponsibility of the commonest of the group. Falstaff's lies, thieving, drinking, and debauchery made him the butt of repeated ludicrous situations. He used any reverse to the advantage of obtaining another bottle of sack, of gratifying his ego by attracting the attention of his cohorts, or of endearing himself, with his sly rascality, to the prince. Because of Falstaff, comedy and history join in this play.

The Story:

King Henry, conscience-stricken because of his part in the murder of King Richard II, his predecessor, planned a pilgrimage to the Holy Land. He declared to his lords that war had been banished from England and that peace would reign throughout the kingdom.

But there were those of differing opinions. Powerful barons in the North remained disaffected after the accession of the new king. Antagonized by his failure to keep promises made when he claimed the throne, they recruited forces to maintain their feudal rights. In fact, as Henry announced plans for his expedition to the Holy Land, he was informed of the brutal murder of a thousand persons in a fray between Edmund Mortimer, proclaimed by Richard as heir to the crown, and Glendower, a Welsh rebel. Mortimer was taken prisoner. A messenger also brought word of Hotspur's success against the Scots at Holmedon Hill. The king expressed his commendation of the young knight and his regrets that his own son, Prince Henry, was so irresponsible and carefree.

But King Henry, piqued by Hotspur's refusal to release to him more than one prisoner, ordered a council meeting to bring the overzealous Hotspur to terms. At the meeting Henry refused to ransom Mortimer, the pretender to the throne, held by Glendower. In turn, Hotspur refused to release the prisoners taken at Holmedon Hill, and Henry threatened more strenuous action against Hotspur and his kinsmen.

In a rousing speech Hotspur appealed to the power and nobility of Northumberland and Worcester and urged that they undo the wrongs of which they were guilty in the dethronement and murder of Richard and in aiding Henry instead of Mortimer to the crown. Worcester promised to help Hotspur in his cause against Henry. Worcester's plan would involve the aid of Douglas of Scotland, to be sought after by Hotspur, of Glendower and Mortimer, to be won over through Worcester's efforts, and of the Archbishop of York, to be approached by Northumberland.

Hotspur's boldness and impatience were shown in his dealing with Glendower as they, Mortimer, and Worcester discussed the future division of the kingdom. Hotspur, annoyed by the tedium of Glendower's personal account of his own ill-fated birth and by the uneven distribution of land, was impudent and rude. Hotspur was first a soldier, then a gentleman.

In the king's opinion, Prince Henry was quite lacking in either of these attributes. In one of their foolish pranks Sir John Falstaff and his riotous band had robbed some travelers at Gadshill, only to be set upon and put to flight by the prince and one companion. Summoning the prince from the Boar's Head Tavern, the king urged his son to break with the undesirable company he kept, chiefly the ne'er-do-well Falstaff. Contrasting young Henry with Hotspur, the king pointed out the military achievements of Northumberland's heir. Congenial, high-spirited Prince Henry, remorseful because of his father's lack of confidence in him, swore his allegiance to his father and declared he would show the king that in time of crisis Hotspur's glorious deeds would prove Hotspur no better soldier than Prince Henry. To substantiate his pledge, the prince took command of a detachment that would join ranks with other units of the royal army—Blunt's, Prince John's, Westmoreland's, and the king's —in twelve days.

Prince Henry's conduct seemed to change very little. He continued his buffoonery with Falstaff, who had recruited a handful of bedraggled, nondescript foot soldiers. Falstaff's contention was that, despite their physical condition, they were food for powder and that little more could be said for any soldier.

Hotspur's forces suffered gross reverses through Northumberland's failure, because of illness, to organize an army. Also, Hotspur's ranks were reduced because Glendower believed the stars not propitious for him to march at that time. Undaunted by the news of his reduced forces, Hotspur pressed on to meet Henry's army of thirty thousand.

At Shrewsbury, the scene of the battle, Sir Walter Blunt carried to Hotspur the king's offer that the rebels' grievances would be righted and that anyone involved in the revolt would be pardoned if he chose a peaceful settlement. In answer to the king's message Hotspur reviewed the history of Henry's double-dealing and scheming in the past. Declaring that Henry's lineage should not continue on the throne, Hotspur finally promised Blunt that Worcester would wait upon the king to give him an answer to his offer.

Henry repeated his offer of amnesty to Worcester and Vernon, Hotspur's ambassadors. Because Worcester doubted the king's sincerity, on account of previous betrayals, he lied to Hotspur on his return to the rebel camp and reported that the king in abusive terms had announced his determination to march at once against Hotspur. Worcester also reported Prince Henry's invitation to Hotspur that they fight a duel. Hotspur gladly accepted the challenge.

As the two armies moved into battle, Blunt, mistaken for the king, was slain by Douglas, who, learning his error, was sorely grieved that he had not killed Henry. Douglas, declaring that he would yet murder the king, accosted him after a long search over the field. He would have been successful in his threat had it not been for the intervention of Prince Henry, who engaged Douglas and allowed the king to withdraw from the fray.

In the fighting Hotspur descended upon Prince Henry, exhausted from an earlier wound and his recent skirmish with Douglas. When the two young knights fought, Hotspur was wounded. Douglas again appeared, fighting with Falstaff, and departed after Falstaff had fallen to the ground as if he were dead. Hotspur died of his wounds and Prince Henry, before going off to join Prince John, his brother, eulogized Hotspur and Falstaff. The two benedictions were quite different. But Falstaff had only pretended lifelessness to save his life. After the prince's departure he stabbed Hotspur. He declared that he would swear before any council that he had killed the young rebel.

Worcester and Vernon were taken prisoners. Because they had not relayed to Hotspur the peace terms offered by the king, they were sentenced to death. Douglas, in flight after Hotspur's death, was taken prisoner. Given the king's permission to dispose of Douglas, Prince Henry ordered that the valiant Scottish knight be freed.

The king sent Prince John to march against the forces of Northumberland and the Archbishop of York. He and Prince Henry took the field against Glendower and Mortimer, in Wales. Falstaff had the honor of carrying off the slain Hotspur.

HENRY THE FOURTH, PART TWO

Type of work: Drama
Author: William Shakespeare (1564-1616)
Type of plot: Historical chronicle
Time of plot: 1405-1413
Locale: England
First presented: 1597

Principal characters:
KING HENRY THE FOURTH
HENRY, Prince of Wales
JOHN OF LANCASTER, another son of the king
EARL OF WESTMORELAND, a member of the king's party
EARL OF NORTHUMBERLAND, enemy of the king
SIR JOHN FALSTAFF, a riotous old knight
SHALLOW, a country justice
THE LORD CHIEF JUSTICE, judge of the King's Bench
MISTRESS QUICKLY, hostess of the Boar's Head Tavern in Eastcheap

Critique:

As in *The History of King Henry IV, Part I,* comedy is an outstanding feature of this sequel. The same devices—puns, hyperbole, coarseness—are used to good effect, and in the earlier scenes of the play the character of Falstaff again sustains the spirit of high comedy. He ambles his way through this second part of *Henry IV* as he did in the first, his lying, drinking, and chicanery still useful to his own ends. In this sequel he becomes further involved with Mistress Quickly, and his promise to marry her is no more binding than are any of his other vows. At the end Falstaff goes on breezily promising great things for his friends, until his death. The pomp and display common to Shakespeare's historical chronicles permeate the serious parts of the drama, and the deathbed scene between Henry IV and Prince Henry is generally considered among the best in dramatic literature.

The Story:

After the battle of Shrewsbury many false reports were circulated among the peasants. At last they reached Northumberland, who believed for a time that the rebel forces had been victorious. But his retainers, fleeing from that stricken field, brought a true account of the death of Hotspur, Northumberland's valiant son, at the hands of Prince Henry, and of King Henry's avowal to put down rebellion by crushing those forces still opposing him. Northumberland, sorely grieved by news of his son's death, prepared to avenge that loss. Hope lay in the fact that the Archbishop of York had mustered an army, because soldiers so organized, being responsible to the Church rather than to a military leader, would prove better fighters than those who had fled from Shrewsbury field. News that the king's forces of twenty-five thousand men had been divided into three units was encouraging to his enemies.

In spite of Northumberland's grief for his slain son and his impassioned threat against the king and Prince Henry, he

1269

was easily persuaded by his wife and Hotspur's widow to flee to Scotland, there to await the success of his confederates before he would consent to join them with his army.

Meanwhile Falstaff delayed in carrying out his orders to proceed north and recruit troops for the king. Deeply involved with Mistress Quickly, he used his royal commission to avoid being imprisoned for debt. With Prince Henry, who had paid little heed to the conduct of the war, he continued his riotous feasting and jesting until both were summoned to join the army marching against the rebels.

King Henry, aging and weary, had been ill for two weeks. Sleepless nights had taken their toll on him, and in his restlessness he reviewed his ascent to the throne and denied, to his lords, the accusation of unscrupulousness brought against him by the rebels. He was somewhat heartened by the news of Glendower's death.

In Gloucestershire, recruiting troops at the house of Justice Shallow, Falstaff grossly accepted bribes and let ablebodied men buy themselves out of service. The soldiers he took to the war were a raggle-taggle lot.

Prince John of Lancaster, taking the field against the rebels, sent word by Westmoreland to the archbishop that the king's forces were willing to make peace, and he asked that the rebel leaders make known their grievances so that they might be corrected.

When John and the archbishop met for a conference, John questioned and criticized the archbishop's dual role as churchman and warrior. Because the rebels announced their intention to fight until their wrongs were righted, John promised redress for all. Then he suggested that the archbishop's troops be disbanded after a formal review; he wished to see the stalwart soldiers that his army would have fought if a truce had not been declared.

His request was granted, but the men, excited by the prospect of their release, scattered so rapidly that inspection was impossible. Westmoreland, sent to disband John's army, returned to report that the soldiers would take orders only from the prince. With his troops assembled and the enemy's disbanded, John ordered some of the opposing leaders arrested for high treason and others, including the archbishop, for capital treason. John explained that his action was in keeping with his promise to improve conditions and that to remove rebellious factions was the first step in his campaign. The enemy leaders were sentenced to death. Falstaff took Coleville, the fourth of the rebel leaders, who was sentenced to execution with the others.

News of John's success was brought to King Henry as he lay dying, but the victory could not gladden the sad old king. His chief concern lay in advice and admonition to his younger sons, Gloucester and Clarence, regarding their future conduct, and he asked for unity among his sons. Spent by his long discourse, the king lapsed into unconsciousness.

Prince Henry, summoned to his dying father's bedside, found the king in a stupor, with the crown beside him. The prince, remorseful and compassionate, expressed regret that the king had lived such a tempestuous existence because of the crown and promised, in his turn, to wear the crown graciously. As he spoke, he placed the crown on his head and left the room. Awaking and learning that the prince had donned the crown, King Henry immediately assumed that his son wished him dead in order to inherit the kingdom. Consoled by the prince's strong denial of such wishful thinking, the king confessed his own unprincipled behavior in gaining the crown. Asking God's forgiveness, he repeated his plan to journey to the Holy Land to divert his subjects from revolt, and he advised the prince, when he should become king, to involve his powerful lords in wars with foreign powers, thereby relieving the country of internal strife.

The king's death caused great sorrow among those who loved him and to those who feared the prince, now Henry V. A short time before, the Lord Chief Justice, acting on the command of Henry IV, had alienated the prince by banishing Falstaff and his band, but the newly crowned king accepted the Chief Justice's explanation for his treatment of Falstaff and restored his judicial powers.

Falstaff was rebuked for his conduct by Henry who stated that he was no longer the person Falstaff had known him to be. Until the old knight learned to correct his ways, the king banished him, on pain of death, to a distance ten miles away from Henry's person. He promised, however, that if amends were made Falstaff would return by degrees to the king's good graces. Undaunted by that reproof, Falstaff explained to his cronies that he yet would make them great, that the king's reprimand was only a front, and that the king would send for him and in the secrecy of the court chambers they would indulge in their old foolishness and plan the advancement of Falstaff's followers.

Prince John, expressing his admiration for Henry's public display of his changed attitude, prophesied that England would be at war with France before a year had passed.

HENRY THE SIXTH, PART ONE

Type of work: Drama
Author: William Shakespeare (1564-1616)
Type of plot: Historical chronicle
Time of plot: 1422-1444
Locale: England and France
First presented: c. 1592

Principal characters:
KING HENRY VI
DUKE OF GLOSTER, uncle of the king and Protector of the Realm
DUKE OF BEDFORD, uncle of the king and Regent of France
HENRY BEAUFORT, Bishop of Winchester, afterward cardinal
RICHARD PLANTAGENET, who becomes Duke of York
JOHN BEAUFORT, Earl of Somerset
EARL OF SUFFOLK
LORD TALBOT, a general, afterward Earl of Shrewsbury
CHARLES, the Dauphin, afterward King of France
THE BASTARD OF ORLEANS, a French general
MARGARET OF ANJOU, afterward married to King Henry
JOAN LA PUCELLE, commonly called Joan of Arc

Critique:

Replete with political intrigue, courtly pomp, grandeur of battle, and the mystery of witchcraft, *King Henry the Sixth, Part I,* is typically Shakespearean historical drama. Also typical, but more flagrant than in most of the other history chronicles are the playwright's gross distortions and inaccuracies in historical detail. A distinguishing factor in the play is the fuller use of melodramatic devices to further character development in instances in which military prowess or statecraft are hardly adequate. Typical, atypical, or distinctive, *Henry the Sixth* is a rousing play, either in print or upon stage. It is a revision of an earlier drama, known by Shakespeare.

The Story:

The great nobles and churchmen of England gathered in Westminster Abbey for the state funeral of King Henry V, hero of Agincourt and conqueror of France. The eulogies of Gloster, Bedford, Exeter, and the Bishop of Winchester, profound and extensive, were broken off by messengers bringing reports of English defeat and failure in France, where

1271

the Dauphin, taking advantage of King Henry's illness, had raised the standards of revolt. The gravest defeat reported was the imprisonment of Lord Talbot, general of the English armies. Bedford swore to avenge his loss. Gloster said that he would also hasten military preparations and proclaim young Prince Henry, nine months old, King of England. The Bishop of Winchester, disgruntled because the royal dukes had asked neither his advice nor aid, planned to seize the king's person and ingratiate himself into royal favor.

In France, the Dauphin and his generals, discussing the conduct of the war, attempted to overwhelm the depleted English forces. Although outnumbered and without leaders, the English fought valiantly and tenaciously. Hope of victory came to the French, however, when the Bastard of Orleans brought to the Dauphin's camp a soldier-maid, Joan La Pucelle, described as a holy young girl with God-given visionary powers. The Dauphin's attempt to trick her was unsuccessful, for she recognized him although Reignier, Duke of Anjou, stood in the Dauphin's place. Next she vanquished the prince in a duel to which he challenged her in an attempt to test her military skill.

The followers of the Duke of Gloster and the Bishop of Winchester rioted in the London streets, as dissension between Church and State grew because of Winchester's efforts to keep Gloster from seeing young Henry. The Mayor of London proclaimed against the unseemly conduct of the rioters.

When the English and the French fought again, Lord Salisbury and Sir Thomas Gargrave, the English leaders, were killed by a gunner in ambush. Meanwhile Lord Talbot, greatly feared by the French, had been ransomed in time to take command of English forces in the siege of Orleans. Enraged by the death of Salisbury, Talbot fought heroically, on one occasion with La Pucelle herself. At last the English swarmed into the town and put the French to rout. Talbot ordered Salisbury's body to be carried into the public market place of Orleans as a token of his revenge for that lord's murder.

The Countess of Auvergne invited Lord Talbot to visit her in her castle. Fearing chicanery, Bedford and Burgundy tried to keep him from going into an enemy stronghold, but Talbot, as strong-willed as he was brave, ignored their pleas. He did whisper to his captain, however, certain instructions concerning his visit.

On his arrival at Auvergne Castle the countess announced that she was making him her prisoner in order to save France from further scourges. Talbot proved his wit by completely baffling the countess with double talk and by signaling his soldiers, who stormed the castle, ate the food and drank the wine, and then won the favor of the countess with their charming manners.

In addition to continued internal strife resulting from Gloster's and Winchester's personal ambitions, new dissension arose between Richard Plantagenet and the Earl of Somerset. Plantagenet and his followers chose a white rose as their symbol, Somerset and his supporters a red rose, and in the quarrel of these two men the disastrous Wars of the Roses began. In the meantime Edmund Mortimer, the rightful heir to the throne, who had been imprisoned when King Henry IV usurped the crown some thirty years before, was released from confinement. He urged his nephew, Richard Plantagenet, to restore the family to the rightful position the Plantagenets deserved.

Youthful King Henry VI, after making Plantagenet Duke of York, much to the displeasure of Somerset, was taken to France by Gloster and other lords to be crowned King of France. In Paris, Talbot's chivalry and prowess were rewarded when he was made Earl of Shrewsbury.

In preparation for the battle at Rouen, La Pucelle won Burgundy over to the cause of France by playing upon his vanity and appealing to what she termed his sense of justice. The immaturity of the king was revealed in his request that Talbot go to Burgundy and chastise him for his desertion.

The Duke of York and the Earl of Somerset finally brought their quarrel to the king, who implored them to be friendly for England's sake. He pointed out that disunity among the English lords would only weaken their stand in France. To show how petty he considered their differences he casually put on a red rose, the symbol of Somerset's faction, and explained that it was merely a flower and that he loved one of his rival kinsmen as much as the other. He appointed York a regent of France and ordered both him and Somerset to supply Talbot with men and supplies for battle. Then the king and his party returned to London.

The king's last assignment to his lords in France was Talbot's death knell; Somerset, refusing to send horses with which York planned to supply Talbot, accused York of self-aggrandizement. York, in turn, blamed Somerset for negligence. As their feud continued, Talbot and his son were struggling valiantly against the better-equipped, more fully manned French army at Bordeaux. After many skirmishes Talbot and his son were slain and the English suffered tremendous losses. Flushed with the triumph of their great victory, the French leaders planned to march on to Paris.

In England, meanwhile, there was talk of a truce, and the king agreed, after a moment of embarrassment because of his youth, to Gloster's proposal that Henry accept in marriage the daughter of the Earl of Armagnac, a man of affluence and influence in France. This alliance, designed to effect a friendly peace between the two countries, was to be announced in France by Cardinal Beaufort, former Bishop of Winchester, who, in sending money to the pope to pay for his cardinalship, stated that his ecclesiastical position gave him status equal to that of the loftiest peer. He threatened mutiny if Gloster

ever tried to dominate him again. The king sent a jewel to seal the contract of betrothal.

The fighting in France dwindled greatly, with the English forces converging for one last weak stand. La Pucelle cast a spell and conjured up fiends to bolster her morale and to assist her in battle, but her appeal was to no avail, and York took her prisoner. Berated as a harlot and condemned as a witch by the English, La Pucelle pleaded for her life. At first she contended that her virgin blood would cry for vengeance at the gates of heaven. When this appeal failed to move York and the Earl of Warwick, she implored them to save her unborn child, fathered, she said variously, by the Dauphin, the Duke of Alençon, and the Duke of Anjou. She was condemned to be burned at the stake.

In another skirmish the Earl of Suffolk had taken as his prisoner Margaret, daughter of the Duke of Anjou. Enthralled by her loveliness, he was unable to claim her for himself because he was already married. He finally struck upon the notion of wooing Margaret for the king. After receiving her father's permission to present Margaret's name to Henry as a candidate for marriage, Suffolk went to London to petition the king. While Henry weighed the matter against the consequences of breaking his contract with the Earl of Armagnac, Exeter and Gloster attempted to dissuade him from following Suffolk's suggestions. Their pleas were in vain. Margaret's great courage and spirit, as described by Suffolk, held promise of a great and invincible offspring.

Terms of peace having been arranged, Suffolk was ordered to conduct Margaret to England. Suffolk, because he had brought Margaret and Henry together, planned to take advantage of his opportune political position and, through Margaret, rule youthful Henry and his kingdom.

HENRY THE SIXTH, PART TWO

Type of work: Drama
Author: William Shakespeare (1564-1616)
Type of plot: Historical chronicle
Time of plot: 1444-1455
Locale: England
First presented: c. 1592

Principal characters:
KING HENRY VI
DUKE OF GLOSTER, his uncle
CARDINAL BEAUFORT, great-uncle of the king
RICHARD PLANTAGENET, Duke of York
EDWARD, and
RICHARD, York's sons
DUKE OF SOMERSET, leader of the Lancaster faction
DUKE OF SUFFOLK, the king's favorite
EARL OF SALISBURY, a Yorkist
EARL OF WARWICK, a Yorkist
BOLINGBROKE, a conjurer
MARGARET, Queen of England
ELEANOR, Duchess of Gloster
MARGERY JOURDAIN, a witch

Critique:

In addition to those features contained in the first part of *King Henry the Sixth* as described in the critique of that play, there are in this second part scenes reflecting social implications. These scenes, within the limits of the five acts, not only make clear the social strata of commoners and nobles but also point up the principal characters. This fuller realism of historical perspective and social content in no way diminishes the picture of ambition, jealousy, love, and courage among the nobility. As is true of the first part of *King Henry the Sixth,* this drama is a revision of an earlier play.

The Story:

The Earl of Suffolk, having arranged for the marriage of King Henry VI and Margaret of Anjou, brought the new queen to England. There was great indignation when the terms of the marriage treaty were revealed. The contract called for an eighteen-months' truce between the two countries, the outright gift of the duchies of Anjou and Maine to Reignier, Margaret's father, and omission of her dowry. As had been predicted earlier, no

good could come of this union, since Henry, at Suffolk's urging, had broken his betrothal to the daughter of the Earl of Armagnac. But Henry, pleased by his bride's beauty, gladly accepted the treaty and elevated Suffolk, the go-between, to a dukedom.

The voices were hardly still from the welcome of the new queen before the lords, earls, and dukes were expressing their ambitions to gain more control in affairs of state. The old dissension between the Duke of Gloster and Cardinal Beaufort continued. The churchman tried to alienate others against Gloster by saying that Gloster, next in line for the crown, needed watching. The Duke of Somerset accused the cardinal of seeking Gloster's position for himself. And these high ambitions were not exclusively for the men. The Duchess of Gloster showed great impatience with her husband when he said he wished only to serve as Protector of the Realm. When she saw that her husband was not going to help her ambitions to be queen, the duchess hired Hume, a priest, to traffic with witches and conjurers in her behalf. Hume accepted

1274

her money; but he had already been hired by Suffolk and the cardinal to work against the duchess.

Queen Margaret's unhappy life in England, her contempt for the king, and the people's dislike for her soon became apparent. The mutual hatred she and the duchess had for each other showed itself in tongue lashings and blows. The duchess, eager to take advantage of any turn of events, indulged in sorcery with Margery Jourdain and the notorious Bolingbroke. Her questions to them, all pertaining to the fate of the king and his advisers, and the answers which these sorcerers had received from the spirit world, were confiscated by Buckingham and York when they broke in upon a seance. For her part in the practice of sorcery the duchess was banished to the Isle of Man; Margery Jourdain and Bolingbroke were executed.

His wife's deeds brought new slanders upon Gloster. In answer to Queen Margaret's charge that he was a party to his wife's underhandedness, Gloster, a broken man, resigned his position as Protector of the Realm. Even after his resignation Margaret continued in her attempts to turn the king against Gloster. She was aided by the other lords, who accused Gloster of deceit and crimes against the State; but the king, steadfast in his loyalty to Gloster, described the former protector as virtuous and mild.

York, whose regency in France had been given to Somerset, enlisted the aid of Warwick and Salisbury in his fight for the crown, his claim being based on the fact that King Henry's grandfather, Henry IV, had usurped the throne from York's great-uncle. Suffolk and the cardinal, to rid themselves of a dangerous rival, sent York to quell an uprising in Ireland. Before departing for Ireland, York planned to incite rebellion among the English through one John Cade, a headstrong, warmongering Kentishman. Cade, under the name of John Mortimer, the name of York's uncle, paraded his riotous followers through the streets of London.

The rebels, irresponsible and unthinking, went madly about the town wrecking buildings, killing noblemen who opposed them, and shouting that they were headed for the palace, where John Cade, the rightful heir to the throne, would avenge the injustices done his lineage. An aspect of the poorly organized rebellion was shown in the desertion of Cade's followers when they were appealed to by loyal old Lord Clifford. He admonished them to save England from needless destruction and to expend their military efforts against France. Cade, left alone, went wandering about the countryside as a fugitive and was killed by Alexander Iden, a squire who was knighted for his bravery.

Gloster, arrested by Suffolk on a charge of high treason, was promised a fair trial by the king. This was unwelcome news to the lords; and when Gloster was sent for to appear at the hearing, he was found in his bed, brutally murdered and mangled. Suffolk and the cardinal had hired the murderers. So was fulfilled the first prophecy of the sorcerers, that the king would depose and outlive a duke who would die a violent death.

Shortly after Gloster's death the king was called to the bedside of the cardinal, who had been stricken by a strange malady. There King Henry heard the cardinal confess his part in the murder of Gloster, the churchman's bitterest enemy. The cardinal died unrepentent.

Queen Margaret became more outspoken concerning affairs of state, especially in those matters on behalf of Suffolk, and more openly contemptuous toward the king's indifferent attitude.

At the request of Commons, led by Warwick and Salisbury, Suffolk was banished from the country for his part in Gloster's murder. Saying their farewells, he and Margaret declared their love for each other. Suffolk, disguised, took ship to leave the country. Captured by pirates, he was beheaded for his treacheries and one of his gentlemen was instructed to return his body to the king.

In London, Queen Margaret mourned her loss in Suffolk's death as she caressed his severed head. The king, piqued by her demonstration, asked her how she would react to his death. Diplomatically evasive, she answered that she would not mourn his death; she would die for him. The witch had prophesied Suffolk's death: she had said that he would die by water.

Returning from Ireland, York planned to gather forces on his way to London and seize the crown for himself. Because he also stated his determination to remove Somerset, his adversary in court matters, the king tried to appease the rebel by committing Somerset to the Tower Hearing that his enemy was in prison, York ordered his army to disband.

His rage was all the greater, therefore, when he learned that Somerset had been restored to favor. The armies of York and Lancaster prepared to battle at Saint Albans, where Somerset, after an attempt to arrest York for capital treason, was slain by crookbacked Richard Plantagenet, York's son. Somerset's death fulfilled the prophecies of the witch, who had also foretold that Somerset should shun castles, that he would be safer on sandy plains. With his death the king and queen fled. Salisbury, weary from battle but undaunted, and Warwick, proud of York's victory at Saint Albans, pledged their support to York in his drive for the crown, and York hastened to London to forestall the king's intention to summon Parliament into session.

HENRY THE SIXTH, PART THREE

Type of work: Drama
Author: William Shakespeare (1564-1616)
Type of plot: Historical chronicle
Time of plot: 1455-1471
Locale: England and France
First presented: c. 1592

Principal characters:
KING HENRY VI
EDWARD, Prince of Wales, his son
LOUIS XI, King of France
RICHARD PLANTAGENET, Duke of York
EDWARD, York's son, afterward King Edward IV
EDMUND, York's son, Earl of Rutland
GEORGE, York's son, afterward Duke of Clarence
RICHARD, York's son, afterward Duke of Gloster
LORD HASTINGS, of the Duke of York's party
THE EARL OF WARWICK, a king-maker
MARGARET, Queen of England
LORD CLIFFORD, Margaret's ally
LADY GREY, afterward Edward IV's queen
LADY BONA, sister of the Queen of France

Critique:

Although the third part of *King Henry the Sixth* is not a tragedy in the classical sense, it is more poignant than many tragic dramas. A revision of an earlier play, it is an outstanding example of writing for unity of impression. Infinite and unswerving ambition in the characters, and situations of plot closely knit to reveal this unrelenting aggression are always apparent, making this play a masterpiece of gripping drama. The plot is so developed that King Henry is made a pawn to the wishes of others. The characterization is handled with finesse, an

1276

occasional line by King Henry showing his true nature. The labels frequently given him — "poltroon," "weak-willed," "willy-nilly"—are unjust and misapplied. Shakespeare's King Henry in this third part is a man caught in the mesh of circumstances and required to exhibit the qualities of leadership, when his only wish was for contentment and tranquillity. Henry's was a life spent in quiet desperation.

The Story:

In the House of Parliament, York, his sons, and the Earl of Warwick rejoiced over their success at Saint Albans. Riding hard, the Yorkists had arrived in London ahead of the routed king, and Henry, entering with his lords, was filled with consternation when he saw York already seated on the throne, to which Warwick had conducted him. Some of the king's followers were sympathetic toward York and others were fearful of his power; the two attitudes resulted in defection in the royal ranks. Seeing his stand weakened, the king attempted to avert disorder by disinheriting his own son and by pledging the crown to York and his sons, on the condition that York stop the civil war and remain loyal to the king during his lifetime.

Annoyed by the reconciliation and contemptuous toward the king because of her son's disinheritance, Margaret deserted the king and raised her own army to protect her son's rights to the throne. The queen's army marched against York's castle as York was sending his sons to recruit forces for another rebellion. York's sons had persuaded their father that his oath to the king was not binding because his contract with the king had not been made in due course of law before a magistrate.

In a battle near Wakefield, Lord Clifford and his soldiers killed Rutland, York's young son, and soaked a handkerchief in his blood. Later, as he joined Margaret's victorious army, which outnumbered York's soldiers ten to one, Lord Clifford gave York the handkerchief to wipe away his tears as he wept for his son's death. York's sorrow was equaled by his humiliation at the hands of Margaret, who, after taking him prisoner, put a paper crown on his head that he might reign from the molehill where she had him placed to be jeered by the soldiers. Clifford and Margaret stabbed the Duke of York and beheaded him. His head was set on the gates of York.

Hearing of the defeat of York's forces, Warwick, taking the king with him, set out from London to fight Queen Margaret at Saint Albans. Warwick's qualities as a general were totally offset by the presence of the king, who was unable to conceal his strong affection for Margaret, and Warwick was defeated. Edward and Richard, York's sons, joined Warwick in a march toward London.

King Henry, ever the righteous monarch, forswore any part in breaking his vow to York and declared that he preferred to leave his son only virtuous deeds, rather than an ill-gotten crown. At the insistence of Clifford and Margaret, however, the king knighted his son as the Prince of Wales.

After a defiant parley, the forces met again between Towton and Saxton. The king, banned from battle by Clifford and Margaret because of his antipathy to war and his demoralizing influence on the soldiers, sat on a distant part of the field lamenting the course affairs had taken in this bloody business of murder and deceit. He saw the ravages of war when a father bearing the body of his dead son and a son with the body of his dead father passed by. They had unknowingly taken the lives of their loved ones in the fighting. As the rebel forces, led by Warwick, Richard, and Edward approached, the king, passive to danger and indifferent toward his own safety, was rescued by the Prince of Wales and Margaret before the enemy could reach him. He was sent to Scotland for safety.

After a skirmish with Richard, Clifford fled to another part of the field, where, weary and worn, he fainted and died. His head, severed by Richard, replaced York's head on the gate. The Yorkists marched on to London. Edward was proclaimed King Edward IV; Richard was made Duke of Gloster, and George, Duke of Clarence.

King Edward, in audience, heard Lady Grey's case for the return of confiscated lands taken by Margaret's army at Saint Albans, where Lord Grey was killed fighting for the York cause. The hearing, marked by Richard's and George's dissatisfaction with their brother's position and Edward's lewdness directed at Lady Grey, ended with Lady Grey's betrothal to Edward. Richard, resentful of his humpback, aspired to the throne. His many deprivations resulting from his physical condition, he felt, justified his ambition; he would stop at no obstacle in achieving his ends.

Because of their great losses, Margaret and the prince went to France to appeal for aid from King Louis XI, who was kindly disposed toward helping them maintain the crown. The French monarch's decision was quickly changed at the appearance of Warwick, who had arrived from England to ask for the hand of Lady Bona for King Edward. Warwick's suit had been granted, and Margaret's request denied, when a messenger brought letters announcing King Edward's marriage to Lady Grey. King Louis and Lady Bona were insulted; Margaret was overjoyed. Warwick, chagrined, withdrew his allegiance to the House of York and offered to lead French troops against Edward. He promised his older daughter in marriage to Margaret's son as a pledge of his honor.

At the royal palace in London, family loyalty was broken by open dissent when King Edward informed his brothers that he would not be bound by their wishes. Told that the prince was to marry Warwick's older daughter, the Duke of Clarence announced that he intended to marry the younger one. He left, taking Somerset, one of King Henry's faction, with him. Richard, seeing in an alliance with Edward an opportunity for his own advancement, remained; and he, Montague, and Hastings pledged their support to King Edward.

When the French forces reached London, Warwick took Edward prisoner. The king-maker removed Edward's crown and took it to re-crown King Henry, who had, in the meantime, escaped from Scotland, only to be delivered into Edward's hands and imprisoned in the Tower. Henry delegated his royal authority to Warwick and the Duke of Clarence, in order that he might be free from the turmoil attendant upon his reign.

Richard and Hastings freed Edward from his imprisonment. They formed an army in York; and while Warwick and Clarence, who had learned of Edward's release, were making preparations for defense, Edward, marching upon London, again seized King Henry and sent him to solitary confinement in the Tower.

Edward made a surprise attack on Warwick near Coventry, where Warwick's forces were soon increased by the appearance of Oxford, Montague, and Somerset. The fourth unit to join Warwick was led by Clarence who took the red rose, the symbol of the House of Lancaster, from his hat and threw it into Warwick's face. Clarence accused Warwick of duplicity and announced that he would fight beside his brothers to preserve the House of York. Warwick, a valiant soldier to the end, was wounded by King Edward and died soon afterward. Montague was also killed.

When Queen Margaret and her son arrived from France, the prince won great acclaim from Margaret and the lords for his spirited vow to hold the kingdom against the Yorkists. Defeated at Tewkesbury, however, the prince was cruelly stabbed to death by King Edward and his brothers. Margaret pleaded with them to kill her too, but they chose to punish her with life. She was sent back to France, her original home. After the prince had been killed, Richard of Gloster stole off to London, where he assassinated King

Henry in the Tower. Again he swore to get the crown for himself.

The Yorkists were at last supreme. Edward and Queen Elizabeth, with their infant son, regained the throne. Richard, still intending to seize the crown for himself, saluted the infant with a Judas kiss, while Edward stated that they were now to spend their time in stately triumphs, comic shows, and pleasures of the court.

HERAKLES MAD

Type of work: Drama
Author: Euripides (c. 485-c. 406 B.C.)
Type of plot: Classical tragedy
Time of plot: Remote antiquity
Locale: Thebes
First presented: c. 420 B.C.

Principal characters:
AMPHITRYON, married to Alcmene, the mother of Herakles
MEGARA, wife of Herakles and daughter of Creon
LYCUS, usurper of Kingdom of Thebes
HERAKLES, son of Zeus and Alcmene
THESEUS, King of Athens
IRIS, messenger of the gods
MADNESS
CHORUS OF THE OLD MEN OF THEBES

Critique:

Herakles Mad, one of the most puzzling of Euripides' plays, begins with a stereotyped situation and weak characters, builds to a powerful climax in the mad scene of Herakles, and is followed by one of the most moving tragic reconciliations in all drama. Some critics see in Euripides' treatment of Herakles the suggestion that he has been deluded all his life and has never really performed his twelve great labors; others have suggested that the madness comes not from Hera, but from Fate. In either case he reaches heroic and tragic stature when, after murdering his wife and children in a fit of madness, he refuses to commit suicide and decides to face whatever life has in store for him.

The Story:

Amphitryon, who together with Megara and the sons of Herakles had sought sanctuary at the altar of Zeus, lamented the fact that while Herakles was in Hades performing one of his twelve labors Lycus had murdered Creon and seized the throne of Thebes. The murderer was bent upon consolidating his position by killing Megara and her children, whose only hope lay in the protection of Zeus until Herakles returned. Lycus came to taunt them with the charge that Herakles was a coward who used a bow and killed only animals and that, in any case, he was dead in Hades and would never return.

Amphitryon, retorting that Lycus was the coward in seeking to kill an old man, a woman, and innocent children, begged that they at least be allowed to go into exile. Enraged, Lycus sent his servants to fetch oak logs in order to burn the relatives of Herakles alive in their sanctuary. The chorus of old men vowed that they would fight with their staves against such a horrible sacrilege.

Megara, however, counseled that it was folly to attempt to escape destiny; Herakles could not emerge from Hades to save them and since they must die they ought to do so without being burnt alive. Amphitryon then begged that he and Megara be killed first so that they would not have to witness the massacre of innocent children, and Megara pleaded for the privilege of dressing the children

1279

in the proper funeral robes. Lycus haughtily granted both wishes. As the group left the sanctuary for the palace, Amphitryon cursed Zeus for being a senseless and unjust god. In their absence the chorus chanted an ode on the glories of Herakles and the sadness of old age.

Returning with the children, Megara woefully recounted the marvelous plans she had made for her sons. Meanwhile, Amphitryon fervently prayed to Zeus for deliverance. Suddenly they were startled by the spectacle of Herakles approaching. The great joy of their meeting was darkened by the fearful tale Megara had to tell her husband. Furious with rage, Herakles swore that he would behead Lycus and throw his carcass to the dogs; but Amphitryon cautioned him to curb his reckless haste, for Lycus had many allies in his treachery. Though deeply moved by the fear that made his children cling to his robes, Herakles agreed to plan his revenge carefully and led his family into the palace. The chorus of ancients once again lamented their old age and praised Zeus for sending deliverance in the person of Herakles, his son.

Lycus, upon encountering Amphitryon emerging from the palace, commanded that he bring Megara with him, but Amphitryon refused on the ground that such a deed would make him an accomplice in her murder. Intent on dispatching Megara, Lycus angrily stormed into the palace. Amphitryon followed to watch Herakles' revenge. As the chorus hailed the death cries of Lycus, the specters of Madness and Iris appeared from above. Iris, the female messenger of the gods, pronounced that although destiny had preserved Herakles until he had finished his twelve labors, Hera had decreed that

he must now suffer lest the powers of man seem greater than those of the gods. She commanded that Madness force Herakles to murder his own wife and children. Reluctantly, Madness sent out her power and described the horrible seizures of Herakles within the palace. When the two specters disappeared, a messenger emerged from the palace to tell how Herakles in a frenzy of madness had murdered his wife and children, believing them to be the kin of his former master, Eurystheus. Amphitryon was saved only by the intervention of Athena, who put the possessed hero to sleep and had him tied to a pillar.

The doors of the palace were opened, revealing Herakles, now awake and puzzled by the awful scene about him. Informed of what he had done, Herakles crouched in shame and wailed in anguish.

Theseus, who had been rescued from Hades by Herakles, arrived with an army for the purpose of aiding his old friend against Lycus. Crushed by the weight of his dishonor, Herakles could not face his friend, and he announced his intention to commit suicide. His compassionate friend Theseus pleaded with him to live and accept his fate; he offered to take Herakles to Athens where, after being purified of his pollution, he would be given great estates and high status. Though he preferred to grow into a stone oblivious of his horrid deed, Herakles reluctantly agreed to harden his heart against death and rose with profound gratitude to accept his friend's offer. As he left, he urged the sorrowful Amphitryon to bury the dead and to follow him to Athens, where they would live out the remainder of their lives in peace.

HERCULES AND HIS TWELVE LABORS

Type of work: Classical myth
Source: Folk tradition
Type of plot: Heroic adventure
Time of plot: Remote antiquity
Locale: Mediterranean region

First transcribed: Unknown

Principal characters:
HERCULES, hero of virtue and strength
EURYSTHEUS, his cousin

Critique:

Hercules is the mighty hero of popular imagination in Western culture. Art galleries feature paintings and sculpture of the splendid body of the hero. The latest engines, the strongest building materials, the most powerful utilities bear his name. Hercules, not born a god, achieved godhood at the time of his death, according to tradition, because he devoted his life to the service of his fellow men. Some authorities link Hercules with legends of the sun, as each labor took him further from his home and one of his tasks carried him around the world and back. His twelve labors have been compared to the signs of the zodiac.

The Story:

Hercules was the son of a mortal, Alcmena, and the god Jupiter. Because Juno was hostile to all children of her husband by mortal mothers, she decided to be revenged upon the child. She sent two snakes to kill Hercules in his crib, but the infant strangled the serpents with ease. Then Juno caused Hercules to be subject to the will of his cousin, Eurystheus.

Hercules as a child was taught by Rhadamanthus, who one day punished the child for misdeeds. Hercules immediately killed his teacher. For this his foster father, Amphitryon, took Hercules away to the mountains, to be brought up by rude shepherds. Early in youth Hercules began to attract attention for his great strength and courage. He killed a lion single-handedly and took heroic part in a war. Juno, jealous of his growing success, called on Eurystheus to use his power over Hercules. Eurystheus then demanded that Hercules carry out twelve labors. The plan was that Hercules would perish in one of them.

The first labor: Juno had sent a lion to eat the people of Nemea. The lion's hide was so protected that no arrow could pierce it. Knowing that he could not kill the animal with his bow, Hercules met the lion and strangled it with his bare hands. Thereafter he wore the lion's skin as a protection when he was fighting, for nothing could penetrate that magic covering.

The second labor: Hercules had to meet the Lernaean hydra. This creature lived in a swamp, and the odor of its body killed all who breathed its fetid fumes. Hercules began the battle but discovered that for every head he severed from the monster two more appeared. Finally he obtained a flaming brand from a friend and burned each head as he severed it. When he came to the ninth and invulnerable head, he cut it off and buried it under a rock. Then he dipped his arrows into the body of the hydra so that he would possess more deadly weapons for use in future conflicts.

The third labor: Hercules captured the Erymanthian boar and brought it back on his shoulders. The sight of the wild beast frightened Eurystheus so much that he hid in a large jar. With a fine sense of humor the hero deposited the captured boar in the same jar. While on this trip Hercules incurred the wrath of the centaurs by drinking wine which they had claimed for their own. In order to escape from them he had had to kill most of the half-horse men.

The fourth labor: Hercules had to capture a stag which had antlers of gold and hoofs of brass. In order to capture this creature Hercules pursued it for a whole year.

The fifth labor: The Stymphalian birds were carnivorous. Hercules alarmed them with a bell, shot many of them with his arrows, and caused the rest to fly away.

The sixth labor: Augeas, king of Elis, had a herd of three thousand oxen whose stables had not been cleansed for thirty years. Commanded to clean the stables, Hercules diverted the rivers Alpheus and Peneus through them and washed them clean in one day. Augeas refused the payment agreed to and as a result Hercules later declared war on him.

The seventh labor: Neptune had given a sacred bull to Minos king of Crete. Minos' wife, Pasiphaë, fell in love with the animal and pursued it around the island. Hercules overcame the bull and took it back to Eurystheus by making it swim the sea while he rode upon its back.

The eighth labor: Like the Stymphalian birds, the mares of Diomedes fed on human flesh. Usually Diomedes found food for them by feeding to them all travelers who landed on his shores. Diomedes tried to prevent Hercules from driving away his herd. He was killed and his body was fed to his own beasts.

The ninth labor: Admeta, daughter of Eurystheus, persuaded her father to send Hercules for the girdle of Hippolyta, queen of the Amazons. The Amazon queen was willing to give up her girdle, but Juno interfered by telling the other Amazons that Hercules planned to kidnap their queen. In the battle that followed Hercules killed Hippolyta and took the girdle from her dead body.

The tenth labor: Geryoneus, a three-bodied, three-headed, six-legged, winged monster possessed a herd of oxen. Ordered to bring the animals to Eurystheus, Hercules traveled beyond the pillars of Hercules, now Gibraltar. He killed a two-headed shepherd dog and a giant herdsman, and finally slew Geryones. He loaded the cattle on a boat and sent them to Eurystheus. He himself returned afoot across the Alps. He had many adventures on the way, including a fight with giants in the Phlegraean fields, near the present site of Naples.

The eleventh labor: His next labor was more difficult, for his task was to obtain the golden apples in the garden of the Hesperides. No one knew where the garden was, and so Hercules set out to roam until he found it. In his travels he killed a giant, a host of pygmies, and burned alive some of his captors in Egypt. In India he set Prometheus free. At last he discovered Atlas holding up the sky. This task Hercules assumed, releasing Atlas to go after the apples. Atlas returned with the apples and reluctantly took up his burden. Hercules brought the apples safely to Eurystheus.

The twelfth labor: This was the most difficult of all his labors. After many adventures he brought the three-headed dog Cerberus from the underworld. He was forced to carry the struggling animal in his arms because he had been forbidden to use weapons of any kind. Afterward he took Cerberus back to the king of the underworld. So ended the labors of this mighty ancient hero.

HEREWARD THE WAKE

Type of work: Novel
Author: Charles Kingsley (1819-1875)
Type of plot: Historical romance
Time of plot: Eleventh century
Locale: England, Scotland, Flanders
First published: 1866

> *Principal characters:*
> HEREWARD THE WAKE, a Saxon thane and outlaw
> LADY GODIVA, his mother
> TORFRIDA, his wife

ALFTRUDA, his second wife
MARTIN LIGHTFOOT, a companion in his wanderings
WILLIAM THE CONQUEROR, Duke of Normandy and King of England

Critique:

Hereward the Wake is one of the very few stories that deal realistically and credibly with the Anglo-Saxon period of English history. Although elements of the chivalric romance, in the more academic sense of that term, are present in this novel, Kingsley has re-created the age and its people in a believable and highly interesting manner. *Hereward the Wake* is both an interesting story and a valuable historical study.

The Story:

Hereward was the son of the powerful Lord of Bourne, a Saxon nobleman of a family close to the throne. A high-spirited, rebellious youth, he was a source of constant worry to his mother, Lady Godiva. Hereward lacked a proper respect for the Church and its priests and lived a boisterous life with boon companions who gave him their unquestioning loyalty.

One day a friar came to Lady Godiva and revealed that Hereward and his friends had attacked him and robbed him of what the priest insisted was money belonging to the Church. Lady Godiva was angry and hurt. When Hereward came in and admitted his crime, she said that there was no alternative. For his own good, she maintained, he should be declared a wake, or outlaw. Upon his promise not to molest her messenger, for Hereward really did not mind being outlawed as he wished to see more of the world, Lady Godiva sent Martin Lightfoot, a servant, to carry the news of Hereward's deed to his father and to the king. Hereward was then declared an outlaw subject to imprisonment or death.

Before he left his father's house, however, he released his friends from their oath of allegiance. Martin Lightfoot begged to be allowed to follow him, not as his servant but as his companion. Then Hereward set out to live among the rude and barbarous Scottish tribes of the north.

His first adventure occurred when he killed a huge bear that threatened the life of Alftruda, ward of a knight named Gilbert of Ghent. For his valorous deed he achieved much renown. But the knights of Gilbert's household, jealous of Hereward's courage and his prowess, tried to kill him. Though he escaped the snares laid for him, he decided that it would be best for him to leave Scotland.

Accordingly, he went to Cornwall, where he was welcomed by the king. There the king's daughter was pledged in marriage to a prince of Waterford. But a giant of the Cornish court had become so powerful that he had forced the king's agreement to give his daughter in marriage to the ogre. Hereward, with the help of the princess and a friar, slew the giant, whose death freed the princess to marry the prince whom she really loved.

After leaving Cornwall, Hereward and his companions were wrecked upon the Flemish coast. There Hereward stayed for a time in the service of Baldwin of Flanders and proved his valor by defeating the French in battle. There, too, Torfrida, a lady wrongly suspected of sorcery, schemed to win his love. They were wed after Hereward had fought in a successful campaign against the Hollanders, and a daughter was born of the marriage.

Meanwhile King Edward had died and Harold reigned in England. A messenger came to Hereward with the news that Duke William of Normandy had defeated the English at the battle of Hastings and that King Harold had been killed. Hereward then decided to return to Bourne, his old home. There, accompanied by Martin Lightfoot, he found the Norman raiders encamped. He found too that his family had been despoiled of all its property and that his mother had been sent away. He and Martin, without revealing their identity, secretly went out and annihilated all the Normans in the area. Hereward swore that he would return with an army that would push the Norman invaders into the sea.

Hereward then went to his mother, who received him happily. Lady Godiva accused herself of having wronged her son and lamented the day she had proclaimed him an outlaw. He took her to a place of refuge in Croyland Abbey. Later he went to the monastery where his aged, infirm uncle, Abbot Brand, was spending his last days on earth. There Hereward was knighted by the monks, after the English fashion. Hereward went secretly to Bourne and there recruited a rebel army to fight against Duke William.

Although there were many men eager to fight the Normans, the English forces were disunited. Another king, an untried young man, had been proclaimed, but because of his youth he did not have the support of all the English factions. Hereward had been promised help from Denmark, but the Danish king sent a poor leader through whose stupidity the Danes were inveigled into positions where they were easily defeated by the Normans at Dover and Norwich. Then, instead of coming to Hereward's aid, the Danes fled. Hereward was forced to confess the failure of his allies to his men, but they renewed their pledge to him and promised to keep on fighting. The situation seemed hopeless when Hereward and his men took refuge on the island of Ely. There, with Torfrida's wise advice, Hereward defeated Duke William's attack upon the beleaguered island. Hereward and his men retreated to another camp of refuge. Shortly afterward Torfrida learned of Hereward's infidelity with Alftruda, the ward of Gilbert of Ghent. She left Hereward and went to Croyland Abbey, where she proposed to spend the last of her days ministering to the poor and to Hereward's mother. Hereward himself went to Duke William and submitted to him. The conqueror declared that he had selected a husband for Hereward's daughter. In order to free herself from Hereward, Torfrida falsely confessed that she was a sorceress, and her marriage to Hereward was annulled by the Church. Hereward then married Alftruda and became Lord of Bourne under Duke William. His daughter, despite her entreaties, was married to a Norman knight.

But Hereward, the last of the English, had many enemies among the French, who continually intrigued against him for the favor of Duke William. As a result, Hereward was imprisoned. The jailer was a good man who treated his noble prisoner as kindly as he could, although, for his own sake, he was forced to chain Hereward.

One day, while Hereward was being transported from one prison to another, he was rescued by his friends. Freed, he went back to Alftruda at Bourne, but his life was not a happy one. His enemies plotted to kill him. Taking advantage of a day when his retainers were escorting Alftruda on a journey, a group of Norman knights broke into Bourne castle. Though Hereward fought valiantly, he was outnumbered. He was killed and his head was exhibited in victory over the door of his own hall.

When she heard of his death, Torfrida came from Croyland Abbey and demanded Hereward's body. All were so frightened, especially Alftruda, by Torfrida's wild appearance and her reputation as a witch, that Hereward's first wife got her way and the body was delivered to her. She carried it away to Croyland for burial. Thus did Hereward, the last of the English, die, and

thus, too, did William of Normandy be-   of England.
come William the Conqueror and King

A HERO OF OUR TIME

Type of work: Novel
Author: Mikhail Yurievich Lermontov (1814-1841)
Type of plot: Psychological romance
Time of plot: 1830-1838
Locale: The Russian Caucasus
First published: 1839

Principal characters:
    "I" supposedly Lermontov, Narrator One
    MAKSIM MAKSIMICH, Narrator Two
    GRIGORIY ALEKSANDROVICH PECHORIN, Narrator Three, the "Hero of
       Our Time"
    BELA, a young princess
    KAZBICH, a bandit
    AZAMAT, Bela's young brother
    YANKO, a smuggler
    PRINCESS MARY, daughter of Princess Ligovskoy
    GRUSHNITSKI, a cadet and suitor to Princess Mary
    VERA, the former sweetheart of Pechorin
    LIEUTENANT VULICH, a Cossack officer, a Serbian

Critique:

This realistic novel of social and military life in nineteenth-century Russia well deserves its renown because of its colorful descriptions and sharp delineations of character. Structurally, the novel is made up of five related short stories, with Narrator One (presumably Lermontov), Maksim Maksimich, and Pechorin in the principal roles. The narrative is skillfully constructed. In "Bela," "I" meets Maksim Maksimich, who refers to Pechorin. Maksim Maksimich, Narrator Two, tells the story bearing his name as its title. Pechorin actually appears, but briefly. In "Taman," "Princess Mary," and "The Fatalist," the narrator is Pechorin himself, the stories being told as extracts from his journal. A second notable feature of the writing, in addition to the involuted time sequence, is Lermontov's habit of letting the reader eavesdrop in order to avoid detailed narrative. This device makes for compact writing, since it is a convenient means of letting the principal characters

learn of events necessary to an understanding of the story. Lermontov felt compelled to preface his novel with the explanation that *A Hero of Our Time* was not a biography of any Russian person, living or dead. Rather, Pechorin was intended to be a collective personification of all the evil and vice then found in Russian life. In creating his portrait of Pechorin, the "superfluous" man, Lermontov pointed to the development of the Russian psychological novel.

The Story:

The Narrator met Maksim Maksimich while on a return trip from Tiflis, the capital of Georgia, to Russia. The season was autumn, and in that mountainous region snow was already falling. The two men continued their acquaintance at the inn where they were forced to take refuge for the night. When the Narrator asked Maksim Maksimich about his experiences, the old man told of his friendship with

A HERO OF OUR TIME by Mikhail Yurievich Lermontov. Translated by Vladimir and Dmitri Nabokov. By permission of the publishers, Doubleday & Co., Inc. Copyright, 1958, by Vladimir and Dmitri Nabokov.

Grigoriy Pechorin, a Serbian who had come from Russia about five years before to join a company of cavalry in the Caucasus:

To relieve their boredom on that frontier post, the soldiers played with Azamat, the young son of a neighboring prince. As a result of this friendship, the prince invited Maksimich and Pechorin to a family wedding. At that celebration Pechorin and Kazbich, a bandit, met and were equally attracted to Bela, the beautiful young daughter of the prince. Azamat, observing this development, later offered to give Bela to Kazbich in exchange for the bandit's horse. Kazbich laughed at the boy and rode away.

Four days later Azamat was back at the camp and visiting with Pechorin, who promised to get Kazbich's horse for the boy in exchange for Bela. The promise was fulfilled. Kazbich, insane with rage at his loss, tried to kill Azamat but failed.

Suspecting that Azamat's father had been responsible for the theft, Kazbich killed the prince and stole his horse in revenge for the loss of his own animal.

Weeks passed, and Pechorin became less attentive to Bela. One day she and Maksimich were walking on the ramparts when Bela recognized Kazbich on her father's horse some distance away. An orderly's attempt to shoot Kazbich failed and he escaped. But Kazbich had recognized Bela, too, and a few days later, when the men were away from camp, he kidnapped her. As Pechorin and Maksimich were returning to camp, they saw Kazbich riding away with Bela. They pursued the bandit, but as they were about to overtake him, he thrust his knife into Bela and escaped.

Although Pechorin seemed to be deeply grieved by Bela's death, when Maksimich tried to comfort him, he laughed.

The Narrator, having parted from Maksim Maksimich, stopped at an inn in Vladikavkaz, where he found life very dull until, on the second day, Maksimich arrived unexpectedly. Before long there was a great stir and bustle in preparation for the arrival of an important guest. The travelers learned that Pechorin was the guest expected. Happy in the thought of seeing Pechorin again, Maksimich instructed a servant to carry his regards to his former friend, who had stopped off to visit a Colonel N——. Day turned to night but still Pechorin did not come to return the greeting. Dawn found Maksimich waiting at the gate again. When Pechorin finally arrived, he prevented Maksimich's intended embrace by coolly offering his hand.

Maksimich had anticipated warmth and a long visit, but Pechorin left immediately. Neither Maksimich's plea of friendship nor his mention of Bela served to detain Pechorin.

Thus Maksimich bade his friend goodbye. To the Narrator's attempt to cheer him the old man remarked only that Pechorin had become too rich and spoiled to bother about old friendships. In fact, he would throw away Pechorin's journal that he had been saving. The Narrator was so pleased to be the recipient of the papers that he grabbed them from the old man and rushed to his room. Next day the Narrator left, saddened by the reflection that when one has reached Maksim Maksimich's age, scorn from a friend causes the heart to harden and the soul to fold up. Later, having learned that Pechorin was dead, the Narrator published three tales from the dead man's journal, as Pechorin himself had written them:

Taman, a little town on the seacoast of Russia, was the worst town Pechorin had ever visited. For want of better lodging, he was forced to stay in a little cottage that he immediately disliked. Greeted at the door by a blind, crippled boy, Pechorin admitted to a prejudice against people with physical infirmities. To him, a crippled body held a crippled soul. His displeasure was enhanced when he learned there was no icon in the house —an evil sign.

In the night Pechorin followed the blind boy to the shore, where he witnessed a rendezvous that he did not comprehend. The next morning a young woman appeared at the cottage and he accused her of having been on the beach the night before. Later, the girl returned, kissed him, and arranged to meet him on the shore.

Pechorin kept the appointment. As he and the girl sailed in a boat, she tried to drown him; he, in turn, thrust her into the swirling, foaming water and brought the boat to shore. He was stunned to find that she had swum to safety and was talking to a man on shore. Pechorin learned that the man was a smuggler. The blind boy appeared, carrying a heavy sack which he delivered to the girl and the smuggler. They sailed away in a boat.

Pechorin returned to the cottage to find that his sword and all his valuables had been stolen.

Quite a different atmosphere pervaded Pechorin's next experience, as described in his journal. While stopping at Elizabeth Spring, a fashionable spa, he met Grushnitski, a wounded cadet whom he had known previously. The two men were attracted to Princess Mary, and Pechorin was angry—though he pretended indifference—because Princess Mary paid more attention to Grushnitski, a mere cadet, than she did to him, an officer. The men agreed that young society girls looked upon soldiers as savages and upon any young man with contempt.

Pechorin opened a campaign of revenge against Princess Mary. On one occasion he distracted an audience of her admirers; again, he outbid her for a Persian rug and then disparaged her sense of values by putting it on his horse. Her fury at these and other offenses gave Pechorin the satisfaction of revenge for her favor of Grushnitski.

Grushnitski wanted Pechorin to be friendly toward Princess Mary so that the cadet might be accepted socially through his association with her. Having seen Vera, a former lover of his but now married, Pechorin decided to court Princess Mary as a cover for his illicit affair with Vera.

As excitement mounted in anticipation of the ball, the major social event of the season, antagonism between Pechorin and Grushnitski and Pechorin and Princess Mary grew. Grushnitski's excitement and pride were the result of his promotion; Princess Mary would see him in his officer's uniform.

Succumbing to Pechorin's attitude of indifference, Princess Mary consented to dance the mazurka with him. Pechorin did not wish to hurt Grushnitski by divulging this news when the new officer later boasted that he intended to have this honored dance with the princess.

When, after the ball, it was rumored that Princess Mary would marry Pechorin, he fled to Kislovodsk to be with Vera. Grushnitski followed, but not to continue his association with Pechorin, whom he deliberately ignored. A short time later the princess and her party arrived in Kislovodsk to continue their holiday.

Still furious at the affront which had caused his disappointment at the ball, Grushnitski enlisted the aid of some dragoons in an attempt to catch Pechorin in Princess Mary's room. When this effort failed, Grushnitski challenged Pechorin to a duel. According to the plan Pechorin would have an empty pistol. Having discovered the plot, Pechorin compelled Grushnitski to stand at the edge of an abyss during the duel. Then he coolly shot the young officer, who tumbled into the depths below. Pechorin labeled Grushnitski's death an accident.

Princess Mary's mother asked Pechorin to marry the girl. He refused and wrote in his journal that a soft, protected life was not his way.

On another occasion, Pechorin and a group of Cossack officers were ridiculing the fatalism of the Moslems. Lieutenant Vulich, a renowned gambler, offered to prove his own faith in fatalism. While Pechorin and the Cossacks watched, aghast, Vulich aimed a pistol at his head and pulled the trigger. No shot was fired. He then aimed at a cap hanging on the wall; it was blown to pieces. Pechorin was amazed that the pistol had misfired on Vulich's first attempt. He was sure he had seen what he called the look of death on Vulich's face. Within a half hour after that demonstration Vulich was killed in the street by a drunken Cossack.

The next day Pechorin decided to test his own fate by offering to take the maddened Cossack alive, after an entire detachment had not dared the feat. He was successful.

Later, when Pechorin discussed the incident with Maksim Maksimich, the old man observed that Circassian pistols of the type which Vulich used for his demonstration were not really reliable. He added philosophically that it was unfortunate Vulich had stopped a drunk at night. Such a fate must have been assigned to Vulich at his birth.

HERSELF SURPRISED

Type of work: Novel
Author: Joyce Cary (1888-1957)
Type of plot: Social comedy
Time of plot: First quarter of the twentieth century
Locale: London and the English southern counties
First published: 1941

> Principal characters:
> SARA MONDAY, a cook
> MATTHEW (MATT) MONDAY, her husband
> GULLEY JIMSON, a painter
> NINA, his supposed wife
> MR. WILCHER, owner of Tolbrook Manor
> BLANCHE WILCHER, his niece by marriage
> MISS CLARISSA HIPPER, her older sister
> MR. HICKSON, a friend of the Mondays

Critique:

Sara Monday, the life-loving, self-indulgent, and generous cook who is the heroine of the first volume of Cary's first trilogy, tells her story sometimes ingenuously, sometimes shrewdly. Both these characteristics are portrayed with Cary's compassion and irony. The vivid, complete characters in Cary's novels are presented through their reactions to difficulties. Thus his books are crowded with incident, but without formal plot. Cary's prose style is simple, his language rich and colorful. Although critics have found it impossible to interpret his philosophy with any certainty, he is considered one of the foremost British novelists of his period.

The Story:

In prison Sara Monday realized that she was indeed guilty as charged. She hoped that other women would read her story and examine their characters before their thoughtless behavior brought them also to ruin.

Sara's first position was that of cook in a medium-sized country house. Matthew Monday, the middle-aged son of Sara's employer, had been dominated all his life by his mother and sister. Then this rather pathetic man fell in love with Sara, who discouraged his attentions, both because she feared he would cause her to lose her job and because she found him slightly ridiculous. Nevertheless, and somewhat to her surprise, when he proposed marriage she accepted him.

At a church bazaar a few months after her marriage, Sara met Mr. Hickson, a millionaire art collector with whom Matthew was associated in business. With Hickson's help she was able to emancipate Matt from the influence of his family. Partly because she was grateful to him for his help, Sara did not rebuke Hickson when he tried to flirt with her. After Sara had been forced to spend a night at Hickson's country house—his car had broken down—Matt supported her against the gossip and disapproval the episode occasioned.

Sara's life with Matt was, except for the death of their son in infancy, a happy one during the first years of their marriage. They had four daughters, and Sara's time was filled with parties, clothes, her nursery, and work on local committees.

Hickson brought an artist to stay with the Mondays. He was Gulley Jimson, who was to compete for the commission to paint a mural in the new town hall. Gulley settled in quickly and soon his forbearing wife, Nina, joined him. After a quarrel over a portrait of Matt, the Jimsons left. Soon afterward Sara visited them in their rooms at the local inn.

In jealousy, Hickson told Matt of these visits and the infuriated man accused his wife of infidelity. After his outburst Matt was very repentant and blamed himself for neglecting Sara. However, the incident caused him to lose all the confidence his marriage had given him.

Sara did not see Gulley for years after this incident. One day during Matt's last illness he reappeared. He looked shabby and he wanted money to buy paints and clothes. After telling her that Nina was dead, he asked Sara to marry him after Matt's death. Although she was shocked, Sara did not stop seeing Gulley immediately. While Matt was dying Gulley repeatedly proposed to her. Finally she sent him away.

After Matt's death and the sale of her house, Sara went to Rose Cottage, where Gulley was staying with Miss Slaughter, one of the sponsors for the church hall in which he was painting a mural. Miss Slaughter encouraged Sara to marry Gul-

ley, and at the end of a week they were engaged. Just before they were to be married, however, Gulley unhappily confessed that he had a wife and had never formally been married to Nina. Sara was furious and also bitterly disappointed, but in the end she agreed to live with Gulley and to say they were married. After an intensely happy honeymoon, they lived with Miss Slaughter while Gulley worked on his mural. During that time Sara tried to persuade Gulley to accept portrait commissions. Infuriated by her interference, Gulley struck Sara, who then left him. She was glad to return, however, when Miss Slaughter came for her.

Although Gulley's completed mural was considered unacceptable, he refused to change it. When Sara wanted him to repair some damage done to the painting, Gulley knocked her unconscious and left. Having exhausted her funds, Sara paid their outstanding bills with bad checks, and she was duly summonsed by the police.

After Sara had thus lost her good character, the only position she could obtain was that of cook at Tolbrook Manor. The owner, Mr. Wilcher, had a bad reputation for molesting young girls and seducing his women servants. Sara, however, pitied him and liked him. Eventually Mr. Wilcher moved Sara to his town house, having persuaded her to serve as housekeeper for both residences. She was glad of the extra money because Gulley had been writing to her asking for loans.

For many years Mr. Wilcher had had a mistress whom he visited every Saturday. During one of many long talks by Sara's fireside, he told her that he was tired of visiting this woman. When he asked Sara to take her place, she was at first slightly hesitant and confused, but in the end she agreed. The arrangement worked well enough for several years.

Mr. Wilcher became worried with family and financial affairs and Sara helped him by economizing on household expenses. At the same time she managed to falsify her accounts and send extra money to Gulley. One day a policeman came to the house with two girls who had complained of Mr. Wilcher's behavior. Mr. Wilcher disappeared, but Sara discovered him hours later hiding behind the chimney stacks on the roof. The family was appalled by this incident. After the impending summons had been quashed, Mr. Wilcher became even more unstable. Haunted by his past misdemeanors, he decided to confess them to the police. He also asked Sara to marry him after he had served his sentence. At this time he had an attack of sciatica. While he was confined to his bed, Blanche Wilcher, his niece by marriage and a woman who had always been suspicious of Sara, dismissed her.

Returning from a visit to her daughter, Sara forgot that she was no longer employed and entered Mr. Wilcher's street. There she found that the house had burned down in the night. Mr. Wilcher had been taken to the house of his niece's sister Clarissa. After he had recovered from shock he continued to see Sara and ignored Blanche. He rushed Sara to a registry office to give notice of their forthcoming marriage and then took a small new house for them to live in.

Sara had recently encountered Gulley once more and had gradually assumed financial responsibility for his new household. She maintained these payments for a time by selling to an antique shop oddments that Mr. Wilcher had told her to throw away.

The evening before her marriage, Sara arrived at the new house to find Blanche and a detective examining her possessions. She did not protest. After they had found receipts from the antique dealer and grocers' bills for supplies for Gulley, she was taken to the police station. She received an eighteen-month prison sentence and did not see Mr. Wilcher again.

A newspaper offered her money for her story. With this she paid Gulley's expenses and planned to become a cook again after she had served her sentence. She knew she could thus regain her "character," and she believed she could keep it now that she had discovered her weaknesses.

HESPERIDES

Type of work: Poetry
Author: Robert Herrick (1591-1674)
First published: 1648

As thou deserv'st, be proud; then gladly let
The Muse give thee the Delphick Coronet.

This brief epigram, one of hundreds Robert Herrick included in his collection of twelve hundred poems, best describes the pride with which he presented his *Hesperides* and the recognition he received after more than one hundred years of neglect. His subtitle, *The Works both Human and Divine of Robert Herrick Esq.*, indicates the inclusion in one volume of his *Hesperides* and his *Noble Numbers*, a group of ecclesiastical poems, prayers, hymns, and apothegms dated 1647. This collection, together with fifteen or so poems discovered by nineteenth-century scholars and about twice the number recovered recently in manuscript, comprise the literary remains of one of the finest lyricists in the English language.

The arrangement of the poems in *Hesperides* (the name itself is a conceit based on the legend of nymphs who guarded with a fierce serpent the golden apples of the goddess Hera) is whimsical. Most of the lyrics were composed in Devonshire, where Herrick was vicar of Dean Prior from 1629 until the Puritan victories caused his removal from his parish in 1647. Restored to his living in 1662, he lived until his death in the West Country which had inspired his pagan-spirited, rustic verse.

The great Herrick scholar, L. C. Martin, has discovered a chronology, from the collation of many manuscripts, which indicates the four general periods in which these poems were composed, carefully rewritten, and then painstakingly published. From his apprenticeship to his goldsmith uncle at least one poem remains, "A Country Life," which may have been one of the reasons why the youthful poet was allowed to terminate his service and go to Cambridge. Though Herrick's activities during his university period are remembered chiefly for the letters he wrote asking his uncle for money, he also composed a variety of commendatory poems and memory verses. One, the longest poem he wrote, is addressed to a fellow student who was ordained in 1623.

The second period, and perhaps the most important, was from 1617 to 1627, when he became the favorite of the "sons" of Ben Jonson. Herrick's famous poem, "His Fare-well to Sack," epitomizes these formative years of good talk, wide reading, witty writing, and good fellowship. In this poem too are the names of the poets who most influenced him—Anacreon, Horace, and by implication, Catullus and Theocritus. The well-known "The Argument of His Book" echoes the pastoral strain in the poet's declaration of his literary interests:

I sing of *Brooks*, of *Blossomes, Birds*, and *Bowers*:
Of *April, May*, of *June*, and *July-Flowers*.
I sing of *May-poles, Hock-carts, Wassails, Wakes*,
Of *Bride-grooms, Brides*, and of their *Bridall-cakes*.
I write of *Youth*, of *Love*, and have Accesse
By these, to sing of cleanly-*Wantonnesse*.
I sing of *Dewes*, of *Raines*, and piece by piece
Of *Balme*, of *Oyle*, of *Spice*, and *Amber-Greece*.
I sing of *Times trans-shifting*; and I write

How *Roses* first came *Red*, and *Lillies White*.
I write of *Groves*, of *Twilights*, and I sing
The Court of *Mab*, and of the *Fairie-King*.
I write of *Hell*; I sing (and ever shall)
Of *Heaven*, and hope to have it after all.

The Dean Prior vicar's hope for heaven seems to be based on his "cleanly-Wantonnesse," even if one considers his many mistresses—Corinna, stately Julia, smooth Anthea, and sweet Electra—as imaginary, the idealized woman of poetic tradition. Herrick's philosophy is Anacreontic, the *carpe d'em* attitude of the Cavalier poets. The best-known example from his work, in his own time as well as ours, is "To the Virgins, to Make Much of Time," which begins: "Gather ye Rosebuds while ye may."

That Herrick was a man of his time may be ascertained by a glance at the rich variety of his poetic subjects. Set in the form of the madrigal, "Corinna's *going a Maying*," catches all the excitement of the festival in the most intricate of singing forms. A ballad in the manner of Campion is "Cherrie-ripe," one which deserves to be better known:

Cherrie-Ripe, Ripe, Ripe, I cry
Full and faire ones; come and buy:
If so be, you ask me where
They doe grow? I answer, There,
Where my *Julia's* lips doe smile
There's the Land, or Cherry-Ile:
Whose Plantations fully show
All the yeere, where Cherries grow.

In the manner of Shakespeare he composed "The mad Maids Song," with the same "Good Morrows" and the strewing of flowers for the tomb, but in this instance the lament is for a lover killed by a bee sting. In the style of Marlowe and then Raleigh, Herrick continues the Elizabethan shepherd-maiden debate in "To Phillis to love, and live with him":

Thou shalt have Ribbands, Roses, Rings,

Gloves, Garters, Stockings, Shooes, and
    Strings
Of winning Colours, that shall move
Others to Lust, but me to Love.
These (nay) and more, thine own shal
    be,
If thou wilt love, and live with me.

A Master of Arts (1620) and a disciple of Jonson, Herrick never forgot his classical background. As an epigrammatist he was without peer, especially since he injected strong originality into a conventional and satiric form. He often made his parishioners models for these satiric verses, as in this comment on one man's discomfiture:

Urles had the Gout so, that he co'd
    not stand;
Then from his Feet, it shifted to his
    Hand:
When 'twas in's Feet, his Charity was
    small;
Now 'tis in's Hand, he gives no Almes
    at all.

Nor does he spare himself and his friends:

Wantons we are; and though our words
    be such,
Our Lives do differ from our Lines by
    much.

An extension of this mode is Herrick's Anacreontic verse. In "To Bacchus, *a Canticle*" he begs the god of revelry and reproduction to show him the way, among thousands, to have more than one mistress. Somewhat more restrained and in the vein of Catullus are his lyrics to Lesbia and the epithalamia with which he greeted his many friends and relatives who, despite all his verses, insisted on getting married. In "The cruell Maid" he echoes, or is echoed by, his contemporary, Andrew Marvell:

Give my cold lips a kisse at last:
If twice you kisse, you need not feare
That I shall stir, or live more here.
Next, hollow out a Tombe to cover
Me; me, the most despised Lover:
And write thereon, *This Reader, know,
Love kill'd this man.* No more but so.

The more humble and bucolic songs of Horace, however, were the poet's abiding love. While he may have wished for the court rather than the parish, his best work was composed amid peaceful surroundings on pleasant rural subjects. His "To Daffadills" is a more delicate and subtle poem than the well-known lyric by Wordsworth:

Faire Daffadills, we weep to see
    You haste away so soone:
As yet the early-rising Sun
    Has not attain'd his Noone.
      Stay, stay,
    Untill the hasting day
      Has run
    But to the Even-song;
And, having pray'd together, we
    Will goe with you along.

In the final period represented in *Hesperides*, "His returne to London" is a significant poem illustrating the sophisticated side of his genius, the pomp and circumstance which made a lasting poetry for this faithful royalist. He sings here of

O Place! O *People!* Manners! fram'd to
    please
All Nations, Customes, Kindreds, Languages!

as he links himself with his Elizabethan patron saints, the Renaissance man who took all life and all things for their province.

"And here my ship rides having Anchor cast," he writes in his concluding poems of the book which he sent forth to find "a kinsman or a friend." He honestly thought and in fact knew "The Muses will weare blackes, when I am dead." Ironically, his death went almost unnoticed, though his verses were recalled in oral tradition for many years before the recovery of his work by modern scholarship—a most appropriate tribute to the man who gives such a vivid picture of the folk and their wassails, harvests, wakes, and loves.

To his Book's end this last line he'd
    have plac't,
*Jocund his Muse was; but his Life was
    chast.*

A HIGH WIND RISING

Type of work: Novel
Author: Elsie Singmaster (Mrs. E. S. Lewars, 1879-   )
Type of plot: Historical chronicle
Time of plot: 1728-1755
Locale: Pennsylvania
First published: 1942

> *Principal characters:*
> ANNA SABILLA SCHANTZ, a pioneer matriarch
> JOHANN SEBASTIAN SCHANTZ, her grandson
> OTTILIA ZIMMER, a young German immigrant, loved by Sebastian
> MARGARETTA, and
> GERTRAUD, their twins
> CONRAD WEISER, a famous interpreter and Indian agent
> SHEKELLIMY, an Oneida chief, friend of Weiser
> SKELET, a half-friendly, half-treacherous Delaware

Critique:

A High Wind Rising deals with a phase of American history which most writers have neglected. It is a story of the Pennsylvania settlements beyond the Schuylkill during the decisive years when French and English battled for control of the Ohio and Conrad Weiser helped to determine the fate of a continent by keeping the Six Nations loyal to their British allies. The writer brings the period dramatically to life in her characterizations of pioneers like Conrad Weiser and Sebastian Schantz, of frontier women like resourceful, devoted Anna Sabilla. Those people live with no self-conscious sense of national destiny, as do so many pioneers in lesser fiction. Their lives illustrate what must have been the daily life of the frontier, the hardships and dangers that they faced no more than a part of their everyday existence. Other figures great in Pennsylvania annals are more briefly viewed in this crowded canvas of people and events—Benjamin Franklin, James Logan, John Bertram, Henry Melchior Muhlenburg, Lewis Evans. The passing of time and the pressures of history shape the plot, but the story itself is as simple and realistic as homely family legend. The novel is an example of the historical chronicle at its best.

The Story:

In 1728, Conrad Weiser, white clan brother of the Mohawks, saw Owkwari-owira—Young Bear—for the first time, a naked small boy daubed with clay and running wild in Chief Quagnant's village. Weiser, his quick eye seeing pale skin under the dirt and grease, bartered for the child and took him back to the German settlement at Schoharie. Young Bear was baptized Johann Sebastian, and found in Anna Eve, Conrad's wife, a second mother. The Weisers believed that Bastian was the grandson of Anna Sabilla Schantz, whose daughter Margaretta had followed an English trader into the forest.

Many of the Schoharie community were preparing to move to Pennsylvania, where there was rich land for thrifty, industrious German settlers. Anna Sabilla had already gone to her own cabin in a clearing beside the Blue Mountains. Sturdy, resolute, she cared for Nicholas, her paralyzed brother, tended her garden, called all Indians thieves and rascals, but fed them when they begged at her door. For trader Israel Fitch she carved wooden puppets in exchange for salt, cloth, tools. Weiser took Bastian to her when he went to claim his own lands along the Tulpehocken.

Growing up, Bastian helped his grandmother with plantings and harvests. From Skelet, a sickly, humpbacked Indian whom Anna Sabilla had nursed back to health, he learned the ways of animals and the deep woods. When old Nicholas died, Bastian moved into his room. Tall and strong for his age, he was the man of the family at fourteen.

The chiefs' road ran through the clearing, and along the trail Delawares and Iroquois traveled to and from the treaty councils in Philadelphia. Bastian knew them all— old Sassoonan of the Delawares, loyal Shekellimy, Weiser's friend, who ruled the Delawares for the Six Nations, Seneca, Oneida, and Mohawk spokesmen —and they remembered Owkwari-owira. Sharp-tongued Anna Sabilla grumbled when he talked with them in their own tongues, but she raised few objections when he went with Weiser and the chiefs to Philadelphia for the great council of 1736.

The city was finer than Bastian had ever imagined it. Whenever he could, he left the State House and wandered through the streets and along the waterfront. He saw a shipload of German immigrants and among them a black-haired girl whose parents had died at sea. Because she had no one to pay her passage, her eyes were like those of a hurt deer, and he gave all his money to a kindly couple who offered to look after her. Bastian heard only that her name was Ottilia before a runner from Weiser summoned him to the council. He went back to look for her later, but the immigrants had gone.

Anna Sabilla hinted that Anna Maria, Weiser's daughter, or the Heils' blonde Sibby would have him quickly enough, but Bastian remembered black hair and dark eyes. Tramping from clearing to clearing looking for her, he found some passengers from the ship who remembered that she had gone away with a family named Wilhelm. Again he went to Philadelphia for a treaty council. There Weiser found the girl's name on a ship's list— Ottilia Zimmer. Bastian's search led him to John Bartram, the Quaker naturalist,

along the Schuylkill, beyond the Blue Mountains. Nowhere did he get word of Ottilia or the Wilhelms. Anna Maria Weiser became engaged to marry Henry Melchior Muhlenburg, a young pastor. Anna Sabilla shook her head over Bastian; in her old age she wanted the comfort of another woman and children in the cabin.

The chiefs of the Six Nations and delegates from Pennsylvania, Maryland, and Virginia met in Lancaster in 1744. Weiser was there because he was needed to hold the Long House in friendly alliance, Bastian because, as the years passed, Weiser counted greatly on his help. The weather was hot, the noise deafening. Weiser and Bastian went to a small inn to escape feasting Indians. The waitress had black hair and dark eyes. She was Ottilia, and she rode home with Bastian when the conference ended. Humpbacked Skelet ran ahead to tell Anna Sabilla that Bastian had found his squaw.

Settlers were moving beyond the Susquehanna. While Delawares and Shewanese signed treaties with the French, Weiser worked to keep the Long House neutral. Bastian went with him to Logstown on the Ohio, where Tanacharison and Scarouady promised to keep their tribes friendly toward the English. As Bastian rode home, neighbors called to him to hurry. In the kitchen of the cabin Anna Sabilla rocked a cradle in which slept the newborn *zwillings,* Margaretta and Gertraud. At last, said Anna Sabilla, they were a real family.

But winds of violence blew from the west. Weiser gave presents at Aughwick, at Carlisle, but his arguments, feasts, and gifts could not hold the Shewanese and the Delawares, angry because their hunting grounds had been taken from them. General Braddock, marching to force the French from the Ohio, was ambushed. Fitch, the trader, brought word of burnings and killings beyond the mountains. Because Pennsylvania lay open to war parties of French and Indians, Bastian was glad when Fitch decided to stay; another man might be needed if Indians appeared on the Tulpehocken.

Bastian had gone to help a sick neighbor when the raiders struck, burning the cabin and barn and leaving Fitch's body where it fell. Anna Sabilla, Ottilia, and the twins were gone. Pretending ferocity, Skelet had taken a small part of Ottilia's scalp and left her unconscious. Anna Sabilla and the twins he took with him to Kitanning, calling Anna Sabilla his squaw. She was indignant, but she realized that his claims kept her alive and the twins safe.

Reviving, Ottilia wandered through the woods for days in company with a small boy whose parents had been killed and scalped. At last, with other fugitives, she made her way to the Moravian settlement at Bethlehem. There Bastian found her on his journey back from Philadelphia, where he and other settlers had gone to demand the formation of militia units and forts to protect the frontier. Leaving Ottilia with the Weisers, he joined the garrison at Fort Henry, built where Anna Sabilla's cabin had once stood.

One night he and a friend captured a young Frenchman who carried the carved figure of a little girl, and Bastian, recognizing Anna Sabilla's work, concluded that she and the twins were still alive. He joined a raiding party marching on Kitanning, but Anna Sabilla and the little girls were not among the white prisoners freed in the attack.

Anna Sabilla and the twins were already on the way home. Knowing that Skelet was vain and greedy, she promised money if he would guide them back to the settlements. They set out, Skelet dreaming of the rum and finery he would buy with the old woman's gold. Then, worn out by hardships on the trail, he died on the ridge above her own clearing.

Suddenly Anna Sabilla smelled chimney smoke, heard voices. She ran, urging the girls before her. Safe within the stockade, and grateful, she declared that the old humpback had been a rascal but that he had been helpful. She intended to bury him among her people.

THE HILL OF DREAMS

Type of work: Novel
Author: Arthur Machen (1863-1947)
Type of plot: Impressionistic romance
Time of plot: Late nineteenth century
Locale: England
First published: 1907

Principal characters:
LUCIAN TAYLOR, a would-be author
THE REVEREND MR. TAYLOR, Lucian's father, a rural clergyman
ANNIE MORGAN, Lucian's sweetheart

Critique:

This novel by Arthur Machen, in part an autobiography, received little notice when it was published. During the 1920's, after Machen's books had won him a reputation, this novel also came in for a share of attention and popularity. Machen himself said, in the introduction to a later edition of the book, that he had begun it as proof to the world and to himself that he was indeed a man of letters and that, even more important, he had thrown off the style of Robert Louis Stevenson, whom he had been accused of imitating, and had found a style of his own to express his ideas. He also related that the writing of the novel was imbedded in the work itself: that many of the trials and weird experiences which have been put into the

THE HILL OF DREAMS by Arthur Machen. By permission of the publishers, Alfred A. Knopf, Inc. Copyright, 1922, by Alfred A. Knopf, Inc. Renewed.

life of the fictional Lucian Taylor were, in reality, the experiences of Machen himself as he wrote the novel. This novel will probably never be a popular one, for it is a somewhat difficult study of a highly introverted character, a man who, while searching for a way to express life, lost both himself and the power to understand humanity. Although such studies are too intense and yet too nebulous to appeal to a widely diversified body of readers, the book is likely to stand as a notable example of its type.

The Story:

Lucian Taylor, son of an Anglican rector in a rural parish, was an extraordinary lad, even before he went to school. He was both studious and reflective, so much so that he was not accepted readily by the boys of the neighborhood. When Lucian went away to school he did very well in his studies, but he formed an acute dislike for athletics and for social life with his fellow students. In his studies he turned toward the less material, preferring to learn of the dim Celtic and Roman days of Britain, of medieval church history, and of works in magic.

In his fifteenth year Lucian returned to his home during the August holidays and found it quite changed. His mother had died during the previous year, and his father's fortunes had sunk lower and lower. As a result his father had become exceedingly moody and Lucian spent much of his time away from the house. His habit was to wander through the rolling countryside by himself.

One bright summer afternoon he climbed up a steep hillside to the site of an old Roman fort. The site was at some distance from any human habitation, and Lucian felt quite alone. Because of the heat, he had an impulse to strip off his sweaty clothing and take a nap. He did, only to be awakened by someone kissing him. By the time he had fully regained his senses, the unknown person had disappeared. Lucian was not sure whether some supernatural being or Annie Morgan, daughter of a local farmer, had awakened him thus.

Soon afterward Lucian went back to school. At last the rector told his son that he could no longer afford to send him to school and that matriculation at Oxford was out of the question. Lucian was disappointed, but he settled down to studying in his father's library or wandering about the countryside in solitary fashion, as he had done during his vacations from school.

As the elder Taylor's fortunes had declined, his popularity in the parish had diminished. Lucian's own reputation had never been high, and his failure to take a job in some respectable business establishment turned the local gentry against him. Everyone felt that his studies and his attempts to write were foolish, since they brought in no money. Nor could the people understand Lucian's failure to maintain their standards of respectability in dress and deportment.

Lucian felt, however, that he could stand beyond such criticism of his habits, but his self-respect suffered a blow when he tried to sell some of his writings. Publishers, refusing to accept his work, pointed out to him that what they wanted was sentimental fiction of a stereotyped kind. Lucian, not wishing to cheapen himself or his literary efforts, refused to turn out popular fiction of the type desired. He felt that he had to express himself in a graver kind of literature.

Lucian's social and intellectual loneliness preyed upon him, plunging him at times into the deepest despair. One afternoon, while sunk in a mood of depression, he went out for a long walk. By dusk he was far from home, or so he thought, and in the midst of a wood. Finally fighting his way clear of the dense brush, Lucian blundered onto a path and there met Annie Morgan. She sensed his mood and fell in with it. Both of them announced their love and pledged one another. Lucian went home feeling better than he had in months.

As the days passed Lucian fell into the

habit of putting himself in a world apart, a world of the past, when Rome held Britain as a distant province. He dreamed that the modern town of Caermaen, near which was his father's rectory, was once again the Roman settlement it had been centuries before. Lucian called his land of make-believe Avallaunius and spent most of his time there, peopling it with men and women, buildings and customs, that he had learned of through his exhaustive studies of Roman times in Britain. He went wandering through the modern town, imagining that the people he met and the scenes before his eyes were those of ancient times. Even Annie Morgan's announcement that she was going away made little impression upon him, for he felt that she had accomplished her mission in his life by showing him how to escape into a better world.

People wondered at the strange behavior of the young man; even his father, not given to noticing anything, became worried because Lucian ate little and grew thin. People who knew him only by sight suspected him of being a drunkard because of his odd behavior and absentmindedness.

But at last Lucian escaped physically from Caermaen; he received notice that a distant cousin who had lived on the Isle of Wight had died and left him two thousand pounds. He immediately gave five hundred pounds to his father and invested the remainder for himself. With the assurance of a small, regular income, Lucian left Caermaen behind and went to London. There he felt he could escape from the moodiness which had held him prisoner in the country. He also hoped that the different mental atmosphere would prove helpful to him in his attempts at writing.

Upon his arrival in the city Lucian found himself a single room in a private home. He soon settled down to a regular existence, writing late each night, sleeping late in the morning, reading over his work of the night before, and walking, in the afternoons. His meals were sketchy, for he was forced to live on as little as fifteen shillings a week. But the regular schedule was not to hold for long. His inspiration was not a regular thing, and Lucian felt that he had to make his writings perfection itself. He threw away as much as he wrote. Disappointment over his efforts soon began to drive him into worse moods than he had known before.

Having been impressed as a boy by the work of De Quincey in *Confessions of an English Opium Eater*, Lucian turned to that drug for solace and inspiration. After he began taking drugs, he knew little that was going on in the world about him. He spent much of his time lying quietly in his room and reliving the past in visions. Once he had a real inspiration to write; his story about an amber goddess was the product of true imagination. But publication of the story did little to generate ambition and the will to create; he was too far gone in his addiction to opium.

A heavy snow and a severe wave of cold struck London and southern England, but the weather made little impression on him; he might just as well have been living in a ghost city. Then one night he took too much opium. His landlady, not hearing him stir for many hours, looked into his room and found him dead at his desk, his writings spread about him. Even she felt little sorrow for him, although he had made over his small fortune to her.

HILLINGDON HALL

Type of work: Novel
Author: Robert Smith Surtees (1803-1864)
Type of plot: Comic romance
Time of plot: Nineteenth century
Locale: England
First published: 1845

JOHN JORROCKS, a wealthy cockney grocer and sportsman
MRS. JORROCKS, his shrewish wife
EMMA FLATHER, a country girl
MRS. FLATHER, her mother
THE DUKE OF DONKEYTON, Jorrocks' neighbor
THE MARQUIS OF BRAY, his son

Critique:

Hillingdon Hall, Or, The Cockney Squire is the final novel of the Jorrocks series. Here the emphasis is on country life and its charms and oddities. John Jorrocks, a London grocer turned sporting country proprietor and agriculturist, is less a clown than he was in previous volumes, although he does meet with many undignified adventures; and the whole tone of the book is more sympathetic than picaresque. There is some good satire in the electioneering scenes and in Emma Flather's attempts to get a husband, and some current farming fads come in for good-natured ridicule. *Hillingdon Hall* is one of the better constructed works in the series, and the cockney speech, as in all of Surtees' work, is accurately represented.

The Story:

Hillingdon Hall was a charming example of the old-style manor house with its many haphazard additions and types of architecture. It was set in a pretty village and the nearby river added to its attractions. Mr. Westbury, the former owner, had been an old-fashioned gentleman of talent and learning who spent his whole time in the country. Since he was a kind of patriarch for the district, the village wondered after his death who would be the new owner of the hall.

When the carriage drew up at the door, curious eyes were fastened on the new arrivals. The chaise was covered with dust. A package of apple trees lay on the roof, the coach boy clutched a huge geranium, and flowers and plants of all kinds were sticking out of the windows. A huge, fat man with roses in his back pocket got out, followed by his wife in stiff brocade. John Jorrocks, the new owner, had arrived.

Mrs. Flather announced the news to her blooming daughter Emma. The two ladies thought it would be only neighborly for them to call right away, especially since there might be a son in the family. Emma at the time had an understanding with James Blake, who had the living at Hillingdon, but she was always on the alert for a better match. Mrs. Trotter, who was, if anything, quicker at gossip than Mrs. Flather, brought the news that Jorrocks was old and married and had no children.

Jorrocks tried hard to be a good gentleman farmer. He visited his tenants faithfully but found them a poor lot. They could scarcely understand his cockney accent and they were full of complaints; besides, they knew much more than he did about farming. Mrs. Jorrocks got on better at first with her country folk. Traditionally the lady of Hillingdon Hall was the patroness of the local school. When she visited the establishment, she was appalled at the drab uniforms worn by the girls. Forthwith she had a friend in London, an actress, design new costumes in the Swiss mode. These she forced on the protesting girls. Unfortunately, when she had a new sign put up at the school the spelling was bad; it announced to the world that the institution was "founder'd" by Julia Jorrocks.

One memorable day a magnificent coach drove up and an impressive footman left a card from the Duke of Donkeyton. The duke fancied himself as a politician. Thinking that Jorrocks might become a person of standing, and feeling sure that he must be a Whig, the duke wanted to make certain of his allegiance.

The Jorrockses were still more astounded to receive an invitation to dine and stay the night at Donkeyton. Although much puzzled by the initials R. S. V. P., Jorrocks wrote a formal acceptance. Mrs. Flather and Emma were also invited, but characteristically they were thinking of the duke's son, the Marquis of Bray, as a possible suitor for Emma.

On the way to Donkeyton, Jorrocks contrived to get in the same carriage with Mrs. Flather and squeezed that poor lady and stole a kiss or two. He continued his boisterous tactics at the castle. The duke was much impressed by Jorrocks' appetite for food and drink. After dinner he made the mistake of trying to keep up with Jorrocks in drinking toasts; consequently, he had to retire early and was unable to appear in time for breakfast.

The elegant and effeminate Marquis of Bray was quite taken with Emma. He fell in with a scheme that Jorrocks and the duke had for founding an agricultural society with Bray as president and Jorrocks as vice-president. He readily agreed to come to an organizational meeting, since there he would see Emma again.

The meeting was a great success. Bray was horrified at the amount of food put away by Jorrocks and his farmers, but he did his best to keep up appearances. Jorrocks' speech sounded good, although some of the farmers did not follow him very well. He advocated the growing of pineapples and the making of drain tile with sugar as the principal ingredient. Bray topped off the occasion by a speech lauding the ancient Romans. Afterward he was able to visit Emma and capture that girl's willing heart.

For some time Jorrocks had had as estate manager a jack-of-all-trades named Joshua Sneakington—Sneak for short. After he had arranged for fees and bribes to add to his income, Sneak thought himself well off. One morning, however, Jorrocks rose very early and decided to make a tour of inspection. In a secluded spot he came upon Sneak netting pheasants.

Furious at the trickery, he had Sneak sent to jail. His new manager was a doughty North Countryman, James Pigg, who had been with Jorrocks at Handley Cross.

The duke showed favor to Jorrocks by giving him a prize bull, which won a ribbon at a fair, and by appointing him magistrate. Bray came again to visit, mostly to see Emma, but Jorrocks dragged him off to a rough farmers' masquerade. Bray, who was a slender youth, made the mistake of dressing as a woman. A loutish farmer who would not be put off tried to kiss him. The boisterous treatment startled Bray so much that he wandered off in the night and got lost. He came upon a sleeping household and, after awaking the inhabitants, found he had blundered on the Flather's house. After staying the night with the family, he had a chance to flirt with Emma at breakfast.

After that adventure Emma and her mother confidently expected an offer from Donkeyton. When no word came, the desperate Mrs. Flather herself went to the castle. The duchess was amused at the idea of her son's marriage with a commoner, but the duke was incensed; he knew that Bray had conducted himself properly, for he had read Chesterfield. The son had no voice in the matter at all. Later Emma and her mother had to admit he had never made an outright profession of love.

The member of Parliament from the district died. The duke immediately sent out a bid for Bray to fill the vacancy, and no opposition was expected. The Anti-Corn-Law League wrote several times to Bray asking his stand on repeal of the grain tariff, but Bray knew nothing of the matter and did not reply. Thereupon the League put up its own candidate, Bill Bowker, a grifting friend of Jorrocks. To avoid a campaign, the duke bought off Bowker for a thousand pounds and endorsed the proposals of the League.

It was a shocking thing for the duke to advocate removal of tariffs on grain.

When next the farmers tried to sell their produce at market, they found that prices had tumbled. In their anger they put forth the willing Jorrocks as their candidate. The duke was hurt that a man to whom he had given a bull and whom he had elevated to a magistracy should run against his son, but Jorrocks was obdurate. At the hustings, although the Marquis of Bray won, Jorrocks' supporters demanded a poll.

The farmers all worked to get every eligible voter to vote. Pigg was a little tricky because he persuaded the Quakers to vote for Jorrocks on the grounds that his candidate was a teetotaler. When the votes were counted, Jorrocks won by a margin of two. Elated at beating a marquis, and glad to go back to London, Jorrocks left Pigg in charge of Hillingdon Hall and went on to bigger things.

HIPPOLYTUS

Type of work: Drama
Author: Euripides (480-406 B.C.)
Type of plot: Classical tragedy
Time of plot: Remote antiquity
Locale: Troezen in Argolis
First presented: 428 B.C.

Principal characters:
THESEUS, King of Athens
HIPPOLYTUS, son of Theseus and Hippolyta, Queen of the Amazons
PHAEDRA, wife of Theseus
APHRODITE, goddess of physical love
ARTEMIS, goddess of spiritual love

Critique:

The *Hippolytus* is probably one of the most provocative of Greek tragedies, and Phaedra, despite her comparatively brief appearance in the play, is one of the most pitiful of tragic heroines. Hippolytus himself is an insufferable prig; but because Phaedra and Theseus are victims of relentless fate our sympathies go out to them. It has been said that this play is Euripides' dramatic treatment of the conflict in the human between physical and spiritual love, although this theory may attribute too much importance to the traditional rivalry between Aphrodite and Artemis in Greek mythology. Racine treated this story in the baroque manner in his *Phèdre.*

The Story:

Aphrodite, goddess of physical love, became angry because Hippolytus, offspring of an illicit union between Theseus and Hippolyta, Queen of the Amazons, alone among the citizens of Troezen refused to do her homage. Instead, the youth, tutored by holy Pittheus, honored Artemis, goddess of the chase and of spiritual love. To punish him for his disdain of love and marriage, Aphrodite, jealous of Artemis and incensed at his neglect of her altars, vowed revenge: she would reveal to Theseus the love his wife, Phaedra, had for her stepson.

Some time before, Hippolytus had gone to the country of Pandion to be initiated into the holy mysteries. There Phaedra, seeing him, had fallen in love with the handsome youth, and because her heart was filled with longing she had dedicated a temple to the Cyprian goddess. Poseidon, ruler of the sea, had once promised Theseus that three of his prayers to the sea god should be answered. Through that promise Aphrodite planned to accomplish her revenge.

Now it happened that Theseus had killed a kinsman, and as punishment for his crime he had been exiled for a year in Troezen. There Phaedra, who had accompanied her husband when he left Athens, was unhappy in her secret love for the young huntsman.

Hippolytus, returning from the chase, paid his respects with song and garlands before the altar of Artemis. Reminded by a servant that an image of Aphrodite stood nearby, he answered impatiently that he acknowledged the power of the Cyprian goddess, but from afar. Dedicated to chastity, he had no desire to become her devotee. The attendant, after Hippolytus had left the shrine, asked Aphrodite to indulge the young man's foolish pride.

Phaedra, meanwhile, moped in her hopeless passion for the young prince, so much so that her servants expressed deep concern over her illness and wondered what strange malady affected her. A nurse, alarmed at Phaedra's restiveness and petulance, was the most concerned of all. When her mistress expressed a desire to hunt wild beasts in the hills and to gallop horses on the sands, the nurse decided that Phaedra was light-headed because she had not eaten food for three days.

At last the nurse swore by the Amazon queen who had borne Theseus a son that Phaedra would be a traitor to her own children if she let herself sicken and die. At the mention of Hippolytus' name Phaedra started; then she moaned pitifully. Thinking how horrible it was that she had been stricken with love for her husband's son, she bewailed the unnatural passions of her Cretan house. At the nurse's urging she finally confessed her true feelings for her stepson. The nurse, frightened at the thought of the consequences possible because of that sinful passion, was horrified. The attendants mourned at what the future seemed to hold for all concerned. Phaedra told them that she was determined to take her own life in order to preserve her virtue and to save Theseus from shame.

But the nurse, having reconsidered, advised her mistress to let matters take a natural course; she would offend Aphrodite if she were to resist her love for Hippolytus. Phaedra was quite scandalized, however, when the nurse suggested that she even see Hippolytus. The nurse said that she had a love charm that would end Phaedra's malady. As it turned out, the potion was ineffectual without a word from Hippolytus' mouth or an item of his clothing or personal belongings.

Phaedra's attendants melodically invoked Aphrodite not to look askance upon them in their concern for their mistress.

The nurse, eager to aid the lovesick woman, went to Hippolytus and told him of Phaedra's love. The young huntsman, shocked, rebuked the nurse for a bawd and expressed his dislike for all mortal womankind. Phaedra, having overheard her stepson's angry reproaches and his condemnation of all women, feared that her secret would be revealed. To make Hippolytus suffer remorse for her death, she hanged herself.

Theseus, who had been away on a journey, returned to discover that Phaedra had taken her life. Grief-stricken, he became enraged when he read a letter clenched in his dead wife's hand. In it she wrote that Hippolytus had caused her death by his attempts to ravish her. Wild with sorrow and rage, Theseus called upon Poseidon to grant the first of his requests: he asked the god to destroy Hippolytus that very day. His attendants, shocked, implored him to be calm, to consider the welfare of his house, and to withdraw his request.

Hippolytus, returning at that moment, encountered his father and was mystified by the passionate words of Theseus. Standing over the body of his dead wife, the king reviled his bastard son and showed him the letter Phaedra had written. Hippolytus, proudly defending his innocence, said that he had never looked with carnal desire upon any woman. Theseus, refusing to believe his son's protestations, banished the young man from his sight. Hippolytus departed, still insisting to his friends that he was the purest of mortals.

Going down to the seashore, Hippolytus entered his chariot after invoking Zeus to strike him dead if he had sinned. As he drove along the strand, on the road leading to Argos, an enormous wave rose out of the sea and from the whirling waters emerged a savage, monstrous bull whose bellowing echoed along the shore. The horses drawing Hippolytus' chariot panicked and ran away, the bull in pursuit. Suddenly one of the chariot wheels struck a rock and the car overturned. Hippolytus, dragged across the rocks, was mortally injured.

Theseus, learning with indifference that his son still lived, consented to have him brought back to the palace. While he waited, Artemis appeared and told him of his son's innocence and of Phaedra's guilty passion for Hippolytus. Aphrodite, she declared, had contrived the young hunter's death to satisfy her anger at his neglect of her shrines.

Hippolytus, his body maimed and broken, was carried on a litter into his father's presence. Still maintaining his innocence, he moaned with shameless self-pity and lamented that one so pure and chaste should meet death because of his frightened horses. They were, he said, the principal means by which he had always honored Artemis, goddess of the hunt. When she told him that Aphrodite had caused his death, he declared that he, his father, and Artemis were all victims of the Cyprian's evil designs.

Knowing the truth at last, Hippolytus, humbled, took pity on broken-hearted Theseus and forgave his father for his misunderstanding and rage. Theseus, arising from the side of the dead prince, miserably faced the prospect of living on after causing the destruction of his innocent, beloved son.

HISTORIA CALAMITATUM

Type of work: Autobiography
Author: Pierre Abélard (1079-1142)
Time: 1079-c.1132
Locale: Paris, Melun, Laon, and St. Gildas, France
First transcribed: c. 1132

Principal personages:

PIERRE ABÉLARD, philosopher, theologian, churchman
FULBERT, Canon of Notre Dame
HÉLOÏSE, Canon Fulbert's niece
WILLIAM OF CHAMPEAUX, Abélard's teacher, a philosopher
ANSELM OF LAON, a teacher
BERNARD OF CLAIRVAUX, Abbot of Clairvaux

Abélard's *History of My Calamity* is an account of the romantic and intellectual misfortunes of one of the significant philosophers of the Middle Ages. As a moderate realist Abélard upheld the Aristotelian idea that names of characteristics do not name independently real universals but merely call attention to certain resemblances in things. This opinion made him a philosophical opponent of his teacher, William of Champeaux. Abélard's reliance on logic and dialectic together with his love of debate resulted in his antagonizing many churchmen,

Bernard of Clairvaux in particular, and he was condemned for heresy. This misfortune took second place to the castration which he suffered as the result of having seduced Héloïse, niece of the Canon of Notre Dame. Abélard's story of his misfortunes is at the same time a personal statement from the Middle Ages and a timeless expression of human trials.

Pierre Abélard was born in the village of Pallet, about eight miles from Nantes. His father was a soldier who had studied letters, and through his influence Abélard acquired a passion for learning. In particular, he delighted in philosophy and in the logical exercise of disputation.

In Paris he studied under William of Champeaux, whom he irritated by besting him in a series of debates. Abélard set up a school of his own at Melun and, later, at Corbeil, near Paris, until he was forced by illness to return to his native province for several years. When he returned to Paris, he resumed study with William of Champeaux, but once again Abélard's skill in overthrowing his master's philosophy of universals gained the enmity of that cleric. Consequently, Abélard reëstablished his school at Melun and attracted many of William's students to his own school. Later, he moved closer to Paris, conducted his school on Mont Ste. Geneviève, and carried on a philosophical feud with William.

After the conversion of his parents to the monastic life, Abélard decided to study under Anselm of Laon, but he was disappointed to discover that Anselm's fame was more a result of custom than of intellect. Anselm had a great flow of words, but the words were all meaningless. Taunted by Anselm's admirers for his desultory attendance at the lectures, Abélard invited the students to hear his own exposition of the Scriptures. The presentation was so successful that, like William, Anselm began to persecute Abélard for surpassing him. When Anselm ordered Abélard to cease the work which was embarrassing him, Abélard returned to Paris.

In Paris he completed the glosses on Ezekiel which he had begun at Laon. As his philosophical fame grew and the numbers of his students increased, his pride and sensuality grew accordingly. Attracted by Héloïse, the young niece of a canon named Fulbert, Abélard determined to possess her. Having persuaded her uncle to take him in as a lodger, he agreed to become Héloïse's tutor and guide.

Abélard's objective was soon reached. Pretending to be engrossed in study, the lovers explored all the avenues of love,

and Abélard gave less and less time to philosophy and to teaching. Instead of writing new lectures, he wrote love poetry which became famous among those who loved the delights of this world. Fulbert dismissed the rumors which came to him because he loved his niece and had faith in the continence of Abélard. The truth becoming finally apparent, even to Fulbert, the lovers were forced to part. Their separation brought them shame, but shame gave way to increased desire. When Héloïse discovered that she was pregnant, Abélard arranged to have her taken to his sister's house. There Héloïse gave birth to a son, Astrolabe.

Fulbert, nearly mad with grief, would have killed or injured Abélard had he not feared that Héloïse might suffer from the vengeance of her lover's family. Then Abélard begged the canon's forgiveness and declared his intention to marry Héloïse. Fulbert agreed to the offer and sealed their agreement with a kiss.

When Abélard told Héloïse of his intention, she objected strenuously, arguing that it would be a loss to the Church and to philosophy if he were to disgrace himself by marrying a girl he had seduced. Furthermore, she argued, if he were to marry he would be going against the advice of the most eminent philosophers, who argued that no one could devote himself to philosophy while compelled to listen to the disturbances of family life. Finally she referred to the examples provided by those who undertook the monastic life in order to serve God.

Abélard refusing to be convinced, he and Héloïse were married secretly in Paris, the ceremony witnessed by her uncle and a few friends. When Héloïse criticized her uncle for telling the secret of her marriage, Fulbert punished her. Abélard, hearing of the punishment, sent Héloïse to a convent at Argenteuil. This act so angered the canon that he and his kinsmen arranged to have Abélard castrated. Two of those who perpetrated this shameful deed were later apprehended and, as punishment, blinded and also castrated.

Abélard suffered not so much from the physical injury as from the grief of the clerics and scholars of Paris. Héloïse took the vows of a religious life at the convent of Argenteuil, and Abélard became a monk at the abbey of St. Denis. There, deploring the scandalous life of the abbot and other monks, he lured their students from them by teaching secular philosophy as well as theology.

Abélard's rivals at the abbey, through the coöperation of Alberic and Lotulphe, apologists for Anselm, arranged to have him called before an ecclesiastical council at Soissons for writing a tract containing what they regarded as heretical views concerning the unity and trinity of God. Although no case against the book could be made, Abélard's enemies convinced the council that the book should be ordered burned. This decision was carried out and Abélard was sent to the abbey of St. Médard as punishment. After a short period of time, however, all who had been involved in punishing Abélard put the blame on others; Abélard was allowed to return to the abbey of St. Denis.

When the envy of the monks of St. Denis prompted more ecclesiastical quarrels, Abélard secured permission to build an oratory at Troyes. This he named the Paraclete, dedicating the church to the Holy Spirit.

Abélard was then called to be abbot of St. Gildas at Ruits, but his suffering continued because of the undisciplined and immoral behavior of the monks.

When the abbot of St. Denis expelled the nuns from the abbey of Argenteuil, where Héloïse served, Abélard arranged to have her and some of her deposed companions take charge of the Paraclete. In this manner he secured Héloïse's happiness. Rumors began to spread that Abélard was acting in her behalf because he was moved by lust, but he defended himself by arguing that the damage done to his person made any base act impossible. Furthermore, he regarded it as his duty to supervise the nuns, and he pointed out passages in scripture in support of his action.

Abélard was constantly threatened by the monks of his abbey, who attempted to poison him and to have him murdered by bandits. Only by exercising great care and by excommunicating the most wicked among the brothers was Abélard able to survive. He wrote the letter giving an account of his misfortunes in order to show how much suffering is possible for one who serves God and to argue that, despite suffering, all persons should trust in God's providence.

THE HISTORY OF COLONEL JACQUE

Type of work: Novel
Author: Daniel Defoe (1661?-1731)
Type of plot: Picaresque adventure
Time of plot: Late seventeenth century
Locale: England, France, Virginia
First published: 1722

Principal characters:
    COLONEL JACQUE, commonly called Jack, a waif
    CAPTAIN JACK, his foster brother
    MAJOR JACK, another foster brother
    WILL, a pickpocket
    COLONEL JACQUE's FOUR WIVES

Critique:

Although in our day Daniel Defoe is remembered chiefly for *Robinson Crusoe*, in its own time *Colonel Jacque* attained great popularity. Defoe declared that his twofold purpose was to show the ruination of youth through lack of proper training and to prove that a misspent life may be redeemed by repentance. The novel opens on a theme similar to that of *Oliver Twist* but follows a line of development modeled after *Gil Blas*. Although a rogue, Colonel Jacque aspires to win back his good name, and in the end he succeeds. Defoe, in the fashion of his day, gave the novel a grandiose title: *The History and Remarkable life of the truly Honourable Colonel Jacque, vulgarly called Col. Jack, who was born a Gentleman, put 'Prentice to a Pick-pocket, flourished six and twenty years as a Thief, and was then Kidnapped to Virginia; came back a Merchant, was five times married to four Whores, went into the Wars, behaved bravely, got preferment, was made Colonel of a Regiment, came over and fled with the Chevalier, is still Abroad Completing a Life of Wonders, and resolves to die a General.* The end of the novel does not fulfill, however, the promise of the title.

The Story:

The illegitimate son of a gentleman and a lady, Colonel Jack, as he was later known, was early in his life given to his nurse to rear. There he was brought up with her own son, Captain Jack, and another unwanted child, Major Jack. She treated the boys well, but she herself had little money and so they were forced to fend for themselves. When Colonel Jack was but ten years of age, the good woman died, leaving the three boys to beg their food. Lodging did not bother them; they slept in ash piles and doorways in the winter and on the ground in summer. Captain Jack soon turned to picking pockets for a living and was so successful that he took Colonel Jack into partnership. The two young rogues preyed on wealthy men who were careless of their money. One of the boys would take the money, extracting only a small note from the whole; then the other would return the rest to its rightful owner and collect a reward for its return. One of the men thus duped was so grateful to honest-

seeming Colonel Jack that upon the return of his wallet he agreed to keep the reward money for the boy and pay him interest on it. Since Colonel Jack had no place to keep the stolen goods safely, he had asked the gentleman to do him that service. Later Colonel Jack took more stolen money to the same man for safekeeping and received his note for the whole amount, to be paid only to Colonel Jack himself. In fairness let it be said that after the scamps had robbed a poor woman of all her savings, Colonel Jack was so ashamed that he later returned her money with interest.

Captain Jack, a real villain, was apprehended and taken to Newgate Prison. Colonel Jack then became a partner of a thief named Will, a really vicious rogue who plundered and robbed and at last killed. He also was caught and taken to Newgate to be hanged, a fate which Colonel Jack knew Will deserved but which made his heart sick and his own conscience a heavy burden.

Captain Jack escaped from prison. Colonel Jack being also in danger because of his deeds, the two journeyed to Scotland. They were almost caught many times, but on each occasion Captain Jack's foresight enabled them to elude capture. When they were ready to return to England, they took work on a ship bound for London, or so they thought. Since they were deserters from the army, which they had joined to save their skins, they could not afford to risk regular means of travel. But the two who had cheated so many were themselves duped. Instead of sailing for England, they found themselves on the high seas bound for America and servitude. Colonel Jack, knowing himself for a villain, accepted his fate calmly, but Captain Jack stormed against it. The defiant Captain Jack abused his master, escaped back to England, resumed his old ways, and some twenty years later was hanged.

In Virginia, Colonel Jack was the property of a good master who told him that after he had served five years he would be freed and given a small piece of land. Thus, if he were industrious and honest, he might benefit from his ill fate. Jack, respecting his master, worked diligently for him. Soon he was made an overseer, and his kind heart and keen mind were responsible for changing the Negro slaves from rebellious fiends to loyal workers. His master was so fond of Jack that he bought for him a small plantation nearby and lent him the money to supply it. He also arranged for Jack to secure his money left in keeping in London. The money was converted into goods for the plantation, goods which were lost at sea. The master offered Jack his freedom before the five years were up, but Jack was loyal and continued to serve his master until that gentleman's death.

Jack's plantation prospered. The original two slaves given to him by his old master were increased by several more slaves and bonded white workers. Jack, always a kind master, won the loyalty of his workmen. Wanting to improve his education, for he could neither read nor write, he took one of his bonded men as a tutor and soon grew to admire him as he himself had been admired by his former master.

Resolving to return to England after an absence of almost twenty years, he tried to get his tutor to travel with him. When the man refused, Jack made him the overseer of his large plantations. It was some time before Jack arrived in his native land. He was first tossed about at sea, then captured by the French, and at last exchanged for a prisoner held by the English.

Soon Jack's heart was taken by a lady who lived nearby and they were married. But she proved unfaithful to him, as well as being a gambler and a spendthrift, and shortly after the birth of their child he left her. He first attacked her lover, however, and so had to flee for his life. Later, learning that she was to have another child, he divorced her and went to France. There he joined an Irish brigade and fought in France, Germany, and

Italy. Captured, he was sent to Hungary and then to Italy, where he married the daughter of an innkeeper. Eventually he was allowed to go to Paris with his wife. There he recruited volunteers to fight against the English. Tiring of war, he returned to Paris unexpectedly, only to find that his second wife had also taken a lover. After almost killing the man, he fled to London and then to Canterbury, where he lived as a Frenchman with the English and as an Englishman with the French.

Still desiring a happy home life, he married again. His wife, at first beautiful and virtuous, became a drunkard and finally killed herself. They had had three children. Wishing to provide for them, Jack married an older woman who had cared for them and whom they loved as a mother. But that good woman, after bearing him children, died from a fall, leaving him a widower once more. After smallpox took all but two of his children, he returned to Virginia. His daughter he left with her grandfather; the remaining son he took with him.

In Virginia he found his affairs in good order, the tutor having made a faithful overseer for twenty-four years. Several slaves and servants had been added to the plantations, and Jack found one of them to be his first wife. Since she had repented wholly of her sins, he married her again and lived happily with her for many years.

But he was not always to live in peace. Several captive servants who knew of his part in the rebellion, when he had served with the Irish brigade, were brought to neighboring plantations. His part in the rebellion becoming known, he had to leave Virginia until he could secure a pardon from the king. He and his wife went to Antigua, from which she later returned to Virginia to await the news of her husband's pardon. Pardoned, he was on his way home when he was captured by the Spanish. After many long months as a hostage he was released, having turned the experience into profit by trading with some of his captors. He continued the trade, which was illegal in the eyes of the Spanish government, and made thousands of pounds. He was often in danger during his voyages, even taken, but each time he turned the situation to his own advantage.

At last he left danger behind, returned to England, and sent for his beloved wife.

There they remained, leaving the Virginia plantations in the hands of the faithful tutor. In his old age Colonel Jack spent many hours contemplating the goodness of the God he had formerly ignored. He believed that his story was one to make others repent of their sins and mend their broken ways.

THE HISTORY OF ENGLAND

Type of work: History
Author: Thomas Babington Macaulay (1800-1859)
Time: 56 B.C.-A.D. 1702
Locale: England
First published: Books I and II, 1848; III and IV, 1855; V, unfinished, 1861

Principal personages:
CHARLES II
JAMES II
WILLIAM III
MARY, wife of William
JOHN CHURCHILL, Duke of Marlborough
WILLIAM PENN

Macaulay knew little about English history before the seventeenth century. He knew almost nothing about foreign history. He was not interested in art, science, philosophy, or religion. As a Whig, he had no sympathy with the Tories and little understanding of James II. He overlooked many of the authoritative books covering the period about which he was writing. Therefore, in *The History of England from the Accession of James the Second* he is sometimes unfair to certain figures or mistaken in facts and interpretations. The result, however, is a vivid and eminently readable history with vivid pictures of the actors and the social and cultural background against which they performed.

Macaulay was a child prodigy who started writing early. Before he was eight, this future historan, poet, and essayist had completed an outline of history and a poem in three cantos modeled after the poetry of Scott. He went to Trinity College, Cambridge, intending to enter law. Before he passed his bar examinations in 1826, he had attracted attention by a

critical essay on Milton, the first of many he contributed to the influential *Edinburgh Review*. Later his essays about the Indian question got him an appointment on a commission to India.

While still in India, he wrote in his diary his intention to compile a five-volume history, the first part to cover the thirty years from the revolution of 1688 to the beginning of Walpole's administration. It would end with the death of George IV and achieve unity by covering "the Revolution that brought the crown into harmony with the Parliament and the Revolution which brought the Parliament into harmony with the nation." Further planning convinced him of the need to precede his account of the revolution by the story of the reign of James II.

When he returned to England, he had barely begun his project before he was named Secretary of War, a post which gave him no time for literary work until the elections of 1841 turned him out of office and into his study. He progressed slowly on his history until the return of his party to power in 1846, when he was

1307

appointed Paymaster General. In spite of public demands on his time the first two volumes of *The History of England from the Accession of James the Second* appeared in November, 1848.

The ten chapters begin with an account of Roman times and bring the story of England down to the crowning of William and Mary on February 13, 1689. Diary entries reveal Macaulay's worry about how to begin. He had to start somewhere and so, in the first paragraph, he bravely announced his purpose to "offer a slight sketch of my country from the earliest times." Romans, Saxons, and Danes move through the first chapter, bringing the reader up to the general elections of 1660 and the return of Charles II to England. In the next chapter Macaulay followed the career of Charles II until his death in 1685. At this point the historian was ready to begin his task in earnest. His announced purpose in the third chapter was to "give a description of the state in which England was at the time when the crown passed from Charles II to his brother, James."

First, Macaulay stressed the small population of the British Isles in 1685, perhaps five million, with half living in England. Then he discussed the revenue available. Excise taxes, taxes on chimneys, and the rest brought in hardly a fifth as much to the crown as France was collecting. Then follows a study of the army and the navy on which the money was largely spent. A discussion of agriculture and mineral wealth introduces the country gentlemen and the yeomanry, with a glance at the clergy. Next, the historian's attention fixes on the towns and their growth, following the expansion of trade and manufacturing, with special attention to London. Discussion of communication with London leads to a section on the postal system, inns, and highwaymen. A study of England's cultural status, both literary and scientific, precedes the final section on the terrible condition of the very poor.

The description of the death of Charles II, in Chapter IV, is a sample of Macaulay's style. The ten pages read like a historical novel, except that the historian has footnotes available for the details of the palace room, the visitors at the bedside, and such bits as the king's dying comment about winding the clock at his bedside. The surreptitious visit of the priest, John Huddleston, and the reaction of the crowd outside the palace bring vividness to the event.

The succession of James II to the throne is the theme of the other six chapters of the first two volumes. The new monarch lacked the political acumen and the general knowledge of the world possessed by Charles II; otherwise, he might not have been so easily duped by his Jesuit adviser, for he did possess administrative ability, more, perhaps, than Macaulay grants him.

The exciting part of this section tells of James's following the invasion of England by William of Orange and of his capture by "rude fishermen of the Kentish coast," who mistook the royal party for Jesuits and the monarch for his hated adviser, Father Petre. Then came his flight to France, the Convention that formulated the Declaration of Rights, and the coronation of William and Mary. Because of this stirring material, excitingly told, thirteen thousand copies of the history were sold in four months.

Such success worried Macaulay. Attempting to make the other volumes dealing with William as colorful, he provided himself with a timetable: two book pages a day, two years to finish the first draft, and another year for revision and polishing. He felt the need for making every sentence clear and precise, for seeing that his paragraphs had continuity. Such labor took longer than he had planned. It was nearly seven years before he had the manuscript of Volumes III and IV ready for the printer. Their twelve chapters brought England's story to the end of the war with France in 1697. The public acceptance justified the time taken in its composition. Within two months 26,-500 copies were sold, and his royalties amounted to twenty thousand pounds.

Macaulay's diary frequently voiced his desire for fame and immortality. "I think posterity will not let my book die," he wrote in 1838. In addition to the wealth it brought, the success of the work replaced the Tory view of English history, as voiced by Hume in his *History of England* (1754-1761), with the Victorian concept originated with Macaulay.

In the new volumes Macaulay showed himself kindly disposed toward Mary in her trying position between her Catholic father and her Protestant husband, who divided his attention between her and Elizabeth Villiers. But William of Orange did love Mary. The last lines of Macaulay's history tell about "a small piece of black silk ribbon," found next to William's skin when his remains were being laid out. "The lords in waiting ordered it to be taken off. It contained a gold ring and a lock of the hair of Mary."

Macaulay admired William. The Dutch king had an enormous task, organizing England, reconquering Ireland, and subduing rebellious Scotland, all the while carrying on a war in France. Macaulay does seem to overestimate William's political genius, and his account of the king's yearning to return to Holland and leave England for Mary to rule is considered by some scholars an exaggeration of William's basic disillusionment with English life. With a rosy picture of the prosperity amid which William rode into London on Thanksgiving Day in November, 1697, and with the promise of a happier age, the volumes published during the writer's lifetime come to an end.

When Macaulay died he had completed only three chapters of the concluding volume, bringing the story up to the prorogation of Parliament, April 11, 1700. His sister, Lady Trevelyan, prepared this material for publication exactly as Macaulay had left it, with "no references verified, no authority sought for or examined," but she did include several fragments, among them six pages describing the death of William with which Macaulay had probably intended to conclude his work. She also compiled a fifty-page, double-column index of the five books.

In his presentation of his characters, Macaulay was often biased. As one who seemed never in doubt, who decided on one of two conflicting stories and frequently did not mention the existence of the other, he saw a man as good or bad. Historians have pointed out his failure to do justice to William Penn. Being a Whig, he used a more severe criterion toward Tories, as is evident in his discussions of James's relations with Catherine Sedley, and William's with Elizabeth Villiers. What was lamentable in William was a crime in James, whom he portrayed as a libertine and black monster.

His villains are sometimes caricatures. The crafty Robert Ferguson and Titus Oates, whose perjury about the Popish Plot brought death to the innocent, are made physically hideous. In Chapter IV, Macaulay writes of Oates's "short neck, his forehead low as that of a baboon, his purple cheeks, and his monstrous length of chin . . ." and features "in which villainy seemed to be written by the hand of God." For Marlborough, even when he was plain John Churchill, Macaulay turned to lampoons for details, though he must have known they were biased. Perhaps his dislike was based on the unproved accusation that Marlborough had tried to overthrow William.

In a work of such magnitude, errors of fact and interpretation were bound to creep in, but even some that were pointed out to Macaulay during his lifetime remained uncorrected. In other cases, he did not have access to the journals and scholarly research now available. Another source of error arose from Macaulay's attitude toward everything outside the British Isles. Except for India, where he had lived for four years, he practically ignored the colonies. American history is brought in chiefly in connection with happenings in England. Captain Kidd and the piratical activities of New England and New York appear to explain the fate of an English ministry, while the Jamaica earthquake of 1692 serves only as one more reason for the unpopularity of William's reign.

Macaulay's style has also come in for some criticism. His efforts toward clearness lead at times to verbosity and his attempts to emphasize sometimes create a paragraph where a sentence would have served. But its basic flaw is that Macaulay thought as an orator. His history is more impressive when read aloud than when read silently; it is more rhetorical than literary.

But no book lacking in inherent worth can outlast its century, and *The History of England* remains a landmark of its kind. As long as people are moved by an exciting story, interestingly told, they will continue to read Macaulay's history with both enjoyment and profit.

THE HISTORY OF MR. POLLY

Type of work: Novel
Author: H. G. Wells (1866-1946)
Type of plot: Comic romance
Time of plot: Early twentieth century
Locale: England
First published: 1909

Principal characters:
MR. POLLY, a shopkeeper
MIRIAM, his wife
THE PLUMP WOMAN
UNCLE JIM, her nephew

Critique:

A timeless comedy, as funny now as when it was first published in 1909, *The History of Mr. Polly* has strangely enough not been one of H. G. Wells' most popular novels. It is the story of a gentle man who rebels at last against the insults heaped upon him by the world and finds the peace of mind that few achieve. Wells' special genius here is in the quiet humor that startles even as it amuses. This is a highly original book, funny, moving, and pathetic.

The Story:

Mr. Polly sat on a stile and cursed. He cursed the world, his wife, and himself. For Mr. Polly was thirty-five and buried alive. He hated his slovenly wife, his fellow shopkeepers, and every other person in the world. His life, he felt, had been nothing but one frustration after another, from babyhood into his middle thirties.

Mr. Polly had been the usual adored baby, kissed and petted by his parents. His mother had died when he was seven. After the routine sketchy schooling of his class, he was apprenticed by his father to the owner of a draper's shop.

Mr. Polly was ill-suited to work in that shop or in any other. But he served out his apprenticeship and then began a progression from one shop to another, being unable to hold one position for very long. He hated the bleak life in dreary dormitories. He hated being told to hustle when he wanted to dream beautiful dreams about adventure and romance. He spent most of his money and all his spare time on books which took him away from the humdrum of socks and neckties. He did not know what it was he really wanted, but to anyone who might have studied him the answer would have been simple. He wanted companions.

When his father died, Mr. Polly found himself in possession of several useless bits of bric-a-brac and three hundred and ninety-five pounds. It seemed at first that a whole new world was open to him with this new wealth. Various relatives had sensible suggestions for him, most of them centering on his opening a little shop. He put them off, for he wanted to spend his time in taking a holiday.

At his father's funeral, which was a proper one, Mr. Polly had met aunts and cousins he did not know existed. Three of his cousins, all female, began to set their caps for their rich relative, and before he was sure of what had happened, Mr. Polly found himself in possession of a wife, his cousin Miriam, and a draper's shop. For the next fifteen years Mr. Polly was a respectable though unhappy shopkeeper. He could get on with none of his neighbors, and before long he hated his slatternly wife as much as he hated the other shopkeepers.

For these reasons Mr. Polly sat on the stile and cursed his luck. For the first time in fifteen years he found himself, in addition to his other troubles, unable to meet the forthcoming rent. As well as he could figure, he was in debt sixty or seventy pounds. He knew how Miriam would greet this news; it was just too much for him.

At that point a plan which had been forming in the back of his mind began to take shape. He would kill himself. Then the struggle would be over for him and Miriam would be provided for by his insurance. He would set fire to the shop, for the fire insurance, and before he burned up would cut his throat. Craftily he waited until a Sunday evening, when almost everyone was at church, and then carried out his plan. It worked so well that half the business area of the village burned down. But when Mr.

Polly saw flames licking the leg of his trousers, he forgot all about cutting his throat and ran screaming down the street.

It was a beautiful fire, and because of it Mr. Polly was for the first time in his life a hero. He rescued a deaf old lady who lived on a top floor and for whose safety he felt responsible because he had started the fire. When the excitement was all over, it dawned on him that he had forgotten to cut his throat. He felt a little guilty.

But that one night of fighting back against the world changed Mr. Polly forever. Taking only twenty-one pounds for himself and leaving the rest for Miriam, he simply disappeared. Wandering through the country, he enjoyed life for the first time. He discovered the world, the beauties of nature, the casual friendship of passing acquaintances. It was wonderful.

After a month Mr. Polly arrived at a little wayside inn run by a cheerful plump woman. They felt an instant closeness, and she offered him a job as handy man. His duties were endless and varied, but there was an unhurried peace about the plump woman and the inn that brought joy to the soul of Mr. Polly. There was, however, a black spot on the peace. The plump woman had a nephew, called Uncle Jim, who was a brute and a villain. He had run off all other males who had ever stopped there, and he beat his aunt and stole her money. She knew that he would return again when he was out of funds. Mr. Polly knew this was not his fight, but he had started fighting on the night of the fire and he would not stop now. Sometimes running when he should have been chasing, hiding when he should have been seeking his adversary, Mr. Polly nevertheless bested the scoundrel in two encounters. Then Uncle Jim disappeared again, taking Mr. Polly's clothing and leaving in his place an uneasy peace.

Uncle Jim did not appear again. After five years at the inn Mr. Polly began to think of Miriam and her sadness at losing her husband. Conscience-stricken, he returned to the village and there found that Miriam and her sisters had opened a tearoom, untidy but successful enough to provide their living. They thought him dead, a body wearing his clothing having been fished out of the river. Miriam, recognizing him in terror, began at once to fret about having to pay back his insurance money. She could have spared herself the worry, however; Mr. Polly had no desire to reappear. He told her to keep her mouth shut and no one would be the wiser.

Mr. Polly made his way back to the inn and the plump woman. With Uncle Jim gone for good, he knew at last a mellow, wonderful peace.

A HISTORY OF NEW YORK, BY DIEDRICH KNICKERBOCKER

Type of work: Humorous pseudo-history
Author: Washington Irving (1783-1859)
Time: 56 B.C. to 1664
Locale: New Amsterdam (New York)
First published: 1809

> *Principal personages:*
> HENDRICK HUDSON, the Dutch explorer
> WOUTER VAN TWILLER, the first governor of New Amsterdam
> WILHELMUS KIEFT, the second governor
> PETER STUYVESANT, the last governor
> GENERAL VON POFFENBURGH, Commander of Fort Casimir
> JAN RISINGH, Governor of the Province of New Sweden

The fun of reading a parody is heightened by acquaintance with the material burlesqued. Although Washington Irving confessed, in the "Author's Apology" added to the edition of 1848, that his idea had been to parody Samuel L. Mitchell's *A Picture of New York* (1807), a knowledge of Mitchell's book is not necessary to the enjoyment of the Irving volume. The parody is only part of the humor of *A History of New York, by Diedrich Knickerbocker*, originally begun as a collaboration of Washington and his older brother Peter, and concluded by Washington alone. The original title was *A History of New York from the Beginning of the World to the End of the Dutch Dynasty.*

The book shows the interest of its twenty-five-year-old author in history, customs, and etymology, and the burlesquing of several literary styles reveals Irving as a literary critic. His notebook supplies the names of some of the authors parodied, names now largely forgotten.

While Irving was in the course of completing the book, his fiancée, Matilda Hoffman, died suddenly, and at first he was too stunned to continue his work. Later he returned to the manuscript as an anodyne for his grief, finished it quickly, and delivered it to his publisher. About the same time he conceived the idea of ascribing the authorship of his book to an imaginary and eccentric Dutchman. The hoax was elaborately contrived. First printed in the public press was a story about the disappearance of a man named Diedrich Knickerbocker. A short time later an advertisement appeared, supposedly signed by the owner of the boarding house where Knickerbocker had lived, offering for sale "a very curious kind of written book," printed to reimburse the landlord for the old gentleman's unpaid rent.

On December 6, 1809, *A History of New York, by Diedrich Knickerbocker*, in seven parts and 130,000 words, was first offered for sale. Legends about its reception spread rapidly. A Dutch woman in Albany threatened to horsewhip the author for his slanderous account of an ancestor. A number of famous New York families were reported ready to sue the publisher. On the other hand, Walter Scott was reported with sore ribs from laughing at it.

The style wanders from playful to erudite. Evidence of Washington Irving's wide reading appears on almost every page, and voluminous footnotes clothe it with pseudo-scholarship. At first readers thought that these references were part of the humor; later scholars began tracing them to actual, though minor, Roman and Greek writers.

The author's pleasantries are apparent from the beginning. Book I, according to him, was "learned, sagacious, and nothing at all to the purpose," and he suggested that the idle reader skip it. More precisely, as Irving embarked on a study of cosmogony or creation of the world he advised the reader to "take fast hold of his skirt or take a short cut and wait for him at the beginning of some smoother chapter."

The first books contain more chatter than matter. It is waggish humor. Noah is mentioned in connection with travel by sea, in order to get the reader to America. In one place the author defends the killing of the Indians because, as the original inhabitants of America, they did not know European procedure to improve ground; therefore they did not use the talents that Providence had bestowed upon them; therefore they had proved careless stewards; therefore they had no right to the soil; and therefore there was Biblical authority for their extermination.

In Book II the author proceeds to the settlement of the Province of Nieuw Nederlandts. He confessed that his was the procedure of Hans von Dunderbottom, who took a running start of three miles to jump over a hill, and arrived at it out of breath. So he "sat down to blow and then walked over it at his leisure."

One source of humor lies in the derivation of names. The four explorers who passed through Hell Gate and reached the Island of Manna-hata ("The Island of Manna") were named Van Kortlandt (Lack-land), Van Zandt (Earth-born), Harden Broeck (Tough Breeches), and Ten Broeck (Ten Breeches or Thin Breeches). Irving usually refers to the governors by his translation of their names. Wouter Van Twiller becomes "Walter the Doubter," living up to his name by smoking his pipe and maintaining silence in every crisis. According to Irving, this man of wisdom, five feet six inches in height and six feet five inches in circumference, settled a suit between debtor and creditor by weighing the papers containing their claims, finding them equally weighty, and decreeing that the accounts were balanced. After he made the constable pay the fees, he had no further law trials.

His successor, Wilhelmus Kieft or "William the Testy," defied the Yanokies ("Silent Men") from Mais-Tchusaeg and Connecticut by bombarding them with proclamations and by building a fortress, garrisoned by a lusty bugler, a flag pole, Quaker guns, and a windmill, to resist them. One of the amusing scenes in the book is the description of the Yankees marching to war at Oyster Bay, where they were defeated by the doughty burghers, who thereupon celebrated on oysters and wine. Later this governor disappeared; either he was lost in the smoke of his pipe or carried away like King Arthur. Peter Stuyvesant, "the Headstrong," then became the governor.

Stuyvesant is the favorite of Diedrich Knickerbocker; three volumes are devoted to him. It was he who built the Battery to hold off the Yankee invasion, though actually their own witch hunting diverted them from their proposed expedition. Then he declared war on Governor Risingh of the Colony of New Sweden, across the Delaware. By treachery Governor Risingh had captured Fort Casimir. (The earlier writer who supplied Irving's model for his flowery description of that campaign is unknown.)

The Dutch fighters paused at noon to eat, and the author advised his readers to do the same. Then the battle was resumed, the only casualty being a flock of geese killed by a wild Swedish volley.

Stuyvesant had other troubles, first the Yankees from Connecticut and later the "roaring boys of Merryland"—King Charles II of England who gave New World territory to his brother, the Duke of York, and lent him a fleet to conquer it. Against the arrival of the British ships the Dutch "fortified themselves—with resolution" and burned everything in the colony of British origin. But their defense was futile. Melancholically the white-haired Knickerbocker narrates the end of his "beloved Island of Manna-hata" on August 27, 1664.

In the 1812 edition of his history Irving presents an additional account of his imaginary author and tells of his return to New York, now a British colony, and his death. He was buried, "say the old records," in St. Mark's Cemetery beside his hero, Peter Stuyvesant.

In the revised 1848 edition Irving added an "apology" and an explanation. In setting down the amusing legends of New York, he declared, he had not intended offense to living descendants of any of the old families. His purpose had been to present the history of that remote and almost forgotten age in the spirit of imaginative fancy and legend. This happy blending is his true contribution in his history, accepted by those who have never seen the book or heard of the original Harmen Knickerbocker, who came from Holland about 1674 and settled in Albany, as well as by those who have read with smiles and chuckles this playful but surprisingly accurate history of the Dutch in New Amsterdam.

HISTORY OF THE CONQUEST OF MEXICO

Type of work: History
Author: William Hickling Prescott (1796-1859)
Time: 1519-1525
Locale: Mexico
First published: 1843

> *Principal personages:*
> Don Diego Velásquez, Governor of Cuba
> Hernando Cortés, conqueror of Mexico
> Pedro de Alvarado, one of Cortés' lieutenants
> Marina, Cortés' Indian mistress
> Montezuma, Emperor of the Aztecs
> Guatemozin, Montezuma's nephew and successor
> Cacama, nephew of the emperor
> Pánfilo de Narváez, Velásquez' lieutenant

Prescott's observations on Spanish efforts to convert the Aztecs betray his rather marked suspicion of the Catholic Church. His personal biases are less pronounced in other matters. Because Prescott deals with his narrative in dramatic terms and with an abundance of background material, particularly on the Aztec civilization, his *History of the Conquest of Mexico* has remained the classic account of the death of a civilization which in many ways rivaled ancient Egypt's.

The success of the Spanish conquest was aided by the Aztec legend of Quetzalcoatl, a benevolent god who, once having lived on earth and departed, was expected to return: tall, white-skinned, dark-bearded. When the first Spanish expeditionary party, led by Juan de Grijalva, made a preliminary exploration of the mainland, it encountered an unfriendly reception on landing. When the Aztecs happened to associate the Spaniards with the legend of Quetzalcoatl, however, they sent Grijalva away with rich gifts. As a result, Velásquez, Governor of Cuba, immediately organized a second expedition, to be led by Hernando Cortés.

Cortés' armada left Cuba on February 10, 1519, and landed on the island of Cozumel. At that time he acquired two valuable aides: a Spanish soldier named Aguilar, who had been taken captive by the natives of Cozumel during the Grijalva expedition, to serve as an interpreter, and Marina, a girl from the mainland whose mother had sold her on Cozumel. Marina became not only an interpreter but Cortés' mistress.

When the Spaniards moved on to the mainland, landing on Good Friday at what is now Vera Cruz, they stepped ashore in a Mexico significantly disunited. Montezuma, Emperor of the Aztecs, was a good warrior and a just ruler, but he was also superstitious and a lover of pleasure, with numerous enemies. There was in addition to this political unrest a vague feeling among the people that the return of Quetzalcoatl was imminent: since the days of Columbus, there had been rumors of the Spaniards, and these rumors had somehow fused with the ancient legend. Dissension among the lesser kingdoms and tribes of Montezuma's empire and the revival of the Quetzalcoatl myth were of great value to the Spaniards in their invasion of Mexico.

Because he sensed mounting resistance to his leadership, Cortés established Vera Cruz as a civil colony rather than a military base; in this way he made the expedition responsible only to the crown, not to the governor of Cuba. Later, when Juan Díaz conspired to turn the expedition back to Cuba, Cortés ordered the destruction of his fleet. With only one small ship left, the men had little to think about but the march forward.

Leaving some men behind to protect the coastal settlement, Cortés began his march toward the capital, Tenochtitlán, now Mexico City. While one of the orig-inal purposes of the expedition was the conversion of the Indians to Catholicism, the expedition, once under way, did not delay for missionary activities. Indeed, Father Olmedo, the expedition's priest, persuaded Cortés not to try to convert all of the heathen along the route.

The first pronounced resistance to the Spaniards took place among the Tlascalans, an agricultural people, but a nation of warriors as well. Two earlier battles with the Tlascalans were indecisive, but a third, fought on September 5, 1519, was in effect a victory for the Spaniards. The Tlascalan leader, Xicotencatl, continued, however, to threaten and to harass the invaders. Cortés forged ahead, his forces plundering as they went, and finally, with Xicotencatl reconciled to submission, the Spaniards arrived at Tlascala itself. In the meantime Montezuma continued in his policy of sending gifts but barring the Spaniards from Tenochtitlán.

At Cholula, Cortés learned through Marina that the natives were planning a conspiracy with Montezuma's help. Profiting from former enmity between the Cholulans and the Tlascalans, Cortés stationed Tlascalans around the city and proceeded to massacre the treacherous Cholulans.

Suspecting still further hostility, Cortés and his men moved on, passing between the mountains named Iztaccihuatl and Popocatepetl. No further resistance was forthcoming, and the expedition was shortly at a point where the fertile Valley of Mexico lay before them. Confounded by their advance and awed by their power, Montezuma at last sent his nephew Cacama with a message of welcome for the conquistadors. On November 8, 1519, Cortés and his men entered Tenochtitlán, a city built in the middle of a great lake, and Montezuma greeted them with pomp and dignity. Although the Aztecs remained outwardly friendly, Cortés continued to be suspicious of his host because he had received reports from Vera Cruz of troubles instigated by the

1315

emperor. Quauhpopoca, governor of the coastal province, was burned for his part in the disturbances, and Montezuma, taken by surprise, was seized and removed to the fortified quarters occupied by the Spaniards. Although a hostage, Montezuma conducted the business of the country as usual.

In 1520, Montezuma formally announced his subservience to Spain: the nobles concurred, and the legend of Quetzalcoatl was revived among the people. Though conditions appeared to be stable, Cortés ordered the rebuilding of his fleet.

Cortés' relations with Velásquez had now deteriorated to such an extent that the governor outfitted a rival expedition under the leadership of Pánfilo de Narváez. Gonzalo de Sandoval, the governor appointed by Cortés at Villa Rica, maintained a close watch over Narváez' attempts to establish a settlement, but Cortés felt compelled to deal with Narváez personally. Leaving the capital in the care of an aide, Pedro de Alvarado, he marched to the coast with a detachment of troops and Indian allies.

With his band of only 226 men and five horses, Cortés surprised Narváez and took him prisoner. In Cortés' absence, revolt broke out in Tenochtitlán. Alvarado, plagued by constant fears of conspiracy, had slaughtered several hundred Aztec nobles during the festival of Huitzilopotchli, the Aztec god of war. Earlier, Cortés had allowed Montezuma's brother, Cuitlahua, to act as the imperial representative during Montezuma's captivity. Bitterly vengeful after the massacre, Cuitlahua led the Aztecs in a retaliatory uprising against the Spaniards.

With his own band reinforced by two thousand Tlascalans, Cortés returned hurriedly to the capital. During the first stages of hostilities following the return of Cortés, Montezuma attempted to intercede and pacify the embattled Aztecs, but his people turned on him and he was fatally wounded. Broken and in despair, Montezuma died on June 30, 1520.

During the uprising the Aztecs had destroyed all bridges on causeways leading to the mainland, and the Spanish retreat from the city became chaotic, with heavy losses. On the plains of Otumba, however, the Spaniards and their Tlascalan allies managed to put the Aztecs to flight. The Spaniards retreated into Tlascalan territory, where they could feel safe once more. But the troops were restless after their harrowing retreat, and for a time there seemed to be some chance that the Tlascalans might join the Aztecs in common cause against the invaders. Fortunately, the Tlascalans remained friendly; in fact, their chief, before he died of smallpox, became a Christian—the first successfully converted heathen.

Guatemozin, Montezuma's nephew and successor, had sworn to drive the Spaniards from his country. As Cortés marched back toward the capital, however, he gathered from friendly tribes more Indian auxiliaries to lead against the Aztecs. Welcomed in Tezcuco by the new prince, Ixtlilxochitl, an enemy of Montezuma, Cortés' forces advanced for the final subjugation of the Aztec civilization.

More cohesive than Prescott's companion study on the conquest of Peru, *History of the Conquest of Mexico* is the author's most brilliant work. Though the book may lack profound philosophical insight, it is a vivid portrayal of a fascinating historical fact: the subjugation of a whole people by a mere handful of alien adventurers—cruel, daring intriguers who played upon the religious superstitions of their victims.

THE HISTORY OF THE DECLINE AND FALL OF THE ROMAN EMPIRE

Type of work: History
Author: Edward Gibbon (1737-1794)
Time: 180-1461
Locale: Italy, Persia, Germany, Constantinople, Greece, Africa, Arabia, Turkey
First published: 1776-1788

Gibbon's *The History of the Decline and Fall of the Roman Empire* is the definitive history of the Roman empire from the end of its golden age to its final political and physical disintegration. The massive character of the work, testifying to the years devoted to its composition by its scholar-author, is the first, but most superficial sign, of its greatness. The style—urbane, dramatic, polished—assures its eminent place in literature. Finally, as history, the work stands or falls on the accuracy and depth of its report of events covering more than twelve centuries; and in this respect *The Decline and Fall of the Roman Empire* continues to prevail as the most authoritative study on this theme ever written. Later scholars have challenged minor points or added to the material of the history, but Gibbon's work stands as the source of all that is most relevant in the story of Rome's declining years.

The account begins with a critical description of the age of the Antonines. Gibbon concentrates on the period from 96 to 180, a time which he describes as "a happy period," during the reigns of Nerva, Trajan, Hadrian, and the two Antonines. The first three chapters are prefatory to the body of the work; they establish the claim that Rome was then at the height of its glory as an Empire— it was strong, prosperous, active, with world-wide influence. After the death of Marcus Aurelius, and with the ascent of Commodus (180-192), the Empire began its long and gradual decline. The body of Gibbon's work is devoted to a careful recital of the events that followed.

Gibbon was more interested in recounting the principal events of the Empire's history than he was in analyzing events in an effort to account for the downfall of Rome. But he did not entirely ignore the question of causes. At the close of his monumental history he reports four principal causes of Rome's decline and fall: "I. The injuries of time and nature. II. The hostile attacks of the barbarians and Christians. III. The use and abuse of the materials. And, IV. The domestic quarrels of the Romans."

It is customary for commentators on Gibbon to emphasize the reference to the opposing influences of Christianity and barbarism; and, in particular, some critics have been inclined to charge Gibbon with a lack of sympathetic understanding of the early Christian church. It is clear from Gibbon's narrative and summary statement, however, that the Christian contribution to the eventual downfall of Rome was only part of a complex of causes, and it seems unlikely that the Christian effort would have succeeded if the Roman Empire had not already been in decline.

In any case, it is not so much what Gibbon says as his way of saying it that has proved irritating. In the first place, Gibbon writes as if he were located in Rome; his view of events is from the Roman perspective, although it does not always exhibit a Roman bias. Secondly, his objectivity, when it is achieved, has been offensive to some who so cherish the Christian church that they cannot tolerate any discussion of its faults; it is as if such critics were demanding that Gibbon maintain historical impartiality about the Romans but not about the Christians.

When the *Decline and Fall* first appeared, the chapters on Christianity— Chapters XV and XVI—immediately became the objects of critical attack. Gibbon seems to have anticipated this response, for he wrote, "The great law of impartiality too often obliges us to reveal the imperfections of the uninspired teachers and believers of the Gospel; and, to a careless observer, *their* faults may seem to cast a shade on the faith which they professed." Perhaps this word of caution would have pacified the critics had not Gibbon immediately brought into play his urbane sarcasm, so distasteful to the insistently pious: "The theologian may indulge the pleasing task of describing Religion as she descended from Heaven, arrayed in her native purity. A more melancholy duty is imposed on the historian. He must discover the inevitable mixture of error and corruption which she contracted in a long residence upon earth, among a weak and degenerate race of beings."

Obviously, there is no truly impartial judge. Gibbon's tone is acceptable, even proper, to those who share his skepticism; but to others more emotionally involved in the Christian faith Gibbon seems cynical to the point of gross distortion.

Gibbon asks how the Christian faith came to achieve its victory over Rome and the other religions of the world. He rejects as unsatisfactory an answer which attributes Christianity's force to the truth of its doctrine and the providence of God. Five causes of the rapid growth of the Christian church are then advanced: "I. The inflexible, and, if we may use the expression, the intolerant zeal of the Christians. . . . II. The doctrine of a future life. . . . III. The miraculous powers ascribed to the primitive church. IV. The pure and austere morals of the Christians. V. The union and discipline of the Christian republic, which gradually formed an independent and increasing state in the heart of the Roman empire."

In his comments on these five causes Gibbon discusses Jewish influences on the Christian faith and explains how the Roman religion had failed to be convincing in its mythology and doctrine of a future life; but although he admits the persuasive power of the Christian use of the claim of immortality, he speaks with skeptical condescension of the efforts of philosophers to support the doctrine of a future life, and he is sarcastic when he mentions "the mysterious dispensations of Providence" which withheld the doctrine from the Jews only to give it to the Christians. When he speaks of the miracles, Gibbon leaves the impression that the pagans failed to be convinced because no such events actually took place. "The lame walked, the blind saw, the sick were healed, the dead were raised," he writes; but he adds that "the laws of Nature were frequently suspended for the benefit of the church."

Gibbon argues that the emperors were not as criminal in their treatments of the Christians as some Christian apologists have argued. He maintains that the Romans acted only with caution and reluctance after a considerable amount of time and provocation, and that they were moderate in their use of punishments. He offers evidence in support of his claim that the stories of martyrdom were often exaggerated or wholly false, and that in many cases the Christians sought martyrdom by provoking the Romans to violence. Gibbon concludes by casting doubt on the numbers of those punished by death, and he insists that the Christians have inflicted more punishments on one another than they received from the Romans.

Discussion of Gibbon's chapters on Christianity sometimes tends to turn attention away from the historian's virtues: the inclusiveness of his survey, the liveliness of his account, and his careful documentation of historical claims. Gibbon did not pretend that he was without moral bias, but his judgments of the tyrannical emperors are defended by references to their acts. It was not enough for Gibbon to discover, for example, that Septimus Severus was false and insincere, particularly in the making of treaties; the question was whether Severus was forced, by the imperious demands of politics, to

1318

be deceitful. Gibbon's conclusion was that there was no need for Severus to be as false in his promises as he was; consequently, he condemns him for his acts. In similar fashion he reviews the tyrannical behavior of Caracalla, Maximin, and other emperors before the barbarian invasion of the Germans.

Gibbon names the Franks, the Alemanni, the Goths, and the Persians as the enemies of the Romans during the reigns of Valerian and Gallienus, when a weakened Empire was vulnerable to attack both from within and without. Perhaps the Empire would have wholly disintegrated at that time had not Valerian and Gallienus been succeeded by Claudius, Aurelian, Probus, and Diocletian, described as "great princes" by Gibbon and as "Restorers of the Roman world."

Several chapters of this massive work are devoted to a recital and discussion of the acts and influence of Constantine I, who reunited the Empire which had been divided under Diocletian and as a consequence of his conversion to the Christian faith, granted tolerance to the Christians by the Edict of Milan. One result of the consequent growth of Christianity was a growing emphasis upon the distinction between temporal and spiritual powers; the result was not that Church and state remained apart from each other, but that the bishops of the Church came to have more and more influence on matters of state. The date 476 is significant as marking the end of the West Roman Empire with the ascent to power of Odoacer, the barbarian chieftain.

The remainder of Gibbon's classic story of Rome's decline is the story of the increase of papal influence, the commencement of Byzantine rule, the reign of Charlemagne as emperor of the West, the sacking of Rome by the Arabs, the retirement of the popes to Avignon, the abortive efforts of Rienzi to restore the government of Rome, the return of the popes and the great schism, and the final settlement of the ecclesiastical state.

HISTORY OF THE PELOPONNESIAN WAR

Type of work: History
Author: Thucydides (455?-c. 400 B.C.)
Time: 431-411 B.C.
Locale: Greece and the Mediterranean
First transcribed: c. 431-400 B.C.

> *Principal personages:*
> PERICLES, founder of Athenian democracy
> THUCYDIDES, an Athenian general and historian
> DEMOSTHENES, the famous orator
> ALCIBIADES, an Athenian general and turncoat
> NICIAS, an Athenian general
> ARCHIDAMUS, King of Sparta
> BRASIDAS, a Spartan general

In writing his *History of the Peloponnesian War,* Thucydides, content to look for human causes behind results, refused to credit the gods with responsibility for the acts of man. Impartially he chronicled the clash of a military and a commercial imperialism: the land empire of the Spartans confronting the Athenian maritime league. Some have attributed to him an attitude of moral indifference, such as is revealed in his report of the debate between Athenian and Melian ambassadors, but he wrote with no intention of either moralizing or producing a cultural history. He was a military man interested in the vastly different political and economic patterns of Athens and Sparta. Seeing in the modes and ideals of their cultures an explanation of their ways of warfare, he wrote for intelligent readers rather than the ignorant masses.

The eight books of Thucydides' history, divided into short paragraph-chapters, provide a few facts about their author. For instance, in Book IV, he refers to himself as "Thucydides, son of Olorus, who wrote this history." He must have been wealthy, for, discussing Brasidas' attack on Amphipolis, he states that the Spartan "heard that Thucydides had the right of working goldmines in the neighboring district of Thrace and was consequently one of the leading men of the city." He also tells frankly of his failure as the commander of a relief expedition to that city and of his twenty years' exile from Athens as punishment. Apparently he spent the years of his exile in travel among the sites of the battles he describes, thereby increasing the accuracy of his details. Students of warfare find that he gives descriptions of the tricks and stratagems of both siege and defense. Not until 404, after the war had ended, did he return to Athens. By tradition he was killed about 400 B.C., either in Thrace for the gold he carried, or in Athens for publicly writing his opinions.

"Thucydides the Athenian wrote the history of the war in which the Peloponnesians and the Athenians fought against one another" are the opening words of this masterpiece of Greek history. "He began to write when they first took up arms, believing it would be great and memorable above all previous wars." After this beginning Thucydides drops into the first person to explain the rivalry of Athens and Sparta, the two great states of Hellas then at the height of their power. He was proud of the advances made by his native Athens over the ways of the barbarians. "In ancient times the Hellenes carried weapons because their homes were undefended and intercourse unsafe." But swords, like the old-fashioned linen undergarments and the custom of binding the hair in knots, had gone out of style by his time.

Rivalry between the two cities was an old story; it had kept Spartans from fight-ing beside Athenians at Marathon. It took a commercial form, however, when the Lacedaemonians demanded that their allies, the Megarians, be allowed to market their products in Athens. Pericles, orator, statesman, and patron of the arts, took the first step toward breaking his own Thirty Years' Truce, agreed upon in 445 B.C. In a fiery oration he declared that to yield to the Spartans would reduce the Athenians to vassals.

The final break, according to Thucydides, came later. He dates the year (431) according to the calendars of the three leading states: Chrysis had been high priestess of Argos for forty-eight years; Aenesias was ephor of Sparta; and Pythodorus was concluding his archonship in Athens. In that year Thebes, at the invitation of disgruntled Plataean citizens, made a surprise attack on Plataea, a Boeotian ally of Athens.

To understand the situation fully, it is necessary to keep in mind a clash of political concepts that the historian does not mention. In 445 B.C., under Pericles, Athens had become a radical democracy whose policy was to send help to any democratically-inclined community. Sparta and its allies were just as eager to promote their conservative oligarchy. To both, self-interest was paramount.

Violation of the truce by Thebes, says Thucydides, gave Athens an excuse to prepare for war. Its walled city could be defeated only by a fleet and Sparta had no fleet. On the other hand, landlocked Sparta could withstand anything except a full-scale land invasion, and Athens had no army. The Lacedaemonians begged their friends in Italy and Sicily to collect and build ships, and Athens sent ambassadors to raise armies and completely surround Sparta. Thucydides was honest enough to admit that public opinion largely favored the Spartans, who posed as the liberators of Hellas.

Sparta moved first by invading the Isthmus of Corinth in 431 B.C. Strife during the winter and summer of the first year (as the historian divided his time) consisted largely of laying waste the fields around the fortified cities. Like many primitive peoples, the Greeks stopped fighting during planting and harvesting. (The entries frequently begin with: "The following summer, when the corn was coming into ear.") The war was also halted for their games, not only the Olympic games of 428, but the Delian, Pythian, and Isthmian games as well.

In the summer of the next year a plague broke out in Athens and raged intermittently for three years. Seven chapters of Book II provide a vivid description, "for I myself was attacked and witnessed the suffering of others." The seriousness of the plague protected Athens because enemy troops were afraid to approach its walls.

The most vivid part of Thucydides' history deals with the Syracuse campaign of 416. An embassy from Egesta, Sicily, sought Athenian help against its rival city of Selinus. The ambitious Alcibiades thought this would be a good excuse for Athens to annex Syracuse. With Alcibiades, Nicias, and Lamachus sharing the command, the best-equipped expeditionary force ever sent from a Greek city sailed for Sicily with 134 triremes, 5,100 hoplites or heavy-armed infantry, 480 archers, and 820 slingers.

Alcibiades had left behind bitter enemies who accused him of defacing sacred statues on the day the fleet sailed. Though there was no evidence against him, he was ordered home to defend himself. Fearing treachery, he fled to Sparta, where he was warmly welcomed. Informed of the Athenian expedition, the Lacedaemonians sent a military adviser to Syracuse. The Persians offered to outfit a fleet for Alcibiades to lead against Athens. His patriotism outweighed his injured pride, however, and eventually he returned to Athens and won several victories for the city before another defeat sent him again into exile. This occurred, however, after the period covered by Thucydides' history.

Meanwhile, in the campaign before Syracuse, Nicias disregarded the advice of Demosthenes and was defeated on both land and sea. "Of all the Hellenic actions on record," writes Thucydides, "this was the greatest, the most glorious to the victor, and the most ruinous to the vanquished. Fleet and army vanished from the face of the earth; nothing was saved, and out of the many who went forth, few returned home. This ended the Sicilian expedition."

The account of the expedition practically ends Thucydides' history. There is another book, but it does not rise to the dramatic pitch of Book VII. Though he lived eleven years after these events and four years after the end of the war, Thucydides did not chronicle its last stages, perhaps because they were too painful. After Alcibiades had been exiled a second time, Sparta starved the Athenians into surrender, and with this defeat their glory faded. For the next thirty years Sparta was the supreme power in Hellas.

As Macaulay wrote, Thucydides surpassed all his rivals as the historian of the ancient world. Perhaps not as colorful as Herodotus, "the Father of History," he was certainly more accurate; and while the annals of Tacitus contain excellent character delineation, the Roman's pages are "cold and poor." Thucydides may be superficial in his observations and shallow in his interpretation of events, but he did accumulate facts and dates and he presented them in a three-dimensional picture of people and places. For this reason his work has survived for more than twenty-three hundred years.

THE HISTORY OF THE PERSIAN WARS

Type of work: History
Author: Herodotus (484-c. 425 B.C.)
Time: 500-479 B.C.
Locale: Greece, Egypt, Asia Minor
First transcribed: c. 430 B.C.

Principal personages:
CROESUS, King of Lydia
SOLON, an Athenian statesman
CYRUS THE GREAT, King of Persia
DARIUS, Cyrus' cousin
XERXES, Darius' son and successor
LEONIDAS, King of Sparta

"Herodotus, beyng of the citye of Halicarnassus in Greece, wrote and compiled an History to the end that nether tract of time might overwhelme and bury in silence the actes of humayne kind; nor the worthye and renowned adventures of the Grecians and Barbarians (as well others as chiefly those that were done in warre) might want the due reward of immortale fame." So did the unknown "B.R." begin his translation of two of the nine books of Herodotus, "entitled with the names of the nine Muses," in 1584.

As the first to use the word "history," Herodotus deserves Cicero's title, "Father of History." To be sure, this son of wealthy upper-class parents did not have the historian's critical attitude toward his sources. Interesting anecdotes of the wars between the Greeks and the Persians of the fifth century B.C. found their way into his pages whether he could verify them or not, but he does sometimes hedge and tag certain items as hearsay. From his quotations, he must have read widely. From the details in his descriptions and the comments like "this I saw," he must have visited most of the places he mentions. The true greatness of Herodotus lies in the fact that he was the first important writer to depart from the verse of Homer and others, to produce Europe's first prose literature. Some predecessors had chronicled the beginnings of their small communities or states, but the writings of Herodotus embrace a vaster panorama, not only Greece, but Egypt,

Sardis, and Babylon as well. And he looked for the reasons back of the events. His aim was to trace the early rivalries between Greek and barbarian; in the process he recounted the story of many tribes, described the lands they inhabited, and reported many of their interesting customs. Those who want greater accuracy can consult Thucydides (c.455-400 B.C.), who wrote a half-century later. His work is more objective, but it lacks the color of Herodotus' account.

The Persians maintained that the Phoenicians originally started the quarrel by kidnapping women from Argos. Later the Hellenes raided the port of Tyre and abducted Europa, the king's daughter. The wars actually started, however, when Croesus, whose magnificent court was visited by Solon, desired to enlarge his empire by conquering some of the Ionian cities of Asia Minor. When he consulted the oracles, he was persuaded at Delphi to gather his allies for an attack on the mainland. The invasion resulted in a stalemate, however, and Croesus returned to Lydia, where his capital, Sardis, was surprised and captured by the Persians. Only a rainstorm, sent by the gods, saved him as he was being burned to death. The same miracle persuaded Cyrus to free his captive after taking possession of some of his vassal states. With them, Cyrus went on to capture Babylon. However the Massagetae, under Queen Tomyris, were too strong in their resistance and strategy. Book I, titled Clio, ends with the death of Cyrus.

Book II, called Euterpe, tells how Cambyses, the son of Cyrus, became king and planned to march against Egypt. The rest of the book is a tourist's guide and history of Egypt from its beginnings to the coronation of Amasis.

Book III, called Thalia, tells how Cambyses marched against Amasis. The Egyptian king having died in the meantime, the mercenary army of his son was no match for the Persian, who then betrayed his incipient insanity by dishonoring his slain enemies.

Book IV, called Melpomene, introduces Darius, cousin of and successor to Cambyses, who let the barbarous Scythians outwit him into making peace with them.

The next volume, whose Muse is Terpsichore, begins with a plan that failed. Two Paeonian nobles, wishing to be named rulers over their people, brought their beautiful sister to Sardis, where Darius saw her, carrying water on her head, leading a horse, and spinning. Anxious to spread such industry throughout his empire, he had the Paeonians sent throughout Asia Minor. But the book deals largely with the revolt in Ionia, the growth of Athens, and its expedition, encouraged by Aristagoras, against Sardis. Although the capital was captured and burned, Darius rallied and defeated the invaders at Salamis, in Cyprus.

Erato is the Muse of Book VI, which tells of a battle fought between 353 Ionian triremes and six hundred Babylonian ships. By dissension among the enemy rather than by his strength Darius defeated them and went on to besiege and conquer Miletus. Again Greek bickering helped him during his march to Athens, but the Athenians, rallying and with a few Plataeans, successfully engaged the forces of Darius at Marathon, on September 14, 450 B.C. The Persians were driven back with a loss of 6,400 dead. The Athenians lost only 192 in the battle.

Book VII, named after Polymnia, Muse

of the Sublime Hymn, tells in considerable detail how Darius prepared to revenge his defeat. Fate delayed him; rebellious Egypt sidetracked him, and death ended all his plans. The uncertain Xerxes, succeeding his father to the throne, undertook the Egyptian campaign. After a quick victory, at the head of twenty thousand soldiers he marched on Athens. It took seven days for his army to cross the Hellespont bridge, erected by his engineers, and he, reviewing them, lamented that none would be alive a hundred years hence.

Many Greek cities were quick to surrender. Only Athens, as Herodotus boasts, dared confront the host of Xerxes. Themistocles interpreted the oracle's counsel to defend the city with "wooden walls" as advice to use the two hundred warships originally built for an attack on Egypt. Nature, however, provided a better defense in an east wind that wrecked four hundred Persian galleys along with uncounted transports and provision carriers. However, neither armed forces nor natural obstacles halted Xerxes' army until it reached the Pass of Thermopylae. There, for a day, the Athenians and Spartans checked the Persian host until a traitor revealed another path to the invader. The next day the Persians were again on the march, leaving all the defenders and twenty thousand of their own troops dead behind them.

In Book VIII, titled Urania, there is an account of Xerxes' march into Athens and the firing of the Acropolis. But the "wooden walls" of the Athenian fleet were victorious at Salamis on September 20, 480 B.C. Winner of the greatest glory was the Persian queen Artemis, who used the confusion of battle to get revenge on another Persian by ramming and sinking his ship. Because Xerxes thought she was attacking an enemy and the Athenians believed she had changed loyalties, everybody lauded her.

Fearing that the Greeks might sail on to destroy his bridge, Xerxes ordered a retreat. From the Asian mainland he sent demands for a peace treaty, promptly refused by both Athens and Sparta.

Calliope is the Muse presiding over Book IX. Here the account tells how Mardonios renewed the attack against the Greeks in the hope of sending word of victory back to Xerxes in Sardis. Though temporarily checked by the Thebans, he again entered Athens, whose citizens had fled to Salamis to assemble their allies. When they marched back, Mardonios burned what was left of Athens and retreated.

Except for cavalry skirmishes, neither side wanted to engage in battle until the sacrifices were propitious, but Mardonios' patience broke first, and he fell into a trap at Plataea, where he was killed and his army routed; there were twenty thousand Persian and Boeotian casualties against ninety-one Spartans and fifty-two Athenians killed.

At Thermopylae, Leonidas, the Spartan king, had been crucified and beheaded by the Persians. Certain Greeks wanted to dishonor Mardonios in the same way, but they were told that dishonoring a dead enemy was worthy only of barbarians. Some of the fleeing Persians were pursued and killed at Mycale. Their defeat ended Xerxes' ambitious plan to crush the Hellenes.

Modern historians have honored Herodotus by translating his history into English. Littlebury's version (1709) is outstanding in style, but reveals the writer's imperfect knowledge of Greek. George Rawlinson translated the work in 1858. The most satisfactory translation is the two-volume work published by G. C. Macaulay in 1890.

HIZA-KURIGE

Type of work: Tales
Author: Jippensha Ikku (1765-1831)
Time: Late eighteenth and early nineteenth centuries
Locale: Japan
First published: 1802-1814

> *Principal characters:*
> YAJIROBEI (YAJI), a picaresque traveler
> KITAHACHI (KITA), his companion

The first of this series, which was published in eight sections, was titled in various ways, the common part being *Hiza-kurige* (literally, "Knee-chestnut-horse"), usually translated as *Shank's Mare*. The publication dates of these sections are (1) 1802; (2) 1803; (3) in two volumes, 1803; (4) in two volumes, 1805; (5) in two volumes and a supplement in one volume, 1806; (6) in two volumes, 1807; (7) in two volumes, 1808; and (8) in three volumes, 1809. The Prologue, in one volume, was published in 1814.

This work was so popular that it is supposed to have raised the price of paper in the city of Edo, now Tokyo, where it was first published. Ikku's important contribution to Japanese literature through this work was the creation of a fresh type of popular literature—the comic novel. Travel accounts had been written ever since the tenth century, but these early models extolled the beauties of nature, emphasized poetry, and appealed to readers among the educated aristocracy. Ikku turned this form into a popular one for the commoner.

The use of two traveling companions was by no means a new device, but whereas in previous works they were merely mechanical and shadowy, Ikku's two characters are robustly alive. They are not even the better educated, more refined of the commoners living and working in the bustling streets of Edo, but deliberately chosen stereotypes of the lower classed Edo-ite: exuberant, emotional, quick to anger and as quick to forget, with little strength of character to resist temptation, whose wit and skills are untrained, but yet knowing and shrewd with a shallow wisdom. By making these two characters fall into predicaments of their own making, Ikku created a broad humor, often bawdy but always good, a humor that was mirth-provoking without the sting of satire.

The story line is extremely simple, the treatment episodic. In downtown Edo there lived one Yajirobei, called Yaji for short. He had been born into a merchant family of some means in the town of Fuchû, in the province of Suruga (Ikku's own birthplace), but indulgence in worldly pleasures involving women and wine had greatly reduced his circumstances. Taking with him an actor named Hana-no-suke (which in modern idiom might be translated "Schnozzola"), later renamed Kitahachi, or Kita for short, whom he patronized, Yaji had come to live in Edo. For a time he sent Kita out in servitude, but the poverty of such circumstances proved boring and anyway, Kita was soon discharged. Yaji then sold the belongings he still possessed and with the proceeds set out with Kita on an extended journey. The route they chose was the Eastern Sea Circuit (Tôkai-dô), extending from Edo to Kyoto, including a trip to Japan's holy Great Shrine of Ise, and ending in the commercial city of Osaka.

Ikku himself had made the same trip. Using material from his own experience, perhaps, he added episodes and occurrences of which he had only heard, and he was not above using material found in the Kyôgen, those comic interludes performed in programs of the Nô drama, some almost in their entirety, others only thinly disguised. These episodes introduce the reader to particular places of interest along the Eastern Sea Circuit, and each ends with a line or two of humorous verse which greatly points up the humor. This humor is also expressed in play on words, puns, and the clever use of pivotal words joining one phrase to the next. The work has been translated into French and into English. An English translation by Thomas Satchell is titled *Hizakurige (Tokaido Circuit)* (Kobe, Chronicle Press. 1929). One section of this translation is included in Donald Keene's *Anthology of Japanese Literature* (New York, 1955).

The twelve parts of the *Zoku Hizakurige (Shank's Mare, Continued)* were published under various titles, each applicable to the part which it represented. Only Parts 11 and 12 contain the title *Zoku Hiza-kurige*. Each part is in two volumes, with the exception of Part 12, which was published in three volumes. The publication dates were: (1) 1810; (2) 1811; (3) 1812; (4) 1813; (5) 1814; (6) 1815; (7) and (8) 1816; (9) 1819; (10) 1820; (11) 1821; and (12) 1822. This work has not yet been translated.

In Ikku's sequel, the two companions go to the island of Shikoku to worship at the Kompira Shrine, back to Honshû to visit Miyajima, then eastward over the back way, the Kiso Road, to Zenkô-ji in Shinano Province, on to the famous Kusatsu Hot Springs, and finally back to Edo. The style and the format of the continuation remain the same as in the original series.

H. M. S. PINAFORE

Type of work: Comic opera
Author: W. S. Gilbert (1836-1911)
Type of plot: Humorous satire
Time of plot: Latter half of the nineteenth century
Locale: Portsmouth harbor, England
First presented: 1878

Principal characters:

JOSEPHINE, the Captain's daughter
RALPH, the lowly sailor who loves Josephine
SIR JOSEPH PORTER, First Lord of the Admiralty, and Josephine's suitor
THE CAPTAIN, Josephine's father
LITTLE BUTTERCUP, who loves the Captain

Critique:

W. S. Gilbert shared the honors of this operetta with his composer-partner, Sir Arthur Sullivan. *H. M. S. Pinafore; or, The Lass That Loved A Sailor* was written to be sung and acted on the stage; it was not meant to be published and read by itself. Gilbert and Sullivan obviously were poking fun at the extravagances of grand opera, and at the improbable plots in particular. The plot of *Pinafore,* which effectively disregards the element of time, is a successful vehicle of comedy and satire. Every song, every scene is full of mischievous and clever rhymes, adroit and ingenious dialogue.

The Story:

Lying at anchor in Portsmouth harbor, the *Pinafore* was the scene of hectic activity, for Sir Joseph Porter, K.C.B., First Lord of the Admiralty, had announced his intention to visit the ship. The sailors swabbed the decks and were inspected by the Captain, who was as content with them as they were with him. One member of the crew, however, was far from happy. Ralph, the lowly foremast hand, was sunk in gloom and despair. He loved Josephine, the Captain's daughter, but because of his low rank she repulsed his advances and rejected his love.

Before Sir Joseph's arrival, Little Buttercup came on board, plying her trade as a seller of ribbons and laces, scissors and knives, treacle and toffee. In a conversation with the Captain she hinted that appearances are often deceiving. The Captain noticed that Little Buttercup had physical charms not displeasing to him.

Sir Joseph's barge approached, and the First Lord was soon on board, accompanied by his sisters, his cousins, and his aunts. After inspecting the crew, he gave them instructions for success. His own formula had been simple enough. He had polished door handles, stuck close to his desk, and never gone to sea. Sir Joseph then proceeded to the purpose of his visit. He had come to ask Josephine to marry him.

Josephine had no intention of marrying Sir Joseph, whom she disliked. Not able to give an outright refusal, she informed him that marriage with such a high-ranking officer was impossible because she was only a captain's daughter. Sir Joseph admired her modesty, but brushed the objection aside. Rank, he assured her, was absolutely no barrier, for love leveled all rank. Josephine hastened to agree with him, and everyone immediately assumed that a marriage would soon take place.

Giving up all hope of winning Josephine, Ralph put a pistol to his head and prepared to pull the trigger. At that moment Josephine rushed in, told him not to destroy himself, and proclaimed her undying love for him. At this turn of events there was general rejoicing among Ralph's messmates, with the exception of an unsavory character by the name of Dick Dead-eye.

The couple laid plans to steal ashore the next evening to be married. Once the ceremony was performed, they reasoned, nobody could do anything about it. But Dick Dead-eye went to the Captain and warned him of the plan. Accordingly, just as the lovers and their accomplices were quietly tiptoeing away, the Captain entered, enraged at Ralph's presumption and at the low company in which he found his daughter. Ralph was thrown into the brig.

Attracted by the Captain's swearing, Sir Joseph came rushing up in time to hear what had happened. The sisters, the cousins, and the aunts were horribly shocked. Sir Joseph was equally shocked, so shocked that he administered a very severe rebuke to the Captain. In the midst of the argument, Little Buttercup appeared. To the astonishment of everyone, she announced that many years ago she had been a baby-farmer. Two infants had been put into her care, one of lowly birth, the other of high position. Because she was very fond of one of them she had changed them around. The Captain was really of low birth, and Ralph was the patrician.

This astounding announcement resulted in a very odd situation which was quickly and amicably arranged. The Captain changed places with Ralph, who became captain instead. Sir Joseph announced that he could not marry Josephine since she was only the daughter of a common sailor. Accordingly, Josephine married Ralph; the Captain married Little Buttercup, and Sir Joseph had no one to marry except a well-born cousin.

THE HOLY TERRORS

Type of work: Novel
Author: Jean Cocteau (1891-   )
Type of plot: Psychological fantasy
Time of plot: The present
Locale: Paris
First published: 1929

Principal characters:
PAUL, a sensitive, imaginative boy
ELISABETH, his sister
GÉRARD, their friend
AGATHA, Gérard's wife, friend of Paul and Elisabeth
MICHAEL, an American

Critique:

Jean Cocteau, a playwright, stage designer, painter, film director, and poet, has been one of the most influential figures in the Paris art world in this century. In this psychological fantasy (*Les Enfants terribles*) he has drawn much on Freudian imagery, and the book is, like his films, informed by romantic imagination. Written with great insight, it is a compassionate account of the creativity and destructiveness of adolescence. The snow scenes at the beginning and the end of the novel provide an image of insulation from the familiar world and of the results of isolation that such alienation may produce.

The Story:

Paul and Elisabeth lived with their paralyzed mother in an old quarter of Paris. They lived as though in a world of vegetable instinct, dissociated from adults by passivity, imagination, and secret, mysterious rites.

One night, when the quarter was transformed by snow, Paul was wandering among the snowballing groups in search of the school hero Dargelos, whom he worshiped. Dargelos, who possessed great charm, was both vicious and beautiful. As Paul moved toward him, Dargelos, perhaps accidentally, knocked him down with a stone-packed snowball. Although he injured Paul, he escaped immediate punishment but was later expelled from the school. Paul was taken home by Gérard who loved him as much for his weakness as Paul loved Dargelos for his strength. Elisabeth was extremely angry with them when they reached Paul's

THE HOLY TERRORS by Jean Cocteau. Translated by Rosamund Lehmann. By permission of the publishers, New Directions. Copyright, 1957, by Rosamund Lehmann.

home. She was then sixteen, two years older than Paul and utterly absorbed by him. She was frequently transported by fury when he appeared to be leaving her sphere of influence.

The three children went into the Room where Paul and Elisabeth ate, slept, read, fought, and played the Game. That Room was the sole material reality in their lives; the Game, their inner world. The Room existed in an established chaos of boxes, clothes, papers, and books. Paul left it only for school and Elisabeth only to look after their mother or to buy magazines. Essentially the Game was daydreaming, a willed withdrawal to an imaginary world of submerged consciousness.

After Elisabeth had sent Gérard away, she undressed Paul and put him to bed. Their doctor decided that Paul was unfit to return to school, a decision which plunged Paul into despair until he learned of Dargelos' expulsion. After that school held no interest for him.

The Room held hidden treasures, the artifacts of their unconscious minds—keys, marbles, aspirin bottles—and when Gérard told Paul that Dargelos had disappeared, a photograph of him dressed as Athalie was added to the collection.

The mother died suddenly. When Paul and Elisabeth saw her, rigid and transfixed in her chair, staring forward, the picture haunted them; it was the one they retained. The mother's nurse, Mariette, remained in the household, content to care for and love Paul and Elisabeth without altering them.

Now an accepted visitor in the Room, Gérard was aware of the almost tangible tension, expressed in fights, recriminations, and reconciliations, between the two. When Paul was well enough, Elisabeth, surprisingly, accepted an invitation from Gérard's uncle to take a holiday by the sea. On the journey she watched Paul while he was sleeping and was disgusted by the air of weakness which his illness had accentuated. She decided to remold him on her own lines.

Once by the sea, they established a Room as much like their own as possible. Paul gained strength under Elisabeth's tutelage, in part through stealing useless objects from local shops while on raids that she had planned. Their booty formed a treasure imitating that in the Paris Room.

When they returned to Paris, Elisabeth was suddenly aware that Paul had outstripped her and that she had become the subordinate party in their relationship. Paul spent his evenings wandering around Montmartre, watching girls, drinking, and finally meeting Gérard and bringing him home for the night. On these occasions Elisabeth would use him as a means of tormenting Paul. The first time she succeeded in rousing her brother came when she declared that she too would go into the world. Her position, she felt, had become untenable, and she subsequently obtained work as a mannequin. This act enraged Paul, who declared that she was prostituting herself; she thought the same about his nightly excursions.

At the dressmaker's establishment where she worked Elisabeth met Agatha, an orphan whose parents, drug addicts, had committed suicide. For Agatha she felt, for the first time, warm affection; but the girl's introduction to the Room precipitated Paul's and Elisabeth's destruction when Agatha became devoted to Paul. The photograph revealed a startling likeness between Dargelos and Agatha, and Paul enthralled her as he had been in thrall to Dargelos. Agatha felt at home in the Room, but at the same time she recognized the strange, dreamlike existence her friends led.

As they matured, the Game failed to absorb Paul and Elisabeth completely. This situation so distressed Elisabeth that when she met Michael, an American friend of Gérard, she transferred her dream life to him. Paul was excluded from this friendship with Michael, but his anger at learning of it evaporated when he discovered that Michael wanted to marry Elisabeth and not, as he had subconsciously feared, Agatha. Elisabeth did marry Michael, but true to Gérard's vision of her the marriage was never consummated: Michael was killed while driving alone in his sports car a few hours after the wedding.

Elisabeth inherited his fortune and his Paris house, into which the four moved. Lonely and disoriented in separate rooms, they gravitated to the Room that Paul finally established in the dining hall. Their lives moved slowly to a climax from the moment that Paul realized he was in love with Agatha. Afraid to tell each other of their love, they each told Elisabeth. Terrified that Paul might leave her, Elisabeth moved tirelessly between them all one night to dissuade them from marrying. Lying, she told Paul that it was Gérard whom Agatha loved, and told Agatha that Paul was too selfish ever to love anyone. She also convinced Gérard that by friendship he had won Agatha's love and that it was his duty to marry her. Elisabeth was so dedicated to the idea of possessing Paul and so trusted by the others that she succeeded completely in her scheme.

A short time after his marriage to Agatha, Gérard met Dargelos. The former schoolmate sent Paul a gift, part of his collection of poisons. Paul and Elisabeth were delighted with the present which, to Agatha's horror, was added to the treasure.

Weeks later when Paris was again covered in snow, Elisabeth dreamed that Paul was dead. She woke to find Agatha at the door. Agatha was convinced Paul had killed himself; she had received a letter from him threatening suicide. They ran to the Room and found Paul choking in poison fumes which filled the screened-in corner where he lay. Although he could barely speak, with Agatha he reconstructed Elisabeth's scheme. When he cursed her, she felt that her heart had died. After admitting her guilt and jealousy, she snatched a revolver; by that violent act she was able to regain their attention and thus to captivate Paul once more. Elisabeth worked to charm him back into their world of the Room and the Game, far from Agatha, who seemed less real to him than the snowstorm outside. The two women watched each other until Paul fell back exhausted. Thinking him dead, Elisabeth shot herself. Crashing against the screens, she destroyed the Room and let in the enemy world. Paul saw visions of snowballers crowding the windows, watching as he died. Theirs was the tragedy of outcasts who, unaware that they lived on borrowed time, died fighting for their private existence.

THE HONEST WHORE, PART ONE

Type of work: Drama
Author: Thomas Dekker (c.1572-1632?) with Thomas Middleton (1580-1627)
Type of plot: Tragi-comedy
Time of plot: Sixteenth century
Locale: Milan, Italy
First presented: 1604

> *Principal characters:*
> GASPARO TREBAZZI, Duke of Milan
> INFELICE, his daughter
> COUNT HIPPOLITO, a nobleman in love with Infelice
> MATHEO, his friend
> CANDIDO, a linen draper
> VIOLA, Candido's wife
> FUSTIGO, Viola's brother
> BELLAFRONT, a harlot

Critique:

This is a minor play by one of the minor Elizabethan dramatists. Thomas Dekker was an extremely prolific writer, working often in collaboration with other playwrights. From a passage in Henslowe's diary, it is known that Middleton had a hand in Part One of this play; but scholars are uncertain as to the precise amount that he contributed. The main plot, as will be seen, has a strangely inverted resemblance to that of *Romeo and Juliet,* while the subplot, although the scene is laid in Milan, gives a realistic glimpse of London shop life of that time. Both plots are, by modern standards, exaggerated and improbable. Lamb found the play "offensively crowded" with diatribes against the harlot's profession; the reader of today, however, will not be shocked. Rather, unless he is a specialist in Elizabethan drama, he is likely to be bored, and he will hardly agree with Hazlitt that the "contrivance" of the main plot is "affecting and romantic."

The Story:

In Milan, at the funeral of Infelice, daughter of Duke Gasparo, Count Hippolito refused to be restrained by his friend Matheo. Frantic with grief over the death of his beloved, he accused her father of having killed her. After a violent altercation between the two noblemen, the hearse was borne off. In Milan, also, Viola's brother, Fustigo, had returned from sea, to find his sister married to Candido, a linen-draper, and unhappy because her husband was such a model of patience and good temper. In order to make Candido angry, Viola proposed to Fustigo—whom Candido had never seen—that he pretend to be her lover, and this plan was agreed upon.

In the meantime, at the ducal palace, it was revealed that Infelice's death was only a trick produced by a sleeping-potion administered at her father's command. Duke Gasparo admitted that Hippolito was a noble youth whom he would have welcomed as a son-in-law had it not

been for a feud between the two families; he had, however, devised the stratagem of her supposed death to break up the love affair between her and the young count. When Infelice awoke, her father told her that Hippolito was dead. He then ordered her to go to Bergamo in order that she might recover from her grief. After she had gone, the duke's physician offered to poison Hippolito and thus relieve the duke's mind forever of the fear of a reunion of the lovers. To this plan the cold-blooded duke assented.

Meanwhile a merry group of Milanese gallants, planning a trick to try the famous patience of Candido, went to his shop and examined his wares, particularly a bolt of lawn at eighteen shillings the yard. When asked the length desired, one of them ordered only a pennyworth and insisted that it be cut from the middle of the piece, thereby ruining the entire bolt. To this fantastic order Candido acceded, to the fury of his wife. But the unruffled Candido served the gallants with wine and even remained calm when one of them walked off with a silver-gilt beaker. He quietly sent for the constable, got his goblet returned, and then invited the gentlemen to dinner.

After the dinner the gentlemen went to the house of a harlot named Bellafront, where they were joined by Hippolito and Matheo. Count Hippolito had never visited the house before and, still in a melancholy mood, he left after a few moments. When he returned to fetch Matheo, he found all the gentlemen gone and Bellafront alone. She immediately fell in love with him, but all she got in return was a long diatribe on the evils of prostitution. Repulsed, she tried to stab herself but was prevented by Hippolito, whose love she vowed to win at any cost.

The attempts to break the patience of Candido continued, as Fustigo put into execution the plan of pretending to be Viola's lover. But the trick miscarried: Candido refused to be offended by his

1330

wife's behavior. His loyal apprentices, not knowing the true situation, gave Fustigo a thorough drubbing. Next, the baffled Viola locked up his formal gown, so that, when he was summoned to a meeting of the city Senate, he lacked the proper clothes to wear. But the imperturbable Candido fashioned a gown out of a tablecloth. Wearing this and with a nightcap on his head, he went to the meeting.

Meanwhile Bellafront, chastened by her love for Hippolito, had resolved to give up her shameless life, and so had turned all the gallants out of her house. Her first seducer had been Matheo, who ironically told her that an honest whore is an impossibility. Still determined to win Hippolito's love, Bellafront gained entrance to his house in the disguise of a page. There she found the count gazing at a picture of the supposedly dead Infelice. When Bellafront revealed her identity, he rudely repulsed her again, and she resolved to leave Milan. As she left the house, Hippolito received a note from the duke's physician asking for an interview.

During these events, the drubbed Fustigo had hired two bullies to take revenge upon Candido's apprentices. Viola had ordered one apprentice to dress in his master's clothes, but again Candido, who returned still wearing the tablecloth, refused to take offense and merely changed his own clothes for those of an apprentice. Just as his wife was declaring him insane, the two bullies entered; seeing Candido in the distinctive garb of an apprentice, they started to beat the poor old man. Again the faithful apprentices came to the rescue, but Candido would not let them hurt his assailants. However, Viola entered with two officers and, under the pretext that Candido was mad, had him bound and carried off to Bethlem Monastery—that is, to the London insane asylum. He meekly submitted.

In the meantime the physician informed Duke Gasparo that he had poisoned Hippolito, but he also warned his master that, having done this deed for gold, he might well be hired to poison the duke. Duke Gasparo instantly banished him with the curt statement that rulers often hate the man by whom their plots are carried out. As soon as he was alone the doctor revealed the true situation: he had not poisoned Count Hippolito. He also informed the count of Infelice's feigned death and promised to bring the lovers together in the chapel of Bethlem Monastery, where they could be married.

Viola, beginning to feel that she had gone too far in her efforts to vex her husband, had repaired to Duke Gasparo's palace to seek a warrant releasing Candido from the madhouse. Unfortunately, just as the duke was about to sign the order for the linen-draper's release, a courier brought the news that Hippolito was not dead and that he and Infelice were to meet at the monastery that afternoon for their marriage. Matheo had carelessly revealed the secret. In a desperate attempt to foil the lovers, Duke Gasparo and his courtiers rode in disguise to the monastery, leaving Viola's warrant unsigned.

Hippolito and Infelice had already arrived at the monastery and were planning to be married that evening. When Matheo arrived with the news that the duke had learned of their intention and was on his way to prevent the wedding, the friar who was to marry them promised to perform the ceremony and to get them out of the building disguised as monks. They were hurried out of sight just as the duke and his followers arrived. The situation became one of great confusion. Bellafront entered, having come to the monastery earlier in the day under pretext of madness. The disguised lovers also came into the room where the duke was, as did Viola, her servant, and Candido. When the various disguises had been thrown off, the duke suddenly relented, forgave Infelice and Hippolito, permitted their marriage, and gave justice to Bellafront by marrying her to

Matheo, the man who had first seduced her. Even Viola knelt to ask Candido's forgiveness for the vexations that she had subjected him to. Patient to the end, he forgave her and then delivered to the assembly a long harangue on patience as the greatest of all virtues.

THE HONEST WHORE, PART TWO

Type of work: Drama
Author: Thomas Dekker (c. 1572-1632?)
Type of plot: Tragi-comedy
Time of plot: Sixteenth century
Locale: Milan, Italy
First presented: c. 1605

Principal characters:
GASPARO TREBAZZI, Duke of Milan
INFELICE, his daughter
COUNT HIPPOLITO, a nobleman, Infelice's husband
BELLAFRONT, a former harlot
ORLANDO FRISCOBALDO, Bellafront's father
MATHEO, Bellafront's husband
CANDIDO, a linen-draper
CANDIDO'S BRIDE

Critique:

Part One of *The Honest Whore* must have been successful on the stage, for Dekker very quickly followed it with a sequel, written entirely by himself. He was obviously endeavoring to capitalize on features of the first play, since in the second part he used all the principal characters save one and continued the subplot of the patient Candido. He ended with a scene in Bridewell, a London prison of his time, to balance the Bethlem Scene in Part One. He also continued the high moral tone of the earlier play, this time, however, making gambling as well as prostitution the object of his strictures. The new character of Friscobaldo, the outwardly stern yet inwardly forgiving father, was extravagantly admired by Hazlitt, and both he and Ernest Rhys considered Part Two superior to Part One. The modern reader will perhaps find that some of the freshness of Part One has worn off and feel that Dekker tried to carry a good thing a bit too far.

The Story:

One day Bellafront, a former prostitute now married to Matheo, the former friend of Count Hippolito, arrived at that nobleman's house with a petition. Her husband had killed a man, but it was in fair fight and the man a notorious villain. Still, Matheo has been condemned to death. Hippolito, who was about to ride out with his wife Infelice, stayed behind to hear the petition. He took the opportunity to remind Bellafront of their old relationship and promised to help Matheo to a pardon and, if possible, to reconcile her with her unforgiving father. But it was significant that Count Hippolito showed much more interest in Bellafront than she in him.

Meanwhile, at the palace of Duke Gasparo, father of Infelice, the courtiers were talking of the marriage of Candido, an old linen-draper still famous in Milan for his patience. Viola had died, and, to the mystification of the gallants, Candido was marrying a young girl. Just as they had decided to attend the wedding feast, Hippolito entered, followed shortly by Orlando Friscobaldo, Bellafront's estranged father. Their meeting gave Hippolito an opportunity to ask the old man

1332

about his daughter. Friscobaldo declared that he had not seen her for seventeen years, that her disgrace had been so great that he no longer considered her his child. But when Hippolito had left, with the parting remark that Bellafront was in dire poverty, the father relented and resolved to rescue his daughter. To this end, he put on the livery of a servant and, thus disguised, went to find his offspring.

At the same time, the wedding of the widowed Candido was taking place, attended by some of the gallants of the city who wished to see what sort of bride the old man had chosen. The first impression was unfavorable: when the bride was handed the wedding goblet, she broke the glass and refused to drink. Candido was as patient as ever, but he did consent to allow a nobleman to disguise himself as an apprentice so that the disguised man might try to cure the bride of her peevishness. The courtiers did not wish to see Candido saddled with another shrew.

Thanks to Hippolito, Matheo had been released from prison and had, somewhat unconvincingly, promised his wife to reform and give up gambling. When Friscobaldo arrived, disguised as a servant, he pretended to be an old family retainer discharged by Bellafront's father. He asked Matheo for a place in his household and insisted on turning over to the latter, for safe-keeping, what he claimed to be his life's savings: twenty pounds. His offer was enthusiastically accepted by Matheo, who took the opportunity to abuse his father-in-law. The outburst was interrupted by the arrival of Hippolito, come ostensibly to congratulate Matheo but in reality to pursue his wooing of Bellafront. He had already sent her gifts; he now left her a purse. To the delight of her disguised father—who was to convey the purse—she rejected all the gifts and resolved to remain honest.

Meanwhile, a rather labored trick was being played at Candido's shop. The nobleman, disguised as an apprentice, ar-

rived as if looking for work. The bride refused to prepare a room for him, whereupon Candido took the unusual step of vowing to tame her. He picked up a yardstick; she armed herself with the longer ell-wand; but before they could come to blows, the bride asked forgiveness and delivered a speech on the proper obedience of wives.

In the interest of saving his daughter from Hippolito's advances, Friscobaldo went to the count's house and revealed to Infelice her husband's infidelity, surrendering to her the gifts sent to Bellafront. When Hippolito returned, Infelice was able to play a neat trick upon him. Kneeling, she made a mock confession of having committed adultery with a servant. The enraged husband delivered a tirade on unfaithful wives, thus giving Infelice the opportunity to turn his own words against him as she displayed the gifts he had sent Bellafront. But her just reproaches succeeded only in making her husband the more determined to pursue his illicit passion.

In the household of Matheo, affairs were going from bad to worse. That unlucky gamester had lost everything at dice, including the money entrusted to him by his feigned servant; so, reduced to nothing, he pawned his wife's clothes and hinted strongly that he would be pleased if she would return to her former profession so as to gain a few ducats. He was, however, temporarily rescued by a friend, who promised to give him both money and clothes fashionable for a gentleman.

Candido's troubles, also, were continuing. Two disreputable characters, Mrs. Horseleech, a bawd, and Botts, a pander, had designs upon his new wife and tried to seduce her for one of their customers; but the plot broke against her honesty. While these events were taking place, Matheo had received his new clothes and was happily showing them to his wife. In the midst of Matheo's display old Friscobaldo appeared, this time in his own person, to be recognized by

Bellafront, who asked his forgiveness. The father startled Matheo by his knowledge of the latter's shady dealings and then left in pretended anger, vowing that he would let the couple starve. While Bellafront and Matheo were quarreling, the father returned in his servant's disguise to hear Matheo's very garbled account of what had just happened and his proposal that they rob Friscobaldo's house. The disguised old man agreed to the plan.

After they had left the house, Bellafront appeared with Hippolito, who was still intent on his wooing. A long debate ensued between them, Hippolito urging his suit and Bellafront describing the miseries of a harlot's life. When she repulsed his advances, he swore to continue until he had succeeded. In the meantime, Friscobaldo had been revealing to Duke Gasparo the villainy of Matheo. The duke agreed to aid the plot of catching Matheo in the robbery and also resolved to cure Hippolito by purging Milan of harlots by imposing such strict laws that Hippolito would be afraid to approach a prostitute, no matter how fair she might be.

The young Milanese gallants, never tired of trying to vex the patient Candido, met at Matheo's house to plan another trick. Matheo suggested that, as a bait, he should offer to sell Candido some lawn, thus accomplishing two purposes at once, for he had stolen the lawn from two supposed peddlers—actually men hired by Friscobaldo. Candido arrived and was persuaded to drink a glass of wine. At that moment the constable entered to arrest Matheo for theft and Candido for receiving stolen goods. Both were taken to Bridewell prison, along with Mrs. Horseleech and Botts, who had been present during the episode. Duke Gasparo, attended by his court, arrived at the prison to administer justice. Hippolito came also, having heard that Bellafront had been arrested in the wholesale sweep of the harlots of Milan. At the trial Matheo's real baseness was revealed: he boldly admitted the robbery but claimed that his wife had inspired it; when this charge was disproved by the disguised Friscobaldo, he accused Bellafront of being a whore and swore that he had found her in bed with Hippolito. To this accusation, Infelice, in order to prolong the stratagem, added that Bellafront had accepted presents from Hippolito. In the midst of these charges and countercharges Friscobaldo at last threw off his disguise and proclaimed his daughter's innocence and Matheo's villainy. All ended happily when, at Bellafront's petition, her unworthy husband was pardoned, Hippolito and his wife were reconciled, and Candido was shown to have been the victim of a cruel joke.

HONEY IN THE HORN

Type of work: Novel
Author: H. L. Davis (1896-   )
Type of plot: Regional romance
Time of plot: 1906-1908
Locale: Oregon
First published: 1935

Principal characters:
    CLAY CALVERT, a migrant worker
    WADE SHIVELEY, his stepfather
    UNCLE PRESS SHIVELEY, Wade's father
    LUCE, Clay's woman
    THE HORSE TRADER, Luce's father

HONEY IN THE HORN by H. L. Davis. By permission of the author. Published by Harper & Brothers. Copyright, 1935, by Harper & Brothers.

The story told in this novel is less important than the character studies of some people who settled Oregon in the early part of this century. In his introduction the author states that he is neither criticizing any social group nor suggesting reforms; rather, he attempts to give an accurate picture of the migrants who were always seeking new homes in better lands. The story itself is excellent, however—fast-moving and interestingly told. There have been many novels of pioneers and early settlers during the last two decades, but few surpass *Honey in the Horn*.

The Story:

Wade Shiveley had killed his own brother in a fight over a squaw and had murdered and robbed old man Howell. Now he had been captured. The officers wanted Uncle Press Shiveley, Wade's father, to try to get Wade to say where he had hidden the money. But Uncle Press had threatened to shoot Wade if he ever laid eyes on him again, and so in his place he sent Clay Calvert, the son of one of Wade's wives. Clay did not want to go because he also hated Wade. Uncle Press gave Clay a gun to slip to Wade in the jail. Having loaded the gun with blank cartridges, he hoped Wade would use the worthless gun to attempt an escape and thus be shot down by the officers.

On the way to the jail, Clay met a horse trader and his wife and daughter. When Clay slipped the gun to Wade in the jail, Wade said that he had not killed Howell, that Howell was killed by a bullet that split when it was fired and that such a bullet did not fit his own gun. Wade had always been a liar, but Clay suspected that this time he might be telling the truth.

Clay left town to hide in Wade's abandoned shack until after Wade had been killed and buried. Later Uncle Press sent a half-breed Indian to tell him that Wade had escaped and that the

sheriff was now looking for Clay as an accomplice. Clay left the shack with the Indian, taking with him Wade's rifle he had found there, and after traveling awhile they met the horse trader and his women again. Clay learned that the girl was called Luce and that she traveled around with her father and stepmother, trading horses, racing them, and picking hops in season. Since he wanted to get out of the immediate territory and because he was strongly attracted to Luce, Clay decided to travel with the horse trader's family. The Indian stole Wade's rifle from Clay and ran away.

Clay and the horse trader's family worked for a time in the hop fields. The trader was a weak man who lost all he and his family earned by gambling, and Luce took the responsibility for the family on her shoulders. Clay and Luce liked each other very much, but they quarreled frequently, and one day Clay moved away from the wagon. When the sheriff appeared at the field one day, Clay became frightened and left hurriedly, traveling toward the coast.

Luce and her folks found him after awhile, and Luce and Clay decided to stay together. There was no place for them to get married. They spent the winter in a little settlement on the coast, in a cabin apart from the horse trader's. Luce rescued some bags of flour which had floated to shore from a wrecked ship, and with money earned by selling the flour to the Indians she and Clay were able to buy a wagon and start on their own.

Clay and Luce left for eastern Oregon, but Clay refused to let her father and stepmother go with them, for he could not stand the sight of the weak horse trader. They traveled across the mountains and into Looking Glass Valley, where they joined another group of settlers led by Clark Burdon. Burdon described to Clay a stranger who was looking for him, and Clay knew the man was Wade. Clay liked Burdon and told him the story of Wade and his killings and escape. Burdon promised to help him get rid of Wade. That night Clay shot a man he thought was Wade, but the dead prowler turned out to be the son of one of the settlers. When Burdon and Clay declared that Wade had shot the boy, the men formed a posse and captured Wade. After Wade tried to kill Clay, the men believed that the outlaw was trying to keep Clay from testifying against him; and the posse vowed to hang Wade. Clay felt guilty, for he doubted that Wade had killed Howell and he knew that he himself had shot the prowler. But it was his life or Wade's, and so he kept silent. He felt dirty and sick when he saw Wade hanged.

The settlers traveled eastward, Clay and Luce with them. Luce had a miscarriage. She would not let Clay go for a doctor, for she was terrified that he would leave her and never come back. The rest of the caravan had gone on and they were alone. Clay finally left Luce, promising to return with help as soon as possible. He came back with an Indian midwife, to find that Luce had gone away in the wagon. There were two sets of wagon wheels, and Clay knew instinctively that her father had come by and that Luce had left with him. Angry and hurt by her desertion, Clay decided to go on alone.

He rode his horse into the threshing country and worked with a mowing crew. There he met the half-breed from the Shiveley ranch and told the Indian to be on the lookout for Luce and her father. The Indian did meet the horse trader and made a large wager on a race with him. The horse trader lost the race and the Indian collected the money. Next day the Indian was found with a bullet in the back of his head and no money in his clothing, and the horse trader and Luce had disappeared. Clay helped bury the Indian, but before the burial he shot Wade's rifle, which the Indian had stolen. The bullet did not split. Clay knew then that Wade had been telling the truth about not killing Howell. He suspected that Luce's father had killed and robbed both Howell and the Indian.

Clay joined a party moving on to a railroad construction camp. On their way there was an accident, and one of the horses had to be killed. When Clay saw the horse, he recognized it as one belonging to Luce's father, and he knew that she was in the group. He volunteered to shoot the horse, but first he found Luce and asked for her rifle. With it he killed the animal and later, examining the bullet, he saw that it was split. When he told her that the trader had murdered Howell and the Indian, she claimed she had done the killings. She said that her father, who was now dead, had lost a lot of money to Howell and that her stepmother and Howell had fought. Luce had shot the old man during the fight and had taken the money her father had lost to him. Later she killed the Indian because he had won her father's money in the horse race.

Clay suspected that Luce was trying to protect her dead father. Besides, he still wanted her. He climbed into her wagon and they joined the long line of settlers who were still seeking a place where they could make real homes. Whatever their past, they would always go on together.

THE HOOSIER SCHOOLMASTER

Type of work: Novel
Author: Edward Eggleston (1837-1902)
Type of plot: Regional romance
Time of plot: About 1850
Locale: Indiana

First published: 1871

Principal characters:
RALPH HARTSOOK, a young schoolmaster
BUD MEANS, Ralph's pupil and friend
HANNAH THOMSON, the Means' bound-girl
DR. SMALL, Ralph's enemy
PETE JONES, Dr. Small's partner in crime
WALTER JOHNSON, Ralph's cousin, one of the robbers
MARTHA HAWKINS, Bud Means' sweetheart
SHOCKY, Hannah's brother

Critique:

Eggleston wrote *The Hoosier Schoolmaster* as a regional study. In it he caught the Hoosiers of his day, with their singular twists of phrasing, their rough frontier conduct. His simple plots, stock characters and thinly-disguised morality were all subordinate to his main purpose. If *The Hoosier Schoolmaster* is not a great book, it certainly is not to be overlooked, for its author faithfully recorded the place and time he wished to describe.

The Story:

Ralph Hartsook had not thought schoolteachers were judged by their muscular ability when he applied for the job as schoolmaster of Flat Creek, Indiana. Before long, however, he learned his competence would be judged by his power to keep his pupils from driving him out of the schoolhouse. His first step was to make friends with Bud and Bill Means, sons of the school trustee, in whose house he was to board for a time. He was tired from the ten miles he had trudged to apply for his job, but he walked almost the same distance that evening when he went coon hunting with the boys.

Ralph Hartsook held his own against the pranks and challenges of his pupils until the night of the big spelling-bee. Then before most of the people in Flat Creek he was defeated by the Means' bound-girl, Hannah Thomson.

Finding himself strongly attracted to the girl, he escorted her home after the spelling-bee.

Kept awake by curiosity about Hannah's past, Ralph had trouble sleeping that night. At two in the morning he got up, restless, and strolled down the road toward the schoolhouse. Three horsemen passed him in the darkness, one riding a horse with white markings. A few minutes later Dr. Small rode by, returning, Ralph supposed, from a night call. He went back to Pete Jones' house, where he was staying at the time. The next morning he discovered that the horse with the white markings stood in Pete's stable, and he learned from Shocky Thomson, Hannah's young brother, that there had been a robbery the night before.

He decided not to tell what he knew. He had no proof that Pete Jones was connected with the housebreaking and it would have been awkward to explain his own ramblings at an early hour. To add to his misery that day, Mirandy Means, who had been casting sheep's eyes at him, informed him that her brother Bud was fond of Hannah.

Squire Hawkins invited Ralph to spend the weekend with him. Walking toward the squire's house with Shocky, who took the same direction home from school, he learned from the boy that his father was dead and his blind mother in the poorhouse. When Hannah went to live with the Means, he himself had been taken in by Mr. Pearson, a basketmaker.

That evening Ralph was surprised to see Dr. Small's horse tied in front of Granny Sander's cabin. She had a reputation as a witch among the people of Flat Creek, and she was a malicious gossip. Ralph did not know that the doctor was busy planting the seeds of rumors in Granny Sander's mind, rumors that Ralph had been a philanderer at home, and that he was somehow implicated in the robbery. Small disliked Ralph, though Ralph had never been able to find any reason for it. Rumor had done its ugly work by Sunday morning. At church Ralph's neighbors had little to say to him.

On Christmas Day, which came the following week, the boys did not follow the custom of asking the teacher for a holiday. Instead Bud and others of the older pupils barricaded themselves in the schoolhouse to keep Ralph from entering and had to be forced out by sulphur thrown down the chimney. Later Bud threatened to thrash Ralph because the schoolmaster had taken the squire's niece, Martha, to church the Sunday before. Bud was jealous. Ralph immediately declared he was really inclined toward Hannah, but had avoided seeing her because of Mirandy's statement. He and Ralph quickly became fast friends. Now, the schoolmaster felt, he had a clear field for courting.

Before Bud and Ralph finished their talk, Shocky burst into the schoolhouse with the news that Mr. Pearson was about to be tarred and feathered by the people of Flat Creek, who had been led by Pete Jones to believe the basket-maker was guilty of the robbery. Pearson, too, had seen three men riding by on the night of the robbery, and Jones had decided the best way to divert suspicion from himself would be to accuse Shocky's benefactor.

Hoping to protect the old man, Bud Means started toward the Pearson home. On the way he met Jones to whom he gave a sound drubbing.

That night Bud helped Pearson to escape to his brother's home in the next county. To thwart Pete Jones' efforts to have Shocky Thomson bound out by declaring the Pearsons paupers, Ralph took the boy to stay with his friend, Miss Nancy Sawyer, in his home town

of Lewisburg. His aunt, Mrs. Matilda White, refused to have Shocky's mother in her house because she was a pauper, and so, at Miss Sawyer's own suggestion, Mrs. Thomson was brought to the Sawyer home to spend the weekend with her son. Through Miss Sawyer's efforts, a collection was taken up at church that Sunday afternoon, and with that donation and the money she earned knitting socks, Mrs. Thompson was able to make a home of her own for Shocky.

That same Sunday Bud, intending to ask Martha to marry him, visited Squire Hawkins' house. Suddenly bashful, he told her only of the spelling-bee to take place at the schoolhouse on Tuesday night. Shortly afterward the squire received an anonymous letter, threatening him with the burning of his barn if Martha associated with Bud, the implication being that Bud was incriminated in the robbery. The squire persuaded Martha to ignore Bud. Chagrined by her refusal to let him escort her home from the spelling-bee, Bud began to cultivate Pete Jones and his friends, among them Dr. Small and Walter Johnson, Ralph's cousin.

Bud soon proved he was still Ralph's friend. One day Hannah brought Ralph a letter Bud had sent warning him that he was suspected of the robbery and that there was a plan afoot to tar and feather him that night. Ralph saved himself from the mob by going to a nearby town and giving himself up to the authorities there. His trial was held the next day.

All of Flat Creek was present to see the schoolmaster convicted. Mrs. Means and Pete Jones, particularly, were willing to offer damaging testimony, the former because Ralph had spurned Mirandy's attentions. It was Dr. Small who vindicated Ralph, however, by overshooting the mark in his anxiety to clear himself of Ralph's testimony that the doctor had been out on the night of the robbery.

Small had Walter Johnson called to the stand to testify they had spent the evening together in the physician's office. But Johnson, at a prayer meeting he had attended with Bud, had been deeply impressed by the minister's warning of eternal damnation for sinners. Summoned before the court, he gave way to his guilty conscience and declared that he, Small, Pete Jones, and Pete's brother had committed the robbery, and that Ralph and Mr. Pearson were innocent.

Walter Johnson went free because of his testimony, but Dr. Small, who had been the ringleader of the band, was hanged. Jones and his brother were given prison sentences.

Ralph Hartsook returned to Lewisburg to teach in a new academy there. Shortly afterward he married Hannah. At Ralph's wedding Bud found his courage at last and proposed to Martha.

HORACE

Type of work: Drama
Author: Pierre Corneille (1606-1684)
Type of plot: Neo-classical tragedy
Time of plot: Remote antiquity
Locale: Rome
First presented: 1640

Principal characters:
> HORACE, the most courageous of the Roman soldiers
> SABINE, his Alban wife
> OLD HORACE, his father, formerly a soldier
> CAMILLE, Horace's sister
> CURIACE, Sabine's brother, in love with Camille
> VALÈRE, a Roman soldier in love with Camille
> JULIE, confidante of both Sabine and Camille
> TULLE, the ruler of Rome

Critique:

After the controversy which raged over The Cid (1636), an extravagant heroic drama, Corneille turned to Livy for his inspiration. In Horace, a tightly constructed play which rigorously followed dramatic precepts, he succeeded in producing a patriotic drama both popular with the audience and acceptable to the critics.

The Story:

Although formerly united by ties of patriotism and blood, for Alba was the birthplace of the founders of Rome, Romulus and Remus, the cities of Rome and Alba were at war. Sabine, the wife of Horace, was divided in her loyalties between the city of her birth, where her brothers still lived, and the city of her famous warrior-husband. The battle was

to be decided by armed combat between three heroes from each side. Sabine drew little comfort from the resolution, which meant the defeat either of her kinsman or of her husband. Camille, the betrothed of Curiace, the Alban warrior-brother of Sabine, felt her loyalties divided between her loved one and her brother Horace. Even though the oracles had been favorable toward her coming marriage, her dreams envisioned the imminent horror.

The battle postponed, Curiace visited Camille at the home of Old Horace, her father. He declared his abiding love for her, though he remained an Alban patriot, loyal to his city. They commented on the oracles and wished for a lasting peace. When the two warriors met, however, Horace was insistent on the out-

HORACE by Pierre Corneille, from CHIEF PLAYS OF CORNEILLE. Translated by Lacy Lockert. By permission of the publishers, Princeton University Press. Copyright, 1952, 1957, by Princeton University Press.

come of the trial by combat. Curiace, who stressed the need for peaceful understanding, was dismayed to hear that his prospective brothers-in-law, Horace and his two brothers, were to represent the Romans. He was even more oppressed in spirit when a messenger announced that he and his two brothers were to defend the honor of Alba.

Horace wanted no sympathy from Curiace, though he bore him no ill will. Curiace saw love of wife and family as paramount over Horace's kind of patriotism.

Horace then gave the lovers a moment together before the debt of honor was to be paid. Camille, mindful of the fact that she was the daughter and the sister of famous warriors, denounced the patriotism that could make her choose between love of family and of her future husband. She begged Curiace to avoid a battle which could only end in tragedy, no matter what the outcome. His first duty, however, was to his country, and he brutally asserted this fact. Sabine and Camille then begged the cause of love of home and family, while Horace and Curiace defended honor and patriotism. The women were unsuccessful in their suit, and Old Horace comforted them as the young men went off to prepare for the combat. Young Horace, loving to his sister and kind to his aged parent, sought glory in battle; Curiace, no less patriotic, felt that he had lost wife, brothers, and brothers-in-law by a grim turn of fate.

Sabine, given at first to confusion and later to bitterness, lamented her sad position as the sister of the Alban warriors and the wife of their adversary. When she inquired of her friend Julie whether her husband or her brothers had been vanquished, she was told that no resolution had been reached; the king had just then arranged the combatants and charged them to fight to the death, that the fate of the two principalities might be determined. Camille, wearied by her solitary wonderings and fears, joined the discussion. She renounced the deceptive oracle, and neither the wife nor the prospective bride could find solace for their anxiety and grief. Sabine declared that a wife was the most bereaved, to which Camille replied that her sister-in-law had never been in love. For the moment the controversy was resolved by Old Horace, who declared that Rome suffered most; all else was in the hands of the gods.

Julie then brought word that the Alban brothers had been victorious, that two of Old Horace's sons were dead, and that Horace had fled the battlefield. The old man was appalled that his son could see his brothers die without drawing new courage from such defeat and either go down to death or glory. Camille felt some relief that both her lover and brother were for the moment spared, and Sabine was content that her husband was alive. Old Horace could share none of these sentiments; his loyalties were for honor, country, manliness.

Valère, dispatched by Tulle to bring comfort to Old Horace, told of the outcome of the battle. He said that Horace had retreated as a ruse in order to attack the Albans at a disadvantage and that he had killed all three. The old man, his family honor vindicated, rejoiced in the face of Camille's great sorrow. Left alone, she lamented the death of her two brothers and her lover and reviled Rome as the symbol of patriotic infamy.

Into this scene of unrestrained grief came the victorious warrior accompanied by his faithful soldier-in-arms bearing the swords of the vanquished brothers. Displaying the arms, now the spoils of war, which had killed their brothers, he taunted Camille with the glory of Rome while she declared his deed murder. When he accused her of disloyalty, her replies inflamed him to murder, and with the sword of Curiace he killed his sister, a deed which he defended as an act of justice. Sabine, shocked by her husband's bloody deed, was comforted crudely by her husband, who felt that he had performed an act of patriotism justified by the insult to his country. The deeds of heroism he recounted only heightened the despair of his wife, who declared her only wish was to die.

Old Horace, proud of his son's achievements but saddened by his vindictiveness, was distressed over the sudden turn of events which might now deprive him of his last offspring. The fate of his son he must now leave to his king. Tulle, in response to the eloquent plea by Valère, allowed Horace to speak for himself. The hero and murderer wanted most to die, knowing that his past glory had been dimmed by the murder of his own sister. Sabine begged the king to kill her that her husband might live; Old Horace wished the king to save the last of his sons. Tulle, after he had heard all the pleas, felt that Horace's fate rested with the gods, that a king could only pardon that which he could not condone.

THE HORSE'S MOUTH

Type of work: Novel
Author: Joyce Cary (1888-   )
Type of plot: Picaresque romance
Time of plot: The 1930's
Locale: London
First published: 1944

      Principal characters:
          GULLEY JIMSON, an unconventional artist
          SARA MONDAY, his one-time model
          COKER, a barmaid
          NOSY, an aspiring artist
          MR. HICKSON, an art collector
          PROFESSOR ALABASTER, a critic
          SIR WILLIAM BEEDER, Jimson's benefactor

Critique:

The Horse's Mouth is one of several novels depicting the life and times of Gulley Jimson, artist and social rebel. Told in the first person singular, the story is a delightful combination of humor, pathos, and down-to-earth philosophy. Whether Gulley was a genius or the greatest rogue in modern art circles is a question which the writer makes no attempt to settle, but there is no doubt that Gulley is one of the most fascinating figures in modern literature. Here is the familiar picaresque romance brought up to date and enlivened by the supple, witty qualities of Mr. Cary's style.

The Story:

Just out of prison, Gulley Jimson looked up his old friend Coker, the ugly barmaid at the Eagle. Coker wanted him to press a lawsuit over some of his paintings, for if Gulley collected Coker would collect from him. At last Gulley managed to get away from her and return to his studio in an old boat shed.

The shack roof leaked and the walls sagged. His paints and brushes had either been stolen or ruined by rain and rats, but the Fall was there. The Fall, depicting Adam and Eve in their fall from grace, would be his masterpiece.

Gulley had a questionable reputation as an artist. Several years back he had painted some nudes of Sara Monday, startling portraits of a lovely girl in her bath. Sara had lived with Gulley as his wife. When the breakup came she had stolen the pictures and sold most of them to a collector named Hickson. One or two she kept for herself. Gulley, past sixty now, had done nothing since the Sara nudes to add to his reputation, but he still had faithful followers of tramps, beggars, and young Nosy. Nosy, wanting to be an artist, worshiped art and Gulley Jimson.

To complete the Fall, Gulley needed paints and brushes. In order to get Gulley to see Sara Monday and secure evidence for a lawsuit to compel Hickson to return the Sara nudes, Coker bought him some paints and brushes. Off and on he worked on the Fall, driven sometimes by compulsion to paint, sometimes by desire for a beer or two.

When Coker pinned him down and took him to see Sara, Gulley was stunned to find her an old hag to whom he felt drawn even while he pitied and despised her. Sara willingly signed a statement that she had given the stolen pictures to Hickson; then she tried to renew her affair with Gulley. Sara had been badly treated by a succession of men, but, like Gulley, she had few complaints. Both felt that the short-lived prosperity and good times they had enjoyed were now being paid for.

Gulley, working intermittently on the Fall, frequently had to trick Coker into buying him paints. Once she forced him to go with her to Hickson, to try to get the pictures or a settlement for them. When Hickson was ready to settle a small sum on Gulley, even though he had legitimately taken the pictures in return for a debt, Gulley slipped some valuable snuffboxes in his pocket and was caught by Hickson and the police. Although that bit of foolishness cost him six months, he bore no malice toward Hickson.

In jail, Gulley received a letter from Professor Alabaster, who planned to write a life history of the painter of the Sara Monday pictures. Gulley thought the idea ridiculous, until he decided there might be money in it. He had had another idea for another masterpiece, and after his release he hurried back to the boat shed to finish the Fall and get started on his new work. He found Coker pregnant and in possession of the shed. Betrayed by her latest lover, her job at the pub lost, she had moved to the shed with her mother. Gulley had to find some way to get the Fall out. Before he had made any plans, he met Professor Alabaster. Alabaster not only wanted to write Gulley's life history but also hoped to sell some of Gulley's work to Sir William Beeder, a collector who admired the paintings possessed by Hickson. Gulley tried to interest Alabaster and Sir William in one of the new masterpieces he was going to do, but Sir William had a great desire for one of the Sara nudes or something similar.

Gulley still hoped to interest Sir William in the Fall, but when he went again to the boat shed he found that Coker's mother had cut it up to mend the roof. Gulley decided there was no use in getting his temper up and doing something foolish; then he would land back in jail before he could do another masterpiece or make a sale to Sir William. Besides, he suddenly realized that he was tired of the Fall.

In the meantime, if Sir William wanted a Sara nude, perhaps Gulley could persuade old Sara to give him one of the small ones she had kept. But Sara, still vain, loved to take out the portraits of her lovely youth and dream over them. Gulley tried every trick he could think of, without success.

When Sir William left London, Gulley wheedled Alabaster into giving him the key to Sir William's apartment. Needing canvas and paints, he pawned the furniture and art collections, and even grudgingly let a sculptor rent one end of the drawing-room to chip away on a piece of marble. Gulley honestly kept the pawn tickets so that Sir William could redeem his possessions. He used one wall for a weird painting he was sure would please Sir William. But when the owner returned unexpectedly, Gulley decided to talk to him from a distance and ducked out before his benefactor found him.

With faithful Nosy, Gulley went to the country for a time. There he worked a new scheme to get money, but another crook beat him up and sent him to the hospital. While recuperating, Gulley had another vision for a masterpiece and wrote Sir William about his idea. Alabaster replied for Sir William, who still insisted on a nude and thanked Gulley for caring for his furniture.

By the time Gulley got back to the boat shed, Coker had had her baby and was firmly installed there. Gulley moved into another empty building and set about preparing the wall for a painting of the Creation. He was aided by Nosy and several young art students he had shanghaied. He tried again to get a nude from old Sara. When Hickson died and gave the Sara pictures to the nation, Gulley was famous. Alabaster found a

backer for the life history, and distinguished citizens called on Gulley to see about buying more pictures from him. Gulley had, in the meantime, copied one of his old pictures of Sara from the original in the Tate Gallery and had sold it on approval to Sir William for an advance payment of fifty pounds.

He made one last try to get a picture from Sara. When she refused, he pushed her down the cellar stairs and broke her back. Knowing the police would soon be after him, he raced back to the Creation and painted like a madman, trying to finish the picture before his arrest. He never completed the painting; his spiteful landlord tore the building down over his head. Thrown from his scaffold, he came to in a police ambulance and learned that he had suffered a stroke. He did not grieve. Rather, he laughed at all the jokes life had played on him, and the jokes he had played on life.

HORSESHOE ROBINSON

Type of work: Novel
Author: John P. Kennedy (1795-1870)
Type of plot: Historical romance
Time of plot: 1780
Locale: The Carolinas
First published: 1835

Principal characters:
SERGEANT HORSESHOE ROBINSON, a colonial patriot
MAJOR ARTHUR BUTLER, his friend
MR. LINDSAY, a Loyalist
MILDRED, Lindsay's daughter
HENRY, Lindsay's son
WAT ADAIR, a Tory
TYRREL, a British officer
MARY MUSGROVE, a patriot
JOHN RAMSAY, Mary's sweetheart

Critique:

Horseshoe Robinson, A Tale of the Tory Ascendency is a love story and a war story. A good narrative description of the effect of the American Revolution on the people of the Carolinas, the novel is unspoiled by flag-waving sentimentality. Horseshoe Robinson is a hunter and a woodsman with a personality much like

that of our common story-book conception of early American pioneers. The love story is important in this novel, but it is trivial compared to the importance of the war itself. From a historical point of view, the book makes a valuable contribution with its portrayal of the confusion caused by divided loyalties be-

1343

tween England and the Colonies.

The Story:

In the secluded back country of South Carolina two men in the service of the revolutionary colonial forces were traveling together. They were Major Arthur Butler and his shrewd sergeant, a man known throughout the region as Horseshoe Robinson, because of his former occupation as a blacksmith. Although they passed as chance travelers, they were on a secret mission to trace the movements of the enemy and to enlist aid for the cause of colonial independence.

Before setting out on their dangerous journey, Arthur Butler was moved to stop near Dove-Cote, the residence of Mr. Lindsay, a Loyalist gentleman who had come to this territory to live because he wished to avoid the conflict between the colonists and the British government. He himself was loyal to the crown because of financial interests in England, but his son Henry was sympathetic to the American cause. Mildred, Lindsay's daughter, was in love with Arthur Butler, but because of the major's connections with the colonial army Mr. Lindsay had forbidden her to see Butler. For this reason they met secretly in a grove not far from Dove-Cote. After the meeting she returned unseen to Mr. Lindsay's house, and Butler and Horseshoe Robinson went to the inn of Mistress Dimock, not far away.

That night at the inn Horseshoe encountered a Tory spy named James Curry, a stealthy rascal who was passing as the servant of Mr. Tyrrel, a guest at Dove-Cote. Tyrrel, a disguised British officer, was often at Mr. Lindsay's home, ostensibly to secure that gentleman's aid for the Loyalists, but in reality to court Mildred, who despised him and everything he stood for. Seeing Curry at the inn, Horseshoe knew that Tyrrel was again visiting Dove-Cote. Although he let the fellow escape, he was afraid that Tyrrel and Curry might cause trouble for Butler and himself on their trip through

South Carolina.

Major Butler had been sent by General Gates on a mission to another rebel general in Georgia. With Horseshoe as a companion, the major felt certain that he could complete his undertaking. On their first night in the forest Horseshoe led Butler to the home of Wat Adair, an old friend whom he thought loyal to the rebel cause. However, Wat was not a true friend. Having been bought off by the Tories, he planned that night to direct Butler and Horseshoe to an ambush in the forest. But a relative of Wat, Mary Musgrove, overheard Wat plotting with another Tory, and being loyal to the rebels she whispered to Butler the plans she had learned.

Through her warning Horseshoe and Butler avoided one trap, only to fall into an ambush of some rough Tories, among them Curry. Fearing that the drunken crew planned to murder Butler and himself, Horseshoe escaped, hoping to rescue Butler later.

The family of Mary Musgrove was a rebel family, and Horseshoe proceeded to their home to get help in his plan. In addition, the family of Mary's sweetheart, John Ramsay, was a rebel family. With the Ramsays and the Musgroves, Horseshoe planned to engage the enemy and bring Butler to safety. Mary, pretending to be a vendor of fruit, was to enter the Tory camp where Butler was being held. There she was to communicate with the major and give him word of his rescuers' plans.

James Curry had charged Butler with conspiring to murder Mr. Lindsay, a loyal subject of the king. In order to disprove this charge, Horseshoe returned to Dove-Cote. Mildred's distress at the news of her lover's arrest had caused her father great grief, and he relented his stern stand against Butler and assured Mildred that he would not punish her for her concern over the major. When Horseshoe found Mildred and her brother Henry at Dove-Cote, Mr. Lindsay had gone off with Tyrrel to a meeting of

Loyalists in a nearby town. Having heard Horseshoe's account of the charges against Butler, Mildred resolved to go to Cornwallis, the English general, and plead with him for Butler's life. Mildred was confident she could prove that Butler could never have had designs on the father of the girl he loved. Accompanied by Henry Lindsay and Horseshoe Robinson, she set out for Cornwallis' headquarters.

John Ramsay and Mary were able to effect Butler's escape from the camp where he was held prisoner, but John was killed before they reached a place of safety. Grief-stricken by the loss of her sweetheart, Mary attended the funeral services, which were conducted by her father, Allen Musgrove. While the services were going on, they were interrupted by some British troops, and Butler was once again taken prisoner.

When Mildred and her two companions succeeded in getting an interview with Cornwallis, the courtly general gave Mildred his promise that no harm would befall Butler. While the general was speaking with Mildred, he received a message that Butler had escaped. Mildred set out for Dove-Cote with Horseshoe and her brother. On their way they met Mary Musgrove, her family, and the Ramsays, who told them of Butler's second capture by British troops from a nearby camp. Again Mildred resolved to intercede on behalf of her lover, and Henry and Horseshoe agreed to accompany her.

While Mildred awaited an opportunity to seek Butler, the forces of the Loyalists and the rebels were engaging in the battle of King's Mountain. During the fighting Horseshoe rescued Butler and brought him safely back to Mildred. Then the two lovers revealed that they had been married for over a year, in a secret ceremony witnessed by Mistress Dimock and Henry Lindsay.

Wat Adair was captured, and Horseshoe saw to it that he received just punishment for betraying his American friends. Wat told Horseshoe that Tyrrel was really an English general who had bribed Wat to lead Butler and Horseshoe into a trap. Henry, who had participated in the battle, found Tyrrel's body lying among the dead and wounded. James Curry was captured by rebel forces. It seemed certain that the Tory ascendency in South Carolina was at an end.

But the happy reunion of the lovers was clouded by the death of Mr. Lindsay. When he learned that Mildred had gone to see Cornwallis, he set out to find her before the battle began. Following Tyrrel toward the scene of the fighting, Mr. Lindsay was fatally wounded and Tyrrel killed. Mildred and Henry were able to speak with their father before he died, however, and he lived long enough to take the hands of Mildred and Butler and forgive them for having disobeyed him. He died shortly afterward in a delirium brought on by his fever.

Mildred and Butler returned to Dove-Cote to live a long and prosperous life together.

THE HOUSE BY THE CHURCHYARD

Type of work: Novel
Author: Joseph Sheridan Le Fanu (1814-1873)
Type of plot: Mystery romance
Time of plot: Late eighteenth century
Locale: Chapelizod, a suburb of Dublin
First published: 1863

Principal characters:
    MR. MERVYN, son of Lord Dunoran
    LORD DUNORAN, an Irish peer convicted of murdering one
        Mr. Beauclerc

PAUL DANGERFIELD, the real murderer of Mr. Beauclerc
ZEKIEL IRONS, Dangerfield's accomplice in the murder
DR. BARNABY STURK, a witness to the murder

Critique:

Le Fanu's career as a novelist dated from the publication of this book, which he began writing after the death of his wife in 1858. He withdrew from society at the time of her death and wrote to keep himself occupied. Le Fanu's novels, including this one, are novels of lush life—and something more. Death, mystery, and the supernatural are the grim twilight materials of his fiction. Constant speculation on death and the supernatural enabled him to communicate a spectral atmosphere to his novels. A master of terror, Le Fanu has been favorably compared in the past with such other masters of the supernatural as Wilkie Collins and Poe. This novel is generally regarded as his masterpiece, although *Uncle Silas* was the most popular during his vogue.

The Story:

Lord Dunoran, an Irish peer, had been executed after his conviction for murdering a man named Beauclerc in London. In addition, his estates were declared forfeit to the crown, and his family was left under a shadow. Eighteen years after his death, his son, who went under the name of Mr. Mervyn, took the body back to Ireland and buried it in the family vault in the Anglican church in Chapelizod, a suburb of Dublin. Following the burial, Mervyn moved into an old house that was reputed to be haunted; several families had moved out of it after having seen strange apparitions and heard strange noises at night. Mervyn hoped that in the neighborhood he might pick up some clues that would lead him to the true murderer of Beauclerc, for the young man still believed his father innocent of the crime for which he had died years before.

About the same time that young Mervyn took up residence in the haunted house, another stranger came to Chapelizod, a man named Paul Dangerfield, who was looking after the affairs of a local nobleman. Dangerfield was a very rich man, and before long he had ingratiated himself in the hearts of the local people by his apparent good sense and his liberality. Of young Mervyn, on the other hand, the villagers were very suspicious, for he kept to himself, and only a few people knew his real identity.

The appearance of Paul Dangerfield caused fears and apprehensions in the minds of two men who lived in Chapelizod. The two were Zekiel Irons, the clerk at the Anglican church, and Dr. Barnaby Sturk, a surgeon at the garrison of the Royal Irish Artillery. Irons had been the accomplice of the man who had actually committed the murder of which Lord Dunoran had been convicted. Dr. Sturk had been a witness to the murder. They both recognized Paul Dangerfield to be a man named Charles Archer, a ruthless wretch who would think as little of taking their lives as he had of taking those of others.

Zekiel Irons, who wanted to live without fear, resolved to help young Mervyn discover the guilt of Archer-Dangerfield, for Irons knew that he could never live securely until the man was in prison or dead. Irons had been present also when Dangerfield had killed his other accomplice, who had tried to blackmail Dangerfield. On two occasions Irons visited Mervyn and imparted a portion of what he knew; on both occasions he warned Mervyn not to tell anyone at all, lest his informant be killed.

Dr. Sturk, meanwhile, also recognized Dangerfield as Charles Archer, the man he had seen commit a murder. Dr. Sturk, pressed for money, was trying to become an agent for Lord Castlemallard, who was represented by Dangerfield. Dr.

Sturk made the mistake, however, of threatening Dangerfield with exposure if the agency were not forthcoming. Dr. Sturk was found terribly beaten about the head one night. Since he was in a deep coma, no one knew who had tried to kill him. Evidence pointed, however, to Charles Nutter, the man Dr. Sturk was trying to replace as the nobleman's agent in Chapelizod, for Nutter had disappeared on the same night that Dr. Sturk was attacked. There was no evidence to indicate that Dangerfield had been the attacker. He had been so helpful to Dr. Sturk that he was under no suspicion.

Dr. Sturk lingered on, and for a time it seemed as if he might recover. Dangerfield arranged for a surgeon to come, at a high fee, to operate on the doctor. Dangerfield had convinced Mrs. Sturk that the operation was the only chance her husband had for life, but actually Dangerfield hoped the operation would be a failure and that Dr. Sturk would die without revealing the identity of his attacker. But the operation was a partial success. Dr. Sturk regained his mind and lived for several days, during which time he made depositions to the magistrates concerning the identity of his attacker and the fact that Dangerfield had murdered another man years before. These events moved Zekiel Irons to go also to the magistrates and tell what he knew about the real identity of Paul Dangerfield and the part he himself had played in the murder of Beauclerc. Even in the face of that evidence, the magistrates found it difficult to believe Dangerfield guilty. The fact that Dangerfield had paid for the operation and had lent money to Mrs. Sturk, as well as the disappearance of Charles Nutter, left them in doubt.

But Charles Nutter, apprehended in Dublin within one day of Dangerfield's arrest, was able to prove that he had been away on other business at the time of the attack on Dr. Sturk. He had, however, gone so close to the scene of the crime that he had frightened off Dangerfield before he could finish the murder.

Nutter had not run away; he had simply been to England and Scotland trying to straighten out his domestic affairs. A woman had attempted to prove he was a bigamist because he had married her several years before his marriage to the woman the people in Chapelizod knew as his wife. He had married the woman, but she herself was a bigamist, having been already married to another man. Nutter had been off to find the true husband, to prove that his marriage to the woman was really no marriage at all. He had been compelled to leave secretly lest he be arrested as a bigamist before he could gather evidence to clear his name.

In another quarter of the village the apprehension of Dangerfield had great implications. He had been engaged to the daughter of the commanding general of the Royal Irish Artillery, even though he was many years older than the girl. Because of his wealth, the general was quite anxious to have his daughter marry Dangerfield. The girl, however, was in love with Mervyn and secretly engaged to him. Dangerfield's arrest prevented the general from marrying his daughter to a man she did not love.

So far as Mervyn was concerned, the apprehension of Dangerfield did more than open the way for his marriage to the general's daughter. The information which Dr. Sturk and Zekiel Irons gave concerning the murder of Beauclerc cleared Mervyn's father, Lord Dunoran. When Parliament met again, it returned to Mervyn his good name, his title, and the estates forfeited at the time of his father's conviction.

Paul Dangerfield, alias Charles Archer, was never convicted, nor was he tried by a court. He died mysteriously in his cell in the county gaol in Dublin while awaiting trial, thus cheating the state of executing him for murder. Not long afterward, the new Lord Dunoran and

THE HOUSE BY THE MEDLAR TREE

Type of work: Novel
Author: Giovanni Verga (1840-1922)
Type of plot: Impressionistic realism
Time of plot: Mid-nineteenth century
Locale: Sicily
First published: 1881

Principal characters:
PADRON 'NTONI, head of the Malavoglia
BASTIANAZZO, his son
LA LONGA, Bastianazzo's wife
'NTONI, their oldest son
LUCA, their second son
MENA, their oldest daughter
ALESSIO, their youngest son
LIA, their youngest daughter
UNCLE CRUCIFIX DUMBBELL, a local usurer
GOOSEFOOT, his assistant
DON MICHELE, brigadier of the coast guard

Critique:

This novel, translated also under the title *The Malavoglia*, is one of the most interesting contributions of Italian literature to modern realism. Its characters are poor, simple people who can never rest from their struggle to keep alive. The message of the novel is that man is continually being pulled apart by his own forces, so that only by working together with his fellow men can he hope to survive. Written in a completely realistic fashion, with no intrusion from the author, this novel bridges the gap between realism and naturalism.

The Story:

In the village of Trezza, on the island of Sicily, the Malavoglia family had once been great. Now the only Malavoglia left were Padron 'Ntoni and his little brood in the house by the medlar tree. But they were happy and prosperous, living well on the income brought in by their boat, the *Provvidenza*.

When the oldest grandson, 'Ntoni, was conscripted, the first sadness fell on the household. In that same year other things went badly, and the market for fish was poor. With 'Ntoni gone, the money that came in had to be divided with extra help that Padron was forced to hire. Eventually Padron 'Ntoni had to arrange a loan with Uncle Crucifix Dumbbell to buy a shipment of coarse black beans on credit from him. The beans were to be resold at Riposto by Padron's son, Bastianazzo. Although La Longa, Bastianazzo's wife was skeptical of this deal, she kept quiet, as befitted a woman. Soon afterward, Bastianazzo sailed away on the *Provvidenza* with the cargo of beans aboard. All the villagers whispered that the beans were spoiled, that Uncle Crucifix had cheated the Malavoglia. It was well known that Uncle Crucifix was an old fox in all money matters.

Nevertheless, if the beans were sold, Padron 'Ntoni's family would be well off. The man whose son was to marry Mena Malavoglia rubbed his hands in anticipation of his boy's good fortune. The women of the village, and others too, agreed that Mena was everything a girl should be. But luck went against the Malavoglia family.

In the early evening a huge storm came up. Down at the tavern Don Michele, the brigadier of the coast guard, predicted the doom of the *Provvidenza*. When word came that the boat had been lost, Bastianazzo with her, grief engulfed the Malavoglia family. To add to their troubles, Uncle Crucifix began to demand his money. All the neighbors who brought gifts of condolence to the house by the medlar tree looked about the premises as if they saw Uncle Crucifix already in possession.

Stubbornly Padron 'Ntoni and his family set to work to repay the loan. It was decided to have Mena married as soon as possible. Alfio Mosca, who drove a donkeycart and often lingered to talk with the girl, was grieved at the news. Then one day the *Provvidenza*, battered but still usable, was towed into port. The Malavoglia rejoiced. At the same time 'Ntoni arrived home. Luca, the second son, was drafted. Each member of the family slaved to make enough money to repay the debt.

Meanwhile Uncle Crucifix was fiercely repeating his demands. At last he decided to pretend to sell his debt to his assistant, Goosefoot; then, when officers were sent to Padron 'Ntoni's house, people could not say that a usurer or the devil's money had been involved in their troubles. A short time later a stamped paper was served on the Malavoglia family. Frightened, they went to a city lawyer who told them that Uncle Crucifix could do nothing to them because the house was in the name of the daughter-in-law, and she had not signed the papers in the deal of beans. Padron 'Ntoni felt guilty, however; he had borrowed the money and it must be paid back. When he asked advice from the communal secretary, that official told him that the daughter-in-law must give dower rights on the house to Goosefoot, who was now the legal owner of the note. Although Goosefoot protested that he wanted his money, he nevertheless accepted a mortgage.

As the family began to gather money to repay the loan, luck again went against them. New taxes were put on pitch and salt, two necessary commodities, and personal relations between Goosefoot and the family were strained when he and young 'Ntoni came to blows over a girl. In the village there was talk of smugglers, and the rumors involved two of 'Ntoni's close friends. Goosefoot enlisted the aid of Don Michele to watch 'Ntoni closely.

When Mena's betrothal was announced, Alfio Mosca sadly left town. Padron 'Ntoni, happy over the approaching marriage of his granddaughter, offered Goosefoot part of the money on the loan. But Goosefoot, demanding all of it, refused to be moved by the fact that Mena needed a dowry. On top of these troubles the Malavoglia family learned that Luca had been killed in the war. Goosefoot began again to send stamped papers. When Padron 'Ntoni appealed to the lawyer, he was told that he had been a fool to let La Longa give up her dower rights on the house but that nothing could be done about the matter now. So the family had to leave the house by the medlar tree and move into a rented hovel.

Somewhat repaired and on a fishing excursion, the *Provvidenza* ran into a storm. When Padron 'Ntoni was injured by a blow from the falling mast, young 'Ntoni had to bring the boat in alone. After the old man had recovered, 'Ntoni announced his decision to leave home; he could no longer stand the backbreaking, dull work of his debt-ridden family. His mother, grief-stricken by his departure, contracted cholera and soon died. Meanwhile Mena's engagement had been called off by her betrothed's father. Everything was against the Malavoglia. Goosefoot and Uncle Crucifix gave the family no rest, but insisted that they too were poor and needed their money.

When young 'Ntoni returned to his home with no fortune and clothing more ragged than ever, the villagers laughed with derision. Alessio, the youngest son, now began to help with the work, and he and 'Ntoni were able to earn a little money to apply on the family debt. 'Ntoni, still discontented, was often drunk coming home from the tavern.

Don Michele told the boy's young sister Lia, whom he secretly admired, that she and Mena must keep their eyes on 'Ntoni because he was involved with the smugglers. Although the frightened girls tried to remonstrate with their brother, he refused to listen to their pleas. One night Don Michele knocked at Lia's door and told her that she must find her brother, for the police were planning to ambush the smugglers. His warning came too late for the sisters to act, and 'Ntoni was caught after he had stabbed Don Michele in a scuffle during the raid.

Padron 'Ntoni spent all his savings in an attempt to rescue his grandson. Then he was told a false version of the incident, that 'Ntoni had stabbed Don Michele because he had learned of an affair between the soldier and Lia. The old man was so horrified by this news that he suffered a stroke from which he never completely recovered. Lia left home immediately, without attempting to make known the true facts of the case, and young 'Ntoni was sent to the galleys for five years.

Gradually, under the direction of the youngest son, Alessio, the affairs of the family began to mend. Uncle Crucifix and Goosefoot finally got their money, and Alessio and his bride regained possession of the house by the medlar tree.

THE HOUSE IN PARIS

Type of work: Novel
Author: Elizabeth Bowen (1899-   )
Type of plot: Psychological realism
Time of plot: After World War I
Locale: France and England
First published: 1936

Principal characters:
> HENRIETTA MOUNTJOY, a brief visitor in Paris, eleven years of age
> LEOPOLD MOODY, another visitor, nine years of age
> MISS NAOMI FISHER, their hostess for a day
> MADAME FISHER, Naomi's invalid mother
> KAREN MICHAELIS, friend of Naomi, former pupil of her mother
> MAX EBHART, a young Parisian, attractive and intellectual

Critique:

Her facility in creating suspense would have stood Elizabeth Bowen in good stead had she chosen to write detective novels. *The House in Paris* gradually unravels a human secret which not only the readers but also the characters of the novel find both absorbing and oppressive. The author's method, however, is not to emphasize physical action but rather to unfold complex relationships of people, evolving slowly into a conclusion that is logical but necessarily incomplete. There are no pat endings to Miss Bowen's books, no perfect dovetailing of desire and fulfillment; as long as people live, she convincingly and calmly implies, there are questions that will be only partially answered, wishes that will be only partially granted. In this book she presents the situation that a child creates by merely existing: an inadvertent love and an inadvertent begetting that become a problem to several people. It is, in short, the problem of an illegitimate boy, and it has rarely been traced with more keenness and candor.

The Story:

Henrietta arrived at the Gare du Nord uncomfortably early in the morning. She

THE HOUSE IN PARIS by Elizabeth Bowen. By permission of the publishers, Alfred A. Knopf, Inc. Copyright, 1935, by Elizabeth D. C. Cameron.

had never been in Paris before; and she was not to be there long this time, for one day only, between two night trains. By a previous arrangement, the eleven-year-old girl was met at the station by Miss Naomi Fisher, an acquaintance of Henrietta's grandmother, who would look after her during her day in Paris.

Clutching her plush toy monkey while the taxi bumped through gray Paris streets, Henrietta drowsily absorbed Miss Fisher's nervous chatter. The flow of comments, however, was not entirely pointless: Henrietta was presently made to comprehend that her stopover would be affected by some rather unusual developments at Miss Fisher's house. For one thing, Miss Fisher's mother was ill, though today she was feeling better and Miss Fisher could still hope to take Henrietta out for a short sightseeing expedition after lunch. A more important complication seemed to be the presence of Leopold.

Leopold, Miss Fisher explained with obvious agitation, was an added responsibility which she had not foreseen when she agreed to meet Henrietta. He was nine years old, and he had come from Italy to see his mother, who was a very dear friend of Miss Fisher. Apparently, Henrietta gathered, he had never seen his mother before, a fact which struck the little girl as being quite odd and mysterious. Miss Fisher agreed that the circumstances were rather unusual, but she evaded a more direct explanation. Leopold, she was careful to bring out, was naturally excited and anxious; Henrietta might play with him, if she liked—but she must not question him about his mother.

After arriving at the house in Paris, Henrietta had breakfast and a nap on the sofa before she awoke to find Leopold standing across the salon and gazing at her curiously. The children made wary approaches to acquaintanceship and tentatively compared notes on their respective journeys. In spite of Miss Fisher's injunction, Henrietta managed to learn that Leopold lived at Spezia with his foster parents. Before she could find out more about him, she was summoned upstairs to meet the ill Madame Fisher. The latter seemed a queer person to Henrietta; her manner was ironic and penetrating, and, to her daughter's distress, she insisted on discussing Leopold's father. Once, Madame Fisher intimated, he had broken her daughter's heart. Now he was dead.

Left alone below, Leopold rummaged through Miss Fisher's purse in a vain search for information about his mother. After Henrietta rejoined him, the children had lunch and played aimlessly at cards. While they were thus occupied, the doorbell rang, and Miss Fisher was heard to go to the door. A few minutes later she entered the room, her face suffused with regret and pity. Leopold struggled manfully to affect nonchalance as she told him that, after all, his mother was not coming—she could not come.

Leopold had no way of knowing that his mother was Karen Michaelis, now married to Ray Forrestier. More than ten years earlier, her engagement to Ray had just been announced, and their friends rejoiced in what seemed an ideal match.

The marriage was to be delayed, however, until Ray's completion of a diplomatic mission in the East. Shortly after his departure from England, Karen visited her aunt in Ireland. Returning home, she found a pleasant surprise awaiting her; Naomi Fisher was spending a few days in London.

Karen and Naomi had been intimate ever since Karen, an English schoolgirl, had spent a year under the roof of Madame Fisher in Paris. There she had been housed, perfected in French, and given Madame's keen-eyed supervision, along with other English and American girls who were accepted into the establishment from time to time. There, too, she had first become conscious of Max Ebhart, a dark, taut, brilliant young man whose

1351

conversation and intellect Madame Fisher found stimulating. Rather unaccountably, Max had now become engaged to the unassuming Naomi and had accompanied her to England to aid in the settlement of an aunt's estate. Karen welcomed the opportunity to see Naomi, but she expressed reluctance to encounter Max, whose strong self-possession and penetrating mind had always affected her strangely.

Naomi's persistence prevailed, however, and on the final day of her stay in London she succeeded in getting Max and Karen together. While Naomi prepared tea inside the almost-emptied house of her dead aunt, Max and Karen sat outside on the lawn. Little was said, but both were conscious of the tension that their presence together always inspired. That night, as Karen said goodbye at the station, she looked at Max, and their eyes exchanged the mutual admission that they were in love.

A month later the Michaelis telephone rang. It was Max, in Paris, asking Karen to meet him in Boulogne the following Sunday. There they walked and talked, the thought of Naomi shadowing their conversation. Before they parted they arranged to meet again, at Hythe, the next Saturday. They spent the night together and decided that they must marry, in spite of their unwillingness to hurt Naomi. Max went back to Paris to impart the difficult news to his fiancée.

Karen never saw Max again; word of his suicide came in a telegram from Naomi. Weeks later Naomi herself crossed the channel to tell Karen how Max had slashed his wrists after a trying interview with Madame Fisher. When Karen confessed that she was going to bear Max's child, the two girls considered the plans she must make. Karen had already tried to break off her engagement with Ray Forrestier, but he had written that he would never give her up. Nevertheless, she intended to be gone when he returned to London; she would travel to Paris with Naomi and then go on to Germany for perhaps a year. She and Naomi would find a good home for the child. Meanwhile no one else—except possibly Karen's mother—should ever know.

These were the facts about his parents that Leopold had never learned. Now, his mother having failed him by not coming to get him at the house in Paris, he stood, for a moment, immovable, lapped in misery. His air of resolution and determined indifference soon gave way. Crossing to the mantelpiece and pressing himself against it, he burst into sobs. Henrietta tried to comfort him, but he ignored her. Recovering from his spasm of grief, he was sent upstairs to endure Madame Fisher's careful scrutiny. He found her surprisingly sympathetic. She told him something of his mother's marriage to Ray Forrestier, and he confided his determination not to return to his foster parents in Italy. Something in the old invalid's inner force seemed to stiffen and encourage him.

Downstairs the doorbell rang once more, and presently Miss Fisher came running swiftly up the steps. She directed Leopold to the salon where he found a tall, pleasant-looking Englishman. It was Ray Forrestier; overruling Karen's doubts, he had come to accept Leopold as his own son and to restore him to his mother.

THE HOUSE OF ATREUS

Type of work: Drama
Author: Aeschylus (525-456 B.C.)
Type of plot: Classical tragedy
Time of plot: After the fall of Troy
Locale: Argos
First presented: 458 B.C.

Principal characters:

AGAMEMNON, the king
CLYTEMNESTRA, his queen
CASSANDRA, a Trojan captive
AEGISTHUS, paramour of Clytemnestra
ORESTES, son of Agamemnon
ELECTRA, his sister

Critique:

In the archonship of Philocles, in 458 B.C., Aeschylus won first prize with his dramatic trilogy, *The House of Atreus.* This story of the doomed descendants of the cruel and bloody Atreus is one of the great tales of classic literature. Aeschylus, building his plays upon themes of doom and revenge, was deeply concerned with moral law in the Greek state. For this reason the moral issues of the plays are clear and steadfast, simple and devastating in implication, especially the working of conscience in the character of Orestes. *Agamemnon, The Libation-Bearers,* and *The Furies* are the individual titles which make up the trilogy.

The Story:

The house of Atreus was accursed because in the great palace at Argos the tyrant, Atreus, had killed the children of Thyestes and served their flesh to their father at a royal banquet. Agamemnon and Menelaus were the sons of Atreus. When Helen, wife of Menelaus, was carried off by Paris, Agamemnon was among the Greek heroes who went with his brother to battle the Trojans for her return. But on the way to Troy, while the fleet lay idle at Aulis, Agamemnon was prevailed upon to sacrifice his daughter, Iphigenia, to the gods. Hearing of this deed, Clytemnestra, his wife, vowed revenge. She gave her son, Orestes, into the care of the King of Phocis, and in the darkened palace nursed her consuming hate.

In her desire for vengeance she was joined by Aegisthus, surviving son of Thyestes, who had returned from his long exile. Hate brought the queen and Aegisthus together in a common cause; they became lovers as well as plotters in crime.

The ship of Menelaus having been delayed by a storm, Agamemnon returned alone from the Trojan wars. A watchman first saw the lights of his ship upon the sea and brought to his queen the news of the king's return. Leaving his men quartered in the town, Agamemnon drove to the palace in his chariot, beside him Cassandra, captive daughter of the king of Troy and an augeress of all misfortunes to come, who had fallen to Agamemnon in the division of the spoils. She had already warned the king that some evil was to befall him.

Agamemnon, however, had no suspicions of his homecoming, as Clytemnestra came to greet him at the palace doorway, her armed retainers about her, magnificent carpets unrolled for the feet of the conqueror of Troy. Agamemnon chided his queen for the lavishness of her reception and entered the palace to refresh himself after his long journey. He asked Clytemnestra to receive Cassandra and to treat his captive kindly.

After Agamemnon had retired, Clytemnestra returned and ordered Cassandra, who had refused to leave the chariot, to enter the palace. When Cassandra persisted in remaining where she was, the queen declared she would not demean herself by bandying words with a common slave and a madwoman. She re-entered the palace. Cassandra lifted her face toward the sky and called upon Apollo to tell her why she had been brought to this cursed house. She informed the spectators in front of the palace that Clytemnestra would murder Agamemnon. She lamented the fall of Troy, recalled the butchery of Thyestes' children, and the doom that hung over the sons of Atreus, and foretold again the murder of Agamemnon by his queen. As she entered the palace, those outside heard the death cry of Agamemnon within.

A moment later Clytemnestra appeared in the doorway, the bloody sword of Aegisthus in her hand. Behind her lay the body of the king, entangled in the rich carpets. Clytemnestra defended herself before the citizens, saying she had killed the king for the murder of Iphigenia, and had also killed Cassandra, with whom Agamemnon had shamed her honor. Her deed, she told the citizens defiantly, had ended the bloody lust of the house of Atreus.

Then she presented Aegisthus, son of Thyestes, who asserted that his vengeance was just and that he intended to rule in the palace of Agamemnon. Reproaches were hurled at the guilty pair. There were cries that Orestes would avenge his father's murder. Aegisthus and Clytemnestra, in a fury of guilty horror, roared out their self-justification for the crime and defied the gods themselves to end their seizure of power.

Orestes, grown to manhood, returned from the land of Phocis, to discover that his mother and Aegisthus had murdered his father. He mourned his father's death and asked the king of the gods to give him ability to take vengeance upon the guilty pair. Electra, daughter of Agamemnon, also mourned and cursed the murderers. Encountering her brother, she did not at first recognize him, for he appeared in the disguise of a messenger who brought word of the death of Orestes. They met at their father's tomb, where he made himself known to his sister. There he begged his father's spirit to give him strength in his undertaking. Electra assured him nothing but evil could befall any of the descendants of Atreus and welcomed the quick fulfillment of approaching doom.

Learning that Clytemnestra had once dreamed of suckling a snake which drew blood from her breast, Orestes saw in this dream the image of himself and the deed he intended to commit. He went to the palace in disguise and killed Aegisthus. Then he confronted Clytemnestra, his sword dripping with the blood of his mother's lover, and struck her down.

Orestes displayed the two bodies to the people and announced to Apollo that he had done the deed required of him. But he realized that he must suffer for his terrible crime. He began to go mad as Furies, sent by his mother's dead spirit, pursued him.

The Furies drove Orestes from land to land. Finally he took refuge in a temple, but the Pythian priestess claimed the temple was profaned by the presence of the horrible Furies, who lay asleep near Orestes. Then Apollo appeared to tell Orestes that he had put the Furies to sleep so the haunted man could get some rest. He advised Orestes to visit the temple of Pallas Athena and there gain full absolution for his crime.

While Orestes listened, the ghost of Clytemnestra spitefully aroused the Furies and commanded them to torture Orestes again. When Apollo ordered the Furies to leave, the creatures accused him of blame for the murder of Clytemnestra and Aegisthus and the punishment of Orestes. The god confessed he had demanded the death of Agamemnon's murderers. He was told that by his demands he had caused an even greater crime, matricide. Apollo said Athena should decide the justice of the case.

In Athens, in the temple of the goddess, Orestes begged Athena to help him. Replying the case was too grave for her to decide alone, she called upon the judges to help her reach a wise decision. There were some who believed the ancient laws would be weakened if evidence were presented, and they claimed Orestes deserved his terrible punishment.

When Orestes asked why Clytemnestra had not been persecuted for the murder of Agamemnon, he was told her crime had not been the murder of a blood relative, as his was. Apollo was another witness at the trial. He claimed the mother was not the true parent, that the father, who planted the seed in the mother's womb, was the real parent, as shown in the tracing of descent through the male line. Therefore, Orestes was not guilty of the murder of a true member of his blood family.

The judges decided in favor of Orestes.

There were many, however, who in an angry rage cursed and condemned the land where such a judgment might prevail. They cried woe upon the younger gods and all those who tried to wrest ancient rights from the hands of established tradition. But Athena upheld the judgment of the court and Orestes was freed from the anger of the Furies.

A HOUSE OF GENTLEFOLK

Type of work: Novel
Author: Ivan Turgenev (1818-1883)
Type of plot: Psychological realism
Time of plot: Nineteenth century
Locale: Russia
First published: 1858

Principal characters:
MARYA DMITRIEVNA, a widow
LAVRETZKY, her cousin
LIZA, her daughter
VARVARA, Lavretzky's wife
PANSHIN, an official

Critique:

A House of Gentlefolk, sometimes translated as *A Nobleman's Nest,* belongs with the simple, powerful group of Turgenev's romances. Here are two characters who stand as symbols of Russia: Lavretzky and Liza. Although their lot is a sad one, they are presented in heroic mold. Indeed, the author in this work exhibits a greater degree of Slavophilism than is usually found in his novels. In this work Turgenev shows little patience with the detractors of Russia, those who exalt the worth of French and German culture. Even the glittering Panshin must admit the worthiness of Lavretzky's aim to cultivate the soil.

The Story:

Marya, since the death of her husband, had become a social leader in her small provincial town. Her daughter Liza spoke French quite well and played the piano. Her other children had the best tutors available. She delighted to receive guests, especially Panshin, who had an important position in Moscow. Her evening gather-

ings were always entertaining when Panshin was there to quote his own poetry.

It was rumored that Lavretzky was returning to the district. Although he was a cousin of the house, Marya scarcely knew how to treat him, for Lavretzky had made an unfortunate marriage. He was separated from his pretty wife, who was reputed to be fast and flighty.

But Lavretzky's visit created no difficulties. He was a rather silent, affable man who noticed Liza with interest. Liza was a beautiful, religious-minded girl of nineteen. It was very evident that the brilliant Panshin was courting her with the full approval of her mother. On the evening of his visit Lavretzky was not impressed with Panshin's rendition of his musical romance, but the ladies were ecstatic.

The following day Lavretzky went on to his small country estate. The place was run-down because it had been uninhabited since his sister's death. Lavretzky, content to sink into a quiet country life, ordered the gardens cleaned up, moved in some newer furniture, and began to take an interest in the crops. He seemed suspended in a real Russian atmosphere close to the land. The new life was particularly pleasing after his residence in France and the painful separation from his wife.

Lavretzky had had a different upbringing. His father, disappointed by his failure to inherit an aunt's fortune, had decided to make his son a strong man, even a spartan. At twelve Lavretzky was dressed in Highland kilts and trained in gymnastics and horsemanship. He ate only one meal a day and took cold showers at four in the morning. Along with the physical culture intended to produce a natural man according to Rousseau's doctrines, the father filled his son full of Voltaire's philosophy.

The father died horribly after enduring pain for two years. During this period he lost all his bravery and atheistic independence; at the end he was a sniveling wreck. His death was a release to Lavretzky, who immediately enrolled, at the age of twenty-three, in a university in Moscow.

At the opera one night he met the beautiful Varvara, daughter of a retired general who lived mostly by his wits. At first the parents had little use for Lavretzky, for they thought him only an unimportant student. When they learned, however, that he came of good family and was a landed proprietor, they favored an early marriage. Since Varvara wanted to travel, Lavretzky wound up his affairs and installed his new father-in-law as overseer of his properties.

In Paris, Varvara began a dizzy social whirl. Her adoring husband, content merely to be at her side, let her indulge her whims freely. She soon had a reputation as a brilliant hostess, but her guests thought her husband a nonentity. Lavretzky had no suspicion that his wife was anything but a devoted wife and mother to their daughter until a letter came by accident into his hands. From it he learned of her lover and their sordid, furtive meetings in obscure apartments. Lavretzky left home immediately and took

up separate residence. When he wrote to Varvara, telling her of the reason for the separation, she did not deny her guilt, but only asked for consideration. Settling an income on his wife, Lavretzky returned to Russia.

After spending some time on his estate, Lavretzky began to ride into town occasionally to call on Marya and her family. After he became better acquainted with Liza, the young girl scolded him for being so hard-hearted toward his wife. According to her religious beliefs, Lavretzky should have pardoned Varvara for her sins and gone on with the marriage. Lavretzky, in turn, warned Liza that Panshin was not the man for her. The gay young official was a diplomat, all surface and no substance. Lavretzky had an ally in Marfa, the old aunt who also saw through Panshin's fine manners and clever speeches. When Panshin proposed to Liza by letter, she postponed making a decision.

Liza's music teacher was an old, broken German named Lemm. Although Lavretsky had little ear for music, he strongly appreciated Lemm's talent. He invited the old man to his farm. During the visit the two men found much in common. Lavretsky was saddened to see that the old music teacher was hopelessly in love with Liza.

One night, in Marya's drawing-room, Panshin was brilliantly holding forth on the inadequacies of Russia. The country was much behind the rest of Europe, he asserted, in agriculture and politics. The English were superior in manufacture and merchandising, the French in social life and the arts, the Germans in philosophy and science. His views were the familiar theme of the aristocratic detractors of Russia. The usually silent Lavretzky finally took issue with Panshin and skillfully demolished his every argument. Liza listened with approval.

In a French paper Lavretzky came upon a brief notice in the society section; his wife was dead. For a while he could not think clearly, but as the import of the news came home to him he realized that he was in love with Liza. Riding into town, he gave the paper quietly to Liza. As soon as he could be alone with her, he declared his love. The young girl received his declaration soberly, almost seeming to regard their love as a punishment. Although troubled at first by her attitude, Lavretzky soon achieved a happiness he had never expected to find.

That happiness, however, was short-lived. His servant announced one day that Varvara had returned with their daughter. His wife told him she had been very ill and had not bothered to correct the rumor of her death. Now she asked only to be allowed to live somewhere near him. Suspecting that her meekness was only assumed, Lavretzky arranged for her to live on a distant estate, far from his own house, and went to break the news to Liza.

Liza was controlled. She might almost have awaited the punishment, for she knew that sorrow was the lot of all Russians. Varvara brazenly called on Marya and completely captivated her with her beauty, her French manners, and her accomplished playing and singing. Liza met Lavretzky's wife with grave composure.

For a time Varvara complied with her promise to stay isolated on the distant estate, where she frequently entertained Panshin. In the winter, when she moved to Moscow, Panshin was her devoted follower. At last she went back to Paris.

Liza entered a convent. Lavretzky saw her once from a distance as she scurried timidly to a prayer service. Taking what strength he could from the soil, he remained on his farm. When he was forty-five, he visited the house where Liza had lived. Marya and all the older people of the household had died. He felt ill at ease among the younger, laughing generation.

THE HOUSE OF MIRTH

Type of work: Novel
Author: Edith Wharton (1862-1937)
Type of plot: Social criticism
Time of plot: Early twentieth century
Locale: New York
First published: 1905

Principal characters:
>   LILY BART, a social schemer
>   MR. SELDEN, her friend
>   MR. ROSEDALE, a financier
>   PERCY GRYCE, an eligible young man
>   GUS TRENOR, a wealthy socialite
>   JUDY TRENOR, his wife
>   BERTHA DORSET, who hated Lily
>   GEORGE DORSET, Bertha's husband

Critique:

The House of Mirth is still popular among readers who enjoy stories about the social life of the early part of this century. The theme of the book is a criticism of the emptiness and folly of life among the idle rich. Lily Bart sacrificed herself, her principles, her chance for real love, and even her life, in a vain attempt to find a life of ease for herself. The conflict arose when her better nature exerted itself. In that respect she was superior to those who scorned her, for most of them had no redeeming qualities of character. The story is easily read, for it is written with Edith Wharton's usual skill.

The Story:

Selden enjoyed watching Lily Bart put a new plan into operation. She was a very beautiful and clever young lady, and no matter how impromptu any action of hers appeared, Selden knew that she never moved without a definitely worked out plan.

Lily had almost no money of her own; her beauty and her good family background were her only assets. Her father had died soon after a reversal of his financial affairs, and her mother had drilled into her the idea that a wealthy marriage was her only salvation. After her mother's death, Lily was taken in by her aunt, Mrs. Peniston. Mrs. Peniston supplied her with fashionable clothes and a good home, but Lily needed jewels, gowns, and cash to play bridge if she were to move in a social circle filled by wealthy and eligible men.

Mr. Rosedale, a Jewish financier, would gladly have married Lily and provided her with a huge fortune, for he wanted to be accepted into the society in which Lily moved. But Lily thought that she still had other prospects less repulsive to her, the most likely one being Percy Gryce, who lived protected from scheming women by his watchful widowed mother.

Lily used her knowledge of his quiet life to her advantage. Selden, Lily, and Gryce were all house guests at the home of Gus and Judy Trenor, and the opportunity was a perfect one for Lily, who assumed the part of a shy, demure young girl. But when Gryce was ready to propose, she let the chance slip away from her, for Lily really hated the kind of person she had become. In addition, although Selden was poor and offered her no escape from her own poverty, she was attracted to him because only he really understood her.

Gus Trenor offered to invest some of Lily's small income, and over a period of time he returned to her more than eight thousand dollars, which he assured her was profit on the transaction. With that amount she was able to pay most of her creditors and reopen her charge accounts. Gus seemed to think, however, that his wise investment on her account should make them better friends than Lily felt was desirable.

In the meantime, Lily unexpectedly got possession of some letters which Bertha Dorset had written to Selden. Bertha had once loved Selden, but George Dorset's fortune was great and she had left Selden for George. She continued to write to Selden after her marriage.

When Gus Trenor began to get more insistent in his demands for Lily's companionship, she became really worried. She knew that people were talking about her a great deal and that her position in society was precarious. She turned to Selden for advice. He told her that he loved her for what she could be, but that he could give her nothing now. He had no money, and he would not even offer her his love because he could not love her as she was, a scheming, ruthless fortune-hunter.

One night Lily received a message that Judy Trenor wanted her to call. When she arrived at the Trenor home, Lily found Gus there alone. He had sent the message. Gus told her then that the money had not been profit on her investment, but a gift from him. When he intimated that she had always known the money was from him personally, Lily was terrified, but at last she managed to get out of the house. She knew then that there was only one thing for her to do. She must accept Rosedale's offer of marriage. But before she wrote to Rosedale accepting his offer, the Dorsets invited her to take a Mediterranean cruise on their yacht. The moment of decision was postponed for a time.

Selden also left New York. Unknown to her, he had seen Lily leave the Trenor house on the night Gus had tricked her into thinking Judy wanted her to call. Selden had always refused to believe the unsavory stories circulating about

Lily, but the evidence of his own eyes, he thought, was too plain to be ignored. When he met Lily abroad, he treated her with courteous disinterest.

Lily returned to New York. Her aunt, Mrs. Peniston, had died, leaving Lily ten thousand dollars. Lily planned to repay Gus Trenor with her inheritance, and she found intolerable the delay in settling her aunt's estate. Meanwhile Bertha Dorset's insinuations about Lily's conduct abroad, coupled with the talk about Lily and Gus Trenor, finished Lily's reputation. She took various positions, until at last she was reduced to working in the factory of a milliner. She had first offered to accept Rosedale's former proposal of marriage, but she was no longer useful to Rosedale since her fall from favor, and he refused to marry her. He knew that Lily had the letters Bertha had written Selden, and he also knew that George Dorset no longer loved his wife and would gladly marry Lily. It seemed to Rosedale that Lily had only two alternatives, either to take George Dorset away from Bertha or to go to Bertha with the letters and force her to receive Lily once more.

At first Lily's feeling for Selden made her shrink from doing anything that would harm him. Then she lost her position. Without money to buy food or to pay for her room in a dingy boarding-house, she reluctantly took the letters and started to the Dorset home. On the way she stopped to see Selden. When he again told her that he loved her, or rather that he would love her if she would only give up her greed for wealth and position, she gave up her plan and, unseen by him, dropped the letters into the fireplace. Then she thanked him for the kindness he, and he alone, had given her, and walked out into the night.

When she returned to her room, she found the check for the ten thousand dollars of her inheritance. She sat down at once and wrote a check to Gus Trenor for the amount she owed him and put it in an envelope. In another envelope she placed the ten thousand dollar check and addressed the envelope to her bank. She put the two envelopes side by side on her desk before she lay down to sleep.

But sleep would not come. At last she took from her bureau a bottle of chloral, which she had bought for those nights when she could not sleep. She poured the contents of the bottle into a glass and drank the whole. Then she lay down again upon her bed.

The next morning, feeling a sudden need to see Lily at once, Selden went early to her rooming-house. There he found a doctor already in attendance and Lily dead from an overdose of chloral. On her desk he saw the two envelopes. The stub of the open checkbook beside them told the whole story of Lily's last effort to get her accounts straight before she died. He knew then that his love for her had been justified, but the words he spoke as he knelt by her bed came too late.

THE HOUSE OF THE SEVEN GABLES

Type of work: Novel
Author: Nathaniel Hawthorne (1804-1864)
Type of plot: Psychological romance
Time of plot: 1850
Locale: Salem, Massachusetts
First published: 1851

Principal characters:
MISS HEPZIBAH PYNCHEON, a spinster
CLIFFORD PYNCHEON, her brother
JUDGE JAFFREY PYNCHEON, a kinsman

PHOEBE PYNCHEON, a distant cousin
MR. HOLGRAVE, Miss Hepzibah's lodger

Critique:

The theme of Hawthorne's justly famous novel is obviously that the sins of the fathers are passed on to the children in succeeding generations. In the ingenious plot of this novel the reader watches the gradual expiation of old Matthew Maule's curse on the Pyncheon family, as youth in the guise of Phoebe and Holgrave enters the old house. Evident in the finely-written pages of *The House of the Seven Gables* is the author's lively interest in New England history, and his increasing doubts about a moribund New England that looked backward to past times.

The Story:

The House of the Seven Gables was a colonial house built in the English style of half-timber and half-plaster. It stood on Pyncheon Street in quiet Salem. The house had been built by Colonel Pyncheon, who had wrested the desirable site from Matthew Maule, a poor man executed as a wizard. Because Colonel Pyncheon was responsible and because he was taking the doomed man's land, Maule at the moment of his execution declared that God would give the Pyncheons blood to drink. But in spite of this grim prophecy the colonel had his house, and its builder was Thomas Maule, son of the old wizard.

Colonel Pyncheon, dying in his great oak chair just after the house had been completed, choked with blood so that his shirt front was stained scarlet. Although doctors explained the cause of his death as apoplexy, the townsfolk had not forgotten old Maule's prophecy. The time of the colonel's death was inauspicious. It was said he had just completed a treaty by which he had bought huge tracts of land from the Indians, but this deed had not been confirmed by the general court and was never discovered by any of his heirs. Rumor also had it that a man was seen leaving the house about the time Colonel Pyncheon died.

More recently another startling event had occurred at the House of the Seven Gables. Jaffrey Pyncheon, a bachelor, had been found dead in the colonel's great oaken armchair, and his nephew, Clifford Pyncheon, had been sentenced to imprisonment after being found guilty of the murder of his uncle.

These events were in the unhappy past, however, and in 1850, the House of the Seven Gables was the home of Miss Hepzibah Pyncheon, an elderly, single woman, who let one wing of the old house to a young man of radical tendencies, a maker of daguerreotypes, whose name was Mr. Holgrave.

Miss Hepzibah was about to open a shop in one of the rooms of her house. Her brother Clifford was coming home from the state prison after thirty years, and she had to earn money in some way to support him. But on the first day of her venture as a storekeeper Miss Hepzibah proved to be a failure. The situation was saved, however, by the arrival of young Phoebe Pyncheon from the country. Soon she was operating the shop at a profit.

Clifford arrived from the prison a broken man of childish, querulous ways. Once he tried to throw himself from a big arched window which afforded him almost his only contact with the outside world. He was fond of Phoebe, but Miss Hepzibah irritated him with her sullen scowling. For acquaintances Clifford had Uncle Venner, a handy man who did odd jobs for the neighborhood, and the tenant of the house, Mr. Holgrave, the daguerreotypist.

The only other relative living in town was the highly-respected Judge Pyncheon, another nephew of the old Jaffrey Pyncheon, for whose murder Clifford had spent thirty years in prison. He was, in fact, the heir of the murdered man and he had been somehow involved with Clifford's arrest and imprisonment. For these reasons Clifford refused to see him when the judge offered to give Clifford and Hepzibah a home at his countryseat.

Meanwhile, Phoebe had become friendly with Mr. Holgrave. In turn, he thought that she brought light and hope into the gloomy old house, and he missed her greatly when she returned to her home in the country. Her visit was to be a brief one, however, for she had gone only to make some preparations before coming to live permanently with Miss Hepzibah and Clifford.

Before Phoebe returned from the country, Judge Pyncheon visited the House of the Seven Gables and, over Miss Hepzibah's protest, insisted on seeing Clifford, who, he said, knew a family secret which meant great wealth for the judge. When at last she went out of the room to summon her brother, Judge Pyncheon sat down in the old chair by the fireplace, over which hung the portrait of the Colonel Pyncheon who had built the house. As the judge sat in the old chair, his ticking watch in his hand, an unusually strong family likeness could be noted between the stern judge and his Puritan ancestor in the portrait. Unable to find Clifford to deliver the judge's message, Miss Hepzibah returned. As she approached the door, Clifford appeared from within, laughing and pointing to the chair where the judge sat dead of apoplexy under the portrait of the old colonel. His shirt front was stained with blood. The wizard's curse had been fulfilled once more: God had given him blood to drink.

The two helpless old people were so distressed by the sight of the dead man that they crept away from the house without notifying anyone and departed on the train. The dead body of the judge remained seated in the chair.

It was some time before the body was discovered by Holgrave. When Phoebe returned to the house, he admitted her.

He had not yet summoned the police because he wished to protect the old couple as long as possible. While he and Phoebe were alone in the house, Holgrave declared his love for her. They were interrupted by the return of Miss Hepzibah and the now calm Clifford. They had decided that to run away would not solve their problem.

The police attributed the judge's death to natural causes, and Clifford, Miss Hepzibah, and Phoebe became the heirs to his great fortune. It now seemed certain that Jaffrey Pyncheon had also died of natural causes, not by Clifford's hand, and that the judge had so arranged the evidence as to make Clifford appear a murderer.

In a short time all the occupants of the House of the Seven Gables were ready to move to the judge's country estate which they had inherited. They gathered for the last time in the old room under the dingy portrait of Colonel Pyncheon. Clifford said he had a vague memory of something mysterious connected with the picture. Holgrave offered to explain the mystery and pressed a secret spring near the picture. When he did so, the portrait fell to the floor, disclosing a recess in the wall. From this niche Holgrave drew out the ancient Indian deed to the lands which the Pyncheons had claimed. Clifford then remembered he had once found the secret spring. It was this secret which Judge Pyncheon had hoped to learn from Clifford.

Phoebe asked how Holgrave happened to know these facts. The young man explained his name was not Holgrave, but Maule. He was, he said, a descendant of the wizard, Matthew Maule, and of Thomas Maule who built the House of the Seven Gables. The knowledge of the hidden Indian deed had been handed down to the descendants of Thomas Maule, who built the compartment behind the portrait and secreted the deed there after the colonel's death. Holgrave was the last of the Maules and

Phoebe, the last of the Pyncheons, would bear his name. Matthew Maule's curse had been expiated.

THE HOUSE WITH THE GREEN SHUTTERS

Type of work: Novel
Author: George Douglas (George Douglas Brown, 1869-1902)
Type of plot: Regional realism
Time of plot: Late nineteenth century
Locale: Rural Scotland
First published: 1901

Principal characters:
JOHN GOURLAY, a wealthy merchant
YOUNG JOHN, his son
MRS. GOURLAY, his slovenly wife
JAMES WILSON, Gourlay's competitor

Critique:

Disgusted with the quaint and sentimental novels in which writers of the kailyard school portrayed his native Scotland, George Douglas Brown attempted to present in his work a more realistic picture of Scottish life in the late nineteenth century. *The House With the Green Shutters* is a forceful book, one alive with characters that grip the reader in their problems. Brown's purpose was to show the true Scottish peasant as he saw him.

The Story:

John Gourlay was proud of his twelve wagons and his many business successes, but mostly he was proud of his House with the Green Shutters. Into it he had put all the frustration he felt for his lack of friends, his slovenly wife, his weakling son. Gourlay's was a pride of insolence. He would have more than his neighbors, his betters; he would make them acknowledge him as their superior. Gourlay had not found a golden touch. He had simply worked hard, turning every shilling into pounds by any method open to him. In the process he became mean, stingy, boastful, and evil.

His son John had inherited all of his characteristics except his courage. As a schoolboy, constantly ridiculed by his mates, he took refuge in boasting of his father's wealth and power. He was no good with his fists, and his only revenge after a sound drubbing was to tell his father. Gourlay hated his son almost as much as he hated everyone else, but he could not let his son be laughed at by the sons of his enemies. Thus John was avenged by the father who despised him.

Gourlay also hated his wife. She who had once been a laughing, pretty lass had become a slattern and a bore whose son was her only reason for living. On him she lavished all the love denied her by her husband. There was one daughter. She was ignored by her mother and favored by her father, each parent taking the opposite point of view from the other.

The whole village bowed to Gourlay, even while they prayed that he would one day meet his match. They were not to be disappointed. One James Wilson returned to the village with money he had earned during his fifteen years' absence. One of the first to meet Wilson was Gourlay. When Wilson had left years before, Gourlay had been then as now the big man in the town. Had Gourlay said a kind word or given one bit of praise for the success of his former acquaintance, Wilson would have been flattered and would have become his friend. But Gourlay was not such a man. He immediately ridiculed Wilson and laughed at the idea that he could be a success at anything. Wilson developed a hatred that was to bring the insolent Gourlay to ruin.

Wilson used his money to set up a general store, which he stocked with many items the villagers had formerly had to send away for and pay Gourlay to haul for them. He also delivered items to neighboring towns and farms. Then he started a regular carting service, cutting prices to get business from Gourlay, just as Gourlay had done to his competitors. The townspeople were glad to patronize Wilson in order to get back at Gourlay for his years of dominance and insolence. Indeed, they even gave Wilson new suggestions for expanding his trade. Gourlay's downfall started slowly, but soon it became a landslide. The peasants began to stand up to the old man, even to laugh openly at him. Gourlay's vows of vengeance were empty talk.

Gourlay turned to his son as his only hope. When Wilson's son went away to high school, John was sent, even though he had no head for books and no ambition. John played truant frequently and was a braggart and a coward as before, but his father still had power enough to keep him in school and in money and in some way the boy was graduated. Wilson sent his son to the university. Gourlay decided that John must go too. Never was a boy more miserable, for he knew he was not suited for advanced study. Gourlay hoped to make the lad a minister; his hope was to recoup some respect, if not money, for the family.

At the university John found little stimulation for his sluggish mind. He had one high spot in his career, indeed in his whole life, when he won a prize for an essay. Since that was the first honor he ever won, he swaggered and boasted about it for months. Because of the prize, also, he won his first and only word of praise from his father. In his second term John fell to his own level and became a drunken sot. Books were too much for him, and people scorned him. The bottle was his only friend.

While John was stumbling through his second term at the university, Gourlay's fortunes reached their lowest ebb. The House with the Green Shutters was mortgaged heavily, all Gourlay's other assets having been lost in wild speculations to recoup his fortunes. But Gourlay still pinned his hopes on the son he had always hated. John would save the family name, the lost fortune, the House. Thus when Gourlay learned that John had been expelled for drunkenness and insubordination, and heard that the whole town knew of the disgrace through a letter of young Wilson to his father, the news was too much for the old man. He returned to the House with the Green Shutters like a madman, as indeed he was. The first sight that greeted him was John, who had sneaked into town in the darkness. Like a cat toying with a mouse, Gourlay tortured his son. He pretended to consider him a great man, a hero. He peered at him from all angles, waited on him with strong whiskey, called him a fine son, a credit to the family. Cowardly John rushed from the house in terror, followed by the screams of his mother and sister and the howls of his father. Then his false courage returned, and he went back into the house after fortifying himself with more whiskey. Picking up a large poker which had been one of his father's prideful purchases, John swung at his father and crushed in his head.

The mother and sister convinced the authorities that Gourlay, falling from a ladder and striking his head, had died accidentally. But John was lost. For days he was haunted by red eyes glaring at him out of space, by unknown things coming to get him. His mother and sister, dependent upon him for their livelihood, tried to get him out of his madness, but nothing soothed him except whiskey, and that only briefly. One day he asked his mother for money, bought his last bottle of whiskey and a vial of poison, and ended his wretched existence.

Completely alone now, aware that even the house must go to the creditors, dying themselves of cancer and consumption, the mother and daughter divided the rest of the poison and joined Gourlay and John in death. The pride, the lust, the greed were gone. The House with the Green Shutters had claimed them all.

HOW GREEN WAS MY VALLEY

Type of work: Novel
Author: Richard Llewellyn (Richard D. V. Llewellyn Lloyd, 1907-   )
Type of plot: Domestic realism
Time of plot Nineteenth century
Locale: Wales
First published: 1940

Principal characters:
>   GWILYM MORGAN, a Welsh miner
>   BETH MORGAN, his wife
>   HUW MORGAN, their son and the narrator
>   IVOR,
>   DAVY,
>   OWEN,
>   IANTO, and
>   GWILYM, other sons
>   ANGHARAD, their daughter
>   BRONWEN, Ivor's wife
>   MARGED, Gwilym's wife
>   IESTYN EVANS, Angharad's husband

Critique:

How Green Was My Valley is a story of the life of a Welsh boy, seen through the eyes of an old man who has only memory to sustain him. The novel was published during the war years, and perhaps the strife that was everywhere then accounted somewhat for its great popularity. There was trouble in the lives of the people we meet in this story, but the kindness of the main characters was so great that even death seemed gentle and not to be feared. The novel is simply and beautifully told.

The Story:

How beautiful and peaceful the valley looked to Huw Morgan when he was ready to leave it! All the memories of a long lifetime came back to him.

Huw's earliest memories were of his father and brothers when they came home from the mines on Saturday night There was trouble brewing at the mines. The men talked of unions and organizing, and the owners were angry.

Huw loved his family very much, and when he learned that his brother Ivor was to marry he was sorry to lose his brother. But from the first moment Huw saw Ivor's Bronwen, he loved her, and that love for his sister-in-law stayed with him all of his life.

Another brother, Ianto, married soon afterward. His wife was a girl from the village, where Ianto went to live.

Trouble came at last to the mines.

The men in the pits went on strike for twenty-two weeks, but the owners were the stronger because they were not watching their families starve. The men finally went back to work for less money than before. After that first strike, the father would never again join the men trying to form a union, for he could not bring himself to lead men out of work. Davy and the other boys, however, were more bitter than ever. When the father ordered his sons never to attend another meeting, Davey, Owen, and Gwilym left home and took a room in a lodging-house. Their mother cried all night, but the father would not change his mind. It was a miserable time for six-year-old Huw. When his sister Angharad found that the three boys were living in filth, she went to the rooming-house to take care of them. Then the father relented and allowed the boys to come home, but he said that they would be lodgers only, not sons.

After the father became superintendent at the mine, Huw heard some of the miners say that his father and Ivor, who agreed with him, might be beaten or even killed by some of the more violent miners. Frightened, he told his mother what he had heard. One winter night she and Huw went to the mountain where the miners were meeting, and she told the men there that she would kill anyone who harmed her husband. On the way home his mother slipped on the bank of a little river. Huw, standing in the icy water, supported his mother on the bank until help came. After that he knew nothing until he awoke in his bed and his father told him that he had saved his mother's life and the life of his new baby sister. Huw had fever in his legs for almost five years and never left his bed during that time.

During his sickness Bronwen nursed him and his brothers read to him until he was far beyond his years in learning. While he was in bed, he first met the new minister, Mr. Gruffydd, who was to become his best friend.

Huw's brother Owen fell in love with Marged Evans. When Marged's father found Owen kissing Marged, he said terrible things to the boy, so that Owen would have nothing more to do with Marged. Gwilym married her, for he had always loved her.

Ianto's wife died and he came home to live. By this time Huw, well once more, went to the National School, over the mountain. He had many fights before he was accepted by the other boys.

Angharad and Iestyn Evans, the son of the mine owner, began to keep company, but Angharad did not seem to be happy. It was some time before Huw learned that Angharad loved Mr. Gruffydd but that he could not take a wife because he was poor. Huw began to think love caused heartache instead of happiness.

One day he took a basket of food to Gwilym's house, and there he found Marged completely mad. Thinking he was Owen, she told him she could not live without him. Huw ran to find Gwilym. Before he returned with his brother, Marged had thrown herself into the fire and burned to death. Afterward Gwilym and Owen went away together, no one knew where.

Iestyn Evans' father died, and soon after Iestyn and Angharad were married in London. Davy was married before they came home, and for the wedding Huw had his first long trousers. Bronwen told him that he was now a man.

Shortly afterward Huw was put out of school for giving the teacher a beating because he had made a small child wear around her neck a sign announcing that she was Welsh. Huw went to work in the pits with his brothers. Owen and Gwilym had returned home and all the boys lived again in the valley. But soon Owen had a telegram from London about an engine he was trying to perfect, and he and Gwilym left again. From London they went to America. Soon afterward Davy went to London on mine union business.

Angharad came home from London alone, Iestyn having gone to Cape Town on business. Soon gossip started because Mr. Gruffydd and Angharad often took carriage rides together. Finally Angharad left the valley and went to Cape Town. Mr. Gruffydd also left the valley.

When Ivor was killed in a cave-in at the mine, Huw's mother sent him to live with Bronwen in her loneliness. Discharged from the mines for striking one of the workmen who made a slurring remark about Angharad and Mr. Gruffydd, Huw became a carpenter. Ianto had already left the pits and only his father and Davy were left in the mines. Davy decided to go to New Zealand. Ianto went to Germany, where he thought he could do better in his trade. The family was now scattered.

One day the workers flooded the mines and Huw's father was crushed by a cave-in. Huw crawled to his father and stayed with him until he died. Huw's heart was as empty as his mother's when he told her the terrible news.

Everyone of whom Huw had thought during this reverie was now dead. He walked slowly away from his valley and from his memories.

HOWARDS END

Type of work: Novel
Author: E. M. Forster (1879-   )
Type of plot: Domestic realism
Time of plot: Early twentieth century
Locale: England
First published: 1910

Principal characters:
    HENRY WILCOX, a British businessman
    RUTH WILCOX, his first wife
    CHARLES WILCOX, his older son
    PAUL WILCOX, his younger son
    MARGARET SCHLEGEL, Henry Wilcox's second wife
    HELEN SCHLEGEL, Margaret's sister
    THEOBALD SCHLEGEL, Margaret's brother
    LEONARD BAST, a poor young man
    JACKY BAST, Leonard's wife

Critique:

E. M. Forster is not a prolific author. He is well known to students of fiction, however, as a thorough critic, as well as an important novelist in his own right, and his *Aspects of the Novel* is a major contribution to study in that field. Prior to his best work of fiction, *A Passage to India, Howards End* was ranked as his most mature novel. Particularly important in Forster's fiction are his subtle and complete characterization, his deft use of irony, the careful plotting of action, the eternal contrast between illusion and reality. *Howards End* is second only to *A Passage to India* in illustrating these characteristics.

The Story:

The Wilcox family met Margaret Schlegel and her sister Helen while both families were vacationing in Germany. Neither group expected the chance acquaintance to amount to anything more, but later, after all had returned to England, Helen Schlegel was invited to visit the Wilcox family at Howards End, their country home near London. While there, Helen fell in love with Paul Wilcox. Both families disapproved of the match, and after hard words on both sides it was broken off.

A few months later the Wilcoxes rented a town flat across the street from the Schlegel home. Both young people were out of the country. Mrs. Wilcox and Margaret Schlegel met and became friends.

Also acquainted with the Schlegels was a young man named Leonard Bast, a seedy fellow whose umbrella had been accidentally taken by Helen at a concert. The young man had interested the girls and their brother by his conversation when he had called to reclaim his umbrella. They did not know that he had an exceedingly frowsy wife, a woman some years older than he who had trapped him into a distasteful marriage.

Some months after the acquaintance between Mrs. Wilcox and Margaret Schlegel had ripened into friendship, Mrs. Wilcox became ill and died. Much to her husband's and sons' surprise, she left a note, in addition to her will, leaving Howards End to Margaret. In their anger at the prospect of letting the house go out of the family, the Wilcoxes disregarded the note, since it was not a part of the official will.

Margaret Schlegel, knowing nothing of the bequest, was really glad that the tie between herself and the Wilcox family had been broken, for she was afraid that her sister was still in love with Paul Wilcox and suffered when she came into contact with other members of the family.

One evening, long after Mrs. Wilcox's death, Margaret and her sister were sitting in the park. There they met Mr. Wilcox, who told them that the firm for which Leonard Bast worked was unreliable. Acting on that information, the girls advised the young man to change jobs. He did so. They did not know that Mr. Wilcox, in love with Margaret, had given them bad advice in order to get rid of a young man he saw as a possible rival for Margaret's love.

A few weeks later the long-term lease on the Schlegels' house was up and they were forced to move. Although they searched a long time, they found nothing suitable. Mr. Wilcox, hearing of their predicament, sent a letter to Margaret offering to lease them his house in London. Margaret went with him to look at the house. While they were there, Mr. Wilcox declared his love. Margaret, who was well into her thirties, was surprised, but without embarrassment or shock. She asked only for a few days to think over the rental of the house and the proposal of marriage. After considering both problems, she agreed to marry Mr. Wilcox, thus making any decision about the rental unnecessary.

Before Margaret's marriage to Mr. Wilcox, his daughter was also married at a house owned by the Wilcoxes near Wales. Shortly after the daughter's wedding Helen Schlegel, who had disapproved of Margaret's approaching marriage, appeared at the house with Leonard Bast and his wife. Helen had learned that through their bad advice Bast had lost everything he had, including his job. Helen thought that Mr. Wilcox ought to recompense the young man. When Mrs. Bast was discovered, rather tipsy, on the lawn, she revealed to Mr. Wilcox and Margaret that she had been Mr. Wilcox's mistress many years before. Margaret was willing to forgive Mr. Wilcox, but she resolved not to help the Basts. Under the circumstances, she felt it was unnecessary and in poor taste to do so.

Helen, who had unwittingly fallen in love with Bast, felt sorry for him. She spent part of one night with him and then remorsefully left England. She tried to give Bast five thousand pounds, most of her fortune, but he refused to accept her aid.

The relationship between her sister and Leonard Bast was unknown to Margaret, who went ahead with her marriage to Mr. Wilcox, despite the fact that his sons did not approve of their father's second marriage. Helen's refusal to return for the ceremony did not surprise her sister. Eight months went by. Helen still had not returned, and Margaret began to worry about her sister.

Helen finally came back to England and sent word that she wanted some books stored in the house at Howards End. She acted so mysteriously that Margaret and Mr. Wilcox planned to encounter her at the house. Because she refused to see them directly, Margaret, worried, thought that Helen might need mental treatment. When Margaret saw Helen, however, the reason for the mystery was plain: Helen was pregnant as the result of the night she spent with Leonard Bast. Helen asked to be permitted to spend one night with her sister in the unoccupied house at Howards End. Mr. Wilcox refused to allow Margaret to do so.

The two sisters stayed in the house in spite of Mr. Wilcox's refusal. The following morning Mr. Wilcox's older son, Charles, went to the house to get them out. A minute or two after his arrival Leonard Bast came to the house in search of Margaret, from whom he hoped to get money. As soon as he saw him, Charles seized a saber that hung on the wall and struck Bast on the shoulders with the flat of the weapon several times. The shock of seeing Helen and the beating were too much for Bast's weak heart. He died suddenly.

Charles was tried for manslaughter and sentenced to three years in prison. The disgrace was too great for his father, who became an invalid. Margaret moved her husband and her sister into the house at Howards End, where Helen's child was born. Mr. Wilcox came to love the baby during his illness and convalescence, and so Helen and the child, much to the displeasure of the other Wilcoxes, were permitted to remain. A few months before Charles' release from prison, Mr. Wilcox called a family conference. He had made a new will giving all his money to the children by his first marriage, but the house at Howards End was to go to Margaret and after her death to Helen's illegitimate child. Thus the mansion, which had played so great a part in all their lives, eventually came to Margaret Schlegel, just as the first Mrs. Wilcox had wished before her death.

HUASIPUNGO

Type of work: Novel
Author: Jorge Icaza (1902-   )
Type of plot: Social criticism
Time of plot: Twentieth century
Locale: Ecuador
First published: 1934

Principal characters:
ALFONSO PEREIRA, a debt-ridden landowner
BLANCA, his wife
LOLITA, his daughter
DON JULIO, his uncle
POLICARPIO, an overseer
ANDRÉS CHILIQUINGA, an Indian laborer
CUNSHI, his wife
PADRE LOMAS, the village priest
JUANCHO CABASCANGO, a well-to-do Indian tenant farmer

Critique:

Stark, brutal realism overlies the art-   istry of this novel of protest against the enslavement of the Indian in rural Ecuador. Icaza is only one of many Latin-American novelists who, influenced by Dostoevski, Gorky, and other European realists, have used the indigenous theme and shown the white man's cruelty toward the Indian, but his *Huasipungo* is the best of these polemic works. Greater as a social document, perhaps, than as a work of fiction, it is made up of a series of episodes whose power lies in a graphic account of the lives and trials of the Indian. Icaza writes carelessly, with a scorn of syntax, but with a keen ear that reproduces the difficult dialect of the Quichua-speaking inhabitants of the Andean region near Quito. Types symbolizing classes rather than clearly realized individuals fill his pages, and in this novel the avaricious, lustful priest has been made especially hateful. In spite of its defects *Huasipungo* is a powerful novel, with many pirated editions in Spanish, an English translation printed in Russia, and even a version in Chinese.

The Story:

Alfonso Pereira was an Ecuadorian landowner plagued by domestic and financial troubles. His wife Blanca nagged him and he was worried over his seventeen-year-old daughter Lolita, who wanted to marry a man who was part Indian. Don Julio, his uncle, added to his difficulties by demanding repayment of a loan of ten thousand sucres, a debt already three months overdue.

When Pereira confessed himself unable to pay the loan, Don Julio suggested that his nephew try to interest Mr. Chapy, a North American promoter, in a timber concession on Pereira's mountain estate. Privately the old man suspected that Mr. Chapy and his associates were on the lookout for oil and used their lumber-cutting activities in the region as a blind. In order to interest the North Americans, however, it would be necessary to build fifteen miles of road and get possession of two forest tracts. Also, the Indians

must be driven off their *huasipungos*, the lands supplied to them in return for working on the master's estate.

Pereira assured his uncle that such a course would be difficult. The Indians, having a deep affection for their lands along both sides of the river, would never willingly give them up. Old Julio ridiculed Pereira's sentimentality and told him to return to the estate at Tomachi and build the road.

Back home, Pereira discussed his problem with Padre Lomas, the village priest. The padre agreed to persuade the Indians to work on the road: he would tell them that the labor was the will of God. They also tried to determine how many *mingas*, brawls in which Indians were plied with drink to make them willing to work, would be necessary before the road could be completed. Jacinto Quintana, proprietor of the village store and saloon, promised that he and his wife Juana would make the home-brew for the first of the *mingas*.

Andrés Chiliquinga, an Indian workman, was unhappy because Pereira had returned, for he had gone against his master's and the priest's wishes by taking Cunshi as his wife. He was one of thirty Indians sent to start cutting wood and clearing the roadbed.

To find a wet nurse for her baby, Blanca Pereira examined some of the dirty Indian mothers. Their undernourished babies were diseased, some with malaria or dysentery; others were idiotic or epileptic. Policarpio, the overseer, finally chose Cunshi, mother of the healthiest child in the village, and took her to the Pereira house. The master, seeing the young Indian woman, forced her to sleep with him.

One night Andrés made the long trip home to see his wife. Finding no one in their hillside shack, he became suspicious and angry. The next day he deliberately let his ax fall on his foot. The Indians treated the cut with spiderwebs and mud, but when the bandage was removed, three days later, the foot was so badly infected that Andrés was sent home. A medicine man who poulticed the sore saved Andrés' life, but the wound left him lame.

One day, while Pereira and the priest were at the Quintana store discussing the building of the road, they sent Jacinto on an errand. After his departure both men forced Juana to accept their attentions.

Pereira gave Padre Lomas one hundred sucres for a big mass. Then he held a *minga* and work on the road was speeded up. Storms made life miserable for the Indians, unprotected as they were in their camps. Some died when they tried to drain a swamp. Others perished in quicksands. Pereira, choosing to risk the Indians rather than follow a longer, safer route, kept the workmen drunk and entertained them with cockfights. The ignorant laborers continued to toil.

The priest went to Juancho Cabascango, an Indian with a prosperous *huasipungo* beside the river, and asked for one hundred sucres to pay for another mass. When the Indian refused, Padre Lomas cursed him. A short time later a flash flood drowned some of the Indians and their cattle. Blaming the disaster on Juancho, his superstitious neighbors beat him to death. The priest declared the affair the will of God and easily collected several hundred sucres for his mass.

At last the road was completed, but the Indians received none of the benefits Padre Lomas had promised. He himself bought a bus and two trucks that took away all transport from those who used to drive mule teams into Quito with the products of the region. Young Indians rode the bus to the city and there ended up as criminals and prostitutes.

Because of easy transportation and the possibility of a profitable sale in Quito, Pereira decided not to give the Indians their customary grain from his plentiful harvest. Policarpio's protests did no good. When the hungry Indians went to Pereira's patio and begged their master to relieve the hunger of their families, he told them that their daily pay of fifty centavos was generous enough. Besides, the ton and a half of corn needed to feed the Indians would help considerably in reducing his debts. He did, however, heed his overseer's warning and asked that guards for his estate be sent from Quito.

Hunger stalked the region and babies and old people perished. When one of Pereira's cows died, the famished Indians begged for the carcass. He refused because they might be tempted to kill other cows, and ordered Policarpio to bury the dead animal. Desperate, Andrés dug it up. After he and his family ate some of the meat, the tainted flesh killed Cunshi. Padre Lomas demanded twenty-five sucres, more than the Indian could ever earn, in payment for burying the dead woman. That same night Andrés stole one of his master's cows and sold it to a nearby butcher. Tracked down by dogs, the Indian was captured and flogged in Pereira's patio. There was no one to protest except his small son, who was almost killed by the white men when he tried to help his father.

A score of foreigners arrived in Tomachi. The Indians welcomed them timorously, thinking that these new white men could certainly be no more cruel than their Spanish masters. But Mr. Chapy's first act was to order the Indians driven from their *huasipungos* to make room for company houses and a sawmill.

When Andrés' son brought news of the order, the Indians rebelled. They had stolidly accepted the white man's cruelty, even his lechery toward their women, but they felt that the land was theirs. Jacinto vainly tried to stop them when they marched on the village. The enraged Indians killed six of the white men. The others, including Mr. Chapy, fled in their autos.

They returned, over the road the Indians had built, with three hundred soldiers under a leader who had killed two thousand Indians in a similar rebellion near Cuenca. Troops hunted down and machine-gunned Indians of all ages and sexes. The few survivors, taking refuge in Andrés' hillside shack, rolled down rocks on the soldiers and shot at them with birdguns. Finally the soldiers set fire to the thatched roof. When the Indians ran from the burning house, the troops shot them without mercy.

HUCKLEBERRY FINN

Type of work: Novel
Author: Mark Twain (Samuel L. Clemens, 1835-1910)
Type of plot: Humorous satire
Time of plot: Nineteenth century
Locale: Along the Mississippi River
First published: 1885

Principal characters:
HUCKLEBERRY FINN
TOM SAWYER, his friend
JIM, a Negro slave

Critique:

Not to have read *The Adventures of Huckleberry Finn* is nearly as sad as never having been to a circus or never having played baseball with the neighborhood gang. Huck is every young boy who ever lived, and he is also an individual worth knowing. He swears and smokes, but he has a set of ethics of his own. Reared haphazardly in the South, he believes that slaves belong to their rightful owners, yet in his honest gratitude toward his friend Jim, he helps him escape his slavery. Huck could not bear to cheat the three Wilks girls, but he did not hesitate to steal food when he was hungry. Huck talks with a lowbrow dialect, but he is keen-witted and intelligent. He tells his story with a straight-faced forwardness, but the reader finds laughter and shrewd, sharp comment on human nature in every chapter of his adventures along the Mississippi.

The Story:

Tom Sawyer and Huckleberry Finn had found a box of gold in a robber's cave. After Judge Thatcher had taken the money and invested it for the boys, each had a huge allowance of a dollar a day. The Widow Douglas and her sister, Miss Watson, had taken Huck home with them to try to reform him. At first Huck could not stand living in a tidy house where smoking and swearing were forbidden. Worse, he had to go to school and learn how to read. But he managed to drag himself to school almost every day, except for the times when he sneaked off for a smoke in the woods or to go fishing in the Mississippi.

Life was beginning to become bearable to him when one day he noticed some tracks in the snow. Examining them closely, he realized that they belonged to the worthless father whom Huck had not seen for over a year. Knowing that his father would be back hunting him when the old man learned about the six thousand dollars, Huck rushed over to Judge Thatcher and persuaded the judge to take the fortune for himself. The judge was puzzled, but he signed some papers, and Huck was satisfied that he no longer had any money for his father to take from him.

Huck's father finally showed up one night in Huck's room at Widow Douglas' home. Complaining that he had been cheated out of his money, the old drunkard took Huck away with him to a cabin in the woods, where he kept the boy a prisoner, beating him periodically

HUCKLEBERRY FINN by Mark Twain. Published by Harper & Brothers.

and half starving him. Before long Huck began to wonder why he had ever liked living with the widow. With his father, he could smoke and swear all he wanted, and his life would have been pleasant if it had not been for the beatings. One night Huck sneaked away, leaving a bloody trail from a pig he had killed in the woods. Huck wanted everyone to believe he was dead. He climbed into a boat and went to Jackson's Island to hide until all the excitement had blown over.

After three days of freedom, Huck wandered to another part of the island and there he discovered Jim, Miss Watson's Negro slave. Jim told Huck that he had run off because he had overheard Miss Watson planning to sell him down south for eight hundred dollars. Huck swore he would not report Jim. The two stayed on the island many days, Jim giving Huck an education in primitive superstition. One night, Huck rowed back to the mainland. Disguised as a girl, he called on a home near the shore. There he learned that his father had disappeared shortly after the people of the town had decided that Huck had been murdered. Since Jim's disappearance had occurred just after Huck's alleged death, there was now a three hundred dollar reward posted for Jim's capture, as most people believed that Jim had killed Huck.

Fearing that Jackson's Island would be searched, Huck hurried back to Jim and the two headed down the Mississippi. They planned to leave the raft at Cairo and then go on a steamboat up the Ohio into free territory. Jim told Huck that he would work hard in the North and then buy his wife and children from their masters in the South. Helping a runaway slave bothered Huck's conscience, but he reasoned that it would bother him more if he betrayed such a good friend as Jim. One night as they were drifting down the river on their raft, a large boat loomed before them, and Huck and Jim, knowing that the raft would be smashed under the hull of

the ship, jumped into the water. Huck swam safely to shore, but Jim disappeared.

Huck found a home with a friendly family named Grangerford. The Grangerfords were feuding with the Shepherdsons, another family living nearby. The Grangerfords left Huck mostly to himself and gave him a young slave to wait on him. One day the slave asked him to come to the woods to see some snakes. Following the boy, Huck came across Jim, who had been hiding in the woods waiting for an opportunity to send for Huck. Jim had repaired the broken raft. That night one of the Grangerford daughters eloped with a young Shepherdson, and the feud broke out once more. Huck and Jim ran away during the shooting and set off down the river.

Shortly afterward, Jim and Huck met two men who pretended they were royalty and made all sorts of nonsensical demands on Huck and Jim. Huck was not taken in, but he reasoned that it would do no harm to humor the two men to prevent quarreling. The Duke and the King were clever schemers. In one of the small river towns they staged a fake show which lasted long enough to net them a few hundred dollars. Then they ran off before the angered townspeople could catch them.

The Duke and the King overheard some people talking about the death of a Peter Wilks, who had left considerable property and some cash to his three daughters. Wilks' two brothers, whom no one in the town had ever seen, were living in England. The King and the Duke went to the three daughters, Mary Jane, Susan, and Joanna, and presented themselves as the two uncles. They took a few thousand dollars of the inheritance and then put up the property for auction and sold the slaves. This high-handed deed caused great grief to the girls, and Huck could not bear to see them so unhappy. He decided to expose the two frauds, but he wanted to insure Jim's safety first. Jim had been hiding in the woods waiting for his companions to return to him. Employing a series of lies, subterfuges, and maneuverings that were worthy of his ingenious mind, Huck exposed the Duke and King. Huck fled back to Jim, and the two escaped on their raft. Just as Jim and Huck thought they were on their way and well rid of their former companions, the Duke and King came rowing down the river toward them.

The whole party set out again with their royal plots to hoodwink the public. In one town where they landed, Jim was captured, and Huck learned that the Duke had turned him in for the reward. Huck had quite a tussle with his conscience. He knew that he ought to help return a slave to the rightful owner, but, on the other hand, he thought of all the fine times he and Jim had had together and how loyal a friend Jim had been. Finally, Huck decided that he would help Jim to escape.

Learning that Mr. Phelps was holding Jim, he headed for the Phelps farm. There, Mrs. Phelps ran up and hugged him, mistaking him for the nephew whom she had been expecting to come for a visit. Huck wondered how he could keep Mrs. Phelps from learning that he was not her nephew. Then to his relief he learned they had mistaken him for Tom Sawyer. Huck rather liked being Tom for a while, and he was able to tell the Phelps all about Tom's Aunt Polly and Sid and Mary, Tom's brother and sister. Huck was feeling proud of himself for keeping up the deception. When Tom Sawyer really did arrive, he told his aunt that he was Sid.

At the first opportunity Huck told Tom about Jim's capture. To his surprise, Tom offered to help him set Jim free. Huck could not believe that Tom would be a slave stealer, but he kept his feelings to himself. Huck had intended merely to wait until there was a dark night and then break the padlock on the door of the shack where Jim was kept. But Tom said the rescue had to be done according to the books, and he laid out a most complicated plan with all kinds of story-book ramifications. It took fully three weeks of plotting, stealing, and deceit to let Jim out of the shack. Then the scheme failed. A chase began after Jim escaped, and Tom was shot in the leg. After Jim had been recaptured, Tom was brought back to Aunt Sally's house to recover from his wound. Then Tom revealed the fact that Miss Watson had died, giving Jim his freedom in her will. Huck was greatly relieved to learn that Tom was not really a slave stealer after all.

To complicate matters still more, Tom's Aunt Polly arrived. She quickly set straight the identities of the two boys. Jim was given his freedom and Tom gave him forty dollars. Tom told Huck that his money was still safely in the hands of Judge Thatcher, but Huck moaned that his father would likely be back to claim it again. Then Jim told Huck that his father was dead; Jim had seen him lying in an abandoned boat along the river.

Huck was ready to start out again because Aunt Sally said she thought she might adopt him and try to civilize him. Huck thought that he could not go through such a trial again after he had once tried to be civilized under the care of Widow Douglas.

HUDIBRAS

Type of work: Poem
Author: Samuel Butler (1612-1680)
Type of plot: Satirical burlesque
Time of plot: 1640-1660
Locale: England
First published: 1663-1678

Principal characters:

SIR HUDIBRAS, a Presbyterian knight
RALPHO, Sir Hudibras' squire, a religious Independent
THE WIDOW, a wealthy woman who befriended Sir Hudibras
SIDROPHEL, an astrologer
CROWDERO, a fiddler
TRULLA, a woman who subdued Sir Hudibras

Critique:

Butler's *Hudibras* was intended to ridicule the Presbyterians, Dissenters, and others who had fought against the crown in the conflict between Charles I and Oliver Cromwell. Published shortly after the restoration of Charles II, the poem had immense popularity for a time. The king himself, one of its most ardent admirers, carried a copy in his pocket and quoted from it. *Hudibras* has sometimes been called a mock-epic. It is more accurate, however, to say that the poem is to an epic what farce is to tragic drama. The burlesque is used with telling effect. Mean and low persons, things, and situations are described in pompous language. By so doing, Butler hoped to unmask the hypocrisy and absurdity of Dissenting reformers in seventeenth-century England and to show them as ridiculous, odious, and obnoxious. He also wanted to draw attention to the pretensions of the false learning rampant in England at the time. Astrology, fortune-telling, alchemy, "sympathetic" medicine, and other pseudo-sciences were presented in such fashion as to show the readers of his time the absurdity of practices and practitioners alike. To *Hudibras* can be ascribed little organization; the best qualities of the poems lie in isolated passages devoted to the satire.

The Story:

Sir Hudibras, a Presbyterian knight, was one of those who had ridden out against the monarchy during the civil war. He was a proud man, one who bent his knee to nothing but chivalry and suffered no blow but that which had been given when he was dubbed a knight. Although he had some wit, he was very shy of displaying it. He knew Latin, Greek, and Hebrew; indeed, his talk was a kind of piebald dialect, so heavily was it larded with Greek and Latin words and tags. He was learned in rhetoric, logic, and mathematics, and he frequently spoke in a manner demonstrating his learning. His notions fitted things so well that he was often puzzled to decide what his notions were and what was reality.

In figure he was thick and stout, both before and behind, and he always carried extra victuals in his hose. He rode a mealy-mouthed, wall-eyed, skinny old nag whose tail dragged in the dust, and he encouraged his horse with a single old spur.

Sir Hudibras had a squire named Ralpho, who was an Independent in religion —a fact which accounted for his partisanship and dogmatic approach to the many discussions and arguments he had with his master on matters of faith. Ralpho was a tailor by trade, but his belief in the efficacy of divine revelation to the individual had made him something of a religious oracle, at least in his own satisfied opinion.

Sir Hudibras and Ralpho rode forth from the knight's home to reform what they called sins and what the rest of the world regarded as mild amusement. After they had gone a few miles on their journey they came to a town where the people danced enjoyably to a fiddle and, worse in Sir Hudibras' eyes, indulged themselves in the sport of bearbaiting. To the knight's resolve to end these activities Ralpho added his agreement that they were certainly unchristian. When the knight advanced, however, he was met by an unsympathetic crowd. With the rabble were several leaders. One was

Crowdero, a fiddler wtih one wooden leg, who played his instrument for the mob in the absence of more martial fifes and drums. Another leader was Orsin, the bear keeper, who led his charge at the end of a rope fastened to the creature's nose. Talgol, a butcher, was also in the van, as was a woman named Trulla, an Amazon of a damsel. When Sir Hudibras called upon the people to disperse and return quietly to their homes, leaving Crowdero a prisoner, a fight began.

Ralpho was soon bucked off his horse when some one put a burr under the animal's tail. Sir Hudibras, pulled from his steed, fell on the bear, who became enraged and escaped from his keeper. The bear's escape scattered the crowd and Crowdero was left behind, the prisoner of Sir Hudibras and Ralpho, for the fiddler's wooden leg had been broken in the melee. Having swooned from fear, Hudibras also lay helpless for a time, but he was soon revived by Ralpho. The pair took their prisoner to the end of the town and placed his good leg in the stocks. They hung his fiddle, bow, and case above the stocks as a trophy of victory.

The people who had been dispersed by the enraged bear, overcoming their fright, planned to attack the knight and release his victim. Hudibras and Ralpho sallied out of their quarters to the attack. A blow on Ralpho's horse caused the animal to unhorse his rider. Hudibras, at first frightened, summoned his courage and charged. The crowd dispersed once again, and Hudibras went to the aid of his squire. When the knight's back was turned, Trulla attacked him from behind and quickly overpowered him. Rejoined by her friends, the woman marched Hudibras to the stocks to take the place of Crowdero. Placed in the stocks, Hudibras and Ralpho discussed and argued their situation and what had occasioned it. Then a widow who had heard of the knight's plight came to see him in the stocks. After much discussion, she agreed to have Hudibras set free if he would

consent to a whipping. He agreed to the condition and was released.

Sir Hudibras, once out of the stocks, was reluctant to keep the bargain he had made. He was anxious for her hand, too, but for her money rather than her love. Hudibras and Ralpho argued long about flagellation. Hudibras suggested that the whipping be administered to Ralpho, as a proxy for the knight. Ralpho refused and an argument ensued. When the two were almost at swords' points, they heard a terrible din. They looked about and saw coming down the road, a party of people making a noisy to-do over a poor man who had let his wife take over his authority. Sir Hudibras tried to break up the crowd, but a volley of rotten eggs and other filth defeated him and cooled his ardor for reform. The knight, going to clean himself after his most recent encounter with sin, decided to lie to the widow about having received a whipping.

Before approaching the widow's house, Sir Hudibras went to consult Sidrophel, an astrologer. Hudibras and Ralpho agreed that a godly man might reasonably consult with such a man if he were on a Christian errand. Hudibras, soon convinced that Sidrophel and his apprentice, Whachum, were frauds, perhaps dabblers with the devil, sent Ralpho off to find a constable. Meanwhile, Hudibras overcame the pair and went through the astrologer's belongings. Instead of going for a constable, however, Ralpho decided to go to the widow. He was afraid that the authorities might think Hudibras involved in black magic.

Ralpho, telling all to the widow, revealed that Hudibras was going to lie about having received a whipping and that he was only after the widow's money. When Hudibras arrived a short time later, the widow hid Ralpho and let the knight tell his long string of half-truths and lies. The widow, knowing the truth, treated him to a somewhat frightening masquerade, with Ralpho as the chief sprite. Hudibras and the squire decided to escape before worse could happen to them. They went hugger-mugger through a window and escaped on their saddleless horses.

The poet then turned in the last part of the poem to talk directly about the religious groups for which Ralpho and Hudibras stood—the Independents and the Presbyterians—and how they had fallen out with one another after the end of the Civil War and had eventually, in their weakness, paved the way for the Restoration of the Stuart line in the person of Charles II.

HUGH WYNNE, FREE QUAKER

Type of work: Novel
Author: Silas Weir Mitchell (1829-1914)
Type of plot: Historical romance
Time of plot: 1753-1783
Locale: Colonial America
First published: 1897

Principal characters:
    JOHN WYNNE, a Quaker
    MARIE, his wife
    HUGH WYNNE, John's son
    JACK WARDER, Hugh's friend
    ARTHUR WYNNE, Hugh's cousin
    DARTHEA PENISTON, who marries Hugh
    GAINOR WYNNE, John's sister

Critique:

Hugh Wynne, Free Quaker is one of the best novels of the American Revolution. The veracity of its events in the historical sense can be judged by any student of history, and its faithfulness to the social history of the time can be judged by reading diaries and chronicles of those who lived through the war years. More than historical fiction, however, the novel is a touching revelation of a child-parent relationship and of the consequences of too much doctrinal discipline.

The Story:

The Wynne family had descended from an ancient Welsh line. That part of the family which had remained in Wales now held the family estate of Wyncote. The American branch, being Quaker, had dissociated itself from the more worldly family at Wyncote, and Hugh Wynne grew up under the stern discipline of John Wynne's orthodoxy.

John's sister, Gainor Wynne, had not become a Quaker. Because Hugh was his aunt's favorite, early in his life he fell under the influence of those who were outside the ways of the Quakers.

Jack Warder was Hugh's closest friend, the two boys having gone to school together. Aunt Gainor often invited both boys to her home in Philadelphia, where she was surrounded by a worldly group of English officers, men upon whom the Quakers frowned. Hugh enjoyed their society, to the delight of his aunt, who wished her nephew to break his Quaker ties. Jack Warder, however, did not like Gainor Wynne's friends. When he and Hugh were old enough to judge moral values for themselves, their friendship became strained. Hugh's father was never fully aware of the way Hugh spent his time away from home.

One night, while drinking and gambling with his worldly friends, Hugh met

HUGH WYNNE, FREE QUAKER by Silas Weir Mitchell. By permission of the publishers, Appleton-Century-Crofts, Inc. Copyright, 1896, by The Century Co. Renewed. 1923, by Langden Elwyn Mitchell.

a cousin, Arthur Wynne, of the family at Wyncote. He instinctively disliked his relative because of his superior ways and his deceitful manner. During the evening Hugh became very drunk. Suddenly his mother and Jack Warder burst into the room.

This incident marked the beginning of Hugh's break with his father's church and the renewal of his friendship with Jack Warder. Hugh, realizing his folly, was thankful that Jack had seen him on the streets and had led his mother to rescue him from the drunken party. He began to realize the depth of his mother's love and understanding. John Wynne was quite different in his attitude. A few nights later he took Hugh to a Quaker meeting, where public prayers were offered to save Hugh's soul. Hugh's embarrassment caused him to lose all of his love for the Quaker religion and to bear a deep resentment against his father.

At Gainor Wynne's home, Jack and Hugh heard much conversation about disagreement between the Americans and the British. Gainor was a Whig, and under her influence Jack and Hugh gained sympathy for their American compatriots. Arthur Wynne too had become part of the society that gathered at Gainor Wynne's house. Jack and Hugh had never liked Arthur, but now they had a new cause for their dislike. Arthur made no secret of his admiration for Darthea Peniston, a schoolmate of Jack and Hugh, and his bragging about Wyncote seemingly won her interest, thus arousing Hugh's jealousy. When Hugh told Darthea of his love, she insisted that she did not love him.

Meanwhile Hugh's parents went abroad. During their absence he stayed with Gainor Wynne. Claiming that the time was not far off when he would need such a skill, she urged him to take fencing lessons. Jack practiced the sport with his friend, although he knew it to be contrary to the laws of the church. Hugh and Jack both knew that soon they would join the American cause for liberty.

While John Wynne and his wife were abroad, Hugh received a letter telling that his mother had died. On his return John showed no signs of his grief at the loss of his wife. Hugh himself felt her loss deeply.

At Gainor's home, where he spent more time than ever since the death of his mother, Hugh quarreled with an English officer and was challenged to a duel. With Jack as his second, Hugh answered the challenge. As a result the Quakers notified both boys that unless they changed their ways and repented for their sins, they could no longer belong to the Society of Friends. Jack and Hugh announced that they intended to join the American army; fighting had already begun at Lexington.

Jack went to join the troops. After a short time Hugh decided to follow him, in spite of his father's crafty excuses that he needed Hugh to conduct his business affairs for him. When he did join the army, Hugh was captured by the British and sent, wounded and sick, to a filthy prison. In the prison Arthur Wynne, now a Tory captain, saw his cousin, but left Hugh to die. Hugh never forgave him for this cruelty and for his subsequent lie concerning the meeting.

Hugh recovered and escaped from prison to return to Gainor Wynne's house. Arthur Wynne was staying at the home of John Wynne and ingratiating himself in the eyes of the old man. Hugh knew that there was something mysterious in relation to the Welsh estate of Wyncote. Supposedly Arthur's father owned the estate, having bought it from John's father. Gainor Wynne urged Hugh to investigate the title of the estate. John Wynne, it seemed, still possessed the title, and out of sympathy for Arthur's alleged poverty had promised to give it to him. Hugh was unable to change his father's decision, even after he told of Arthur's cruel desertion when Hugh lay near death in prison. His father refused to believe Hugh's story.

Hugh could not tell Darthea about Arthur's behavior, for he felt that she would rush to Arthur's defense if he said anything against his cousin.

Once, while Hugh was at home, his father, thinking Hugh was Arthur, handed him the deed to Wyncote. Knowing that his father's mind had often misled him of late, Hugh tried to convince the old man that he was not Arthur, but John insisted that Hugh take the deed. Hugh took it to Gainor Wynne.

After a rest of a few months, Hugh rejoined the American troops. He was able to perform a courageous service for General Washington, for which he received praise and a captaincy. Jack, too, had become an officer.

When Hugh and Jack returned to Philadelphia on leave, Gainor Wynne managed to expose Arthur to Darthea. Although the young girl had lost her earlier love for the Tory officer, she had been unwilling to break her promise to him. But with proof of Arthur's villainy before her, she felt that she was free at last to break her engagement.

Again Hugh asked her to marry him and she surprised him by accepting. Hugh still did not want the title to Wyncote, and Darthea agreed with him that after he had taken Arthur's betrothed it would not become Hugh to take his inheritance from him as well. Although Gainor Wynne wished to press the legality of the ancient deed, Darthea threw it into the fire, and so destroyed any claim Hugh might have upon the ancestral estate.

John Wynne, who had ceased to live for Hugh when he had lost his mental faculties, died soon after the war ended. Darthea and Hugh were happily married, and they lived long years together to watch their children and their grandchildren grow up unburdened by the rigorous religious control which Hugh had known in his youth.

THE HUMAN COMEDY

Type of work: Novel
Author: William Saroyan (1908-   )
Type of plot: Sentimental romance
Time of plot: Twentieth century
Locale: Ithaca, California
First published: 1943

Principal characters:
    KATEY MACAULEY, a widow
    HOMER,
    ULYSSES, and
    MARCUS, her sons
    BESS, her daughter
    MARY ARENA, Marcus' sweetheart
    THOMAS SPANGLER, manager of the telegraph office
    MR. GROGAN, assistant in the telegraph office
    TOBEY GEORGE, Marcus' friend from the army
    LIONEL, Ulysses' friend

Critique:
This novel has for its theme the idea that no human can ever die as long as he lives in the hearts of those who loved him. The story deals with the family of a soldier who died in the war. Frankly sentimental, *The Human Comedy* is one of the most touching of Saroyan's works.

The Story:
Mr. Macauley was dead and his wife

and children had to take care of themselves. When Marcus went into the army, Homer, the next oldest, obtained a job on the night shift in the telegraph office at Ithaca, California. He worked at night because he was still attending school during the day. Little Ulysses watched his family and wondered what was going on, for his baby's mind could not comprehend all the changes that had taken place in his home.

Every morning Homer arose early and exercised in his room so that he would be physically fit to run the two-twenty low hurdles at high school. After he and Bess had eaten their breakfast, Mary Arena, who was in love with Marcus, came from next door, and she and Bess walked to school together.

In the ancient history class, taught by Miss Hicks, Homer and Hubert Ackley the Third insulted each other, and Miss Hicks kept the boys after school. But Coach Byfield had picked Hubert to run the two-twenty low hurdles that afternoon, and Hubert told Miss Hicks that the principal had asked that he be excused. Indignant at the deceit, Miss Hicks also sent Homer to run the race. Although Hubert was the winner, Homer felt that justice had been done.

Thomas Spangler was in charge of the telegraph office and Mr. Grogan, an old man with a weak heart, was his assistant. Because Mr. Grogan got drunk every night, one of Homer's duties was to see to it that Mr. Grogan stayed awake to perform his duties. A problem which had weighed on Homer's mind ever since he had taken his new job and had grown up overnight was whether the war would change anything for people. Mr. Grogan and Homer often talked about the world, Homer declaring that he did not like things as they were. Seeing everyone in the world mixed up and lonely, Homer said, he felt that he had to say and do things to make people laugh.

Mrs. Macauley was happy that her children were so human. Ever since her husband had died, Katey Macauley had pretended to see him and discuss with him problems that arose concerning the rearing of her family. She felt that the father was not dead if he lived again in the lives of his children. One afternoon she had a premonition of Marcus' death, for she imagined that her husband came to her and told her he was going to bring Marcus with him.

Little Ulysses had a friend, Lionel, who was three years older than Ulysses. The older boys chased Lionel away from their games because they said that he was dumb. When Lionel came to Mrs. Macauley to ask her whether he was stupid, the kind woman assured him that he was as good as everyone else. Lionel took Ulysses to the library with him to look at all the many-colored books on the shelves. Ulysses, who spent his time wandering around and watching everything, was pleased with the new experience.

Marcus wrote to Homer from an army camp somewhere in the South, and Homer took the letter back to the telegraph office with him. The letter told about Marcus' friend, an orphan named Tobey George. Marcus had described his family, Homer, Ulysses, Bess, his mother, and his sweetheart, Mary, to Tobey. Because Tobey had no family of his own, he was grateful to Marcus for bringing to him second-hand the Macauley family. Marcus had told Tobey that after the war he wanted Tobey to go to Ithaca and marry Bess. Tobey was not so certain that Bess would want to marry him, but he felt for the first time in his life that he had a family that was almost his own. Marcus had written to Homer, as the new head of the family, to tell him about Tobey George and to ask him to look after his mother and Bess.

Homer was moved by his brother's letter. When he had finished reading it, he told Mr. Grogan that if Marcus should be killed he would spit at the world. Homer could express his love for Marcus in no other way.

1379

The same events repeated themselves many times in Ithaca. Ulysses continued to watch everything with increasing interest. Mary and Bess sang their songs and went for their evening walks. Telegrams came, and Homer delivered them. Soldiers began coming home to Ithaca, to their mothers and to their families.

Homer had been working at the telegraph office for six months. One Sunday night, while he was walking downtown with Lionel and Ulysses, he saw through the window of the telegraph office that Mr. Grogan was working alone. He sent the two small boys home and went in to see if Mr. Grogan needed him. The old man had suffered one of his heart attacks, and Homer ran to the drug store to get some medicine for him. Mr. Grogan attempted to type out one more telegram, a message for Katey Macauley telling her that her son Marcus had been killed in action. When Homer returned with the medicine, he found Mr. Grogan slumped over the typed-out message. He was dead. Homer went home with the message that Marcus had been killed.

That night a soldier had got off the train at Ithaca. He was Tobey George. He walked around for a time before he went to see Marcus' family. When he came to the Macauley porch, he stood and listened to Bess and Mary singing inside the house. Bess came outside and sat next to him while he told her that Marcus had sent him to be a member of the family. When Homer came to the porch with the telegram, Tobey called him aside and told him to tear up the message. Tobey assured him that Marcus was not dead; Marcus could never die. Mrs. Macauley came onto the porch, and Ulysses ran to Tobey and took his hand. For a while the mother looked at her two remaining sons. Then she smiled at her new son as the family walked into the house.

HUMPHRY CLINKER

Type of work: Novel
Author: Tobias Smollett (1721-1771)
Type of plot: Social satire
Time of plot: Mid-eighteenth century
Locale: England, Scotland, Wales
First published: 1771

   Principal characters:
   MATTHEW BRAMBLE, a Welsh squire
   MISS TABITHA BRAMBLE, his sister
   LYDIA MELFORD, his niece
   JERRY MELFORD, his nephew
   WINIFRED JENKINS, a maid
   HUMPHRY CLINKER, a servant, discovered to be Mr. Bramble's natural son
   LIEUTENANT OBADIAH LISMAHAGO, an adventurer and sportsman
   MR. DENNISON, a country gentleman
   GEORGE DENNISON, his son, the actor known as Wilson

Critique:

This novel, written in the form of letters, is easy to read and continually amusing. The characters of the writers of the letters are shown by the variation of their descriptions of the same events. The picture is one of a realistic if somewhat eccentric family, whose members display the manners and customs of eighteenth-century society. *The Expedition of Humphry Clinker,* to use its full title, has often been called the greatest of the letter-novels, and an outstanding example of English humor.

The Story:

Squire Matthew Bramble was an eccentric and skeptical gentleman with large estates in Wales. With him lived his sister, Miss Tabitha Bramble, a middle-aged maiden of high matrimonial hopes that were greater than her expectations. Painfully afflicted with the gout, the squire set out for Bath to try the waters, but with few hopes of their healing properties. With him went his sister; her servant, Winifred Jenkins; his own manservant, and, at the last minute, his niece and nephew, Lydia and Jerry Melford.

The young Melfords were orphans and Squire Bramble's wards. Lydia had been in boarding-school, where, unfortunately, she had fallen in love with an actor—a circumstance Squire Bramble hoped she would soon forget among the gay and fashionable gatherings at Bath. Her brother, who had just finished his studies at Oxford, had tried to fight a duel with the actor, but an opportunity to defend his sister's honor had not presented itself to his satisfaction.

On the way to Bath a Jewish peddler made his way into Squire Bramble's lodgings on the pretext of selling glasses, and in a whisper made himself known to Lydia as George Wilson, the strolling player. The lovesick girl ordered Winifred Jenkins to follow the actor and talk with him. The maid came back in a great flurry. He had told her that Wilson was not his real name, that he was a gentleman, and that he intended to sue for Lydia's hand in his proper character. But, alas, the excited maid had forgotten Wilson's real name. There was nothing for poor Lydia to do but to conjecture and daydream as the party continued on toward Bath.

Arriving at Bath without further incident, the party entered the gay festivities there with various degrees of pleasure. Tabitha tried to get proposals of marriage out of every eligible man she met, and the squire became disgusted with the supposed curative powers of the waters which were drunk and bathed in by people with almost any infirmity in hopes of regaining their health. Lydia was still languishing over Wilson, and Jerry enjoyed the absurdity of the social gatherings. In an attempt to lighten his niece's spirits, Squire Bramble decided to go on to London.

They had traveled only a short way toward London when the coach accidentally overturned and Miss Tabitha's lapdog, in the excitement, bit the squire's servant. Miss Tabitha made such loud complaint when the servant kicked her dog in return that the squire was forced to discharge the man on the spot. He also needed another postilion, as Miss Tabitha declared herself unwilling to drive another foot behind the clumsy fellow who had overturned the coach. The squire hired a ragged country fellow named Humphry Clinker to take the place of the unfortunate postilion, and the party went on to the next village.

Miss Tabitha was shocked by what she called Humphry's nakedness, for he wore no shirt. The maid added to the chorus of outraged modesty. Yielding to these female clamors, the squire asked about Humphry's circumstances, listened to the story of his life, gruffly read him a lecture on the crimes of poverty and sickness, and gave him a guinea for a new suit of clothes. In gratitude Humphry refused to be parted from his new benefactor and went on with the party to London.

In London they were well entertained by a visit to Vauxhall Gardens as well as by several public and private parties. Squire Bramble was disconcerted by the discovery that Humphry was a preacher by inclination, and had begun giving sermons in the manner of the Methodists. Miss Tabitha and her maid were already among Humphry's followers. The squire attempted to stop what he considered either hypocrisy or madness on Humphry's part. Miss Tabitha, disgusted with her brother's action, begged him to allow Humphry to continue his sermons.

The family was shocked to learn one day that Humphry had been arrested as a highway robber, and was in jail. When the squire arrived to investigate the case, he discovered that Humphry was obviously innocent of the charge against him, which had been placed by an ex-convict who made money by turning in criminals to the government. Humphry had made a fine impression on the jailer and his family and had converted several of his fellow prisoners. The squire found the man who supposedly had been robbed and got him to testify that Humphry was not the man who had committed the robbery. In the meantime Humphry preached so eloquently that he kept the prison taproom empty of customers. When this became evident he was hurriedly released, and Squire Bramble promised to allow him to preach his sermons unmolested.

Continuing their travels north after leaving London, the party stopped in Scarborough, where they went bathing. Squire Bramble undressed in a little cart which could be rolled down into the sea, so that he was able to bath nude with the greatest propriety. When he entered the water, he found it much colder than he had expected and gave several shouts as he swam away. Hearing these calls from the squire, Humphry thought his good master was drowning, and rushed fully clothed into the sea to rescue him. He pulled the squire to shore, almost twisting off his master's ear, and leaving the modest man shamefaced and naked in full view upon the beach. Humphrey was forgiven, however, because he had meant well.

At an inn in Durham, the party made the acquaintance of Lieutenant Lismahago, who seemed somewhat like Don Quixote. The lieutenant, regaling the company with tales of his adventures among the Indians of North America, quite captured the heart of Miss Tabitha. Squire Bramble was also charmed with the crusty conversation of the retired soldier, and made plans to meet him later on in their journey. The group became more and more fond of Humphry as time

went on, especially Winifred. After a short and frivolous flirtation with Jerry's part-time valet, she settled down to win Humphry as a husband.

The party continued its trip through Scotland. In Edinburgh Lydia fainted when she saw a man who looked like Wilson, an action which showed her uncle that she had not yet forgotten the affair. After visiting several parts of Scotland and enjoying the most gracious hospitality everywhere, they continued by coach back to England. As they were traveling south, Lieutenant Lismahago rejoined the party and Miss Tabitha renewed her designs on him.

Just outside Dumfries the coach was overturned in the middle of a stream. Jerry and Lismahago succeeded in getting the women out of the water after a struggle, and Humphry staged a heroic rescue of the squire, who had been caught in the bottom of the coach. They found lodgings at a nearby inn until the coach could be repaired. While all were gathered in the parlor of a tavern, Squire Bramble was accosted by an old college friend named Dennison, a successful farmer of the county. Mr. Dennison had known the squire only as Matthew Lloyd, a name he had taken for a while in order to fulfill the terms of a will. When Humphry heard his master called Lloyd, he rushed up in a flutter of excitement and presented the squire with certain papers he had always carried with him. These papers proved that Humphry was the squire's natural son. In a gracious way, Squire Bramble welcomed his offspring, and presented him to the rest of his family. Humphry was overcome with pleasure and shyness. Winifred was afraid that his discovery would spoil her matrimonial plans, but Humphry continued to be the mild religious man he had been before.

The squire was also surprised to learn that the actor who had called himself Wilson was really Dennison's son, a fine proper young man who had run away from school and become an actor only to escape a marriage his father had planned for him long before. He had told his father about his love for Lydia, but Dennison had not realized that the Mr. Bramble who was her uncle was his old friend Matthew Lloyd. Now the two young lovers were brought together for a joyous reunion.

Lieutenant Lismahago was moved to ask for Miss Tabitha's hand in marriage, and both the squire and Miss Tabitha eagerly accepted his offer. The whole party went to stay at Mr. Dennison's house while preparations were being made for the marriage of Lydia and George. The coming marriages prompted Humphry to ask Winifred for her hand, and she also said yes. The three weddings were planned for the same day.

George and Lydia were a most attractive couple. The lieutenant and Tabitha seemed to be more pleasant than ever before. Humphry and Winifred both thanked God for the pleasures He saw fit to give them. The squire planned to return home to the tranquility of Brambleton Hall and the friendship of his invaluable doctor there.

THE HUNCHBACK OF NOTRE DAME

Type of work: Novel
Author: Victor Hugo (1802-1885)
Type of plot: Historical romance
Time of plot: Fifteenth century
Locale: France
First published: 1831

Principal characters:
QUASIMODO, the hunchback of Notre Dame
ESMERELDA, a gipsy dancer
CLAUDE FROLLO, archdeacon of Notre Dame
PHOEBUS DE CHATEAUPERS, Esmerelda's sweetheart
GRINGOIRE, a stupid and poverty-stricken poet

Critique:

Victor Hugo, leader of the French romantic movement, not only could tell a gripping story, but also could endow his essentially romantic characters with a realism so powerful that they have become monumental literary figures. *The Hunchback of Notre Dame* has every quality of a good novel: an exciting story, a magnificent setting, and deep, lasting characterizations. Perhaps the compelling truth of this novel lies in the idea that God has created in man an imperfect image of Himself, an image fettered by society and by man's own body and soul, but one which, in the last analysis, has the freedom to transcend these limitations and achieve spiritual greatness.

The Story:

Louis XI, King of France, was to marry his oldest son to Margaret of Flanders, and in early January, 1482, the king was expecting Flemish ambassadors to his court. The great day arrived, coinciding both with Epiphany and the secular celebration of the Festival of Fools. All day long, raucous Parisians had assembled at the great Palace of Justice to see a morality play and to choose a Prince of Fools. The throng was supposed to await the arrival of the Flemish guests, but when the emissaries were late Gringoire, a penniless and oafish poet, ordered the play to begin. In the middle of the prologue, however, the play came to a standstill as the royal procession passed into the huge palace. After the procession passed the play was forgotten, and the crowd shouted for the Prince of Fools to be chosen.

The Prince of Fools had to be a man of remarkable physical ugliness. One by

1383

one the candidates, eager for this one glory of their disreputable lives, showed their faces in front of a glass window, but the crowd shouted and jeered until a face of such extraordinary hideousness appeared that the people acclaimed this candidate at once as the Prince of Fools. It was Quasimodo, the hunchback bell-ringer of Notre Dame. Nowhere on earth was there a more grotesque creature. One of his eyes was buried under an enormous wen. His teeth hung over his protruding lower lip like tusks. His eyebrows were red bristles, and his gigantic nose curved over his upper lip like a snout. His long arms protruded from his shoulders, dangling like an ape's. Though he was deaf from long years of ringing Notre Dame's thunderous bells, his eyesight was acute.

Quasimodo sensed · that he had been chosen by popular acclaim, and he was at once proud and suspicious of his honor as he allowed the crowd to dress him in ridiculous robes and hoist him above their heads. From this vantage point he maintained a dignified silence while the parade went through the streets of Paris, stopping only to watch the enchanting dance of a gipsy girl, La Esmerelda, whose grace and charm held her audience spellbound. She had with her a little trained goat that danced to her tambourine. The pair were celebrated throughout Paris, though there were some who thought the girl a witch, so great was her power in captivating her audience.

Late that night the poet Gringoire walked the streets of Paris. He had no shelter, owed money, and was in desperate straits. As the cold night came on, he saw Esmerelda hurrying ahead of him. Then a black-hooded man came out of the shadows and seized the gipsy. At the same time, Gringoire caught sight of the hooded man's partner, Quasimodo, who struck Gringoire a terrible blow. The following moment a horseman came riding from the next street. Catching sight of Esmerelda in the arms of the black-hooded man, the rider demanded that he free the girl or pay with his life. The

attackers fled. Esmerelda asked the name of her rescuer. It was Captain Phoebus de Chateaupers. From that moment Esmerelda was hopelessly in love with Phoebus.

Gringoire did not bother to discover the plot behind the frustrated kidnaping, but had he known the truth he might have been more frightened than he was. Quasimodo's hooded companion had been Claude Frollo, archdeacon of Notre Dame, a man who had once been a pillar of righteousness, but who now, because of loneliness and an insatiable thirst for knowledge and experience, had succumbed to the temptations of necromancy and alchemy.

Frollo had befriended Quasimodo when the hunchback had been left at the gates of Notre Dame as an unwanted baby, and to him Quasimodo was slavishly loyal. He acted without question when Frollo asked his aid in kidnaping the beautiful gipsy. Frollo, having admired Esmerelda from a distance, planned to carry her off to his small cell in the cathedral, where he could enjoy her charms at his leisure.

As Quasimodo and Frollo hurried back to the cathedral, Gringoire continued on his way and found himself in a disreputable quarter of Paris. Captured by thugs, he was threatened with death if none of the women in the thieves' den would marry him. When no one wanted the pale, thin poet, a noose was lowered about his neck. Suddenly Esmerelda appeared and volunteered to take him. But Gringoire enjoyed no wedding night. Esmerelda's heart belonged to Phoebus; she had rescued the poet only out of pity.

In those days the courts of Paris often picked innocent people from the streets, tried them, and convicted them with little regard for justice. Quasimodo had been seen in his role as the Prince of Fools and had been watched as he stood before the gipsy girl while she danced. It was rumored that Esmerelda was a witch, and most of Paris suspected that Frollo, Quasimodo's only associate, was a sorcerer. Consequently Quasimodo was brought into a court, accused of keeping questionable company, and sentenced to a severe flogging and exposure on the pillory. Quasimodo endured his disgrace, stoically, but after his misshapen back had been torn by the lash, he was overcome with a terrible thirst. The crowd jeered and threw stones. They hated and feared Quasimodo because of his ugliness.

Presently Esmerelda mounted the scaffold and put her flask to Quasimodo's blackened lips. This act of kindness moved him deeply and he wept. At that same time Frollo had happened upon the scene, caught sight of Quasimodo, and departed quickly. Later Quasimodo was to remember this betrayal.

One day Phoebus was entertaining a lady in a building overlooking the square where Esmerelda was dancing. The gipsy was so smitten with Phoebus that she had taught her goat to spell out his name with alphabet blocks. When she had the animal perform this trick, the lady called her a witch and a sorceress. But Phoebus followed the gipsy and arranged for a rendezvous with her for the following night.

Gringoire, meanwhile, happened to meet Frollo, who was jealous of the poet because he was rumored to be Esmerelda's husband. But Gringoire explained that Esmerelda did not love him; she had eyes and heart only for Phoebus.

Desperate to preserve Esmerelda for himself, Frollo trailed the young gallant and asked him where he was going. Phoebus said that he had a rendezvous with Esmerelda. The priest offered him money in exchange for an opportunity to conceal himself in the room where this rendezvous was to take place, ostensibly to discover whether Esmerelda were really the girl whose name Phoebus had mentioned. It was a poor ruse at best, but Phoebus was not shy at love-making and he agreed to the bargain. When he learned that the girl was really Esmerelda, Frollo leaped from concealment and wounded

Phoebus with a dagger. Esmerelda could not see her lover's assailant in the darkness and when she fainted Frollo escaped. A crowd gathered, murmuring that the sorceress had slain Phoebus. They took the gipsy off to prison.

Now tales of Esmerelda's sorcery began to circulate. At her trial she was convicted of witchcraft, sentenced to do penance on the great porch of Notre Dame and from there to be taken to a scaffold in the Place de Greve and publicly hanged.

Captain Phoebus was not dead, but he had kept silence rather than implicate himself in a case of witchcraft. When Esmerelda was on her way to Notre Dame, she caught sight of him riding on his beautiful horse, and called out to him, but he ignored her completely. She then felt that she was doomed.

When she came before Frollo to do penance, he offered to save her if she would be his; but she refused. Quasimodo suddenly appeared on the porch, took the girl in his arms, and carried her to sanctuary within the church. Esmerelda was now safe as long as she remained within the cathedral walls.

Quasimodo hid her in his own cell, where there was a mattress and water, and brought her food. He kept the cell door locked so that if her pursuers did break the sanctuary, they could not reach her. Aware that she would be terrified of him if he stayed with her, he entered her cell only to bring her his own dinner.

Frollo, knowing that the gipsy was near him in the cathedral, secured a key to the chamber and stole in to see Esmerelda one night. She struggled hopelessly, until suddenly Quasimodo entered and dragged the priest from the cell. With smothered rage, he freed the trembling archdeacon and allowed him to run away.

One day a mob gathered and demanded that the sorceress be turned from the cathedral. Frollo was jubilant. Quasimodo, however, barred and bolted the great doors. When the crowd charged the cathedral with a battering ram, Quasimodo threw huge stones from a tower where builders had been working. The mob persisting, he poured melted lead upon the crowd below. Then the mob secured ladders and began to mount the façade, but Quasimodo seized the ladders and pushed them from the wall. Hundreds of dead and wounded lay below him.

The king's guards joined the fray. Quasimodo, looking down, thought that the soldiers had arrived to protect Esmerelda. He went to her cell, but to his amazement he found the door open and Esmerelda gone.

Frollo had given Gringoire the key to her chamber and had led the poet through the cathedral to her cell. Gringoire convinced her that she must fly, since the church was under siege. She followed him trustingly, and he led her to a boat where Frollo was already waiting. Frightened by the violence of the priest, Gringoire fled. Once more, Frollo offered to save Esmerelda if she would be his, but she refused him. Fleeing, she sought refuge in a cell belonging to a madwoman. There the soldiers found her and dragged her away for her execution the next morning at dawn.

Quasimodo, meanwhile, roamed the cathedral searching for Esmerelda. Making his way to the tower which looked down upon the bridge of Notre Dame, Quasimodo came upon Frollo, who stood shaking with laughter as he watched a scene far below. Following the direction of the priest's gaze, Quasimodo saw a gibbet erected in the Place de Greve and on the platform a woman in white. It was Esmerelda. Quasimodo saw the noose lowered over the girl's head and the platform released. The body swayed in the morning breeze. Then Quasimodo picked up Frollo and thrust him over the wall on which he had been leaning. At that moment Quasimodo understood everything that the priest had done to ensure the death of Esmerelda. He looked at the crushed body at the foot of the tower and then at the figure in white upon the gallows. He wept.

After the deaths of Esmerelda and Claude Frollo, Quasimodo was not to be found. Then in the reign of Charles VIII the vault of Montfaucon, in which the bodies of criminals were interred, was opened to locate the remains of a famous prisoner who had been buried there. Among the skeletons were those of a woman who had been clad in white and of a man whose bony arms were wrapped tightly around the woman's body. His spine was crooked, one leg was shorter than the other, and it was evident that he had not been hanged, for his neck was unbroken. When those who discovered these singular remains tried to separate the two bodies, they crumbled into dust.

HUNGER

Type of work: Novel
Author: Knut Hamsun (Knut Pedersen Hamsund, 1859-1952)
Type of plot: Impressionistic realism
Time of plot: Late nineteenth century
Locale: Norway
First published: 1890

Principal character:
THE NARRATOR, a young writer

Critique:

Hunger was the work that immedi- ately brought Hamsun to the attention

HUNGER by Knut Hamsun. Translated by George Egerton. By permission of the publishers, Alfred A. Knopf, Inc. Copyright, 1920, by Alfred A. Knopf, Inc. Renewed, 1948, by Alfred A. Knopf, Inc.

of a wide literary audience, and the novel has been reprinted and translated many times. Realistic in subject, its form and treatment are highly impressionistic. Hamsun has given us a striking study of a man's mind under stress, but it is not a clinical study; it is an artistic piece of literature.

The Story:

I awoke at six o'clock and lay awake in my bed until eight. Hungry, I searched in my packet of odds and ends, but there was not even a crumb of bread. I knew that I should have gone out early to look for work, but I had been refused so often I was almost afraid to venture out again.

At last I took some paper and went out, for if the weather permitted I could write in the park. There were several good ideas in my head for newspaper articles. In the street an old cripple with a big bundle was using all his strength to keep ahead of me.

When I caught up with him he turned around and whined for a halfpenny to buy milk. Not having a cent on me, I hurried back to the pawnbroker's dark shop. In the hall I took off my waistcoat and rolled it in a ball. The pawnbroker gave me one and six for it. I found the old cripple again and gave him his halfpenny. He stared at me with his mouth open as I hurried away.

Two women, one of them young, were idly strolling about. When I told the young woman that she would lose her book, she looked frightened and they hurried on. Seeing them standing before a shop window, I went up to them again and told the younger woman that she was losing her book. She looked herself over in a bewildered way; she had no book. I kept following them, but they put me down as a harmless madman.

In the park I could not write a thing. Little flies stuck to my paper. All afternoon I tried to brush them off. Then I wrote an application for a job as book-keeper. After a day or two I went to see the man in person. He laughed at my desire to become a bookkeeper because I had dated my letter 1848, years before I was born. I went home discouraged.

On my table was a letter. I thought it a notice from my landlady, for I was behind in my rent. But no, my story had been accepted. The editor said it would be printed right away. He had included a half sovereign in payment. I had written a masterpiece and I had a half sovereign.

A few weeks later I went out for an evening walk and sat in a churchyard with a new manuscript. At eight o'clock, when the gates were closed, I meant to go straight home to the vacant tinker's workshop which I had permission to occupy, but I stumbled around hardly knowing where I was. I felt feverish because I had not eaten for several days. At last I sat down and dozed off. I dreamed that a beautiful girl dressed in silk waited for me in a doorway and led me down a hall, she holding my hand. We went into a crimson room where she clasped me tightly and begged me to kiss her.

A policeman woke me up and advised me to go to the police barracks as a homeless man. When I got there, I lied about my name and said that it was too late for me to get back to my lodgings. The officer believed me and gave me a private room. In the morning, thinking I was only a young rake instead of a destitute, the police gave me no breakfast ticket. I drank a lot of water but I could scarcely keep it down.

Faint with hunger, I cut the buttons from my coat and tried to pawn them, but the pawnbroker laughed at me. On the way out I met a friend bringing his watch to pawn. He fed me and gave me five shillings.

I went to see an editor who critically read my sketch on Corregio. He was kind, saying that he would like to publish my work but that he had to keep his subscribers in mind. He asked if I could write something more to the common taste. When I prepared to leave, he also asked me if I needed money. He was sure I could write it out. Although I had not eaten a real meal for some time, I thanked him and left without an advance payment.

A lady in black stood every night on the corner by my tinker's garret. She would look intently at my lodging for a while and then pass on. After several days I spoke to her and accompanied her on her walk. She said she had no special interest in my poor garret or in me. When she lifted her veil, I saw she was the woman I had followed and spoken to about the book. She was merry with me and seemed to enjoy my company.

One night she took me to her home. Once inside, we embraced; then we sat down and began to talk. She confessed that she was attracted to me because she thought I was a madman. She was an adventurous girl, on the lookout for odd experiences. I told her the truth about myself, that I acted queerly because I was so poor. Much of the time I was so hungry that I had a fever. She found my story hard to believe, but I convinced her. She was sympathetic for a moment. I had to leave, for her mother was returning, and I never saw her again.

I awoke sick one morning. All day I shivered in bed. Toward night I went down to the little shop below to buy a candle, for I felt I had to write something. A boy was alone in the store. I gave him a florin for my candle, but he gave me change for a crown. I stared stupidly at the money in my hand for a long time, but I got out without betraying myself.

I took a room in a real hotel and had a chamber to myself and breakfast and supper. About the time my money was gone I started on a medieval play. The landlady trusted me for quite a while, for I explained that I would pay her as soon as my play was finished. One night she brought a sailor up to my room and turned me out, but she let me go down and sleep with the family.

For some time I slept on a sofa in the entryway, and once in a while a servant gave me bread and cheese. In my nervous condition it was hard to be meek and grateful. The break came one evening when the children were amusing themselves by sticking straws into the nose and ears of the paralyzed grandfather who lay on a bed before the fire. I protested against their cruel sport. The landlady flew at me in a rage and ordered me out.

I wandered down to the docks and got a berth on a Russian freighter going to England. I came back to the hotel for my possessions and on the step met the postman. He handed me a letter addressed in a feminine hand. Inside was a half sovereign. I crumpled the envelope and coin together and threw them in the landlady's face.

HUON DE BORDEAUX

Type of work: Chanson de geste
Author: Unknown
Type of plot: Chivalric romance
Time of plot: Ninth century
Locale: Paris, Jerusalem, Rome, the fairy kingdom of Mommur
First transcribed: First half of the thirteenth century

Principal characters:
    HUON OF BORDEAUX, older son of the dead Duke of Guienne
    GERARD, his younger brother
    CHARLEMAGNE, King of France

CHARLOT, his older son
EARL AMAURY, Charlot's evil adviser
DUKE NAYMES, Charlemagne's adviser
THE ABBOT OF CLUNY, uncle to Huon and Gerard
GERAMES, a loyal hermit
OBERON, king of fairyland
GAWDIS, Amir of Babylon
CLARAMOND, his daughter

Critique:

In this lengthy example of medieval French verse romance, we see a *chanson de geste*—a "tale of a deed"—in a developed and perhaps impure form. The unknown author, thought to be a writer of the first half of the thirteenth century and perhaps a resident of the town of St. Omer, combines in a somewhat ununified tale different sorts of materials. The events are supposed to take place late in the reign of Charlemagne, after the betrayal and defeat of Roland at Roncesvalles and therefore early in the ninth century. The Charlemagne of this poem bears a celebrated historical name but few of the attributes of the great king of the Dark Ages. He is petulant, suspicious, and ill-advised in important decisions: the wisdom, temperance, and heroism of the historical figure is gone, and a fairy tale personage—an inferior King Lear—remains; on his vacillating decisions much of the story rests. Although the imagination of the author of *Huon de Bordeaux* did respond to the actual social conditions of his time, he drew also on conventional but highly fanciful narrative materials to which any medieval storyteller had access. Stories of the dwarf fairy-king, Oberon, rise from both Celtic tale and Germanic story. Tales about the crusaders made available to the writer confused details about "paynim" countries that bulk large in the main portion of Huon's adventures, but it is plain to any reader that these details mask a very sketchy knowledge. In leaving France behind, the medieval rhymer left reality behind; and the extensive travels of the hero take us into realms as fantastic and nonexistent as those of Prester John.

The Story:

King Charlemagne, grown old and wishing to relinquish the burden of government, summoned his court and consulted with his nobles to determine the succession to his throne. His plan was to abdicate in favor of his two sons, but the nobles of France were not willing to accept his favorite, Charlot, partly because of the young prince's association with Earl Amaury, kinsman of the infamous Ganelon who had betrayed Roland to his death. The earl, the partisan of Charlot, took the occasion to get revenge on the noble house of Guienne. His suggestion was that Charlot be given a province to govern before he took over the responsibilities of a state. It was called to Charlemagne's doting attention—for the king had become violent and unreasonable in his judgments and punishments—that the two sons of the dead duke had not yet come to Paris to pay their respects and render homage. Earl Amaury's hope was to see them dispossessed and their lands given to Charlot.

Sent to conduct the heirs of the dead duke to Charlemagne's court, messengers discovered that what the king's wise adviser, Duke Naymes, had stated was indeed the case: the brothers, Huon and Gerard, had been too young to come to court before. The messengers, pleased with their reception by the duchess, the boys' mother, and with the manly bearing of young Huon of Bordeaux, the older son, returned with word that the young noblemen would soon follow them to swear fealty to the king.

Huon and Gerard set out on their journey to Paris, stopping on the way at the monastery of Cluny where their uncle was abbot. The noble churchman decided to accompany his nephews to Charlemagne's court.

In the meantime Charlot had been persuaded by Earl Amaury to ambush the boys and kill them. Because their lands were extensive and tempting, the prince agreed. But in the fray Charlot was killed when Huon struck him with his sword, severing the prince's helmet. In spite of the abbot's testimony, however, Charlemagne refused to believe that Huon had acted in self-defense and without knowledge of his assailant's identity. In a trial by combat with Earl Amaury, Huon killed that wretched knight before he could gasp out, at death's verge, a true account of his villainy. Still unenlightened, the angry king sent Huon on a pilgrimage to Jerusalem and also ordered him to kiss three times the beautiful Claramond, the daughter of Gawdis, Amir of Babylon, and to return with white hairs from the amir's beard and teeth from his mouth.

Obedient to Charlemagne's command, Huon parted company with his brother Gerard, in whose care he left his lands. Although there had been love between the brothers in the past, Gerard straightway became false to his trust and plotted great evil against his distant brother. For Huon's return was greatly delayed. Though fortune often favored him and provided him with kinsmen in odd corners of the world, the wicked paynims abused him, imprisoned him, and on many occasions carried him far from his destination. Gerames, a hermit, became his loyal follower after chance threw them together, and he was close at Huon's heels when the Christian knight kissed Claramond and got the teeth and the hair from the severed head of the amir after that ruler had received the bowstring from the dread Caliph of Arabia. Huon secreted the teeth and hair in the side of the hermit for safekeeping.

Huon was aided in his adventures by two gifts from Oberon, the dwarf king of the Otherworld, born of an ancient union between Julius Caesar and Morgan le Fay. Gerames, the wise hermit, had warned Huon not to speak to Oberon, but Huon, ignoring his advice, spoke to the dwarf and so won the protection of the white magic of that strange little creature. Huon was able to carry with him the gifts from Oberon. One was a cup that filled up at the sign of the cross and emptied when it was held in the hand of a wicked person. The other was a horn which Huon was supposed to blow to summon Oberon's help when grave danger threatened. Huon, like the boy who cried wolf in Aesop's fable, blew the horn too frequently, and Oberon was sometimes tempted not to respond. Moreover, Huon's dignity and prudence sometimes left him. Despite warnings, he embraced the lovely Claramond before they were married and so brought about an interminable separation; and he once imprudently allowed a giant to arm himself before a contest. But at last, with the combined help of the hermit and the fairy king, Huon and Claramond reached Rome, where their marriage was blessed by the Pope himself, who was the uncle of Huon.

On his return to France with his bride, Huon found that his brother was now his foe and that well-wishers like Duke Naymes could not protect him from the anger and dotage of Charlemagne. But Oberon could. The fairy king made his appearance, humbled great Charlemagne, and saw to it that Huon and Claramond were secure in all their rights. Though Huon interceded for his brother's life and made the court weep by his display of generosity, Oberon was obdurate, and Gerard and his fellow conspirators were hanged. As a final favor, Huon was promised that he would someday inherit Oberon's kingdom.

HYDE PARK

Type of work: Drama
Author: James Shirley (1596-1666)
Type of plot: Comedy of manners
Time of plot: Early seventeenth century
Locale: London
First presented: 1632

Principal characters:
> LORD BONVILE, a sporting peer
> TRIER, his friend, betrothed to Julietta
> FAIRFIELD, favored suitor to Mistress Carol
> RIDER, and
> VENTURE, her rejected suitors
> BONAVENT, a merchant returned after seven years' absence
> MISTRESS BONAVENT, his wife, who thinks herself a widow
> LACY, Mistress Bonavent's suitor
> JULIETTA, Fairfield's sister, pursued by Lord Bonvile
> MISTRESS CAROL, Mistress Bonavent's cousin and companion

Critique:

Hyde Park, the second of Shirley's sprightly comedies, paved the way for the later Restoration drama. The play, honoring the opening of Hyde Park to the public by the first Earl of Holland, presented to the audience of that time interesting gaming talk as well as the manners of the fashionable world. Pepys reports that live horses were led across the stage in a production of Hyde Park some years after the playwright's death in the Great Fire of London. Though the play itself looks forward to a more sophisticated drama, it is still firmly based in the delightful fancies of Shakespeare, Jonson, and other Elizabethan and Jacobean playwrights, of whom Shirley was the last of note.

The Story:

Because her husband, a merchant, had been missing for seven years, Mistress Bonavent had for some time considered a second marriage to Lacy, her persistent suitor. Mistress Carol, her cousin and companion, urged her not to give away so lightly the independence she had won. Mistress Carol herself swore never to marry, even though she carried on flirtations with Rider, Venture, and Fairfield. Rider and Venture, vying with each other for the lady's favor, had each given her a gift which she in turn presented to his rival. Comparing notes, they concluded that Fairfield must be the favored suitor.

Lacy, summoned by Mistress Bonavent's servant, felt certain that his suit was now successful. Into this confused arena of love arrived Lord Bonvile, a sportsman who admired both horses and women, and Bonavent, disguised in order to find out what had happened during his absence.

Though Fairfield's overtures to Mistress Carol were rejected, Lacy's to Mistress Bonavent were accepted, and the wedding was set for that very morning. Mistress Carol told her cousin that she was acting rashly, no man being worth the candle.

Bonavent soon learned that the sound of merriment in his own house augured no good for that returned merchant who, held captive by a Turkish pirate, had only recently been ransomed. Lacy, perhaps too merry with wine and anticipation, bade the stranger welcome and asked, then demanded, that he dance with and, finally, for them. Bonavent's dancing was ridiculed, especially by sharp-tongued Mistress Carol. Lacy tried to

1391

make amends by inviting him to join additional revels in Hyde Park that very day.

In the meantime Fairfield, despairing because of his love for Mis'ress Carol, said farewell to his sister Julietta and wished her well in her coming marriage to Jack Trier. But it was soon apparent to the young woman that her suitor was not in earnest in his avowals of love, for he introduced her to his friend Lord Bonvile and then left them. Before his departure Trier had whispered in the lord's ear that he was in a sporting house and the lady was a person of easy virtue. As a woman of good breeding, and aware only that her fiancé had shown poor manners, Julietta invited Lord Bonvile to accompany her to the park, an invitation which provided her betrothed with an opportunity to try her chastity.

When the two aggrieved lovers, Rider and Venture, appealed to Mis'ress Carol not to make sport of them by passing their gifts on to their rival, she declared that she had no interest in them and had always told them so; in their persis'ence, however, they had paid little attention to her. Fairfield, coming to say goodbye, first asked her to swear to one agreement without knowing what it was. Convinced at last that the agreement would not commit her to love, marry, or go to bed with him, she agreed; at his request she then swore never to desire his company again or to love him. The oath sealed with a kiss, he departed, leaving her in a state of consternation.

Julietta, courted by a baffled lord whose very propositions were turned into pleasantries, remained aloof from her still more baffled suitor, who could not determine how far the flirtation had gone in Hyde Park.

Still in disguise, Bonavent learned that Lacy and his wife were indeed married but that the marriage had not yet been consummated—to the pleasure of his informant, Mis'ress Carol, who by now was distressed by affection for the previously spurned Fairfield. She sent a message by Trier asking Fairfield to come to see her, but on his arrival she denied that she had sent for him. Fairfield, in turn, offered to release her from her oath if she would have him, but she turned coquette and rejected his proposal. Consequently, he refused to believe her when she protested that she now loved him.

Lord Bonvile, torn between his desire to play what he thought was a sure thing and the horses which were a gamble, pushed his suit too far, and for his brashness received a lecture on titles and good breeding, a remonstrance which he took to heart.

The disconsolate Mistress Carol met Julietta, who informed the spurned one that Fairfield was as disconsolate as she. Mis'ress Carol then concocted a stratagem at the expense of Venture, a poet, horseman, and singer. She goaded him into writing a poem on the lengths to which he would go for her love, and to this effusion she later affixed the name of Fairfield. Meanwhile, in Hyde Park, Bonavent hired a bagpipe and made the bridegroom dance to the tune of a sword at his legs, a return for the courtesy extended at the wedding festivities. In a note to his wife, the merchant informed her of his return but urged her to secrecy for the time being.

Mistress Carol, who now pretended to believe that Venture's hyperbole was a suicide note from Fairfield, summoned her recalcitrant suitor. Thinking that she was still making fun of him, he denied any intention of doing away with himself and in turn accused her of duplicity. He added that he would make himself a gelding so that women would no longer concern him—a threat more real to Mistress Carol than that of suicide. On the spot she abandoned all pride and proposed marriage to him. He immediately accepted.

Lord Bonvile, having learned too late from Trier that he was the victim of a jealous lover, was accepted by Julietta as a worthy suitor, now that his thoughts were as lofty as his position in society.

Bonavent, to show himself unresentful, proposed a merry celebration and placed willow garlands on the heads of the disappointed lovers: Trier, Lacy, Rider, and Venture. He received the good wishes of Lacy and pledged himself to entertain the whole party at supper with tales of his captivity.

All this, however, had been prophesied earlier in Hyde Park, when Lord Bonvile and his Julietta, Fairfield and Mistress Carol, and Mr. and Mistress Bonavent had heard the song of Philomel, the nightingale. The others had heard only the cuckoo.

HYPATIA

Type of work: Novel
Author: Charles Kingsley (1819-1875)
Type of plot: Historical romance
Time of plot: Fifth century
Locale: Egypt and Italy
First published: 1853

Principal characters·
   PHILAMMON, a young monk
   HYPATIA, a female Greek philosopher and teacher
   RAPHAEL ABEN-EZRA, a young Jew, Hypatia's pupil
   MIRIAM, an old Jewish crone
   AMAL, a young Gothic chief
   PELAGIA, Amal's mistress
   ORESTES, Roman prefect of Alexandria

Critique:

In Alexandria in the fifth century after Christ's death, there were many forces, Pagan, Christian, and Jewish, all struggling for the souls of men. *Hypatia* is the story of that conflict, which ended with the disintegration of a victorious Christian faction that used violence to gain its ends. The larger background of the novel is the dissolving Roman Empire.

The Story:

Philammon might never have left the little colony of monks three hundred miles above Alexandria if he had not strayed into an ancient temple in search of kindling. There, on the temple walls, he saw paintings of a life undreamed of in his monastic retreat, and he longed to visit the greater outside world. That very day, against the advice of the abbot and Aufugus, a monk whom he highly respected, he started out in a small boat and traveled down the river toward Alexandria.

In that splendid city at the mouth of the Nile lived Hypatia, the beautiful philosopher and teacher, one of the last to champion the ancient Greek gods. As she sat with her books one day, she was visited by the Roman prefect, Orestes, with the news that Pelagia, a beautiful courtesan who was Hypatia's rival for the hearts and souls of men, had left the city. Pelagia had transferred her affections to Amal, a Goth chieftain, and had joined him on a trip up the Nile in search of Asgard, home of the old Gothic gods.

Cyril, the patriarch of Alexandria, had reported to Orestes that the Jews of the city were about to rise and slaughter the Christians, but Orestes chose to ignore the matter and let events take their course. Hypatia, who also had reason to oppose the Christian patriarch, suggested that Cyril make his charges before the Roman tribunal, which would, of course, postpone action against the Jews.

1393

A wealthy young Jew, Raphael Aben-Ezra, whom Orestes met on his way to the palace, suggested that the prefect plead ignorance of any plot in his reply to Cyril. Raphael disclosed to the Roman that Heraclian, a Roman leader, had recently sailed for Italy, where he planned to destroy the Gothic conquerors of Rome and make himself emperor. His news led Orestes to think of the power he might hold south of the Mediterranean if the expedition succeeded.

Sailing down the Nile, Philammon met Pelagia and the party of Goths traveling in the opposite direction. He helped the men kill a hippopotamus. When he warned them that they could never cross the cataracts to the south, the Goths decided to turn back. Philammon was given a place in their boat.

Orestes sent Hypatia a letter delivered by the old Jewish crone, Miriam. It contained Raphael's news and a proposal that Hypatia marry the prefect and share the throne he was planning to create for himself in Egypt. Hypatia's reply was that she would accept the offer if Orestes would renounce his Christian 'faith and aid her in restoring the Greek gods.

Orestes, having no desire to face excommunication, was disturbed by her answer. At Raphael's suggestion, he decided to wait for a month in the hope that Hypatia's desire to marry a future emperor would overcome her religious zeal.

When they arrived in Alexandria, Philammon left the Goths and went to deliver to the Patriarch Cyril the letters of introduction he carried. While waiting to see the patriarch, Philammon overheard a plot to raid the Jewish quarter the next day.

That night, as he lay in bed in the patriarch's house, Philammon heard cries that the Jews were burning Alexander's Church. Joining a crowd of monks hurrying toward that edifice, he was attacked by a band of Hebrew marauders. But the report of the conflagration was false; it had been a trick of the Jews to lure the Christians into ambush. During the street fighting the Roman constabulary, which was supposed to keep order, remained aloof.

The next morning Miriam, who took a mysterious interest in Raphael's welfare, hastened to his quarters to warn him to flee. Christians, attacking the Jewish quarter, were pillaging the houses and expelling their inhabitants. To Miriam's exasperation, Raphael showed no interest in the fate of his wealth. Calmly exchanging his rich robes for a Christian's tattered rags, he prepared to leave the city. Miriam was left to save what she could of his possessions.

Philammon was one of the Christians who aided in despoiling the Jews. During the rioting he began to compare the conduct of the monks of Alexandria with the principles of charity and good works he himself had been taught. Hearing of Hypatia and her teachings, he naïvely went to the museum where she lectured, in the hope of converting her to Christianity by his arguments. Nearly put out of the building by her pupils when he rose to dispute with her, he was spared at Hypatia's request. After the lecture she invited him to visit her the following day.

The Alexandrian monks were incensed when they learned that one Philammon had been to listen to the discourse of a pagan. When he visited Hypatia again, they accused him of being a heretic, and the young monk barely escaped being murdered. Philammon, charmed by Hypatia's beauty and purity, begged to become her pupil.

Raphael, who had fled to Italy, found himself in a devastated Rome. Heraclian, after his defeat by the Goths, was preparing to reëmbark for Africa. After Raphael had saved one member of the ill-fated expedition and his daughter, Victoria, from two barbarian soldiers, he sailed with them from Ostia to Berenice, a port on the coast of Africa.

Meanwhile, in Alexandria, Philammon had become Hypatia's favorite pupil. Aufugus, learning that the youth had deserted his Christian brethren, went to the city to find him. One day the two men met in the street. Aufugus, seeing that Philammon was determined to remain with his mentor, declared that the young monk was actually his slave, and he appealed to Orestes, who was passing by, to force Philammon to go with his legal owner. Philammon fled to take temporary refuge with the Goths in Pelagia's house.

After Philammon had returned to his own rooms, he received a summons from Miriam. She confirmed the fact that he was Aufugus' slave, for she had seen Philammon bought in Athens fifteen years before. Although Miriam had received the report of Heraclian's defeat by fast messenger, she wrote a letter which declared that Heraclian had been the victor. She sent Philammon to deliver the letter to Orestes.

The prefect immediately planned a great celebration, in which the beautiful Pelagia should dance as Venus Anadyomene. Philammon hotly objected to the plan, for when Miriam told him he was a slave she had implied also that Pelagia was his sister. Annoyed, Orestes ordered the monk to be thrown into jail. There Philammon was held prisoner until the day of the celebration. Released, he hurried to the arena in time to witness the slaughter of some Libyan slaves by professional gladiators. Orestes, with Hypatia beside him, watched from his box.

When Pelagia was carried into the amphitheater by an elephant and introduced as Venus, Orestes' hirelings tried to raise a cry to proclaim him Emperor of Africa. No one responded. Pelagia danced before her audience until Philammon, overcome by shame, could bear the sight no longer. Running to stop her shameful dance, he was caught up by the elephant's trunk and would have been dashed to death if Pelagia had not persuaded the animal to put him down.

Pelagia left the amphitheater. Philammon was hustled away by the guards.

Orestes, however, was determined that his plan should succeed. When the uproar caused by Philammon began to die down, he stepped forward and offered himself as emperor. As had been prearranged, the city authorities began a clamor for him; but hardly had they started their outcry when a monk in the topmost tiers shouted that Heraclian had been defeated. Orestes and Hypatia fled.

Philammon, when he returned home, found Pelagia in his quarters. He begged his sister, as he now called her, to leave the Goth, Amal, and repent her ways, but the courtesan refused. Instead, she entreated him to ask Hypatia to accept her as a pupil, so that Amal, whose affection for her was failing, would love and respect her as the Greek woman was respected. But Hypatia had no pity for her hated rival. Philammon, carrying the news of her refusal to his sister, could not help thinking fondly of his own religion, with its offer of pity to all transgressors.

Hypatia knew the populace would soon be clamoring for her blood and that she would be forced to flee. In one last desperate effort to hold to her creed, she forced herself into a trance that she might have a visitation from the gods. The only face she saw, however, was Pelagia's.

When Miriam visited Hypatia the same day with the promise that she should see Apollo that night if she would visit the house of the Jewess, the distraught philosopher agreed. But the Apollo the crone showed her was Philammon, stupefied by drugged wine. As Miriam had foreseen, Hypatia realized at last that the only gods she would ever see were those that existed in her own mind. Shamed and angry, she went away. The final blow to fall on Hypatia was the news Raphael brought her on his return to Alexandria the next day. Under the persuasion of Augustine, the famous philosopher-monk, he had become a converted Catholic before leaving Berenice, and he had married Victoria. That afternoon, as she started for the museum to give her farewell lecture, Hypatia was torn to pieces by some of Cyril's monks.

Philammon, when he learned of Hypatia's fate, visited Pelagia and pleaded with her to flee with him. By chance he met Amal, and in a struggle that ensued they fell from a tower together, and the Goth was killed. After Amal's death, Pelagia was willing to leave the city. Together they returned to the desert, where Pelagia lived in solitary penitence and Philammon became abbot, eventually, of the community he had left. Brother and sister died at the same time and were buried in a common grave.

Before he departed from Alexandria forever, Raphael learned from Miriam that she was his mother. A Jewess by birth, she had been converted to Christianity and had lived in a convent until it was sacked by the heathen. Afterward she had renounced her faith and had sworn the destruction of everyone not of her own race. Raphael had been given to a rich Jewess, who had represented him to her husband as her own child. After confessing her relationship to her son, Miriam died on his shoulder. She had been mortally wounded by the Goths after the death of their leader.

The victory which the Patriarch Cyril gained by Hypatia's death was only temporary. Though it marked the end of her creed in Egypt, it also signified the decline of the Egyptian Church, for the Christians, splitting into many factions, did not hesitate to use on each other the same violence they had once displayed toward the Greek philosopher.

THE HYPOCHONDRIAC

Type of work: Drama
Author: Molière (Jean Baptiste Poquelin, 1622-1673)
Type of plot: Romantic comedy
Time of plot: Seventeenth century
Locale: Paris, France
First presented: 1673

Principal characters:
ARGAN, an imaginary invalid
BÉLINE, his second wife
ANGÉLIQUE, Argan's daughter
CLÉANTE, her lover
BÉRALDE, Argan's brother
THOMAS DIAFOIRUS, the doctor's son
TOINETTE, Argan's maidservant

Critique:

Turning his satirical pen to the medical profession, Molière almost surpasses even his own bitterness as displayed in his earlier plays. *The Hypochondriac (Le Malade Imaginaire)* was his last comedy, and he was unmerciful in his attack on all doctors and pharmacists. His usual wit and humor are not lost in the irony, but they are secondary to it. It is now almost three hundred years since Molière's death, but his literary stature has not diminished with the years. He is still studied and imitated as he was in his own time.

The Story:

Argan was the worst sort of hypochondriac. Each day saw him trying a new drug of some sort, so that the doctor and apothecary could exist almost exclusively on their profits from Argan. Toinette, his maidservant, tried in vain to persuade him to end his worries about his health, for she was certain that there was absolutely nothing the matter with her master. But he would not listen to her; he was determined to be an invalid.

He was encouraged in his supposed illness by his doctor and by Béline, his second wife, who used his weakness to further her schemes to get his money. Because the law said that a second wife could not inherit, it was essential to Béline that Argan make a settlement on her while he still lived. To that end also she tried to get him to place his two daughters in a convent, so that they could not interfere by claiming money for themselves.

Argan had other plans for his older daughter, Angélique. He was going to force her betrothal to his doctor's son in order to have a doctor in the family. He told the girl that a dutiful daughter would take a husband useful to her father. But Angélique, loving a young man named Cléante, begged her father not to force her marriage to Thomas Diafoirus, the doctor's son. Argan was firm because the young man would also inherit a large sum of money from his father and another from his uncle, the apothecary. If Angélique would not obey his wishes, he threatened to place her in a convent, as her stepmother wished him to do. Toinette scolded him severely for forcing his daughter to marry against her wishes, but he would not be moved. Toinette, wishing to help Angélique, got word to Cléante that his beloved was to be given to another.

Cléante disguised himself as the friend of Angélique's singing-master and told Argan that he had been sent to give her her singing lesson. Toinette pretended to change her mind and sympathize with Argan's position regarding the marriage. In that way she could offer to guard Angélique, while in reality giving the young lovers an opportunity to be alone together.

As the supposed teacher, Cléante had to witness the meeting between Thomas and Angélique. Thomas was a great boob of a boy, quoting memorized speeches to Argan, Angélique, and Béline. His father, the doctor, was quite proud that Thomas had always been a little slow in learning and that he followed blindly the opinions of the ancients, not accepting any of the new medical discoveries—for example, the thesis that blood circulated through the system.

Poor Angélique knew that she could never marry such a stupid oaf. She begged her father at least to give her time to become acquainted with Thomas, but the most he would give her was four days. At the end of that period she must either marry Thomas or go into a convent. In order to be assured of Argan's money, Béline continued to plead with him to choose the convent for his daughter.

Argan's brother, Béralde, called on him and also pleaded Angélique's cause. He thought it wicked to force her to marry against her wishes. He knew that Argan was not really ill and did not need a doctor in the family. In fact, he knew that the doctor would soon cause his brother's death by the constant "drenching" of his abdomen. Béralde sent the medicines away, causing the doctor to renounce his patient and to predict his death within four days. The apothecary canceled his contract to give his nephew a marriage settlement, and neither of the professionals would be soothed by Argan's protestations that it was his brother and not he who had denounced them and their treatments. Argan believed that he would surely die without their attention.

Toinette and Béralde then schemed to trick the hypochondriac. Toinette disguised herself as a physician and told Argan that his former doctor had been entirely mistaken in his diagnosis of Argan's illness. His liver and bowels were not ailing, but his lungs were; he must cut off his arm and pluck out his eye because they were drawing all his strength to them. Even Argan would not take such a drastic remedy. The poor man felt that he was doomed.

Still Argan would not relent concerning Angélique. Since the doctor and the apothecary had broken their marriage contracts, Angélique must go to a convent and become a nun. When Béralde accused him of being influenced by his wife, Argan agreed to Toinette's suggestion that he allow his wife to prove her love for him. Toinette knew the greed of Béline, but she pretended to Argan that if he acted dead he would see that she loved him and not his money. In this way he could convince his brother of Béline's true love.

The plan was carried out, but when Toinette cried to Béline that Argan was dead, the wife praised heaven that she was rid of her dirty, disgusting husband. Then she tried to bribe Toinette to help her keep Argan's death a secret until she could get certain papers and money into her possession. At that Argan rose up from his supposed deathbed to confront his wife. She fled in terror.

Toinette persuaded Argan to try the same plan with his daughter. When Angélique was told that her father was dead, she wept for him. Cléante came into the room and Angélique told him that now she could not marry him. Her father was dead, and she could make amends for her previous refusals to obey him only by carrying out his wishes now. Argan again rose from his deathbed, this time to bless his daughter for her faithfulness. Toinette and Béralde reminded him of his daughter's love and of his duty to reward her by allowing her to marry the man of her choice. Argan agreed that she could marry Cléante if he would become a doctor and minister to Argan's needs. Cléante was willing, but Béralde had a better idea. Argan should become a doctor himself; then he could give himself constant attention. All that was needed was for him to don cap and gown. He could then spout gibberish and make it sound learned. So the matter was settled, and the old hypochondriac gave his blessing to the young lovers.

I, CLAUDIUS

Type of work: Novel
Author: Robert Graves (1895-   )
Type of plot: Historical chronicle
Time of plot: 10 B. C.-A. D. 41
Locale: Rome
First published: 1934

Principal characters:

TIBERIUS CLAUDIUS DRUSUS NERO GERMANICUS, Emperor of Rome after Caligula
AUGUSTUS CAESAR, first Emperor of Rome
LIVIA, his wife, Claudius' grandmother
TIBERIUS, Claudius' uncle, successor to Augustus
GERMANICUS, Claudius' brother
CALIGULA, Germanicus' son, successor to Tiberius

Critique:

I, Claudius is a semi-fictional reconstruction of an interesting period in the history of the Roman empire. In it are snatches of history, records of conquest, Roman scenes, and names famous in history books. It is told in an informal manner, Claudius going to great lengths to reveal plot after plot, and the narrative method obscures in part the scholarly research and historical accuracy of the author.

The Story:

Claudius, Emperor of Rome, was held in little esteem because he was a stammerer. He was, moreover, a scholar in a nation which worshipped soldiering. He had compiled state histories but he realized that they were dull, sententious drivel. At last he decided to tell the true story of his own life. As the source of his inspiration he cited the Cumaean sibyl whom he had visited in her inner cavern. She had said that eventually he would speak clearly.

From the beginning, the Claudian family felt ashamed of young Claudius because he was a lame stammerer who seemed unlikely to carry on the family tradition of power. For that reason he developed into a scholarly person interested in the lives of others. His teachers told him stories about famous people and from many sources he picked up stray scraps of knowledge about them as he grew up.

He was greatly interested in his grandmother, the Empress Livia. Bored with her husband, she had secured a divorce, arranged her own marriage with the Emperor Augustus, and poisoned thereafter anyone who interfered with her plans. Power was her sole delight.

Another of the infamous people about him was Tiberius, who was for years the successor-to-be of Augustus. Son of Livia by an early marriage, he married the wanton Julia, daughter of Livia and Augustus. When Tiberius, having offended Augustus, was banished, Livia insisted that Julia be banished too. Tiberius, tired of his banishment, promised that if Livia would secure his return he would agree with her every wish thereafter. About that time the two sons of Julia and Tiberius died mysteriously.

Between Claudius' ninth and sixteenth years he occupied himself with affairs of his older relatives. He was married early to a girl named Urgulanilla, who detested him as much as he detested her. Claudius' first love had been mysteriously poisoned and Claudius suspected Livia, who later forced him to marry Urgulanilla. Claudius' scholarship and stability eventually brought him into the good graces of Augustus and Livia. They made him a priest of Mars and showed by public interest in him that he was an accepted member of the imperial family.

Grain shortage caused rioting accompanied by arson. Augustus distributed grain according to the usual custom, banished such people as did not hold property in Rome, and rationed what food was available. Livia staged a sword fight in the arena to restore the good will of the populace. Because Claudius fainted publicly at the brutal sports, Livia decided that never again might he show his face in public. Soon afterward the last of Augustus' sons was banished for life. Tiberius was proclaimed the adopted son and successor of Augustus.

Tiberius and young Germanicus, brother of Claudius, campaigned against the barbarians, but Tiberius was not popular in spite of his victories with the army. Augustus suffered stomach disorders and died. Claudius knew that about a month before his death he had decided to restore his banished son, Postumus, grant money and honor to Claudius, and replace Tiberius. Claudius suspected Livia of the emperor's death.

Postumus was reported killed by a captain of the guard which had been placed around him. Livia slowly starved Julia to death. Because Germanicus was too honorable to seize the empire from Tiberius, there remained only the proof that Postumus was really dead to make Tiberius safe upon the throne. When Postumus returned, to disprove reports of his death, Tiberius had him tortured and killed.

Germanicus continued his successful campaign against the Germans. Tiberius, jealous, insisted that Germanicus return to Rome for his triumph. In A. D. 17 Germanicus returned. By that time Livia suspected Claudius and Germanicus of plotting against Tiberius. She sent Claudius to Carthage to dedicate a temple to Augustus, who had been deified by the Roman Senate.

Germanicus was next dispatched to the East to command the armies there. But Livia and Tiberius began to fear that Germanicus would win favor in the East as he had already done in the West. Germanicus was finally poisoned. His wife, Agrippina, sought protection from Claudius.

Claudius promised his thirteen-year-old son in marriage to the daughter of Sejanus, the friend of Tiberius. A few days later his son was found dead. Again he suspected Livia. Shortly afterward a divorce was arranged for Claudius by Sejanus, who was anxious to have Claudius marry Aelia, his sister by adoption. Claudius knew better than to oppose the wills of those in power and he accepted his new wife with practically no concern.

Tiberius set Livia aside. She was now growing old and he no longer had great reason to fear her. Bitter at the removal of her power, she began to make plans for his successor. She determined that Caligula, the son of Germanicus, should succeed him. She called in Claudius to declare a truce with him on the condition that he would have her declared a goddess after her death. In return, she told Claudius most of her state secrets; she said that all the murders she had planned were committed solely for the good of the state.

Tiberius, sixty-seven years old, seemed destined to die before long. He was living on Capri with a court of scholars, doctors, confidants, and entertainers, Sejanus having been left in Rome with authority to rule for him. When Livia finally died at the age of eighty-six, Tiberius refused to return to Rome even for her funeral.

Tiberius began a reign of terror against all members of Livia's faction. When Sejanus attempted to rebel against the emperor's cruel decrees, Tiberius ordered his execution. His children were also put to death. Claudius was ordered to divorce Aelia.

At last the mad Tiberius lay dying at Misenum. Macro, commander of the guards, and Caligula, next in line for the throne, planned to take over the country. Caligula, already infamous among people who knew him, was still popular with the Romans. In too great a hurry they took command of the army. Then, learning that Tiberius was still alive, they smothered him.

In order to establish himself, Caligula pretended sympathy and generosity, but Claudius wrote in his history that Caligula held the record for infamy among princes up to that time. He began by spending the money Tiberius and Livia had hoarded so long. Then he fell ill. When he began to recover, he announced to Claudius that he had been transformed into a god, in fulfillment of the many prophecies that a god was soon to be given to the earth.

Caligula celebrated his godhood by wholesale assassination. Claudius' mother committed suicide because of Caligula's infamies. Soon Macro was forced to kill himself. At last the people began to turn against Caligula because of levies forced from the populace and the indescribable depravities of the palace brothel. Caligula, deciding to become a general, led an expedition into Germany. On his return he forced Claudius to marry his cousin Messalina. Calpurnia, Claudius' only true friend, was banished. The Romans were now plotting, almost openly, the assassination of Caligula. Before long he was murdered, and Claudius, the retiring scholar, was named Emperor of Rome.

I SPEAK FOR THADDEUS STEVENS

Type of work: Biography
Author: Elsie Singmaster (Mrs. E. S. Lewars, 1879-   )
Type of plot: Historical chronicle
Time of plot: 1792-1868
Locale: Vermont, Pennsylvania, Washington, D. C.
First published: 1947

Principal characters:
THADDEUS STEVENS, lawyer and statesman
SALLY MORRILL STEVENS, his mother
JOSHUA,
MORRILL, and
ALANSON, his brothers
LYDIA SMITH, his housekeeper
ABRAHAM LINCOLN
ANDREW JOHNSON
MEMBERS OF CONGRESS, the CABINET, and the ARMED FORCES

Critique:

I Speak for Thaddeus Stevens is a biography in the form of a novel, a work making understandable as a man the complex and often contradictory character of the famous partisan statesman of the Civil War period. The author tells the story of his life as a series of dramatic episodes, each under its proper date and each presenting some crisis, either a triumph or a defeat, in his private affairs or public career. Much of the material in the book is based upon Stevens letters and papers previously unused by historians; the result is a carefully detailed portrait of the man against the unsettled age in which he lived. A native of Pennsylvania, Elsie Singmaster has presented faithfully in her novels and short stories the regional patterns of Pennsylvania German life and the history of the state through three decisive periods in our national life—the frontier in French and Indian days, the American Revolution, and the Civil War.

The Story:

In a Vermont cabin, on April 4, 1792, neighbor women had looked pityingly at a sleeping young mother while they wrapped the deformed foot of her newborn child. There was no need,

however, to pity Sally Morrill Stevens, whose brave spirit was greater than her frail body. She would care for her second son as tenderly as she had looked after little Joshua, his father's namesake and a cripple at birth. She called the baby Thaddeus, after Thaddeus Kosciusko—a hero's name.

When Joshua Stevens, shiftless cobbler and surveyor, disappeared at last into the wilderness, there were two more children in the cabin. Morrill and Alanson stood up straight and were quick on their feet, but lame Thaddeus was Sally's favorite. Ambitious for her sons, she never complained as she worked and planned for their future.

Thaddeus struggled to excel. One day he limped through deep snow, his legs cut and bleeding on the icy crust, to speak before patrons and students of the grammar school in Peacham. His subject was free and universal education. Sensitive because of his own deformity, he learned to hate suffering and to sympathize with the weak. Swimming and riding gave him an athlete's body. His teachers and books borrowed from John Mattocks, Peacham lawyer, had trained him well by the time he was ready for Dartmouth College. Sally had hoped he would preach. He thought of Webster, already famous, and told her that he wanted to be a lawyer.

Vermont seemed a sparse land to her ambitious sons. Crippled Joshua traveled west with his bride. Thaddeus went to York, Pennsylvania, to teach and read for the law. Too impatient and poor to complete another year's residence before he could practice in York County, he rode south across the state line and became a member of the Maryland bar.

Returning, he settled in Gettysburg. At first no clients found their way to his office and few Gettysburgians wanted to hear his frank opinions on slavery and education, but children flocked around him to hear his stories of the Vermont woods. Blacks watched him on the street and whispered that he was their friend as well.

Defense lawyer in a murder trial, he lost his first case in court, but his townsmen praised him after he made his plea for justice and mercy. As his reputation grew men could measure his success by his fine house in Gettysburg and the great tract of mountain land providing ore and charcoal for Caledonia Forge, of which he was a partner. Sally Stevens now owned a fine farm in Peacham; he gave openhandedly to his brothers— Joshua in Indiana; Morrill, a doctor in Vermont; Alanson, with Sally on the farm. He fought Masons and Jackson Democrats and men cheered all night under his windows when he was elected to the Legislature. He was forty-one. There was still time for Washington, for Congress, perhaps the White House.

In 1837 word came to him in Philadelphia that the free education bill was about to be repealed. By train and stagecoach he hurried to Harrisburg and risked his political future with his proposed amendment to strike out the bill of repeal and to insert after the clause, "Be it enacted," the words "To establish a General System of Education by Common Schools." Speaking on that motion, he saved the free school system of Pennsylvania.

His fame spread. Men respected and hated and feared the blunt, shrewd orator whose voice was heard everywhere. In Philadelphia, during the Buckshot War, a mob attacked an assembly hall and he and his friends escaped through a window. Campaigning for Harrison, he hoped for a Cabinet appointment. But Harrison died and Tyler forgot campaign promises. Ruined by his partner's failure in 1842, he moved to Lancaster. There he made money and paid his debts. Young men begged the opportunity to read law in his office. He became an ironmaster, owner of a great furnace at Caledonia. Sometimes Washington seemed a long way off. He waited.

Free-Soil Whigs elected him to Congress in 1848. Fighting the compromise measures and the Fugitive Slave Law, he spoke for gentle Sally Stevens, for old John Mattocks, lover of justice, for slaves fleeing northward along the Underground Railroad. He defended the three white men and thirty-eight Negroes accused after the death of a Maryland farmer in the Christiana riot; later he was to recall how Lucretia Mott and other Quakers had dressed the Negroes alike, to the confusion of witnesses and prosecution. Retired from Congress, he traveled to Vermont in 1854. Sally Stevens was dead, Morrill and Alanson before her. The slander of his enemies could never hurt her now. Joshua was soon to die. Thaddeus was sixty-two and failing, but men were mistaken when they said he was too old for public life.

In 1855 he helped to launch the Republican Party in Lancaster. In 1858 he returned to Congress. In Chicago, in 1860, he heard Abraham Lincoln nominated.

He rode the war years like an eagle breasting a whirlwind. Abraham Lincoln was President, but Thaddeus Stevens spoke for the Republican Party. Often impatient with the sad-eyed, brooding man in the White House, he steered through Congress the bills which gave

1402

Lincoln men and money to fight the Civil War. Lydia Smith, the decent mulatto at whom men sneered, kept his house on B Street. Sometimes he thought of the Cabinet post or Senate seat he believed his due, but usually more important matters filled his mind. Confederate troops, marching toward Gettysburg, had burned Caledonia Furnace. A nephew died at Chickamauga. Unbowed by personal misfortune, he argued for the Thirteenth Amendment, insisted upon education and suffrage for the Negro. There was little time for the card games he loved; he read more often when he went to bed at night—Shakespeare, Homer, the Bible.

Hating weakness and compromise, he fought Andrew Johnson after Lincoln's death. Congress, he thundered, should be the sovereign power of the nation. Sick and weak, he proposed Article

Eleven by which the House hoped to impeach Johnson. Too ill to walk, he was carried into the Senate to hear that decisive roll call. He heard around him whispers of relief, anger, and despair as the telling votes were cast. Friends asked him if he wished to lie down after his ordeal. He answered grimly that he would not.

Although bitter in defeat, he would not let his fellow Republicans punish Vinnie Ream, the little sculptress involved in Johnson's trial, and he angrily insisted that she keep her studio in the Capitol. His detractors claimed he was too mean to die when he refused to take to his bed during that hot Washington summer, but by August the end was near. Devoted son, generous kinsman, loyal friend, harsh enemy, he died at midnight on August 11, 1868. The telegraph clicked the news to the world.

AN ICELAND FISHERMAN

Type of work: Novel
Author: Pierre Loti (Julien Viaud, 1850-1923)
Type of plot: Impressionistic romance
Time of plot: Nineteenth century
Locale: Brittany and at sea
First published: 1886

>   *Principal characters:*
>   SYLVESTER, a young Breton
>   YVONNE, his grandmother
>   GAUD, his cousin
>   YANN, a fisherman

Critique:

The number of translations and editions of *An Iceland Fisherman* are indicative of the warmth created by the reading of this beautiful story. Pierre Loti, of the French Academy, exemplified in this unadorned tale the virtues of French literature: clarity, simplicity, power. The exotic always appealed to Loti, and *An Iceland Fisherman* reflects this appeal in the descriptions of the fishing fleet in Iceland waters. The love interest is well presented and well within

bounds. The characters of little Sylvester, big Yann, and serious Gaud are those of real people, whose fortunes are of genuine concern to the reader.

The Story:

In the foc's'l head, a hollow, pointed room like the inside of a gigantic sea gull, five men were sitting around the massive table which filled almost all the space between the bulkheads. They were waiting to take their turn on watch, for

AN ICELAND FISHERMAN by Pierre Loti. Published by Alfred A. Knopf, Inc.

it was nearly midnight. They had cracked some biscuit with a hammer and had eaten. Now they were drinking wine and cider.

Around the room little pigeonholes near the ceiling served as bedchambers, for these fishermen were outside so much they seemed to need no air while they slept. A murky lamp swung back and forth with the gentle swell of the sea.

Sylvester, who was only seventeen, was impatient for the appearance of Yann. They were celebrating in honor of their patron, the Virgin Mary, and Yann had to take part in the toasts. Finally Yann opened the little hatch in the deck and came down the narrow ladder. Yann, in his late twenties, and a giant of a man, was a hero to Sylvester. The whole company brightened on his arrival.

It was midnight. The toasts were quickly drunk. Then the watch went on deck for their turn to fish. Outside it was daylight, for in those latitudes it never got dark in summer. It was monotonous and soothing to fish in the daylight.

At the rail Yann and Sylvester baited their hooks and dropped their lines. Behind them William waited with sheath knife and salt. Regularly, in turn, Yann and Sylvester brought up their hooks, passed the plump cod to William, and rebaited. Quickly William slit the fish, cleaned them, and packed them in the salt barrel. The pile of kegs in the hold represented the income of whole Breton families for a year. For his share of the catch Yann would bring home fifteen hundred francs to his mother.

While they were fishing Sylvester talked of marriage. Although still a boy, he was already engaged to Yann's sister. He did his best, as he had done all summer, to talk Yann into the idea of marriage with Gaud. Always Yann shook his head; he was engaged to the sea, he said, and some day he would celebrate that wedding.

Gentle and serious Gaud, Sylvester's cousin, was attracted to Yann. She was, however, a mademoiselle with fine hands and good clothes. Her father was rich. Yann could scarcely help knowing that Gaud liked him, but with Breton stubbornness and simplicity he could not think of pretending seriously to a young woman of the upper class.

In September the fishing boat returned to Paimpol in Brittany. The return of the Iceland fleet was the signal for quickened life among these simple folk. The women and children and the old men spent the whole spring and summer raising small gardens and waiting. Then in the fall, when the men came back, there were weddings and engagements and feasts and pardons. Too often a ship did not return, and several families would wear black that winter.

That fall there was a big wedding with the traditional procession to the seashore and afterward a ball. Yann went to the ball and danced the whole evening with Gaud. Yann told her of his life at sea and of his big family in Pors-Even. Part of the time Yann watched his little sister, who danced with Sylvester. The seriousness of the engaged children amused Yann. Gaud was greatly pleased, for at last Yann had unbent and his talk seemed to her too gentle for casual conversation.

Gaud waited all that winter in her rich home with its fine furniture, but Yann never came to see her. At length, overcoming her modesty, she went on a business errand for her father to Yann's house, in the hope of seeing him. She paid a sum of money to Yann's father and waited longer than she should have, but Yann did not come home. Later, she knew, Yann would come to see her father to conclude the business, and she resolved to talk with him then. But when Yann came to see her father, he prepared to leave without inquiring for her. As he came into the hall, Gaud stopped him. Yann simply told her he could not court her because she was rich and he was poor.

In the spring Yann and Sylvester sailed again with the Iceland fleet. Gaud, during that summer, felt an occasional thrill when she wrote letters to Sylvester for his grandmother, Yvonne. Often the doting old woman would dictate a short message to Yann. So Gaud was not completely out of touch with her simple, stubborn fisherman.

Events were soon to bring Gaud and Yann close together. Sylvester, the next winter, had to leave for his military service. His grandmother, Yvonne, visited him once at the barracks just before he left for French Indo-China. He was to be gone five years, and Yvonne was inconsolable.

Sylvester made a brave sailor in the French navy. On shore in the East he was sent with an armed patrol to reconnoiter. When the small band was surprised and surrounded by a large detachment of Tonkinese, Sylvester led a spirited counter-attack, until he was cut down by a sharpshooter. He was buried far from the rocky Breton coast in a green, strange land. An efficient, soulless government sent back his poor effects to Yvonne. She was now really alone, with only a memory growing dimmer as time passed.

Gaud's father committed one folly after another and lost more money trying to recoup earlier losses. Finally, at his death, he was a ruined man. Gaud, the rich man's daughter, became a seamstress. With quick sympathy she went to live with Yvonne, so that the two bereft women could comfort each other.

Yvonne, infirm of limb and mind, was unmercifully teased by a group of small boys who thought she was drunk. Falling into the mud, she vainly tried to regain her footing. Gaud came along to set the old woman on her feet again and brush the mud from her clothes. Just then Yann happened on the scene and chased the tormentors away. He escorted the two women home.

Yann was slowly changing his mind. Now that Gaud was poor, he felt a barrier between them had been removed. He also felt a great bond of sympathy for Yvonne because of her grandson, and Gaud was part of that sympathy. At the urging of his relatives and Yvonne, he proposed to Gaud. Much of that winter the couple sat by the fire in Yvonne's poor hut while the old woman slept. Six days before the fleet was to leave in March, Gaud and Yann were married.

When the fishermen departed on their summer cruise, Gaud for the first time was part of the busy, weeping crowd. Yann's ship was towed out into the harbor to wait a favorable wind. During the delay Yann came ashore again for a final three hours. Gaud watched the ship disappear in the twilight.

The summer passed uneventfully enough. Gaud made fair wages from her sewing, enough to refurnish Yvonne's poor cottage. In September the fishing fleet came straggling back. Yann's ship was not among them. At the end of the month Gaud still had hope. Each masculine step along the path sent her scurrying to the window. Yann's father, also worried, called to comfort her. He told her many stories of ships delayed by fog until December. The fall and early winter came and went, and still Gaud waited.

She never saw Yann again. In August his ship had become separated from the others and was blown north. Somewhere off Iceland, Yann had kept a tryst, his wedding with the sea.

THE IDES OF MARCH

Type of work: Novel
Author: Thornton Wilder (1897-   )
Type of plot: Historical chronicle
Time of plot: 45 B. C.
Locale: Ancient Rome
First published: 1948

Principal characters:
JULIUS CAESAR
POMPEIA, his second wife
CALPURNIA, his third wife
LADY CLODIA PULCHER, a conspirator
CATULLUS, a famous poet
CLEOPATRA, Queen of Egypt
MARCUS BRUTUS, another conspirator

Critique:

When an author writes a novel whose plot is already well-known, and that novel becomes a best seller, we must assume that his style is superior or that the story is so loved that we want to hear it again and again. In *The Ides of March* we have both factors. Thornton Wilder has retold the events of the last months of Caesar's life with warmth and depth of feeling. From imaginary letters and documents he has reconstructed the plots and intrigues leading to the fatal stabbing of the great Roman.

The Story:

There were so many different groups plotting to assassinate Caesar that it was impossible for him to guard himself from all of them. Each day new leaders rose to incite the people against him. Many of the leaders were friends of Caesar; some were relatives; some were merely ambitious men; and some were citizens who sincerely believed that Rome was suffering under Caesar's rule and wanted to free her. The last group had Caesar's admiration. He knew that he had restricted the freedom of the people, but he knew, too, that the masses of people shrink from accepting responsibility for their actions. They want to be ruled by one who will make all important decisions for them, yet they resent that ruler because he has taken their freedom from them. Caesar knew that he would one day be assassinated, but he hoped that he would see in the face of his murderer a love for Rome.

Among the most persistent of the plotters was the mother of Marcus Brutus. She had long hated Caesar and wanted her son to assume the place of the dictator. Many Romans said that Brutus was the illegitimate son of Caesar, but no one had ever been able to prove the accusation. Brutus was loyal to Caesar until the very end; only his mother's repeated urging led him at last to join the conspirators.

Another important figure among Caesar's enemies was Clodia Pulcher, a woman of high birth, great wealth, and amazing beauty. Because of her ambitions and lusts she had become a creature of poor reputation, so much so that her name was scribbled on public walls, accompanied by obscene verses. She was aided in her plots by her brother and by Catullus, the most famous poet in Rome. Catullus was a young man so much in love with Clodia that he would do anything she asked, and he wrote many poems and tracts against Caesar. Clodia spurned Catullus and his love, but her ridicule of him only strengthened his passion for her.

While all these plots against Caesar were taking shape, he and the rest of Rome were preparing for the visit of Cleopatra, Queen of Egypt. She, too, suffered from a bad reputation, for her many conquests in love were well-known in Rome. Most of the high ladies planned to receive her only because Caesar had so ordered, among them Pompeia, Caesar's wife, who knew of his earlier relations with the queen. But at Caesar's command Cleopatra was accorded the honor due a queen. He visited her many times, always in disguise, and on one of his visits barely missed being killed. He could never be sure whether Cleopatra knew of the plot. Marc Antony had begun to find favor in the eyes of Cleopatra, and as Marc Antony was involved in the attempted assassination, Caesar suspected that she too might be involved.

After Cleopatra's arrival, all Rome began to plan for the mysteries of the Good Goddess. This festival took place each year on December 11, and every Roman woman of high birth and moral virtue took part in the ceremonies. The Vestal Virgins participated in the festival also, and only women whose reputations were above reproach were allowed to attend the mysteries. Clodia's recent actions had given rise to the possibility that she might be rejected. In fact, petitions had been sent to Lady Julia Marcia, Caesar's aunt and a directress of the mysteries, to debar Clodia. Caesar interfered in behalf of Clodia, however, for just as he could understand the reasoning of his enemies, he could understand Clodia. She felt that she was fated to live the life she did and blamed the gods for her actions rather than herself.

But Clodia was vengeful. When she learned a compromise had been reached —she was to be allowed to attend the mysteries only until the Vestal Virgins appeared—she arranged to have her brother dress in the robes of a woman and attend the ceremonies with her. No man had ever been present at that sacred rite, and the profanation was the greatest scandal ever to reach the streets of Rome. The two criminals, for so they were called, were arrested, but Caesar pardoned them, thus adding another reason for public resentment. Once again it was suspected that Cleopatra knew of the plot, for she too had wanted to attend the mysteries and had been told she would have to leave when the Virgins appeared. It was rumored that Pompeia had known of Clodia's plan, and for these rumors Caesar divorced Pompeia, his reason being that regardless of whether the rumors were true Pompeia should have conducted herself so that no rumors could be started about her.

After his divorce Caesar married Calpurnia. Catullus had died in the meantime, and Caesar reflected much on the poet's death. He was not sure about his own beliefs concerning the gods and their influence on the world. Often he felt that there were no gods, that each man was the master of his own destiny. He wished that he were not guided by fear and superstition concerning life and death, but he continued to employ soothsayers and magicians and hoped daily for good omens from the heavens.

There were few good omens for Caesar at that time. His chief soothsayer had warned him of several dangerous days, but as all of them had passed uneventfully Caesar began to be less careful; and he planned to leave for the Parthian battlefront on March 17. He asked Brutus and his wife to care for Calpurnia while he was gone. He knew Brutus had been among his enemies, but he loved the younger man and believed that Brutus was now his friend.

Brutus promised Caesar to care for Calpurnia; but Brutus was to play a different role within a few days. The fateful Ides of March came. Caesar walked to the Senate chambers to make his farewell speech before leaving for the war. Approaching the capitol, he was surrounded by the conspirators. One plunged his dagger into Caesar's throat as the others closed in. Caesar was stabbed twenty-three times. When he saw that he was surrounded, he sat down and wrapped his robe about him. He did not cry out, but there are those who say that when he saw Brutus he said, "You, too, Brutus?" and ceased to struggle. Perhaps he was satisfied with his assassin.

THE IDIOT

Type of work: Novel
Author: Fyodor Mikhailovich Dostoevski (1821-1881)
Type of plot: Psychological realism
Time of plot: Mid-nineteenth century
Locale: St. Petersburg, Russia
First published: 1868-1869

Principal characters:
PRINCE LEF NICOLAIEVITCH MYSHKIN
PARFEN ROGOZHIN, friend of the prince
MME. EPANCHIN, friend and relative of the prince
AGLAYA EPANCHIN, her daughter
NATASYA FILIPOVNA, Aglaya's rival
GANYA ARDALIONOVITCH, secretary to General Epanchin

Critique:

Because this book was written by the author of *Crime and Punishment* and *The Brothers Karamazov,* it will always have a significant place in literature. Like so many characters in Russian fiction, however, the people in this novel exhibit a behavior so foreign to the American temperament that the majority of readers may find the entire story rather incredible. Perhaps the most serious handicap lies in the author's portrayal of Prince Myshkin. It would seem that he is meant to be the foil for the other characters, the person who seems foolish but is, in reality, very wise and good. But the fact that the prince suffers from epilepsy confuses the issue, and one wonders if he really is an idiot. However, as a panorama of Russian morals, manners, and philosophy of the period, *The Idiot* is an interesting and informative novel.

The Story:

After four years spent in Switzerland, where he was treated for epilepsy at a sanitarium, Prince Myshkin returned to St. Petersburg. On the train the thread-bare shabbiness of his clothing attracted the attention of the other passengers. One of these, Parfen Rogozhin, began to question him. By the time they reached St. Petersburg, the prince and Rogozhin were well-informed about one another, and Rogozhin offered to take the prince to his home and to give him money.

Myshkin, however, first wanted to introduce himself to General Epanchin, whose wife was distantly related to him. At the Epanchin home he met the general and his secretary, Ganya, who invited him to become one of his mother's boarders. The prince interested the general, who gave him some money, and he also fascinated the general's wife and three daughters. His lack of sophistication, his naïveté, his frankness, charmed and amused the family. Soon they began to call him "the idiot," half in jest, half in earnest, but he remained on good terms with them.

Ganya, a selfish young man given to all kinds of scheming, wanted to marry the beautiful Aglaya Epanchin, chiefly for her money. At the time he was also

THE IDIOT by Fyodor Mikhailovich Dostoevski. Published by The Modern Library, Inc.

involved in an affair with the notorious Natasya, an attractive young woman who lived under the protection of a man she did not love. Extremely emotional and neurotic, Natasya was really innocent of the sins charged against her. Myshkin realized her helplessness and pitied her. At a drinking party one night soon after his arrival, he asked her to marry him, saying that he had received an unexpected inheritance. She refused, declaring that she had no desire to cause his ruin. Instead she went with Rogozhin, who had brought her a hundred thousand roubles.

More than ever, Natasya became the object of spirited controversy among the Epanchins and their circle. Myshkin alone remained unembittered and always kind-hearted. Ganya and Rogozhin poured out their troubles to him, bared the sordidness and shamelessness of their lives, and swore undying friendship for him. Nevertheless, they distrusted Myshkin and plotted against him. When Natasya left Rogozhin, he swore that he would kill "the idiot" because he was sure that Natasya had fled from him because she really loved Myshkin.

Myshkin then became the victim of an extortion attempt. During a violent, repugnant scene, at which the Epanchins were present, he successfully refuted the charge that he had deprived Rogozhin's supposed illegitimate son of his rightful heritage. Having proved that the individual who sought the money was not the illegitimate son, he then, to the disgust of Mme. Epanchin, offered to give money to the extortionist and to become his friend. Mme. Epanchin considered the prince more of an idiot than ever.

Meanwhile, Aglaya Epanchin fell in love with Myshkin, but she continued to treat him scornfully and at first refused to admit that she was in love with him. When her true feelings at last became apparent, Mme. Epanchin gave reluctant consent to their betrothal and planned an evening party to introduce Myshkin to St. Petersburg society. Worried lest he should commit some social blunder, she and her daughter advised him to sit quietly and to say nothing during the evening. But at the party Mme. Epanchin herself drew out the prince, so that he was soon launched on one of his wild and peculiar conversations. The staid, conservative guests were astounded. In the midst of the discussion he knocked over a huge and priceless vase, then stared at the debris like "an idiot." A few minutes later he fell into an epileptic fit and had to be carried to his home. For several days the Epanchins were cold to him, but Mme. Epanchin finally relented and invited him to their home once more.

In the meantime Aglaya had been corresponding with Natasya, and a friendship had strangely developed between them. One evening Aglaya asked Myshkin to go with her to see Natasya.

In Natasya's apartment a hectic and turbulent argument developed, so that the two women showed their anger and bitterness against each other. For the first time Aglaya revealed fully her love for Myshkin. During the argument Natasya fainted. When Myshkin rushed to her aid, Aglaya considered herself rejected and angrily left the house. The scene between the two women became a scandal, and the Epanchins barred their home to Myshkin. Natasya agreed to marry him and made preparations for the wedding. But on the day of the wedding, while Myshkin waited at the church, Natasya fled with Rogozhin, still haunted by her own helplessness and his terrible possessiveness.

Myshkin received the news calmly. Although there were many who laughed at "the idiot," there were some who were sorry for him when he attempted to discover Natasya's whereabouts. He left the village where the ceremony was to have been performed and went to the city. There he inquired among Natasya's acquaintances, but nobody knew where she was. Finally he went to Rogozhin's apartment and learned from a porter

that Rogozhin had slept there the previous night. Myshkin continued his search,
convinced that Rogozhin would kill him
if he could. But Rogozhin himself
stopped him on the street and took him
to the apartment, where Myshkin found
Natasya lying on the bed. Rogozhin
had killed her.

Filled with compassion for the miserable Rogozhin, Myshkin spent that night
with the body of Natasya and her murderer. At daybreak Natasya's worried
friends and the police broke into the
apartment. Rogozhin confessed to the
murder. Myshkin was questioned by the
police, but he was not implicated in the
crime. He was sent back to the sanitarium
in Switzerland, where he was visited,
from time to time, by the Epanchin
family and other friends. There was
little hope that he would ever recover
from his epilepsy.

THE IDYLLS OF THE KING

Type of work: Poem
Author: Alfred, Lord Tennyson (1809-1892)
Type of plot: Chivalric romance
Time of plot: Fifth century
Locale: England
First published: Separately, 1859-1885

> Principal characters:
> KING ARTHUR
> QUEEN GUINEVERE
> SIR LANCELOT,
> GARETH,
> GERAINT,
> BALIN,
> BALAN,
> GAWAIN,
> SIR GALAHAD,
> SIR BORS,
> SIR PELLEAS,
> SIR PERCIVALE,
> SIR MODRED,
> SIR TRISTRAM, and
> SIR BEDIVERE, Knights of the Round Table
> MERLIN, a magician
> LYNETTE, who married Gareth
> ENID, who married Geraint
> VIVIEN, an enchantress
> ELAINE, the lily maid of Astalot
> ETTARRE, loved by Pelleas and Gawain
> ISOLT, of the white hands, Tristram's wife

Critique:

Divided into twelve sections, each
symbolic of one month of the year, these
poems present to the reader the span of
a man's life, extending from the coming
of Arthur to his passing. If one cared
to search into the symbolism of this long
narrative poem, he would find it filled
with mystic and spiritual meanings. Although Tennyson's stories of King Arthur
and the Knights of the Round Table lack
the realism and vitality of Malory's
tales, *The Idylls of the King* have a
poetic compactness and allegorical significance lacking in the original.

The Stories:

THE COMING OF ARTHUR

Gorloïs and Ygerne had borne one

1410

daughter, Bellicent. King Uther overcame Gorloïs in battle and forced the
widow to marry him immediately. Shortly afterward King Uther died. Ygerne's
son, Arthur, was born at a time when
he could have been the son of Gorloïs
or the son of Uther born too soon.

The birth of Arthur was shrouded
in great mystery. Merlin the magician
reared the prince until it was time for
him to take over Uther's kingdom and
to receive from the Lady of the Lake the
magic sword, Excalibur. After the marriage of Arthur and Guinevere, the king
and his loyal members of the Round
Table, in twelve battles, drove the enemy
out of the kingdom.

GARETH AND LYNETTE

Bellicent, Arthur's sister, allowed her
youngest son to join his two brothers in
King Arthur's court on the condition
that Gareth serve as a kitchen knave
under the surly directions of Sir Kay
the seneschal. When the young boy presented himself to King Arthur, Gareth
made the king promise to give him the
first quest which came along without
revealing his identity. One day Lynette
came to the court asking for Sir Lancelot
to save her sister from wicked knights
who held her captive. King Arthur sent
Gareth questing with Lynette, who
grumbled disdainfully at the kitchen
knave ordered to serve her.

The first knight Gareth overcame was
the Morning Star. Lynette still sneered
at the knave. After Gareth had defeated
another knight, Lynette began to relent.
When he conquered a third strong
knight, she allowed him to ride at her
side. Next Gareth encountered a terrible knight, Death, who proved to be
a mere boy forced by his brothers to
assume a fierce appearance. Gareth returned to the Round Table victorious
and married Lynette.

THE MARRIAGE OF GERAINT and GERAINT AND ENID

Geraint, on a quest for Guinevere,
came to the impoverished castle of Earl
Yniol and his daughter Enid, a girl
whose faded brocades spoke of former
wealth and family pride. There Geraint
learned that the rejected suitor of Enid
had caused the ruin of Yniol. The earl
gave Geraint Enid for his wife.

Geraint, fearing that the sin of the
queen's love for Lancelot would taint
Enid's love, went to his own castle and
there idled away the hours in company
with his wife until neighbors began to
gossip that Geraint had lost his courage.
Enid feared to tell her lord about the
gossip, and Geraint, observing her strange
attitude, decided that she had fallen in
love with some knight of the Round
Table. One morning, bidding Enid to
don her faded brocade gown, Geraint
set out with his wife after ordering her
not to speak to him. Riding ahead of
Geraint, Enid encountered men who
would attack her husband, and each time
she broke his command by warning him
of his danger. After a while Enid was
able to prove her love to her suspicious
husband. They returned to Camelot,
where Guinevere warmly welcomed Enid
to the court.

BALIN AND BALAN

Balan left the care of Balin, his mad
brother, and went on a mission to quell
King Pellam, who had refused to pay
his yearly tribute to King Arthur. With
his brother gone, Balin was left alone
in his gloomy moods. He worshipped
the purity of Lancelot and the faithfulness of Guinevere until one day he saw
his two idols speaking familiarly in the
garden. Disillusioned, Balin fled to the
woods. There he met Vivien, a wanton
woman of the court, who further poisoned his mind against Lancelot and
Guinevere. He left hanging on a tree
the shield Guinevere had given him
years before. Hearing Balin's mad shrieks
among the trees, Balan rushed at Balin,
whom he did not recognize without the
shield of Guinevere. In the struggle
Balin killed Balan and then was crushed
by his own horse.

VIVIEN

Vain and coquettish Vivien set out

to ensnare the most chivalric man in all the kingdom, King Arthur, but her wiles failed to win the attention of a king whose mind could harbor no evil thoughts. Vivien then turned to Merlin, who she knew possessed a magic spell. She tried to charm the magician with her beauty, pretending to love the ancient, bearded man, but he knew that she was not to be trusted. When she asked him to teach her the spell, he refused. But Vivien was not to be denied. At last, tricked by her beauty, Merlin taught her his magic powers. She enchanted him and caused him to disappear forever, a prisoner in a hollow tree.

LANCELOT AND ELAINE

Lancelot in disguise went to Astalot, where he left his shield with Elaine and rode off with her brother Lavaine to the tournaments. Lancelot won the jousts; then, wounded, he fled before anyone could discover who he was. King Arthur sent Gawain to search for the winner of the tournament. Gawain rode to Astalot, where he lingered because he had fallen in love with Elaine. She told him that she loved the knight who had left his shield with her. When Gawain saw the shield, he identified it as that of Lancelot.

Elaine nursed Lancelot back to health in the hope that he would return her love. Recovered, he sadly told her that he could never marry any woman. After he had gone, Elaine became ill and finally died in her grief. Her dying wish was to be put into a boat and sent to Camelot, in her hand a letter to Lancelot.

In Camelot Guinevere coldly rejected Lancelot, for Gawain had told of the affair between Lancelot and Elaine. When the body of Elaine floated to Camelot, King Arthur and Lancelot found the beautiful maiden in her boat, the letter in her hand.

Lancelot authorized a fitting burial for the lily maid. He unhappily lamented his hopeless love for the queen, not knowing that he would die a monk.

THE HOLY GRAIL

One day while Sir Galahad, the youngest and purest of all the knights, sat in Merlin's chair, the Holy Grail descended upon the Round Table in a flash and then was gone. When the knights swore to go on a quest for the Holy Grail, King Arthur gloomily predicted that the search would end in disaster for many of his knights because none was pure enough, save Galahad or Percivale, to see the holy vessel.

To Galahad the Grail appeared in all its splendor. Percivale, who followed him, also saw the holy sign. Sir Bors returned to King Arthur to report that he had viewed the Grail; but Lancelot had seen only a sign of it. Some of the other knights never returned to the Round Table from their perilous quest.

PELLEAS AND ETTARRE

Pelleas had given Ettarre a trophy he had won in a tournament, but she, scorning the young knight, barred him from her court. Gawain, meeting Pelleas in his despair, offered to help him. After telling the knight to hide in the forest, Gawain went to Ettarre and told her he had killed Pelleas. As the days passed, Pelleas became impatient. One night, stealing into the castle, he found Gawain and Ettarre sleeping together and placed his naked sword across the throats of the sleeping lovers. Then in a mad rage he rode through the forest until he met Percivale, who accidentally revealed to Pelleas the scandal about Lancelot and Guinevere. Disillusioned, the young knight returned to the Round Table, where his rude manner to the queen foreshadowed evil to Lancelot and Guinevere. Sir Modred saw that the ruin of the Round Table was near at hand.

THE LAST TOURNAMENT

To a tournament at Camelot came Tristram, who had left his bride, Isolt of the white hands. Her name was the same as that of his beloved, Isolt, the wife of King Mark of Cornwall. Lancelot, laboring under the guilt of his sinful love for Guinevere, decided to fight with the similarly guilty Tristram, who won the tournament. Tristram then went to Isolt of Cornwall. King Mark was away on a hunting trip. He returned unexpectedly, found the lovers together, and killed Tristram.

In the north a knight rebelled against King Arthur's rule and charged that the Round Table was a thing of falseness and guilt where harlots and adulterers lived disguised as ladies and knights. King Arthur rode to quell the revolt and the guilty man was killed; but King Arthur was heavy in heart when he returned to Camelot.

GUINEVERE

Fearing exposure of her love for Lancelot, Guinevere asked him to leave Camelot. On the night of their farewell Modred trapped the lovers together, and Guinevere, feeling that she was shamed forever, went to Almesbury and took refuge in a nunnery. There she recalled how Lancelot had brought her from her father's home to marry Arthur, how she had thought Arthur cold and had fallen in love with the courtly, gay Lancelot.

King Arthur went to Almesbury. To Guinevere he spoke of his pride in the marvelous truths which the Round Table had upheld, and which Guinevere had

inspired. Now all was lost, but he forgave Guinevere before he went off to fight against Modred and his traitor knights.

Filled with remorse, Guinevere asked the nuns to accept her in their order. There she gave her services until they made her abbess. After three years in that rank she died.

THE PASSING OF ARTHUR

In Modred's revolt King Arthur was wounded. As he lay dying he told Sir Bedivere to cast the sword Excalibur into the lake. When Bedivere finally brought to King Arthur the tale that amid flashing and strange sights an arm reached out from the lake to receive the sword, King Arthur knew that Bedivere had truly sent Excalibur back to the Lady of the Lake. Next King Arthur told Bedivere to carry him to the shore. There three maidens came in a barge to take King Arthur away. As Bedivere stood weeping, King Arthur assured him that the old order of the Round Table must pass to give way to something new.

So King Arthur passed, in the manner of his legendary beginning, back across the waters to Avalon, but many men believed that some day he would return to his people in their need. Bedivere watched on the shore until the wintry dawn broke bringing a new year.

IF WINTER COMES

Type of work: Novel
Author: A. S. M. Hutchinson (1880-   )
Type of plot: Social criticism
Time of plot: 1912-1919
Locale: Southern England
First published: 1920

Principal characters:
    MARK SABRE, an idealist
    MABEL SABRE, his wife
    LADY NONA TYBAR, a friend
    MR. FORTUNE, Mark's employer
    MR. TWYNING, a business associate
    HAROLD TWYNING, Twyning's son
    EFFIE BRIGHT, Sabre's friend

The very least that can be said about *If Winter Comes* is that it is a beautiful and heart-warming novel. It is the story of a man who loved all humanity, but who was persecuted and betrayed by those who did not understand him. Although the book makes no pretensions to great literature, it is a perennial favorite among all classes of readers.

The Story:

Most of his friends thought Mark Sabre a queer sort, in spite of the normal life he led. He was married to a girl of his own class and he worked in the very respectable firm of Fortune, East, and Sabre, suppliers for the best churches and schools in England. It was his attitude toward life that seemed queer. He had no definite convictions about anything, and he could always see both sides of any controversy. He hated the restrictions that convention placed on people, but at the same time he believed that conventions were based on sound principles. Mabel Sabre, one of the most conventional women alive, was totally unable to understand anything her husband tried to discuss with her.

The only person who understood him well was Lady Nona Tybar, with whom Sabre had once been in love. Nona's husband, Lord Tybar, was a charming man, but completely without moral principles. When he flaunted other women in Nona's face, she turned to Sabre for comfort in his friendship, but Mabel, Sabre's wife, could not understand their friendship any better than she could understand anything else about her husband. After five years of marriage Mabel and Sabre were living almost as strangers under one roof. Mark Sabre's employer, Mr. Fortune, and his business associate Mr. Twyning, despised him because they did not understand him, and so Sabre felt that he lived only as he bicycled between his home and his office, for then he could know himself as he really was. Sabre felt that there was a mystery to life which he could unlock if he found the right key. And his life was almost dedicated to finding that key.

In addition to Nona, Sabre had three friends with whom he liked to spend his time. They were his neighbors, Mr. Fargus and old Mrs. Perch and her son. When the war came, young Perch wanted to enlist, but he could not leave his invalid mother alone. Sabre knew that Effie Bright, daughter of an employee at his office, wanted a position as a companion, and he arranged to have her stay with Mrs. Perch after her son went to the army. Young Perch was killed, and when his mother received the news she died too. Shortly after the old lady's death, Sabre himself joined the army. Because Mabel did not want to stay alone, she employed Effie to stay with her. However, she treated Effie as a servant.

Lord Tybar was a hero in the war, winning the Victoria Cross before he was killed. Nona went to France after her husband's death and drove an ambulance for the rest of the war years. When Sabre came home on leave, Mabel discharged Effie. She said that the girl was impertinent and unreliable.

Late in 1917, Sabre was wounded and sent home to stay. Mabel took no more interest in him than she had before, until the day she received a letter from Effie. Effie begged to come back to the Sabres. She now had an illegitimate child and no one, including her father, would take her in. Mabel was righteously angry at the proposal, and when Sabre tried to defend the girl she began to suspect that he might have a reason to help Effie. Before they reached a decision Effie, having no other place to go, arrived with her baby. When Sabre insisted that she stay, Mabel left, declaring she would not return until the girl and her baby had gone. Mr. Fortune and Mr. Twyning, who had been made a partner in the firm, would not allow Sabre to return to the firm unless he sent Effie away. They feared scandal would hurt their business. But Sabre would not be forced to do what he felt would be an injustice and a sin. For he had found the key to the puzzle; he knew that the solution to the mystery of the world is simply that God is love. Love for one's fellow men could set the world right again. He loved Effie as he loved all mankind, as he loved even his wife and the others who hated him.

But keeping Effie in the face of criticism brought only disaster to him and to the girl. Mabel sued for divorce on grounds of adultery, naming Effie. Sabre was away from his home when the papers were served, and before he could quite comprehend that his wife could believe such a foul thing he was arrested. Effie had taken poison, first killing her baby. She had learned of Mabel's suit and thought she could help Sabre best by committing suicide. Sabre's enemies were not satisfied. He was taken to court and accused of being responsible for her death. Effie's father, Mabel, and Mr. Twyning all claimed that he was the father of Effie's baby and that he had bought the poison which she drank. It was proved that he could have been the father of the child. Only one voice was raised in his defense. Nona returned from France and appeared at the trial. But there was little she could do.

The verdict made Sabre responsible for Effie's suicide. Sabre went home, but he would not allow Nona to go with him. In his house he found a letter from Effie. In it she told him that she was taking her life and that of her baby because she had caused him so much trouble. She also named the father of her baby; it was Harold Twyning, the son of Sabre's enemy. The boy had been afraid of his father's anger and had not claimed his responsibility.

Enraged, Sabre went to his old office prepared to kill Mr. Twyning. But when he reached the office, he learned that his enemy had just received word of Harold's death in battle. Sabre dropped Effie's letter in the fire and offered his sympathy to the man mainly responsible for ruining him. Then he went into his old office and collapsed from a cerebral hemorrhage. Nona found him there and took him home. For many months he could remember nothing that had happened to him, but gradually he began to piece together the sordid, tragic story. He learned that Mabel had secured her divorce and remarried. He learned to know Nona again, but he asked her to go away because he had accepted disgrace rather than reveal the story of Effie's letter. Nona refused to leave him, and after a year they were married. Sabre knew then that he had really found the key to the mystery of existence in that dark season of life before winter gives way to spring.

THE ILIAD

Type of work: Poem
Author: Homer (c. ninth century B. C.)
Type of plot: Heroic epic
Time of plot: Trojan War
Locale: Troy
First transcribed: Sixth century B. C.

> *Principal characters:*
> PRIAM, King of Troy
> HECTOR, a Trojan warrior, Priam's son
> HELEN OF TROY
> PARIS, Hector's brother and Helen's lover
> MENELAUS, Helen's husband
> AGAMEMNON, Menelaus' brother
> ACHILLES, a Greek warrior
> PATROCLUS, Achilles' friend

1415

Homer has been hailed as the father of all poetry, and the *Iliad* has survived as a masterpiece for all time. The *Iliad,* within a three-day period of the Trojan wars, tells the story of the wrath of Achilles against King Agamemnon. The battle episodes reveal the true characters of the warriors, their strength and their weaknesses. These figures step out of unrecorded history as human beings, not of one era, but of all eras and for all time.

The Story:

The Greeks were camped outside the walls of Troy, in the tenth year of their siege on that city. Agamemnon, king of the Achaians, wanted the maid, Briseis, for his own, but she was possessed by Achilles, the son of Zeus. When Achilles was forced to give up the maid, he withdrew angrily from the battle and returned to his ship. But he won from Zeus the promise that the wrong which he was enduring would be revenged on Agamemnon.

That evening Zeus sent a messenger to the Greek king to convey to him in a dream an order to rise and marshal his Achaian forces against the walls of Troy. When the king awoke, he called all his warriors to him and ordered them to prepare for battle. All night long the men armed themselves in battle array, making ready their horses and their ships. The gods appeared on earth in the disguise of warriors, some siding with the Greeks, some hastening to warn the Trojans. With the army mustered, Agamemnon began the march from the camp to the walls of the city, while all the country around was set on fire. Only Achilles and his men remained behind, determined not to fight on the side of Agamemnon.

The Trojan army came from the gates of the city ready to combat the Greeks. Then Paris, son of King Priam and Helen's lover, stood out from the ranks and suggested that he and Menelaus settle the battle in a fight between them, the winner to take Helen and all her possessions, and friendship to be declared between the warring nations. Menelaus agreed to these words of his rival, and before the warriors of both sides, and under the eyes of Helen, who had been summoned to witness the scene from the walls of Troy, he and Paris began to battle. Menelaus was the mightier warrior. As he was about to pierce his enemy, the goddess Aphrodite, who loved Paris, swooped down from the air and carried him off to his chamber. She summoned Helen there to minister to her wounded lord. Then the victory was declared for Menelaus.

In the heavens the gods who favored the Trojans were much disturbed by this decision. Athena appeared on earth to Trojan Pandarus and told him to seek out Menelaus and kill him. He shot an arrow at the unsuspecting king, but the goddess watching over Menelaus deflected the arrow so that it only wounded him. When Agamemnon saw that treacherous deed, he revoked his vows of peace and exhorted the Greeks once more to battle. Many Trojans and many Greeks lost their lives that day, because of the foolhardiness of Pandarus.

Meanwhile Hector, son of King Priam, had returned to the city to bid farewell to Andromache, his wife, and to his child, for he feared he might not return from that day's battle. He rebuked Paris for remaining in his chambers with Helen when his countrymen were dying because of his misdeeds. While Paris made ready for battle, Hector said goodbye to Andromache, prophesying that Troy would be defeated, himself killed, and Andromache taken captive. Then Paris joined him and they went together into the battle.

When evening came the Greeks and the Trojans retired to their camps. Agamemnon instructed his men to build a huge bulwark around the camp and in front of the ships, for fear the enemy would press their attack too close. Zeus then remembered his promise to Achilles to avenge the wrong done to him by Agamemnon. He summoned all the gods and forbade them to take part in the war. The victory was to go to the Trojans.

The next day Hector and the Trojans swept through the fields slaughtering the Greeks. Hera, the wife of Zeus, and many of the other goddesses could not be content to watch the defeat of their mortal friends. But when they attempted to intervene, Zeus sent down his messengers to warn them to desist.

Fearing his armies would be destroyed before Achilles would relent, Agamemnon sent Odysseus to Achilles and begged the hero to accept gifts and be pacified. But Achilles, still wrathful, threatened to sail for home at the break of day. Agamemnon was troubled by the proud refusal of Achilles. That night he stole to the camp of the wise man, Nestor, to ask his help in a plan to defeat the Trojans. Nestor told him to awaken all the great warriors and summon them to a council. It was decided that two warriors should steal into the Trojan camp to determine its strength and numbers. Diomedes and Odysseus volunteered. As they crept toward the camp, they captured and killed a Trojan spy. Then they themselves stole into the camp of the enemy, spied upon it, and as they left, took with them the horses of one of the kings.

The next day the Trojans pressed hard upon the Greeks with great slaughter. Both Diomedes and Odysseus were wounded and many warriors killed. Achilles watched the battle from his ship but made no move to take part in it. He sent his friend Patroclus to Nestor to learn how many had been wounded. The old man sent back a despairing answer, pleading that Achilles give up his anger and help his fellow Greeks. At last the Trojans broke through the walls of the enemy, and Hector was foremost in an attack upon the ships.

Meanwhile many of the gods plotted to aid the Greeks. Hera lulled Zeus to sleep, and Poseidon urged Agamemnon to resist the onrush of the Trojans. In the battle that day Hector was wounded by Aias, but as the Greeks were about to seize him and bear his body away the bravest of the Trojans surrounded their hero and covered him with their shields until he could be carried to safety.

When Zeus awakened and saw what had happened, his wrath was terrible, and he ordered Apollo to restore Hector to health. Once again the walls were breached and the Trojans stormed toward the ships, eager to fire them. Zeus inspired the Trojans with courage and weakened the Greeks with fear. But he determined that after the ships were set afire he would no longer aid the Trojans but would allow the Greeks to have the final victory.

Patroclus went to his friend Achilles and again pleaded with him to return to the fight. Achilles, still angry, refused. Then Patroclus begged that he be allowed to wear the armor of Achilles so that the Greeks would believe their hero fought with them, and Achilles consented. Patroclus charged into the fight and fought bravely at the gates of the city. But there Hector mortally wounded Patroclus and stripped from his body the armor of Achilles.

All that day the battle raged over the body of Patroclus. Then a messenger carried to Achilles word of his friend's death. His sorrow was terrible, but he could not go unarmed into the fray to rescue the body of Patroclus.

The next morning his goddess mother, Thetis, brought him a new suit of armor from the forge of Hephaestus. Then Achilles decked himself in the glittering armor which the lame god of fire had prepared for him and strode forth to the beach. There he and Agamemnon were reconciled before the assembly of the Greeks, and he went out to battle with them. The whole plain was filled with men and horses, battling one another. Achilles in his vengeance pushed back the enemy to the banks of the River Xanthus, and so many were the bodies of the Trojans choking the river that at length the god of the river spoke to Achilles, ordering him to cease throwing their bodies into his waters. Proud Achilles mocked him and sprang into the river to fight with the god. Feeling himself overpowered, he struggled out upon the banks, but still the wrathful god pursued him. Achilles then called on his mother to help him, and Thetis, with the aid of Hephaestus, quickly subdued the angry river god.

As Achilles drew near the walls of Troy, Hector girded on his armor. Amid the wailing of all the Trojan women he came from the gates to meet the Greek warrior. Not standing to meet Achilles in combat, he fled three times around the city walls ·before he turned to face Achilles' fatal spear. Then Achil-

les bound Hector's body to his chariot and dragged it to the ships, a prey for dogs and vultures.

In the Trojan city there was great grief for the dead hero. The aged King Priam resolved to drive in a chariot to the camp of Achilles and beg that the body of his son Hector be returned to him. The gods, too, asked Achilles to curb his wrath and restore the Trojan warrior to his own people, and so Achilles received King Priam with respect, granted his request, and agreed to a twelve-day truce that both sides might properly bury and mourn their dead. Achilles mourned for Patroclus as the body of his friend was laid upon the blazing funeral pyre. In the city the body of mighty Hector was also burned and his bones were buried beneath a great mound in the stricken city.

IMAGINARY CONVERSATIONS

Type of work: Dialogues
Author: Walter Savage Landor (1775-1864)
First published: 1824-1848

Landor once said, "Poetry was always my amusement, prose my study and business." When he was forty-five, after having devoted many years to poetic composition, he began the *Imaginary Conversations,* and in this work he found the form best suited to the peculiar aim and direction of his art. His poetry, although some of it attains a gem-like perfection, suffers by comparison with the work of his more famous contemporaries. While the major Romantic writers, with their emphasis on imagination, were bringing new life to poetry, Landor chose not to go beyond ideas that could be clearly grasped. Thus his poetry lacks the emotional appeal necessary to the highest attainment in this form. In prose writing, however, where clarity and restraint are more to be desired, Landor deserves consideration with the best of his age.

By the very nature of his character

Landor was drawn for guidance and inspiration to the classical tradition. One side of his personality admired balance, moderation, and precision, qualities admirably displayed in his writing. The other side was irascible, impractical, and impulsive; these traits are revealed in some of his personal relationships. Like Mozart, Landor appears to have found in his restrained and faultless art a counterpoise to his external world of turbulence.

Landor was a true classicist, not a belated adherent of neo-classicism with its emphasis on rules over substance. He was rigorously trained in youth and continued his scholarly pursuits throughout his adult life. His knowledge was no mere surface phenomenon; he was so immersed in the ancients that he took on their characteristic habits of thought. Thus the volumes of the *Imaginary Con-*

1418

versations not only make use of events and characters from the Greco-Roman civilization, but are infused with classical ideals of clarity and precision in style and tough intellectualism in content.

The *Imaginary Conversations,* written in five series, are grouped into classical dialogues, dialogues of sovereigns and statesmen, dialogues of literary men, dialogues of famous women, and miscellaneous dialogues. The conversations, usually between two people, cover many centuries, ranging from the time of the Trojan War to Landor's own period, and they include people from many geographical areas. Many of the scenes are based on suggestions from history or mythology, but the actual remarks of the individuals are never used. Landor did not attempt to re-create a sense of the past by use of artificial or archaic language. He did, however, endeavor to represent faithfully the spirit of the age and the essential nature of the personage presented.

In the *Imaginary Conversations,* Landor was above all concerned with interpretation of character. While he displayed brilliant insights into human nature, his aim was not toward fully developed characters, but for abstractive idealizations. They are products not of observation directly reported but of observation, especially that gained from reading, filtered through a long process of reflection. Never are the predilections of the author —his sympathies and his aversions—far from the surface.

The manly, heroic character is depicted in many of the dialogues. Two examples of this type are found in "Marcellus and Hannibal." History records the death of Marcellus in the Second Punic War and the respect paid him by Hannibal. Landor created a scene in which Marcellus survived long enough to converse with the Carthaginian leader. When the wounded Marcellus was brought to the camp, Hannibal made every effort to save his life and to make him comfortable. A contrast to Hanni-

bal's chivalric behavior was provided by that of his ally, a Gallic chief who thought only of revenge and of glory to Gaul. Marcellus welcomed death as an escape from capture and politely declined Hannibal's request that Rome agree to a peace treaty. Although under great suffering, he avoided any outward expression of pain. In return for Hannibal's kindness, Marcellus presented him with a ring that might benefit him with the Romans, if his fortunes changed. As Marcellus was dying, the two men were more closely united by their common nobility and respect for nobility in others than were they divided by the exigencies of war.

Women of praiseworthy character are depicted in several of the conversations. In "Lady Lisle and Elizabeth Gaunt," Landor portrayed the remarkable idealism of two women who were condemned to death for sheltering adherents of Monmouth. They had acted through simple Christian charity. Confronted with a choice between the law of the king and the commandment of Jesus, they embraced the latter. Lady Lisle had no blame for the jury that under duress had convicted her. Elizabeth, serene about her own fate, felt sorrow for her companion. Betrayed by the very man she had concealed, she felt no anger toward him, but pitied him for his having to suffer a guilty conscience. Both viewed execution as the avenue to eternal bliss and wished that others might have their perfect serenity.

A more complex character study is found in "Oliver Cromwell and Walter Noble." Cromwell was controlled by conflicting emotions—ambition, pride, compassion, vindictiveness, humility, fear. In response to the practically irrefutable arguments of Noble against regicide, Cromwell constantly shifted position and even contradicted himself. As a last refuge, he justified his proposed action as the carrying out of God's will.

Although Landor sometimes used crucial situations as settings for his conver-

1419

sations, he seldom revealed character in truly dramatic fashion. His dialogues, unlike Browning's monologues, do not have a close causal relationship between the stresses of the moment and the disclosures of the speaker. Nor do Landor's speakers often reveal their inner natures unwittingly. While Browning's works are subtle and require reading between the lines, Landor's are direct and leave little to implication. In the treatment of characters with whom he was unsympathetic, Landor used an irony that is unmistakable, even too obvious at times.

In some of the dialogues, especially the long discursive ones, the characters are not important in themselves, but serve as vehicles for the ideas of the author. Not a systematic philosopher nor a highly original thinker, Landor was alive to the whole range of man's thought, past and present. A wise and judicious man, he expressed his opinions felicitously.

Love of freedom is a leading theme in the *Imaginary Conversations*. Fighters for liberty, such as Washington and Kosciusko, who combined modesty with valor, evoked Landor's highest admiration. Equally fervid was his detestation of tyrants, as expressed, for example, in "Peter the Great and Alexis," a dialogue in which Peter, having failed to make his son as brutal as he, callously orders the boy's execution. Landor believed in a republican form of government and opposed pure democracy because of the corruption, intemperance, and anti-intellectualism that such a system fostered. His expression of political ideas seldom went beyond a statement of general principles.

Landor was often critical of religious leaders and he showed his antipathy to fanaticism in such dialogues as "Mahomet and Sergius" and "Melanchthon and Calvin." Hypocrisy is attacked in other dialogues, such as "Fra Filippo Lippi and Pope Eugenius IV," which is, in part, a satire on the Pope, who makes an outward show of piety and displays great zeal in maintaining the forms of religion, but who is essentially a worldly and sensual man. Also, in this conversation, the Christian-spirited barbarians of Tunisia are, with heavy irony, contrasted with the barbaric Christians of Rome. Landor favored a simple religion that stayed close to its basic tenets. Believing in the limitation of human reason in such matters, he disliked dogmatism and theological quibbling.

His philosophy was influenced by Epicurus and by the Stoics. He believed in meditation, in detachment, in freedom from the ambition and envy of the world. These sentiments are expressed in "Epicurus, Leontion, and Ternissa." Feeling that man's happiness depends on his use of reason to overcome doubts and worries, in many of his character portrayals Landor revealed his belief in self-control, fortitude, sympathy, and humanitarianism.

A significant part of the *Imaginary Conversations* is devoted to literary criticism. Classical standards were Landor's guide. He disapproved of unnecessary ornamentation in writing. "Never try to say things admirably, try only to say them plainly." "Whatever is rightly said, sounds rightly." But Landor was not a narrow classicist in his tastes; he admired a variety of authors, his favorites being Milton, Bacon, Shakespeare, Dante, and Pindar. Among his contemporaries he most respected Wordsworth and Southey.

Landor predicted that only a small, select group of people would prize his writings. He was correct. One reason for the failure of the *Imaginary Conversations* to attract a large audience is the fact that the dialogues lack direction and cohesive development. The absence of dramatic motivation and the presence of disconcerting gaps and shifts in argument create difficulties for the reader.

This weakness, which is a considerable one, has prevented the high merits of the *Imaginary Conversations* from being widely appreciated. The aphorisms scattered throughout the work are among the best in the language. The range of Landor's thought is impressive. His prose style is unexcelled in vigor and purity.

THE IMITATION OF CHRIST

Type of work: Religious meditations
Author: Thomas à Kempis (c. 1380-1471)
First transcribed: c. 1400

Although arguments have been brought forward through the centuries in an effort to show that Thomas à Kempis did not really write *The Imitation of Christ (Imitatio Christi),* evidence to the contrary has never been widely accepted and Thomas à Kempis is usually regarded as the author of the famous work. Aside from the Bible, *The Imitation of Christ* is undoubtedly the most famous religious work of the Christian world, having been translated into more than fifty languages and printed in more than six thousand editions. Widely known in manuscript, it was being circulated as early as 1420. Its first publication in English was in 1696. The original language of *The Imitation of Christ* was Latin, not the classical Latin of Rome, but medieval Latin considerably changed from the language of Cicero and Vergil. Many later writers have praised it. Fontenelle said it was the finest piece of writing ever done by man. John Wesley thought so highly of it that he published an English translation under the title *The Christian's Pattern* (1735). Matthew Arnold thought that it was, next to the Bible, the most eloquent expression of the Christian spirit ever penned.

The substance of *The Imitation of Christ* is that God is all and man is nothing, that from God flows the eternal Truth which man must seek, and that by imitating the spirit and actions of Christ man may be helped to achieve a state of grace with God. But as many writers have pointed out, the greatness of Thomas à Kempis' book does not lie in any originality, for there is little that is new in the matter of the work. It is the expression of a spirit that makes *The Imitation of Christ* a piece of great religious literature. Traceable are most of the strands of Christian philosophy and theology of the time, including those which Christians took over, at least in part, from the great pagan thinkers of Greece and Rome. The book has sometimes been described as a mosaic of matter and ideas taken from the early and medieval Christian mystics, the Bible, and writings of the Church fathers. Borrowings from St. Bernard, St. Gregory, St. Ambrose, St. Thomas Aquinas, Plato, Aristotle, Seneca, and even Ovid can be found within the pages of *The Imitation of Christ,* each contributing in a way to the spirit of Christian example. No reader can ever miss, even within a few pages, the eloquence and sincerity of the author. The religious feeling has been expressed so ardently that it is unmistakably a call to the reader to heed the call of Christ and to follow in His steps.

Although he calls the reader to a Christian, hence otherworldly, life, Thomas à Kempis is eminently practical in his insights into human beings, their motivations, and their psychology. More than once the author points out that virtue is only to be claimed by those who have been tempted and have proved themselves equal to denying worldly vanities and other devil's snares in order to remain in act, thought, and spirit a follower of Christ's doctrines and example. Thomas à Kempis also realized that established custom is not easily relinquished by the individual or the community and is thus always a means of keeping one from a Christian life. Thomas certainly was not a man to truckle to the moment; relativism and Christianity could not go hand

1421

in hand in his philosophy. Though strict in his admonitions that there was no worldly good, nor any love of man, which could be sufficient reason for doing evil, he admitted that for the help of the suffering, or for a better work, a good work might sometimes be postponed.

The palpable faith of Thomas in philosophical idealism is constantly before the reader. There may be doubt, however, as to whether this idealism is entirely Christian or whether there is a direct influence from Plato or the later neo-Platonists of Alexandria. Though the author's faith in the ideal of God is a mystic belief, intuitive in nature, with little of the rational core of thought behind it upon which Plato insisted, Thomas à Kempis, like Plato, believes that the real world, the world of ideality, is the only true world. But in Thomas' case the method by which Truth is achieved is not through reason; rather, the immediate source is grace acquired through the sacraments of the Church, and through revelation acquired by abstinence from worldly matters, the application of prayer, and the use of contemplation. In answer to his own rhetorical question as to how the Christian saints became so perfect, Thomas points out the fact that their perfection lay in their contemplation of divinity. The greatness of the saints, he adds, came from the fact that they steadfastly sought to abstain from all worldly considerations and to cling with their whole hearts to God and thoughts of Him.

The power of God is, for Thomas à Kempis, in divine love, a good above all others which makes every burden light and equalizes all opportunity. He wrote:

> Love is swift, sincere, pious, pleasant, gentle, strong, patient, faithful, prudent, long-suffering, manly, and never seeking her own; for wheresoever a man seeketh his own, there he falleth from love. Love is circumspect, humble, and upright; not weak, not fickle, nor intent on vain things; sober, chaste, steadfast, quiet, and guarded in all senses. Love

is subject and obedient to all that are in authority, vile and lowly in its own sight, devout and grateful towards God, faithful and always trusting in Him even when God hideth His face, for without sorrow we cannot live in love.

The pious author suggests in *The Imitation of Christ* that there were four rules for the accomplishment of peace and true liberty: that we should try to do another's will rather than our own, that we should seek always to have less than more, that we should seek the lowest place, and that we should wish and pray always to fulfill the will of God.

The Imitation of Christ was arranged in four parts. Book I deals with "Admonitions Profitable for the Spiritual Life"; Book II, "Admonitions Concerning the Inward Life"; Book III, "On Inward Consolation"; Book IV, "Of the Sacrament of the Altar." The last, a kind of manual for the devout, gives instruction, advice, and guidance on preparing for the sacrament of communion. In the third book are many prayers noted for their eloquence and sincerity of devotion. The last paragraph of a prayer for the spirit of devotion is one of the best examples:

> How can I bear this miserable life unless Thy mercy and grace strengthen me? Turn not away Thy face from me, delay not Thy visitation. Withdraw not Thou Thy comfort from me, lest my soul 'gasp after Thee as a thirsty land.' Lord, teach me to do Thy will, teach me to walk humbly and uprightly before Thee, for Thou are my wisdom, who knowest me in truth, and knewest me before the world was made and before I was born into the world.

Although a monk, devoted to his order, his vocation, and God's service through most of his life, Thomas à Kempis was gifted with a keen insight into the world and what it can do to men. He inculcated submission to divine will and recognized at the same time that most men would have difficulty in making such submission. He advocated an ascetic, otherworldly life and point of view, and yet he also recognized the worth of practical goodness. The rules and suggestions he wrote in *The Imitation of Christ* are clear-sighted; the analysis is keen; the tone is humane. The seriousness of its message, the sincerity of its tone, and the humility and compassion of its author make understandable the place that this great devotional work has held in the hearts of men for generations.

THE IMPORTANCE OF BEING EARNEST

Type of work: Drama
Author: Oscar Wilde (1856-1900)
Type of plot: Comedy of manners
Time of plot: Late nineteenth century
Locale: London and Hertfordshire
First presented: 1895

Principal characters:
ALGERNON MONCRIEFF (ALGY), a man about town
LADY AUGUSTA BRACKNELL, his aunt
GWENDOLEN FAIRFAX, her daughter
JACK WORTHING, in love with Gwendolen
CECILY CARDEW, his ward
MISS LETITIA PRISM, Cecily's governess
THE REVEREND CANON CHASUBLE, D.D.

Critique:

This play is built on a pun and the plot turns on a misunderstanding over the name Ernest. The theme is an attack on *earnestness*, that is, the Victorian solemnity of a false seriousness which results in priggishness, hypocrisy, and so-called piety. Unlike Shaw, who used his conventional plots to reinforce his iconoclastic ideas, Wilde used his wit as an ironic counterpoint to the absurdity of the action.

The Story:

Algernon Moncrieff, nephew of the aristocratic Lady Bracknell, was compelled by necessity to live a more or less double life, or he would have been completely at the mercy of his Aunt Augusta. To escape from her incredibly dull dinner parties, he had emulated that lady's husband by inventing a wholly fictitious friend named Bunbury, whose precarious state of health required Algy's absence from London whenever his aunt summoned him to attendance.

Algy's friend, Jack Worthing, was also forced by circumstances into a similar subterfuge for quite a different reason. He had under his care a young ward named Cecily Cardew, who lived at Jack's country place in Hertfordshire under the admirable tutelage of a stern governess, Miss Prism. Jack thought it necessary to preserve a high moral tone in the presence of Cecily and her governess. To escape from this atmosphere of restraint, he invented an imaginary brother named Ernest, who was supposed to be quite a reprobate, and whose name and general mode of behavior Jack took over during his frequent trips to London.

To complicate matters, Jack had fallen in love with Gwendolen Fairfax, the daughter of Algy's aunt, Lady Bracknell. Moreover, Gwendolen had fallen in love with him, particularly with his name, Ernest, of which she was very fond. When Lady Bracknell learned "Ernest's" intentions toward Gwendolen, she naturally wanted to know something of his family history. But since "Ernest" could supply nothing more definite than the fact that he had been found in a leather bag at the Victoria Railway Station, and that his

1423

true parentage was quite unknown, Lady Bracknell refused to consider his marriage to her daughter.

Jack realized that the time had come to put an end to Ernest. He even went so far as to appear at the manor house in Hertfordshire in deep mourning for his brother Ernest. But his friend Algy, "Bunburying" as usual, had preceded him, posing as Ernest. Cecily took an immediate interest in Algy, the supposed brother of her guardian. When Jack and Algy came face to face, Jack promptly announced that his brother Ernest had been unexpectedly called back to London and was leaving at once. But Algy, having fallen in love with Cecily, refused to leave. Cecily, in turn, confessed that it had always been her dream to love someone whose name was Ernest.

Algy, realizing that his hopes of marrying Cecily depended on his name, decided to have himself rechristened Ernest, and to that effect he called upon the local clergyman, the Reverend Canon Chasuble, D.D. But Jack had preceded him with a like request. Dr. Chasuble had an engagement for two christenings at five-thirty that afternoon.

In the meantime Gwendolen arrived at the manor house. Because of the mix-up in names, both Gwendolen and Cecily believed that they were in love with the same man, the non-existent Ernest.

When Jack and Algy appeared together, the real identities of the two pretenders were established. Both girls became furious. At first Jack and Algy upbraided each other for their mutual duplicity, but they finally settled down to tea and consoled themselves by vying with one another to see who could eat the last muffin on the plate. Cecily and Gwendolen at last decided to forgive their suitors, after Algy had admitted that the purpose of his deception was to meet Cecily, and Jack maintained that his imaginary brother was an excuse to go to London to see Gwendolen. Both girls agreed that in matters of grave importance—such as marriage—style and not sincerity was the vital thing.

Lady Bracknell, arriving in search of her daughter, discovered her nephew engaged to Cecily. Afraid that the girl, like her guardian, might possibly have only railway station antecedents, Lady Bracknell demanded to know Cecily's origin. She was informed that Cecily was the granddaughter of a very wealthy man and the heiress to one hundred and thirty thousand pounds. When she willingly gave her consent to the marriage, Jack refused to allow the match, pointing out that Cecily could not marry without his consent until she came of age, and that according to her grandfather's will she would not come of age until she was thirty-five. However, he said he would give his consent the moment Lady Bracknell approved of his marriage to Gwendolen.

There were, however, some objections to Jack as a suitable husband for Gwendolen, the main one being the question of his parentage. But the mystery was cleared up to Lady Bracknell's satisfaction by the revelation that Miss Letitia Prism, Cecily's governess, was the nurse who had left Lord Bracknell's house with a perambulator containing a male infant which she had placed in a leather handbag and left in the cloakroom of the Victoria Station. The infant was the son of Lady Bracknell's sister, a circumstance which made Jack Algy's older brother. Jack's Christian name still had to be determined. It turned out to be—Ernest. The Reverend Chasuble was relieved of his two christenings that afternoon, and Gwendolen was happy that she was actually going to marry a man named Ernest.

IN DUBIOUS BATTLE

Type of work: Novel
Author: John Steinbeck (1902-   )
Type of plot: Social criticism
Time of plot: The 1930's
Locale: California
First published: 1936

Principal characters:

MAC, a Communist labor organizer
JIM NOLAN, his assistant and friend
LONDON, leader of the fruit pickers
DOC BURTON, a friend of the strikers
AL TOWNSEND, a man sympathetic to the strikers

Critique:

With the possible exception of *The Grapes of Wrath, In Dubious Battle* is the most successful proletarian novel yet written in the United States. More sharply focused than the former, and more vivid in its characterizations, its effect is probably more forceful. Although the story springs directly from the clash of social and economic forces during the early part of the depression decade, it remains considerably more than a propaganda piece. An intensely vital narrative, exhibiting both the social awareness and artistic craftsmanship of the author, this book stands among the best of Steinbeck's novels.

The Story:

Jim Nolan's father was a workingman driven to his death by the blows of police clubs and pistol butts. As a youngster Jim witnessed both his father's courage and his despair; he saw his mother lose even her religious faith as poverty and starvation overwhelmed the family.

Older, but still keenly remembering his youth, with the scars of brutality and starvation deeply embedded in his heart, Jim Nolan became a member of the Communist Party. He was assigned to work with Mac, an able, experienced organizer. Together they became fruit pickers, at a time when the fruit growers had cut wages even lower than the workers

had thought possible. A strike was brewing and Mac and Jim determined to hurry it along and to direct its course.

Luck was with them. Shortly after their arrival at the camp of the workers, Mac, by giving the impression that he was a doctor, delivered Lisa, daughter of the camp leader, of a baby. Word of his accomplishment spread throughout the area. After Mac and Jim became friendly with London, leader of the camp, and the other workers, they persuaded the fruit pickers to organize and to strike for higher wages and better living conditions. This was not easy to do. As usual, the orchard owners had made effective use of Communism as a bogey. Furthermore, the vigilantes were a constant menace, not to mention deputies, troops, and strikebreakers, all hirelings of the fruit growers. In addition, the authorities could always close down the camp by maintaining that it violated the sanitation laws and was a menace to public health. There was also the problem of money and food; the poor migrant workers desperately needed work to supply their daily necessities.

But at last a strike was called. On the night that the strikers were to sneak out to meet the strikebreakers called in by the owners, Mac and Jim were ambushed by vigilantes. They succeeded in escaping, but Jim was shot in the arm. Word of their plan for the next morning had leaked out, and they suspected that a stool pigeon was in their midst. Nevertheless, the next day they marched out to meet the strikebreakers at the railroad station, and to implore them not to fight against their fellow workers.

Although the police had assembled in force, they seemed afraid of the strikers. During the encounter, Joy, an old and crippled comrade, was shot and killed. The strikers carried the body back to the camp, and over the body of their comrade Mac delivered a fiery and eloquent speech, exhorting the strikers to carry on and to fight to the finish. This action proved to be the best of all possible spurs to bring the workers together, and the strikers were aroused to carry on the struggle even more fiercely.

Luck was with them in other ways. They had persuaded the father of Al Townsend, who owned a lunch cart and gave handouts to Party members, to allow them to camp on his farm, after they promised him that his crop would be picked and that his property would be protected. Doc Burton, a philosopher and skeptic, took charge of the sanitation, thus protecting the camp against the health inspectors. Dick, a handsome comrade, used his charms on women in order to get money and food for the strikers.

Meanwhile the owners tried everything to break up the strike. They attempted to intimidate the workers, to divide them, to bribe London, but all their efforts failed. Then another problem arose. The owners had an article published in which it was stated that the county was feeding the strikers. The report was not true, but those who sympathized with the strikers believed it and stopped helping them altogether. Dick was getting far fewer results from his endeavors, and the situation became desperate.

Mac was often on the point of losing his head, of letting his anger get the best of him, so that the strategy of the strike was sometimes imperiled. By contrast, Jim grew more able, more hardened. He ignored the women of the camp who sought to lure him into their tents, and did not allow his feeling for Lisa to become anything more than a casual, friendly relationship. Thus he provided a sort of balance for his emotional comrades.

Conditions grew worse. The strikers had practically no money, no food. Dick finally managed to get a cow and some beans, but the food sufficed for only a few days. Meanwhile, Doc Burton had vanished. Without his help, the sick and the wounded could not be attended to, and the sanitation of the camp grew progressively worse. One night someone managed to outwit the guards and set a barn afire. The barn and an adjacent kennel housing some favorite pointers were totally destroyed. The next day the owner called in the sheriff to evict the strikers.

The strike seemed lost. The spirits of the men were at a very low ebb, and they gave signs of yielding. On the following night a boy came and told Jim and Mac that Doc Burton was lying wounded in a field. They rushed out, only to realize, when they were fired upon, that they had fallen into a trap. Mac called out a word of warning and fell to the ground. When he got up, after the firing had stopped, he called out to Jim. He got no answer. Jim was dead. By that time the shots had aroused the others and they came forward. Over the body of his comrade and friend, Mac made a strong and rousing speech, urging the workers to stick together, to fight on, and to win the strike.

IN THE WILDERNESS

Type of work: Novel
Author: Sigrid Undset (1882-1949)
Type of plot: Historical chronicle
Time of plot: Early fourteenth century
Locale: Norway
First published: 1927

Principal characters:
OLAV AUDUNSSON, master of Hestviken
EIRIK, his heir
CECILIA, Olav's daughter
BOTHILD ASGERSDATTER, Olav's foster daughter
LADY MÆRTA, Bothild's grandmother
TORHILD BJÖRNSDATTER, mother of Olav's son Björn
SIRA HALLBJÖRN, a priest

Critique:

When Sigrid Undset was awarded the Nobel Prize for Literature in 1928, that award was made, according to the citation, "principally with regard to her powerful pictures of Northern life in medieval times." No one who has read *Kristin Lavransdatter* or *The Master of Hestviken* will deny the justice of that statement. Those not familiar with her novels must be prepared to find a writer who, while true to the life and spirit of a past age, pays little attention to the historical personages and actual events so necessary to the historical romancer. Madame Undset's stories of medieval life are so full bodied and rich in detail that there is little need in her books for a parade of names and dates. *In the Wilderness*, the third volume of the Hestviken series, is the one exception to her usual practice, however, for the closing episode of this novel deals with the invasion of Norway by Duke Eirik of Sweden in 1308.

The Story:

Olav Audunsson had little desire to stay on at Hestviken through the summer following his wife's death, and when the sons of the English armorer in Oslo asked him to be shipmaster of their boat on a trading voyage to London it was plain that the idea pleased him. Eirik, Ingunn's

son by the Icelander, wanted also to go on the trip, but Olav told him nay—he must remain at Hestviken and be companion to little Cecilia, the daughter Ingunn had borne in her last years.

In England two adventures befell Olav. At evensong in the Dominican's church he saw a woman so much like dead Ingunn that for a moment his breath failed him. So like she was, and yet young enough to be his daughter. With her was a blind man, apparently her husband. Olav saw her again, at mass and evensong, and after a time they began to exchange glances and smiles. One night her serving-woman stopped him after the service and led him to a great house outside the walls. The strange woman was in the garden, her only dress a thin silk shift. For a moment Olav felt that he was about to clasp Ingunn again. Then he realized that she was only a wanton wife seeking sport with a stranger. Thrusting her from him, he ran away.

At another time he went with his shipmates to a famous shrine north of London. Separated from his companions, he wandered in the woods until he encountered some men beside a brook. That night they attacked him for his rich dress and jewels. While Olav fought with the robbers in the dark, he felt the battle-surge he had known in his outlawed youth. Later it seemed to him that he had been tempted by pleasures of the flesh and of violence, sent to lead him from the path of redemption he must follow to atone for the secret slaying of Teit, Eirik's father.

When Olav sailed home in late summer, he found Eirik grown taller and strong for his age and Cecilia fairer than ever, with promise of great beauty. Resolving that Liv, the slatternly serving-woman, was unfit to train the daughter of Hestviken, he wed Liv to Arnketil, his house-carl, and sent the pair to live at Rundmyr, the farm he carried on for Torhild Björnsdatter, who had borne him a son out of wedlock two years before. One day he went across the fjord to Auken, where Torhild was living, to discuss his arrangement. Seeing his son and Torhild again, he was minded to ask the woman to return and keep his house, but he sadly put the thought out of his mind.

After Liv and Arnketil moved to Rundmyr, the place began to have a bad reputation because of the dicing, wenching, and worse that went on there. At last Sira Hallbjörn, the priest, warned Olav to keep Eirik away from that thieves' den. For years Olav had been of two minds about Eirik. He wanted to like the boy whom he had claimed as his heir, yet he could not abide Eirik's insolence and boasting. He realized that he should give more time to his training but shrank from that duty because of the old clash of wills between them. Urged to marry again, he wanted no other wife beside him at table and bed.

His problem was solved in part when Asger Magnusson, an old friend, died in Tunsberg after asking Olav to foster his daughter Bothild and provide for his mother-in-law, Mærta Birgersdatter. Lady Mærta was grim and gaunt but capable. Never had Hestviken been better kept than it was under her charge. Cecilia and Bothild, close in age, lived as sisters. Lady Mærta dressed them well, and people said that in the whole southland there were no fairer maids than those at Hestviken.

But Eirik set himself against Lady Mærta from the first, and Olav was always angry when he was drawn into their rows and forced to rebuke the boy for the sake of a stranger. In the winter of Eirik's sixteenth year they quarreled after Olav found him in rude sport with a serving-girl. That night Eirik left Hestviken without farewell. There was no report of him at Rundmyr or among Olav's distant kin, but at last word came that he was in Oslo, among the men-at-arms who served Sir Ragnvald Torvaldsson. Knowing Sir Ragnvald a gentle knight from whom Eirik would learn the skills of weapons and courtly ways, Olav was satisfied. He went to Oslo and gave the runaway money and a squire's gear. There was much kindness between them when they parted, Olav almost in envy for Eirik's youth.

Three years passed more quietly than any Olav had known since boyhood. Cecilia was his great delight, with little in her nature to recall her weak-willed, sickly mother. One night some men from another parish came to Hestviken. After the drinking in the hall one of the men tried to seize Bothild and Cecilia. Bothild was terrified, but Cecilia drew her knife and slashed at the man until the blade was red. Olav felt that she should have been the boy of the house.

Olav, beginning to grow restless, was often in the company of Sira Hallbjörn, a priestly lover of falconry and hunting. One night, while they supped at a wedding feast, Olav's ancient Viking ax, Kin-fetch, rang. For a moment they saw in one another's eyes old pagan stirrings that neither could have spoken aloud. Riding home later that night, Olav went into the graveyard and called to Ingunn to arise. On another day he went to Auken, where he found Torhild married to Ketil, a young man on the farm. Olav asked her to send Björn, their son, to live with him. She refused.

The snows lay deep that December

when Duke Eirik crossed the border from Sweden to lead his troops against his father-in-law, King Haakon. Torhild brought word of the invasion to Hestviken one frosty dawn. After sending Cecilia, Bothild, and Lady Mærta to Auken for safety, Olav rode off to warn his neighbors. When the franklins tried to ambush the Swedes, they were routed by the mailed horsemen. Olav and Sira Hallbjörn were among the few who made their way to the manor at Sundrheim and there spent the Yule. Meanwhile the Swedes occupied Oslo and besieged Akershus, the royal fortress. Olav was in that great fight at Aker church and at Frysja bridge, where there was hard fighting to keep Duke Eirik from taking the castle. Sira Hallbjörn was killed at the bridge, and in the press a crossbow-bolt shattered Olav's jaw.

Olav lay in fever for days. After Duke Eirik withdrew from the siege, a merchant took Olav into Oslo and cared for him there. One day he looked at himself in a mirror. His cheek was furrowed and scarred and his hair was gray. When he went back to Hestviken in the spring, Olav felt that he had become an old man.

INAZUMA-BYÔSHI

Type of work: Novel
Author: Santô Kyôden (1761-1816)
Type of plot: Feudal romance
Time of plot: Fifteenth century
Locale: Japan
First published: 1806

Principal characters:

SASAKI SADAKUNI, feudal Lord of Yamato Province
SASAKI KATSURA, his first-born son, by his deceased first wife
SASAKI HANAGATA, his second son, by his present wife
KUMODE NO KATA (LADY SPIDER), his present wife, Hanagata's mother
ICHÔ NO MAE (LADY GINKGO), Katsura's wife
TSUKIWAKA (YOUNG-MOON), son of Katsura and Lady Ginkgo
FUWA DÔKEN (ROAD-DOG), steward to the House of Sasaki
FUWA BANZAEMON, Dôken's son
HASEBE UNROKU, a disloyal retainer
NAGOYA SABUROZAEMON, a loyal retainer
NAGOYA SANSABURÔ, his son
FUJINAMI (WISTERIA-WAVE), a dancing girl
SASARA SAMPACHIRÔ, a loyal retainer, also known as Namuemon
KURITARO (CHESTNUT-SON), his son
KAEDE (MAPLE), his daughter
YUASA MATAHEI, Fujinami's brother
UMEZU KAMON (GOOD-GATE), a recluse
SARUJIRO (MONKEY-SON), Sampachirô's servant
SHIKAZÔ (DEER), Sansaburô's servant

Critique:

Using the central theme of rivalry for succession to a great feudal house, and the triumph of good over evil, right over wrong, Santô Kyôden took his materials from traditional *Kabuki* plays and wrote *Inazuma-byôshi* (*Trouble in the House of Sasaki*) with stage production obviously in mind. The scenes change rapidly, and the plot is complicated by the appearance of a large number of secondary characters who disrupt the unity of the story. Thus the principal theme tends to move away from the succession intrigues to a depiction of the feudal loyalty of a secondary character, Sasara Sampachirô. That this novel was soon produced on the *Kabuki* stage was a matter of course, and it was staged under various titles, the first being in Osaka in 1808, and in Edo in 1809. As a novel the work comprised a unit in itself, but Kyôden wrote a sequel, the *Honchô Sui-bodai Zenden,* which was published in 1809. This later work, making greater use of syllabic meter, has little in connection with the original, and is thin in plot; but it carries the reader on through the author's sheer writing ability.

The Story:

During the mid-fifteenth century, under the shogunship of Ashikaga Yoshimasa, there lived a warrior lord by the name of Sasaki Sadakuni, lord of the Province of Yamato. He had two sons. One, twenty-five years old and named Katsura, was the son of Sadakuni's first wife; the other, twelve-year-old Hanagata, was the son of Sadakuni's second and present wife, Lady Spider. Katsura, a handsome young man, was taken into the luxurious and self-indulgent service of the shogun at Kyoto. There, at the instigation of one of Katsura's retainers, Fuwa Banzaemon, Katsura fell in love with a dancing girl, Wisteria-wave, and began to lead a life of pleasure.

A retainer of the House of Sasaki, Nagoya Sansaburô, was sent to Kyoto to present a treasured painting to the shogun. Learning how matters stood with Katsura, he did his best to make the young lord mend his ways, but to no avail. Meanwhile, Banzaemon himself had been discovered to be in love with Wisteria-wave, and he was discharged from feudal service. Sansaburô was sent back to the Sasaki provincial headquarters. At the same time a loyal retainer, Sasara Sampachirô, killed Wisteria-wave and went into hiding. On the same night a disloyal retainer, Hasebe Unroku, stole the treasured painting and disappeared.

The next day Banzaemon's father, Road-dog, steward to the House of Sasaki, arrived as Sadakuni's emissary, severely reprimanded Katsura for his dissolute

ways, and discharged Katsura's retinue as being disloyal. Behind Road-dog's outwardly righteous actions lay a deeper plan, a plot to take over his lord's domain with the connivance of Governor General Hamana. Knowing Lady Spider's hope that her own son Hanagata would succeed to the lordship of Sasaki, Road-dog had joined forces with her. With the backing of an evil sorcerer, the two attempted to do away with Katsura's wife, Lady Ginkgo, and her son Young-moon, who were living in the Sasaki villa in Heguri, guarded by Sansaburô and his father, Nagoya Saburozaemon. Although their plot failed, Sadakuni was deceived and troops were dispatched against Lady Ginkgo and her young son.

In the meantime Banzaemon, who held a grudge against Sansaburô, killed Saburozaemon. Sansaburô placed Young-moon in the care of Young-moon's elderly nurse and helped them escape; he himself fought valiantly in defense of Lady Ginkgo, but in spite of his courage and efforts his lord's lady was abducted. He himself escaped into Kawachi Province.

The old woman in charge of Young-moon had met with difficulty in escaping with her charge. Young-moon was saved, however, by Sasara Sampachirô, who meanwhile had changed his name to Namuemon, and was hidden in Tamba Province.

Namuemon was still haunted by the spirit of the dead Wisteria-wave whom he had killed for the sake of his lord; his son, Chestnut-son, became blind, and his daughter Maple was haunted by a serpent. When it was known that Namuemon was secretly watching Road-dog's movements with the idea of killing him, warriors were sent against Namuemon, who beheaded his own son and then, in order that Young-moon's life might be spared, identified the head as Young-moon's. Namuemon's daughter Maple sold herself for the painting. Namuemon, with his wife and Young-moon, sought refuge in Kawachi Province. Leaving the two in a place of safety, he himself set

1430

out to find his master Katsura and Katsura's wife, Lady Ginkgo.

Meanwhile, Lady Ginkgo, who had fallen into Road-dog's hands, was about to be murdered, but she was saved by a hero-recluse by the name of Umezu Good-gate. Katsura, who had become an itinerant Buddhist priest, was about to meet his death at a temple festival in Ōmi Province, when his life was saved by Monkey-son, Sansaburō's son who had become a street preacher. After his delivery Katsura was hidden in the home of Wisteria-wave's older brother, Yuasa Matahei, a painter living in Ōtsu. By chance, Namuemon was also staying there. Matahei, becoming aware that Namuemon was his own sister's murderer, was at the same time deeply impressed by the quality of Namuemon's loyalty. Matahei's wife confessed that six years ago she had attempted to hang herself because a ruffian had robbed her of twenty pieces of gold. At the time Namuemon had not only saved her from death but he had even given her twenty gold pieces to make up for her loss. Torn between revenge and gratitude, Matahei drew his sword, cut Namuemon's traveling hat in place of Namuemon's head, and offered the sundered hat to Wisteria-wave's departed but still vengeful spirit. With past wrongs thus redressed, Matahei repaid his gratitude by bringing Namuemon to Katsura. At that point Hasebe Unroku appeared on the scene and was recognized by Matahei's wife as the man who had robbed her six years before. Namuemon forced Unroku to commit suicide to expiate his sins.

Maple, meanwhile, had joined a traveling theatrical troupe which had come to those parts. Namuemon, now revealed as Sampachirō, met his daughter, whose affliction from serpents that always accompanied her had been healed by the painting she had so dearly bought. Matahei, for the first time, realized that he had attained the inner secret which he had striven for in his art—its magical power.

On the following day Katsura and his party left Ōtsu for Kawachi Province. He acquired a book on military strategy and tactics belonging to Good-gate, who had saved Lady Ginkgo's life. Intending to seek the assistance of the new governor general, Katsumoto, the party arrived at Good-gate's secluded abode on Diamond Mountain to find that Katsumoto was already there in an attempt to persuade Good-gate to accept the position of chief of military strategy. It was also revealed that Good-gate was related to Katsura by marriage. Katsura was reunited with Lady Ginkgo, who had been staying there under Good-gate's protection. With the governor general's and Good-gate's backing, Katsura prepared to return to his home province of Yamato.

Meanwhile, in Kyoto, Sansaburō, accompanied by his faithful servant Deer, had been searching for Fuwa Banzaemon and his gang in the brothels of that city. Finally he found them and with the assistance of a courtesan and Good-gate, who had been a friend of his slain father Saburozaemon, Sansaburō achieved his revenge. Good-gate, appointed the governor general's deputy, received orders to go to the headquarters of the House of Sasaki. Requesting the attendance of Sadakuni's wife, Lady Spider, and his steward, Road-dog, as well, Good-gate told Lord Sasaki Sadakuni that Katsura had not only mended his former ways but had displayed great military valor. He requested Sadakuni to pardon his son and to name Katsura his heir and successor; Sadakuni would then retire in Katsura's favor as head of the clan. Good-gate also revealed Lady Spider's and Road-dog's plot to take over the House of Sasaki by conniving for the succession of the second-born, Lady Spider's son Hanagata. With Road-dog under arrest in a caged carriage, and his mission accomplished, Good-gate took his leave amid the low and reverent bows of the House of Sasaki.

1431

INDEPENDENT PEOPLE

Type of work: Novel
Author: Halldór Laxness (1902-   )
Type of plot: Social chronicle
Time of plot: Twentieth century
Locale: Iceland
First published: 1934-1935

Principal characters:
 BJARTUR, a crofter
 ROSA, his first wife
 FINNA, his second wife
 ASTA SOLLILJA, Rosa's daughter
 GVENDUR, Bjartur's son
 NONNI, his younger son
 INGOLFUR ARNARSON, Asta's father

Critique:

Independent People is one of the few novels to give us a faithful and artistic picture of the essentially unrewarding life in bleak, small Iceland. In addition to the background, Laxness has written in a style and with a scope approaching the epic. We get some of the feeling of the traditions of the Vikings, and we see the old give way to the new. Only the hard, barren life of the crofter is unchanging, for the Icelander in the remoter sections of his country lives on about the plane of the primitive savage.

The Story:

After working for eighteen years for Bailiff Jon, Bjartur was at last able to buy, with a heavy mortgage, the croft called Winterhouses. Proud of his new status as a landowner and fiercely independent, Bjartur promptly renamed the place Summerhouses. It was a poor place, fit only for sheep grazing. The house, which Bjartur rebuilt, consisted of one room over the stable. The walls were of sod, and the roof was made of a few sheets of corrugated iron covered with turf. But it was his own place, and Bjartur was determined to be hired workman for no man and to put his trust in sheep.

For his wife he chose the twenty-six year-old Rosa, a small sturdy girl with a cast in one eye, who had also been in service to the bailiff.

Rosa was disappointed in her house, and Bjartur was disappointed in Rosa. He soon found that she was far from innocent, and worse, she was already pregnant. He suspected, and was sure much later, that the man had been the bailiff's son, Ingolfur.

After a few months of marriage Bjartur left on a cold winter day to look for his sheep. Seeing a buck reindeer in the woods, he jumped on the animal's back and attempted to subdue him. But the reindeer was too strong and took off in mad flight for the river. With Bjartur still holding on, the animal swam downstream and finally landed on the other shore. Bjartur, nearly frozen to death, stayed to recuperate at a nearby croft.

He returned home after several days to find his wife dead from childbirth and a baby daughter still alive. Disregarding the parentage of the girl, he proudly named her Asta Sollilja. The bailiff's wife sent pauper Finna and her mother to look after Bjartur and the baby. Finna was nearly forty but strong and well preserved. To settle the problem of the child's care, Bjartur married her.

Each year Finna had another child,

INDEPENDENT PEOPLE by Halldór Laxness. Translated by J. A. Thompson. By permission of the publishers, Alfred A. Knopf, Inc. Copyright, 1946, by Halldór Laxness.

usually stillborn. But after some years there were Helgi, Gvendur, and Nonni, and their sister Asta. The croft was crowded, and the beds were all dirty and filled with vermin, but the land was clear of debt.

A southerner came to the croft one day to ask permission to camp and hunt. The stranger delighted Asta, who was awkward and uncouth but bursting with love. The stranger hardly noticed her, however, and each night he was gone most of the night. The reason for his visit came out later, when the bailiff's daughter left the country in great haste.

After little Helgi was lost on the moor, the tie between Asta and Bjartur became closer. When Finna died from poor diet and rapid childbearing, the father tried his best to make life easier for the girl. He refused to let Asta go to school, but he did teach her much of the old Icelandic poetry.

Bjartur took Asta on his yearly trip to town, where, after doing the shopping, they stayed overnight in a lodging-house for country folk. To save money, father and daughter both slept in the same bed. Asta was unhappy. The town people had laughed at her homely clothes, and the snores of the drunken farmers in the nearby beds were terrifying. She snuggled closer to her father and kissed him. He put his arms around her, but to his horror found that she was kissing him repeatedly. Abruptly Bjartur got up and went out for their horse. Father and daughter left for home in the rainy night.

Then a series of misfortunes, which the Icelanders laid to a witch buried near Summerhouses, greatly reduced Bjartur's flock of sheep, and he went to town to work. Trying to meet his obligations to his children, Bjartur sent a schoolmaster to instruct Asta, Gvendur, and Nonni during the winter. But Bjartur's choice of teacher was unfortunate. After getting drunk one night the schoolmaster took Asta. When Bjartur came home in the spring, Asta was pregnant.

In his rage Bjartur cast out his daughter, who went gladly, full of romantic notions of her lover. She walked to his fine town house, which turned out to be a shack. There she learned that he had many children and that his wife was again pregnant.

Nonni, just before the World War, went to America to join his uncle. Only Gvendur and Bjartur were left, in addition to the old mother-in-law. The war boom raised the price of lambs and Bjartur prospered. He now had two cows and three horses. At the same time, a cooperative movement, with Ingolfur at its head, was organized. In the parish only Bjartur held out; he remained loyal to the merchants who had been gouging him for years.

Nonni sent two hundred dollars from America to pay for Gvendur's passage. In spite of his father's objections, Gvendur, who was seventeen and big and strong for his age, decided to emigrate. He put on his best clothes and went to town to take the coastal steamer. There he was admired because he was going to America. During the day and night Gvendur had to wait before his ship sailed, he met the bailiff's granddaughter. She took him riding on the moor, where they spent the night together. Hoping to win her love, Gvendur renounced his emigration and went back to Summerhouses.

In spite of the depression following the war, Bjartur resolved to build his new house. He went deeply into debt to buy great supplies of stone and timber. That year he got the walls and roof completed, but there were no doors and windows. Before he could finish the house, the mortgage was foreclosed and Summerhouses passed into the hands of the bank.

The only place left for the family was the mother-in-law's old croft, long since abandoned. During the moving Bjartur met Asta and was reconciled to her. Asta had a second child by another man, and she was carrying a third. The family was complete again, except for Nonni.

Asta, like Bjartur, was independent. Ingolfur, now rich and a member of Parliament, had revealed to her that he was her father. His offer of support had been soundly rejected.

Bjartur fell in with some strikers who had struck against the government's low wages. For a while he was sympathetic with the men, who were, in a way, Communist led. Gvendur was even more sympathetic. But they both rejected in principle the idea of collective action. They were independent farmers and herders.

So they moved to the wretched hovel far to the north, with only Blesi, their twenty-five-year-old horse, to do the hauling. By hard work they could continue their old way of life. They would have one room in a turf-covered hut. Their diet would be refuse fish. With luck they would be only a little less comfortable than savages in a jungle.

INDIAN SUMMER

Type of work: Novel
Author: William Dean Howells (1837-1920)
Type of plot: Domestic realism
Time of plot: Shortly after the American Civil War
Locale: Florence, Italy
First published: 1886

Principal characters:
> THEODORE COLVILLE, a middle-aged bachelor
> MRS. LINA BOWEN, a middle-aged friend of Colville
> IMOGENE GRAHAM, a girl chaperoned by Mrs. Bowen
> EFFIE BOWEN, Mrs. Bowen's thirteen-year-old daughter
> MR. MORTON, an admirer of Imogene Graham

Critique:

Many readers will find echoes in this novel of *A Hazard of New Fortunes* and the novels Howells wrote featuring Mr. and Mrs. Basil March in their later lives. In novels dealing with cultured older people, Howells was considerably more successful at sympathetic characterization than he was in such novels as *The Rise of Silas Lapham.* That he was infringing on the realm of Henry James, the master of fiction featuring American expatriates in Europe, Howells was well aware, for he comments jokingly about their work in one passage of this novel. As ever, Howells is in this novel a master of the realism of the commonplace. The details of life in the American colony in Florence at the time, the events of the pre-Lenten carnival season, and the background of the city are set forth explicitly.

The Story:

Theodore Colville studied architecture as a young man and in order to continue his professional education he spent some months in Italy. While there he went about with two young women and fell in love with one of them. The girl rejected his suit. Soon afterward he went back to the United States at the request of his older brother, who had recently purchased a newspaper. Returning to America, Colville became the editor of his brother's paper and finally purchased it. He entered politics in his fortieth year. After his defeat he left his home in Indiana and went at once again to Italy.

In Italy he tried to resume the study of architecture, but his interest was soon diverted by his meeting with Mrs. Bowen, who had been one of his companions in Italy years before, the one with whom he had not fallen in love. Mrs. Bowen, now a widow, invited Colville to visit at her home. When he went there, Colville met Mrs. Bowen's thirteen-year-old daughter Effie, who quickly became fond of him, and Imogene Graham, a twenty-year-old American woman whom Mrs. Bowen was chaperoning.

In company with Mrs. Bowen, Imogene Graham, and Effie Bowen, Mr. Colville spent a number of pleasant days and evenings. At first Imogene regarded him as an old man, since he was twice her age, but she soon realized that she enjoyed his company much more than that of many men her own age. In an effort to be companionable with her, Colville danced and went about socially as he had not done for many years. Mrs. Bowen also enjoyed Colville's company; the result was that they were together a great deal.

Mrs. Bowen chose carefully the places where she and her charges went. During the carnival season she permitted Colville to take them all to a masked ball. At the ball little Effie became ill and had to be taken home unexpectedly. As a result, Imogene and Colville were together unchaperoned during much of the evening. At that time they began to realize their affection for each other.

Mrs. Bowen quickly realized that a love affair was developing. She also realized that no one, least of all herself, had expected it. She tactfully pointed out to Imogene the differences between the girl and a man so much older. When she said, rather less tactfully, that she thought Colville had been trying only to be amusing, the girl reported the conversation to Colville. Hurt, he went to Mrs. Bowen and talked with her, finally agreeing to her suggestion that for propriety's sake he leave Florence. Unfortunately, it was a weekend, and Colville, having insufficient funds to leave the city after settling his hotel bills, was forced to wait until the following Monday. By that time Imogene had decided that it was unfair to make him leave the city because of her. She requested that he stay. He decided to do so.

A few days later Colville and Imogene met accidentally in a public park. Quickly coming to an agreement that they loved one another, they went back to Mrs. Bowen's residence and told her that they had decided to be married. Mrs. Bowen, as Imogene's chaperone, told them she would be forced to write immediately to the girl's parents to inform them of this recent development. The lovers, agreeing to her plan, also promised to say nothing about an official engagement until they heard from America. Imogene warned her chaperone, however, that she would marry Colville, even without her parents' consent.

While they were awaiting word from America, a young minister named Morton, also in love with Imogene, returned to Florence to pay her court. Both Colville and Mrs. Bowen wished to let the young man know the state of affairs, but the girl refused to permit them to tell Mr. Morton of her engagement. To make the situation appear normal, the four— Mrs. Bowen, Mr. Morton, Imogene, and Colville—went about together. Finally word came from Imogene's parents. Her mother had decided to sail for Europe, to see Colville for herself before giving her decision.

During the intervening days before Mrs. Graham's arrival, the four people went on an excursion to Fiesole to see the Etruscan ruins there. At one interval Colville and the young minister walked a short distance beside the carriage. While they were doing so, a peasant driving a band of sheep came over the brow of a hill. The horses, frightened at the sight of the sheep, began to back the carriage dangerously close to a precipitous drop at the side of the road. The two men rescued the women from the carriage. While Mr. Morton was taking Imogene from the vehicle, Colville ran to the horses' heads in an attempt to hold them. Unable to do so, and with his hand caught in the curb strap, he was dragged with the team when the carriage plunged over the edge of the road.

For two weeks Colville lay very ill. When he was finally able to have visitors, Imogene's mother came to see him. She told him that she was taking her daughter to America immediately, even though she felt that Colville had acted as a gentleman in the entire affair. She then gave her reason for preventing the marriage. Her daughter, she said, was not really in love with Colville, although she thought too much of him to break the engagement. The shock was a great one to Colville, but he immediately saw that the girl's departure was the only answer to the problems that the situation had developed. After her mother left, Imogene herself came into the sickroom and bade Colville a hasty goodbye.

Some time later Mrs. Bowen and Colville talked over the affair. During the conversation they both admitted their love for each other. Mrs. Bowen refused to marry Colville, however, because of the embarrassing position in which she had been placed during his affair with Imogene. She had hated herself the whole time she tried to prevent the affair because, although she hoped she could see the situation objectively, she had always feared that her actions and thinking had been colored by her feeling for Colville.

Little Effie Bowen, having formed a very strong attachment for Colville, refused to hear of his departure. Within a few months, under the influence of their mutual love and Effie's attitude toward her mother's suitor, Mrs. Bowen was reconciled to a marriage. They were married quietly and then moved to Rome, where no one who knew them could spread gossip about the affair with Imogene. Not long after their marriage they heard that Mr. Morton, who had been deeply in love with Imogene, had been appointed to a church in a community near Buffalo, where the Grahams lived. Both Mr. and Mrs. Colville hoped that he and Imogene Graham would make a match of their own.

INDIANA

Type of work: Novel
Author: George Sand (Mme. Aurore Dudevant, 1804-1876)
Type of plot: Sentimental romance
Time of plot: Early nineteenth century
Locale: France
First published: 1832

> Principal characters:
> INDIANA, a young Creole
> MONSIEUR DELMARE, her husband
> NOUN, her foster sister and maid
> RODOLPHE BROWN (SIR RALPH), Indiana's cousin
> RAYMON DE RAMIÈRE, her lover

Critique:

Written at the height of the French romantic movement, *Indiana* exhibits all the conventions and idiosyncrasies of the most pronounced romanticism. For this reason modern readers find the characters unbelievable, their words and actions more laughable than tragic, despite the basic tragedy underlying the greater part of the story. The chief value of the book derives from the fact that it typifies a popular literary form and a philosophy which still survive, though in lesser degree, in contemporary literature.

The Story:

Indiana was married to pompous, quick-tempered Monsieur Delmare, a retired army officer no longer young. Loyal to her suspicious and jealous husband, she had lived a discontented, uneventful life. Her cousin, Sir Ralph Brown, himself unhappy and frustrated, was her only companion. Although Monsieur Delmare kept a watchful eye over the young couple, there was nothing untoward in the relationship between them. As a matter of fact, Sir Ralph had secured the good graces of Monsieur Delmare and was accepted as one of the household. If not an intimate friend, he was at least a close companion. Indiana was as reserved in her behavior toward Sir Ralph as she was toward her husband, but to a close observer it was clear that in a friendly, inarticulate manner, Sir Ralph was fond of Indiana.

The submerged tensions of the household erupted one evening when someone was discovered scaling the garden wall and entering the grounds of the estate. Monsieur Delmare rushed out and fired in the darkness at the intruder. When the wounded prowler was brought into the house, he revealed himself as Raymon de Ramière, a young man who, so he maintained, wished to see Monsieur Delmare about the latter's manufacturing enterprise. De Ramière said that his brother had a similar business in another part of the country and would profit by Delmare's information.

Delmare's suspicions were dissolved. He had not, however, noticed the behavior of Noun, Indiana's friend and maid. Noun had become extremely agitated at the entrance of de Ramière, a fact which nobody noticed in the excitement. She knew that de Ramière had come to the estate not to see Delmare on business, but to keep a rendezvous with her. Noun had been his mistress for some time. Once in the house, however, he was immediately attracted to Indiana, especially so since he was already tiring of Noun.

De Ramière began systematically his suit for Indiana's affections and to that end he enlisted the aid of both his mother and Indiana's aunt. Before long Indiana began to reciprocate his attentions and the affair became the subject of much discussion in Parisian salons. Delmare remained ignorant of the gossip. But in spite of de Ramière's urgent avowals and protestations, Indiana refused to yield herself to him because she preferred a pure and spiritual love. Upset by her refusals, de Ramière contracted a fever which kept him confined to his bed for several days. Indiana, too, was strongly affected and experienced several spells of swooning.

One night, impatient to achieve his desire, de Ramière impetuously entered the Delmare house. Indiana was away, but Noun was there awaiting the return of her mistress. The two met in Indiana's room and Noun, as passionate as ever, enticed the young man's surrender. Aroused by the return of Indiana, Noun escaped, leaving de Ramière to face her mistress alone. Indiana, disturbed to find her suitor in her room, ordered him to leave before his presence was discovered.

A short time later, Noun's body was discovered floating in a nearby stream. Pregnant, she had taken her life because of de Ramière's refusal to marry her or even to continue their relationship. Indiana was broken-hearted at the death of her maid and de Ramière himself was greatly perturbed. By that time he had tired of his pursuit of Indiana and had determined to forget her. One night Indiana, having decided at last to become his mistress in fact, went to his rooms. Learning that he was not at home, she waited until he returned at dawn. Then she offered herself to him. Unfortunately, while they were talking, dawn broke. Compromised by her presence in de Ramière's rooms at that hour, Indiana returned to her home, where Delmare, agitated by the discovery of her absence, received her with cold suspicion.

Soon afterward Delmare suffered business reverses and faced complete ruin. Indiana contritely went with him to the Isle of Bourbon, where he hoped to make another fortune. Unhappy in her new home, she lived only for the letters de Ramière wrote her. At last she decided to leave Delmare and arranged for her secret passage back to France. On her arrival in

Paris, she learned that fickle de Ramière had recently married.

For weeks she lived a miserable existence. Penniless and starving, she decided to die. When she and Sir Ralph, who had followed her to Paris, were strangely reunited, they agreed to commit suicide by drowning. At the last minute, however, they changed their minds. Moved by Sir Ralph's devotion, Indiana realized that he was the man she truly loved. Together they forsook civilization and lived as recluses, away from all people and society, but satisfied and happy at last.

INÊS DE CASTRO

Type of work: Drama
Author: António Ferreira (1528?-1569)
Type of plot: Romantic tragedy
Time of plot: 1354-1360
Locale: Portugal
First presented: c. 1558

Principal characters:
ALFONSO IV, King of Portugal
PRINCE PEDRO, his son
INÊS DE CASTRO, secretly married to Pedro
SECRETARY TO THE PRINCE
DIOGO LOPES PACHECO,
PERO COELHO, and
GONZALVES, King Alfonso's advisers

Critique:

The love story of Inês de Castro was popular with poets and historians long before a Lisbon humanist dramatized it as the first dramatic tragedy in Portuguese, and preceded in all European literature by only one other, *Sofonisba* (1515), by the Italian Gian Trissino (1478-1550). The dramatist, António Ferreira, was the younger son of a noble at the court of the Duke of Coimbra. In construction, *Inês de Castro* follows Greek models, with a chorus that appears in all five acts, both as Ideal Spectator and as the Voice of Fate. This tragedy has flaws. The lengthy exposition by Inês in blank verse is hardly inspiring, and the simple plot allows little on-stage action. Even the murder of Inês must be inferred from the words of the Chorus and the messenger's report. But there are, in spite of these defects, moments of dramatic brilliance and scenes of suspense and charged emotion, with moving poetry to give the drama other reasons for permanence besides its interest as a pioneer effort.

The Story:

On a lovely spring day in the middle of the fourteenth century, Inês de Castro felt especially happy as she walked in her garden in Portugal. Though an illegitimate daughter of a famous Galician noble, she had won the love of Prince Pedro, son of Alfonso IV of Portugal; at last she felt sure the world was about to learn that he loved her too. Theirs had been a star-crossed love. Pedro's father, trying his best to destroy his son's love for a woman unsuitable to rule Portugal, had compelled his heir to marry the Princess Constanza of Castile. But, as Inês confided to her nurse, fate had been on the side of true love. The birth of Constanza's son, heir to the crown of Portugal, had cost his mother her life. At last Pedro was free. He had carried out his father's command. He had insured a continuation of the dynasty, and now he was coming back to the woman he really loved. Surely King Alfonso would now relent. The beauty of the day seemed an omen, and Inês was weeping with joy as

1438

she waited for her lover to appear.

The old nurse was less sure, however, that her mistress' tears were an omen of joy; they might be a foreboding of tragedy. She begged Inês not to count on happiness until everything was settled. Inês, hearing Pedro approaching, would listen to no warnings.

The prince greeted her with an assurance that all would go well. To himself, however, he wondered why he was not loved by the common people of Portugal and why his father had been so incensed by his sincere love for Inês. Nevertheless, he was confident, like Inês, that their four children would move the stern old king to pity. Pedro hoped for the royal acceptance of the love between them and a state wedding to show King Alfonso's recognition of his grandchildren.

Pedro's secretary tried to disillusion him. In spite of the nobility of her famous father, the irregularity of Inês' birth was cause enough for King Alfonso's repeated orders that Pedro must put her out of his mind. The secretary begged Pedro, for the good of the state, to let reason conquer desire and to give up the passion that enslaved him and made him disobedient to the royal will. The prince refused. He had obeyed his father in marrying Constanza. Events had proved that Inês was fated to be his real wife.

King Alfonso, meanwhile, was pacing his throne room. His three advisers, Diogo Lopes Pacheco, Pero Coelho, and Gonzalves, were deaf to his complaints that a king had more woes than pleasures. They preached the obligation of power, pointing out that an officially sanctioned marriage between Pedro and Inês, whose children were older than the recently-born son of Constanza's, might jeopardize the succession of the young child. One of the advisers, the dominating Pacheco, argued that the removal of Inês would solve all difficulties. In spite of King Alfonso's basic agreement with the suggestion, much argument was needed before the king finally gave the trio orders to kill his son's mistress.

That night Inês had a dream in which she was about to die. She interpreted it as proof that Pedro was dead; otherwise he would have been quick to defend her. Before she could discover what truth there was in her dream, the king arrived with a sentence of death. He was accompanied by Pacheco, who intended to block any appeals for royal mercy. Inês pleaded so touchingly, however, insisting on her innocence and the helplessness of her four children related through Pedro to King Alfonso, that the king, reminded of his love for his own child, finally agreed to spare her.

But the reprieve did not last long. Once more the king's advisers, selfishly hoping for more gratitude from the King of Castile than revenge by a mere Galician nobleman, worked on the king, in their determination that Constanza's child should inherit the throne. Though they could not get his consent to the death of Inês, King Alfonso did not actually forbid it. Twisting his indefiniteness into permission, the evil trio hurried away to murder the innocent Inês de Castro.

In the meantime Pedro, hurrying eagerly to join her and confident that the king would consider his son's happiness and permit their official marriage, was met by a messenger who told the prince that the three advisers had sought out Inês and killed her. Out of his mind with grief, Pedro swore to have revenge on all concerned, including his father. He would cast him from the throne and then hunt down and torture the three evil murderers, and he would not only see to it that a child of Inês should be named his successor, but when he was crowned he would also have Inês' corpse exhumed and seated on the throne beside him to receive the honors of a royal coronation.

THE INFORMER

Type of work: Novel
Author: Liam O'Flaherty (1896-   )
Type of plot: Psychological melodrama
Time of plot: The 1920's
Locale: Dublin
First published: 1925

Principal characters:
    FRANCIS JOSEPH McPHILLIP, a political murderer
    GYPO NOLAN, the informer
    DAN GALLAGHER, a revolutionist
    KATIE FOX, a prostitute

Critique:

The Informer, an outstanding example of modern Irish realism and a masterpiece of suspense, has had a popular as well as a critical success. Part of its merit consists of its adherence to the classical unities of time, place, and action, for the entire story covers only a single night in Dublin. O'Flaherty has given a realistic picture of the slum and its people, and of the tight-knit revolutionary organization which could flourish so completely only in Ireland.

The Story:

Francis McPhillip came to the door of the public lodging-house. He was unobtrusively and shabbily dressed. With the caution born of necessity, he waited in the doorway until he was sure he was not followed. He kept his hand inside his raincoat to touch the reassuring butt of his pistol. For six months he had been a hunted man, hiding out in the wild mountains.

It was in October that he had killed the secretary of the Farmers' Union. He had orders from the revolutionary organization to use his gun only if he had to; after the killing the organization had disavowed his act and expelled him. So he had been a lone fugitive. Now he was back in Dublin to see his family once more.

He searched among the public rooms crowded with Dublin's poor. In the din-ing-room he found the man he had come to see: Gypo Nolan. Gypo was eating from a huge plate of cabbage and bacon he had stolen from a locker. Francis sat down and inquired hoarsely of Gypo if the police were still watching his parents' house. Gypo gave only grunts at first, and then said he thought the coast was clear. After eating voraciously from Gypo's plate, Francis slipped out.

Gypo thought stolidly of his former companion in the organization. Then he thought bitterly of his empty pockets; he could not buy a bed tonight. He tried to link up these two facts, but Gypo thought only with great difficulty. The organization had expelled him too, for he had been Francis' companion at the time of the murder. Without Francis' agile brain he could make no plans. At last a light came. He marched off to the police station and told the officers where they could find Francis. For his information he received twenty pounds. Shortly afterward, Francis shot himself as police officers surrounded his father's house.

In a public house Gypo met Katie Fox, a prostitute who took care of him occasionally when he was destitute. He bought her a few glasses of gin and told her he had no need of her bed that night. She was suspicious because he was in funds and accused him of robbing a church. During the quarrel she accidentally let drop the word "informer." Gypo was startled. He was glad to leave her and go out in the night.

To keep up appearances, Gypo went to the McPhillip house. He quarreled with Francis' father, who blamed him for the wild life Francis had led. Francis' mother and his sister Mary, however, upheld Gypo for his visit of sympathy. As he left he gave Mrs. McPhillip four silver coins.

Bartly followed him out. Bartly was an organization member sent out to bring Gypo in. After Bartly made a taunting reference to the coins he had given Francis' mother, Gypo choked Bartly, and only the arrival of an armed friend saved his life. By threats and persuasion Gypo was led to the organization headquarters, where he met the feared and respected Dan Gallagher, the revolutionists' leader.

Because of his stupidity and his great strength, Gypo had no fear of men or guns, but Dan was intelligent and soon overcame Gypo's hostility. If Gypo could only give them a lead on the person who had informed the police of Francis' return, he would be taken back into the organization. Dan brought out a bottle and gave Gypo several drinks. Under their influence Gypo concocted a story: Rat Mulligan had a grudge against Francis for betraying his sister, and Gypo declared he had seen Rat following Francis away from the lodging-house. Though he was skeptical, Dan sent for Rat and ordered Gypo to appear for the hearing that night at one-thirty.

Followed by his shadow Bartly, Gypo went out confidently. In a street fight he knocked out a policeman from sheer exuberance. Trailed by an admiring rabble, he went to a lunch stand and bought food for all his admirers. In the confusion he slipped away from Bartly.

Gypo was elated. He had money; he was safe; he would be back in the organization. He went to a superior brothel and spent money recklessly. A well-dressed woman with a scar on her face held aloof. She refused Gypo's advances, saying she was the wife of an army officer and wanted to get back to London. Gypo gave her the fare and accepted the companionship of another girl, Maggie. Bartly found him with her and reminded him of the inquiry. Gypo gave Maggie a pound to take to Katie and followed Bartly willingly.

Meanwhile Dan had been at the McPhillip house to take the family's statements. He made love briefly to Mary and induced her to accompany him to the inquiry, a kangaroo court held in the wine cellar of a ruined house. Dan acted as prosecutor and three of his men were judges.

First Rat Mulligan was questioned, but it soon developed that Rat could not possibly have been the informer. When Gypo was brought in, Dan made a convincing case: Gypo knew where Francis was going, Gypo had left the lodging-house at the right time, Gypo had been squandering money all night. At last Gypo broke down and confessed his guilt. Dan had him imprisoned in a cellar room with armed guards at the door.

Long ago Francis had discussed with Gypo how to get out of the cell. In the ceiling there was a trapdoor covered with dirt. Exerting his great strength, Gypo seized an iron ring with his hands, and with his legs forced up both trapdoor and covering earth. As he scrambled out the alerted guards shot at him, but he got away. Dan was terrified. Gypo might go to the police and the secret organization would be broken up. Mary was astonished at the weakness of resourceful Dan. When he pulled himself together, he sent agents to cover the roads leading out of the area. Gypo was trapped.

Every time Gypo tried to leave the slum district, he found waiting guards. His only refuge was Katie's room. She let him stay, and he thankfully fell into brutish sleep. Somehow Katie began to think of her own lost and vicious life, and she identified her misery with Gypo. With a notion that she would be canonized, she crept off to inform the organization of Gypo's hiding place.

As four armed men closed in on him, Gypo awoke just in time to fight them off. He crippled two of them in a struggle on the stairs, but he was wounded several times as he ran to escape execution.

Gypo became weaker as he fled. Dan saw him but shrugged as he turned away. He knew the informer was done for. In growing confusion Gypo went into a church where early mass was being celebrated. With dimming vision he made out Mrs. McPhillip. He fell in front of her seat and confessed his treachery. When she forgave him, Gypo stood up and in a loud voice called to Francis that his mother had forgiven him. With a gurgle he fell forward and shivered as blood gushed from his mouth.

THE INNOCENT VOYAGE

Type of work: Novel
Author: Richard Hughes (1900-   )
Type of plot: Psychological realism
Time of plot: Early nineteenth century
Locale: Jamaica, the high seas, England
First published: 1929

Principal characters:
MR. BAS-THORNTON, a plantation owner in Jamaica
MRS. BAS-THORNTON, his wife
JOHN,
EMILY,
EDWARD,
RACHAEL, and
LAURA, their children
MARGARET FERNANDEZ, Emily's friend
HARRY FERNANDEZ, her brother
CAPTAIN JONSEN, captain of a pirate ship
A DUTCH SEA CAPTAIN, murdered by Emily

Critique:

The Innocent Voyage, equally well-known under its alternate English title, A High Wind in Jamaica, is an unusual novel on which the author has realistically shown the effect—or lack of effect —of a series of horrible experiences upon the minds of seven young children. These experiences include a hurricane, capture by pirates, seduction, murder, and a trial at Old Bailey. Written with varied humor that runs from macabre playfulness to biting satire, the novel ranks as a minor classic because of its convincing insights into the childhood psyche. For the world of childhood, as the writer makes plain, is quite different from the adult one, and also different from what most grownups suppose. The Bas-Thornton children are not young monsters, as some mistaken readers have supposed. They are children protected and insulated by the amorality of their own innocence from an adult world of compulsions, frustrations, and fears.

The Story:

Five young Bas-Thorntons lived on the family's run-down sugar plantation in Jamaica. On the day after Emily's tenth birthday they were allowed to make their first visit away from home. They went to meet Margaret and Harry Fernandez, children of creole neighbors, on a nearby plantation. The Fernandez children often ran around barefoot, like Negroes; Emily thought it quite wonderful. During their visit the region was shaken by a slight quake. Emily, wildly excited, galloped her pony into the sea. For the first time she realized that there were forces in the world over which neither she nor adults had any control.

If the earthquake was the most thrilling event of Emily's life, the death of a pet cat was soon to be the most terrible. The next evening, back home, a hurricane struck the island. While the house shook under the force of wind and rain, Tabby streaked through the house and dashed out into the storm pursued by a pack of wild jungle cats. That night the house and the surrounding countryside were blown flat, but the destruction was nothing compared with the mystery of Tabby's horrible fate.

Mr. and Mrs. Bas-Thornton had no way of knowing what was passing through the children's minds. Fearing that the hurricane must have been a shock to them, the parents reluctantly decided to send them back to England to school. They and the Fernandez children were shortly put aboard the *Clorinda,* in care of Captain James Marpole.

Off the Cuban coast pirates boarded the vessel. Her stores and valuables were seized, and the children removed to the marauder for their supper. Captain Marpole, mistaking efforts to return the children for the splash of bodies thrown overboard, left the scene under full sail. Later he wrote the Bas-Thorntons that the pirates had callously murdered the children. Actually, Captain Jonsen, leader of the pirate crew, was surprised to find himself the custodian of seven young travelers.

The *Clorinda's* cargo was auctioned off at Santa Lucia, Cuba. While playing, Emily's older brother John fell forty feet to his death from a warehouse doorway. The vessel presently put to sea with the surviving children.

For weeks the pirate ship sailed aimlessly over the ocean in search of booty.

The children, allowed to do much as they pleased, amused themselves with two pigs and a monkey the vessel carried. Emily began to be aware of her identity as a separate personality; shipboard life which she had accepted unquestioningly at first began to disturb her. One night Captain Jonsen, drunk, came into the children's quarters. When he tried to stroke Emily's hair she bit his thumb. Margaret, more mature, was sick after the incident, but a few days later she went to the captain's cabin to live. From that time on she avoided the other children.

As both bore an individual weight of guilt, Emily and the captain evaded each other after the drunken incident, until a thigh wound Emily received from a marlin spike dropped by Rachel brought about a reconciliation. Captain Jonsen carried her to his cabin, dressed the gash, and gave her his bunk.

Emily was still confined to bed, her wound healing, when the pirates captured a Dutch steamer carrying a cargo of wild animals. Her captain was bound and left tied on the floor of Emily's cabin while Captain Jonsen and his crew amused themselves with the animals aboard their prize.

While Emily screamed futilely, the Dutch captain managed to roll toward a knife lying in a corner. He was not a handsome man. He seemed to have no neck and he reeked of cigar smoke; the fact that he was tied up like an animal added to Emily's terror. His fingers were groping for the blade when she threw herself out of her bunk. Seizing the knife, she slashed at him until he was covered with wounds. Leaving him to bleed to death, she then hurled the weapon toward the door and dragged herself back to the bunk.

Margaret was the first to enter the cabin, and so the first boatload of pirates to return from the captured steamer thought she had committed the crime. Horrified, they dropped her overboard to drown. The freebooters in the second boat, assuming that she had accidentally fallen in, picked her up. In the excitement caused by the murder no one noticed her come aboard, and she was not disturbed when she rejoined the younger children in the hold.

With the captain's death hanging over their heads, intimacy between children and pirates came to an end. Realizing the wantonness of her deed, Emily had to bear the double burden of her conscience and the fear that Margaret would identify the real culprit.

The sight of a man-of-war on the horizon finally brought Captain Jonsen to a decision; it was time he and the children parted company. With his ship disguised as a shabby cargo vessel, the *Lizzie Green*, he persuaded the captain of a passing steamship to relieve him of his young passengers. The children were laying their own plans for capturing another prize when the mate called Emily aside to coach her in what he hoped would be the children's story. Emily willingly promised to say that the captain of the *Lizzie Green* had rescued them from pirates; but it was she who, in a childish burst of confidence to the stewardess aboard the steamer, told the secret of the pirate vessel. On that information, a gunboat apprehended Captain Jonsen and his men; they were imprisoned in Newgate. The young Bas-Thorntons were reunited with their parents, who had sold the plantation and moved to England. Margaret and Harry Fernandez went to stay with relatives.

Although Emily had revealed their captors' identities readily enough, the prosecuting attorney had good reason for doubting his ability to obtain a conviction. The children told about the pirates' monkey and some turtles the *Clorinda* had carried, but of life aboard the pirate ship they had little to say. All memory of John seemed obliterated from their minds. It was accepted by the grownups, and gradually by the children, that he had died trying to protect the girls. This conclusion was substantiated by Margaret's condition of shock and loss of memory.

Emily became the chief witness for the Crown. Asked about the Dutch captain and the possibility that he had been murdered, she became hysterical but managed to say she had seen him lying in a pool of blood. Her statement was enough for a conviction. As she left the courtroom she saw in Captain Jonsen's eyes the same desperate and despairing look she had seen in Tabby's the night of the hurricane. Captain Jonsen was condemned to be hanged.

A few days later Emily was taken to her new school by her parents. The head mistress spoke feelingly of the experiences Emily had undergone, but anyone else, looking at her, would have found that Emily's innocent young face blended perfectly with the others as she stood chattering with the quiet-mannered young ladies who were to be her new friends.

THE INSPECTOR GENERAL

Type of work: Drama
Author: Nikolai V. Gogol (1809-1852)
Type of plot: Political satire
Time of plot: Early nineteenth century
Locale: Russia
First presented: 1836

Principal characters:
ANTON ANTONOVICH SKVOZNIK-DMUKHANOVSKY, prefect of a small provincial town
ANNA, his wife
MARIA, his daughter
IVAN ALEXANDROVICH HLESTAKOV, a traveler

Critique:

This comedy, the high point of Gogol's work in the drama, represents an effective protest on his part against the fumbling, venal bureaucracy of Russia's small towns. Under the tsars, favoritism was rife, and the practice of giving and accepting bribes and favors is here satirized. The characters in the play are numerous but unimportant. The situation, which is credibly presented, and the system of government portrayed are what make this comedy live. The resemblances to modern manners and customs are close enough for us to enjoy the basic similarity to bureaucratic institutions in our own time.

The Story:

The prefect of the town, Anton Antonovich, had received a disquieting letter. A friend wrote that an inspector was coming to visit the province and particularly his district. The inspector would probably travel incognito. The friend advised the prefect to clean up the town and hide evidence of any bribes that might discredit him. Anton in haste called a meeting of the local dignitaries and instructed them how to make a good impression on the official from the capital.

Artemy Filippovich Zemlyanika, the hospital manager, was advised to put clean nightcaps on the patients and take away their strong tobacco for a time. The manager was thoughtful; he had always proceeded on the theory that if a patient were going to die, he would die anyway. He decided, however, to clean up both the patients and the hospital and to put up a sign in Latin over each bed to tell the patient's malady.

Ammos Fedorovich Lyapkin-Tyapkin, the judge, spent most of his time hunting. He kept a whip and other sporting equipment in his courtroom, and in the vestibule the porter kept a flock of geese. His assessor always smelled of liquor. Ammos protested that the assessor was injured as a baby and had smelled of brandy ever since. Anton suggested that he be made to eat garlic to cover the smell.

Luka Lukich Hlopov, the head of the school, was advised to cover up the more obvious foibles of his teachers. The one with a fat face, for instance, always made horrible grimaces when a visitor came and pulled his beard under his necktie, and the history teacher jumped on his desk when he described the Macedonian wars.

Piqued by a recital of their weaknesses, the others turned on Anton and reminded him that he took money bribes and only recently had had the wife of a non-commissioned officer flogged. During the wrangle the postmaster came in to see if they had had any news of the inspector's arrival. Anton advised the postmaster to open all letters in an attempt to discover who the inspector might be and when he would arrive. The advice was superfluous, for the postmaster always read all the letters anyway.

Two squires of the town, Bobchinsky and Dobchinsky, rushed in with exciting news. A mysterious stranger, obviously a high-born gentleman, was at that moment lodging in the local inn, and had been there a fortnight. His servant had let it out that his master was from St. Petersburg. Sure that the stranger was the inspector, the company trembled to think what he might already have learned. They scattered to repair any damage they could.

At the inn Osip was lying on his master's bed and ruminating on the queerness of gentlefolk. His gentleman was always gambling, always broke, always selling his clothes to get funds. They were stuck in this wretched inn because there was no money to pay their bill. At this point, Ivan Alexandrovich burst in, loudly calling for supper.

When the waiter was summoned, he insolently refused to serve Ivan until the guest had paid his bill. After a long argument, some watery soup and a tough hen were brought, and perforce Ivan dined poorly. As the dishes were being removed amidst a tussle between Osip and the waiter for the remains of the supper, visitors were announced.

Nervous and apologetic, the prefect stood before Ivan's august person. Ivan thought, however, that he was to be put in jail. For a time the conversation was at cross purposes, but Ivan had the nimbler wit and allowed the prefect to do most of the talking. When he began to suspect what Anton was trying to say, he coolly accepted two hundred roubles to pay his bill, an invitation to stay at the prefect's house, and a nomination as the guest of honor at an official dinner at the hospital.

Anna and Maria were arguing about clothes, as usual, when Dobchinsky rushed in to announce the arrival of the inspector and his fine condescension in coming to stay at their house. Dobchinsky thought that he was being honest when he assured them their guest was a general. Thrilled at the idea of entertaining a general, the two ladies began to primp and preen.

When the men came in, Anton tried to impress the inspector by saying that he never played cards. Ivan approved; he especially abhorred gambling. Osip snickered at his master's remark, but fortunately he was not noticed. To impress the household Ivan then informed them that he was an author; besides writing for the papers he composed poetry and novels. When he referred casually to his high political connections, his hearers were agog, particularly the ladies. Meanwhile Ivan was steadily drinking wine. At last he fell into a drunken sleep in his chair.

With only Osip remaining, Anton tried to pump the servant as to his master's habits and tastes, while the ladies tried to find out something about Ivan's love life. Since Anton kept giving him money, Osip obliged by telling many details of his master's place in high society.

Ivan was put to bed to sleep off the wine. When he awoke, the dignitaries of the town waited on him one by one. Ammos, the judge, introduced himself and asked for the inspector's orders. Ivan carelessly promised to speak well of the judge to his friends, and just as carelessly

borrowed money from his suppliant. The postmaster was impressed with Ivan's friendliness and was glad to lend him three hundred roubles. Both Luka and Artemy were glad to lend the inspector three or four hundred roubles, but Bobchinsky and Dobchinsky together could raise only sixty-five roubles.

When the petitioners left, Osip begged his master to leave while the pickings were still good. Ivan, agreeing that immediate departure might be prudent, sent the servant to make arrangements. Osip wangled the best coach the town could offer. In the meantime several shopkeepers also came in to protest against the prefect, who was making them pay tribute. From them Ivan borrowed five hundred roubles.

When Maria came in, Ivan was so elated at his successes that he made love to her and finally kissed her on the shoulder. The daughter scurried away as her mother came in, and Ivan ogled the older lady, too. The daughter came back, full of curiosity, and in his confusion Ivan proposed marriage to Maria, who accepted him graciously. After writing a letter to a friend, in which he detailed his humorous adventures, Ivan left town. He promised, however, to return the next day.

In the morning Anton and his wife received the envious congratulations of friends. The ladies, green with envy, assured Maria that she would be a belle in St. Petersburg society. The parents, much taken with the idea, decided that their new son-in-law would insist on taking the whole family to live in the capital. Anton was sure that he would be made a general at least.

At that moment the postmaster arrived with Ivan's letter. When he read the frank description of the pretended inspector's love-making and his franker opinion of the muddle-headed town officials, the tremendous hoax gradually dawned on the company.

As the crestfallen crowd was counting up the losses, a gendarme came in with an official announcement. An inspector from St. Petersburg had just arrived and desired them all to wait upon him immedi-   ately. He was staying at the inn.

THE INTERPRETATION OF DREAMS

Type of work: Psychological study
Author: Sigmund Freud (1856-1939)
First published: 1900

In March, 1931, in a foreword to the third English edition of *The Interpretation of Dreams,* Freud expressed the opinion that the volume contained the most valuable of all the discoveries he had been fortunate enough to make.

The author's estimation of his work concurs with that of most students and critics. The ideas that dreams are wish-fulfillments, that the dream disguises the wishes of the unconscious, that dreams are always important, always significant, and that they express infantile wishes—particularly for the death of the parent of the same sex as that of the dreamer—all appear in this masterpiece of psychological interpretation. Here the Oedipus complex is first named and explained and the method of psychoanalysis is given impetus and credibility by its application to the analysis of dreams.

It is common criticism of Freud to say that the father of psychoanalysis, although inspired in this and other works, went too far in his generalizations concerning the basic drives of the unconscious. Freud is charged with regarding every latent wish as having a sexual object, and he is criticized for supposing that dreams can be understood as complexes of such universally significant symbols as umbrellas and boxes.

Although Freud argues that repressed wishes that show themselves in disguised form in dreams generally have something to do with the unsatisfied sexual cravings of childhood—for dreams are important and concern themselves only with matters we cannot resolve by conscious deliberation and action—he allows for the dream satisfaction of other wishes that reality has frustrated: the desire for the continued existence of a loved one already dead,

the desire for sleep as a continuation of the escape from reality, the desire for a return to childhood, the desire for revenge when revenge is impossible.

As for the charge that Freud regarded dreams as complexes of symbols having the same significance for all dreamers, this is clearly unwarranted. Freud explicitly states that "only the context can furnish the correct meaning" of a dream symbol. He rejects as wholly inadequate the use of any such simple key as a dream book of symbols. Each dreamer utilizes the material of his own experience in his own way, and only by a careful analytical study of associations—obscured by the manifest content of the dream—is it possible to get at the particular use of symbols in an individual's dream. It is worth noting, Freud admits, that many symbols recur with much the same intent in many dreams of different persons; but this knowledge must be used judiciously. The agreement in the use of symbols is only partly a matter of cultural tendencies; it is largely attributable to limitations of the imagination imposed by the material itself: "To use long, stiff objects and weapons as symbols of the female genitals, or hollow objects (chests, boxes, etc.) as symbols of the male genitals, is certainly not permitted by the imagination."

It is not surprising that most of the symbols discussed by Freud, either as typical symbols or as symbols in individual cases, are sexually significant. Although Freud did not regard all dreams as the wish-fulfillments of repressed sexual desires, he did suppose that a greater number of dreams have a sexual connotation: "The more one is occupied with the solution of dreams, the readier one becomes to acknowledge that the majority

1447

of the dreams of adults deal with sexual material and give expression to erotic wishes." But Freud adds, "In dream-interpretation this importance of the sexual complexes must never be forgotten, though one must not, of course, exaggerate it to the exclusion of all other factors."

The technique of dream-interpretation is certainly not exhausted, according to Freud, by the technique of symbol interpretation. Dreams involve the use of the images dreamed, the *manifest* dream-content, as a way of disguising the unconscious "dream-thoughts" or *latent* dream-content. The significance of a dream may be revealed only after one has understood the dramatic use of the symbolism of the dream, the condensation of the material, the displacement of the conventional meaning of a symbol or utterance, or even a displacement of the "center" of the dream-thoughts; i.e., the manifest dream may center about a matter removed from the central concern of the latent dream. As Freud explains the problems of dream-interpretation, making numerous references to dream examples, it becomes clear that dream interpretation must be at least as ingenious as dream-work—and there is nothing more ingenious.

Freud begins *The Interpretation of Dreams* with a history of the scientific literature of dream problems from ancient times to 1900. He then proceeds to make his basic claim: that dreams are interpretable as wish-fulfillments. To illustrate his point, he begins with an involved dream of his own, justifying his procedure by arguing that self-analysis is possible and, even when faulty, illustrative.

A problem arises with the consideration of painful dreams. If dreams are wish-fulfillments, why are some dreams nightmares? Who wishes to be terrified? Freud's answer is that the problem arises from a confusion between the manifest and the latent dream. What is painful, considered as manifest, may, because of its disguised significance, be regarded as

satisfactory to the unconscious. When one realizes, in addition, that many suppressed wishes are desires for punishment, the painful dream presents itself as a fulfillment of such wishes. To understand the possibility of painful dreams it is necessary to consider Freud's amended formula: "The dream is the (disguised) fulfilment of a (suppressed, repressed) wish."

In describing the method most useful in enabling a person to recall his dream both by facilitating memory and by inhibiting the censorship tendency of the person recounting the dream, Freud presents what has become familiar as the psychoanalytic method of free association. He suggests that the patient be put into a restful position with his eyes closed, that the patient be told not to criticize his thoughts or to withhold the expression of them, and that he continue to be impartial about his ideas. This problem of eliminating censorship while recounting the dream is merely an extension of the problem of dealing with the censorship imposed by the dreamer while dreaming. The dreamer does not want to acknowledge his desires; for one reason or another he has repressed them. The fulfillment of the suppressed desire can be tolerated by the dreamer only if he leaves out anything which would be understandable to the waking mind. Consequently, only a laborious process of undoing the dream-work can result in some understanding of the meaning the censor tries to hide.

Among the interesting subsidiary ideas of Freud's theory is the idea that the dream-stimulus is always to be found among the experiences of the hours prior to sleeping. Some incident from the day becomes the material of the dream, its provocative image. But although the dream-stimulus is from the day preceding sleep, the repressed wish which the dream expresses and fulfills is from childhood, at least, in the majority of cases: "The deeper we go into the analysis of dreams, the more often are we put on to the track

1448

of childish experiences which play the part of dream-sources in the latent dream-content." To explain the difficulty of getting at the experiences in childhood which provide the latent dream-content, Freud argues for a conception of dreams as stratified: in the dream layers of meaning are involved, and it is only at the lowest stratum that the source in some experience of childhood may be discovered.

Among the typical dreams mentioned by Freud are the embarrassment dream of nakedness, interpreted as an exhibition dream, fulfilling a wish to return to childhood (the time when one ran about naked without upsetting anyone); the death-wish dream in which one dreams of the death of a beloved person, interpreted as a dream showing repressed hostility toward brother or sister, father or mother; and the examination dream in which one dreams of the disgrace of flunking an examination, interpreted as reflecting the ineradicable memories of punishments in childhood.

Of these typical dreams, the death-wish dream directed to the father (by the son) or to the mother (by the daughter) is explained in terms of the drama of *Oedipus* by Sophocles. In the old Greek play, Oedipus unwittingly murders his own father and marries his mother. When he discovers his deeds, he blinds himself and exiles himself from Thebes. The appeal of the drama is explained by Freud as resulting from its role as a wish-fulfillment. The play reveals the inner self, the self which directed its first sexual impulses toward the mother and its first jealous hatred toward the father. These feelings have been repressed during the course of our developing maturity, but they remain latent, ready to manifest themselves only in dreams somewhat more obscure than the Oedipus drama itself. Freud mentions *Hamlet* as another play in which the same wish is shown, although in *Hamlet* the fulfillment is repressed. Freud accounts for Hamlet's reluctance to complete the task of revenge by pointing out that Hamlet cannot bring himself to kill a man who accomplished what he himself wishes he had accomplished: the murder of his father and marriage to his mother.

In his discussion of the psychology of the dream process, Freud calls attention to the fact that dreams are quickly forgotten—a natural consequence, if his theory is correct. This fact creates problems for the analyst who wishes to interpret dreams in order to discover the root of neurotic disturbances. However, the self that forgets is the same self that dreamed, and it is possible by following the implications of even superficial associations to get back to the substance of the dream.

Realizing that many persons would be offended by his ideas, Freud attempted to forestall criticism by insisting on the universal application of his theory and by claiming that dreams themselves—since they are not acts—are morally innocent, whatever their content.

There seems little question but that Freud's contribution to psychology in *The Interpretation of Dreams* will remain one of the great discoveries of the human mind. Whatever its excesses, particularly in the hands of enthusiastic followers, Freud's central idea gains further confirmation constantly in the experiences of dreamers and analysts alike.

INTRUDER IN THE DUST

Type of work: Novel
Author: William Faulkner (1897-   )
Type of plot: Social realism
Time of plot: Early 1930's

INTRUDER IN THE DUST by William Faulkner. By permission of the publishers, Random House, Inc. Copyright, 1948, by Random House, Inc.

Locale: Jefferson, Mississippi
First published: 1948

Principal characters:
CHARLES ("CHICK") MALLISON, a sixteen-year-old boy
GAVIN STEVENS, his uncle, a lawyer
LUCAS BEAUCHAMP, an old Negro
ALECK SANDER, Chick's young colored friend
MISS HABERSHAM, an old woman
HOPE HAMPTON, the sheriff

Critique:

In *Intruder in the Dust,* Faulkner juxtaposed his views regarding the problem of the Negro in the South against a bizarre tale involving murder, grave robbing, and lynching. Before the publication of this novel, in such works as "The Bear" and *Light in August,* he had only hinted at his concept of the problem, with the result that his views were often misunderstood, but in *Intruder in the Dust* he set forth his views boldly, often reinforcing them with italics and using one of his characters as his spokesman. Faulkner's main tenet, developed by Lawyer Gavin Stevens, is that the South must be left alone to solve its own problem; that any interference in the form of federal legislation will only strengthen the South's historic defiance of the North. Lifted from context, however, the plot resembles nothing so much as a rather far-fetched murder mystery; isolated, Gavin Stevens' commentaries on the plot sound like so much propaganda. But within the framework of the novel the plot is credible and Lawyer Stevens' harangues are appropriate. After all, the story is oriented around a boy. It is quite conceivable that a sixteen-year-old could get himself into just such a situation; it stands to reason that a rhetorical lawyer should try to clarify a confused nephew's thinking. *Intruder in the Dust* is a successful novel because Faulkner succeeds in making the reader believe in its central character, understand him, and sympathize with him.

The Story:

On a cold afternoon in November, Chick Mallison, twelve years old, accompanied by two Negro boys, went rabbit hunting on Carothers Edmonds' place. When he fell through the ice into a creek, an old Negro, Lucas Beauchamp, appeared and watched while the boy clambered awkwardly ashore. Then Lucas took the white boy and his companions to the old colored man's home. There Chick dried out in front of the fire and ate Lucas' food. Later, when Chick tried to pay the old man for his hospitality, Lucas spurned his money. Chick threw it down, but Lucas made one of the other boys pick it up and return it. Chick brooded over the incident, ashamed to be indebted to a black man, especially one as arrogant as Lucas Beauchamp. Again trying to repay the old man, he sent Lucas' wife a mail-order dress bought with money he had saved; again refusing to acknowledge payment and thus admit his inferiority as a Negro, Lucas sent Chick a bucket of sorghum sweetening.

Some four years later when Lucas was accused of shooting Vinson Gowrie in the back, Chick still had not forgotten his unpaid debt to the Negro. Realizing that Vinson's poor-white family and friends were sure to lynch Lucas, Chick wanted to leave town. But when Sheriff Hope Hampton brought Lucas to the jail in Jefferson, Chick, unable to suppress his sense of obligation, was standing on the street where the old colored man could see him. Lucas asked Chick to bring his uncle, Gavin Stevens, to the jail.

At the jail the old man refused to tell Stevens what happened at the shooting, whereupon the lawyer left in disgust. But Lucas did tell Chick that Vinson Gowrie had not been shot with his gun—a forty-

1450

one Colt—and he asked the boy to verify this fact by digging up the corpse. Although the body was buried nine miles from town and the Gowries would be sure to shoot a grave robber, Chick agreed to the request; he knew that Lucas would undoubtedly be lynched if someone did not help the old man. Barbershop and poolroom loafers had already gathered while waiting for the pine-hill country Gowries to arrive in town.

Stevens laughed at the story, so Chick's only help came from a Negro boy—Aleck Sander—and Miss Habersham, an old woman of good family who had grown up with Lucas' wife, now dead. And so the task of digging up a white man's grave in order to save a haughty, intractable, but innocent Negro was left to two adolescents and a seventy-year-old woman who felt it her obligation to protect those more helpless than she. The three succeeded in opening the grave without incident. In the coffin they found not Vinson Gowrie but Jake Montgomery, whose skull had been bashed in. They filled the grave, returned to town, wakened Stevens, and went to the sheriff with their story.

This group, joined by old man Gowrie and two of his sons, reopened the grave. But when they lifted the lid the coffin was found to be empty. A search disclosed Montgomery's body hastily buried nearby and Vinson's sunk in quicksand. When the sheriff took Montgomery's body into town, the huge crowd that had gathered in anticipation of the lynching of Lucas Beauchamp soon scattered.

Questioning of Lucas revealed that Crawford Gowrie had murdered his brother Vinson. Crawford, according to the old Negro, had been cheating his brother in a lumber deal. Jake Montgomery, to whom Crawford had sold the stolen lumber, knew that Crawford was the murderer and had dug up Vinson's grave to prove it. Crawford murdered Montgomery at the grave and put him in Vinson's coffin. When he saw Chick and his friends open the grave, he was forced to remove Vinson's body too. Sheriff Hampton soon captured Crawford, who killed himself in his cell to avoid a trial.

At last, Chick thought, he had freed himself of his debt to the old Negro. A short time later, however, Lucas appeared at Stevens' office and insisted on paying for services rendered. Stevens refused payment for both himself and Chick but accepted two dollars for "expenses." Proud, unhumbled to the end, Lucas Beauchamp demanded a receipt.

THE INVISIBLE MAN

Type of work: Novel
Author: H. G. Wells (1866-1946)
Type of plot: Mystery romance
Time of plot: Late nineteenth century
Locale: England
First published: 1897

Principal characters:
GRIFFIN, the Invisible Man
MR. HALL, landlord of the Coach and Horses Inn
MRS. HALL, his wife
DR. KEMP, a Burdock physician
COLONEL AYDE, chief of the Burdock police
MARVEL, a tramp

Critique:

The Invisible Man belongs to that series of pseudo-scientific romances which

H. G. Wells wrote early in his literary career. The plot is one of sheer and fantastic invention, but it achieves an air of probability by means of the homely and realistic details with which it is built up. The characters involved in Griffin's strange predicament are also in no way remarkable; their traits, habits, and fears are revealed convincingly. The novel has outlived the time of its publication because of the psychological factors arising from the central situation and the suspense created by the unfolding of an unusual plot.

The Story:

The stranger arrived at Bramblehurst railway station on a cold, snowy day in February. Carrying a valise, he trudged through driving snow to Iping, where he stumbled into the Coach and Horses Inn and asked Mrs. Hall, the hostess, for a room and a fire. The stranger's face was hidden by dark-blue spectacles and bushy side-whiskers.

He had his dinner in his room. When Mrs. Hall took a mustard jar up to him, she saw that the stranger's head was completely bandaged. While she was in his room, he covered his mouth and chin with a napkin.

His baggage arrived the next day—several trunks and boxes of books and a crate of bottles packed in straw. The drayman's dog attacked the stranger, tearing his glove and ripping his trousers. Mr. Hall, landlord of the inn, ran upstairs to see if the stranger had been hurt and entered his room without knocking. He was immediately struck on the chest and pushed from the room. When Mrs. Hall took up the lodger's supper, she saw that he had unpacked his trunks and boxes and set up some strange apparatus. The lodger was not wearing his glasses; his eyes looked sunken and hollow.

In the weeks that followed the villagers made many conjectures as to the stranger's identity. Some thought he suffered from a queer disease that had left his skin black-and-white spotted. Unusual happenings also mystified the village. One night the vicar and his wife were awakened by a noise in the vicar's study and the clinking of money. Upon investigation, they saw no one, although a candle was burning and they heard a sneeze.

In the meantime Mr. Hall found clothing and bandages scattered about the lodger's room; the stranger had disappeared. The landlord went downstairs to call his wife. They heard the front door open and shut, but no one came into the inn. While they stood wondering what to do, their lodger came down the stairs. Where he had been or how he had returned to his room unnoticed was a mystery he made no attempt to explain.

A short time later, the stranger's bill being overdue, Mrs. Hall refused to serve him. When the stranger became abusive, Mr. Hall swore out a warrant against him. The constable, the landlord, and a curious neighbor went upstairs to arrest the lodger. After a struggle, the man agreed to unmask. The men were horror-stricken; the stranger was invisible to their view. In the confusion the Invisible Man, as the newspapers were soon to call him, fled from the inn.

The next person to encounter the Invisible Man was a tramp named Marvel. The Invisible Man frightened Marvel into accompanying him to the Coach and Horses Inn to get his clothing and three books. They arrived at the inn while the vicar and the village doctor were reading the stranger's diary. They knocked the two men about, snatched up the clothes and books, and left the inn.

Newspapers continued to print stories of unnatural thefts; money had been taken and carried away, the thief invisible but the money in plain view. Marvel always seemed to be well-supplied with funds.

One day Marvel, carrying three books, came running into the Jolly Cricketers Inn. He said that the Invisible Man was after him. A barman, a policeman, and a cabman awaited the Invisible Man's arrival after hiding Marvel. But the Invisible Man found Marvel, dragged him into the inn kitchen, and tried to force him through the door. The three men struggled with the unseen creature while Marvel crawled into the bar-parlor. When the voice of the Invisible Man was heard in the inn yard, a villager fired five shots in the direction of the sound. Searchers found no body in the yard.

Meanwhile, in Burdock, Dr. Kemp worked late in his study. Preparing to retire, he noticed drops of drying blood on the stairs. He found the doorknob of his room smeared with blood and red stains on his bed. While he stared in amazement at a bandage that was apparently wrapping itself about nothing in midair, a voice called him by name. The Invisible Man had taken refuge in Kemp's rooms.

He identified himself as Griffin, a young scientist whom Kemp had met at the university where both had studied. Griffin asked for whiskey and food. He said that except for short naps he had not slept for three days and nights.

That night Kemp sat up to read all the newspaper accounts of the activities of the Invisible Man. At last, after much thought, he wrote a letter to Colonel Adye, chief of the Burdock police.

In the morning Griffin told his story to Kemp. He explained that for three years he had experimented with refractions of light on the theory that a human body would become invisible if the cells could be made transparent. Needing money for his work, he had robbed his father of money belonging to someone else and his father had shot himself. At last his experiments were successful. After setting fire to his room in order to destroy the evidence of his research, he had begun his strange adventures. He had terrorized Oxford Street, where passersby had seen only his footprints. He discovered that in his invisible state he was compelled to fast, for all unassimilated food or drink was grotesquely visible. At last, prowling London streets and made desperate by his plight, he had gone to a shop selling theatrical supplies. There he had stolen the dark glasses, side-whiskers, and clothes he wore on his arrival in Iping.

Griffin planned to use Kemp's house as a headquarters while terrorizing the neighborhood. Kemp believed Griffin mad. When he attempted to restrain Griffin, the Invisible Man escaped, and shortly thereafter a Mr. Wicksteed was found murdered. A manhunt began.

The next morning Kemp received a note which announced that the reign of terror had begun; one person would be executed daily. Kemp himself was to be the first victim. He was to die at noon; nothing could protect him.

Kemp sent at once for Colonel Adye. While they were discussing possible precautions, stones were hurled through the windows. The colonel left to return to the police station for some bloodhounds to set on Griffin's trail, but outside the house Griffin snatched a revolver from Adye's pocket and wounded the police officer. When Griffin began to smash Kemp's kitchen door with an ax, the doctor climbed through a window and ran to a neighbor's house. He was refused admittance. He ran to the inn. The door was barred. Suddenly his invisible assailant seized him. While they struggled, some men came to the doctor's rescue. Kemp got hold of Griffin's arms. A constable seized his legs. Someone struck through the air with a spade. The writhing unseen figure sagged to the ground. Kemp announced that he could not hear Griffin's heartbeats. While the crowd gathered, Griffin's body slowly materialized, naked, dead. A sheet was brought from the inn and the body was carried away. The reign of terror was ended.

1453

IOLANTHE

Type of work: Comic opera
Author: W. S. Gilbert (1836-1911)
Type of plot: Humorous satire
Time of plot: Nineteenth century
Locale: England
First presented: 1882

Principal characters:
THE LORD CHANCELLOR
STREPHON, an Arcadian shepherd
QUEEN OF THE FAIRIES
IOLANTHE, Strephon's fairy mother
PHYLLIS, a shepherdess and ward in Chancery
THE EARL OF MOUNTARARAT, and
EARL TOLLOLLER, her suitors
PRIVATE WILLIS, a palace guard

Critique:

The story of a shepherd lad, the top of him a fairy but his feet mired in human form, *Iolanthe, Or, The Peer and the Peri* is a light-hearted satire on many human foibles. In particular, the drama pokes fun at the House of Lords, but it is such gentle fun that no one in Victorian England could take offense. *Iolanthe* is a delightful comedy, one of many from the pen of Sir William Schwenck Gilbert, whose name will always be associated with that of his composer-collaborator, Sir Arthur Seymour Sullivan.

The Story:

The Fairy Queen had banished Iolanthe because she had married a mortal. Normally the punishment for such an act was death, but the queen so loved Iolanthe that she had been unable to enforce a penalty so grave. Iolanthe had been sentenced to penal servitude for life, on the condition that she never see her mortal husband again. At last the other fairies begged the queen to relent, to set aside even this punishment, for Iolanthe had served twenty-five years of her sentence by standing on her head at the bottom of a stream.

The queen, unable to resist their pleas, summoned the penitent Iolanthe and pardoned her. Iolanthe explained that she had stayed in the stream to be near her son Strephon, an Arcadian shepherd who was a fairy to his waist and a human from the waist down. While they spoke, Strephon entered, announcing that he was to be married that day to Phyllis, a ward of Chancery. The Lord Chancellor had not given his permission, but Strephon was determined to marry his Phyllis anyway. He was delighted when he learned that his mother had been pardoned, but he begged her and all the fairies not to tell Phyllis that he was half fairy. He feared that she would not understand.

The queen determined to make Strephon a member of Parliament, but Strephon said that he would be no good in that august body, for the top of him was a Tory, the bottom a Radical. The queen solved that problem by making him a Liberal-Unionist and taking his mortal legs under her particular care.

Phyllis talked with Strephon and warned him that to marry her without the Lord Chancellor's permission would mean lifelong penal servitude for him. But Strephon could not wait the two years until she was of age. He feared that the Lord Chancellor himself or one of the peers of the House of Lords would marry her before that time had passed.

Strephon's fears were well founded; the Lord Chancellor did want to marry

1454

his ward. Fearing that he would have to punish himself for marrying her without his permission, however, he decided to give her instead to one of the peers of the House of Lords. Two were at last selected, the Earl of Mountararat and Earl Tolloller, but there was no agreement as to the final choice. Phyllis herself did not wish to accept either, for she loved only Strephon. Then she saw Strephon talking with Iolanthe, who, being a fairy, looked like a young and beautiful girl, even though she was Strephon's mother. Phyllis was filled with jealousy, augmented by the laughter of the peers when Strephon in desperation confessed that Iolanthe was his mother. Weeping that he had betrayed her, Phyllis left Strephon. No one had ever heard of a son who looked older than his mother.

The Fairy Queen herself told the Lord Chancellor and the peers that they would rue their laughter over Iolanthe and her son. To punish them, Strephon would change all existing laws in the House of Lords. He would abolish the rights of peers and give titles to worthy commoners. Worst of all, from then on peers would be chosen by competitive examinations. Strephon would be a foe they would not soon forget.

The queen's prediction came true. Strephon completely ruled the House of Lords. Every bill he proposed was passed, the fairies making the other members vote for Strephon even when they wanted to vote against him. The peers appealed to the fairies, but although the fairies admired the peers, they could not be swayed against Strephon.

The Earl of Mountararat and Earl Tolloller tried to decide who should have Phyllis. Each wanted the other to sacrifice himself by giving up all rights to her. Both had a family tradition that they must fight anyone who took their sweethearts, and since a fight meant that one of them would die and the survivor would be left without his friend, each wanted to make the sacrifice of losing his friend. At last the two decided that friendship was more important than love. Both renounced Phyllis.

Strephon and Phyllis met again, and at last he convinced her that Iolanthe was really his mother. Phyllis still could not believe that Strephon looked like a fairy, and she could not quite understand that his grandmother and all his aunts looked as young as his mother. She was sensible, however, and promised that whenever she saw Strephon kissing a very young girl she would know the woman was an elderly relative. There was still the Lord Chancellor to contend with. When they went to Iolanthe and begged her to persuade him to consent to their marriage, Iolanthe told them that the Lord Chancellor was her mortal husband. He believed her dead and himself childless, and if she looked on him the queen would carry out the penalty of instant death.

Iolanthe could not resist the pleas of the young lovers. As she told the Lord Chancellor that she was his lost wife, the queen entered and prepared to carry out the sentence of death against Iolanthe. Before she could act, however, the other fairies entered and confessed that they too had married peers in the House of Lords. The queen grieved, but the law was clear. Whoever married a mortal must die. But the Lord Chancellor's great knowledge of the law saved the day. It would now read that whoever did *not* marry a mortal must die. Thinking that a wonderful solution, the queen took one of the palace guards, Private Willis, for her husband. Knowing that from now on the House of Lords would be recruited from persons of intelligence, because of Strephon's law, the peers could see that they were of little use. Sprouting wings, they all flew away to Fairyland.

1455

ION

Type of work: Drama
Author: Euripides (c. 485-c. 406 B.C.)
Type of plot: Tragi-comedy
Time of plot: Remote antiquity
Locale: The temple of Apollo at Delphi
First presented: Fifth century B.C.

Principal characters:

HERMES, speaker of the prologue
ION, son of Apollo and Creusa
CREUSA, daughter of Erechtheus, King of Athens
XUTHUS, Creusa's husband
AGED SLAVE TO CREUSA
A PRIESTESS OF APOLLO
PALLAS ATHENA, goddess of wisdom
CHORUS OF CREUSA'S HANDMAIDENS

Critique:

In *Ion,* Euripides fashioned a curious and compelling drama out of a legend which, so far as we know, no other ancient playwright touched. Although several lines of action threaten to culminate in tragedy, as when the outraged Creusa sends her slave to poison Ion and when Ion attempts to retaliate, the play ends happily and must be described as a comedy. Indeed some critics claim that the technique of the recognition scene, the identity of Ion being established by his miraculously preserved swaddling clothes, is the basis of the New Comedy which developed in the fourth century B.C. A tantalizing ambiguity in *Ion* concerns Euripides' attitude toward the gods. On the one hand the action of the play demands that we accept Apollo's existence and his power; on the other, the sly way in which he is presented seems to suggest that he is ridiculously anthropomorphic, a knave caught cheating and forced to concoct a way out for himself.

The Story:

(Years before Phoebus Apollo had ravished Creusa, daughter of King Erechtheus, who subsequently and in secret gave birth to a son. By Apollo's command she hid the infant in a cave where Hermes was sent to carry him to the temple of Apollo. There he was reared as a temple ministrant. Meanwhile, Creusa had married Xuthus as a reward for his aid in the Athenian war against the Euboeans, but the marriage remained without issue. After years of frustration, Xuthus and Creusa decided to make a pilgrimage to Delphi and ask the god for aid in getting a son.)

At dawn Ion emerged from the temple of Apollo to sweep the floors, chase away the birds, set out the laurel boughs, and make the usual morning sacrifice. Creusa's handmaidens came to admire the temple built upon the navel of the world and to announce the imminent arrival of their mistress. At the meeting of Creusa and Ion, Creusa confirmed the story that her father had been drawn from the earth by Athena and was swallowed up by the earth at the end of his life. The credulous Ion explained that his own birth, too, was shrouded in mystery, for he had appeared out of nowhere at the temple and had been reared by the priestess of Apollo. The greatest sorrow of his life, he said, was not knowing who his mother was. Creusa sympathized and cautiously revealed that she had a friend with a similar problem, a woman who had borne a son to Apollo, only to have the infant disappear and to suffer childlessness for the rest of her life.

Ion, shocked and outraged at the insult to his god, demanded that Creusa end her accusation of Apollo in his own temple, but the anguished woman assailed the god with fresh charges of injustice, breaking off only at the arrival of her husband. Xuthus eagerly took his wife into the temple, for he had just been assured by the prophet Trophonius that they would not return childless to Athens. The perplexed Ion was left alone to meditate on the lawlessness of gods who seemed to put pleasure before wisdom.

Xuthus, emerging from the temple, fell upon the startled Ion and attempted to kiss and embrace him. He shouted joyfully that Ion must be his son, for the oracle had said that the first person he would see upon leaving the temple would be his son by birth. Stunned and unconvinced, Ion demanded to know who his mother was, but Xuthus could only conjecture that possibly she was one of the Delphian girls he had encountered at a Bacchanal before his marriage. Ion, reluctantly conceding that Xuthus must be his father if Apollo so decreed, begged to remain an attendant in the temple rather than become the unwelcome and suspicious heir to the throne of Athens—for Creusa would surely resent a son she had not borne. Xuthus understood his anxiety and agreed to hide his identity; however, he insisted that Ion accompany him to Athens, even if only in the role of distinguished guest. He then gave orders for a banquet of thanksgiving and commanded that the handmaidens to Creusa keep their silence on pain of death. As they departed to prepare the feast, Ion expressed the hope that his mother might still be found and that she might be an Athenian.

Accompanied by the aged slave of her father, Creusa reappeared before the temple and demanded from her handmaidens an account of the revelation Xuthus had received from Apollo. Only under relentless cross-examination did the fearful servants reveal what had passed between Xuthus and Ion. Overcome by a sense of betrayal, Creusa cursed Apollo for his cruelty but dared not act upon the old slave's suggestion that she burn the tem-

ple or murder the husband who had, after all, been kind to her.

But the murder of the usurper, Ion, was another matter. After some deliberation Creusa decided upon a safe and secret method of eliminating the rival of her lost son. From a phial of the Gorgon's blood which Athena had given to Creusa's grandfather and which had been passed down to her, the old slave was to pour a drop into Ion's wineglass at the celebration feast. Eager to serve his master's daughter, the slave departed, and the chorus chanted their hope for success.

Some time later a messenger came running to warn Creusa that the authorities were about to seize her and submit her to death by stoning, for her plot had been discovered. He described how at the feast a flock of doves had dipped down to drink from Ion's cup and had died in horrible convulsions and how Ion had tortured a confession out of the old slave. The court of Delphi had then sentenced Creusa to death for attempting murder of a consecrated person within the sacred precincts of the temple of Apollo. The chorus urged Creusa to fling herself upon the altar and remain there in sanctuary.

A short time later Ion arrived at the head of an infuriated crowd, and he and Creusa began to hurl angry charges and counter-charges at each other. Suddenly the priestess of the temple appeared, bearing the cradle and the tokens with which the infant Ion had been found years before. Slowly and painfully the truth emerged: Ion was the lost son of Creusa and Apollo. Creusa was seized with a frenzy of joy, but the astounded Ion remained incredulous. As he was about to enter the temple to demand an explanation from Apollo himself, the goddess Athena appeared in mid-air and confirmed the revelation. She urged that Xuthus not be told the truth so that he might enjoy the delusion that his own son was to be his heir, while Creusa and Ion could share their genuine happiness. Creusa renounced all her curses against

Apollo and blessed him for his ultimate wisdom. As she and Ion departed for Athens the chorus called upon all men to reverence the gods and take courage.

IPHIGENIA IN AULIS

Type of work: Drama
Author: Euripides (480-406 B.C.)
Type of plot: Classical tragedy
Time of plot: Beginning of Trojan War
Locale: Aulis, on the west coast of Euboea
First presented: 405 B.C.

Principal characters:
AGAMEMNON, King of Mycenae
CLYTEMNESTRA, his wife
IPHIGENIA, their daughter
ACHILLES, a Greek warrior
MENELAUS, King of Sparta

Critique:

In *Iphigenia in Aulis,* Agamemnon, the co-commander of all the Greek forces in the Trojan War, impresses one as being essentially the civilian executive, the upper middle-class husband and father who would rather be dictating business, not military policies. Likewise, Clytemnestra, his wife, resembles the society-conscious suburban matron, rather than a queen. Hence, despite its heroic background and despite the nominally heroic aspects of its characters, the play is in many respects a domestic tragedy. Lacking are the terrible and compulsive passions which motivate the story of Clytemnestra and Agamemnon in the dramas of Aeschylus.

The Story:

At Aulis, on the west coast of Euboea, part of Greece, the Greek host had assembled for the invasion of Ilium, the war having been declared to rescue Helen, wife of King Menelaus, after her abduction by Paris, a prince of Troy. Lack of wind, however, prevented the sailing of the great fleet.

While the ships lay becalmed, Agamemnon, commander of the Greek forces, consulted Calchas, a seer. The oracle prophesied that all would go well if Iphigenia, Agamemnon's oldest daughter, were sacrificed to the goddess Artemis. At

first Agamemnon was reluctant to see his daughter so destroyed, but at last Menelaus, his brother, persuaded him that nothing else would move the weather-bound fleet. Agamemnon wrote to Clytemnestra, his queen, and asked her to conduct Iphigenia to Aulis, his pretext being that Achilles, the outstanding warrior among the Greeks, would not embark unless he were given Iphigenia in marriage.

The letter having been dispatched, Agamemnon had a change of heart; he felt that his continued popularity as co-leader of the Greeks was a poor exchange for the life of his beloved daughter. In haste he dispatched a second letter countermanding the first, but Menelaus, suspicious of his brother, intercepted the messenger and struggled with him for possession of the letter. When Agamemnon came upon the scene, he and Menelaus exchanged bitter words. Menelaus accused his brother of being weak and foolish, and Agamemnon accused Menelaus of supreme selfishness in urging the sacrifice of Iphigenia.

During this exchange of charge and countercharge a messenger announced the arrival of Clytemnestra and Iphigenia in Aulis. The news plunged Agamemnon into despair; weeping, he regretted his kingship and its responsibilities. Even

Menelaus was affected, so that he suggested disbanding the army. Agamemnon thanked Menelaus but declared it was too late to turn back from the course they had elected to follow. Actually, Agamemnon was afraid of Calchas and of Odysseus, and he believed that widespread disaffection and violence would break out in the Greek army if the sacrifice were not made. Some Chalcian women who had come to see the fleet lamented that the love of Paris for Helen had brought such stir and misery instead of happiness.

When Clytemnestra arrived, accompanied by Iphigenia and her young son, Orestes, she expressed pride and joy over the approaching nuptials of her daughter and Achilles. Agamemnon greeted his family tenderly; touching irony displayed itself in the conversation between Agamemnon, who knew that Iphigenia was doomed to die, and Iphigenia, who thought her father's ambiguous words had a bearing only on her approaching marriage. Clytemnestra inquired in motherly fashion about Achilles' family and background. She was scandalized when the heartbroken Agamemnon asked her to return to Argos, on the excuse that he could arrange the marriage details. When Clytemnestra refused to leave the camp, Agamemnon sought the advice of Calchas. Meanwhile the Chalcian women forecast the sequence of events of the Trojan War and hinted in their prophecy that death was certain for Iphigenia.

Achilles, in the meantime, insisted that he and his Myrmidons were impatient with the delay and anxious to get on with the invasion of Ilium. Clytemnestra, meeting him, mentioned the impending marriage, much to the mystification of Achilles, who professed to know nothing of his proposed marriage to Iphigenia. The messenger then confessed Agamemnon's plans to the shocked Clytemnestra and Achilles. He also mentioned the second letter and cast some part of the guilt upon Menelaus. Clytemnestra, grief-stricken, prevailed upon Achilles to help her in saving Iphigenia from death by sacrifice.

Clytemnestra then confronted her husband, who was completely unnerved when he realized that Clytemnestra was at last in possession of the dreadful truth. She rebuked him fiercely, saying that she had never really loved him because he had slain her beloved first husband and her first child. Iphigenia, on her knees, implored her father to save her and asked Orestes, in his childish innocence, to add his pleas to his mother's and her own. Although Agamemnon was not heartless, he knew that the sacrifice must be made. He argued that Iphigenia would die for Greece, a country and a cause greater than them all.

Achilles, meanwhile, spoke to the army in behalf of Iphigenia, but he admitted his failure when even his own Myrmidons threatened to stone him if he persisted in his attempt to stop the sacrifice. At last he mustered enough loyal followers to defend the girl against Odysseus and the entire Greek host. Iphigenia refused his aid, however, saying that she had decided to offer herself as a sacrifice for Greece. Achilles, in admiration, offered to place his men about the sacrificial altar so that she might be snatched to safety at the last moment.

Iphigenia, resigned to certain death, asked her mother not to mourn for her. Then she marched bravely to her death in the field of Artemis. Clytemnestra was left in prostration in her tent. Iphigenia, at the altar, said farewell to all that she held dear and submitted herself to the sacrifice.

The Chalcian women, onlookers at the sacrifice, invoked Artemis to fill the Greek sails now with wind so that the ships might carry the army to Troy to achieve eternal glory for Greece.

1459

IPHIGENIA IN TAURIS

Type of work: Drama
Author: Euripides (480-406 B.C.)
Type of plot: Romantic tragedy
Time of plot: Several years after the Trojan War
Locale: Tauris, in the present-day Crimea
First presented: c. 420 B.C.

Principal characters:

IPHIGENIA, a priestess of Artemis
ORESTES, her brother
PYLADES, Orestes' friend
THOAS, King of Tauris
ATHENA, goddess of the hunt

Critique:

Actually, *Iphigenia in Tauris* is not a tragedy in the classic sense at all; instead, it is a romantic melodrama. Iphigenia, after years in a barbaric land, may still have felt hatred for the Greeks, but her sentimental longing to return to Argolis, her birthplace and the scene of her happy childhood, was intense. Her feelings are described most touchingly by Euripides. The play abounds in breathtaking situations of danger and in sentimental passages of reminiscence. The recognition scene is perhaps the most thrilling, if not the most protracted in the classic Greek drama. Goethe dramatized this story in his *Iphigenie auf Tauris* (1787).

The Story:

When the Greek invasion force, destined for Ilium, was unable to sail from Aulis because of a lack of wind, Agamemnon, the Greek commander, appealed to Calchas, a Greek seer, for aid. Calchas said that unless Agamemnon gave Iphigenia, his oldest daughter, as a sacrifice to Artemis, the Greek fleet would never sail. By trickery Agamemnon succeeded in bringing Clytemnestra, his queen, and Iphigenia to Aulis, where the maiden was offered up to propitiate the goddess. At the last moment, however, Artemis substituted a calf in Iphigenia's place and spirited the maiden off to the barbaric land of Tauris, where she was doomed to spend the rest of her life as a priestess of Artemis. One of Iphigenia's duties was to prepare Greek captives—any Greek

who was apprehended in Tauris was by law condemned to die—for sacrifice in the temple of the goddess.

Iphigenia had been a priestess in Tauris for many years when, one night, she had a dream which she interpreted to mean that her brother Orestes had met his death; now there could be no future for her family, Orestes having been the only son.

Orestes, however, was alive; in fact, he was actually in Tauris. After he and his sister Electra had murdered their mother to avenge their father's death at her hands, the Furies had pursued Orestes relentlessly. Seeking relief, Orestes was told by the Oracle of Delphi that he must procure a statue of Artemis which stood in the temple of the goddess in Tauris and take it to Athens. Orestes would then be free of the Furies.

Orestes and his friend Pylades reached the temple and were appalled at the sight of the earthly remains of the many Greeks who had lost their lives in the temple. They resolved, however, to carry out their mission of stealing the statue of Artemis.

Meanwhile Iphigenia, disturbed by her dream, aroused her sister priestesses and asked their help in mourning the loss of her brother. In her loneliness she remembered Argos and her carefree childhood. A messenger interrupted her reverie with the report that one of two young Greeks on the shore had in a frenzy slaughtered Taurian cattle which had been led to the sea to bathe. The slayer

1460

was Orestes, under the influence of the Furies. In the fight which followed Orestes and Pylades held off great numbers of Taurian peasants, but at last the peasants succeeded in capturing the two youths. The Greeks were brought to Thoas, the King of Tauris.

Iphigenia, as a priestess of Artemis, directed that the strangers be brought before her. Heretofore she had always been gentle with the doomed Greeks and had never participated in the bloody ritual of sacrifice. Now, depressed by her dream, she was determined to be cruel.

Orestes and Pylades, bound, were brought before Iphigenia. Thinking of her own sorrow, she asked them if they had sisters who would be saddened by their deaths. Orestes refused to give her any details about himself, but he answered her inquiries about Greece and about the fate of the prominent Greeks in the Trojan War. She learned to her distress that her father was dead by her mother's treachery and that Orestes was still alive, a wanderer.

Deeply moved, Iphigenia offered to spare Orestes if he would deliver a letter for her in Argos. Orestes magnanimously gave the mission to Pylades; he himself would remain to be sacrificed. When he learned that Iphigenia would prepare him for the ritual, he wished for the presence of his sister to cover his body after he was dead. Iphigenia, out of pity, promised to do this for him. She went to bring the letter. Orestes and Pylades were convinced that she was a Greek. Pylades then declared that he would stay and die with his friend. Orestes, saying that he was doomed to die anyway for the murder of his mother, advised Pylades to return to Greece, marry Electra, and build a temple in his honor.

Iphigenia, returning with the letter, told Pylades that it must be delivered to one Orestes, a Greek prince. The letter urged Orestes to come to Tauris to take Iphigenia back to her beloved Argos; it explained how she had been saved at Aulis and spirited by Artemis to Tauris.

Pylades, saying that he had fulfilled the mission, handed the letter to Orestes. Iphigenia, doubtful, was finally convinced of Orestes' identity when he recalled familiar details of their home in Argos. While she pondered escape for the three of them, Orestes explained that first it was necessary for him to take the statue of Artemis, in order to avoid destruction. He asked Iphigenia's aid.

Having received a promise of secrecy from the priestesses who were present, Iphigenia carried out her plan of escape. As Thoas, curious about the progress of the sacrifice, entered the temple, Iphigenia appeared with the statue in her arms. She explained to the mystified Thoas that the statue had miraculously turned away from the Greek youths because their hands were stained by domestic murder. She declared to King Thoas that it was necessary for her secretly to cleanse the statue and the two young men in sea water. She commanded the people of Tauris to stay in their houses lest they too be tainted.

When Orestes and Pylades were led from the temple in chains, Thoas and his retinue covered their eyes so that they would not be contaminated by evil. Iphigenia joined the procession and marched solemnly to the beach. There she ordered the king's guards to turn their backs on the secret cleansing rites. Fearful for Iphigenia's safety, the guards looked on. When they beheld the three Greeks entering a ship, they rushed down to the vessel and held it back. The Greeks beat off the Taurians and set sail. The ship, however, was caught by tidal currents and forced back into the harbor.

Thoas, angry, urged all Taurians to spare no effort in capturing the Greek ship. Then the goddess Athena appeared to Thoas and directed him not to go against the will of Apollo, whose Oracle of Delphi had sent Orestes to Tauris to get the statue of Artemis. Thoas meekly complied. Iphigenia, Orestes, and Pylades returned to Greece, where Orestes, having set up the image of the Taurian Artemis in Attica, was at last freed from the wrath of the Furies. Iphigenia continued, in a new temple, to be a priestess of Artemis.

ISRAEL POTTER

Type of work: Novel
Author: Herman Melville (1819-1891)
Type of plot: Social satire
Time of plot: 1774-1826
Locale: Vermont, Massachusetts, England, France, the Atlantic Ocean
First published: 1855

Principal characters:
ISRAEL POTTER, a wanderer
ISRAEL'S FATHER
KING GEORGE III
BENJAMIN FRANKLIN
JOHN PAUL JONES
ETHAN ALLEN
SQUIRE WOODCOCK, an American agent
THE EARL OF SELKIRK

Critique:

Facetiously dedicated to the Bunker Hill Monument, *Israel Potter* is a mock picaresque novel. The hero, Israel Potter, wanders about America and Europe for over fifty years, never settling, never successful, providing a vehicle through which Melville satirizes a great many ideas and institutions. The pious morality of Benjamin Franklin, tidied into sugar-coated aphorisms, is one of Melville's principal targets. Other targets are the brutality of all wars, the idiocy of jingoistic patriotism, the barbarous quality lurking behind supposedly civilized behavior; neither American energy nor European polish can protect man from brutality or from the ridiculous patriotism around him. Despite the serious nature of Melville's theme, the novel is frequently very funny. Israel, the innocent, frequently stumbles into difficult situations and out of them by changing clothes, masquerading as a ghost, feigning madness, or pretending a polite worldliness he does not possess. The novel was not well received when it was written, for mid-nineteenth-century American taste did not relish the picaresque or the mocking treatment of America's noble fight for freedom. Although generally appreciated by those who have read it, *Israel Potter* has not yet received the attention accorded to many of Melville's other novels nor the attention that it deserves because of its genuine comedy and its astringent defense of civilized values.

The Story:

Born among the rugged stones of the New England hills, in the Housatonic Valley, Israel Potter grew up with all the virtues of the hard, principled, new land. After an argument with his father over a girl whom his stern parent did not think a suitable match, Israel decided to run away from home while his family was attending church. He wandered about the countryside, hunting deer, farming land, becoming a trapper, dealing in furs. During his wanderings he learned that most men were unscrupulous. He also hunted whales from Nantucket to the coast of Africa.

In 1775, Israel joined the American forces and took part in the Battle of Bunker Hill. He fought bravely, but the battle, as he saw it, was simply disorganized carnage. Wounded, Israel enlisted aboard an American ship after his recovery. Once at sea, the ship was captured by the British. Israel was taken prisoner and conveyed to England on the British ship, but on his arrival in London he managed to make his escape.

Wandering about London, Israel met various Englishmen who mocked his American accent. Some of the English were kind and helpful to him; others cuffed him about and berated the scurrilous Yankee rebels. He found various odd jobs, including one as a gardener working for a cruel employer. He escaped from this job and found one as a gardener on the king's staff at Kew Gardens. One day Israel met King George III. The king, completely mad, realized that Israel was an American and was ineffectually kind to him. Eventually, in a slack season, Israel was discharged. He then worked for a farmer, but when neighboring farmers discovered that he was an American, he was forced to run away.

Israel met Squire Woodcock, a wealthy and secret friend of America, who sent him on a secret mission to Benjamin Franklin in Paris. Israel carried a message in the false heel of his new boots. On his arrival in Paris, while he was looking for Benjamin Franklin, a poor man tried to shine his boots on the Pont Neuf. Israel, in fright, kicked the man and ran off. At last he found Benjamin Franklin, who took the message and then insisted that Israel return and pay damages to the bootblack.

In this fashion Israel, under the tutelage of Franklin, learned his first lesson in European politeness and consideration. From this incident Franklin proceeded to instruct Israel in the ways of proper behavior, deriving many of his lessons from the simple maxims in *Poor Richard's Almanack*. Israel, still innocent, absorbed the teaching carefully, although none of it ever applied to his later experiences. Franklin promised that Israel would be sent back to America, if he would first return to England with a message. While still in Paris, Israel met the stormy and ferocious Captain John Paul Jones, who also visited Franklin.

John Paul Jones found Israel a bright and likely young man.

Israel made his way back across the Channel and went to Squire Woodcock. The squire urged him to hide in the dungeon cell for three days, since their plot was in danger of discovery. When Israel emerged from the cell, he recognized that the good squire must have been killed for his activities in the American cause.

Having appropriated some of the squire's clothes, Israel masqueraded as Squire Woodcock's ghost and escaped from a house filled with his enemies. He then traded clothes with a farmer, wandered to Portsmouth, and signed on as a foretopman on a British ship bound for the East Indies. In the Channel, his ship met another ship whose captain had authority to impress some of the men; Israel was among those taken. That same night the ship was captured by an American ship under the command of John Paul Jones. Having revealed himself to his old friend, Israel soon became the quartermaster of the *Ranger*. With John Paul Jones, Israel engaged in piracy, capturing and looting ships.

In Scotland they called on the Earl of Selkirk in order to rob him, but the nobleman was not at home. Israel impressed the earl's wife with his Parisian manners, drank tea with her, and assured her that he and John Paul Jones did not intend to do the lady any harm. The crew, however, insisted that plunder was a part of piracy, and so Israel and John Paul Jones were forced to allow the men to take the family silver and other valuables. Israel promised to restore all articles of value, and when he received a large sum of money from another exploit, he and John Paul Jones bought back all the earl's articles from the men and returned them to the Selkirk family.

Other adventures did not end so cheerfully. The sea fight between the *Bon Homme Richard* and the *Serapis* was a violent and bloody battle, fought along national lines and devoid of all the amenities of piracy. Both ships were lost, and Israel and John Paul Jones, still hoping to get to America, sailed on the *Ariel*. The *Ariel* was captured by the British and Israel was again impressed into the British Navy. By feigning madness to hide his Yankee origins, he got back to England safely.

In England, Israel met Ethan Allen, a strong, heroic, Samson-like figure, held prisoner by the English. Israel tried to help Allen escape but was unsuccessful. Disguised as a beggar, he went to London, where he remained for over forty years. During that time he worked as a brick-maker and laborer, always hoping to save enough money to return to America but never finding the economic situation in London stable enough to permit saving. A wanderer in an alien land, he became part of the grime and poverty of London. During those years he married a shopgirl who bore him a son. Finally, in 1826, he secured some credit and, with the help of the American consul, sailed for America with his son.

Israel arrived in Boston on July 4, during a public celebration of the Battle of Bunker Hill. No one recognized him or acknowledged his right to be there. Instead, people laughed at him and thought he was mad. He returned to his father's farm, but the homestead had long since disappeared. Old Israel, his wanderings ended, found no peace, comfort, or friendship in his old age. Although heroes of the Revolution were publicly venerated, the aged man could not even get a small pension.

IT IS BETTER THAN IT WAS

Type of work: Drama
Author: Pedro Calderón de la Barca (1600-1681)
Type of plot: Cape-and-sword comedy
Time of plot: Seventeenth century
Locale: Vienna
First presented: 1631

Principal characters:
  CARLOS COLONA, son of the Governor of Brandenburg
  DON CÉSAR, a Viennese magistrate
  FLORA, his daughter
  LAURA, Flora's friend
  FABIO, Laura's brother
  ARNALDO, Laura's suitor
  DINERO, Carlos' servant

Critique:

In his early days, Calderón, as the inheritor of the good and the bad of sixteenth-century drama, followed Lope de Vega's formula for comedy, but with a tightening of the plot and the illumination of some of the extra threads. His cape-and-sword plays dealt with veiled women, secret rooms, and the hoodwinking of fathers and guardian brothers by sweethearts who, like Lope's heroines, are frequently motherless, lest fooling a mother might be regarded as disrespect for womanhood. Calderón's servants, derived from the *gracioso* invented by Lope, are a combination of a shrewd rascal faithful to his master and a character added to the cast to provide humor. During his ten years of service in Spanish armies (1625-1635) Calderón sent back from Flanders and Italy about ten plays, including *It Is Better than It Was,* an optimistic contrast to the earlier *It Is Worse than It Was.* In the celebrated letter to the Duke of Veragua, written ten months before his death and listing the 111 plays from his pen, Calderón men-

1464

tioned it as among those still unpublished. There is little philosophy in this drama, aside from the shrewd wisdom and salty comments of the skeptical servant. It is a comedy of love-making among the nobility, with the outcome not definitely known until the lines spoken just before the hero puts in a good word for the author to end the play.

The Story:

Flora and her friend Laura, both motherless, went out veiled into the streets of Vienna to witness the city's welcome to the Spanish princess María. Unfortunately, they were recognized by Arnaldo, in love with Laura, and by Licio, chosen by Flora's father as the future husband of his daughter. Flora became intrigued by the attempts of a handsome stranger to talk to her. When a quarrel between him and Licio seemed imminent, both ladies fled to their homes.

Into Flora's home rushed the stranger, Carlos Colona, in search of asylum. He said that he had been forced into a duel over a veiled woman and had killed his challenger. Without identifying herself, Flora promised him protection and hid him in a closet as Arnaldo appeared, seeking to kill the man who had murdered Licio. Her father, Don César, also came in, having learned from Dinero, the stranger's servant, that the murderer was the son of his old friend, the Governor of Brandenburg. He faced a predicament. His ties of friendship required that he help the young fugitive, but as magistrate he must hunt him down and execute him.

In the meantime Arnaldo had carried the news to Laura as an excuse to enter her house without objections from her brother and guardian, Fabio; but Fabio warned the young man never again to try to talk to Laura while she was unchaperoned. Then, seeing in Flora's grief a chance to further his own courtship, Fabio left to visit her and in doing so interrupted her plans to get Don Carlos to a place of safety.

Because there were too many people around the house, visitors come to see the magistrate, Flora and her servant Silvia decided to hide Don Carlos in the tower of the building, formerly the town jail. Later Silvia returned to tell the fugitive that a heavily muffled woman wanted to talk to him. Flora, the caller, knew that it was impossible for her to go openly calling on the man who had just killed her fiancé. Don Carlos decided that the women of Vienna were kind to strangers. The visitor, after making him promise not to try to discover her identity, explained that she had come because she was the cause of all his trouble, the motive for the duel, and she wanted to make amends. He answered that he was leaving Vienna as soon as possible in order not to harm her reputation. But the arrival of Dinero again delayed his escape. The servant, learning Flora's identity, prevented her father's discovery of her secret by claiming that he had brought a cloak which the girl was merely trying on.

Don César having gone to post guards at the gates, Don Carlos gave Flora a jewel as a token and then slipped over the wall into the next house. There he interrupted the love-making of Arnaldo and Laura, but he won their sympathy by telling a story about fleeing from a jealous husband. Arnaldo, having boosted the fugitive over a high fence to safety, was himself caught by Don César, who was pursuing the fugitive, and by Fabio, who had been awakened by the noise. By keeping muffled, Arnaldo tricked the magistrate into believing him the escaping Don Carlos. Don César ordered a jailer to return the fugitive to the tower prison.

Don Carlos had already taken refuge there, convinced it was the safest place in which he could hide. The young man's presence now offered Don César a triple problem of honor: his conflicting duties as father, friend, and magistrate. Meanwhile, Arnaldo, finding Don Carlos in the tower, started a quarrel. The noise of the fight brought Don César to the scene.

He scoffed at Arnaldo's accusations that the young man was secretly visiting Flora; his own jailer had brought the young man there. Denounced as a scandalmonger, Arnaldo was thrown out of the house.

Laura, veiled, was an early morning visitor to the tower. At first Flora, also in disguise, saw in her friend a possible rival; but Laura, thinking that the prisoner was Arnaldo, had come to confess her indiscretion, if necessary, in order to free him. The others, bursting in, found the two veiled women. Arnaldo, realizing that one was Laura, confessed his misdeeds and asked to marry her, but only after he had killed Don Carlos. The prisoner then concocted a story that placated everybody. Laura's honor was now safe. Don Carlos also assured Don César that he had sought asylum in the house of his father's friend, not of his sweetheart's father; and he pointed out his marriage to Flora would resolve all problems. So all ended happily with a double wedding.

IT IS WORSE THAN IT WAS

Type of work: Drama
Author: Pedro Calderón de la Barca (1600-1681)
Type of plot: Cape-and-sword comedy
Time of plot: Seventeenth century
Locale: Gaeta, Italy
First presented: 1630

Principal characters:
> César Ursino, a fugitive from justice
> Camacho, his servant
> Flérida Colona, whom César loves
> Juan de Aragón, Governor of Gaeta
> Lisarda, his daughter
> Celia, her servant
> Don Juan, Lisarda's suitor and César's friend

Critique:

In his early days, Calderón imitated the complicated plots of Lope de Vega's cape-and-sword plays with their disguises and mistaken identities. A good example is *It Is Worse than It Was (Peor está que estaba)*, first presented in 1630 and appearing in the first "Parte" of twelve plays by Calderón published in 1635. Later it was corrected and reprinted in 1682 by Calderón's friend, Juan de Vera Tassis. Because many seventeenth-century Spanish dramatists were competing with Lope for popularity, the Jesuit-trained Calderón, to make his plays different, added an interest in philosophy and logic. His characters, as one critic has put it, make love like debaters. Lisarda, inquiring how César can love her without having seen her, is answered by an exposition of how blind people can admire what they cannot see. For additional differentiation, Calderón borrowed from the Gongoristic literary practice, then popular, and provided word puzzles for his audiences, as when he refers to a diamond bribe given a servant as an "errant star," or played with metaphors, as when César speaks of the dawn "crowned with roses and carnations." But Calderón was also a skilled poet and dramatist, even in his early days. His thoughts are clothed in word music, and his plots, in spite of their complications, are mechanically correct and exciting to follow.

The Story:

When Juan de Aragón, Governor of Gaeta, received a letter from his old friend Alonso Colona of Naples, saying that his daughter had run off with a murderer, César Ursino, that official was so upset and incoherent that his daughter Lisarda was sure that her own guilty secret had been discovered, for she had been going veiled to assignations with a romantic wooer. This gallant, who called himself Fabio, was really César. He was deeply interested in the veiled girl whom he was meeting, much to the dismay of his servant Camacho, who remonstrated with his master and reminded him that he was to marry Flérida.

One day César ran across his old friend, Don Juan, who had returned from Flanders to visit an old soldier friend of his and to pay court to Lisarda. About the same time Flérida Colona arrived in Gaeta from Naples and appealed for help to the governor's daughter. Calling herself Laura, she explained that her sweetheart was in flight after having killed a man who had molested her, and that she was following him.

During her next meeting with César, Lisarda was persuaded to unveil herself. Her maid Celia, flirting with Camacho, also revealed herself. At that moment they were discovered by the governor, who was searching for César. The fugitive declared: "Things are worse than they were." The governor sent him a prisoner to the tower, and ordered the veiled girl, whom he took for the daughter of his old friend, to be taken under guard to his own house.

Returning home before her father, Lisarda was able to make him believe on his arrival that his captive had been Flérida, the girl whom Lisarda was already sheltering in the house. Satisfied with the way matters had turned out, the governor dispatched a messenger to his friend in Naples and promised to keep the runaway girl out of mischief until she was safely married. Meanwhile, Don Juan had been accepted as Lisarda's suitor and was being entertained in the governor's house.

Lisarda, remorseful that César had been jailed because of his passion for her, sent Celia to him with a note arranging for another meeting that night. The servant found him and Camacho comparing Flérida and his new lady. César, immediately accepting the invitation, promised to bribe the jailer for a night of freedom. Bribery was not necessary, however. Don Juan, on his arrival to visit the prisoner, announced that the jailer was his old military comrade, who would let César out on parole. César had hoped to keep his friend from learning about the veiled woman, but was glad of Don Juan's help when his pistol went off unexpectedly, revealing his presence in Lisarda's room. Don Juan, who was staying in the governor's house, arrived first on the scene, recognized César, and aided him to escape.

Don Juan debated all night whether to challenge César as a rival or to aid him as a friend. Unable to make up his mind, he hesitated about accepting the governor's offer of immediate marriage to Lisarda. While he was debating with himself, the early-rising Flérida found him in the patio. Her general remarks about César and their adventures together in the past convinced Don Juan that she had been the girl in César's company the night before. During their discussion Flérida learned for the first time that César was in the Gaeta jail.

When her attempts to visit him aroused Lisarda's jealousy, the governor, overhearing part of the conversation between the girls, almost uncovered the truth about Lisarda's secret meetings. But Lisarda managed to keep her secret from her father. She also promised Flérida a full explanation of everything that had happened.

Once more Don Juan visited César in jail. Camacho, by his quick wit, managed to save Lisarda's good name, but all was nearly discovered when the governor arrived with news that he had made arrangements for César's immediate marriage to Flérida. Unable to understand the young man's surprise at news of his sweetheart, he insisted that he had found them together the previous night.

To get the truth, Don Juan gathered everyone concerned at the governor's house. There Lisarda, to escape scandal, was compelled to see Flérida paired off with César while she had to be satisfied with Don Juan. To complete the round of weddings, Celia and Camacho were paired off with each other.

THE ITALIAN

Type of work: Novel
Author: Mrs. Ann Radcliffe (1764-1823)
Type of plot: Gothic romance
Time of plot: 1758
Locale: Italy
First published: 1797

Principal characters:
VINCENTIO DI VIVALDI, a young nobleman of Naples
ELLENA DI ROSALBA, loved by Vincentio
THE MARCHESE DI VIVALDI, and
THE MARCHESA DI VIVALDI, Vincentio's parents
SCHEDONI, the marchesa's confessor, formerly the Count di Bruno
SIGNORA BIANCHI, Ellena's aunt
SISTER OLIVIA, formerly the Countess di Bruno
PAULO MENDRICO, Vincentio's faithful servant

Critique:

In *The Journal of a Tour,* an account of a journey through Holland and Germany with her husband in 1794, Mrs. Radcliffe told how on her trip up the Rhine she had encountered two Capuchins "as they walked along the shore, beneath the dark cliffs of Boppart, wrapt in the long black drapery of their order, and their heads shrouded in cowls, that half concealed their faces. . . ." She saw them as "interesting figures in a picture, always gloomily sublime." This vision is commonly believed to have inspired the character of Schedoni, the most sinister villain in that gallery of villains, the Gothic novel. As in her other books, *The Italian, or, The Confessional of the Black Penitents* mingles the wild or idyllic beauty of nature with scenes of nightmare and terror. The novel is wholly a work of the romantic imagination, lacking both the fantastic supernaturalism and the turgid sensationalism of her rivals in this specialized genre.

The Story:

Vincentio di Vivaldi saw Ellena di Rosalba for the first time at the Church of San Lorenzo in Naples. So impressed was he by the sweetness of her voice and the grace of her person that at the end of the service he followed the girl and her elderly companion in the hope that the fair unknown would put aside her veil so that he might catch a glimpse of her features. When the elderly woman stumbled and fell, Vivaldi seized the opportunity to offer her his arm, a gallant gesture which gave him the excuse to accompany the two women to the Villa Altieri, their modest home on an eminence overlooking the bay of Naples.

The next day he returned to ask after the health of Signora Bianchi, as the older woman was named. Although the matron received her guest courteously, Ellena did not appear. Thrown into a mood of despondency by her absence, he inquired of his acquaintances into the girl's family, but learned only that she was an orphan, the niece and ward of her aged relative.

That night, resolved to see Ellena again, he left a reception given by his mother and repaired to the Villa Altieri. The hour was late and only one window was lighted. Through a lattice he saw Ellena playing on her lute while she sang a midnight hymn to the Virgin. Entranced, he drew near the lattice and heard her pronounce his name; but when he revealed himself the girl closed the lattice and left the room. Vivaldi lingered in the garden for some time before returning to Naples. Lost in reverie, he was passing under a shattered archway extending over the road when a shadowy figure in a monk's robe glided across his path and in a ghostly whisper warned him to beware of future visits to the villa.

Thinking that the warning had been given by a rival, he returned the next night in the company of his friend Bonorma. Again the dark figure appeared and uttered a sepulchral warning. Later, as the two young men were passing under the arch, the figure showed itself once more. Vivaldi and Bonorma drew their swords and entered the ancient fortress in search of the mysterious visitant. They found no trace of anyone lurking in the ruins.

Still believing that these visitations were the work of a rival, Vivaldi decided to end his suspense by making a declaration for Ellena's hand. Signora Bianchi listened to his proposal and then reminded him that a family as old and illustrious as his own would object to an alliance with a girl of Ellena's humble station. Vivaldi realized that she spoke wisely, but with all the fervor of a young man in love he argued his suit so eloquently that at last Signora Bianchi withdrew her refusal. After Vivaldi had made repeated visits to the villa, a night came when the aged woman placed Ellena's hand in his and gave them her blessing. To Vivaldi's great joy it was decided that the marriage would be solemnized during the coming week.

The Marchese and Marchesa di Vivaldi, in the meantime, had not remained in ignorance of their son's frequent visits at the Villa Altieri. On several occasions the marchese, a man of great family pride and strict principles, had remonstrated with his son and assured him that any

expectation of marriage to one so far below him in station was impossible. To this argument Vivaldi answered only that his affections and intentions were irrevocable. His mother, a haughty and vindictive woman, was equally determined to end what she regarded as her son's foolish infatuation. Realizing that the young man could not be moved by persuasion or threats, she summoned her confessor and secret adviser, the monk Schedoni, and consulted him on measures to separate Ellena and Vivaldi.

Schedoni, a monk at the Convent of the Santo Spirito, was a man of unknown family and origins. His spirit appeared haughty and disordered; his appearance conveyed an effect of gloom that corresponded to his severe and solitary disposition. Because of his austere manners, brooding nature, and sinister appearance he was loved by none, hated by many, and feared by most. Vivaldi disliked the monk and avoided him, even though he had no presentiment of what Schedoni was preparing for him and Ellena.

On the morning after his acceptance as Ellena's suitor Vivaldi hastened to the villa. In the darkened archway the ghostly figure again appeared and told him that death was in the house. Deeply disturbed, Vivaldi hurried on, to learn on his arrival that Signora Bianchi had died suddenly during the night. When Beatrice, the old servant, confided her suspicions that her mistress had been poisoned, Vivaldi grew even more concerned. His own suspicions falling on Schedoni, he confronted the monk in the marchesa's apartment on his return to Venice, but the confessor cleverly parried all the questions Vivaldi put to him. Vivaldi, apologizing for his conduct and accusing speech, failed to realize that he had made an enemy of Schedoni and that the monk was already planning his revenge.

Meanwhile, it had been decided that Ellena was to find a sanctuary in the Convent of Santa Maria della Pieta after her aunt's funeral, and Vivaldi was in agreement with her desire to withdraw to that shelter during her period of mourning. While Ellena was packing in preparation for her departure the next day, she heard Beatrice screaming in another room. At that same moment three masked men seized Ellena and in spite of her protests carried her from the house. Thrust into a closed carriage, she was driven throughout the night and most of the next day into the mountainous region of Abruzzo. There her captors conducted her to a strange religious establishment where she was turned over to the care of the nuns. Almost distracted, the girl was led to a cell where she was at last able to give way to the extremities of her terror and grief.

Knowing nothing of these events, Vivaldi had decided that same night to explore the ruined fortress and to discover, if possible, the secret of the strange visitant he had encountered there. With him went Paulo Mendrico, his faithful servant. When they were within the archway the figure of the monk suddenly materialized, this time telling Vivaldi that Ellena had departed an hour before. Paulo fired his pistol, but the figure eluded them. Following drops of blood, Vivaldi and Paulo came at last to a chamber into which the figure had disappeared. As they entered, the great door shut behind them. In the chamber they found only a discarded, bloody robe. During the night they spent as prisoners in that gloomy room Paulo told his master of a muffled penitent who had appeared at the Church of Santa Maria del Pianto and made a confession apparently so strange and horrible that Ansaldo di Rovalli, the grand penitentiary, had been thrown into convulsions. During this recital they were startled by hearing groans close by, but they saw no one. In the morning the door of the chamber stood open once more, and Vivaldi and Paulo made their escape.

Alarmed for Ellena's safety, Vivaldi went at once to the villa. There he found Beatrice tied to a pillar and learned from her that her mistress had been carried off by abductors. Convinced that the strange happenings of the night were part of a plot to prevent his intended marriage, he again confronted Schedoni at the Convent of the Santo Spirito and would have assaulted the monk if others had not seized the distraught young man and restrained him by force. That night, by accident, Vivaldi heard from a fisherman that early in the day a closed carriage had been seen driving through Bracelli. Hopeful that he could trace the carriage and find Ellena, he set off in pursuit in the company of faithful Paulo.

On the fourth day of her imprisonment Ellena was conducted to the parlor of the abbess, who informed her that she must choose between taking the veil or the person whom the Marchesa di Vivaldi had selected as her husband. When Ellena refused both offers she was taken back to her cell. Each evening she was allowed to attend vespers and there her attention was attracted to Sister Olivia, a nun who tried to reconcile her to the hardships of her confinement. For this reason, perhaps, Sister Olivia was the nun chosen by the abbess to inform Ellena that if she persisted in refusing a husband proper to her station she must take holy orders immediately.

Vivaldi, meanwhile, was continuing his search for Ellena. On the evening of the seventh day he and Paulo fell in with a company of pilgrims on their way to worship at the shrine of a convent about a league and a half distant. Traveling with this company, Vivaldi arrived at the convent in time to witness the service at which Ellena was to be made a novitiate. Hearing her voice raised in protest, he rushed to the altar and caught her as she fainted. Unable to secure Ellena's freedom, Vivaldi left the convent in order to try another plan to set her free. Though he did not know it, there was need of haste; the abbess had decided to punish Ellena by confining her in a chamber from which none had ever returned alive. Alarmed for the girl's life, Sister Olivia promised to help her escape from the convent that night.

Dressed in the nun's veil, Ellena attended a program of music given in honor of some distinguished strangers who were visiting the convent. There Vivaldi, disguised as a pilgrim, passed her a note in which he told her to meet him at the gate of the nuns' garden. Guided by Sister Olivia, Ellena went to the gate where Vivaldi was waiting with Brother Jeronimo, a monk whom he had bribed to lead them from the convent by a secret path. Brother Jeronimo tried to betray them, however, and Ellena would have been recaptured if an aged monk whom they disturbed at his solitary prayers had not pitied them and unlocked the last door standing between the lovers and freedom.

Once in the open air, Vivaldi and Ellena descended the mountains to the place where Paulo waited with the horses for their escape. Instead of taking the road toward Naples, the fugitives turned westward toward Aquila. That day, as they were resting at a shepherd's cabin, Paulo brought word that they were being pursued by two Carmelite friars. Eluding their pursuers, they rode toward Lake Celano, where Ellena took refuge for the night in the Ursuline convent and Vivaldi stayed in an establishment of Benedictines.

While these events were taking place, the marchese, who knew nothing of his wife's scheming with Schedoni, was suffering great anxiety over his son's possible whereabouts and welfare. The marchesa, on the other hand, was apprehensive only that Ellena would be found and her plans undone. When Schedoni suggested in his sly, indirect fashion that Ellena be put out of the way for good, she was at first horrified by his suggestion. Later she reconsidered and at last she and the sinister monk came to an understanding. Ellena was to die. Schedoni, who had spies everywhere, was not long in locating the fugitives. As Vivaldi and Ellena were about to be married in the chapel of San Sebastian at Celano, armed men broke into the church and arrested the two under a warrant of the Holy Inquisition. Ellena was charged with having broken her nun's vows and Vivaldi with having aided her escape. Vivaldi, although wounded in his struggle to prevent arrest, was carried to Rome and after a short hearing before the Inquisitor was imprisoned to await future trial and possible torture to extort a confession. Paulo, protesting against separation from his master, was also confined.

After the agents of the Inquisition had taken Vivaldi and Paulo away, Ellena's guards put her on a waiting horse and set out on a road which led toward the Adriatic. After traveling with little interruption for two nights and two days they came to a lonely house on the seashore. There she was turned over to a villainous-looking man whom the guards called Spalatro and locked in a room in which the only furnishing was a tattered mattress on the floor. Exhausted, she fell asleep. Twice during the next day Spalatro came to her room, looked at her with a gaze that seemed a mixture of impatience and guilt, and then went away. At another time he took her to walk on the beach, where she met a monk whose face was hidden by his cowl. The monk was Schedoni. When he spoke to her, Ellena realized that he was neither a friend nor a protector but an enemy; and she fainted. Revived, she was returned to her room.

Schedoni was determined that Ellena should die that night. When Spalatro confessed pity for the girl and refused to be the executioner, Schedoni swore to do the deed himself. Going to the room where the girl was sleeping, he stood, dagger in hand, over her. Suddenly he bent to look closely at a miniature she wore about her neck. Agitated, he awoke Ellena and asked her if she knew whose portrait she wore. When she answered that it was the miniature of her father, Schedoni was even more shaken. He was convinced that he had discovered his lost daughter.

1471

Overcome by remorse for his persecution of Ellena and the accusation which had exposed Vivaldi to the tortures of the Inquisition, Schedoni now tried to make amends. He and Ellena traveled as quickly as possible to Naples. After leaving the girl at the Villa Altieri, the monk hastened to the Vivaldis' palace and in an interview with the marchesa begged, without disclosing his connection with Ellena, that objections to Vivaldi's suit be withdrawn. When the marchesa proved inattentive, he determined to solemnize, without her consent, the nuptials of Vivaldi and Ellena.

Called a second time before the tribunal of the Inquisition, Vivaldi heard again among those present at the trial the voice which had warned him on earlier occasions against his visits to the Villa Altieri. That night a strange monk visited him in his cell and asked how long he had known Schedoni. The monk then instructed Vivaldi to reveal to the Inquisition that Schedoni was actually Count Ferando di Bruno, who had lived fifteen years in the disguise of a Dominican monk. He was also to ask that Ansaldo di Rovalli, the grand penitentiary of the Black Penitents, be called to testify to a confession he had heard in 1752. When Vivaldi was again brought before the Inquisition he did as he had been told, with the result that Schedoni was arrested on his way to Rome to intercede for Vivaldi's freedom.

At Schedoni's trial the mystery that linked the sinister father confessor and the two lovers was made clear. Years before, Schedoni, then a splendthrift younger son known as the Count di Marinella, had schemed to posses himself of his brother's title, his unencumbered estate, and his beautiful wife. He had arranged to have his brother, the Count di Bruno, assassinated by Spalatro and had contrived a story that the count had perished while returning from a journey to Greece. After a proper season of mourning he had solicited the hand of his brother's widow. When she rejected

him his passion had caused him to carry her off by force. Although the lady had retrieved her honor by marriage, she continued to look on her new husband with disdain, and in his jealousy he became convinced that she was unfaithful. One day, returning unexpectedly, he found a visitor with his wife. Drawing his stiletto with the intention of attacking the guest, he struck and killed his wife instead. This was the confession which had so agitated the grand penitentiary, for he himself had been the guest and for him an innocent woman had died.

Further proof was the dying confession of Spalatro, whose death had been caused by a wound inflicted by Schedoni. Condemned to die for plotting his brother's death, Schedoni still persisted in his declaration that Ellena was his daughter. This mystery was cleared up by Sister Olivia, who in the meantime had removed to the Convent of Santa Maria della Pieta; the nun was the unfortunate Countess di Bruno and the sister of Signora Bianchi. Her wound had not been mortal, but the report of her death had been given out in order to protect her from her vengeful husband. Wishing to withdraw from the world, she had entrusted her daughter by the first Count di Bruno and an infant daughter by the second to Signora Bianchi. The infant had died within a year.

Ellena, who knew nothing of this story, had been mistaken in her belief that the miniature was that of her father, and it was on her word that Schedoni had claimed her as his daughter. It was also revealed that Father Nicola, who had collected the evidence against Schedoni, had been the mysterious monk whose ghostly warnings Vivaldi heard under the arch of the old fortress. Appalled by the father confessor's villainy, he had turned against him after being wounded by Paulo's pistol on the night of the midnight search.

Schedoni had his final revenge. In some manner he administered a fatal dose of poison to Father Nicola and then died of the same mysterious drug. In his last moments he boasted that he was escaping an ignominious death at the hands of the Inquisition.

Because of Schedoni's dying confession, Vivaldi was immediately set free. During his imprisonment the marchesa had died repentant of the harm she had plotted against Ellena. Now the marchese, overjoyed to be reunited with his son, withdrew all objections to Vivaldi's suit. With all doubts of Ellena's birth and goodness removed, he went in person to the Convent of Santa Maria della Pieta and asked Sister Olivia for her daughter's hand in the name of his son. Vivaldi and Ellena were married in the convent church in the presence of the marchese and Sister Olivia. As a mark of special favor Paulo was allowed to be present when his master took Ellena for his wife. If it had not been for the holy precincts and the solemnity of the occasion the faithful fellow would have thrown his cap into the air and shouted that this was indeed a happy day.

THE ITCHING PARROT

Type of work: Novel
Author: José Joaquín Fernández de Lizardi (1776-1827)
Type of plot: Picaresque satire
Time of plot: The 1770's to 1820's
Locale: Mexico
First published: 1816

Principal characters:
PEDRO SARMIENTO, The Itching Parrot, or Poll, a young Mexican
DON ANTONIO, Poll's prison mate and benefactor
JANUARIO, Poll's schoolmate
AN ARMY COLONEL, Poll's superior and benefactor

Critique:

This novel, written by the most rabid controversialist among Mexican authors during the unsettled years when Mexico was seeking to become independent of Spain, was suppressed after the publication of the eleventh chapter in 1816, and the complete novel was not published until three years after the author's death. Scholars have viewed it as the first Spanish-American novel, and it is reputed to have sold over one hundred million copies. Lizardi managed to smuggle into the novel most of the polemical tracts which had earned him nationwide fame as The Mexican Thinker, pamphlets directed against whoever sat at the head of the Mexican government, whether he was Spanish viceroy or revolutionist dictator. Lizardi, like his fictional hero, spent many months in jail. He considered himself a no-party man, and many Mexican regimes resorted to prison sentences to silence him; but Lizardi, always placing Mexico above its rulers, alternately satirized and advised them.

The Story:

Pedro Sarmiento was born to upper middle-class parents in Mexico City between 1771 and 1773; of the actual date, he was not sure. As a child he was willful, and his mother's excessive devotion only made him worse. He became such a scamp that at last his father sent him off to school. At school he was nicknamed Parrot. A little later, when he contracted the itch, his schoolmates nicknamed him The Itching Parrot, or Poll for short, and the name stuck to him through most of his life.

THE ITCHING PARROT by José Joaquín Fernández de Lizardi. By permission of the publishers, Doubleday & Co., Inc. Copyright, 1942, by Doubleday & Co., Inc.

In addition to his nickname, Poll acquired many vicious habits from his schoolfellows. Poll's father resolved to put Poll out as an apprentice in a trade, but Poll's mother, not wishing her son to disgrace her family by becoming a vulgar tradesman, insisted that the boy be sent to college. Against his better judgment, the father agreed, and so Poll was sent off to study for a college degree. After learning some Latin, some Aristotle, some logic, and a little physics, Poll was awarded a baccalaureate degree by the College of San Ildefonso.

Shortly after receiving his degree, Poll went into the countryside to visit a hacienda owned by the father of a former schoolmate. At the hacienda he earned the hatred of his schoolmate, Januario, by making advances to the latter's cousin, with whom Januario was infatuated. Januario took his revenge by tempting Poll into a bullfight. Poll, who lost both the fight and his trousers, became the laughingstock of the hacienda. Still unsatisfied, Januario tricked Poll into trying to sleep with the girl cousin. Through Januario, the girl's mother discovered the attempt, beat Poll with her shoe, and sent him back to Mexico City in disgrace.

Upon his return to the city Poll was told by his father that he had to find some means of earning a livelihood. Poll, searching for the easiest way, decided he would study theology and enter the Church. Theology quickly proved uninteresting, and Poll gave up that idea. Trying to escape his father's insistence that he learn a trade, Poll then decided to enter a Franciscan monastery. There he soon found that he could not stand the life of a monk; he was glad when his father's death gave him an excuse to leave the monastery. After a short period of mourning Poll rapidly exhausted his small inheritance through his fondness for gambling, parties, and women. The sorrow he caused his mother sent her, also, to an early death. After his mother died, Poll was left alone. None of his relatives, who knew him for a rogue, would have anything to do with him.

In his despair Poll fell in with another schoolmate, who supported himself by gambling and trickery. Poll took up a similar career in his schoolmate's company. A man he gulled discovered Poll's treachery and beat him severely. After his release from the hospital Poll went back to his gambling partner and they decided to turn thieves. On their very first attempt, however, they were unsuccessful. Poll was caught and thrown into prison.

Because he had no family or friends to call upon, Poll languished in jail for several months. He made one friend in jail who helped him; that friend was Don Antonio, a man of good reputation who had been unjustly imprisoned. Although Don Antonio tried to keep Poll away from bad company, he was not entirely successful. When Don Antonio was freed, Poll fell in with a mulatto who got him into all kinds of scrapes. By chance Poll was taken up by a scrivener who was in need of an apprentice and was pleased with Poll's handwriting. The scrivener had Poll released from prison to become his apprentice.

Poll's career as a scrivener's apprentice was short, for he made love to the man's mistress, was discovered, and was driven from the house. The next step in Poll's adventures was service as a barber's apprentice. He left that work to become a clerk in a pharmacy. After getting into trouble by carelessly mixing a prescription, Poll left the pharmacy for the employ of a doctor.

Having picked up some jargon and a few cures from his doctor-employer, Poll set out to be a physician. Everything went well until he caused a number of deaths and was forced to leave the profession.

Trying to recoup his fortunes once more, Poll returned to gambling. In a game he won a lottery ticket which, in its turn, won for him a small fortune. For a time Poll lived well: he even married a girl who thought he had a great deal of money. But the life the couple led soon exhausted the lottery money, and they were almost

1474

and rich in the world's goods.

Not long after his first wife died, Jack remarried, the second time to a young woman. The wife was a poor choice, even though he had the pick of the wealthy women of his class in the county. Not many months passed after the marriage, which had been a costly one, before James, King of Scotland, invaded England while King Henry was in France. The justices of the county called upon Jack to furnish six men-at-arms to join the army raised by Queen Catherine. Jack, however, raised a company of a hundred and fifty foot and horse, which he armed and dressed at his own expense in distinctive liveries. Jack himself rode at the head of his men. Queen Catherine was greatly pleased and thanked Jack Winchcomb personally for his efforts, although his men were not needed to achieve the English victory at Flodden Field. In reward for his services, Jack received a chain of gold from the hands of the queen herself.

In the tenth year of his reign King Henry made a trip through Berkshire. Jack Winchcomb introduced himself in a witty way to the king as the Prince of the Ants, who was at war with the Butterflies, a sally against Cardinal Wolsey. The king, vastly pleased, betook himself to Newberry, along with his train, where all were entertained by Jack at a fabulous banquet. After the banquet the king viewed the weaving rooms and warehouses Jack owned. Upon his departure the king wished to make Jack a knight, but the weaver refused the honor, saying he would rather be a common man and die, as he had lived, a clothier.

In his house Jack of Newberry had a series of fifteen paintings, all denoting great men whose fathers had been tradesmen of one kind and another, including a portrait of Marcus Aurelius, who had been a clothier's son. Jack kept the pictures and showed them to his friends and workmen in an effort to encourage one and all to seek fame and dignity in spite of their humble offices in life.

Because of the many wars in Europe during King Henry's reign, trade in general was depleted. The lot of the clothiers and weavers being particularly bad, they joined together and sent leaders to London to appeal to the government on their behalf. One of the envoys they sent was Jack Winchcomb of Newberry. The king remembered Jack and in private audience assured him that measures would be taken to alleviate the hardships of the clothiers. Another man who had not forgotten Jack was the Lord Chancellor, Cardinal Wolsey. In an attempt to circumvent the king's promise, he had Jack and the other envoys thrown into prison for a few days. Finally the Duke of Somerset intervened and convinced the cardinal that the clothiers meant no harm.

Some time later an Italian merchant named Benedick came to the house of Jack of Newberry to trade. While there, he fell in love with one of Jack's workers, a pretty girl named Joan. But she paid no attention whatever to Benedick and asked a kinsman to tell the Italian not to bother her. When the kinsman did as he was asked, he angered the Italian, who vowed to make a cuckold of the kinsman for his pains. With gifts and fair speech the Italian finally had his way with the weaver's wife, although the woman was immediately sorry. She told her husband, who had his revenge on the Italian by pretending that he would see to it that the Italian was permitted to go to bed with Joan. The Italian fell in with the scheme and found himself put to bed with a pig, whereupon all the Englishmen laughed at him so heartily that he left Newberry in shame.

Jack's second wife was a good young woman, but she sometimes erred in paying too much attention to her gossipy friends. At one time a friend told her that she was wasting money by feeding the workmen so well. She cut down on the quantity and the quality of the food she served the workers, but Jack, who remembered only too well the days when he had been an apprentice and journeyman forced to eat whatever was placed in front of him, became very angry and made her change her ways again. His workers were gratified when he said that his wife's friend was never to set foot in his house again.

At another time Jack of Newberry went to London, where he found a draper who owed him five hundred pounds working as a porter. Learning that the man, through no fault of his own, had become a bankrupt, Jack showed his confidence in the man by setting him up in business again. Friends warned him that he was sending good money after bad, but Jack's judgment proved correct. The man paid back every cent and later became an alderman of London.

Jack was always proud of his workers. One time a knight, Sir George Rigley, seduced a pretty and intelligent girl who worked for Jack. Jack vowed that he would make it right for her. He sent the woman, disguised as a rich widow, to London. There Sir George fell in love with her, not knowing who she was, and married her. The knight was angry at first, but he soon saw the justice of the case and was very well pleased with the hundred pounds Jack gave the girl as a dower. Still knowing their places in life, Jack and his wife gave precedence to Sir George and his new lady, even in their own house.

JACK SHEPPARD

Type of work: Novel
Author: William Harrison Ainsworth (1805-1882)
Type of plot: Picaresque romance
Time of plot: 1702-1724
Locale: London and its environs
First published: 1839

Principal characters:
JACK SHEPPARD, a housebreaker and popular jailbreaker
JOAN SHEPPARD, his mother
OWEN WOOD, a London carpenter
MRS. WOOD, his wife
WINIFRED, their daughter
SIR ROWLAND TRENCHARD, an aristocrat
THAMES DARRELL, Sir Rowland's nephew and foster son of Owen Wood
JONATHAN WILD, a thief-taker
BLUESKIN, devoted henchman of Jack Sheppard

Critique:

Jack Sheppard differs from most of Ainsworth's work in that it has a rogue instead of a historical figure for its title character. Extremely popular in its own day, it has remained the most widely read of this author's novels. The plot is based on the life of a famous English criminal who so appealed to the public imagination that both Hogarth and Sir James Thornhill used him as a model in their paintings. Abounding in characters, circumstantial incident, obviously delineated protagonists and antagonists, and scattered references to historical incident, the novel illustrates the typically Victorian treatment of the rogue theme in fiction. Thackeray, critical of Ainsworth's characterization of Sheppard, wrote *Catherine* in protest against this book.

The Story:

When Owen Wood went to offer his condolence to Joan, the widow of Tom Sheppard, who had been executed for stealing from Wood, he found the woman living in misery near the Old Mint, a haven for mendicants, thieves, and debtors. Joan told Wood that Van Galgebrok, a Dutch seaman and conjurer, had prophesied that her baby, Jack, would be

1480

executed as his father had been. The prophecy was based on the presence of a mole behind Jack's ear. Wood offered to take the infant out of that sordid environment in order to avert fulfillment of the prophecy, but the mother refused to part with her child.

Left alone with the infant while Joan went to the attic to get a key which her deceased husband had ordered given to Wood, the carpenter was accosted by a mob led by Sir Rowland Trenchard, in pursuit of a young man named Darrell. In the confusion Jonathan Wild, a thief-taker, picked up the key which Joan was to return to Wood.

While a great storm raged, Darrell, the fugitive, with a baby in his arms, was again pursued by Sir Rowland. The chase continued to the flooded Thames, where Darrell was drowned after a struggle with Sir Rowland. Wood, on his way home, rescued the baby from drowning. Some falling bricks saved him and the baby from Sir Rowland's wrath. Wood, understanding little of the night's strange events, took the child home with him. He named the boy Thames Darrell.

Twelve years later Wood had taken Jack Sheppard as an apprentice in his carpenter shop, but he found the boy indifferent and listless in his work. Thames Darrell, reared by the Woods, was a model apprentice. A third child in the household was Winifred, Wood's daughter, a charming, beautiful girl. The three twelve-year-olds were very fond of each other.

Mrs. Wood, a termagant, had long berated her husband for his kindness to Jack and to Joan Sheppard, who lived modestly and respectably in Willesden. Following an episode in which Thames was injured while trying to prevent injury to Jack, Mrs. Wood reprimanded Jack and predicted that he would come to the same end that his father had met. Her chastisement was strong enough to arouse a spirit of misdemeanor and criminality in Jack.

Jonathan Wild, who had hanged Tom Sheppard, boasted that he would hang the son as well. A resolute and subtle plotter, he worked slyly to bring about the boy's ruin. One day he gave Jack the key which he had found on the floor of the Mint twelve years before. It was Wood's master key; his hope was that Jack would rob the carpenter. Investigating Thames' parentage, Wild learned also that Thames was the child of Sir Rowland Trenchard's sister, Lady Alvira, whose husband Sir Rowland had drowned and whose child he had tried to destroy on the night of the great storm. Later Lady Alvira had been forced to marry her cousin, Sir Cecil Trafford. Lady Trafford was dying, in which event the estates would revert to her brother if she left no other heir. Wild promised Sir Rowland that he would remove Thames in order that Sir Rowland could inherit the entire estate. As a hold over the nobleman, he told him also that he knew the whereabouts of Sir Rowland's other sister, Constance, carelessly lost in childhood to a gipsy.

Wild and Sir Rowland trapped Thames and Jack in Sir Rowland's house and accused them of robbery. Imprisoned, Jack and Thames made a jail break from Old Giles' Roundhouse, the first of innumerable and difficult escapes for Jack, and the last for Thames, who was sent off to sea to be disposed of by Van Galgebrok, the Dutch seaman and conjurer.

Jack was soon fraternizing with the patrons of the Mint, much to the pleasure of the derelicts, prostitutes, and gamblers, who gathered there. It was in this environment that Joan saw Jack as the criminal he had become. When she went there to admonish her son to live a life of righteousness, she was answered by the taunts and sneers of the patrons, who reminded her that she had at one time enjoyed the life of the Mint. Jack, egged on by two prostitutes, spurned her pleas. Joan returned to her little home in Willesden to pray for Jack.

Jonathan Wild, having rid himself of Thames, one obstacle in the thief-taker's scheme to get control of the fortune of Sir Montacute Trenchard, Thames' grandfather, set about to remove Sir Rowland as well. Wild, plotting against the aristocrat, had him arrested for treason in connection with a proposed Jacobite uprising against the crown.

Jack Sheppard used the key given him by Wild to rob Wood's house. Caught and jailed in the Cage at Willesden as he was going to visit his mother, he soon escaped from the supposedly impregnable structure. At his mother's house Jack declared his undying love for her but announced that he could not return to honest living. Questioned by Joan as to how long he would wait to execute his threat against Jack, Wild, who had followed Jack to Willesden, answered boldly and confidently, "Nine."

Nine years later, in 1724, Jack had become the most daring criminal and jailbreaker of the day. By that time the Woods were affluent citizens living in Willesden. Joan Sheppard, insane because of worry over Jack, had been committed to Bedlam, a squalid, filthy asylum. Sir Rowland had been released from prison. Thames Darrell, thrown overboard by Van Galgebrok, had been picked up by a French fishing boat and carried to France, where he was employed by and subsequently commissioned by Philip of Orleans. Wild had continued in his pleasures of execution and collecting keepsakes of his grisly profession.

Jack Sheppard and Blueskin, one of Wild's henchmen, quarreled with Wild because he would not help Thomas Darrell get his rightful share of the estate which Sir Rowland had confiscated, and Blueskin became Jack's loyal henchman. The two robbed the Wood home again, Blueskin slashing Mrs. Wood's throat as she attempted to detain him.

Jack went to see his mother, a haggard, demented object of human wreckage, in chains and on a bed of straw. Wild followed Jack to the asylum. During a brawl Wild struck Joan and the blow restored the poor woman's senses. After her release from Bedlam, Wild divulged to Sir Rowland Trenchard the fact that Joan was his long-lost sister and an heir to the Trenchard estates.

Wild disposed of Sir Rowland by bludgeoning him and throwing him into a secret well. Sir Rowland, almost dead from the beating, attempted to save himself by catching hold of the floor around the opening of the well, but Wild trampled his fingers until the nobleman dropped to his watery grave. The thieftaker, still plotting to secure the Trenchard wealth, took Joan captive, but she killed herself rather than be forced into a marriage with the villain. At her funeral Jack was apprehended after a jail break that required passage through six bolted and barred doors and the removal of innumerable stones and bricks from the prison walls.

In the meantime Thames Darrell had returned from France to visit in the Wood household. Through information contained in a packet of letters which reached him in circuitous fashion, he learned that his father, the fugitive known only as Darrell, had been the French Marquis de Chatillon. His paternity proved, he inherited the Trenchard estates as well. He married Winifred Wood.

Jack Sheppard, after his seizure at his mother's funeral, was executed at Tyburn. As his body swung at the end of the rope, Blueskin cut him down in an attempt to save his life. A bullet from Wild's gun passed through Jack's heart. The body was buried beside Joan Sheppard in Willesden cemetery; and in later years the Marquis de Chatillon and his wife tended the grave and its simple wooden monument. Jonathan Wild eventually paid for his crimes; he was hanged on the same gallows to which he had sent Jack Sheppard and his father.

JALNA

Type of work: Novel
Author: Mazo de la Roche (1885-   )
Type of plot: Domestic realism
Time of plot: The 1920's
Locale: Canada
First published: 1927

Principal characters:
RENNY WHITEOAK, head of the family
MEG, his sister
EDEN,
PIERS,
FINCH, and
WAKEFIELD, their half-brothers
PHEASANT VAUGHAN, Piers' wife
MAURICE VAUGHAN, her father
ALAYNE ARCHER, Eden's wife
GRANDMA WHITEOAK

Critique:

One of a series of novels dealing with the Whiteoak family, *Jalna* describes the violent passions of a household that is as familiar to many readers as John Galsworthy's fictional Forsytes. The brothers and sisters are strangely different from each other, but all are bound together by family ties which few of them can understand. Over all towers the somewhat frightening figure of Grandma Whiteoak, binding them to her with the uncertain terms of her will and her unyielding spirit. This indomitable old woman is a character lifting the Jalna novels above the level of popular fiction.

The Story:

The Whiteoaks of Jalna were quite a family. The parents were dead, and the children, ranging in age from eight to over forty, were held together by Renny, the oldest son, and tyrannized by Grandma Whiteoak, a matriarch of ninety-nine years. The family estate of Jalna had been founded by Grandfather Whiteoak, but it had dwindled somewhat from its original greatness. By common consent Renny managed the farms and the family, although he frequently encountered resistance from both.

Meg, the oldest daughter, had in her youth been engaged to Maurice Vaughan, a neighbor and a friend of the family. But while he waited out the long engagement insisted upon by Meg, he had become entangled with a low-class girl and fathered a child, Pheasant. The girl had disappeared and Maurice had grudgingly raised Pheasant. Meg, deaf to the pleas of Maurice and her family for a forgiving heart, had broken the engagement and gone into almost complete retirement. Maurice was never allowed at Jalna again, although he and Renny served in the war together and remained friends.

Renny had remained a bachelor, the head of the family, and a man with quite a reputation with the women. Only his passions had been involved in these affairs, however, and thus it seemed that he would never marry. Renny accepted his power and his position but seemed not greatly to enjoy either.

The rest of the children were half-brothers to these two. Eden was a poet and a dreamer. Farm life disgusted him, and since he had recently had a book of poetry accepted by a New York publisher, he hoped to get away from Jalna and make his way with his writing. However, work of any kind was so distasteful to Eden that it seemed unlikely he could ever break the ties which held him to Jalna.

Piers was a plodder, with no flights of fancy or dreams of grandeur. Doing most of the manual work on the farms, he took orders from Renny in a lethargic way. Renny, learning that Piers had been seen with Pheasant Vaughan, warned the boy that such an alliance could lead only to trouble for both.

Finch was the real problem. Still in school, he barely managed to return each term. Different from the rest, he had no ambition, no drive of any kind. The family obviously considered him useless, but they stuck by him because he was family. Finch brooded. On his lonely walks through the woods and fields, he often saw through matters other members of the family tried to conceal.

Wakefield was just eight, and thus greatly spoiled. He had a heart condition which allowed him to get his own way without effort.

Over them Grandma Whiteoak held a whip. Her will had been made—and often changed—to be used as a weapon over the children and her two sons, who also lived at Jalna. She was ninety-nine and a despot. In many ways she was evil, using her power to force the children to obey her whims.

The first to cause a real stir at Jalna was Piers. He and Pheasant eloped. When they returned home, both Maurice and the Whiteoaks scorned them. Meg became hysterical and swore she would not have Maurice's daughter in her house. Grandma hit Piers over the head with her cane and would have hit Pheasant, but Renny quieted them and said that Pheasant was now part of the family and would be treated accordingly. Instantly everyone, even Meg, accepted his authority.

Eden went to New York to see his publisher and there met and married Alayne Archer, a reader for the publishing house. She felt she had discovered him through his poetry and could inspire him. An orphan, she looked forward to being part of such a large family. But when they reached Jalna, she felt an unexplained coldness. She was warmly welcomed by all but Piers, who resented the difference between her reception and Pheasant's, but she could feel tensions that were just under the surface. Grandma was revolting to the gentle Alayne, who knew she must make the old tyrant like her if she was to know any peace at Jalna.

With Alayne, Finch found his first real happiness. Seeing the artistic need in the boy, she tried to encourage the others to help him. Only Renny listened to her, and because of her arranged to have Finch take music lessons from a good teacher. The boy drove the rest of the family crazy with his practicing, but for the first time he began to be less restless.

Eden, reluctant to get down to serious writing, began to accuse Alayne of nagging him when she tried to encourage him. She wanted to get away from Jalna, for the place was exerting an uneasy hold on her. Worse, she and Renny were unwillingly drawn to each other. He kissed her once, and although they both pretended it was only a brotherly kiss, each knew it was more. At last they confessed their love for each other, but both knew that they would never bow to it because Eden was Renny's brother.

Eden grew troublesome about working at his writing or anything else. When he was injured in a friendly family scuffle, Alayne nursed him tenderly, hoping to hurry him back to health so that they could leave Jalna and Renny. Pheasant also helped nurse Eden, spending hours in his room. When they fell in love, they too tried to fight it because Pheasant's husband was family. At last Eden was able to be about again. Finch, during one of his wanderings, saw Pheasant in Eden's arms. He ran to Piers and told him about his wife and brother. Piers went prepared to kill them, but Pheasant escaped to her father's house. Renny and Piers followed her there. Piers, deciding that she was his wife and therefore his responsibility, took her back to Jalna, where he locked her in her room and allowed no one to see her for weeks. Eden fled, leaving Pheasant and Alayne to face disgrace alone.

When Piers took Pheasant back to Jalna, Meg, refusing to stay in the same house with Pheasant, moved into an abandoned hut on the farm. After a few weeks, Maurice Vaughan went to see her and persuaded her to forgive him his old sin. Soon afterward they were married, trying to make up quickly for all the years they had lost. Alayne prepared to return to New York alone. There would be no divorce, no marriage to Renny. The scandal would be too much for the family — whose pattern would never change.

JANE EYRE

Type of work: Novel
Author: Charlotte Brontë (1816-1855)
Type of plot: Psychological romance
Time of plot: 1800
Locale: Northern England
First published: 1847

> *Principal characters:*
> JANE EYRE, an orphan
> MRS. REED, mistress of Gateshead Hall
> BESSIE LEAVEN, a nurse
> EDWARD ROCHESTER, owner of Thornfield
> ST. JOHN RIVERS, a young clergyman
> MARY, and
> DIANA RIVERS, his sisters

Critique:

Charlotte Brontë published *Jane Eyre* under the pseudonym of Currer Bell, a name chosen, she said, because it was neither obviously feminine nor masculine. But the emotions behind the book are purely feminine. Literary criticism may point to the extravagance, melodrama, and faulty structure of the novel, but lasting popularity is sufficient evidence of its charm and character for generations of readers. Charlotte Brontë wrote wisely when she cast her novel in the form of an autobiography. The poetry and tension of *Jane Eyre* marked a new development in adult romanticism, just as Jane herself brought to English fiction a new type of heroine, a woman of intelligence and passion.

The Story:

Jane Eyre was an orphan. Both her father and mother had died when Jane was a baby, and the little girl passed into the care of Mrs. Reed of Gateshead Hall. Mrs. Reed's husband, now dead, had been the brother of Jane Eyre's mother, and on his deathbed he had directed Mrs. Reed to look after the orphan as she would her own three children. At Gateshead Hall Jane knew ten years of neglect and abuse. One day a cousin knocked her to the floor. When she fought back, Mrs. Reed punished her by sending her to the gloomy room where Mr. Reed had died. There Jane lost consciousness. Furthermore, the experience caused a dangerous illness from which she was nursed slowly back to health by sympathetic Bessie Leaven, the Gateshead Hall nurse.

Feeling that she could no longer keep her unwanted charge in the house, Mrs. Reed made arrangements for Jane's admission to Lowood School. Early one morning, without farewells, Jane left Gateshead Hall and rode fifty miles by stage to Lowood, her humble possessions in a trunk beside her.

At Lowood, Jane was a diligent student, well-liked by her superiors, especially by Miss Temple, the mistress, who refused to accept without proof Mrs. Reed's low estimate of Jane's character. During the period of Jane's schooldays at Lowood an epidemic of fever caused many deaths among the girls. It resulted, too, in an investigation which caused improvements at the institution. At the end of her studies Jane was retained as a teacher. When Jane grew weary of her life at Lowood, she advertised for a position as governess. She was engaged by Mrs. Fairfax, housekeeper at Thornfield, near Millcote.

At Thornfield the new governess had only one pupil, Adele Varens, a ward of Jane's employer, Mr. Edward Rochester. From Mrs. Fairfax, Jane learned that Mr. Rochester traveled much and seldom came to Thornfield. Jane was pleased with the quiet country life, with the beautiful old house and gardens, the book-filled library, and her own comfortable room.

Jane met Mr. Rochester for the first time while she was out walking, going to his aid after his horse had thrown him. She found her employer a somber, moody man, quick to change in his manner toward her, brusque in his speech. He commended her work with Adele, however, and confided that the girl was the daughter of a French dancer who had deceived him and deserted her daughter. Jane felt that this experience alone could not account for Mr. Rochester's moody nature.

Mysterious happenings occurred at Thornfield. One night Jane, alarmed by a strange noise, found Mr. Rochester's door open and his bed on fire. When she attempted to arouse the household, he commanded her to keep quiet about the whole affair. She also learned that Thornfield had a strange tenant, a woman who laughed like a maniac and who stayed in rooms on the third floor of the house. Jane believed that this woman was Grace Poole, a seamstress employed by Mr. Rochester.

Mr. Rochester attended numerous parties at which he was obviously paying court to Blanche Ingram, daughter of Lady Ingram. One day the inhabitants of Thornfield were informed that Mr. Rochester was bringing a party of house guests home with him. In the party was the fashionable Miss Ingram. During the house party Mr. Rochester called Jane to the drawing-room, where the guests treated her with the disdain which they thought her humble position deserved. To herself Jane had already confessed her interest in her employer, but it seemed to her that he was interested only in Blanche Ingram. One evening while Mr. Rochester was away from home the guests played charades. At the conclusion of the game a gipsy fortune-teller appeared to read the palms of the lady guests. Jane, during her interview with the gipsy, discovered that the so-called fortune-teller was Mr. Rochester in disguise.

While the guests were still at Thornfield, a stranger named Mason arrived to see Mr. Rochester on business. That night Mason was mysteriously wounded by the strange inhabitant of the third floor. The injured man was taken away secretly before daylight.

One day Bessie Leaven came from Gateshead to tell Jane that Mrs. Reed, now on her deathbed, had asked to see her former ward. Jane returned to her aunt's home. The dying woman gave Jane a letter, dated three years before, from John Eyre in Madeira, who asked that his niece be sent to him for adoption. Mrs. Reed confessed that she had let him believe that Jane had died in the epidemic at Lowood. The sin of keeping from Jane news which would have meant relatives, adoption, and an inheritance had become a heavy burden on the conscience of the dying woman.

Jane went back to Thornfield, which she now looked upon as her home. One night in the garden Edward Rochester embraced her and proposed marriage. Jane accepted and made plans for a quiet ceremony in the village church. She wrote also to her uncle in Madeira, explaining Mrs. Reed's deception and telling him she was to marry Mr. Rochester.

Shortly before the date set for the wedding Jane had a harrowing experience. She awakened to find a strange, repulsive-looking woman in her room. The intruder tried on Jane's wedding veil and then ripped it to shreds. Mr. Rochester tried to persuade Jane that the whole incident was only her imagination, but in the morning she found the torn veil in her room. At the church, as the vows were being said, a stranger spoke up declaring the existence of an impediment to the marriage. He presented an affirmation, signed by the Mr. Mason who had been wounded during his visit to Thornfield. The document stated that Edward Fairfax Rochester had married Bertha Mason, Mr. Mason's sister, in Spanish Town, Jamaica, fifteen years before. Mr. Rochester admitted this fact; then he conducted the party to the third-story chamber at Thornfield. There they found the attendant Grace Poole and her charge, Bertha Rochester, a raving maniac. Mrs. Rochester was the woman Jane had seen in her room.

Jane felt that she must leave Thornfield at once. She notified Mr. Rochester and left quietly early the next morning, using all her small store of money for the coach fare. Two days later she was set down on the moors of a north midland shire. Starving, she actually begged for food. Finally she was befriended by the Reverend St. John Rivers and his sisters, Mary and Diana, who took Jane in and nursed her back to health. Assuming the name of Jane Elliot, she refused to divulge anything of her history except her connection with the Lowood institution. Reverend Rivers eventually found a place for her as mistress in a girl's school.

Shortly afterward St. John Rivers received from his family solicitor word that John Eyre had died in Madeira, leaving Jane Eyre a fortune of twenty thousand pounds. Because Jane had disappeared under mysterious circumstances, the lawyer was trying to locate her through the next of kin, St. John Rivers. Jane's identity was now revealed through her connection with Lowood School, and she learned, to her surprise, that St. John and his sisters were really her own cousins. She then insisted on sharing her inheritance with them.

When St. John decided to go to India as a missionary, he asked Jane to go with him as his wife—not because he loved her, as he frankly admitted, but because he admired her and wanted her services as his assistant. Jane felt indebted to him for his kindness and aid, but she hesitated to accept his proposal.

One night, while St. John was awaiting her decision, she dreamed that Mr. Rochester was calling her name. The next day she returned to Thornfield by coach. Arriving there, she found the mansion gutted—a burned and blackened ruin. Neighbors told her that the fire had broken out one stormy night, set by the madwoman, who died while Mr. Rochester was trying to rescue her from the roof of the blazing house.

Mr. Rochester, blinded during the fire, was living at Ferndean, a lonely farm some miles away. Jane Eyre went to him at once, and there they were married. For both, their story had an even happier ending. After two years Mr. Rochester regained the sight of one eye, so that he was able to see his first child when it was put in his arms.

JASON AND THE GOLDEN FLEECE

Type of work: Classical legend
Source: Folk tradition
Type of plot: Heroic adventure
Time of plot: Remote antiquity
Locale: Ancient Greece
First transcribed: Unknown

Principal characters:
JASON, Prince of Iolcus
KING PELIAS, his uncle
CHIRON, the Centaur who reared Jason
ÆETES, King of Colchis
MEDEA, his daughter

Critique:

The story of *Jason and the Golden Fleece* has been repeated in story and song for more than thirty centuries. Jason lived when great heroes lived and gods supposedly roamed the earth in human form. The story of the golden ram and his radiant fleece is read and loved by adults as it is by children. The story has been told in many different forms, but its substance remains unchanged.

The Story:

In ancient Greece there lived a prince named Jason, son of a king who had been driven from his throne by a wicked brother named Pelias. To protect the boy from his cruel uncle, Jason's father took him to a remote mountaintop where he was raised by Chiron the Centaur, whom many say was half man and half horse. When Jason had grown to young manhood, Chiron the Centaur told him Pelias had seized his brother's crown. Jason was instructed to go and win back his father's kingdom.

Pelias had been warned to beware of a stranger who came with one foot sandaled and the other bare. It happened that Jason had lost one sandal in a river he crossed as he came to Iolcus, where Pelias ruled. When Pelias saw the lad he was afraid and plotted to kill him. But he pretended to welcome Jason. At a great feast he told Jason the story of the golden fleece.

In days past a Greek king called Ath-

amas banished his wife and took another, a beautiful but wicked woman who persuaded Athamus to kill his own children. But a golden ram swooped down from the skies and carried the children away. The girl slipped from his back and fell into the sea, but the boy came safely to the country of Colchis. There the boy let the king of Colchis slaughter the ram for its golden fleece. The gods were angered by these happenings and placed a curse on Athamus and all his family until the golden fleece should be returned to Colchis.

As Pelias told Jason the story, he could see that the young prince was stirred, and he was not surprised when Jason vowed that he would bring back the golden fleece. Pelias promised to give Jason his rightful throne when he returned from his quest, and Jason trusted Pelias and agreed to the terms. He gathered about him many great heroes of Greece—Hercules, the strongest and bravest of all heroes; Orpheus, whose music soothed savage beasts; Argus, who with the help of Juno built the beautiful ship *Argo;* Zetes and Calais, sons of the North Wind, and many other brave men.

They encountered great dangers on their journey. One of the heroes was drawn under the sea by a nymph and was never seen again by his comrades. They visited Salmydessa where the blind King Phineus was surrounded by Harpies, loathsome creatures, with the faces of women and the bodies of vultures. Zetes and Calais chased the creatures across the skies, and the heroes left the old king in peace.

Phineus had warned the heroes about the clashing rocks through which they must pass. As they approached the rocks they were filled with fear, but Juno held the rocks back and they sailed past the peril. They rowed along the shore until they came to the land of Colchis.

Æetes, King of Colchis, swore never to give up the treasure, but Jason vowed that he and his comrades would do battle with Æetes. Then Æetes consented to yield the treasure if Jason would yoke to the plow two wild, fire-breathing bulls and sow a field with dragon's teeth. When a giant warrior sprang from each tooth, Jason must slay each one. Jason agreed to the trial.

Æetes had a beautiful daughter Medea, who had fallen in love with the handsome Jason, and she brewed a magic potion which gave Jason godlike strength;

thus it was that he was able to tame the wild bulls and slay the warriors. Æetes promised to bring forth the fleece the next day, but Jason saw the wickedness in the king's heart and warned his comrades to have the *Argo* ready to sail.

In the night Medea secured the seven golden keys that unlocked the seven doors to the cave where the golden fleece hung and led Jason to the place. Behind the seven doors he found a hideous dragon guarding the treasure. Medea's magic caused the dragon to fall asleep, and Jason seized the fleece. It was so bright that night seemed like day.

Fearing for her life, Medea sailed away from her father's house with Jason and the other heroes. After many months they reached their homeland, where Jason placed the treasure at the feet of Pelias. But the fleece was no longer golden. Pelias was wrathful and swore not to give up his kingdom. But in the night the false king died. Afterward Jason wore the crown and the enchantress Medea reigned by his side.

JAVA HEAD

Type of work: Novel
Author: Joseph Hergesheimer (1880-1954)
Type of plot: Period romance
Time of plot: 1840's
Locale: Salem, Massachusetts
First published: 1919

Principal characters:
GERRIT AMMIDON, a Yankee sea captain
TAOU YUEN, Gerrit's Chinese bride
NETTIE VOLLAR, Gerrit's former sweetheart
EDWARD DUNSACK, Nettie's uncle
JEREMY AMMIDON, Gerrit's father

Critique:

Java Head is a novel of colorful detail and romantic incident, its scene laid in a historic port town during the period when the clipper ship was making America the mistress of the seas. In this novel Hergesheimer recaptures the spirit of an era, and by placing the exotic Taou Yuen against a late Puritan background

he presents also a contrast of civilizations. One of the interesting features of the book is the fact that each chapter is written from the point of view of a different character.

The Story:

In Salem, Massachusetts, one spring

in the early 1840's, there was concern because the ship *Nautilus*, owned by Ammidon, Ammidon, and Saltonstone, was seven months overdue. The captain of the ship was young Gerrit Ammidon, son of Captain Jeremy Ammidon, senior partner of the firm. Nettie Vollar grew more disturbed as the weeks passed. On the day the *Nautilus* left Salem, her grandfather had ordered Gerrit from the house before he reached the point of announcing his love for Nettie and asking her to marry him. The old man's reason for his action had been that Nettie was an illegitimate child and, as such, did not deserve to be married and lead a normal life. His theory was that the girl had been placed on earth only as a punishment for her mother.

Old Jeremy Ammidon also awaited the return of the *Nautilus*, for Gerrit was the favorite of his two sons. The other son, William, was primarily a tradesman interested in making money. Old Jeremy and William clashed regularly over the kind of trade the firm was to take, the liberty to be given its captains in trading, and whether the ships of the firm should be replaced by the swift new clippers that were revolutionizing the Pacific trade. William had never told old Jeremy that the firm had two schooners engaged in carrying opium, a cargo the older man detested. The atmosphere at Java Head, the Ammidon mansion in Salem, was kept more or less in a state of tension because of the disagreements between the father and son. Rhoda Ammidon, William's cheerful and sensible wife, was a quieting influence on both men.

Not many days later the *Nautilus* was sighted. When it cast anchor off the Salem wharves, Gerrit asked that the Ammidon barouche be sent to carry him to Java Head. The reason for his request became clear when the carriage discharged at the door of the mansion not only Gerrit but also his Manchu wife, Taou Yuen. The sight of her resplendent clothes and lacquered face was almost too much for Gerrit's conservative New England family. Only William's wife was able to be civil; the father said nothing, and William declared that the painted foreign woman was an unpleasant surprise.

Gerrit's first difficulty came when he assured his family that the Chinese marriage ceremony which had united him with Taou Yuen was as binding as the Christian service of William and Rhoda. The people of Salem wished to look upon the Chinese noblewoman as a mistress rather than as a wife. Nor did they understand that Taou Yuen was from one of the finest families of China, as far removed from the coolies and trading classes of Chinese ports as the New Englanders themselves.

The first Sunday afternoon after the arrival of the *Nautilus* Edward Dunsack appeared to thank Gerrit Ammidon for bringing a chest from China for him. The sight of Taou Yuen stirred Dunsack, largely because he was homesick for China. When he left Java Head, his mind was filled with a sense of injustice that Gerrit Ammidon should have the Manchu woman as his bride instead of Edward Dunsack and that Gerrit had married the Chinese woman instead of Dunsack's niece, Nettie Vollar.

Back in port, Gerrit saw to the refitting of the *Nautilus*. He did not see Nettie Vollar. Then, on the Fourth of July, the Ammidons met Nettie on the street and took her back to Java Head for the evening, lest she be injured or insulted by rough sailors on the streets. She did not see Taou Yuen, however, for the Chinese woman had remained in her room during the day. When it was time for Nettie to return home, Gerrit escorted her. It was the first time they had been alone together since he had been ordered from her home months before. Gerrit returned to the Ammidon house realizing that he had done Nettie a great wrong when he married Taou Yuen.

The following morning misfortune

struck the Ammidons. Old Jeremy accompanied his son William down to the offices of the firm to inspect the specifications for two new clipper ships, and among some papers he discovered a bill of lading for one of the firm's two schooners engaged in the opium trade. His anger was roused to such an extent that his heart could not carry the strain. He collapsed and died in the office.

After the funeral, Gerrit, sick of the life ashore, took the *Nautilus* as his share in the estate, left the company, and prepared to return to sea as an independent trader. Even his wife had become unbearable to him since he had renewed his friendship with Nettie. Nevertheless, he determined to take Taou Yuen back with him and to establish their household in Shanghai, where he would no longer face the complications which arose from residence in Salem.

One day Edward Dunsack appeared at the Ammidon home to ask Gerrit to pay a call on his niece Nettie, who had been severely injured by a carriage. Gerrit left immediately, and Dunsack took the opportunity to attempt the seduction of Taou Yuen. Failing in his design, he poisoned her mind with an account of the love affair between his niece and Gerrit. In the meantime Gerrit, after a regretful interview with Nettie, had gone down to the *Nautilus* to regain his peace of mind.

The next day Taou Yuen was driven in the Ammidon carriage to pick up Rhoda Ammidon at the Dunsack home, where the latter had made a call on Nettie Vollar. Rhoda had already left. On an impulse Taou Yuen went into the house to see her rival. Angered because she thought Nettie commonplace and plain, Taou Yuen began to contemplate suffocating the girl. Suddenly Edward Dunsack, drug-crazed, entered the room and locked the door. Nettie fainted. When Taou Yuen repelled Edward, he threatened to strangle her so as to leave marks on her throat. To escape such disfiguration, forbidden by Confucius, Taou Yuen quickly swallowed some opium pills lying on the table beside the invalid Nettie's bed.

When help came a short time later, Taou Yuen was already unconscious. She died soon afterward. Edward Dunsack had gone mad.

Several days later, after the Christian burial of Taou Yuen, the *Nautilus* sailed from Salem harbor. It carried its young captain and his new wife, Nettie, to what they hoped would be a happier life.

JEAN-CHRISTOPHE

Type of work: Novel
Author: Romain Rolland (1866-1944)
Type of plot: Social chronicle
Time of plot: Late nineteenth and early twentieth centuries
Locale: Germany, France, Switzerland
First published: 1904-1912

> *Principal characters:*
> JEAN-CHRISTOPHE KRAFFT, a musician
> MELCHIOR, his father
> JEAN MICHEL, his grandfather
> LOUISA, his mother
> ANTOINETTE, a French girl
> OLIVIER, her brother
> GRAZIA, Jean-Christophe's friend

JEAN-CHRISTOPHE by Romain Rolland. Translated by Gilbert Cannan. By permission of the publishers, Henry Holt & Co., Inc. Copyright, 1910, 1911, 1913, 1938, by Henry Holt & Co., Inc.

Critique:

Jean-Christophe is a two-thousand-page novel originally published in ten volumes, the painstaking record of the artistic development of a musical genius. Romain Rolland set out to portray the adventures of the soul of his hero and succeeded magnificently; in addition he broke down the artistic barrier between France and Germany. The experiences of Jean-Christophe are those of every genius who turns from the past to serve the future. In 1915 Rolland was awarded the Nobel Prize for Literature, in great part for *Jean-Christophe.*

The Story:

Melchior Krafft was a virtuoso, his father Jean Michel a famous conductor. It was no wonder that Melchior's son, Christophe, should be a musician.

Louisa, Melchior's wife, was a stolid woman of the lower class. Her father-in-law had been furious at his son for marrying beneath him, but he was soon won over by the patient goodness of Louisa. It was fortunate that there was a strong tie between them, for Melchoir drank and wasted his money. Often the grandfather gave his little pension to Louisa because there was no money for the family.

Melchior by chance one day heard his three-year-old Christophe playing at the piano. In his drunken enthusiasm, Melchior conceived the idea of creating a musical prodigy. So began Christophe's lessons. Over and over he played his scales; over and over he practiced until he was letter perfect. Often he rebelled. Whipping only made him more rebellious, but in the end the piano always pulled him back.

His grandfather noticed that he would often improvise melodies as he played with his toys. Sitting in a different room, he would transcribe those airs and arrange them. Christophe showed real genius in composition.

At the age of seven and a half Christophe was ready for his first con-cert. Dressed in a ridiculous costume, he was presented at court as a child prodigy of six. He played works of some of the German masters and then performed with great success his own compositions gathered into an expensive privately printed volume, *The Pleasures of Childhood: Aria, Minuetto, Valse, and Marcia, Opus 1,* by *Jean-Christophe Krafft.* The grand duke was delighted and bestowed the favor of the court on the prodigy.

Before reaching his teens, Christophe was firmly installed as official second violinist in the court orchestra, where his father was concert master. Rehearsals, concerts, composition, lessons to give and take—that was his life. He became the mainstay of the family financially, even collecting his father's wages before Melchior could get his hands on them. All the other phases of his life were neglected; no one even bothered to teach him table manners.

When Melchior finally drowned himself, his death was a financial benefit to the Kraffts. But when Jean Michel died, it was a different matter. Christophe's two brothers were seldom home, and only Louisa and her musician son were left. To save money, they moved into a smaller, more wretched flat.

Meanwhile Christophe was going through a series of love affairs which always terminated unhappily because of his unswerving honesty and lack of social graces. In his early twenties he took Ada, a vulgar shop girl, for his mistress. Because of gossip, he found it much harder to get and keep pupils. When he dared to publish a criticism of the older masters, he lost his standing at court. He had almost decided to leave Germany.

At a peasant dance one night he protected Lorchen, a farm girl, from a group of drunken soldiers. In the ensuing brawl, one soldier was killed and two were seriously injured. With a warrant out for his arrest, Christophe escaped to

Paris.

Once in France, a country he greatly admired, Christophe found it difficult to acclimate himself. He met a group of wealthy and cynical Jews, Americans, Belgians, and Germans, but he judged their sophistication painful and their affectations boring. His compositions, although appreciated by a few, were not generally well received at first.

After a time, with increasing recognition, he found himself alternately praised and blamed by the critics. But he was noticed, and that was the important thing. Although he was received in wealthy homes and given complimentary tickets for theaters and concerts, he was still desperately poor.

At the home of the Stevens family, where he was kindly received, he instructed Colette, the coquettish daughter, and the younger, gentler Grazia, her cousin. Without falling in love with Colette, he was for a time her teacher and good friend. Grazia, who adored him, was only another pupil.

One night a blushing, stammering young man of letters was introduced to him. It was Olivier, who had long been a faithful admirer of Christophe's music. Christophe was immediately attracted to Olivier, although at first he was not quite sure why. Olivier's face was only hauntingly familiar.

It turned out that Olivier was the younger brother of Antoinette, a girl whose image Christophe cherished. Before he left Germany, a Jewish friend had given Christophe tickets for a box at the theater. Knowing no one to ask to accompany him, he went alone and in the lobby saw a French governess who was being turned away from the box office. Impulsively, Christophe took her in with him. The Grunebaums, the girl's employers, had expected to be invited also, and they were angry at the fancied slight. Antoinette was dismissed from their employ.

As she was returning to France, Christophe caught a glimpse of her on the train. That was all the contact he ever had with Antoinette. Now he learned that she had worn herself out by supporting Olivier until he could enter the École Normale. When he finally passed the entrance examinations, she had already contracted consumption, and she died before Christophe came to Paris.

Finding a real friend in Olivier, Christophe took an apartment with him. The house was only middle-class or less; but in that house and its inhabitants, and with Olivier's guidance, Christophe began to find the real soul of France. Away from the sophisticated glitter of Paris, the ordinary people lived calm and purposeful lives filled with the ideal of personal liberty.

Olivier became a champion of Christophe and helped establish his reputation in the reviews. Then some one, an important person, worked anonymously on Christophe's behalf. In a few years he found himself famous in France and abroad as the foremost composer of the new music.

Olivier's marriage to the shallow Jacqueline separated the two friends. In his eventful life Christophe made many more friends, but none so dear as Olivier. He did, however, discover his anonymous benefactor. It was Grazia, no longer in love with him and married to a secretary of the Austrian legation.

Jacqueline left Olivier, and he and Christophe became interested in the syndicalist movement. They attended a May Day celebration which turned into a riot. Olivier was fatally stabbed. After killing a soldier, Christophe fled the country.

During his exile in Switzerland, Christophe went through an unhappy love affair with Anna, the wife of a friend, and the consequent sense of guilt temporarily stilled his genius. But with the help of the now widowed Grazia, Christophe spent ten fruitful years in Switzerland.

When he returned to France, he was sought after and acclaimed. He was

vastly amused to find himself an established master, and even considered out
of date by younger artists.

Although Grazia and Christophe never
married, they remained steadfast and

consoling friends. Grazia died in Egypt,
far from her beloved Christophe. He
died in Paris. To the end, Christophe
was uncompromising, for he was a true
artist.

JENNIE GERHARDT

Type of work: Novel
Author: Theodore Dreiser (1871-1945)
Type of plot: Naturalism
Time of plot: The last two decades of the nineteenth century
Locale: Chicago and various other Midwestern cities
First published: 1911

Principal characters:
JENNIE GERHARDT
WILLIAM GERHARDT, her father
MRS. GERHARDT, her mother
SEBASTIAN GERHARDT, her brother
SENATOR BRANDER, Jennie's first lover
VESTA, Jennie's daughter
MRS. BRACEBRIDGE, Jennie's employer in Cleveland
LESTER KANE, a carriage manufacturer, Jennie's second lover
ROBERT KANE, Lester's brother
MRS. LETTY PACE GERALD, a widow, Lester's childhood sweetheart,
later his wife

Critique:

Jennie Gerhardt, like other of Dreiser's
novels, tells the story of a beautiful and
vital young girl who is beaten by the
forces of life. Jennie's nobility, her willingness to sacrifice herself for her family
and others, is part of the reason why she
finds herself cast off by society and vic-
timized by the accident of her humble
birth. The forces that defeat Jennie are
not malign or cruel (her seducers, for
example, do not toy with her cynically
and cast her aside); rather, these forces
are accidental and inevitable, yielding
the notion that all human life is diverted
from its purpose and its self-control by
the casual forces of nature. Jennie, in
Dreiser's terms, neither sins nor is over-
whelmingly sinned against; things simply
do not work out happily for the heroine
in Dreiser's naturalistic world. This novel
again demonstrates the inevitable play of
external forces that are stronger than
man's will or purpose. The full social and

economic details of the work provide an
interesting picture of urban life in the
Middle West at the end of the nineteenth
century.

The Story:

Jennie Gerhardt, the beautiful and
virtuous eighteen-year-old, was the eldest
of six children of a poor, hard-working
German family in Columbus, Ohio, in
1880. Her father, a glass blower, was ill,
and Jennie and her mother were forced
to work at a local hotel in order to provide for the younger children in the family. Jennie did the laundry for the kind
and handsome Senator Brander (he was
fifty-two at the time), and attracted his
eye. Senator Brander was kind to Jennie
and her family. When he was able to
keep Jennie's brother Sebastian out of
jail for stealing some needed coal from
the railroad, Jennie, full of gratitude,
allowed him to sleep with her. Senator

Brander, struck by Jennie's beauty, charm, and goodness, promised to marry her. He died suddenly, however, while on a trip to Washington.

Left alone, Jennie discovered that she was pregnant. Her father, a stern Lutheran, insisted that she leave the house, but her more understanding mother allowed her to return when her father, now in better health, left to find work in Youngstown. Jennie's child was a daughter whom she named Vesta. At Sebastian's suggestion, the family moved to Cleveland to find work. While her mother looked after Vesta, Jennie found a job as a maid in the home of Mrs. Bracebridge. One of Mrs. Bracebridge's guests, Lester Kane, the son of a rich carriage manufacturer, found Jennie temptingly attractive. When he tried to seduce Jennie, the girl, though greatly attracted to him, managed to put off his advances.

Mr. Gerhardt was injured in a glass-blowing accident and lost the use of both of his hands. Again, the family needed money badly, and Jennie decided to accept Lester's offer of aid for her family. The price was that she become his mistress, go on a trip to New York with him, and then allow him to establish her in an apartment in Chicago. Although Jennie loved Lester, she knew that he did not intend to marry her because his family would be horrified at such an alliance, but once again she sacrificed her virtue because she felt that her family needed the offered aid. After Jennie had become Lester's mistress, he gave her family money for a house. Jennie was afraid, however, to tell Lester about the existence of her daughter Vesta.

Jennie and Lester moved to Chicago and lived there. Her family began to suspect that, contrary to what Jennie had told them, she and Lester were not married. When Mrs. Gerhardt died, several years later, Jennie moved Vesta to Chicago and boarded the child in another woman's house. One night Jennie was called because Vesta was seriously ill,

and Lester discovered Vesta's existence. Although upset at first, when Jennie told him the story, Lester understood and agreed to allow Vesta to live with them. They soon moved to a house in Hyde Park, a middle-class residential district in Chicago. Mr. Gerhardt, now old and ill and willing to accept the situation between Jennie and Lester, also came to live with them and to tend the furnace and the lawn.

Although they were constantly aware of the increasing disapproval of Lester's family, Jennie and Lester lived happily for a time. Lester's father, violently opposed to the relationship with Jennie, whom he had never met, threatened to disinherit Lester if he did not leave her. Lester's brother Robert urged his father on and attempted to persuade Lester to abandon Jennie. Nevertheless, Lester felt that he owed his allegiance, as well as his love, to her, and he remained with her in spite of the fact that they were snubbed by most of Lester's society connections.

When Lester's father died, still believing that his son's relationship with Jennie demonstrated irresponsibility, he left Lester's share of the estate in trust with Robert. Lester was given three alternatives: he could leave Jennie and receive all his money; he could marry Jennie and receive only $10,000 a year for life, or he could continue his present arrangement with the knowledge that if he did not either abandon or marry Jennie within three years, he would lose his share of the money. Characteristically, Lester hesitated. He took Jennie to Europe, where they met Mrs. Letty Pace Gerald, a beautiful and accomplished widow who had been Lester's childhood sweetheart and who was still fond of him. In the meantime Robert had expanded the carriage business into a monopoly and eased Lester into a subordinate position. When Lester returned to Chicago, he decided to attempt to make an independent future for himself and Jennie. He put a good deal of money into a real estate deal and lost it. Mrs. Gerald also moved to Chicago in pursuit of Lester.

After old Mr. Gerhardt died, Jennie found herself in a difficult situation. Lester, out of the family business because of her, was finding it difficult to earn a living. Mrs. Gerald and Robert's lawyers kept pressing her to release him, claiming this suggestion was for his own economic and social good. Jennie, always altruistic, began to influence Lester to leave her. Before long both were convinced that separation was the only solution so that Lester could return to the family business. Finally Lester left Jennie. Later he set up a house and an income for her and Vesta in a cottage an hour or so from the center of Chicago.

Once more established in the family business, Lester married Mrs. Gerald. Six months after Lester had left Jennie, Vesta, a fourteen-year-old girl already showing a good deal of sensitivity and talent, died of typhoid fever.

Jennie, calling herself Mrs. Stover, moved to the city and adopted two orphan children. Five years passed. Jennie, although still in love with Lester, accepted her quiet life. At last she was able to cope with experience in whatever terms it presented itself to her, even though she had never been able to impose her will on experience in any meaningful way.

One night, Lester, having suffered a heart attack while in Chicago on some business matters, sent for Jennie; his wife was in Europe and could not reach Chicago for three weeks. Jennie tended Lester throughout his last illness. One day he confessed that he had always loved her, that he had made a mistake ever to permit the forces of business and family pressure to make him leave her. Jennie felt that his final confession, his statement that he should never have left her, indicated a kind of spiritual union and left her with something that she could value for the rest of her life. Lester died. Jennie realized that she would now be forced to live through many years that could promise no salvation, no new excitement—that would simply impose themselves upon her as had the years in the past. She was resolved to accept her loneliness because she knew there was nothing else for her to do.

Jennie went to see Lester's coffin loaded on the train. She realized then, even more clearly, that man was simply a stiff figure, moved about by circumstance. Virtue, beauty, moral worth could not save man; nor could evil or degeneracy. Man simply yielded and managed the best he could under the circumstances of his nature, the society, and the economic force that surrounded him.

JERUSALEM DELIVERED

Type of work: Poem
Author: Torquato Tasso (1544-1595)
Type of plot: Historical romance
Time of plot: Middle Ages
Locale: The Holy Land
First published: 1580-1581

Principal characters:
GODFREY DE BOUILLON, leader of the Crusaders
CLORINDA, a female warrior
ARGANTES, a pagan knight
ERMINIA, princess of Antioch
ARMIDA, an enchantress
RINALDO, an Italian knight
TANCRED, a Frankish knight

Critique:

Jerusalem Delivered is one of the great poems to come out of the Italian Renaissance, and since that time the work has remained a landmark of heroic literature. The treatment of the Crusades is highly romantic, with both God and Satan freely taking an active part and magicians, angels, and fiends frequently changing the course of events. The descriptions of the fighting are in the typical romantic, chivalric vein. The action is rapid, scene following scene in kaleidoscopic review. In all, we have here an absorbing tale.

The Story:

For six years the Crusaders had remained in the Holy Land, meeting with success. Tripoli, Antioch, and Acre were in their hands, and a large force of Christian knights occupied Palestine. Yet there was a lassitude among the nobles; they were tired and satiated with fighting. They could not generate enough warlike spirit to continue to the real objective of their Crusade, the capture of Jerusalem.

In the spring of the seventh year, God sent the Archangel Gabriel to Godfrey de Bouillon, ordering him to assemble all his knights and encouraging him to begin the march on Jerusalem. Obeying the Lord's command, Godfrey called a council of the great nobles and reminded them stirringly of their vows. When Peter the Hermit added his exhortations, the Crusaders accepted their charge, and all preparations were make to attack the Holy City.

Within the walls of Jerusalem the wicked King Aladine heard of the projected attack. At the urging of Ismeno the sorcerer he sent soldiers to steal the statue of the Virgin Mary, hoping to make the Christian symbol a palladium for Jerusalem. But next morning the statue had disappeared. Enraged when he could not find the culprit who had spirited away the statue, Aladine ordered a general massacre of all his Christian

subjects. To save her co-religionists, the beautiful and pure Sophronia confessed to the theft. Aladine had her bound to the stake. As her guards were about to light the fire, Olindo, who had long loved Sophronia in vain, attempted to save her by confessing that he himself had stolen the statue.

Aladine ordered them both burned. While they were at the stake, Sophronia admitted her love for Olindo. They were saved from burning, however, by the arrival of Clorinda, a beautiful woman warrior who knew that both were admitting the theft to save the other Christians from death. Released, Sophronia and Olindo fled from the city.

Clorinda was a great warrior who scorned female dress. On a previous campaign she had met Tancred, a mighty Christian noble, and Tancred had fallen in love with her; but she rejected his love. On the other hand, Erminia of Antioch had become enamored of Tancred when he had taken her city, but Tancred felt only friendship for her.

The Christians came within sight of Jerusalem. A foraging party encountered first a small force under Clorinda. She was so valorous that she defeated them.

The King of Egypt, whose army was advancing to the aid of Jerusalem, sent Argantes to parley with Godfrey. The Crusader chief haughtily rejected the overtures of the Egyptians, and Argantes angrily joined the infidel defenders of the Holy City. Although the Crusaders met with some initial successes, Argantes was always a formidable opponent.

Satan was annoyed at the prospect of the fall of Jerusalem. He induced Armida, an enchantress, to visit the Christian camp and tell a false story of persecution. Many of the knights succumbed to her wiles and eagerly sought permission to redress her wrongs. Godfrey was suspicious of her, but he allowed ten knights chosen by lot to accompany her. In the night forty others slipped away to join her, and she led the fifty to her castle where she changed them into fishes. Their loss was a great blow to Godfrey because the pagans were slaying many of his men.

Rinaldo, one of the Italian knights among the Crusaders, sought the captaincy of a band of Norwegian adventurers. Gernando, who sought the same post, quarreled with him, and in a joust Gernando was killed. For this breach of discipline Rinaldo was banished.

When Argantes challenged to personal combat any champion in the Crusaders' camp, Tancred was chosen to meet him. On the way to the fight, Tancred saw Clorinda and stopped to admire her. Otho, his companion, took advantage of his bemusement and rushed in ahead to the battle. Otho was defeated by Argantes and taken prisoner. Then Tancred, realizing what had happened, advanced to meet the pagan knight. Both men were wounded in the mighty, daylong duel. They retired to recuperate, agreeing to meet again in six days.

When Erminia heard of Tancred's wounds, she put on Clorinda's armor and went to his camp to attend him. He heard of her coming and waited impatiently, thinking his beloved Clorinda was approaching. But Erminia was surprised by the sentries, and in her maidenly timidity she ran away to take refuge with a shepherd.

When the supposed Clorinda did not arrive, Tancred went in search of her and came to the castle of Armida, where he was cast into a dungeon.

Godfrey received word that Sweno, Prince of Denmark, who had been occupying Palestine, had been surprised by pagan knights and killed with all his followers. The messenger announced that he had been divinely appointed to deliver Sweno's sword to Rinaldo. Although Rinaldo was still absent, Godfrey set out to avenge the Palestine garrison.

Godfrey and his army fought valiantly, but Argantes and Clorinda were fighters too powerful for the shaken Christians to overcome. Then Tancred and the fifty knights, who had been freed from Armida's enchantment, arrived to rout the pagans with great losses. Godfrey learned that the missing men had been liberated by Rinaldo. Peter the Hermit was then divinely inspired to foretell the glorious future of Rinaldo.

In preparation for the attack on Jerusalem the Christians celebrated a solemn mass on the Mount of Olives before they began the assault. Wounded by one of Clorinda's arrows, Godfrey retired from the battle while an angel healed his wound. The Christians set up rams and towers to break the defense of the city.

At night Clorinda came out of the city walls and set fire to the great tower by which the Christians were preparing to scale the wall. She was seen, however, by the Crusaders, and Tancred engaged her in combat. After he had run his sword through her breast, he discovered to his sorrow that he had killed his love. He had time to ask her pardon and baptize her before her death.

Godfrey was taken in a vision to heaven where he talked with Hugh, the former commander of the French forces. Hugh bade him recall Rinaldo, and Godfrey sent two knights to find the banished Italian. On the Fortunate Islands the messengers discovered the Palace of Armida where Rinaldo, having fallen in love with the enchantress, was dallying with his lady love. The sight of the two knights quickly reminded him of his duty. Leaving his love, he joined the besieging forces of Godfrey.

With the arrival of Rinaldo, the Christians were greatly heartened. Then the Archangel Michael appeared to Godfrey and showed him the souls of all the Christians who had died in the Crusades. With this inspiration, the Crusaders redoubled their efforts to capture Jerusalem.

The walls of the city were breached. Tancred met Argantes and killed him in single combat. Finally the victorious invaders stormed through the streets and sacked the Holy City. When the Egyptians arrived to help the pagan defenders of Jerusalem, they too were beaten and their king was slain by Godfrey. Armida, all hope gone, surrendered herself to Rinaldo, who had been the most valorous of the conquerors.

After the fighting was over, Godfrey and all his army worshipped at the Holy Sepulchre.

THE JEW OF MALTA

Type of work: Drama
Author: Christopher Marlowe (1564-1593)
Type of plot: Romantic tragedy
Time of plot: Fifteenth century
Locale: Malta
First presented: c. 1589

Principal characters:
BARABAS, a Jewish merchant
ABIGAIL, his daughter
ITHAMORE, a slave
THE GOVERNOR OF MALTA

Critique:

The Machiavellian character of Barabas dominates *The Jew of Malta;* the other characters are merely sketched in. The plot of the play seems to have come wholly from the fertile mind of Marlowe, whose exotic plots and romantic heroes set a pattern which was followed by subsequent Elizabethan playwrights, including Shakespeare. Mechanically, *The Jew of Malta* begins well, but it degenerates into an orgy of blood after the second act.

The Story:

Barabas, a Christian-hating merchant of Malta, received in his counting-house a party of merchants who reported the arrival of several vessels laden with wealth from the East. At the same time three Jews arrived to announce an important meeting at the senate.

The import of the meeting was that the Turkish masters of Malta had demanded tribute long overdue. The Turkish Grand Seignior had purposely let the payment lapse over a period of years so that the Maltese would find it impossible to raise the sum demanded. The Maltese had a choice of payment or surrender. The Christian governor of the island, attempting to collect the tribute within a month, decreed that the Jews would have to give over half of their estates or become Christians. All of the Jewish community except Barabas submitted to the decree of the governor in one way or another. The governor seized all of Barabas' wealth as punishment and had the Jew's house turned into a Christian convent.

Barabas, to avoid complete ruin, purposely failed to report part of his treasure hidden in the foundation of his house. Then he persuaded his daughter, Abigail, to pretend that she had been converted to Christianity so that she might enter the convent and recover the treasure. Abigail dutifully entered the nunnery as a convert and subsequently threw the bags of money out of the window at night to her waiting father.

Martin Del Bosco, vice-admiral of Spain, sailed into the harbor of Malta for the purpose of selling some Turkish slaves he had aboard his ship. The governor was reluctant to allow the sale because of the difficulties he was having with the Grand Seignior. Del Bosco, by promising military aid from Spain, persuaded the governor to defy the Turks and to permit the sale.

Barabas bought one of the slaves, an

1499

Arabian named Ithamore. During the sale, Barabas fawned upon Don Lodowick, the governor's son, and Don Mathias. He invited the two young men to his house and ordered Abigail, now returned from the convent, to show favor to both. In his desire for revenge, Barabas arranged with each young man, separately, to marry his daughter. He then sent forged letters to Don Lodowick and Don Mathias, and provoked a duel in which the young men were killed. Meanwhile Barabas trained his slave, Ithamore, to be his creature in his plot against the governor and the Christians of Malta.

Because of her father's evil intentions, Abigail returned to the convent. Barabas, enraged, sent poisoned porridge to the convent as his gesture of thanks on the Eve of St. Jacques, the patron saint of Malta. All in the convent were poisoned, and Abigail, before she died, confessed to Friar Jacomo, disclosing to him all that Barabas had done and all that he planned to do.

When the Turks returned to Malta to collect the tribute, the governor defied them and prepared for a siege of the island.

Meanwhile the friars, in violation of canon law, revealed the information they had gained from Abigail's confession. Barabas, again threatened, pretended a desire to become a convert and promised all of his worldly wealth to the friars who would receive him into the Christian faith. The greediness of the friars caused differences to arise among them; Barabas took advantage of this situation and with the help of Ithamore strangled a friar named Bernardine. He then propped up Bernardine's body in such a way that Friar Jacomo knocked it down. Observed in this act, Friar Jacomo was accused of the murder of one of his clerical brothers.

Ithamore met a strumpet, Bellamira, who, playing upon the slave's pride and viciousness, persuaded him to extort money from his master by threatening to expose Barabas. His master, alarmed by threats of blackmail, disguised himself as a French musician, went to the strumpet's house, and poisoned Bellamira and Ithamore with a bouquet of flowers.

Before their deaths, they managed to communicate all they knew to the governor, who, despite his preoccupation with the fortifications of Malta, threw Barabas into prison. By drinking poppy essence and cold mandrake juice, Barabas appeared to be dead. His body was placed outside the city. Reviving, he joined the Turks and led them into the city. As a reward for his betraying Malta, Barabas was made governor. He now turned to the conquered Maltese, offering to put the Turks into their hands for a substantial price.

Under the direction of Barabas, explosives were set beneath the barracks of the Turkish troops. Then Barabas invited the Turkish leaders to a banquet in the governor's palace, after planning to have them fall through a false floor into cauldrons of boiling liquid beneath. On signal, the Turkish troops were blown sky-high, but the Christian governor, who preferred to seize the Turkish leaders alive, exposed Barabas' scheme. The Jew of Malta perished in the trap he had set for the Turks.

THE JEWESS OF TOLEDO

Type of work: Drama
Author: Franz Grillparzer (1791-1872)
Type of plot: Historical tragedy
Time of plot: About 1195
Locale: Toledo and vicinity
First presented: 1872

THE JEWESS OF TOLEDO by Franz Grillparzer. Translated by Arthur Burkhard. By permission of the publishers, Register Press, Yarmouth Port, Mass. Copyright, 1953, by Register Press.

Principal characters:

ALFONSO VIII, King of Castile
ELEANOR OF ENGLAND, daughter of Henry II, his wife
ISAAC, the Jew
ESTHER, and
RACHEL, his daughters
MANRIQUE, Count of Lara, Almirante of Castile
DON GARCERAN, his son
DOÑA CLARA, lady in waiting to the queen

Critique:

Few writers since Shakespeare have managed to use the dramatic form with the poetic clarity and tragic force exhibited by the Austrian playwright, Franz Grillparzer. Usually the form is too much for the content or the content overburdens the play, giving to exposition the prominence that the expression of passion should have. Grillparzer avoids these faults, and contributes new psychological and moral perspectives which give his work its distinctive quality. *The Jewess of Toledo* tells of a monarch's lapse from duty because of his sudden passionate affection for a beautiful but vain young Jewess. With a simplicity of effect that defies analysis, Grillparzer makes the king's discovery of his own foolish bondage credible, without in the least detracting from the impression that Rachel, the Jewess, for all her faults, was undeniably charming and even to be pitied.

The Story:

Isaac, a Jew, found himself in the royal gardens of Toledo with his two daughters, Rachel and Esther. Realizing that the king was about to visit the gardens and that no Jews should be there during the royal outing, he urged his daughters to hurry from the gardens. Rachel laughingly refused, declaring that she would stay and see if the king was as young and handsome as she had heard. Isaac answered that Rachel was like her mother, for his second wife had found the Christians charming and had had eyes for nothing but fine clothing, jewels, and banquets. Esther, on the other hand, was like her mother, Isaac's first wife, who had been as good as she was poor.

Rachel sang and danced about while waiting for the king. She told her father that perhaps the monarch would find her charming, would pinch her cheek, and make the queen jealous. Isaac, frightened more than ever, hastened to leave the gardens with Esther.

When King Alfonso appeared, he invited the crowds to draw near him. He explained that the people had made him king while he had been still a child, that they had rallied around him in order to depose his uncle, a tyrant, and that they had then taught him the duties of one who would be just and good. Count Manrique turned to Queen Eleanor and told her of the people's affection for their ruler. The count declared that the present king was the noblest of all who ever ruled in Spain, turning aside petty criticism with wisdom and justice. The king, half jesting, replied that he might be an even better king if he were forced to overcome some fault. He suggested that the protection of the people might have kept him from developing the moral strength a ruler should have.

The king also urged everyone to enjoy the respite between wars, for the Moors were about to start another attempt to invade Spain. He called his wife's attention to the English-type garden he had ordered; he was disappointed that she had not noticed it.

A messenger, Don Garceran, the son of Count Manrique, brought news of the military preparations being made by Jussuf, the ruler of Morocco. Don Garceran was making his first appearance before the king since being assigned to a frontier post for having stolen into the women's quarters of the palace to view Doña Clara, his betrothed.

When the king suggested that the peasants pray to God for victory, Don Garceran replied that the churches were crowded, such was the religious zeal of the people. One sign of mistaken zeal, however, was the rough treatment sometimes given the Jews.

As the king was vowing to protect the Jews and all other of his subjects, he received word that a Jew and two girls were being pursued by the guards. Rachel came running to the group for protection. When Queen Eleanor refused to take her hands, she threw down her bracelet and necklace as ransom and clasped the king's knees. King Alfonso asked Esther, who had joined them, whether Rachel was always timid, and Esther replied that her sister was often too bold, too much the clown. The king, attracted by Rachel, ordered Don Garceran to shelter her in one of the garden houses until night, when there would be no danger of mob action.

After Don Garceran had escorted Isaac and his daughters to a shelter in the garden, the king accosted Don Garceran, questioning him about the family, praising the Jews for their long history, and begging for information about the art of casual love. Isaac, scolding his daughters for not attempting to leave, came from the garden house. He told Don Garceran that Rachel was her old self again, laughing and singing, and amusing herself by dressing herself as a queen with some masquerade costumes she had found.

Vowing Don Garceran and Isaac to silence, the king entered the garden house in time to observe Rachel, dressed as a queen, pretending to address a portrait of Alfonso which she had removed from its frame. In the role of the queen, Rachel accused the king in the portrait of having been attracted to the Jewess. The monarch interrupted this play and assured the frightened girl that he did indeed like her and that after the war he might ask for her. He asked her to return the portrait to its frame, but she refused. At that moment the arrival of the queen and the royal party forced the king to hide in another room. Count Manrique would have discovered him had not Don Garceran intercepted his father and, in the king's name, put an end to the search.

When the king reappeared after the queen's departure, he realized how he had already shamed himself because of the Jewess, and he asked her to return the portrait and leave with Don Garceran. After she had gone, he found that she had put her own portrait in the frame. The king was instantly stirred by the picture as if some magical spell surrounded it. In confusion, he first ordered his servant to go after Don Garceran and demand the return of his portrait; then he decided to go himself. He also asked about the Castle Retiro where a former king had kept a Moorish girl, but he could not copy such baseness. Finally, giving in to his passion, he went after Rachel.

Later, at Castle Retiro, Isaac was dealing with petitioners to the king, forcing them to pay heavily for the privilege of having their messages conveyed. Rachel complained that King Alfonso did not give enough time to her, and she was upset because her dallying with Don Garceran did not make him jealous. Esther arrived with the news that Queen Eleanor, Count Manrique, and other noblemen were joining in counsel, apparently plotting a revolt against the king. The king, already feeling guilty about neglecting the preparation for war, quickly left with Don Garceran for Toledo. Rachel, convinced that the king had never loved her, found no satisfaction in her perfumes and jewels.

Count Manrique and the noblemen, with the queen present, considered how to deal with the Jewess. Buying her off with gold was suggested, but the king had gold to give her. Imprisoning her would be useless, for the king had the power to release her. Finally, Count Manrique turned to the queen, who softly suggested that death was the answer, death for the woman who had broken the laws of God. Don Garceran interrupted the proceedings with an order from the king to dissolve the meeting. Count Manrique, dismissing the nobles, told them to be prepared for action. He then urged his son to join the rebellion, but Don Garceran refused. The count and the others left.

The king then prevailed upon the queen to listen to him. In a heartfelt conversation he admitted his guilt, calling attention to the changes of heart and mind that are inevitable for man. But the queen was reluctant to place the entire blame on her husband. She accused the girl of using shameless magic. In anger, King Alfonso defended Rachel as one who, for all her faults, had never pretended to a lifeless virtue that made life empty of warmth. He criticized the queen for encouraging his nobles to conspire against him.

The king discovered that the queen had left while he was talking. In growing apprehension he pursued the vassals to Castle Retiro. He arrived too late. The castle was in ruins, and Isaac and Esther told him that Rachel had been killed. To fire his desire for vengeance, the king viewed her body, but the sight of her reminded him not of her charm but of her wanton guile. Reaffirming his duty to the people, he forgave Count Manrique and the others when they appeared, swordless, to learn their punishment. He made his infant son king, with the queen as regent, and set forth for war against the Moors. Esther, at first cynical about the quick atonement of the Christian king, was appalled to find that her father was more concerned about his gold than he was over the tragic event that had involved them all. She confessed that she, her father, and Rachel were as guilty as the Christians.

JOANNA GODDEN

Type of work: Novel
Author: Sheila Kaye-Smith (1888-   )
Type of plot: Domestic realism
Time of plot: Early twentieth century
Locale: Rural England
First published: 1921

> Principal characters:
> JOANNA GODDEN, a wealthy landowner
> ELLEN GODDEN, her younger sister
> ARTHUR ALCE, Joanna's perennial suitor
> MARTIN TREVOR, Joanna's betrothed
> ALBERT HILL, Joanna's betrayer

Critique:

Joanna Godden is the powerful story of a strong and vibrant woman who ruled her sister and her farm with an iron hand. She herself, however, was often bewildered by emotions she did not understand. When tragedy involved her, she did not let it ruin her as it might have lesser women. She simply marshaled all her forces and went to meet it. That was

Joanna's way. The novel is also notable for its atmosphere of the English countryside in all weathers and seasons.

The Story:

After her father's funeral, Joanna Godden took immediate command of her sister Ellen and of the prosperous farm, Little Ansdore. She had always had many notions about making the farm even more productive, and she proposed now to execute these ideas, even though her neighbors and her advisers thought her a stubborn and foolish woman. Her perennial suitor, Arthur Alce, stuck by her, although he knew he could never change Joanna's mind about the farm or about accepting him as a husband.

In addition to the farm, her sister Ellen consumed much of Joanna's energy. Ellen must be a lady. To this end she was sent to school and humored in many other ways. But Joanna was the boss. No matter how much she babied Ellen, Joanna still made all decisions for her. Ellen was pliable, but she secretly planned for the day when she could escape her sister's heavy hand.

Little Ansdore prospered under Joanna. She shocked her neighbors by painting her house and wagons in bright colors and by appearing in loud clothing and jewels as soon as the period of mourning was over. In spite of their distrust of her, they were forced to admire her business acumen. Many men failed while she accumulated money in the bank. Through it all, Arthur stood by her and ran her errands. Once she felt stirrings of passion for one of her farm hands, but she quickly subdued the feeling because the ignorant lad was unsuitable. Joanna knew vaguely that she was missing something every woman wanted, something she did not completely understand but still longed for.

When Joanna met Martin Trevor, the son of a neighboring squire, she knew almost at once that Martin was the kind of man she had waited for. Although they were at first antagonistic, they soon were drawn together in real love and announced their engagement. Joanna was happy; Martin made her feel she was a woman first and a successful farmer second. The sensation was novel for Joanna. Martin's father and clergyman brother accepted her, in spite of a social position lower than theirs. Poor Arthur Alce grieved to lose her, even though

he had never possessed more than her friendship. He sincerely wished her happiness.

The only thing that dimmed their happiness was Joanna's insistence upon waiting for the wedding until there should be a slack time on the farm. Martin knew that if he gave in to her he would forever play second fiddle to Ansdore. On a walk, one rainy day, he begged her to marry him at once, both to please him and to show him that he was first in her heart. She refused, but at home a few nights later she knew that she must give in, for herself as well as for Martin. When she hurried to his home to see him the next day, she found Martin gravely ill. He had not been strong and the walk in the rain had caused a serious lung congestion. Joanna, realizing that her happiness was not to last, felt no surprise when Martin died. Her grief was so deep that she could feel nothing, only numbness. She felt that she had missed the only real happiness of her life.

The farm claimed her once more, and to it she gave all her energy and hope. Ellen also felt Joanna's will. Seventeen and finished with school, she was a lady. But Joanna was not pleased with her. Ellen had more subdued taste than Joanna, and the two girls clashed over furnishings, clothing, manners, and suitors for Ellen. Ellen usually submitted, but her one ambition was to get out from under Joanna's domination. Marriage seemed her only course. When Joanna began to ask Arthur to escort Ellen various places so that the young girl would not be so bored, Ellen thought it would be a good joke to take Arthur away from Joanna. However, Joanna herself thought a match between Ellen and Arthur would be a good thing. Unknown to Ellen, she asked Arthur to marry her sister. Arthur protested that he loved and would always love Joanna. She, in her usual practical way, overrode his objections and insisted that he marry Ellen. Finally he proposed to Ellen and was accepted. Ellen believed that she had stolen her sister's lover.

At first Ellen was happy with Arthur, for she was genuinely fond of him, but she resented his continuing to run errands for Joanna. She attributed these acts to Joanna's domineering ways, never realizing that her husband still loved her sister. Because Ellen also resented not meeting any of the gentlefolk of the area, Joanna arranged for her to meet Squire Trevor, Martin's father. It was an unfortunate meeting. Ellen became infatuated with the old man, left Arthur, and followed the squire to Dover. When she asked for a divorce, Arthur refused. Joanna was alternately furious with Ellen for her immorality and sorry for her heartbreak. At last Ellen went home to Little Ansdore. Joanna took her in and treated her like a little girl again.

When a neighboring estate, Great Ansdore, was put on the market, Joanna bought it. Her triumph was now complete; she was the wealthiest farmer in the area. New power went with the land. She chose the rector for the village church and in other ways acted as a country squire. But she still longed for Martin; or perhaps only for love. At any rate, when Arthur refused to stay after Ellen came home, Joanna for the first time saw him as a man she might love. Too sensible to risk more trouble from that quarter, however, she brushed off his goodbye kiss and turned her mind back to Ansdore.

After a time Arthur was killed in a hunting accident at his new home. His will, leaving his old farm to Joanna, made Ellen dependent on her sister as before. Ellen was furious, but Joanna could see no harm in Arthur's having left his money to his friend rather than to his faithless wife. Meanwhile Joanna would take care of Ellen, who would no doubt marry again.

Time began to take its toll of Joanna. Following her doctor's advice, she combined a business trip and a vacation. During that time she met Albert Hill, a young man thirteen years her junior. Thinking herself in love with Albert, Joanna the strong, the moral, the domineering, gave herself to the young man. They planned to marry, but Joanna, on second thought, realized that she did not love Albert, could never marry him. Learning that she was pregnant, she confessed to Ellen, who demanded that she marry Albert to protect their family name. But Joanna wanted her baby to grow up in happiness and peace, not in the home of parents who did not love each other. She would sell Ansdore and go away. As she made her plans, Martin's face came back to her and gave her strength. He would have approved. The past seemed to fuse with the years ahead. Joanna Godden, her home, her sister, her good name, and her lover all gone, still faced the years with courage and with hope.

JOHN BROWN'S BODY

Type of work: Poem
Author: Stephen Vincent Benét, (1898-1943)
Type of plot: Historical romance
Time of plot: 1858-1865
Locale: The United States
First published: 1928

Principal characters:
JACK ELLYAT, a soldier from Connecticut
CLAY WINGATE, a soldier from Georgia
LUKE BRECKINRIDGE, a Southern mountaineer
MELORA VILAS, Jack Ellyat's beloved

JOHN BROWN'S BODY by Stephen Vincent Benét. By permission of Brandt & Brandt and the publishers, Rinehart & Co., Inc. Copyright, 1927, 1928, by Stephen Vincent Benét.

SALLY DUPRÉ, Clay Wingate's fiancée
LUCY WEATHERBY, Sally's rival
SHIPPY, a Union spy
SOPHY, a Richmond hotel employee

Critique:

John Brown's Body, which won the Pulitzer Prize for 1929, tells, in free and formal verse, the tragic story of the Civil War and its effects upon the nation. Benét achieves an effective counterpoint by weaving several small plots concerned with fictional characters into the main plot which we know as the actual history of the time. He manipulates his characters so that important phases of the war are interfused with his minor plots, and the two are carried forward simultaneously. His re-creation of the atmosphere of a burgeoning, adolescent United States is excellent.

The Story:

Jack Ellyat, a Connecticut youth, had premonitions of trouble as he walked with his dog in the mellow New England Indian summer. He and his family were Abolitionists. The influence of Emerson and Thoreau was felt in Concord, where they talked about an ideal state. But in Boston Minister Higginson and Dr. Howe waited for reports of a project planned for Harper's Ferry. In Georgia young Clay Wingate also received a premonition of impending disaster and great change.

John Brown, rock-hard fanatic, believing he was chosen by God to free the black man in America, led his troop of raiders to seize the United States arsenal at Harper's Ferry, Virginia. The first man killed in the fracas was Shepherd Heyward, a free Negro. The South was alarmed. Federal troops under Robert E. Lee subdued the Brown party in fifteen minutes; all was ended but the slow, smoldering hates and the deaths to come.

At Wingate Hall in Georgia all was peaceful. Sally Dupré and Clay Wingate were expected to marry. When Cudjo, the major-domo of the Wingate plantation, heard of the Harper's Ferry raid and John Brown, he opined that the Negro's business was not the white man's business. In Connecticut Mrs. Ellyat prayed for John Brown.

Brown was tried at Charles Town, Virginia. During the trial he denied the complicity of anyone but himself and his followers in the raid. He insisted that he had done what he thought was right. A legend grew around his name and mushroomed after he was hanged. Songs were sung. John Brown's body rested in its grave, but his spirit haunted the consciences of North and South alike.

Fort Sumter surrendered, and the Confederate States of America elected gaunt, tired Jefferson Davis president. Lank, sad-faced Abraham Lincoln, the frontier wit and small-time politician, was President of the United States. He ordered conscription of fighting men. Clay Wingate, loyal to Dixie, joined the Black Horse Troop and rode away to the war. Jack Ellyat marched off with the Connecticut volunteers.

Raw soldiers of North and South met at Bull Run under the direction of Generals McDowell, Johnston, and Beauregard. Congressmen and their ladies drove out from Washington to watch the Union victory. While they watched, the Union lines broke and retreated in panic. A movement to treat with the Confederacy for peace got under way in the North. Lincoln was alarmed, but he remained steadfast.

Jack Ellyat was mustered out after Bull Run. Later he joined the Illinois volunteers in Chicago and became known as "Bull Run Jack." Near Pittsburg Landing, in Tennessee, he lost his head and ran during a surprise attack. He was captured but escaped again during a night march. Hungry and worn out,

Jack arrived at the Vilas farm, where he stayed in hiding and fell in love with Melora Vilas. At last he left the farm to seek the manhood he had lost near Pittsburg Landing, but not before he had got Melora with child. He was recaptured soon afterward.

Meanwhile Clay Wingate returned to Georgia on leave. At Wingate Hall the war seemed far away, for the successful running of the Union blockade of Southern ports made luxuries still available. Lucy Weatherby, a Virginian whose sweetheart had been killed at Bull Run, attended a dance at Wingate Hall and replaced Sally Dupré in Clay's affections. Spade, a slave on the nearby Zachary plantation, escaped that same night.

New Orleans was captured. Davis and Lincoln began to bow under the burdens of the war. McClellan began his Peninsular campaign. Lee inflicted defeat after defeat on the Army of the Potomac. Jack Ellyat was sent to a prison in the deep South. The fortunes of the Union were at their lowest ebb after the Confederate victory at the Second Manassas, and the spirit of John Brown was generally invoked by editors and preachers. Lincoln issued the Emancipation Proclamation. In the meantime, Spade made his way north and swam across a river to freedom, but when he arrived in the land of the free he was railroaded into a labor gang. McClellan was relieved by Burnside, who, in turn, was relieved by Hooker, as commander of the Army of the Potomac. Jack Ellyat, sick, was returned to the North in an exchange of prisoners of war.

Slowly the Confederacy began to feel the effects of the blockade and the terrible cost of war. Clay Wingate thought of his next leave—and of Lucy Weatherby. Jack Ellyat spent the dark winter of 1862-63 convalescing at his home in the cold Connecticut hills. He had been assigned to the Army of the Potomac as soon as his recovery was complete. In Tennessee, Melora Vilas gave birth to a baby boy.

Grant and Sherman led the Union forces to victory in the West; Vicksburg was surrounded. Hunger and anti-inflation riots broke out in Richmond. America, meanwhile, was expanding. New industries sprang up in the North, and the West was being developed. In Richmond, Shippy, a Union spy posing as a peddler, promised Sophy, a servant at the Pollard Hotel, to bring her some perfume from the North. Sophy knew that Clay Wingate and Lucy Weatherby had stayed together in the hotel. Luke Breckinridge, Sophy's rebel suitor, was a member of a patrol that stopped Shippy to search him. When they found incriminating papers in his boots, Luke gloated, for he was jealous of Shippy.

Stonewall Jackson was killed by his own pickets, and Lee, desperate for provisions, invaded the North. Jack Ellyat was in the Union army that converged on Gettysburg and was wounded during a battle there. After three days of bloody fighting at Gettysburg, Lee fell back to Virginia. Then Vicksburg surrendered. Defeated, the South continued to hang on doggedly. Sheridan marched through the Shenandoah Valley and left it bare and burned. Petersburg was besieged. Luke, along with thousands of other rebel troops, deserted from the Confederate Army, and when he headed back toward his laurel-thicket mountains he took Sophy with him. Melora and her father, John Vilas, traveled from place to place in search of Jack Ellyat; they became a legend in both armies.

General Sherman captured Atlanta and marched on to the sea. During Sherman's march, Wingate Hall caught fire accidentally and burned to the ground. Clay Wingate was wounded in a rear-guard action in Virginia. The war came to an end when Lee surrendered to Grant at Appomattox.

Spade, who had gone from the labor gang into the Union Army and who had been wounded at the Petersburg crater, hired out as a farm laborer in

Cumberland County, Pennsylvania. Clay Wingate returned to his ruined home in Georgia, where Sally Dupré was waiting. And in Connecticut Jack Ellyat heard stories of strange gipsy travelers who were going from town to town looking for a soldier who was the father of the child of the woman who drove the creaking cart. One day he was standing beneath the crossroads elms when he saw a cart come slowly up the hill. He waited. The woman driving was Melora.

JOHN HALIFAX, GENTLEMAN

Type of work: Novel
Author: Dinah Maria Mulock (Mrs. George Craik, 1826-1887)
Type of plot: Domestic realism
Time of plot: Turn of the nineteenth century
Locale: Rural England
First published: 1857

> Principal characters:
> JOHN HALIFAX, one of Nature's gentlemen
> URSULA, his wife
> GUY, their oldest son
> MAUD, a daughter
> ABEL FLETCHER, John's benefactor
> PHINEAS FLETCHER, his invalid son
> LORD RAVENEL, a landowner

Critique:

The story of John Halifax is one depicting the simple pleasures of lower middle-class life in rural England. In the book there is also a plea that a man be judged by his merits, not by his social class or his birth. But primarily the story is one of simple domesticity, of the real love that exists among members of a simple family who place the happiness and security of others above themselves. The theme was common among nineteenth-century authors, one that found immediate reception from readers who were slowly awakening to a new social order. Shortly after its publication the book was translated into French, German, Italian, Russian, and Greek.

The Story:

When Phineas Fletcher and his father, Abel, first saw John Halifax, they were immediately struck with his honest face and worthy character. For although the boy was only fourteen and an orphan, he would accept help from no one. Instead, he preferred to make his own way, even though it meant that he was always half-starved. Phineas, just sixteen, and an invalid, would have enjoyed having John for a companion, but Abel Fletcher, a wealthy Quaker, put the boy to work in his tannery. Although Abel was a real Christian and wanted to help others, he knew that the boy would be better off if he helped himself. Then, too, there was a class distinction between Phineas and John that even Abel could not entirely overlook.

Phineas and John became good friends, the orphan being the only friend Phineas ever loved as a brother. John rose rapidly in the tannery because of his honesty and his willingness to work at any job. He also had the ability to handle men, an ability ably proved when a hungry mob would have burned down the Fletcher home and the mill which the Quaker owned. John arranged to have the workers get wheat for their families, and from then on they were loyal to him through any crisis.

When they were in their early twenties, Phineas and John took a cottage in the country so that Phineas might have the advantage of the country air. While there they met a lovely girl, Ursula March, who had taken her dying father to the same spot. John was from the first attracted to the modest girl, but since she was a lady he felt that he could not tell her of his feelings. After the death of her father, it was learned that she was an heiress, and to John even more unattainable. However, John knew himself to be a gentleman, even if others did not, and at last circumstances brought him an opportunity to let her know his heart. When Ursula saw his true character and gladly married him, everyone was shocked but Phineas. Ursula's kinsman, a dissolute nobleman, refused to give her her fortune, and John would not go to court to claim the fortune, as was his legal right as Ursula's husband.

After the death of Abel Fletcher, Phineas lived with John and Ursula and their children, the oldest of whom was a lovely blind girl. Abel had made John a partner in the tannery, and since John did not like the tan-yard and also since it was losing money, he sold it and put the money into the operation of the mill. Times were often hard during the next few years, but finally, for political reasons Ursula's kinsman released her fortune to John. After settling a large amount on his wife and children, he used the rest to lease a new mill and expand his business interests. His hobby was a steam engine to turn the mill, and before long he began to see his project materialize. The family moved to a new home in the country and lived many long years there in peace and happiness. John, becoming influential in politics, used his power by choosing honorable men for office. He made some powerful enemies too, but his concern was only for the right. During this time his income grew until he was a very wealthy man. He continued to use his money to help others.

The steam engine, built and put into operation, gave John new advantages, but he provided generously for his workmen so that they would not suffer because of the machine. Then tragedy struck the family. Shortly after the birth of their last child, a daughter, the blind child was taken by death. It was a sorrow from which John never completely recovered. The years brought other troubles to his household. Two of his sons loved the same girl, the governess of their little sister. The brothers had a bitter quarrel, and the loser, who was the oldest son, Guy, left home and went abroad, almost breaking his mother's heart. After two or three years they learned that Guy had almost killed a man in Paris and had fled to America. From that time on, Ursula aged, for Guy was her favorite son.

Shortly afterward, John learned from Lord William Ravenel that that nobleman was in love with the youngest daughter, Maud. Lord Ravenel was not only the son of a worldly family; he himself had led a useless and sometimes wild life. John would not listen to the man's pleas, and Lord Ravenel, agreeing that he was unworthy of her, left without telling Maud of his love. But John was to revise his opinion somewhat when, after the death of his father, Lord Ravenel gave up his inherited fortune to pay his father's debts. After this incident Lord Ravenel was not heard from for many years. Maud did not marry. Her parents knew that she had never lost her affection for Lord Ravenel, although she did not know that he had returned her feelings.

Years passed. The married children gave John and Ursula grandchildren. John could have had a seat in Parliament, but he rejected it in favor of others. He continued to do good with his money and power, even when suffering temporary losses. And always he longed for his lost blind child, just as Ursula longed for her missing oldest son. Their own love grew even deeper as they reached their twilight years. John often suffered attacks that left him gasping in pain and breathlessness, but in order to spare his family any unnecessary worry he kept this information from all but Phineas.

Then came wonderful news: Guy was coming home. All of the family rejoiced, Ursula more than any other. They had six anxious months when he did not appear and his ship was not accounted for, but at last he arrived. He had been shipwrecked and lost, but had eventually made his way home. With him was Lord Ravenel, who had gone to America after being rejected by John. Both men had done well there, but had lost everything in the shipwreck. In their happy reunion, the money seemed of little importance. John knew now that Lord William Ravenel had proved himself worthy of Maud,

and the two lovers were at last allowed to express their love for each other. Guy, too, began to show interest in a childhood friend, and another wedding in the family seemed likely.

John felt that his life was now complete, his peace and happiness being broken only by longing for his dead child. He was soon to join her. One day he sat down to rest, and so his family found him in the peaceful sleep of death. That night, as she sat by her husband's body, Ursula must have felt that she could not lose him, for the children and Phineas found her lying dead beside her husband. They were buried side by side in the country churchyard.

JOHN INGLESANT

Type of work: Novel
Author: Joseph Henry Shorthouse (1834-1903)
Type of plot: Historical-philosophical romance
Time of plot: Seventeenth century
Locale: England and Italy
First published: 1881

Principal characters:

JOHN INGLESANT, an Englishman interested in spiritual affairs
EUSTACE INGLESANT, his materialistic twin brother
FATHER ST. CLARE, a Jesuit and John's mentor
CHARLES I, King of England, who used John's services as an agent
LAURETTA CAPECE, John's Italian wife
CARDINAL CHIGI, John's Italian patron

Critique:

John Inglesant, a philosophical and historical romance, was done, according to its author, in the style of the great American writer of romances, Nathaniel Hawthorne. In all literature there is probably no better picture of the complicated political and ecclesiastical affairs in England during the stormy years of the reign of Charles I and the ensuing Civil War. In this novel many of the historical personages of the time—King Charles, Archbishop Laud, John Milton, Thomas Hobbes, and others—make their appearance, adding to the realism of the story and demonstrating the parts they played in seventeenth-century England. While Shorthouse, in his author's introduction

to the second edition, laid the greatest emphasis on the philosophical content of the novel, the modern reader is likely to find the historical aspects considerably more important and certainly more interesting than the nebulous philosophical gropings adumbrated in the story.

The Story:

The family of Inglesant had long been loyal to the British crown, which had conferred lands and honors upon it, and yet the family also had strong leanings toward the Roman Catholic Church. Such inclinations were dangerous during the sixteenth and seventeenth centuries, when the whole of England was forced to

1510

change religions several times, according to the monarch who sat on the throne. In 1622 two sons were born to the family, twins whose mother died at their birth. One was named Eustace, after his father; the other, born a few minutes later and therefore the younger son of the family, was named John.

In boyhood the twins saw little of one another. Eustace, the older, was given a worldly training, for his father, outwardly conforming to the Anglican Church under James I and Charles I, wished him to make a place for himself at court. The younger son, John, was given bookish training in the classics and philosophy by various tutors. At the age of fourteen, John was placed under the tutelage of Father St. Clare, who was in England on a political and ecclesiastical mission for his order. The priest saw in the highly intelligent and cultured young lad the prospects of a fine instrument that his order might use; in addition, he felt that the boy deserved the training which would make him fitted for that unquestioning discipline of the highest order, as the Jesuits saw it: the discipline that is enforced from within the individual but controlled from without.

After several years of study and training, John Inglesant became a page in the train of the queen at the court of Charles I. Father St. Clare had sent him to court that he might come to the attention of the Roman Catholic nobles and serve to further the interests of the Roman Church in England.

As the country became more and more troubled, and civil war threatened because of rivalry between the Puritans and the adherents to the crown and the Anglican Church, the Roman Catholics felt themselves in a rather strong position with the king and everyone loyal to him. It was the dream of Father St. Clare, as a member of the Society of Jesus, to return England to the domination of Rome. With that end in view, he did all he could to aid the crown against the Puritans. Because John Inglesant, who came from a family long noted for its loyalty to the king, was active as an agent between Roman Catholic leaders and the crown, he was often employed on secret missions by the king. Father St. Clare, who saw Inglesant as having greater value as an Anglican communicant with papist leanings, advised the young man against conversion to the Roman Church. Inglesant, puzzled, followed his mentor's wishes.

When fighting broke out between the Cavaliers and the Puritans, Inglesant spent much of his time on missions for the king and Father St. Clare. Eustace Inglesant, after marrying a rich woman some ten years his senior, believed the king's cause doomed to failure and left England for France. John Inglesant was sent on a secret mission to Ireland, where Lord Glamorgan was attempting to raise an Irish army to aid the royal cause in England. From Ireland, young Inglesant was sent to bear tidings of imminent relief to the royal garrison at Chester, which was under siege.

Inglesant reached Chester and gave his message to Lord Biron, the commander. Weeks went by, but the relief did not appear. At last the garrison learned that the king had been forced to deny any part in the plan for an Irish invasion of England, because of popular outcry against the project. Chester was given up to the Puritans, and Inglesant, wishing to protect his monarch, permitted himself to be sent to London as a prisoner charged with treason.

Weeks turned into months; still Inglesant languished in prison. Meanwhile the Puritans were trying to implicate the king in the charge against Inglesant. Finally the king's forces were utterly defeated and Charles I was taken prisoner. In an effort to make him give evidence against the king, Inglesant was condemned and actually taken to be executed, but, true to his Jesuit training, he remained steadfast.

Through the good offices of Father St. Clare, Inglesant was released after the beheading of Charles I. One day Eustace Inglesant, who had returned to England

1511

under the protection of his wife's Puritan kinsmen, brought his brother's pardon to the Tower of London. Immediately, the two brothers set out for the estate of Eustace's wife.

Eustace, in the meantime, had been warned by an astrologer that his life was in danger, and he was murdered during the journey by an Italian, an enemy whom he had encountered while traveling in Italy years before. John Inglesant, after a period of sickness and recuperation spent at his sister-in-law's estate, left for France, where he hoped to find Father St. Clare and to gather information about his brother's murderer, whom he had resolved to kill in revenge.

Arriving in France, he was not immediately successful in finding Father St. Clare. In the interval he tried to evaluate his spiritual life. A Benedictine acquaintance tried to encourage him to enter that order, but Inglesant felt that his spiritual answers did not lie in that direction. He believed that somehow he had been singled out by heaven to find salvation more independently. When he finally found Father St. Clare, the priest told him to go to Rome and there continue his spiritual search under the protection of the Jesuits, who were indebted to him for the many missions he had undertaken in their cause.

On the way to Rome, a journey taking several months, Inglesant stopped many times. He spent several weeks in Siena as a guest of the Chigi family. One of the Chigis was a cardinal who had hopes of being elected pope when the incumbent died. From Siena, Inglesant journeyed to Florence. There he met Lauretta Capece, with whom he fell in love.

After his eventual arrival in Rome, Inglesant was sent to the Duke of Umbria on a mission by influential Jesuits who wished the nobleman to turn his lands over to the Papal See after his death. His mission accomplished, Inglesant married Lauretta Capece. He returned to Rome as a temporary aide to Cardinal Chigi during the conclave to elect a new pope. The cardinal was elected. Inglesant retired to an estate given to him by the Duke of Umbria.

Inglesant and his wife lived in Umbria for several years, until a great plague broke out in Naples. Inglesant went to that city in an effort to save his brother-in-law, who had been in hiding there. In Naples, also, he found his brother's murderer; the man had become a monk after having been beaten and blinded by a mob. Now, with his brother's murderer in his power, Inglesant had lost his desire for revenge. In company with the blind monk, he continued his search and finally discovered his dying brother-in-law. After the sick man had died, Inglesant returned home, only to learn that his family had been wiped out by the plague.

Once again he journeyed to Rome in search of spiritual consolation, but because of his independent attitudes he got into serious trouble with the Inquisition. Because of Jesuit influence, he was not condemned to prison or death. Instead, he was sent back to England, where he lived out his days in philosophical contemplation.

JONATHAN WILD

Type of work: Novel
Author: Henry Fielding (1707-1754)
Type of plot: Social criticism
Time of plot: Late seventeenth century
Locale: England
First published: 1743

Principal characters:
JONATHAN WILD, a "great man"
LAETITIA, his wife
LA RUSE, a rogue

HEARTFREE, a good man
MRS. HEARTFREE, his good wife

Critique:

Although *The History of Jonathan Wild the Great* is possibly the least known of Fielding's novels, it is the one likely to appeal most to those who enjoy barbed satire and pure irony. Jonathan was a "great man"—not a good man. Fielding makes it quite clear that greatness and goodness are never to be found in one person. A "great man" is a pure villain, with none of the minor virtues with which ordinary villains are endowed. The characters are vivid; the plot is sure and swift. *Jonathan Wild* is, in all ways, a delightful book.

The Story:

Jonathan Wild was prepared by nature to be a "great man." His ancestors were all men of greatness, many of them hanged for thievery or treason. Those who escaped were simply shrewder and more fortunate than the others. But Jonathan was to be so "great" as to put his forefathers to shame.

As a boy he read about the great villains of history. At school he learned little, his best study being to pick the pockets of his tutors and fellow students. When he was seventeen, his father moved to town, where Jonathan was to put his talents to even better use. There he met the Count La Ruse, a knave destined to be one of the lesser "greats." La Ruse was in prison for debt, but Jonathan's skill soon secured his friend's freedom. Together they had many profitable ventures, picking the pockets of their friends and of each other. Neither became angry when the other stole from him, for each respected the other's abilities.

Jonathan, for unknown reasons, traveled in America for seven or eight years. Returning to England he continued his life of villainy. Since he was to be a truly "great" man, he could not soil his own hands with too much thievery because there was always the danger of the gal-

lows if he should be apprehended. He gathered about him a handful of lesser thieves who took the risks while he collected most of the booty. La Ruse joined him in many of his schemes, and the two friends continued to steal from each other. This ability to cheat friends showed true "greatness."

Jonathan admired Laetitia Snap, a woman with qualities of "greatness" similar to his own. She was the daughter of his father's friend, and she too was skilled in picking pockets and cheating at cards. In addition, she was a lady of wonderfully loose morals. But try as he would, Jonathan could not get Laetitia to respond to his passion. The poor fellow did not at first know that each time he approached her she was hiding another lover in the closet. Had he known, his admiration would have been even greater.

Jonathan's true "greatness" did not appear until he renewed his acquaintance with Mr. Heartfree, a former schoolmate. Heartfree would never be a "great" man because he was a good man. He cheated no one, held no grudges, and loved his wife and children. These qualities made him the sort of person Jonathan liked to cheat. Heartfree was a jeweler who by hard work and honest practices had become moderately prosperous. With the help of La Ruse, Jonathan was able to bring Heartfree to ruin. They stole his jewels and his money and hired thugs to beat him unmercifully, all the time convincing the good man that they were his friends.

La Ruse approached the greatness of Jonathan by leaving the country after stealing most of their booty. Poor Heartfree was locked up for debt after the two scoundrels had ruined him. Then Jonathan performed his greatest act. He had also a strong passion for Mrs. Heartfree, a good and virtuous woman, and he persuaded her that her husband had asked him to take her and some remaining jewels to Holland until her husband could obtain his release. So cleverly did he talk that the woman did not even tell her husband goodbye, though she loved him dearly. Instead, she put her children in the hands of a faithful servant and accompanied the rogue on a ship leaving England immediately.

When a severe storm arose, Jonathan was sure that death was near. Throwing caution aside, he attacked Mrs. Heartfree. Her screams brought help from the captain. After the storm subsided, the captain put Jonathan adrift in a small boat. The captain did not know that Jonathan was a "great" man, not destined to die in ignoble fashion. After a while he was rescued. He returned to England with tall tales of his adventure, none of which were the least bit true.

In the meantime Heartfree had begun to suspect his friend of duplicity. When Jonathan returned, he was for a time able to persuade Heartfree that he had done everything possible to help the jeweler. He told just enough of the truth to make his story acceptable, for in "greatness" the lie must always contain some truth. But Jonathan went too far. He urged Heartfree to attempt an escape from prison by murdering a few guards. Heartfree saw his supposed friend as the rogue he was and denounced Jonathan in ringing tones. From that time on Jonathan lived only to bring Heartfree to complete destruction.

While Jonathan was plotting Heartfree's trip to the gallows, Laetitia's father finally gave his consent to his daughter's marriage to the rogue. It took only two weeks, however, for his passion to be satisfied; then the couple began to fight and cheat each other constantly.

After his marriage Jonathan continued in all kinds of knavery, but his most earnest efforts were directed toward sending Heartfree to the gallows. At last he hit upon a perfect plan. He convinced the authorities that Heartfree himself had plotted to have his wife take the jewels out of the country in order to cheat his creditors. Mrs. Heartfree had not returned to England. Although Jonathan hoped she was dead, he thought it better to have her husband hanged at once in case she should somehow return. Before Heartfree's sentence was carried out, however, Jonathan was arrested and put in jail. He was surprised by a visit from Laetitia. She came only to revile him. She, having been caught picking pockets, was also a prisoner. Her only wish was that she could have the pleasure of seeing Jonathan hanged before her turn came to die on the gallows.

On the day that Heartfree was to be hanged his wife returned. After many adventures and travel in many lands, she came back in time to tell her story and to save her husband from hanging. She had brought with her a precious jewel which had been given to her by a savage chief she met on her travels. Heartfree was released and his family was restored to prosperity. It was otherwise with Jonathan, whose former friends hastened to hurry him to the gallows. On the appointed day he was hanged, leaving this world with a curse for all mankind. His wife and all his friends were hanged, save one. La Ruse was captured in France and broken on the wheel. Jonathan Wild was a "great" man because he was a complete villain.

JORROCKS' JAUNTS AND JOLLITIES

Type of work: Tales
Author: Robert Smith Surtees (1803-1864)
Type of plot: Comic romance
Time of plot: The 1830's
Locale: England and France
First published: 1838

Critique:

This volume of Jorrocks' adventures differs from the others in that there is no connecting plot; the work is simply a series of tales given unity by the irrepressible and immortal Jorrocks. The satire here is double-edged; first there is the pretentious cockney aping his aristocratic betters; second, sporting life comes in for uncomfortably keen depiction. The wealth of detail furnishes us with a good contemporary account of town and country life in Victorian England.

The Story:

When they went out to hunt, the members of Jorrocks' Surrey fox hunt did not always keep their minds on the sport. As they gathered, their talk included shouts to the dogs and quotations on the price of cotton, advice on horses, and warnings of bank policies. While waiting for the dogs to run the fox closer, they all eagerly pulled out bread and meat from their capacious pockets.

One morning a swell joined the veteran Surrey hunters. He was plainly an aristocrat. While the others were paunchy and stooped, he was thin and straight. His handsome mount contrasted sharply with their skinny nags. They all watched him enviously. He was new in Surrey evidently, for he drove his horse at a fast clip through the bottom lands, heedless of the numerous flints. The riders were glad when he had to retire from the chase with a lame horse.

As he left, Jorrocks rushed up with the news that the stranger was no less a personage than a Russian diplomat. The whole hunt joined in heartily wishing him back in Russia for good.

In town Jorrocks ran into agreeable Mr. Stubbs, a footloose Yorkshireman and invited him to go to the hunt on Saturday morning. So long as Jorrocks paid the bills, the Yorkshireman was glad for any entertainment. On the appointed foggy morning Jorrocks was on time. He was riding his own bony nag and leading a sorry dray horse for his guest. The fog was so thick that they bumped into carriages and sidewalk stands right and left. The Yorkshireman would have waited for the fog to lift, but doughty Jorrocks would countenance no delay. Mrs. Jorrocks had a fine quarter of house-lamb for supper and her husband had been sternly ordered to be back at five-thirty sharp. Jorrocks was never late for a meal.

On the way Jorrocks' horse was nearly speared by a carriage pole. The resourceful hunter promptly dismounted and chaffered a bit with a coach driver. When he remounted, he had a great coach lamp tied around his middle. Thus lighted, the two horsemen got safely out of town.

The hunt that day held an unexpected surprise for both of them. Thinking to show off a little for his younger friend, Jorrocks put his horse at a weak spot in a fence. He wanted to sail over in good time and continue after the fox. Instead, he landed in a cesspool. His bright red coat was covered with slime and mud for the rest of the day. But the Yorkshireman noted that Jorrocks carried on till the end of the hunt and got home in time for his house-lamb.

As usual, Jorrocks went hunting in Surrey on a Saturday. When his horse went lame, he stopped at the smith's shop for repairs, and his five-minute delay made him lose sight of the pack. Consequently, he lost out on a day's sport. As he sat in a local inn nursing a grouch and threatening to withdraw his subscription to the Surrey hunt, in came Nosey Browne. Jorrocks was delighted to see his old friend and willingly accepted an invitation to a day's shooting on Browne's estate.

A few days later he collected the Yorkshireman and set out eagerly for the shooting. He was dashed to find that Nosey's big estate was little more than a cramped spot of ground covered with sheds and other outbuildings. Squire Cheatum, learning that Nosey was a bankrupt, had forbidden his neighbor to hunt in his woods, and so Jorrocks was forced to hunt in the yard behind sheds. Soon he saw a rabbit. In his excitement he took a step forward and shot the animal. As he was about to pick up his prize, a gamekeeper arrived and accused him of trespassing. After an extended argument it was shown that Jorrocks' toe had indeed at the moment of shooting been over the line on Squire Cheatum's land; and so the wrathy Jorrocks was fined one pound one.

He was no man to accept calmly a fine so obviously unfair. He hired a lawyer and appealed the case to the county court. On the day of the trial Jorrocks beamed as his own attorney pictured him as a substantial citizen with a reputation for good works. He squirmed as the squire's lawyer described him as a cockney grocer who was infringing on the rights of countryfolk. At the end the judges woke up and sustained the fine.

After the fox-hunting season ended, Jorrocks accepted an invitation to a stag hunt. The Yorkshireman came to breakfast with him on the appointed morning. Jorrocks led him down into the kitchen, where the maid had set out the usual fare. There were a whole ham, a loaf of bread, and a huge Bologna sausage. There were muffins, nine eggs, a pork pie, and kidneys on a spit. The good Betsy was stationed at the stove, where she deftly laid mutton chops on the gridiron.

As the two friends ate, Mrs. Jorrocks came in with an ominous face. She held up a card, inscribed with a woman's name and address, which she had found in her spouse's pocket. Jorrocks seized the card, threw it into the fire, and declared it was an application for a deaf and dumb institute.

The men set out for the hunt in Jorrocks' converted fire wagon. Ahead of them was a van carrying a drowsy doe. They were shocked to learn on arriving that their "stag" was that same tame deer imported for the day. She had to be chased to make her stop grazing on the common. Jorrocks' disappointment was complete when he learned that he had been invited only for his contribution to the club fund.

Abandoning the hunt for a while, Jorrocks took a boat trip to Margate with the Yorkshireman. That expedition was also a failure, for he left his clothes on the beach when he went for a swim and the tide engulfed them. The unhappy grocer was forced to go back to London in hand-me-downs.

Seeing numerous books for sale at fancy prices, Jorrocks determined to write a four-volume work on France that would sell for thirty pounds. With little more ado he collected the Yorkshireman and set out for Dover.

He was charmed with Boulogne, for the French were gay and the weather was sunny. On the coach to Paris he met the Countess Benwolio, as Jorrocks, in cockney fashion, called her. She was quite receptive to the rich grocer. The countess seemed a beautiful, youthful woman until she went to sleep in the coach and her teeth dropped down. Once in Paris, Jorrocks was snugly installed as the favored guest in her apartment. He began to collect information for his book.

The countess was avid for presents, and before many days Jorrocks began to run short of money. He tried to recoup at the races, but the Frenchmen were too shrewd for him. Finally he offered to race fifty yards on foot, with the Yorkshireman perched on his shoulders, against a fleet French baron who was to run a hundred yards. Jorrocks took a number of wagers and gave them to the countess to hold. He won the race easily. When he regained his breath and looked about for the countess, she had disappeared.

With little money and no French, the

Englishmen were quite some time getting back to the countess' apartment. By the time they arrived, a gross Dutchman was installed as her favorite. When Jorrocks tried to collect his wagers, she presented him with a detailed board bill. Pooling his last funds with the Yorkshireman's hoard, he was barely able to pay the bill. Chastened by his sojourn among the French, Jorrocks returned to England.

JOSEPH ANDREWS

Type of work: Novel
Author: Henry Fielding (1707-1754)
Type of plot: Comic epic
Time of plot: Early eighteenth century
Locale: England
First published: 1742

> *Principal characters:*
> JOSEPH ANDREWS, a footman to Lady Booby
> PAMELA ANDREWS, his sister, wife of Squire Booby
> LADY BOOBY, aunt of Squire Booby
> FANNY, Joseph's sweetheart
> MRS. SLIPSLOP, Lady Booby's maid
> PARSON ADAMS, parson of Booby parish and friend of Joseph

Critique:

The History of the Adventures of *Joseph Andrews, and of his Friend Mr. Abraham Adams* is the full title of the work often called the first realistic novel of English literature. Henry Fielding turned aside from the episodic sentimental writing of the age to give an honest picture of the manners and customs of his time and to satirize the foibles and vanities of human nature. In particular, he ridiculed affectation, whether it stemmed from hypocrisy or vanity. Although the structure of the novel is loose and rambling, the realistic settings and the vivid portrayal of English life in the eighteenth century more than compensate for this one weakness. Joseph is presented as the younger brother of Samuel Richardson's heroine, Pamela.

The Story:

Joseph Andrews was ten or eleven years in the service of Sir Thomas Booby, uncle of the Squire Booby who married the virtuous Pamela, Joseph's sister. When Lord Booby died, Joseph remained in the employ of Lady Booby as her footman. This lady, much older than her twenty-one-year-old servant, and apparently little disturbed by her husband's death, paid entirely too much attention to pleasant-mannered and handsome Joseph. But Joseph was as virtuous as his famous sister, and when Lady Booby's advances became such that even his innocence could no longer deny their true nature, he was as firm in resisting her as Pamela had been in restraining Squire Booby. Insulted, the lady discharged Joseph on the spot, in spite of the protests of Mrs. Slipslop, her maid, who found herself also attracted to the young man.

With very little money and fewer prospects, Joseph set out from London to Somersetshire to see his sweetheart, Fanny, for whose sake he had withstood Lady Booby's advances. The very first night of his journey, Joseph was attacked by robbers, who stole his money, beat him soundly, and left him lying naked and half dead in a ditch. A passing coach stopped when the passengers heard his cries, and he was taken to a nearby inn.

Joseph was well cared for until the innkeeper's wife discovered that he was penniless. He was recognized, however, by another visitor at the inn, his old tutor and preceptor, Parson Adams, who was on his way to London to sell a collection of his sermons. He paid Joseph's bill with his own meager savings; then, discovering that in his absent-mindedness he had forgotten to bring the sermons with him, he decided to accompany Joseph back to Somersetshire.

They started out, alternately on foot and on the parson's horse. Fortunately, Mrs. Slipslop overtook them in a coach on her way to Lady Booby's country place. She accommodated the parson in the coach while Joseph rode the horse. The inn at which they stopped next had an innkeeper who gauged his courtesy according to the appearance of his guests. There Joseph was insulted by the host. In spite of the clerical cassock he was wearing, Parson Adams stepped in to challenge the host, and a fist fight followed, the ranks being swelled by the hostess and Mrs. Slipslop. When the battle finally ended, Parson Adams was the bloodiest looking, since the hostess in the excitement had doused him with a pail of hog's blood.

The journey continued, this time with Joseph in the coach and the parson on foot, for with typical forgetfulness the good man had left his horse behind. However, he walked so rapidly and the coach moved so slowly that he easily outdistanced his friends. While he was resting on his journey, he heard the shrieks of a woman. Running to her rescue, he discovered a young woman being cruelly attacked by a burly fellow, whom the parson belabored with such violence that he laid the attacker at his feet. As some fox hunters rode up, the ruffian rose from the ground and accused Parson Adams and the woman of being conspirators in an attempt to rob him. The parson and the woman were quickly taken prisoners and led off to the sheriff. On the way the parson discovered that the young woman whom he had aided was Fanny. Having heard of Joseph's unhappy dismissal from Lady Booby's service, she had been on her way to London to help him when she had been so cruelly molested.

After some uncomfortable moments before the judge, the parson was recognized by an onlooker, and both he and Fanny were released. They went to the inn where Mrs. Slipslop and Joseph were staying.

Joseph and Fanny were overjoyed to be together once more. Mrs. Slipslop, displeased to see Joseph's display of affection for another woman, drove off in the coach, leaving Parson Adams and the young lovers behind.

None of the three had any money to pay their bill at the inn. Parson Adams, with indomitable optimism, went to visit the clergyman of the parish in order to borrow the money, but with no success. Finally a poor peddler at the inn gave them every penny he had, just enough to cover the bill.

They continued their trip on foot, stopping at another inn where the host was more courteous than any they had met, and more understanding about their financial difficulties. Still farther on their journey, they came across a secluded house at which they were asked to stop and rest. Mr. and Mrs. Wilson were a charming couple who gave their guests a warm welcome. Mr. Wilson entertained the parson with the story of his life. It seemed that in his youth he had been attracted by the vanity of London life, had squandered his money on foppish clothes, gambling, and drinking, and had eventually been imprisoned for debt. From this situation he was rescued by a kindly cousin whom he later married. The two had retired from London to this quiet country home. They had two lovely children and their only sorrow, but that a deep one, was that a third child, a boy with a strawberry mark on his shoulder, had been stolen by gipsies and had never been heard of since.

After a pleasant visit with the kindly family, the travelers set out again. Their adventures were far from ended. Parson Adams suddenly found himself caught in the middle of a hare hunt, with the hounds inclined to mistake him for the hare. Their master goaded on the dogs, but Joseph and the parson were victorious in the battle. They found themselves face to face with an angry squire and his followers. But when the squire caught sight of the lovely Fanny, his anger softened, and he invited the three to dine.

Supper was a trying affair for the parson, who was made the butt of many practical jokes. Finally the three travelers left the house in great anger and went to an inn. In the middle of the night, some of the squire's men arrived, overcame Joseph and the parson, and abducted Fanny. On the way, however, an old acquaintance of Fanny, Peter Pounce, met the party of kidnapers, recognized Fanny, and rescued her.

The rest of the journey was relatively uneventful. When they arrived home however, further difficulties arose. Joseph and Fanny stayed at the parsonage and waited eagerly for the publishing of their wedding banns. Lady Booby had also arrived in the parish, the seat of her summer home. Still in love with Joseph, she exerted every pressure of position and wealth to prevent the marriage. She even had Fanny and Joseph arrested. At this point, however, Squire Booby and his wife Pamela arrived. That gentleman insisted on accepting his wife's relatives as his own, even though they were of a lower station, and Joseph and Fanny were quickly released from custody.

All manner of arguments were presented by Pamela, her husband, and Lady Booby in their attempts to turn Joseph aside from his intention of marrying Fanny. Her lowly birth made a difference to their minds, now that Pamela had made a good match and Joseph had been received by the Boobys.

Further complications arose when a traveling peddler revealed that Fanny, whose parentage until then had been unknown, was the sister of Pamela. Mr. and Mrs. Andrews were summoned at this disclosure, and Mrs. Andrews described how, while Fanny was still a baby, gipsies had stolen the child and left behind them a sickly little boy she had brought up as her own. Now it appeared that Joseph was the foundling. However, a strawberry mark on Joseph's chest soon established his identity. He was the son of the kindly Wilsons.

Both lovers were now secure in their social positions, and nothing further could prevent their marriage, which took place, to the happiness of all concerned, soon afterward.

JOSEPH VANCE

Type of work: Novel
Author: William De Morgan (1839-1917)
Type of plot: Simulated autobiography
Time of plot: Mid-nineteenth century
Locale: England
First published: 1906

Principal characters:
> JOSEPH VANCE, who wrote his memoirs
> MR. CHRISTOPHER VANCE, his father
> DR. RANDALL THORPE, Joseph's foster father
> LOSSIE THORPE, Dr. Thorpe's daughter
> JOE THORPE (BEPPINO), her brother
> VIOLET THORPE, her sister
> NOLLY THORPE, another brother
> BONY MACALLISTER, Joseph's business partner

GENERAL DESPREZ, Lossie's husband
JANEY SPENCER, Joseph's wife
PHEENER, a maid

Critique:

Joseph Vance is an early example of the now popular type of autobiographical novel. It is the story of the life of Joseph Vance from his earliest recollections until the last years of his life. As the author tells us through the words of his main character, there is much that might have been left out, since there are many threads of the plot which are unimportant to the story. Humor and pathos are successfully mixed; the humor particularly is the quiet kind that makes us chuckle to ourselves. It comes largely from the character of Vance's father, whose firm belief it is that to be a success a person must know absolutely nothing about doing the job he is hired to do. De Morgan gave his novel a subtitle, *An Ill-Written Autobiography*, but few of his readers will agree with him.

The Story:

Joseph Vance's father was more often drunk than sober. But he was a good man, never mean when he was drunk. Having lost several positions because of his drinking, he was in no way depressed. He took Joe with him to visit a pub on the night of his discharge from his last position, and while there he quarreled with a chimney sweep and had the poor end of the fight. Forced to spend some time in the hospital after the affair, he decided to give up his excessive drinking.

After his release from the hospital he set himself up as a builder and drain repairman, by virtue of acquiring a signboard advertising the possessor as such a workman. Mr. Vance knew nothing about the building trade, but he believed that it was his ignorance which would cause him to be a success at the business. He appeared to be right. His first job was for Dr. Randall Thorpe, of Poplar Villa, and Dr. Thorpe was so pleased with the work that he recommended Mr. Vance for more jobs until his reputation was such that he was much in demand. Mr. Vance took Joe with him on his first call at Poplar Villa, and there Joe met Miss Lossie Thorpe, the first real young lady he had ever seen. At this time Joe was nine and Lossie fifteen, but he knew from the first meeting that she was to be his lady for the rest of his life.

When Dr. Thorpe learned that Joe was a bright boy, he sent him to school and made him almost one of the family. Lossie was like a sister to him; in fact, she called him her little brother and encouraged him in his studies. In the Thorpe household were also young Joe Thorpe, called Beppino, a sister Violet, and another brother named Nolly. With these young people Joe Vance grew up, and Dr. Thorpe continued to send him to school, even to Oxford when he was ready. Although Dr. Thorpe had hoped that Joe Vance might excel in the classics, the boy found his interest in engineering. Beppino did grow up to be a poet, but he wrote such drivel that his father was disgusted. Meanwhile a deep friendship had developed between Joe Vance and Lossie, a brother-and-sister love that made each want the other's happiness above all else.

Mr. Vance's business prospered so much that he and his wife took a new house and hired a cook and a maid. After Joe had finished at Oxford, he joined his old school friend, Bony Macallister, and they established an engineering firm. Their offices were in the same building with Mr. Vance. By that time Lossie had married General Desprez, a wealthy army officer, and had moved with him to India. Joe suffered a great deal at the loss of his dear friend, but he knew that General Desprez was a fine man who would care for Lossie and love her tenderly.

Shortly after Lossie sailed for India, Joe's mother died, and his father began to drink once more. Joe tried to think of some way to help his father. Joe thought that if he married his wife might influence his father, and he asked Janey Spencer, a friend of Lossie, to marry him. She accepted, but when she learned that Joe wanted to marry her only for the sake of his father, she broke the engagement and did not relent until two years later. By that time Joe knew he really loved her, and she married him. In the meantime, Joe's father had married Pheener, his housemaid, and for a time she kept him from the bottle.

After Janey and Joe had been married for five years, they took a trip to Italy. The ship caught on fire and almost all on board were lost. When Janey refused to get into a lifeboat without her husband, they tried to swim to shore. Janey was drowned. Joe's life was empty without her, and only his visits with Dr. Thorpe and his letters from Lossie gave him any comfort.

Joe's business prospered, as did his father's. But one day Mr. Vance, while drunk, caused an explosion and a fire in the building. He was seriously injured, and he seemed to be ruined because he had let his insurance lapse. But before the catastrophe he had given Pheener a tiara worth fifteen thousand pounds, and with the money received from the sale of the jewels he was able to start his business anew.

In the meantime Beppino was grieving his family by an affair with a married woman. For the sake of the Thorpes, Joe took Beppino to Italy. On Joe's return Beppino remained behind. When Beppino returned, he met and married Sibyl Perceval, an heiress, and the family believed he had changed his ways. But Beppino died of typhoid fever shortly after his marriage, and then Joe learned what Beppino had done while

in Italy. He had married an Italian girl, using the name of Joe Vance, and she had had a child. The Italian girl had died, too, and her relatives wrote to Joe in the belief that he was the father. Joe told General Desprez of Beppino's duplicity, the General and Lossie having come home for a visit, and the two men agreed that Lossie must never know of her brother's deed. Joe went to Italy and told the girl's relatives that he was a friend of the baby's father. He arranged to send money for the boy's care.

Shortly afterward Joe went to Brazil on an engineering project. While there, he sent for Beppino's boy and adopted him. The next twenty years of his life he spent in Brazil. He heard from Lossie and Dr. Thorpe frequently, but otherwise he had no connection with England. His father died and Pheener remarried. While Joe was in Brazil, Lossie heard rumors from Italy that he was the baby's real father. She was so disappointed in her foster brother that she never wrote again. Joe returned to England. Living near Lossie, he did not see her or let her know he was back in the country. The boy was attending school in America. Lossie's husband died without telling the real story about the child, and Joe would not tell the truth even to save himself in Lossie's eyes. He wrote the story in his memoirs, but left his papers to be burned after his return to Brazil.

But a maid burned the wrong package, and a publisher's note completed Joe's story. Lossie found a letter from Beppino in some of her husband's papers and surmised the truth. She found Joe Vance before he left for Brazil and made him confess that he had acted only to save her feelings. She begged Joe to forgive her. Reunited, the two friends went to Italy and spent their remaining days together.

JOURNEY TO THE END OF THE NIGHT

Type of work: Novel
Author: Louis-Ferdinand Céline (Louis Ferdinand Destouches, 1894-   )
Type of plot: Naturalism
Time of plot: World War I and following years
Locale: France
First published: 1932

> *Principal characters:*
> FERDINAND, a rogue
> LÉON, his friend
> MADELON, engaged to Léon

Critique:

In tone *Journey to the End of the Night* is pessimistic, in style abrupt and whittled down, in form experimental. The action is seen through the eyes of a neurotic narrator who reduces all his experience to a cynical level. In a way the approach can be called symbolical; that is, impressions are suggested rather than realistically described. The abrupt, fragmentary recounting of important events lends a tough, terse quality to the work. The philosophy is that of post-war disillusionment.

The Story:

Ferdinand, an indifferent student of medicine in Paris, was violently pacifistic, even anarchistic in his reaction to authority. Just prior to World War I he was expounding his cynical disregard for nationalistic pride in a café. Down the street came a colonel at the head of a military band. Because the music and the uniforms captured Ferdinand's fickle fancy, he rushed off to enlist. During the fighting he was a runner constantly exposed to scenes of savage brutality and to dangerous errands. On one mission he met Léon, who was always to be a kind of incubus to him.

When Ferdinand suffered a slight wound in his arm, he was given convalescent leave in Paris. There he met Lola, an American Red Cross worker who idolized the French. She romanticized his wound, became his temporary mistress, and filled him with stories of the United States. When she finally discovered Ferdinand's cowardice and cynicism, she left him.

The thought of losing Lola was more than Ferdinand could bear. When his mind gave way, he was sent to a variety of mental hospitals, where he quickly learned to ingratiate himself with the psychiatrists by agreeing with everything they said. His tactics at last procured his release as cured but unfit for active duty.

In Paris he led a precarious life for a time, but later he bettered his existence considerably by acting as a go-between for Musyne, a dancer who was greatly sought after by rich Argentine meat dealers. The thought of all that beef to be sold at high prices was too much for Ferdinand after some months with Musyne, and he left for Colonial Africa.

In French West Africa he was assigned to a trading post far in the interior. He made the ten-day trip by canoe into the hot, lush jungle, where his trading post turned out to be a cozy shack anchored by two big rocks. The mysterious trader he had come to relieve was frankly a thief, who told Ferdinand that he had no goods left to trade, very little rubber, and only canned stew for provisions. The rascal gave Ferdinand three hundred francs, saying it was all he had, and left in the direction of a Spanish colony. Only after he had gone did Ferdinand realize that his predecessor had been Léon.

After several weeks of fever and canned stew, Ferdinand left the trading post. The shack having accidentally burned, his only baggage was the three hundred francs and some canned stew. His overland safari was a nightmare. His fever rose dangerously high, and during much of the trip he was delirious. At last his black porters stole his money and left him with a Spanish priest in a seaport. The priest, for a fee, delivered him to a captain of easy scruples. Ferdinand, still sick, was shanghaied on a ship bound for the United States.

When he attempted to jump ship in New York, he was caught by the immigration authorities. Pretending to be an expert on flea classification, he was put to work in a quarantine station catching and sorting fleas for the Port of New York. After gaining the confidence of his chief, he was sent into the city to deliver a report, although technically he was still under detention. In New York he looked up Lola, now older but still attractive, who gave him a hundred dollars to get rid of him. With the money he took a train to Detroit. Soon he was employed by the Ford Motor Company.

In Dearborn he fell in love with Molly, who lived in a brothel. Each day he escorted her to the bordello in the early evening. Then he rode streetcars until she was through for the night. On one of his nightly trips he met Léon again. Léon was unhappy in America because he could not learn enough English to get along. He had to be content with a janitor's job. Ferdinand learned that Léon also wished to return to France.

Although he loved Molly very much, Ferdinand left her and Detroit to go back to Paris. Completing his medical course, he was certified as a doctor, and he settled down to practice in a poor suburb. All his patients were poor and rarely paid him. Mostly he was called in on shady abortion cases.

One day the Henrouilles summoned him to attend the old grandmother who lived in a hut behind their house. They hated to spend the money necessary to feed the old woman and Mme. Henrouille offered Ferdinand a thousand francs if he would certify that the grandmother was insane. Through conscience or fear, Ferdinand refused. Then Léon was called in on the same case. He agreed to set a bomb next to the old woman's hut so that she would kill herself when she opened the door. But clumsy Léon bungled the job; he accidentally detonated the bomb and lost his sight.

With the help of the Abbé Protiste, the family worked out a scheme to get rid of both the old woman and Léon. They proposed to send the two to Toulouse, where there was a display of mummies connected with a church. Léon would be a ticket seller and old Mme. Henrouille would be the guide. For persuading Léon to accept the proposition, Ferdinand received a fee of a thousand francs.

Ferdinand's practice grew smaller. At last he went to the Montmartre section of Paris, where for a time he was well pleased with his job as supernumerary in a music hall. The Abbé Protiste looked him up after some months and offered to pay his expenses to Toulouse, where Ferdinand was to see if Léon were likely to make trouble for the Henrouilles on the score of attempted murder.

In Toulouse Ferdinand learned that Léon was regaining his sight. He had also become engaged to Madelon. The old lady was a vigorous and successful guide. Ferdinand dallied a little with the complaisant Madelon, but decided to leave before their intimacy was discovered. Old Mme. Henrouille fell, or was tripped, on the stairs and was killed in the fall. It was a good time for Ferdinand to leave—hurriedly.

Dr. Baryton ran a genteel madhouse. By great good luck Ferdinand was hired on his staff. He ingratiated himself with his employer by giving him English lessons. Dr. Baryton read Macaulay's *History of England* and became so enamored of things English that he departed for foreign lands and left Ferdinand in charge. Shortly afterward Léon showed up, broke and jobless. He had run away from Madelon. Ferdinand took him in and gave him a job.

Madelon came looking for Léon and haunted the hospital gate. Hoping to appease her, Ferdinand arranged a Sunday party to visit a carnival. In the party were Léon, Madelon, Ferdinand, and Sophie, Ferdinand's favorite nurse. After a hectic day they took a taxi home. On the way Léon declared he no longer loved Madelon. The spurned girl took out her revolver and killed him. Ferdinand knew that the time had arrived for him to move on once more.

JOURNEY'S END

Type of work: Drama
Author: Robert C. Sherriff (1896-   )
Type of plot: Impressionistic realism
Time of plot: March, 1918
Locale: A battlefield in France
First presented: 1929

Principal characters:
CAPTAIN DENNIS STANHOPE, a British company commander
LIEUT. OSBORNE, Stanhope's middle-aged second-in-command
LIEUT. RALEIGH, Stanhope's school friend, his fiancée's brother
2ND LIEUT. HIBBERT, a cowardly officer in Stanhope's company

Critique:

Originally Robert Sherriff had no literary ambitions, and *Journey's End* was written to be used by a group of amateurs who were interested in dramatics. At that time Sherriff was an insurance claims adjuster. The play grew out of letters Sherriff had written to his family during World War I, when he served as an officer in the British Army. On a chance suggestion, *Journey's End* was sent to George Bernard Shaw, who helped to get the play produced. It was an immense success; at one time there were nine companies playing it in the United States and England. The play made the author famous, and he became a professional writer. Although he has written other plays and novels, none has been as successful as *Journey's End*.

The Story:

Captain Stanhope's infantry company entered the front lines on Monday, March 18, 1918, at a time when the Allied Powers were expecting a strong German attack near St. Quentin. Lieutenant Os-borne, a middle-aged officer who had been a schoolmaster in civilian life, met Lieutenant Raleigh, a new officer, when the latter arrived at the headquarters dugout. Discovering that Raleigh was an ardent hero worshiper of Captain Stanhope, who was absent at the time, Osborne tried to make the new officer realize that Stanhope's three years in the lines had made a different man of him.

Raleigh could barely realize just how much his friend had changed. Stanhope had become a battle-hardened, cynical infantry officer who drank whiskey incessantly in order to keep his nerves together.

After supper that evening Stanhope confided to Osborne that he was fearful of young Raleigh's opinion, and he declared that he meant to censor all the young officer's mail, lest Raleigh reveal to his sister the kind of man Stanhope, her fiancé, had become. Stanhope was bitter that Raleigh had landed in his company when there were so many others in France to which he might have been assigned. He was also concerned over

Lieutenant Hibbert, another officer who was malingering in an effort to get sent home to England. Stanhope, who hated a quitter, resolved that Hibbert should be forced to stay.

The following morning the company prepared for the expected German attack. Stanhope sent out parties to put up a barbed wire enclosure in case neighboring units were forced to withdraw. Stanhope, having received orders to stand, meant to do so. During the morning Raleigh and Osborne had a long talk and became very friendly. After their talk Raleigh went to write a letter to his sister. When he finished, Stanhope made him hand it over for censoring. Raleigh, after some bitter words, did so. Stanhope, angry with himself for insisting, could not bring himself to read the letter. Osborne, anxious to keep harmony in the company, read it and reported to Stanhope that Raleigh had written only praise of the captain to his sister.

That afternoon word from regimental headquarters reported that the German attack was sure to occur on Thursday morning, and Stanhope hurried up preparations for the expected attack. As he finished a conference with his sergeant major, the colonel commanding the regiment stepped into the company headquarters for a conference. He had come because the matter was a serious one; he wanted Stanhope to send a raiding party to capture prisoners, from whom the colonel expected to gain information about the Germans' disposition for the attack. The raid would be a dangerous one because it had to be made in daylight.

The officers selected to lead the raid were Osborne, because of his experience, and Raleigh, because of his youthful vitality. Stanhope hated to send either, for he needed Osborne and he was afraid that Raleigh was too inexperienced. Above that, there was the possibility that they would never return.

After the colonel had gone, Hibbert told Stanhope that he was going to the doctor to be relieved from duty. Stanhope, realizing that the man was feigning illness, threatened to shoot him if he left. Having bullied the man into behaving himself, Stanhope, to show that he held no ill will, promised to stand duty with Hibbert that night.

Later in the afternoon Osborne and Raleigh were told the details of the proposed raid. Osborne was quiet, knowing what they were in for; Raleigh, not knowing how dangerous the raid would be, took the assignment as a great adventure.

By the next afternoon preparations for the raid had been completed. A gap had been made in the barbed wire between the lines by trench mortars. The Germans, to let the British know they realized what was coming, had gone out and hung red rags on the gap, and they had zeroed in their machine guns on the gap. Stanhope tried to get the raid called off, but the colonel insisted that it was necessary. The mortars laid down a barrage of smoke shells to hide the rush of the raid. While Osborne and his party went to the German parapet and kept the way clear, Raleigh and another group of men clambered into the trench to capture a prisoner.

The raid went as well as could be expected. Raleigh and his men returned with a prisoner from whom they obtained valuable information on the disposition of German troops. Osborne and several of his enlisted men had been killed by the Germans, and Raleigh was crushed by the death of his newly made friend The other officers, trying to pass off the incident, had a chicken dinner with champagne that night to celebrate the success of the raid. Raleigh, thinking them barbarous in their conduct, remained away from the dugout. He could not see that the other officers were simply trying to forget what had happened; any one of them might be killed during the next raid.

After the dinner Stanhope gave Raleigh a violent tongue-lashing for his conduct and tried to explain to the young officer why it had been necessary for the living to celebrate, even though Osborne had been killed.

The next morning the German attack began. During the first bombardment several men in the company, including Raleigh, were wounded. Stanhope ordered Raleigh to be brought into the dugout, where the captain tried to comfort him with word that the wound was serious enough to require evacuation to England for treatment and convalescence. For the first time since Raleigh's arrival at the company the two were able to meet as friends. Their renewed friendship was short-lived, however, for Raleigh was wounded so severely that he died within a few minutes. Stanhope, turning his back on his friend's body, went out to direct the defense against the Germans.

A JOVIAL CREW

Type of work: Drama
Author: Richard Brome (?-1652 or 1653)
Type of plot: Farce
Time of plot: Seventeenth century
Locale: England
First presented: 1641

>   *Principal characters:*
>   OLDRENTS, a country squire
>   SPRINGLOVE, his steward
>   RACHEL, Oldrents' older daughter
>   MERIEL, his younger daughter
>   VINCENT, Rachel's lover
>   HILLIARD, Meriel's lover
>   MASTER CLACK, a justice
>   AMIE, the justice's niece

Critique:

A Jovial Crew; or, The Merry Beggars is a good-natured, unpretentious comedy. It presents a world filled with pleasantly unreal problems that permit equally unreal solutions, a world populated with eccentric gentry and philosophic beggars. Light, gay entertainment was the author's goal, and he attained it.

The Story:

Squire Oldrents had ample reason to be happy: he owned a large estate from which he received a good income; he was beloved by the rich for his warm hospitality and by the poor for his generosity; he had two lovely daughters who were being courted by two very presentable young gentlemen. But the joy that he derived from these blessings was suddenly destroyed by a fortune-teller's prediction that Oldrents' daughters would become beggars. Oldrents' friend Hearty, a gentleman who had seen better days but who always looked on the bright side of things, tried to cheer up the old man. As a result of his persuasiveness, Oldrents resolved to put on, at least, an outward show of good spirits.

A second source of worry for the squire was his steward, Springlove. As a youth Springlove had been a beggar, until Oldrents took him in and schooled him. During winters, Springlove had always been very diligent in his work. But with the arrival of May, every year he found some pretext to leave home. One year Oldrents met Springlove begging on the highway and thus discovered how his summers were spent. To break the young man of his wanderings, Oldrents had made him his steward, a position in which Spring-love had done well. But now it was nearly May again, and Springlove announced that the call of nature was too insistent, and he must go a-begging.

One of Oldrents' charities was the maintenance of an old barn as a guest house for wandering beggars. Rachel and Meriel, his daughters, had long watched these beggars and envied them their complete freedom. The girls were bored with their home life and further depressed by the low spirits of their father. Thus developed their plan for going with the beggars. Their two lovers, Vincent and Hilliard, who were afraid of losing the girls, agreed to accompany them. When they announced their intention to Spring-love, he revealed the prophecy Oldrents had received. Now the girls felt that a brief sojourn with the beggars would have the additional advantage of bringing peace of mind to their father. In a letter to the old man they disclosed their project, but he, fearing that its contents might destroy his resolution to be happy, refused to open it.

The first night on the road dispelled any romantic notions that the four amateur beggars had about their new life. The two men, having spent an uneasy and sleepless night, would have gladly returned home, but they did not wish to give the appearance of softness. The girls, having been housed in a pigsty, were equally disillusioned, but they resolved not to be the first to show signs of weakening.

Despite Springlove's instructions, the amateurs had little success in their first attempts at begging because they lacked the requisite humility. Approaching two gentlemen, Vincent, after first being tongue-tied, asked for such a large sum that they drove him off with their swords. Hilliard, also asking for a large sum, was switched; thereupon, in very unbeggarly manner, he demanded satisfaction of his chastiser, a man named Oliver. This same Oliver had noticed the two girls and had been filled with lust. Finding them alone,

he gave them money, kissed them, and then tried to drag Rachel behind some bushes. But his intentions were frustrated by the arrival of the men in response to her screams. After he had restrained Vincent and Hilliard, Springlove, knowing that Oliver would be too ashamed to do so, suggested that he get a beadle to punish the girls.

The next travelers the beggars encountered were Martin and Amie. Amie had left home to escape marriage with Master Talboy, a marriage that her uncle, Master Clack, had tried to force upon her. Martin, the justice's clerk, seeing a chance to advance his own position, had agreed to run away with her. Now that she had had a better opportunity to observe Martin, she had begun to doubt the wisdom of her action. When they encountered the beggars, they were hungry and unhappy. Springlove gave them food and offered to get a curate to marry them. Amie, impressed by his solicitude, decided to remain temporarily with the beggars.

Meanwhile, a search for the runaways was in progress. Among the searchers was Oliver and the rejected lover, Talboy. Their pursuit brought them to the home of Oldrents. The squire, still doggedly attempting to banish sorrow from his life, despite the loss of his daughters, welcomed them with song and drink. But Talboy, with his incessant weeping and sighing, disturbed the old man. On a sudden whim, Oldrents decided to visit Master Clack, who he had heard was an odd character.

Officials, in the meantime, stopped and questioned the beggars on suspicion of harboring the fugitives. This trouble with the law was the final blow to the four amateurs, who now gave up any further pretense of liking this kind of life. When the constable threatened to beat Spring-love until he disclosed Amie's whereabouts, she, having fallen in love with him, revealed herself. Amie was then returned home, and the beggars were arrested.

1527

When the beggars were brought to Master Clack's home, Oldrents was there. The justice at first contemplated dire punishment for the vagrants; but, when he heard that they could present a drama, he saw a chance to entertain Oldrents without expense. In a play concerning two lost daughters and a vagrant steward, Rachel, Meriel, and Springlove played the leading roles. Oldrents was ecstatic at being reunited with his daughters, and his joy was increased by the revelation that Springlove was, in reality, his illegitimate son. Springlove, because of this disclosure and because of his intention of marrying Amie, announced that he would beg no more. Thus, the last of Oldrents' worries was over, and the old man again had his full measure of contentment.

JUDE THE OBSCURE

Type of work: Novel
Author: Thomas Hardy (1840-1928)
Type of plot: Philosophical realism
Time of plot: Eighteenth century
Locale: Wessex
First published: 1894

Principal characters:
JUDE FAWLEY, a stonemason
ARABELLA DONN, a vulgar country girl
SUE BRIDEHEAD, Jude's cousin, a neurotic free-thinker
LITTLE FATHER TIME, Jude's son by Arabella
RICHARD PHILLOTSON, a schoolmaster
DRUSILLA FAWLEY, Jude's great-grandaunt

Critique:

Jude the Obscure marks the peak of Hardy's gloom and deterministic philosophy. Sunshine never breaks through the heavy clouds of tragedy that smother this narrative of war between the flesh and the spirit. The gloom becomes steadily heavier as circumstances conspire to keep the hero from realizing any happiness he seeks. The plot is believable; the characters are three-dimensional. The story itself is a vehicle for Hardy's feelings toward contemporary marriage laws and academic snobbery. His sexual frankness, his unconventional treatment of the theme of marriage, and his use of pure horror in scenes like the deaths of Little Father Time and the younger children outraged readers of his generation.

The Story:

In the nineteenth century eleven-year-old Jude Fawley said goodbye to his schoolmaster, Richard Phillotson, who was leaving the small English village of Marygreen for Christminster, to study for a degree. Young Jude, hungry for learning, yearned to go to Christminster too, but he had to help his great-grandaunt, Drusilla Fawley, in her bakery. At Christminster, Phillotson did not forget his former pupil. He sent Jude some classical grammars which the boy studied eagerly.

Anticipating a career as a religious scholar, Jude apprenticed himself, at nineteen, to a stonemason engaged in the restoration of medieval churches in a nearby town. Returning to Marygreen one evening, he met three young girls who were washing pigs' chitterlings by a stream bank. One of the girls, Arabella Donn, caught Jude's fancy and he arranged to meet her later. The young man was swept off his feet and tricked into marriage, but he soon realized that he had married a vulgar country girl with whom he had nothing in common. Embittered, he tried unsuccessfully to commit suicide; when he began to drink, Arabella left him.

Jude, now free, decided to carry out his original purpose. With this idea in mind, he went to Christminster, where he took work as a stonemason. He had heard that his cousin, Sue Bridehead, lived in Christminster, but he did not seek her out because his aunt had warned him against her and because he was already a married man. Eventually he met her and was charmed. She was an artist employed in an ecclesiastical warehouse. Jude met Phillotson, again a simple schoolteacher. Sue, at Jude's suggestion, became Phillotson's assistant. The teacher soon lost his heart to his bright and intellectually independent young helper. Jude was hurt by evidence of intimacy between the two. Disappointed in love and ambition, he turned to drink and was dismissed by his employer. He went back to Marygreen.

At Marygreen Jude was persuaded by a minister to enter the church as a licentiate. Sue, meanwhile, had won a scholarship to a teacher's college at Melchester; she wrote Jude asking him to come to see her. Jude worked at stonemasonry in Melchester in order to be near Sue, even though she told him she had promised to marry Phillotson after her schooling. Dismissed from the college after an innocent escapade with Jude, Sue influenced him away from the church with her unorthodox beliefs. Shortly afterward she married Phillotson. Jude, despondent, returned to Christminster, where he came upon Arabella working in a bar. Jude heard that Sue's married life was unbearable. He continued his studies for the ministry and thought a great deal about Sue.

Succumbing completely to his passion for Sue, Jude at last forsook the ministry. His Aunt Drusilla died, and at the funeral Jude and Sue realized that they could not remain separated.

Phillotson, sympathizing with the lovers, released Sue, who now lived apart from her husband. The lovers went to Aldbrickham, a large city where they would not be recognized. Phillotson gave Sue a divorce and subsequently lost his teaching position. Jude gave Arabella a divorce so that she might marry again.

Sue and Jude now contemplated marriage, but they were unwilling to be joined by a church ceremony because of Sue's dislike for any binding contract. The pair lived together happily, Jude doing simple stonework. One day Arabella appeared and told Jude that her marriage had not materialized. Sue, jealous, promised Jude that she would marry him. Arabella's problem was solved by eventual marriage, but out of fear of her husband she sent her young child by Jude to live with him and Sue, This pathetic boy, nicknamed Little Father Time, joined the unconventional Fawley household.

Jude's business began to decline, and he lost a contract to restore a rural church when the vestry discovered that he and Sue were unmarried. Forced to move on, they traveled from place to place and from job to job. At the end of two and a half years of this itinerant life, the pair had two children of their own and a third on the way. They were five, including Little Father Time. Jude, in failing health, became a baker and Sue sold cakes in the shape of Gothic ornaments at a fair in a village near Christminster. At the fair Sue met Arabella, now a widow. Arabella reported Sue's poverty to Phillotson, who was once more the village teacher in Marygreen.

Jude took his family to Christminster, where the celebration of Remembrance Week was under way. Utterly defeated by failure, Jude still had a love for the atmosphere of learning which pervaded the city.

The family had difficulty finding lodgings and they were forced to separate. Sue's landlady, learning that Sue was

1529

an unmarried mother and fearful lest she should have the trouble of childbirth in her rooming-house, told Sue to find other lodgings. Bitter, Sue told Little Father Time that children should not be brought into the world. When she returned from a meal with Jude, she found that the boy had hanged the two babies and himself. She collapsed and gave premature birth to a dead baby.

Her experience brought about a change in Sue's point of view. Believing she had sinned and wishing now to conform, she asked Jude to live apart from her. She also expressed the desire to return to Phillotson, whom she believed, in her misery, to be still her husband. She re-turned to Phillotson and the two remarried. Jude, utterly lost, began drinking heavily. In a drunken stupor, he was again tricked by Arabella into marriage. His lungs failed; it was evident that his end was near. Arabella would not communicate with Sue, whom Jude desired to see once more, and so Jude traveled in the rain to see her. The lovers had a last meeting. She then made complete atonement for her past mistakes by becoming Phillotson's wife completely. This development was reported to Jude, who died in desperate misery of mind and body. Fate had grown tired of its sport with a luckless man.

JUDITH PARIS

Type of work: Novel
Author: Hugh Walpole (1884-1941)
Type of plot: Historical chronicle
Time of plot: Nineteenth century
Locale: England
First published: 1931

Principal characters:
    JUDITH HERRIES, later Judith Paris, daughter of Rogue Herries
    DAVID HERRIES, her half-brother
    FRANCIS HERRIES, her nephew
    JENNIFER, Francis' wife
    REUBEN SUNWOOD, Judith's cousin
    GEORGES PARIS, Judith's husband
    WILLIAM HERRIES, Francis' brother
    CHRISTABEL, William's wife
    WALTER HERRIES, William's son

Critique:

Judith Paris is the second of four novels dealing with the history of the Herries family. Like the others, it contains many characters and covers about half a century. While *Judith Paris* is an independent novel, it should be read in sequence with the others, or many of the allusions may confuse the reader. Like the preceding *Rogue Herries* and the succeeding *The Fortress* and *Vanessa,* Judith Paris is long and comprehensive in scope, with many references to the political and social background of the period.

The Story:

On the wild winter night Judith Herries was born in the gloomy old house at Herries in Rosthwaite, her aged father and young gipsy mother both died. The country midwife laid out the parents with as much respect as she thought Rogue Herries and his strange wife deserved. The baby she wrapped up warmly, for it was bitterly cold. Then to fortify her own thin blood she sat down

JUDITH PARIS by Hugh Walpole. By permission of the Executors, estate of Sir Hugh Walpole, and the publishers, Messrs. MacMillan & Co., London. Copyright, 1931, by Doubleday, Doran & Co., Inc.

with a bottle of strong drink. The wind rose and a loose windowpane blew in. The snow drifted in upon the cradle, but the midwife slept on.

Squire Gauntry, tough and taciturn, came by tired from hunting. He stopped when he heard the child's thin wail above the howling wind. Failing to arouse the stupid countrywoman, he took the baby home to his masculine hall until her half-brother, David Herries, arrived to claim her.

Judith Herries grew up at Fell House, near Uldale, with David Herries and his family. But David was fifty-five years older than Judith and often he clashed with his young sister. She was spanked many times; the most serious punishment came when she danced naked on the roof. Judith frequently visited Stone Ends, Squire Gauntry's place, where there were no restrictions.

One significant visit came in her eleventh year, when she ran away from Fell House after being punished for disobedience. Rough Gauntry welcomed her to a strange gathering. With the gentlemen who were drinking and playing cards, there were two women. One was vast Emma, Gauntry's mistress, who was always to be Judith's friend, and the other was beautiful Madame Paris, the mother of Georges. Georges, only a year or so older than Judith, came up to her and enticed her away on a childish prank. He kissed her soundly and she slapped his face.

That night, when Judith went to bed, she entered the room she usually slept in at Stone Ends. There she saw Georges' beautiful mother standing naked beside the bed. On his knees before her, dressed only in his shirt, knelt a gentleman who was kissing Madame Paris' knees. From that night on Judith thought as a woman.

When she was fourteen, she saw Georges again at a display of fireworks by the lake. Disobeying orders, she went out in a boat with him. His kisses that night were more grown-up.

When she was seventeen, Judith married Georges. It was a bad match in every way, except that Judith really loved her husband. Georges installed her at Watendlath, a remote northern farm. There she lived a lonely life. Georges, a smuggler, spent little time at home.

After some years Georges and Judith went to London, where the smuggler turned gambler and intriguer to recoup their fortunes. During a comparatively harmonious interval, they attended the famous ball given by Will Herries.

Jennifer Cards was the belle of the ball. She was a strikingly beautiful woman of twenty-six, still single by preference. Many of the married Herries men followed her like sheep. Christabel, Will's wife, was much upset and scolded Jennifer for being without a chaperon. Jennifer answered roughly and in her anger she seized Christabel's fan and broke it. That was the occasion for the great Herries quarrel. Ever after Will and then his son Walter were intent on destroying Jennifer.

Their quarrel eventually involved Francis, Judith's well-loved nephew, for Francis, thirty-six years old and a pathetic, futile man of deep sensibility, married Jennifer soon afterward.

Georges at last seemed to be serious in attempting to advance his fortunes. Judith never knew exactly what he was doing, but part of his project meant standing in well with Will Herries, who was a real power in the city. Mysterious men came and went in the Paris' shabby rooms. Stane was the one whom Judith distrusted most, and often she begged Georges to break with him. Her suspicions were verified one day when Georges came home exhausted and in wild despair. All his projects had failed, and Stane had lied his way into Will's favor.

Despondent, Georges and Judith went back to Watendlath, and Georges returned to smuggling. After one of his mysterious trips Georges appeared haggard and upset, to tell her that off Norway he choked Stane to death. Then he had overturned the small boat, to make the death appear an accident, and swam ashore. Although Georges was unsuspected, he needed Judith now. She had him to herself at last.

Then old Stane came, professing to seek shelter with his dead son's friend. When he had satisfied his suspicion of Georges' guilt, the powerful old man threw Georges over the rail and broke his back, killing him.

Now a widow, Judith left Watendlath and at their strong urging went to stay with Francis and Jennifer. The beautiful Jennifer now had two children, John and Dorothy. Since she had never loved Francis, Jennifer felt no compulsion to keep his love. She gave herself to Fernyhirst, a neighbor. Although most of the people in the neighborhood knew of her infidelity, Francis shut his eyes to it.

Then came the news that Will Herries had bought Westaways, only eight miles away from Fell House, where Judith lived in the uneasy home of Jennifer and Francis. They were sure that Will meant to harm them for the slight to his wife years before, and indeed Will hated them savagely. It was Walter, however, who was to be the agent for his father's hate.

Warren Forster brought the news of Will's plans to Fell House. He was a tiny, kindly man who had long admired Judith. The two went riding one day, and out of pity and friendship Judith gave herself to Warren, whose wife had left him years before.

When Judith, who was nearly forty, knew that she was carrying Warren's child, she went to Paris with blowzy Emma, now on the stage. It was just after Waterloo, and Paris was filled with Germans and Englishmen. When Warren finally found them, he was a sick man. In their little apartment, he died with only Judith and Emma to attend him.

One night, while Judith was dining in a café, a vengeful Frenchman shot a Prussian sitting at the next table. The shock unnerved Judith, and there, behind a screen, her son Adam was born.

In England, Walter was determined to harm Jennifer. He knew of her affair with Fernyhirst and he knew also of a journey Francis was taking. After he sent a note of warning to the inn where Francis was staying, Francis returned unexpectedly to Fell House. There he found his wife's lover in her room and fell on him savagely. Later he overtook the fleeing Fernyhirst and fought a duel with him, but Fernyhirst ran away. In futile despair Francis killed himself.

Now Judith had to manage a shaken and crumpled Jennifer and fight a savage Walter. A riot, incited by Walter, caused the death of Reuben Sunwood, Judith's kinsman and staunch friend, and a fire of mysterious origin broke out in the stables. Judith gave up her plan to return to Watendlath. For Jennifer's sake she and Adam went back to Fell House to stay.

JULIUS CAESAR

Type of work: Drama
Author: William Shakespeare (1564-1616)
Type of plot: Romantic tragedy
Time of plot: 44 B.C.
Locale: Rome
First presented: 1601

Principal characters:
JULIUS CAESAR, dictator of Rome
MARCUS ANTONIUS, his friend
MARCUS BRUTUS, a conspirator against Caesar
CAIUS CASSIUS, another conspirator against Caesar

PORTIA, wife of Brutus and Cassius' sister
CALPURNIA, Caesar's wife

Critique:

Actually, *The Tragedy of Julius Caesar* tells the story of Brutus rather than that of Caesar. At Shakespeare's hands the mighty dictator of Rome emerges as little more than a braggart whose chief activity, at least in this play, is a consistent refusal to read the handwriting on the wall. Brutus himself is a forerunner of Hamlet. Since Cassius, the so-called villain of this play, is presented rather sympathetically, some of our respect for Brutus is lost near the end of the play.

The Story:

At the feast of Lupercalia all Rome rejoiced, for the latest military triumphs of Julius Caesar were being celebrated during that holiday. Yet tempers flared and jealousies seethed beneath this public gaiety. Flavius and Marallus, two tribunes, coming upon a group of citizens gathered to praise Caesar, tore down their trophies and ordered the people to go home and remember Pompey's fate at the hands of Caesar.

Other dissatisfied noblemen discussed with concern Caesar's growing power and his incurable ambition. A soothsayer, following Caesar in his triumphal procession, warned him to beware the Ides of March. Cassius, one of the most violent of Caesar's critics, spoke at length to Brutus of the dictator's unworthiness to rule the state. Why, he demanded, should the name of Caesar have become synonymous with that of Rome when there were so many other worthy men in the city?

While Cassius and Brutus were speaking, they heard a tremendous shouting from the crowd. From aristocratic Casca they learned that before the mob Marcus Antonius had three times offered a crown to Caesar and three times the dictator had refused it. Thus did the wily Antonius and Caesar catch and hold the devotion of the multitude. Fully aware of Caesar's methods and the potential danger that he

embodied, Cassius and Brutus, disturbed by this new turn of events, agreed to meet again to discuss the affairs of Rome. As they parted Caesar arrived in time to see them, and suspicion of Cassius entered his mind. Cassius was not contented-looking; he was too lean and nervous to be satisfied with life. Caesar much preferred to have fat, jolly men about him.

Cassius' plan was to enlist Brutus in a plot to overthrow Caesar. Brutus himself was one of the most respected and beloved citizens of Rome; if he were in league against Caesar, the dictator's power could be curbed easily. But it would be difficult to turn Brutus completely against Caesar, for Brutus was an honorable man and not given to treason, so that only the most drastic circumstances would make him forego his loyalty. Cassius plotted to have certain false papers denoting widespread public alarm over Caesar's rapidly growing power put into Brutus' hands. Then Brutus might put Rome's interests above his own personal feelings.

Secretly, at night, Cassius had the papers laid at Brutus' door. Their purport was that Brutus must strike at once against Caesar to save Rome. The conflict within Brutus was great. His wife Portia complained that he had not slept at all during the night and that she had found him wandering, restless and unhappy, about the house. At last he reached a decision. Remembering Tarquin, the tyrant whom his ancestors had banished from Rome, Brutus agreed to join Cassius and his conspirators in their attempt to save Rome from Caesar. He refused, however, to sanction the murder of Antonius, planned at the same time as the assassination of Caesar. The plan was to kill Caesar on the following morning, March fifteenth.

On the night of March fourteenth, all nature seemed to misbehave. Strange lights appeared in the sky, graves yawned, ghosts walked, and an atmosphere of terror pervaded the city. Caesar's wife Calpurnia dreamed she saw her husband's statue with a hundred wounds spouting blood. In the morning she told him of the dream and pleaded that he not go to the Senate that morning. When she had almost convinced him to remain at home, one of the conspirators arrived and persuaded the dictator that Calpurnia was unduly nervous, that the dream was actually an omen of Caesar's tremendous popularity in Rome, the bleeding wounds a symbol of Caesar's power going out to all Romans. The other conspirators then arrived to allay any suspicion that Caesar might have of them and to make sure that he attended the Senate that day.

As Caesar made his way through the city, more omens of evil appeared to him. A paper detailing the plot against him was thrust into his hands, but he neglected to read it. When the soothsayer again cried out against the Ides of March, Caesar paid no attention to the warning.

At the Senate chamber Antonius was drawn to one side. Then the conspirators crowded about Caesar as if to second a petition for the repealing of an order banishing Publius Cimber. When he refused the petition, the conspirators attacked him, and he fell dead of twenty-three knife wounds.

Craftily pretending to side with the conspirators, Antonius was able to reinstate himself in their good graces, and in spite of Cassius' warning he was granted permission to speak at Caesar's funeral after Brutus had delivered his oration. Before the populace Brutus, frankly and honestly explaining his part in Caesar's murder, declared that his love for Rome had prompted him to turn against his friend. Cheering him, the mob agreed that Caesar was a tyrant who deserved death. Then Antonius rose to speak. Cleverly and forcefully he turned the temper of the crowd against the conspirators by explaining that even when Caesar was most tyrannical, everything he did was for the people's welfare. Soon the mob became so enraged over the assassination that the conspirators were forced to flee from Rome.

Gradually the temper of the people changed, and they became aligned in two camps. One group supported the new triumvirate of Marcus Antonius, Octavius Caesar, and Aemilius Lepidus. The other group followed Brutus and Cassius to their military camp at Sardis.

At Sardis, Brutus and Cassius quarreled constantly over various small matters. In the course of one violent disagreement Brutus told Cassius that Portia, despondent over the outcome of the civil war, had killed herself. Cassius, shocked by this news of his sister's death, allowed himself to be persuaded to leave the safety of the camp at Sardis and meet the enemy on the plains of Philippi. The night before the battle Caesar's ghost appeared to Brutus in his tent and announced that they would meet at Philippi.

At the beginning of the battle the forces of Brutus were at first successful against those of Octavius. Cassius, however, was driven back by Antonius. One morning Cassius sent one of his followers, Titinius, to learn if approaching troops were the enemy or the soldiers of Brutus. When Cassius saw Titinius unseated from his horse by the strangers, he assumed that everything was lost and ordered his servant Pindarus to kill him. Actually, the troops had been sent by Brutus. Rejoicing over the defeat of Octavius, they were having rude sport with Titinius. When they returned to Cassius and found him dead, Titinius also killed himself. In the last charge against Antonius, the soldiers of Brutus, tired and discouraged by these new events, were defeated. Brutus, heartbroken, asked his friends to kill him. When they refused, he commanded his servant to hold his sword and turn his face away. Then Brutus fell upon his sword and died.

THE JUNGLE

Type of work: Novel
Author: Upton Sinclair (1878-   )
Type of plot: Social criticism
Time of plot: Early twentieth century
Locale: Chicago
First published: 1906

Principal characters:
    JURGIS RUDKUS, a stockyards worker
    ANTANAS RUDKUS, his father
    ONA, Jurgis' wife
    ELZBIETA, Ona's stepmother
    JONAS, Elzbieta's brother
    MARIJA, Ona's orphan cousin

Critique:

The Jungle is an indignant book, written in anger at the social injustices of the meat-packing industry, and from this anger the novel derives its power. At the time of publication the book served its purpose in arousing public sentiment against unfair practices in the meat industry. It is still an honestly told and gripping story.

The Story:

While he was still a peasant boy in Lithuania, Jurgis Rudkus had fallen in love with a gentle girl named Ona. When Ona's father died, Jurgis, planning to marry her as soon as he had enough money, came to America with her family. Besides the young lovers, the emigrant party was composed of Antanas, Jurgis' father; Elzbieta, Ona's stepmother; Jonas, Elzbieta's brother; Marija, Ona's orphan cousin, and Elzbieta's six children.

By the time the family arrived in Chicago they had very little money. Jonas, Marija, and Jurgis at once got work in the stockyards. Antanas tried to find work, but he was too old. They all decided that it would be cheaper to buy a house on installments than to rent. A crooked agent sold them a ramshackle house which had a fresh coat of paint and told his ignorant customers that it was new.

Jurgis found his job exhausting, but he thought himself lucky to be making forty-five dollars a month. At last Antanas also found work at the plant, but he had to give part of his wages to the foreman in order to keep his job. Jurgis and Ona saved enough money for their wedding feast and were married. Then the family found that they needed more money. Elzbieta lied about the age of her oldest son, Stanislovas, and he too got a job at the plant. Ona had already begun to work in order to help pay for the wedding.

Antanas worked in a moist, cold room where he developed consumption. When he died, the family had scarcely enough money to bury him. Winter came, and everyone suffered in the flimsy house. When Marija lost her job, the family income diminished. Jurgis joined a union and became an active member. He went to night school to learn to read and speak English.

At last summer came with its hordes of flies and oppressive heat. Marija found work as a beef trimmer, but at that job the danger of blood poisoning was very great. Ona had her baby, a fine boy, whom they called Antanas after his grandfather. Winter came again, and Jurgis sprained his ankle at the plant. Compelled to stay at home for months, he became moody. Two more of Elzbieta's children left school to sell papers.

When Jurgis was well enough to look for work again, he could find none, because he was no longer the strong man he had been. Finally he got a job in a fertilizer plant, a last resource, for men lasted only a few years at that work. One of Elzbieta's daughters was now old enough to care for the rest of the children, and Elzbieta also went to work.

Jurgis began to drink. Ona, pregnant again, developed a consumptive cough and was often seized with spells of hysteria. Hoping to save the family with the money she made, she went to a house of prostitution with her boss, Connor. When Jurgis learned what she had done, he attacked Connor and was sentenced to thirty days in jail. Now that he had time to think, Jurgis saw how unjustly he had been treated by society. No longer would he try to be kind, except to his own family. From now on he would recognize society as an enemy rather than a friend.

After he had served his sentence, Jurgis went to look for his family. He found that they had lost the house because they could not meet the payments, and had moved. He found them at last in a rooming-house. Ona was in labor with her second child, and Jurgis frantically searched for a midwife. By the time he found one, Ona and the child had died. Now he had only little Antanas to live for. He tried to find work. Blacklisted in the stockyards for his attack on Connor, he finally found a job in a harvesting machine factory. Shortly afterward he was discharged when his department closed down for a lack of orders.

Next he went to work in the steel mills. In order to save money he moved near the mills and came home only on weekends. One weekend he came home to find that little Antanas had drowned in the street in front of the house. Now that he had no dependents, he hopped a freight train and rode away from Chicago. He became one of the thousands of migratory farm workers; his old strength came back in healthful surroundings.

In the fall Jurgis returned to Chicago. He got a job digging tunnels under the streets. Then a shoulder injury made him spend weeks in a hospital. Discharged with his arm still in a sling, he became a beggar. By luck he obtained a hundred-dollar bill from a lavish drunk. When he went to a saloon to get it changed, however, the barkeeper tried to cheat him out of his money. In a rage Jurgis attacked the man. He was arrested and sent to jail again. There he met a dapper safe-cracker, Jack Duane. After their release, Jurgis joined Duane in several holdups and became acquainted with Chicago's underworld. At last he was making money.

Jurgis became a political worker. About that time the packing plant workers began to demand more rights through their unions. When packing house operators would not listen to union demands, there was a general strike. Jurgis went to work in the plant as a scab. One day he met Connor and attacked him again. Jurgis fled from the district to avoid a penitentiary sentence. On the verge of starvation, he found Marija working as a prostitute. Jurgis was ashamed to think how low he and Marija had fallen since they came to Chicago. She gave him some money so that he might look for a job.

Jurgis was despondent until one night he heard a Socialist speak. Jurgis believed that he had found a remedy for the ills of the world. At last he knew how the workers could find self-respect. He found a job in a hotel where the manager was a Socialist. It was the beginning of a new life for Jurgis, the rebirth of hope and faith.

1536

THE JUNGLE BOOKS

Type of work: Short stories
Author: Rudyard Kipling (1865-1936)
Type of plot: Beast fables
Time of plot: Nineteenth century
Locale: India
First published: 1894, 1895

Principal characters:

MOWGLI, an Indian boy
FATHER WOLF
MOTHER WOLF
SHERE KHAN, the tiger
AKELA, leader of the wolf pack
BAGHEERA, the black panther
BALOO, the bear
KAA, the rock python
THE BANDAR-LOG, the monkey people
HATHI, the elephant
MESSUA, a woman who adopted Mowgli for a time
MESSUA'S HUSBAND
BULDEO, a village hunter
GRAY BROTHER, a young wolf

Critique:

Rudyard Kipling, winner of the Nobel Prize in 1907, wrote these stories for children while living in Brattleboro, Vermont. *The Jungle Book* and *The Second Jungle Book* are children's classics which attempt to teach the lessons of justice, loyalty, and tribal laws. It is evident from reading these books that here is a master writer who loved children and could tell them a good story with an underlying meaning that adults can appreciate as well.

The Stories:

Shere Khan, the tiger, pursued a small Indian boy who had strayed from his native village, but Shere Khan was lame and missed his leap upon the child. When Father Wolf took the boy home with him to show to Mother Wolf, Shere Khan followed and demanded the child as his quarry. Mother Wolf refused. The tiger retired in anger. Mowgli, the frog, for such he was named, was reared by Mother Wolf along with her own cubs.

Father Wolf took Mowgli to the Council Rock to be recognized by the wolves. Bagheera, the panther, and Baloo, the bear, spoke for Mowgli's acceptance into the Seeonee wolf pack. Thus Mowgli became a wolf.

Baloo became Mowgli's teacher and instructed him in the lore of the jungle. Mowgli learned to speak the languages of all the jungle people. Throughout his early life the threat of Shere Khan hung over him, but Mowgli was certain of his place in the pack and of his friends' protection. But some day when Akela, the leader of the wolves, would miss his kill, the pack would turn on him and Mowgli. Bagheera told Mowgli to get the Red Flower, or fire, from the village to protect himself. When Akela missed his quarry one night and was about to be deposed and killed, Mowgli attacked all of their mutual enemies with his fire sticks and threatened to destroy anyone who molested Akela. That night Mowgli realized that the jungle was no place for him, and that some day he would go to live with men. But that time was still far off.

One day Mowgli climbed a tree and made friends with the Bandar-Log, the monkey tribe, who because of their stupidity and vanity were despised by the other jungle people. When the Bandar-Log carried off Mowgli, Bagheera and Baloo went in pursuit, taking along Kaa, the rock python, who loved to eat monkeys. Mowgli was rescued at the old ruined city of the Cold Lairs by the three pursuers, and Kaa feasted royally upon monkey meat.

One year during a severe drought in the jungle, Hathi the elephant proclaimed the water truce; all animals were allowed to drink at the water hole unmolested. Shere Khan announced to the animals gathered there one day that he had killed a Man, not for food but from choice. The other animals were shocked. Hathi allowed the tiger to drink and then told him to be off. Then Hathi told the story of how fear came to the jungle and why the tiger was striped. It was the tiger who first killed Man and earned the human tribe's unrelenting enmity, and for his deed the tiger was condemned to wear stripes. Now for one day a year the tiger was not afraid of Man and could kill him. This day was called, among jungle people, the Night of the Tiger.

One day Mowgli wandered close to a native village, where he was adopted by Messua, a woman who had lost her son some years before. Mowgli became a watcher of the village herds, and so from time to time he met Gray Wolf, his brother, and heard the news of the jungle. Learning that Shere Khan intended to kill him, he laid plans with Akela and Gray Brother to kill the tiger. They lured Shere Khan into a gully and then stampeded the herd. Shere Khan was trampled to death. Stoned from the village because he was believed to be a sorcerer who spoke to animals, Mowgli returned to the jungle resolved to hunt with the wolves for the rest of his life.

Buldeo, the village hunter, followed the trail of Mowgli, Gray Brother, and Akela. Mowgli overheard Buldeo say that Messua and her husband were imprisoned in their house and would be burned at the stake. Messua's husband had saved some money and he had one of the finest herds of buffaloes in the village. Knowing that the imprisonment of Messua and her husband was a scheme for the villagers to get their property, Mowgli laid plans to help his friends. Entering the village, he led Messua and her husband beyond the gates in the darkness. Then the jungle people began to destroy, little by little, the farms, the orchards, and the cattle, but no villager was harmed because Mowgli did not desire the death of any human. Finally, just before the rains, Hathi and his three sons moved into the village and tore down the houses. The people left and thus the jungle was let into the village.

Kaa took Mowgli to Cold Lairs to meet the guardian of the king's treasure, an old white cobra who had expressed a desire to see Mowgli. The old cobra showed them all the treasure, and when he left Mowgli took a jeweled elephant goad, a king's ankus, with him, even though the cobra had said it brought death to the person who possessed it.

Back in the jungle Mowgli threw the ankus away. Later that day he went with Bagheera to retrieve the ankus and discovered that it was gone. They followed the trail of the man who had picked it up and found that altogether six men who had had possession of the ankus had died. Believing it to be cursed, Mowgli returned the ankus to the treasure room in the Cold Lairs.

Sometimes fierce red dogs called dholes traveled in large packs, destroying everything in their paths. Warned of the approach of the dholes, Mowgli led the marauders, by insults and taunts, toward the lairs of the Little People, the bees. Then he excited the bees to attack the dholes. The destruction of the red dogs that escaped the fury of the bees was completed by the wolves lying in ambush a little farther down the river which flowed under the cliffs where the Little People lived. But it was the last battle of old Akela, the leader of the pack when Mowgli was a little boy. He crawled out slowly from under a pile of carcasses to bid Mowgli goodbye and to sing his death song.

The second year after the death of Akela, Mowgli was about seventeen years old. In the spring of that year Mowgli knew that he was unhappy, but none of his friends could tell him what was wrong. Mowgli left his own jungle to travel to another, and on the way he met Messua. Her husband had died, leaving her with a child. Messua told Mowgli that she believed he was her own son lost in the jungle years before and that her baby must be his brother. Mowgli did not know what to make of the child and the unhappiness he felt. When Gray Brother came to Messua's hut, Mowgli decided to return to the jungle. But on the outskirts of the village he met a girl coming down the path. Mowgli melted into the jungle and watched the girl. He knew at last that the jungle was no longer a place for him and that he had returned to the Man-pack to stay.

JUNO AND THE PAYCOCK

Type of work: Drama
Author: Sean O'Casey (1884-   )
Type of plot: Satiric realism
Time of plot: 1922
Locale: Dublin
First presented: 1924

> *Principal characters:*
> "Captain" Jack Boyle, a ne'er-do-well
> Juno Boyle, his wife
> Johnny Boyle, their son
> Mary Boyle, their daughter
> "Joxer" Daly, the Captain's pal
> Jerry Devine, Mary's suitor
> Charlie Bentham, a schoolteacher
> Mrs. Maisie Madigan, a neighbor
> "Needle" Nugent, a tailor

Critique:

Sean O'Casey's plays mark the culmination of the Irish dramatic renaissance, which had begun as a part of the European movement toward realistic theater in opposition to the French romantic drama, but which diverged from the dramaturgic techniques of Ibsen and Shaw. Believing that Continental and English dramas were too intellectualized, O'Casey, along with his compatriots Yeats and Synge, tried to make the drama individualistic and realistic by drenching it in Irish local color. Formlessness—ignoring formal dramatic technique to reflect the vigor and vitality of life—was O'Casey's unique contribution to the Irish movement. In *Juno and the Paycock* he reached a new peak of realism. He dispensed with an elaborate plot, ideas, and consistency of character, content merely to show characters, Irish characters, in action.

The Story:

Waiting for "Captain" Jack Boyle to come in from his morning visit to the pub, Mary Boyle and her mother, Juno, discussed the newspaper account of the murder of Robbie Tancred, a fanatic Irish Republican. Johnny Boyle, who himself had been shot in the hip and had lost an arm fighting against the Free State, left the living room of the tenancy after denouncing the two women for their morbid insensitivity. Juno scolded Mary for participating in the Trades Union Strike, especially at a time when the family was in debt for food; but Mary defended her activities, and her brother's as well, as matters of principle.

When Jerry Devine rushed in with a message from Father Farrell, who had found a job for Boyle, Juno sent Jerry to look for her husband at his favorite bar. Soon afterward she heard her husband and his crony, "Joxer" Daly, singing on the stairs. She hid behind the bed curtains so as to catch them talking about her. Disclosing herself, she frightened Joxer away and berated her husband for his laziness and malingering. Jerry returned and delivered his message to Boyle, who immediately developed a case of stabbing pains in his legs. Juno, not deceived, ordered him to change into his working clothes. She then left for her own job.

Jerry accosted Mary, complained of her unfriendliness, and once again proposed to her. Although Jerry offered her love and security, Mary refused him, and both left in a huff.

Ignoring his wife's instructions to apply for the job, Boyle, leisurely proceeding to get his breakfast, was rejoined by Joxer. Absorbed in their talk, they refused to acknowledge a loud knocking at the street door, though the continuance of it seemed to upset young Johnny Boyle. Their rambling discourse on family life, the clergy, literature, and the sea was interrupted by Juno and Mary, who had returned with Charlie Bentham, a school-teacher and amateur lawyer, to announce that a cousin had bequeathed £2,000 to Boyle. Boyle declared that he was through with Joxer and the like, whereupon Joxer, who had been hiding outside the window, reappeared, expressed his indignation, and left.

Two days later the two cronies had been reconciled, Joxer having served as Boyle's agent for loans based on expectations of the inheritance. The entrance of Juno and Mary with a new gramophone was followed by that of Bentham, now Mary's fiancé. Over family tea, Bentham explained his belief in theosophy and ghosts. Johnny, visibly upset by this conversation about death, left the room but quickly returned, twitching and trembling. He was convinced that he had seen the bloody ghost of Robbie Tancred kneeling before the statue of the Virgin.

The arrival of Joxer with Mrs. Madigan, a garrulously reminiscent neighbor, smoothed over the incident. A party featuring whiskey and song ensued. The revelry was interrupted by Mrs. Tancred and some neighbors, on their way to Robbie Tancred's funeral. Soon thereafter the merriment was again dispelled, this time by the funeral procession in the street. A young man, an Irregular Mobilizer, came looking for Johnny, whom he reproached for not attending the funeral. He ordered Johnny to appear at a meeting called for the purpose of inquiring into Tancred's death.

Two months later, Juno insisted on taking Mary to the doctor, for the girl seemed to be pining away over Bentham, who had disappeared.

After the women had left, Joxer and Nugent, a tailor, slipped into the apartment. Having learned that Boyle would not receive the inheritance, Nugent had come to get the suit which he had sold to Boyle on credit. Taking the suit from a chair, Nugent scoffed at Boyle's promise to pay and his order for a new topcoat as well.

Joxer, who had sneaked out unseen, returned, hypocrite that he was, to commiserate with Boyle. Mrs. Madigan, who had also heard that Boyle would not receive his inheritance, arrived to collect the three pounds she had lent him. Rebuffed, she appropriated the gramophone and left, followed by Joxer.

News of Boyle's misadventure spread rapidly; two men arrived to remove the new, but unpaid-for, furniture. Mrs. Boyle ran out to find her husband.

Mary having returned, Jerry Devine came to see her. Again he proposed. Although he was willing to forget that Mary had jilted him for Bentham, he recoiled at her admission that she was pregnant.

Left alone with the two moving men, Johnny imagined that he felt a bullet wound in his chest. At that moment two armed Irish Irregulars entered the apartment and accused Johnny of informing on Robbie Tancred to the gang that had murdered him. Ignoring Johnny's pro-testations of innocence and loyalty, the men dragged him out. A little later, Mrs. Madigan notified Mary and Juno that the police were waiting below, requesting that Juno identify a body. Juno and Mary left, vowing never to return to the worthless Boyle.

Soon Boyle and Joxer stumbled into the abandoned apartment, both very drunk and unaware of Johnny's death or Juno and Mary's desertion. Joxer stretched out on the bed; Boyle slumped on the floor. With thick tongues they stammered out their patriotic devotion to Ireland, and Boyle deplored the miserable state of the world.

JURGEN

Type of work: Novel
Author: James Branch Cabell (1879-   )
Type of plot: Fantasy
Time of plot: Middle Ages
Locale: Poictesme, a land of myth
First published: 1919

Principal characters:
> JURGEN, a middle-aged pawnbroker
> DAME LISA, his wife
> DOROTHY LA DÉSIRÉE, his childhood sweetheart
> QUEEN GUENEVERE
> DAME ANAÏTIS
> CHLORIS, a Hamadryad
> QUEEN HELEN of Troy
> MOTHER SEREDA
> KOSHCHEI, the maker of things as they are

Critique:

Jurgen, A Comedy of Justice, is one of a series dealing with the mythical country of Poictesme. Although it was once charged in the courts with being an obscene book, it is by no means merely an erotic tale. This novel can be read on many levels; as a narrative of fantastic love and adventure, as a satire, and as a philosophic view of life. The book is an interesting product of a romantic imagination and a critical mind.

The Story:

Once in the old days a middle-aged pawnbroker named Jurgen said a good word for the Prince of Darkness. In gratitude, the Prince of Darkness removed from the earth Dame Lisa, Jurgen's shrewish wife. Some time later Jurgen heard that his wife had returned to wander on Amneran Heath; consequently the only manly thing for him to do was to look for her.

It was Walburga's Eve when Jurgen

met Dame Lisa on the heath. She led him to a cave, but when he followed her inside she disappeared and Jurgen found a Centaur instead. Jurgen inquired for his wife. The Centaur replied that only Koshchei the Deathless, the maker of things as they are, could help Jurgen in his quest. The Centaur gave Jurgen a beautiful new shirt and started off with him to the Garden between Dawn and Sunrise, the first stopping place of Jurgen's journey to find Koshchei.

In the garden Jurgen found Dorothy la Désirée, his first sweetheart, who retained all the beauty he had praised in his youthful poetry. She no longer knew him, for she was in love only with Jurgen as he had been in youth, and he could not make her understand that in the real world she also had become middle-aged and commonplace. So he parted sadly from her and found himself suddenly back in his native country.

His friend the Centaur had now become an ordinary horse. Jurgen mounted and rode through a forest until he came to the house of Mother Sereda, the goddess who controlled Wednesdays and whose job it was to bleach the color out of everything in the world. By flattery Jurgen persuaded her to let him live over a certain Wednesday in his youth with Dorothy la Désirée. But when the magic Wednesday ended, Dorothy la Désirée turned into the old woman she really was, and Jurgen quickly departed.

He wandered again to Amneran Heath and entered the cave to look for Koshchei and Dame Lisa. There he found a beautiful girl who said that she was Guenevere, the daughter of King Gogyrvan. Jurgen offered to conduct her back to her home. When they arrived at the court of King Gogyrvan, Jurgen, pretending to be the Duke of Logreus, asked for the hand of Guenevere as a reward for her safe return. But she had already been promised to King Arthur. Jurgen stayed on at court. He had made the discovery that he still looked like a young man; the only trouble was that his

shadow was not his shadow; it was the shadow of Mother Sereda.

King Arthur's envoys, Dame Anaïtis and Merlin, had arrived to take Guenevere to London. Jurgen watched her depart for London without feeling any sorrow because of a magic token Merlin had given him. Then Dame Anaïtis invited Jurgen to visit her palace in Cocaigne, the country where Time stood still. There Jurgen participated with her in a ceremony called the Breaking of the Veil, to learn afterwards that it had been a marriage ceremony and that Dame Anaïtis was now his wife. Dame Anaïtis, a myth woman of lunar legend, instructed Jurgen in every variety of strange pleasures she knew.

Jurgen visited a philologist, who said that Jurgen had also become a legend; consequently he could not remain long in Cocaigne. When the time came for him to leave the country, Jurgen chose to go to Leukê, the kingdom where Queen Helen and Achilles ruled. Jurgen's reason for wishing to go there was that Queen Helen resembled his first sweetheart, Dorothy la Désirée.

In Leukê, Jurgen met Chloris, a Hamadryad, and married her. He was still curious about Queen Helen, however, and one evening he entered her castle and went to her bedchamber. The sleeping queen was Dorothy la Désirée, but he dared not touch her. Her beauty, created from the dreams of his youth, was unattainable. He left the castle and returned to Chloris.

Shortly afterward the Philistines invaded Leukê and condemned all its mythical inhabitants to limbo. Jurgen protested because he was flesh and blood and he offered to prove his claim by mathematics. Queen Dolores of the Philistines agreed with him after he had demonstrated his proof to her by means of a concrete example. However, he was condemned by the great tumble-bug of the Philistines for being a poet.

After Chloris had been condemned to limbo, Jurgen went on to the hell of his

1542

fathers. There he visited Satan and learned that Koshchei had created hell to humor the pride of Jurgen's forefathers. Then he remembered that he was supposed to be looking for Dame Lisa. Learning that she was not in hell, he decided to look for her in heaven. Mistaken for a pope by means of the philologist's charm, he managed to gain entrance to heaven. Dame Lisa was not there. St. Peter returned him to Amneran Heath.

On the heath he again met Mother Sereda, who took away his youth and returned him to his middle-aged body. Actually, it was a relief to Jurgen to be old again. Then for the third time he entered the cave in search of Dame Lisa. Inside he found the Prince of Darkness who had taken her away. The Prince was really Koshchei; Jurgen was near the end of his quest. He asked Koshchei to return Dame Lisa to him.

Koshchei showed him Guenevere, Dame Anaïtis, and Dorothy la Désirée again. But Jurgen would not have them. He had had his youth to live over, and he had committed the same follies. He was content now to be Jurgen the pawnbroker.

Koshchei agreed to return Jurgen to his former life, but he asked for the Centaur's shirt in return. Jurgen gladly gave up the shirt. Koshchei walked with him from the heath into town. As they walked, Jurgen noticed that the moon was sinking in the east. Time was turning backward.

It was as if the past year had never been. For now he approached his house and saw through the window that the table was set for supper. Inside, Dame Lisa sat sewing and looking quite as if nothing had ever happened.

JUSTICE

Type of work: Drama
Author: John Galsworthy (1867-1933)
Type of plot: Social criticism
Time of plot: 1910
Locale: London
First presented: 1910

Principal characters:
WILLIAM FALDER, a solicitor's clerk
COKESON, a senior clerk
RUTH HONEYWILL, with whom Falder is in love

Critique:

Since 1910, when this play was written, prison reforms have progressed considerably. The play is a protest against dehumanized institutionalism, with particular attention directed toward the evils of solitary confinement and the strict parole system. The problem of making a convicted man into a useful citizen once more is complex. Galsworthy thought rehabilitation likely only if all who came into contact with the man accepted their share of the responsibility.

The Story:

Cokeson, managing clerk for the firm of James and Walter How, solicitors, was interrupted one July morning by a woman asking to see the junior clerk, Falder. The woman, Ruth Honeywill, seemed in great distress, and though it was against office rules, Cokeson permitted her to see Falder.

Falder and Ruth Honeywill were planning to run away together. Ruth's husband, a drunken brute, had abused her until she would no longer stay with him. Falder arranged to have Ruth and her two children meet him at the railway station that night. Ruth left and Falder went back to work.

Young Walter How came to the office. Cokeson was skeptical of the young man's desire to keep the firm not only on the right side of the law but also on the right side of ethics. James How entered from the partners' room. He and Walter began to check the firm's balance, which they decided was below what they remembered it should have been. Then they discovered that a check written the previous Friday had been altered from nine to ninety pounds.

The check had been cashed on the same day that another junior clerk, Davis, had gone away on some firm business. Cokeson was quickly cleared. When it became certain that the check stub had been altered after Davis had started on his trip, suspicion fell on Falder.

The bank cashier was summoned. He recognized Falder as the man who had cashed the check. James How accused Falder of the felony. Falder asked for mercy, but How, convinced that the felony had been premeditated, sent for the police. Falder was arrested.

When the case came to court, Frome, Falder's counsel, tried to show that Falder had conceived the idea and carried it out within the space of four minutes, and that at the time he had been greatly upset by the difficulties of Ruth Honeywill with her husband. Frome called Cokeson as the first witness, and the managing clerk gave the impression that Falder had not been himself on the day in question. Ruth Honeywill was the most important witness. She indicated that Falder had altered the check for her sake. Cleaver, the counsel for the prosecution, tried his utmost to make her appear an undutiful wife.

In defense of Falder, Frome tried to press the point that Falder had been al-most out of his mind. Cleaver questioned Falder until the clerk admitted that he had not known what he was doing. Then Cleaver declared Falder had known enough to keep the money he had stolen and to turn in the sum for which the check originally had been written. The jury found Falder guilty and the judge sentenced him to three years.

At Christmas time Cokeson visited the prison on Falder's behalf. He attempted to have Falder released from solitary confinement and asked for permission to bring Ruth Honeywill to see Falder. Cokeson's visit accomplished nothing. Both the chaplain and the prison governor were indifferent to his appeal.

When Falder was finally released on parole, Ruth Honeywill went to intercede for him at How's office. She intimated that she had kept herself and her children alive by living with another man after she left her husband. Falder went to tell Cokeson that his relatives wanted to give him money to go to Canada. He was depressed and ill at ease; he had seen Ruth only once since his release. James How made it clear that if Falder refused to abide by strict standards of justice there would be no hope that the firm would take him back.

James How, aware that Ruth Honeywill had been living with another man, crudely broke the news to Falder. He did, however, give Falder and Ruth an opportunity to talk over their predicament. While they were talking in a side room, a detective sergeant came looking for Falder. Falder was to be arrested again because he had failed to report to the police according to the parole agreement. Although How and Cokeson refused to disclose Falder's whereabouts, the detective discovered Falder in the side room. As he was rearresting Falder, the clerk suddenly broke loose and killed himself by jumping from the office window.

THE KALEVALA

Type of work: Poem
Author: Elias Lönnrot (1802-1884)
Type of plot: Folk epic
Time of plot: Mythological antiquity
Locale: Finland and Lapland
First published: 1835

Principal characters:
VÄINÄMÖINEN, the Son of the Wind and the Virgin of the Air, the singer-hero
ILMARINEN, the smith-hero
LEMMINKÄINEN, the warrior-hero
LOUHI, ruler of Pohjola, the North Country
AINO, a young Lapp maiden
JOUKAHÄINEN, a Laplander, Aino's brother
KULLERVO, an evil, sullen slave, very powerful
THE DAUGHTER OF LOUHI, Ilmarinen's wife

Critique:

The *Kalevala*, which may be roughly translated as "The Land of Heroes," is a long narrative poem fashioned by the Finnish scholar, Elias Lönnrot, from the folk legends and oral traditions of his country. It is the national epic of Finland and as such ranks with those of other nations whose mythologies are better known. In legend, the ancestor of all the heroes is Kaleva, but he never appears in the stories. Aside from giving the poem its title, Kaleva constitutes one of its few unifying principles; for, like most folk epics, the work lacks unity and cohesion, being the product of many hands and voices over hundreds of years. Nevertheless, the tales of Väinämöinen, Ilmarinen, and Lemminkäinen are told with great beauty, simplicity, and poetic force. Lönnrot performed a tremendous task in gathering the many tales, editing them, arranging them, and even writing connective material. From a purely literary standpoint, his monumental production, peculiar because of its relatively late formation, stands as a worthy representation of the early culture of a civilization little known to Western readers.

The Story:

After his mother had created the land, the sun, and the moon out of sea duck eggs, Väinämöinen was born, and with the help of Sampsa Pellervoinen he made the barren land fruitful by sowing seeds and planting trees. By the time Väinämöinen was an old man he had gained great fame as a singer and charmer. When a brash young man named Joukahäinen challenged him to a duel of magic songs, Väinämöinen easily won and forced the young man to give him his sister Aino for a wife. But Aino was greatly saddened at having to marry an old man and so she drowned herself, to Väinämöinen's sorrow. He looked all over the sea for her and found her at last in the form of a salmon, but in that form she escaped him forever.

In time he heard of the beautiful daughters of Louhi in the far North Country and he decided to seek them out. On the way to Pohjola, the land of Louhi, his horse was killed by the bold young man whom he had defeated in the duel of songs, and Väinämöinen was forced to swim to Pohjola. Louhi, the witch, found him on the beach, restored his health, told him that he would have to forge a magic Sampo in order to win a daughter, and then sent him on his way.

Väinämöinen found one of Louhi's daughters seated on a rainbow and asked her to become his wife. She gave him three tasks to do. After completing two, he was wounded in the knee while trying to complete the third. The wound, which bled profusely, was healed by a magic ointment prepared under the directions of an old man skilled in leechcraft. Väinämöinen went home and raised a great wind to carry Ilmarinen, the mighty smith who had forged the sky, into the North Country to make the Sampo for Louhi. Ilmarinen forged the Sampo, but still Louhi's daughter refused to marry and leave her homeland. Ilmarinen, also in love with the maiden, went sadly home.

A gallant youth, Lemminkäinen, was famous for winning the love of women. Having heard of Kyllikki, the flower of Saari, he was determined to win her for his wife. When he arrived in Esthonia she refused him, and he abducted her. They lived happily together until one day she disobeyed him. In retaliation he went north to seek one of Louhi's daughters as his wife. In Pohjola, Lemminkäinen charmed everyone except an evil herdsman whom he scorned. Like Väinämöinen, he was given three tasks and performed the first two without much difficulty; but while trying to complete the third he was slain by the evil herdsman. Alarmed by his long absence, his mother went searching for him, found him in pieces at the bottom of a river, and restored him finally to his original shape.

Meanwhile, Väinämöinen was busy building a ship by means of magic, his third task for Louhi's daughter, when he found that he had forgotten the three magic words needed to complete the work. He searched everywhere for them and was almost trapped in Tuonela, the kingdom of death. Then he heard that the giant Vipunen might know them. When they met, Vipunen swallowed him, but Väinämöinen caused the giant so much pain that the creature was forced to release him and reveal the magic charm. With the charm Väinämöinen completed his ship and again set sail for Pohjola.

Ilmarinen, learning of Väinämöinen's departure, started after him on horseback. When they met they agreed to abide by the maiden's choice. On their arrival at Pohjola, Louhi gave Ilmarinen three tasks to perform: to plow a field of snakes, to capture a bear and a wolf, and to catch a great pike. Ilmarinen performed these tasks. Since Väinämöinen was old, Louhi's daughter chose Ilmarinen for her husband. There was great rejoicing at the marriage. Väinämöinen sang for the bridal couple. A gigantic ox was slain and mead was brewed, and the bride and groom were both instructed in the duties of marriage. At last Ilmarinen took his new bride to his home in the south.

Meanwhile, Lemminkäinen had not been invited to the festivities because of his quarrelsome nature, and he was therefore angry. Although his mother warned him of the dangers he would have to face on the journey and of Louhi's treachery, he insisted on going to Pohjola. With his magic charms he was able to overcome all dangers along the way. In Pohjola, Louhi tried to kill him with snake-poisoned ale, but Lemminkäinen saw through the trick. Then he and Louhi's husband engaged in a duel of magic which ended in a tie. Finally they fought with swords and Lemminkäinen slew Louhi's husband. Lemminkäinen then turned into an eagle and flew home. In fear of retribution he took his mother's advice and went to live for several years on an obscure island where the only inhabitants were women, their warrior husbands being away from home.

Forced to flee when the time came for the husbands to return, Lemminkäinen set out for his own land in a boat. The craft turned over and he was forced to swim to shore. On reaching home he found the country desolate and his mother missing. At last he found her hiding in the forest. Swearing to avenge himself on the warriors of Pohjola who had desolated the land, he set sail with Tiera, a warrior companion, but Louhi sent the frost to destroy him. Although Lemminkäinen managed to charm the frost, he and his companion were shipwrecked and were forced to retreat.

The wife of Kalervo had been carried off by her brother-in-law, Untamöinen, who then laid waste to Kalervo's land. In the cradle Kullervo, born to Kalervo's wife, swore to be avenged on his uncle. Kullervo grew up strong, but so stupid and clumsy that he broke or ruined everything he touched. He tried to kill his uncle and his uncle tried to kill him. Finally, the uncle gave him to Ilmarinen. Ilmarinen's wife immediately disliked the boy and gave him a loaf of bread with a stone in it. In return, while Ilmarinen was away from home, Kullervo had her killed by wild beasts. He then fled into the forest, where he found his parents and lived with them for a long time. He performed all his chores badly. After a time he set out on a journey. Two women having refused him, he ravished a third, only to learn that she was his sister. In anguish she killed herself and Kullervo returned home in sorrow. When his family rejected him, he set off to attack Untamöinen. After killing his uncle he returned to find his family dead and the countryside desolate. He wandered off into the forest and killed himself by falling on his sword.

Ilmarinen, after weeping for his dead wife, made up his mind to get another in his forge. He fashioned a woman out of gold and silver, but she remained cold and lifeless; so Ilmarinen went north again to Pohjola. When Louhi refused to give him a wife, he abducted one of her daughters. This wife soon proved unfaithful and in anger he turned her into a seagull.

Meanwhile, Väinämöinen had been thinking about the Sampo, that magic mill which ground out riches. Determined to steal it from Louhi, he built a ship and Ilmarinen forged a sword for him, and the two heroes started for Pohjola. On the way Lemminkäinen called to them from the shore and asked to accompany them. They took him along. During the voyage the boat struck a giant pike. Väinämöinen killed the great fish and from its bones fashioned a harp with which he sang everyone in Pohjola to sleep. With the help of an ox the three heroes took the Sampo and sailed for home. In the meantime Louhi had awakened and sent fog and wind after the heroes. During the storm Väinämöinen's harp fell overboard.

Louhi and her men followed in a warboat. The two boats met in a great battle. Although Väinämöinen was victorious, Louhi dragged the Sampo from his boat into the lake. There it broke into pieces, most of which sank to the bottom. Only a few smaller pieces floated to shore. After making violent threats against Kalevala, Louhi returned home with only a small and useless fragment of the Sampo. Väinämöinen collected the pieces on the shore and planted them for good luck; the land became more fruitful. Having searched in vain for his lost harp, Väinämöinen made another of birchwood and his songs to its music gave joy to everyone.

Vexed because her land was barren after the loss of the Sampo, Louhi sent a terrible pestilence to Kalevala, but Väinämöinen healed the people by magic and salves. Next she sent a great bear to ravish the herds, but Väinämöinen killed the savage beast.

Louhi stole the moon and the sun, which had come down to earth to hear Väinämöinen play and sing. She also stole the fire from all the hearths of Kalevala. When Ukko, the supreme god, kindled a new fire for the sun and the moon, some of it fell to earth and was swallowed by a fish in a large lake. Väinämöinen and Ilmarinen finally found the fish and Ilmarinen was badly burned. The fire escaped and burned a great area of country until it was at last captured and returned to the hearths of Kalevala. Ilmarinen, recovered from his burns, prepared great chains for Louhi and frightened her into restoring the sun and the moon to the heavens.

Marjatta, a holy woman and a virgin,

swallowed a cranberry and a son was born to her in a stable. The child was baptized as the King of Carelia despite Väinämöinen's claim that such an ill-omened child should be put to death. Angered because the child proved wiser than he, Väinämöinen sailed away to a land between the earth and the sky, leaving behind him, for the pleasure of his people, his harp and his songs.

DAS KAPITAL

Type of work: Political economy
Author: Karl Marx (1818-1883)
First published: Vol. I, 1867; Vols. II and III, edited by Friedrich Engels, 1885-1894

If Marx was right, the Russian revolution was inevitable and the world-wide growth of communism is also inevitable; therefore, even if *Das Kapital* had never been written, the world would have been split by revolution and by the emergence of communism as a dynamic political force. But it may be that Marx was mistaken, and that the emergence of communism would not have been possible had it not been for the labors of Marx in the British Museum which resulted in the writing and publication of *Das Kapital.* Even if economic unbalance had resulted in a revolutionary uprising of the proletariat in Russia or elsewhere, it probably would not have taken the form it did, or occurred when it did, or had the subsequent world-wide effect that it has had, had Marx not written *Das Kapital.* To write that this book has been world-shaking, then, is but to speak the truth.

Many of Marx's revolutionary ideas had already been expressed in the *Communist Manifesto* (1848) which he wrote with Friedrich Engels, but *Das Kapital* was more than another call to arms; it was an attempt to base communism on a theory of political economy which could be scientifically and dialectically defended. The *Manifesto* is a passionate document, an outline of a political philosophy, and something of a prophecy; but *Das Kapital* is a scholar's treatise, the product of years of research and reflection, a work of economic theory that continues to challenge professional economists. This contrast is illuminating, for the Communist movement has always

been characterized by contrast: the intellectual leads the laborers; the reasoned defense is supplemented by violence and murder, and the scholar's program comes alive in revolution and the threat of war.

In the *Manifesto,* Marx and Engels argued that the history of all societies has been a history of class struggles, that the struggle had become one between the bourgeois class and the proletariat, that all the injustices of society result from the economic advantage the bourgeoisie have over the proletariat, that the proletariat would finally rebel and take over the means of production, forming a classless society, a dictatorship of the proletariat.

In *Das Kapital,* Marx uses a dialectic method which was inspired by Hegel, even though it is put to a different use. Marx claimed that his dialectic method was the "direct opposite" of Hegel's, that with Hegel the dialectic "is standing on its head" and "must be turned right side up again, if you would discover the rational kernel within the mystical shell." The method is not mysterious; it involves attending to the conflicting aspects of matters under consideration in order to be able to attain a better idea of the whole. Thus, Marx describes his "rational" dialectic as including "in its comprehension and affirmative recognition of the existing state of things, at the same time, also, the recognition of the negation of that state, of its inevitable breaking up. . . ." He went on to maintain that his account regarded "every historically developed social form as in fluid movement, and therefore takes into account its transient nature not less than its momentary existence. . . ."

In Marx the dialectic method led to "dialectical materialism," the theory that history is the record of class struggles, the conflict of economic opposites.

Das Kapital begins with a study of commodities and money. Marx distinguishes between *use* value and value, the latter being understood in terms of exchange value but involving essentially the amount of labor that went into the production of the commodity; thus, "that which determines the magnitude of the value of any article is the amount of labour socially necessary, or the labourtime socially necessary for its production."

Money results from the use of some special commodity as a means of exchange in order to equate different products of labor. Money serves as "a universal measure of value." According to Marx, it is not money that makes commodities commensurable, but the fact of their being commensurable in terms of human labor that makes money possible as a measure of value.

Money begets money through the circulation of commodities: this is Marx's general formula for capital. Money is the first form in which capital appears precisely because it is the end product of a circulatory process which begins with the use of money to purchase commodities for sale at higher than the purchase price.

Capital would not be possible without a change of value. If money were used to purchase a commodity sold at the initial price, no profit would be made, no capital made possible. To explain the surplus value that emerges in the process, Marx reminds the reader that the capitalist buys labor power and uses it. The material of production belongs to the capitalist; therefore the product of the productive process also belongs to him. The product has a use-value, but the capitalist does not intend to use the product; his interest is in selling it for a price greater than the sum of the costs of its production, including the cost of labor. The realization of surplus value is possible, finally, only by some sort of exploitation of the laborer; somehow or other the capitalist must manage to make the cost of labor less than the value of labor.

One way of increasing surplus value is by increasing the productiveness of labor without decreasing the work day, but the problem which then arises is the problem of keeping the price of commodities up. One solution takes the form of using large numbers of laborers and dividing them for special tasks. The capitalist takes advantage of lower prices of commodities by paying labor less and purchasing materials more cheaply. At the same time, through a division of labor, he achieves greater productiveness without a corresponding rise in labor cost. In other words, the capitalist hires an individual and puts him to work in coöperation with others; he pays for the labor power of that individual, but he gains the value that comes from using that power coöperatively.

Marx rejects the idea that machinery is introduced in order to make work easier. He argues that "Like every other increase in the productiveness of labour, machinery is intended to cheapen commodities, and, by shortening that portion of the working day, in which the labourer works for himself, to lengthen the other portion that he gives, without an equivalent, to the capitalist. In short, it is a means for producing surplus value."

Marx concluded that the possibility of the growth of capital depended upon using labor in some way that would free the capitalist from the need to pay for the use of labor power. He decided that capital is "the command over unpaid labour. All surplus value . . . is in substance the materialisation of unpaid labour."

Capitalist production, according to Marx, "reproduces and perpetuates the condition for exploiting the labourer. It incessantly forces him to sell his labour-power in order to live, and enables the capitalist to purchase labour-power in order that he may enrich himself." Accordingly, the division between men which is described in terms of classes is inevitable in a capitalistic society.

Marx explains the self-destruction of the capitalistic society by arguing that from the exploitation of laborers the capitalist, if he has the economic power, passes to the exploitation of other capitalists and, finally, to their expropriation. "One capitalist always kills many." The monopolistic tendencies of capitalists finally hinder the modes of production, and the mass exploitation of workers reaches such a peak of misery and oppression that an uprising of the proletariat destroys the capitalist state. Thus, "capitalist production begets, with the inexorability of a law of Nature, its own negation." The transformation into the socialized state is much quicker and easier than the transformation of the private property of the workers into capitalist private property, for it is easier for the mass of workers to expropriate the property of a few capitalists than for the capitalists

to expropriate the property of the laborers.

Das Kapital has often been criticized as an economic study written in the style of German metaphysics. It is generally regarded, particularly by those who have never read it, as an extremely difficult book, both in content and style. By its nature it is a complex, scholarly work, but it is also clear and direct in the exposition of Marx's ideas; and it is lightened by numerous hypothetical cases which illustrate in a vivid manner the various points which Marx makes. In its consideration of the work of other scholars it is respectful if not acquiescent. Perhaps the primary fault of this momentous work is not that it is too difficult, but that it is too simple. To argue that capital is made possible by exploitation of labor may be to ignore the ways in which profit can be realized and labor paid to the satisfaction of both the capitalist and the laborer. But impartial criticism of such a thesis is impossible. Whether a capitalist economic system gives cause for revolution is something that is shown by history but only recommended by men.

KATE FENNIGATE

Type of work: Novel
Author: Booth Tarkington (1869-1946)
Type of plot: Domestic realism
Time of plot: Twentieth century
Locale: The Middle West
First published: 1943

> Principal characters:
> KATE FENNIGATE, a managing woman
> AUNT DAISY, her aunt
> MARY, Aunt Daisy's daughter
> AMES LANNING, Mary's husband
> CELIA, their daughter
> LAILA CAPPER, Kate's schoolmate
> TUKE SPEER, Ames' friend
> MR. ROE, owner of Roe Metal Products

Critique:

Twenty years intervene between the publication of *Alice Adams* and *Kate Fennigate*. By comparing the two, one observes the great improvement of the latter over the former. A single protagonist is offered to the reader in each novel; but the technique of *Kate Fennigate* is vastly superior to that of *Alice Adams*. In *Kate Fennigate* the chief characters have more of a third dimension; the background seems more realistic, and, as a whole, the novel is a more unified work.

The Story:

Kate Fennigate was a manager, even as a young child; she influenced her mother, her schoolmates, and, particularly, her father. But because of her good manners Kate was never offensive in her desire to lead. Her father, who had showed great promise as a lawyer when he was young, had permitted both women and liquor to interfere with his career. Mrs. Fennigate had no great interest in life except eating, and Mr. Fennigate had no great interest in her. Kate grew into a pretty, quiet, well-mannered girl with a managing complex. Her only intimate was Laila Capper, a self-centered, unintelligent, but beautiful girl who attended Miss Carroll's day school with Kate. Kate found it flattering to help Laila with her homework, and to get for her invitations to parties to which Laila would not otherwise have been invited.

At a school dance, just before she graduated, Kate first became aware of her love for Ames Lanning, her cousin Mary's husband. Not long after Kate's graduation, her mother died, and she and her father sold the house and went to Europe for two years. Her father, who had been ill even before they left America, died and was buried in Europe. When Kate returned home, Aunt Daisy, the tyrant of her family, insisted that Kate stay with her. With the excuse of protecting Kate, she made a household drudge of her. Kate was nurse to Mary, Aunt Daisy's daughter, governess to Mary's child, Celia, and maid-of-all-work about the house. In return, she received only her room and board. Kate

realized what Aunt Daisy was doing, but she preferred to stay on. She wanted to help Ames make something of his talents as a lawyer and to get him from under his mother-in-law's thumb.

Ames introduced Kate to Tuke Speer, his friend. But Laila also took an interest in Tuke, who fell deeply in love with Kate's friend. Aunt Daisy taunted Kate for losing out to Laila, but since Aunt Daisy did not guess where Kate's true feelings lay, the girl did not mind.

When Mary, a semi-invalid for years, died, Aunt Daisy was inconsolable. Her whole life had been wrapped up in her child, her money, and her house. The first of her interests was gone. Kate convinced Ames that he could now take the position he wanted with Mr. Bortshleff, an established lawyer. The second blow fell on Aunt Daisy not long afterward, when the stock market crashed and she lost everything. Her mind broken, she had a fall from the roof and lay an uncomprehending invalid for years afterwards.

Kate obtained a position at the Roe Metal Products. She and Ames shared the expenses of caring for Aunt Daisy and the house, which no one would buy. Tuke asked Kate to renew her friendship with Laila because Laila would need someone now that her family was moving out of town. Laila became a frequent visitor at the house and soon tried her wiles on Ames. When he asked Laila to marry him, she agreed, but later she changed her mind and eloped with Tuke Speer. Ames, hurt and disillusioned, asked Kate to marry him. She accepted.

Ten years later their life together was running smoothly enough. Officially, Ames was Mr. Roe's chief adviser at the plant. War was threatening, and Roe Metal Products, which had been expanding all during the depression, would soon open its fifth plant. Mr. Roe thought highly of both Ames and Kate, and they planned a party to introduce his twin grandchildren, Marjie and Marvin,

1551

to society. Miley Stuart, a new young engineer at the plant, met Celia at the party and the two became good friends. After the party Ames informed Kate that he was tired of her efforts to manage his life. She then and there silently resolved to offer him no more suggestions.

Laila, who in the passing years had lost none of her beauty, had also lost none of her selfishness. She had hounded poor Tuke for more money and a better position, until the good-looking young redhead he had been was no longer visible in the gaunt, hollow-cheeked, graying man. Laila tormented Tuke by once again trying her charms on Ames. Having built up among their friends the idea that she was a martyr to Tuke's drunken moods, she nagged him into an insulting remark while they were calling on the Lannings. Laila turned to Ames for comfort. He took her into the library, where she threw herself, weeping, into his arms. Ames tried to console her and ended up by kissing her. Two interested observers of that scene were Tuke, who was looking in the window from outside, and Celia, who was passing the library door. Celia also saw Tuke's face while he watched Laila and Ames in each other's arms.

Celia, thoroughly frightened, asked Miley Stuart to keep an eye on Tuke for fear he would do something violent. Planning to divorce Tuke, Laila asked Ames to divorce Kate so that he would be free to marry her. When she revealed her intention to Ames in his office, he was aghast, for he regarded her only as a good friend who needed help. Laila was furious when he refused to do as she wished, and she threatened to ruin him with false gossip.

It was necessary for Kate to become a manager once more, to save Ames from disaster. She proposed to Ames and Mr. Roe that Tuke be offered the opportunity of managing the New York office for the firm. Tuke accepted the position, which provided enough money to allow Laila to live in the manner she desired. It also took her far away from Kate and Ames.

KENILWORTH

Type of work: Novel
Author: Sir Walter Scott (1771-1832)
Type of plot: Historical romance
Time of plot: 1575
Locale: England
First published: 1821

    Principal characters:
        DUDLEY, Earl of Leicester
        RICHARD VARNEY, his master of horse
        AMY ROBSART, wife of Dudley
        EDMUND TRESSILIAN, a Cornish gentleman, friend of Amy Robsart
        WAYLAND SMITH, his servant
        THE EARL OF SUSSEX
        QUEEN ELIZABETH
        SIR WALTER RALEIGH
        MICHAEL LAMBOURNE, nephew of Giles Gosling, an innkeeper
        DOCTOR DOBOOBIE, alias Alasco, an astrologer and alchemist
        DICKIE SLUDGE, alias Flibbertigibbet, a bright child and friend of Wayland Smith

Critique:

    Kenilworth is evidence that Scott spoke the truth when he said that the sight of a ruined castle or similar relic of the medieval period made him wish to reconstruct the life and times of what he saw. Scott spends much time and space in setting the stage for the action. However, this scene setting is not without literary merit, for it offers a detailed historical background for his novel. Although the plot itself is very slight, the characters are well portrayed.

The Story:

Michael Lambourne, who in his early youth had been a ne'er-do-well, had just returned from his travels. While drinking and boasting in Giles Gosling's inn, he wagered that he could gain admittance to Cumnor Place, a large manor where an old friend was now steward. It was rumored in the village that Tony Foster was keeping a beautiful young woman prisoner at the manor. Edmund Tressilian, another guest at the inn, went with Michael to Cumnor Place. As Tressilian had suspected, he found the woman there to be his former sweetheart, Amy Robsart, apparently a willing prisoner. At Cumnor Place he also encountered Richard Varney, her supposed seducer, and a sword fight ensued. The duel was broken up by Michael Lambourne, who had decided to ally himself with his old friend, Tony Foster.

Contrary to Tressilian's idea, Amy was not Varney's paramour but the lawful wife of Varney's master, the Earl of Leicester, Varney being only the go-between and accomplice in Amy's elopement. Leicester, who was a rival of the Earl of Sussex for Queen Elizabeth's favor, feared that the news of his marriage to Amy would displease the queen, and he had convinced Amy that their marriage must be kept secret.

Tressilian returned to Lidcote Hall to obtain Hugh Robsart's permission to bring Varney to justice on a charge of seduction. On his way there he employed as his manservant Wayland Smith, formerly an assistant to Dr. Doboobie, an alchemist and astrologer. Later he visited the Earl of Sussex, through whom he hoped to petition either the queen or the Earl of Leicester in Amy's behalf. While there, Wayland Smith saved Sussex's life after the earl had been poisoned.

When the earl heard Tressilian's story,

he presented the petition directly to the queen. Confronted by Elizabeth, Varney swore that Amy was his lawful wife, and Leicester, who was standing by, confirmed the lie. Elizabeth then ordered Varney to present Amy to her when she visited Kenilworth the following week.

Leicester sent a letter to Amy asking her to appear at Kenilworth as Varney's wife. She refused. In order to have an excuse for disobeying Elizabeth's orders regarding Amy's presence at Kenilworth, Varney had Alasco, the former Dr. Doboobie, mix a potion which would make Amy ill but not kill her. This plan was thwarted, however, by Wayland Smith, who had been sent by Tressilian to help her. She escaped from Cumnor Place and with the assistance of Wayland Smith made her way to Kenilworth to see Leicester.

When she arrived at Kenilworth, the place was bustling in preparation for Elizabeth's arrival that afternoon. Wayland Smith took Amy to Tressilian's quarters, where she wrote Leicester a letter telling him of her escape from Cumnor Place and asking his aid. Wayland Smith lost the letter and through a misunderstanding he was ejected from the castle. Amy, disappointed that Leicester did not come to her, left her apartment and went into the garden. There the queen discovered her. Judging Amy to be insane because of her contradictory statements, she returned Amy to the custody of Varney, her supposed husband.

Leicester decided to confess the true story to the queen. But Varney, afraid for his own fortunes if Leicester fell from favor, convinced the earl that Amy had been unfaithful to him, and that Tressilian was her lover. Leicester, acting upon Varney's lies, decided that the death of Amy and her lover would be just punishment. Varney took Amy back to Cumnor Place and plotted her death. Leicester relented and sent Michael Lambourne to tell Varney that Amy must not die, but Varney killed Lambourne in order that he might go through with his murder of Amy. Leicester and Tressilian fought a duel, but before either harmed the other they were interrupted by Dickie Sludge, the child who had stolen Amy's letter. Reading it, Leicester realized that Amy had been faithful to him and that the complications of the affair had been caused by the machinations of Varney.

Leicester immediately went to the queen and told her the whole story. Elizabeth was angry, but she sent Tressilian and Sir Walter Raleigh to bring Amy. to Kenilworth. Unfortunately, Tressilian arrived too late to save Amy.

She had fallen through a trapdoor so rigged that when she stepped upon it she plunged to her death.

Tressilian and Sir Walter Raleigh seized Varney and carried him off to prison. There Varney committed suicide. Elizabeth permitted grief-stricken Leicester to retire from her court for several years but later recalled him and installed him once more in her favor. Much later in life he remarried. He met his death as a result of poison he intended for someone else.

KIDNAPPED

Type of work: Novel
Author: Robert Louis Stevenson (1850-1894)
Type of plot: Adventure romance
Time of plot: 1751
Locale: Scotland
First published: 1886

> Principal characters:
> DAVID BALFOUR, who was kidnapped
> EBENEZER BALFOUR OF SHAW, his uncle
> MR. RANKEILLOR, a lawyer
> ALAN BRECK, a Jacobite adventurer

Critique:

For a tale of high adventure, told simply but colorfully, there are few to equal *Kidnapped*. Stevenson was a master story-teller. He wove this tale around the great and the small, the rich and the poor, men of virtue and scoundrels, and each character was truly drawn. A stolen inheritance, a kidnapping, a battle at sea, several murders—these are only a few of the adventures that befell the hero. It is easily understood why *Kidnapped* is a favorite with all who read it.

The Story:

When David Balfour's father died, the only inheritance he left his son was a letter to Ebenezer Balfour of Shaw, who was his brother and David's uncle. Mr. Campbell, the minister of Essendean, delivered the letter to David and told him that if things did not go well between David and his uncle he was to return

to Essendean, where his friends would help him. David set off in high spirits. The house of Shaw was a great one in the Lowlands of Scotland, and David was eager to take his rightful place among the gentry. He did not know why his father had been separated from his people.

As he approached the great house, he began to grow apprehensive. Everyone of whom he asked the way had a curse for the name of Shaw and warned him against his uncle. But he had gone too far and was too curious to turn back before he reached the mansion. What he found was not a great house. One wing was unfinished and many windows were without glass. No friendly smoke came from the chimneys, and the closed door was studded with heavy nails.

David found his Uncle Ebenezer even more forbidding than the house, and he began to suspect that his uncle had cheated his father out of his rightful inheritance. When his uncle tried to kill him, he was sure of Ebenezer's villainy. His uncle promised to take David to Mr. Rankeillor, the family lawyer, to get the true story of David's inheritance, and they set out for Queen's Ferry. Before they reached the lawyer's office, David was tricked by Ebenezer and Captain Hoseason into boarding the *Covenant,* and the ship sailed away with David a prisoner, bound for slavery in the American colonies.

At first he lived in filth and starvation in the bottom of the ship. The only person who befriended him was Mr. Riach, the second officer. Later, however, he found many of the roughest seamen to be kind at times. Mr. Riach was kind when he was drunk, but mean when he was sober; while Mr. Shuan, the first officer, was gentle except when he was drinking. It was while he was drunk that Mr. Shuan beat to death Ransome, the cabin boy, because the boy had displeased him. After Ransome's murder, David became the cabin boy, and for a time life on the *Covenant* was a little better.

One night the *Covenant* ran down a small boat and cut her in two. Only one man was saved, Alan Breck, a Highlander of Scotland and a Jacobite with a price on his head. Alan demanded that Captain Hoseason set him ashore among his own people, and the captain agreed. When David overheard the captain and Mr. Riach planning to seize Alan, he warned Alan of the plot. Together the two of them held the ship's crew at bay, killing Mr. Shuan and three others and wounding many more, including Captain Hoseason. Afterwards Alan and David were fast friends and remained so during the rest of their adventures. Alan told David of his part in the rebellion against King George and of the way he was hunted by the king's men, particularly by Colin of Glenure, known as the Red Fox. Alan was the king's enemy while David was loyal to the monarch, yet out

of mutual respect they swore to help each other in time of trouble.

It was not long before they had to prove their loyalty. The ship broke apart on a reef, and David and Alan, separated at first, soon found themselves together again, deep in the part of the Highlands controlled by Alan's enemies. When Colin of Glenure was murdered, the blame fell on Alan. To be caught meant they would both hang. So began their attempt to escape to the Lowlands and to find Mr. Rankeillor, their only chance for help. They hid by day and traveled by night. Often they went for several days without food and only a flask of rum for drink. They were in danger not only from the king's soldiers, but also from Alan's own people. There was always the danger that a trusted friend would betray them for the reward offered. But David was to learn what loyalty meant. Many of Alan's clan endangered themselves to help the hunted pair.

When David was too weak to go on and wanted to give up, Alan offered to carry him. They finally reached Queen's Ferry and Mr. Rankeillor. At first Mr. Rankeillor was skeptical when he heard David's story, but it began to check so well with what he had heard from others that he was convinced of the boy's honesty; and he told David the whole story of his father and his Uncle Ebenezer. They had both loved the same woman, and David's father had won her. Because he was a kind man and because Ebenezer had taken to his bed over the loss of the woman, David's father had given up his inheritance as the oldest son in favor of Ebenezer. The story explained to David why his uncle had tried to get rid of him. Ebenezer knew that his dealings with David's father would not stand up in the courts, and he was afraid that David had come for his inheritance.

With the help of Alan and Mr. Rankeillor, David was able to frighten his uncle so much that Ebenezer offered him two-thirds of the yearly income from the land. Because David did not want to submit his family to public scandal in the courts, and because he could better help Alan if the story of their escape were kept quiet, he agreed to the settlement. In this way he was able to help Alan reach safety and pay his debt to his friend.

So ended the adventures of David Balfour of Shaw. He had been kidnapped and sent to sea; he had known danger and untold hardships; he had traveled the length of his native island; but now he had come home to take his rightful place among his people.

KIM

Type of work: Novel
Author: Rudyard Kipling (1865-1936)
Type of plot: Adventure romance
Time of plot: Late nineteenth century
Locale: British India
First published: 1901

Principal characters:
KIMBALL O'HARA (KIM), a street boy
A TIBETAN LAMA, Kim's teacher
MAHBUB ALI, a horse trader
COLONEL CREIGHTON, director of the British Secret Service
HURREE CHUNDER MOOKERJEE, a babu

Critique:

Kim gives a vivid picture of the complexities of India under British rule. It shows the life of the bazaar mystics, of the natives, of the British military. The dialogue, as well as much of the indirect discourse, makes use of Indian phrases, translated by the author, to give the flavor of native speech. There is a great deal of action and movement, for Kipling's vast canvas is painted in full detail. There are touches of irony as well as a display of native shrewdness and cunning.

The Story:

Kim grew up on the streets of Lahore. His Irish mother had died when he was born. His father, a former color-sergeant of an Irish regiment called the Mavericks, died eventually of drugs and drink, and left his son in the care of a half-caste woman. So young Kimball O'Hara became Kim, and under the hot Indian sun his skin grew so dark that one could not tell he was a white boy.

One day a Tibetan lama, in search of the holy River of the Arrow that would wash away all sin, came to Lahore. Struck by the possibility of exciting adventure, Kim attached himself to the lama as his pupil. His adventures began almost at once. That night, at the edge of Lahore, Mahbub Ali, a horse trader, gave Kim a cryptic message to deliver to a British officer in Umballa. Kim did not know that Mahbub was a member of the British Secret Service. He delivered the message as directed, and then lay in the grass and watched and listened until he learned that his message meant that eight thousand men would go to war.

Out on the big road the lama and Kim encountered many people of all sorts. Conversation was easy. One group in particular interested Kim, an old lady traveling in a family bullock cart attended by a retinue of eight men. Kim and the lama attached themselves to her party. Toward evening, they saw a group of soldiers making camp. It was the Maverick regiment. Kim, whose horoscope said that his life would be changed at the sign of a red bull in a field of green, was fascinated by the regimental flag, which was just that, a red bull against a background of bright green.

Caught by a chaplain, the Reverend Arthur Bennett, Kim accidentally jerked loose the amulet which he carried around his neck. Mr. Bennett opened the amulet and discovered three papers folded inside, including Kim's baptismal certificate and a note from his father asking that the boy be taken care of. Father Victor arrived in time to see the papers. When Kim had told his story, he was informed that he would be sent away to school. Kim parted sadly from the lama, sure, however, that he would soon escape. The lama asked that Father Victor's name and address, and the costs of schooling Kim, be written down and given to him. Then he disappeared. Kim, pretending to prophesy, told the priests what he had heard at Umballa. They and the soldiers laughed at him. But the next day his prophecy came true, and eight thousand soldiers were sent to put down an uprising in the north. Kim remained in camp.

One day a letter arrived from the lama. He enclosed enough money for Kim's first year at school and promised to provide the same amount yearly. He requested that the boy be sent to St. Xavier's for his education. Meanwhile the drummer who was keeping an eye on Kim had been cruel to his charge. When Mahbub Ali came upon the two boys, he gave the drummer a beating, and began talking to Kim. While they were thus engaged, Colonel Creighton came up and learned from Mahbub Ali, in an indirect way, that Kim would be, when educated, a valuable member of the secret service.

At last Kim was on his way to St. Xavier's. Near the school he spied the lama, who had been waiting a day and a half to see him. They agreed to see

each other often. Kim was an apt pupil, but he disliked being shut up in classrooms and dormitories. When vacation time came, he went to Umballa and persuaded Mahbub Ali to let him return to the road until school reopened.

Traveling with Mahbub Ali, he played the part of a horse boy and saved the trader's life when he overheard two men plotting to kill the horse dealer. At Simla, Kim stayed with Mr. Lurgan, who taught him a great many subtle tricks and games and the art of make-up and disguise. For, as Mahbub Ali had said, he was now learning the great game, as the work of the secret service was called. At the end of the summer Kim returned to St. Xavier's. He studied there for a total of three years.

In conference with Mr. Lurgan and Colonel Creighton, Mahbub Ali advised that Kim be permitted once more to go out on the road with his lama. Kim's skin was stained dark and again he resumed the dress of a street boy. Given the password by Hurree Chunder Mookerjee, a babu who was another member of the secret service, Kim set out with his lama after begging a train ticket to Delhi.

Still seeking his river, the lama moved up and down India with Kim as his disciple. The two of them once more encountered the old woman they had met on the road three years before. A little later Kim was surprised to see the babu, who told him that two of the five kings of the north had been bribed and that the Russians had sent spies down into India through the passes that the kings had agreed to guard. Two men, a Russian and a Frenchman, were to be apprehended, and the babu asked Kim's aid. To the lama Kim suggested a journey into the foothills of the Himalayas, and so he was able to follow the babu on his mission.

During a storm the babu came upon the two foreigners. Discovering that one of their baskets contained valuable letters, including a message from one of the traitorous kings, he offered to be their guide, and in two days he had led them to the spot where Kim and the lama were camped. When the foreigners tore almost in two a holy drawing made by the lama, the babu created a disturbance in which the coolies, according to plan, carried off the men's luggage. The lama conducted Kim to the village of Shamlegh. There Kim examined all of the baggage which the coolies had carried off. Everything except letters and notebooks he threw over an unscalable cliff. The documents he hid on his person.

In a few days Kim and the lama set out again. At last they came to the house of the old woman who had be-friended them twice before. When she saw Kim's emaciated condition, she put him to bed, where he slept many days. Before he went to sleep, he asked that a strongbox be brought to him. In it he deposited his papers; then he locked the box and hid it under his bed. When he woke up, he heard that the babu had arrived, and to him Kim delivered the papers. The babu told him that Mahbub Ali was also in the vicinity. They assured Kim that he had played his part well in the great game. The old lama knew nothing of these matters. He was happy because Kim had brought him to his river at last, a brook on the old lady's estate.

A KING AND NO KING

Type of work: Drama
Authors: Francis Beaumont (1585?-1616) and John Fletcher (1579-1625)
Type of plot: Tragi-comedy
Time of plot: Indefinite
Locale: Armenia and Iberia
First presented: 1611

Principal characters:
ARBACES, King of Iberia
TIGRANES, King of Armenia
GOBRIAS, Lord-Protector of Iberia and Arbaces' father
BACURIUS, an Iberian nobleman
MARDONIUS, an honest old captain in Arbaces' army
BESSUS, a cowardly braggart
LYGONES, an Armenian courtier, Spaconia's father
ARANE, Queen-Mother of Iberia
PANTHEA, her daughter
SPACONIA, an Armenian lady, Tigranes' sweetheart

Critique:

A good example of baroque sensibility, *A King and No King* depends for its success on an extremely skillful manipulation of emotional effects rather than on the moral or logical implications of the narrative. For this reason the play employs an impressive array of technical devices for the creation and maintenance of emotional intensity. Chief among these are contrasts and parallels of character, sudden emotional reversals within scenes, the speeding up or retarding of action with little reference to narrative logic, and the use of surprise information which resolves serious difficulties in the plot. So cleverly were these devices used that *A King and No King* was one of the most popular plays of its time, possibly ranked, after *Philaster,* as Beaumont and Fletcher's most successful tragi-comedy. It has been unfavorably criticized because of its neglect of the moral issues raised and particularly because the tragic dilemma is avoided by means of a trick. But Beaumont and Fletcher were not much concerned with the solution of moral problems; rather, they were interested in providing entertainment for a sophisticated audience.

The Story:

Arbaces, the valiant young king of Iberia, had just ended a long war against Armenia by defeating in single combat Tigranes, the king of that country. But Arbaces, though a hero in war, was also an intensely passionate man; honest and outspoken Mardonius commented that he was capable of the wildest extremities of emotion and that he could move through the entire emotional range with the greatest speed. Inflamed by his victory, Arbaces illustrated the qualities Mardonius ascribed to him. In a series of blustering speeches he showed himself to be inordinately proud. When Mardonius took him to task for boasting, he became, after a few gusts of ranting, temporarily contrite and amiable, and he resolved to give his beautiful, virtuous sister Panthea, whom he had not seen since her childhood, in marriage to the defeated but valorous Tigranes. But Tigranes protested because he had already plighted his troth to Spaconia, a lady of his own land.

Messages arrived from Gobrias, in whose care the government of Iberia had been left, telling that a slave sent by Arane to poison Arbaces had been taken and executed. Instead of flying into a rage, Arbaces, in a burst of magnanimity and pity, forgave the queen-mother's unnatural act. Thus he swung from the objectionable boastfulness of moments before to the opposite emotional pole.

Meanwhile, Tigranes, who was to accompany Arbaces home as a prisoner, arranged with Bessus, a fatuous and cowardly captain in the Iberian army, for him to convey Spaconia to Iberia and secure for her a place as one of Panthea's ladies in waiting. There, according to Tigrane's plan, it was to be Spaconia's task to set the princess' heart against a match with him.

In Iberia, where Arane had been put under guard for her attempt on Arbaces'

life, Panthea was deeply torn between her love for her mother on the one hand and her loyalty and devotion to the king, her brother, on the other. Although the reason for Arane's crime was unexplained, her conversation with Gobrias revealed that there were secrets between them having an important bearing on her relationship with Arbaces. Bessus, accompanied by Spaconia, arrived with messages from the king, including a pardon for Arane. Importuned by the courtiers, the braggart gave an amusing account of the duel between Arbaces and Tigranes, contriving to make himself the central figure. Panthea, interrupting Bessus' tale frequently, revealed agonized concern for her brother's safety. Even though she had not yet seen him, she nevertheless felt a powerful attraction to him. Spaconia then revealed to Panthea her reason for coming to Iberia, and the virtuous princess vowed to reject the proposed match with Tigranes.

After a triumphal passage through the city, Arbaces and his company arrived at the court. When Panthea presented herself to her brother, Arbaces, overwhelmed by her beauty, realized that at first sight he had fallen hopelessly in love with her. Frantically he tried to convince himself that she was not really his sister but a lady of the court; however, he was unable to escape the guilty feeling that he had become the victim of an incestuous love.

At last, succumbing to his passion, he kissed her; then, overcome with guilt and shame, he violently ordered the weeping Panthea imprisoned. But as time passed, his love for Panthea increased, and at last he begged Mardonius to act as his bawd. When Mardonius indignantly rejected Arbace's plea, the king turned to Bessus, whom he found more willing to undertake such a task. Revolted by Bessus' ready acquiescence, and probably also by the image of himself that he saw in the minion, Arbaces swore to keep his sin within his own breast in spite of the torture his desire inflicted upon him.

Bessus, meanwhile, discovered that the

reputation for bravery he had created for himself had serious drawbacks. Now that he was worthy of challenge, he was being called to account by all of the gentlemen he had insulted before leaving for the wars. He was just dismissing the second of his two hundred and thirteenth challenger when Bacurius appeared, demanding satisfaction for a past wrong. Bessus, attempting to put him off, pleaded a lame leg; but Bacurius, recognizing the braggart's poltroonery, browbeat him unmercifully and took away his sword. Bessus, after enlisting the aid of two professional swordsmen who were in reality as absurd and as cowardly as he, allowed himself to be convinced by a very peculiar exercise in logic that he was, after all, a valiant man. He was on the way to deliver this news to Bacurius when he encountered Lygones, who had journeyed from Armenia in search of his daughter Spaconia. Believing him to be Spaconia's seducer, Lygones gave Bessus a drubbing before the braggart could explain. Parting from Lygones, bruised Bessus located Bacurius, who, over Bessus' loud protests that he was no coward, mocked his logic and cudgeled his two hired companions. During this time Lygones had located Spaconia and Tigranes in prison; and he learned joyfully that his daughter, whom he had thought guilty of a disgraceful alliance with Bessus, was actually to be married to Tigranes and thus was to become the queen of Armenia.

Indirectly urged on by Gobrias and nearly mad with desire, Arbaces visited Panthea in her prison and at once begged her to yield and not to yield herself to his lust. Although she rejected his proposal, she confessed that she too had felt unsisterly desire for him. After they parted, Arbaces attempted to govern himself but finally concluded wildly that he could bear the situation no longer. He resolved to murder Mardonius, ravish Panthea, and then kill himself. At that moment, however, Gobrias and Arane revealed their secret: Arbaces was really the son of Gobrias. As an infant he had been adopted for political reasons by the barren Arane, who later conceived and bore Panthea. He was thus "no king." But Gobrias, who had protected his son against Arane's attempts to dispose of him so that Panthea could rule and who had subtly encouraged Arbaces' love for Panthea, found his complicated plan a success. Arbaces, now totally without pride of majesty, was overjoyed to learn that he was actually an impostor. His and Panthea's passion now became legitimate, and by marrying her he would once more assume the crown. Thus a happy ending was brought about, and to fill the moment completely Tigranes and Spaconia were released from prison and reunited.

KING JOHN

Type of work: Drama
Author: John Bale (1495-1563)
Type of plot: Historical allegory
Time of plot: Early thirteenth century
Locale: England
First presented: c. 1548

> *Principal characters:*
> ENGLAND, a widow
> KING JOHN,
> NOBILITY,
> CLERGY,
> CIVIL ORDER, and
> COMMUNALITY, betrayers of King John
> SEDITION, the Vice
> DISSIMULATION

PRIVATE WEALTH
USURPED POWER
THE POPE (INNOCENT III)
TREASON
VERITY
IMPERIAL MAJESTY
STEPHEN LANGTON, churchman and statesman
CARDINAL PANDULPHUS

Critique:

John Bale, Bishop of Ossory, one of the most outspoken champions of the English Reformation, claimed to have written some forty plays in his lifetime. Of these, five are extant, and of these five *King John* is the most important. Although far too long and tedious for dramatic effectiveness, being in structure two plays or one play in two parts, it is interesting as a scathing and uncompromising attack on the Church of Rome and as a version of history different from that usually accepted. Challenging those historians—Polydore Virgil in particular—who made King John a knave, Bale depicts the king as a virtuous protector of the realm who was betrayed by the covetousness and viciousness of the Church. Bale's history may be altered and revised to suit his cause, but the fact that he used it at all is of concern to us, for *King John* announces the beginning of the great tradition of the English history play. It is, actually, a piece that shows the transition from the old to the new—an allegorical play using the techniques of the medieval morality (Sedition, for instance, is an example of the morality "vice"), but using them to dramatize historical events.

The Story:

England complained to King John that she had been stripped of her rights and her wealth by the rapacious clergy who had driven her husband, God, from the realm. King John promised to right her wrongs but was mocked by Sedition, the comic vice, and the foremost agent of the Church.

Sedition, demonstrating the way in which he and the Church subverted the government of kings, introduced Dissim-

ulation, his right-hand man. Dissimulation worked with Private Wealth and Usurped Power. Private Wealth was the darling of the religious orders; he gave strength to Usurped Power, who sustained the arrogance of Popes.

King John defied Sedition and his cohorts. He called Nobility, Clergy, and Civil Order to him and prevailed on them for their support. Nobility and Civil Order gave theirs willingly, but Clergy was reluctant. King John had been too harsh on him. When the king reminded him of the temporal rights of rulers as outlined in the Gospel, Clergy, still reluctant, consented.

The allegiance of the three was shortlived, however, for Sedition and his minions had little trouble convincing them that the actual power of Rome was stronger than any abstract claim based on the Gospel. Besides, the Church had the sole right of interpreting the Gospel. Nobility, Clergy, and Civil Order were forsworn.

King John, now bereft of his three strongest allies, placed all his hopes on Communality, his one sure support. Communality, the true son of England, was brought to King John by his mother, and the king was dismayed to learn that he was both impoverished and blind. He was impoverished, his mother explained, because the Church had stolen all his goods; his blindness symbolized his spiritual ignorance, an ignorance in which he was kept by the conspiracy of Clergy who was supposed to open his eyes. Still, for all his failings, Communality was faithful to the king who had always seen to his welfare. He willingly reasserted his faith.

In the end, however, he was no more stanch than his more exalted brothers. Clergy had too strong a hold on him, and he too became a victim of Sedition's plottings.

King John now stood alone in his attempt to save the widow England. Assured now of his vulnerability, the Pope sent his agents to bring the king to his knees. King John's old enemy, Stephen Langton, the Archbishop of Canterbury, returned. The interdict was proclaimed with bell, book, and candle, and the vindictive Cardinal Pandulphus arrived to enforce it.

Still King John stood firm, defying the Pope to do his worst. Claiming that he would not betray England, he turned to history and the scriptures to defend his rights; he pointed out the ways in which the Church perverted the true faith and he cited the corruptions of the holy orders. Sedition mocked him and promised that his defiance would end.

End it did, for the Pope gathered a strong alliance and threatened to invade England. Rather than see his country devastated and his people killed, King John submitted. He surrendered his crown to the Pope and received it back as a fief of the Holy See. When England protested, she was reviled by Sedition and his aides.

King John ruled for a number of years as the vassal of the Pope. If he tried to assert his power, Sedition and his agents were on hand to thwart it. Treason ran through the land with impunity, and when the king tried to punish him he pleaded benefit of clergy and was released. Nevertheless, King John was determined to hang him.

Cardinal Pandulphus and Sedition conceived a plan to curb King John's power. Cardinal Pandulphus would not release England from the interdict until King John had handed over to the Papacy a third of his lands as a dowry for the bride of Richard, his late brother. Although King John protested, Cardinal Pandulphus insisted on these harsh terms. Providentially, the king was released when it was announced that Julyane, the lady in question, was dead.

The forces of the Church were now determined to get rid of King John completely. Dissimulation, in the guise of Simon of Swinsett, a monk, concocted a poison cup from the exudations of a toad. When he offered John the draught, the king forced the monk to drink first and then drained the cup. Both died in agony.

Upon the death of King John, Verity appeared and proclaimed that all the evils that had been attributed to King John were false, the lies of slandering monks. He listed all of the good things the king had done for the benefit of the common people and asserted that for three hundred years that good had been undone by the corrupt Church. But now, he announced, Imperial Majesty (symbolizing Henry VIII) had arrived to crush the Church and save the widow England.

Imperial Majesty confronted Nobility, Clergy, and Civil Order. Verity pointed out to them the error of their ways, and, contrite, they swore their eternal allegiance to Imperial Majesty. England was safe from the evils of Rome.

KING JOHN

Type of work: Drama
Author: William Shakespeare (1564-1616)
Type of plot: Historical chronicle
Time of plot: Early thirteenth century
Locale: England and France
First presented: c. 1594

Principal characters:
JOHN, King of England

PRINCE HENRY, his son
ARTHUR OF BRETAGNE, the king's nephew
WILLIAM MARESHALL, Earl of Pembroke
GEFFREY FITZ-PETER, Earl of Essex
WILLIAM LONGSWORD, Earl of Salisbury
HUBERT DE BURGH, Chamberlain to the king
ROBERT FAULCONBRIDGE, an English baron
PHILIP FAULCONBRIDGE, his half-brother, and natural son of King Richard I
CARDINAL PANDULPH, papal legate
LOUIS, Dauphin of France
ELINOR, King John's mother
CONSTANCE, Arthur's mother
BLANCH OF CASTILE, King John's niece

Critique:

The Life and Death of King John, based on a play of which the authorship is unknown, has as its strongest feature the depiction of character. In a number of long, unbroken scenes, this aspect of the play is achieved by the stream-of-consciousness presentation. Mother-love plays a major part in this superficial plot of political vacillation. *King John,* one of the earliest histories by Shakespeare, is one of his weaker dramas.

The Story:

King John sat on the throne of England without right, for the succession should have passed to Arthur of Bretagne, the fourteen-year-old son of King John's older brother. John and Elinor, his mother, prepared to defend England against the forces of Austria and France, after Constance of Bretagne had enlisted the aid of those countries to gain the throne for her son Arthur.

As John and Elinor made ready for battle, Philip Faulconbridge, the natural son of Richard the Lion-Hearted by Lady Faulconbridge, was recruited by Elinor to serve John's cause in the war. The Bastard, weary of his half-brother's slights regarding his illegitimacy, willingly accepted the offer and was knighted by King John.

The French, Austrian, and British armies met at Angiers in France, but the battle was fought with words, not swords. To John's statement that England was ready for war or peace, King Philip of France answered that for the sake of right-

doing France would fight for Arthur's place on the throne. When Elinor accused Constance of self-aggrandizement in seeking the throne for her son, Constance accused her mother-in-law of adultery. The Bastard and the Archduke of Austria resorted to a verbal volley.

Louis, the Dauphin of France, halted the prattle by stating Arthur's specific claims, which John refused to grant. The citizens of Angiers announced that they were barring the gates of the city to all until they had proof as to the actual kingship. The leaders prepared for a battle.

After excursions by the three armies, heralds of the various forces appeared to announce their victories to the citizens of Angiers, but the burghers persisted in their demands for more definite proof. At last the Bastard suggested that they batter the walls down and then continue to fight until one side or the other was conquered. Arrangements for the battle brought on more talk, for the citizens suggested a peace settlement among the forces and promised entrance to the city if Blanch of Castile were affianced to the Dauphin of France.

John gladly offered certain provinces as Blanch's dowry, and it was agreed the vows should be solemnized. The Bastard analyzed John's obvious motives: it was better to part with some parcels of land and keep the throne than to lose his kingdom in battle.

Constance, displaying the persistence and tenacity of a mother who wished to see justice done her child, doubted that

1563

the proposed alliance would succeed; she wished to have the issue settled in battle. Her hopes rose when Cardinal Pandulph appeared to announce John's excommunication because of his abuse of the Archbishop of Canterbury. John, unperturbed by the decree of excommunication, denounced the pope. The alliance between France and England, the outgrowth of Louis' and Blanch's marriage, could not stand, according to Pandulph, if France hoped also to avoid excommunication. King Philip wisely decided that it would be better to have England as an enemy than to be at odds with Rome.

His change of mind made war necessary. The battle ended with the English victorious. The Bastard beheaded the Archduke of Austria. Arthur was taken prisoner. When Hubert de Burgh pledged his unswerving support to the king, John told him of his hatred for Arthur; he asked that the boy be murdered.

Grieved by her separation from Arthur, Constance lamented that she would never see her son again. Even in heaven, she said, she would be denied this blessing because Arthur's treatment at the hands of the English would change him from the gracious creature he had been.

Pandulph, unwilling to let John have easy victory, persuaded Louis to march against the English forces. The cardinal explained that with Arthur's death—and news of French aggression would undoubtedly mean his death—Louis, as Blanch's husband, could claim Arthur's lands.

In England, Hubert de Burgh had been ordered to burn out Arthur's eyes with hot irons. Although Hubert professed loyalty to John, he had become attached to Arthur while the boy was in his charge. Touched by Arthur's pleas, he refused to carry out King John's orders. After hiding Arthur in another part of the castle, he went to tell John of his decision. On his arrival at the palace, however, he found Pembroke and Salisbury, in conference with the king, pleading for Arthur's life. The people, they reported, were enraged because of John's dastardly action; they threatened to withdraw their fealty to the cruel king. John's sorrow was increased by the information that a large French army had landed in England and that Elinor was dead.

The Bastard, who had been collecting tribute from monks, appeared with Peter of Pomfret, a prophet. When Peter prophesied that John would lose his crown at noon on Ascension Day, John had Peter jailed and ordered his execution if the prophecy were not fulfilled.

Told of Hubert de Burgh's refusal to torture Arthur, the king, overjoyed, sent his chamberlain in pursuit of Pembroke and Salisbury to tell them the good news. But Arthur, fearful for his welfare, had attempted escape from the castle. In jumping from the wall, he fell on the stones and was killed. When Hubert overtook the lords and blurted his tidings, he was confronted by information and proof that Arthur was dead. Pembroke and Salisbury sent word to John that they could be found with the French.

Harried at every turn—deserted by his nobles, disowned by his subjects, attacked by his former ally—John, on Ascension Day, surrendered his crown to Cardinal Pandulph, thus fulfilling Peter's prophecy. He received it back only after he had acknowledged his vassalage to the pope: In return, Pandulph was to order the French to withdraw their forces. Opposed to such arbitration, however, the Bastard secured John's permission to engage the French. King Louis rejected Pandulph's suit for peace. His claim was that officious Rome, having sent neither arms, men, nor money for France's cause in opposing John's hereticism and deviltry, should remain neutral.

Under the direction of the Bastard, the English made a strong stand against the French. The defaulting barons, advised by Melun, a dying French lord, that the Dauphin planned their execution if France won the victory, returned to the king and received his pardon for their disloyalty. But John's graciousness to his barons and his new alliance with Rome brought him only momentary happiness. He was poisoned at Swinstead Abbey and died after intense suffering.

After his death Cardinal Pandulph was able to arrange a truce between the English and French. Prince Henry was named King of England. King Louis returned home to France. The Bastard, brave, dashing, vainglorious, swore his allegiance to the new king. His and England's pride was expressed in his words that England had never been and would never be at a conqueror's feet, except when such a position might lead to future victories.

KING LEAR

Type of work: Drama
Author: William Shakespeare (1564-1616)
Type of plot: Romantic tragedy
Time of plot: First century B.C.
Locale: Britain
First presented: c. 1605

Principal characters:
LEAR, King of Britain
KING OF FRANCE
DUKE OF CORNWALL
DUKE OF ALBANY
EARL OF KENT
EARL OF GLOUCESTER
EDGAR, Gloucester's son
EDMUND, natural son of Gloucester
GONERIL,
REGAN, and
CORDELIA, Lear's daughters

Critique:

Despite the 300-year-old debate regarding the lack of unity in the plot of *King Lear*, it is one of the most readable and gripping of Shakespearean dramas. The theme of filial ingratitude is so keenly present in the depiction of two different families, although circumstances do eventually bring the families together to coördinate the plot for unity, that *King Lear* is not only an absorbing drama but a disturbing one as well. The beauty of diction and the overwhelming pathos of the treatment given to innocence and goodness add to the tragic sadness of this poignantly emotional play. Like the great tragic dramas, the story of Lear and his folly purges the emotions by terror and pity.

The Story:

King Lear, in foolish fondness for his children, decided to divide his kingdom among his three daughters. Grown senile, he scoffed at the foresight of his advisers

and declared that each girl's statement of her love for him would determine the portion of the kingdom she would receive as her dowry.

Goneril, the oldest and the Duchess of Albany, spoke first. She said that she loved her father more than eyesight, space, liberty, or life itself. Regan, Duchess of Cornwall, announced that the sentiment of her love had been expressed by Goneril, but that Goneril had stopped short of the statement of Regan's real love. Cordelia, who had secretly confided that her love was more ponderous than her tongue, told her father that because her love was in her heart, not in her mouth, she was willing to sacrifice eloquence for truth. Lear angrily told her that truth alone could be her dowry and ordered that her part of the kingdom be divided between Goneril and Regan. Lear's disappointment in Cordelia's statement grew into a rage against Kent, who tried to reason Cordelia's case with his foolish king. Because of Kent's blunt speech he was given ten days to leave the country. Loving his sovereign, he risked death by disguising himself and remaining in Britain to care for Lear in his infirmity.

When Burgundy and France came as suitors to ask Cordelia's hand in marriage, Burgundy, learning of her dowerless fate, rejected her. France, honoring Cordelia for her virtues, took her as his wife, but Lear dismissed Cordelia and France without his benediction. Goneril and Regan, wary of their father's vacillation in his weakened mental state, set about to establish their kingdoms against change.

Lear was not long in learning what Goneril's and Regan's statements of their love for him had really meant. Their caustic comments about the old man's feebleness, both mental and physical, furnished Lear's Fool with many points for his philosophical recriminations against the king. Realizing that his charity to his daughters had made him homeless, Lear cried in anguish against his fate. His prayers went unanswered, and the abuse he received from his daughters hastened his derangement.

The Earl of Gloucester, like Lear, was fond of his two sons. Edmund, a bastard, afraid that his illegitimacy would deprive him of his share of Gloucester's estate, forged a letter over Edgar's signature, stating that the sons should not have to wait for their fortunes until they were too old to enjoy them. Gloucester, refusing to believe that Edgar desired his father's death, was told by Edmund to wait in hiding and hear Edgar make assertions which could easily be misinterpreted against him. Edmund, furthering his scheme, told Edgar that villainy was afoot and that Edgar should not go unarmed at any time.

To complete his evil design, he later advised Edgar to flee for his own safety. After cutting his arm, he then told his father that he had been wounded while he and Edgar fought over Gloucester's honor. Gloucester, swearing that Edgar would not escape justice, had his son's description circulated so that he might be apprehended.

Edmund, meanwhile, allied himself with Cornwall and Albany to defend Britain against the French army mobilized by Cordelia and her husband to avenge Lear's cruel treatment. He won Regan and Goneril completely by his personal attentions to them and set the sisters against each other by arousing their jealousy.

Lear, wandering as an outcast on the stormy heath, was aided by Kent, disguised as a peasant. Seeking protection from the storm, they found a hut where Edgar, pretending to be a madman, had already taken refuge. Gloucester, searching for the king, found them there and urged them to hurry to Dover, where Cordelia and her husband would protect Lear from the wrath of his unnatural daughters.

For attempting to give succor and condolence to the outcast Lear, Gloucester was blinded when Cornwall, acting on information furnished by Edmund, gouged out his eyes. While he was at his grisly work, a servant, rebelling against the cruel deed, wounded Cornwall. Regan killed the servant. Cornwall died later as the result of his wound. Edgar, still playing the part of a madman, found his father wandering the fields with an old retainer. Without revealing his identity, Edgar promised to guide his father to Dover, where Gloucester planned to die by throwing himself from the high cliffs.

Goneril was bitterly jealous because widowed Regan could receive the full attention of Edmund, who had been made Earl of Gloucester. She declared that she would rather lose the battle to France than to lose Edmund to Regan. Goneril's hatred became more venomous when Albany, whom she detested because of his kindliness toward Lear and his pity for Gloucester, announced that he would try to right the wrongs done by Goneril, Regan, and Edmund.

Cordelia, informed by messenger of her father's fate, was in the French camp near

1566

Dover. When the mad old king was brought to her by faithful Kent, she cared for her father tenderly and put him in the care of a doctor skilled in curing many kinds of ills. Regaining his reason, Lear recognized Cordelia, but the joy of their reunion was clouded by his repentance for his misunderstanding and mistreatment of his only loyal daughter.

Edgar, protecting Gloucester, was accosted by Oswald, Goneril's steward, on his way to deliver a note to Edmund. After Edgar had killed Oswald in the fight which followed, Edgar delivered the letter to Albany. In it Goneril declared her love for Edmund and asked that he kill her husband. Gloucester died, feeble and broken-hearted after Edgar had revealed himself to his father.

Edmund, commanding the British forces, took Lear and Cordelia prisoners. As they were taken off to prison, he sent written instructions for their treatment.

Albany was aware of Edmund's ambition for personal glory and arrested him on a charge of high treason. Regan, interceding for her lover, was rebuffed by Goneril. Regan, suddenly taken ill, was carried to Albany's tent. When Edmund,

as was his right, demanded a trial by combat, Albany agreed. Edgar, still in disguise, appeared and in the fight mortally wounded his false brother. Learning from Albany that he knew of her plot against his life, Goneril was desperate. She went to their tent, poisoned Regan, and killed herself.

Edmund, dying, revealed that he and Goneril had ordered Cordelia to be hanged and her death to be announced as suicide because of her despondency over her father's plight. Edmund, fiendish and diabolical always, was also vain. While he lay dying he looked upon the bodies of Goneril and Regan and expressed pleasure that two women were dead because of their jealous love for him.

Albany dispatched Edgar to prevent Cordelia's death, but he arrived too late. Lear refused all assistance when he appeared carrying her dead body in his arms. After asking forgiveness of heartbroken Kent, whom he recognized at last, Lear, a broken, confused old man, died in anguish.

Edgar and Albany alone were left to rebuild a country ravaged by bloodshed and war.

THE KING OF THE GOLDEN RIVER

Type of work: Fairy tale
Author: John Ruskin (1819-1900)
Type of plot: Heroic adventure
Time of plot: The legendary past
Locale: Stiria
First published: 1851

Principal characters:
SCHWARTZ, and
HANS, evil brothers
GLUCK, their good brother
THE SOUTH-WEST WIND
THE KING OF THE GOLDEN RIVER

Critique:

First written for the enjoyment of a little girl and not intended for publication, *The King of the Golden River, Or, The Black Brothers, a Legend of Stiria* has become one of the most popular of

Ruskin's works. The plot is not new: the good youngest brother triumphs after the evil older brothers fail and are punished. But just as the stories of Cinderella and Aladdin are always new, so is this story of ancient Stiria and Treasure Valley.

The Story:

In the ancient country of Stiria, there lay a beautiful and fertile valley called Treasure Valley. Surrounded on all sides by high mountainous peaks, the region never knew famine. No matter what droughts or floods attacked the land beyond the mountains, Treasure Valley produced bountiful crops of apples, hay, grapes, and honey. Above the valley beautiful cataracts fell in torrents. One of these shone like gold in the sunlight and thus was named the Golden River.

Treasure Valley was owned by three brothers, Schwartz, Hans, and Gluck. Schwartz and Hans, the older brothers, were stingy and mean. They farmed the valley and killed everything that did not bring them money. They paid their servants nothing, beating them until the servants could stand no more and then turning them out without wages. They kept their crops until they were worth double their usual value in order to sell them for high profits. Gold was stacked up on the floors, yet they gave never a penny to charity. Often people starved at their doorstep without receiving even a morsel of food. Neighbors nicknamed them the Black Brothers.

The youngest brother, Gluck, was a good and honest lad of twelve. Although his heart was filled with pity for the poor, he was helpless against his brothers. He did all their scrubbing and cooking, getting nothing for his pains but an educational cuffing or kicking. One year, when all the country was flooded and only the brothers had a harvest, Schwartz and Hans left Gluck alone one day to turn the roast. A terrible storm was raging. Suddenly Gluck was startled to hear a knock at the door. Investigating, he saw the most peculiar little man imaginable, a creature only about four feet six inches tall, dressed in queer, old-fashioned clothing, who begged to come in out of the rain. Gluck, knowing what his brothers would do if they returned and found a stranger using their fire for warmth, was afraid to open the door. But his heart was so good and tender that he could not long refuse the stranger. The little man dripped so much water that he almost put out the fire. When he asked for food, Gluck feared to give him any. However, his brothers had promised him one slice of the mutton, and he prepared to give the stranger that piece. Before he could finish cutting it, the brothers came home. Furious, they attempted to throw the stranger out, but when Schwartz struck at him, the stick was thrown from his hand. Each of the evil brothers attempted to strike the old man, only to be thrown back upon the floor. Wrapping his long cloak about him, the old man told them that he would come back at midnight, and then never call again.

That night the evil brothers awoke to hear a terrible storm. The roof was gone from their room, and in the darkness, bobbing around like a cork, was the old man. He told them that they would find his calling card on the kitchen table. At dawn they went downstairs to find that the whole valley was in ruin; everything had been flooded and swept away. Their cattle, crops, and gold were all gone. On the table they found a card. Their caller had been the South-West Wind.

He was true to his word. Neither he nor the other winds blew again to bring rain to the valley. The land became a desert, the brothers penniless, and at last they left the valley and went to the city to become goldsmiths, taking with them all that was left of their inheritance, some curious pieces of gold plate. When they mixed copper with the gold to fool the public, the people would not buy the substitute. What little they did make they spent for drink, and soon there was no money left. At last their only possession was a drinking mug belonging to Gluck. On the mug was a face which seemed to peer at whoever was looking at the mug. It broke Gluck's heart when his brothers told him to melt down the mug, but he knew better than to refuse.

1568

After they left him to go to the tavern, Gluck put his mug into the furnace. To his surprise he heard a voice speak to him from the flames. Gluck had thought aloud that it would be wonderful if the Golden River really turned to gold, but the voice told him that it would not be good at all. Opening the furnace, Gluck saw the face on the mug emerge on another little man. When the man came out of the furnace, he told Gluck that he was the King of the Golden River. Imprisoned on the mug by a rival, he was now free because of Gluck. Then he told Gluck that whoever should climb to the top of the mountain and cast three drops of holy water into the Golden River would turn the river to gold. But the first attempt must succeed, and should anyone cast unholy water into the river, he would be turned to a black stone. So saying, the king evaporated.

The brothers returned and beat Gluck unmercifully for losing the last of the plate. When he told them the story, however, they decided to try their luck, and they got into a terrible fight to see who should go first. The constable, hearing the noise, went to arrest them. Hans escaped, but Schwartz was carried off to prison. Then Hans stole some holy water, for no priest would give any to such a scoundrel, and journeyed to the mountain. There he found almost impossible obstacles, but he climbed on. Three times he stopped to drink some of the holy water, for he was about to die of thirst. Each time, as he started to drink, a child or an old man or a dog appeared on the path and begged for a few drops of water, for each was dying of thirst. But Hans scorned them and drank the water himself. At last he reached the top and threw the water into the river. Instantly he was turned to a black stone.

Back home, good Gluck worked to pay his brother's fine. When he was freed, Schwartz also left for the Golden River. He bought holy water from a bad priest. Like his brother, he was beset with many difficulties. And like his brother, he met the three who begged a few drops of water; but he passed on, keeping the water for himself. Then he reached the top and threw his three drops into the stream. He too was turned to black stone.

When Schwartz did not come back, Gluck decided to try his luck. A priest gladly gave him holy water, for he was a good boy. The mountain was even more difficult for him than it had been for his brothers, for he was young and weak. But when he stopped to drink and the old man appeared and asked for water, Gluck shared with him. His way grew lighter. He stopped again and saw the child lying in the path. Again he shared his water, and again the way became less difficult. When he had almost reached the top, he saw the dog gasping for breath, needing water. He had very little left and at first thought he would pass by, but then he looked into the beast's eyes and his heart was moved. He poured the remaining drops into the dog's open mouth. Then the dog disappeared and in his place stood the King of the Golden River. He told Gluck that his brothers had been turned to stone because their water had been unholy through their refusal to help the weak and the dying. Then the king plucked a flower containing three drops of dew and told Gluck to cast them into the river. As he did so the king disappeared. At first Gluck was disappointed because the river did not turn to gold. Instead, it began to disappear. Descending into the valley, as the king had told him to do, he heard the water gurgling under the ground. Green grass and plants began to grow as if by magic. Then Gluck understood that the river had turned to gold by making the land fertile and valuable again. He went to live in the valley and prospered. The poor were always welcomed at his door. To this day the people point out the spot where the river turned into the valley, a place still bordered by the two black brothers.

1569

THE KING OF THE MOUNTAINS

Type of work: Novel
Author: Edmond François About (1828-1885)
Type of plot: Adventure romance
Time of plot: Mid-nineteenth century
Locale: Greece
First published: 1856

Principal characters:

HERMANN SCHULTZ, a botanist
JOHN HARRIS, a fellow lodger and friend
PHOTINI, a Greek girl
DMITRI, a Greek boy who loves Photini
HADGI-STAVROS, a Greek bandit
MRS. SIMONS, an Englishwoman
MARY ANN, her daughter

Critique:

Practically unknown in this country, About's novel deserves to be more widely read, for it is ingenious, clever, and witty. Edmond About, who was well-known and honored in his own country, is the equal of many French writers whom we consider great. It would be difficult to find a book by any of his contemporaries that is so completely enjoyable as this one.

The Story:

While the German botanist, Hermann Schultz, was lodging with a Greek family in Athens, he learned of a notorious Greek bandit so powerful that the government could not destroy his band and so cruel that he had decapitated two young girls he had been holding for ransom. Hadgi-Stavros, the King of the Mountains, was greatly feared, but he was also greatly admired by many of his countrymen. John Harris, an American who was Hermann's fellow lodger, snorted in disgust as the landlord recited with admiration all the exploits of the bandit. Harris was so indignant he was unaware that when he spoke Photini, a young Greek girl who came to the house in order to learn foreign languages from the lodgers, looked at him with love in her eyes.

The newspapers announced the defeat of Hadgi-Stavros and his brigands, and

Hermann believed it safe to leave Athens in order to continue his botanical research. Unfamiliar with the territory, however, he lost his way. Finally he met the landlord's son, Dmitri, who was acting as guide for two Englishwomen, Mrs. Simons and her daughter Mary Ann. Hermann joined their party. When Mrs. Simons, arrogant and querulous, demanded that they stop to eat, Dmitri told her they could find food at the next village. But when they arrived there, the village was deserted; everyone had fled. Dmitri said they could stop at a monastery, only a ten-minute walk away. At the monastery a monk told them that bandits were in the district and he advised them to flee for their lives.

A few minutes later the brigands appeared and surrounded them, despite Mrs. Simons' indignant assertion that she was English. They were led to the hideout of the chief, where Hadgi-Stavros was sitting dictating letters to business firms, to clients, to his daughter who was away at school. When he was through, he ordered food for the captives and Mrs. Simons felt much better.

By clever questioning, Hadgi-Stavros learned that Mrs. Simons was extremely wealthy, and he ordered that she should be held for ransom. When Hermann protested that he was without money or in-

1570

fluential friends, Hadgi-Stavros said that he could take Mrs. Simons' note back to Athens. But when the bandit learned that Hermann was a scientist, a learned man, he decided to hold him for ransom as well.

Mrs. Simons insisted that she would pay nothing, that the soldiers would follow and rescue them. Hermann was discouraged, for he knew that the soldiers would do nothing of the kind. One day a troop of soldiers appeared, and the leader, Captain Pericles, was received with affection. While the bandits went off on a raid, Pericles kept guard over the prisoners. Pretending that he had rescued them, he collected as evidence against the bandit the valuables of the two women. When Hermann protested, he was put under guard. Only after the brigands had returned and were seen in friendly activity with the soldiers was Mrs. Simons convinced that Captain Pericles was in league with Hadgi-Stavros.

Hermann planned to escape by going down a ravine and across a stream, but the plan was abandoned because he could help only one of the women down the steep slope to safety. Later he had another idea. He had heard Hadgi-Stavros dictate to his English bankers, the company owned by Mrs. Simons and her brother. He had Hadgi-Stavros sign two receipts, one for the ransom of Mrs. Simons and Mary Ann, another for his own. The idea was that the banker would deduct the sum from Hadgi-Stavros' account and by the time the bandit discovered that he had been swindled they would be far away. The plan worked, except that Mrs. Simons' brother did not honor the receipt for the botanist. Hermann was condemned to stay. But Mrs. Simons, who had hinted at matrimony for her daughter and Hermann, told him that surely he could escape. She insisted that the first thing he must do when he returned to Athens was to call on her.

Hermann's opportunity to escape came a few days later, when the bandit allowed him, in company with two guards, to go out looking for plants. Hermann ran away from the guards and would have outdistanced his pursuers if his suspenders had not broken. He was recaptured and put under guard. Then he succeeded in getting his guard drunk and escaping across the ravine. Coming face to face with one of the dogs guarding the camp, he fed it some of the arsenic he carried in his specimen box. In his escape he had accidentally drowned his drunken guard, and when the man's body was discovered the bandits set out in pursuit. Hermann was captured once more. Hadgi-Stavros ordered Hermann struck twenty times across the toes and twenty times across the fingers. In anger and pain Hermann told Hadgi-Stavros that he had been duped in the payment of the ransom money. The bandit was furious. Hermann had robbed him, ruined him, he declared.

He offered a reward to any of his men who would devise horrible tortures for Hermann. Meanwhile the prisoner had his hair plucked from his head; later he was put near an open fire to roast. While there, he succeeded in putting arsenic into the food. Then Dmitri arrived in the camp with a letter from John Harris. Hadgi-Stavros read it and turned pale. Harris was holding his daughter as a hostage aboard a ship until Hermann was released, and the daughter was the homely Photini who had loved Harris since she met him at the boarding-house. In anxiety for his daughter, Hadgi-Stavros ordered Hermann to be treated for his wounds and then set free. Before Hermann left the camp, however, Hadgi-Stavros and those who had eaten fell ill, poisoned by the arsenic.

Fighting broke out among the bandits. Some wished to kill the unconscious king and Hermann as well. Those loyal to Hadgi-Stavros defended their leader while Hermann attempted to cure the sick bandit. The fighting ended when Harris and some friends arrived to rescue

Hermann and the king.

Hadgi-Stavros went back to Athens and Photini. At a ball Harris and Hermann saw Mrs. Simons and Mary Ann, but Mrs. Simons treated Hermann with icy politeness. The next day Harris and Hermann went to call on them, but the women had left suddenly for Paris. Hermann gave up all hopes of marriage with the beautiful Mary Ann.

KING PARADOX

Type of work: Novel
Author: Pío Baroja (1872-   )
Type of plot: Social satire
Time of plot: Early twentieth century
Locale: Spain, Tangier, and the imaginary Bu-Tata, in Uganga, Africa
First published: 1906

> *Principal characters:*
> SILVESTRE PARADOX, a modern adventurer
> AVELINO DIZ, his skeptical friend
> ARTHUR SIPSOM, an English manufacturer of needles
> EICHTHAL THONELGEBEN, a scientist
> HARDIBRÁS, a crippled soldier
> UGÚ, a friendly Negro
> BAGÚ, a jealous medicine man

Critique:

Pío Baroja y Nessi believes that fiction must parallel life. Therefore his writing is abrupt, episodic, simple, unrevised, with a wealth of unselected details. His Basque temperament shows in his underlying melancholy and pessimism. At the same time he has deep sympathy for the underdog and the disinherited; he has written a great deal about the needy and the oppressed. His plots, lacking proportion, are not unified or well rounded, and his ideas often become the chief protagonists in his books. Three times he stops *King Paradox* with interludes which, like classical Greek choruses, tie the story together, and in frequent soliloquies he points out that life is a commonplace, monotonous melody played before a limitless horizon. Even in his imaginary Utopia it is impossible to escape the evils of contemporary culture and civilization. Except for a series of twenty-two volumes called *Memories of a Man of Action,* the story of a nineteenth-century soldier of fortune related to the author, Baroja conceived most of his books as trilogies. One of the nine he has written is *The Fantastic Life,* of which *Paradox Rey* is the third and best volume.

The Story:

After many adventures Dr. Silvestre Paradox, a short, chubby man of about forty-five, settled in a small Valencian town. Tiring at last of his quiet life, he announced one morning to his friend, Avelino Diz, his intention of taking a trip to Cananí, on the Gulf of Guinea. A British banker, Abraham Wolf, was setting out on his yacht *Cornucopia* with a party of scientists and explorers for the purpose of establishing a Jewish colony in Africa, and he had invited Paradox to go with him. Paradox suggested that Diz join the expedition.

In Tangier they met several other members of the party, including General Pérez and his daughter Dora, and a crippled, scarred soldier named Hardibrás. They drank to the success of the venture in whiskey. When one of the company fed whiskey to a rooster, the fowl broke

KING PARADOX by Pío Baroja. By permission of the publishers, The Macmillan Co. Copyright, 1937, by The Macmillan Co.

into human speech and deplored what humans drink. Paradox declared that only Nature is just and honorable. He was eager to go where people lived naturally.

They boarded the yacht, Hardibrás swinging himself aboard by the hook he wore in place of his lost hand. There Paradox and Diz met others of the expedition: Mingote, a revolutionist who had tried to assassinate the King of Portugal; Pelayo, who had been Paradox's secretary until his employer fired him for crooked dealings; Sipsom, an English manufacturer; Miss Pich, a feminist writer and ex-ballet dancer, and "The Cheese Kid," a former French cancan dancer. Wolf himself was not on board. He was conferring with Monsieur Chabouly, a French chocolate king who was also Emperor of Western Nigritia, in an attempt to establish peaceful diplomatic relations between Chabouly's domain and the new state of Cananí.

The yacht put out to sea. On the third day stormy waves washed the captain overboard. Because the mate and the crew were drunk, Paradox and two others were forced to take over the yacht. Paradox, alone at the wheel, conversed with the wind and the sea, who told him that they had wills of their own. Yock, his dog, admired his master's resolution and strength, and declared that he was almost worthy of being a dog.

The storm increasing in fury, the mast broke and crashed upon the deck. Paradox called the passengers together and suggested that one of them, Goizueta, be made captain because of maritime experience he had had. Goizueta was elected. His first act, after saving one bottle of brandy for medicine, was to throw the rest overboard.

For a week they sailed through heavy fog that never lifted to reveal their position. At last the coal gave out and they drifted. One night some of the passengers and crew, Miss Pich, Mingote, and Pelayo among them, stole the only lifeboat and deserted the ship.

When the fog lifted, the passengers saw a beach not far away. The yacht struck a rock, but all were able to save themselves on rafts which they loaded with supplies from the ship. The next morning the yacht broke up, leaving the party marooned on a desert island.

It was then proposed that Paradox be put in charge. After modestly protesting, he accepted and assigned jobs to all the survivors. But he failed to make provisions for their defense. The next night a band of Negroes came in two canoes, surprised the sleepers, and took them bound to Bu-Tata.

The first demand Prime Minister Funangué made was for rum. One of the party, Sipsom, explained that they could provide rum only if they were allowed to return to their base of supplies. In his greed Funangué decided to ignore the advice of Bagú, the medicine man, who wanted all the whites slain. A friendly native, Ugú, was assigned to instruct the prisoners in tribal language and customs. From Ugú the captives learned Bagú's prejudices and superstitions. When the witch doctor later appeared, Sipsom declared that one of the prisoners was a wizard fated to die on the same day as Bagú. If Bagú sided with them, however, the white magician would help the medicine man to marry Princess Mahu, King Kiri's daughter. Bagú agreed.

King Kiri, engaged in his favorite pastime of killing subjects whom he disliked, paused in his diversion long enough to receive the prisoners. After a conversation about vested interests, he ordered that their lives be spared. Giving them permission to get supplies from their camp, he dispatched them under guard in two canoes. During the trip the prisoners, having lulled the suspicions of the guards, were about to take their guns and free themselves, but Paradox objected. He said that he had other plans. Diz scoffed at the way his friend put on airs.

After damaging one canoe, the prisoners used the delay to impress the Negroes with their white superiority by working magic tricks. A Frenchman in the party led a discussion on the rights of man. The scheme worked. After two weeks the Negroes agreed to desert their king and accompany the whites to Fortunate Island, a defensible plateau suggested by Ugú. Although Paradox preached the virtues of life out of doors, the others built Fortune House, a communal dwelling.

When King Kiri's army appeared, Paradox's machine gun quickly repulsed them and a searchlight finally put the natives to flight. Peace having come to Fortune House, the Negroes built huts and spent their evenings at magic-lantern shows. The *Fortune House Herald* began publication.

Prime Minister Funangué and two attendants, appearing under a flag of truce, brought King Kiri's appeal for help. The Fulani were attacking Bu-Tata. Paradox and Thonelgeben, the engineer, returned to the capital with the Negroes. At Paradox's suggestion, the river was dynamited to turn Bu-Tata into an island. Bagú objected to such interference with nature and discussed the change with fish, serpents, and frogs. Only the bat refused to voice an opinion.

One day warriors from Bu-Tata appeared at Fortune House with the head of King Kiri and begged one of the whites

to become their ruler. At a meeting all debated monarchial theories. When they failed to agree, Sipsom showed Paradox to the natives and announced that he had been chosen by popular vote. All returned to Bu-Tata for a coronation feast.

But by that time Paradox, reconciled to the advantages of civilization over life close to nature, was tired of Africa. At a session of Congress he argued against state support of art and criticized formal education.

Pelayo and Mingote, captured by Moors after the storm, arrived in Bu-Tata. Miss Pich had been violated by savages. The others had been eaten.

Political life continued. Two couples of the whites got married. Sipsom held law court and gave judgment in complicated cases. Then the French captured Bu-Tata and burned it. The whites were released at the request of "The Cheese Kid." Bagú was shot.

Three years later an epidemic filled the Bu-Tata Hospital. French doctors declared the outbreak the result of civilization, for one of the doctors had unknowingly taken smallpox to a native village while fighting another epidemic. Civilization had also driven Princess Mahu to dancing nude in a night club. As an enterprising journalist stated in *L'Echo* of Bu-Tata, the French army had brought civilization to that backward country.

KING SOLOMON'S MINES

Type of work: Novel
Author: H. Rider Haggard (1856-1925)
Type of plot: Adventure romance
Time of plot: Nineteenth century
Locale: Africa
First published: 1886

> *Principal characters:*
> ALLAN QUATERMAIN, an English explorer
> SIR HENRY CURTIS, his friend
> CAPTAIN JOHN GOOD, Curtis' friend
> UMBOPA, a Zulu, in reality Ignosi, hereditary chieftain of the Kukuanas
> TWALA, ruler of the Kukuanas
> GAGOOL, a native sorceress

Critique:

This story of the search for King Solomon's legendary lost treasure, hidden in the land of the Kukuanas, provides absorbing reading for children and adults alike. The slaughter provoked by the cruelty of King Twala and the character of the ancient sorceress, Gagool, make *King Solomon's Mines* a book which is not soon forgotten.

The Story:

Returning to his home in Natal after an unsuccessful elephant hunt, Allan Quatermain met aboard ship Sir Henry Curtis and his friend, retired Captain John Good. Sir Henry inquired whether Quatermain had met a man named Neville in the Transvaal. Learning that he had, Sir Henry explained that Neville was his younger brother, George, with whom he had quarreled. When Sir Henry inherited his parents' estate, George had taken the name Neville and had gone to Africa to seek his fortune. He had not been heard from since.

Quatermain said that Neville was reported to have started for King Solomon's Mines, diamond mines reputed to lie far in the interior. Ten years before he himself had met a Portuguese, José Silvestre, who had tried unsuccessfully to cross the desert to the mines and had dragged himself into his camp to die. Before he expired, José had given him a map showing the location of the treasure. It was written on a piece of a shirt which had belonged to his relative, another José Silvestre, three hundred years before. That Silvestre had seen the mines, but had died in the mountains while trying to return. His servant had brought the map back to his family, and it had been passed down through succeeding generations of the Silvestre family. By the time the ship reached Natal, Quatermain had agreed to help Sir Henry Curtis find his brother.

In Natal, Quatermain got their equipment together, and the trio chose the five men who were to go with them. Besides the driver and the leader for the oxen which were to pull their cart, they hired three servants; a Hottentot named Ventvögel, and two Zulus, Khiva and Umbopa. Umbopa explained that his tribe lived far to the north, in the direction in which they were traveling, and that he was willing to serve for nothing if he might go with the party. Quatermain was suspicious of the native's offer, but Sir Henry agreed to take Umbopa as his servant.

On the journey from Durban they lost Khiva when, trying to save Captain Good from attack by a wounded bull elephant, the native was torn in two by the animal. At Sitandra's Kraal, at the edge of the desert, the men left all the equipment they could not carry on their backs. Quatermain's plan was to travel at night so as to avoid the heat of the sun and to sleep during the day. On the third day out, however, the men could find no shelter from the heat. They decided that trekking was more comfortable than trying to rest. By the fourth day they were out of water, but on the following day Ventvögel discovered a spring. Refreshing themselves, they started off again that night. At the end of the next night they reached the lower slope of a mountain marked on the map as Sheba's left breast. On the other side of the mountain lay King Solomon's road, which was supposed to lead to the diamond mines.

The climb up the mountain was not an easy one. The higher they ascended, the colder it grew. At the top of the ridge they found a cave and climbed into it to spend the night. Ventvögel froze to death before morning.

Ventvögel was not the only dead man in the cave. The next morning, when it grew light, one of the party saw the body of a white man in its rocky recesses. Quatermain decided that it was the body of the first José Silvestre, preserved by the cold.

Leaving the bodies in the cave, the remaining men started down the mountain slope. As the mist cleared they could distinguish fertile lands and woods below them. Reaching King Solomon's road, they followed it into the valley. The road was a magnificent engineering feat which crossed a ravine and even tunneled through a ridge. In the tunnel the walls were decorated with figures driving in chariots. Sir Henry declared the pictures had been painted by ancient Egyptians.

When Quatermain and his party had descended to the valley, they stopped to eat and rest beside a stream. Captain Good undressed to shave and bathe. Suddenly Quatermain realized that they were being observed by a party of natives. As the leader of the band, an old man stepped up to speak to them, Quatermain saw that he greatly resembled Umbopa.

If it had not been for Captain Good's peculiarities, the four men would surely have been killed. Luckily, Captain Good's false teeth, bare legs, half-shaven face and monocle fascinated the savages so that they were willing to believe Quatermain's story that he and his friends had descended from the stars. To make the story more credible, he shot an antelope with what he declared was his magic tube. At Quatermain's insistence, the old man, whose name was Infadoos, agreed to lead the men to Twala, King of the Kukuanas. After a three-day journey Quatermain and his party reached Loo, where Twala was holding his summer festival. The white men were introduced to the hideous one-eyed giant before an assemblage of eight thousand of his soldiers.

Before Twala's annual witch hunt began that evening, the four travelers had a conference with Infadoos. From him they learned that Twala and his son, Scragga, were hated for their cruelty. Umbopa then revealed that he was, in reality, Ignosi, son of the rightful king, whom Twala had murdered. On the death of her husband his mother had fled across the mountains and desert with her child. As proof of his claim, Ignosi displayed a snake which was tattooed around his middle. The snake was the sign of Kukuana kingship.

All the men, including Infadoos, agreed that they would help him overcome Twala and gain the throne. Infadoos declared that he would speak to some of the chiefs after the witch hunt and win them to Ignosi's cause. He was certain that they could have twenty thousand men in their ranks by the next morning.

That night Gagool and her sister sorceresses helped Twala search out over a hundred of his men charged with evil thoughts or plots against their sovereign. When in their wild dances they stopped before any one of the twenty thousand soldiers who were drawn up in review, the victim was immediately stabbed to death. Gagool did not hesitate, in her blood thirst, to stop in front of Ignosi. Quatermain and his friends fired their guns to impress Twala and persuade him that Ignosi's life should be spared.

Infadoos was true to his word. He brought the chiefs he could muster, and Ignosi again exhibited the tattooing around his waist. The men feared he might be an impostor, however, and asked for a further sign. Captain Good, who knew from his almanac that an eclipse of the sun was due, swore that they would darken the sun the following day.

King Twala, continuing his festival, had his maidens dance before him the next afternoon. When they had finished, he asked Quatermain to choose the most beautiful, it being his custom to have the loveliest of the dancers slain each year. The girl Foulata was selected, but before she could be killed the white men interfered on her behalf. As they did so, the sun began to darken. Scragga, mad with fear, threw his spear at Sir Henry, but the Englishman was luckily wearing a mail shirt, a present from Twala. Seizing the weapon, he hurled it back at Scragga and killed him.

Quatermain and his friends, including Infadoos and the girl, took advantage of the eclipse to flee from the town with the chiefs who had rallied to them. On a hill about two miles from Loo approximately twenty thousand men prepared for battle.

Twala's regiments, numbering about thirty thousand soldiers, attacked the next day. They were driven back and then set upon by their enemies who, driving at them from three directions, surrounded and slaughtered many of the Kukuanas. The vanquished Twala was slain in a contest with Sir Henry, who lopped off his head with a battle-ax.

In return for the help which his white friends had given him, the new king, Ignosi, ordered Gagool to lead them to King Solomon's mines, which lay in the mountains at the other end of the great road. Deep into the hills they went, past three enormous figures carved in the rock, images which Quatermain believed might be the three false gods for whom Solomon had gone astray. To reach the treasure room they had to pass through a cave which Gagool called the Place of Death. There, seated around a table, were all the dead kings of the Kukuanas, petrified by siliceous water dripping upon them.

While the men stood dumbfounded by the sight, Gagool, unobserved moved a lever which caused a massive stone to rise. On the other side of it were boxes full of diamonds and stores of ivory.

As the men stood gloating over the treasure, Gagool crept away. After stabbing Foulata fatally, she released a lever to bring the door down again. Before she could pass under it to the other side, however, it dropped and crushed her.

For several hours Quatermain and his friends believed that they were buried alive, for they had no idea where to find the secret of the door. At last, in the dark, they found a lever which disclosed a subterranean passage. Through it they found their way once more to the outside and to Infadoos, who was waiting for them.

A few weeks later some of Ignosi's men guided them out of Kukuanaland, across the mountains, and on the first stage of their trip back across the desert. The only treasure they had with them was a handful of diamonds Quatermain had stuffed into his pockets before they found a way out of the treasure room.

Their guides who knew of a better trail than that by which the travelers had come, led them to an oasis from which they could pass on to other green spots along their way.

On their return trip they found, near the bank of a stream, a small hut and in it Sir Henry's lost brother, George. He had been badly injured by a boulder, two years before, and had not been able to travel since that time. Quatermain and his friends supported George across the desert to Sitandra's Kraal, and then on to Quatermain's home. According to their agreement before setting out on the expedition, the diamonds were divided. He and Captain Good each kept a third, and the rest of the stones they gave to George, Sir Henry's brother.

THE KING, THE GREATEST ALCALDE

Type of work: Drama
Author: Lope de Vega (Lope Félix de Vega Carpio, 1562-1635)
Type of plot: Tragi-comedy
Time of plot: Sixteenth century
Locale: Spain

THE KING, THE GREATEST ALCALDE by Lope de Vega. By permission of the publishers, Charles Scribner's Sons. Copyright, 1918, by The Poet Lore Company. Copyright, 1936, by John Garrett Underhill.

First presented: 1635

Principal characters:

SANCHO, a poor laborer
NUNO, a farmer
ELVIRA, his daughter
DON TELLO DE NEIRA, a nobleman
FELICIANA, his sister
PELAYO, a swineherd
DON ALFONSO VII, King of Leon and Castile

Critique:

Today we would call The King, the Greatest Alcalde, a social drama, for it portrays vividly the struggle of the peasantry against the nobility. The power is on the side of the aristocracy, but honor on the side of the poor. There is tragedy here, the tragedy of honor lost in spite of bitter fighting to retain it. But there is comedy also, Pelayo being one of the best clowns in all literature. That Lope de Vega loved the common people is evident throughout the play. Justice triumphs in the end, but too late to save the honor of the virtuous Elvira. The playwright intended that his audience should weep for her and for all the poor of his country, even while rejoicing at the happy conclusion of the story.

The Story:

Sancho, a poor peasant, was in love with an equally poor girl, Elvira, the daughter of Nuno, a farmer. When the old man gave Sancho permission to wed his daughter, he insisted that Sancho secure also the consent of Don Tello, master of all the surrounding lands, and of Don Tello's sister, Feliciana. In obedience to Nuno, Sancho went with Pelayo, a swineherd, to the castle to ask his lord's approval of the marriage. Both Don Tello and his sister Feliciana readily gave their consent and their blessing, and declared that they themselves would attend the wedding.

But when Don Tello saw the beautiful Elvira, he was filled with such passion for her that he decided to postpone the wedding, take Elvira to satisfy his own lust, and then give her to Sancho for his wife. Dismissing the priest, he told the as-sembled guests that the wedding must wait until the next day. Sancho and Elvira felt themselves already married, however, since the priest had heard them declare their true love for each other, and Sancho planned to go to Elvira's room that night. When Elvira opened her door, she confronted not her lover but Don Tello and his attendants, all masked, who carried her off to the castle.

Sancho and Nuno, learning of this betrayal, were ready to die. Nuno cautioned Sancho not to despair, however, for he knew his daughter would die rather than lose her honor. Nuno knew his daughter well. Although Don Tello pleaded with her and threatened her, she would not give herself to him. Feliciana begged him to remember his good name and his honor and not to force the girl.

Sancho and Nuno, going to Don Tello, pretended that they had heard but could not believe that he had stolen Elvira away. Don Tello pretended also that he was outraged at such a story and would have whipped those who told such lies to defame his honor. But when Elvira entered the room, Don Tello flew into a rage and ordered Sancho and Nuno beaten to death. They fled for their lives. Don Tello then vowed that he would force Elvira to submit to him or be killed. Again Sancho wanted to die, but once more Nuno persuaded him that there was still hope. He sent Sancho and Pelayo to the court of Alfonso, King of Castile, for the king was a good man and well-known for his justice in dealing with high and low alike.

When the king heard Sancho's story, he immediately wrote a letter to Don Tello, ordering him to release Elvira at once. Don Tello ignored the letter and declared that on his own land his people would do only his will. Pelayo assured Sancho that Don Tello had not yet possessed Elvira, for he would have obeyed the king had his lust been satisfied. Sancho and Pelayo went again to the king, to tell him that Don Tello had not obeyed his orders. The king promised to go in person to Don Tello and force him to return Elvira to her father and husband-to-be. He intended to go in disguise, taking with him only two attendants.

Don Tello, filled with wild rage and passion at Elvira's refusal to accept him, swore that he would take her by force. Nuno spoke with her through the bars of the room where she was confined and told her that Sancho had gone for help, and she promised again to die rather than lose her virtue. When Sancho and Pelayo returned with word that the king was sending help, Nuno was not much encouraged, for he knew that Don Tello kept his castle well guarded and could not be overcome by just three men. What Nuno did not know was that the king himself was coming, even though Pelayo was hard put to it to keep the secret.

When King Alfonso arrived, he questioned Nuno's servants and was convinced that Sancho and Nuno told the truth. Then he went in disguise to Don Tello's castle. There he was rudely received by that haughty nobleman. At last the king revealed himself and ordered Elvira brought before him. Elvira told her story, of her pure love for Sancho, of obtaining her father's and Don Tello's permission, of her seizure by Don Tello and his men, and finally of her lost honor. For Don Tello had carried out his vow. He had ordered her taken into a wood and there, even though she fought until she was weak, he had ravished her. She declared that she could never know joy again, for her honor was lost forever.

The king ordered Don Tello beheaded, both for his treatment of the innocent girl and for his failure to obey the king's command sent in his earlier letter. Although Feliciana pleaded for her brother, the king refused to be moved by her tears. Don Tello confessed that he deserved the penalty, for he had sinned twice, against his own honor and against the king. Then the king pronounced his final sentence. He would wed Elvira to Don Tello, then execute him. As his widow Elvira would inherit half his lands and gold. These would be her dowry when she married Sancho. Feliciana he would take to court, to wait on the queen until a noble husband could be secured for her. The peasants blessed the king's wisdom and actions, for he had righted all their wrongs.

THE KINGDOM OF GOD

Type of work: Drama
Author: Gregorio Martínez Sierra (1881-1947)
Type of plot: Social criticism
Time of plot: Early twentieth century
Locale: Spain
First presented: 1915

> *Principal characters:*
> SISTER GRACIA
> DON LORENZO, her influential father
> MARÍA ISABELA, her worldly mother
> SISTER MANUELA, Mother Superior of the old men's asylum
> TRAJANO,
> GABRIEL, and
> LIBORIO, old men in the asylum

THE KINGDOM OF GOD by Gregorio Martinez Sierra. Translated by Helen and Harley Granville-Barker. By permission of the publishers, E. P. Dutton & Co., Inc. Copyright, 1923, by E. P. Dutton & Co., Inc. Copyright renewed, 1951, by C. D. Medley, Executor of the Estate of Harley Granville-Barker.

MARGARITA,
CANDELAS, and
QUICA, three unwed mothers
Dr. ENRIQUE, the physician at the maternity home
SISTER CRISTINA, Mother Superior of the maternity home
SISTER DIONISIA, cook and housekeeper of the orphanage
FELIPE, a rebellious orphan
JUAN DE DIOS, a bullfighter from the orphanage

Critique:

Though perhaps less widely known and admired than the author's *Cradle Song*, *The Kingdom of God* is in some respects an even more interesting play. Among its features are a large canvas and the wide range of its characterizations; but the chief source of its appeal is a vital theme, relentlessly pursued through three carefully presented scenes. This theme is illustrated in the career of Sister Gracia; it strongly asserts that mankind must not turn a deaf ear to the sufferings of the unfortunate, that the aged, the sinners, and the orphans make claims on the rest of humanity which can neither be denied nor evaded. The scenes of the play show three stages in Sister Gracia's devotion to what she considers her duty. She appears first as a girl of nineteen, then as a woman of twenty-nine, and finally as an old woman of seventy. Though the vows of her particular sisterhood are not irrevocable, being renewable annually, she feels bound to her work by unbreakable threads of conscience and consecration. Her moving story is in the Maeterlinckian mold of quiet drama, "the theatre of kindliness," which made the Spanish stage of the early twentieth century one of international importance.

The Story:

A beautiful young girl, daughter of a prominent family, Gracia had decided to renounce the world in order to enter the benevolent order of St. Vincent de Paul. Her first assignment was in a home for poverty-stricken old men. Among these aged pensioners, her favorite was Gabriel, formerly valet to her own grandfather; but she gave freely of her love and energy to them all. Gradually she became well acquainted with Trajano, a superannuated anarchist, and with Liborio, a half-witted Cuban, whose only escape from melancholy was accomplished by Gracia's gifts of cigars and the personal attention she gave him.

She found true happiness in this unselfish service, but her family felt otherwise about her choice of a career. They thought that Gracia was wasting herself on old men who were dull and repulsive —her mother and sister did not see how she could bear to go near them. Visiting Gracia at the institution, they begged her to return home. Her father, whom Gracia dearly loved and respected, added his pleas; but the girl, though shaken by this emotional tug of war, still firmly declared that she must dedicate her life and happiness to help atone for the world's misery.

Ten years passed. Gracia was no longer at the asylum for old men. Halfway through this period of time, she had been transferred to another institution, this one a maternity home for unwed mothers. Here her fidelity to her vows met a stern test, for Gracia found herself sorely tried by the confusion and heartbreak which she saw all about her. The outcasts of society to whom she tried to minister were all different—even though it was the same kind of misstep which had brought them to the home—and they reacted to her advances in ways which were painfully unpredictable. Some of the girls were incorrigible; Quica, for example, was a perennial visitor, shedding the reproaches of the good sisters as casually as a duck sheds water. Others were girls whose characters were fundamentally good, like the fiercely independent Candelas. Neither Quica nor Candelas, however, presented such a problem as the aristocratic and embittered Margarita, whose wall of resentment could no longer be pierced by any gesture of compassion or sympathy. In trying to cope with the hysteria of Margarita, Sister Gracia underwent such strain that she herself soon reached the verge of emotional collapse.

At that point young Dr. Enrique, the physician at the home, decided that it was time to intervene. He had long loved Gracia in silence, respecting her vow, but now he urged her to marry him and leave an atmosphere which was proving so harmful to her. In becoming his wife, he pointed out, Gracia could take up another life as selfless and charitable as the one she now led, but it would be in a domestic framework much more wholesome and natural.

Gracia could not help recoiling at the doctor's suggestion. Still unnerved by her ordeal with Margarita, she did not think it possible or seemly to speak of love amid such surroundings, and she repeated to the doctor those views on life and service that she had expressed to her parents ten years before. As Dr. Enrique regretfully withdrew, she heard Candelas singing a ballad of love. Gracia could endure no more; frantically she rushed to Sister Cristina, her Mother Superior, and asked for a transfer, offering the reason that it was a matter of conscience.

The years crept up on Sister Gracia, but never again was she tempted to turn her back on the life which she had adopted. At seventy she was still battling the problems found in an imperfect world. By now she herself was a Mother Superior, in charge of an orphanage which was sadly neglected by its indifferent directors. Unperturbed, the old woman made the best of the situation. Aided only by the rather earthy Sister Dionisia, Sister Gracia steered the institution through one small crisis after another. Indignantly, she protected a small orphan from the mistreatment of his

brutal employer, a drunken tailor. Another situation involved two orphans, an older boy and a girl who had become sweethearts and were on the point of eloping. This affair of the heart was handled with an amused tolerance which softened—without completely disguising —the firmness of Sister Gracia's decision that marriage must wait.

Once in a while a colorful interlude would lighten the orphanage routine. One day, to the great delight of the children, a former inmate of the orphanage came back to pay his respects. Now an aspiring bullfighter, Juan de Dios brought with him the ears of his first bull; these, with a flourish, he presented to Sister Gracia. The latter managed a suitable response to this rather unexpected offering, though she could not resist adding to her expression of gratitude a few gentle admonitions to the ebullient young man; then she was swept to the outside gate in triumph. It was a great occasion and the sister was moved by Juan's open pride in having been one of her foundlings, even if the bull's ears seemed a gift of rather dubious value. More to the purpose, she considered ruefully, was the young bullfighter's promise to buy a good dinner for the whole orphanage after his next victory.

But Sister Gracia was soon brought back to everyday reality by a sudden revolt of the older boys. Touched off by their meager fare and led by the fiery Felipe, the mutiny threatened to flare into real trouble as the rebels set off to steal good food and to break any heads or doors which they found in their way. Undaunted, though hard pressed, Sister Gracia rallied all her resources of authority and faith. She commanded the boys to return to their unpalatable soup and to be thankful for what they had. To Felipe she gave earnest assurances— God did not condone injustice, she told him, but the way to overcome injustice was through love. Finally she led the orphans in an inspired prayer, pledging them all to God's love. When they became adults, later, they must not allow children to be forsaken or mothers to be wronged, and they must help build on this earth the Kingdom of God. As the chastened children left the table, Sister

Gracia offered additional counsel to the despondent Felipe. Men do not cry or complain, she told him. Even though they suffer, they must always work and hope.

KINGS IN EXILE

Type of work: Novel
Author: Alphonse Daudet (1840-1897)
Type of plot: Political romance
Time of plot: Nineteenth century
Locale: Paris
First published: 1879

Principal characters:
CHRISTIAN II, exiled King of Illyria
FREDERICA, Queen of Illyria
PRINCE LEOPOLD, their son
ELYSÉE MÉRAUT, the prince's tutor
SÉPHORA LEVIS, Christian's mistress

Critique:

More tragic than its successors, *Kings in Exile* is a forerunner of the highly imaginative and popular Graustarkian romance. As a novel, this book is interesting and satisfying. Daudet's style is a marvelous combination of the simple and the grand, the archaic and the new.

The Story:

When a revolution broke out in Illyria, King Christian II and Queen Frederica fought bravely against the rebels, and after the story of the siege of Ragusa became known throughout Europe much was said about the wonderful bravery of the king. In reality, most of the credit for the defense of the city should have gone to Frederica, who was in every way a queen. Christian was a king who had never had any great desire to wear the crown or occupy the throne.

At last the deposed rulers fled to Paris, where they took rooms in a hotel. There they were greeted by the Duke of Rosen, his son, and his daughter-in-law. Three years before, the duke, a former Illyrian minister, had been deposed by the king to placate the liberal elements of the country. Now he had come to offer his services to his sovereign once more. They

were accepted.

The monarchs thought that their stay in Paris would be brief, that the new republic would soon collapse and the monarchy be restored. Accordingly, Frederica refused to unpack anything. There was an air of the temporary and transitory about their lodgings.

Later it became clear that the republic would last and that the monarchy was doomed. Frederica resigned herself to a long exile from Illyria. The royal family purchased a house and settled down to wait. As time passed, Christian became more and more a frequenter of Parisian theaters and cafés until his activities were known all over the city and the subject of much conversation and scandal. The Duke of Rosen's daughter-in-law became his mistress.

Following the recommendations of two priests, the queen had engaged a tutor for the young prince. He was Elysée Méraut, who was supposed to teach the prince all that he would need to know to be a good sovereign. But the prince was not particularly intellectual. Furthermore, his father did not encourage the lessons, for he had given up all hope of ever regaining his lost throne; in fact, he

1582

was glad to escape the responsibilities of the crown.

Although the Duke of Rosen tried to do his best with the royal finances, the monarchs were, in reality, bankrupt. Elysée discovered that fact when he learned that the king was selling decorations, citations, and military orders to cover his debts. When the queen learned of the situation, she consulted the duke, who admitted that he had been using his own funds to support the monarchs in a regal style. She forbade him to continue his expenditures and the household took on an air of austerity.

In the meantime the king had given up his mistress and had become enamored of Séphora Levis, the wife of Tom Levis, a broker who posed as an Englishman and who had made a fortune out of catering to the whims and needs of exiled royalty. Séphora did not love the king. She promised him, however, that she would become his mistress after he had abdicated his throne. She wished to show him, she insisted, that she loved him for himself and not for his title. In reality, Séphora, Levis, and one of the king's councillors were involved in a plot to profit handsomely by Christian's abdication, for the Illyrian diet had offered the king a large private fortune if he would renounce the throne for himself and his descendants.

At first the king was unwilling to abdicate because he enjoyed too much the privileges of royalty without being willing to assume the responsibilities of his position. But at last he gave Séphora a title and promised her that he would give up his claim to the throne. Elysée, learning of his intention, notified the queen. She and Leopold went at once to the king's room, where he had just signed the act of renunciation. After informing him of a plan to invade Illyria, a plot hitherto kept from the pleasure-loving monarch, Frederica threatened to jump from the window with her child unless Christian destroyed the document he had signed. The king yielded to her desperate demands.

But the invasion attempt failed, for the Illyrian authorities had been warned in advance of the conspirators in Paris. Frederica came to the conclusion that there was only one course for Christian to take; he should abdicate in favor of his son. The king signed an act of abdication by which the young prince became King Leopold V of Illyria and Dalmatia.

Meanwhile a feeling very close to love had grown up between the neglected queen and the loyal tutor. One day, while the prince and Elysée were shooting at a mark in the garden, Leopold was accidentally wounded in one eye. The queen, in sorrow and anger, banished the tutor, and he went back to his dingy apartment.

Frederica took her son to consult a famous Parisian oculist. The doctor told her that the prince had lost the sight of one eye, that he would certainly lose the sight of the other eye, and that an operation was impossible because it would imperil his life. The queen was in despair.

A short time later she heard that Elysée Méraut was dying. As he lay on his deathbed, he heard the door open. Then there came to him a familiar voice—the voice of the young King Leopold, whom the loyal monarchist had loved. Frederica had brought him to see his old tutor. Elysée Méraut died a happy man.

KING'S ROW

Type of work: Novel
Author: Henry Bellamann (1882-1945)
Type of plot: Social criticism
Time of plot: Late nineteenth century

KING'S ROW by Henry Bellamann. By permission of Ann Watkins, Inc. Published by Simon & Schuster, Inc. Copyright, 1940, by Henry Bellamann.

Locale: The Middle West
First published: 1940

Principal characters:
PARRIS MITCHELL, of King's Row
DRAKE McHUGH, Parris' friend
RANDY MONAGHAN, who married McHugh
CASSANDRA TOWER (CASSIE), Parris' friend
ELISE SANDOR, newcomer to King's Row, Parris' friend

Critique:

Although Parris Mitchell is the hero of this novel, the story is also that of his home town, King's Row. For the struggle is always between Parris and the town. Life in King's Row is more tragic than happy, and Henry Bellamann has vividly depicted the town and its people. The result is an extremely skillful and moving story.

The Story:

Parris Mitchell lived with his German-born grandmother. Speaking English with a decided accent, he seemed different from the other boys his own age, and he was, consequently, much alone. He had only a few friends. There was Jamie Wakefield, whom Parris liked but who made him feel uncomfortable. There was Renée, with whom he went swimming and experienced his first love affair. Renée suddenly moved away. Later Cassandra Tower gave herself to him. Although he always remembered Renée, he was also in love with Cassie. But his best friend was another orphan like himself, Drake McHugh, a young idler whose life was almost completely concerned with women.

Parris studied with Cassie's father, Dr. Tower, a mysterious figure in King's Row, but a doctor who other physicians admitted was superior to them in knowledge. Parris' grandmother, Madame von Eln, saw to it, too, that he studied the piano with Dr. Perdorff. His grandmother arranged her affairs so that he could go to Vienna for his medical studies.

He knew that his grandmother was dying because Cassie Tower told him so.

Shortly after her death, Cassie herself died, shot by Dr. Tower, who later committed suicide, leaving his money and property to Parris. Parris went to stay with Drake McHugh, who lived by himself following the deaths of his aunt and uncle. Drake told Parris not to mention to anyone his connection with the Towers. No one knew why Dr. Tower had killed himself and Cassie. While going through Dr. Tower's papers, Parris discovered that Dr. Tower had been having incestuous relations with his daughter.

While Parris was in Europe, Drake continued his life of pleasure. His romance with Louise Gordon, daughter of a local doctor, was forbidden by her parents. Drake made plans to invest in a real estate development. In the meantime, he became friendly with Randy Monaghan, daughter of a railroad employee. Then Drake's guardian absconded with his money and he was left penniless. For weeks he haunted the saloons and drank heavily. One morning, unkempt and weary, he went to Randy's home. Shortly afterward Randy's father got him a job on the railroad. One day he had an accident. Dr. Gordon was summoned, and he immediately amputated both of Drake's legs.

Meanwhile Parris had known nothing of what had happened to his friend, for Drake asked Randy and Jamie Wakefield not to mention his misfortunes in their letters to Parris. But after the accident Randy wrote to Parris, who answered and gave instructions for taking care of Drake. A short time later, Randy and Drake were married. Parris cabled congratulations and turned over the Tower property to them.

With that money, Drake and Randy went into the real estate business. Then Parris came back to King's Row as a staff physician at the insane asylum. Louise Gordon suddenly accused her father of having been a butcher, of having performed needless operations and amputations. When Mrs. Gordon called in Dr. Mitchell to attend Louise, he was advised by his superior, Dr. Nolan, that Louise would fall in love with him. In fact, local gossip was already linking Dr. Mitchell's name with Louise.

Parris investigated Louise's charges and found them to be true. With that discovery, he realized that Drake's legs had been cut off perhaps needlessly. Parris told Randy that at the bottom of every tragedy in King's Row the hand of Dr. Gordon could probably be found. Drake and Randy made Parris a silent partner in their business. While he was away on another trip to Europe, a local newspaper published a story charging he had profited from the sale of land to the hospital. Following the advice of Dr. Nolan, Parris kept silent and nothing came of the charges.

Parris became friendly with Elise Sandor, whose father had bought his grandmother's house, and soon he was spending much of his time there. Then Drake McHugh became seriously ill, and it seemed clear that his illness resulted from the amputation. Parris knew that his friend had no chance to survive. Drake died several weeks later.

Randy, only thirty-two years old, was a widow. She decided to sell the business and look after her brother Tod, who was mentally incompetent. Those happenings were all matters of concern to Dr. Parris Mitchell on the night he walked towards the Sandor home where Elise was waiting for him.

KIPPS

Type of work: Novel
Author: H. G. Wells (1866-1946)
Type of plot: Domestic romance
Time of plot: Early twentieth century
Locale: England
First published: 1905

Principal characters:
    ARTHUR KIPPS, a simple soul
    ANN PORNICK, a neighbor girl
    HELEN WALSINGHAM, a "lady"
    MR. CHITTERLOW, Kipps' friend

Critique:

When H. G. Wells gave *Kipps* a subtitle, *The Story of a Simple Soul,* he summarized the novel briefly and concisely. Kipps was certainly simple, but he was also delightful. His rise in the world brought little change in his character, although he tried valiantly to make the change. Thus his downfall caused him little heartache and in one sense brought him happiness, for he could be himself at last.

The Story:

Young Arthur Kipps knew there was something mysterious about his birth, but his memories of his mother were so vague that they were all but meaningless. He knew only that she had gone away, leaving him in the care of his aunt and uncle and providing a small sum for his education. His was a bleak childhood spent in a wretched school in which he learned nothing. His vacations were dominated by his aunt's notions of what was proper.

His unhappy childhood was lightened somewhat, however, by his friendship with a boy of "low" class and the boy's sister, Ann Pornick. One day he and Ann tore a sixpence note in two, each keeping a half. This was Kipps' first venture in love, but it was short-lived. When he finished school he was apprenticed to a draper. Soon afterward the Pornicks moved away and Ann went into domestic service.

His life as an apprentice was as dull as his childhood. After seven years he was given a position in the firm at twenty pounds a year. He was engaged several times, that being the custom among his friends. But his next real infatuation, after Ann, was for Miss Helen Walsingham, a lady in the true sense. She taught woodcarving in a class he attended for self-improvement. Kipps felt keenly his ignorance about the ways of the world. Helen was so far above him in station that he could only stare at her in awe, for he could neither talk nor act in any way other than clumsily.

But Kipps' fortunes were soon to change. Through an accident he made the acquaintance of Mr. Chitterlow, a would-be playwright and actor. Because Chitterlow poured whiskey into Kipps at an alarming rate, the young man got drunk and stayed away from his residence, which was also his business address, all night, and he found himself the next morning with a month's notice. As he cursed himself for a fool, Chitterlow burst upon him again with news that a person answering Kipps' description was being advertised for by a solicitor. When Kipps investigated, he found that he had inherited a fortune, twelve hundred pounds a year and a handsome house, to be exact. He learned then that he had been the illegitimate son of a gentleman whose father would not let him marry Kipps' mother. Both his parents were dead, as was his grandfather. The old gentleman had relented before his death and left his fortune to his unknown grandson.

Bewildered by his new wealth, Kipps could do nothing constructive for some time. He felt a great need for knowledge of things of which he was dismally ignorant. He was besieged by requests for charity and by salesmen of all descriptions. Chitterlow persuaded him to buy a quarter interest in a play which he was writing, and his uncle invested money for him in all sorts of bargains in antiques which might one day be valuable.

Soon after he became wealthy Kipps met Helen Walsingham again. He felt as unsure of himself as ever, but there was a definite change in her attitude. Formerly she had been aloof; now she was warm and friendly. Before long she had maneuvered him into a proposal and agreed to teach him the things he needed to know in his new position. Kipps found himself scrutinized and instructed on every move he made, for Helen attempted to change his speech, his habits of dress, his social manners, and his attitudes. At first he was grateful, but although he was not aware of it, his infatuation was changing to gloom. Helen even persuaded him to change solicitors and to give his business to her brother, who had a short time before opened an office.

While visiting his aunt and uncle, Kipps met Ann Pornick again, She was not aware of his new fortune, even though he had recently seen her brother and told him the news. Pornick had turned Socialist, and his contempt for Kipps' new wealth, coupled with jealousy, had prevented his telling Ann of his old friend's good luck. Ann, acting naturally with Kipps, made him yearn for the simple life he had once known. The fact that she was in service bothered his new feeling of class superiority, however, and he tried to put her out of his mind. When he met her again, as a servant in the house in which he was a guest, he could control himself no longer. He threw caution and caste to the winds and asked her to marry him. She, having now learned of his position,

1586

protested feebly at the difference in their stations, but soon succumbed to his pleas and married him.

Their married life settled into the humdrum made necessary by idleness. He had let his fine house, and they prepared to build a home. Ann wanted a small house in which she could do her own work, but Kipps planned a larger one of about six rooms. But by the time the architect and Kipps' uncle finished with him, he found himself committed to a house of eleven bedrooms. Ann felt so inferior to him and longed so much for a simpler life that she often wept. Kipps felt the same longings but, convinced that he ought to live well and in society, did not identify them as such.

An abrupt change took place in their lives when he learned from Helen Walsingham that her brother had used Kipps' money for speculation and had lost everything before fleeing the country. Expecting to be penniless again, Kipps and Ann were satisfied when they learned that they still had about four thousand pounds, perhaps more. He fulfilled an ambition of some duration by opening a little bookshop. He knew nothing about books but he prospered enough to meet their now simple wants. The unfinished mansion was sold, and the happy couple settled down to a simple life that pleased them both. Then Chitterlow hit a stroke of luck and sold his play in which Kipps had bought a quarter interest. The play was a huge success, and Kipps collected many times his original investment of one hundred pounds.

When Ann presented him with a son, Kipps' joy was overflowing. Although he was almost as rich as he had been when he had his twelve hundred a year, he longed no more for self-improvement. He thought himself the happiest man alive. Who knows? Perhaps he was.

THE KNIGHT OF THE BURNING PESTLE

Type of work: Drama
Author: Francis Beaumont (1584?-1616)
Type of plot: Mock-heroic comedy
Time of plot: Early seventeenth century
Locale: England and Moldavia
First presented: c. 1607

Principal characters:
GEORGE, a London greengrocer
NELL, his wife
RALPH, an apprentice to George
VENTUREWELL, a London merchant
JASPER MERRYTHOUGHT, his apprentice
MASTER HUMPHREY, a slow-witted youth
LUCE, Venturewell's daughter
MERRYTHOUGHT, a carefree old gentleman

Critique:

Francis Beaumont, the son of a knight, could well have been cruel in a dramatic treatment of the workaday citizens of London, but in *The Knight of the Burning Pestle,* he reveals, beneath the hilarious burlesque of the plot, a warm sympathy for and a large understanding of the London lower middle classes, as represented by George, the greengrocer, his wife Nell, and Ralph, their apprentice. An outstanding feature of the play is the farcical audience participation. This device, a startling innovation in 1607, survives to the present day in semi-dramatic situations of broad humor. *The Knight of the Burning Pestle* was probably written under the influence of the keen interest taken by the literate of James I's time in

1587

Spanish prose fiction; surely Beaumont had heard of, if he had not read, Cervantes' *Don Quixote,* echoes of which mark the play.

The Story:

A production in a London theater was abruptly interrupted when George, a greengrocer, declared that he wanted to see a new kind of play, one in which the common man of London was glorified. Sitting beside him in the audience, George's wife Nell further suggested that there be a grocer in the play and that he kill a lion with a pestle. The indulgent speaker of the prologue agreed to these demands after George had offered his own apprentice, Ralph, to play the part of the commoner-hero. So the play began.

For presuming to love Luce Venturewell, the daughter of his master, apprentice Jasper Merrythought was discharged. Old Venturewell had chosen Master Humphrey, a foolish young citizen, for his daughter, but Luce, in league with Jasper, told the gullible Humphrey that to win her love he must abduct her and take her to Waltham Forest, where she planned to meet Jasper. (In the audience, Nell, the grocer's wife, commented that Humphrey was a fine young man.)

In a grocer's shop Ralph read a chivalric romance and, yearning for the olden times, determined himself to become a knight-errant. He enlisted his two apprentices, Tim and George, to be his foils; the one, his squire; the other, his dwarf. Dubbing himself The Knight of the Burning Pestle, Ralph explained the rules of knight-errantry to his amused followers. (Nell, pleased with Ralph's first appearance on the stage, clamored for his immediate return.)

In the meantime Jasper went home and collected his patrimony—all of ten shillings—from his indigent but carefree father, old Merrythought. Mrs. Merrythought, sick of hard times, packed her few valuables into a small chest and, with her younger son, Michael, left home to seek a better fortune. (In the pit, George

and Nell grew impatient for the reappearance of Ralph, their prodigious apprentice.)

Simple-minded Humphrey told old Venturewell of Luce's whimsical conditions for their marriage, and the old man consented to the plan.

Mrs. Merrythought and Michael, traveling afoot, arrived in Waltham Forest. While resting, they grew frightened and ran away when Ralph, as the Knight of the Burning Pestle, appeared with his retainers. (George and Nell, from their places at the edge of the stage, shouted a welcome to Ralph.) Ralph, assuming that Mrs. Merrythought had fled from some evil knight, followed her in order to rescue her from her distress. Jasper, arriving in the forest to meet Luce, picked up the casket containing Mrs. Merrythought's valuables. (Nell, scandalized, declared that she would tell Ralph what Jasper had done.)

When Mrs. Merrythought reported her loss to Ralph, he, in extravagantly courteous language, promised to assist her in regaining her valuables. (George and Nell commended themselves for having trained such a polite and virtuous apprentice.)

Humphrey and Luce came also to the forest, where they found Jasper waiting. Jasper, after thrashing Humphrey soundly, departed with Luce. (George and Nell, sorry for Humphrey, offered to call back Ralph to fight Jasper. The protests of the theater boy notwithstanding, the grocer and his wife wanted to change the plot to see Jasper properly punished.) Ralph immediately abandoned his search for Mrs. Merrythought's valuables and set out after the runaways. Overtaking them, he challenged Jasper in the language of knight-errantry. (Nell, at this juncture, exhorted Ralph to break Jasper's head.) Jasper, taking Ralph's pestle from him, knocked down the Knight of the Burning Pestle. (George tried to explain Ralph's defeat by saying that Jasper was endowed with magical powers.)

Ralph, his retainers, Mrs. Merrythought, and Michael put up for the night at the Bell Inn in Waltham. When they mistook the inn for a castle, the innkeeper indulgently joined them in their make-believe.

Humphrey, meanwhile, had returned to old Venturewell, to whom he complained of his treatment at the hands of Jasper. Irate, Venturewell went to old Merrythought and threatened to kill Jasper. (George and Nell at this point were so taken with the plot of the play that they believed it to be real.) Old Merrythought, carefree as usual, paid no heed to Venturewell's vengeful threats.

That night, while Luce was asleep in Waltham Forest, Jasper decided to test her love for him. Drawing his sword, he aroused the girl with threats that he intended to kill her because her father had discharged him. (Nell excitedly urged George to raise the London watch, to prevent what appeared to her to be certain violence.) As Luce trustingly submitted to Jasper's threats, Venturewell, Humphrey, and their men appeared and rescued her. Jasper, hopeful that he might somehow explain his behavior to Luce, followed them.

Next morning, at the Bell Inn, Ralph, unable to pay the reckoning, was threatened by the landlord. (George gave Ralph twelve shillings so that he could pay.) Mrs. Merrythought and Michael, disenchanted, went home. But Ralph, still in search of romantic adventure, was directed by the innkeeper to a barber shop in the town, where, he said, a giant named Barbaroso committed enormities every day. (At this point Mrs. Merrythought returned to the stage, only to be dragged off by George and Nell, who could not wait to see Ralph's fight with the barber.)

Ralph, after challenging the barber to mortal combat, knocked him down. While he begged for mercy, Ralph directed his retainers to liberate the barber's victims. One was a knight whose face was covered with lather. Another was a man on whom the barber had done minor surgery. As other victims appeared, the barber was

spared on the condition that he no longer subject humans to such indignities. (George and Nell beamed with pride at Ralph's conquest of the giant Barbaroso, and Nell allowed Mrs. Merrythought and Michael to appear on the stage.)

Mrs. Merrythought despaired because she was unable to get old Merrythought to have a serious thought. (Nell, furious at the old man's carefree indifference, ordered a beer to calm her temper. Then the action of the play became somewhat too pedestrian for the tastes of George and Nell. The couple next requested that Ralph be involved in a truly exotic adventure.)

Ralph suddenly found himself an honored guest at the court of Moldavia. Courteously rejecting Princess Pompiana's favors, he declared that he was promised to Susan, the daughter of a cobbler in London. (George gave Ralph a handful of small coins to distribute as largess to the royal household. Nell commended Ralph's loyalty and patriotism in preferring a London girl to a princess of a foreign land.)

Luce, meanwhile, was confined to her room with the prospect of marriage to Humphrey in three days' time. Mrs. Merrythought sought aid, unsuccessfully, from old Venturewell. Venturewell received a letter of repentance from Jasper, allegedly written by the youth as he lay dying of a broken heart, with the request that his body be conveyed to Luce. Hard upon the letter came a coffin, which was carried to Luce's room. Jasper, quite alive, sprang from the coffin, made explanations to Luce, placed her in the coffin, and had it removed from the room. He hid in the closet. Venturewell, still vengeful, ordered the coffin to be delivered to old Merrythought, who by that time was penniless, although still merry. (George, no respecter of plot, demanded that Ralph appear again.) Ralph, in the guise of Maylord, presented the month of May to the city of London.

Jasper, meanwhile, covered his face with flour and, appearing as a ghost, told

old Venturewell that he would never see his daughter again. Thoroughly frightened and repentant of his past actions, the old man thrashed Humphrey, who had come to see Luce, and sent him away. (George and Nell, their interest flagging, demanded diversion in which Ralph would be the center of attention.) Ralph appeared as a highly efficient captain leading a parade of London volunteers.

The coffin containing Luce was delivered to old Merrythought, who continued to be indifferent. When Jasper appeared and revealed Luce's presence, the young people prevailed upon old Merrythought to take back Mrs. Merrythought and Michael. Venturewell, still mindful of Jasper's ghost, told old Merrythought that he forgave all Jasper's transgressions. Jasper and Luce then confronted Venturewell, who offered them his blessings. (George and Nell, unaware of dramatic proprieties, asked for the stage death of Ralph so that the play could end properly.) Ralph, with a forked arrow through his head, delivered an absurd speech about Princess Pompiana and Susan. (Highly pleased with the sad ending, Nell invited the audience to partake of tobacco and wine at her house.)

THE KNIGHTS

Type of work: Drama
Author: Aristophanes (c. 448-385 B.C.)
Type of plot: Political satire
Time of plot: Fifth century B.C.
Locale: Athens
First presented: 424 B.C.

Principal characters: •
DEMUS, a slave master, a personification of the Athenian people
DEMOSTHENES, slave of Demus
NICIAS, another slave
CLEON THE PAPHLAGONIAN, a favorite slave and a personification of the Athenian tyrant
A SAUSAGE-SELLER, later called Agoracritus

Critique:

In 426 B.C., Cleon, tyrant of Athens, accused Aristophanes of fraudulently using the privileges of his citizenship. In this play, presented two years later, the playwright attacked and ridiculed his powerful enemy, whom he presents as a fawning slave to his master but insolent and arrogant to his fellow slaves. As political satire, the play is one of wit and wisdom. Aristophanes' message is that as long as men will not look beyond their noses, they will continue to sell each other short, never realizing that at the same time they are giving themselves the shortest weight.

The Story:

Demus, a selfish and irritable old man, a tyrant to his slaves, had purchased a tanner, who was nicknamed the Paph- lagonian. This slave, a fawning, foxy fellow, quickly ingratiated himself with his new master, to the dismay of all the other slaves in Demus' household, Demosthenes and Nicias in particular. Because of the Paphlagonian's lies, Demosthenes and Nicias received many floggings. The two at one time considered running away, but decided against this course because of the terrible punishment they would receive if caught and returned to their owner. They also considered suicide, but in the end they decided to forget their troubles by tippling. Going for the wine, Nicias found the Paphlagonian asleep in a drunken stupor. While the drunken man slept, Nicias stole the writings of the sacred oracle that the Paphlogonian guarded carefully. In the prophecies of the oracle, Demos-

1590

thenes and Nicias read that an oakum-seller should first manage the state's affairs; he should be followed by a sheep-seller, and he in turn should be followed by a tanner. At last the tanner would be overthrown by a sausage-seller.

As they were about to set out in search of a sausage-seller, a slave of that butcher's trade came to the house of Demus to sell his wares. Nicias and Demosthenes soon won him over to their cause, flattering him out of all reason and assuring him that his stupidity and ignorance fitted him admirably for public life.

When the Paphlagonian awoke, he loudly demanded the return of the oracle's writings. The Sausage-Seller, however, was able to out bawl him. Spectators became involved. Some of the citizens protested against the Paphlagonian's unjust accusations of the Sausage-Seller. Others claimed that the state was falling into ruin while this shameless name-calling continued. Others accused the Paphlagonian of deafening all Athens with his din. The Sausage-Seller accused the Paphlagonian of cheating everybody. A few citizens gloated that someone even more arrogant and dishonest than the Paphlagonian had been found in the person of the Sausage-Seller. Others feared that this new demagogue would destroy all hope of defending Athens from her enemies.

While the citizens clamored, the Sausage-Seller and the Paphlagonian continued to out-boast, out-shout, and out-orate each other. The Sausage-Seller said that he would make meatballs out of the Paphlagonian. Demus' pampered slave threatened to twitch the lashes off both the Sausage-Seller's eyes. Demosthenes broke in to suggest that the Sausage-Seller inspect the Paphlagonian as he would a hog before butchering it.

At last both began to clamor for Demus, asking him to come out of his house and decide the merits of their claims. When he answered their calls, both boasted of a greater love to do him service. Convinced by the assurances of the Sausage-Seller, Demus decided to dismiss the Paphlagonian and demanded that his former favorite return his seal of office. Both continued their efforts to bribe Demus for his favor. At last the rivals ran to consult the oracles, to prove to Demus the right of their contentions.

Each brought back a load of prophetic writings and insisted upon reading them aloud to Demus. In their prophecies they continued to insult one another, at the same time flattering Demus. The Sausage-Seller related a dream in which Athena had come down from Olympus to pour ambrosia upon Demus and the sourest of pickles upon the Paphlagonian.

Demus sent them off on another foolish errand, laughing meanwhile because he had duped both of them into serving him. But at last the Sausage-Seller convinced the Paphlagonian that he had the right of stewardship by the word of an ancient oracle in whom both believed. Having won his victory, the Sausage-Seller, now calling himself Agoracritus, began to browbeat his new master and to accuse him of stupidity and avarice. He boasted that he would now grow wealthy on bribes the Paphlagonian had formerly pocketed. To show his power, he ordered Cleon the Paphlagonian to turn sausage-seller and peddle tripe in the streets.

THE KREUTZER SONATA

Type of work: Novel
Author: Count Leo Tolstoy (1828-1910)
Type of plot: Social criticism
Time of plot: Late nineteenth century
Locale: Russia
First published: 1889

Principal characters:
VASYLA POZDNISHEF, a Russian aristocrat
MME. POZDNISHEF, his wife
TRUKHASHEVSKY, lover of Mme. Pozdnishef

Critique:

This book has been much misunderstood as representing Tolstoy's own views on marriage and the relationships of the sexes in Russian society. Actually, the story is the confession of an insane man who had murdered his wife in a fit of jealousy brought on by his insanity. Most important, however, is the Christian aspect of sexual morality which underlies the book. Explaining his novel, Tolstoy said that he wanted to do away with the false conception that sexual relationships were necessary for health, to bring to public attention the fact that sexual immorality was based in part on a wrong attitude toward marriage, and to restore the birth of children to a proper place in the sphere of marriage.

The Story:

One spring night a railway train was speeding across Russia. In one of the cars a sprightly conversation about the place of women, both in public and in the home, was in progress among a group of aristocrats. One of the listeners finally broke into the conversation with the statement that Russians married only for sexual reasons and that marriage was a hell for most of them unless they, like himself, secured release by killing the other party to the marriage. With that remark he left the group and retired to his own seat in the car. Later on he told his story to his seat companion.

His name was Pozdnishef and he was a landed proprietor. As a young man he had learned many vices, but he had always kept his relationships with women on a monetary basis, so that he would have no moral responsibility for the unfortunates with whom he came in contact. His early life had taught him that people of his class did not respect sex. The men looked on women only in terms of pleasure. The women sanctioned

such thoughts by openly marrying men who had become libertines; the older people by allowing their daughters to be married to men whose habits were known to be of a shameful nature.

At the age of thirty Pozdnishef fell in love with a beautiful woman of his own class, the daughter of an impoverished landowner in Penza. During his engagement to the girl he was disturbed because they had so little about which to converse when they were left alone. They would say one sentence to each other and then become silent. Not knowing what should come next, they would fall to eating bonbons. The honeymoon was a failure, shameful and tiresome at the beginning, painfully oppressive at the end. Three or four days after the wedding they quarreled, and both realized that in a short time they had grown to hate each other. As the months of marriage passed, their quarrels grew more frequent and violent. Pozdnishef became persuaded in his own mind that love was something low and swinish.

The idea of marriage and sex became an obsession with him. When his wife secured a wet-nurse for their children, he felt that she was shirking a moral duty by not nursing her offspring. Worse, Pozdnishef was jealous of every man who came into his wife's presence, who was received in his home, or who received a smile from his wife. He began to suspect that his wife had taken a lover.

The children born to Pozdnishef and his wife were a great trouble to him in other ways as well. They were continually bothering him with real or fancied illnesses, and they broke up the regular habits of life to which he was accustomed. They were new subjects over which he and his wife could quarrel.

In the fourth year of their marriage, the couple had reached a state of complete disagreement. They ceased to talk over anything to the end. They were almost silent when they were alone, much as they had been during their engagement. Finally the doctors told the woman she could have no more children with safety. Pozdnishef felt that without children to justify their relations, the only reason for their life together was the other children who had been born and who held them like a chain fastening two convicts.

In the next two years the young woman filled out and bloomed in health, after the burden of bearing children was taken from her. She became more attractive in the eyes of other men, and her husband's jealousy sharply increased.

Mme. Pozdnishef had always been interested in music, and she played the piano rather well. Through her musical interest she met a young aristocrat who had turned professional musician when his family fortune had dwindled away. His name was Trukhashevsky. When he appeared on the scene the Pozdnishefs had passed through several crises in their marriage. The husband had at times considered suicide and the wife had tried to poison herself. One evening, after a violent scene in which Pozdnishef had told his wife he would like to see her dead, she had rushed to her room and swallowed an opium compound. Quick action on the part of the husband and a doctor had saved her life, but neither could forget her desperate attempt.

One evening Trukhashevsky came to Pozdnishef's home in Moscow. He and Mme. Pozdnishef played during the evening for a number of guests. The first piece they played together was Beethoven's Kreutzer Sonata. The first movement, a rapid allegro, worked upon the highly-strung emotions of the husband until he began to imagine that there was already an understanding between the musician and his wife. The idea obsessed him so that he could hardly wait until the other man was out of the house.

Never in his life had music affected Pozdnishef in that manner. Between it and his jealousy, he was almost violently insane.

Two days later Pozdnishef left Moscow to attend a meeting. He went away fearful of what might happen while he was gone. On the second day of his absence, Pozdnishef received a letter from his wife saying that the musician had called at the house.

Jealousy immediately seized the husband. He rushed back to Moscow as fast as carriage and trains could carry him. He arrived at his home after midnight. Lights were burning in his wife's apartment. Taking off his shoes, he prowled about the house. He soon discovered the musician's overcoat. He went to the nursery and the children's rooms, but found everyone there asleep. Returning to his study, he seized a dagger and made his way to his wife's apartment. There he found his wife and the musician seated at a table, eating. He rushed at the man, who escaped by ducking under the piano and then out the door. Pozdnishef, beside himself with anger and jealousy, seized his wife and stabbed her. When she dropped to the floor, he ran from the room and went to his study. There he fell asleep on a sofa.

A few hours later his sister-in-law awakened him and took him to see his dying wife. Shortly afterward the authorities carried Pozdnishef away to prison. He went under police escort to his wife's funeral. It was only after he had looked at the waxen face of the corpse that he realized he had committed a murder. Then, at his trial, Pozdnishef was found innocent because he had murdered while in the heat of anger at finding his wife unfaithful to him.

Now judged insane, Pozdnishef declared that if he had it to do over, he would never marry. Marriage, he insisted, was not for true Christians with strong sensibilities and weak moral restraints.

KRISTIN LAVRANSDATTER

Type of work: Novel
Author: Sigrid Undset (1882-1949)
Type of Plot: Historical chronicle
Time of plot: Fourteenth century
Locale: Norway
First published: 1920-1922

Principal characters:

KRISTIN LAVRANSDATTER
LAVRANS BJÖRGULFSÖN, Kristin's father, owner of Jörundgaard
RAGNFRID IVARSDATTER, Kristin's mother
ULVHILD, and
RAMBORG, Kristin's sisters
ERLEND NIKULAUSSÖN, owner of Husaby
SIMON ANDRESSÖN, son of a neighboring landowner
LADY AASHILD, Erlend's aunt
NIKULAUS (NAAKVE),
BJÖRGULF,
GAUTE,
SKULE,
IVAR,
LAVRANS
MUNAN, and
ERLEND, sons of Erlend and Kristin

Critique:

Kristin Lavransdatter is a trilogy—*The Bridal Wreath, The Mistress of Husaby,* and *The Cross*—for which Sigrid Undset received the Nobel Prize in Literature. Madame Undset's work is characterized by consummate artistry in her delineation of character, in her selection of detail, and above all in her ability to tell a story. These three novels laid in medieval Norway, a period little known to the general reader, make possible the reader's acquaintance with many characters who lived long ago, but who faced many of the same great problems that the world knows today.

The Story:

Lavrans Björgulfsön and his wife Ragnfrid Ivarsdatter were descended from powerful landowners. Although Kristin had been born at her father's manor Skog, she spent most of her childhood at Jörundgaard, which fell to Lavrans and Ragnfrid upon the death of Ragnfrid's father. Kristin's childhood was exceedingly happy.

A second daughter, Ulvhild, was crippled at the age of three. Lady Aashild, a declared witch-wife, was sent for to help the child. Kristin became well acquainted with Lady Aashild that summer.

When she was fifteen, Kristin's father betrothed her to Simon Andressön of Dyfrin. One evening Kristin slipped away to bid goodbye to a childhood playmate, Arne Gyrdsön, and on her way home Bentein, Sira Eirik's grandson, accosted her. She escaped after a fight with him, physically unharmed but mentally tortured. Later that year Arne was brought home dead after having fought with Bentein over Bentein's sly insinuations regarding Kristin. Kristin persuaded her father to put off the betrothal feast and permit her to spend a year in a convent at Oslo.

Soon after entering the Convent of Nonneseter, Kristin and her bed-partner, Ingebjörg Filippusdatter, went into Oslo to shop, accompanied by an old servant. When they became separated from the old man, they were rescued by a group of men riding through the woods. In that manner Kristin met Erlend Nikulaussön, the nephew of Lady Aashild. In July, Kristin and Erlend met once more at the St. Margaret's Festival and that night vowed to love each other. The following morning Kristin learned from Ingebjörg of Eline Ormsdatter, whom Erlend had stolen from her husband, and by whom Erlend had had two children. Later that summer, while visiting her uncle at Skog, Kristin and Erlend met secretly and Kristin surrendered to Erlend. During the following winter Kristin and Erlend managed to meet frequently. In the spring, Kristin told Simon of her love for Erlend and her desire to end their betrothal. He agreed, much against his will. Lavrans and Ragnfrid unwillingly accepted Kristin's and Simon's decision.

When Erlend's kinsmen brought suit for Kristin's hand in marriage, Lavrans refused. During the winter Erlend and Kristin planned to elope to Sweden. While they were making their plans at Lady Aashild's home, Eline Ormsdatter overtook them. Discovered by Erlend when she was trying to give poison to Kristin, she stabbed herself. Erlend and Sir Björn, Lady Aashild's husband, put her on a sled and took her south to be buried. Kristin returned home.

The following spring Erlend's relatives again made a bid for Kristin's hand, and worn out with suffering—Ulvhild's death and Kristin's unhappiness—Lavrans agreed to the betrothal. During Erlend's visit at Whitsuntide, Kristin became pregnant. On the night of the wedding Lavrans realized that Kristin already belonged to Erlend. He had given to Erlend what Erlend had already possessed.

After her marriage Kristin moved to Erlend's estate at Husaby. She was quick to notice the neglect everywhere evident. In the next fifteen years she bore Erlend seven sons—Nikulaus, Björgulf, Gaute, the twins Ivar and Skule, Lavrans, and Munan. At the same time she struggled to save her sons' inheritance by better management of Husaby. But Erlend, intent on becoming a great man, sold land to pay his expenses and granted tenants free rent in exchange for supplies for his military musters.

Simon Andressön who lived at Formo with his sister Sigrid and his illegitimate daughter, Arngjerd, made suit to Lavrans for Kristin's youngest sister, Ramborg. The following year Lavrans died, followed two years later by Ragnfrid. Kristin's part of the inheritance was Jörundgaard.

There was much unrest in the country at that time. A boy, Magnus VII, had been named king of both Sweden and Norway, and during his childhood Erling Vidkunssön was made regent of Norway. When Magnus reached the age of sixteen, Sir Erling resigned and soon Norway had little law or order. During those years of unrest Erlend conspired to put another claimant on the throne of Norway. Arrested, he was tried for treason by a king's-men's court. Erlend came off with his life, but he had to forfeit all his lands.

Erlend went with Kristin and his sons to Jörundgaard to live; but he cared little for farming or for the people of the dale, and the neighbors avoided Jörundgaard. As the children grew to manhood, Kristin became more fearful for their future. In her desire to further their fortunes, she and Erlend came to harsh words and she told him he was not a fit lord of Jörundgaard. He left her and went to Haugen, the farm where Lady Aashild had spent her last days. Kristin, although she longed to have Erlend back, felt that she had been in the right and struggled along with the help of Ulf, a servant, to make Jörundgaard produce.

The following winter her brother-in-law Simon died as a result of a cut on the arm, sustained while separating two drunken fighters. Before he died, he asked Kristin to go to Erlend and settle their quarrel. Kristin promised to do so. Ramborg gave birth to her son six weeks early, and upon Simon's death named the child Simon Simonssön.

Kristin kept her promise and went to Haugen to ask Erlend to return to Jörundgaard, but he refused. She stayed at Haugen that summer and then returned home to her sons. Finding herself again with child, she sent her sons to tell her husband. When the child was born, Erlend still did not come to her. The child died before it was three months old. Soon thereafter, when Bishop Halvard came to the parish, Jardtrud, Ulf's wife, went to him and charged Ulf with adultery with Kristin. Lavrans, unknown to the rest of the family, rode to Haugen to get his father. Erlend returned immediately with his son, but in a scuffle in the courtyard he was wounded and he died. The same year Munan died of a sickness which went around the parish. Thus Kristin was left with six sons, each of whom must make his way in the world.

Ivar and Skule, the twins, took service with a distant kinsman. Ivar married Signe Gamalsdatter, a wealthy young widow. Nikulaus and Björgulf entered the brotherhood at Tautra. Gaute fell in love with Jofrid Helgesdatter, heiress of a rich landowner. The two young people eloped and were not married until the summer after the birth of their child, Erlend. During that winter they lived at Jörundgaard and after their marriage Kristin relinquished the keys of the manor to Jofrid. Lavrans took service with the Bishop of Skaalholt and sailed to Iceland.

Kristin, who felt out of place in her old home after she was no longer mistress there, decided to go to Nidaros and enter a convent. In the year 1349, after Kristin had been in the cloister for about two years, her son Skule went to see her. From him she received the first news of the Black Plague. The disease soon engulfed the whole city, carried off her two sons in the convent, Nikulaus and Björgulf, and finally caused Kristin's own death.

THE LADY FROM THE SEA

Type of work: Drama
Author: Henrik Ibsen (1828-1906)
Type of plot: Psychological realism
Time of plot: Nineteenth century
Locale: A small town in northern Norway
First presented: 1889

Principal characters:
>   DOCTOR WANGEL, a physician
>   ELLIDA, his second wife
>   BOLETTA, and
>   HILDA, his daughters by a former marriage
>   ARNHOLM, a schoolmaster
>   LYNGSTRAND, a sculptor
>   A STRANGER

Critique:

The Lady from the Sea was the first of the psychological dramas written by Ibsen, who had formerly devoted himself almost entirely to social criticism. Here the characters are not merely part of a class, for they are strongly and finely drawn in their own right. Also, there are two subplots, another departure from the great dramatist's usual style. Technically, the play does not measure up to the perfection of the social dramas, largely because the treatment of his material was new to Ibsen. The story is intensely moving, however, and worthy of the attention of all readers. The drama was published in 1888, prior to its first presentation.

The Story:

There was no real affection between Ellida Wangel and her two stepdaughters, Boletta and Hilda. She had married their father, Doctor Wangel, several years before, soon after the death of his first wife. He had met Ellida in the seacoast town in which she lived, a town she loved because it was near the sea. In fact, the sea seemed to dominate her whole life, and she felt stifled in her new home, which was surrounded by mountains.

Arnholm, Boletta's former tutor, paid a visit to the Wangel home. He had known and loved Ellida before her marriage to Doctor Wangel, but she had refused his suit because, as she told him, she was betrothed to another. As the two former friends talked, a traveling sculptor, Lyngstrand, stopped to tell them of a group he hoped to model. Lyngstrand had been at sea and there had met a sailor who told him a strange story. The sailor had married a woman who had promised to wait for him, but three years ago he had read that his wife had married another man. The sailor had told Lyngstrand that his wife was still his, that he would have her even though she had broken her vows.

This strange tale moved Ellida, seemed even to frighten her. Her moodiness following the telling of the story made her husband believe she was unhappy because she was away from the sea, and he offered to move his family to the seashore so that Ellida could regain her peace of mind. But Ellida knew that this move would not bring her happiness, while it would make him and the girls unhappy to leave their home. And so she told him the real cause of her misery.

Some years before she had come under the spell of a sailor whose ship was in port for only a few days. He too loved the sea and seemed to be part of it. Indeed, he and Ellida seemed to be animals or birds of the sea, so closely did they identify themselves with the vast waters. Then the sailor murdered his captain, for a reason unknown to Ellida, and he was forced to flee. Before he left, he took his ring and one from her hand, joined them together, and threw them into the sea. He told her that his act joined them in marriage and that she was to wait for him.

At the time she seemed to have no will of her own in the matter, but to be completely under his spell. Later she regained her senses and wrote to tell him that all was over between them, that the joining of the rings was not a lasting bond. But he ignored her letters and continued to write that he would come back to her.

Ellida told her husband that she had forgotten the sailor until three years ago, when she was carrying the doctor's child. Then, suddenly, the sailor seemed very close to her. Her child, who lived only a few months, was born—or so she believed—with the eyes of the stranger. She had felt such guilt that from that time on she had not lived with her husband as his wife. The anguish she had suffered was affecting her mind and she feared that she would go mad. She loved her husband, but she was drawn to the man of the sea whom she had not seen in ten years.

Doctor Wangel, trying to comfort his wife, was also worried about her sanity. One day a Stranger appeared in their garden. He was the sailor, come to claim Ellida. He told her that he had come to hold her to the vow she had taken years before. Ellida said that she could never leave her husband, but the Stranger would not listen. Then the doctor told the Stranger that he would never allow his wife to leave him, that the Stranger could not force her to go against her will. The Stranger said that he would never force her, but she would come to him of her own free will. Those words, of her own free will, seemed to fascinate Ellida. She repeated them over and over and gained strength from them. The Stranger left, saying that he would return for her answer the next night and telling her that if she refused to join him, she would never see him again.

Ellida begged her husband to save her from the Stranger. He tried to persuade her that her mind had been conditioned by the story of the sailor and his unfaithful wife that Lyngstrand had told her. He reminded her also that the sailor did not even look as she had remembered him. But Ellida would not be comforted. She told her husband that there was only one way she could ever make the right decision and save her sanity. The doctor must release her from her marriage vows, not by divorce but only by a verbal release. Then she would be free to choose between her husband and the Stranger. She said that she had never been free. First she had been under the will of the Stranger, then under the will of her husband.

The doctor refused her request because he thought he must save her from the Stranger and from herself. He felt that the Stranger had an evil influence over his wife, and he wanted to save her from disaster. He promised her, however, that after the Stranger left, he would release her from her vow to him and give her the freedom she wished.

The next night the Stranger came again, as he had promised, and Ellida and her husband met him in the garden. When the Stranger asked Ellida to come with him of her own free will, the doctor ordered the Stranger to leave the country or be exposed as a murderer. The Stranger showed them a pistol which he said he would use to take his own life rather than give up his freedom.

Then Ellida told her husband again that he must release her from her marriage vows, for although he could keep her body tied in this place he could not fetter her soul and her desires. Seeing that she was right and that his refusal would drive his wife out of her reason, the doctor told her that he would release her from her bargain with him. She saw that he loved her enough to put her happiness above his own. She turned to the Stranger, who was pleading with her to leave with him on the ship standing offshore, and told him that now she could never go with him. The Stranger, realizing that there was something between these two that was stronger than his will, left them after promising never to return again.

Ellida assured her husband that her mind was whole once more and that she would never again long for the Stranger or the sea. The unknown no longer had a power over her, for at last she had made a decision of her own free will. Because she had been free to choose or reject the fascination of the Stranger, she had found the will to reject him. Now she could go with her husband and live again as his wife. She knew too that she could win his daughters to her and think of them as her own. Ellida would never again feel like the wild, eager birds of the sea. She would bind herself forever to the land, and in her bondage she would find freedom.

LADY INTO FOX

Type of work: Novelette
Author: David Garnett (1892-   )
Type of plot: Fantasy
Time of plot: 1880
Locale: England
First published: 1923

MR. RICHARD TEBRICK
SILVIA FOX TEBRICK, his wife

Critique:

Lady Into Fox is a story in which its author, like Coleridge in *The Rime of the Ancient Mariner,* attempts to make the unreal seem probable. Perhaps many a bridegroom, and as suddenly, has found himself married to a vixen. The book is fantasy, but fantasy written with scrupulous regard for realistic detail. So far as the book's underlying meaning is concerned, the reader may make whatever interpretation he will. It is first of all an entertaining story.

The Story:

Silvia Fox married Richard Tebrick in 1879 and went to live with him at Rylands, near Stokoe, Oxon. The bride was oddly beautiful, a woman with small hands and feet, reddish hair, brownish skin, and freckles. Early in the year 1880, while the two were still very much in love, Silvia accompanied her husband on a walk. Hearing the sounds of a hunt, Mr. Tebrick pulled his bride forward to get a good view of the hounds. Suddenly she snatched her hand away and cried out. Beside him on the ground where his wife had stood Mr. Tebrick saw a small red fox.

Even in her changed form, he could still recognize his wife. When she began to cry, so did he, and to soothe her he kissed her on the muzzle. Waiting until after dark, he buttoned her inside his coat and took her home. First he hid her in the bedroom; then he announced to the maid that Mrs. Tebrick had been called to London. When he carried her tea to the bedroom and found his poor fox trying to cover herself with a dressing gown, he dressed her properly, set her up on some cushions, and served her tea, which she drank daintily from a saucer while he fed her sandwiches.

Because the dogs had all that time been making a clamor, he went out into the yard and shot them. Then he dismissed the servants and retired to bed, sleeping soundly with his vixen in his arms. The next morning their daily routine started. First he would cook breakfast; later he would wash and brush his wife. Next they would eat breakfast together, the same food Silvia had enjoyed before her transformation. Once he started reading to her from *Clarissa Harlowe,* but he found her watching a pet dove in its cage nearby. Soon Mr. Tebrick began to take his vixen outdoors to walk. On such occasions her chief joy was chasing ducks near the pond.

One day after tea she led him to the drawing-room with gestures that showed she wished him to play the piano. But when she continued to watch the bird, he freed the dove from its cage and tore his wife's picture into bits. He also found himself disgusted by the way she ate a chicken wing at the table. One night she refused to share his bed and pranced about the room all night.

The next morning the poor husband tried an experiment. From town he brought her a basket containing a bunch of snowdrops and a dead rabbit. Silvia pretended to admire the flowers; but when her husband left the room purposely, she devoured the rabbit. Later she repented and showed by motions that she wanted him to bring out the stereoscope so that she could admire the views. She refused to sleep with him again that night. Next day she pulled off her clothes and threw them into the pond. From that time on she was a naked vixen, and Richard Tebrick drank frequently to drown his sorrows.

At last Mr. Tebrick decided that to avoid scandal he must move to another location with his vixen, and he chose the cottage of Nanny Cork, Silvia's old nurse, as his place of retreat. He drove over in a dog cart with his wife in a wicker basket on the seat beside him. The best feature of their new home was a walled garden in which the fox could enjoy the air without being seen, but she soon began to dig under the walls in her attempts to escape. Once, thwarted in an attempt to escape, she bit her husband on the hand. Finally he gave his vixen her freedom, and allowed her to run wild in the woods.

Stricken with grief over the loss of his wife, Mr. Tebrick hired a jockey named Askew to follow the hunts and report on the foxes killed. He shot two fox hounds who strayed on his land.

One night Mr. Tebrick heard a fox bark. He heard the barking again in the morning. His vixen had returned to lead him to her earth and proudly display her litter of five tiny cubs. Mr. Tebrick was jealous, but at last he overcame his scruples and went each day to visit the young foxes. Able to identify the cubs

by that time, he christened them Sorel, Kaspar, Selwyn, Esther, and Angelica. Of the whole litter, Angelica was his favorite because she reminded him of her mother.

The Reverend Canon Fox arrived to visit Mr. Tebrick. After hearing Mr. Tebrick's story, the clergyman decided that the man was insane. As the cubs grew older, Mr. Tebrick spent most of his time in the woods, hunting with the vixen and her young by day and sleeping outside with them at night. Once he purchased and brought to them a beehive of honey.

One winter day Mr. Tebrick was outside listening to the sounds of a hunting chase that ended at his own gate. Suddenly the vixen leaped into his arms, the dogs so close after her that Mr. Tebrick was badly mauled. Silvia was dead. For a long time Mr. Tebrick's life was despaired of; but he recovered to live to a hale old age, and may be still living.

THE LADY OF THE LAKE

Type of work: Poem
Author: Sir Walter Scott (1771-1832)
Type of plot: Semihistorical romance
Time of plot: Sixteenth century
Locale: Scottish Highlands
First published: 1810

Principal characters:
JAMES OF DOUGLAS, a banished nobleman
ELLEN DOUGLAS, his daughter
MALCOLM GRAEME, loved by Ellen
RODERICK DHU, a rebel Highland chief
JAMES FITZ-JAMES, a nobleman of royal birth
ALLAN-BANE, a minstrel

Critique:

As the poet of Scottish history and legend Sir Walter Scott stands in a class alone. His poetry is in a sense painting, for his descriptions are so vivid and intense that his readers cannot fail to see the scenes he reveals to them. It is obvious that he loved the locale he described and understood the people who inhabited the wild Highlands. In *The Lady of the Lake* he delved into Gaelic history, to

retell a legend that had been popular for generations. The result was one of his best-known poems, loved by readers of all ages.

The Story:

As he followed a stag during a hunt, James Fitz-James became lost in the Highlands. He wandered around until he came to Loch Katrine, a beautiful lake sur-

1600

rounded by steep mountains. There he met the lovely Ellen, who told him that his coming had been foretold by Allan-Bane, an ancient minstrel who served her father. When she offered the hunter food and shelter for the night, Ellen did not volunteer to tell him her name or anything of her family history, and courtesy forbade his asking questions. Fitz-James was disturbed, however, because she bore such a marked resemblance to members of the Douglas clan, a family banished by the king. When he departed the next morning, he still knew nothing about the young girl whose beauty and grace had deeply touched his heart.

Fitz-James was correct in his fear that Ellen was of the Douglas clan. Her father was James of Douglas, once a powerful friend of the king, but now hunted and with a price on his head. He and Ellen and his sister were protected by Roderick Dhu, a rebel against the king and the leader of a large and powerful Highland clan. Roderick Dhu wanted Ellen's hand in marriage, but although she honored him for the aid he gave her father she detested him for his many cruel and merciless deeds. He killed and plundered at will, trying to avenge himself on the king and the Lowlanders who he felt had robbed him and his people of their land and wealth. Among the men he hated was Malcolm Graeme, a young nobleman, Ellen's former suitor, whom she loved. After Ellen's refusal of his proposal, Roderick Dhu called his clan together to fight Malcolm and the other supporters of the king. His excuse was that he feared Malcolm would lead the king to the hiding place of Douglas.

Like lightning, burning beacons and swift-riding messengers carried through the Highlands word that the clan was gathering. Young men left their brides at the church door and mere boys replaced fathers who had died since the last gathering. The women and children were placed on a lonely and protected island for safety, for a fierce and dangerous battle was to be fought. A hermit monk prophe-sied that the party who spilled the first foe's blood would be the victor. The prophecy suited Roderick Dhu, whose men had seen a spy lurking in the mountains and even now had lured the stranger into paths which would lead him into a trap. He would be killed by Roderick Dhu's men and thus the Highlanders would be assured of victory.

James of Douglas left Ellen. Although he did not tell her his destination, she knew that he had gone to give himself up to the king in order to prevent the bloodshed of a great battle. Allan-Bane tried to cheer Ellen by telling her that his harp sang of glad tidings, but she would not hear him. As she sat grieving, Fitz-James appeared again. Ellen knew that he had been tricked by Roderick Dhu's men, for no one could gain entrance to a place so hidden and secret without their knowledge. But Fitz-James, refusing to heed her warning, asked her to return to the court with him. She refused, telling him of her love for Malcolm Graeme. Then Fitz-James gave her his ring which had been given to him by the king. He said the king owed him a favor and would grant any request made by the bearer of the ring. It would also promise a safe journey through the Lowlands to anyone wearing it. Fitz-James placed the ring on Ellen's finger and then departed quickly.

His guide led him through the mountain paths until they came upon a crazed woman who sang a warning song to Fitz-James. The guide thrust his sword into her. Fitz-James then killed the guide and returned to the side of the crazed woman who, before she died, told him that Roderick Dhu had killed her lover and caused her to lose her sanity. Fitz-James vowed that he would meet Roderick Dhu and avenge the woman. Having been warned by her as well as by Ellen, he was traveling cautiously when he stumbled on a guard stationed by a watch fire. The sentry called him a spy, wanted by Roderick Dhu, but offered him rest and safety, for the laws of the clansmen demanded courtesy even to one's enemy.

The guard, after promising to lead Fitz-James safely through Roderick Dhu's lines, kept his word, even though Fitz-James called Roderick Dhu a coward and a murderer. When they reached a place of safety, the sentry revealed himself as Roderick Dhu. His promise fulfilled, he then challenged Fitz-James to a duel. In personal combat Roderick Dhu proved the stronger, but Fitz-James, who was more skilled, overcame the rebel. Then Fitz-James blew his horn and called his men to carry Roderick Dhu to a prison cell.

In the meantime James of Douglas went to the court to give himself up. First, however, he took part in some games being staged that day and won every event he entered. The whisper went through the crowds that only a Douglas could possess such skill and strength. Then Douglas offered himself to the king as a ransom for his friends and clansmen. When the king ordered him thrown into prison, the people sided with Douglas and would have risen against the king. Douglas quieted them, for he would not act against his monarch, and allowed himself to be taken. The king sent messengers to the Highlanders with word that there was no need to fight; Douglas had sur-rendered and Roderick Dhu was a prisoner.

Ellen and Allan-Bane went to the court to seek the release of her father. The ring given her by Fitz-James afforded her safety along the way. Before news came that a truce had been arranged, Allan-Bane went to Roderick Dhu's cell and sang to him of a fierce battle that had been fought. Roderick Dhu died with a smile, for he believed that his clansmen had fought bravely.

Ellen prepared for her audience with the king. Fitz-James went to her quarters to conduct her to the court, but when they arrived she noted that everyone bowed before Fitz-James. It was not until then that she knew Fitz-James was in reality the king. He told her to claim the favor promised by the ring, but there was nothing she could ask. The king had already restored her father to favor and Roderick Dhu was dead, so that she could not plead mercy for him. She tried to stammer something about Malcolm Graeme, but the king read her heart and called Malcolm to her side. He forgave Malcolm for trying to aid the rebels and redeemed the ring Ellen wore by joining her with her beloved.

LADY WINDERMERE'S FAN

Type of work: Drama
Author: Oscar Wilde (1856-1900)
Type of plot: Comedy of manners
Time of plot: Nineteenth century
Locale: London
First presented: 1892

Principal characters:

LADY WINDERMERE, a proper woman
LORD WINDERMERE, her husband
LORD DARLINGTON, a man about town
MRS. ERLYNNE, an adventuress
LORD AUGUSTUS LORTON, Mrs. Erlynne's fiancé

Critique:

This play is noted for one of the wittiest and best constructed first acts in the history of drama. The exposition, terse and interesting, leads inevitably to the scene in which Lady Windermere threatens to strike with a fan her own mother, whose true relationship she does not know. The plot of the drama is dated today, but it still conveys, to an amazing degree, Wilde's central idea that the "good woman" often costs a great deal more than she is worth.

The Story:

On her birthday Lord Windermere presented his wife with a very beautiful and delicately wrought fan with her name, Margaret, engraved upon it. She intended to carry the fan at a ball she was giving that evening, a ball to which everyone of importance in London had been invited.

That afternoon the Duchess of Berwick called on Lady Windermere, to tell her friend of a rumored affair between Lord Windermere and Mrs. Erlynne, a fascinating but notorious woman not received in the best houses. According to the duchess' story, Lord Windermere had for some months been supplying Mrs. Erlynne with funds for her support, and the old dowager's suggestion was that Lady Windermere should take immediate steps to learn the relationship between the two.

Lady Windermere was naturally upset. Determined to find out if there were any truth in the gossip, she opened her husband's desk. In a locked bank book, which she ripped open, she found evidence of her husband's duplicity, a record of checks issued to Mrs. Erlynne over a long period of time.

Angry and hurt at Lord Windermere's apparent failure to appreciate love and virtue, she turned on him the moment he appeared. His main concern was annoyance that his wife had dared tamper with his property behind his back. He informed her that his relations with Mrs. Erlynne were perfectly honorable, that she was a fine but unfortunate woman who wished to win the regard of society once more. Moreover, Lord Windermere explicitly ordered his wife to send Mrs. Erlynne an invitation to the ball. When Lady Windermere refused, her husband wrote an invitation. Angered at his act, Lady Windermere threatened to strike Mrs. Erlynne with the fan if she dared cross the threshold of Windermere House.

But when Mrs. Erlynne appeared at the ball, Lady Windermere lost her resolution and let the fan drop to the floor. The guests, believing that Mrs. Erlynne had been invited by Lady Windermere herself, naturally accepted her. She was lionized by all the men, and the women, curious because of the many stories they had heard, wanted to see at first hand what she was really like. Among her special admirers was Lord Augustus Lorton, the Duchess of Berwick's disreputable brother, to whom she had just become engaged to be married. Mrs. Erlynne was not the only woman greatly admired that evening. Lord Darlington was persistently attentive to Lady Windermere. Mrs. Erlynne's presence at the ball having put Lady Windermere into a reckless mood, Lord Darlington succeeded in persuading his hostess to leave her husband and come to him.

After the guests had gone, Lady Windermere had a violent struggle with herself, the outcome being a letter informing Lord Windermere that she was leaving his house forever. She gave the letter to a servant to deliver and left for Lord Darlington's apartments.

Mrs. Erlynne, who with Lord Augustus had remained behind to talk with Lord Windermere, discovered the letter Lady Windermere had written, and the thought of that lady's rash act brought back old memories. Twenty years before Mrs. Erlynne had written a similar letter to her husband, and had left him and their child for a lover who had deserted her. Her years of social ostracism had made her a stranger to her own daughter. Perhaps, however, she could keep her daughter from making the same mistake. Lady Windermere should never feel the remorse that her mother, Mrs. Erlynne, had known.

Mrs. Erlynne took Lady Windermere's letter and hurried to Lord Darlington's apartments, first persuading Lord Augustus to take Lord Windermere to his club and keep him there for the rest of the night. In Lord Darlington's rooms, without revealing her identity, Mrs. Erlynne managed to persuade Lady Windermere to think of her child and go back to her husband. Out of the depths of her own bitter experience, Mrs. Erlynne insisted that Lady Windermere's first duty was not to her husband but to her child.

As Lady Windermere was leaving, Lord Darlington returned, accompanied by Lord Windermere and Lord Augustus. Mrs. Erlynne, after hurrying her daughter to a waiting carriage, remained to face the gentlemen. It was an ordeal, for in her haste Lady Windermere had forgotten her fan and Lord Windermere, discovering it, became suspicious. Mrs. Erlynne appeared from behind a curtain with the explanation that she had taken the fan in mistake for her own when she left Windermere House. Her explanation saved Lady Windermere at the cost of her own reputation. Lord Windermere was furious, for he felt that he had in good faith befriended and helped a woman who was beneath contempt. Lord Augustus promptly declared that he could have nothing further to do with Mrs. Erlynne.

Lady Windermere alone defended Mrs. Erlynne. She realized at last that by some strange irony the bad woman had accepted public disgrace in order to save the good one. Lord Windermere, knowing nothing of what had happened, resolved to learn the whole truth when Mrs. Erlynne arrived to return the fan. But the mother, not wanting to shatter Lady Windermere's illusions, refused to reveal herself to the daughter. Waiting for Mrs. Erlynne outside the house, however, was Lord Augustus, who had accepted her explanation that his own interests had taken her to Lord Darlington's rooms. Lord Windermere felt that Lord Augustus was marrying a very clever woman. Lady Windermere insisted that he was marrying someone rarer, a good woman.

THE LADY'S NOT FOR BURNING

Type of work: Drama
Author: Christopher Fry (1907-   )
Type of plot: Poetic comedy
Time of plot: About 1400
Locale: The small market town of Cool Clary
First presented: 1948

Principal characters:
RICHARD, an orphaned clerk
THOMAS MENDIP, a discharged soldier
HEBBLE TYSON, mayor of Cool Clary
MARGARET DEVIZE, his sister
NICHOLAS, and
HUMPHREY, her sons
ALIZON ELIOT, betrothed to Humphrey
JENNET JOURDEMAYNE, a witch

Critique:

A poetic drama set in the late Middle Ages, *The Lady's Not for Burning* is a strange mixture of comedy and poetry. The excellent humor is in the lines of the play, however, as much as in the development of situation and plot. The discharged soldier, egoist and misanthrope, is a character whom Shaw might have created, but the situation into which he projects himself is one of un-Shavian

THE LADY'S NOT FOR BURNING by Christopher Fry. By permission of the publishers, Oxford University Press, Inc. Copyright, 1949, 1950, by Oxford University Press, Inc.

whimsy and symbolism. The play has been successful here and abroad. Christopher Fry has restored poetry and humor to the modern stage.

The Story:

Thomas Mendip wanted to be hanged, but he could get no one to take an interest in his case because everyone in Cool Clary was interested in a witch who was accused of having turned old Skipps, the rag and bone man, into a dog. Thomas begged the mayor's clerk, Richard, to get him an audience with the mayor so that he could confess his crime. But Richard had other things on his mind. The mayor's nephew, Humphrey Devize, had been betrothed to Alizon Eliot, and the girl was due to arrive any minute. No one had time for a fool who wanted to be hanged.

Alizon was one of six daughters whose father feared he had too many girls to marry off. He had placed Alizon in a convent, but after he had got rid of his other daughters easily enough he changed his mind about her and promised her to Humphrey. Humphrey's brother Nicholas had read in the stars that Alizon belonged to him, however, and so he knocked his brother down, hoping to kill him and take Alizon for himself. Humphrey, although he was not dead, lay still. He had not knocked himself down and so he would not pick himself up. Their mother, Margaret Devize, sister of the mayor, sometimes thought motherhood was too much for any woman. Since the boys had become untidy from lying in the rain and mud, she feared Humphrey's unclean linens might discourage Alizon.

When Mayor Hebble Tyson found Thomas waiting to be hanged, he was very much upset. Hebble was a little tired of strangers dropping into town with such ridiculous requests. It was all very irregular. Suspecting that someone was making a mockery of his authority, he threatened to have Thomas tortured if he did not go away and stop his bother.

But Thomas held out for hanging or nothing. He confessed to killing old Skipps and a worthless pander. He did not expect to get the favor of hanging for nothing; he knew the rules, all right.

Thomas' interview with Hebble was interrupted by the announcement from Nicholas that a witch was waiting to see the mayor. Poor Hebble, upset at that news, insisted that he would not have his honor toyed with.

The witch was young and beautiful. Her name was Jennet Jourdemayne, a wealthy young orphan whose property would be confiscated if she were condemned for witchcraft. Jennet thought the accusations a joke, for she had been accused of turning old Skipps into a dog and of doing other evil deeds besides. She had come to Hebble for the protection of his laughter at the crimes of which the mob outside accused her. Hebble, not amused, sent for the constable to arrest her. Thomas tried to divert attention from her to himself by insisting that he had murdered Skipps and the pander, but no one paid the least attention to him. He even told all assembled that the end of the world would come that night. All he got for his pains was to be thrown into the cellar with Jennet, to await her burning on the morrow.

Hebble and his associates had a problem on their hands. Jennet would admit nothing and Thomas would not stop confessing. Thomas was a poor ex-soldier and Jennet had property; she had to be the guilty one. At last Hebble had an idea. They would leave the two together while he and the others listened at an open door. The two were brought forth from the cellar, Thomas still wearing thumb screws to make him stop confessing. Jennet told Thomas of her father, a scientist who had given his life to his dreams. She would have no such nonsense. Facts and facts alone would rule her life—until tomorrow, when she would be burned. Fancy and imagination, she said, had caused her present trouble. Overhearing this conversation, Hebble was convinced that Jennet was a witch. At any rate she was wealthy, and her property would go to the city when she was burned.

From the conversation Hebble also learned that Thomas wanted to be hanged because he found life mean and dull. Therefore his punishment was to spend the night in joy and revelry at the party which would announce the betrothal of Humphrey and Alizon. Thomas would not agree to attend until Jennet was allowed to go to the party with him. Dressed in one of Margaret's old gowns, she was sent to the party, where Humphrey, the bridegroom-to-be, no longer wanted Alizon. Since Humphrey would not claim her, neither would Nicholas. Unknown to them, Alizon had found that she loved Richard and that Richard returned her love. They slipped away and were married by the priest who had found Richard in the poor box when he was just a tiny baby.

Unhappily for Thomas, he had fallen in love with Jennet and she with him.

He had no wish to be in love; life was miserable enough. Jennet, on the other hand, did not want to renounce her factual world for one of love and fancy. But Jennet knew now that Thomas had not committed murder, that he had heard the mobs accusing her of turning Skipps into a dog and said he murdered the ragman only to divert suspicion from her. Then Humphrey went to Jennet and offered to get her free from the charge of witchery if she would entertain him in her cell that night. Although her body loved the thought of living, her mind and heart rebelled, and she turned down his offer. She loved Thomas too much to take life at such a price.

Fortunately for all, old Skipps was found alive. Hebble, still coveting Jennet's property, would not be satisfied, but a soft-hearted justice allowed Thomas and Jennet to slip out of town in the dark. Thomas hated to face living again, but he decided to forego the pleasure of dying for another fifty years and spend his time of waiting with Jennet.

L'AIGLON

Type of work: Drama
Author: Edmond Rostand (1868-1918)
Type of plot: Historical romance
Time of plot: 1830-1832
Locale: Austria
First presented: 1900

Principal characters:
> FRANZ, Duke of Reichstadt and Napoleon's son, called L'Aiglon
> EMPEROR FRANZ, his grandfather
> MARIE-LOUISE, Duchess of Parma, his mother
> COUNTESS CAMERATA, his cousin
> THE ARCHDUCHESS, his aunt
> PRINCE METTERNICH, an Austrian statesman
> SERAPHIN FLAMBEAU, one of Napoleon's soldiers
> COUNT SEDLINSKY, director of police
> THÈRESE OF LORGET, a French exile whom Franz loved
> FANNY ELSSLER, a dancer

Critique:

Edmond Rostand's sympathetic treatment of sensitive people is as evident in his portrait of Napoleon's idealistic but hesitant son as it is in that of his ugly

L'AIGLON by Edmond Rostand. Translated by Louis N. Parker. By permission of the publishers, Harper & Brothers. Copyright, 1900, by Robert Howard Russell. Renewed. All rights reserved.

but unselfish Cyrano de Bergerac. *L'Aiglon* is a verse drama in six acts, much of which must be cut, because of time limitations, when the play is presented on the modern stage. Either way, in print or on the stage, *L'Aiglon* is an impressive play. Perhaps the reason *Cyrano de Bergerac* is better known is that the historical feeling is not there so binding, whereas in *L'Aiglon* the character presented will always be known in history as the weak son of a dominant father.

The Story:

Marie-Louise, daughter of the Emperor Franz of Austria, had rented a villa at Baden, near Vienna, for herself, her retinue, and her son Franz. Franz had been given the title of Duke of Reichstadt by the Austrians as a sop to his feelings when they all but imprisoned him in that country to keep him from arousing the French to follow Napoleon's son as they had followed Napoleon himself.

Marie-Louise pretended a greater sorrow for her husband's death than she truly felt; actually she would have been happy enough living again at the Austrian court if it had not been for Franz, whose sorrow was so deep that he took no interest in anything his mother suggested.

Count Metternich was Franz's official jailer, though such a term was never used. It was he who arranged the police guard, under Count Sedlinsky, to spy on every move L'Aiglon made. Metternich allowed Franz to ride his horses where he would, but always there was an unseen guard along. Metternich also provided tutors for the lad, but they were warned never to speak Napoleon's name. Even the boy's history lessons were given without mention of Napoleon's exploits.

L'Aiglon was then a frail, blond lad of eighteen. He was not strong, his cough leaving him strength only to ride the horses he loved and to find a way to learn his father's history. But there were many people in Austria who were willing to back his bid to return as François, Emperor of France. The Austrian soldiers in his regiment admired his spirit and were known to cry out, "Long live Napoleon!" against the orders of those who wanted them to call out only, "Long live the duke!" The French exiles, hoping against hope, noted in reports from Paris that all the theaters were running plays about Napoleon, and that there was a cry going up to take his ashes back to Paris. The tailor and the fitter L'Aiglon's mother brought from Paris turned out to be Bonapartists, the fitter being his cousin, the Countess Camerata. But the real history of his father he learned from a little dancer, Fanny Elssler, who memorized the stories of Napoleon's campaigns and recited them to him.

A year later, after he had found a cache of books on Napoleon in Franz's room at Schoenbrunn, Metternich allowed Franz to read all the books he pleased, but he set the guards even stronger around the young duke. For a while he deprived Franz of Prokesch, a Bonapartist friend, but Franz's aunt, the archduchess, persuaded Metternich to let Prokesch come back. In return she exacted a promise from Franz that he would ask the emperor, his grandfather, to let him go back to France before he made any other plans with his friends.

Franz and Prokesch began plotting, however, using wooden soldiers on a table top to map battle strategy. The soldiers, which had been in Austrian colors heretofore, were now painted in French uniforms, exact to the last button. Metternich surprised the boys while they planned their battles and had the soldiers thrown away. At the same time Franz realized that the lackey who had guarded him most was also a friend, a man who had been a foot soldier in Napoleon's army for seventeen years. He had repainted the wooden soldiers and he raised the most hope in Franz's heart. Though Franz himself knew he was like a child with his nose pressed against a glass wishing for things in a store window, Flambeau, the lackey, gave him enough confidence to vow that he would return to France.

In the meantime Emperor Franz, having come to Schoenbrunn, held an audience for his subjects. In a grandfatherly way he granted many requests including one from his disguised grandson, who asked to go to his father's land. When Franz threw off his Tirolean disguise, the emperor closed the audience chamber. Just as Franz had persuaded his grandfather to let him go back to France as emperor, Metternich appeared. He seemed to agree that Franz might rule in France, but he set up so many obstacles that Franz realized he had been tricked.

That night Franz left one of his father's old tricorn hats on his table as a signal to Flambeau that he would enter the plot to return to Paris. Overjoyed at seeing the hat, Flambeau took off his lackey's suit to show his old French uniform beneath. Metternich, having come into the room with his private key, was almost persuaded by Flambeau that Napoleon himself was sleeping in the next room. The shock of seeing the slender, trembling Franz instead of his heavy-set father appear was nearly as bad for Metternich as it was for Flambeau. Flambeau escaped through a window.

Then Metternich tore Franz's pride to ribbons as he stood the boy in front of the mirror and pointed out how weak he looked, how feeble his brow and hands were, how like the Hapsburgs—but not at all like Napoleon.

Metternich gave a fancy dress ball in the Roman ruins in the park at Schoenbrunn. Among the costumed crowds it was easy for Franz's confederates, Flambeau and Fanny Elssler, to have him change cloaks with his cousin, the Countess Camerata, who was dressed in a uniform exactly like L'Aiglon's. While the ever-vigilant guards followed her, Franz went with Flambeau to Wagram Field, where horses were to be waiting for their escape.

But they were early and the horses were not ready. Then, as Franz was getting into his saddle to ride for the border, he heard of a plot against him. Realizing that the killers would find the countess in his place, he started to turn back. The countess herself, having escaped, came up begging him to flee. Too late he realized that the police had caught up with him. His fellow conspirators crept away, except for Flambeau, who killed himself rather than face a firing squad. As he was dying, Flambeau thought he was back in the thick of the battle fought on Wagram Field many years before. Franz, carrying on the pretense, told him where each regiment stood, which advanced, which won, how Napoleon raised his hand in sign of victory. As Flambeau breathed his last, voices of Napoleon's long-dead troops sounded across the field. Franz realized he would have to make a great sacrifice to match those the French soldiers had made there long ago.

A short time later, as Franz lay on his deathbed, his family tried to keep from him the seriousness of his condition. He realized something was wrong when the archduchess got up from her own sickbed to see him. When Franz and his aunt went into a smaller room for mass, the Austrian royal family gathered quietly in his bedroom; it was the Austrian custom for the whole family to be present at a royal death. Prokesch came with the countess, bringing Thérèse, the little French exile Franz loved. An old general, who had been the duke's aide, watched at the door to see when Franz would partake of the Holy Bread. Then he opened the door quietly so the family could see the lad for the last time. A sob, escaping from Thérèse, reached the duke's ears and he realized that his time had come.

After sending away the Austrian family, but keeping the Frenchmen with him, François, Prince of France, had the old general read to him the account of the christening in Paris of Napoleon's son. With the Te Deum following that account, François died.

LALLA ROOKH

Type of work: Poem
Author: Thomas Moore (1779-1852)
Type of plot: Oriental romance
Time of plot: c. 1700
Locale: India
First published: 1817

Principal characters:
AURUNGZEBE. Emperor of Delhi
LALLA ROOKH, Aurungzebe's daughter
FERAMORZ. a young poet of Cashmere
ABDALLA, King of Lesser Bucharia
ALIRIS, young King of Bucharia and Abdalla's son
FADLADEEN, chamberlain of the harem

Critique:

A fitting description of this romantic tale told in poetry and prose may be borrowed from Leigh Hunt's description of the author of the piece. Hunt wrote that Moore's "face, upon the whole, is bright, not unruffled with care and passion; but festivity is the predominant expression." Moore's writing is festive with rich descriptions of persons and places; his style is graceful; his narrative is never broken. The romantic interest is admirably sustained, with continued humor. Fadladeen's abilities as a pseudo-critic add to the real pleasure of the whole story.

The Story:

Aurungzebe, Emperor of Delhi, entertained Abdalla, who had recently abdicated his throne to his son Aliris and was on a pilgrimage to the Shrine of the Prophet. Aurungzebe had promised his daughter Lalla Rookh (Tulip Cheek) in marriage to Aliris. The lonely princess was to journey to Cashmere, where she and Aliris would meet and be married.

Lalla Rookh's caravan, of the finest and most comfortable equipment, was manned by the most loyal and efficient of servants, the entire cavalcade having been sent by Aliris to conduct his bride to him. Among the servants sent by Aliris was a young poet of Cashmere, Feramorz.

Feramorz captivated all the women with his beauty and charming musical ability as he sang and recited to the accompaniment of his kitar. Lalla Rookh, not immune, became enamored of the young poet.

Fadladeen. the chamberlain traveling as Lalla Rookh's protector, was a bumptious, all-knowing, perspicacious authority on any subject: food, science, religion, and literature. And his criticisms were so detailed and harsh that the person being assessed was reduced to a virtual ignoramus. He expressed himself freely after Feramorz told the tale of "The Veiled Prophet of Khorassan": Azim and Zelica were young lovers who lived in the province of Khorassan. After Azim went off to fight in the wars in Greece. Zelica was enticed into the harem of Mokanna, the "veiled prophet of Khorassan," in the belief that she would gain admission into Paradise; there she would be reunited with Azim, whom she believed killed in the Greek wars. Mokanna was a dastardly, cruel ruler, who had gained the throne through his powers of magic. When Azim learned, in a dream, of Zelica's plight, he returned to his country to join the army of the veiled prophet. Discovering that his vision of Zelica's unhappy state was true, he joined the troops of an enemy caliph and fought against

Mokanna.

Mokanna, defeated, committed suicide by plunging into a vat of corrosive poison. In her remorse for having become Mokanna's wife and by sadness in seeing her young lover but not being able to be his, Zelica put on the veil of Mokanna and confronted the caliph's army. Azim, mistaking her for Mokanna, killed her. The lovers exchanged vows of devotion and forgiveness as Zelica died. Azim grew old grieving by Zelica's grave, where he finally died after another vision in which Zelica appeared and told him she was blessed.

Feramorz, unaccustomed to criticism, was taken aback by Fadladeen's reactions to this beautiful love poem. For Fadladeen was caustic. He belabored the subject of long speeches by the characters in the story; he contrasted Feramorz' poem with the fluency and tone of poems of other writers of the day; he analyzed the meter of specific lines in the poem. Feramorz did not attempt another story for some days.

Encouraged to sing by Lalla Rookh, he began his second poem only after an appealing look at Fadladeen as he explained that this tale, "Paradise and the Peri," was in a lighter and humbler vein than the first: The Peri, wishing to be admitted to Paradise, was told to bring as her passport the gift most treasured by heaven. Her first offering was a drop of blood from a dying Indian patriot; this unacceptable gift was followed by the last sigh of an Egyptian maiden as she died of grief at the loss of the lover whom she had nursed through the plague. Rejected for this gift, the Peri was finally admitted to Paradise when she presented the penitential tear of a hardened criminal of Balbec. The criminal's tear had been shed as he heard a child's prayer.

Fadladeen, even more outspoken in his criticism of Feramorz' second story, combined petty sarcasm and scholarly jargon in his comments. He refused to be halted by Lalla Rookh.

By the time the party had arrived in Lahore, Lalla Rookh realized that not only was she in love with Feramorz but also that the handsome singer was in love with her, and she resolved that he should not be admitted to her presence again. Although the heart she was to give to her bridegroom would be cold and broken, it must be pure.

As they journeyed on, the travelers came upon the ruins of an ancient tower, a structure that aroused the curiosity of the entire group. Fadladeen, who had never before been outside Delhi, proceeded learnedly to show that he knew nothing whatever about the building. Despite Lalla Rookh's admonition that Feramorz not be called to identify the ruins for them, he was brought before her.

The tower, he said, was the remains of an ancient Fire-Temple, built by Ghebers, or Persians, of an old religion, who had fled to this site from their Arab conquerors in order to have liberty in a foreign country rather than persecution in their own land. This historical detail gave rise to Feramorz' third song, "The Fire-Worshippers": Hafed, the leader of the resisting Gheber forces in the mountains, fell in love with Hinda, the daughter of the Arabian emir who had come to rout out the insurrectionists. Hafed, his identity concealed, gained access to Hinda's quarters and won her love before he was captured by the Ghebers.

The Arabs defeated the Ghebers in a sudden attack, and Hafed sacrificed himself on a funeral pyre. As Hinda was being escorted back to her father's camp, she plunged into a lake and was drowned. On this occasion Fadladeen decided to forego criticism of Feramorz' tale, but to report the profane reciting to Aliris. He hoped in this manner to bring about punishment for Feramorz and to secure for himself a place in Aliris' court.

In the tranquil, beautiful valley of Hussun Abdaul, Feramorz sang his last song, "The Light of the Haram." This was an account of married love reconciled after a misunderstanding between husband and wife.

The "light of the haram" was Sultana Nourmahal, the favorite wife of the Emperor Selim, son of the great Acbar. During the celebration of the Feast of Roses, Nourmahal quarreled with Selim. The couple's period of sadness and remorse because of their harsh words to each other ended when Nourmahal learned a magic song from an enchantress, Namouna. Masked, Nourmahal sang the song to Selim at the emperor's banquet, and they were reunited in undying love for each other.

After considerable hardship the party crossed the mountains that separate Cashmere from the rest of India. At a temple where they rested, the young king came to welcome his bride into his kingdom.

Lalla Rookh, seeing his face full view for the first time, fainted. The king was the young singer, Feramorz. Disguised as a poet, Aliris had traveled from Delhi with the party in order to win Lalla Rookh's love.

Learning the real identity of the man whose songs he had criticized so caustically, Fadladeen recanted immediately and declared that Aliris was the greatest poet of all time. In his new position of prestige, bestowed on him by Aliris, Fadladeen recommended the whip for anyone who questioned Aliris' poetic ability.

It was reported that to her dying day, Lalla Rookh never called the king by any name other than Feramorz.

L'AMOROSA FIAMMETTA

Type of work: Novel
Author: Giovanni Boccaccio (1313-1375)
Type of plot: Psychological romance
Time of plot: Fourteenth century
Locale: Naples
First transcribed: 1340-1345

> *Principal characters:*
> FIAMMETTA, a lady of Naples (Maria d'Aquino)
> PANFILO, a poet (Boccaccio)

Critique:

In the tradition of the Italian masters of literature, Boccaccio found inspiration in the love of a lady. Unlike Petrarch and Dante, however, he pursued his lady to her bedchamber and entered upon a passionate romance. She was Maria d'Aquino, rumored to be the daughter of King Robert of Anjou. In her youth she had considered a religious life, but her beauty drew many admirers who soon awakened her interest in more worldly matters. She was married, but she discovered that love outside the bonds of marriage had a delightful charm of its own. Boccaccio discovered her in church and ambushed her in her chamber while her husband was absent. Although she grew weary of him and took another lover, Boccaccio wrote *L'Amorosa Fiammetta* partly to argue that, in fact, it was he who left her. The novel,

which presents little action, is distinguished by its psychological revelation of fourteenth-century life and manners. The study of Fiammetta, who is Boccaccio's Maria, reveals her as a passionate but sensitive woman, intelligent and fanciful. Despite Boccaccio's imitative style and his labored references to mythological figures, *L'Amorosa Fiammetta* manages to present a realistic image of two lovers in fourteenth-century Naples.

The Story:

Fiammetta had a dream that a serpent bit her while she was lying in a meadow and that, as darkness came, the wound festered and brought her close to death. When she woke she discovered that she had no injury and, failing to realize that the dream was a warning and a prophecy, she dismissed it from her thoughts.

Fiammetta was admired by the ladies and gentlemen who surrounded her when she went to church on a certain festival day, but of all her admirers none struck her fancy until she saw a young gentleman leaning against a marble pillar of the church. The glances which she and the young man exchanged proved that the attraction was mutual.

Fiammetta, realizing that she had been overtaken by love, spent hours in her chamber picturing the young man and hoping to see him again. As other chance meetings increased her interest in him, she became so disturbed and changed by love that her nurse commented on it and warned her of the dangers of passion and of betraying her husband. But Fiammetta, too much enamored of the young man to heed her nurse's warnings, imagined in a dream that Venus came to her and told her of the delight and power of love, urging her to ignore the nurse's warnings and to submit to love's promptings.

Encouraged by her fond glances, the young man became familiar with Fiammetta's friends and with her husband, so that he and Fiammetta might converse together and hide their love. The young man taught her by his example how to converse in the company of others so as to reveal their love only to each other; he pretended to be telling of two Grecian lovers, Fiammetta and Panfilo, in order to show how deeply his own passion moved him. Although Fiammetta herself grew adept at this word game, she knew that their love could not forever be kept within the bounds of reason.

Despite Fiammetta's refusals, which Panfilo took as coy signs of encouragement, he finally gained what all lovers desire. He and Fiammetta spent innumerable nights together, learning new delights of love. Nothing else mattered to Fiammetta. She thanked Venus for encouraging her in love, and she laughed at other gentlewomen who imagined that they knew what passion was.

But there was to be an end to her happiness. One night, while Fiammetta and Panfilo were together in her chamber, Fiammetta awoke to find Panfilo weeping. She hesitated to inquire into the cause of his distress for fear that he would reveal some other love for whom he was secretly longing. Pretending that she had not seen him weeping, she suddenly cried out as if in her sleep. When he wiped his tears and turned to her, she told him that she had suddenly feared that she had lost him. He answered that neither fortune nor death could change his love for her; he then began to sob and sigh again. Answering her question concerning his sorrow, Panfilo told her that he must leave Naples for four months because of his father's illness.

Fiammetta argued that if he loved her he would not leave her. Now that she knew his love, she could not bear to part with it; as one so desperately in love, she deserved his presence more than his father did. She feared for his health and safety if he were to leave her. Finally, she concluded, a storm was coming; no man of sense would go out in such weather.

In spite of her protests Panfilo insisted that it was his duty to see his dying father, but he assured her that he would return at the end of four months. After a long and loving farewell she accompanied him to the gate. Then, overcome with sorrow, she fainted and had to be revived by her maid.

During the first four months of Panfilo's absence Fiammetta spent her days remembering the delights she had shared with him, wondering whether he was falling in love with someone else, counting the days and scolding the moon for being slow in its course, and imagining and dreaming that he had returned to her.

Even the satisfaction of daydreaming was denied to Fiammetta when she learned from the conversation of a merchant that Panfilo was married. She was plunged into jealousy and grief, but as time went on she began to hope that Panfilo might not find happiness with his wife; and she offered prayers to Venus asking that he be stricken again with love for her so that he would return.

Fiammetta's husband noticed that she had lost her appetite and was having difficulty sleeping. Ignorant of the cause, he at first had medicines prescribed for her and then took her on a vacation to some beautiful islands. But the medicines had no effect on her passion, and the islands only reminded her of the delightful times she had spent with Panfilo. Feasts and shows failed to please her, and she spent her days sighing and praying to the gods of love and fortune.

From one of her servants Fiammetta learned that Panfilo was not married, as she had supposed from the merchant's tale, but was in love with a beautiful gentlewoman who loved him. Her misery intensified more than ever by this news, she found no comfort in her husband's loving and compassionate words, nor

could her nurse bring her to her senses. She considered many ways of suicide, all of which seemed too painful or difficult to be considered. She then reasoned that if she killed herself she would never see Panfilo again. Finally, fearing that worse torments were to come, she attempted to leap from the house, but she was stopped by the nurse and other servants.

After her nurse told her that Panfilo was returning to Naples, Fiammetta, for a time, hoped to see him again. But the rumor had confused her Panfilo with another man having the same name, and Fiammetta was forced to realize that she had lost him forever. She compared her condition to that of other betrayed lovers, supposing herself to be more unfortunate than they. Finally she told her story in order that others might take it as an example of what misery may befall an amorous gentlewoman.

THE LAST ATHENIAN

Type of work: Novel
Author: Viktor Rydberg (1829-1895)
Type of plot: Historical romance
Time of plot: Fourth century
Locale: Athens
First published: 1859

Principal characters:

CHRYSANTEUS, archon of Athens, a pagan and a philosopher
HERMIONE, Chrysanteus' daughter
PETER, Bishop of Athens, enemy of Chrysanteus
ANNAEUS DOMITIUS, Roman proconsul at Athens
CHARMIDES, a young Epicurean, lover of Hermione
CLEMENS, a young priest, foster son of Bishop Peter

Critique:

Rydberg has been translated into English more than any other Swedish novelist of the nineteenth century. In addition to this historical novel dealing with the early history of Christianity, he wrote several non-fictional volumes about the Church Fathers and the history of Christianity. The obvious doctrine of this novel is a strong plea for freedom of religious conscience and worship. While it is a glorification of the Greek ideals of reason, wisdom, truth, and harmony, it is not an anti-Christian novel directed

against the principles and ideals of Christianity. It is really a thesis against bigotry, cruelty, and intolerance, as personified in the early leaders of the Church in Athens.

The Story:

Athens in the fourth century, during the reign of the Roman Emperor Constantius, was divided by three factions. Dominant among the three was one Christian faction headed by Bishop Peter of Athens. Opposing them, though less

1613

in number, was the faction which adhered to the heresy of Athanasius. The third faction was the group which still clung to the gods of ancient Greece and the reasonable philosophy of Plato. The last group was headed by Chrysanteus, archon of Athens and its richest citizen. Representing Rome in the city was Annaeus Domitius, the proconsul, who by traveling a middle path hoped to keep some semblance of order in and about the city. His efforts were hindered by the fact that Julian the Apostate was about to succeed Constantius as the emperor of Rome; Constantius, a Christian, had favored the non-Athanasian Christians, but Julian, who was a pagan, favored the people who clung to the old gods.

Under the favor of Constantius, Bishop Peter and his followers practically ruled Athens and dictated orders to the proconsul. When the Athanasians were accused of killing Bishop Peter's father, a hermit who lived at the top of a pillar, Domitius turned over the troops of Rome to the bishop and discreetly left Athens to evade responsibility for what might happen. He did not want to take sides in the quarrel, and he feared that the hatred of the Christians might be turned against the pagans, including Chrysanteus. Domitius knew that if Constantius succeeded in retaining the empire, Chrysanteus' death would be of little moment; but if Julian were to succeed in becoming emperor, his old tutor, for Chrysanteus had been that, would be a very important person, one whom the proconsul did not want as a corpse about his neck.

As Domitius feared, riot and slaughter broke out in Athens, for Bishop Peter turned the troops and his followers against the heretic Christians and against the pagans. Word came to Domitius at his country villa, however, that Julian was emperor, Constantius having died. Domitius immediately went back to Athens with the news, arriving in time to prevent a Christian mob from entering Chrysanteus' dwelling to pillage and murder. Within a few hours the Roman troops, returned to the proconsul's command, restored quiet in Athens and published Julian's order·that freedom of worship and belief were to be accorded all men. Bishop Peter and his Christian faction were reduced, to all appearances, to a position no better than that of any other group. They were ordered to restore to the pagans all the temples they had taken over and to replace treasures they had plundered and destroyed.

Actually, the bishop was more dangerous than ever. He had many spies within and without the city; he had, in addition, a large body of devoted and obedient fanatics at his call. Furthermore, he had as his foster son a young man who was actually Chrysanteus' long-lost son, Clemens. Reared as a Christian, the boy had become a priest. Through Clemens, Bishop Peter plotted to destroy Chrysanteus. The bishop also plotted to convert Hermione, Chrysanteus' daughter, to Christianity, not through any pious motives but simply to undermine the position of Chrysanteus and to secure his immediate wealth.

Fate seemed to go against Bishop Peter when Chrysanteus discovered, quite by chance, that Clemens was his son and that Bishop Peter was an escaped slave who had once belonged to the household of Chrysanteus. The bishop was thrown into prison by the archon and Clemens was restored to his father's home. But Clemens was so fanatic a Christian that he soon left his father's house and became a hermit, dwelling in a cave on the outskirts of the city.

In the meantime Charmides, an Epicurean betrothed to Hermione, fell into the bad graces of both Hermione and her father because of his profligate habits. He also fell prey to a Jewish broker, to whom he owed large sums of money, for the Jew became his enemy when he learned that his daughter was in love with Charmides. At the moment of his greatest despair, he was befriended by Bishop Peter, whose followers had succeeded in securing his release from prison. Bishop Peter saw in Charmides another tool in his battle against paganism and Chrysanteus. Upon Charmides' promise to turn Christian, the bishop interceded with the Jew, showing the Jew that a reformed Charmides would still have an opportunity to marry Chrysanteus' daughter. The Jew, seeing a chance to recoup all the money he had lent to the penniless Charmides, agreed to the bishop's plan.

The plan worked smoothly. Charmides, reformed, was received again by Chrysanteus and Hermione, and a date was set for the wedding. Nothing was said of the fact that Charmides had been baptized as a Christian. But on his wedding night Charmides was killed, murdered by a young Jew who had discovered that Charmides had seduced the usurer's daughter, to whom the assassin had been betrothed. After the death of Charmides, much to Chrysanteus' discomfiture, the Christians claimed the body of Charmides for burial and proved by documents that the dead man had been one of their number.

Further disaster overtook pagan Chrysanteus when his son went mad after being attacked by another hermit. As if that were not enough, Julian the Apostate was killed in a battle with the Persians. The new emperor, Jovian, was not only a Christian, but also an adherent to that branch of the Church represented by Bishop Peter. The bishop, supported by Roman troops and the proconsul, was again the real ruler of Athens.

Immediately upon hearing of Julian's death, Chrysanteus and Hermione fled to the mountains, where they were befriended by another small sect of Christians, a group that had been declared heretics by the bishop and consequently had no love for him. Learning that Chrysanteus and Hermione had taken asylum with the outcasts, Bishop Peter, still avaricious for Chrysanteus' great wealth, prevailed upon the proconsul to lead a crusade into the mountains against the heretics. Domitius was willing to do so, hoping thereby to win acclaim and honors from the new emperor. There was a short but bloody campaign. In it, Chrysanteus was killed and Hermione taken prisoner. Hermione was forced to submit to baptism. Rather than remain alive as a Christian under those circumstances, she killed herself immediately. Her death left the wealth of Chrysanteus in the hands of Bishop Peter. A short time later his reasons for desiring the wealth became known; with it he intended to buy the bishopric of Rome, which even then was regarded as the seat of the Church. His superior at Constantinople suspected that Bishop Peter must intend to turn heretic, for the bishopric of Rome had turned to the beliefs of the Athanasians.

These suspicions being confirmed by agents sent to Athens, orders were sent to Bishop Peter's fellow priests to kill him. He was given a draught of poison which did not cause immediate death; he lived, ironically enough, to receive emissaries from Rome who offered him the coveted bishopric just before he died.

THE LAST CHRONICLE OF BARSET

Type of work: Novel
Author: Anthony Trollope (1815-1882)
Type of plot: Domestic realism
Time of plot: Mid-nineteenth century
Locale: "Barsetshire," England
First published: 1867

> *Principal characters:*
> MR. CRAWLEY, Curate of Hogglestock
> MRS. CRAWLEY, his wife
> GRACE CRAWLEY, their daughter

Mr. Proudie, Bishop of Barchester
Mrs. Proudie, his wife
Henry Grantly, Grace's suitor
Lily Dale, Grace's friend
John Eames, Lily's suitor

Critique:

To readers who are familiar with Trollope's novels the shire of Barset undoubtedly exists and should be shown on the maps. Barchester and its towers, Plumstead Episcopi, and Hogglestock seem as real as if they had actually stood for a thousand years. Mrs. Proudie, the Thornes of Ullathorne, Archdeacon Grantly and his wife, and the weak Quiverfuls are among Trollope's characters who make up an ever-living community. The genius of Anthony Trollope lies in his understanding of human wisdom and human ignorance.

The Story:

In the community of Hogglestock the citizens were upset because Mr. Crawley, the curate, had been accused of stealing a check for twenty pounds. In Archdeacon Grantly's home, where there was concern lest Henry Grantly might marry Grace Crawley, the curate's schoolteacher daughter, feeling was high.

Bishop Proudie and his wife were set against the unfortunate Crawley. Mrs. Proudie, who exerted great power over her husband, persuaded the bishop to write a letter forbidding Mr. Crawley to preach in his church until the case should have been settled one way or another. Mr. Crawley refused the injunction. Mr. and Mrs. Proudie quarreled over the answer, and Mr. Proudie sent for Mr. Crawley to attend him in the bishop's palace at once. When Mr. Crawley arrived, he was hot and tired from walking. He repeated what he had stated in his letter and left the bishop and his wife amazed at his boldness.

Mr. Crawley was not kept from performing his duties on Christmas morning. Since he could not recall how he had come into possession of the money in question, he informed his wife that he had but two choices—either to go to jail or to bedlam.

At last Henry Grantly decided to ask Grace Crawley to marry him, even though he should be going against his parents' wishes. At the same time Lily Dale, Grace Crawley's friend, was being wooed by young John Eames, a clerk in the Income Tax Office in London and a suitor, once rejected, whom Lily's mother favored. Eames was the friend of a London artist named Conway Dalrymple, who was painting a portrait of Miss Clara Van Siever, a mutual friend, in the sitting-room of Mrs. Dobbs Broughton. Meanwhile the aged Mrs. Van Siever was engaged in forcing Dobbs Broughton to pay money he owed to her.

Not long afterward John Eames met Henry Grantly. Neither liked the other at first. John, meeting Lily in Lady Julia de Guest's home, where Grace was also a guest, discussed his unfavorable meeting with Henry Grantly in front of Grace. When Henry proposed to Grace, she refused him and returned home to be with her father during his trial. Lily told John that she planned to die an old maid, her heart having been broken by Adolphus Crosbie, a former suitor.

Mr. Toogood, a distant relative, was to defend Mr. Crawley. John Eames was brought into the Crawley case by Mr. Toogood, who wanted John to go to Florence and attempt to persuade Mr. Arabin, an influential clergyman, to come to Mr. Crawley's rescue. There was another reason why Arabin should return to England. Mrs. Arabin's father, Mr. Harding, was ailing and growing weaker each day.

Conway Dalrymple worked on Miss Van Siever's picture, which was still a secret from Dobbs Broughton, in whose house it was being painted. Although

Broughton had ordered the artist out of his house, Mrs. Broughton wanted the picture painted, regardless of her jealous husband's reactions.

The clerical commission summoned by Bishop Proudie reached no decision concerning Mr. Crawley. It was resolved that nothing should be done until the civil courts had decided his case.

Archdeacon Grantly tried to engage the help of Lady Lufton to prevent the marriage of his son to Grace Crawley, but Lady Lufton refused. The archdeacon finally promised that he would no longer oppose the marriage if Mr. Crawley should be found innocent of any crime.

Dobbs Broughton was being pressed hard for money by old Mrs. Van Siever. Clara Van Siever was to marry Musselboro, Broughton's former partner. Dalrymple, still hoping to marry Clara, was putting the last touches to the canvas when Mrs. Van Siever entered the Broughton house. At her word he destroyed the portrait. Over Clara's objections, Mrs. Van Siever announced that her daughter was to marry Musselboro. After the Van Sievers left, Musselboro arrived with news that Dobbs Broughton had killed himself that morning. Clara and Dalrymple resolved to face Mrs. Van Siever's wrath together.

Mrs. Proudie continued her fight to have Mr. Crawley removed. After a quarrel between the bishop and Mrs. Proudie, she retired to her room and there died of a heart attack. True to the resolution imposed upon him by Mrs. Proudie before her death, Mr. Crawley preached a final sermon in his church and never again entered it as the curate.

On the continent John Eames learned from Mrs. Arabin the cause of Mr. Crawley's troubles. Mrs. Arabin, who had received the check from a tenant, had turned it over to Mr. Crawley without telling her husband, the dean, of the transaction. She had only recently heard of the charges and she was hurrying home to England to do what could be done to straighten out the matter. In the meantime Mr. Toogood traced the theft of the check to the tenant who had forwarded it to Mrs. Arabin.

Mr. Toogood and Henry Grantly took the good news to Mr. and Mrs. Crawley. When she heard their story, Mrs. Crawley, who had defended her husband from the beginning, broke into tears. The messengers had to explain the situation carefully to Mr. Crawley, who could not at first believe that his innocence was about to be proved. Then Mr. Harding, the aged incumbent in St. Ewold's, died. Archdeacon Grantly offered the living to Mr. Crawley as a recompense for all he had suffered. In midsummer Grace Crawley became Mrs. Henry Grantly.

John Eames did not marry Lily Dale after all, for Lily was unable to make her decision, but Dalrymple married Clara Van Siever as he had planned. Musselboro, who had lost Clara, proceeded to marry the widow of his old partner and thus Mrs. Broughton's sorrows were brought to an end.

THE LAST DAYS OF POMPEII

Type of work: Novel
Author: Edward George Earle Bulwer-Lytton (1803-1873)
Type of plot: Historical romance
Time of plot: A.D. 79
Locale: Pompeii
First published: 1834

    Principal characters:
        GLAUCUS, a wealthy young Greek
        ARBACES, Egyptian priest of Isis
        IONE, his Greek ward
        APAECIDES, her brother
        NYDIA, a blind flower girl

Critique:

This novel has found many readers among those who are interested in the classical civilization which ended when barbarians took over the Mediterranean world. Bulwer-Lytton's handling of plot, character, and passion followed a tradition which has not maintained its hold. It is the tradition of nineteenth-century drama, direct, obtuse, fiery. Concerned with indirection today, the reader finds the descriptions of the characters' thoughts unrealistic. Their passions are too apparent, their actions too much explained. Cast in a different mold from novels of today, *The Last Days of Pompeii* offers one of the longest, most sustained views of the world we call classic.

The Story:

Late one afternoon in the ancient city of Pompeii the fashionable rich young men were congregating for the daily rite of the public baths. Among them were Clodius, a foppish Roman, and Glaucus, a popular young Greek. Together the two strolled toward the baths, mingling with slaves bearing bronze buckets, idlers gowned in purple robes. Along the way they saw the beautiful blind flower girl, Nydia. She, too, was from Greece and for that reason Glaucus took an interest in her. It was still too early for the baths, and the two friends walked along the sea front as Glaucus described a Neapolitan girl of Greek birth with whom he had fallen in love. Unfortunately, he had lost contact with the girl and was now morose. While they talked, Arbaces, the evil-looking Egyptian priest of Isis, intercepted them. The two young men were barely able to conceal their dislike for the Egyptian.

Arbaces secretly defied the Romans and the Greeks, and prayed for the day when Egypt would once more be powerful. He revealed to a lesser priest his interest in the brother and sister, Apaecides and Ione, his wards. He hoped to make a priest of Apaecides, and he planned to marry Ione. They had been

in Naples, but recently he had brought them to Pompeii, where he could influence them.

Glaucus met Ione at a party. She was the girl he had seen and lost in Naples. At the same time Arbaces developed his hold over Apaecides, who was growing more and more confused after coming in contact with the sophistries of the corrupt priest of Isis. Meanwhile the blind flower girl, Nydia, was falling hopelessly in love with Glaucus.

It happened that Glaucus and Clodius were loitering in the establishment of Burbo, the wine-seller, when the innkeeper and his wife were beating Nydia, whose slave she was. Glaucus, hearing the girl's cries, bought her; he planned to give her to Ione. Nydia realized Glaucus could never love her after he gave her a letter to deliver to Ione. In this letter he accused Arbaces of false imputations. On reading his letter, Ione decided to go at once to Arbaces' palace and to face him with Glaucus' charges.

Knowing the danger to Ione at Arbaces' palace, Nydia warned both Ione's brother and Glaucus. Glaucus hurried to the palace to confront the priest. An earthquake interrupted the quarrel between the two men. When the goddess Isis fell from a pedestal, striking Arbaces, Glaucus and Ione ran from the building to join the throng in the street. Alone, deserted, the blind slave wept bitterly.

The next day, the earthquake having passed with but little damage, the people of Pompeii took up again the threads of their varied lives. Apaecides became a convert to Christianity. Glaucus and Ione remained together.

Julia, daughter of a wealthy freedman named Diomed, was also in love with Glaucus and sought to interfere between him and Ione. She went to the house of Arbaces, where the two plotted together. Arbaces had a drug prepared which was administered to Glaucus. The drug drove him into a demented stupor so that he ran from his house into a cemetery. To this cemetery came Apaecides and

Arbaces. They quarreled and Arbaces stabbed Apaecides, killing him. Then, hoping to kill Glaucus indirectly, the priest summoned the crowd and declared that Glaucus in his drunken rage had killed Apaecides. Glaucus and a Christian who attempted to defend him were arrested. They were condemned to be given to wild beasts at the public games.

After the funeral of her brother, Ione resolved to declare her belief in the innocence of Glaucus. But before she could carry out her plan Arbaces had seized her and carried her off to his palace. The only one who knew of Arbaces' guilt was a priest who was also his prisoner. But Arbaces reckoned without Nydia, who as a dancing girl had learned most of the secrets of his palace. Nydia, contacting the priest imprisoned by Arbaces, agreed to carry his story to the authorities. Unfortunately, she too was captured. She persuaded a slave to carry the message to Sallust, a friend of Glaucus. But the message was delivered while Sallust was drunk and he refused to read it.

The last day of Pompeii arrived. It was also a day of celebration in the arena, for which the populace had been waiting. The games began with gladiatorial combat which the audience watched listlessly, bored because the deaths did not come fast enough or with enough suffering. After one combat an unpopular gladiator was condemned to death by the action of the crowd. His body was dragged from the arena and placed on the heap with those previously slain. Unfortunately for the crowd's amusement, the lion turned loose in the arena with Glaucus crept with a moan back into its cage. Before the lion could be prodded into action Sallust appeared demanding the arrest of Arbaces. A slave had called his attention to Nydia's letter, which he had thrown aside the night before. Reading it, he had hurried to lay his information before the praetor. The mob, not to be cheated after Glaucus had been set free, demanded that Arbaces be thrown to the lion.

Then the famous fatal eruption began. The whole gladiatorial scene became chaos as terrified thousands poured out of the doomed amphitheater, crushing the weakest in their hurry to escape. Looting began in the temples. Nydia reached Glaucus. Together they hurried to the house of Arbaces to discover and save Ione. It was too dark to see, but Nydia, accustomed to darkness, was able to lead Ione and Glaucus through the streets. Arbaces was killed in the earthquake. At last Glaucus, Ione, and Nydia gained the safety of the seaside and put out to sea in a small ship.

All night they slept in the boat. In the morning Glaucus and Ione discovered that before they had awakened, the heartbroken Nydia had cast herself into the sea.

THE LAST OF SUMMER

Type of work: Novel
Author: Kate O'Brien (1897-)
Type of plot: Naturalism
Time of plot: 1939
Locale: Eire
First published: 1943

> *Principal characters:*
> ANGÈLE MAURY, an actress
> HANNAH KERNAHANS, her aunt
> TOM KERNAHANS, and

THE LAST OF SUMMER by Kate O'Brien. By permission of the author's agent, Ann Watkins, Inc. Published by Doubleday & Co., Inc. Copyright, 1943, by Kate O'Brien.

MARTIN KERNAHANS, Hannah's sons
NORRIE O'BYRNE, in love with Tom

Critique:

Against a background of imminent
war, Angèle Maury struggled against the
iron will of the aunt who had never admitted her existence and who was determined to keep this stranger out of her
family and her life. The story is a dramatic one, tense and stark, but told with
great restraint and simplicity. The personal struggle between Angèle and Hannah seems only to reflect the greater
struggle between those peoples who wanted to be free and the political despots
who would not let go their hold.

The Story:

Angèle Maury was an actress, half
French, half Irish, who had taken her
mother's name as her stage name in preference to Kernahans, her Irish father's
name. Both her parents were dead. On
an impulse she stopped to visit her father's people when her company toured
Ireland. She found her aunt, Hannah
Kernahans, strangely hostile to her and
learned that Aunt Hannah had never told
her three children of their uncle's marriage or of his daughter.

It was obvious that Aunt Hannah was
fiercely jealous of any intruders from the
outside world. She loved all her children,
but Tom, the oldest son, was tied to her
by a silver cord so strong it seemed unlikely the bond would ever be broken.
Tom had long been loved by Norrie
O'Byrne, but he was not sensitive to her
love. Martin, the second son, had grown
up quite independent. A student, he
had traveled all over Europe on scholar-
ships and had lived wildly at times. His
mother either could not or did not care
to tie him to her so closely.

What none of the children knew, and
Angèle did not learn, was that her father and their father had both loved Aunt
Hannah. She had accepted Angèle's father, but before the wedding he had
discovered her steel will and had asked
to be released from the engagement. She
then married his brother, giving the impression that it was she who had changed
her mind. But she never forgave Angèle's
father for embarrassing her, and she
would never forgive Angèle for being her
father's child. She sensed in Angèle an
enemy to the isolated life she lived with
Tom.

Soon after her arrival Martin told
Angèle that he wanted her and offered
her anything but marriage; he was not
yet ready for those ties. Angèle, not taking him seriously, thought that she was
only someone new whom he would soon
forget. The fact that they were first cousins also stood in the way of a serious
proposal. But Martin brooded over her
treatment of him and worried also about
the impending war. Hitler, having taken
Czechoslovakia, stood on the threshold
of Poland. Ireland was neutral, but Martin knew that he could not stand idly
by while the world blew up under his
feet. Only Martin and Angèle took the
war seriously. Knowing that her mother's
people would be deeply affected by the
war, she was annoyed to see Aunt Hannah brush aside the whole affair with
a shrug. Tom refused to see that no one
could remain completely neutral when
war finally came.

One day Tom told Angèle that he
loved her. Unused to strong emotion,
he had not recognized his feelings until
they were too intense to ignore. Angèle,
returning his love, realized that Aunt
Hannah would not like their engagement,
lest Tom get away from her. Aunt Hannah was clever enough to make Tom
believe she was delighted, but she subtly
put obstacles in their way. Since they
were first cousins, they would have to
get special dispensations from Rome.
Angèle wanted to return to France on
their honeymoon, in spite of the dangers
of war. Aunt Hannah used her weapons

cleverly, fooling Tom but not deceiving Angèle at all. She sensed that it would take more will power than Tom had ever shown for him to overcome these obstacles and see his mother's hold on him. Angèle's hope was that Tom would shake off his chains and be free and independent.

Martin brought matters to a head. It angered him to hear Angèle talk of returning to France before war broke out, for he realized that Germany would soon march into Poland. If Angèle wanted to see France, to act like a Frenchwoman, she should return to her people and help them in their time of crisis. Aunt Hannah encouraged the idea, all the time acting considerate and loving. She knew that if she could once get Angèle away from Tom, he would come back to the fold easily enough. Martin, of course, hoped for the separation so that he could have time to make Angèle love him. He knew that she could never win against his mother, and he sincerely felt that she and Tom were not suited to each other.

When Church officials failed to hurry dispensation proceedings, Angèle fretted at the time lost. She even considered going by herself to France. Aunt Hannah tried to goad her into leaving alone, but she did not wish to hurt Tom just to please his mother. Tom kept promising Angèle that he would find a way to hurry matters, but she took little hope; fast action was not in his nature.

Martin, too Irish to sign up with the British, prepared to leave to join the French army. Angèle even wished that she were a man so that she would have to go back to France. Then the issue would be clear, not muddled in emotional reactions. Before he left, Martin told Angèle again that he loved her. He told her too that she did not really love his brother, that she was too strong a person

to love anyone as weak as Tom. He warned her that Hannah would win, that she would never let Tom go. Martin begged her to return to France with him the next day. Although she rejected the plan, Angèle thanked Martin for his honesty and allowed him to kiss her goodbye.

In the meantime Hannah made her final play for Tom. Pretending to feel sorry for Angèle because she was so torn between Tom and France, she told him that Angèle and Martin were the same kind, that Martin was desperately in love with his cousin. She said also that Angèle had fallen in love with Tom because he was attractive and because she thought that he and Martin were much alike. Although it hurt her to tell him, Hannah declared, she knew that Angèle would never be happy with Tom in Ireland, and it was only the girl's sense of obligation that made her stick to her promise. Hannah, knowing that she could handle that problem when she got to it, played too on the suitability of Norrie O'Byrne.

Shortly after his talk with his mother Tom saw Martin and Angèle kissing goodbye. He thought then that his mother had been right, as usual. He went to Angèle, released her from her betrothal to him, and apologized for being a selfish fool in taking her love. Angèle knew then that she was beaten. She told Tom that she really loved him but that she realized their marriage would never work out. It was futile to try to make him see his mother as she really was.

Angèle also told Aunt Hannah why she was leaving—that she did love Tom but knew she could never fight the bond or restore Tom's confidence in himself. She went away with Martin, to return for good to France, and left Tom lost forever, the silver cord unbroken.

THE LAST OF THE BARONS

Type of work: Novel
Author: Edward George Earle Bulwer-Lytton (1803-1873)
Type of plot: Historical romance
Time of plot: 1467-1471
Locale: England
First published: 1843

Principal characters:
EARL OF WARWICK, the kingmaker
ISABELLA, his older daughter
ANNE, his younger daughter
KATHERINE DE BONVILLE, his sister
EDWARD IV, King of England
WILLIAM DE HASTINGS, a royal chamberlain
ADAM WARNER, an alchemist
SIBYLL, his daughter
NICHOLAS ALWYN, a goldsmith
MARMADUKE NEVILE, kinsman of the Earl of Warwick

Critique:

The Last of the Barons is a complex, involved, and fascinating novel of a troubled period in English history. After the Wars of the Roses the House of York seemed secure, the leaders of the House of Lancaster being dead or in exile. Edward IV was a popular ruler who might have enjoyed a peaceful reign if he had not insulted the Earl of Warwick, the last of the great lords whose power overshadowed the king's. A dramatic moment in history has been recaptured by Bulwer-Lytton in this novel.

The Story:

Just outside London a crowd had gathered to watch an archery contest. Several shot at the white cloth on the butt, but no one hit the mark squarely. Then in a haughty and preoccupied way a commoner stepped up, fitted his arrow, and pierced the center of the white field. While his fellow tradesmen applauded, he dropped back into the crowd.

A young noble, who was not entered in the contest, borrowed a bow. With sure aim he hit fairly the little peg that secured the cloth to the butt. Gallantly he returned the bow and strode away. As he was leaving, the commoner who had hit the cloth stopped him. At once

their recognition was mutual, and they began to talk delightedly of past times.

The commoner was Nicholas Alwyn, a goldsmith who had been the younger son of a good family. He had rejected the monk's habit, the usual lot of younger sons, and had chosen to go into trade. He was shrewd enough to see that the future greatness of England lay in the prosperous middle class and that the day of feudal nobility was nearly over. He had taken part in the tournament simply to advertise his profession, not through love of decadent sport. The young noble, who was his foster brother, was Marmaduke Nevile. He had come from his northern estate to seek service with his kinsman, the powerful Earl of Warwick, who was known as the kingmaker.

On Alwyn's advice, Marmaduke went up to Lord Montagu, the Earl of Warwick's brother, and made known his errand. The nobleman repulsed Marmaduke in full view of his retinue, for Marmaduke's father had fought on the side of Lancaster in the recent wars, and the Warwicks had successfully supported the Yorkists.

Feeling abashed, Marmaduke accompanied Alwyn into the city. Alwyn advised him to go to see the earl in person, and Marmaduke resolved to do so the very next day.

On the road to his inn he met a gentle girl surrounded by a screaming mob of women who earned their living by dancing and playing timbrels for fair crowds. Accusing the girl of trying to earn money by playing her gittern at the tournament, they would have harmed her if Marmaduke had not come to her rescue. He escorted the frightened girl away, but through faint-heartedness he did not take her all the way home. As soon as he left her, the women set upon her again. She was rescued by an older man, a true knight who saw her to her ruined dwelling.

It was dusk when Marmaduke left the city. Shortly afterward he was attacked by a band of robbers who slashed him severely and left him to die. He managed to make his way to a nearby house, and there he was cared for by the girl whom he had deserted a short time before. She was Sibyll Warner, daughter of Adam Warner, a philosopher and alchemist who spent all his time in his laboratory. He had, after years of labor, nearly completed a crude model of a small steam engine. In those superstitious days Adam was accounted a sorcerer and his daughter was suspected of witchcraft.

During his convalescence Marmaduke was greatly attracted to Sibyll, but her superior learning was a barrier between them. Alwyn, who came to the house many times, also fell in love with the girl. But Sibyll thought always of the great knight who had brought her to her door.

When Marmaduke was well and able to leave the house, he at once sought an audience with the mighty Earl of Warwick. Warwick welcomed him and made him a courtier. There he met Isabelle, Warwick's haughty older daughter, and Anne, her gentle young sister.

Warwick was preparing to go to France on a mission to the court of Louis XI. On Warwick's advice, King Edward IV had agreed to marry his sister Margaret to one of the French princes. During Warwick's absence Marmaduke served in the king's household.

As soon as Warwick had left the country, Edward's wife and all her kinsmen of the Woodville family began to work on the king's pride. The Woodvilles, intensely jealous of Warwick, encouraged the king to defy the king-maker's power. They proposed that Edward hastily affiance his sister to the Duke of Burgundy. Edward, persuaded by his wife, at once invited the illegitimate brother of the Burgundian ruler to England and concluded the alliance.

Warwick, hurrying back when he heard the news, felt keenly the slight to his honor. When he found Edward at a hunting party, he immediately demanded Edward's reasons for his step. Edward was frightened, but he assumed an air of confidence and declared that he had followed what seemed the best policy of diplomacy. Although he was much mortified, Warwick magnanimously forgave the king and withdrew. His many followers sought him out and offered to rebel, but Warwick withdrew entirely from court and went into seclusion on his own estate.

Meanwhile Adam Warner had been brought to the court as alchemist to the Duchess of Bedford. Sibyll fitted in well with court life, and Lord Hastings became attached to her. In time they became engaged, and Lord Hastings awaited only the king's permission to marry her. Katherine de Bonville, Warwick's sister, had been his first love, but Warwick had refused his consent to a marriage because Lord Hastings then was not powerful enough to aspire to a connection with the Warwicks. Although Katherine had later married another, Lord Hastings still loved her; his attachment to Sibyll was only temporarily the stronger.

As Warwick had forseen, the Duke of Burgundy proved an unworthy ally of England and the incensed French king never ceased to make trouble for the

English. At last Edward had to confess that he could not rule the kingdom without Warwick to advise him. The king swallowed his pride and invited Warwick back to London with more honors and power than he had held before. The gallant earl, as a gesture of friendship, brought his daughter Anne to live in the queen's retinue.

Anne chose Sibyll as her companion and the two girls became close friends. One night the lecherous Edward accosted Anne in her bedroom. The girl screamed with fright and ran to Adam Warner for help. There the king found her and abjectly begged her pardon, but Anne was still hysterical. Marmaduke smuggled Anne out of the castle and told her father what had happened.

Warwick at once put Marmaduke at the head of a hundred men who tried to capture the king, but Edward stayed secure in his tower. Warwick then withdrew his followers from the court and embarked for France.

In London, Lord Hastings and Sibyll continued to meet. Then Katherine de Bonville's husband died and she was free once more. Lord Hastings' old love revived and he married her secretly in France.

Margaret of Anjou, the Lancastrian queen in exile, joined forces with Warwick in France. When the mighty earl returned to England, the people welcomed him and joined his cause. Edward fled without fighting a battle. Warwick restored Henry VI to the throne.

The success of his kingmaking made Warwick careless. Edward's power lay not with the nobles but with the merchants, and a coalition of the rich merchants and the adherents of the House of York soon put Edward back into power. On the battlefield of Barnet Warwick was killed and his chiefs were either executed or exiled. Somehow Adam Warner and Sibyll died together in the same fight. Alwyn, an adherent of Edward, took Marmaduke prisoner but later tried to secure his freedom. History does not tell whether he succeeded.

THE LAST OF THE MOHICANS

Type of work: Novel
Author: James Fenimore Cooper (1789-1851)
Type of plot: Historical romance
Time of plot: 1757
Locale: Northern New York State
First published: 1826

  Principal characters:
    NATTY BUMPPO, a frontier scout known as Hawkeye
    CHINGACHGOOK, Hawkeye's Indian friend
    UNCAS, Chingachgook's son
    MAJOR DUNCAN HEYWARD, an English soldier, Hawkeye's friend
    MAGUA, a renegade Huron
    CORA MUNRO, daughter of the commander of Fort William Henry
    ALICE MUNRO, her sister

Critique:

The battles and exciting pursuits which constitute the plot of *The Last of the Mohicans* are rounded out by interesting Indian lore and the descriptive style of the author. In spite of Cooper's awkward characterizations, this novel remains the most popular of the Leatherstocking Tales, a classic story of the French and Indian wars.

The Story:

Major Duncan Heyward had been ordered to escort Cora and Alice Munro from Fort Edward to Fort William

Henry, where Colonel Munro, father of the girls, was commandant. In the party was also David Gamut, a Connecticut singing-master. On their way to Fort William Henry they did not follow the military road through the wilderness. Instead, they placed themselves in the hands of a renegade Huron known as Magua, who claimed that he could lead them to their destination by a shorter trail.

It was afternoon when the little party met the woodsman, Hawkeye, and his Delaware Mohican friends, Chingachgook and his son Uncas. To their dismay, they learned they were but an hour's distance from their starting point. Hawkeye quickly decided Magua had been planning to lead the party into a trap. His Mohican comrades tried to capture the renegade, but Magua took alarm and fled into the woods.

At Heyward's urging the hunter agreed to guide the travelers to their destination. The horses were tied and hidden among some rocks along a river. Hawkeye produced a hidden canoe from among some bushes and paddled the party to a rock at the foot of Glenn's Falls. There they prepared to spend the night in a cave.

That night a band of Iroquois led by Magua surprised the party. The fight might have been a victory for Hawkeye if their supply of powder and ball had held out. Unfortunately, their ammunition had been left in the canoe which, unnoticed until it was too late, was stolen by one of the enemy who had ventured to swim the swirling river. The only hope then lay in the possibility of future rescue, for the capture of the rock and the little group was a certainty. Hawkeye, Chingachgook, and Uncas escaped by floating downstream, leaving the girls and Major Heyward to meet the savages.

Captured, Cora and Alice were allowed to ride their horses, but Heyward and David were forced by their captors to walk. Although they took a road paralleling that to Fort William Henry, Heyward could not determine the destination

the Indians had in mind. Drawing close to Magua, he tried to persuade him to betray his companions and deliver the party safely to Colonel Munro. The Huron agreed, if Cora would come to live with him among his tribe as his wife. When she refused, the enraged Magua had everyone bound. He was threatening Alice with his tomahawk when Hawkeye and his friends crept silently upon the band and attacked them. The Iroquois fled, leaving several of their dead behind them. The party, under David's guidance, sang a hymn of thanksgiving, and then pushed onward.

Toward evening they stopped at a deserted blockhouse to rest. Many years before it had been the scene of a fight between the Mohicans and the Mohawks, and a mound still showed where bodies lay buried. While Chingachgook watched, the others slept.

At moonrise they continued on their way. It was dawn when Hawkeye and his charges drew near Fort William Henry. They were intercepted and challenged by a sentinel of the French under Montcalm, who was about to lay siege to the fort. Heyward was able to answer him in French and they were allowed to proceed. Chingachgook killed and scalped the French sentinel. Then, through the fog which had risen from Lake George, and through the enemy forces which thronged the plain before the fort, Hawkeye led the way to the gates of the fort.

On the fifth day of the siege, Hawkeye, who had been sent to Fort Edward to seek help, was intercepted on his way back and a letter he carried was captured. Webb, the commander of Fort Edward, refused to come to the aid of Munro.

Under a flag of truce, Montcalm and Munro held a parley. Montcalm showed Webb's letter to Munro and offered honorable terms of surrender. Colonel Munro and his men would be allowed to keep their colors, their arms, and their baggage, if they would vacate the fort the next morning. Helpless to do otherwise, Munro accepted these terms. During one of the parleys Heyward was surprised to see Magua in the camp of the French. He had not been killed during the earlier skirmish.

The following day the vanquished English started their trip back to Fort Edward. Under the eyes of the French and their Indian allies they passed across the plain and entered the forest. Suddenly an Indian grabbed at a brightly-colored shawl worn by one of the women. Terrified, she wrapped her child in it. The Indian darted to her, grabbed the child from her arms, and dashed out its brains on the ground. Then under the eyes of Montcalm, who did nothing to discourage or to hold back his savage allies, a monstrous slaughter began.

Cora and Alice, entrusted to David Gamut's protection, were in the midst of the killing when Magua swooped down upon them and carried Alice away in his arms. Cora ran after her sister, and faithful David dogged her footsteps. They were soon atop a hill, from which they watched the slaughter of the garrison.

Three days later, Hawkeye, leading Heyward, Munro, and his Indian comrades, traced the girls and David with the help of Cora's veil which had caught on a tree. Heyward was particularly concerned for the safety of Alice. The day before the massacre he had been given her father's permission to court her.

Hawkeye, knowing that hostile Indians were on their trail, decided to save time by traveling across the lake in a canoe which he discovered in its hiding place nearby. He was certain Magua had taken the girls north, where he planned to rejoin his own people. Heading their canoe in that direction, the five men paddled all day, at one point having a close escape from some of their intercepting enemies. They spent that night in the woods and next day turned west in an effort to find Magua's trail.

After much searching Uncas found the trail of the captives. That evening, as the party drew near the Huron camp, they met David Gamut wandering about. He told his friends that the Indians thought him crazy because of his habit of breaking into song, and they allowed him to roam the woods unguarded. Alice, he said, was being held at the Huron camp. Cora had been entrusted to the care of a tribe of peaceful Delawares a short distance away.

Heyward, disguising his face with paint, went to the Huron camp in an attempt to rescue Alice, while the others set about helping Cora. Heyward was in the camp but a short time, posing as a French doctor, when Uncas was brought in, a captive. Called to treat an ill Indian woman, Heyward found Alice in the cave with his patient. He was able to rescue the girl by wrapping her in a blanket and declaring to the Hurons that she was his patient, whom he was carrying off to the woods for treatment. Hawkeye, attempting to rescue Uncas, entered the camp disguised in a medicine man's bearskin he had stolen. Uncas was cut loose and given the disguise, while the woodsman borrowed David Gamut's clothes. The singer was left to take Uncas' place while the others escaped, for Hawkeye was certain the Indians would not harm David because of his supposed mental condition. Uncas and Hawkeye fled to the Delaware camp.

The following day Magua and a group of his warriors visited the Delawares in search of their prisoners. The chief of that tribe decided the Hurons had a just claim to Cora because Magua wished to make her his wife.

Under inviolable Indian custom, the Huron was permitted to leave the camp unmolested, but Uncas warned him that in a few hours he and the Delawares would follow his trail.

During a bloody battle Magua fled with Cora to the top of a cliff. There, pursued by Uncas, he stabbed and killed the young Mohican, and was in his turn sent to his death by a bullet from Hawkeye's long rifle. Cora, too, was killed by a Huron. Amid deep mourning by the Delawares, she and Uncas were laid in their graves in the forest. Colonel Munro and Heyward conducted Alice to English territory and safety. Hawkeye returned to the forest. He had promised to remain with his sorrowing friend Chingachgook forever.

THE LAST OF THE VIKINGS

Type of work: Novel
Author: Johan Bojer (1872-   )
Type of plot: Regional realism
Time of plot: Early nineteenth century
Locale: Norway
First published: 1921

> *Principal characters:*
> KRISTÀVER MYRAN, owner of the fishing boat *Seal*
> LARS, his son
> ELEZEUS HYLLA,
> HENRY RABBEN,
> KANELES GOMON, and
> ARNT AWSON, fishermen with Kristàver
> PETER SUZANSA, owner of the *Sea-fire*
> JACOB DAMNIT-ALL-WITH-A LIMP, owner of the *Sea-bird*

Critique:

The Last of the Vikings tells the story of a Lofoten fisherman, Kristàver Myran, as simply as Knut Hamsun tells the story of Isak, the farmer and builder in *Growth of the Soil*. Both types are obsolete in the modern world since the fisherman now goes to sea in a motor-driven ship and the farmer has little new land to break to his plow, but both characters are powerfully drawn. It is hard to forget the rigors of the Lofoten fishing season after reading about Kristàver and his crew. The novel is as simple in design and style as it is compelling in its picture of people, local in time and place, but universal in their qualities of courage and endurance.

The Story:

When Kristàver Myran brought home his own Lofoten boat, his oldest son Lars was tall and strong enough to join the next fishing trip to the islands off the coast of Norway. Lofoten men thought of their boats as descendants of dragon-prowed Viking ships, and Lars dreamed that he was an early Norseman who would do battle when the time came to sail north.

Kristàver had bought the *Seal* cheaply at auction, though even that low price was more than he could pay without guarantors. People said he must want to die early, to have bought that boat which had capsized during the last three winters. Kristàver was sure he could tame her.

His crew consisted of Lars; Elezeus Hylla, a brother-in-law; Henry Rabben, who was always combing his beard; Kaneles Gomon, boyish except for his yellow mustache; and Arnt Awson, a shoreman who had never before sailed on a Lofoten boat. The boats to travel with them were Peter Suzansa's *Sea-fire*, Andreas Ekra's *Storm-bird*, and Jacob Damnit-all-with-a-limp's *Sea-bird*. Kristàver has some trouble keeping the *Seal* up with the other boats as they sailed through the fjord to the open sea. As he and the rest lay in the long bunk on deck after their first day's sailing, he slept, but even in sleep he was working

THE LAST OF THE VIKINGS by Johan Bojer. Translated by Jessie Muir. By permission of the author and his agent, Curtis Brown, Ltd., New York. Published by Appleton-Century-Crofts, Inc. Copyright, 1922, 1923, by The Century Co. Copyright, 1923, by Johan Bojer. Renewed, 1950, by Jessie Muir.

on his problem. Half-awake, he got up and moved some of the cargo back a few yards. The next day the boat, in better humor, pleased Kristàver's crew as she plowed steadily past the other boats. For days they sailed through the snow and anchored at night. The men began to look alike, snow-covered, and to learn to stand wind and cold.

As they passed Helgeland, the Nordland boats came out to join them. Soon the waters were covered with sailing ships and a few steamers. Held over by the weather at Bodö, Jacob was nearly killed in a fight. Henry Rabben carried him on board and the next day Jacob was sailing along with the rest. Whenever the Southlanders met the Nordlanders, there was likely to be a fight in which everybody joined.

One day, across the West Fjord, they sighted Lofoten, a long chain of snow-streaked mountains. At the foot of the mountain wall lay the fishing station from which rose the odor of fish-oil, pitch, and fish. Peter's crew and Kristàver's were to share a hut there for the winter.

When the Inspector raised the signal-flag for the first sea-going day, everybody was ready to head for the banks. It was a great day when they first put out the nets. Each man knew that only plenty of cod in those nets could make it worth while to bear the wind, snow, and sea for months in that frozen place. The first day's catch was poor, and the men were discouraged when bad weather kept them imprisoned at the station. They slept all day. When it was time for supper, each man went to his own chest to take out the flat bread, cheese, and butter his own wife or mother had put in for him; the fishermen felt that they were paying a short visit home. After the storm they found their nets torn and tangled; a bad beginning.

When the cod came, there was no time for rest. The men pulled on their nets and filled their boats until they lay far down in the water. There was hardly time to rest after cleaning the fish before

Kristàver had the men out for the next day's fishing. Even with their big woolen gloves, their hands were rubbed raw, and ice clung to their clothes. But, with fourteen hundred cod in a day, each man figured he would be wealthy by spring. They worked until Saturday night, when they dropped into a heavy sleep that lasted until dark on Sunday. Then, rousing themselves, they called for "Melja," a dish fit for a wedding. They broke flat bread, put boiled fish-liver over it, then grated goat's milk cheese, and long streams of treacle. They had lived on coffee and bread for so long they could not get enough "Melja," and Henry Rabben had to make more and more for them.

Lars was not yet a full-fledged Lofoten man; he was a "scaurie" until he stood treat. To save him embarrassment, his father gave him money to buy French brandy for all who came to the hut. Then he could hold up his head among the fishermen.

As the fishing slackened, the men began to wonder whether this would be a golden year after all. After weeks passed with no cod running, Kristàver listened to the inner voice that had led him right before; this time it told him to turn east. He spoke to Peter about it and then led his men silently down to the *Seal* at night to row away. As dawn came, they saw a host of boats coming out of harbors, all hurrying as though they had news of fish. Then they saw a whale spouting. Where there is a whale, there are herring; where there are herring, there are cod.

After the whale had been driven into a fjord, trouble began because the steamers came and blocked the entrance to keep the fishermen out. The fishermen, seeing shoals of fish just inside the fjord, were frantic to get them. The cod were gold just outside their reach. Men cannot stand back under such circumstances, and so they began to fight the men on the steamers. Driven back by streams of boiling water from hoses, the fishermen were about to give up when Kaneles swam under the steamer and came up on the other side to turn the hoses on the steamer men. Then the fight started all over the ships until the fishermen drove their little boats past the steamers. Soon the fjord was packed with boats. The fish were so thick that nets filled immediately, but the boats were so close that the nets fouled. Not until the next day, when the Inspector brought law into the fjord, could the fishermen pull in their nets. Then Arnt came into his own. He built a cabin on the shore so that Kristàver's men would not freeze while they slept at night. Elezeus was nearly frozen that first night and he never recovered, but Henry Rabben gave him the sacrament and he died in peace.

Sailing back to the fishing station, the *Seal* heeled over in a storm. Kaneles was knocked unconscious, but Kristàver held him while the others clung to the keel. Peter Suzansa, in the *Sea-fire*, was swept by them in the storm. Jacob Damnit-all-with-a-limp was able to tack around and drive his boat over the keel while his own men pulled in the survivors, all but Kaneles.

When his boat was recovered after the storm, Kristàver put his new mast four inches farther aft than it had been before. After that he was able to make her stand up. When he sailed home in the fair spring winds, he felt that she was a Viking ship and he a chieftain.

THE LAST PURITAN

Type of work: Novel
Author: George Santayana (1863-1952)
Type of plot: Social criticism
Time of plot: Early twentieth century
Locale: Connecticut, Massachusetts, England
First published: 1936

Principal characters:
OLIVER ALDEN, the last puritan
PETER ALDEN, his father
HARRIET ALDEN, his mother
FRAULEIN IRMA SCHLOTE, Oliver's governess
JIM DARNLEY, Oliver's friend
ROSE DARNLEY, Jim's sister
MARIO VAN DE WEYER, Oliver's cousin
EDITH VAN DE WEYER, another cousin
BOBBY, Jim's illegitimate son

Critique:

Although he is best known as a philosopher and essayist, George Santayana has invaded the field of fiction with great success. *The Last Puritan* is his first novel; but, unlike most first novels, it is the work of a mature mind. In the story of Oliver Alden, Santayana has given us a character sketch of an almost extinct type of American, a puritan.

The Story:

Young Peter Alden was educated in America but left Harvard before he had completed his studies and went abroad with a tutor. After he had come of age and had inherited his money he wandered aimlessly about the world, studying occasionally. He was in his early middle years before he completed any one course. Licensed to practice medicine, his practice was limited to himself, for he had burdened himself with many ills, some real but most of them imaginary. Once he consulted Dr. Bumstead, a psychiatrist whose main concern was Peter's money. Dr. Bumstead convinced Peter that a home and a wife would be the best treatment possible and, as a consequence, Peter married the doctor's daughter Harriet. Oliver was their only child.

Little Oliver was a puritan from the beginning. He accepted things as they were, never complaining, never wondering why. There were no other children with whom he could play because his mother feared that other children might be dirty or vulgar. And there were no stories, songs, or prayers for the boy, as Mrs. Alden would not have him filled with nonsensical ideas. His father was no more than a polite stranger to little Oliver, for he spent most of his time traveling about the world.

Fraulein Irma Schlote, a German, became Oliver's governess, and from her he had what little brightness there was in his childhood. On their long walks together, Irma instilled in Oliver his first love of nature and a love for the German language. But even with Irma, Oliver remained a stoical little puritan. If he were tired or his foot hurt, there was no use to complain. They had come for a walk, and they must finish that walk. One must do his duty, even an unpleasant one. As he grew older, Oliver hated human weakness with the hatred of a true puritan.

When Oliver was fifteen, he went to high school, where he excelled in scholarship and in athletics because it was his duty to keep his body strong and because it was his duty to do everything that the school demanded.

During one holiday season Oliver joined his father on his yacht. There he met Jim Darnley, the captain, who had been a British sailor before he became involved in a scandal. Jim was an entirely new type of person in Oliver's world. Oliver knew that the sailor was worldly and had no sense of duty, but strangely enough Oliver was always to consider Jim his dearest friend.

After his graduation from high school, Oliver joined his father and Jim in England. There, while visiting Jim's family, he learned to respect Jim's minister father and to enjoy the company of Rose, Jim's young sister. He learned also that Jim had an illegitimate child, Bobby, who lived with Mrs. Bowler, his tavern-keeping mother.

While in England, Oliver also met his distant cousin, Mario Van de Weyer, a worldly young man dependent upon his rich relatives for his education and livelihood. Mario also puzzled Oliver. Mario had nothing, not even much real intelligence, yet he was happy. Oliver, who had everything, was not consciously happy; he merely lived as he felt it his duty to live.

Before they left England, Oliver's father committed suicide. He felt that Oliver needed to be free of him and as much as possible of his own mother. Rather than see the boy torn between his conflicting duties to both parents, Peter took his own life.

Back in America, Oliver entered Williams College. While playing football, he broke his leg. In the infirmary he was visited by his cousin Mario and another cousin, Edith Van de Weyer. Mario, who attended Harvard on Oliver's money, seemed to feel no reluctance about living extravagantly on his cousin's bounty. Oliver began to think of Edith as a possible wife. Like his father, he did not consider love an important element in marriage, but he felt it his duty to marry and have children.

In his last year of college, Oliver transferred to Harvard University. There he spent much time with Mario, until that young man was forced to leave college because he had been found in his room with a young woman. When he went to Edith's home to tell her about Mario, Oliver found that Edith's family had already heard the story from Mario and had forgiven him. Oliver also learned that Edith had great affection for Mario. But because he thought a match between

1630

himself and Edith a sensible one, he proposed to her anyway, forgetting to mention love. Edith refused him. She knew that marriage with Oliver would be a dutiful experience only, and she wanted more than duty.

When he had finished college, Oliver took a cruise around the world. Then he settled in England and lived for a time near Jim Darnley's family. War was coming closer, but Oliver felt no duty toward either side. Mario enlisted at once, for Mario was romantic. The war became more personal for Oliver when he learned that Jim had been killed. Jim's death seemed proof of war's useless waste. More practically, Jim's death meant that Bobby and Rose were now Oliver's responsibility.

When the United States entered the war, Oliver felt that it was his duty to go home and join the army. After his training he was sent to France. Before he went to the front, he wrote to Rose Darnley, asking her to marry him at once, so that she would be his wife and would be cared for if he were killed. But Rose, like Edith, wanted love, and she refused to marry him. She knew, too, that Oliver should never marry, because love should be unreasoning and illogical at times, conditions which Oliver could never accept.

After Rose's refusal, Oliver seemed free for the first time. No one needed him any longer. Jim was dead. Mario was in the army and provided for in case of Oliver's death. Bobby had been made secure financially. Edith was engaged to be married. Rose was provided for in Oliver's will. All his life he had acted in accordance with duty, in his parental relations, in school, in the army. At least he would not be a dutiful husband. Now he need be true only to himself. That night he slept peacefully.

Oliver was killed, but not in battle. He was a post-Armistice casualty, the victim of a motorcycle accident. His will told the story of his life. He had left adequate, but not extravagant, provisions for Mario, Rose, Mrs. Darnley, Fraulein Irma, and Bobby. The bulk of his fortune he left to his mother because he had believed it his duty to provide for her.

So Oliver Alden ended his life a true puritan, doing what must be done without flinching, taking little pleasure in worldly things, yet not withdrawing from the world. He did not believe in puritanism, for he knew that those who lived selfishly were often more happy than he. He was not a prig. He had been a puritan in spite of himself, and for that reason, perhaps, the last true puritan.

THE LAST TYCOON

Type of work: Novel
Author: F. Scott Fitzgerald (1896-1940)
Type of plot: Social criticism
Time of plot: The 1930's
Locale: Hollywood
First published: 1941

Principal characters:
MONROE STAHR, a film producer
KATHLEEN MOORE, his mistress
PAT BRADY, Stahr's partner
CECILIA BRADY, his daughter

Critique:

This unfinished novel is perhaps the most highly regarded fragment in American literature, for in it Fitzgerald's prose is said to have achieved its greatest power, flexibility, and economy. As edited by Edmund Wilson, *The Last Tycoon* has six completed chapters (about half the book), a summary conclusion, and a selection of the author's notes; but since Fitzgerald was a painstaking reviser, it is by no means certain that the completed chapters are in their final form. Nevertheless, it is clear that the heart of the novel is the deathly tired Stahr's poignant love affair with Kathleen. Of considerable technical interest is the use of Cecilia as a narrator who is allowed to imagine fully events she does not actually witness.

The Story:

Cecilia Brady was flying to California for a summer vacation from college. On the plane she met Wylie White, an alcoholic screenwriter, and Schwartz, a ruined producer. Monroe Stahr, the partner of Cecilia's father, was also aboard, though traveling as Mr. Smith. When the plane was grounded at Nashville, Schwartz sent a note to Stahr, warning him about Pat Brady, Cecilia's father. When the plane took off again, Schwartz stayed behind and committed suicide.

Stahr had been the boy wonder of the film industry. He had been in charge of the studio in his twenties, almost dead from overwork at thirty-five. Indeed, he was half in love with death for the sake of his dead wife, Minna Davis, a great star with whom he had been deeply in love. Since her death he had increased his work load, often remaining in his office around the clock. In contrast to Stahr's highly developed sense of responsibility, Brady was mean and selfish. Lacking taste and understanding little of the technical end of the industry, Brady had acquired his share of the studio through luck and had retained it through shrewdness.

One night, while Cecilia was visiting the studio, there was an earthquake. Stahr, working with his trouble-shooter, Robinson, to clear away the mess, saw a sightseer perched on top of a floating idol. The girl reminded him of his dead wife, and he tried to discover her identity. That night Cecilia also fell in love with Stahr, but she felt that her attachment was hopeless.

A self-made, paternalistic employer, Stahr personally managed almost every detail at the studio, from picking the stories to passing on the rushes. Though not an educated man, he had raised the artistic level of the movies and did not hesitate to make good pictures that would lose money. As a result he had incurred the distrust of the stockholders, exploiters who saw the movies only as a business. Their distrust, however, was mixed with a genuine respect for the producer's many abilities. In addition to the opposition of the stockholders, Stahr was concerned because Communists were trying to organize the writers; he worked closely with his writers and wanted them to trust him. Wylie White, in particular, enjoyed his favor, although White resented him. At this time White hoped to marry Cecilia for the sake of her father's influence. Typical of Stahr's interest in his employees was his investigation of the attempted suicide of a cameraman, Pete Zavras. Stahr learned that Zavras had been unable to find work because of a rumor that he was going blind. Stahr was able to scotch the rumor by providing Zavras with a statement from an oculist.

By this time Stahr had succeeded in locating the girl who resembled his wife. She was Kathleen Moore. Though she was at first reluctant to meet him, they later had a brief, passionate affair. Stahr learned that she had been the mistress of a deposed monarch who had undergone a personality deterioration and that now she was about to marry an American who had rescued her from that situation. Stahr realized that marriage to Kathleen could give him the will to go on living. While he hesitated, her fiancé arrived ahead of schedule, and she went through with the marriage from a sense of obligation.

Cecilia, knowing nothing of these matters, was still desperately hoping to attract Stahr, her pull toward him increased by a break with her father after she had discovered him with his nude secretary. At Stahr's request she arranged a meeting with a Communist organizer. Then Stahr got drunk and tried to beat him up.

At this point the manuscript ends, but the rest of the story may be pieced together from the author's notes. Because the studio had been in financial difficulties, Brady had tried to push through a wage cut. Stahr, opposing this plan, had gone east to convince the other stockholders to postpone the wage slash. Brady cut the salaries and betrayed the writers while Stahr was sick in Washington. Although he broke with Brady after that, Stahr agreed to go along with Brady's plan for a company union, chiefly because Stahr felt personally responsible for the welfare of his employees. Wylie White had also turned on Stahr.

In the meantime Kathleen and Stahr resumed their relationship. When Brady tried to blackmail Stahr, the producer threatened him with some information about the death of Brady's wife. At one time Fitzgerald had considered having Brady persuade Robinson to undertake Stahr's murder; however, Fitzgerald rejected this idea in favor of having Brady inform Kathleen's husband, a movie technician involved with the union organizers, of Kathleen's affair with Stahr. An alienation-of-affection suit resulted from that, but Stahr was somehow saved by Zavras, the cameraman.

Stahr became alienated from Kathleen and was no longer able to dominate his associates at the studio. Nevertheless, he continued to oppose Brady. Finally Stahr felt that he had to eliminate Brady before Brady had him killed. After hiring gangsters to murder Brady, Stahr flew east to provide himself with an alibi; but he changed his mind on the plane and decided to call off the killers at the next airport. The plane crashed before he could carry out his intention.

Fitzgerald was uncertain about including an episode in which the plane's wreckage was plundered by three children who discovered it, the idea being that each child's personality was reflected by the items he stole. Stahr's funeral would have been a powerful, detailed, ironic arraignment of Hollywood sham. It would have included the incident of a has-been cowboy actor who was invited to be a pallbearer by mistake and consequently enjoyed a return of good fortune.

Cecilia later had an affair, probably with Wylie White, and then suffered a complete breakdown. At the end of the novel the reader was to learn that she was telling the story while a patient in a tuberculosis sanitorium.

THE LATE GEORGE APLEY

Type of work: Novel
Author: John P. Marquand (1893-   )
Type of plot: Simulated biography
Time of plot: Late nineteenth and early twentieth centuries
Locale: Boston
First published: 1937

> Principal characters:
> GEORGE APLEY, a proper Bostonian
> JOHN, his son

ELEANOR, his daughter
CATHARINE, his wife
MR. WILLING, George Apley's biographer

Critique:

Satire has been said to require the utmost of great minds. In a sense it requires a man to have two visions: one of society as it might be and one as it is. The range between those two points offers the opportunity for satirical comparisons. In *The Late George Apley* the satire is double-edged because of the method of telling the story. The novel is sub-titled "A Novel in the Form of a Memoir." Mr. Willing, the supposed biographer of these memoirs, is as much a source of satire as George Apley himself, for without Mr. Willing, the staid, polished, and politely-dull annotator, the book would be only one more realistic novel.

The Story:

George William Apley was born on Beacon Hill, on January 25, 1866. The Apleys were an old family in Massachusetts. Thomas, known in the old records as Goodman Apley, had emigrated from England to America and settled in Roxbury in 1636. Goodman Apley's son, John, had graduated from Harvard in 1662. From his time there had been an Apley in Harvard in each succeeding generation. John Apley's son, Nathaniel, established himself in Boston. A later Apley, Moses, became a shipping master and laid the foundation of the Apley fortune. Moses Apley was George Apley's grandfather.

George Apley grew up in a quiet atmosphere of wealth and social position. He learned his parents' way of living calmly and with fortitude. In an orderly way he was introduced to the polite world, at first through visits to relatives; later, through study at Harvard.

His Harvard days were probably the high point of his life. He was sent to Harvard to weld those qualities of gentlemanly behavior which private grammar school and parents together had tried

to encourage. His parents were anxious that he should make friends with the right people. George was carefully instructed in the ways of high-minded gentlemen. His training was indicated by a theme in which he wrote a description of a Boston brothel in terms expressing his repulsion and shock. In the gymnasium George won distinction as a boxer. Moreover, he became a member of the Board of the Harvard *Lampoon*. He was taken into the Club, an honor his father appreciated greatly. In his junior and senior years he took part in the musical extravaganzas of the Hasty Pudding Club. In spite of these activities he never neglected his studies and he was known as a respectable student with grades placing him in the middle of his class at graduation.

While in college, he fell in love with an impossible girl, Mary Monahan. The affair was cut short by the Apleys and never referred to publicly. Shortly thereafter his family prescribed a sea voyage for him. When he returned home he took up the study of law, and became a member of the board for the Boston Waifs' Society.

George was instructed in the shrewd businesslike manners and knowledge of tne Apleys. He was sent to work with his Uncle William for one summer. William sensed that his nephew would never make a good businessman and advised that George should be put into law or made a trustee of other peoples' money, not his own. As a result George, like many of his friends, never went actively into business, but spent his lifetime clipping coupons.

In February, 1890, George followed his parents' wishes and suitably became engaged to Catharine Bosworth. Both his father-in-law and his own father saw to it that the young couple had a summer cottage and a house for the winter.

The two mothers were equally solicitous. George discovered that he had married not only Catharine but also her family.

As the years passed, George devoted his time to charitable groups, learned societies, and to writing for his clubs. One of his papers, "Jonas Good and Cow Corner," was said to be among the best papers read before the Browsers in fifty years.

His first child's name was a subject for debate in his own and Catharine's family. The name, John, common to both families, was finally chosen. His second child was a daughter, Eleanor.

Shortly after his sister Amelia's marriage, George's father died of an apoplectic stroke. He left a million dollars to Harvard, other large sums to his charities, and the remainder of his fortune in trust for his family. George had to pay a sum of money to a woman who claimed she had borne a son to his father. Although he did not believe the charge, he paid rather than cause scandal in the family.

George invested in a place known as Pequod Island and there he took his friends when he wanted to get away from Boston. On the island he and his friends condescended to share the campfire with their guides. Planned as a male retreat, the island was soon overrun with literary lights of the times invited by George's wife and sister.

As his son grew up, George noted an increasing desire on the part of the younger generation to be wild and careless with money. Later, George began to realize that he and his generation had let much slip and that Boston was going to the Irish. He gave his name to the "Save Boston Association" as he considered his membership an Apley duty. He also interested himself in bird lore and philosophy and took as much personal concern as possible in the affairs of his children. When his mother died in 1908, George counted her death one of his most poignant tragedies.

When George's son entered Harvard,

George took a new interest in the university and noted many changes he did not like.

Old Uncle William, now over eighty, still controlled the Apley mills and held out successfully against the new labor unions. One day the old man shocked his family by marrying his nurse, a Miss Prentiss.

His daughter Eleanor's marriage was completely unsatisfactory to George because she did not induce her husband to give up his job for a position in the Apley mills and to take up residence near her family. But George was proud of his son John for his service at the front. George himself belonged to the Home Guards. When John married a girl of good connections after the war, George was doubly pleased.

At last George came into opposition with a man named O'Reilly, whom George planned to have brought before criminal court on charges of extortion. However, O'Reilly tricked George into a scandal. George intended to have the whole case cleared in court, but before the trial he received a note from his one-time sweetheart, Mary Monahan. After an interview with her, he settled the case quietly and bought off his opponents.

In 1928 he became a grandfather. As soon as the baby had been born, George telegraphed Groton to include his grandson's name among the entrance applicants.

In his last years George took interest in the new novels, condemning those too blatant in their description of sex and fighting against the inclusion of some of them in the Boston libraries. His own copy of *Lady Chatterly's Lover* he hid in the silver safe to keep his daughter from seeing it. He defied prohibition as an abuse of his rights and kept a private bootlegger on principle because he thought it important to help break the prohibition law.

He thought, too, that the colossal fortunes being gathered by the uneducated should be handed over to the government. In the autumn of 1929 he and his wife made a trip to Rome, where they visited Horatio Apley, recently appointed to a diplomatic post there. George was absent from America when the stock market crash came. His financial affairs did not suffer greatly, but, his health breaking, he began to plan his will and his funeral.

George Apley died in December, 1933.

THE LATE MATTIA PASCAL

Type of work: Novel
Author: Luigi Pirandello (1867-1936)
Type of plot: Psychological realism
Time of plot: Early twentieth century
Locale: Italy
First published: 1904

Principal characters:
    MATTIA PASCAL, a young Italian
    ROBERTO PASCAL, his brother
    ROMILDA PESCARONE, Mattia's wife
    MALAGNA, manager of the Pascal estates
    ADRIANA, a young girl in love with Mattia

Critique:

Outside of Italy, Pirandello has been much better known for his dramas than for his novels, although his fiction has always been highly regarded in his native land. In this particular case, part of the plot of the novel was also used in a play, as the first part of the novel formed the basis for Pirandello's Sicilian comedy, *Liola.* When the novel appeared, some critics objected to it, saying that the action was impossible in terms of real life. In 1921, Pirandello wrote a preface to the book in which he pointed out that a similar happening had actually occurred in Buffalo, New York, in that same year. He went on to state that it was his opinion this type of criticism should not be used in evaluating a work of the creative imagination; he said that the novel, like any other medium of art, dealt not with individuals but with mankind and all of the incidents and individuals which make up the total composite of man. He felt that the illusion of the present might very possibly be the reality of the future.

The Story:

As boys, Mattia Pascal and his brother Roberto lived an easy life with their wealthy widowed mother. While the boys were growing up, however, the fortune their merchant father had left them was gradually acquired by a dishonest man named Malagna, to whom the mother confided all her business affairs. One by one the farms and city property belonging to the Pascals were mortgaged and then sold. Everyone except the widow Pascal realized how dishonest Malagna was. Her confidence in her agent enabled him to rob her of everything over a period of many years.

When he was in his teens, Mattia Pascal fell in love with a beautiful young girl, Romilda Pescarone. Unfortunately for the affair, Malagna, whose two wives had failed to give him any children, had his eye on Romilda for himself. A bad situation developed when Romilda became pregnant; her mother, a termagant who seized any opportunity to improve her position, saw a chance to capitalize on the evil. She advised Romilda to take Malagna as her lover and let him think the child was his. The mother thought that he would be so happy to have his impotence seemingly disproved that he would at least make Romilda, her mother, and the child very comfortable.

Although Romilda told Malagna the truth, the two kept the whole affair a secret. Malagna's wife discovered, through Mattia Pascal, what had happened. In revenge on her husband, whom she had suspected of playing her false, she in turn became pregnant by Mattia. The husband, realizing what had happened as soon as his wife told him of her pregnancy, was furious. In his anger he refused to help Romilda, saying it was bad enough that he should be compelled to support one of Mattia Pascal's bastards. In a way the prospect pleased him, for the Pascal fortune he had stolen would now go eventually to Mattia's child by Malagna's wife.

Mattia and Romilda were married, but their marriage was a most unhappy one. Because Malagna had foreclosed on the last bit of property owned by the Pascals, the newlyweds and Mattia's mother were forced to move into the hovel owned by Romilda's mother. Mattia's aunt finally took pity on his mother and took her away, but Mattia, who was unable to find a job, and his wife continued to live with his shrewish mother-in-law. Their situation was relieved somewhat by Mattia's success in getting a political appointment as the caretaker of a municipal library in the town. The post was a sinecure; Mattia spent most of his time reading and catching rats that infested the place.

Mattia's mother and his child both died suddenly and within a day of one another. A few days after his mother's burial Mattia received several hundred lire from his brother, who had married into a rich family. The funeral expenses were already paid for and Mattia put the money away. One day he suddenly decided to travel. He took the money his brother had sent and went to Monte Carlo. There he won a fortune. Although he lost most of it again, he stopped playing after seeing the corpse of a destitute young gambler who had shot himself.

On his way home with the eighty-two thousand lire he had won, Mattia read in a newspaper an account of his death and burial. The people in his village, it appeared, had discovered a body some days after his secret departure, and his relatives had identified it as his. When the shock of the story wore off, Mattia realized how lucky he was: he had been released suddenly from an unhappy marriage and a mountain of debts; in addition, he had enough money in his pockets to live comfortably for many years.

Instead of going back to his native village, Mattia went to Rome and assumed a new identity. He shaved off his beard, had his hair cut shorter, and called himself Adriano Meis. The only part of his appearance he could not change was a crossed eye; to disguise that identifying characteristic, he began wearing dark glasses.

As Adriano Meis, Mattia rented a room in a private home and spent his days walking and reading. But he gradually discovered that his lack of a past was bothersome; he hated to live a literal lie. He discovered also that without an official record, any proof of identity, he was limited in his activities. He could not even buy a dog, lest he get into trouble in buying a license for it. At the same time he could not afford to have his real identity become known because he would be sent to prison for deserting his wife and evading his debts. Most discouraging of all, he fell in love with the daughter of his landlord, a girl named Adriana. He could not marry her, however, for he could not prove his own existence. His life was that of a shadow in the world of men.

The circumstance which finally convinced him that he could not go on masquerading as Adriano Meis was the theft of twelve thousand lire by his landlord's son-in-law. Everyone knew that the man had taken the money, but the victim was unable to go to the police, for fear they would investigate him and ask embarrassing questions. When he did not go to the police, everyone became suspicious, even the girl who loved him. Mattia took his money one evening and wandered about town while he tried to decide what to do with himself. He realized that his position was untenable; he could not go on living as he had.

As he was about to leap into the river and commit suicide, Mattia had a brilliant idea. Deciding to die as Adriano Meis and return to his identity as Mattia Pascal, he left his hat and other evidence to make it seem as if Adriano Meis had jumped into the river. Within a day or two the newspapers carried accounts of the suicide of Adriano Meis. Quite happy to regain his original identity, Mattia went to visit his brother Roberto. At his brother's home Mattia learned that Romilda had married a childhood sweetheart and had had a child. Mattia was even more disconcerted to learn that he would have to take his wife and her mother back again. According to the law, his return from the dead voided the second marriage.

Disturbed by that news, Mattia returned to his native village. There he found his wife and her new husband quite happy and his hateful mother-in-law alive. In spite of the law they all decided that it was best for the current arrangements to continue, and so Mattia relinquished unofficially his marital rights and responsibilities. He found himself some rooms in the village and lived there quietly, spending his days reading and preparing an account of his strange adventures, a story which was to be published after what he termed his third and final death.

LAVENGRO

Type of work: Novel
Author: George Henry Borrow (1803-1881)
Type of plot: Simulated autobiography
Time of plot: Nineteenth century
Locale: England, Scotland, Ireland
First published: 1851

Principal characters:
LAVENGRO, a scholar, journalist, and tinker
JOHN, his brother
JASPER PETULENGRO, his gipsy friend
MRS. HERNE, an old crone
THE FLAMING TINMAN, a bully of the roads
ISOPEL BERNERS, Lavengro's companion
PETER WILLIAMS, an evangelist
WINIFRED, his wife

Critique:

Lavengro; The Scholar—The Gipsy—The Priest is a long novel, in part fiction and in part the autobiography of its eccentric author, which gives an interesting and unusual picture of England during the early part of the last century. The autobiographical method of the narrative has aroused the interest of scholars as to what is fact in the book and what is pure imagination. To the general reader, *Lavengro* is most interesting for its accounts of nomadic gipsy life and character studies of tinkers, beggars, and thieves who roamed the English highways more than a hundred years ago.

The Story:

Lavengro was the son of an army officer who had fought against Napoleon, and the boy spent his early years at army garrisons in various parts of England, Scotland, Ireland, and Wales. When he was six years old, Lavengro discovered *Robinson Crusoe*, a book which stimulated his imagination and aroused in him a desire to read and to study languages. One day, wandering on the outskirts of a garrison town, he met a group of gipsies who threatened to do him harm. They drew back, however, when he showed them a tame snake which he was carrying. The gipsies, becoming friendly, nicknamed him Sapengro, or snake tamer. A young gipsy named Jasper declared that they would always be brothers. He met also at the gipsy camp a Romany whom he saw hanged fifteen years later at Newgate.

A few years later he began the study of Latin. About the same time his father was ordered to Edinburgh. In Scotland, Lavengro took part in several bickers, or fights, with his schoolmates and learned mountain climbing. Then in 1815 his father was ordered to Ireland. Lavengro went to a seminary at Clonmel and studied more Latin and Greek and, in an incidental fashion, learned to speak Irish. His brother John was made an ensign and transferred to a post some few miles away. After peace was signed with the French, opportunities for military employment were few. John had always wanted to paint; therefore, his father allowed him to go to London to study his art.

Lavengro again met Jasper, his gipsy friend, and discovered that Jasper's last name was Petulengro. Jasper was now a Romany Kral—or gipsy king—a horseshoer, pugilist, jockey, and soothsayer. Through Jasper, Lavengro made the acquaintance of a malignant old crone named Herne, who hated him because she believed that he was stealing the Romany tongue. It was Jasper who named him Lavengro, which means "word-master," because he learned the gipsy language so rapidly. All of the gipsies departed for London, except Mrs. Herne, who went to Yorkshire. Lavengro remained at home with his parents while his father tried to decide what to do with him. It was finally agreed that Lavengro would enter a solicitor's office

to study law. But Lavengro neglected his Blackstone while he studied Welsh and translated the poetry of Ab Gwilym. About the same time, Lavengro obtained a Danish book and learned to read it by first studying the Danish Bible. One day Lavengro was sent to deliver a thousand pounds to a magistrate with whom he had a very entertaining conversation concerning the manly art of self-defense. In spite of the magistrate's fondness for boxing, however, he refused a place on his land for a match.

Lavengro met Jasper again and put on the gloves with him for a friendly bout. Later he returned home and discovered that his father was seriously ill. His brother John also arrived home just before his father died. Shortly afterward Lavengro went to London to seek his fortune as a writer, taking with him a letter of introduction to a noted publisher. The publisher seemed delighted to be able to employ him, but was not interested in such things as Lavengro's translations of the songs of Ab Gwilym and his translations of Danish songs. Lavengro was informed that the reading public scoffed at works like these. Instead, the publisher recommended a story somewhat along the line of *The Dairyman's Daughter*.

While walking through Cheapside one day, Lavengro climbed upon the balustrade of a bridge in order to see something below. An old woman selling apples nearby thought he was trying to commit suicide and begged him not to fling himself over. The old lady had a partiality for a book about the "blessed" Mary Flanders. Lavengro returned from time to time to see her and to talk with her.

Lavengro, invited to dinner at the publisher's house one Sunday, discovered that the publisher did not believe in eating meat or drinking wine. After dinner Lavengro heard what was to be his new assignment since the publisher had now decided not to publish anything like *The Dairyman's Daughter*. He was to prepare a collection of the stories of the lives and trials of famous criminals incarcerated at Newgate. In addition, he was to translate the publisher's book of philosophy into German and to write an article about it for the *Review*.

In the company of an acquaintance named Francis Ardry, Lavengro visited many of the underworld spots of London and this experience, together with the series on criminals which he was preparing, gave him a wide and practical knowledge of the underworld. Then Lavengro's brother came to London and introduced him to a painter of the heroic. The peculiar thing about this painter's pictures was the short legs of the people in his paintings. When Lavengro's stories of crime were finished, he took them to the publisher. But the publisher was displeased because Lavengro had omitted several of the publisher's favorite criminal histories.

Lavengro went to visit the apple-woman again and his despondent appearance led her to think that he had been caught stealing. The apple-woman never became aware of Lavengro's profession. He talked her into letting him read her cherished copy of the life of Mary Flanders.

The publisher's speculations failed and left Lavengro without money, but Lavengro finally obtained all the wages that were due him. Taggart, the publisher's assistant, told Lavengro that Glorious John, another printer, would publish his ballads and the songs of Ab Gwilym. But Lavengro never offered his ballads to Glorious John. In midwinter he went again to visit the apple-woman and found that she had moved her stall to the other side of the bridge. He promised to take her book and trade it in for a Bible. However, he lost the book and had nothing to trade. He decided to purchase a Bible and never let her know about his negligence.

About this time Lavengro saved an Armenian from pickpockets. The Armenian wished him to translate some Armenian fables into English, but Lavengro refused. The Armenian, who had inherited a hundred thousand pounds from his father, was intent upon doubling the amount through his speculation. The Armenian ran into a bit of luck and came into possession of two hundred thousand pounds. Lavengro's advice to the Armenian was to take his fortune and fight the Persians.

Lavengro decided, when his money got short, to do the translations for the Armenian but the man had already departed to invest his money in a war against the Persians.

Lavengro left London after having some small success writing fiction. He met and talked with many and various people on his travels about England. On his rambles he heard the stories concerning the Flaming Tinman, who held a great repute as a fighter and who had forced Jack Slingsby, another tinker, out of business on threats of death. Lavengro met Slingsby and bought him out. He decided to become a tinker himself in the hope of meeting the Flaming Tinman.

One day, while he was mending pots and pans, he encountered Mrs. Herne and Leonora, a thirteen-year-old girl who was traveling with the old woman. Leonora brought him cakes made by Mrs. Herne. He ate one of them and that night became seriously ill. When the evil old crone came to gloat over him, he realized that the cakes had been poisoned. Then the sound of wheels frightened the old woman away, and Lavengro was saved by the timely arrival of Peter Williams, a traveling Welsh preacher, and Winifred, his wife. Peter Williams told Lavengro the sad story of his life and related how he had been led to commit the sin against the Holy Ghost, a sin for which there was no redemption. Peter had become a preacher to warn other people against the unforgivable sin. Lavengro journeyed with Peter and his wife as far as the Welsh border, where he left them to join Jasper Petulengro and his band of gipsies.

Jasper told Lavengro how Mrs. Herne had hanged herself because of her failure to poison him. Since Jasper was a blood-kinsman of Mrs. Herne, it was required by Romany law that he obtain revenge from Lavengro. Lavengro, however, was really only indirectly responsible for the old woman's death, a fact of which Jasper was well aware. They retired to a place where they could fight, and there Jasper received full satisfaction when he made Lavengro's nose bleed.

Soon after his friendly tussle with Jasper, Lavengro met the Flaming Tinman, Moll, his wife, and Isopel Berners, child of a gipsy mother and a noble father and now a free woman of the roads. Isopel was responsible for Lavengro's victory in a brawl with the Flaming Tinman, for she had told him to use his right hand and to strike at the bully's face. The Flaming Tinman and Moll departed, leaving the territory to Lavengro the tinker, but Isopel remained behind with her belongings. The story of the Flaming Tinman's defeat was soon known throughout the neighborhood, and Lavengro became a hero of the roads. At a public house he met a priest whom he called the Man in Black. He and Lavengro had many conversations concerning religion and the attempt to establish Catholicism as the religion in England.

On a wild stormy night Isopel and Lavengro helped a coachman right his coach which had overturned. Later the coachman told them the story of his life, and his tale was proof that in those days romance journeyed on the highways and adventure waited around the turn of any English lane.

THE LAY OF THE LAST MINSTREL

Type of work: Poem
Author: Sir Walter Scott (1771-1832)
Type of plot: Semihistorical romance
Time of plot: Mid-sixteenth century
Locale: The Scottish Border
First published: 1805

Principal characters:
  LADY BUCCLEUCH, widow of the Lord of Branksome
  MARGARET, her daughter
  THE MASTER OF BUCCLEUCH, her son
  LORD CRANSTOUN, Margaret's lover
  SIR WILLIAM OF DELORAINE, a knight in Lady Buccleuch's service
  THE DWARF, an evil magician
  THE GHOST OF MICHAEL SCOTT, a wizard

Critique:

As Scott himself tells us in his introduction to *The Lay of the Last Minstrel*, his purpose was to describe the manners and the scenery of the Scottish Border country during the middle of the sixteenth century. He was concerned more with these than he was with the story itself and often left the narrative for several stanzas in order to portray customs of the Scottish clans. As in his other metrical romances, Scott had here the touch of the artist; the scenes he painted are as real to us as if we were seeing them for ourselves. Scott's ability to tell a picturesque, rousing story in verse is almost as great as his achievement in the novel.

The Story:

As an old minstrel, the last of his kind, wandered through the country, he was treated kindly by a duchess at whose mansion he asked food and shelter. Later he

1641

rewarded her by singing a song of days gone by. This is the tale he sang:

Bold Lord Buccleuch had been killed in battle with the English, but his widow and children were well protected in their castle at Branksome by a group of brave knights who had followed their dead leader. Although a truce had been declared, there were skirmishes between the English and the Scots throughout the Border country.

The widow, Lady Buccleuch, was the daughter of a magician; before he died he had taught her to talk with the spirits. One night she heard the spirits predicting that the stars would show no favor to Branksome castle until pride should die and make love free. Lady Buccleuch knew this omen was meant for her, for her daughter Margaret loved the young Lord Cranstoun, who had fought against Lord Buccleuch. But Lady Buccleuch swore that Margaret should never wed a foeman, no matter what the spirits might say. She sent William of Deloraine to Melrose Abbey, there to secure the mystic book of Michael Scott, a wizard long dead and buried in the abbey crypt. She ordered William of Deloraine not to look into the book on peril of his life.

The monk at the abbey, although he quavered at the request made by Deloraine, obeyed without question Lady Buccleuch's command. Leading him deep into the vaults, he took the knight to the wizard's tomb. Deloraine, bravest of knights in battle, shivered with dread as he looked at the body of the magician. The man lay as if he had not been dead a day, and when the knight took the book from his hand, he seemed to frown. As Deloraine left the vault, he heard noises like the laughter and sobbing of fiends.

On the same day, while Deloraine went to the abbey, Margaret slipped out of the castle to meet her lover, Lord Cranstoun. Cranstoun was accompanied by a Dwarf, who had some time before attached himself to Cranstoun and now would not leave his side. Since the Dwarf served him well, Cranstoun had

ceased his efforts to rid himself of the little page. The Dwarf warned the lovers of the approach of a horseman. The traveler was Deloraine, returning from his mission, and while Margaret fled, the two knights battled. Deloraine was seriously wounded. Cranstoun ordered the Dwarf to take Deloraine to Branksome Hall so that his wounds could be properly tended. The Dwarf found the book but could not open it until after he had smeared the cover with the blood of Deloraine, who was almost an infidel. While he was reading one of the spells described in the book, an unseen hand struck him on the cheek and knocked him to the ground. The book snapped shut and could not be opened again. The Dwarf, hiding it under his cloak, proceeded to Branksome Hall with the wounded Deloraine.

At the castle the Dwarf spied the young Master of Buccleuch. Changing himself and the boy into dogs, he led the child into the woods. There, after they had resumed their real shapes, the child was captured by the English soldiers patrolling the Border. At the castle his absence was not known, for the Dwarf returned there and, taking the child's shape, made mischief for everyone. Lady Buccleuch, busy tending the wounds of her faithful Deloraine, failed to notice the child's strange behavior.

Suddenly watchers in the castle sighted signal fires. Their meaning was clear; the English were gathering to attack the Scots. From the castle messengers were sent hurriedly to summon friendly clans of the Border to the defense of Branksome Hall. In the confusion the Dwarf, still in the form of the Master of Buccleuch, escaped from the knight assigned to watch him.

The English, arriving before the castle, made their demands. They wanted Deloraine turned over to them, for they accused him of murdering the brother of one of their group. They also demanded that two hundred English knights be quartered in Branksome, to prevent the Scotsmen from making raids on the English side of the Border. If these demands were not met, they declared, the castle would be stormed and the young heir of Buccleuch, who was held by the English, would be sent to the English court to serve as a page.

Lady Buccleuch would not meet the demands. She could not send her faithful knight to his doom, though her deed might cost her her son, her castle, and perhaps her life. She proposed that Deloraine meet the brother of the slain man in combat and settle the dispute in that knightly fashion. The English leaders, refusing to accept these terms, were preparing to attack the castle when one of their number brought word that strong Scottish clans were approaching the castle. Fearful of a trap, the English agreed to accept the proposal for a settlement by mortal combat between the two knights concerned, or by the wronged man and a substitute for Deloraine should his wounds not be healed by the next day. Then English and Scots joined together in feasting and revelry until the time appointed for the combat.

As the time approached, other knights argued over the right to represent Deloraine, who was still weak from his wounds. But at the last minute Deloraine appeared in full armor, ready to defend himself. The fighting was long and fierce, and both knights lost much blood before the Englishman fell wounded. Deloraine,

standing triumphantly over his victim, did not remove his visor. Then the spectators saw with amazement that Deloraine was approaching from the castle. Quickly the supposed Deloraine was uncovered. In his place stood young Lord Cranstoun. He had stolen Deloraine's armor so that he might defend the home and save the brother of Margaret. At first Lady Buccleuch would not greet him, but at last she thought of the prophecy of the spirits and knew that she must forget pride and allow love to prevail. Yielding, she gave her daughter to the knight who had been her husband's enemy. She also swore to herself that she would return the book to Michael Scott's tomb.

At the wedding feast the Dwarf continued to make trouble. In order to undo the mischief he caused, all the minstrels sang songs of days gone past. As the last song died away, the banquet hall grew suddenly dark. A great flash of lightning streaked through the room and struck the Dwarf. The evil page was seen no more. Deloraine was terrified, for in the unearthly light he had seen the shape of the dead wizard. Lady Buccleuch renounced forever the magic of her father, and all the knights made pilgrimages to pray for peace and rest for Michael Scott's soul.

Thus ended the song of the ancient minstrel.

LAZARILLO DE TORMES

Type of work: Novel
Author: Unknown
Type of plot: Picaresque romance
Time of plot: Sixteenth century
Locale: Spain
First published: 1553

Principal character:
LAZARILLO DE TORMES, an adventurer

Critique:

This early work is the first of many picaresque tales. *The Life of Lazarillo de Tormes* antedates Cervantes, and LeSage drew heavily on this entertaining story of a rogue. The narrator, in a series of brief sketches, gives a vivid picture of the stratagems used by the poor merely to stay alive. Without a trace of self-pity he shows us the humorous side of continual penury and want. The tales are scarcely developed into a unified whole. This novel was once credited to the sixteenth-century writer, Diego Hurtado de Mendoza, but his authorship is now regarded as extremely doubtful.

The Story:

Lazarillo's surname came from the peculiar circumstance of his birth. His mother happened to stay the night at the mill where his father was employed. Lazarillo was born on the mill floor just over the river Tormes, after which he was named.

He had reached his ninth year when his father was caught taking flour from customers' sacks. After being soundly punished, the father joined an army getting ready to move against the Moors. He became a mule driver for a gentleman soldier and was killed in action.

Lazarillo's mother opened an eating house near a nobleman's estate. The widow soon made the acquaintance of Zayde, a colored groom who frequently visited them. At first Lazarillo was afraid of the black man, but he quickly learned that Zayde's visits meant food and firewood. One consequence was a bit displeasing: Lazarillo acquired a small, dark brother to look after.

The nobleman's steward began to miss horseshoes and brushes as well as other supplies. When he was asked directly about the thefts, Lazarillo told all he knew of Zayde's peccadillos. Zayde was soundly flogged and boiling fat was poured on his ribs. Lazarillo's mother, to avoid further scandal, set up a new eating house in a different neighborhood.

When Lazarillo was fairly well grown, his mother apprenticed him to a blind man who wanted a boy to lead him about. Though old, the blind man was shrewd and tough. As they were leaving the city, they passed by a stone bull. When the blind man told the boy to put his ear to the statue and listen for a peculiar noise, Lazarillo obeyed. Then the old man knocked the boy's head sharply against the stone, hard enough so his ears rang for three days. Lazarillo was forced to learn a few tricks for himself in order to survive.

The blind man, when they squatted over a fire to cook a meal, kept his hand over the mouth of his wine jug. Lazarillo bored a tiny hole in the jug, and, lying down, let the liquid trickle into his mouth. Then he stopped up the hole with beeswax. But when the suspicious old man felt the jug, the wax had melted and he found the hole. Giving no sign, the next night he again put the jug in front of him and Lazarillo again lay down expecting to guzzle wine once more. Suddenly the blind man raised the jug and brought it down with great force in Lazarillo's face. All the boy's teeth were loosened.

On another occasion Lazarillo seized a roasting sausage from the spit and substituted a rotten turnip. When the blind man bit into his supposed sausage he roared with rage and scratched the boy severely with his long nails. Resolved to leave his master, Lazarillo guided him to the shores of a brook. Telling the blind man he must run and leap, he placed his master behind a stone pillar. The old man gave a mighty jump, cracked his head on the stone, and fell down senseless. Lazarillo left town quickly.

His next master was a penurious priest who engaged him to assist at mass. Unfortunately, the priest watched the collection box like a hawk, and Lazarillo had no chance to filch a single coin. For food, the priest allowed him an onion every fourth day. If it had not been for an occasional funeral feast, the boy would have starved to death.

The priest kept his fine bread securely locked in a chest. Luckily, Lazarillo met a strolling tinker who made him a key. Then to avoid suspicion, he gnawed each loaf to make it look as if rats had got into the chest. The alarmed priest nailed up the holes securely, but Lazarillo made new holes. Then the priest set numerous traps from which Lazarillo ate the cheese. The puzzled priest was forced to conclude that a snake was stealing his bread.

Fearing a search while he was asleep, Lazarillo kept his key in his mouth while he was in bed. One night the key shifted so that he was blowing through the keyhole. The resulting whistle awoke the priest. Seizing a club, he broke it over Lazarillo's head. After his head had been bandaged by a kind neighbor, Lazarillo was dismissed. Thinking to find employment in a larger city, he sought further fortune in Toledo.

One night while his pockets were full of crusts he had begged on the city streets, a careless young dandy, a real esquire, engaged Lazarillo as a servant. Thinking himself lucky to have a wealthy master, Lazarillo followed him to a bare, mean house with scarcely a stick of furniture. After waiting a long time for a meal, the boy began to eat his crusts. To his surprise his master joined him. So the days went by, both of them living on what Lazarillo could beg.

At last the esquire procured a little money and sent Lazarillo out for bread and wine. On the way he met a funeral procession. The weeping widow loudly lamented her husband and cried out that the dead man was going to an inhospitable house where there was no food or furniture. Thinking they were going to bring the corpse to his esquire's house, Lazarillo ran home in fear. His master disabused him of his fear and sent him back on his errand.

At last the master left town and Lazarillo was forced to meet the bailiffs and the wrathful landlord. After some difficulty he persuaded the bailiffs of his innocence and was allowed to go free.

His next master was a bulero, a dealer in papal indulgences, who was a most accomplished rogue. Rumors began to spread that his indulgences were forged, and even the alguazil accused him publicly of fraud. The wily bulero prayed openly for his accuser to be confounded, and forthwith the alguazil, falling down in a fit, foamed at the mouth and grew rigid. The prayers and forgiveness of the bulero were effective, however, and little by little the alguazil recovered. From that time on the bulero earned a rich harvest selling his papal indulgences. Lazarillo, now wise in roguery, wondered how the bulero worked the trick; but he never found out.

Four years of service with a chaplain who sold water enabled Lazarillo to save a little money and buy respectable clothes. At last he was on his way to some standing in the community. On the strength of his new clothes he was appointed to a government post which would furnish him an income for life. All business matters of the town passed through his hands.

The archpriest of Salvador, seeing how affluent Lazarillo had become, gave him a wife from his own household. The woman made a useful wife, for the archpriest frequently gave them substantial presents. Lazarillo's wife repaid the holy man by taking care of his wardrobe. But evil tongues wagged, and the archpriest asked Lazarillo if he had heard stories about his wife. Lazarillo disclosed that he had been told that his wife had borne three of the archpriest's children. The archpriest advised him sagely to think of his profit more and his honor less. So Lazarillo was content, for surely the archpriest was an honorable man.

Lazarillo was now so influential that it was said that he could commit any crime with impunity. His happiness increased when his wife presented him with a baby daughter. The good lady swore that it was truly Lazarillo's child.

LEAVES OF GRASS

Type of work: Poetry
Author: Walt Whitman (1819-1892)
First published: 1855

The total effect of Walt Whitman's *Leaves of Grass* has been compared to that of a symphony, with interwoven and recurring themes that are scored for a full orchestra, from gentle strings to raucous brass; actually, if one compares his poetry to music, Whitman's work seems closer to a Wagnerian opera, for Wagner employs not only the great melodic themes and the contrast of soft and harsh music but also a human element, the actors and singers on the stage. And while Whitman is famed as a champion of democratic ideas, he rarely presents them in the abstract, rarely strays from the individual man or woman. Even the *en-masse* "I" of his "Song of Myself" becomes particular in the dramatic incidents of the runaway slave who is "limpsy and weak" from his journey, of the woman who peeks from behind the blinds of her windows and mentally projects herself among the twenty-eight young men who splash naked on the seashore, and of the brave captain in the sea battle who has just begun to fight. Whitman is also like Wagner in that his triumphs and failures are similar to those of the composer; both are capable of unmatched eloquence and both fail when they become overblown and pretentious.

So broad is Whitman's scope in *Leaves of Grass* that any short discussion of his work must be divided into compartments (which may be arbitrary and incomplete) or degenerate into random comments. Because of his breadth, Whitman may be considered as four men: philosopher, propagandist, humorist, and poet.

Whitman the Philosopher: In the short poem which opens *Leaves of Grass* Whitman bluntly states the core of his philosophy:

> One's-Self I sing—a simple, separate
>   Person;

Yet utter the word Democratic, the
    word *En-masse.*

Of Physiology from toe to toe I sing;
Not physiognomy alone, nor brain
    alone, is worthy for the muse—I say
    the Form complete is worthier far;
The Female equally with the male I sing.

O Life immense in passion, pulse, and
    power,
Cheerful—for freest action form'd, under
    the laws divine,
The Modern Man I sing.

Having stated the paradox, the dilemma, Whitman expands upon this theme so persuasively that by the time the reader has finished the volume he accepts the paradox as reasonable and true. In the strident "Song of the Open Road," Whitman seems to emphasize the individual at the expense of society, telling us to throw off all conventions and responsibilities, to strike out on our own:

Afoot and light-hearted I take to the
    open road,
Healthy, free, the world before me,
The long brown path before me, lead-
    ing wherever I choose.

Henceforth I ask not good fortune—I
    am good fortune,
Henceforth I whimper no more, post-
    pone no more, need nothing,
Strong and content, I travel the open
    road.

The earth—that is sufficient,
I do not want the constellations any
    nearer,
I know they are very well where they
    are,
I know they suffice for those who be-
    long to them.

Still here I carry my old delicious
    burdens,

I carry them, men and women—I carry
them with me wherever I go,
I swear it is impossible for me to get
rid of them,
I am filled with them, and I will fill
them in return.

In "Crossing the Brooklyn Ferry," the individual merges into crowds that in turn merge with the stream of life. When Whitman examines his position in "I Hear It Was Charged Against Me," he seems to evade the paradox by proclaiming that he has nothing to do with any institution except that "of the dear love of comrades"; but the reader may reflect that these comrades are the individuals who make up a complex world society.

Many themes appear in *Leaves of Grass*. Whitman celebrates the brotherhood of man, democracy, America as a symbol of both brotherhood and democracy, and Lincoln as a symbol of the lonely individual deeply involved in humanity; as natural outgrowths of these themes come Whitman's insistence on the "normality" of sex, the equality of male and female, and the oneness of man with all things in the universe, from great stars to tiny ants. All these ideas are consistent with the poet's viewpoint, all a part of the primary dilemma. One of his greatest poems, "When Lilacs Last in the Dooryard Bloom'd," presents Lincoln as the solitary figure who is also the man of the people; and when the funeral train slowly bears his body across the country, Whitman describes not only the great grief of the masses but also the mourning of the poet, the individual:

Coffin that passes through lanes and
streets,
Through day and night, with the great
cloud darkening the land,
With the pomp of the inloop'd flags,
with the cities draped in black,
With the show of the States themselves,
as of crapeveil'd women, standing,
With processions long and winding,
and the flambeaus of the night,
With the countless torches lit—with the

silent sea of faces and the unbared
heads,
With the waiting depot, the arriving
coffin, and the sombre faces,
With dirges through the night, with
the thousand voices rising strong and
solemn;
With all the mournful voices of the
dirges, pour'd around the coffin,
The dim-lit churches and the shudder-
ing organs—
Where amid these you journey,
With the tolling, tolling bells' perpetual
clang;
Here! coffin that slowly passes,
I give you my sprig of lilac.

Whitman the Propagandist: In this role, Whitman, like his contemporary Whittier, seems least successful. While it is natural for a poet in a time of crisis to feel his responsibilities, to turn his talent to a cause, only rarely does he produce great poetry in so doing. The section of *Leaves of Grass* called "Memories of President Lincoln" is above the realm of propaganda and ranks with the finest elegies written in the English language; but many of the selections in "Drum-Taps," which is concerned with the Civil War, are "forced" poems, written as if the poet felt himself compelled to comment on the events taking place. For instance, in "Beat! Beat! Drums!" the first few lines are:

Beat! beat! drums!—Blow! bugles! blow!
Through the windows—through doors
—burst like a force of ruthless men,
Into the solemn church, and scatter the
congregation;
Into the school where the scholar is
studying:
Leave not the bridegroom quiet—no
happiness must he have now with
his bride;
Nor the peaceful farmer any peace,
ploughing his field or gathering his
grain;
So fierce you whirr and pound, you
drums—so shrill you bugles blow.

Here Whitman is merely superimposing the spirit and technique of "Song of the

Open Road" on an entirely different subject. However, in a few of the war poems —such as "Come Up from the Fields Father" and "Give Me the Splendid Silent Sun," in which Whitman is writing about the fringes of the war—he seems more at ease and is consequently more successful.

Whitman the Humorist: This aspect of Whitman's talent is rarely recognized and almost never discussed fully. *Leaves of Grass* contains much sly humor, many passages in which the reader suspects Whitman of poetic playfulness. Although Whitman wrote no purely comical poems, he often expresses his ideas in a witty manner. In "To a Common Prostitute" he seriously accepts the girl as a part of the human scene, but surely in the last line he has his tongue in his cheek: "Till then I salute you with a significant look that you do not forget me." The first line of "Salut au Monde"—"O take my hand Walt Whitman"—and the other passages in which the poet talks to himself and makes poetry of his own name are certainly the affectation of a "character." Even the justly celebrated section in "Song of Myself" about the nature of grass can become, with a slightly unsympathetic reading, a deadpan masterpiece of comic simplicity. And Whitman's humor is intentional. In Richard Chase's *Walt Whitman Reconsidered*, the poet is quoted as having said to his Camden friends: "I pride myself on being a real humorist underneath everything else." Here is a poet who is alternately comic and serious—and sometimes both at the same time. Whitman will always be chiefly remembered as a poet of force and eloquence, a prophet of high ideals, but his wit must also be reckoned a part of his genius.

Whitman the Poet: The range of Whitman's skill in poetic technique is remarkable. In his carol in praise of death, from "When Lilacs Last in the Dooryard Bloom'd," he creates an effect as soft as a summer night; and in the love song of the grieving bird in "Out of the Cradle Endlessly Rocking" the music is gentle, poignant, haunting:

> Soothe! Soothe!
> Close on its wave soothes the wave behind,
> And again another behind, embracing and lapping, every one close,
> But my love soothes not me.
>
> Low hangs the moon—it rose late,
> O it is lagging—O I think it is heavy with love.
>
> O madly the sea pushes upon the land,
> With love—with love.
>
> O night!
> O do I not see my love fluttering out there among the breakers?
> What is that little black thing I see there in the white?
>
> . . . .
>
> O rising stars!
> Perhaps the one I want so much will rise with some of you.

At other times he sounds his "barbaric yawp," which many casual readers have labeled the uncontrolled outpourings of an undisciplined poet. True, there are times when the repetition, the ceaseless cataloguing, the too Biblical rhythms, the artificial combination of Quakerisms and first-reader French seem hardly worth wading through; but these passages contain the flaws to be found in the collected works of any poet. At his best Whitman is a master of precise diction. The opening twenty-two lines of "Out of the Cradle Endlessly Rocking" not only contain a stirring rhythm and a perfectly timed climax but also are characterized by an exquisite choice of words. In a much shorter poem, "When I Heard the Learn'd Astronomer," Whitman's form is the usual heavily accented free verse, but here again there seems hardly a word that could be changed or omitted.

Whitman has been called a "line poet" because among his many virtues is the ability to pack the memorable into a single line. Frequently these lines open his poem and he lets them double as titles: "As Toilsome I Wander'd Virginia's Woods," "Give Me the Splendid Silent Sun," "I Hear America Singing," "Goodbye My Fancy," and "I Sing the Body Electric." Whitman is so famed as the breaker of tradition, the iconoclast who broke the way for the "modern poetry" of our time, that we tend to forget his rank among the master craftsmen of English verse. Whitman underestimated himself when he said, in "Poets To Come,"

I but write one or two indicative words for the future,
I but advance a moment, only to wheel and hurry back in the darkness.

I am a man who, sauntering along, without fully stopping, turns a casual look upon you, and then averts his face,
Leaving it to you to prove and define it,
Expecting the main things from you.

Many of these "main things" are already fulfilled in *Leaves of Grass*.

THE LEGEND OF GOOD WOMEN

Type of work: Poem
Author: Geoffrey Chaucer (c. 1343-1400)
First transcribed: 1380-1386

Principal characters:
CHAUCER, the dreamer
CUPID
ALCESTE, wife of Admetus, King of Pherae
CLEOPATRA, Queen of Egypt
THISBE loved by Pyramus
DIDO, Queen of Carthage
HYPSIPYLE, Queen of Lemnos, betrayed by Jason
MEDEA, princess of Colchis, betrayed by Jason
LUCRETIA Roman matron ravished by Tarquin
ARIADNE, Cretan princess betrayed by Theseus
PHILOMELA, Athenian princess ravished by Tereus
PHYLLIS, Greek maiden betrayed by Demophon
HYPERMNESTRA, daughter of Danaüs, King of Egypt

The Legend of Good Women, a poem recounting the stories of women from history and myth who were martyrs to love, is written in the tradition of medieval love poetry. Unlike Chaucer's masterpieces, *Troilus and Criseyde* and *The Canterbury Tales,* this work only occasionally rises above the limitations imposed by the artificial conventions of the times and is, therefore, inferior to these other works. Chaucer's greatness as a poet resulted not so much from his ability to perfect the current modes of writing as it did from his capacity to transcend them. Although his debt to contemporary thought and literary practice was considerable, his high position among English writers depends largely on his gift

for bringing reality to a literature that was customarily unrealistic. In *The Legend of Good Women,* however, he constructed a framework so restricting that he was unable to infuse it with the richness and subtle shadings of human existence.

The most engaging part of the poem is the prologue, in which Chaucer revealed his elation at the arrival of spring. He delighted in roaming through the meadows, listening to the small birds, and gazing at the flowers. He was especially attracted to the daisy, which he could observe for hours without becoming bored. One spring day, after a walk in the fields, he fell asleep and had a vision in which the God of Love and the beautiful Alceste, dressed in the colors of the daisy, appeared before him. Cupid denounced the dreamer for committing heresy against the laws of love by writing of Criseyde's infidelity and by translating *The Romance of the Rose* with its disparaging remarks about womankind. But Cupid's companion (the same Alceste whom Hercules rescued from Hades after she had given her life to redeem her husband from death) rose to the poet's defense by contending that he, having appropriated his plots from other writers, acted out of ignorance, not malice. She concluded that he might gain Cupid's forgiveness by writing a legendary of wives and maidens who had been faithful in love all their lives.

The prologue is filled with literary devices popular in the fourteenth century. The religion of love—with its sins, penances, self-abnegation, and sanctity, with its Cupid and Alceste analogous to God and the Virgin Mary—closely paralleled the Christian religion. The daisy, having recently replaced the rose, was the symbol of love. The question of whether the flower or the leaf was superior, apparently a hotly debated issue in courtly circles, Chaucer touches upon, but without committing himself. The dream-vision used here had been a very popular device ever since the appearance of *The Romance of the Rose*, Chaucer himself employing it in several works. Despite this elaborate machinery, which today is mainly of historic interest, the prologue has about it a universal appeal; cheerfulness, humor, and a tinge of ironic detachment preserve it from mediocrity. Also of special excellence is Chaucer's expression of his delight in nature.

According to the prologue, Chaucer planned to write twenty tales concerning good women. He finished eight and left a ninth just short of completion. The theme of all the legends is the fidelity of women in love. All the heroines suffer for, and the majority die for, their love. All are treated as wholly admirable, even saintly, without regard to the illicit nature of some of the relationships presented. Events in their lives not concerned with their fidelity are omitted or hastily summarized. With the exception of the first two legends, the women suffer as the result of the treachery of men, who generally are as thoroughgoing in their villainy as the women are in their virtue.

The longest and one of the best of the legends retells the story of Dido's love for Aeneas. After Aeneas had landed on the Libyan coast, he met Venus, his mother, who instructed him to go to the court of Dido, Queen of Carthage. Dido greeted him cordially and, knowing his flight from Troy, felt great pity for the disinherited hero. And with her pity, came love. For comfort and entertainment during his visit, she provided everything riches could command.

One day, when Aeneas, Dido, and her retinue were hunting, a thunderstorm burst upon them. Everyone rushed for shelter, and Dido and Aeneas found themselves in the same cave. There the perfidious Aeneas protested his love for her; and she, upon much importuning, had pity and yielded herself to him. For a time, Aeneas performed all the duties of a courtly lover, but finally, becoming weary, he made plans to leave. When Dido, noting his lessened ardor, asked what was wrong, he told her of a vision (a pure fabrication, Chaucer implied) in which his father reminded him of his destiny to conquer Italy. Ignoring her pleas, Aeneas stole away to his ships without her. As soon as she discovered his absence, she had her sister build a funeral pyre upon which, using Aeneas' sword, she stabbed herself.

Chaucer's principal source for this tale was Vergil's *Aeneid.* With slight modifications of the plot, Chaucer made substantial changes in characterization. Dido, who did not escape Vergil's censure, was made blameless by Chaucer, mainly by his elaboration of the scene in the cave. With a minimizing of the intervention of the gods and a degrading of his motives, the pious Aeneas of Vergil became in

Chaucer's hands a mere seducer. Thus a story of tragic struggle between love and duty was transformed into one of man's treachery and woman's loyalty.

Chaucer's source for "The Legend of Lucretia" was Ovid's *Fasti*, which he followed rather closely. To prove the virtues of his wife Lucretia, Collatinus offered to accompany Tarquin, the king's son, to Rome to see her. Secreted outside her chamber door, they found her spinning among her servants and expressing concern for her husband's safety. Tarquin, observing her natural beauty, conceived a great desire for her. The next day, his lust increasing, he determined to return to Collatinus' house and make Lucretia his lover. Stealing into her room at night, he threatened her at sword's point and, while she lay in a swoon, ravished her. After he had left, Lucretia dressed in mourning, called her friends about her, and revealed to them the vile deed. Telling them that her husband should not gain a foul name from her guilt, she brought forth a knife and stabbed herself.

"The Legend of Hypsipyle and Medea" recounts the double treachery of Jason. On his expedition to recover the Golden Fleece, Jason, accompanied by Hercules, stopped at the island of Lemnos, where they met Queen Hypsipyle, and conspired in capturing her affections for Jason. While Jason counterfeited modesty, his virtues were extolled by Hercules. Thus Hypsipyle was ensnared and consented to marry him. After making use of her wealth and begetting two children upon her, he left. Although he ignored her letter imploring him to return, she remained true to him and died of a broken heart.

Arriving at Colchis, Jason was entertained by King Aeëtes. Medea, the king's daughter, became enamored of Jason and revealed to him that the Golden Fleece could be secured only with her help. They agreed to marry, and Jason made a solemn promise never to be untrue. Later, after the expedition had been successful, Jason again proved false and left her to marry Creüsa.

Toward the end of *The Legend of Good Women*, Chaucer indicated a definite weariness with his subject. By adhering to his original plan, he wrote tales that have a tiresome sameness about them. Committed to perfect women and, in most instances, evil men, he found it difficult to develop his characters. A further deterrent to good characterization was his effort to keep the tales brief; some, as a result, are little more than plot summaries. Upon Dido he lavished more attention than on his other heroines, and she is his most lifelike portrait. There are good touches in other female characters; for example, the pathos of Lucretia in her death scene and the mingled fear and courage of Thisbe. His men, however, are little more than abstractions.

These tales mark a step toward Chaucer's later work, for in this poem he first used the decasyllabic couplet, afterward employed so successfully in *The Canterbury Tales*. His juxtaposing of *The Legend of Good Women* with *Troilus and Criseyde* prepared him for the more subtle contrasts of the Marriage Group. The work may have been left unfinished because of Chaucer's growing absorption with *The Canterbury Tales*. Although *The Legend of Good Women* is not without merit, this redirection of his efforts can hardly be regretted.

THE LEGEND OF SLEEPY HOLLOW

Type of work: Tale
Author: Washington Irving (1783-1859)
Type of plot: Regional romance
Time of plot: Eighteenth century
Locale: New York State

First published: 1819-1820

Principal characters:
ICHABOD CRANE, a schoolteacher
KATRINA VAN TASSEL, a rustic heiress
ABRAHAM VAN BRUNT, known as Brom Bones

Critique:

Washington Irving, the first professional writer in America, was by inclination an amused observer of people and customs. By birth he was in a position to be that observer. Son of a New York merchant in good financial standing, he was the youngest of eleven children, several of whom helped him to take prolonged trips to Europe for his health and fancy. He was responsible for two trends in American literature: one, toward the local color, legendary tale; the other, toward the historical novel. "The Legend of Sleepy Hollow" belongs to the first trend. It was first published in Irving's *The Sketch Book of Geoffrey Crayon, Gent.*, the book which established his reputation at home and abroad.

The Story:

Near Tarry Town on the Hudson is a little valley which, years ago, was the quietest place in the world. A drowsy influence hung over the place and people so that the region was known as Sleepy Hollow, and the lads were called Sleepy Hollow boys. Some said that the valley was bewitched. True it was that marvelous stories were told there.

The main figure to haunt the valley was one on horseback, without a head. Some said the specter was the apparition of a Hessian horseman who had lost his head to a cannon ball, but, whatever it was, it was often seen in the valley and adjacent countryside in the gloom of winter nights. The specter was known to all as the Headless Horseman of Sleepy Hollow.

In the valley, years ago, there lived a schoolteacher called Ichabod Crane. He looked like a scarecrow because of his long, skinny frame and his snipe-like nose.

As was the custom in that fertile Dutch countryside, he boarded with the parents of his pupils a week at a time. Fortunately for him the Dutch larders were full and the tables groaning with food, for the schoolmaster had a wonderful appetite. He was always welcome in the country homes because in small ways he made himself useful to the farmers. He was patient with the children, and he loved to spend the long winter nights with the families of his pupils, exchanging tales of ghosts and haunted places while ruddy apples roasted on the hearths.

Ichabod believed heartily in ghosts, and his walks home after an evening of tale-telling were often filled with fear. His only source of courage at those times was his voice, loud and nasal as it made the night resound with many a psalm tune.

The schoolteacher picked up a little odd change by holding singing classes. In one of his classes he first became aware of a plump and rosy-cheeked girl named Katrina Van Tassel. She was the only child of a very substantial farmer, and that fact added to her charms for the ever-hungry Ichabod. Since she was not only beautiful but also lively, she was a great favorite among the lads in the neighborhood.

Abraham Van Brunt was Katrina's favorite squire. The Dutch first shortened his name to Brom, and then called him Brom Bones when he became known for the tall and powerful frame of his body. He was a lively lad with a fine sense of humor and a tremendous amount of energy. When other suitors saw his horse hitched outside Katrina's house on a Sunday night, they went on their way. Brom Bones was a formidable rival for the gaunt and shaggy Ichabod. Brom would have liked to carry the battle into the open, but the schoolteacher knew better than to tangle with him physically. Brom Bones could do little but play practical jokes on lanky Ichabod.

The whole countryside was invited one fall evening to a quilting-frolic at Mynheer Van Tassel's. For the occasion Ichabod borrowed a horse from the farmer with whom he was then living. The horse, called Gunpowder, was as gaunt as Ichabod himself, but the steed still had a fair amount of spirit. The two of them were a sight as they jogged happily along to the party.

Ichabod was well pleased by every prospect he saw on the Van Tassel farm, the most prosperous holding for miles around. Perhaps Ichabod might be able to sell it and, with the proceeds, go farther west. It was a pretty picture he saw as he passed fields full of shocks of corn and pumpkins, granaries stuffed with grain, and meadows and barnlots filled with sleek cattle and plump fowls.

The party was a merry one with many lively dances. Ichabod was at his best when he danced with Katrina. After a time he went out on the dark porch with the men and exchanged more Sleepy Hollow ghost stories. But the food was best of all. Ichabod did credit to all the cakes and pies, meats and tea.

After the others left, he tarried to pay court to Katrina, but it was not long before he started home crestfallen on the gaunt Gunpowder. All the stories he had heard came back to him, and as he rode along in the darkness he became more dismal. He heard groans as the branches of the famed Major André tree rubbed against each other. He even thought he saw something moving beneath it.

When he came to the bridge over Wiley's Swamp, Gunpowder balked. The harder Ichabod urged him on, the more the horse bucked. Then, on the other side of the marsh, Ichabod saw something huge and misshapen.

The figure refused to answer him when he called. Ichabod's hair stood straight on end. Because it was too late to turn back, however, the schoolmaster kept to the road. The stranger—it looked like a headless horseman, but it seemed to hold its head on the pommel—kept pace with him, fast or slow. Ichabod could not stand going slowly and he whipped Gunpowder to a gallop. As his saddle loosened, he nearly lost his grip, but he hugged the horse around the neck. He could not even sing a psalm tune.

When he reached the church bridge, where by tradition the headless specter would disappear in a flash of fire and brimstone, Ichabod heard the horseman close in on him. As he turned to look, the spirit threw his head at him. Ichabod tried to dodge, but the head tumbled him into the dust.

In the morning a shattered pumpkin was found near the bridge. Gunpowder was grazing at the farmer's gate nearby. But Ichabod was never seen in Sleepy Hollow again. In the valley they say that Brom Bones, long after he had married the buxom Katrina, laughed heartily whenever the story was told of the horseman who had thrown his head at the schoolteacher during that ghostly midnight pursuit.

LEGEND OF THE MOOR'S LEGACY

Type of work: Tale
Author: Washington Irving (1783-1859)
Type of plot: Folklore
Time of plot: Seventeenth century
Locale: Granada, Spain
First published: 1832

PEDRO GIL, called PEREGIL, a water carrier
HIS WIFE
A MOORISH SHOPKEEPER
PEDRILLO PEDRUGO, a prying barber
THE ALCADE
A CONSTABLE

Critique:

In 1829, during his first visit to Spain, Washington Irving lived for three months in the Alhambra, the historic fortress from which the Moors had been expelled by Ferdinand and Isabella in 1492. Irving's interest in Spanish history and legend appears in many of his writings, but his Spanish material received its most finished form in *The Alhambra*, published in 1832. The book, a collection of stories drawn from actual history and from folk imagination, includes the well-known "Legend of the Moor's Legacy." Like the more familiar "Rip Van Winkle" and "The Legend of Sleepy Hollow," this tale shows Irving's love of the picturesque and his interest in the fantastic and legendary stories of many lands. The combined qualities of reverie, genial humor, and romantic imagination made him a perfect writer of traveler's tales. This legend undoubtedly goes back beyond its Spanish origins to the unknown storytellers of *The Arabian Nights' Entertainments.*

The Story:

In the Square of the Cisterns, fronting the royal palace in the fortress of the Alhambra, was a deep Moorish well of clear, cold water. So famous was the well throughout all Granada that to it repaired water carriers from every quarter of the city, some bearing great earthen jars on their own sturdy shoulders, others, more prosperous, driving donkeys similarly burdened. The well was also a great place for meeting and gossip. Each day housewives, lazy servants, beggars—idlers of every age and condition—gathered on the stone benches to talk over the doings of their neighbors and to exchange rumors which were afloat in the city.

Among the carriers who drew water from the ancient well of the Alhambra there was once a strong-backed, bandy-legged little fellow named Pedro Gil, called Peregil for short. He had begun his trade with only a single water jar, but since no one in all Granada was more industrious than he, it was not long before he was able to purchase a donkey to do his carrying for him. All day long he trudged the streets calling his wares, and for every woman, old or young, he had a merry smile and a pleasing compliment. It was not surprising that everyone thought him the happiest of men. But Peregil's heart was often heavy and sad. He had a brood of ragged children who were ravenous as young birds, so that it was all he could do to fill their mouths with food. His wife, grown slatternly and fat, nagged poor Peregil even while she spent his hard-earned money for fripperies they could not afford. Subdued to patience by his matrimonial yoke, Peregil made the best of things and concealed his frequent dejection with merry quips and songs.

Late one summer night he made one last trip to the well in hopes of adding to his small store of coppers for meat to put in the Sunday pot. He found the square empty except for a stranger in Moorish dress. When the man said that he was a traveler taken suddenly ill, Peregil, touched with compassion, gave the stranger a ride back to the city on his donkey. On the way the man confessed that he had no lodgings in the town, and he asked that he be allowed to rest under Peregil's roof. He promised that the carrier would be well repaid.

Peregil had little desire to deal in this manner with an infidel, but in the kindness of his heart he could not refuse aid to the stranger. Ignoring his wife's protests, the carrier spread a mat in the coolest part of his hovel for the sick man. Before long the Moor was seized with convulsions. Knowing that his end was near, he gave Peregil a small sandalwood box and told him that it contained the secret to a great treasure. He died before he could reveal the nature of the secret.

Peregil's wife, afraid that the body would be found in their house and that they would be charged with murder, railed at her husband for his folly. Equally disturbed, the carrier tried to mend matters by taking the dead Moor, under cover of darkness, to the bank of the river and there burying it.

Now it happened that Peregil lived opposite to a barber named Pedrillo Pedrugo, whose greatest pleasure was to spy on his neighbors and tattle their affairs. Having seen Peregil arriving with the Moor, he was still on watch when the carrier took away the body of the dead man. Following stealthily, he spied on the secret burial. Early the next morning he hurried off to the alcalde, who was one of his daily customers, and told what he had seen.

The alcalde, who put so high a value on justice that he sold it only for gold, sent a constable to bring Peregil before him. Frightened, the water carrier called upon the saints to witness his innocence and frankly related the whole story. When he produced the sandalwood box, the alcalde expected to find it filled with gold or jewels. Instead, it contained only a parchment scroll and the end of a wax taper. Disappointed, he returned the box to Peregil, but kept the carrier's donkey to pay for the trouble the poor wretch had caused.

At home, Peregil became so disgusted with his wife's taunts over the loss of his donkey that he threw the sandalwood box to the floor. When the parchment rolled out, he picked it up and found on it some writing in Arabic. Curious to know what the meaning might be, he took it to a Moorish shopkeeper of his acquaintance. The Moor said that the scroll contained an incantation for the recovery of a treasure hidden under the Alhambra.

At first Peregil was skeptical. Several days later, however, he heard loiterers by the well talking about a treasure supposed to be buried under the Tower of the Seven Floors in the old fortress. Once more he went to the Moor and proposed that they search for the treasure together. The Moor replied that the incantation was powerless without a magic candle to burn while the charm was being read. Peregil said that the taper was also in his possession.

Later that night he and the Moor went secretly to the Tower of the Seven Floors and descended into the damp, musty vault beneath. There they lit the taper and the Moor began to read the words on the parchment. As he finished, the floor opened with a noise like thunder. Descending the steps thus revealed, they found themselves in another vault, where stood a chest and several great jars filled with gold coins and precious stones, over which two enchanted Moorish warriors stood guard. Amazed and fearful, they filled their pockets with valuables. Then they climbed the stairs and blew out the taper. The floor closed again with a ponderous crash.

Peregil and the Moor hoped to keep their secret safe, but the carrier could conceal nothing from his wife. She bought herself expensive clothing and put on so many fine airs that her neighbors became curious. One day the barber saw her after she had decked herself with some of the jewels Peregil had found. Once more Pedrillo hurried to the alcalde to tell his story. The alcalde, convinced that Peregil had tricked him, ordered the trembling water carrier dragged into his presence.

After Peregil's story had been confirmed by the Moor, the alcalde's greed for gold became almost more than he could bear. That night, taking Peregil and the Moor with them as prisoners, the alcalde, the constable, and the prying barber went to the tower. With them they took the donkey Peregil had once owned. There in the vault the taper was lighted and the Moor read the incantation. Again the floor rolled aside, revealing the treasure vault beneath. The alcalde and his friends were too frightened to descend, but they ordered Peregil to bring up two immense jars filled with gold and gems and to strap them on the donkey which they had brought to carry away the spoils. When they learned that the vault also contained a chest filled with treasure, the alcalde, the constable, and the barber overcame their fears sufficiently to go down the stairs to secure the riches for themselves. After they had entered the lower vault, the Moor blew out the taper, and the floor closed over the men below, leaving them entombed in darkness. The Moor, assuring Peregil that such was the will of Allah, threw away the magic taper.

Peregil and the Moor divided the treasure equally between them. A short time later the Moor returned to his native city of Tangier. Peregil, with his wife, his brood of children, and his sturdy donkey, went to Portugal, where his wife used his riches to make him a man of consequence, known to all as Don Pedro Gil. As for the greedy alcalde, the constable, and the prying barber, they remain under the Tower of the Seven Floors to this day.

THE LEGEND OF TYL ULENSPIEGEL

Type of work: Novel
Author: Charles Théodore Henri de Coster (1827-1879)
Type of plot: Historical romance
Time of plot: Sixteenth century
Locale: The Low Countries
First published: 1867

Principal characters:
>   TYL ULENSPIEGEL, the wanderer
>   CLAES, his father
>   SOETKIN, his mother
>   NELE, his wife
>   LAMME GOEDZAK, his companion
>   KATHELINE, a midwife
>   HANS DUDZEELE, Katheline's betrayer
>   PHILIP, King of Spain

Critique:

The glorious adventures of Tyl Ulenspiegel and Lamme Goedzak are well-known to readers of most countries of the world. De Coster's book is a heroic epic based on folk legend and history, a story complete with visions, high adventures, traitors, and heroes. Ulenspiegel was the spirit of his native land, and he had been born to deliver her from her oppressors. Always the parallel between him and King Philip is carefully drawn: Philip a destroyer and Ulenspiegel a savior. De Coster preserved the old legends of Flanders, and his account of the Flemish hero maintains its great popularity even today.

The Story:

Tyl Ulenspiegel was born with two marks, one the sign of a lucky star, the other the print of the devil's finger. Katheline, the midwife, had a vision in which she saw Ulenspiegel as the incarnated spirit of his native Flanders. At the same time Philip of Spain was born.

In her vision Katheline saw Philip as the butcher of Flanders. She was afraid.

As a boy Ulenspiegel roamed the fields of Flanders. His playmate was Nele, illegitimate daughter of Katheline the midwife. But as the children played, gloom gathered over the lowlands. The father of Philip fished in the pockets of the people, and each day new edicts announced torture and death for heretics. The Inquisition was beginning, and neighbor turned against neighbor in order to inherit half his possessions. Katheline was tortured as a witch on the complaint of a neighbor. As a result of this experience the poor woman went mad.

Ulenspiegel, as a young man living by his wits, traveled into many lands. Sometimes he was hard pressed to escape with his life, but his high spirit and great strength served him well. When he returned at last to his homeland he had to put his youthful follies behind him, for trouble had come to his family. Claes had been convicted of heresy on the testimony of a fishmonger who wanted to inherit part of his wealth. The good man was tortured and burned to slow death. Soetkin and Ulenspiegel wept, helpless to save him. Ulenspiegel took ashes from Claes' heart and wore them in a bag around his neck after swearing eternal vengeance upon the murderers. Because Soetkin and Nele had hidden Claes' money, the searchers looked for it in vain. Then Soetkin and Ulenspiegel were put to torture, but although they were broken on the wheel and burned they would not reveal their secret. Meanwhile Claes' ashes beat against Ulenspiegel's heart.

In spite of their courage the money was lost. Mad Katheline told Hans, her evil lover, and Nele's father, where the money was hidden. Hans and a friend robbed the widow and son of their inheritance. Then Hans, not knowing that mad Katheline watched him, killed his accomplice. Ulenspiegel, meeting the lying fishmonger, threw his enemy into the water. Philip, now King of Spain, robbed and murdered his people and the people of Flanders.

After Soetkin died of her grief and her torture, Ulenspiegel vowed to avenge her and Claes and all of his loved homeland. Mad Katheline conjured up a vision from which Ulenspiegel learned that he could be avenged if he sought and found the Seven. Not knowing who the Seven were, he left Nele to seek them. With him went Lamme Goedzak, a fat buffoon seeking his wife, who had left him because she had been told by a monk to give up lusts of the flesh and enter a nunnery. Lamme drowned his grief in food and wine, but the ashes of Claes burned against Ulenspiegel's heart. Knowing no peace, he looked only for the Seven.

He and Lamme joined the army of William of Orange, leader of the forces against Philip and the Inquisition. They traveled over many lands, sometimes alone and sometimes with Prince William's troops. Often they were in danger of death by torture, but God protected them and kept them safe. Several times Lamme or Ulenspiegel caught glimpses of Lamme's wife, but Lamme could not catch up with her. The two friends saw much blood spilled, until they were weary of war and torture. Still Ulenspiegel looked for the Seven.

Ulenspiegel served Orange well. In spite of all resistance, however, Philip conquered all of the Low Countries and the people suffered and starved. When Hans returned to Katheline for more money, the mad woman, not knowing what she did, accused him of witchery. He was tortured and condemned to slow death by fire. Katheline, too, was given a witch's trial by water. Although she sank to the bottom, proving her innocence, the poor madwoman died three days later from the chill and the shock.

Nele, now an orphan, left Flanders and traveled to Holland. There she saved the life of Ulenspiegel, who was on the gallows for accusing his commander of false promises. The two lovers were married. Together they traveled with Lamme, who continued to seek his wife. Still the robbery and killings went on, and still Ulen-

1657

spiegel searched for the Seven who could tel him how to avenge his family and save Flanders. William of Orange began to gain victories. Philip, enraged, demanded more and more bloodshed.

Ulenspiegel was placed in command of a ship, with Lamme for his cook. After a battle in which Lamme was injured, they brought on board a captive monk who was fat and lustful. His torture was that he must eat all that Lamme prepared for him, seven times a day, and he must live in a cage just big enough to enclose his great bulk. Before Lamme could get the monk fat enough to burst, Lamme's wound reopened and in his delirious condition he had to be tied to the ship so that he would not fall into the sea.

One night Lamme's wife came aboard the ship, treated his wound, and cured it. He pursued her as she fled in her boat, caught her, and heard her story. A monk, the one whom Lamme had imprisoned in a cage, had preached to her and ordered her to give up lusts of the flesh and follow him. In her innocence she had deserted her husband and gone away with the monk. Lamme feared that she had given herself to the monk, but when he learned that she had not, he took her again as his wife. The two happy lovers left Ulenspiegel and Nele and went to restore their lost home.

After William of Orange lost his life, his son carried on the battle for liberty and the lowlands were soon freed. In a vision Nele and Ulenspiegel saw at last the Seven that were and the Seven that should be, if their native land was to be free. The Seven that were now were Pride, Gluttony, Idleness, Avarice, Anger, Envy, and Lust. In the vision Ulenspiegel was told to burn the Seven. When he burned them, they were reduced to ashes and blood ran. Then from Pride came forth Noble Spirit; from Gluttony, Appetite; from Idleness, Reverie; from Avarice, Economy; from Anger, Vivacity; from Envy, Emulation, and lastly from Lust sprang forth Love. Then a mighty hand hurled Nele into space and came again and hurled Ulenspiegel into space after her. Nele awoke from the vision, but Ulenspiegel lay as one dead for two days and two nights. When a priest passed by on the way to a burial, he ordered a grave dug that Ulenspiegel might be buried by the church. But Ulenspiegel rose up from the grave and threw off the dirt, for he knew that his motherland was free at last. The new Seven would be her salvation. He knew, too, that Nele was the heart and he was the spirit of the new Flanders, and that they could never die.

LETTERS FROM AN AMERICAN FARMER

Type of work: Epistolary essays
Author: Michel-Guillaume Jean de Crèvecœur (1735-1813)
First published: London, 1782; Philadelphia, 1793

When, in 1759, Voltaire published his *Candide*, Crèvecœur was already planning to cultivate his garden, hewn out of the Pennsylvania frontier. Like Voltaire's naïve hero, he had seen too much of the horrors of the civilized world and was more than ready to retire to his bucolic paradise, where for nineteen years he lived in peace and happiness until the civilized world routed him and his family with the outbreak of the American Revolution. The twelve essays that make up his *Letters from an American Farmer* are an unfamiliar pen. The opening letter presents the central theme quite clearly: the decadence of European civilization makes the American frontier one of the great hopes for a regeneration of mankind. He wonders why men travel to Italy to "amuse themselves in viewing the ruins of temples . . . half-ruined amphitheatres and the putrid fevers of the Campania must fill the mind with most melancholy reflections." By contrast, he delights in the humble rudiments and embryos of societies spreading everywhere in the colonies, men converting large forests into pleasing fields and creating thirteen provinces of easy subsistence and political harmony. He has his interlocutor say of him, "Your mind is . . . a *Tabula rasa* where spontaneous and strong impressions are delineated with felicity." Similarly, he sees the American continent as a clean slate on which men can inscribe a new society and the good life. It may be said that Crèvecœur is a Lockian gone romantic, but retaining just enough practical good sense to see that reality is not rosy. "Men are like plants;" the crude, occasionally eloquent, testimony of a man trying desperately to convince himself and his readers that it was possible to live the idealized life advocated by Rousseau.

With a becoming modesty, appropriate to a man who had learned English at sixteen, Crèvecœur begins with a confession of his literary inadequacy and decides simply to write down what he would say. But his style is not smoothly colloquial. Except in a few passages in which conviction generates enthusiasm, one senses the strain of the unlettered man wielding he says, "the goodness and flavour of the fruit proceeds from the peculiar soil and exposition in which they grow."

The first image Crèvecœur presents is perhaps a bit too idyllic for modern taste. He dandles his little boy on the plow as his wife sits at the edge of the field knitting and praising the straightness of the furrows, while birds fill the air with summer melodies. "Who can listen unmoved to the sweet love tales of our robins told from tree to tree?" Nevertheless, this is the testimony of a man who for nineteen years actually lived at the edge of the wilderness, three hundred miles from the Atlantic. He was no Thoreau at Walden Pond within easy walking distance of friends, family, and a highly developed New England culture at Concord. He was, instead, a responsible man, who cleared 371 acres of virgin land and raised enough crops and animals to provide for his family, Negro

hands, and all peaceful strangers who chanced to appear at his door. Also unlike Thoreau (with whom he inevitably invites comparison), he was acutely aware of his social responsibilities and enormously proud of the superior way in which they could be fulfilled in the New World. No doubt it was the third epistle, "What Is An American?" that caught the attention of Benjamin Franklin and the Europeans of the Age of Enlightenment:

> [America] is not composed, as in Europe, of great lords who possess everything, and of a herd of people who have nothing. Here are no aristocratical families, no courts, no kings, no bishops, no ecclesiastical dominion, no invisible power giving to a few a very visible one; no great manufacturers employing thousands, no great refinements of luxury. The rich and the poor are not so far removed from each other as they are in Europe. . . . We are the most perfect society now existing in the world.

Enthusiastic as this description is, it is not as extravagant as it might be; Crèvecœur does not claim that the colonies had founded the best of all possible worlds. He is, for example, acutely aware of the paradox that religious influence gradually declines as one goes west; instead of liberating men, it reduces them to a perfect state of war, man against man. Yet he rejoices that there are almost no concentrated religious sects preying upon each other: "Zeal in Europe is confined . . . a grain of powder enclosed; here it burns away in the open air, and consumes without effect."

Furthermore, not every man succeeds after arriving in the New World—only the sober, the honest, the industrious. In his "History of Andrew, the Hebridean," Crèvecœur presents a case history of the Horatio Alger hero in primitive America, the story of a simple illiterate Scotchman who after four years of sweat and toil became a prospering freeholder. Franklin had occasion to caution his friends in France that Crèvecœur's was a highly colored account.

Part of the coloring is contributed by the pervasive nature imagery. The freedom and beauty of birds seem to symbolize the condition man might achieve when he immerses himself in nature. Crèvecœur describes hours spent in quiet admiration of the hummingbirds, tells regretfully of shooting a kingbird to rescue bees (of 171 removed from its craw, 54 returned to life), describes the feeding and care of quail in the winter. Insects, too, fascinated him; he kept a hornet's nest in the house. The letter on rattlers and copperheads is as horrendous and awesome as anything in Bartram. Here Crèvecœur tells of copperheads enticing birds by the power of their eyes, of a defanged rattler trained as a pet, of a pair of snakes in mortal combat. Most curious of all is the account of a farmer who kicked away a snake that had thrust its fangs into his boot. After pulling off his boots that night, he suddenly became violently ill, writhed horribly, and died. His son, inheriting the boots, suffered the same fate. A neighbor, next in succession, almost died, too, but was saved when a shrewd doctor located the poison-filled fangs stuck in the boot. Crèvecœur in these passages reveals an exciting narrative power.

Apart from the agricultural life inland, Crèvecœur praises most the industry and sobriety of the coastal fishing communities at Nantucket and Martha's Vineyard, where "perfect equanimity prevails." At Nantucket (which, oddly, he locates north of Boston), five thousand prosperous people inhabited a place which in Europe would have housed a few simple fishermen. Their Yankee ingenuity and sound business sense had enabled them to build—beginning with one whale boat —a whaling fleet that ranged even to the South Seas. And Martha's Vineyard was already the "nursery" of seamen for the entire east coast. So detailed is Crèvecœur's description of the chase, the ferocity of the whale's struggle, the dangers from sharks and thrasher whales,

the processing of blubber into whale oil —in short, the entire experience, that one wonders how Melville could have overlooked it in compiling the extracts in *Moby Dick* (1851).

Crèvecœur found Nantucket such a model community that it contained only one minister (a Presbyterian, for the Quakers, much to Crèvecœur's delight, do not have special ministers), two doctors, one lawyer (seldom employed), no soldiers, no governors. "Happy the people who are subject to so mild a government; happy the government which has to rule over such harmless and such industrious subjects! . . . I wish I had it in my power to send the most persecuting bigot I could find in —— to the whale fisheries; in three or four years you would find him a much more tractable man and therefore a better Christian." But colonial Nantucket was apparently not perfect; the Quakers persisted in their ungrammatical English, did not tolerate any deviation from their sober customs and homespun dress, sternly prohibited music, singing, and dancing. "Such an island . . . is not the place where gay travellers should resort in order to enjoy the variety of pleasures the more splendid towns of this continent afford." Crèvecœur also reports, obviously misled by some notorious gossip, that the women were addicted to opium. "But," he philosophizes, "where is the society perfectly free from error and folly?"

Crèvecœur's criticism is reserved for the most European of American cities, Charles-Town, "gayest in America . . . centre of our beau monde." Lawyers, planters, and merchants make up the population, all addicted to dangerous excesses of all kinds. At the heart of this social corruption, Crèvecœur finds the brutal institution of slavery. He tells the horrifying tale of his chance encounter with a Negro who had been driven to kill an overseer. As his punishment he had been suspended from a tree in a cage for two days. Vicious birds had already plucked out his eyes and bared his cheekbones. No sooner were the birds dispersed than swarms of insects covered him. The miserable man begged for water and hoped it was poisoned. "Gracious God!" cries Crèvecœur, "to what end is the introduction of so many beings into [such] a mode of existence! . . . Is there then no superintending power who conducts the moral operations of the world?"

Some of Crèvecœur's faith is restored by the spectacle of the humble, kind, and generous aspect of William Bartram, the Quaker botanist, whose Negroes were salaried free men, workers on his plantation, companions at his table, and worshipers at the Friends' meeting house.

But the *Letters from an American Farmer* end in ominous tones of impending tragedy. Unwilling to commit his allegiance to either the British or the colonists, Crèvecœur finds it necessary to flee: "Must I in order to be called a faithful subject, coolly and philosophically say it is necessary for the good of Britain that my children's brains should be dashed

against the walls of the house in which they were reared; that my wife should be stabbed and scalped before my face; that I should be either murdered or captivated?" To escape such a fate, Crèvecœur develops an intricate plan to take his family to join an Indian settlement in the uncultivated wilderness (a plan which he never actually carried out). It is, of course, tragically ironic that this mild Frenchman's absolute certainty of the blessings of life in the colonies should be so violently shattered after nineteen years of expending all his energies to make a decent life possible. But it is also ironically appropriate that his final impulse is to immerse himself deeper into nature by joining the Indians. Whatever flaws it may have, *Letters from an American Farmer* is the most sympathetic and thoughtful of all eighteenth-century analyses of frontier life and its shaping influence on the emerging American character.

LETTERS FROM THE UNDERWORLD

Type of work: Novel
Author: Fyodor Mikhailovich Dostoevski (1821-1881)
Type of plot: Impressionistic realism
Time of plot: Mid-nineteenth century
Locale: St. Petersburg, Russia
First published: 1864

      Principal characters:
        THE NARRATOR
        SIMONOV, his acquaintance from school days
        ZVERKOV, a young Russian officer
        LIZA, a prostitute

Critique:

Letters from the Underworld, sometimes called also *Notes from Underground,* is actually more than an extended and bitter prose fiction. The first part constitutes a philosophical statement; the second part is the morbid illustration from life of this statement. The "underworld" of the title apparently is the depths of

degradation and humiliation to which the too acutely conscious human being can descend because of a perverse human quality, a factor which, according to Dostoevski, scientists will never neatly label. This quality resists fruition, completion, and whatever we tend to call the normal state of happiness. Dostoevski's arrestingly paradoxical affirmation, in the first part of this work, of the stupendous force of individuality in human nature may provide consolation for the present-day man who feels that modern social forces are molding him more and more into an uncomfortable sameness with his neighbors. The book was written after Dostoevski's return from exile in Siberia. It serves as an arrow to point the direction of his later novels.

The Story:

The Narrator, addressing an imaginary group of acquaintances, declared that after many years of life as a rude and spiteful government official, and after many years as a recluse, he was not really bitter in his heart. Something perverse in him, his acute consciousness, had led him to find pleasure in the pain of humiliating experiences.

From experience, he advised against intellectual acuteness. The intellectual, when faced with revenge, surrounded himself with a legion of doubts; then he would crawl into his self-imposed rat's nest and torture himself with petty spite. The direct man, in wreaking revenge, might with dispatch hit his head against a wall, but he would accept the wall. But the intellectual would not accept the wall. Indeed, he would feel responsibility for the presence of the wall.

The Narrator declared that he had always had to feign taking offense and that he had had, in the face of life's transiency, to pretend to love. Life to him was a colossal bore. He could never avenge wrongs done him because the culprit, the culprit's motives, and the very misdeed itself were all phantoms in his doubting intellect.

Given another chance at life, he would have chosen a career of complete laziness, one in which he might have reveled among good and beautiful things. He declared that even if man knew absolutely what things in life were to his best advantage, he would perversely avoid these things.

The Narrator advanced the idea that

man may be destined for creativeness, and for this reason, conscious of his fate, he perversely practiced destruction to individuate himself. Perhaps man was fearful of completion, of perfection; perhaps he found final attainment distasteful: life consisted in the attaining, not in the attainment. He concluded his philosophical soliloquy by pointing out that conscious inertia was the ideal state. He provocatively insisted that he did not believe a word he had written, that he had written only because the written word seemed imposing and dignified. He was oppressed by memories which were evoked by the fall of snow outside.

At the age of twenty-four the Narrator had an inchoate character. He talked to no one. His intense self-consciousness caused him to be vain at one moment and self-loathing the next. He tried to look intelligent and feared any eccentricity in himself. This acute awareness of self made him lonely, yet he felt superior to others. He became a recluse. He read voraciously and began to walk the streets at night.

One night he saw a man thrown out of the window of a billiard parlor. In envy, he went into the parlor in the hope that he, too, might be thrown out. He was humiliated when an officer shoved him aside without noticing him. He returned the next night, but, morally fearful that all the fools in the parlor would jeer at his being thrown out, he did not enter. Dedicated to revenge, he followed the officer about for months. He learned the officer's name and wrote a satirical novel in which the officer was the principal character. The novel was rejected; its style was out of date.

Two years passed. He wrote a letter challenging the officer to a duel, but he did not mail the letter. Instead, he began to take regular walks along the river promenade, where he reveled in his resentment. One Sunday he was rudely pushed aside by the officer. Maddened at his weakness, he conceived the idea of not giving way next time. He gloated over his idea. He practiced pushing aside an imaginary officer. His courage had failed him once, but he finally stood his ground when the officer tried again to push him aside. Actually, the officer did not notice him at all, but he was delirious with happiness in having gained back his self-respect.

The Narrator now began to daydream. In his fantasies, he brought beauty and good to the world. During the fever pitch of his dream life, feeling the need of companionship, he visited his immediate superior, Anton, and sat in silence with Anton's family for hours.

He called on an old schoolmate, Simonov, and found Simonov planning, with two other old schoolmates, a farewell dinner for Zverkov, a fellow student of the direct, not too acutely-conscious type, whom he hated. Zverkov, a wealthy man, was successful in the army. The Narrator, greeted coldly by his boyhood acquaintances, invited himself to the dinner party. The other young men agreed reluctantly; he was obviously not a favorite with them. Later he detested himself for consciously having opened himself up to humiliation, but secretly he rather enjoyed having discomfited his companions.

The next day he dressed for the dinner with doubt and misgiving. He wanted to make a great impression; he wanted to eclipse the popular Zverkov. Yet he knew that he really did not want to do this either. He arrived too early and was humiliated by his wait. During the dinner he antagonized everyone and drank incontinently. Having thoroughly degraded himself, he offered conciliation and sought the love of his companions. When he apologized to Zverkov for insulting him, Zverkov humiliated him by saying that such as he could not possibly

insult him. Filled with a wild, unreasonable intention of slapping Zverkov and fighting a duel with him, he followed the others to a brothel.

Here, a young girl was brought into the parlor to him; he was pleased with the prospect of being repulsive to her. He slept off his drunkenness, awoke, and delivered a bookish, insincere sermon to Liza, the prostitute, on the hazards of her profession. He was attitudinizing and he knew it to his shame. He told her of the importance of human love, something about which he actually knew nothing. Liza, to prove to him that she was not entirely lost, showed him a love letter that she had received from a young gentleman. He gave her his address and left her.

The next day he regretted having given Liza his address. He hated himself for his insincerity with her; he feared her coming. But she did not come. He imagined an idyllic relationship between himself and Liza. He would be her tutor and would mold her into a perfect creature.

When Liza finally came, she was confused by the wretched conditions in the poor Narrator's rooms. She said that she had left the brothel. Alarmed, he confessed his insincerity and declared that he had sought power over someone because he himself had been humiliated. Liza understood his inner turmoil and took him in her arms.

Liza's intuition soon told her, however, that he was despicable and that he was incapable of love. After she left his rooms, he ran after her to seek her forgiveness, but he never saw her again. He derived some consolation from the thought that her resentment of him would give her pleasure for the rest of her life.

THE LETTERS OF WALPOLE

Type of work: Letters
Author: Horace Walpole (1717-1797)
Collected editions published: Letters, edited by Peter Cunningham, 1857-1859 (9 vols.); Letters, edited by Mrs. Paget Toynbee, 1903-1905 (16 vols.); *The Yale Edition of Horace Walpole's Correspondence*, edited by W. S. Lewis, 1937-continuing

No student, not even a general reader, interested in the eighteenth century and its culture in England can afford to overlook Horace Walpole and his works. Walpole's life spanned eighty years of that century, and the man himself engaged in most of the activities of the times in one way or another. His interests lay in many areas—political, literary, artistic, antiquarian, horticultural, architectural, and social. He was novelist, playwright, historian, member of Parliament, the son of a prime minister, an arbiter of artistic excellence, a publisher, a collector, and, among other things, an inveterate letter writer. It is anticipated that the monumental collected edition of the letters, the Yale edition now in progress, will eventually reach a total of fifty volumes.

In the realm of literature alone, Walpole had an amazing record of production, even for an age notorious for its prolific writers. Walpole wrote a novel, a comedy, a tragedy, some poetry, memoirs of the eighteenth-century Hanoverian kings of England, a volume on the career of the infamous Richard III, a catalogue of royal and noble English authors, a work on painting in England, and other writings. Although his novel, *The Castle of Otranto,* has always had some vogue, his letters have received more attention in the past hundred years. Walpole would probably approve, for he himself said that letters were the best key to the history of an age. Indeed, it seems that he wrote his correspondence with posterity in mind and according to something resembling a plan. That the letters have had continued popularity is due to their intrinsic worth, as well as their historical significance. Walpole had a pleasant style, and it must have been a pleasure to have been a recipient of his letters, as Horace Mann was, for example, over a period of more than forty years.

The language of Walpole's letters seems modern, for the idiom is attractive and anything but dated. And they are never boring. One reason for their effect is the fact that the letters are seldom about the author himself. Walpole wrote, rather, about the world, its main outlines as he knew them and its details as he observed them. He saw the world in its larger relationships, but he also had an eye and mind that were cognizant of little things. A chronic victim of the gout in later life, he seldom used his letters to indulge in self-pity. Though a thoughtful man, he did not inject into the letters a mass of subjective philosophizing; though an active man, he did not expatiate upon his activities from a personal point of view. There is always a conversational tone to the letters. They read much the same way that an eighteenth-century salon conversation probably sounded. Occasional improprieties, slight bursts of anger, the gossip, the wit, even the diction, are those which one probably would have heard among the well bred people with whom Walpole was familiar.

The subject matter of the letters is almost universal, though centered in the strata of the world that Walpole knew, the world of the Whig aristocracy of eighteenth-century England, a gay, intelligent, if somewhat superficial world from the twentieth-century viewpoint.

Certain letters have achieved eminence above others. In the main, they are those letters frequently referred to as "set pieces." They include the letters describing the trial of rebellious Jacobite peers, after the abortive revolution of 1745, of which Walpole gives an almost day-to-day account. They include a description of the executions, which Walpole apparently did not witness, of Balmerino and Lord Kilmarnock. Two funerals are also famous in Walpole's correspondence: one the funeral of George II of England, the other the funeral in Paris of the Duke de Tresmes, governor of Paris and a marshal of France.

While the "set pieces" have their place, it is the very bulk and scope of subject matter that is most important in Walpole's letters, a bulk which is impossible merely to catalogue, for somewhere in the letters Walpole seems to have hit upon almost every subject significant (and some not so significant) in his time. Highwaymen, prisons, slavery, Strawberry Hill, the ins and outs of politics, London gossip, dueling, Benjamin Franklin, George Washington, General Howe and his army, marriages, divorces, masquerades, dinner parties, the weather (usual and unusual), balloons, Captain Cook's voyages, sea-bathing, the French Revolution—all these and many more are to be found as subjects in the letters. Some readers may argue that the correspondence is too large in bulk and too slightly organized, but perhaps those supposed weaknesses are the very strength of the *Letters*. Plato wrote his philosophy in the form of dialogues so that the reader would have to participate and learn actively; in somewhat similar fashion the reader of Walpole's letters must in a sense participate in the writer's account of eighteenth-century life, filling in the larger outline from the smaller items presented.

Walpole's purposes in writing the letters now seems clear. He was reporting the age to selected friends, many of whom were recipients of his letters for many years. At the same time Walpole seems to have been careful to write so that a larger audience might eventually appreciate what he wrote. He lived in an age when letter writing was decidedly an art, and yet the polish of his letters, the careful selection of details, and the superb control of the prose rhythms in many of them indicate that extraordinary care was lavished upon his correspondence. so that it became in Walpole's mind the best means for presenting a history of his time, being immediate, flexible, and open to varying levels of formality and tone. The letters were written in the main to selected people, a circumstance which made it easier for him to write what he did and as he did. And scholars have

pointed out, in a sense Walpole's correspondence substituted space for time. The largest number of letters went to Horace Mann, British envoy at Florence. Writing to a man he met but once, a man who lived at considerable distance, culturally as well as geographically, Walpole had a fine recipient for letters containing what may be termed the main strand, of his social history.

In the letters to Mann, the outlines of the social history could be given, while specific areas of interest could be, and apparently were, allotted to other recipients of portions of the correspondence. The various friends who received large numbers of Walpole's letters were each written to from a somewhat different viewpoint. Thomas Gray, the poet, a lifelong friend of Walpole (despite occasional differences), received letters on matters of artistic and antiquarian interest. When Gray died, the man who became his biographer, the Reverend William Mason, became the recipient, so that the thread was not broken. Lady Ossory received letters containing gossip, especially after the death of George Montagu, who had for some years been a Walpole correspondent.

Although there is a certain element of satire in the letters, Walpole was almost never bitter. He had the well-bred man's ability to see the humor and the absurdity in human conduct without having to regard foolishness as wickedness. For more than fifty years Walpole recorded what he saw, and in such a manner that the reader feels the immediacy of what happened long ago. On the scene himself at the time, Walpole was able to write for the modern reader, as well as for the eighteenth-century recipients of the correspondence, and in such fashion that the glow of reality lights up the history.

LETTERS TO HIS SON

Type of work: Courtesy letters
Author: Philip Dormer Stanhope, Lord Chesterfield (1694-1773)
First published: 1774

On the periphery of literature exists a valuable and fascinating genre, the personal letter which, like the private diary, reveals a man and an age far more intimately than any other form of writing. Probably no era practiced the epistolary art more widely than the eighteenth century and no man more skillfully than the fourth Earl of Chesterfield. Though the good earl had served his country unimpeachably as a member of Parliament, Lord Lieutenant of Ireland, and ambassador to Holland, and though his name designates an overcoat and a couch, it is generally conceded that Lord Chesterfield would have remained an inconspicuous figure in the eighteenth-century historical scene had it not been for the unintended publication of some four hundred letters to his illegitimate son, Philip Stanhope. No doubt the very fact that these letters were strictly private, intended to develop the education and manners of a young man who was expected to take a significant place in government and cultivated society, endows them with a frankness and honesty that betrays the cultivated self-seeking and the hypocritical morality of the upper-class society of the time. Eugenia Stanhope, whose secret marriage with young Philip was only one of the many disappointments Lord Chesterfield suffered at the hands of his intractable son, was so incensed at being excluded from the earl's will that against the family's wishes she sold the *Letters* to Dodsley for £1,575, thus infuriating English society and securing for Lord Chesterfield minor but recognized importance in the history of English prose.

The early letters are charmingly didactic essays addressed to a pre-adolescent mind, expected to become "not only the best scholar but the best bred boy in England of your age." "Dear boy," they all begin, and then proceed to shape little lessons on language, literature, geography, history, and good manners. They conclude with admonitions to obey Maittaire, his seventy-year-old tutor, and promises of "very pretty things" to reward him for industrious study. There is irony in Lord Chesterfield's explanation of irony—"Suppose that I were to commend you for your great attention to your book, and for your retaining and remembering what you have once learned; would you not plainly perceive the irony, and see that I laughed at you?" Reasons for such laughter were to come, but it was never bitter or audible ("there is nothing so illiberal, and so ill-bred as audible laughter"). Lord Chesterfield's optimism and faith in rationalism may have diminished somewhat, but it was never extinguished completely. After his failure in making an outstanding figure of young Philip, in 1761 he began the whole process over again with his godson, to whom he wrote almost three hundred letters in a decade.

It is not the early letters to his son but the later ones—addressed to "My Dear Friend"—that have aroused controversy. A strong believer in Locke's educational theory that a man's mind is wax to be molded into shape by environmental influences, Lord Chesterfield sent his son at fourteen not to a university but on the grand tour accompanied by a new tutor, the Reverend Walter Harte, supplied with letters of introduction into the highest social circles of great European cities, spied upon by the earl's agents, and pursued by affectionate but earnest epistles from an anxious father. How earnest they were can be gauged from this excerpt written to Lausanne in 1746: "I do not so much as hint to you how absolutely dependent you are on me; and that, as I have no womanish weakness for your person, your merit must and will be the only measure of my kindness." Nevertheless, it would

1666

be unfair to observe that even if the father never displayed warmth, love, or understanding, his kindness far exceeded the boy's merit.

The controversy concerns Lord Chesterfield's realistic observations on those aspects of life that he constantly urges his son to explore:

Search, therefore, with the greatest care, into the characters of those whom you converse with; endeavor to discover their predominant passions, their prevailing weaknesses, their vanities, their follies, and their humours, with all the right and wrong, wise and silly springs of human actions, which make such inconsistent and whimsical beings of us rational creatures. . . . This is the true knowledge of the world; and the world is a country which nobody ever yet knew by description; one must travel through it oneself to be acquainted with it.

Having well-traveled that country, Lord Chesterfield could advise his son with a somewhat cynical sophistication. A man who never knew love and who married for a dowry that would repair his fortunes, he wrote: "Women are merely children of a larger growth. . . . A man of sense only trifles with them . . . . They will greedily swallow the highest [flattery], and gratefully accept the lowest . . . [but] They have, from the weakness of men, more or less influence in all courts. It is therefore necessary to manage, please and flatter them." It is this worldly self-interest that constitutes the dominant tone of the letters, "without some dissimulation no business can be carried on at all." There was no trace

of mysticism or sentimentality about him; "religion must still be allowed to be a collateral security, at least, to Virtue." But virtue, apparently, was not an end in itself. Rather, it was a means to worldly success, a dependable means, if Lord Chesterfield's own career based on honesty and integrity is any measure. Nevertheless, worldly success was the goal and though "learning, honour, and virtue are absolutely necessary to gain you the esteem and admiration of mankind, politeness and good breeding are equally necessary to make you welcome and agreeable in conversation and common life." Elsewhere he urges his son to be neat and clean, to avoid obesity, to care for his teeth, and never under any circumstances to stick his finger into his nose.

The ultimate purpose was that young Stanhope should become—at the very least—a successful diplomat; but the principal objective of that occupation was "to get into the secrets of the court at which he resides" through any means including flattery or intimacy with a king's or minister's mistresses.

On the Continent, publication of the *Letters* was met with acclaim, their greatest admirer probably being Lord Chesterfield's old friend Voltaire: "I am not certain that it is not the best book on education which has ever been written." But in England the reaction was sternly condemnatory, even virulent. One periodical declared that as a man, he was "certainly solely actuated by pride, vanity, and ambition," and in her own letters Mrs. Montagu expressed her belief that "tho' many admired, no one ever esteem'd Lord Chesterfield."

LEVIATHAN

Type of work: Philosophy of politics
Author: Thomas Hobbes (1588-1679)
First published: 1651

To appreciate the range of Hobbes' subject matter in the *Leviathan* one may first consider the entire title: *Leviathan, or the Matter, Form, and Power of a* *Commonwealth Ecclesiastical and Civil.* In considering the "matter, form, and power" of the commonwealth, or state, Hobbes was doing far more than de-

1667

scribing governments as he found them. His goal was to explain the origin of political institutions and to define their powers and right limits. To this end he thought it necessary to draw an analogy between the art of nature, productive of man, and the art of man, productive of the commonwealth. In drawing the analogy he first explained man himself, giving to the description a thoroughly mechanistic bias. He then proceeded to explain the state as man's artful creation, designed to put an end to the war of all against all.

The state, "that great Leviathan," is but an "Artificial Man," wrote Hobbes. The sovereign is an artificial soul, the officers of the state are artificial joints, reward and punishment are nerves, wealth and riches are strength; the people's safety is the business of the artificial man; the laws are its reason and will; concord, its health; sedition, its sickness; and civil war, its death.

All of men's ideas originate in sense, according to Hobbes—that is, they are derived from sense impressions. All sensation is a result of external bodies pressing upon the sense organs. Imagination is "nothing but *decaying sense*," the effect of sense impressions after the external body has ceased to press upon the organs. If we want to emphasize the past cause of the impression, we call the fading image a "memory" image; but if we want to emphasize the image as one not now related to any present cause, we call it "fancy" or "imagination."

Hobbes was led by his mechanistic psychology to deny content to such a term as "infinite." He argued that when we say something is infinite we merely show that we cannot conceive its boundaries. Consequently, such a term as "God" is used not to conceive any being, but only to honor something incomprehensible.

Common names, such as "man," "horse," and "tree" may be applied to a number of individual things, yet there is nothing universal but names. In making this claim Hobbes was denying the Platonic belief that individual objects share a certain common character, or universal, in virtue of which they are similar. According to Hobbes, then, reasoning is simply the manipulation—the addition and subtraction—of names.

The passions are the "interior beginnings of voluntary motions," writes Hobbes. Since he argued that everything can be understood in terms of bodies in motion, it is not surprising that even the emotions are simply notions inside the body. Motion toward something is desire; motion away, aversion. In terms of these two basic motions Hobbes defined the other passions.

After considering the intellectual virtues and defects, the two kinds of knowledge (knowledge of observed fact, and the conditional knowledge of science), and the powers and manners of men, Hobbes turned his analytical mind to religion. Religion, he writes, is man's invention, the result of his ignorance and fear. Religious power and dogma are used to serve the interests of the priests. It is not surprising that, with these views, Hobbes was constantly in trouble both at home and abroad.

When Hobbes finally comes to the point of declaring that men are by nature equal, he does so with no tone of ringing idealism. He means only that the differences between men are not so marked as the similarities, and he means also that there is no natural sanction for one man's assuming authority over another. Because men are similar, they sometimes come to desire the same thing; and if they cannot both enjoy the object of their desire, they become enemies and war over the object. There are three principal causes of fights between men: competition, diffidence, and glory. While men have no common power over them to keep them all in check, they are in "that condition which is called Warre; and such a warre, as is of every man, against every man." There are many inconveniences to war, and the fact that in a state of war there is no injustice (since there is no natural law governing action) in no way makes that state of affairs satisfactory. In order to secure peace men enter upon certain agreements by which they bring about a transferring of rights. It is possible for men to make such agreements, or contracts, because they have certain natural rights to use their power however they choose in order to preserve themselves.

Having discussed men, their nature, and their rights, Hobbes argued, in the second part of *Leviathan,* that the commonwealth is brought into being in order to enable men to escape from the state of war. Loving liberty and dominion over others, men agree to make some person sovereign over them all to work for their peace and benefit. The sovereign is not bound by the contract or covenant; the contract is among those who are to be ruled. If the ruler turns out to be a despot, it must be remembered that it is better to be ruled in a commonwealth than to be in a state of nature and, consequently, a continual state of war.

Hobbes considers three kinds of commonwealth: monarchy, democracy, and aristocracy, the latter being ruled by an assembly of part of the commonwealth. There are certain advantages to the monarchial form of government, according to Hobbes: a monarch combines the private and public interest; he is better able to consult with men who have knowledge he needs; the only inconstancy the monarch has to put up with is his own; he cannot disagree with himself; and although it is sometimes inconvenient to have power vested in one man, particularly when the monarch may be an infant because of succession, the disadvantages are no greater than they are in other forms of government.

The subjects in a commonwealth are not entirely subject to the sovereign. The basic principle is that they cannot be compelled to act against that natural inclination toward self-preservation which the commonwealth is supposed to serve.

They cannot be bound to injure themselves or to wage war—although this is a dubious right since the sovereign is free to imprison or execute them for disobedience. If the sovereign is not able to protect his subjects, the subjects are absolved of obedience to him.

The civil law of a commonwealth is made up of all those rules which prescribe what is right and wrong for the subjects; and since the commonwealth itself is no lawmaker, the sovereign must be the legislator. He is not subject to civil law, and only he can abrogate the law. Since an undeclared law is no law at all, and since law is not binding unless it is clearly commanded by the sovereign, the sovereign must make the law known and understood, and he must see to it that it be known as his law. The only laws that need not be published are laws of nature, and they can be contained in one sentence: "Do not that to another, which thou thinkest unreasonable to be done by another to thy selfe."

Hobbes regarded crime as resulting from some defect of the understanding, or from some error of reasoning, or from some force of the passions. He declares that "No law, made after a Fact done, can make it a Crime," and that although ignorance of natural law is no excuse, ignorance of civil law may excuse a man provided he had not the opportunity to hear the law declared. Punishment is not fundamentally retributive in Hobbes' scheme: "A Punishment, is an Evill inflicted by publique Authority, on him that hath done, or omitted that which is Judged by the same Authority, to be a Transgression of the Law; to the end that the will of men may thereby the better be disposed to obedience."

Like anything made by men, a commonwealth can perish. Its infirmities result from what Hobbes calls an "Imperfect Institution"—errors in the creation of the commonwealth. Perhaps the sovereign is not given enough power, or every man is allowed to be a judge, or conscience is authoritative in moral judgment, or supernatural inspiration is given precedence over reason, or the sovereign is held to be subject to civil law, or it is supposed that every man has some absolute property which the sovereign cannot touch, or it is supposed that sovereign power can be divided. Other difficulties, such as the lack of money, the presence of monopolies and corrupt politicians, the popularity of certain subjects, the greatness of a town, or the invasion by a foreign power can lead to the dissolution of the commonwealth.

Part III of *Leviathan* is concerned with showing the relations between a Christian commonwealth and commonwealths in general. Hobbes uses hundreds of Biblical references, as interpreted by him, to support his conclusion that it is possible to reconcile our obedience to God with our obedience to a civil sovereign, for the sovereign is either a Christian or he is not. If he is a Christian, then, even if he may sometimes err in supposing that some act is God's will, the proper thing for the subject, who has no right to judge, is to obey. If the sovereign is an infidel, then the subject must obey because the law of nature justifies the sovereign's power in a common-wealth, and to disobey would be to disobey the laws of nature which are the laws of God. No church leader, even a Pope, can rule the sovereign; and this situation is not contrary to God's law, for the Church works through civil government.

The concluding section, "Of the Kingdome of Darknesse," argues that spiritual darkness has not been completely eliminated from the Church—by which Hobbes means the Church of Rome. His principal attack on the Church of Rome is based on his claim that the Scripture is misinterpreted in order to justify the assumption of temporal power by the Popes.

Although Hobbes maintains that his entire argument is based upon a study of nature and of man's natural inclinations, it is clear that a large part of his discourse is an expression of his own preference for absolute monarchy. On this account he tends to overlook the possibility of restraining the power of a sovereign by democratic procedures. Nevertheless, the *Leviathan* is a remarkable attempt to explain and justify the institution of government, and it remains one of the masterpieces of political thought.

LIBER AMORIS

Type of work: An autobiographical account of a love affair
Author: William Hazlitt (1778-1830)
Time: 1820 1822
Locale: London and Scotland
First published: 1823

Principal personages:
    H. (WILLIAM HAZLITT), the lover, a writer
    S. (SARAH WALKER), the beloved
    M. W. (MICAIAH WALKER), her father, a landlord and tradesman
    C. P. (PETER GEORGE PATMORE), Hazlitt's friend
    J. S. K. (JAMES SHERIDAN KNOWLES), another of Hazlitt's friends

Since William Hazlitt was a writer, it was not enough that he found himself passionately attracted to his landlord's daughter; he had to write about it. *Liber Amoris, or, The New Pygmalion* appeared in 1823, slightly disguised by initials in place of names, as the anonymous account of a writer's foolish passion; but it was not long before the secret was out. A reviewer for *John Bull* claimed that the review in the *Times*, favorable to the book, had been written by Hazlitt himself, and an effort was made to picture the girl of the account as a young, innocent child and Hazlitt as an "impotent sensualist."

The fact is that *Liber Amoris* was properly subtitled *The New Pygmalion*, for Hazlitt allowed his quite natural passion for an attractive and compliant young lady to lead him into flights of creative imagination whereby he sought to give her traits of character and depth of feeling to match her physical charms. His conversations with the landlord's daughter, delightfully transcribed at the beginning of the work, show Hazlitt to have been as much dazzled by his own literary facility in expressing her charms as he was with the charmer herself, seated upon his lap day after day and returning his kisses. By the end of the affair, after he had discovered that she was no more than a flirt—and not an innocent one at that—what impressed him most of all was that she was not what she had *seemed*. What she seemed to be is what, in his writer's imagination, he made her; and what he discovered, when he realized her true nature, was that reality does not bother to copy the images of poets, even when they write a *Liber Amoris*.

The Pygmalion theme is never explicitly developed in the book, but Hazlitt speaks of Sarah as "the statue." In the first of his letters to C. P., Esq. written from Scotland, Hazlitt wrote in a footnote, "I have begun a book of our conversations (I mean mine and the statue's) which I call *Liber Amoris*." Later, in Letter XIII, the next to last letter of Part II of the *Liber Amoris*, he wrote to Patmore again concerning Sarah: "Since I wrote to you about making a formal proposal, I have had her face constantly before me, looking so like some faultless marble statue, as cold, as fixed and graceful as ever statue did. . . ."

The book begins with a series of conversations, apparently the result of Hazlitt's attempt to re-create the substance and feeling of amatory moments spent with Sarah. Then a series of letters to Patmore carry the narrative forward, telling of Hazlitt's hopes and doubts while in Scotland awaiting a divorce from his wife. The book closes with some letters to J. S. K. which, unlike the letters to Patmore, were never actually sent but were composed to complete the book.

Hazlitt became acquainted with Sarah Walker after his separation from his wife. Sarah, the second daughter of his landlord, Micaiah Walker, a tailor, was in her late teens when he met her. According to the *Liber Amoris* account, Sarah let him kiss her the first time they met, and during the first week of their acquaintance she sat upon his knee, and, in his words to her, "twined your arms round me, caressed me with every mark of tenderness consistent with modesty. . . ."

Later Hazlitt was to tell her father that Sarah had made a habit of sitting on his knee and kissing him. The father had supposed that the occasion upon which he had surprised the two lovers together was perhaps the only time such a thing occurred, but Hazlitt, trying to win sympathy for himself when he could not convince Sarah to marry him, assured Walker that "It was a constant habit; it has happened a hundred times since, and a thousand before. I lived on her caresses as my daily food, nor can I live without them."

The conversations are convincing and lively, more self-revealing than Hazlitt probably supposed. They show a man convinced of his ability to charm with language one whom he had so often kept busy with embraces. By the brief answers which Sarah gives we can guess that she found him something of a chatterbox and wished that he would pay more attention to the physical side of love and less to the spiritual and literary aspects of the experience.

For Hazlitt the overwhelming problem of his affair with Sarah was how to reconcile their hours of intimacy with her refusal to marry him or, at least, to live with him "in friendship." He asks her for an answer; he asks his friends; he asks her mother and father. But Sarah had the answer all along, only he lacked the ability to recognize its truth: "I told you my regard could amount to no more than friendship." Of course, it was the friendship of a healthy girl who enjoyed nothing more than being fondled by the lodgers in her father's house; but Hazlitt had the conventional notion that a girl who *seems* innocent and demure makes love only because she wishes to signify an intention to accept a proposal of marriage.

The course of the affair is simply told. Hazlitt met the tailor's daughter, kissed her on their first meeting, and held her on his lap. The entertainment continued for hundreds of performances. Hazlitt, as a writer, spent a good part of the time expressing his love in elaborate, literary ways which, for the most part, Sarah failed to appreciate. He kept making the effort to win from her a declaration of love to match his own, but she insisted that he could never be more than a friend to her. He gave her various books, including several he had written—and a small bronze figure of Napoleon which she treasured because it reminded her of a man she had cared for, a nobleman who considered the social distance between himself and Sarah too great to be overcome.

After Hazlitt went to Scotland to await a divorce from his wife, he wrote entreating letters to Sarah which were either not answered or were answered perfunctorily. His doubts and hopes were expressed at great length in letters to his friend Patmore.

Upon returning to London, after the divorce, Hazlitt again tried to persuade Sarah to marry him; but on the pretext that he had insulted her in a quarrel before his journey, when he had suggested vaguely that she was easy in her favors, she not only refused to marry him but returned the books and the statuette, which he promptly smashed. He finally discovered that she was playing the same game with another gentle-

man, C——, and that she had been doing so during the very period when he thought he had her embraces to himself alone. His final opinion of her, contrasting with the image of her as she *seemed* to be, was that she was "a practiced, callous jilt, a regular lodging-house decoy, played off by her mother upon the lodgers, one after another, applying them to her different purposes, laughing at them in turns, and herself the probable dupe and victim of some gallant in the end."

Despite Hazlitt's literary flights shown in both the conversations and the letters, *Liber Amoris* is a convincing and compelling account of an ordinary love affair. The style is mannered, in the fashion of a time when literary elaboration of ordinary passion was as much a sport as holding the landlord's daughter on one's knee. Yet beneath the poetry and the banter there is something of the English spirit and attitude which gives a dignity to what would otherwise be too trivial to be worth writing about, whatever the joys and pains of the participants. Hazlitt shows himself to be a divided man, worldly enough to realize that the girl, for all her demureness, allowed him liberties which she could not have allowed were she all she seemed to be, yet romantic enough and idealistic enough to suppose that somehow the fault was in himself and that all he had to do was to make himself worthy of her love and esteem. In this division of self Hazlitt shows himself to be the romantic Englishman—cynical and hopeful at the same time.

It is not enough to say that the portrait of Hazlitt and his "statue" is convincing and typical. Considered as a piece of literary work, *Liber Amoris* is remarkable in that it sustains interest with material so slight. What accounts for Hazlitt's success is the spirit of the piece; it is amusing, lively, sophisticated, and revealing of human foibles—all at once. It is a minor piece, and perhaps it is better to remember Hazlitt as a critical essayist; but it is from such minor pieces that English literature acquires its dis-tinctive flavor and enduring charm.

LIEH KUO CHIH

Type of work: Novel
Author: Feng Meng-lung (1574?-1645?)
Type of plot: Historical romance
Time of plot: 770-220 B.C.
Locale: China
First published: Probably early seventeenth century

Principal personages:
KING YU, the last king of the Western Chou dynasty
KING P'ING, the first king of the Eastern Chou dynasty
DUKE HUAN OF CH'I, the first overlord
KUAN CHUNG, a philosopher and statesman
DUKE WEN OF CHIN, an overlord
KING CHUAN OF CH'U, an overlord
DUKE HSIAO OF CH'IN, a powerful feudal lord
SHANG YANG, a statesman and political reformer
SU CH'IN, a diplomat
CHANG I, a diplomat
CHING K'O, an assassin
SHIH-HUANG-TI, "The First Emperor" of Ch'in, a tyrant

Critique:

A popularized history, based entirely on Chinese classics, the *Lieh Kuo Chih* or *Tung Chou Lieh Kuo Chih* (*Chronicles of Divers Feudal States under the Eastern Chou Dynasty*) contains no fictitious figures. Its *dramatis personae* are numerous, including almost all the kings, princes, feudal lords, heroes, and villains throughout China from the early eighth century to the end of the third century B.C. This period of 550 years is probably the most important in Chinese history. We see how feudalism flourished, how the seven "contending kingdoms" fought bloody wars, and how China was reunified under the tyrant Ch'in Shih-huang. Much of the political institutions and strategic ideas of the succeeding centuries had their origins in the statesmen and generals of this period, just as Laotzu, Confucius, and leaders of other schools, all of whom appear in the text, marked the beginnings of systematic philosophical thought in China. Side by side with the shocking accounts of political assassination, incest, and massacre, heroic actions and noble deeds are recounted,

to be remembered by posterity as the supreme lessons of practical morality. The classic version of this novel is credited to Feng Meng-lung, a prolific anthologist who edited and rewrote earlier fiction and drama, interspersing them with original work of his own.

The Story:

For hundreds of years the kings of Chou ruled China. King Yu-wang (781-771 B.C.) had a beautiful concubine whom he loved dearly. But the girl always looked depressed. The king would pay any price to make her smile. One day he lighted the fire beacon, a signal to announce the approach of an enemy. As the feudal lords with their troops hurried to the rescue, they found the king drinking with his concubine. They were forced to lead their troops back. The concubine enjoyed the practical joke so much that for the first time she gave a hearty laugh.

The Marquis of Shen, father of the lawful queen, resented the treatment of his daughter and grandson by the king,

1673

and he allied himself with the barbarians. Together they marched on the capital. The fire beacon was again lighted, but this time no rescuing troops appeared. King Yu-wang was killed and the beautiful concubine carried away by the barbarians.

The capital was also sacked and destroyed. When the heir-apparent, P'ing-Wang, was raised to the throne, he moved the government to Loyang, a city to the east. This was the beginning of the Eastern Chou dynasty (770 B.C.). From that time on, the royal house was weakened, and several feudal states rose to unprecedented power. The territory in the west, the present province of Shensi, was given up to the State of Ch'in, which gradually aggrandized itself as a result of the conquest of the neighboring tribes of barbarians, and became the force to reunify China centuries later.

The first feudal lord to attain to imperial importance was Duke Huan of Ch'i (685-643 B.C.) who occupied the northeast of the present province of Shangtung. His prime minister, Kuan Chung, on whom the duke relied heavily, launched a program of economic reconstruction. With his people enjoying economic prosperity at home and placing full confidence in him, the duke began a series of diplomatic moves which successfully bound various other states by treaty and he became an overlord, the leader of the feudal lords, defender of the royal house, and protector of weaker states.

The great menace to the allied states, with the King of Chou as their nominal head, was Ch'u, occupying, roughly, the present provinces of Hupeh and Hunan, a mere viscountship in the south, generally considered barbarous, but grown so formidable in its military strength and vast in its territory that its rulers defied the royal house and called themselves kings. The utmost Duke Huan of Ch'i accomplished with regard to the potential enemy in the south, though he had chased the barbarians in the northeast up

to the border of Manchuria during a military campaign to help the much harassed state of Yen, was to bring about a pact of amity. The smaller states, under the pressure of circumstances, were often compelled to choose between joining the allies led by Ch'i or paying allegiance to Ch'u.

The first severe blow to Ch'u was dealt by Duke Wen of Chin, another prince who had become an overlord. Nearly a thousand chariots of war on either side, each with its allies, were engaged in a battle at a place called Ch'engp'u (632 B.C.) and Ch'u was defeated. This was the first great battle in Chinese history, and it is said to have saved Chinese civilization. Chin (occupying the present province of Shansi) for two centuries remained a great state in the north, but the power of the duke was usurped by his hereditary ministers until he had as little authority over his retainers as did the King of Chou over the feudal lords. The retainers fought fiercely among themselves and the houses of Wei, Han, and Chao emerged as the victors. These three retainers were recognized as hereditary feudal lords by the king, in 403 B.C. In 376 B.C. they divided among them the territory of Chin.

The power and prestige of Ch'u reached its zenith under King Chuan (613-591 B.C.), who defeated Chin. A hundred years later two other states in the south, hitherto obscure, extended their influence to the north. The first was Wu (now Kiangsu) whose armies in one campaign reached as far as the capital of Ch'u (506 B.C.) but were forced to withdraw before the intervention of Ch'in from the northwest. Though it had also defeated Ch'i, the glory of Wu soon faded; it was conquered by Yueh (now Chekiang) in 473 B.C., and in 334 B.C. Yueh was annexed by Ch'u.

After endless internal disturbance within most of the states and wars among them, seven "great powers" were left: Ch'in, Ch'u, Ch'i, Wei, Han, Chao, and Yen. The smaller and weaker states grad-

1674

ually became extinct, to the aggrandizement of the powers. The authority of the royal house was now utterly disregarded. The potentates of the great powers followed the once-detested example of Ch'u to assume kingship in the fourth century B.C. It was an age of the test of strength, when each state had to fight with every possible resource, military, diplomatic, material, and ideological, for survival if not to win supremacy.

Of the seven, Ch'in was considered geographically unassailable. Having annexed a large territory in the west, it was ready to bid for supremacy in China. Under Duke Hsiao (361-338 B.C.), organization of the peoples, which had been remarkable, was further strengthened by the policies of the prime minister, Shang Yang. The foundations of a totalitarian empire had been laid.

The military strength of Ch'in having struck such terror into the other states, their main problem was how to deal with the power in the west. At one time an alliance of six was formed to contend against Ch'in, acting upon the strategy of the diplomat Su Ch'in, who also became the chancellor of the confederation. But Su's scheme was obstructed by his former fellow-student, Chang I, who was work-ing hard for Ch'in. With crafty maneuvers, bribery, and threats, Ch'in succeeded in dividing the allies who were either to accept defeat or to place their inter-allied jealousy above their common cause. In 317 B.C. Su Ch'in was assassinated.

The conquest of the six states by Ch'in was delayed by the efforts of the Four Statesmen of Ch'i, Ch'u, Chao and Wei. Able administrators and diplomats, they also gained great fame as patrons who threw open their doors to the scholars and men of ability who were wandering all over China seeking employment. Their popularity and ability enabled their states to hold out against Ch'in while they lived; after their deaths, none was able to stop the advance of the conqueror.

Ching K'o of Yen made a heroic attempt to assassinate the man then sitting on the throne of Ch'in (227 B.C.). His effort failed, however, and the king of Ch'in was crowned as Shih-huang-ti, "The First Emperor," known to posterity as the builder of the Great Wall and the burner of the books, after the conquest of his six rivals (220 B.C.). The last shadow monarch of the Chou Dynasty died in 256 B.C.

THE LIFE AND DEATH OF MR. BADMAN

Type of work: Allegorical dialogue
Author: John Bunyan (1628-1688)
First published: 1680

> Principal characters:
> MR. BADMAN, a sinner
> MR. WISEMAN, who tells about Badman's career
> MR. ATTENTIVE, a listener

Practically every literate speaker of English has heard of *The Pilgrim's Progress* and its author, John Bunyan. Less well-known to readers, however, are Bunyan's other writings, including *The Life and Death of Mr. Badman.* There are reasons, of course, for modern neglect of Bunyan's other works. For one, there are relatively few readers attracted to the vast bulk of seventeenth-century religious writings in our time. For another, *The Life and Death of Mr. Badman,* being a didactic work, seems to the modern reader sententious and dull. Thirdly, the moral viewpoints expressed by Bunyan in *The Life and Death of Mr. Badman* sound strange in this century, so foreign are the writer's ideas to those prevalent in our time.

Yet in one sense *The Life and Death*

of Mr. Badman is a companion piece to *The Pilgrim's Progress*. The latter work shows the Christian, devoted and obedient, winning his way to the rewards of righteousness, while the former illustrates what happens to the sinner who steadfastly refuses to acknowledge his evil ways and insists upon leading a depraved existence throughout a life that can be characterized only as evil, regardless of whether one agrees wholeheartedly with Bunyan's code of ethics in its entirety. The protagonist of the story, as it is related in dialogue, is Mr. Badman. He has all the evil in his heart one could possibly ask. Unlike the typical hero of picaresque fiction, Mr. Badman has no aspect which can endear him to the reader. Bunyan expected his readers to feel that the sooner Mr. Badman received punishment the better; there is no need to shed tears over such a character.

Bunyan's technique in presenting the story of Mr. Badman is to have Mr. Wiseman, the author's spokesman, relate the story of Badman's life shortly after the sinner's death. Mr. Wiseman's listener, aptly named Mr. Attentive, not only listens carefully but also draws out the details of the narrative when Mr. Wiseman lags. The dialogue form is an old one, used for ages to bring edifying material to the reader and force him into the role of a passive participant.

Possibly the most striking characteristic in *The Life and Death of Mr. Badman* is the insistence upon moral free choice and the assurance on the part of John Bunyan that all moral responsibility rests with the individual. Bunyan had no room in his theories for environmental determinism. The idea that the environment —family, the community, society in general—could be blamed for an individual's wrongdoing could not be fitted into Bunyan's moral philosophy. In the early pages of the dialogue between Mr. Wiseman and Mr. Attentive, putting the words into Mr. Wiseman's mouth as he speaks of Mr. Badman, Bunyan wrote:

"I will tell you that from a child he was very bad; his very beginning was ominous, and presaged that no good end was in likelihood to follow thereupon. There were several sins that he was given to when he was but a little one, that manifested him to be notoriously infected with original corruption; for I dare say he learned none of them of his father or mother, nor was he admitted much to go abroad among other children that were vile, to learn to sin of them; nay, contrariwise, if at any time he did get abroad amongst others, he would be as the inventor of bad words and an example in bad actions. To them all he used to be, as we say, the ringleader and master sinner from a child."

To this kind of theory voiced by Mr. Wiseman, Mr. Attentive agrees wholeheartedly, saying that certainly evil ways come from within the individual rather than, as most people believe today, from without.

The burden of the career of Mr. Badman is that one sin begets another. As a small child Badman, who has, says Bunyan, a host of equivalents in every generation, begins by lying and stealing from other members of the household, and he goes on to invest himself with almost the entire catalogue of sinfulness. Swearing, whoring, drinking, faithlessness in marriage, hypocrisy, and many other sins are committed by Badman during his lifetime.

Each mention of a new sin as the story of Mr. Badman's life progresses sends Mr. Wiseman or Mr. Attentive off into a kind of sermon or into a series of examples. Scholars have pointed out that the examples Bunyan used in the dialogue were often borrowed from other writers, in whose books Bunyan had found them during his own reading. Bunyan accepted the stories he used as examples as fact, just as Cotton Mather was willing to accept signs of "Divine Providences" when they helped him to prove a point to his congregation or his readers.

There is no need to wonder why Bunyan wrote this dialogue of a sinner's progress, for he makes his purpose abundantly clear in an address to the "Courteous Reader." The world, says Bunyan again and again, is full of sinful people, and Mr. Badman has his relatives in every family and household. Convinced that there are so many sinners, Bunyan hopes to spread a word that may either convert or confound. Even Bunyan's Courteous Reader is viewed by the author as a possible (even probable) sinner, and he is asked to consider carefully whether he is treading in Mr. Badman's path to perdition.

LIFE IN LONDON

Type of work: Novel
Author: Pierce Egan (1772-1849)
Type of plot: Picaresque romance
Time of plot: Early nineteenth century
Locale: London
First published: 1821

Principal characters:
CORINTHIAN TOM, a man of fashion
JERRY HAWTHORN, his cousin
BOB LOGIC, their friend

Critique:

Tom and Jerry is a title commonly given to Pierce Egan's *Life in London; or the Day and Night Scenes of Jerry Hawthorn, Esq., and his Elegant Friend, Corinthian Tom, accompanied by Bob Logic, the Oxonian, in their Rambles and Sprees Through the Metropolis.* The book is a minor masterpiece. Any student of history who wishes to know of life in Regency London must read it, for it is the best single source of its kind. Pierce Egan, a sporting gentleman who observed keenly the life around him, put into his picaresque narrative a detailed account of boxing, cock fighting, masquerades, and taverns. In this work can be found much of the slang of the day—some of it still seems new—carefully explained in footnotes. At the time of publication the innumerable puns added to the liveliness of the novel, but to most modern readers the plays on words are often obscure and they can be disregarded. Egan's comic spirit made him a forerunner of Surtees and Dickens.

The Story:

Corinthian Tom, as he was later known, had been born into a rich family with loving parents, who watched after his welfare and provided for his every want. As he grew older he was a little uneasy at their solicitude, for the gay life in the capital appealed to him; and he would have liked to savor life without restrictions of any kind. Gradually instances of the many different facets of London life came under his observation: the hungry man who counted the trees in St. James's Park to while away the dinner hour; the rake who crossed the street to avoid his tailor; the pawnshop customers. As Tom's knowledge increased, his impatience to savor the whole of life became keener.

He became very friendly with Bob Logic, a one-time student at Oxford. That merry fellow, with a comical face and an aptitude for puns, was rich, and he had already been orphaned. With no strictures of purse or parents, Bob's life was one long prank. For a time Tom envied him.

Tom's mother died first, and when his father also passed away, Tom's grief was genuine. With rare tact, Bob left him to face his sorrow alone, but after a decent wait he turned up again with his usual jests and puns. Tom then embarked on the life he most desired under Bob's shrewd tutelage. In short order Corinthian Tom was known at boxing matches, the society parades, the opera, and in slum dens. His career was crowned by the acquisition of the most desirable mistress in town, lovely and talented Catherine. As their connection became known, inevitably she was called Corinthian Kate.

His gay life was halted, temporarily, when Tom fell ill. He called in Doctor Pleas'em, a knowing doctor with the perfect approach for gay young blades. Doctor Pleas'em prescribed a country rest for his weary patient. Searching through his invitations, Tom found one from an uncle who lived at Hawthorn Hall, and immediately he set out to visit him.

At the hall Tom met his young cousin Jerry, a strong and quick lad who was dazzled by his city relative. Soon country life worked its wonders, and on the last day of his stay Tom accompanied Jerry on a twenty-six mile fox hunt. Both young men were in at the kill. That afternoon, when an agreeable party met to say their farewells to Tom, it was decided that Jerry should return to London with his cousin to acquire a city polish.

Jerry, much impressed by the appointments of Corinthian House, was a willing pupil in learning social graces. The first step was to call in a good tailor. Tom's man was Mr. Primefit, who was the most accomplished tailor in town. Mr. Primefit had built up his vast custom by never pressing for a bill; in return, the young blades never questioned the amount of a bill when they finally paid it. In his new clothes Jerry saw his first panorama of society when Tom took him riding in Rotten Row and Hyde Park.

With Tom and Bob as guides, Jerry saw the gambler, the tradesman, the sharper—all decked in finery well beyond their purses. The lively Lady Wanton and her sister, Miss Satire, were attracted by Jerry's fresh face and manly bearing. When Miss Satire made an unkind remark about Jerry's lack of polish, Lady Wanton warmly defended Jerry. The most beautiful woman they saw was the dazzling Duchess of Hearts. With his happy felicity for knowing everyone, Tom introduced Jerry to her. Jerry was struck dumb: her lovely face, her intelligent eyes, her warm heart were too much for him to comprehend.

Another person they met was Trifle, the thinnest and slightest dandy in London. To Jerry he seemed an absolute oddity. Then a calm older woman, warm of smile and respectable of appearance, drove by with three bewitching girls. Jerry hoped for an introduction to the charming family, for they spoke to Bob. But he learned that introductions were not in order; the woman, madam of a select bawdy house, was advertising three of her most recent acquisitions.

Jerry's rusticity wore off quickly. Every afternoon and evening Bob and Tom took him out. They attended gatherings of all sorts. One afternoon Tom proposed an evening visit to the theater. Jerry assented eagerly, but Bob begged off; the theater was a bit high-toned for him. That evening Tom and Jerry went to Drury Lane. There Tom took a quick look at the stage and a longer one at the audience. Seeing few friends, the two cousins went on to Covent Garden, where the company seemed more congenial. After a glance at the play, they pushed into the Saloon. Jerry was struck by the crowds of laughing girls who were so very friendly. Tom had to tell him that the girls were on the lookout for customers.

Although Jerry was reluctant to leave the Saloon, Tom induced him to visit a coffee house. There the raffish hangers-on decided to have a bit of fun with the two swells. In the fight that followed Tom and Jerry were acquitting themselves well when the watch broke up the riot. Unfortunately, the cousins continued to battle the watch. They were finally subdued and hauled off to jail. Released on bail, they had to appear before a magistrate the next day. Their fine was supposed to pay the watch for the damage they had done.

In turn Tom, Jerry, and Bob went to a boxing establishment, a fencing salon, the dog fights, the condemned yard at Newgate. A highlight was a masquerade supper at the opera. Jerry, attracted by a coquettish woman dressed as a nun, was importunate in trying to learn her name. Finally the nun wrote an acrostic to supply the information. With Bob's help, Jerry finally learned that his companion had been Lady Wanton.

Tom was reluctant for some time to introduce Corinthian Kate, but he finally arranged a meeting with her for Bob and Jerry. Kate, glad to see them, presented her very good friend Sue. Jerry was interested in analyzing the two women, both beautiful. Kate was self-possessed and inclined to dramatic settings; an accomplished belle. Sue seemed much warmer and more genuinely sympathetic. While Bob played the piano for them, Jerry and Sue had a pleasant tête-à-tête. Jerry was reluctant to leave.

Tom arranged a special trip for the two ladies about which he was quite mysterious. He warned them to be dressed by eleven sharp, for the success of the trip depended on punctuality, and so the ladies were ready when Tom and Jerry called. They were whisked away in a cab to Carleton Palace. There the friends went through the succession of fine rooms and examined the appointments at their leisure.

One of their memorable jaunts was an evening spent among cadgers. Disguising themselves as beggars, they visited a tavern frequented by professional alms takers, where they saw the crippled woman descend a ladder in a lively manner without her crutches. All manner of frauds came to light in that dismal gathering.

But all pleasant excursions were drawing to an end; Bob was put in debtors' prison. Although he was as merry as ever when Tom and Jerry went to see him, he did promise to put his affairs in better order, for he was confident he would soon be released. When Jerry caught a cold which he could not seem to get rid of, Doctor Pleas'em told him that he could not expect to lead such a life indefinitely, and he must return to Hawthorn Hall for a rest. Then he could come back and plunge into London life once more. Vowing to be back soon, and asking Tom to give his best wishes to Sue, Jerry returned to the country.

LIFE IS A DREAM

Type of work: Drama
Author: Pedro Calderón de la Barca (1600-1681)
Type of plot: Romantic melodrama
Time of plot: Sixteenth century
Locale: Poland
First presented: 1635

Principal characters:
BASILIO, King of Poland
SEGISMUNDO, his son
ASTOLFO, Basilio's nephew and a duke of Muscovy
ESTRELLA, the infanta, Basilio's niece
CLOTALDO, a Polish general
ROSAURA, a Russian noblewoman disguised as a man
FIFE, her servant

Critique:

Before Calderón's *La vida es sueño* was freely adapted by Edward Fitzgerald in

1679

1853, it had been known to most English and European readers through the medium of French translations from the original Spanish. In spite of their richness of imagination, however, Calderón's plays are still little known outside the Spanish-speaking world. All of this playwright's work has vigor and brilliance; in *Life Is a Dream,* for example, he used his Polish setting and period as freely as Shakespeare used the seacoast of Bohemia or the forest of Arden. There is also a Gothic quality in the mountain scenes which suggests the popular atmosphere of much eighteenth-century fiction, and there is considerable psychological insight into character as well. This play reveals admirably the personality of its writer, who was a soldier, an ardent patriot, an artist, and a devout son of the Church. It has also been translated as *Such Stuff as Dreams Are Made Of.*

The Story:

One night, in the wild, mountainous country between Poland and Russia, a Russian noblewoman, Rosaura, and her servant, Fife, found themselves in distress. Their horses had bolted, and they feared that they would have to make on foot the remainder of their journey to the royal court of Poland. Rosaura, for protection through that barbarous frontier country, was disguised as a man.

Their weary way brought them at last to a forbidding fortress. There they overheard a young man, chained to the doorway of the castle, deliver a heart-rending soliloquy in which he lamented the harshness of his life. Rosaura approached the youth, who greeted her eagerly, with the excitement of one who had known little of sympathy or kindness during his brief span of years. At the same time he warned her to beware of violence. No sooner had he spoken these words than a shrill trumpet blast filled the night. Rosaura tossed her sword to the captive before she and Fife hid themselves among the rocks.

Clotaldo, a Polish general and the keeper of the youth, galloped up to the young man. Seeing the sword in his prisoner's hand, he ordered his men to seek the stranger who must be lurking nearby. Apprehended, Rosaura explained that she and Fife were Russian travelers on their way to the Polish court and that they were in distress because of the loss of their horses. Fife inadvertently hinted that Rosaura was really a woman. But the sword interested Clotaldo most of all, for he recognized the weapon as one which he had owned years before and which he had left in the keeping of a young noblewoman with whom he had been deeply in love. He decided that Rosaura must be his own son, but, torn between his sworn duty to his king and his paternal obligation toward his supposed son, he decided at last to say nothing for the time being. The fact that Rosaura possessed the sword obligated him to protect the travelers and to escort them safely through the mountains.

Meanwhile, in King Basilio's royal castle, the problem of succession to the Polish throne was to be decided. To this purpose, the king welcomed his nephew Astolfo and his niece Estrella, cousins. The problem of the succession existed because it was generally believed that the true heir, King Basilio's son, had died with his mother in childbirth many years before. The need for a decision was pressing; both Astolfo and Estrella were supported by strong rival factions which in their impatience were threatening the peace of the realm.

King Basilio greeted his niece and nephew with regal ceremony and then startled them with the news that his son Segismundo was not really dead. The readings of learned astrologers and horrible portents which had accompanied Segismundo's birth had led the superstitious king to imprison the child in a mountain fortress for fear that otherwise the boy might grow up to be a monster who would destroy Poland. Now, years later, King Basilio was not sure that he had done right. He proposed that Segismundo be brought to the court in a drug-induced sleep, awakened after being dressed in attire befitting a prince, and observed carefully for evidence of his worthiness to wear his father's crown. Astolfo and Estrella agreed to that proposal.

In accordance with the plan, Segismundo, who dressed in rough wolfskins in his captivity, was drugged, taken to the royal castle, and dressed in rich attire. Awaking, he was disturbed to find himself suddenly the center of attention among obsequious strangers. Force of habit caused him to recall sentimentally his chains, the wild mountains, and his former isolation. Convinced that he was dreaming, he sat on the throne while his father's officers and the noble courtiers treated him with the respect due his rank. When they told him that he was the heir to the throne, he was mystified and somewhat apprehensive, but before long he began to enjoy his new feeling of power.

Clotaldo, his former guard and tutor, appeared to confirm the fact that Segismundo was really the prince. The young man then demanded an explanation of his lifelong imprisonment. Clotaldo patiently explained King Basilio's actions in terms that Segismundo might understand, but the youth, blinded by the sudden change in his fortunes, could see only that he had been grievously mistreated by his father. Declaring that he would have revenge for his unwarranted imprisonment, he seized Clotaldo's sword, but before he could strike the old general Rosaura appeared out of the crowd, took the weapon from him, and reproved him for his rashness.

Segismundo, in a calmer mood, was introduced to Astolfo, whose courtly bearing and formal speech the prince could not bear. Sick of the whole aspect of the court, he ordered the guards to clear the audience hall. But again he was mollified, this time by the appearance of Estrella and her ladies in waiting. Unaccustomed to feminine society, he behaved in a boorish manner, even attempting to embrace Estrella. The courtiers advised him to behave in a manner befitting a prince, and Astolfo, who hoped to marry his beautiful cousin, cautioned Segismundo about his

behavior toward the princess. Unfamiliar with the formalities of court life, Segismundo lost all patience. Holding all present responsible for his long exile, he reminded them of his exalted position and defied anyone to touch Estrella. When Astolfo did not hesitate to take her by the hand, Segismundo seized Astolfo by the throat.

At this crucial moment in Segismundo's test, King Basilio entered the throne room and saw his son behaving like a wild beast. Crushed, he feared that the forecast had been true after all. Segismundo faced his father with shocking disrespect. Pressed for an explanation of his son's imprisonment, the king tried to prove that it had been written in the stars. Segismundo scoffed at the folly of man in putting responsibility for his actions on the disinterested heavens. Then he cursed his father and called the guards to seize the king and Clotaldo. But at a trumpet blast the soldiers quickly surrounded Segismundo himself and took him prisoner.

Having failed the test of princehood, Segismundo was drugged and returned in chains to the mountain fortress. In his familiar surroundings once more, he had full opportunity to reflect on his late experiences. When he spoke to Clotaldo about them, the old general assured him that all had been a dream. Since the prince had been drugged before he left the fortress and before he returned, he was quite convinced that he had suffered an unpleasant dream. Clotaldo assured him that dreams reveal the true character of the dreamer. Because Segismundo had conducted himself with violence in his dream, there was great need for the young man to bridle his fierce passions.

Meanwhile Rosaura, aware of Segismundo's plight and anxious to thwart the ambitions of Astolfo, who had once promised to marry her, stirred up a faction to demand the prince's release. The rebels invaded the mountains and seized the fortress· they failed, however, to seize Clotaldo, who had already returned to the

1681

royal castle to report to King Basilio. When the rebel army carried the sleeping Segismundo out of the fortress and awakened him with trumpet blasts, the unhappy prince would not be persuaded that his new experience was real, and he doubted the assurance that he had been rescued from his imprisonment. The rebel leader finally convinced him that it would be well for him to join the dream soldiers and fight with them against King Basilio's very real army, which was approaching.

Clotaldo was taken prisoner by Segismundo's forces, but the young prince, remembering the advice to curb his passions, ordered the old general's release. A great battle then took place, in which Segismundo proved his princely valor and chivalric bearing. King Basilio, defeated but refusing Clotaldo's and Astolfo's pleas to flee to safety, in admiration surrendered his crown to his son.

King of Poland in his own right, Segismundo ordered the marriage of Astolfo to Rosaura, who had, in the meantime, been revealed as Clotaldo's daughter. Estrella became Segismundo's queen. The young king made Clotaldo his trusted adviser.

LIFE OF NELSON

Type of work: Biography
Author: Robert Southey (1774-1843)
Time: 1758-1805
Locale: England, the British colonies, the Continent, the high seas
First published: 1813

Principal personages:
  VISCOUNT HORATIO NELSON, English naval hero
  EDMUND NELSON, his father
  LADY EMMA HAMILTON, his mistress
  LADY FRANCES NELSON, his wife
  MAURICE SUCKLING, Nelson's uncle, a naval captain, later Comptroller of the Navy
  SIR WILLIAM HAMILTON, English ambassador to Naples
  THOMAS TROUBRIDGE,
  ALEXANDER BALL,
  SAMUEL HOOD,
  BENJAMIN HALLOWELL,
  HYDE PARKER,
  THOMAS GRAVES,
  EARL ST. VINCENT (SIR JOHN JERVIS), and
  CUTHBERT COLLINGWOOD, English naval officers

"What has poor Horatio done, who is so weak, that he, above all the rest [of your children], should be sent to rough it out at sea? But let him come, and the first time we go into action, a cannon-ball may knock off his head, and provide for him at once."

Had Nelson's uncle, Captain Maurice Suckling, been prophetic in this letter to Nelson's father, the course of English history subsequent to the Napoleonic Wars (1803-1815) might well have been quite different from what it has been.

The weakness of the twelve-year-old Horatio that Captain Suckling referred to was only physical. Weak though he was, Nelson had already given proof of the resoluteness of heart and nobleness of mind that were to characterize his distinguished career.

Always a stranger to fear and a companion of honor, Nelson led the exemplary life that his father foresaw for his son. Nelson's father had always marked him for success in whatever profession he might follow. Through his indomitable spirit, his seafaring abilities, and his acumen in personal relationships, Nelson was a lieutenant at nineteen, a captain at twenty-one, and an admiral before he was thirty.

From his maiden voyage to India early in his career, Nelson, reduced almost to a skeleton by tropical disease, was returned home. Dejected by his physical condition and the diminished promise of success in his career, he considered suicide for a time. But from this state of mind he suddenly rallied with a feeling bordering on the religious, so obsessed was he by the "sudden glow of patriotism . . . presented by king and country as my patron."

Southey's explanation of this fervor and determination that spurred Nelson on to become a hero is compatible in its beauty with the exquisite qualities of a man who surmounted obstacles to have his name become as well known as that of the country for which he achieved heroism:

He knew to what the previous state of dejection was to be attributed; that an enfeebled body, and a mind depressed, had cast this shade over his soul; but he always seemed willing to believe, that the sunshine which succeeded bore with it a prophetic glory, and that the light which led him on was "light from heaven."

Though heroes are often seen in an aura of celestial light and divine guidance, Nelson was most cognizant of mundane matters that need attending to, even though one confides in Providence. His readiness in political strategy was a factor in the first of his three greatest naval successes, the defeat of Napoleon's fleet at Aboukir in 1798. For more than a month Nelson's fleet had sought the French fleet in the Mediterranean. Thwarted at every attempt to get information concerning the French position or to secure supplies, Nelson turned at last to Lady Emma Hamilton, the wife of the English ambassador to Naples. Through her influence with the Queen of Naples, Nelson secured supplies at Syracuse and began again his pursuit of the French.

Contrary to his command to his men that they obey orders implicitly without questioning their propriety, Nelson, sometimes seeing circumstances in a different light from that of his superiors, did not always obey orders. In the victory at Copenhagen, in 1801, against the armed neutrality of the Baltic, Nelson, second in command, ignored his commander's order to cease action. Putting his telescope to his blind eye when he was told the signal giving the order had been raised (Nelson had lost the sight of one eye in battle at Calvi), he continued the attack, saying he could not see the signal.

Acting without orders from his commander, Sir John Jervis, Nelson was largely responsible for the defeat of the Spanish fleet at Cape St. Vincent (1797). In that engagement the enemy fleet far outnumbered the English ships, twenty-seven to fifteen. This victory destroyed a threatened invasion of England.

Another practical personal qualification contributing to Nelson's success was his ability as a leader, especially his attention to effective communication. He had marked confidence in his officers' abilities, but he was sure in every case possible that everyone knew his principles of tactics.

In keeping with his confidence in Providence, Nelson seemed obsessed with the assurance of victory. This attribute was inculcated into his men. Quite pleased with the scope of the plan of an attack against the French, one of Nelson's captains asked, "If we succeed, what will the world say?" "There is no *if* in the case," Nelson exclaimed. "That we shall succeed is certain: who may live to tell the story is a very different question."

After destroying thirteen French ships at Aboukir, making useless the French army in Egypt, placed there in preparation for Napoleon's projected conquest of the East, Nelson became an international hero. He was showered with congratulations, rewards, and honors by all countries which, because of his military success, had escaped Napoleon's aggression. Such accolades, received before he was thirty, were to become commonplace to England's greatest naval hero.

Southey's biography is no mere chronological recital of events. His descriptions of naval battles are sufficiently developed and detailed enough to provide the excitement of adventure stories. But in these, as in the more ordinary incidents, emphasis is on persons—their abilities and weaknesses, their hopes and disappointments. The writing has a poet's tone and spirit without poetic devices. This quality in the prose serves to convey the spirit of self-reliance, nonconformity, and courage that constitutes a hero. Clarity and conciseness are the keynotes of the style.

In his choice of biographical detail, Southey never lost sight of the fact that Nelson was first a man and then a naval hero. The strong bond of love and admiration between Nelson and his father, for example, is a warming thread throughout the book. The son's deliberate adherence to his father's counsel and the father's pride in the son's accomplishments add to the stature of the hero. It was fitting, in the light of this lifelong devotion between Nelson and his father, that a few months before the father's death the older Nelson came to accept Nelson's affair with Lady Hamilton. Perhaps in blind love for his son, he saw in his son's mistress a woman described by Southey as "a character which, both in its strength and in its weakness, resembled his own." This reconciliation meant much to Nelson because his association with Lady Hamilton had brought sorrow and displeasure to his father, especially when Nelson was separated from Lady Nelson.

Southey treats Nelson's marital situation in a matter of fact manner as another facet of the admiral's life. This is no love idyl, developed by a poet.

The affair began in Naples, where Sir William Hamilton was English ambassador and Nelson was in charge of a squadron during the French occupation of Naples (1798-1799). Nelson and the Hamiltons became inseparable friends; they returned to England together in 1800. At Sir William's death, he was holding Nelson's hand and entrusting Lady Hamilton to his care.

Nelson did arrange a pension for Lady Hamilton and Horatia Nelson Thompson, "believed to be his [Nelson's] daughter," as Southey discreetly identified the child, born to Lady Hamilton about the time Nelson was separating from Lady Nelson.

Nelson's third and last great victory was the sea battle fought off Cape Trafalgar, where in 1805 he destroyed both the French and Spanish fleets. This success culminated two years of strategic naval maneuvering and warfare, with Nelson in command of the fleet in the Mediterranean. During that time he blockaded the French fleet at Toulon for twenty-two months. The English victory at Trafalgar resulted in the capture of twenty enemy ships—not an English vessel was lost— and the end of Napoleon's power of the sea. But in that battle Nelson lost his life. His immortal words "England expects that every man will do his duty" were among his last.

Nelson's stature is admirably established in Southey's description of his death:

> The most triumphant death is that of the martyr; the most awful, that of the martyred patriot; the most splendid, that of the hero in the hour of victory; and if the chariot and the horses of fire had been vouchsafed for Nelson's translation, he could scarcely have departed in a brighter blaze of glory. He has left us, not indeed his mantle of inspiration, but a name and an example, which are at this hour inspiring hundreds of the youth of England: a name which is our pride, and an example which will continue to be our shield and our strength.

The eminence of the subject and the cogency of Southey's writing make it easy to see why the American government published a special edition of the *Life of Nelson* and issued a copy to every seaman and officer in the American navy.

Although Southey was poet laureate of England for thirty years, he is remembered for only a few of his vigorous short poems, "The Battle of Blenheim" being one of his best. Ironically, the poet is best known today for his prose writing, this model among short biographies and a classic in English literature.

THE LIFE OF SAMUEL JOHNSON, LL.D.

Type of work: Biography
Author: James Boswell (1740-1795)
Time: The eighteenth century
Locale: England
First published: 1791

Principal personages:
> SAMUEL JOHNSON, author, critic, and lexicographer
> JAMES BOSWELL, the biographer, Johnson's friend
> DAVID GARRICK,
> SIR JOSHUA REYNOLDS,
> MR. AND MRS. THRALE,
> DAVID HUME, and
> OLIVER GOLDSMITH, members of the Johnson circle

James Boswell's life of Samuel Johnson has usually been considered the greatest biography yet produced in the English language, and it has undoubtedly commanded more readers than any other biography written in English. There are more massive biographies in our literature, such as David Masson's *Life of Milton* and J. G. Lockhart's *Memoirs of the Life of Sir Walter Scott,* but none has ever achieved the critical acclaim or the popularity or the prestige lavished justly upon Boswell's biography of Samuel Johnson.

During his lifetime Boswell published three great works: *The Life of Samuel Johnson, LL.D., The Journal of a Tour to the Hebrides with Samuel Johnson, LL.D.,* and *An Account of Corsica: The Journal of a Tour to That Island; and Memoirs of Pascal Paoli.* Of these three works, the *Life of Johnson* stood out as the greatest for almost a century and a half. Within the last thirty years, however, a new estimate of James Boswell's work has had to be taken, for much of Boswell's writing was lost in manuscript until the 1920's. During the period between 1927 and 1949 Colonel Isham, an American and a collector, brought together the papers which had been stored at Malahide Castle, near Dublin, Ireland, and the Forbes collection, which had accidentally passed into the hands of one of Boswell's executors and descended to the latter's heirs. Some of the papers were published by Isham, who sold the entire collection to Yale University in 1949 and 1950. The university has published several volumes of the papers under the general title of *The Yale Editions of the Private Papers of James Boswell.* Through such volumes of Boswell's writing as *Boswell's London Journal, 1762-1763* (1950), *Boswell in Holland, 1763-1764* (1952), and *Boswell on the Grand Tour: Germany and Switzerland, 1764* (1953), Boswell has emerged as a splendid writer of journals. This fact, however, does not yet detract from his stature as the author of the biography of Johnson, nor will these newer works replace the biography as the most important of Boswell's books, even though critical opinion may be modified to grant him greater stature in literature than he once had.

We now know that the *Life of John-*

son was based upon what Boswell had recorded in copious journals which he kept during the greater part of his adult life. This is not to say, however, that the biography was merely a transcription of materials from those journals. From present knowledge of the papers it can be seen that Boswell was an artist in biography, choosing carefully what suited his needs and goals. Even those who feel that Boswell intruded himself too much into the biography must now recognize that he was at some pains to omit much material about Johnson in which he himself figured. Those who felt that Boswell intruded too much into the work possibly overlooked the fact that during Johnson's life Boswell was Johnson's friend and spent from four hundred to five hundred days with his subject, thus becoming himself a part of Johnson's life and the Johnsonian environment.

Boswell's method was to record materials about Johnson in his journals. Sometimes the material was recorded daily, but on occasion Boswell fell behind and had to rely upon his memory—a phenomenal one—to recall materials he had garnered in a period of four or five days and evenings. It is notable, too, that Boswell was careful to prompt Johnson into conversation, often asking what seem to be obvious or absurd questions in order to goad Johnson into making remarks worthy of record. One such question noted by critics is that in which Boswell asked Johnson what he would do if given the solitary care of a small infant; the question, seemingly absurd, led Johnson to reply in such fashion as to comment on rearing and educating children and to set forth a philosophy of education. The more we learn about Boswell and his work, the more we understand that he was not a mere transcriber, as critical legend held for some time, but that he was a skillful writer who shaped his materials in every way he could, instead of accepting them as he found them. The casual reader may even miss some of the more obvious points of care and artistry, such as notations on how Johnson looked and spoke when delivering comments and opinions.

Johnson was a man of many achievements. He single-handedly brought forth the first recognized dictionary of the English language; he also made himself famous as a writer by means of *The Rambler* papers, his tragedy *Irene*, his poetry, and his moral essays. As a moralist Johnson also won fame as the author of the didactic novel, *The History of Rasselas, Prince of Abyssinia*. As a critic he was famous for his *Lives of the Poets* and his preface to an edition of Shakespeare's plays. People great and small admired Johnson, including many of the famous and remarkable Englishmen of his time, men like Hume, Reynolds, Goldsmith, and Garrick. In addition, he was a picturesque, at times even ludicrous, figure; and this fact Boswell did not attempt to hide, taking to himself the task of writing "not his panegyrick, which must be all praise, but his Life; which great and good as he was, must not be supposed to be perfect." In further defense of his way of writing biography, Boswell wrote near the beginning of his biography:

> I am fully aware of the objections which may be made to the minuteness on some occasions of my detail of Johnson's conversation, and how happily it is adapted for the petty exercise of ridicule by men of superficial understanding, and ludicrous fancy; but I remain firm and confident in my opinion, that minute particulars are frequently characteristick, and always amusing, when they relate to a distinguished man. I am therefore exceedingly unwilling that anything, however slight, which my illustrious friend thought it worth his while to express, with any degree of point, should perish.

Boswell realized, as we know from what he himself said and wrote, that the function and art of biography is to focus on the subject and keep him constantly before the reader. This Boswell did in his biography of Johnson. To do so he carefully gathered together more than what he knew at first-hand of the man who was his friend and subject. He exercised diligence and care in collecting letters written by Johnson, including the text of the famous letter to Lord Chesterfield. He collected, too, letters written about Johnson, as well as anecdotes about his subject's life, trying at the same time to establish the authenticity of these reports he had of Johnson. These materials are presented in the biography in chronological order. If the results have some defects, the defects are more or less forgivable in view of their sparseness. Seldom did Boswell record facts which later biographers needed to correct.

If the account of Johnson's life before meeting Boswell is relatively short, this fact may be excused on the ground that Boswell used only what information about Johnson's early life that he could gather and trust. Naturally, he had a much larger fund of materials from the period during which he knew Johnson person-

ally. Some critics have noted Boswell's reluctance to interpret. Of this reluctance, it must be said that interpretation was not Boswell's way. Upon occasion he generalized upon Johnson perceptively, but he preferred, as he carefully stated, to present the particulars, rather than the generalizations. The result is that Johnson is "alive" in the *Life* as few biographical subjects are, with his personality and character borne out by his own spoken and written words. On occasion the reader may feel that Johnson's written words, usually letters, have been inserted where they fit none too well, seeming to interfere with the flow of the book. And yet they are a part of the scheme Boswell worked out and put together.

Samuel Johnson has been the subject of many biographies; five, for example, appeared after Johnson's death and before Boswell's work. Others have been written since, but none has ever equaled in merit Boswell's *Life of Samuel Johnson, LL.D.*

LIFE ON THE MISSISSIPPI

Type of work: Reminiscence
Author: Mark Twain (Samuel L. Clemens, 1835-1910)
Type of plot: Regional romance
Time of plot: Mid-nineteenth century
Locale: Mississippi River region
First published: 1883

Principal characters:
MARK TWAIN
MR. BIXBY, a river pilot

Critique:

It is extraordinary that a book with so many defects should have become one of the classics of our national heritage. There is, for example, a sharp and obvious division between the first twelve or fourteen chapters and the rest of the book. It is clear that it was not written all at one time, and the effects of bad composition are evident. The chapters are badly organized and there are many labored passages. Despite this lack of craftsmanship, *Life on the Mississippi* is a vivid, dramatic, and extremely interesting collection of reminiscences. Like the

mighty river with which it is concerned, the book has become part of the American tradition, part of our national pride and history.

The Story:

When Mark Twain was a boy, he and his comrades in Hannibal, Missouri, had one great ambition; they hoped to become steamboatmen. They had other ambitions, too, such as joining the circus or becoming pirates, but these soon passed. Only the ambition to be a steamboatman remained, renewed twice each

1687

day when the upriver and the down-river boats put in at the rickety wharf and woke the sleepy village to bustling life. Through the years, boy after boy left the river communities, to return later, swaggering in his importance as a worker on a steamboat. Mark Twain saw these boys often, and the fact that some of them had been considered as undeniably damned in the eyes of the pious folk shook Twain's convictions profoundly. He wondered why these boys who flouted Sunday School maxims and ran away from home should win the rewards of adventure and romance that meeker town boys never knew.

Mark Twain, too, had this dream of adventure. His ambition was a lofty one. He determined to become a cub-pilot. While in Cincinnati, he heard that a government expedition was exploring the Amazon. With thirty dollars he had saved he took a boat bound for New Orleans. His intention was to travel on to the headwaters of the Amazon. But the ship was grounded at Louisville, and during the delay Mark came to the attention of Mr. Bixby, the most famous pilot on the Mississippi River. He prevailed upon Bixby to teach him how to navigate.

At first the adventure was a glorious one. But soon Mark found that the more he knew about the river, the less romantic it seemed. Though he was a dutiful student, he discovered that he could not remember everything Bixby told him, regardless of how important this information seemed to be. Furthermore, to his astonishment and despair, his instructor told him that the river was changing its course continually; that there were no such things as permanent landmarks; that the river channel was never the same, but always variable. There were times when the young cub-pilot was frightened, especially when he narrowly missed hitting another ship, or trimmed the boat too close to shore. But worse was the experience of piloting in the dead of night, with no landmarks to observe and only deep blackness all around.

Bixby claimed the secret of navigation was not to remember landmarks, which changed, but to learn the shape of the river, and then to steer by the shape in one's head.

It was undeniably an interesting life. The pilot had to be on the lookout for rafts sailing the river at night without lights. Often a whole family would be on a raft, and they would shout imprecations at the steamboat which had just barely missed dumping them all into the river. Then there was the fascinating behavior of the river itself. Prosperous towns would be isolated by a new cut-off and reduced to insignificance; towns and islands in one state would be moved up or down and into another state, or, as sometimes happened, into an area that belonged to no state at all!

The river pilot reigned supreme on his boat. The captain was theoretically the master; but as soon as the boat got under way, the pilot was in charge, and only a very foolhardy captain would have interfered. The importance of the pilot in river navigation eventually led to the formation of a pilots' association. At first the idea seemed ridiculous. But the union grew as, one by one, all the good pilots joined. As a result pilots could make their own terms with the owners. Not only were wages guaranteed, but pilots secured better working conditions, pensions, and funds for their widows and orphans. Within a few years the association was the most indestructible monopoly in the country. But its days were numbered. First of all, the railroads came in and river transportation was gradually abandoned in favor of rail traffic. Then, too, the Civil War reduced navigation to a mere trickle and dealt a deathblow to river commerce. The steamboat was no longer an important means of transportation.

From then on the river was different. It seemed very different to Mark Twain when he returned after many years away from it, and saw the changes with nostalgic regret. He traveled once more on the Mississippi, but this time as a passenger and under an assumed name. He listened tolerantly to the man who told him wild and improbable stories about the river, and to a fellow traveler who explained, very explicitly, how everything worked.

Mark Twain decided to search for a large sum of money left by a murderer whom he had met in Germany. He and his companions made plans about the ten thousand dollars soon to be in their possession, and they asked to get off their boat at Napoleon to look for it. Unfortunately, the Arkansas River, years before, had swept the whole town into the Mississippi!

On his return to the river, Mark Twain learned many things he had not known. He witnessed the vast improvements in navigation and in the construction of the boats, improvements that made navigation easier and safer. He talked to the inhabitants of Vicksburg, who described their life during the bombardment of the town by Union forces. He visited Louisiana and expressed horror at the sham castles that passed for good architecture. He read Southern newspapers and saw in them, as in so many Southern traditions, the romantic sentimentality of Sir Walter Scott, an influence that he regretted, hated, and held responsible for the South's lack of progress. He came in contact with a cheerful and clever gambler; he heard about senseless feuds that wiped out entire families; he saw new and large cities that had grown up since he had left the river; he met such well-known writers as Joel Chandler Harris and George W. Cable; he had an experience with a spiritualist who grew rich on the credulous and the superstitious; he witnessed tragedy, and lost friends in steamboat explosions.

The river would never be the same again. The age of mechanization had arrived to stay. The days of the old river pilots, such as Mr. Bixby, were now a thing of the past. America was growing up, and with that growth the color and romance of the Mississippi had faded forever.

LIFE WITH FATHER

Type of work: Short stories
Author: Clarence Day, Jr., (1874-1935)
Type of plot: Humorous satire
Time of plot: Late nineteenth century
Locale: New York City
First published: 1935

Principal characters:
CLARENCE DAY, SR.
MRS. CLARENCE DAY, his wife
CLARENCE DAY, JR., the narrator

Critique:

This narrative of personal recollections is a humorous commentary on American manners in the Victorian age. Father is a domestic tyrant whose bark is considerably worse than his bite. His crotchety behavior is the last resort of masculine aggressiveness in a woman-dominated world.

The Story:

The Day household existed under the eccentric domination of Clarence Day, Sr., a Wall Street businessman who was convinced that he was always right. His son stood in awe of him. The boy's greatest treat was to be taken to his father's office on Saturday mornings. With Father dressed formally in silk hat and tailed coat, they rode downtown on the elevated and the boy gaped curiously into the windows of flophouses and wished that he could enjoy the luxury and freedom of being a tramp. That ambition he did not reveal to his father. Once he ventured to suggest that he would like to be a cowboy, but Father retorted that cowboys were shiftless people.

Father's office seemed very mysterious to the boy, and he enjoyed the privilege of filling inkwells and running errands. Later there would be luncheon at Delmonico's. Father and his favorite waiter always chatted in French about the menu, and Father enjoyed himself greatly. But the boy did not think highly of the food. There was too little of it, scarcely enough to satisfy his appetite. Seeing the starved look on his face, Father would order a large chocolate éclair for him.

One of Father's chief worries was the fear of becoming fat. The members of his club recommended long walks, but Father was already taking long walks. Then they suggested horseback riding. Accordingly, Father became a member of the Riding Club on East Fifty-eighth Street. Apart from stabling conveniences, the club had a park for riding, really only a little ring. But it was tame enough for Father, who liked things to be orderly and suitably arranged for his use. In a very short time he felt as if the park belonged to him, and if the leaves were not raked, if papers were lying around, he would take the neglect as a personal affront.

The first horse Father bought was an independent, rebellious creature. There was little love lost between them. The climax came one morning when the horse refused to obey. It reared and reared until Father gave up in disgust and went back to the club. Since the rest of the family wanted a horse of their own, Father gave them that one. He bought another for himself.

Having never been sick, Father be-

came very annoyed whenever anybody else was ill; and he had no sympathy whatever for people whose illnesses he considered to be simply imaginary. Whenever he was unlucky enough to catch a cold, his method of treating it was to blow his nose loudly or to sneeze. Whenever he had a sick headache, he would not eat. After he had starved out his illness, he would eat again and triumphantly light up a cigar.

Father's laws were regarded as edicts not to be challenged. Accordingly, young Clarence was amazed when anyone did not respond to Father's whims and orders. While out in the country one summer, the family ran out of ice. Because Father's wine must always be chilled, the crisis was a grave one. Nothing the family could do was successful. But when Father came home, he went down to the village, intimidated a dealer into selling him an icebox, provided he would somehow get it filled with ice, and argued the iceman into delivering a load immediately.

Father got things done in his own way. The family could never keep servants for very long. One day the cook left. Father stormed into an employment agency, looked over the assembled girls, and then, over the manager's protests, picked out the one he liked. Although she had not wanted to be a cook, the girl went with him meekly and stayed on in the Day household for twenty-six years. Her name was Margaret.

In the summer Margaret always stayed in New York to look after the house, and each year there arose the problem of a temporary cook during the time that the family was in the country. One year they hired Delia. Before long Father insisted that she was starving him to death. Delia was replaced by a Japanese. At the first meal prepared by the Japanese, Father moaned with pain and declared that he was poisoned. Margaret was hastily summoned from the city, and Father was happy again.

What really vexed Father was Mother's inability to keep household accounts according to the system he tried to teach her. The money always inexplicably disappeared, and the bills were always high. In addition, Mother was fond of charge accounts. It was so easy to buy things that way, and the first of the month seemed far off in the distance. When the bills came in, however, Father always raged—and then gave in.

When Mother went on a trip to Egypt, Father could not understand why she should want to go off to the far corners of the world just to see pyramids. When she came back with part of her expense money unaccounted for, Father was curious. At last Mother admitted that she had not spent it, but intended to keep it. Father, wanting to know what good it would do her to keep it, demanded its return. But again he lost out. Mother kept the money.

Young Clarence witnessed many examples of Father's behavior. He was urged to be prompt for breakfast and bribed with the offer of a watch. He suffered whenever Father opened his mail, particularly when the letters were from young ladies. Father could never understand that letters could ever be for anyone else. When Father finally agreed to have a telephone installed, he likewise assumed that all calls were for him. Once he was very perturbed when a young lady, thinking she was speaking to young Clarence, invited him to lunch.

Women, Father insisted, did not know anything about politics. When Mother came under the influence of Miss Gulick, an emancipated young woman, he snorted contemptuously. Though he liked to dine out with friends, he did not like company in his own house. Once he startled a group of Mother's friends by uttering a lone, monosyllabic word as he stamped past the dining-room on his way upstairs.

Because he had disliked some members of his family buried in the family plot in the cemetery, he did not wish to be buried there after his death. Mother reminded him that such matters are not important to the dead. But Father insisted that he was going to buy a new plot in the cemetery, one all for himself, and in a corner where he could get out. Mother looked at him in astonishment. She whispered to young Clarence that she almost believed he could do it.

LIGEIA

Type of work: Short story
Author: Edgar Allan Poe (1809-1849)
Type of plot: Gothic romance
Time of plot: Early nineteenth century
Locale: Germany and England
First published: 1838

Principal characters:
THE NARRATOR
LIGEIA, his first wife
LADY ROWENA TREVANION, his second wife

Critique:
Poe himself called "Ligeia" his best story. It is a tale of terror combined with pure fantasy. As always in the prose tales of this genius of American literature, plot, character, and setting are fused into one. It was Poe's literary creed that all elements should be subordinated to the total effect desired. Nowhere does he better demonstrate this belief than in the fantastic story of Ligeia. Many critics have read deeper moral significance into this Gothic work.

The Story:

He could not remember when he had first met Ligeia, and he knew nothing of her family except that it was old. Ligeia herself, once his wife, he could remember in every detail. She was tall and slender. Ethereal as a shadow, her face was faultless in its beauty, her skin like ivory, her features classic. Crowning the perfect face and body was raven-black, luxuriant hair. But her eyes, above all else, held the key to Ligeia's mystery. Larger than ordinary, those black eyes held an expression unfathomable even to her husband. It became his all-consuming passion to unravel the secret of that expression.

In character, Ligeia possessed a stern will that never failed to astound him. Outwardly she was placid and calm, but she habitually uttered words of such wildness that he was stunned by their intensity. Her learning was immense. She spoke many tongues, and in metaphysical investigations she was never wrong. Her husband was engrossed in a study of metaphysics, but it was she who guided him, she who unraveled the secrets of his research. With Ligeia he knew that he would one day reach a goal of wisdom undreamed of by others.

Then Ligeia fell ill. Her skin became transparent and waxen, her eyes wild. Knowing that she must die, he watched her struggles against the grisly reaper, a conflict frightening in its passion. Words could not express the intense resistance with which she fought death. He had always known she loved him, but in those last days she abandoned herself completely to love. From her heart she poured fourth phrases of idolatry. And on the last day of her life she bade him repeat to her a poem she had composed not long before. It was a morbid thing about death, about the conquering of Man by the Worm. As he finished repeating the melancholy lines, Ligeia leaped to her feet with a shriek, then subsided on her deathbed. In a scarcely audible whisper she repeated a proverb that had haunted her before: that man did not yield to death save through the weakness of his own will. So Ligeia died.

Crushed with sorrow, her husband left his desolate home by the Rhine and retired to an old and decayed abbey in a deserted region in England. The exterior of the building he left in its sagging state, but inside he furnished the rooms lavishly and weirdly. He had become the slave of opium, and the furnishings took on the shapes and colors of his fantastic dreams. One bedchamber received the most bizarre treatment of all, and to this chamber he led his new bride, the blue-eyed Lady Rowena Trevanion of Tremaine.

The room was in a high turret of the abbey. It was of immense proportions, lighted by a single huge window. The pane had a leaden hue, giving a ghastly luster to all objects within the room. The walls, the floors, the furniture were all covered with a heavy, arabesque tapestry, black figures on pure gold. The figures changed as one looked at them from different angles, their appearance being changed by an artificial current of air that stirred the draperies constantly.

In rooms such as this he spent a bridal month with Lady Rowena. It was easy to perceive that she loved him but little, and he hated her with a passion more demonic than human. In his opium dreams he called aloud for Ligeia, as if he could restore her to the earthly life she had abandoned. He reveled in memories of her purity and her love.

In the second month of her marriage Rowena grew ill, and in her fever she spoke of sounds and movements in the chamber, fantasies unheard and unseen by her husband. Although she recovered, she had recurring attacks of the fever and it became evident that she would soon succumb. Her imaginings became stronger, and she grew more insistent about the sounds and movements in the tapestries.

One night in September she became visibly weaker and unusually agitated. Seeking to calm her, her husband stepped across the room to get some wine. But he was arrested midway by the sense of something passing lightly by him. Then he was startled to see on the gold carpet a shadow of angelic aspect. Saying nothing to Rowena, he poured the wine into a goblet. As she took the vessel, he distinctly heard a light footstep upon the carpet and saw, or thought he saw, three or four drops of a ruby-colored liquid fall into the goblet from an invisible source.

Immediately Rowena grew worse, and on the third night she died. As he sat by her shrouded body in that bridal chamber, he thought of his lost Ligeia. Suddenly he heard a sound from the bed upon which the corpse of his wife lay. Going closer, he perceived that Rowena had a faint color. It was unmistakable; Rowena lived. Unable to summon aid, he watched her with mounting terror. Then a relapse came, and she subsided into a death pallor more rigid than before. All night this phenomenon recurred. Rowena returned briefly from the dead, only to sink once more into oblivion. Each time he saw again a vision of Ligeia.

Toward morning of that fearful night the enshrouded figure rose from the bed and tottered to the center of the chamber. Terrified, he fell at her feet. She unwound the burial cerements from her head and there streamed down raven-black hair unknown to the living Rowena. Then the spectral figure slowly opened her eyes. He screamed in one last mad shout. He could not be mistaken. Staring at him were the full black eyes of his lost love, the Lady Ligeia.

LIGHT IN AUGUST

Type of work: Novel
Author: William Faulkner (1897-   )
Type of plot: Psychological realism
Time of plot: Early twentieth century
Locale: Mississippi
First published: 1932

> *Principal characters:*
> Joe Christmas, a white Negro
> Doc Hines, his grandfather
> Mr. McEachern, his foster father
> Joanna Burden, his benefactress and mistress
> Joe Brown, alias Lucas Burch, his partner
> Lena Grove, mother of Brown's child
> Byron Bunch, in love with Lena

Critique:

This novel makes a study of the race problem in the South and psychological obsession with the Civil War. It is a fascinating narrative told with little regard for strict time sequence. Sometimes the author's sentence structure becomes obscure; sometimes the exact meaning of his poetic compression is lost. But the novel is important in its vivid treatment of a theme of widespread social signficance.

The Story:

Joe Christmas was the illegitimate son of a circus trouper of Negro blood and a white girl named Milly Hines. Joe's grandfather, old Doc Hines, killed the circus man, let Milly die in childbirth, and put Joe—at Christmas time; hence his last name—into an orphanage, where the children learned to call him "Nigger." Doc Hines then arranged to have Joe adopted by a religious and heartless farmer named McEachern, whose cruelties to Joe were met with a matching stubbornness that made of the boy an almost subhuman being.

One day in town McEachern took Joe to a disreputable restaurant, where he talked to the waitress, Bobbie Allen. McEachern told the adolescent Joe never to patronize the place alone. But Joe went back. He met Bobbie at night and became her lover. Night after night, while the McEacherns were asleep, he would creep out of the house and hurry to meet her in town.

One night McEachern followed Joe to a country dance and ordered him home. Joe reached for a chair, knocked McEachern unconscious, whispered to Bobbie that he would meet her soon, and raced McEachern's mule home. There he gathered up all the money he could lay his hands on and went into town. At the house where Bobbie stayed he encountered the restaurant proprietor and his wife and another man. The two men beat up Joe, took his money, and left for Memphis with the two women.

Joe moved on. Sometimes he worked. More often he simply lived off the money women would give him. He slept with many women and nearly always told them he was of Negro blood.

At last he went to Jefferson, a small town in Mississippi, where he got work shoveling sawdust in a lumber mill. He found lodging in a long-deserted Negro cabin near the country home of Miss Joanna Burden, a spinster of Yankee origin who had few associates in Jefferson because of her zeal for bettering the lot of the Negro. She fed Joe and, when she learned that he was of Negro blood, planned to send him to a Negro school. Joe was her lover for three years. Her reactions ranged from sheer animalism to evangelism, in which she tried to make Joe repent his sins and turn Christian.

A young man who called himself Joe Brown came to work at the sawmill, and Joe Christmas invited Brown to share his cabin with him. The two began to sell bootleg whiskey. After a while Joe told Brown that he was part Negro; before long Brown discovered the relations of Joe and Miss Burden. When their bootlegging prospered, they bought a car and gave up their jobs at the lumber mill.

One night Joe went to Miss Burden's room half-determined to kill her. That night she attempted to shoot him with an antiquated pistol that did not fire. Joe cut her throat with his razor and ran out of the house. Later in the evening a fire was discovered in Miss Burden's house. When the townspeople started to go upstairs in the burning house, Brown tried to stop them. They brushed him aside. They found Miss Burden's body in the bedroom and carried it outside before the house burned to the ground.

Through a letter in the Jefferson bank, the authorities learned of Miss Burden's New Hampshire relatives, whom they notified. Almost at once word came back offering a thousand dollars reward for the capture of the murderer. Brown tried to tell the story as he knew it, putting the blame on Joe Christmas, so that he could collect the money. Few believed his story, but he was held in custody until Joe Christmas could be found.

Joe Christmas remained at large for several days, but at last with the help of bloodhounds he was tracked down. Meanwhile old Doc Hines had learned of his grandson's crime and he came with his wife to Jefferson. He urged the white people to lynch Joe, but for the most part his rantings went unheeded.

On the way to face indictment by the grand jury in the courthouse, Joe, handcuffed but not manacled to the deputy, managed to escape. He ran to a Negro cabin and found a gun. Some volunteer guards from the American Legion gave chase, and finally found him in the kitchen of the Reverend Gail Hightower, a one-time Presbyterian preacher who now was an outcast because he had driven his wife into dementia by his obsession with the gallant death of his grandfather in the Civil War. Joe had gone to Hightower at the suggestion of his grandmother, Mrs. Hines, who had had a conference with him in his cell just before he escaped. She had been advised of this possible way out by Byron Bunch, Hightower's only friend in Jefferson. The Legionnaires shot Joe down; then their leader mutilated him with a knife.

Brown now claimed his reward. A deputy took him out to the cabin where he had lived with Joe Christmas. On entering the cabin, he saw Mrs. Hines holding a new-born baby. In the bed was a girl, Lena Grove, whom he had slept with in a town in Alabama. Lena had started out to find Brown when she knew she was going to have a baby. Traveling most of the way on foot, she had arrived in Jefferson on the day of the murder and the fire. Directed to the sawmill, she had at once seen that Byron Bunch, to whom she had been sent, was not the same man as Lucas Burch, which was Brown's real name. Byron, a kindly soul, had fallen in love with her. Having identified Brown from Byron's description, she was sure that in spite of his new name Brown was the father of her child. She gave birth to the baby in Brown's cabin, where Byron had made her as comfortable as he could, with the aid of Mrs. Hines.

Brown jumped from a back window and ran away. Byron, torn between a desire to marry Lena and the wish to give her baby its rightful father, tracked Brown to the railroad grade outside town and fought with him. Brown escaped aboard a freight train.

Three weeks later Lena and Byron took to the road with the baby, Lena still searching for Brown. A truck driver gave them a lift. Byron was patient, but one night tried to compromise her. When she repulsed him, he left the little camp where the truck was parked. But next morning he was waiting at the bend of the road, and he climbed up on the truck as it made its way toward Tennessee.

LILIOM

Type of work: Drama
Author: Ferenc Molnar (1878-1952)
Type of plot: Fantasy
Time of plot: Early twentieth century
Locale: Budapest
First presented: 1909

> *Principal characters:*
> LILIOM, a merry-go-round barker
> MRS. MUSKAT, his employer
> JULIE, his wife
> MARIE, her friend
> WOLF, Marie's husband
> MRS. HOLLUNDER, Julie's aunt
> FICSUR, Liliom's friend
> LINZMAN, the cashier whom Ficsur suggests robbing
> LOUISE, daughter of Julie and Liliom

LILIOM by Ferenc Molnar. Translated by Benjamin F. Glazer. By permission of the author and his agent Dr Edmond Pauker, of Paramount Pictures, Inc., and the publishers, Liveright Publishing Corp. Copyright, 1921, by Boni & Liveright, Inc. Renewed, 1949, by Ferenc Molnar.

Critique:

This play is a popular favorite on the stages of Europe and America. The author's purpose was to tell a story of love and loyalty among the working classes. As literature the play is not profound, but as an entertainment piece it will probably enjoy a long life.

The Story:

Liliom was a barker for Mrs. Muskat's merry-go-round at an amusement park on the edge of Budapest. As a barker he was a great success, for he had a stock of funny jokes that kept the customers laughing, and he had a playful way with the girls.

One day two young servant girls, Marie and Julie, came to the merry-go-round. To Mrs. Muskat's indignation, Liliom followed Julie onto the merry-go-round and put his arm around her. Mrs. Muskat warned Julie that if she ever came near the merry-go-round again she would be thrown out, as she did not wish to lose her license because of questionable behavior in the park. Liliom, however, told Julie to come back any time and she would be welcome. Although Mrs. Muskat was reluctant to let Liliom go, she could not ignore his insolence, and she dismissed him.

Liliom, to show his independence, announced that he was going to get some beer. While he was collecting his belongings, Marie disclosed to Julie that she was in love with a man in a uniform, a porter, however, not a soldier. When Liliom returned, he turned Marie away and began to discuss love with Julie, bragging and bullying all the while. Julie showed that she was deeply in love, for she had forfeited her job by staying out so late. Two policemen looking for vagrants interrupted their conversation. After asking routine questions and warning Julie that Liliom was a notorious ne'er-do-well, the policemen continued on their rounds. Though Julie protested that she did not love Liliom, it was obvious that she did. So they were married.

They moved into a run-down photographer's shop operated by the Hollunders, mother and son, at the edge of the park. Mrs. Hollunder, Julie's aunt, provided them not only with shelter but also with food and fuel. She grumbled all the time, but she was good-hearted beneath her gruffness. Marie, meanwhile, was falling more deeply in love with Wolf, the porter. One day, while the two girls were exchanging confidences, Mrs. Hollunder came in and said that Julie's other suitor, a widowed carpenter with two children and a respectable income, still wanted to take her out of the poverty in which she lived. Julie preferred to stay where she was. Then Mrs. Muskat came and offered to take Liliom back, but he refused. He and a friend named Ficsur had a scheme for getting a great deal of money; he was no longer interested in his old job at the merry-go-round.

Ficsur was planning a robbery. Each Saturday a cashier for a leather factory passed a nearby railway embankment, with the workmen's wages in a leather bag. Liliom was to accost the man and ask him what time it was while Ficsur was to come up from behind and stab the man. Ficsur encouraged Liliom to steal a knife from Mrs. Hollunder's kitchen. Julie, knowing that the two men were up to no good, begged Liliom not to go out with Ficsur, for she had arranged to have the carpenter come that evening and offer Liliom work. After Liliom had gone, Mrs. Hollunder missed her knife and suspected Liliom of taking it. Julie lied, saying that she had gone through Liliom's pockets and had found only a pack of cards.

Liliom and Ficsur arrived at the embankment just as the six o'clock train passed. Being early, they started a game of twenty-one and Ficsur won from Liliom his share in the loot they hoped to take from the cashier. Liliom accused Ficsur of cheating. Then their victim appeared and Liliom accosted him. As

Ficsur was about to strike, however, the cashier seized Ficsur's arm. He pointed a pistol at Liliom's breast. Ironically, he had come from the factory, where he had just finished paying off the workers, and if Ficsur had killed him the robbers would have got no money. As the cashier called out to two policemen in the distance, Liliom broke away and stabbed himself with the kitchen knife.

The policemen attempted to take him to a hospital, but his condition was too critical. They took him back to the photographer's studio, where he died with Julie by his side holding his hand.

Dying, Liliom had a vision. Two heavenly policemen came to him and told him to follow them. They reminded him that death was not the end, that he was not through with earth until his memory had also passed away. Then they led him to the heavenly court assigned to suicide cases. There he learned that after a period of purification by fire, suicides were sent back to earth for one day to see whether they had profited by their purification. Liliom was sentenced to sixteen years in the fires.

At the end of that time Liliom returned to earth to find his wife and sixteen-year-old daughter Louise about to lunch in the garden of their dilapidated little house. Liliom was unrecognized. Julie gave him some food. He learned from Louise that her father, a handsome man, had gone to America before she was born, and had died there. When Liliom accused her husband of having struck her, Julie denied that he had ever mistreated her, and she dismissed Liliom as an ungrateful wretch. Liliom tried to please his daughter with card tricks and with a beautiful star which he had stolen from heaven, but Louise would have nothing more to do with him. As he left he struck her hard on the hand, but the blow felt as tender as a caress to her. Her mother told her that there had been times when she, too, had experienced that sort of reaction from a blow. So Liliom left in the company of the two policemen, who shook their heads in profound regret at Liliom's failure.

THE LINK

Type of work: Drama
Author: August Strindberg (1849-1912)
Type of plot: Social criticism
Time of plot: Late nineteenth century
Locale: Sweden
First presented: 1893

> *Principal characters:*
> BARON SPRENGEL
> BARONESS SPRENGEL, his wife
> THE JUDGE
> THE PASTOR
> ALEXANDERSSON, a farmer
> TWELVE JURORS

Critique:

The Link, a one-act play in sixteen scenes, is one of Strindberg's briefer attempts to deal dramatically with the problems of marriage and divorce—problems which concerned him personally through-out his adult life. (He had experienced the first of his three divorces in 1891, and there are undoubtedly autobiographical connections here.) The "link," which gives the play its title, is the child of the

THE LINK by August Strindberg, from PLAYS BY AUGUST STRINDBERG. Translated by Edwin Björkman. By permission of the publishers, Charles Scribner's Sons. Copyright, 1912, by Charles Scribner's Sons. Renewed. All rights reserved.

two people who wish to be separated. The child holds them together when everything else is gone between them; the desire to prevent the child from becoming a ward of the court unites them, their old antagonisms still alive, in a common bond of enmity against the unfeeling powers of the state. In this, the play becomes something more than merely a commentary on divorce. It becomes an exposé of modern justice. Once the conflict of Baron Sprengel and his wife is placed before the court, it is no longer theirs. In the hands of the youthful Judge and the callous jurors, it is stripped of its human qualities and reduced to the cold terms of abstract argument. This is a social evil, but the ever-present moralist in Strindberg seems to imply that it is fit punishment for the sins of the erring husband and wife.

The Story:

The courtroom was crowded, for popular interest in the two cases about to be heard—a false accusation charge brought against the farmer Alexandersson by his servant girl, Alma Jonsson, and a separation suit between Baron and Baroness Sprengel—was running high. The young Judge, only twenty-seven years old, was uneasy: he was taking the bench for the first time. He conferred at length with the Pastor before opening the proceedings.

The Alexandersson-Jonsson case was first. The old farmer admitted accusing the girl of theft; he had, he claimed, caught her red-handed. There were, however, no witnesses; and, as the charges could not be proved, his accusations were false—so the girl's lawyer asserted. While the court was cleared, Judge and jury conferred. All agreed that the farmer, though actually in the right, was nevertheless technically guilty. Had he denied accusing the girl, nothing could have been done to him; by being honest, however, he had lost his case. Finally the Judge called Alexandersson in and sentenced him to a fine of a hundred crowns— enough, Alexandersson claimed, to cause

the loss of his farm.

The divorce case came next. The Sprengels had planned to handle things as amicably as possible. The baron was to bring the complaint against his wife, charging her with a disposition incompatible with his. She was to have a sizable annuity and the custody of their one child, a son. The baron, however, was to retain the right to supervise the child's education. These were to be the terms, and none of the personal details of their quarrel were to be brought out.

Such was their agreement; but, once the proceedings began, they found that the agreement was not to be honored. The court, the young Judge curtly informed them, would decide the disposition of the child. Meanwhile, the separation case must be decided: the husband, as complainant, must substantiate his claim.

Confused by the attitude of the court and sensing the possibility of losing her child, the baroness responded emotionally to the planned charges of her husband. The baron, realizing that his right to have charge of the boy's education was threatened by the attitude of the court, asserted that the baroness, by her feminine methods of child-rearing, was undermining the boy's masculinity.

Here the agreement for an amicable settlement broke down completely. Under the goading of the court, the two became overt enemies. All of the sordid details were dragged into the open. The baroness, turning complainant, charged the baron with adultery and produced letters to prove her accusation. The baron met this charge with a stream of vilification, which the baroness emotionally returned. Enraged, the baron announced a countercharge of adultery. The baroness defied him to prove his accusation. The baron promised that he would.

At that point the young Judge adjourned the proceedings and sought help from the elderly Pastor. The Judge, despairing of doing justice, threatened to give up his profession. The Pastor advised him always to adhere to the strict, abstract letter of the law and never to consider the human involvements in a case—else he would go mad. Meanwhile, the baron and the baroness were exchanging personal vituperations.

When the proceedings resumed, the baroness agreed to testify under oath that she was not guilty of adultery. Technical quibblings on her right to testify followed. Then the farmer Alexandersson, probably as a false witness, piqued by the injustice done him, arose and claimed that he had actually observed the baroness' infidelities. While the validity of his testimony was being argued, the baron produced copies of incriminating letters, the originals of which the baroness had seen him destroy.

Again the court was cleared so that Judge and jury could confer. As they waited, the husband and wife realized that they both had lost, that they both

had been defeated by the inhuman forces of a hostile society. Their child, they knew, would be taken from them and brought up ignobly in the name of peasant morality. This realization brought them temporarily together. The baron left to take the child to his mother, out of the court's hands.

He returned just in time to hear the verdict. The two were to be separated for a year and the child placed in the custody of a peasant couple. The baron informed his wife that he had not spirited the child away but had left him at the Pastor's house in preparation for appealing the verdict to a higher court. He predicted the wranglings and heartaches they would endure in the course of the appeal and suggested that it all was a judgment of God upon them for the years that they had lived together unmarried before the child had been born.

THE LION OF FLANDERS

Type of work: Novel
Author: Hendrik Conscience (1812-1883)
Type of plot: Historical romance
Time of plot: 1298-1305
Locale: Flanders
First published: 1838

Principal characters:
PETER DECONINCK, dean of the clothworkers' guild at Bruges
JAN BREYDEL, dean of the butchers' guild at Bruges
COUNT ROBERT DE BETHUNE, called the Lion of Flanders
COUNT GUY OF FLANDERS, Count Robert's elderly father
LADY MATILDA, Count Robert's daughter
ADOLF OF NIEWLAND, a Flemish knight in love with Lady Matilda

Critique:

Hendrik Conscience is regarded as the father of modern Flemish literature, for it was he who first used the Flemish language in his fiction, thus reviving what was a dying literary language. Writing soon after Belgium had become a nation, before his death Conscience gained recognition as a leader of culture in that country, honored by his government in many ways. His books, including *The Lion of Flanders,* his first great success, have been translated into other languages. Like other

novels by Conscience, this work presents a period in the history of Flanders and the Flemish-speaking people in a manner similar to that of Sir Walter Scott in his fiction; and in its ample historical detail and pageant-like descriptions, it is typical of Conscience's work. Students of Flemish culture assert that the pictures of medieval life in Flanders are highly accurate. Others will find that plot and atmosphere combine to give the book a romantic sweep that adds to the interest and pleas-

1699

ure of the reader.

The Story:

At the beginning of the fourteenth century Philip the Fair ruled as King of France, along with his queen, Joanna of Navarre. At the time the French treasury was almost depleted from the cost of many wars, and Philip hoped to refill it with treasure and tax money from the rich cities of Flanders. The burghers, jealous of their privileges, refused to pay, even when asked to do so by Count Guy of Flanders, who was Philip's vassal. Count Guy found himself the victim of the king's displeasure, with his lands confiscated and his daughter Philippa imprisoned in the Louvre. In hopes of aiding Count Guy, Charles de Valois, King Philip's brother, took the Flemish barons to the king to effect a reconciliation. Despite the safe conduct guaranteed by his brother, the king imprisoned the nobles. He was led to that unworthy deed by his queen, who hated the Flemings, nobles and commoners alike. Chagrined by his royal brother's unknightly conduct, Charles de Valois broke his sword and vowed not to serve France until his brother's reign was ended.

Only one Flemish noble, Sir Diederik die Vos, nicknamed the Fox, escaped. Disguising himself as a palmer, he set out to return to his native province where he hoped to lay plans to help his fellow Flemings. The French took over Castle Wynandael, the home of Count Guy. Lady Matilda, Count Robert's daughter, fled to Bruges and found asylum in the home of Adolf of Niewland. Another of her protectors was Peter Deconinck, powerful dean of the great clothworkers' guild in the city.

At the time the Flemings were divided into three groups. One, the Lilyards, favored collaboration with the French. Another, made up chiefly of commoners, favored supporting Count Guy and independence, even though the count was the French king's prisoner; this group was known as the Clawards, after the claws of

the heraldic device of Flanders, a lion. The third group, made up of nobles, held back from participation in the disagreements; because the commoners were involved they did not consider this a conflict in which they could become involved with honor.

Determined to subjugate the Flemings, Philip the Fair entered Bruges with a military force and appointed his queen's uncle governor of Flanders. After the king left a per capita tax was laid on the citizens to pay for the cost of the visit. Peter Deconinck advised his clothworkers not to pay the tax; for his rebellious counsel he was placed in prison. To Deconinck's rescue went Jan Breydel, dean of the butchers, and freed him. In retaliation the Lilyards and the French governor planned to hang both Deconinck and Breydel as the first step in forcing the guilds and the people to submit entirely. The two deans of the guilds made battle plans and met force with force. The Lilyards were forced into the confines of the castle, but at last the threat of pillage by the French forces outside the city forced the Clawards to submit. The French entered the city, freed the Lilyards, and held the people of Bruges at their mercy.

One day as Adolf of Niewland walked in the countryside outside the city walls he met Sir Diederik die Vos in the disguise of a friar. The nobleman brought word that the French vassal who guarded Count Robert de Bethune, called the Lion of Flanders, was willing to grant Count Robert freedom for a time if someone else would take his place. Adolf of Niewland agreed to do so.

Some weeks later the French, led by a disloyal clothworker, arrested Lady Matilda and prepared to take her off to prison in France. Lady Matilda had displeased Queen Joanna, and this was the queen's revenge. As soon as he learned what had happened, Jan Breydel set off to rescue Lady Matilda. Captured, he managed to escape. Returning with several hundred followers, he burned the castle at Male. A small band of French knights escaped, taking Lady Matilda with them. A short time later they met a knight in black armor who rescued the girl. The knight was Count Robert in disguise. He was so pleased with the conduct of Deconinck and Breydel that he left word that they were to be knighted at the first opportunity.

On his return to Bruges, Breydel found that many citizens were fleeing to the country, the Clawards deeming it unsafe to remain in the city. They were led by Deconinck, who hoped to join forces with some nobles who were ready to support actively the cause of Count Guy of Flanders. At a council of war Count Robert advised that they prepare as quickly as possible as large a force as they could, for the French king was gathering an army of seventy thousand men to subdue Flanders. He also brought word that his sister Philippa had been poisoned in prison.

Meanwhile, the Clawards left in Bruges were badly mistreated. On May 13, 1302, in an attempt to cow the population, the French governor and the Lilyards picked out eight men to be hanged. Only one of the eight was saved —the father of Jan Breydel, rescued by his son at the last minute. In immediate retaliation the French killed all the Clawards they could find and pillaged their homes; among the victims were the mother and sister of Jan Breydel. Then the Clawards returned to the city in force and killed seven thousand Frenchmen and many Lilyards. Only a handful of the French escaped. When the city was restored to order, Lady Matilda and Adolf of Niewland returned to the latter's home. Soon after, Lord Guy, the younger brother of Count Robert, arrived with a body of troops to help protect the city.

Philip the Fair, undaunted by the setback at Bruges, raised a large army for the invasion of Flanders. The Flemings, seeing that their land must be laid waste by the French or defended to the utmost, took an oath to stand together and gathered their forces to resist the French.

Soon the two armies, each in excess of sixty thousand men, advanced to meet in battle. The Flemish took up a defensive position before the city of Courtrai. There, in full view and hearing of all, Lady Matilda and Lord Guy, her uncle, invested Peter Deconinck and Jan Breydel with knighthood, as Count Robert had commanded. The French army,. meanwhile, had camped near Lille. The French leader, Count Robert d'Artois, was so eager to do battle that he failed to reconnoiter the Flemish position. His vows of bloody revenge were so terrible that part of his force deserted, preferring to fight with the Flemings rather than dishonor themselves.

The French advanced from Lille to the attack. At first the advantage was on their side, but their failure to make a reconnaissance left a trap for their cavalry. Before the city of Courtrai was a large, deep marsh, into which wave after wave of the French horsemen sank, to be ridden over by their comrades who followed and to be decimated by weapons of the Flemish forces. Even so, for a time the battle seemed to go against the Flemings, until a knight in gold appeared. He was Count Robert, the Lion of Flanders, freed again from his prison for a time and hurrying to the aid of his people. Under his leadership the Flemings won the victory. After the battle Count Robert returned to his prison, knowing that the French would not dare kill him, lest hostages held by the Flemish army be killed in reprisal. Before he left, Count Robert promised that Lady Matilda should become the bride of Adolf of Niewland. The young knight had fought bravely in the battle. Badly wounded, he was recovering in the monastery in which Lady Matilda had taken refuge.

After the battle at Courtrai, called the Battle of the Golden Spurs, Flanders was safe; trade and commerce flourished again. The French still tried to subdue the Flemish people, but several such attempts ended in failure. Philip the Fair dishonored himself in one truce to write

1701

a treaty, but additional French defeats forced him finally to give up all hope of subduing the stubborn, independent Flemish. Old Count Guy of Flanders died while waiting for the treaty to be signed and so was never released from his prison. But Count Robert, the Lion of Flanders, was set free after the signing of the treaty in 1305, and until his death seventeen years later he ruled over his free people.

THE LITTLE CLAY CART

Type of work: Drama
Author: Shudraka (fl. 100 B.C.)
Type of plot: Tragi-comedy
Time of plot: Fifth century B.C.
Locale: Ancient Hindu city of Ujjayinī
First presented: Unknown

Principal characters:

CHĀRUDATTA, an impoverished young Brāhmana
VASANTASENĀ, a courtesan in love with Chārudatta
MAITREYA, a poor Brāhmana, Chārudatta's friend
SAMSTHĀNAKA, King Pālaka's brother-in-law
ĀRYAKA, an exiled prince
SARVILAKA, a Brāhmana and a thief
MADANIKĀ, Vasantasenā's slave and confidante

Critique:

The Little Clay Cart is regarded by students of literature in the Western world as one of the two best extant Sanskrit plays, the other being Kalidasa's *Sakuntala*. Many critics have pointed out that *The Little Clay Cart* is more like Western drama than any other Sanskrit play, in structure, characterization, and tone. This similarity to Occidental drama may account for the fact that its Indian critics have been less enthusiastic than those of the Western world. *The Little Clay Cart* is noteworthy for being the only known Sanskrit play to show a courtesan in love with a Brāhmana, as it is the only known one also to contain important characters from various strata of Hindu society, not from the upper castes only. It is the seemingly realistic and vivid presentation of these characters which probably has appealed most to Western readers. In the original the title is *Mrcchakatikā*.

The Story:

Chārudatta was a Brāhmana who had impoverished himself by spending his substance on the public welfare and in helping those individuals who sought his aid. Though dwelling in poverty in a broken-down house, he still enjoyed a fine reputation in Ujjayinī as an honest and upright man of rare wisdom. This reputation eased somewhat the fact that he had been deserted by most of his friends and was embarrassed by his lack of wealth.

Although married happily and the proud father of a small son, Rohasena, Chārudatta was enamored of Vasantasenā, a courtesan of great wealth and reputation who, having seen him at a temple, was also in love with him. One evening as Chārudatta and his friend Maitreya sat discussing Chārudatta's misfortunes and the efficacy of devotion to the gods, Vasantasenā found herself pursued by Samsthānaka, a half-mad brother-in-law of King Pālaka, and one of his henchmen. The men offered to do violence to Vasantasenā, but she escaped from them in the darkness and found safety in the house of Chārudatta, where a meeting between the two increased the love they already felt for each other. The courtesan, before she left to return to her own palace, entrusted a casket of jewelry to Chārudatta, as an excuse to see him again.

During the night a thief, Sarvilaka, entered Chārudatta's house and stole the jewelry to buy his love, Madanikā, who was Vasantasenā's slave and confidante. The courtesan accepted the jewels and freed Madanikā to marry Sarvilaka, intending to see that Chārudatta should learn that the jewels had been recovered. In the meantime, Chārudatta sent a rare pearl necklace of his wife's to Vasantasenā to recompense the courtesan for the loss of the less valuable jewels. His friend Maitreya, fearing that Vasantasenā's attentions could bring only bad luck and disaster, cautioned Chārudatta against doing so. Maitreya, knowing courtesans, believed that Vasantasenā was merely scheming to take from Chārudatta the few possessions he still had.

After leaving Vasantasenā's palace with his newly freed bride, Sarvilaka learned that his friend, Prince Āryaka, had been arrested by King Pālaka and placed in a dungeon. The king, neither a popular nor a just monarch, feared that the people might rise up, as a soothsayer had predicted, to place Prince Āryaka on the throne. After Sarvilaka succeeded in freeing the prince from prison, Āryaka sought help from Chārudatta, who aided him in escaping the pursuing guards.

Vasantasenā, having proved her love for Chārudatta by becoming his mistress, met his small son and gave him some jewels with which to purchase a golden toy cart to replace the unsatisfactory clay cart Chārudatta had been able to afford. She made arrangements to meet Chārudatta in Pushpakarandaka Park, outside the city, for a day's outing, but by mistake she entered the wrong vehicle and found herself in the gharri belonging to Samsthānaka, who still pursued her and was madly jealous of the love and favors she bestowed freely upon Chārudatta. When Vasantasenā arrived at the park, she was discovered in the gharri by Samsthānaka, who at first was overjoyed at seeing her because he thought she had come to him voluntarily. When she

spurned him and declared her love for Chārudatta, Samsthānaka tried to make his henchmen kill her, but they refused. Samsthānaka sent his followers away and choked her himself. Believing her dead, he hid the body under a pile of leaves. Then, hoping to escape the penalty for his crime, Samsthānaka decided to go to a court and accuse Chārudatta of murdering Vasantasenā.

When Samsthānaka first appeared at court, the judges, who knew him to be somewhat mad, refused to see him or take him seriously; but when he threatened to go to King Pālaka, the judges became frightened and sent for Chārudatta. Falsely accused, Chārudatta proclaimed his innocence. But circumstances were against him. He admitted having been in the park, and the jewels of Vasantasenā were found at his home, offering a motive for the poverty-stricken man to have killed the girl. The judges, in spite of his previous reputation, were forced to find Chārudatta guilty. Although his status as a Brāhmana exempted him from the death penalty for any crime, King Pālaka ordered Chārudatta put to death. No one knew that the body identified as Vasantasenā's was that of another woman or that Vasantasenā, befriended by a Buddhist monk, was recovering near the park from Samsthānaka's attack.

Chārudatta was taken through the city by two executioners, who stopped several times to announce the name of the condemned man and the nature of his crime. Although the people of the city loved Chārudatta, they dared not intervene on his behalf, even though he steadfastly maintained his innocence. Samsthānaka's slave tried to tell that his master had really committed the crime, but no one believed him, and so Chārudatta and his executioners, accompanied by a crowd, continued on their way to the place of execution, a cemetery south of the city.

The executioners, thinking to be merciful, offered to decapitate Chārudatta, but a miracle prevented their sword from touching him, and so they prepared the

1703

victim for the slow, agonizing death by impalement upon a pike. Fortunately, Vasantasenā, seeing the excited crowd as she made her way back to the city, intervened in time. When she told who had really attacked her, though unsuccessfully, Samsthānaka was arrested. The excitement was not ended, however, for word came that Chārudatta's wife, believing herself a widow, was about to cast herself upon a funeral pyre. Chārudatta

reached her in time to prevent her death, and she and Vasantasenā met and accepted one another. Word came, too, that Prince Āryaka had deposed King Pālaka and was now king. One of his first deeds was to restore Chārudatta's fortune and make him an important official of the court. Chārudatta, still a man of conscience and charity, forgave Samsthānaka's villainy and caused him to be set free.

LITTLE DORRIT

Type of work: Novel
Author: Charles Dickens (1812-1870)
Type of plot: Sentimental romance
Time of plot: Early nineteenth century
Locale: England
First published: 1855-1857

Principal characters:
    LITTLE DORRIT, a child born and reared in debtors' prison
    WILLIAM DORRIT, her father
    FANNY, her older sister
    ARTHUR CLENNAM, Little Dorrit's friend
    MRS. CLENNAM, Arthur's mother and Little Dorrit's employer
    MONSIEUR BLANDOIS, a blackmailer
    MR. MERDLE, a banker and Fanny Dorrit's father-in-law

Critique:

This book, which has never had the popularity of most of Dickens' other novels, was the product of the author's "middle period," which came prior to his great successes with *A Tale of Two Cities* and *Great Expectations.* To a modern reader the book is dreary because of the scenes in the Marshalsea debtors' prison. In addition, the very concept of a debtors' prison is so far removed from modern experience that we have difficulty in picturing the setting. To Dickens' contemporaries, however, there was probably a great deal of interest in the sections dealing with the red tape and inefficiency of the Circumlocution Office, by which Dickens satirized the inefficiency of the British government during the Crimean War.

The Story:

Amy Dorrit, or, as she was better known, Little Dorrit, was born while her mother stayed with her father, a bankrupt,

in Marshalsea debtors' prison. Although her mother died soon after, the little girl, along with her older brother and sister, continued to live in the prison. As she became older, Little Dorrit went outside the prison to do sewing, for only the debtor himself was not permitted to leave the place.

One of the women for whom Little Dorrit sewed was Mrs. Clennam, a widow carrying on a place of business, even though she had been confined to her room by illness for fifteen years. Mrs. Clennam's son, who was forty, had gone to the Orient twenty years before and had joined his father, who looked after the company's business in the East. After his father's death Arthur Clennam returned. He told his mother that he would take his part of the inheritance and fend for himself; he did not want to remain in the business with his miserly, grasping, and rather inhuman mother. Mrs. Clennam, confronted by her son's decision, took her old clerk into partnership with her.

While he was staying at his mother's house, Arthur noticed Little Dorrit and made inquiry about her. Having been struck by the girl's sweet disposition and appearance, he went to Marshalsea debtors' prison and tried to help the Dorrit family. He even said that he would try to get Mr. Dorrit out of the place. Everyone thought such a course impossible, for some of Mr. Dorrit's debts were owed through the Circumlocution Office, a place of endless red tape, to the crown.

Arthur found that he had a confederate, though an unusual one, in a clerk named Pancks, a queer creature who collected rents for Arthur's former fiancée's father. Pancks was aided in turn by John Chivery, the son of a turnkey, who was also in love with Little Dorrit, and by Mr. Rugg, an elderly lawyer.

In addition to helping Little Dorrit by putting in motion action to have her father released from prison, Arthur aided her by getting her more sewing clients, by getting her brother out of trouble, and by sending small amounts of money to defray the expenses of the Dorrit household in the prison.

At last Pancks brought unusual advice. He had discovered that Mr. Dorrit, who had been in prison over twenty years, was the only surviving heir to a large fortune which had gone unclaimed for years. Within a short time Mr. Dorrit was released, his debts having been paid, and he immediately set himself up as a man of fortune. Mr. Dorrit and his two oldest children, determined to live up to the new social position that their fortune had given them, tried to forget everything in the past. They even convinced themselves that Arthur Clennam had insulted them and refused to have anything more to do with the man. Only Little Dorrit remained unspoiled, merely surprised at the good fortune which had been thrust upon them.

As quickly as possible the Dorrit family went to the continent, where they could successfully carry out the fiction that they had never seen a debtor's prison. Because of their money they were admitted to the society of Britons who were living away from England. Fanny Dorrit, the older of the two daughters, was pursued by Mr. Sparkle, stepson of Mr. Merdle, who was supposed to be the richest and most influential banker in England. Fanny, although not in love with Sparkle, considered with pleasure the prospect of marrying into a wealthy family. The Merdles, who saw only that the Dorrits had a fortune, agreed to the match, even though Mrs. Merdle was well aware of the fact that her son had fallen in love with Fanny when the latter was a dancer on the stage in London.

After the marriage Fanny and her husband went to live in London. Mr. Dorrit visited them there and became a close friend of Mr. Merdle. The banker even proposed to help Mr. Dorrit increase his already large fortune through shrewd and well-paying investments. Mr. Dorrit, the former debtor, was in seventh heaven because of his new prospects.

Little Dorrit wondered at the change in her family but remained her own self. She wrote to Arthur at intervals, for she, at least, was still grateful for all he had done to help her. Besides, she was in love with him.

Arthur, still in London, was trying to fathom certain mysterious people who had been seen about his mother's house and also attempting to keep his own business on solid financial ground. Neither task was easy. Mrs. Clennam was visited on two occasions by a Monsieur Blandois, whom Arthur knew to be a knave and probably a murderer. He wondered what business his mother could have with such a person. He also distrusted Flintwinch, the clerk who had become his mother's partner. Flintwinch, a grubbing miserly fellow who mistreated his wife, had taken a great dislike to Arthur.

While trying to unravel the mystery, Arthur became financially insolvent. Like many others, he had become convinced that the business ventures of Mr. Merdle were the safest and quickest way to make a fortune. As a result, he had put his money and his company's money into Merdle's ventures. When Merdle and his bank failed, Arthur became a bankrupt and was sent to the Marshalsea debtors' prison, where he was housed in Mr. Dorrit's old quarters.

Mr. Rugg and Pancks did their best to make Arthur's imprisonment a short one, but he seemed to have lost all desire to live, much less to leave the prison. Only after Little Dorrit returned to England and took up quarters within the prison, to comfort him as she had comforted her father, did Arthur take any interest in life.

Learning that Monsieur Blandois had disappeared from Mrs. Clennam's house,

Pancks tracked down the man and brought him back to London. Then the reason for his attempt to blackmail Mrs. Clennam was revealed. Mrs. Clennam, realizing that she had to make known the mystery to her son unless she intended to pay blackmail, rose from her wheelchair and left her house for the first time in almost twenty years. She went to the prison to tell Arthur that he was not her child and that she had for many years been keeping money from him and from Little Dorrit.

When that mystery had been solved, and the money was forthcoming, Arthur was soon released from prison. Shortly afterward he and Little Dorrit were married. Little Dorrit, after a quarter century of misfortune, was at last about to embark upon a quiet and comfortable life.

THE LITTLE FOXES

Type of work: Drama
Author: Lillian Hellman (1905-   )
Type of plot: Social realism
Time of plot: 1900
Locale: The Deep South
First presented: 1939

Principal characters:
REGINA GIDDENS, a predatory woman
BENJAMIN HUBBARD, and
OSCAR HUBBARD, her brothers
HORACE GIDDENS, her husband
ALEXANDRA, daughter of Regina and Horace
BIRDIE HUBBARD, Oscar's wife

Critique:

The Little Foxes is usually considered the major achievement of Lillian Hellman, and many critics place it high on the list of American plays. In the first place, it is technically a well-knit piece of writing: her dialogue crackles and her characters convince; there is no extraneous matter present, so that The Little Foxes is brilliantly compact and effective theater. Secondly, in the chicanery of the Hubbard family, we have what is probably an accurate picture of one aspect of

the rise of industrialism in the post-Civil War South.

The Story:

William Marshall, a Chicago businessman, came South to negotiate with Benjamin and Oscar Hubbard and their sister, the striking Regina Giddens, over matters concerning the construction of a cotton mill. The Hubbard brothers and Regina foresaw a glittering future for them all. No longer would the cotton have to come to the machines; instead, at long last, it would be the other way around. They firmly believed that millions awaited them: the Hubbards would be the richest family in the South. Ben foresaw a stable of race horses, Oscar speculated on a new home, and the hapless Birdie, whom Oscar had married for her father's cotton fields, longed to see Lionnet, her old family home, restored to its former grace and beauty. Birdie continually sought a return to the genteel, refined behavior of earlier days, before the rise of materialistic ruthfulness.

Later, certain difficulties arose. The brothers lacked seventy-five thousand dollars, Regina's third of the sum which the Hubbards were to put up. Presumably this amount would come from Horace, Regina's husband, who lay in a Baltimore hospital with a fatal heart ailment. Though Regina had given Ben and Oscar her promise that Horace would put up the money, no word had yet reached them. Horace, away five months, had failed to acknowledge Regina's demands for his return. Regina suggested, however, that he was possibly holding out for a larger share of the profits; when one's money was badly needed, one should be entitled to a bigger share of the eventual returns. After crafty manipulation, Regina extracted from Ben a promise of a greater share of the profits if she could get Horace home within two weeks. Regina immediately dispatched Alexandra, her daughter, to Baltimore.

When Horace arrived a week later, in response to his daughter's summons, the Hubbards and Regina descended on him. No one in his right mind, the argument ran, would refuse a seventy-five thousand dollar investment that would garner a million. Ben explained how water power would be cheap and how the men of the mountains and small towns would be happy to work for low wages. Thus the profits would be tremendous. But Horace, though sourly admitting that the venture was a good deal for the Hubbards, stated that he and Regina had

enough money already. The truth was that Horace had had enough of his scheming wife and her equally conniving family, who, having made a sizable sum already through their exploitation of the poor, were now on their way to greater fortune in identical fashion.

Regina protested furiously, but to no avail. However, Ben and Oscar were not too upset. Oscar's son Leo, through a young banking employee, had discovered that Horace had eighty-eight thousand dollars in bonds in his safe deposit box, securities which he checked only once in six months. Assuming that Horace would never miss them for a few months, Ben had Oscar seize the bonds—more than enough to meet the sum required by Marshall—and leave for Chicago to complete negotiations. Regina, after a fierce argument with Horace, learned that Oscar had gone. Ben now held the upper hand; he simply told Regina that everything had been settled. Horace, an onlooker, was quietly amused. Now, he thought, he would not be a party to the wrecking of the town. He would at least die honestly. To the watching Alexandra's horror, Regina calmly informed him that she hoped he would indeed die as quickly as possible.

Two weeks later, Horace went to his now estranged wife's part of the house. Knowing that he was to be short-lived, he had had his deposit box brought to him, and had discovered the theft. This he told Regina, along with his accurate suspicions as to the thieves' identity. To Regina's surprise, however, he stated that he intended to say nothing unless forced to, and then he would simply call the theft a loan. Horace planned to make a new will, leaving Regina eighty-eight thousand dollars in bonds. Thus she would eventually inherit his bonds, but she would not receive a single cent of the millions ·Ben and Oscar prophesied for the Hubbard family. For once Horace had tied the hands of his cunning wife.

Recalling their unhappy married life, Regina shrewishly revealed her contempt for Horace from the start. Horace, feeling an attack coming on, broke his bottle of medicine. Regina, hoping that his efforts to climb the stairs would prove fatal, cruelly refused to go upstairs for his second bottle. Horace staggered from his wheelchair and collapsed on the stair landing.

In an interview with her brothers after Horace was carried to his room, Regina revealed what she had learned from her husband. Should he die, she would blackmail them for a seventy-five percent share of the profits in exchange for the bonds. Soon word came, in the person of the silent Alexandra, that Regina's plan had worked. Horace was dead. Regina then announced her plans for seeing the judge the next day. Any jury would be swayed

by a woman whose brothers had stolen from her. Regina also declared that there were not twelve men in the state whom the brothers had not cheated. A philosophical Ben gave in to Regina's demands, but as he left he was wondering what Horace, who had been in a wheelchair, was doing on the landing. Perhaps in the future he might find out. And when he did, he would let Regina know.

Realizing that Alexandra loved her father very much, Regina tried to be sympathetic. However, her saddened, sickened daughter defied her plans for their future in Chicago. Alexandra announced her final departure from Regina and the Hubbards because she believed that her father would have wanted it that way.

THE LITTLE MINISTER

Type of work: Novel
Author: James M. Barrie (1860-1937)
Type of plot: Sentimental romance
Time of plot: Mid-nineteenth century
Locale: The village of Thrums in Scotland
First published: 1891

Principal characters:
    GAVIN DISHART, the little minister of Thrums
    MARGARET DISHART, his mother
    MR. OGILVY, the schoolmaster, Margaret's second husband, and the narrator
    ROB DOW, a drunkard converted by Gavin
    BABBIE, a gipsy who loves Gavin
    NANNY WEBSTER, an old woman saved from the poorhouse by Babbie
    LORD RINTOUL, Babbie's guardian and her betrothed

Critique:

Barrie's sensitivity and deep appreciation of human values explain the popularity of this novel. The quiet, reserved humor appeals to the intellect and the heart rather than to a ludicrous sense of buffoonery, and the frequent note of sentiment is delicate and restrained. The book displays Barrie's gift for character portrayal and his lack of self-consciousness in his whimsical, ironic style.

The Story:

Mr. Ogilvy, the schoolmaster of Glen Quharity, had not seen Margaret Dishart for eighteen years until that day when he stood in the crowd that had gathered to welcome Gavin Dishart, the new minister of Auld Licht parish in Thrums. When the dominie saw Margaret again, he knew that all her happiness lay in her son Gavin. The schoolmaster did not allow Margaret to see him, as he never would even in the disturbed days to come. He knew that he was best out of her life, that he could bring her only unhappiness. When he

THE LITTLE MINISTER by James M. Barrie. Published by Charles Scribner's Sons.

heard Gavin deliver his first sermon at Auld Licht, the dominie knew that the little minister, who was just twenty-one, had indeed received the "call."

Lord Rintoul's castle stood in the Spittal on the hill above Glen Quharity. It was rumored that he had in his household a young girl whom he expected to marry soon, but no one had seen the girl except the sheriff of Thrums, who stopped at the castle to tell Lord Rintoul that a detachment of militia was coming to Thrums to arrest some insurgent weavers. Dressed as a gipsy, the young bride-to-be ran to the village to warn the people that soldiers were on their way.

Gavin Dishart met her that night as he was walking through Windyghoul toward Caddam. She ran dancing and singing, and laughed at him as she darted past him toward Thrums. When Gavin caught up with her, they became rivals as Gavin attempted to calm the workers whom the gipsy had aroused against the soldiers. Her activities on the night the militia came was a topic of discussion in Thrums for days afterward—this mysterious gipsy whose origin no one could guess. Even Gavin spent more hours than was proper pondering over the girl who had brazenly claimed, when the soldiers had tried to arrest her, that she was his wife.

Gavin's next meeting with the gipsy was in the cottage of old Nanny Webster, a parish charge. This story the schoolmaster heard through village gossip. The story of how Gavin had gone with Dr. McQueen to take old Nanny to the poorhouse, and how the gipsy girl, Babbie, interrupted the proceedings by offering to provide Nanny with an income for the old woman's support, reached the dominie only in rumor. Most of the villagers believed that the little minister had done the good work; few knew about the gipsy's part in the story.

Gavin could have avoided ever seeing Babbie again, but he did not. He even went so far as to tell her when he would be walking through Caddam woods. Bab-

bie was not like the people of Thrums. She horrified old Nanny with her impertinence to the little minister of Auld Licht. She embarrassed Gavin by teasing him about his height, a fact which had caused him great distress all his life. Ever on the lookout for the pair was Rob Dow, who skulked among the pines of Windyghoul spying on his beloved minister and the witch who had cast a spell on Gavin. Rob, a drunkard whom Gavin had converted, feared for his minister after he had seen the gipsy nearly succeed in her attempt to make the minister kiss her. Rob jealously guarded his secret, for he was no gossip. To his death, Rob protected the little minister who had saved him from drink.

While the dominie feared lest Margaret be hurt by this woodland courtship, Gavin was troubled by his love for the brazen gipsy. As she gradually became aware of his devotion, the gipsy girl began to love him in turn. No one had ever loved her before. Lord Rintoul only played at watching her beauty. When Gavin stated that he would marry her, Babbie protested that he would be banished from Thrums and so break his mother's heart.

One night the lovers walked together through Windyghoul. Unknown to anyone, the dominie, Mr. Ogilvy, often strolled through the same wood so that he could gaze at the manse where Margaret lived. That night he met Gavin and Babbie. Immediately sensing their relationship and thinking only of Margaret, Ogilvy stepped into the affair and there he remained until it ended, not for Gavin's sake but for Margaret's protection. There were no words exchanged that night, but each knew that the dominie was aware of the love between Gavin and Babbie.

In Windyghoul, the next day, Babbie met Micah, Rob Dow's small son. Sobbing, the child told her that his father had taken to drink again because the little minister had been bewitched by the gipsy. If only she would go away, Rob

1709

could regain his faith in the minister and stop his drinking once more. Babbie realized then that Gavin's duty called him from her. She never laid eyes again on her lover until the terrible day of the great rain.

On the day of the great rain plans were being made at the Spittal for Lord Rintoul's wedding to his young bride. On this same day there was a fight in Thrums, and false news spread that Gavin had been killed by a drunken Highland piper. When the news traveled as far as the Spittal, Babbie, alarmed for Gavin and Margaret, ran to Mr. Ogilvy to ask his aid. The schoolmaster went with her to Windyghoul, where they encountered Gavin. When the two lovers were reunited, Babbie told Gavin that this was the day of her wedding to Lord Rintoul. Again Gavin asserted that he would marry her.

They hurried away to a gipsy camp and there the gipsy king married them over the tongs. Meanwhile Lord Rintoul, searching for his bride, had followed her in time to witness the ceremony. In the confusion of the gipsy camp, Babbie cried out to Gavin that she heard Lord Rintoul's voice. As Gavin rushed to encounter his rival, Babbie was suddenly snatched away. Assuming that Lord Rintoul would bring her back to the Spittal, Gavin headed toward Glen Quharity. The increasing rain drove him to Mr. Ogilvy's house for shelter.

The dominie ordered Gavin to end his fruitless pursuit, but the little minister insisted that he would take Babbie back to the manse as his bride. Then Mr. Ogilvy had to tell Gavin about Margaret. The schoolmaster—his name was Gavin also—had married Margaret after her first husband, Adam Dishart, had disappeared at sea. Six years after little Gavin's birth Adam Dishart had returned to claim his wife and little Gavin as his own. Mr. Ogilvy, perceiving the sorrow in Margaret's eyes as she faced the two men who claimed her, had disappeared and had sworn never to allow

Margaret to know of his existence again. It was too late for the little minister and his real father to find any filial love after the schoolmaster's painful revelation. Gavin acknowledged his father, but he claimed that it was more God's will that he find Babbie again. As Gavin set out toward the Spittal, Mr. Ogilvy started toward Thrums to protect Margaret from village gossip that might reach her.

Babbie had not been captured by Lord Rintoul. Rob Dow, resolved to destroy the cause of his minister's downfall, had seized her. The gipsy eluded him during the severe storm, however, and ran to the manse to find Gavin.

Gavin, meanwhile, had lost all trace of Lord Rintoul in the rain-swept darkness. While he was making his way across the storm-flooded countryside, he came upon a ravine where some men shouted to him that Lord Rintoul was stranded on a small islet which was being washed away by the swiftly-flowing water. He could be saved if a man would jump down onto the island with a rope. Although he had no rope, Gavin jumped in the hope that he could help Lord Rintoul to maintain his foothold on the tiny piece of dwindling turf. As the villagers gathered at the brink of the ravine, their minister shouted to them that he had married Babbie the gipsy and that Mr. Ogilvy was to carry the news of his death to his mother and his wife. Then a man leaped into the ravine with a rope. It was Rob Dow, who performed his last living act to save the little minister whom he loved.

Gavin, followed by his admiring congregation, returned to the manse. There he found his mother and Babbie, who now could reveal herself, not as the wild gipsy of Windyghoul, but as the lady whom Lord Rintoul had planned to wed. Gavin and Babbie were married again under the prayers of a real minister, but Gavin always felt that he had really married her under the stars in the gipsy camp.

Mr. Ogilvy told the story of Gavin and

1710

Babbie to the eager little girl who was the daughter of the little minister and his wife. At the schoolmaster's request, Margaret Dishart had never learned of his part in Gavin's love affair. But after her death Gavin Ogilvy heard Babbie's and Gavin's daughter call him grandfather.

LITTLE WOMEN

Type of work: Novel
Author: Louisa May Alcott (1832-1888)
Type of plot: Sentimental romance
Time of plot: Nineteenth century
Locale: A New England village; New York City; Italy
First published: 1868

> *Principal characters:*
> MEG,
> JO,
> BETH, and
> AMY, the March sisters
> MRS. MARCH (MARMEE), their mother
> MR. MARCH, their father
> THEODORE LAWRENCE (LAURIE), a young neighbor
> PROFESSOR BHAER, a tutor, in love with Jo

Critique:

Little Women is one of the best-loved books of all time, as popular today as when it was written eighty years ago. Although it is actually a children's book, it appeals to grownups as well, who see in it a mirror of their own childhood, or at least the childhood they would have preferred. The story is largely autobiographical, the March girls being Louisa's own sisters, with herself as Jo.

The Story:

The March family lived in a small house next door to the Lawrence mansion, where young Theodore Lawrence and his aged grandfather had only each other for company in the great house. Old Mr. Lawrence was wealthy and he indulged every wish of his grandson, but often Laurie was lonely. When the lamp was lit and the shades were up in the March house, he could see the four March girls with their mother in the center seated around a cheerful fire. He learned to know them by name before he met them, and in his imagination he almost felt himself a member of the family.

The oldest was plump Meg, who had to earn her living as governess of a group of unruly youngsters in the neighborhood. Next was Jo, tall, awkward, and tomboyish, who liked to write, and who spent all her spare time devising plays and entertainments for her sisters. Then there was gentle Beth, the homebody, content to sit knitting by the fire, or to help her mother take care of the house. The youngest was curly-haired Amy, a schoolgirl who dreamed of someday becoming a famous artist like Michelangelo or Leonardo da Vinci.

At Christmas time the girls were confronted with the problem of what to do with the dollar Marmee, as they called their mother, had said they might spend. At first each thought only of her own pleasure, but all ended by buying a gift for Marmee instead. On Christmas morning they insisted on sharing their breakfast with the Hummels, a poor family in the neighborhood, and for this unselfishness they were rewarded when rich Mr. Lawrence sent over a surprise Christ-

LITTLE WOMEN by Louisa May Alcott. Published by Little, Brown & Co.

mas feast consisting of ice cream, bonbons, and four bouquets of flowers for the table.

Many happy days followed, with Laurie, who had met Jo at a fashionable New Year's Eve dance, becoming a part of the March family circle. But in November of that same year a telegram brought a message that their father, an army chaplain in the Civil War, was critically ill. Mrs. March did not know what to do. She felt that she should go to her husband at once, but she had barely five dollars in her purse. She was hesitant about going to wealthy, irascible Aunt March for help. Jo solved the problem by selling her beautiful, long, chestnut hair, which was her only vanity, for twenty-five dollars. She made the sacrifice willingly, but that night, after the others had gone to bed, Marmee went to her daughter's room and found her weeping. Marmee asked if she were crying over her father's illness, and Jo sobbed that it was not her father she was crying for now, but for her hair.

During Marmee's absence dark days fell upon the little women. Beth, who had never been strong at best, contracted scarlet fever, and for a time it looked as if Jo were going to lose her dearest sister. Marmee was sent for, but by the time she arrived the crisis had passed and her little daughter was better. By the next Christmas, Beth was her old contented self again. Mr. March surprised them all when he returned home from the front well and happy. The little family was together once more.

Then John Brooke, Laurie's tutor, fell in love with Meg. This fact was disclosed when Mr. Brooke surreptitiously stole one of Meg's gloves and kept it in his pocket as a memento. Laurie discovered the glove and informed Jo. To his great surprise, she was infuriated at the idea that the family circle might be disturbed. But she was quite reconciled when, three years later, Meg became Mrs. Brooke.

In the meantime, Jo herself had grown up. She began to take her writing seriously, and even sold a few stories which helped with the family budget.

Her greatest disappointment came when Aunt Carrol, a relative of the Marches, decided she needed a companion on a European trip, and asked not Jo but the more lady-like Amy to accompany her. Then Jo, with Marmee's permission, decided to go to New York. She took a job as governess for a Mrs. Kirke, who ran a large boarding-house. There she met Professor Bhaer, a lovable and eccentric German tutor, who proved to be a good friend and companion.

Upon her return home, Laurie, who had always loved Jo, asked her to marry him. Jo, who imagined that she would always remain an old maid, devoting herself exclusively to her writing, tried to convince Laurie that they were not made for each other. He persisted, pointing out that his grandfather and her family both expected them to marry. When she made him realize that her refusal was final, he stamped off, and shortly afterward went to Europe with his grandfather. In Europe he saw a great deal of Amy, and the two became close friends, so that Laurie was able to transfer to her younger sister a great deal of the feeling he previously had for Jo.

In the meantime Jo was at home caring for Beth, who had never fully recovered from her first illness. In the spring, Beth died, practically in Jo's arms, and after the loss of her gentle sister Jo was lonely indeed. She tried to comfort herself with her writing, and with Meg's two babies, Daisy and Demi, but not until the return of Amy, now married to Laurie, did she begin to feel her old self again. When Professor Bhaer stopped off on his way to a university appointment in the Midwest, Jo was delighted. One day, under an umbrella he had supplied to shield her from a pouring rain, he asked her to marry him, and Jo accepted. Within a year old Aunt March died and willed her home, Plumfield, to Jo. She decided to open a boys' school, where she and her professor could devote their lives to instructing the young.

So the little women reached maturity, and on their mother's sixtieth birthday they all had a great celebration at Plumfield. Around the table, at which there was but one empty chair, sat Marmee, her children and her grandchildren. When Laurie proposed a toast to her, she replied by stretching out her arms to them all and saying that she could wish nothing better for them than this present happiness for the rest of their lives.

LIVES OF THE CAESARS

Type of work: Biography
Author: Gaius Suetonius Tranquillus (c. 70-c. 140)
Time: c. 86 B.C.-A.D. 96
Locale: The Roman world
First transcribed: c. 120

Principal personages (in historical order):
JULIUS CAESAR (CAIUS JULIUS CAESAR), c. 102-44 B.C.
AUGUSTUS (CAIUS OCTAVIUS), 63 B.C.-A.D. 14
TIBERIUS (TIBERIUS CLAUDIUS NERO), 42 B.C.-A.D. 37
GAIUS CALIGULA (CAIUS CAESAR GERMANICUS), 12-41
CLAUDIUS (TIBERIUS CLAUDIUS DRUSUS), 10 B.C.-A.D. 54
NERO (NERO CLAUDIUS CAESAR), 37-68
GALBA (SERVIUS SULPICIUS GALBA), 3 B.C.-A.D. 69
OTHO (MARCUS SALVIUS OTHO), 32-69
VITELLIUS (AULUS VITELLIUS), 15-69
VESPASIAN (TITUS FLAVIUS VESPASIANUS), 9-79
TITUS (TITUS FLAVIUS SABINUS VESPASIANUS), 41-81
DOMITIAN (TITUS FLAVIUS DOMITIANUS), 51-96

Perhaps Suetonius, like other biographers and historians, made mistakes; perhaps he retained ancedotes and bits of gossip that a less lively writer would have discarded; but he made the Caesars mortal men, though some of them carried the title of god, and he showed them in defeat and victory, virtue and vice, as they were or, at least, as some men reputed them to be. So colorful are the details of murders and lustful acts that even the most extravagant of Hollywood representations of ancient Rome are calm and temperate by comparison.

The beginning of the life of Julius Caesar is missing, the account beginning in his sixteenth year, but otherwise the book is complete. Like the other biographies there is more emphasis on Julius the person and on his relationships with the people about him than there is on the great historical moments of his life. But the major events were bound to be reported in great detail in ordinary works; Suetonius performs the service of filling out the cold lines of history with an impartial account of the personal traits of the Caesars.

After the death of his father, Julius married Cornelia, daughter of the consul Cinna, who bore him a daughter, Julia. Since by this act—which allied Julius with the popular party—he irritated the dictator Sulla, he was forced to go into hiding; but Caesar's friends interceded for him and at last he was forgiven. Sulla warned, however, that Caesar would "one day deal the death blow to the cause of the aristocracy."

Brief statements are made about Caesar's campaigns in Asia and about his service in Cilicia under Servilius Isauricus. Julius then returned to Rome and began his political career by bringing a charge of extortion against Cornelius Dolabella. After Dolabella had been ac-

1713

quitted Caesar went to Rhodes to study oratory under Apollonius Molo. On the way he was kidnapped by pirates; after being freed upon payment of ransom, he returned to capture and punish the pirates.

Julius became military tribune and gained an increasing reputation as an orator. After the death of his wife he married Pompeia, but he divorced her on suspicion that she had committed adultery with Publius Clodius.

By his political acts Caesar made himself popular with the masses, an advantage he made secure by arranging gladiatorial shows and stage plays for their amusement. By resorting to bribery, he won the election to the office of pontifex maximus. His efforts to secure mercy for Catiline after the conspiracy was detected almost cost him his life, for the address of Marcus Cato kept the Senate committed to the extreme penalty and Julius was threatened by the Roman knights who stood as guards in the Senate.

After becoming consul in 60 B.C., Caesar made a compact with Gnaeus Pompeius and Marcus Crassus, thus securing power over the Senate.

Suetonius carefully describes the political moves by which Julius continued to increase his own power while battling for the popular party against the Senate. After the nine-year campaign in Gaul, Caesar decided that only civil war could settle the political dissension. Crossing the Rubicon, he marched on Rome. After his victory he rewarded his troops, entertained the masses with shows, and undertook a reform of the Senate and of the calendar. His victory over Pompey, who had led the opposition, made the subsequent defeat of the senatorial party an easier task. As dictator, Caesar began with reforms but ended with such an assumption of power and infallibility, together with complete disdain of the Senate, that a conspiracy was formed against him which included Brutus, Cassius, Cimber, Casca, and other friends of Caesar who had turned against him. He died by their daggers on the Ides of March, after being warned by a series of signs.

Suetonius devotes the bulk of his essay on Julius to an account of Caesar's personal characteristics. Julius is described as having been "tall of stature, with a fair complexion, shapely limbs, a somewhat full face, and keen black eyes. . . . He was somewhat overnice in the care of his person, being not only carefully trimmed and shaved, but even having superfluous hair plucked out. . . ." Lengthy consideration is given to the charge that Julius had been intimate with King Nicomedes. Suetonius writes that he will take no account of various invectives and reproaches made against Caesar on this matter; he then proceeds to quote, with great detail, all gossip he disdains. Julius drank very little wine, according to Suetonius; he seduced many women, had love affairs with queens—including Cleopatra—excelled in the art of war, wrote his memoirs with simplicity and skill, rode a horse that was "almost human," treated his friends with kindness and consideration, and was so merciful that when he captured the pirates who had kidnapped him, he cut their throats before crucifying them. Suetonius declares that Julius Caesar "was numbered among the gods, not only by a formal decree, but also in the conviction of the common people."

The life of Augustus, like that of Julius, is first summarized by Suetonius, who then proceeds to tell of Augustus the man. Born Caius Octavius, he inherited power from Julius, although he had to join with Antony and Lepidus and fight a series of battles in order to become undisputed ruler of the Empire. The name "Augustus" was a title conferred by the Senate to honor him.

Suetonius mentions some of the acts Augustus committed while triumvir, deeds by which he incurred "general detestation." He ordered a Roman knight stabbed to death for taking notes; he so abused Tedius Afer, consul elect, that Afer "hurled himself headlong," committing suicide; he tortured Quintus Gallius because of the suspicion that Gallius had a sword under his cloak, and he tore out the man's eyes with his own hands after ordering his execution.

On the more constructive side, Augustus is credited with having built many public works, revising the wards of the city and the system of night watches, building up a library of Sibylline books after burning prophetic writings of little repute, adding to the public security, revising existing laws, rebuilding roads, and surpassing his predecessors in the magnificence of public shows.

He won the affection of the people and the Senate, and was named "Father of his Country" by the latter. He had few friends, but he was faithful to them. He gambled and made love to other men's wives, although this latter practice is partly excused by Suetonius on the ground that it was pursued not from passion but from a desire for information about the ladies' husbands. In other respects he was temperate, furnishing his house simply and eating simple food. He is described as handsome, although he had teeth that were "wide apart, small, and ill-kept. . . ." Augustus died painlessly and without disturbance, as he had wished, from an illness.

Suetonius' treatment of the lives of the other Caesars is similar to that of Julius and Augustus, although with most of the Caesars, beginning with Tiberius, murders and sexual excesses were so common that most of the accounts are taken up with a recital of monstrous deeds. Although Nero is the most infamous of the Caesars—and probably deserves to be remembered as almost entirely depraved—it would be difficult to decide which of the others was the worst.

After a few years of attention to the duties of emperor, Tiberius openly gave way to his vices, drowning himself in wine, consorting at banquets attended by nude girls, killing those who offended him or who were about when something angered him, and finally arranging matters so that every day was execution day and every crime a capital one. He drove his sister-in-law to suicide by starvation. He devised elaborate systems of torture and, to insure the death of his victims, had them thrown over a cliff to the rocks where guards broke up the bodies with boathooks. When he died there was general rejoicing and cries of "Tiberius to the Tiber!"

After writing of some of Caligula's accomplishments—great public games, the building of public works—Suetonius comments, "So much for Caligula as emperor; we must now tell of his career as a monster." He demanded that he be worshipped as a god; he built temples to himself and invited the moon to his embraces. He lived in incest with his sisters, stole the wives of other men, and had a series of wives. He murdered his friends and those who helped him to power. He matched worthless gladiators against wild beasts, and in random fashion chose prisoners to be devoured by savage animals in the arena. He enjoyed watching executions while eating his lunch, and at a banquet he ordered the hands of a slave cut off and hung about his neck so that the wretched man could be led about the banquet hall as a warning against stealing. These are simply samples of Caligula's deeds. He was stabbed to death when he was twenty-nine years old, after almost four years of rule.

Claudius began his rule in such manner that he won the love and devotion of his subjects, and he accomplished many worthwhile objectives; but he was a cruel and suspicious man, and he died by poison.

Even a summary statement of Nero's crimes is difficult. He was cruel, vain, and lustful. Ordinary entertainment and ordinary modes of sexual intercourse were displaced by extravagant orgies of various sorts. Regarding himself as a musician and singer, he forced great audiences to listen to him for hours on end, forbidding anyone to leave, so that women sometimes gave birth to children while he performed. He enjoyed fires and burned great sections of Rome. He wandered the streets in disguise, indulging in revels and fights. Boys, men, married women, prostitutes, and wives—all fed his lust, sometimes in violent and dramatically contrived ways. He murdered his mother after several attempts, and it was Suetonius' opinion that he had something to do with the poisoning of Claudius. Hundreds of other persons—his family, his companions, and others—died by his hand or by his orders. Suetonius writes that Nero "showed neither discrimination nor moderation in putting to death whomso-

ever he pleased on any pretext whatsoever." When the Senate finally sent men to capture him for execution, he killed himself by cutting his own throat, but only after considerable wailing and postponement.

Nero was the last Caesar by family connection; the others bore the name "Caesar" as a designation of rank. Suetonius' account of the remaining Caesars—Galba, Otho, Vitellius, Vespasian, Titus, and Domitian—gives considerably less space to their exploits; but the style continues to be lively and informative.

LIZA OF LAMBETH

Type of work: Novel
Author: W. Somerset Maugham (1874-   )
Type of plot: Naturalism
Time of plot: Late nineteenth century
Locale: England
First published: 1897

> *Principal characters:*
> LIZA KEMP, a street girl
> TOM, who loved her
> JIM BLAKESTON, Liza's lover
> SALLY, her friend

Critique:

Liza of Lambeth is the first novel of W. Somerset Maugham. One of the least known to readers of his more popular novels, it belongs to the school of naturalism which flourished in English fiction about the turn of the century. There is virtually no development of character, and the plot is no more remarkable than the commonplace lives of the people in the novel. Here, more than in any other of his novels, Maugham drew directly upon his own observations and experiences as a young doctor serving his internship among the poor of the London slums. The novel is as blunt and unsparing as a clinical report.

The Story:

Liza Kemp spent most of her free time

on the streets of Lambeth. She was not exactly a loose girl, but her dress and actions provoked whistles and jeers whenever she appeared. Liza's father was dead, and her mother, living on a small pension, earned enough as a charwoman to keep herself in beer. She never spoke a kind word to her daughter, although she expected Liza to hand over all her money and spend all her time with her mother. Like most girls of her class, Liza worked in a factory and made only enough money to live and to buy a few items of cheap finery.

After a gay dance in the streets of Lambeth, Liza was chased by several young men trying to kiss her. As she fled, only half in earnest, she ran straight into the arms of a stranger and was soundly kissed. Flouncing off, she found herself strangely moved by the unexpected experience. That night Tom, her earnest and persistent suitor, called on her as usual. Liza liked Tom but she did not love him, and so she tried to send him away without hurting his feelings. But Tom was stubborn. He begged her to take time to consider his proposal. When he asked her to go on an outing the next day, she refused. She did not want him to spend his money or his hopes on her.

Later her friend Sally also begged her to go on the outing. When she learned that the stranger who had kissed her would be one of the party, Liza relented, but against her better judgment. She had learned that the stranger was Jim Blakeston, a married man and the father of five children. Jim's wife went on the outing too, but Jim paid little attention to her. Instead, he spent most of his time following Liza and Tom around. Jim's actions angered Tom, but that poor young man was too much in love to blame Liza for encouraging the older man.

After the excursion Jim followed Liza home and kissed her passionately. She knew that she should be angry, but she was also flattered and pleased. From that night on Liza was lost. When Jim asked her to walk with him or to meet him at a show, she refused; then she kept the appointment anyway. Although she knew they were both wrong, she seemed powerless to withdraw from his influence. They tried to avoid people they knew, but Liza was afraid that they would be seen sooner or later. At last, grown reckless, she allowed Jim to seduce her.

The next few weeks were heaven for Liza. She loved Jim deeply, and he returned her love. But Liza knew that people were beginning to talk about her. Young men and girls yelled insults after her. Even Tom cut her once, and that fact hurt her because she knew that Tom was good and kind and she hated to lose his former opinion of her. Her love was too strong, however, to be permanently affected by the insults she received. Jim even offered to leave his wife and take her away to another part of the city, but Liza knew that they would always be in danger of being caught. She also realized that Jim loved his children and would be unhappy away from them. Furthermore, Liza felt that she could not leave her mother. Although the old woman had never been much of a mother, Liza thought it her duty to stay with her. There seemed nothing for Liza and Jim to do but to continue as they were or to part entirely. Neither could think of parting.

After Liza's friend Sally was married, her happiness made Liza even more miserable in her own shame. Later she learned that Sally's happiness was only superficial. Her husband beat her regularly, but the girl was too proud to let anyone but Liza know. Liza also had a shock. Once she was late for an appointment with Jim and he drank too much while he waited for her. When she tried to keep him from going back into the pub for more beer, he struck her in the eye. He was instantly contrite, but the damage to Liza's heart never quite mended.

Sally warned Liza one day that Jim's wife was looking for her. To avoid a public scene, Liza tried to keep clear of Mrs. Blakeston, who was much the larger and stronger of the two. In a fight, Liza realized, she would be bested. But at last they met and Mrs. Blakeston gave Liza a horrible beating. Outclassed from the beginning, the girl fought gamely. Tom and Jim appeared almost simultaneously and stopped the fight, Tom carrying Liza home tenderly and Jim threatening to kill his wife for hurting Liza.

Tom loved Liza so much that he wanted to marry her, although he knew all the gossip about her; he had cut her in the past because of his hurt. Even when she told him that she was going to have Jim's baby, Tom still wanted to have her for his wife. Liza refused him again, however; Tom was too good to be tied to a woman of her reputation.

1717

Jim himself almost killed his wife. He was prevented from doing so only by the intervention of a neighbor woman.

Later that night Liza awoke with a burning fever and intense pain. For the next day or two she suffered terribly, and at last her mother became worried enough to send for a midwife. The woman knew at once that Liza had miscarried and was gravely ill. Although they sent for a doctor, the midwife knew that there was little hope for the girl. Tom called regularly, out of his mind with worry. Liza, when she was conscious, looked only for Jim. He came as soon as he heard about her condition, but he was too late to give any comfort to the dying girl. She lay unconscious for several hours, then quietly died. As the doctor covered her face, Jim turned away, weary and defeated.

THE LONG JOURNEY

Type of work: Novel
Author: Johannes V. Jensen (1873-1950)
Type of plot: Cultural epic
Time of plot: The Age of Man
Locale: The world
First published: 1923-1924

    Principal characters:
        FYR, typical of the earliest users of fire
        CARL, typical of the early Stone Age man in the glacial period
        WHITE BEAR, typical of the later Stone Age man
        WOLF, typical of the horse-riding and horse-breeding man
        NORNA GEST, typical of the man who entered the Iron Age and lingered to the fall of the Roman Empire
        CHRISTOPHER COLUMBUS, typical of the Renaissance man
        CHARLES DARWIN, typical of modern man

Critique:

In 1944 the Nobel Prize in Literature was awarded to Johannes V. Jensen "because of the exceptional vigor and fertility of his poetic imagination, combined with an all-embracing intellectuality and bold creative expression." All those qualities are certainly manifest in *The Long Journey*, a prose epic published in translation as *Fire and Ice* (1923), *The Cimbrians* (1923), and *Christopher Columbus* (1924). Yet to call *The Long Journey* a novel is to understate its value; rather, it is a great work of cultural mythology, a new integration and an ultra-sensitive reinterpretation of the progress Man has made in the world since that remote age when he first began to walk upon the earth. At least one writer has termed it a "bible of evolution." Perhaps no less comprehensive category can hold a work which ranges from before the Ice Age to the twentieth century. This work was published in Denmark as six novels over the period 1909 to 1922.

The Story:

In the north of what is now Europe, in the prehistoric days before the glaciers came from the North, Man lived in fear and trembling—in fear of the elements, the beasts of the jungles, and his own primitive leaders. Into one of those herd-like groups was born a boy who was named Fyr. As the child grew older he was seized with a desire to climb to the top of Gunung Api, a vast volcano quiet but not extinct. There on the slopes of the volcano, wandering by himself, Fyr

THE LONG JOURNEY by Johannes V. Jensen. Translated by A. G. Chater. By permission of the publishers, Alfred A. Knopf, Inc. Copyright, 1923, 1924, by Alfred A. Knopf, Inc. Renewed, 1952, by Alfred A. Knopf, Inc.

learned to make use of the flames and their heat to keep himself warm, to cook his meat, to provide himself with a deity, and to enhance his own importance.

Attracted first by his songs and then by his person, women joined Fyr, until he, like other leaders, was the head of a primitive family group. After the women came children and, finally, other men who made themselves subservient to Fyr. Under his leadership the tribe became a band of hunters, using the pits, spears, and bows which Fyr devised for them. Wherever they went, they took with them burning wood to re-create their god and household symbol: the fire. Soon all the forest folk bowed to the authority of Fyr, bound to him by his fire and by the tools of wood and stone which he created to make their lives more bearable. One day, however, the god seemed to demand a sacrifice, and the people, making Fyr their scapegoat, placed him in the fire he had brought them. Although he was roasted and eaten, he lived on, a representative of human ingenuity which they could not understand.

As ages passed, Gunung Api became extinct. Still later, the northern ice cap, beginning to move over the land, brought cold to the tropic jungles. After other ages had passed, a small band of hunters lay crouched in the same forest. The seasons were much colder, and the tribe and most of the animals had moved to the South, until a hunting expedition had brought them back to the old territory. One of their number, Carl, was the fire-tender. He was thrown out of the band, an outcast, when he let the fire die.

Carl fled to the North, somehow keeping himself alive in the winter by wrapping himself in skins and burrowing into the ground or building rude huts of stone. High on the extinct volcanic cone he traveled. Everywhere he saw only desolation and ice. He sought for the enemy of his tribe, the cold, but did not find him. He was joined in his wanderings by a dog; the animal slowly joined into a comradeship with the man, al-

though not without some trembling and hesitancy on the part of each. As the winters passed, Carl learned to prepare for them by laying in a supply of food and building a shelter. He even learned to foretell when the great cold was coming and where he would find food and shelter as its ice and snows moved gradually to the South. When he did find an occasional human being, the encounter served only as an opportunity for Carl to eat a different kind of meat. One day he gave chase to a human being who turned out to be a woman. He captured her by the sea, and the lure of the sea was to call him again.

Carl's wife was Mam. She brought new habits of gathering and storing, as well as children. She added vegetables to Carl's diet, and their home became a permanent one. Carl was still aware of fire, a possession which he had lost and not regained. Gathering many stones, he chipped them against one another in his efforts to strike fire from them. At last, successful, he bequeathed fire to his children.

The children of Carl and their wives added pottery work to their skills; with ceramics came boiling, a new way of cooking. Among the descendants of Carl there arose a group of priests, against whom rebels were sometimes pitted. Such a rebel was White Bear. Denied a certain woman for his wife, he killed the leader of the priestly clan. Like Carl before him, White Bear became an outcast, taking May, his woman, with him. White Bear became a seaman, building small boats and sailing them, in company with his sons, while May and the daughters remained at home to farm and care for the cattle.

White Bear began to use horses. He built a chariot, with horses to draw it. His sons, more adventurous, learned to ride. One of the sons, Wolf, became so enamored of the horses that he rode them away to become a nomad, forerunner of the Golden Horde of Genghis Khan.

Ages later a new man appeared. He

1719

was Norna Gest, son of the matriarch Gro. While he was still a young boy dwelling at the edge of the sea on an island, he built himself a dugout canoe and sailed away, carrying with him a young girl who was, after a time, to become his mate. They and their child explored a new land to the north, now Sweden, but returned to the home island in after years. Gest himself was not an ordinary mortal; he was to live as long as he kept a partially burned candle. After his return to his original home, he and his companions went on many voyages and made use of sails as well as paddles.

As years passed, Gest found he had outlived his companions. He awoke one day to find himself in a changed Sealand, a place where men were either thralls or earls. Disturbed at the changes and despised because he had taken a new wife in the person of a milkmaid, one of the thralls, he wandered sadly about the land.

Unhappy in the changed Sealand, Gest and his bondwoman-wife sailed to Sweden to found a new colony in which they were to be the leaders. With them they took new techniques of smelting and forging metals. In their new home they gradually acquired domestic animals —horses, sheep, and cattle. Their sons and daughters married, and thus the colony grew. The mother died, and one day Gest disappeared, to wander again over the globe. Unnoticed but noticing, he traveled through central Europe and floated down the Danube. He traversed the Mediterranean lands, where his life began in the early Stone Age. Finding something wanting in the lands of the South, Gest turned his face once again toward his homeland, where he became a wandering skald.

Arriving in Jutland, he was welcomed by Tole, a leader who was guardian of the ancient god of the Jutlanders. This was a wooden idol which Tole wished to enclose in a great bronze bull. Tole welcomed Gest as the bringer of

skills with metals and as a man of great wisdom. The two men made plans to cast the bronze bull at the time of the great spring festivals, before the flocks and herds were taken up to the summer pastures. The bull was successfully cast, and the festivities ended with human sacrifices of slaves and thralls. Gest wandered off afoot after the festival.

In later years floods rose up in the seas about Jutland, and the younger men wished to leave the country to search for a homeland safe from the ever-encroaching sea. The entire tribe left, except for elderly Tole. With the tribe went the bronze bull, destined now to long journeying across the face of central and southern Europe.

Back and forth across the lands went the Cimbrians, enlisting other tribes in their search for better lands. At last they traveled far enough to come to the notice of the Romans.

Failing to obey the warning of the Romans to remain out of their dominions, the Cimbrians and their allies of the North became enemies of the Empire. As enemies they decided to strike at Rome itself. Victorious at first, they became proud and reckoned not at all on the strategy of the Roman generals, strategy which defeated them. In their defeat the Cimbrians and their allies were ruined. Those who were not killed or who did not commit suicide were sold into bondage to the Romans, to live miserably as captives in the South, where eventually their blood blended with the blood of their conquerors.

Norna Gest saw these things happening. Finally, knowing that his time was at an end, he once again left Rome in his boat and glided slowly toward the sea, there to burn his candle to its end.

After the fall of the Roman Empire, barbarians from the North were gradually assimilated into the Christian religion. The ancient ship of the North, inverted on land, became the Gothic cathedral, a compound of the mariner's vessel and the stately forests through which earlier man had roamed. Among the descendants of the barbaric tribes of the North were the Langobards. One of the descendants of the latter group was a man named Christopher Columbus, who was to lead mankind farther on its journey of discovery across the seas and into a whole new hemisphere then undreamed of, or at least forgotten by the descendants of the early Northmen who had once visited it.

Columbus saw himself as a veritable Christopher, one who carried the Christ into the world. While others caroused before setting out across the ocean with him, he prepared himself by attending masses in the cathedral. He had faith in divine help and a divine purpose. When the qualities which his faith gave him proved insufficient to meet the demands of leadership, he could also call upon an amazing strength of body which his northern forebears had bequeathed him.

Although he reached the islands of the West Indies, other men carried man's long journey into the New World; Columbus was doomed to be only a leader pointing the way. To later conquistadors, men like Cortés and Pizarro, went the credit for gaining the mainland for European culture. Those men faced the odds of sheer numbers when they met the strength of the late Stone Age men, the followers of Montezuma and the Incas, who still existed in America, savages caught in the lag where European culture had left them many ages before. In Mexico, for example, Cortés was to find human sacrifices and worship of volcanic spirits, examples of culture-progress which had long since ceased to exist in the Old World. The light which Columbus saw from his ship at night was a symbol of the fire worship met throughout the New World.

The Indians believed that the coming of the white men marked the return of their great sun god, Quetzalcoatl. Perhaps the god might have been Norna Gest, visiting the New World during his travels. But the savages soon lost their superstitious awe of men with fair skins and hair, and many Europeans were sacrificed on the altars of Mexico and other southern countries.

The great battle of the New World was fought in Mexico. There the journey of the European culture was most seriously threatened. In the north the Indians seemed to fade away before the white culture; in the West Indies disease had killed them like summer flies at the first autumn frost. But in Mexico there was warfare between the eagle and the serpent, symbols of Man's migrations and his conflicting cultures. Cortés and his soldiers were like eagles swooping down on the snake, insignia of the Aztecs.

Even though Cortés was temporarily successful, with the help of a woman who turned against her own people, and even though he was able to send the idol of Huitzilopochtli toppling down the long flights of stairs which led to its temple, the Spaniards were doomed to temporary defeat. Cortés had to hack his way out of Tenochtitlán while the screams of Spaniards sacrificed alive echoed in his ears.

Years later a young man named Darwin, a naturalist on H. M. S. *Beagle,* was to become a new symbol in man's journey from the past, through the present, into the future. Those on the *Beagle* thought they saw the Flying Dutchman. Perhaps that dread captain, doomed to sail forever, will become the symbol of Man's long journey as it continues. Or perhaps the long journey is now almost ended. No one knows.

THE LONG NIGHT

Type of work: Novel
Author: Andrew Lytle (1902-   )
Type of plot: Historical romance
Time of plot: 1857-1862
Locale: Alabama, Mississippi, Tennessee
First published: 1936

Principal characters:
LAWRENCE McIVOR, the narrator, William McIvor's son
CAMERON McIVOR, his grandfather, an Alabama planter
PLEASANT, Cameron McIvor's favorite son and avenger
WILLIAM, and
LEVI, Pleasant's brothers
ELI McIVOR, Pleasant's uncle
TYSON LOVELL, leader of a gang of slave speculators
LIEUTENANT ROSWELL ELLIS, Pleasant's friend
ALBERT SIDNEY JOHNSTON, Confederate general

Critique:

A remarkable first novel based in part on actual characters and events, *The Long Night* is a work of originality and true historical imagination. After the murder of his father by a gang of desperadoes modeled more or less upon the notorious Murrell gang of actual history, a young Alabaman embarks upon a grim career of revenge, but with the outbreak of the Civil War his desire for private vengeance becomes submerged in the greater and bloodier issues of that conflict. At last, facing a tragic dilemma, he makes his own desperate and separate peace and goes into hiding. In spite of minor structural defects the novel achieves its purpose with considerable stylistic vigor and imaginative power, and the account of the battle of Shiloh is a vivid piece of war reporting. In addition, the writer presents a realistic and convincing regional picture of ante-bellum life on the southern frontier. These qualities combine to give *The Long Night* its definite distinction among more conventional novels dealing with the Civil War theme.

The Story:

Lawrence McIvor was twenty-two when he heard his family's story for the first time. Just out of college, he had been summoned to his Uncle Pleasant's house deep in the coves of Winston County, Alabama. There through all of one dark winter night he listened to his kinsmen's tale of hatred and grim vengeance.

The McIvor troubles began in Georgia, at a militia muster where powerful old Cameron McIvor refused to wrestle one of the reckless Caruthers twins. Several days later Job Caruthers attacked McIvor and the planter broke the young man's arm. After his recovery Job and his brother Mebane returned a borrowed team of horses in a wind-broken condition. Furious, McIvor shot Job. The brother then started a lawsuit which left the planter almost ruined. McIvor decided to move to Texas. Pleasant, his favored son, was sixteen at the time.

The McIvors traveled by wagon, with their cattle and remaining slaves. Near Wetumpka, Alabama, they met Tyson Lovell, a wealthy landowner who offered McIvor five hundred acres of good land to crop on shares. Not long after they had settled in their new home William, the oldest son, married a storekeeper's daughter and went to live in town. Pleasant and his younger brother Levi helped their father and the hands in the fields. There was something mysterious and

THE LONG NIGHT by Andrew Lytle. By permission of the author and the publishers, The Bobbs-Merrill Co., Inc. Copyright, 1936, by The Bobbs-Merrill Co., Inc.

sinister about Lovell. After McIvor and Pleasant, tracking a lost mule, found a shack in which two neighbors named Wilton were guarding several strange slaves, the father became convinced that Lovell was a speculator, head of a gang of slave stealers and horse thieves, an organization to which most of their neighbors belonged. Lovell, becoming alarmed, tried to frighten the McIvors into leaving the country, first by having the sheriff discover two stolen slaves in the planter's smokehouse, later, after McIvor and Lovell quarreled, by swearing out a bench warrant which named McIvor an outlaw.

Defying Lovell, the planter waited for his enemy to act. William came to stay at the farm, but he was called away suddenly by false news of his wife's illness. That night Pleasant was waylaid and locked in an old church. Before daylight armed men broke into the McIvor house. While the Wilton brothers held the old planter in his bed, a man named Fox shot him.

The McIvor kin gathered in secret. A few, William among them, argued that the murderers should be punished by the law. Others clamored for an open feud. Grief-crazed over his father's death, Pleasant revealed that he had tracked the gang to its meeting place and learned the names of its forty members. After the court dismissed charges brought by McIvor's widow, she and her family quietly left the country. Pleasant, a young uncle named Eli, and Bob Pritchard, a cousin, swore to answer violent death with violence.

Pleasant and his kinsmen began to terrorize the region. A dishonest district attorney, Lovell's tool, was killed in a fall from an inn balcony. One Wilton was dragged to death by his horse. Another was found shot. Lovell's house burned, his overseer's charred body in the ruins. Fox ran away. After Sheriff Botterall's posse trapped and killed Pritchard, Pleasant resolved to kill secretly and alone. Forcing Botterall into a wild stallion's stall, he lashed the animal until

it trampled Lovell's henchman to death. Several of the gang fled to Texas, but Pleasant followed and killed them. He and Eli built a cabin in the wilds of Winston County. From there he planned to carry on his stealthy, deadly raids around Wetumpka.

Two years after his father's death he went one night to a house Lovell owned near Buyckville. In hiding, he had not known that Fort Sumter had been fired on until he found Lovell in his study and learned from his mocking enemy that the Civil War had begun. Lovell declared that the army would soon swallow the survivors of his gang; besides, Pleasant had walked into a trap. Hearing bloodhounds baying in the distance, Pleasant boasted that he still intended to make Lovell the last of his victims. After knocking the man unconscious with a pistol, he ran from the house before his trackers could surround it.

Pleasant and Eli joined the Confederate Army, and as a result Pleasant continued his work of revenge. At Corinth, while on outpost duty, he killed a sergeant and four men from Lovell's gang and arranged the bodies to make them appear as if shot by Federal scouts. Summoned to General Albert Sidney Johnston's headquarters to give his version of the attack, he met Lieutenant Roswell Ellis, on the staff of Colonel Armistead McIvor, Pleasant's cousin from Kentucky. In an army in which there were few binding distinctions of rank Pleasant and Ellis became friends. Pleasant learned that Fox, his father's murderer, had offered to have Andrew Johnson assassinated and that General Johnston had scornfully rejected the offer. Knowing that Fox was in the neighborhood, he bided his time.

The march toward Shiloh Church began through pouring rain. Two nights before the battle Pleasant and Ellis were detailed to scout duty along the Federal lines. After Ellis returned to report, Pleasant spent the night in the woods. All the next day he watched the Federal encampment and waited for the battle to begin. But there were delays in bringing up Confederate troops and equipment and the battle of Shiloh was not joined until Sunday morning, April 6, 1862. Pleasant, wandering through the acrid battle haze, found his own company in time to join in a wild charge in which Eli was killed. The Federal troops retreated. Pleasant, shot in the hand, spent the night with a wounded major from Ohio. The next day the reinforced Federal lines advanced and the Confederates, with General Beauregard in command after General Johnston's death, began their retreat to Corinth.

Pleasant was with the army at Murfreesboro when he heard that his brother William had been killed. Levi, after nursing his wounded brother, died three days later. Pleasant went to meet his mother at Chattanooga when she drove through the Federal lines to claim her sons' bodies. On his way back to Murfreesboro, Pleasant was glad to have Roswell Ellis' friendship. Ellis was of the living, and Pleasant had seen too many deaths. After Shiloh woods he was beginning, despairingly, to doubt his vows of hatred and revenge.

Scouting near La Vergne, Pleasant did not return to camp immediately because he was on the track of a Lovell man named Awsumb, but when he looked at his enemy through his gunsights he was unable to pull the trigger. On his arrival at headquarters he learned that after his failure to report at once a brigade had been sent to test the enemy strength at La Vergne. Ellis had been killed in the engagement. Pleasant felt that his delay had caused his friend's death. Ellis had given him back his humanity and he had destroyed his friend. Following dark and bloody trails of reprisal, he had loved the dead too much and the living too little, and he himself was doomed. He thought of the hills and hidden coves of Winston County. There a deserter from whatever cause he fled could hide forever.

THE LONGEST JOURNEY

Type of work: Novel
Author: E. M. Forster (1879-   )
Type of plot: Social criticism
Time of plot: Early twentieth century
Locale: England
First published: 1907

Principal characters:
> RICKIE ELLIOT, a student at Cambridge
> AGNES PEMBROKE, an old friend
> HERBERT PEMBROKE, her brother
> STEWART ANSELL, a friend of Rickie at Cambridge
> EMILY FAILING, his aunt
> STEPHEN WONHAM, his half-brother

Critique:

In this novel Forster is primarily concerned with the story of a sensitive young man and the problems he encounters on his introduction into the world. The author is somewhat satiric as he views his characters but, as usual, he does not present the world as a completely dreary and uninteresting place. Men, in general, are portrayed as rather weak individuals who are fighting against superior forces, but the reader is not meant completely to lose his love and respect for them. Here, in a novel which is probably autobiographical in part, we see several characters who try without success to live happily in a world of weak and misguided ideals.

The Story:

Frederick Elliot, who was a student at Cambridge and almost alone in the world, had finally attained some degree of contentment in his life after a rather unhappy childhood. He had been born with a lamed left foot which kept him from most of the normal activities of children, and he had grown up virtually without friends. Early in his life his father had begun to call him Rickie because of its close similarity to rickety, and the name had stayed with him. Besides his deformity there was another, more serious, difficulty. He found out quite early that his father and mother did not love each other and that he was loved not at all by his father and only a little by his mother. Both his parents died when he was fifteen, leaving him comfortably well off so far as finances were concerned but without anyone who wanted to give him a home.

At Cambridge he had shown himself to be a capable student but one without any scholarly pretensions. He had made several friends among the non-athletic groups and spent much of his time in long discussions on topics of literary or philosophical interest. One day, during such a discussion, he was interrupted by the arrival of his old friends, Agnes and Herbert Pembroke, whom he had invited for the weekend. In the meantime he had completely forgotten about them. Because these two people were part of that very small group which took an interest in Rickie's career, they spent a great part of their time at Cambridge encouraging him to decide on a particular course for his life, even if he did nothing more than write, the only thing he admitted having an interest in. They pointed out that money was not important as long as he met a certain standard of ideals.

At Christmas of that same year Rickie saw his friends again. He had stayed several days with Stewart Ansell, a friend from Cambridge, but felt it was necessary to spend a part of his vacation with the Pembrokes as well. He rather dreaded this part of his vacation because Agnes' fiancé, a man whom Rickie had known at public school, was to be there. Rickie not only disliked Gerald Dawes but he also hated to witness the lovers' happiness; he felt that such happiness was forever to be denied him because of his lame foot which he considered a hereditary disorder. During this time Gerald was killed while playing football, and it was Rickie who was able to offer the most comfort to Agnes by convincing her that she *should* suffer since her love for Gerald had been the greatest thing she could ever experience.

Two years later, when she came again to visit him at Cambridge, Rickie realized that he was also in love with Agnes, although he still felt that he could never marry because of his deformity. She convinced him, however, that they should be married. Rickie was about to finish his work at Cambridge, but they felt a long engagement was necessary for him to settle himself. Ansell immediately opposed the marriage because he sensed that Agnes was not a sincere person. She laid constant claim to honesty and forthrightness, but Ansell could not be convinced that these qualities revealed the true Agnes. He knew immediately that she would force Rickie into a dull and conventional life, convincing him at the same time that he was taking the proper step.

Soon after their engagement Rickie and Agnes visited his aunt, Mrs. Emily Failing, at her country home. Rickie had never particularly liked his aunt, but since she was his only known relative he and Agnes felt that they should go to see her. Mrs. Failing was a woman who liked for people to do what she wanted and she was never happier than when they were obviously uncomfortable while carrying out her desires. While there they also saw Stephen Wonham, a young man whom Rickie had met before but whose relation to Mrs. Failing had never been made clear. However, after Rickie had been so bold as to engage in an argument with his aunt, she informed him that Stephen was actually his brother. It was not until later that Rickie found out that Stephen was the son of his mother, whom he had loved very much, and not of his father. Not even Stephen himself knew who he was, but the matter had never greatly concerned him.

After their marriage Rickie and Agnes went to live with Herbert at Sawston School. The arrangement had been worked out between Herbert and Agnes because Herbert needed help in his duties as a house master. Although Rickie soon realized that Herbert was basically stupid and that they disagreed on many points, he adapted himself to whatever course Herbert and Agnes chose. His marriage, in which he had hoped to find certain spiritual ideals, never reached a very intimate level, and before long his life became a shell. Ansell would have no more to do with him, and he was cut off from the one intellect at the school because of Herbert's feelings and aspirations.

Two years later, after Rickie had apparently succumbed completely to the forces playing on him, Stephen Wonham again entered his life. It became apparent immediately that Agnes, who had kept up a connection with Mrs. Failing, had been instrumental in having Stephen thrown out of her house, all because of her desire to inherit the money from the estate. Rickie was furious but again he submitted. Stephen, who had finally been told the truth about himself, came to Sawston expecting to find the kind of love which he had never known before. But when Rickie refused to see him and Agnes offered him money never to say anything about his parentage, he left immediately.

Stephen wandered around London for several days doing odd jobs and supporting himself as well as he could. Before long he had saved enough money for a drunken spree. During his drunkenness, determined to wreck Rickie's house, he returned to Sawston. In the process he might have killed himself if Rickie had not saved him. By this time Rickie, under the influence of Ansell, had begun to see how foolish he had been. Now he decided to give Stephen a home. Although Stephen would have none of this idea, he managed to convince Rickie that they should go away together.

Thus Rickie began the regeneration of his soul. Unfortunately it was of short duration. On a subsequent visit to his aunt, at which time Stephen insisted on accompanying him, he again saved Stephen's life but lost his own. Stephen, who had promised not to drink, got drunk and collapsed on the railroad crossing. Rickie managed to get him off, but he himself was killed. Just before he died he realized that he had been betrayed a second time by his belief in the individual.

LOOK HOMEWARD, ANGEL

Type of work: Novel
Author: Thomas Wolfe (1900-1938)
Type of plot: Impressionistic realism
Time of plot: 1900 to 1920
Locale: North Carolina
First published: 1929

Principal characters:
EUGENE GANT

LOOK HOMEWARD, ANGEL by Thomas Wolfe. By permission of Edward C. Aswell, Administrator, Estate of Thomas Wolfe, and the publishers, Charles Scribner's Sons. Copyright, 1929, by Charles Scribner's Sons.

ELIZA GANT, his mother
OLIVER GANT, his father
BEN GANT, his brother
MARGARET LEONARD, his teacher
LAURA JAMES, his first sweetheart

Critique:

The work of Thomas Wolfe contains two invariable elements. One is a reliance on characters of exceptional brilliance and vitality. The other is the portrayal of a central character who is the sensitive artist isolated in a hostile world. The latter character is generally Thomas Wolfe himself. In his fiction Wolfe attempted to re-create the whole American experience in his own image, and beneath the sprawling, often chaotic mass of his novels there are firm outlines of the naked and innocent story of the American land and its people. Although his emotional range is limited to the adolescent and the romantic, he stands plainly in the succession of American writers who have expressed in their work the symbols of a haunted inner world of thought and feeling.

The Story:

Eugene, the youngest child in the Gant family, came into the world when Eliza Gant was forty-two years old. His father went on periodic drinking sprees to forget his unfulfilled ambitions and the unsatisfied wanderlust which had brought him to Altamont in the hills of old Catawba. When Eugene was born, his father was asleep in a drunken stupor.

Eliza disapproved of her husband's debauches, but she lacked the imagination to understand their cause. Oliver, who had been raised amidst the plenty of a Pennsylvania farm, had no comprehension of the privation and suffering which had existed in the South after the Civil War, the cause of the hoarding and acquisitiveness of his wife and her Pentland relations in the Catawba hill country.

Eliza bore the burden of Oliver's drinking and promiscuousness until Eugene was four years old. Then she departed for St. Louis, taking all the children but the oldest daughter, Daisy, with her. It was 1904, the year of the great St. Louis Fair, and Eliza had gone to open a boarding-house for her visiting fellow townsmen. The idea was abhorrent to Oliver. He stayed in Altamont.

Eliza's sojourn in St. Louis ended abruptly when twelve-year-old Grover fell ill of typhoid and died. Stunned, she gathered her remaining children to her and went home.

Young Eugene was a shy, awkward boy with dark, brooding eyes. He was, like his ranting, brawling father, a dreamer. He was not popular with his schoolmates, who sensed instinctively that he was different, and made him pay the price; and at home he was the victim of his sisters' and brothers' taunts and torments. His one champion was his brother Ben, though even he had been conditioned by the Gants' unemotional family life to give his caresses as cuffs. But there was little time for Eugene's childish daydreaming. Eliza believed early jobs taught her boys manliness and self-reliance. Ben got up at three o'clock every morning to deliver papers. Luke had been a *Saturday Evening Post* agent since he was twelve. Eugene was put under his wing. Although the boy loathed the work, he was forced every Thursday to corner customers and keep up a continuous line of chatter until he broke down their sales resistance.

Eugene was not yet eight when his parents separated. Eliza had bought the Dixieland boarding-house as a good investment. Helen remained at the old house with her father. Daisy married and left town. Mrs. Gant took Eugene with her. Ben and Luke were left to shift for themselves, to shuttle back and forth between the two houses. Eugene grew to detest his new home. When the Dixieland was crowded, there was no privacy, and Eliza advertised the Dixieland on printed cards which Eugene had to distribute to customers on his magazine route and to travelers arriving at the Altamont station.

But although life at the boarding-house was drabness itself, the next four years were the golden days of Eugene's youth, for he was allowed to go to the Leonards' private school. Margaret Leonard, the tubercular wife of the schoolmaster, recognized Eugene's hunger for beauty and love, and was able to find in literature the words that she herself had not the power to utter. By the time he was fifteen Eugene knew the best and the greatest lyrics almost line for line.

Oliver Gant, who had been fifty when his youngest son was born, was beginning to feel his years. Although he was never told, he was slowly dying of cancer. Eugene was fourteen when the World War broke out. Ben, who wanted to join the Canadian Army, was warned by his doctor that he would be refused because he had weak lungs.

At fifteen, Eugene was sent to the university at Pulpit Hill. It was his father's plan that Eugene should be well on his way toward being a great statesman before the time came for old Oliver to die. Eugene's youth and tremendous height made him a natural target for dormitory horseplay, and his shy, awkward manners were intensified by his ignorance of the school's traditions and rituals. He roomed alone. His only friends were four wastrels, one of whom contributed to his social education by introducing him to a brothel.

That summer, back at the Dixieland, Eugene met Laura James. Sitting with her on the front porch at night, he was trapped by her quiet smile and clear, candid eyes. He became her lover on a summer afternoon of sunlit green and gold. But Laura went home to visit her parents and wrote Eugene that she was about to marry a boy to whom she had been engaged for nearly a year.

Eugene went back to Pulpit Hill that fall, still determined to go his way alone. Although he had no intimates, he gradually became a campus leader. The commonplace good fellows of his world tolerantly made room for the one who was not like them.

In October of the following year Eugene received an urgent summons to come home. Ben was finally paying the price of his parents' neglect and the drudgery of his life. He was dying of pneumonia. Eliza had neglected to call a competent doctor until it was too late, and Oliver, as he sat at the foot of the dying boy's bed, could think only of the expense the burial would be. As the family kept their vigil through Ben's last night, they were touched with the realization of the greatness of the boy's generous soul. Ben was given, a final irony, the best funeral money could buy.

With Ben went the family's last pretenses. When Eugene came back to the Dixieland after graduation, Eliza was in control of Oliver's property and selling it as quickly as she could in order to use the money for further land speculations. She had disposed of their old home. Oliver lived in a back room at the boarding-house. His children watched each other suspiciously as he wasted away, each concerned for his own inheritance. Eugene managed to remain unembroiled in their growing hatred of each other, but he could not avoid being a target for that hatred. Helen, Luke, and Steve had always resented his schooling. In September, before he left for Harvard to begin graduate work, Luke asked Eugene to sign a release saying that he had received his inheritance as tuition and school expenses. Though his father had promised him an education when he was still a child and Eliza was to pay for his first year in the North, Eugene was glad to sign. He was free, and he was never coming back to Altamont.

On his last night at home he had a vision of his dead brother Ben in the moonlit square at midnight; Ben, the unloved of the Gants, and the most lovable. It was for Eugene as well a vision of old, unhappy, unforgotten years, and in his restless imagination he dreamed of the hidden door through which he would escape forever the mountain-rimmed world of his boyhood.

LOOKING BACKWARD

Type of work: Novel
Author: Edward Bellamy (1850-1898)
Type of plot: Utopian romance
Time of plot: A.D. 2000
Locale: Boston, Massachusetts
First published: 1888

Principal characters:
JULIAN WEST, a traveler in time
EDITH BARTLETT, his nineteenth century fiancée
DR. LEETE, a twentieth century citizen
EDITH LEETE, his daughter

Critique:

The main value of *Looking Backward: 2000-1887* lies in its credible presentation of a socialist Utopia, and the book has served to introduce many famous people to the theory of socialism. Bellamy was not merely a follower of Marx and other economists; he rationalized for himself the case for economic revolution. The prophecies he makes for the world by A.D. 2000 are sometimes strikingly shrewd, and his judgments made of modern society are pointed and witty. Bellamy's idea was to present the ideas of socialism, as he saw them, in a way which would appeal to a wide reading public, both of yesterday and today.

The Story:

Julian West had a hard time sleeping. In order to have complete quiet he had built a sound-proof room with thick cement walls in the cellar of his house. He was also in the habit of having a quack doctor named Pillsbury put him to sleep by hypnosis.

One night he went to dinner with his fiancée's family and spent an enjoyable evening with Edith and her father, Mr. Bartlett. He went home, had the doctor give him a treatment, and went to sleep. He awoke to find strange people in the room. They asked him who he was, and when he had gone to sleep. Julian was amazed when he realized that he had been asleep one hundred and thirteen years, three months, and eleven days.

From much questioning, Julian learned what must have happened. During the night that he last remembered, his house had burned down except for the sealed room in which he slept; and apparently everyone assumed that he had died in the fire. Because of his hypnotic state, his body had remained the same. He was still a young man of thirty when he was discovered by Dr. Leete in the year 2000. Dr. Leete and his daughter, Edith, were very kind to their guest from the past and tried to explain the changes in the world since he had last seen it.

Boston was a new city with only the bay and the inlets as he remembered them. The city was beautiful, with attractive buildings and spacious parks. The strikes and labor troubles of the nineteenth century had resulted in a bloodless revolution, and now a socialized government controlled all business. There was no smoke because all heating was done by electricity. All the people were healthy and happy.

Dr. Leete tried to explain the world of A.D. 2000. There was no money. The state gave everyone, no matter what

1729

his job, a card which contained the same amount of credit for a year's expenses. There was no chance, however, for anyone to spend his credit foolishly and starve. If a person proved incapable of handling his credit card intelligently, the government took care to see that he was supervised. Julian was taken to one of the big stores to see how goods were sold. The store had nothing but samples, representing every type of material made in or imported by the United States. The buyer picked out the items he wanted, called a clerk, gave the order, and the clerk relayed the order to the central warehouse from which the item was delivered to the buyer's home before he returned from the store. Julian was much impressed with this system.

He learned from Dr. Leete how education was handled. Everyone was given a full education until he was twenty-one. A broad cultural course was taught so that there was no intellectual snobbery among the people. At twenty-one, the student went into menial service for three years. During this time he waited on tables in the large public eating houses, or did some other simple task. After three years, he was given an examination to qualify him for one of the government professional schools. If he failed, he was helped to find the job for which he was best suited and which he would most enjoy. If this job proved to be the wrong one, he could change his position. In order that all necessary jobs would be chosen by enough people to do the essential work, the jobs were arranged so as to be equally attractive. If one job was so boring that few people would want to choose it, the hours were made shorter so that enough applicants could be found. Whether a citizen was a doctor or a bricklayer, he was given the same amount of credit for his work.

Crime was treated as a mental disease; criminals were put in hospitals and treated as mental cases. Julian learned that crime had been cut down amazingly as soon as money was abolished. Theft became silly when everyone had the right and power to own the same things. At the head of the government was the President, who was controlled by Congress. Education and medicine were controlled by boards made up of older professional advisers to the President. A woman chosen by the women of the country had the power to veto any bill concerning the rights of the female population. There was no public discontent with government, and there was wonderful international cooperation.

Julian asked Dr. Leete what he had done in life, and learned that the doctor had practiced medicine until he was forty-five years old. At that time he had retired. Now he studied and enjoyed various kinds of recreation.

Edith Leete took great pleasure in showing Julian the various advances the world had made in culture since his day. She showed him how music was carried into all the homes in the country by telephone. She showed him the public libraries in which Julian learned that his old favorites were still read. Dickens was especially popular, as the new world thought him one of the wisest men in judging the sadness of the old capitalistic system. When an author wrote a book, it was published at his own expense by the government. If it proved a success, he received royalties in additional credit cards. Works of art were voted on by the public in the same way. When Julian commented that this plan would not have worked in his day because of the lack of public taste, Edith told him that with general education the taste of the people had developed greatly. Julian became very fond of Edith, and thought how strange it was that she should have the same name as his long-dead fiancée.

When Julian became worried about a means of support, Dr. Leete told him that he had arranged for him to take a college lectureship in history, as Julian knew much about the past which even historians would be delighted to learn. Knowing that he was secure in this new world, Julian asked Edith to marry him. She told him that she had always loved him.

When Julian asked how this was possible, she explained that she was the great-granddaughter of Edith Bartlett. She had found some of Julian's old love letters to the other Edith, and had been charmed by them. She had always told her parents that she would marry only a man like the lover who had written them. Julian was pleased at this unexpected turn of affairs, and the two planned to marry and live happily in the wonderful world of the twenty-first century.

LORD JIM

Type of work: Novel
Author: Joseph Conrad (Teodor Józef Konrad Korzeniowski, 1857-1924)
Type of plot: Psychological romance
Time of plot: Late nineteenth century
Locale: Ports and islands of the East
First published: 1900

>   Principal characters:
>   LORD JIM, a British sailor
>   MARLOW, his friend
>   STEIN, a trader
>   DAIN WARIS, a native

Critique:

Lord Jim first ran as a magazine serial that puzzled many readers. Conrad claimed that he had planned the narrative as a novel. Critics claimed that he had written a short story which had run away from him. The fact remains that the story is told in a unique framework. At its beginning it seems to skip haphazardly backward and forward through time at no one's direction. It is told partly by Conrad, partly in narrative by Marlow, and partly through a letter written by Marlow. The reader must solve for himself the problem of Jim's character. Certainly, Conrad was attempting to illustrate in Jim's weakness and strength the mystery of human character and to reveal the hidden springs of human conduct.

The Story:

Jim was an outcast, a wanderer. Hired as water clerk in seaports throughout the East, he would keep his job only until his identity became known. Then he would move on. The story of Lord Jim began when he determined to leave home to go to sea. Accordingly, his father obtained a berth for him as an officer candidate and he began his service. Although he loved the sea, his beginning was not heroic. Almost at once he was injured and was left behind in an Eastern port. When he recovered, he accepted a berth as chief mate aboard an ancient steamer, the *Patna,* carrying Moslem pilgrims on their way to Mecca.

The steamer was unseaworthy, her German captain a gross coward, her chief engineer liquor-soaked. One sultry night in the Red Sea the ship struck a floating object. The captain sent Jim to check.

A month later Jim testified in court that when he went to investigate he found the forward hold rapidly filling with sea water. Hearing his report, the captain declared the *Patna* would sink quickly and gave orders to abandon ship.

At first Jim was determined to stand by his post. At the last minute, on sudden impulse, he jumped to join the other white men in the lifeboat they had launched. The pilgrims were left aboard the sinking vessel.

But the *Patna* had not sunk. A French gunboat overtook the vessel and towed it and the abandoned passengers into port without its chief officers aboard.

Marlow, a white man, sat at the inquiry. Later, he took up the thread of the story as he had learned it from Jim. Something in Jim was fixed to Marlow's memory so that he was forced to recall the event and to tell the story to friends as long as he lived; it became a part of his own life.

It always began the same way. First there had come a cable from Aden telling that the *Patna,* abandoned by its officers, had been towed into port. Then two weeks later the captain, the two engineers, and Jim had come ashore, their boat having been picked up by a steamer of the Dale Line. They were whisked into court at once for the investigation. The captain lost his papers for deserting his ship, and he stormed away declaring that his disgrace did not matter; he would become an American citizen.

The chief engineer went to a hospital. There, raving in delirium tremens, he declared he had seen the *Patna* go down. The *Patna* was full of reptiles when she sank, he declared. He also declared that the space under his bed was crammed with pink toads. The second engineer, his arm broken, was also in the hospital. Neither was called to testify.

Jim, with his recollection of his family and his father's teaching, as well as his own deeply established sense of honor, was a marked man for the rest of his life. Marlow told how he had dinner with Jim during the trial. The boy seemed of a different stamp from the other officers of the *Patna.* Marlow was determined to fathom the boy's spirit, just as Jim was determined to regain his lost moral identity.

Jim told Marlow how the disgraceful affair had happened. After he had investigated the damage, he had felt that the ship could not remain afloat, for her plates were rust-eaten and unable to stand much strain. There were eight hundred passengers and seven boats, and not enough time to get into the boats the few passengers who could be carried to safety. Shortly afterward he discovered the captain and the engineers making ready to desert the ship. They insisted that he join them; the passengers were doomed anyway. The acting third engineer had a heart attack in the excitement and died. Jim never knew when— or why—he had jumped into the lifeboat the other officers had launched. Jim told Marlow how they had agreed to tell the same story. Actually, he and his companions thought that the *Patna* had gone down. Jim said that he had felt relief when he had learned that the passengers were safe. The whole story made sailor-talk in all ports where seamen met and talked. After the inquiry Marlow offered to help Jim, but Jim was determined to become a wanderer, to find out by himself what had happened to his soul.

Jim began his wanderings, to Bombay, to Calcutta, to Penang, Batavia, and the islands of the East. For a time he found work with an acquaintance of Marlow's, but he gave up his job when the second engineer of the *Patna* turned up unexpectedly. Afterward he became a runner for some ship chandlers, but he left them because he had heard one of the owners discussing the case of the *Patna.* He moved on, always toward the East, from job to job.

Marlow continued his efforts to help Jim. He sought out Stein, a trader who owned a number of trading posts on the smaller islands of the East Indies. Stein made Jim his agent at Patusan, an out-of-the-way settlement where he was sure Jim might recover his balance. There, in that remote place, Jim tried to find some answer to his self-hatred. Determined never to leave Patusan, he associated with the natives, and by his gentleness and consideration became their leader. They called him Tuan Jim— Lord Jim. Dain Waris, the son of Doramin, the old native chief, was his friend.

The rumor spread in the ports that Jim had discovered a valuable emerald, and that he had presented it to a native woman. There was a story about a native girl who loved him and who had given him warning when some jealous natives came to murder him.

Marlow followed Jim to Patusan. When Marlow prepared to leave, Jim accompanied him part of the way. He explained to Marlow that at last he felt as though his way had been justified. Somehow, because the simple natives trusted him, he felt linked again to the ideals of his youth. Marlow felt there was a kind of desperateness to his conviction.

The end came when Gentleman Brown, a roving cutthroat, determined to loot Lord Jim's stronghold. He arrived while Jim was away. Led by Dain Waris, the natives isolated Brown and his marauders on a hilltop but were unable to capture them. Lord Jim returned and after a long talk with Brown became convinced that Brown would leave peaceably if the siege were lifted. He persuaded the reluctant natives to withdraw. The vicious Brown repaid Lord Jim's magnanimity by vengefully murdering Dain Waris. Lord Jim went unflinchingly to face native justice when he offered himself to the stern old chieftain as the cause of Dain Waris' death. Doramin shot Jim through the breast.

Marlow, who had watched Jim's life so closely, felt that Jim had at last won back his lost honor.

LORNA DOONE

Type of work: Novel
Author: R. D. Blackmore (1825-1900)
Type of plot: Historical romance
Time of plot: Late seventeenth century
Locale: England
First published: 1869

> *Principal characters:*
> JOHN RIDD, yeoman of the parish of Oare in Somerset
> SIR ENSOR DOONE, head of the outlaw Doone clan
> LORNA DOONE, his ward
> CARVER DOONE, his son
> TOM FAGGUS, a highwayman
> JEREMY STICKLES, king's messenger
> REUBEN HUCKABACK, John Ridd's great-uncle

Critique:

R. D. Blackmore, in his preface to *Lorna Doone: A Romance of Exmoor*, was content to call his work a "romance," because the historical element was only incidental to the work as a whole. Secret agents, highwaymen, clannish marauders, and provincial farmers figure against a background of wild moor country. A feeling for the old times, for great, courageous people, for love under duress made the novel popular with Victorian readers. People who have read it in their youth remember it with nostalgia, for the book has a penetrating simplicity. Told in the first person by John Ridd, the main character in the novel, it has an authentic ring, the sound of a garrulous man relating the adventures of his youth.

The Story:

John Ridd was engaged in a schoolboy fight in the yard of old Blundell's school when John Fry, employed by Ridd's father, called for the boy to summon him

LORNA DOONE by R. D. Blackmore. Published by Dodd, Mead & Co., Inc.

home. Before the two left, however, young John completed his fight by knocking out his opponent. On their way home through the moorlands they were nearly captured by members of the outlaw Doone band, who had been ravaging the countryside, stealing and killing. When John Ridd reached his father's farm, he learned that only a few days before, the Doones had set upon and murdered his father. This incident stimulated the desire for revenge by all the members of the parish of Oare, for the murdered man had been greatly respected.

John settled down to the responsibilities which the death of his father had thrust upon him. At first his time was greatly taken by farm work, as he grew and matured into the largest and strongest man in the Exmoor country. As he grew up, John learned much about the wild Doone clan. There was one Doone, however, for whom he felt no animosity. This was the beautiful child of the man supposed to be the murderer of John's father. At first sight John had been stirred by the beauty of Lorna Doone. Thereafter he was in great conflict when he understood that his passion was directed toward the girl whom he ought for his father's sake to hate.

When John's great-uncle, Master Reuben Huckaback, was attacked and robbed by the Doones, he went with John to swear out a warrant for their arrest, but he had no luck because the magistrates were unwilling to incur the enmity of the Doones.

John was drawn deeper into his relationship with Lorna Doone. At their secret meetings in Doone Valley she told him the story of her life with the outlaws; how she always had loved her grandfather, Sir Ensor Doone, but feared and lately had come to hate the rough, savage sons, nephews, and grandsons of Sir Ensor. This hatred was increased when Carver Doone cold-bloodedly murdered Lord Alan Brandir, a distant relative, who had come to take her away from the Doones.

About this time John was called to London to serve the cause of James II's tottering throne. There he disclosed all he knew of the Doones' activities and of the false magistrates who seemed to be in league with them. He was warned that Tom Faggus, a highwayman who was John's own cousin, might go to the gallows before long. He returned to his mother and his farm no penny richer or poorer than when he left, because of his refusal to accept bribes or to become the dupe of sly lawyers in the city.

In the meantime concern over Lorna, who had two suitors among the Doones themselves, had almost unhinged John's mind. He was delighted to discover that Lorna, still only seventeen, held off the two Doones. At the same time he feared more than ever his chance of winning the ward of the outlaws he was pledged to help the king destroy. However, he at last won Lorna over to his suit, and with her agreement he felt nothing could stop him.

At home the love of his sister Annie for her cousin, Tom Faggus, reminded John of his duties as his father's son and plunged him into the worries over his mother and Annie and the farm. John's mother had other plans for his marriage, but when he revealed the only course his love must take, he won her over. In the meantime Master Jeremy Stickles brought news of the rising of the Duke of Monmouth and of troubles brewing for the king.

Suddenly, Lorna's signals stopped. John made his will and descended into the Doone hideout and there at great risk discovered that Lorna had been kept in her rooms because she would not marry Carver Doone. John managed to talk to her and she pledged never to give in to her family. He narrowly escaped capture, and at the same time managed to save the life of Jeremy Stickles, king's messenger, by overhearing the outlaws as they plotted to kill Jeremy when he should be crossing the valley bridge. The

Doones' plot to kill Stickles brought further plans for retaliation from the king's men.

Old Sir Ensor Doone was close to death. Before he died, he gave John Ridd and Lorna Doone his blessing and to Lorna he presented the glass necklace he had kept for her since childhood. Then John took Lorna home with him to his mother's farm. Jeremy Stickles went south to muster forces for the destruction of the Doone clan.

The counselor of the Doones took advantage of his absence to visit the Ridd farm in order to make a truce with John Ridd. His offer was rejected, but he threw trouble into the paths of the lovers by telling them that Lorna's father had murdered John's father and that his own father was the murderer of Lorna's father. Moreover, he tricked them out of Lorna's necklace, which by now, through the word of Tom Faggus, they knew to be made of diamonds.

Uncle Reuben Huckaback grew interested in having John marry his granddaughter Ruth, and took John to see the gold mine he had just bought. Upon his return, John learned that Lorna had disappeared. She had been taken away by the Dugals, who claimed her as their missing heiress.

When Tom Faggus joined the rebels against the king, John, at his sister Annie's request, went to find him and to bring him back to safety. John discovered Tom almost dead. John was taken prisoner and was nearly executed. He was saved only by the arrival of his friend, Jeremy Stickles.

John went to London and there saw Lorna. By good chance and virtue of his great strength he overcame two villains who were attempting to rob and kill a nobleman. The man happened to be Lorna's relative. In return for this deed, the king gave John the title of knight. Moreover, he had the court of heralds design a coat of arms for John's family. The coat of arms was soundly made and the queen herself paid for it, the king declining.

When John returned from London, covered with honors, he discovered the Doones had been raiding once more. Then came the long awaited revenge. The Doones were routed, their houses were burned, and their stolen booty was divided among those who put in claims for redress. The counselor revealed that it was Carver Doone who had killed John's father. The necklace was recovered.

Arrangements for the wedding of John and Lorna were made. At the end of the ceremony in the church, Carver Doone, out of his great jealousy, shot Lorna. Without a weapon in his hand, John rushed out in pursuit of Carver and found him at Barrow Down. There took place the greatest battle between two men ever told of in books. It was a fight of giants. As John felt his ribs cracking in Carver's tremendous hug, he fastened his own iron grip upon his enemy's arm and ripped it loose. Then he threw his crushed and bleeding enemy into the bog and saw Carver Doone sucked down into its black depths.

Thus the greatest enemy of John Ridd was at last destroyed and John returned to his bride to find that she might live. She did survive and in peace and plenty John Ridd lived among his friends to a hearty old age.

LOST HORIZON

Type of work: Novel
Author: James Hilton (1900-1954)
Type of plot: Adventure romance

Time of plot: 1931
Locale: Tibet
First published: 1933

Principal characters:
HUGH CONWAY, a British consul
RUTHERFORD, his friend
HENRY BARNARD, an American embezzler
MISS BRINKLOW, a missionary
CAPTAIN MALLISON, another British consul
CHANG, a Chinese lama
FATHER PERRAULT, the High Lama

Critique:

Shangri-La, the name for the setting of this novel, has come to mean to most Americans a place of peace and contentment. Such was the strange Utopia James Hilton described in *Lost Horizon*, making it seem like a real place, peopled b y living beings, rather than the land of an impossible ideal.

The Story:

When Rutherford had found Hugh Conway, a former schoolmate, suffering from fatigue and amnesia in a mission hospital, Conway had related a weird and almost unbelievable story concerning his disappearance many months before.

Conway was a member of the consulate at Baskul when trouble broke out there in May, 1931, and he was considered something of a hero because of the efficiency and coolness he displayed while white civilians were being evacuated. When it was his turn to leave, he boarded a plane in the company of Miss Roberta Brinklow, a missionary; Henry Barnard, an American, and Captain Charles Mallison, another member of the consulate. The plane was a special high-altitude cabin aircraft provided by the Maharajah of Chandapore. Conway, thirty-seven years old, had been in the consular service for ten years. His work had not been spectacular and he was expecting to rest in England before being assigned to another undistinguished post.

After the plane had been in the air about two hours, Mallison noticed that their pilot was the wrong man and that they were not headed toward Peshawur, the first scheduled stop. Conway was undisturbed until he realized they were flying over strange mountain ranges. When the pilot landed and armed tribesmen refueled the plane before it took off again, Conway began to agree with Mallison and Barnard, who thought they had been kidnaped and would be held for ransom.

When Conway tried to question the pilot, the man only pointed a revolver at him. A little after midnight the pilot landed again, this time narrowly averting a crackup. Climbing out of the plane, the passengers found the pilot badly injured. Conway believed that they were high on the Tibetan plateau, far beyond the western range of the Himalaya Mountains. The air was bitterly cold, with no signs of human habitation in that region of sheer-walled mountains. The pilot died before morning, murmuring something about a lamasery called Shangri-La. As the little group started in search of the lamasery, they saw a group of men coming toward them.

When the men reached them, one introduced himself in perfect English; he was a Chinese named Chang. Following the men, Conway and his friends arrived at the lamasery of Shangri-La that evening. There they found central heat, plumbing, and many other luxuries more commonly found only in the Western Hemisphere. They were given fine rooms and excellent food. They learned that there was a High Lama whom they would not be privileged to meet. Although Chang told them porters would arrive in a few weeks to lead them back to the outer world, Conway had the strange feeling that their coming had not been an accident and that they were not destined soon to leave.

Presently Chang told them that Conway was to be honored by an interview with the High Lama. Mallison begged him to force the High Lama to provide guides for them, for Mallison had learned that Barnard was wanted for fraud and embezzlement in the United States and he was anxious to turn Barnard over to the British authorities. But Conway did not discuss their departure with the High Lama, whom he found a very intelligent, very old man. Instead, he listened to the lama's remarkable story of Father Perrault, a Capuchin friar lost in the mountains in 1734, when he was fifty-three years old. Father Perrault had found sanctuary in a lamasery and had stayed there after adopting the Buddhist faith. In 1789 the old man lay dying, but the miraculous power of some drugs he had perfected, coupled with the marvelous air on the plateau, prolonged his life. Later tribesmen from the valley helped him build the lamasery of Shangri-La, where he lived the life of a scholar. In 1804 another European came to the lamasery; then others came from Europe and from Asia. No guest was ever allowed to leave.

Conway learned then that the kidnaping of their plane had been deliberate. But, more important, he learned that the High Lama was Father Perrault and that he was two hundred and fifty years old. The old man told Conway that all who lived at Shangri-La had the secret of long life. He had sent the pilot for new people because he believed a war was coming which would destroy all known civilization and Shangri-La would then be the nucleus of a new world. His picture of life in the lamasery pleased Conway. He was content to stay.

Conway, knowing that the others would find it hard to accept the news, did not tell them that they could never leave. Mallison continued to talk of the coming of the porters, but Barnard and Miss Brinklow announced that they intended to pass up the first opportunity to leave Shangri-La and wait for a later chance. Barnard faced jail if he returned, and Miss Brinklow thought she should not miss the opportunity to convert the lamas and the tribesmen in the valley.

The weeks passed pleasantly for Conway. He met a Frenchman called Briac, who had been Chopin's pupil. He also met Lo-Tsen, a Chinese girl who seemed quite young, but Chang told him she was really sixty-five years old. Conway had more meetings with the High Lama; at one of them the old man told Conway that he knew he was going to die at last and that he wanted Conway to take his place as ruler of the lamasery and the valley and to act wisely so that all culture would not be lost after war had destroyed Western civilization.

While he was explaining these matters, the old lama lay back in his chair, and Conway knew he was dead. Conway wandered out into the garden, too moved to talk to anyone. He was interrupted by Mallison, with the news that the porters had arrived. Although Barnard and Miss Brinklow would not leave, Mallison had paid the porters to wait for him and Conway. Mallison said that the Chinese girl was going with them, that he had made love to her and that she wanted to stay with him. Conway tried to tell Mallison that the girl was really an old woman who would die if she left the valley, but Mallison refused to listen. At first Conway also refused to leave Shangri-La, but after Mallison and the girl started and then came back because they were afraid to go on alone, Conway felt that he was responsible for them as well and he left the lamasery with them. He felt that he was fleeing from the place where he would be happy for the rest of his life, no matter how long that life might be.

Rutherford closed his manuscript at

that point, for Conway had slipped away and disappeared. Later Rutherford met a doctor who told him that Conway had been brought to the mission by a woman, a bent, withered, old Chinese woman.

Perhaps, then, the story was true. Convinced that Conway had headed for the hidden lamasery, Rutherford hoped that his journey had been successful, that Conway had reached Shangri-La.

LOST ILLUSIONS

Type of work: Novel
Author: Honoré de Balzac (1799-1850)
Type of plot: Naturalism
Time of plot: Early nineteenth century
Locale: Angoulême, France
First published in three parts: 1837, 1839, 1843

Principal characters:
DAVID SÉCHARD, a printer
EVE, his wife
LUCIEN CHARDON, his brother-in-law
MADAME DE BARGETON, loved by Lucien

Critique:

This longest of all Balzac's novels is a study of a hero who is too innocent even to understand all the machinations of his enemies. The tone is somber and cynical. Virtue is rewarded in a way, but chicanery is always triumphant. Although the plot is marred by the lavish details with which the past histories of the characters are presented, Balzac has achieved in this novel considerably more suspense than usual. *Lost Illusions* is perhaps the high point of the author's "Scenes of Country Life."

The Story:

Angoulême was divided into two social classes: the aristocrats of fashionable society and the bourgeois. David Séchard and Lucien Chardon were scarcely aware that they belonged to the less privileged class. Lucien was the brilliant, handsome, unstable son of a chemist. David was the sober, kind son of a printer.

David's father had sent him to Paris to learn all the latest innovations in the printing trade. The illiterate father, avaricious and mean, hoped that David would learn how to make more money from the old-fashioned printery shop of Séchard and Son. When David returned from Paris, his father quickly sold him the business at a high price and retired to his vineyard.

Partly because of his friendship for poetic Lucien and partly because of his temperament, David did not prosper. He was always discussing a grand project with Lucien or dreaming of Eve, Lucien's beautiful sister.

Lucien wrote some verses which attracted attention. Even the aristocrats of the town heard of him, and Madame de Bargeton, a woman of thirty-six married to an old husband, invited him to one of her famous evening gatherings. Eve scrimped to buy Lucien the proper clothes for the occasion. The evening was not an entire success. Few except Madame de Bargeton listened to Lucien's poetry, but he made a real conquest of his hostess.

While Lucien did his best to break into society and win the heart of Madame de Bargeton, David and Eve were quietly falling in love. David strained his resources to the utmost to furnish rooms over the print shop for his wife-to-be, a room at the rear for his mother-in-law, and a comfortable room on the street for Lucien. David had determined to promote Lucien's literary talent by supporting him.

Two days before the wedding, Lucien was surprised in Madame de Bargeton's boudoir. Her husband, old as he was, fought a duel with a man who had gossiped about Madame de Bargeton. Not wishing to face the scandal, Madame de Bargeton decided to go to Paris, and Lucien was to follow her. With a heavy heart, for he knew Lucien's weaknesses, David drove his friend at night along the Paris road. Safely away from Angoulême, Lucien joined his mistress.

David and Eve, married, settled into their new rooms. Eve was a devoted wife, though foolishly fond of her scapegrace brother. Before her child was born she began to grow uneasy. Lucien wrote very seldom and David paid little attention to his business. He was too busy working on an experiment to find a new way to make paper without rags. If he could invent a new process they would all be rich. Meanwhile the family was desperately in need, for Lucien's demands for money kept them poor. At last Eve herself took charge of the print shop.

She had her first small success when she hit on the idea of printing a *Shepherd's Calendar,* a cheap almanac to peddle to farmers. But the firm of Cointet Brothers, rivals in the printing trade, gave her so much unfair competition that she made only a small profit from her printing venture. After her baby came she had to give up her efforts for a while. David was more than ever wrapped up in his attempts to find a new process for making paper.

Meanwhile Lucien had failed completely to make his way in Paris. He had quarreled with his rich mistress, and they had parted. He could find only odd jobs as a journalist. He borrowed continually from David to lead the dissolute life of a man-about-town. Finally, when he went to live openly with Coralie, an actress, he lost all chances for any real success.

Pressed for money, Lucien forged David's name to notes for three thousand francs. When the firm of Cointet Brothers, acting as bankers, presented the notes to David for payment, he was unable to raise the money. The law suit that followed disturbed Eve so much that she had to hire a wet nurse for her baby; in that small French town she was disgraced.

Cointet Brothers promised a rich marriage to Petit-Claud, David's lawyer, if he would prolong the suit, increase the costs to David, and eventually force him into debtor's prison. During the delays Eve and David both appealed to his father for help, but the old miser refused aid to his son. He was mainly interested in collecting rent for the building where David had his shop. With all help denied, David went into hiding and worked feverishly on his paper process.

In Paris, Coralie died, leaving Lucien without a place to live. Having no money, he began the long walk home. One night he caught a ride among the trunks of a carriage and went to sleep on his precarious perch. When he awoke the carriage had stopped. As he got off he saw that he had been riding with his former mistress, Madame de Bargeton, now Madame la Comtesse Châtelet, wife of the new prefect of the district. She and her husband laughed openly as the disheveled Lucien stalked away.

A few miles from Angoulême Lucien became ill and sought refuge with a miller. Thinking him about to die, the miller sent for a priest. When Lucien begged for news of his family, the priest told him of David's troubles. Lucien hurried to town to see what he could do for the brother-in-law he had helped to ruin.

In Angoulême, Lucien was sorrowfully received by his sister. To add to the distress of David and his family, Cointet Brothers published in the paper a glowing account of Lucien's successes in Paris. There was a parade in Lucien's honor, and the du Châtelet's even invited him to dinner.

Realizing that he still had a hold over Madame du Châtelet, Lucien tried to get David released from his debts through her influence. Meanwhile, after seeing some samples of David's work, the Cointets offered to pay off his debts, buy his print shop, and develop his invention for him. The offer was intended, however, to bring David out of hiding. Then a letter from

Lucien to his friend was intercepted and a forged note substituted, appointing a place of meeting. David, on the way to the meeting, was arrested and thrown into prison.

Lucien, after a despairing farewell to his sister, left Angoulême. He intended to kill himself, but on the road he was picked up by a Spanish priest, an emissary traveling between Madrid and Paris. The envoy saw promise in Lucien and offered him fifteen thousand francs in return for Lucien's promise to do as the priest wished. The Spaniard meant to acquire power through Lucien's attraction for women and his poetic fervor. The bargain sealed, Lucien sent the fifteen thousand francs to David.

The money arrived just after David had signed away his shop and his paper-making process to the Cointets. David and Eve retired to the country and in due time inherited money and a vineyard from his father. Petit-Claud, the double crossing lawyer, became a famous prosecutor. The Cointets made a great fortune from David's process, and one of them became a deputy and a peer.

A LOST LADY

Type of work: Novel
Author: Willa Cather (1876-1947)
Type of plot: Regional realism
Time of plot: Late nineteenth century
Locale: Nebraska
First published: 1923

Principal characters:
　　CAPTAIN FORRESTER, a railroad constructor
　　MRS. FORRESTER, his wife
　　JUDGE POMMEROY, his friend and legal adviser
　　NIEL HERBERT, the judge's nephew
　　IVY PETERS, a shyster lawyer

Critique:

This book, which is marked by a studied attention to form, achieves an epic-like tone. In part this is derived from the theme as well as from the viewpoint of the novel. The theme expresses a feeling of admiration which most Americans share for the builders who opened the West, a herculean task which could not be done twice. The viewpoint is that of a young man whose youth claims the right of sentimental ardor which makes youth so delightful. Moreover, Miss Cather captured the tone of many women of the generation about which she was writing. Mrs. Forrester possessed more valiant self-reliance than many of her contemporaries. As such she was able to be a lost lady and still keep her own personality intact.

The Story:

The Forrester home at Sweet Water was a stopping off place for railroad magnates riding through the prairie states along the Burlington line. Old Captain Forrester liked to drive his guests from the station and watch them as they approached his estate. He enjoyed their praise of his stock farm and their delight when his charming wife met them at the front door. Everyone from railroad presidents to the village butcher boy and the kitchen maids liked Mrs. Forrester; her manner was always one of friendliness and respect.

Niel Herbert's acquaintance with Mrs. Forrester began when he fell from a tree while playing with some village boys on the captain's property and Mrs. Forrester summoned a doctor. He did not know it at the time, but Mrs. Forrester had already singled him out from the others because he was Judge Pommeroy's nephew. After his recovery he was often invited to the Forrester home with his uncle.

The boy who had caused Niel's fall was Ivy Peters. He had winged a woodpecker and then had slit its eyes. The bird had fumbled back into its hole, and Niel was trying to reach the creature to put it out of its misery when he lost his balance and fell.

During a period of hard times Niel's father went out of business and left Sweet Water. Niel stayed on to read law in his uncle's office. A few days before Christmas, Mrs. Forrester invited Niel to her home to help entertain Constance Ogden, the daughter of one of the captain's friends, who was coming to spend the holidays with the Forresters. Also included in the party was Frank Ellinger, a bachelor of forty. The dinner was a gay one. Niel decided that Constance was neither pretty nor pleasant. It was plain that she had designs on Frank Ellinger.

The following day Niel was asked to stay with Constance during the afternoon, while Mrs. Forrester and Frank took the small cutter and went after cedar for the Christmas decorations. The Blum boy, out hunting, saw Mrs. Forrester and Frank after he came upon the deserted cutter beside a thicket, but he did not give away their secret. The doings of the rich were not his concern and Mrs. Forrester had been kind to him on many occasions.

During that winter Judge Pommeroy and his nephew often went to play cards with the Forresters. One night, during a snowstorm, Mrs. Forrester revealed to Niel how much she missed the excitement and glamour of former winters at fashionable resorts. She mocked the life of quiet domesticity in which she and the captain were living.

In the spring the captain went to Denver on business and while he was gone Frank Ellinger arrived for a visit. One morning Niel cut a bouquet of wild roses to leave outside the windows of Mrs. Forrester's bedroom. Suddenly he heard from the bedroom the voices of Mrs. Forrester and Frank Ellinger. The first illusion of his life was shattered by a man's yawn and a woman's laugh.

When the captain came home from Denver, he announced that he was a poor man. Having satisfied his creditors, he had left only his pension from the Civil War and the income from his farm. Shortly afterward the captain had a stroke.

Niel continued to visit the sick man and his wife. He realized that Mrs. Forrester was facing her new life with terror she tried to hide for her husband's sake. Niel, having decided to become an architect, left Sweet Water to spend two years at school in the East. When he returned, he learned that Ivy Peters, shrewd and grasping, had become an important person in the town. Niel, who despised Peters, was disappointed to learn that Peters, now the captain's tenant, had drained the marsh where the boys had gone fishing years before. The captain himself had become wasted and old. Most of the time he sat in his garden staring at a strange sundial he had made.

Niel learned that Mrs. Forrester, who seemed little older, was still writing to Frank Ellinger. He observed, too, that Mrs. Forrester treated Peters with easy familiarity, and he wondered how she could be on friendly terms with the pushing young lawyer.

That summer a storm flooded the fields along the creek. Niel went to Judge Pommeroy's office to read. He thought of an item he had seen in the Denver paper earlier in the day; Frank Ellinger had finally married Constance Ogden. Close to midnight Mrs. Forrester, drenched to the skin, appeared at the office. At her demand Niel made the telephone connection with Ellinger in Colorado Springs. Mrs. Forrester began to talk politely, as though complimenting Ellinger on his marriage. Then she became hysterical. When she began to scream reproaches, Niel cut the wires.

Mrs. Forrester recovered after her collapse, but the gossipy town telephone operator pieced together a village scandal from what she had managed to overhear.

Captain Forrester died in December. None of his wealthy friends attended the funeral, but old settlers and former employees came to do honor to the railroad pioneer who had been one of the heroes of the early West.

One day Mr. Ogden stopped in Sweet Water. He thought that Judge Pommeroy ought to send to Washington a claim to have Mrs. Forrester's pension increased. Niel was forced to explain that Mrs. Forrester had turned her affairs over to Ivy Peters.

After her husband's death Mrs. Forrester began to entertain Ivy Peters and other young men from the village. At her urging Niel went to one party, but he was disgusted with the cheap manners of both hostess and guests. He could not bear to see the old captain's home thus abused.

Niel felt that an era was ending. The great old people, such as the judge and the captain and their friends, were passing, the men who had built the railroads and the towns. The old men of gallant manners and their lovely ladies had gone forever. In their place was a new type of man, the shrewd opportunist, like Ivy Peters. On the day Niel saw Peters putting his arms around Mrs. Forrester, he decided to leave Sweet Water.

As long as his uncle lived, however, he had news of Mrs. Forrester. The judge wrote that she was sadly broken. Then his uncle died and Niel heard no more for many years.

A long time afterward a mutual friend told him what had happened to his lost lady. She had gone to California. Later, she had married a rich Englishman and had gone with him to South America. She had dyed her hair and had dressed expensively in an effort to keep her youth.

Finally, one year, the G.A.R. post received a letter from Mrs. Forrester's English husband. It enclosed money for the continued care of Captain Forrester's grave. His gift was a memorial to his late wife, Marian Forrester Collins.

THE LOST WEEKEND

Type of work: Novel
Author: Charles Jackson (1903-   )
Type of plot: Psychological melodrama
Time of plot: Twentieth century
Locale: New York City
First published: 1944

Principal characters:
DON BIRNAM, an alcoholic
WICK, his brother
HELEN, his friend

Critique:

Although *The Lost Weekend* is in some respects more a case history than a novel, it is nevertheless a vivid and convincing story of a maladjusted personality. Jackson shows considerable insight into alcoholism as a social problem without destroying the personal quality of his hero's experience and the desperation of his struggle during a long weekend when he is thrown upon his own resources. In this novel the drama remains objective; the underlying cause of Don Birnam's alcoholism is dramatized rather than analyzed.

The Story:

Don Birnam was an unsuccessful writer who drank too much. Time and again, his brother Wick and his friend Helen tried to break him of the habit. They kept money out of his reach so that he could not buy liquor. They warned neighbors and bartenders against his habits. They sent him to a rest farm for the cure. But even there he managed to get something to drink.

One weekend Don was left alone while Wick went to the country. As soon as his brother had gone, Don took the money Wick had left for the housekeeper and went out to buy liquor. He went into a bar and chatted with Gloria, the hostess. He told her about his life, about his wife who was frigid, his children, and other details all equally fantastic and imaginary. He asked Gloria to meet him later. After being convinced that he was not joking, she accepted.

That night Don went into another bar and began drinking heavily. While there, idly watching a young couple, he suddenly decided to steal the girl's purse. He would do it only as a joke, he told himself. Later he could return the purse and they would all laugh at his prank. He picked up the purse and slipped it under his coat, acting calmly and naturally all the time, but as he was walking out a waiter stopped him. Luckily, the girl did not want to press charges. Don was pushed out into the street.

He went from one bar to another. When he drifted back to Sam's bar, Gloria was angry because he had forgotten his date with her. He could not understand why she asked him about his wife and his children, because he had neither. Next morning he found that his money had disappeared and that there was no money in the apartment. He decided to pawn his typewriter. He walked up and down the streets, but all the pawnshops were closed because it was a Jewish holiday. He went home, changed his clothes, and borrowed ten dollars from a nearby merchant. He went out to drink again. Coming back, he fell down a flight of stairs and lost consciousness.

When he awoke, he was in the alcoholic ward of a hospital. With him were a doctor and Bim, a male nurse. He wanted his clothes, he insisted; he wanted to go home. At last the doctor told him that he could go if he would sign a paper absolving the hospital of all responsibility.

Leaving the hospital, Don went straight to his apartment, where he fell asleep. The ringing of the telephone awoke him. He could not remember when he had last eaten. When he tried to get up, he almost collapsed, and he sank, exhausted, into a chair. After a while he heard a key in the lock. It was Helen, coming to see how he was getting along while Wick was away. She helped him to get dressed and took him to her apartment. When the maid came in, Helen went out on an errand. Don tried to get the key to the closet, but the maid pretended that she had no idea where it was. Don was growing more and more desperate for liquor. Before Helen left the apartment, he had called to her in terror because he thought a bat was devouring a mouse in the room. His thirst was growing worse. Seeing Helen's fur coat, he seized it and ran out of the apartment. He pawned the coat for five dollars and bought several pints of whiskey. He went back to his own apartment. Afraid that Wick might return, he hid one bottle in the bathroom and suspended the other on a string outside his window.

He lay down on the bed and took a long drink of whiskey. He felt wonderful. The ordeal was over; he had come through once more. There was no telling what might happen the next time, but he saw no reason to worry now.

LOVE FOR LOVE

Type of work: Drama
Author: William Congreve (1670-1729)
Type of plot: Comedy of manners
Time of plot: Seventeenth century
Locale: London
First presented: 1695

Principal characters:
> SIR SAMPSON LEGEND, a foolish old gentleman
> VALENTINE, his son, an indigent gallant
> BENJAMIN, another son, a sailor
> FORESIGHT, an old man given to astrology
> ANGELICA, his niece
> PRUE, his daughter
> MRS. FORESIGHT, his young second wife
> MISTRESS FRAIL, her sister

Critique:

Love for Love, generally considered one of Congreve's finest plays, is marked by a relatively simple but not particularly original plot. For the most part, the Restoration writers of comedy seemed to be content to follow their Elizabethan and Jacobean predecessors in matters of plot and of stock characters. Whatever grossness—and it is comparatively trifling—is present in this play is far overbalanced by clever and amusing dialogue and by several pairs of well-conceived and variously-contrasted characters. Surely Ben Jonson's theory of humors is quite alive in Sir Sampson Legend's penchant for tall tales of travel and in old Foresight's obsession for prognostication.

The Story:

Young Valentine Legend, having squandered all of his money in riotous living, was destitute and deeply in debt. With no property left but his books, he declared his intention of becoming a playwright, for his love for Angelica had indeed compelled him to take desperate measures. On hearing of his intention, Jeremy, his knavish manservant, showed alarm and said that Valentine's family would surely disown him.

Among Valentine's creditors was Trapland, a lecherous old scrivener who persisted in dunning him. When Valentine, who had been joined by his friend Scandal, subtly threatened Trapland with blackmail concerning a wealthy city widow the old man suddenly forgot the money owed him.

Sir Sampson Legend's steward told Valentine that he could be released from all debts by signing over his rights as Sir Sampson's heir to Ben, his younger brother. If he signed, he would receive four thousand pounds in cash.

In the meantime Foresight, an old fool given to the science of prognostication, recalled Prue, his bumpkin daughter, from the country. Foresight planned to marry her to Ben Legend.

Angelica, wealthy, young, and clever, reproved her uncle for his belief in astrology. Irate, Foresight threatened to end her friendship with Valentine. Angelica, piqued, insinuated that Mrs. Foresight, the old man's young second wife, was not true to him.

Sir Sampson Legend, a great teller of tall tales of world travel, arranged with Foresight for the marriage of Ben and Prue. When Sir Sampson playfully hinted to Foresight that Mrs. Foresight might not be a faithful wife, Foresight threatened to break off the marriage agreement. Sir Sampson quickly made amends.

Valentine, seeking Angelica, encountered his father at Foresight's house. He was indignant when his father disowned him as a son and he begged his father to change his mind about the conditions under which he could be freed of debt.

When Mrs. Foresight rebuked her sister for her indiscretion in frequenting the haunts of gamesters and gallants, Mistress Frail revealed her knowledge of Mrs. Foresight's own indiscretions. Mistress Frail then declared her intention of marrying Ben and enlisted her sister's aid in the project. Prue, meanwhile, found herself charmed by Tattle, a voluble young dandy. When Mrs. Foresight and Mistress Frail encouraged Tattle to court Prue, he was mystified because he knew of the marriage arranged between Prue and Ben. Even so, he gave Prue a lesson in the art of love, a lesson which progressed as far as her bedchamber. Tattle, having grown tired of dalliance with the rude country girl, was relieved when Prue's nurse found them.

Ben, returning from a sea voyage, declared that marriage did not interest him at the moment, but he visibly changed his mind when Mistress Frail flattered him. Left alone, he and Prue expressed dislike for each other. Ben declared that he talked to Prue only to obey his father.

Scandal, in Valentine's behalf, ingratiated himself with Foresight by pretending a knowledge of astrology. His scheme succeeding, he convinced Foresight that it was not in the stars for Valentine to sign over his inheritance or for Ben and Prue to marry. Attracted to Mrs. Foresight, Scandal hoodwinked old Foresight in order to pay gallant attentions to his young wife. Meanwhile Ben and Mistress Frail confessed their love and decided to marry.

Because Scandal had reported that Valentine was ill, Angelica went to his lodgings. In spite of Scandal's insistence that her acknowledgment of love for Valentine would cure the young man, she quickly detected a trick and departed. Sir Sampson and a lawyer named Buckram arrived to get Valentine's signature to the documents they had prepared. Jeremy insisted that Valentine was out of his mind. Buckram said that the signature would be invalid under the circumstances, but Sir Sampson forced his way into his son's presence. Valentine, pretending complete lunacy, called himself Truth and declared that he would give the world the lie. After the frightened Buckram left, Valentine showed clarity of mind, but, when the lawyer was called back, Valentine again seemed to lapse into lunacy.

Mistress Frail, having learned that there was little chance of Ben's getting the whole estate, broke off their engagement. Sir Sampson, frustrated by Valentine, decided to marry and beget a new heir. Mrs. Foresight plotted with Jeremy to marry Mistress Frail, disguised as Angelica, to Valentine during one of his fits of madness. When Jeremy revealed the scheme to Valentine and Scandal, the friends, in their turn, planned to marry Mistress Frail to Tattle by means of another disguise.

After Valentine had confessed his feigned madness to Angelica, she expressed disappointment; she had thought him really mad for love of her. She then went to Sir Sampson, learned his new state of mind, and suggested that he and she go through with a mock marriage ceremony in order to bring Valentine to his senses. When foolish Sir Sampson suggested that they actually get married so that she could inherit his estate, Angelica said that his plan would not be advisable since the papers leaving the estate to Ben were already drawn up.

Jeremy tricked foolish Tattle into believing that he, disguised as a friar, might marry Angelica, who would be disguised as a nun. Prue, forsaken by Tattle, asserted that she would marry Robin, the butler, who had professed his love for her.

Mistress Frail, thinking that she was marrying Valentine, and Tattle, thinking that he was marrying Angelica, were thus tricked into wedlock. Told by Angelica that she intended to marry his father, Valentine in despair declared that he was ready to sign over his inheritance. Impressed by this indication of his love for her, Angelica tore up the bond, which Sir Sampson had given her, and she brought the doting old man to his senses by revealing that she had always intended to marry Valentine. Sir Sampson and old Foresight consoled each other; they admitted that they had acted like fools.

LOVE IN A WOOD

Type of work: Drama
Author: William Wycherley (1640-1716)
Type of plot: Comedy of manners
Time of plot: Seventeenth century
Locale: London
First presented: 1671

Principal characters:
MR. RANGER, a young man about town
LYDIA, his cousin and betrothed
MR. VALENTINE, a gallant lately returned to London
CHRISTINA, his betrothed
MR. VINCENT, a confidant of all the lovers
ALDERMAN GRIPE, an elderly usurer
MISTRESS MARTHA, his daughter
LADY FLIPPANT, his sister, in London to find a husband
SIR SIMON ADDLEPLOT, an indomitable fortune hunter
MR. DAPPERWIT, a fop and a would-be gentleman
MRS. JOYNER, a matchmaker and procuress
MRS. CROSSBITE, a blackmailer and procuress
LUCY, her daughter

Critique:

The first of three satiric comedies, *Love in a Wood; or, St. James's Park,* as it was popularly known, shows brilliantly the genius of William Wycherley, who gained his insight as an intimate in high society on both sides of the Channel. It was this play which gained for the young man the favor of a king and the love of the king's mistress, the Duchess of Cleveland.

The Story:

Lady Flippant, a widow disappointed in her efforts to find a new husband, berated her matchmaker, Mrs. Joyner, for not finding a wealthy young man to relieve her impecunious position. The lady's brother, Alderman Gripe, had grown tired of her foppish visitors, especially the witless Mr. Dapperwit.

Sir Simon Addleplot, at the suggestion of the cozening Mrs. Joyner and the double-dealing Dapperwit, disguised himself and gained employment as a clerk to the miserly Gripe in order to woo the usurer's daughter Mistress Martha and through her to secure her father's fortune. Not realizing that he had been gulled into becoming Jonas the clerk, Sir Simon was again duped into believing that he was loved by Lady Flippant, who was really enamored of Dapperwit.

Mr. Ranger, with Mr. Vincent, his friend and confidant, was about to go into St. James's Park in search of some amorous adventure when his cousin and betrothed, Lydia, discovered his whereabouts. He avoided her, however, and dined for diversion with the gulled Sir Simon, Dapperwit, and Lady Flippant in order to watch the work of Mrs. Joyner, who had already made twenty crowns through introductions and would obtain a hundred if Sir Simon got Mistress Martha or fifty if he got Lady Flippant. The widow spurned Sir Simon,

1746

flirted with Dapperwit, and hinted at matrimony to both the young gallants, Ranger and Vincent.

Later, all promenaded through St. James's Park in the hope of discovering one another's intrigues. Lydia, recognizing Ranger, ran into the house of her friend Christina in order to avoid a compromising meeting with her betrothed. Ranger pursued her, only to become enamored of Christina, who was faithfully waiting the return to London of Mr. Valentine, her fiancé. Christina, in order to help Lydia, had pretended to be the young woman he had pursued from the park. Her little act quickly over, she sent the impertinent Ranger away. Ranger, in despair because he had not learned the fair unknown's name, did not know that Lydia had heard his gallant speeches to Christina.

Ranger went to the home of his friend Vincent. Valentine, in danger of his life from a rival, was in hiding there; he wished no one else to know of his return from France before his loved one did. Valentine, concealed, overheard Ranger ask the name of the young woman whom he pursued into her apartment. When Vincent named the apartment as Christina's, Valentine became convinced that his beloved one had been untrue to him.

In contrast to this sequence of mistaken and confused identities, the busy Mrs. Joyner was more positive in identifying Lucy, the daughter of her friend Mrs. Crossbite, as the object of hypocritical old Gripe's lust. The solicitous mother, pleased with this development, ordered her recalcitrant daughter to give up her love for Dapperwit. When Dapperwit, thinking to cure Ranger's melancholy over Christina, brought him to see Lucy, the girl repulsed him for his infidelity and what she thought was his intention of procuring her for Ranger. The jilted fop recovered his spirits, however, when he received a message delivered by Jonas, the supposed clerk. The message held out the promise of a later assignation which might lead, Dapperwit hoped, to a wedding.

As the gallants departed, the ever-busy Mrs. Joyner brought furtive Alderman Gripe to see Lucy. His hasty lust frightened the lass, however, and she screamed. Though he dickered for the sake of salving his miserly conscience, Gripe was coerced into paying five hundred pounds of hush money to Mrs. Crossbite. Lady Flippant, at the same time, was making advances to the defenseless Dapperwit, and the nimble-footed lovers, Ranger and Lydia, were busy at double deception. Lydia denied that she had been in the park jealously searching for him; Ranger assured her that he had called for her as he had promised.

The Gripe household was at this time in an uproar. The sly old man was busily attempting to hide his shame and regain his money, and Mrs. Joyner virtuously pretended horror at the treatment he had received at the hands of Mrs. Crossbite. Jonas, meanwhile, made love to Lady Flippant, who protested only after she learned that her seducer was really Sir Simon Addleplot, the man she hoped finally to marry. So the poor man, undone by his own deceit, lost Mistress Martha through his dissembling ways and Dapperwit's roguery.

Lydia, desirous of testing Ranger, sent him a letter to which she signed Christina's name, asking the gallant to meet her that evening at St. James's Gate. The wronged Christina, however, had since learned of her lover's return, and Valentine was at that time trying to reassure himself of her innocence. Overhearing Ranger's new plans unsettled his mind again, though his eavesdropping on a conversation between Christina and Vincent and then on one between Christina and her supposed lover finally set his mind at rest. Lydia also confessed her part in this lovers' plot and counterplot. The two couples, thus reunited, decided that matrimony was the only sure solution to love's equation.

But the false lovers found no such

1747

easy solution, so addle-witted and dapper-plotted had their intrigues become. Sir Simon, still passing as Jonas, escorted Mistress Martha to Dapperwit; he thought their embraces inopportune and inappropriate. But Sir Simon's arrangements for a parson, a supper, and a reception in nearby Mulberry Garden were not completely wasted. Propelled to the same garden by the two scheming procuresses, Alderman Gripe married Lucy to be revenged on his son-in-law, that Dapperwit who took a bride six months pregnant. Sir Simon took widowed Lady Flippant as his wife, just as she had intended.

Thus were all the honest ladies made wives and all the bawds made honest, up in St. James's Park.

LOVE'S LABOUR'S LOST

Type of work: Drama
Author: William Shakespeare (1564-1616)
Type of plot: Comedy of manners
Time of plot: Sixteenth century
Locale: Navarre, Spain
First presented: c. 1594

Principal characters:
FERDINAND, King of Navarre
BEROWNE,
LONGAVILLE, and
DUMAINE, lords of Navarre
DON ADRIANO DE ARMADO, a foolish Spaniard
COSTARD, a clown
THE PRINCESS OF FRANCE
ROSALINE,
MARIA, and
KATHERINE, ladies attending the princess
JAQUENETTA, a country wench

Critique:

There is little wonder that *Love's Labour's Lost* is not among the popular favorites of most readers of Shakespeare. The play is slow-moving, in places dull, and it shows neither the perfection of plot nor the fineness of characterization which distinguish most of the later plays. At the same time it is filled with clever talk and it exhalts, in the romantic manner of the sonneteers, the theme of love. The note of seriousness apparent beneath the surface cleverness of the dialogue makes this play an early comedy of manners, in which the ladies try to teach the young noblemen the value of sincerity and faithfulness to vows. The foolish Armado and the stupid clown enliven many of the scenes with their wit. All in all, this drama is not a poor play; an early work, it is not so good as most readers expect from the master dramatist.

The Story:

The King of Navarre had taken a solemn vow and forced three of his attending lords to take it also. This vow was that for three years they would fast and study, enjoy no pleasures, and see no ladies. None of the three noblemen wanted to take the vow; Berowne, in particular, felt that it would be impossible to keep his promise. He pointed out this fact to the king by reminding him that even at that very time the Princess of France was approaching the court of Navarre to present a petition from her father, who was ill. The king agreed that he would be compelled to see her, but he added that in such cases the vow must be broken by necessity. Berowne foresaw that "necessity" would often cause the breaking of their vows.

The only amusement the king and his lords would have was provided by

Costard, a clown, and by Don Adriano De Armado, a foolish Spaniard attached to the court. Armado wrote the king to inform him that Costard had been caught in the company of Jaquenetta, a country wench of dull mind. Since all attached to the court had been under the same laws of abstinence from earthly pleasures, Costard was remanded to Armado's custody and ordered to fast on bran and water for one week. The truth was that Armado also loved Jaquenetta. He feared the king would learn of his love and punish him in the same manner.

The Princess of France arrived with her three attendants. All were fair and lovely, and they expected to be received at the palace in the manner due their rank. But the king sent word that they would be housed at his lodge, since under the terms of his vow no lady could enter the palace. The princess, furious at being treated in this fashion, scorned the king for his bad manners. When she presented the petition from her father, she and the king could not agree, for he vowed he had not received certain monies she claimed had been delivered to him.

At that first meeting, although each would have denied the fact, eight hearts were set to beating faster. The king viewed the princess with more than courteous interest. Berowne, Longaville, and Dumaine, his attendants, looked with love on the princess' ladies in waiting, Rosaline, Maria, and Katherine. A short time later Berowne sent a letter to Rosaline, with Costard as his messenger. But Costard had also been given a letter by Armado, to be delivered to Jaquenetta. The obvious happened. Costard, mixing up the letters, gave Jaquenetta's to Rosaline and Rosaline's to the country wench.

Berowne had been correct in thinking the vow to leave the world behind would soon be broken. Hiding in a tree, he heard the king read aloud a sonnet which proclaimed his love for the princess. Later the king, in hiding, overheard Longaville reading some verses he had composed to

Maria. Longaville, in turn, concealed himself and listened while Dumaine read a love poem inscribed to Katherine. Then each one in turn stepped out from hiding to accuse the others of breaking their vows. Berowne all that time had remained hidden in the tree. Thinking to chide them for their broken vows, he revealed himself at last and ridiculed them for their weakness, at the same time proclaiming himself the only one able to keep his vow. But at that instant Costard and Jaquenetta brought to the king the letter Berowne had written Rosaline, the letter Costard had mistakenly delivered to the country girl.

Then all confessed that they had broken their vows. Berowne provided an excuse for all when he declared that one could learn much by studying women and the nature of love. Their honor saved, the four determined to woo the ladies in earnest, and they made plans to entertain their loves with revels and dances.

Each lover sent his lady a token to wear in his honor. But when the ladies learned from a servant that the lovers were, for a joke, coming in disguise to woo the princess and her companions, the girls in turn planned to discomfit the king and the three lords by masking themselves and exchanging tokens. The men arrived, also masked and disguised as Russians. Each man tried to make love to the lady wearing his token, but each was spurned and ridiculed. The ladies would not dance or sing, but would only mock the bewildered gentlemen.

Finally the suitors departed, hurt and indignant at the treatment they had received. Before long they returned in their own dress. The ladies then unmasked and told of the lunatic Russians who had called on them. Although the men confessed their plot and forswore all such jokes forever, the ladies still did not stop teasing them. Since each man had made love to the wrong girl because of the exchange of tokens, the ladies pretended to be hurt that each man had broken his vows of love and constancy by protesting love for another. The poor suitors suffered greatly for their merriment before they learned that the ladies had anticipated their coming in disguise and thus had planned a joke of their own.

The king ordered a play presented for the entertainment of all. But in the midst of the gaiety word came that the princess' father, the King of France, had died. She must sail for home immediately, accompanied by her attendants. When the king and his lords pleaded with the ladies to stay in Navarre and marry them, the ladies refused to accept their serious protestations of love; they had jested too much to be believed. Each man vowed that he would remain faithful, only to be reminded of the former vows he had broken.

Then each lady made a condition which, if met, would reward her lover a year hence. The king must retire for twelve months to a hermitage and there forsake all worldly pleasures. If at the end of that time he still loved the princess, she would be his. In the same fashion the other three lords must spend a year in carrying out the wishes of their sweethearts. Even the foolish Armado was included in the plan. He joined the others, announcing that Jaquenetta would not have him until he spent three years in honest work.

Thus all the swains tried with jests and fair speech to win their ladies, but without success. Now as the price of their folly they must prove in earnest that they deserved the hearts of their beloveds.

LOVING

Type of work: Novel
Author: Henry Green (Henry Vincent York, 1905-   )
Type of plot: Domestic comedy
Time of plot: World War II
Locale: Eire
First published: 1945

> *Principal characters:*
> CHARLEY RAUNCE, an English butler
> MRS. TENNANT, Raunce's employer
> MRS. JACK TENNANT, Mrs. Tennant's daughter-in-law
> EDITH, a maid in love with Raunce
> ALBERT, Raunce's assistant

Critique:

The novels of Henry Green have not found favor with American readers as readily as they have in Great Britain. Green combines modern techniques with Dickensian humor and sly social criticism. In this novel he conducts his readers to the little known world below stairs, the world of the servants which few masters or mistresses ever see. The qualities of depth and perception revealed in this and other of Green's books have made him a novelist better known to other writers than he is to the public at large.

The Story:

The great mansion owned by Mrs.

Tennant had been thrown into turmoil by the death of old Eldon, the butler. In the servants' quarters no one knew quite what arrangements would be made after his death, for the mansion and its inhabitants formed an isolated bit of England in Eire. None of the servants could guess what Mrs. Tennant, who was a widow and very vague, might do in rearranging their duties. Only the footman, Charley Raunce, kept any purpose in his behavior.

Immediately after Eldon's death, Raunce went into the butler's room and took two small notebooks, one filled with the butler's monthly accounts and the other containing a set of special memoranda about visitors to the mansion, information which had helped the old man to solicit generous tips from Mrs. Tennant's guests. That same day Raunce went to his mistress and asked for the post of butler. She agreed to give him the post, but without any extra pay. Raunce knew, however, that by juggling the accounts he could make up whatever pay rise he deemed sufficient. That evening he solidified his position by successfully taking over the old butler's place at the head of the table in the servants' dining-room.

There were two upstairs maids in the Tennant mansion, Edith and Kate. Raunce insisted that Edith, with whom he was in love, continue her practice of bringing the butler his morning tea. The housekeeper, Mrs. Burch, was scandalized, but was forced to give in.

Raunce's usurpation of the old butler's position immediately upon the latter's death soon appeared a minor matter, for a scandal rocked the mansion within a few days. Mrs. Tennant's daughter-in-law, Mrs. Jack, was found in bed with a neighbor, Captain Davenport. The discovery was made by Edith, who went to open the curtains and lay out Mrs. Jack's clothes in the morning. Even though Mrs. Tennant was unaware of her daughter-in-law's indiscretion, the episode created consternation and nervousness in the servants' quarters.

To add to the uneasiness among the servants, a blue sapphire ring belonging to Mrs. Tennant disappeared. Mrs. Tennant, who was always losing valuables, did not blame the servants, but the loss made them feel ill at ease.

A few days afterward Mrs. Tennant and her daughter-in-law went to England to visit Jack Tennant, who had been given a few days' leave from military duty. The English servants almost gave their notice when they learned that they were being left in sole charge of the mansion, for they were well aware of the unfriendly attitudes of the Irish about the countryside and were also in fear of an invasion of the district by German troops. Raunce, who had a great sense of duty, as well as a realization of what a good place he had, prevailed upon them to remain, despite the general dissatisfaction.

In Mrs. Tennant's absence Raunce paid court to Edith and discovered that she was in love with him. They spent many pleasant hours together, for Raunce was kept from his duties by a sore throat and Edith spent much of her time nursing him. They, like the other servants, were worried by the absence of their mistress and by their failure to find Mrs. Tennant's missing ring. Edith finally found it, but she and Raunce were at a loss to know where to keep it until Mrs. Tennant's return. They decided to hide it in the upholstering of a chair.

Much to their dismay, the ring was taken from the chair. Shortly after they discovered its loss a second time, an investigator from an insurance company called at the mansion. All the servants refused to answer his questions, for his presence during their mistress' absence bothered them and they did not know what to say in order to protect her and her interests. The investigator left in a suspicious mood, saying that his company would not pay for the loss. After his departure the servants discovered that the initials of the insurance company were like those of the militant, revolutionary Irish Republican Army. The discovery almost panicked them completely. Only the thought of military service and short rations in England kept them from giving up their jobs immediately.

In the remaining days before Mrs. Tennant's return, Edith learned that Mrs. Tennant's grandchildren and the cook's nephew had found the sapphire ring while playing. Not realizing the value of the piece of jewelry, the youngsters

1751

had taken it out and hidden it on the lawn. By pretending to want it as a wedding present from one of the little girls, Edith persuaded the child to bring it to her.

When Mrs. Tennant returned, the ring was restored to her, and the matter of its loss and the ugliness of the insurance investigator soon became matters of the past, almost forgotten after Raunce's helper, a young lad named Albert, gave his notice and left the mansion because Mrs. Tennant had implied that he had taken the ring in the first place. He went back to England to enter the military service and become an aerial gunner.

Raunce was made restless by the realization, brought home to him by Albert's departure, that he had no part in the war effort. He also felt remorseful be-cause his mother, who was exposed to the bombings by the Germans, refused to come to Ireland to live with her son and Edith after their marriage. These influences, plus the many dissensions among the servants and the domestic crises that were occurring at the mansion, assumed larger and larger proportions as he thought about them. At last he admitted to Edith that he was dissatisfied and wanted to leave. His announcement made Edith unhappy, for she thought at first that he was trying to get out of marrying her.

When he convinced her that he wanted her to go with him, they decided that, unlike good servants, they would leave without giving notice to Mrs. Tennant. One night they eloped and went back to England to be married and to live.

THE LOWER DEPTHS

Type of work: Drama
Author: Maxim Gorky (Aleksei Maksimovich Peshkov, 1868-1936)
Type of plot: Naturalism
Time of plot: Late nineteenth century
Locale: Russia
First presented: 1902

Principal characters:
 KOSTILYOFF, the landlord
 VASSILISA, his wife
 NATASHA, her sister
 VASKA, a young thief
 KLESHTCH, a locksmith
 ANNA, his wife
 NASTYA, a street-walker
 THE BARON, a former nobleman
 LUKA, a tramp
 SATINE, a cardsharp
 THE ACTOR, an alcoholic

Critique:

The Lower Depths, also translated as *A Night's Lodging* and *At the Bottom,* is generally accounted the best of Gorky's plays and one of the most vital of Russia's dramatic pieces. The play was pure naturalism in its day, but to modern taste it may appear more romantic. Gorky presents little of positive affirmation, but he observes shrewdly an unfortunate people. Perhaps more than any other document, the play explains the Russian revolution of 1917.

THE LOWER DEPTHS by Maxim Gorky. By permission of the publishers, Coward-McCann, Inc. Copyright, 1922, by Morris Gest. Renewed.

The cellar resembled a cave, with only one small window to illuminate its dank recesses. In a corner thin boards partitioned off the room of Vaska, the young thief. In the kitchen lived Kvashnya, a vendor of meat pies, the decrepit Baron, and the streetwalker Nastya. All around the room were bunks occupied by a succession of lodgers.

Nastya was reading a story called *Fatal Love*. She was absorbed in the novel with her head bent down. The Baron, who lived largely on her earnings, seized the book and read its title aloud. Then he banged Nastya over the head with it and called her a lovesick fool. Satine raised himself painfully from his bunk at the noise. His memory was vague, but he knew he had been beaten up the night before. Bubnoff cruelly told him he had been caught cheating at cards. The Actor stirred in his bed on top of the stove. He predicted that some day Satine would be beaten to death.

The Actor awakened enough to remind the Baron to sweep the floor. The landlady was strict and made them clean every day. The Baron loudly announced that he had to go shopping. He and Kvashnya left to make the day's purchases.

The Actor climbed down from his bunk and declared that the doctor had told him he had an organism poisoned by alcohol. Sweeping the floor would be bad for his health.

Anna coughed loudly in her bunk. She was dying of consumption and there was no hope for her. Kleshtch, her husband, was busy at his bench, where he fitted old keys and locks. Anna sat up to call her husband. Kvashnya had left her some dumplings in the pot, and she offered them to her husband. Kleshtch agreed there was no use to feed a dying woman, and so with a clear conscience he ate the dumplings.

The Actor helped Anna down from her high bed and out to the draughty hall. The sick woman was wrapped in rags. As they went through the door, the landlord, Kostilvoff, nearly knocked them over

Kostilvoff looked around the dirty cellar and glanced several times at Kleshtch, working at his bench. The landlord asserted loudly that the locksmith occupied too much room for two roubles a month and henceforth the rent would be two roubles and a half. Then Kostilvoff edged toward Vaska's room and inquired furtively if his wife had been in. He had good reason to suspect that Vassilisa was sleeping with Vaska.

At last Kostilyoff got up enough courage to call Vaska. The thief came out and denounced the landlord for not paving his debts, saying that Kostilyoff still owed seven roubles for a watch he had bought. Ordering Kostilvoff to produce the money immediately, Vaska sent him roughly out of the room.

The others admired Vaska for his courage and urged him to kill Kostilvoff and marry Vassilisa; then he could be landlord. Vaska thought over the idea for a time, but decided that he was too soft-hearted to be a landlord. Besides, he was thinking of discarding Vassilisa for her sister Natasha. Satine asked Vaska for twenty kopecks, which the thief was glad to give immediately; he was afraid Satine would want a rouble next.

Natasha came in with Luka. She put him in the kitchen to sleep with the three already there. Luka was a merry fellow who began to sing, but he stopped when all the others objected. The whole group sat silent when Vassilisa came in, saw the dirty floor, and gave orders for an immediate sweeping. She looked over the new arrival, Luka, and asked to see his passport. Because he had none, he was more readily accepted by the dissolute company.

Miedviedeff, who was a policeman and Vassilisa's uncle, entered the cellar to check up on the lodging. He began to question Luka, but when the tramp called him sergeant, Miedviedeff left him alone.

That night Anna lay in her bunk while a noisy, quarrelsome card game went on. Luka talked gently to the consumptive woman as Kleshtch came from time to time to look at her. Luka remarked that her death would be hard on her husband, but Anna without emotion accused Kleshtch of causing her death. She hoped for the rest and peace she had never known. Luka assured her there would be peace after her death.

The card players became louder and Satine was accused of cheating. Luka quieted the rioters; they all respected him even if they thought him a liar. He told Vaska he could reform in Siberia, and he assured the Actor that at a sanatorium he could be cured of alcoholism.

Vassilisa came in. When the others left, she told Vaska that if he would kill Kostilvoff and set her free she would give him three hundred roubles. Then Vaska would be free to marry Natasha, who at the moment was recovering from a beating given by her jealous sister. Vaska was about to refuse when Kostilyoff entered in search of his wife. He was violently suspicious, but Vaska pushed him out of the cellar.

There was a noise on top of the stove. Luka had overheard the whole thing. He was not disturbed greatly, and he even warned Vaska not to have anything to do with the vicious Vassilisa. Walking over to Anna's bunk, Luka saw that she was dead. When they got Kleshtch out of the saloon, he came to look at the body of his dead wife. The others notified him that he would have to remove the body, because in time dead people smell.

Kleshtch agreed to take her outside.

The Actor began to cavort in joy, and he talked excitedly. He had made up his mind to go to the sanatorium for his health. Luka had told him he would even be cured at state expense.

In the back yard that night, as Natasha was telling romantic stories to the crowd, Kostilyoff came out and gruffly ordered Natasha in to work. When she went in, Vassilisa poured boiling water on her feet. Vaska went to the rescue of Natasha and knocked Kostilyoff down. Somehow in the brawl Kostilyoff was killed. At once Vassilisa blamed Vaska for the murder as the crowd slunk away. Natasha thought that Vaska had murdered Kostilyoff for the sake of Vassilisa. Natasha was almost in delirium as she wandered about accusing Vaska of murder and calling for revenge.

In the excitement Luka wandered off; he was never seen again. Vaska escaped a police search. Natasha went to the hospital. In the lodging things went on much as they had before. Satine cheated at cards, and the Baron tried to convince the others of his former affluence. They all agreed that Luka was a kind old man, but a great liar.

During a bitter quarrel with Nastya, the Baron stepped out in the yard. Satine and the others struck up a bawdy song. They broke off when the Baron hurried back to announce that the Actor had hanged himself. Satine thought the suicide was too bad—it broke up the song.

LOYALTIES

Type of work: Drama
Author: John Galsworthy (1867-1933)
Type of plot: Social criticism
Time of plot: Early 1920's
Locale: London
First presented: 1922

> Principal characters:
> FERDINAND DE LEVIS, a rich young Jew
> CAPTAIN RONALD DANCY, D. S. O., retired
> MABEL, his wife

LOYALTIES by John Galsworthy, from PLAYS by John Galsworthy. By permission of the publishers, Charles Scribner's Sons. Copyright, 1909, 1910, by John Galsworthy, 1928, by Charles Scribner's Sons.

Loyalties is one of the first plays to deal honestly and openly with the problem of anti-Semitism. Galsworthy takes such pains to deal fairly with both sides of the question, however, that he comes close to destroying his own thesis. The most completely drawn character is probably Captain Dancy, a man of action trying to adjust himself to a static society and finding an outlet in anti-social behavior. Although he does not ask us to condone Dancy's behavior, Galsworthy certainly enables us to understand it.

The Story:

Having retired from His Majesty's service, young Captain Ronald Dancy, D.S.O., was at loose ends as to what to do with himself. Accustomed to a life of action, he at first absorbed himself in horses and women, but he found in neither the violent excitement he craved. His stable was so expensive that he was at last forced to give his Rosemary filly to his friend, Ferdinand De Levis, because he could no longer afford to keep her. As for his women, he decided to throw them all over and marry a woman who admired him, and who had the spirit which Ronny desired in his wife.

In spite of the fact that he was obviously penniless, Ronny managed to keep his memberships in his favorite London clubs, and friends invited him and his wife to their weekend parties in the country. At Meldon Court, the home of his old friend, Charles Winsor, Ronny discovered that De Levis had sold for a thousand pounds the horse Ronny had given him. He was naturally embittered by the discovery, and later in the evening his resentment prompted him to bet De Levis ten pounds that he could jump to the top of a bookcase four feet high. He won his bet, but De Levis was contemptuous of a man who would indulge in such parlor games for the sake of a little money.

Around midnight, Winsor and his wife were awakened by De Levis, who announced that the thousand pounds he had received for the sale of the filly had been stolen from under his pillow. De Levis demanded an investigation. The Winsors were reluctant to incriminate either their servants or their guests, but at the insistence of De Levis the police were called.

Ronny's friends immediately arrayed themselves against De Levis for his tactlessness in handling the matter. He instantly interpreted their attitude as the result of prejudice because he was a Jew, and Ronny substantiated his conclusion by taunting De Levis with his race. Although they tried desperately to be fair, Ronny's friends had to admit that De Levis had behaved badly, and they suddenly remembered that his father had sold carpets wholesale in the city. After all, De Levis was a little too pushing; in spite of his money he did not exactly belong to the Mayfair and country set.

De Levis carried into the club to which both men belonged the enmity aroused by Ronny's insult to his race, and he openly accused Ronny of the theft. Ronny immediately challenged him to a duel, but since such barbaric customs were no longer tolerated among gentlemen, De Levis was saved.

Ronny urged his wife Mabel to go with him to Nairobi. But she, believing in her husband's innocence, begged him to remain and fight for his good name. Realizing that to do otherwise would be an admission of guilt, Ronny consulted a lawyer and entered a suit against De Levis for defamation of character. However, the lawyer selected to defend Ronny's case was the worst choice that a man in Ronny's position could possibly have made. Old Jacob Twisden, senior partner of the firm of Twisden and Graviter, was a lawyer of the old school who believed that simple justice should take precedence over all loyalties, whether they were racial, economic, social, political, or merely personal.

In addition to the fact that he had stolen De Levis's money, Ronny had also withheld from his wife and his friends his relations with an Italian girl before his marriage. The girl's father, a wine dealer named Ricardos, had threatened to inform Ronny's wife of the relationship unless he provided for the girl. Out of fear, Ronny had been prompted to make a daring jump from his room to that of De Levis to obtain the money with which to pay Ricardos. The stolen notes were eventually identified as having passed through these different hands. When Twisden learned the true circumstances on which the case he was defending were based, he advised Ronny to drop the suit and leave the country as soon as possible. In that proposal he was seconded by Ronny's own superior officer, General Canynge, who offered Ronny a way out with a billet in the Spanish war.

When De Levis discovered that the suit was to be dropped, he appeared willing to let bygones be bygones because he felt that he had been vindicated; he wanted no money in return. But Ronny's problems were still unsolved. When he confessed to his wife the truth about all that had happened, she at first refused to believe his story. At last she agreed to follow Ronny wherever he might choose to go. Before Ronny could make his escape, however, the police arrived with a warrant for his arrest. He fled to his room and called to the officers to come and get him. Before they could reach him, he had shot himself.

What Ronny never knew was that both he and De Levis were victims of social conventions. Because Ronny belonged, his friends had been loyal. But loyalty, as they now realized, was not enough.

LUCIEN LEUWEN

Type of work: Novel
Author: Stendhal (Marie-Henri Beyle, 1783-1842)
Type of plot: Psychological romance
Time of plot: The 1830's
Locale: France
First published: 1894

Principal characters:
    LUCIEN LEUWEN, a serious young man
    MONSIEUR LEUWEN, his father
    MADAME DE CHASTELLER, a beautiful widow
    MADAME GRANDET, an ambitious woman
    DR. DU POIRIER, a physician

Critique:

Published posthumously, *Lucien Leuwen* is a long unfinished work divided into two novels: *The Green Huntsman* and *The Telegraph.* In it Stendhal gives a subtle, penetrating analysis, Freudian in tone, of a young commoner in the difficult days after the revolution of 1830. Lucien is considered an idealized portrait of Stendhal. The novel, though rewarding, is frustrating, for Stendhal never revised the manuscript; indeed, parts of the narrative were not completed. The grand passion of Lucien for Bathilde, for example, is not concluded; from his notes we know that the author intended them to marry. Despite these imperfections the novel is regarded in France as Stendhal's third masterpiece.

LUCIEN LEUWEN by Stendhal. Translated by Louise Varèse. By permission of the publishers, New Directions. Book I, THE GREEN HUNTSMAN, copyright, 1950, by Louise Varèse. Book II, THE TELEGRAPH, copyright, 1950, by Louise Varèse.

The Story:

The revolution of 1830 was not a success; the armed rabble were victorious in the fighting, but afterward the rich bourgeoisie came to power. Although the king had lost much of his authority, France was not yet a true republic. The absolute monarchists remained loyal to the vanished power of the Bourbons, the people still hoped for a democratic rule, and the middle class steered a cautious, unsatisfactory path between the two extremes.

Lucien, son of a rich banker, had mild republican leanings. For daring to air his views, he was expelled from the Ecole Polytechnique, and for a time he remained idle at home. His indulgent, wealthy father tried to induce him to work in the family bank, and his mother presented him to the polite, gay society of her Parisian salon. But Lucien was dull and preoccupied. In despair his father filled his pockets with money and bade him entertain the light ladies at the Opera.

As a way out, Lucien took a commission as second lieutenant in a regiment of lancers going to maintain order in Nancy. Lucien liked his uniform with the magenta stripes, but he found his fellow officers insufferable. His lieutenant-colonel, especially, was a man of honorable reputation, but a bore. Only the soldiers in the ranks seemed genuine and unaffected.

The regiment was depressed on entering the town of Nancy. The land was flat; sewage ditches ran down the narrow, crooked streets, and the houses were mean. Lucien felt that he made an unsoldierly appearance because his mount, furnished by the regiment, was a mean-looking nag. As they passed a more pretentious house, a woman standing at an upstairs window seemed interested in Lucien, but as luck would have it, he was thrown from his horse just as he was trying to see her more clearly.

Lucien soon bought a good horse and rented a comfortable apartment, once occupied by a lieutenant-colonel who had left the regiment. In spite of his servants, his wine, and his stable, he was quite unhappy. His commanding officer, resenting his wealth, made his life miserable; the other officers had little to do with him. The townspeople held aloof from the military. One faction consisted of the aristocrats who were opposed to the moderate monarchy, and the other faction was the republican majority who smarted under any kingly rule. None of the officers was received in society; few of the enlisted men made friends with people of the suspicious working class.

Backed by his father's money and his own Parisian graces, Lucien set out determinedly to be accepted by the nobility. He cultivated the wily Dr. du Poirier, the leader of the monarchist set. Little by little Lucien was welcomed to the various salons. Only his military life irked him now. Government spies even reported that he had gone into a republican reading room; to quiet rumors of political unreliability Lucien fought and won two duels.

Several of the salons were presided over by beautiful, high-born women who accepted Lucien on friendly terms. The most beautiful of all, however, was Madame de Chasteller; and for long Lucien did not meet her. He heard of her in some detail, however, a rich widow dominated by a miserly father. She had had only one lover, so the gossips said, the lieutenant-colonel whose apartment Lucien had rented. When he finally met her, Lucien was smitten. Bathilde de Chasteller was lonely, proud, and shy.

Bathilde was an aristocrat, Lucien a commoner. As their love grew, they were both troubled. Bathilde felt that a marriage was impossible, and Lucien hesitated to try to make her his mistress. Unhappy much of the time, they were together so much that gossip soon spread. At a dinner at a country tavern, The Green Huntsman, they came to an open confession of their love.

The aristocratic young men were much displeased. They were afraid that Lucien, a commoner, would marry the rich Bathilde and take her away. Some of the more hot-headed ones proposed to challenge Lucien to a duel. Scheming Dr. du Poirier guaranteed to rid them of the hated Lucien.

Bathilde, ill for days, was under the treatment of Dr. du Poirier, and Lucien had been given permission to visit her. As he waited in the hall, the doctor brought a baby in swaddling clothes from Bathilde's chamber. From a conversation Lucien understood that Bathilde's illness had been a confinement. Sure that the lieutenant-colonel was the father, Lucien obtained leave and left Nancy.

In Paris, through his father, he secured his release from the army. Then, through his father's influence, he obtained a post as Master of Petitions in the Ministry of the Interior. Although he could not forget lovely Bathilde, Lucien threw himself into politics and soon was a valuable aid to the minister. At first he had little idea of the trickery so common in high office, but his knowledge grew rapidly. The minister had speculated successfully with money borrowed from M. Leuwen. When there was some danger the transaction would come to light, Lucien managed to hide all traces of the affair.

Another incident added to his standing. The government hired *agents provocateurs* to harass the military. One agent made the mistake of trying to intimidate a sentry, who shot him in the abdomen. Gravely wounded, the agent was taken to a hospital. Afraid that he would make a deathbed statement as to who had employed him, a government spy tried to induce a doctor to poison the wounded man. When the doctor objected, the minister gave Lucien the job of hushing up the scandal. Lucien succeeded in bribing the dying man and his wife so that they both maintained silence.

Lucien was sent to Caen to try to influence an election. On the way he was set upon by a mob and spattered with mud. Heartsick at the way people reacted to the corrupt government, he nevertheless did his best. By paying a hundred thousand francs to bribe the legitimist party, he almost prevented the election of a favored candidate.

The minister showed his displeasure by passing over Lucien on the honors list. Not willing to have his son slighted, M. Leuwen went into politics himself and became a deputy. With his wealth and charm, he soon was powerful enough to dictate who should be in the cabinet. He arranged to have the fatuous Grandet made a minister if his beautiful and ambitious wife would become Lucien's mistress. Madame Grandet accepted the proposition and soon fell really in love with Lucien.

M. Leuwen made the mistake of revealing the bargain to Lucien, who thought he had won by his own merit the most beautiful woman in Paris. He was greatly upset and even thought himself unfaithful to his lost Bathilde. Taking leave from the ministry, he left for a stay in the country.

M. Leuwen died suddenly, leaving his affairs in bad state. Lucien, insisting on paying all creditors in full, saved only a modest income for his mother and himself. He got an appointment to the embassy at Capel. He was happy in his new post, and felt only a faint melancholy for Bathilde.

THE LUCK OF ROARING CAMP AND OTHER SKETCHES

Type of work: Short stories
Author: Bret Harte (1836-1902)
Time: 1850-1865
Locale: California
First published: 1870

Relatively few authors ever achieve the astonishing literary success that Bret Harte did during his lifetime. His stories of California life, enormously popular, were in great demand by magazine editors all over the country, and the *Atlantic Monthly* bid the unheard-of amount of ten thousand dollars for the sole rights to one year of Harte's literary production.

However, this flash in the pan popularity is seldom consistent with a lasting literary reputation, and in Harte's case the line between literary value and entertainment is often thin. That Harte reached his artistic maturity at the age of thirty-one and began to decline five years later indicates this fact. During these few years Harte produced some stories of genuine literary value. The majority of them are collected in *The Luck of Roaring Camp and Other Sketches,* and it is mainly on this volume that Harte's literary reputation rests.

Harte's vision of life goes far to explain the meteoric popularity of his stories. The local color, the picturesque characters, and the trick endings all added to Harte's attraction, certainly, but they were surface attractions. The heart of his success lay in his particular vision of life and his ability to convey that vision to his readers.

Harte was, essentially, an optimist and an uplifter. This does not mean that Harte believed in a shallow doctrine of social or moral reform. Rather, he believed in the potential goodness of man and in the possibility of redemption for every sinner. Harte saw life as a purgatory for the human soul. He saw life as a test for men, as a trial in which the ultimate goal is salvation. Salvation, however, was to be achieved in this life, although, paradoxically, it was frequently to be gained at the cost of death. In other words, death, rather than being an end of the trial, was to be seen as the final consummation of the trial, as a selfless act of devotion on the part of his heroes. Redemption for Harte was an act of selfless heroism, of love, of devotion. Such an act lifted one above the petty world of grasping self-interest and redeemed one from the sin of self-involvement. This is the spirit that pervades Harte's most memorable stories.

This spirit raises Harte's best characters from local stereotypes and picturesque caricatures to people of real feelings and semi-heroic stature, and it helps to explain Mark Twain's statement that "Bret Harte got his California and his Californians by unconscious absorption, and put both of them into his tales alive." He wove the experiences of his people into his private theme of redemption and thereby gave them life.

The people Harte wrote about were people seeking salvation from themselves, people who longed to wipe their past clean, and people who had come West to lose their identity, as is indicated by the fact that very few of his characters retained their given names. His characters have had their identities and pasts wiped clean with names like Cherokee Sal, Kentuck, Yuba Bill, Tennessee's Partner, and the Duchess. People like these were ripe material for redemption by virtue of their self-dissatisfaction. In order to be saved, one must first have sinned.

This theme is the core of Harte's most successful stories. In the title story of the collection, "The Luck of Roaring Camp," which first appeared in the *Overland Monthly* in 1868, a dissolute prostitute works out her salvation by giving birth to a baby and dying. The miners in the camp work out their salvation by giving the baby love and generous gifts in the absence of a mother.

One miner in particular, Kentuck, works out his salvation by giving his life in a futile attempt to save the baby. The baby, of course, is incidental because of its innocence. What matters is that the baby brought out the generous qualities of the people involved and thereby redeemed them from their own pettiness. In the second story of the collection, "The Outcasts of Poker Flat," the theme is the same. A gambler and two prostitutes are saved from themselves by virtue of their devotion to a pair of innocent youngsters who had eloped. In the third story, "Miggles," a pretty young woman is redeemed by virtue of her devotion to a helpless invalid.

The theme of love's power to save turns Harte's best stories into human interest tales, which Harte did a good deal to popularize. This theme was the source of Harte's uplift, optimism, and popularity.

Harte's vices as well as his virtues can be attributed to this same theme. It quickly lapses into sentimentalism, and it also tends to gloss over the sharp frictions and discordances of everyday life with a nonexistent glamor and romance. In "Brown of Calaveras" the image of gambler Jack Hamlin riding off into the rosy sunset after having handsomely refused to run away with a man's beautiful young wife certainly strikes one as unnecessarily romantic and sentimental. Again, this theme of redemption through love and death lends itself too easily to theatrical endings in which death seems to be an easy way to end the story.

At his best, however, Harte avoids these tendencies. The sentimentality of the story is balanced frequently by an ironic, humorous narrative style. In his most memorable stories Harte employs an ironic prose that maintains a distance between himself and his subject matter. This prose is clear and restrained, giving his fiction a sweet-sour flavor that blends well with his vision of things. Thus his skillful prose gives the reader the impression that his characters do not deserve one's full sympathy until they succeed in redeeming themselves. It reminds us that his characters are human and, as such, are subject to human failings. This fact does not mean that Harte is ever self-righteous. On the contrary, he was always humane in his treatment of character. It was just that he realized human limitations as well as human virtues. In his preface to *The Luck of Roaring Camp* he wrote:

I might have painted my villains of the blackest dye. . . . I might have made it impossible for them to have performed a virtuous or generous action, and have thus avoided that moral confusion which is apt to rise in the contemplation of mixed motives and qualities. But I should have burdened myself with responsibility of their creation, which . . . I did not care to do.

Even in his preface Harte's use of irony is skillful. Actually, he was a shrewd judge of character with a talent for "the contemplation of mixed motives and qualities."

Harte put this talent to good use in his sketches. He was an admirable craftsman in blending virtue and vice, humor and pathos, the ridiculous and the sublime. He had a good eye for contrasts, particularly for the contrast between nature and man. Nature, like man, was ambivalent for Harte. On the one hand, he saw nature as serene, remote, and passionless; on the other, it could be violent, deadly, and passionate. In Harte's stories the moods of nature are usually in juxtaposition to the moods of his people. In "The Luck of Roaring Camp," for example, nature becomes still for a moment at the birth and the first cry of the baby. Later, when everything in the human realm seems calm and settled, nature in the form of a flood overwhelms the mining camp and takes several lives, including the baby's. The same occurs in "The Outcasts of Poker Flat." When the gambler, the thief, and the two prostitutes are driven out of town, everything is calm, but when these four begin to find some measure of peace, a snowstorm overwhelms them and their two innocent companions.

It has been pointed out that Harte's literary techniques were borrowed from writers like Irving and Dickens. To be sure, Harte did adapt his techniques from the Eastern writers and from Europeans. Also, he had a romantic tradition behind him. Harte was, essentially, an Easterner who had come West for his literary materials. But to hold the fact that Harte borrowed from other writers against him is to miss the point. Harte transformed these techniques with his own personal merits and limitations. He transmuted them with his own personal vision of life.

Both Harte's virtues and vices as a storyteller derive from his optimistic vision of human redemption. On the debit side, his bitter-sweet endings are patently stylized, and there is a tendency to coat his situations with sentiment. On the asset side, Harte's endings have a good measure of dramatic impact. Then, too, he frequently balances the senti-

ment and glamor with a healthy humor and irony. Again, Harte was an effective stylist and his sentences are sharp and lucid. Furthermore, Harte opened the field for human interest and local color stories, thus paving the way for a flourishing school of regional fiction. Finally, Harte's happy talent for characterization and caricature blended very well with his style of writing and his personal outlook on life, thus forming a fortunate fusion of form and content. For these reasons he retains an assured place in a minor tradition.

THE LUSIAD

Type of work: Poem
Author: Luis Vaz de Camoëns (1524?-1580)
Type of plot: Epic
Time of plot: Fifteenth century
Locale: Europe, Africa, and Asia
First published: 1572

          Principal characters:
              VASCO DA GAMA, Portuguese sea captain and explorer
              VENUS, goddess of love, patroness of the Portuguese
              BACCHUS, god of revelry, patron of Asia

Critique:

Descended from an ancient Galician family, Camoëns was distantly related to the hero of his epic narrative. In addition, the author had covered part of Vasco da Gama's route when he went to the Orient as an agent of the crown. On his return trip from Macao Camoëns was shipwrecked, saving nothing but a faithful Javanese slave and the manuscripts of *The Lusiad*. The poem was, like all great epics, the product of a man of action during a period of great national activity, at a time when the national spirit of Portugal had reached a high point. In the epic tradition, the poem finds the gods of Olympus siding for and against the Portuguese heroes; there is a descent into the underworld of Neptune. The "famous weapon" in this poem is the Portuguese ships' cannon. All of the other hallmarks of the epic are present, too, for those who would seek them.

The Story:

The gods and goddesses, called together by Jove, assembled on Olympus. When they had taken their places, Jove announced to them that the Fates had decreed that the men of Lusitania, or Portugal, should outdo all the great conquerors of ancient times by sailing around Africa to Asia, there to become the rulers of a new continent. Of all the assembled pantheon only Bacchus, who looked upon Asia as his own, dissented. Venus, friendly toward the Portuguese, however, took their side, aided by Mars.

Vasco da Gama was the captain chosen to head the voyage of exploration. Having sailed southward to the Cape of Good Hope, the Portuguese ships made their way around it and then sailed northward along the African coast, until they arrived at the island of Mozambique. The natives of that island pretended friendliness but tried to ambush the sailors when they put

1761

ashore for water; fortunately, the Portuguese escaped. Leaving the island behind, da Gama sailed northward along the African coast in search of India. He tried to land on another coast but there, too, the natives were unfriendly. When they tried to lay an ambush, Venus interceded on behalf of da Gama and his men.

Guided by Mercury, da Gama set sail for a point still farther north. Arriving off Mombassa, the Portuguese ships dropped sails and anchors. The Moorish King of Mombassa made the Portuguese welcome to his domain, as Jove had told Venus he would, and gave the men of Portugal needed supplies. While paying a visit to da Gama's ship, he asked the Portuguese leader to tell him about Portugal's history and the history of the voyage thus far. Da Gama was only too glad to give an account of his long and troublesome voyage and to tell of his nation's history.

Da Gama told the king where Portugal lay on the map of Europe and related how the Moors had at one time overrun the land. He described the great battles of Portuguese kings against the Moors: how the first Alphonso had first pushed the Moors back toward the shores of the Mediterranean and how his grandson, also named Alphonso, had continued the wars against the Moors and defeated with a small army five hosts of Moors under five Moorish kings. The second Alphonso was succeeded by Sancho, who, continuing the wars against the Moors, drove them from Europe and then fought against them in the Holy Land. Da Gama also told of the wars between the Spanish kings and the descendants of the great Alphonsos.

After ending his narrative of the martial history of Portugal, da Gama described his own adventures since leaving the mouth of the Tagus River. He told how his ships had sailed past the Canary Islands, past the Hesperides, and past the mouth of the mighty Congo. He told the king of the strange waterspouts they had seen, the terrible storms they had endured, and the awesome sea creatures they had met. He related how they had tried to make friends of the black people of the African coast by giving them odd knick-knacks and how the blacks in return had tried to kill them after pretending friendship. Da Gama told of the experiences of one of his men, Veloso, who had wandered too far inland and had almost been killed by blacks, and how Veloso had claimed that he returned quickly only because he thought the ships in danger.

Da Gama also narrated his adventure with the spirit of the Cape of Good Hope. The spirit appeared to the Portuguese as his ships sighted the cape and told them that they were the first men to sail in those waters. In return for their daring, the spirit prophesied, some of them would have to die, and that many of these men who followed them would also die for venturing so far into strange lands. The spirit told da Gama that he was one of the Titans who had fought against Jove and that his name had been Adamastor. The Titan had pursued a nymph, a chase which ended when divine wrath changed him into a range of mountains forming the cape at Africa's foot.

Da Gama next told of the plague which had struck his crew, of the shortage of drinking water, of the loss of necessary food through spoilage. He also told of battles and ambushes in which the Portuguese fought with unfriendly natives of the east African coast.

After hearing his account of Portuguese history and da Gama's fabulous voyage, the king thought he could not do enough to show his friendliness toward the great men who represented Portugal. The Mombassans sent a pilot to da Gama and also the provisions and water necessary for a voyage across the Indian Ocean to the city of Calcutta.

Bacchus, meanwhile, was furious at the success of da Gama and his ships. Determined to prevent Asia from falling into the hands of the Portuguese, Bacchus went into the depths of the sea to the court of Neptune, there to seek the aid of the sea god. He told Neptune that the men of Portugal were despoiling his kingdom and that the Portuguese spoke of the ruler of the sea only in terms of insolence. Neptune, angered at the report, sent storms to destroy their ships, but Venus interceded once more on behalf of the Portuguese and saved them from the storms unleashed by Neptune.

The Portuguese, arriving on the Indian coast, landed on the shore near Calcutta. One of the first to meet the men of Portugal was a Mohammedan who was glad to see them because he himself was from the northwestern part of Africa. He sent word to the Emperor of Malabar, informing him of the white strangers and of the distance they had traveled. The emperor quickly gave audience to da Gama, who told the ruler that he wished to trade for products of the eastern lands. Arrangements went forward to exchange Portuguese goods for spices and other products of India. The Mohammedan peoples in India became aroused and tried to bribe the king's council to halt the trading. Failing in that plan, they tried to delay da Gama's departure, for they hoped to destroy the Portuguese ships in battle with a fleet sailing from Arabia. Da Gama outwitted his enemies, however, and set out on the return voyage before the Arabian fleet had arrived.

As the Portuguese ships sailed westward toward home, Venus moved an island into their path. Needing a rest from their travels, da Gama and his men anchored off the island and went ashore. There, under the guidance of Venus, nymphs charmed away the hours for the sailors, and the goddess herself took da Gama to a castle high on a hill and showed him a vision of the future in which he saw later Portuguese—Albuquerque, Sampoyo, Noronia, and others—completing the conquest of Asia for their king and nation.

LYSISTRATA

Type of work: Drama
Author: Aristophanes (c. 448-385 B.C.)
Type of plot: Utopian comedy
Time of plot: Fifth century B.C.
Locale: Athens
First presented: 411 B.C.

> *Principal characters:*
> LYSISTRATA, an Athenian woman
> CLEONICE, her friend
> LAMPITO, a Spartan woman
> MYRRHINÉ, a Greek woman
> A MAGISTRATE
> CINESIAS, a Greek husband
> OLD MEN OF ATHENS, the Chorus

Critique:

The basic assumption on which the *Lysistrata* is based is highly comic; indeed, Aristophanes reveals, in the very weakness of the average woman in the play, his knowledge that the supposition was not only comic but also impossible. Yet the assumption that women, by concerted determination not to lie with their men, could effect peace and government reform is not entirely comic. This idea was probably an ancient one even in the time of Aristophanes, but he was able to blend the alarming logic and the delightful illogic of it to produce an amusing if somewhat bawdily skeptical work of art. Lysistrata herself is the archetype of the militant feminist, the woman who has managed through the ages to keep alive the war of the sexes.

The Story:

The Second Peloponnesian War was in progress when Lysistrata, an Athenian

1763

woman, summoned women from Athens, Sparta, and all other Greek cities involved in the war. She wished to have them consider her carefully thought out plan for ending hostilities between Athens and Sparta. The women arrived one by one, curious about the purpose of the meeting. Since their husbands were all away at war, they looked with enthusiasm for any scheme which would bring their men back to them.

Lysistrata declared that the war would end immediately if all the Greek women refrained, from that time on, until the fighting stopped, from lying with their husbands. This suggestion took the women by complete surprise, and they objected strenuously. But Lampito, a Spartan woman, liked the idea. Although the others finally agreed to try the plan, they did so without enthusiasm.

Over a bowl of Thracian wine, Lysistrata led her companions in an oath binding them to charm their husbands and their lovers, but not to lie with them unless forced. Some of the women returned to their native lands to begin their continent lives. Lysistrata went to the Acropolis, citadel of Athens.

While the younger women had been meeting with Lysistrata, the older women had marched upon the Acropolis and seized it. The old men of the city laid wood around the base of the Acropolis and set fire to it with the intention of smoking out the women, who, in turn, threatened the old men with pots of water. During an exchange of scurrilous vituperation the women threw water on their opponents.

When a magistrate and his men attempted to break open a gate of the citadel, Lysistrata, now in command, emerged and suggested that the magistrate use common sense. When the indignant magistrate ordered his Scythians to seize Lysistrata and bind her hands, the Scythians advanced reluctantly and were soundly trounced by the fierce defenders. Asked why they had seized the Acropo-

lis, the women replied that they had done so in order to possess the treasury. Since they now controlled the money, and since it took money to wage war, they believed that the war must soon end.

The male pride of the old men was deeply wounded when Lysistrata declared that the women had assumed all civil authority and would henceforth provide for the safety and welfare of Athens. The magistrate could not believe his ears when he heard Lysistrata say that the women, tired of being home-bodies, were impatient with the incompetence of their husbands in matters which concerned the commonweal. For rebuking the women, the magistrate received potfuls of water poured on his head. The ineffectual old men declared that they would never submit to the tyranny of women. The women answered that the old men were worthless, that all they could do was to legislate the city into trouble.

Despite their brave talk and their bold plan, however, the women proved to be weak in the flesh, and disaffection thinned their ranks. Some, caught as they deserted, offered various excuses in the hope of getting away from the strictures imposed by Lysistrata's oath. One woman simulated pregnancy by placing the sacred helmet of Athena under her robe. Some of the women claimed to be frightened by the holy snakes and by the owls of the Acropolis. As a last desperate measure, Lysistrata resorted to a prophecy, which was favorable to their project, and the women returned reluctantly to their posts.

When Cinesias, the husband of Myrrhiné, one of Lysistrata's companions, returned from the war and sought his wife, Lysistrata directed Myrrhiné to be true to her oath. Begging Myrrhiné to come home, Cinesias used various appeals, without success. Although Myrrhiné consented to his request for a moment of dalliance with her, she put him off with trifling excuses. At last, in spite of his pleas, she retired into the citadel.

1764

A messenger arrived from Sparta, where Lampito and her cohorts had been successful, and declared that the men of Sparta were prepared to sue for peace. As the magistrate arranged for a peace conference, the women looked once more upon the old men of Athens with a kindness that cooled the ire of the indignant old fellows.

On their arrival in Athens, the Spartan envoys were obviously in need of the favors of their wives. Indeed, so desperate were they that they were ready to agree to any terms. Lysistrata rebuked the Spartans and the Athenians for warring upon each other; they had, she declared, a common enemy in the barbarians, and they shared many traditions. While she spoke, a nude maiden, representing the goddess of peace, was brought before the frustrated men. Lysistrata reminded the men of the two countries that they had previously been friends and allies and again insisted that war between the two was illogical. The men, their eyes devouring the nude maiden, agreed absently with everything Lysistrata said, but when she asked for an agreement contention immediately arose because one side asked for conditions unsatisfactory to the other.

The women, seeing that any appeal to reason was futile, feasted the envoys and filled them with intoxicating liquors. Sated, and eager for further physical satisfaction, the men signed a peace agreement and dispersed hastily, with their wives, to their homes.

THE MABINOGION

Type of work: Tales
Author: Unknown
Type of plots: Heroic romances
Time of plots: The Middle Ages
Locale: Arthurian Britain, mainly Wales
First transcribed: Twelfth and thirteenth centuries; first translation published, 1838-1849

Principal characters:
PWYLL, Prince of Dyved
RHIANNON, his wife
PRYDERI, their son
KICVA, Pryderi's wife
BENDIGEID VRAN, King of the Island of the Mighty, Llyr's son
BRANWEN, Llyr's daughter
MATHOLWCH, King of Ireland, Branwen's husband
MANAWYDAN, another of Llyr's sons, Pryderi's stepfather
KING MATH
GWYDION, one of King Math's warriors
LLEW LLAW GYFFES, Gwydion's favorite son
BLODEUWEDD, Llew Llaw Gyffes' elfwife
MACSEN WLEDIG, Emperor of Rome
LLUDD, King of Britain
LLEVELYS, his brother, King of France
KING ARTHUR
KILHWCH, one of King Arthur's knights
YSBADDADEN, a crafty giant
OLWEN, his daughter, loved by Kilhwch
RHONABWY, a dreamer
OWAIN, the new Knight of the Fountain
PEREDUR, one of King Arthur's knights

THE MABINOGION. Translated by Gwyn Jones. By permission of the translator. Published by J. M. Dent & Sons, Ltd. Copyright, 1949. All rights reserved.

GERINT, another of King Arthur's knights, later a king
ENID, his wife

Critique:

Paradoxically, the title of this collection of Welsh tales, written in the twelfth and thirteenth centuries and preserved in the fourteenth-century manuscript titled *Red Book of Hergest*, is a relatively modern one. When Lady Charlotte Guest, the translator, called these tales *The Mabinogion* she used a misnomer for the most part, for her title applies only to the first four stories. These tales, among the finest of medieval literature, represent the best of Celtic culture. The world they disclose to our modern eyes is one of great heroes, black villains, incomparable battles, women of great beauty, old crones, magnificent splendor, wretched squalor, landscapes of matchless glamour, wizards, and warlocks—a world of chivalric romance and harsh brutality. Undoubtedly, this world and these stories have their roots in primitive Celtic mythology that was translated into folklore and eventually into romantic tales. Although the poet-authors are unknown, they show considerable artistry and craftsmanship in the treatment of their subjects.

The Stories:

PWYLL, PRINCE OF DYVED

Pwyll, the Prince of Dyved, was caught stealing a dying deer. In order to redeem himself Pwyll agreed to exchange lands and appearances with the chieftain who had caught him and to slay the chieftain's enemy after a year's time. That year each prince ruled the other's land wisely and well, and each remained faithful to his own true wife. At the year's end Pwyll slew the enemy, returned home on good terms with the other prince, and eventually gained the other's lands. From a hill one day Pwyll saw a lovely lady ride by. She eluded him three times, but on the fourth he spoke to her. She told him that her name was Rhiannon and invited him to her castle a year from that day. Pwyll went with his men, subdued her other suitor, and won the lady. Some time thereafter Rhiannon bore a son who disappeared the first night after his birth. The women on watch accused her of killing it, and so Pwyll made her pay a heavy penance. Meanwhile, a farmer had taken the baby from a monster. Eventually he restored the boy to Pwyll, who then released his wife from her penance and named his son Pryderi.

BRANWEN, DAUGHTER OF LLYR

Bendigeid Vran, son of Llyr and King of the Island of the Mighty, made a pact with Matholwch, King of Ireland, and gave him his sister Branwen to wed. When the King of Ireland suffered an insult at the hands of one of Bendigeid Vran's men, Bendigeid Vran made good the loss; but because of the insult Matholwch and Branwen were made to suffer heavily at the hands of the Irishmen. Bendigeid Vran learned of their treatment, sailed to Ireland, and made war on the Irish. Both sides suffered great losses. Bendigeid Vran was killed by a poisoned spear; his last request was that his head be buried in the White Mount in London. Branwen died of sorrow. Finally, only seven of Bendigeid Vran's men were left alive to bury the heads of their chief, and only five pregnant Irish women.

MANAWYDAN, SON OF LLYR

Two of the men left living after the war in Ireland were Pryderi and Manawydan, the brother of Bendigeid Vran. These two went to live on Pryderi's lands, and Manawydan married Pryderi's mother. The two men and their wives, for Pryderi had a wife named Kicva, lived pleasantly until the countryside was magically laid desolate and everyone else had disappeared. They left their lands and tried to earn a living at various trades, but were always driven off by their envious competitors. When they returned to their own lands, Pryderi and his mother entered a magic castle that vanished with them. Manawydan then tried farming, and again his crops were magically desolated. Determined to get to the bottom of the mystery, Manawydan stayed up to watch his last field. When he saw thousands of mice ravaging the field, he caught one and declared that he would hang it. Pryderi's wife tried to dissuade him along with three churchmen, but he was still determined to hang the mouse. At last the third churchman disclosed himself as the one who had cursed Manawydan and his friends in revenge for an insult from Pryderi's father years before. He promised to restore everything, including Pryderi and his mother, if Manawydan would release the mouse. Manawydan insisted that the magician never touch his lands again, and he returned the mouse, who happened to be the churchman's wife. Everything was restored, and the four companions returned to their former happiness.

MATH, SON OF MATHONWY

Gwydion's brother, Gilvaethwy, loved King Math's footmaiden, Goewin. Hoping to secure the maiden for his brother, Gwydion tricked Pryderi into exchanging some pigs for twelve phantom steeds and twelve phantom greyhounds. Pryderi and his men pursued them. While King Math and his men were preparing to fight this army, Gwydion and his brother raped the footmaiden before they returned to the fight and won the battle for King Math. The king then punished the brothers by turning them into animals for three years. After his penance Gwydion had two sons. Their mother cursed Gwydion's favorite son, named Llew Llaw Gyffes, by saying that he would never have a human wife. To thwart this curse King Math and Gwydion created for him an elfwife, Blodeuwedd, out of flowers. The wife proved unfaithful by

taking a lover. Determined to get rid of her husband, she asked him how he might be killed. Foolishly, he told her and she told her lover, who tried to kill Llew Llaw Gyffes. Gwydion's son did not die, however, but was turned into an eagle. Gwydion then searched for his son, found him, and restored him to his former shape. Gwydion and Llew Llaw Gyffes then took revenge on the wife and her lover by turning her into an owl and killing him.

THE DREAM OF MACSEN WLEDIG

Macsen Wledig, the Emperor of Rome, dreamed one night of a lovely maiden in a strange and wonderful land. Awaking, he sent his messengers all over the world in search of her. After wandering in many lands they found her in a castle in Britain, and they guided the emperor to her. He found everything as it had been in his dream. The maiden accepted him, and for her maiden portion he gave her father the island of Britain and caused three castles to be built for her. Macsen Wledig lived with his wife in Britain for seven years. Meanwhile, the Romans had chosen a new emperor, who sent a note to Wledig warning him not to return. Wledig then marched on Gaul, fought his way through Italy, and reconquered Rome.

LLUDD AND LLEVELYS

Three plagues ravaged Britain. The first was a crafty foreign people; the second was a yearly midnight scream that made everything barren; and the third was the habitual disappearance of food at the king's court. Lludd, the great King of Britain, asked help from his wise and well-beloved brother, Llevelys, who was King of France. Llevelys told him to mash insects in water and sprinkle the solution over the foreigners to kill them. To get rid of the screaming dragon Lludd would have to lure it with mead, put it in a sack, and bury it in a stone coffer. To keep the food Lludd would have to capture a magician who put everyone to sleep. The king performed these tasks and Britain was rid of the plagues.

KILHWCH AND OLWEN

Kilhwch's stepmother had spitefully prophesied that Kilhwch would not have a woman until he won Olwen, the daughter of Ysbaddaden, a crafty and powerful giant. Straightway, Kilhwch, who had fallen in love with Olwen without having seen her, set out for King Arthur's court, where King Arthur accepted the young man as his knight. Kilhwch then set out to seek Ysbaddaden; with him went all of King Arthur's gallant warriors. After a long journey Kilhwch met Olwen, the most beautiful woman he had ever seen. He and King Arthur's men proceeded to Ysbaddaden's court to ask for Olwen. After fighting for three days and wounding the giant three times, Kilhwch learned that he could win Olwen and slay her father after performing forty nearly impossible tasks for the giant. By dint of brute force, cunning, and magic, Kilhwch, King Arthur, and his men succeeded in completing the tasks. Kilhwch then slew Ysbaddaden, married Olwen, and lived happily ever after.

THE DREAM OF RHONABWY

While seeking a man who had ravaged the land, Rhonabwy and his companions found themselves in a dark hall where the floors were covered with dung. After trying to talk to the strange people inhabiting the hall and failing, Rhonabwy lay down on an ox-skin and began to dream. He dreamed of the heroic Arthurian age when men were demigods who lived in splendor in a land where life was full. He found himself in King Arthur's court watching a game between King Arthur and Owain. While the game was in progress, three servants informed Owain that his ravens were being killed by King Arthur's men, but the king insisted that the game continue. Owain told his men to raise his banner, whereupon the ravens revived and began to slaughter the men. Three servants came to tell King Arthur how his men were being killed, but Owain insisted that the game continue. At last the king begged Owain to call off the ravens. He did so and there was peace. Many men then brought tribute to King Arthur. At that point Rhonabwy awakened.

THE LADY OF THE FOUNTAIN

While at King Arthur's court Owain learned from Kynon of a powerful Knight of the Fountain who overthrew all challengers. Upon being taunted by Kai, Owain went in search of this knight, challenged him, and slew him. Then with the help of a maiden Owain escaped the angry townsmen who were seeking to avenge the death of their lord and he married the dead knight's wife. He ruled the land well for three years. Meanwhile, King Arthur and his knights had come in search of Owain. Upon arriving at the fountain, King Arthur's men all challenged the new Knight of the Fountain and were overthrown by him. The king and Owain were finally reunited, and Owain returned to King Arthur's court after promising his wife that he would return at the end of three years. Owain was reminded of his promise when his wife came to King Arthur's court and removed the ring which she had given him as a token by which to remember her. Then Owain went in search of his wife. After restoring a lady's kingdom, killing a serpent about to destroy a lion, saving the maiden who had aided him six years earlier, and killing her tormentors, Owain was restored to his wife. Another feat was defeating and transforming the Black Oppressor. Thereafter Owain and his wife lived happily at King Arthur's court.

PEREDUR, SON OF EVRAWG

Peredur lived a sheltered life with his mother; nevertheless he grew up strong and swift. Although his mother did not want him to become a knight, nothing could keep him from fulfilling his desire. When he prepared to leave his mother and journey to King Arthur's court, she instructed him in the chivalric code. Peredur was an ungainly sight as he entered King Arthur's court, for he was still awkward and naïve. However, he soon showed his prowess in battle, and through many adventures he acquired polish and skill in the arts of hunting, war, and love. Many reports of his strength and bravery reached King Arthur's ears. Peredur spent his time defending and loving maidens, restoring kingdoms to the wronged, avenging insults, killing monsters and evil men, protecting the weak, and ridding the land of plagues. In short, he was a matchless knight. When, in the course of his adventures, he inadvertently caused a kingdom to wither and grow barren, he restored it to fertility by dint of strength and courage. In the end he rid the land of seven evil witches.

GERINT, SON OF ERBIN

While King Arthur and his men were hunting, Gerint rode with the queen and her maids. When a dwarf insulted Gerint and one of the maids, the knight challenged the dwarf's lord to a contest and defeated him. Afterward Gerint restored a kingdom to its proper lord and won the king's daughter, Enid, as his wife. Gerint then traveled back to King Arthur's court and received a stag head for his reward. In time Gerint, having inherited a kingdom from his father, went with Enid to rule the land. Because he devoted more time to his wife than he did to jousts or battles, his subjects complained bitterly. When Enid learned of their grievance, she inadvertently told him. In anger, Gerint set out on a journey with his wife to prove his strength and valor. He performed superhuman feats and slaughtered belligerent knights and caitiffs in vast numbers, but he nearly died in the attempt. Finally, having proved himself to his wife and subjects, he returned home to rule once more.

MACBETH

Type of work: Drama
Author: William Shakespeare (1564-1616)
Type of plot: Romantic tragedy
Time of plot: Eleventh century
Locale: Scotland
First presented: 1606

Principal characters:
MACBETH, a Scottish thane
LADY MACBETH, his wife
DUNCAN, King of Scotland
MALCOLM, his son
BANQUO, a Scottish chieftain
MACDUFF, a rebel lord

Critique:

The Tragedy of Macbeth, one of Shakespeare's shortest dramas, is the story of a highly imaginative, ambitious and conscience-stricken nobleman whose wife drove him to murder. Macbeth, at first a man of honor and integrity, had one major flaw — ambition. When the opportunity for power was presented to him, he committed his first crime. Later he was forced into utter degradation in order to conceal that first evil step. The macabre settings of *Macbeth*, the gloomy castle and the eerie heath, are in keeping with the weird tone of the whole play.

The Story:

On a lonely heath in Scotland, three witches sang their riddling runes and said that soon they would meet Macbeth.

Macbeth was the noble thane of

1769

Glamis, recently victorious in a great battle against Vikings and Scottish rebels. For his brave deeds, King Duncan intended to confer upon him the lands of the rebellious thane of Cawdor.

But before Macbeth saw the king, he and his friend Banquo met the three weird witches upon the dark moor. The wild and frightful women greeted Macbeth by first calling him thane of Glamis, then thane of Cawdor, and finally, King of Scotland. Too, they prophesied that Banquo's heirs would reign in Scotland in years to come.

When Macbeth tried to question the three hags, they vanished. Macbeth thought very little about the strange prophecy until he met one of Duncan's messengers, who told him that he was now thane of Cawdor. This piece of news stunned Macbeth, and he turned to Banquo to confirm the witches' prophecy. But Banquo, unduped by the witches, thought them evil enough to betray Macbeth by whetting his ambition and tricking him into fulfilling the prophecy. Macbeth did not heed Banquo's warning; the words of the witches as they called him king had gone deep into his soul. He pondered over the possibility of becoming a monarch and set his whole heart on the attainment of this goal. If he could be thane of Cawdor, perhaps he could rule all of Scotland as well. But as it was now, Duncan was king, with two sons to rule after him. The problem was great. Macbeth shook off his ambitious dreams to go with Banquo to greet Duncan.

A perfect ruler, Duncan was kind, majestic, gentle, strong; Macbeth was fond of him. But when Duncan mentioned that his son, Malcolm, would succeed him on the throne, Macbeth saw the boy as an obstacle in his own path, and he hardly dared admit to himself how this impediment disturbed him.

On a royal procession, Duncan announced that he would spend one night at Macbeth's castle. Lady Macbeth, who knew of the witches' prophecy, was even more ambitious than her husband, and she saw Duncan's visit as a perfect opportunity for Macbeth to become king. She determined that he should murder Duncan and usurp the throne.

That night there was much feasting in the castle. After everyone was asleep, Lady Macbeth told her husband of her plan for the king's murder. Horrified at first, Macbeth refused to do the deed. But on being accused of cowardice by his wife, and having bright prospects of his future dangled before his eyes, Macbeth finally succumbed to her demands. He stole into the sleeping king's chamber and plunged a knife into his heart.

The murder was blamed on two grooms whom Lady Macbeth had smeared with Duncan's blood while they were asleep. But the deed was hardly without suspicion in the castle, and when the murder was revealed, the dead king's sons fled — Malcolm to England, Donalbain to Ireland. Macbeth was proclaimed king. But Macduff, a nobleman who had been Duncan's close friend, also carefully noted the murder, and when Macbeth was crowned king, Macduff suspected him of the bloody killing.

Macbeth began to have horrible dreams; his mind was never free from fear. Often he thought of the witches' second prophecy, that Banquo's heirs would hold the throne, and the prediction tormented him. Macbeth was so determined that Banquo would never share in his own hard-earned glory that he resolved to murder Banquo and his son, Fleance.

Lady Macbeth and her husband gave a great banquet for the noble thanes of Scotland. At the same time, Macbeth sent murderers to waylay Banquo and his son before they could reach the palace. Banquo was slain in the scuffle, but Fleance escaped. Meanwhile in the large banquet hall Macbeth pretended great sorrow that Banquo was not present. But Banquo was present in spirit, and his ghost majestically appeared in Macbeth's own seat. The startled king was so frightened that he almost betrayed his guilt when he alone saw the apparition. Lady Macbeth quickly led him away and dismissed the guests.

More frightened than ever, thinking of Banquo's ghost which had returned to haunt him, and of Fleance who had escaped but might one day claim the throne, Macbeth was so troubled that he determined to seek solace from the witches on the dismal heath. They assured Macbeth that he would not be overcome by man born of woman, nor until the forest of Birnam came to Dunsinane Hill. They warned him to beware of Macduff. When Macbeth asked if Banquo's children would reign over the kingdom, the witches disappeared. The news they gave him brought him cheer. Macbeth felt he need fear no man, since all were born of women, and certainly the great Birnam forest could not be moved by human power.

Then Macbeth heard that Macduff was gathering a hostile army in England, an army to be led by Malcolm, Duncan's son, who was determined to avenge his father's murder. So terrified was Macbeth that he resolved to murder Macduff's wife and children in order to bring the rebel to submission. After this slaughter, however, Macbeth was more than ever tormented by fear; his twisted mind had almost reached the breaking point, and he longed for death to release him from his nightmarish existence.

Before long Lady Macbeth's strong will broke. Dark dreams of murder and violence drove her to madness. The horror of her crimes and the agony of being hated and feared by all of Macbeth's subjects made her so ill that her death seemed imminent.

On the eve of Macduff's attack on Macbeth's castle, Lady Macbeth died, depriving her husband of all courage she had given him in the past. Rallying, Macbeth summoned strength to meet his enemy. Meanwhile, Birnam wood had moved, for Malcolm's soldiers were hidden behind cut green boughs, which from a distance appeared to be a moving forest. Macduff, enraged by the slaughter of his innocent family, was determined to meet Macbeth in hand-to-hand conflict.

Macbeth went out to battle filled with the false courage given him by the witches' prophecy that no man born of woman would overthrow him. Meeting Macduff, Macbeth began to fight him, taunting him at the same time about his having been born of woman. But Macduff had been ripped alive from his mother's womb. The prophecy was fulfilled. Macbeth fought with waning strength, all hope of victory gone, and Macduff, with a flourish, severed the head of the bloody King of Scotland.

McTEAGUE

Type of work: Novel
Author: Frank Norris (1870-1902)
Type of plot: Naturalism
Time of plot: 1890's
Locale: San Francisco and Death Valley
First published: 1899

> *Principal characters:*
> McTeague, a dentist
> Trina, his wife
> Marcus Schouler, McTeague's friend and Trina's cousin

Critique:

McTeague, generally considered the best of Norris' novels, falls into the category of naturalism, a mode popular in the early 1900's. Two characteristics of this school were the hero of much brawn and few brains, and the influences of heredity and environment upon character. McTeague, Trina, and Marcus are drawn inevitably to catastrophe through their own inherited qualities acted upon by environmental forces. The novel is at once powerful and terrifying.

The Story:

McTeague, born in a small mining town, worked with his unambitious father in the mines. But his mother saw in her son a chance to realize her own dreams. The opportunity to send him away for a better education came a few years after McTeague's father had died. A traveling dentist was prevailed upon to take the boy as an apprentice.

McTeague learned something of dentistry, but he was too stupid to understand much of it. When his mother died and left him a small sum of money, he set up his own practice in an office-bedroom in San Francisco. McTeague was easily satisfied. He had his concertina for amusement and enough money from his practice to keep him well supplied with beer.

In the flat above McTeague lived his friend, Marcus Schouler. Marcus was in love with his cousin, Trina Sieppe, whom he brought to McTeague for some dental work. While they were waiting for McTeague to finish with a patient, the cleaning woman sold Trina a lottery ticket.

McTeague immediately fell in love with Trina. Marcus, realizing his friend's attachment, rather enjoyed playing the martyr, setting aside his own love in order that McTeague might feel free to court Trina. He invited the dentist to go with him to call on the Sieppe family. From that day on McTeague was a steady visitor at the Sieppe home. To celebrate their engagement, McTeague took Trina and her family to the theater. Afterward they returned to McTeague's flat, to find the building in an uproar. Trina's lottery ticket had won five thousand dollars.

In preparation for their wedding, Trina was furnishing a flat across from McTeague's office. When she decided to invest her winnings and collect the monthly interest, the dentist was disappointed, for he had hoped to spend the money on something lavish and exciting. But Trina's wishes prevailed. With that income and McTeague's earnings, as well as the little that Trina earned from her hand-carved animals, the McTeagues could be assured of a comfortable life.

Marcus slowly changed in his attitude toward his friend and his cousin. One day he accused McTeague of stealing Trina's affection for the sake of the five thousand dollars. In his fury he struck at his old friend with a knife. McTeague was not hurt, but his anger was thoroughly aroused.

In the early months after their wedding, McTeague and Trina were extremely happy. Trina was tactful in the changes she began to make in her husband. Gradually she improved his manners and appearance. They both planned for the time when they could afford a home of their own. Because of those plans they had their first real quarrel. McTeague wanted to rent a nearby house, but Trina objected to the high rent. Her thriftiness was slowly turning into miserliness. When McTeague, unknown to her, rented the house, she refused to move or to contribute to the payment of the first month's rent which signing of the lease entailed.

Some days later they went on a picnic to which Marcus was also invited. Outwardly he and McTeague had settled their differences, but jealousy still rankled in Marcus. When some wrestling matches were held, Marcus and the dentist were the winners in their bouts. It now remained for the two winners to compete. No match for the brute strength of McTeague, Marcus was thrown. Furious, he demanded another match.

1772

In that match Marcus suddenly leaned forward and bit off the lobe of the dentist's ear. McTeague broke Marcus' arm in his anger.

Marcus soon left San Francisco. Shortly thereafter an order from City Hall disbarred McTeague from his practice because he lacked college training. Marcus had informed the authorities.

Trina and McTeague moved from their flat to a tiny room on the top floor of the building, for the loss of McTeague's practice had made Trina more niggardly than ever. McTeague found a job making dental supplies. Trina devoted almost every waking moment to her animal carvings. She allowed herself and the room to become slovenly, she begrudged every penny they spent, and when McTeague lost his job she insisted that they move to even cheaper lodgings. McTeague began to drink, and drinking made him vicious. When he was drunk, he would pinch or bite Trina until she gave him money for more whiskey.

The new room into which they moved was filthy and cramped. McTeague grew more and more surly. One morning he left to go fishing and failed to return. That night, while Trina was searching the streets for him, he broke into her trunk and stole her hoarded savings. After his disappearance Trina learned that the paint she used on her animals had infected her hand. The fingers of her right hand were amputated.

Trina took a job as a scrub woman, and the money she earned together with the interest from her five thousand dollars was sufficient to support her. Now that the hoard of money that she had saved was gone, she missed the thrill of counting over the coins, and so she withdrew the whole of her five thousand dollars from the bank and hid the coins in her room. One evening there was a tap on her window. McTeague was standing outside, hungry and without a place to sleep. Trina angrily refused to let him in. A few evenings later, drunk and vicious, he broke into a room she was cleaning. When she refused to give him any money, he beat her until she fell unconscious. She died early next morning.

McTeague took her money and went back to the mines, where he fell in with another prospector. But McTeague was haunted by the thought that he was being followed. One night he stole away from his companion and started south across Death Valley. The next day, as he was resting, he was suddenly accosted by a man with a gun. The man was Marcus.

A posse had been searching for McTeague ever since Trina's body had been found, and as soon as Marcus heard about the murder he volunteered for the manhunt. While the two men stood facing each other in the desert, McTeague's mule ran away, carrying on its back a canteen bag of water. Marcus emptied his gun to kill the animal, but its dead body fell on the canteen bag and the water was lost. The five thousand dollars was also lashed to the back of the mule. As McTeague went to unfasten it, Marcus seized him. In the struggle McTeague killed his enemy with his bare hands. But as he slipped to the ground, Marcus managed to snap one handcuff to McTeague's wrist, the other to his own. McTeague looked stupidly around, at the hills about a hundred miles away, and at the dead body to which he was helplessly chained. He was trapped in the parching inferno of the desert that stretched away on every side.

MADAME BOVARY

Type of work: Novel
Author: Gustave Flaubert (1821-1880)
Type of plot: Psychological realism
Time of plot: Mid-nineteenth century
Locale: France
First published: 1857

Principal characters:
CHARLES BOVARY, a provincial doctor
EMMA, his wife
LÉON DUPUIS, a young lawyer
RODOLPHE BOULANGER, a wealthy landowner

Critique:

Flaubert's genius lay in his infinite capacity for taking pains, and *Madame Bovary,* so true in its characterizations, so vivid in its setting, so convincing in its plot, is ample testimony to the realism of his work. This novel was one of the first of its type to come out of France, and its truth shocked contemporary readers. Condemned on the one hand for picturing the life of a romantic adulteress, he was acclaimed on the other for the honesty and skill with which he handled his subject. Flaubert does not permit Emma Bovary to escape the tragedy which she brings upon herself. Emma finds diversion from the monotony of her life, but she finds it at the loss of her own self-respect. The truth of Emma's struggle is universal and challenging.

The Story:

Charles Bovary was a student of medicine who married for his own advancement a woman much older than himself. She made his life miserable with her nagging and groundless suspicions. One day Charles was called to the bedside of M. Rouault, who had a broken leg, and there he met the farmer's daughter, Emma, a beautiful but restless girl whose early education in a French convent had given her an overwhelming thirst for broader experience. Charles found his patient an excellent excuse to see Emma, whose charm and grace had captivated the young doctor. But his whining wife, Héloise, soon began to suspect the true

reason for his visits to the Rouault farm. She heard rumors that in spite of Emma's peasant background, the girl conducted herself like a gentlewoman. Angry and tearful, Héloise made Charles swear that he would not visit the Rouault home again. Then Héloise's fortune was found to be non-existent. There was a violent quarrel over her deception and a stormy scene between her and the parents of Charles brought on an attack of an old illness. Héloise died quickly and quietly.

Charles felt guilty because he had so few regrets at his wife's death. At old Rouault's invitation, he went once more to the farm and again fell under the influence of Emma's charms. As old Rouault watched Charles fall more deeply in love with his daughter, he decided that the young doctor was dependable and perfectly respectable, and so he forced the young man's hand, told Charles he could have Emma in marriage, and gave the couple his blessing.

During the first weeks of marriage Emma occupied herself with changing their new home, and busied herself with every household task she could think of to keep herself from being utterly disillusioned. Emma realized that even though she thought she was in love with Charles, the rapture which should have come with marriage had not arrived. All the romantic books she had read during her early years had led her to expect more from marriage than she received, and the dead calm of her feelings was a bitter disappointment. The intimacy of marriage disgusted her. Instead of a perfumed, handsome lover in velvet and lace, she found herself tied to a dull-witted husband who reeked of medicines and drugs.

As she was about to give up all hope of finding any joy in her new life, a noble patient whom Charles had treated invited them to a ball at his chateau. At the ball Emma danced with a dozen partners, tasted champagne, and received compliments on her beauty. The contrast between the life of the Bovarys and that of the nobleman was painfully evident. Emma became more and more discontented with Charles. His futile and clumsy efforts to please her only made her despair at his lack of understanding. She sat by her window, dreamed of Paris, moped, and became ill.

Hoping a change would improve her condition, Charles took Emma to Yonville, where he set up a new practice and Emma prepared for the birth of a child.

When her daughter was born, Emma's chief interest in the child was confined to laces and ribbons for its dresses. The child was sent to a wet nurse, where Emma visited her, and where, accidentally, she met Léon Dupuis, a law clerk bored with the town and seeking diversion. Charmed with the youthful mother, he walked home with her in the twilight, and Emma found him sympathetic to her romantic ideas about life. Later Léon visited the Bovarys in company with Homais, the town chemist. Homais held little soirees at the local inn, to which he invited the townsfolk. There Emma's acquaintance with Léon ripened. The townspeople gossiped about the couple, but Charles Bovary was not acute enough to sense the interest Emma took in Léon.

Bored with Yonville and tired of loving in vain, Léon went to Paris to complete his studies. Broken-hearted, Emma deplored her weakness in not giving herself to Léon, fretted in her boredom, and once more made herself ill.

She had not time to become as melancholy as she was before, however, for a stranger, Rodolphe Boulanger, came to town. One day he brought his farm tenant to Charles for bloodletting. Rodolphe, an accomplished lover, saw in Emma a promise of future pleasure. When he began his suit, Emma realized that if she gave herself to him her surrender would be immoral. But she rationalized her doubts by convincing herself that nothing as romantic and beautiful as love could be sinful.

Deceiving Charles, Emma met Rodolphe, rode over the countryside with him, listened to his urgent avowals of love, and finally succumbed to his persuasive appeals. At first she felt guilty, but later she identified herself with adulterous heroines of fiction and believed that, like them, she had known true romance. Sure of Emma's love, Rodolphe no longer found it necessary to continue his gentle lover's tricks. He no longer bothered to maintain punctuality in his meetings with Emma; and though he continued to see her, she began to suspect that his passion was dwindling.

Meanwhile Charles became involved in Homais' attempt to cure a boy of a clubfoot with a machine Charles had designed. Both Homais and Charles were convinced that the success of their operation would raise their future standing in the community. But after weeks of torment, the boy contracted gangrene, and his leg had to be amputated. Homais' reputation was undamaged, for he was by profession a chemist, but Bovary, a doctor, was looked upon with suspicion. His practice began to fall away.

Disgusted with Charles' failure, Emma, in an attempt to hold Rodolphe, scorned her past virtue, spent money recklessly on jewelry and clothes, and involved her husband deeply in debt. She finally secured Rodolphe's word that he would take her away, but on the very eve of what was to be her escape she received from him a letter so hypocritically repentant of their sin that she read it with sneers. Then, in horror over the realization that she had lost him, she almost threw herself from the window. She was saved when Charles called to her. But she became gravely ill with brain-fever, and lay near death for several months.

Her convalescence was slow, but she was finally well enough to go to Rouen to the theater. The tender love scenes behind the footlights made Emma breathless with envy. Once more, she dreamed of romance. In Rouen she met Léon Dupuis again.

This time Léon was determined to possess Emma. He listened to her complaints with sympathy, soothed her, and took her driving. Emma, whose thirst for romance still consumed her, yielded herself to Léon with regret that she had not done so before.

Charles Bovary grew concerned over his increasing debts. In addition to his own financial worries, his father died, leaving his mother in ignorance about the family estate. Emma used the excuse of procuring a lawyer for her mother-in-law to visit Léon in Rouen, where he had set up a practice. At his suggestion she secured a power of attorney from Charles, a document which left her free to spend his money without his knowledge of her purchases.

Finally, in despair over his debts, the extent of which Emma only partly revealed, Charles took his mother into his confidence and promised to destroy Emma's power of attorney. Deprived of her hold over Charles' finances and unable to repay her debts, Emma threw herself upon Léon's mercy with all disregard for caution. Her corruption was so complete that she had to seek release and pleasure or go out of her mind.

In her growing degradation, Emma began to realize that she had brought her lover down with her. She no longer respected him, and she scorned his faithfulness when he was unable to give her money she needed to pay her bills. When her name was posted publicly for a debt of several thousand francs, the bailiff prepared to sell Charles' property to settle her creditors' claims. Charles was out of town when the debt was posted, and Emma, in one final act of self-abasement, appealed to Rodolphe for help. He, too, refused to lend her money.

Knowing that the framework of lies with which she had deceived Charles was about to collapse, Emma Bovary resolved to die a heroine's death and swallowed arsenic bought at Homais' shop. Charles, returning from his trip, arrived too late to save her from a slow, painful death.

Charles, pitiful in his grief, could barely endure the sounds of the hammer as her coffin was nailed shut. Later, feeling that his pain over Emma's death had grown less, he opened her desk, to find there the carefully collected love letters of Léon and Rodolphe. Broken with the knowledge of his wife's infidelity, scourged with debt, and helpless in his disillusionment, Charles died soon after his wife, leaving a legacy of only twelve francs for the support of his orphaned daughter. The Bovary tragedy was complete.

MADEMOISELLE DE MAUPIN

Type of work: Novel
Author: Théophile Gautier (1811-1872)
Type of plot: Sentimental romance
Time of plot: Early nineteenth century
Locale: France
First published: 1835
    Principal characters:
        M. D'ALBERT, a young esthete

ROSETTE, his mistress
THÉODORE DE SÉRANNES, in reality Mademoiselle Madelaine de Maupin

Critique:

France, in the 1830's, was going through one of those occasional periods of high morality which at intervals excite the world, and Gautier, disgusted with the hypocrisy of many of the period's defenders, wrote this romance of passion as his challenge to the period. In a long and boastful preface he pleads the cause of moral freedom in art. The novel is highly sensual, its plot based partly on history and partly on Shakespeare's *As You Like It.*

The Story:

D'Albert was a young Frenchman of twenty-two, handsome, well-educated, artistic, and well-versed in the affairs of the world. He loved beauty, especially female beauty. All his life he had dreamed of women, but he had never met the girl of his dreams, who would combine the beauty of a Ruben's nude with that of a Titian nude. It was little wonder that he had not found her.

The one thing lacking in d'Albert's life was a mistress. One day his friend de C—— offered to take him around the town and discourse on the various ladies of his acquaintance so that d'Albert could make a choice. The expedition was a delightful one, as de C—— seemed to have precise and full information on every beauty, not only on her outward circumstances, but also on the very quality of her mind. D'Albert, after some hesitation, finally decided to lay siege to Rosette, a beautiful young woman who seemed the most likely to bring his romantic and poetic mind down to earth.

It did not take d'Albert long to win the love of Rosette, and they were soon acknowledged lovers. Rosette was pliable, versatile, and always entertaining. She did not let d'Albert alone long enough for him to go off into musing daydreams. Variety was the spice of their love.

For five months the two continued to be the happiest of lovers, but at last d'Albert began to tire of Rosette. As soon as she noticed the cooling of his ardor, Rosette knew that she must do something different if she wished to keep his love. If he were growing tired of her in the solitary life they were leading, perhaps he would regain his interest if he saw her among a group of people. For this reason Rosette took d'Albert to her country estate for a visit. There she planned parties, dinners, and visits to keep him amused, but he remained bored.

One day a visitor, an old friend of Rosette, arrived. The guest was an extremely handsome young man named Théodore de Sérannes, whose conversation, riding, and swordsmanship all entranced d'Albert. The two men met every day and went hunting together, and the more d'Albert saw of Théodore the more fascinated he became. In time d'Albert was forced to admit to himself that he was in love with Théodore.

He was in love with a man, and yet he always thought of him as a woman. D'Albert's mind grew sick with the problem of Théodore's true identity. Some days he would be sure that Théodore was a woman in disguise. Then, seeing him fencing or jumping his horse, d'Albert would be forced to conclude that Théodore was a man. Rosette, he knew, was also in love with Théodore, and her infatuation kept her from noticing d'Albert's interest in the same young man.

One day d'Albert mentioned that his favorite play was Shakespeare's *As You Like It.* The rest of the company immediately decided to present the play. At first Rosette was chosen for the part of Rosalind, the heroine who dressed as a man in order to escape from her uncle, but when she refused to wear men's clothes the part was given to Théodore.

As soon as d'Albert saw Théodore dressed in woman's clothes, he guessed rightly that Théodore really was a woman. What he did not know was that Théodore, who was really named Madelaine de Maupin, had decided that she would have nothing to do with men until she had found a good and noble lover. She knew that as a woman she would have no chance to see men as they really were, and so she had hit upon the device of learning about them by dressing as a man. But she had found perfidy and falseness in every man she met. Mademoiselle de Maupin had with amusement seen d'Albert fall in love with her, and she had watched the tortures of his mind when he could not decide whether she was male or female.

As the rehearsals of the play went on, the parallels between the play and real life became even more amusing to both d'Albert and Mademoiselle de Maupin. At last, after the play had been presented, d'Albert wrote Mademoiselle de Maupin a letter. In it he said that he was sure she was a woman, and that he loved her deeply.

She took so long to reply to his letter that d'Albert again became afraid that she really was a man. One night, however, as d'Albert stood at a window a hand gently touched his shoulder. He looked around and beheld Mademoiselle de Maupin dressed in her costume as Rosalind. He was struck dumb with amazement. Mademoiselle de Maupin told him her story, and said that since he was the first man to see through her disguise, he should be the man to first have her as a woman.

That night d'Albert learned that she was truly the woman of his dreams. In the morning he found himself alone. Mademoiselle de Maupin had gone, leaving a letter in which she told d'Albert and Rosette that they would never see her again. She wrote to d'Albert that they had known one perfect night. She had answered his dream, and to fulfill a dream once was enough. Her letter ended by telling d'Albert to try to console Rosette for the love she had wasted on the false Théodore, and she hoped that the two would be very happy for many years to come.

THE MADRAS HOUSE

Type of work: Drama
Author: Harley Granville-Barker (1877-1946)
Type of plot: Social criticism
Time of plot: Early twentieth century
Locale: London
First presented: 1910

Principal characters:
    HENRY HUXTABLE
    KATHERINE, his wife
    CONSTANTINE MADRAS, Katherine's brother
    AMELIA MADRAS, his wife
    PHILIP MADRAS, their son
    JESSICA, Philip's wife
    MAJOR HIPPISLY THOMAS, Philip's friend
    MARION YATES, an employee at the Madras House
    EUSTACE PERRIN STATE, an American, a prospective buyer of the
        Madras House
    MISS CHANCELLOR, and
    MR. BRIGSTOCK, also employees at the Madras House

Critique:

The Madras House is a dramatic work still interesting in the contemporary theater. A problem play of the type popularized by Ibsen and Shaw at the turn of the century, it attempts to deal realistically with several related themes: the contrast between sexual honesty and sexual hypocrisy, the contrast between bourgeois respectability and real honesty in human dealings, the inevitability of social change even in connection with a long-established commercial institution like the Madras House, and the contrast in all personal relations between expressed motive and real motive. As in his other works, the playwright asked his audiences to think about themselves and the standards of the world which they at the time were far too likely to take for granted. If Granville-Barker's dramas seem a little old-fashioned to some persons today, the causes are simple: we enjoy certain freedoms because the characters on his stage talked about them at length. Further, we have had full experience of enjoying those freedoms and find that pursuit of them may at one and the same time free us from old restrictions and plunge us into new ones, ambiguities of human action that the author of *The Madras House* did not foresee.

The Story:

Henry Huxtable, his wife, and six spinster daughters lived in dreary middle-class respectability, supported by the income from a great store, the Madras House. Their lives were in sharp contrast to that of the sales persons who were required to "live in" at store dormitories closely supervised to make sure that the store was actually as respectable as it seemed to be. Another owner was Constantine Madras, Katherine Huxtable's brother, who had retreated from England and respectability and had lived for many years in Moslem countries.

The time had come for the sale of the Madras House; such a sale had been necessitated by confusion in family affairs. On an October Sunday, Philip Madras, Constantine's son, heard that his father had returned to England, and he was distressed by this news of the reappearance of the elderly black sheep. But this was not the only problem that Philip wished to discuss with his uncle, Henry Huxtable. The morale of the store had been upset by the discovery that one of the closely supervised girls at the store, Marion Yates, was pregnant. It was suspected that her betrayer was Mr. Brigstock, another sales person, for he had been seen kissing the disgraced girl. The old immorality of Constantine—who, it was soon learned, had lived as the master of a harem in Arabia—and the current immorality of Marion were threats to what the Huxtables called decency.

First, the Marion Yates situation was inquired into. It was immediately apparent that the young woman would refuse to name the father of her child. Instead, she planned to bear it and bring it up as her nephew or niece; the child, at least, would not be affected by family pressures for which the Huxtables stood.

Another problem that came up concerned the prospective buyer of the store, an American named State. Mr. State distressed everyone by talking in excessively naïve terms. All his phrases—such as "the Needs of the Gentler Sex" and "Woman's Noble Instinct to Perpetuate the Race"— seemed to come from his mouth in capital letters; he was a grotesque representative of an early stage of modern advertising. Furthermore, he insultingly believed that his methods were in advance of British ones and that his presence in England would change for the better the English system of merchandising.

To State's unconscious hypocrisy and to the self-conscious respectability of the Huxtables, Constantine Madras opposed himself and his own nature. At great length he defended his own pattern of life, one in which man was free to do what he liked and in which woman

1779

learned to like what man did. He pointed out that Arabian culture had not been feminized and intellectualized as, he claimed, had happened in England. To all such remarks, his hearers lent a shocked ear.

A further complication arose when Philip learned that he had a problem of his own: his wife Jessica felt neglected and was ready to fall in love with Philip's best friend, Major Thomas. For the first time Philip was forced to recognize that his wife was a woman and an individual as well as a wife. His reaction to Jessica's problem was complicated by the fact that he felt contempt for sentimentalities displayed during his mother's fruitless interview with her estranged husband Constantine.

Philip's moderately respectable soul was still more disturbed when he learned that his father was the father of Marion Yates's unborn child. But Constantine did not blush at this revelation; he merely demanded care and protection for Marion and favored the company with a discourse on English priggishness. But Constantine, in turn, was distressed when Marion refused any assistance from him. Confused by her lack of social docility and feminine meekness, Constantine retreated to a cab and, eventually, to his Arabian household.

Still unresolved was the relationship between Philip and his wife. He finally recognized her as a person. To please her as well as himself, he gave up his interest in the Madras House, leaving it to Mr. State, the American. His plan was to talk matters over with his wife and to engage in activities useful to society. Both he and Jessica found themselves united by a hope that they could work together to improve the conditions of a faulty society which the sale of the Madras House had called to their attention.

THE MADWOMAN OF CHAILLOT

Type of work: Drama
Author: Jean Giraudoux (1882-1944)
Time: A little before noon in the spring of next year
Locale: The Chaillot District of Paris
First presented: 1945

> *Principal characters:*
> COUNTESS AURELIA, the Madwoman of Chaillot
> MME. CONSTANCE, the Madwoman of Passy
> MLLE. GABRIELLE, the Madwoman of St. Sulpice
> MME. JOSEPHINE, the Madwoman of La Concorde
> THE RAGPICKER
> THE PRESIDENT
> THE BARON
> THE BROKER
> THE PROSPECTOR

In *The Madwoman of Chaillot*, Jean Giraudoux orchestrates three of his most constantly recurring themes: the inscrutability of woman, the love of humanity, and the abhorrence of materialism. For one who is familiar with all of Giraudoux's plays, the anti-war theme is implied in the latter. Stylistically, Giraudoux employs two of his favorite devices: the fantastic parable and the duality of character. The resulting impact of *The Madwoman of Chaillot* is that it possesses a remarkable unity of both form and idea, the unifying theme being the writer's love and faith in the triumph of the human entity in a time of despair.

As in several of Giraudoux's other plays, *The Madwoman of Chaillot* extends into the realm of fantasy, leaving irritating reality far behind. It differs from his other plays, however, in that it involves some forty acting parts and depends to some extent upon mere motion rather than upon typical plot complications for its effect.

The basic framework of the plot is simple. A mighty syndicate of financiers wishes to exploit the untouched deposits of oil under the streets of Paris, and they ignore humanity, beauty, and truth in the process. The free souls of Paris oppose them and eventually triumph by literally removing them from the scene.

In depicting the opposing forces in the battle for humanity, Giraudoux has weighted the scales in favor of the human element. On the one side are Presidents, Prospectors, Barons, Press Agents, Brokers, and Ladies of the Street. On the other side are the Waiter, the Little Man, the Street Singer, the Flower Girl, the Shoelace Peddlar, the Ragpicker, and other folk. In the middle, and significantly devoted to the gentle souls, is the Madwoman of Chaillot, aided by her compatriots, the Madwomen of Passy, St. Sulpice, and La Concorde. The capitalistic forces are stereotypes who function as well-oiled machinery; they are devoid of characteristics which would set them apart or elicit for them the least bit of empathic reaction. The people of Paris are all recognizable types, but each possesses some quality of individuality. Their vocations are of little concern; what matters is their love of life and mankind. The situation is basically mad, for the forces are utterly extreme.

The Madwoman tips the scales. She is both mad and frighteningly sane. Hers is an almost obligatory characterization, and Giraudoux has constructed the fabric of Countess Aurelia in such a fashion as to envelop the viewer in the sheer logic of her reasoning, making him captive of her every move. At the same time he suspends his belief in the situation through its sheer madness, so that a detachment from reality is effected. (Giraudoux's plays usually abound in understated truths made in situations of extreme agitation or tension.) He endows Countess Aurelia with telling powers of observation. Her comments are frequently so simply and mercilessly clear and true that we wish we might have said them ourselves. But our sanity renders us incapable of such guileless simplicity.

A less facile playwright than Giraudoux might easily have succumbed to the practice of constructing the parable with idealized characters lacking reality and acting within a metaphysical framework. Or another writer might have developed the situation realistically, carefully couching his thesis among the intricacies of plot and character relationships. Although *The Madwoman of Chaillot* is not exactly a compromise between these two extremes, Giraudoux employs the best techniques of both. In this play he shows the value of revealing two levels of thought within the same character.

Countess Aurelia's very insanity is sane, for she is caught up in a moment of fantastic ideals, of powerful and inhuman forces, of incredible economic stratagems which require sanity of a kind. Success ignores life and beauty in a headlong momentum toward some indefinable goal. The mad countess has captured and held her sanity in an attempt to love life and beauty to the fullest. For this gentle woman, time has stopped when life was at its loveliest.

The Madwoman encounters the menace in the form of the President, the Baron, the Prospector, and the Broker at a sidewalk café in the Chaillot district. Her friends are all aware that something terrible is afoot and inform her of the plot to drill for oil beneath the streets. The Prospector has sent his agent with a bomb to destroy the city architect, the only obstacle to the drilling. Pierre, the young assassin, is rescued by the Policeman as he is about to throw himself into the river rather than carry out his task. He is revived and convinced by the Madwoman that life is really worth living.

It is apparent to the Madwoman that the only way to combat the encroachment of the materialistic interests is to annihilate them. Because she and her friends have little chance of opposing them if commonly interpreted methods of justice were used, she decides upon an infallible plan and sends her confederates scurrying about on errands to help her carry it out.

She retires to her quarters in the Rue de Chaillot where she will receive the delegation of capitalists. They dare not resist her invitation, for she has informed them that a large deposit of oil rests under her basement. To prove it, she has prepared a sample; a bottle of mixed kerosene and mange cure is waiting for the Prospector, who professes to be able to detect the existence of oil deposits by merely sniffing the air.

Some years before, the Madwoman had rescued a Sewer Man who promised to show her a secret entrance from her basement into the sewers of Paris. She summons him now and he willingly presses the stone concealing the entrance. The other Madwomen, Mme. Constance, who takes her invisible lap dog with her everywhere; Mlle. Gabrielle, who talks to nonexistent friends; and Mme. Josephine, who is an expert at jurisprudence because her brother-in-law was a lawyer, all arrive for a delightful tea scene. They are indeed mad, but this in no way prejudices the trial which follows.

Mme. Josephine is called upon to conduct a court, for it is only just and proper that the financiers have a fair hearing before they are sent to oblivion. The Ragpicker agrees to speak in their defense, and a damning testimony it is, with money at the root of this materialistic evil. The verdict of the tribunal is unanimous; the accused are guilty on all charges. The Madwoman may proceed with the extermination.

The guests begin to arrive, and in a wonderful scene of comic irony each group in turn is sent through the door into the sewer. First come the Presidents, next the Prospectors, then the Press Agents, and so on until all, like sheep, have followed the infallible nose of the Prospector down the dark stairway, never to return again.

Immediately all the wrongs of the world are righted. Giraudoux ends his play with a paean to the Madwoman of Chaillot and to life itself. The pigeons fly again; the air is pure; the sky is clear; grass sprouts on the pavements; complete strangers are shaking hands. Humanity has been saved, and the friends of friendship thank the Madwoman, the triumphant feminine force, who expresses Giraudoux's philosophy in a simple statement that any sensible woman can set right in the course of a single afternoon whatever is wrong in this muddled world.

MAGGIE: A GIRL OF THE STREETS

Type of work: Novel
Author: Stephen Crane (1871-1900)
Type of plot: Social criticism
Time of plot: Late nineteenth century
Locale: New York
First published: 1893

Principal characters:
MAGGIE, a girl of the slums
JIMMY, her brother
PETE, Jimmy's friend and Maggie's lover
THE MOTHER

MAGGIE: A GIRL OF THE STREETS, by Stephen Crane. By permission of the publishers Alfred A. Knopf, Inc.

Critique:

The importance of *Maggie* is primarily historical, for it was the first novel to deal realistically and straightforwardly with the sordid life of the slums. It is, therefore, the first naturalistic novel in America of any real value, and in spite of its many faults of style and structure it gave rise to the naturalistic fiction of our day. For this contribution to our literature we owe Stephen Crane a great debt.

The Story:

In the slum section of New York City, Maggie and her two brothers grew up in the squalor and corruption, both moral and physical, of that poverty-stricken area. Her father usually came home from work drunk, and her mother, too, was fond of the bottle. The children were neglected. When the drunken parents ranted at each other, the children hid in terror under the table or the bed.

Somehow Maggie managed to remain untouched by that sordidness. Her younger brother died. Jimmy, her older brother, went to work after the father died. He fought, drank, and had many affairs with women. From time to time he was hounded by some of the women, who demanded support for themselves and the illegitimate children he had fathered. Jimmy brushed them aside.

When Jimmy brought his best friend home with him, Maggie fell in love. Pete, a bartender, was handsome, flashy, and exciting. One night he took her out to show her the night life of the city. Maggie's wonder knew no bounds, for to her the experience was the height of luxury. On the doorstep she allowed Pete to kiss her goodnight. Pete was

disappointed, but not discouraged. He took Maggie out again. The next time she surrendered and went to live with him.

But Pete soon grew tired of Maggie, and she was compelled to return home. In furious indignation, her mother ordered her out of the house. She had done everything, the mother insisted, to bring Maggie up to be a fine, decent girl. She had been an excellent mother and had spared no pains to keep her daughter on the path of virtue. Now her daughter would be dead to her. The neighbors joined in, denouncing Maggie. Jimmy, the seducer of other men's sisters, became indignant. He and a companion went to the bar where Pete worked, intent upon beating him up. When they failed, Jimmy contented himself by shrugging his shoulders and condemning his sister.

Maggie was now homeless and penniless. She went to see Pete, but he sent her away, irritated and fearful lest he should lose his job. She turned to prostitution, plying her trade by night, accosting poor and wealthy alike. But she did not have much luck. One night she walked forlornly and unsuccessfully in the waterfront district. Resignedly she trudged on, toward the pier and the black, murky depths of the river.

A short time later, Jimmy came home from one of his prolonged absences. Maggie, the mother wailed, was dead. With the neighbors around her, she sobbed and moaned. What the Lord had given the Lord had taken away, the neighbors told her. Uncomforted, Maggie's mother shrieked that she forgave her daughter; oh yes, she forgave Maggie her sins.

THE MAGIC MOUNTAIN

Type of work: Novel
Author: Thomas Mann (1875–1955)
Type of plot: Philosophical chronicle
Time of plot: 1907-1914
Locale: Davos, Switzerland

First published: 1924

> *Principal characters:*
> HANS CASTORP, a German engineer
> JOACHIM ZIEMSSEN, his cousin
> SETTEMBRINI, a patient at Davos
> NAPHTA, Settembrini's friend
> CLAVDIA, Hans' friend

Critique:

The Magic Mountain is a novel concerned with perspectives of history and philosophy in our time. In it the modern age has become the International Sanatorium Berghof high in the Swiss Alps, and to this institution gravitate various and conflicting currents of thought and activity in the persons of a group of invalids exiled by disease to a pinnacle of the "magic mountain." The magic it exercises in their lives is to cut them off from calendar time. Time flows through their days and years with quiet nothingness and perceptions of reality stretch into eternity. Modern ideologies and beliefs are represented by characters like the Italian humanist, the absolutist Jewish Jesuit, a German doctor, a Polish scientist, and hedonistic Mynheer Peeperkorn. The magic mountain is the sick world of Europe, and its people are various aspects of the modern consciousness.

The Story:

Hans Castorp had been advised by his doctor to go to the mountains for a rest. Accordingly, he decided to visit his cousin, Joachim Ziemssen, who was a patient in the International Sanatorium Berghof at Davos-Platz in the mountains of Switzerland. He planned to stay there for three weeks and then return to his home in Hamburg. Hans had just passed his examinations and was now a qualified engineer; he was eager to get started in his career. His cousin was a soldier by profession. His cure at the sanatorium was almost complete. Hans thought Joachim looked robust and well.

At the sanatorium, Hans soon discovered that the ordinary notions of time did not exist. Day followed day almost unchangingly. He met the head of the institution, Dr. Behrens, as well as the other patients, who, at dinner, sat in groups. There were, for instance, two Russian tables, one of which was known to the patients as the bad Russian table. A couple who sat at the latter table had the room next to Hans. Through the thin partitions, he could hear them— even in the daytime—chase each other around the room. Hans was rather revolted, inasmuch as he could hear every detail of their love-making.

There was another patient who interested him greatly, a gay Russian woman, supposedly married, named Clavdia Cauchat. Every time she came into the dining-room she would bang the door, an act which annoyed Hans a great deal. Hans also met Settembrini, an Italian, a humanist writer and philosopher. Settembrini introduced him to a Jew, Naphta, who turned out to be a converted Jesuit and a cynical absolutist. Because the two men spent their time in endless discussions, Settembrini finally left the sanatorium to take rooms in the village, in the house where Naphta lodged.

From the very first day of his arrival, Hans felt feverish and a bit weak. When his three weeks were almost up, he decided to take a physical examination. The examination proved that he had tuberculosis. So he stayed on as a patient. One day, defying orders, he went out skiing and was caught in a snowstorm. The exposure aggravated his condition.

His interest in Clavdia was heightened when he learned that Dr. Behrens, who liked to dabble in art, had painted her picture. Further, the doctor gave Hans an X-ray plate of Clavdia's skeletal structure. The plate Hans kept on his bureau in his room.

Most of his free time he spent with Joachim or with Settembrini and Naphta. The Italian and the Jesuit were given to all sorts of ideas, and Hans became involved in a multitude of philosophical discussions on the duration of time, God, politics, astronomy, and the nature of reality. Joachim, who was rather humorless and unimaginative, did not enjoy those talks. But Hans, since he himself had become a patient at the sanatorium, felt more at home and was not quite so attached to Joachim. Besides, it was Clavdia who interested him.

On the occasion of a carnival, when some of the restrictions of the sanatorium had been lifted, Hans declared his love for Clavdia. She thought him foolish and refused his proposal. The next day she left for Russia. Hans was in despair and became listless. Joachim grew even more impatient with the progress of his cure when the doctor told him that he was not yet well and would have to remain on the mountain for six more months. Wanting to rejoin his regiment, Joachim, in defiance of the doctor's injunctions, left the sanatorium. The doctor told Hans that he could leave too; but Hans knew that the doctor was angry when he said it, and he remained.

Before long Joachim returned, his condition now so serious that his mother was summoned to the sanatorium. He died shortly afterward. Clavdia Cauchat also returned. She had been writing to the doctor and Hans had heard of her from time to time. But she did not return alone. As a protector, she had found an old Dutchman named Mynheer Peeperkorn, an earthy, hedonistic planter from Java. Hans became very friendly with Peeperkorn, who soon learned that the young engineer was in love with Clavdia. The discovery did not affect their friendship at all, a friendship that lasted until the Dutchman died.

For a time the guests amused themselves with spiritualist seances. A young girl, a new arrival at the sanatorium, claimed that she was able to summon anyone from the dead. Hans took part in one meeting and asked that Joachim be called back from the dead. But Dr. Krokowski, the psychologist at the sanatorium, was opposed to the seances and the sessions broke up. Then Naphta and Settembrini got into an argument. A duel was arranged between the two dialecticians. When the time came, the Italian said he would fire into the air. When he did so, Naphta became more furious than ever. Realizing that Settembrini would not shoot at him, Naphta turned the pistol on himself and pulled the trigger. Dying, he fell face downward in the snow.

Hans Castorp had come to the sanatorium for a visit of three weeks. That stay turned out to be more than seven years. During that time he saw many deaths, many changes in the institution. He became an old patient, not just a visitor. The sanatorium became another home in the high, thin air of the mountaintop. For him time, as measured by minutes, or even years, no longer existed. Time belonged to the flat, busy world below.

Then an Austrian archduke was assassinated. Newspapers brought the world suddenly to the International Sanatorium Berghof, with news of war declared and troop movements. Some of the patients remained in neutral Switzerland. Others packed to return home. Hans Castorp said goodbye to Settembrini, who was his best friend among the old patients, and the disillusioned humanist wept at their parting. Hans was going back to Germany to fight. Time, the tragic hour of his generation, had overtaken him at last, and the sanatorium was no longer his refuge. Dodging bullets and bombs in a front line trench, he disappeared into the smoky mists that hid the future of Europe.

1785

MAGNALIA CHRISTI AMERICANA

Type of work: History
Author: Cotton Mather (1663-1728)
Time: 1620-1698
Locale: New England
First published: 1702

Cotton Mather's *Magnalia Christi Americana; or The Ecclesiastical History of New England from Its First Planting, in the Year 1620, Unto the Year of Our Lord 1698* is commonly referred to, and dismissed, as a fairly authoritative and substantial picture of the Puritan theocracy in New England. It is a history of Puritanism in the New World and much of it is true; but it is the product of a dogmatic, neurotic, tyrannical clergyman who failed to discriminate between facts and legends, the laws and the superstitions, of the early colonial period. Mather gives as much prominence and weight to accounts of witches and repentant criminals as he does to the biographies of church leaders, and the entire history is conditioned by the belief that God's will was done in early New England.

If the book is taken not as a history but as an impassioned product of the Puritan character in all of its dedication and its blindness, the experience of reading the book becomes a time-experiment by which one can gaze into the working of a mind three hundred years removed from our own. Great writers do not allow such strange, backward glimpses; their comments have a timelessness that makes their minds contemporary. But Mather is no great writer, and when he speaks he reveals himself as his times made him: pedantic, intemperate, and superstitious, yet an educated, religious man. From such personalities much of the distinctive character of America developed, and if the historian uses the *Magnalia* as source material for a study of the early American character and its formative influence, more will be gained than if the book is taken as simply an account of New England Calvinism in its beginnings.

Mather was pastor of the North Church in Boston only after the book appeared; during its writing he was assistant minister. He was a prolific writer, and critics generally agree in recognizing the quantity of his work without granting any worth, other than ordinary, to its literary quality.

The *Magnalia* is divided into two volumes; the first contains three books, the second, four. The first book, titled "Antiquities," reports, in Mather's words, "the design where-on, the manner wherein, and the people where-by the several colonies of New England were planted." The second book contains the lives of the governors and the names of the magistrates of New England, and the third presents the lives of "sixty famous divines." Volume II begins with an account of the history of Harvard College, proceeds to an account of the "acts and monuments" of the New England churches, their discipline and principles, then records a number of "illustrious discoveries and demonstrations of the Divine Providence"—including "sea-deliverances . . . remarkables done by thunder . . . an history of criminals, executed for capital crimes; with their dying speeches," —and concludes with "the wonders of the invisible world, in preternatural occurrences. . . ." The last book, "A Book of the Wars of the Lord," deals with early religious controversies, with the "molestations given to the churches of New England by that odd sect of people called Quakers," with impostors who pretended to be ministers, and with an account of the Indian wars.

The historical account of the discovery and founding of New England begins with a critical consideration of the claims of various countries as discoverers of the New World. Mather finally gives the

Cabots of England the credit for the discovery of the North American continent, but he declares that regardless of who first discovered America, it was the English who did the most for the new colonies.

Mather writes of the early settlements in Florida and Virginia and of their difficult days. He then provides a dramatized recital of the voyage of the *Mayflower*. The landing at Cape Cod is taken by Mather as a sign of God's providence; had the voyagers landed somewhere along the Hudson River, he declares, they would have been massacred by the Indians.

Mather's story of the founding of the various colonies is enlivened by zestful and partly imaginary accounts of Indian raids, of storms and droughts, and of quarrels with England and among the colonists themselves. The difficulties of the early settlers are interpreted as signs of God's providence working to produce men of strong faith in a new land. To the history of the establishment of the colonies and of churches within the colonies Mather attaches an "ecclesiastical map" which is a list of the congregations and ministers in the Plymouth, Massachusetts, and Connecticut colonies in 1696. The churches were erected, Mather writes, "on purpose to express and pursue the Protestant Reformation."

After some "historical remarks" on Boston, a lecture given in 1698 and designed to warn the Bostonians that their town had fallen on evil ways and that only with the help of God could it be returned to its former state of power and piety, Mather presents the lives of the governors of the colonies, commencing with William Bradford, governor of Plymouth colony. Other governors whose lives are included are John Winthrop, governor of Massachusetts colony; Edward Hopkins, the first governor of Connecticut colony; Theophilus Eaton, governor of New Haven colony; John Winthrop (the son), governor of Connecticut and New Haven, and other successors.

His stories of the clergy are so punctuated with moralizing passages and anecdotes that it is difficult to distinguish one divine from another. Despite Mather's pious tone, it is possible to appreciate the courage and religious devotion of the colonial ministers.

Mather is at his informative best in recording the decisions of the early churchmen concerning matters of faith. He objected to the opinion that the churches of New England simply followed the doctrines professed in England. A copy is given of the "Confession of Faith" agreed upon at Boston on May 12, 1680. The predominant feature of the document is the declaration of reliance on Holy Scripture, which is taken to be the word of God, interpretable by reference to the Scripture itself. Man's corruption is definitely admitted and is related to the fall of Adam, as seduced by Satan. Christ is the mediator between God and man. Man has free will, but since he does not always will the good, he is a sinner, to be saved only by the grace of God. The laws of God are for the direction of man, but they do not bind God Himself. The report of these points of dogma is supplemented by an account of the practices of the churches concerning such matters as church membership, election of officers, ordination, and the communion of churches with one another.

Mather becomes more human, almost gay, in the section titled "Remarkables of the Divine Providence." He begins with sea-deliverances: "I will carry my reader upon the huge Atlantick, and, without so much as the danger of being made sea-sick, he shall see 'wonders in the deep.'" The first story concerns Ephraim Howe, who lost two sons during a voyage from New Haven to Boston, was buffeted by storms for weeks, was shipwrecked and forced to live on gulls, crows, and ravens, and was rescued only after his friends had died and he had been isolated on an island near Cape

Sables for over three months. Other tales of deliverances after prayer include the story of a man preserved on the keel of an overturned boat, an incident of "twelve men living five weeks for five hundred leagues in a little boat," and several incidents of rescue at sea involving the calming of storm-tossed waters, the changing of wind, or the chance passage of a rescuing boat.

To his accounts of sea-deliverances Mather adds stories of other acts of God —of flocks of birds arriving to end a plague of caterpillars, of the relief of droughts and floods, of persons rescued from drowning or other dangers. Mather was impressed by wounds which would have been fatal, in his opinion, had not Divinity intervened. He tells, for example, of Abigail Eliot:

> One Abigail Eliot had an iron struck into her head, which drew out part of her brains with it: a silver plate she afterwards wore on her skull where the orifice remain'd as big as an half crown. The brains left in the child's head would swell and swage, according to the tides; her intellectuals were not hurt by this disaster; and she liv'd to be a mother of several children.

In the hope of correcting ordinary sinners, Mather included a number of dying speeches of criminals. A verbatim report is given of the conversation between Hugh Stone, who cut his wife's throat, and a minister. The conversation was lengthy, but the criminal continued his confession of sins in a discourse and prayer almost as long as the conversation. He directed his remarks to "young men and maids," and warned that "If you say, when a person has provok'd you, 'I will kill him;' 'tis a thousand to one but the next time you will do it."

In writing of witches, Mather had few reservations concerning the truth of the charges against them. He believed in molestations from evil spirits, as directed by Satan, and he regarded the evidence of such possession as beyond any reasonable doubt. He wrote of women who claimed to have made pacts with the devil, who rode on broomsticks and put curses on others, causing endless trouble. Execution was the proper punishment for such persons, according to Mather— although he did admit that there was "a going too far in this affair."

Perhaps the wonder is that the Christian spirit survived the passionate dogmatism and superstitions of colonial days. Mather's *Magnalia* is a curious and fascinating hodgepodge of history, didacticism, and fatal error combining to give an authentic reflection of a seventeenth-century American mind.